COMPLETE ADVANCED LEVEL MATHEMATICS

Pure Mathematics

Andy Martin • Kevin Brown • Paul Rigby • Simon Riley

STANLEY THORNES

First published in 2000 by
Stanley Thornes (Publishers) Ltd
Delta Place
27 Bath Road
Cheltenham
Glos GL53 7TH

A catalogue record for this book is available from the British Library.

ISBN 0 7487 3558 5

Book plus *Advanced Level Mathematics Tutorials Pure Mathematics CD-ROM sample (Trade Edition)*
ISBN 0 7487 4523 8

Advanced Level Mathematics Tutorials Pure Mathematics CD-ROM
Multi-user version ISBN 0 7487 3914 9
Single-user version ISBN 0 7487 3918 1

00 01 02 03 04 / 10 9 8 7 6 5 4 3 2 1

Cover photograph, STP Archive
Photograph, p 106, STP Archive

Typeset by The Alden Group, Oxford
Printed and bound in Italy by STIGE, Turin

Contents

Examination Papers

We are grateful to the following Awarding Bodies for permission to reproduce questions from their past examination papers:

- Assessment and Qualifications Alliance (AQA), including Northern Examinations and Assessment Board (NEAB), Associated Examining Board (AEB), Secondary Mathematics Project (SMP) and Joint Matriculation Board (JMB).
- The Edexcel Foundation, including University of London Examinations and Assessment Council (ULEAC).
- Oxford, Cambridge and RSA (OCR), including University of Cambridge Local Examinations Syndicate (UCLES), Oxford & Cambridge Schools Examination Board (OCSEB) and Mathematics in Education and Industry (MEI).
- Northern Ireland Council for the Curriculum, Examinations and Assessment (NICCEA).
- Welsh Joint Education Committee (WJEC).

All answers and worked solutions provided for examination questions are the responsibility of the authors.

Graphical calculator support

An icon ( ) is shown in the margin feature of this book to denote areas where the work can be further developed or demonstrated with a graphical calculator. A *Graphical Calculator Support Pack* is also available to use alongside this book (ISBN: 07487 4524 6), containing key sequences and calculator settings for Texas, Sharp and Casio machines. Additional questions that build on the activities are also provided. Where there is a link on the page of this book to the pack this is indicated next to the icon in the margin.

Advanced Level Mathematics Tutorials Pure Mathematics

Advanced Level Mathematics Tutorials Pure Mathematics is a new CD-ROM resource. It is designed to provide further and valuable extra practice and additional support to your Pure Mathematics work. There are two versions of this programme, each providing Live Authored™ worked solutions to exercises from this book. The Multi-user version provides worked solutions to 120 exercises; the Single-user version provides worked solutions to 75 exercises. Each worked solution is supported by an additional two new exercises to try.

An icon  is shown in the margin feature of the pages in this book to denote where a worked solution to an exercise on that page is provided on the CD-ROM. The relevant exercise number(s) is shown with the icon.

For further details of this new resource, contact Stanley Thornes (Publishers) Ltd, Ellenborough House, Wellington Street, Cheltenham, Glos GL50 1YW. Tel: 01242 267272. Fax: 01242 253695. e-mail: cservice@thornes.co.uk

Multi-user version: A set of three identical disks containing 120 Live Authored™ worked solutions. Each disk is licensed to three users.

ISBN 0 7487 3914 9

Single-user version: A single disk containing 75 Live Authored™ examples. The disk is licensed to one user.

ISBN 0 7487 3918 1

About the Authors

- **Andy Martin** is currently Head of Mathematics in a Doncaster school. He has also been a Pure Mathematics Examiner and Coursework Moderator since 1994 as well as a member of the Examination Board's subject committee. Andy is also the National Project Officer for a National Curriculum Development project.
- **Kevin Brown** is currently Head of Mathematics at a school in St Helens. Kevin has many years' teaching experience at a comprehensive school in Liverpool. He has also previously written material for a Mathematics multimedia package.
- **Paul Rigby** is currently Second in the Mathematics department of a high school in Bolton. Paul has worked previously at a comprehensive school in Oldham.
- **Simon Riley** is currently Head of Mathematics at a school in Leeds. He is also an assistant Examiner.

Introduction

Complete Advanced Level Mathematics is an exciting new series of mathematics books, Teacher Resource Files and other support materials (see page viii) from **Stanley Thornes** for those studying at Advanced Level. It has been developed following an extensive period of research and consultation with a wide number of teachers, students and others. All the authors are experienced and practising teachers and, in some cases, Advanced Level Mathematics Examiners. Chapters have been trialed in schools and colleges. All the requirements for complete success in Advanced Level Mathematics are provided by this series.

This book covers all the requirements for **Pure Mathematics** from all the latest Advanced Level specifications and course requirements for AS and A Level mathematics. It will provide you with:

- Material that builds on work done at GCSE level, where appropriate.
- Comprehensive coverage and clear explanations of all Pure Mathematics topics and skills.
- Numerous exercises and worked examples with questions and clear diagrams.
- Precise and comprehensive teaching text with clear progression.
- Margin notes that provide supporting commentary on key topics, formulas and other aspects of the work.
- In text highlighted 'hints' to assist with important areas, such as specific calculations in worked examples and key formulas.
- Margin icons for topics requiring the use of a graphical calculator or computer. Topics that can be developed with IT are included throughout.
- A comprehensive list of formulas that students need to know, with chapter references, and a full index.

Chapters in this book contain a number of **key features**:

- **What you need to know** sections covering prerequisite knowledge for a chapter.
- **Review** sections with practice questions on what you need to know.
- **Worked Examples** and supporting commentary.
- **Technique** and **Contextual Exercises** to give thorough practice in all Pure Mathematics concept areas and skills.
- **Consolidation A** and **B Exercises**, which include actual examination questions, to build on the work in a chapter and provide practice in a variety of question types.
- **Applications and Activities** as a support to coursework.
- A **Summary** of all the key concepts covered.

Companion volumes for ***Mechanics*** (0 7487 3559 3) and ***Statistics*** (0 7487 3560 7) and a ***Pure Mathematics Teacher Resource File*** (0 7487 3561 5) are also available in this series.

1 Algebra I

What you need to know

- How to use index form.
- How to evaluate $\sqrt{a} \times \sqrt{a}$.
- How to collect like terms.
- How to expand brackets.
- How to solve linear equations.
- How to factorise algebraic expressions.
- How to use a division algorithm (method) without a calculator.

Review

1 Write the following in index form:

a $x \times x$
b $7 \times 7 \times 7$
c $x \times x \times x$
d $a \times a \times b \times b \times b$
e $2x \times 2x$
f $3a \times 2a \times 2a$

2 Find the exact value of the following:

a $\sqrt{36} \times \sqrt{36}$
b $\sqrt{4} \times \sqrt{4}$
c $\sqrt{9} \times \sqrt{9}$
d $\sqrt{16} \times \sqrt{16}$
e $\sqrt{a} \times \sqrt{a}$
f $\sqrt{x} \times \sqrt{x}$

3 By collecting like terms simplify the following expressions:

a $2x + 3x$
b $9x^2 + 3x^2 - 2x^2$
c $6y - 3y + 4x$
d $4xy + 3yx$
e $2x^2 - 3x + 4$
f $2x + 9x - 3x$

4 Multiply out, or expand, the following terms in brackets, simplifying the answer where possible:

a $3(x + 2)$
b $2(x - 3)$
c $-2(x + 2)$
d $-3(x - 3)$
e $-5(x + 2y - 3)$
f $6(2x - 2y - 12)$
g $(x + 1)(x + 2)$
h $(x - 2)(x + 3)$
i $(x + 4)(x - 1)$
j $(x + 3)(x + 5)$
k $(x - 2)(x - 3)$
l $(x - 4)^2$

5 Solve the following equations:

a $5x = 25$

b $3x - 3 = 12$

c $7x - 2 = 11x - 22$

d $3(x + 2) = 21$

e $2(x + 1) = 18$

f $-7(x - 4) = -49$

6 Factorise the following expressions:

a $2x + 2y$

b $3x - 3y$

c $7x + 14y$

d $8x - 12y$

e $18x^2 - 6xy$

f $12x^3y^2 + 6x^2y^3$

7 Without using a calculator evaluate the following (leaving remainders in fraction form where necessary):

a $3000 \div 24$

b $4064 \div 32$

c $3096 \div 17$

d $5997 \div 13$

e $4539 \div 14$

f $9077 \div 16$

1.1 The Number System and Surds

In its historical development mathematics started out from the numbers 1, 2, 3, ... and from the figures of geometry such as points, lines, angles, plane shapes, and so on. The numbers 1, 2, 3, 4, ... are known as the **natural numbers** and are denoted by the symbol $\mathbb{N}$. Mathematically, this can be written $\mathbb{N} = \{1, 2, 3, \ldots\}$.

The set of **integers** is denoted by $\mathbb{Z}$ (which stands for *Zahl*, the German word for number). Mathematically, this can be written $\mathbb{Z} = \{\ldots, -2, -1, 0, 1, 2, \ldots\}$. Notice how the set of integers $\mathbb{Z}$ includes the set of natural numbers $\mathbb{N}$.

Integers are simply whole numbers, both positive and negative.

The number system can be further expanded. The set of all **rational numbers** is denoted by $\mathbb{Q}$. Mathematically this can be written,

$$\mathbb{Q} = \left\{\frac{m}{n} : m \in \mathbb{Z}, n \in \mathbb{Z}, n \neq 0\right\}$$

The symbol $\in$ means 'is contained in', so m and n must both be integers.

This means a number can belong to the set $\mathbb{Q}$ provided it can be written as a fraction where both numerator and denominator are integers.

Example 1

Which of the following numbers belong to the set $\mathbb{Q}$?

a 7 **b** 0.4 **c** $2\frac{1}{2}$
d 0.333... **e** 2.13

Solution

a $7 = \frac{7}{1}$ **b** $0.4 = \frac{4}{10}$ **c** $2\frac{1}{2} = \frac{5}{2}$
d $0.333\ldots = \frac{1}{3}$ **e** $2.13 = \frac{213}{100}$

Since all the numbers can be written in the required form, they are all members of $\mathbb{Q}$.

Example 2

Show that the number 0.813 813 81 ... belongs to $\mathbb{Q}$.

Solution

Let $x = 0.813\,813\,81\ldots$ call this equation [1]

Then $1000x = 813.813\,81\ldots$ call this equation [2]

Recall that $\times 1000$ has the effect of changing the place value of the figures by three places. The decimal point is now between the first 3 and the second 8.

So $999x = 813$

Subtract equation [1] from equation [2].

$x = \frac{813}{999}$

Since $0.813\,813\,81\ldots = \frac{813}{999}$, it is of the required form and is a member of $\mathbb{Q}$.

Irrationals and surds

There are some numbers that cannot be written in this form. These numbers have a decimal expansion that doesn't terminate, but goes on forever without repeating. These numbers are known as **irrational numbers**. Some examples of irrational numbers are π, $\sqrt{2}$, $\sqrt{5}$ and $\sqrt{7}$. They cannot be evaluated exactly; calculators simply give an approximation to 8, 10 or 12 decimal places. The ancient Greeks called numbers like $\sqrt{2}$, $\sqrt{5}$ and $\sqrt{7}$ **incommensurables**. Now they are often referred to as **surds**. Not all irrationals are surds; π is not a surd.

They were called incommensurables because although they could be constructed with a ruler and a pair of compasses they couldn't be measured exactly.

Surds are used to give exact answers instead of an approximation to many decimal places (in much the same way as fractions are preferred to decimals). Surds can also be manipulated using the following properties.

$\sqrt{ab} = \sqrt{a} \times \sqrt{b}$ Property 1 ◀ **Learn these properties.**

$\sqrt{\frac{a}{b}} = \frac{\sqrt{a}}{\sqrt{b}}$ Property 2

$a\sqrt{b} + c\sqrt{b} = (a + c)\sqrt{b}$ Property 3

$a\sqrt{b} - c\sqrt{b} = (a - c)\sqrt{b}$ Property 4

Properties 3 and 4 demonstrate how surds behave in the process of factorisation.

Example 3

Simplify:

a $\sqrt{45}$ **b** $\sqrt{24}$ **c** $6\sqrt{7} + 2\sqrt{7}$ **d** $5\sqrt{3} - \sqrt{27}$

Solution

a $\sqrt{45} = \sqrt{9 \times 5}$

$= \sqrt{9} \times \sqrt{5}$ ◀ **Using property 1.**

$= 3\sqrt{5}$

Note the square number, 9.

b $\sqrt{24} = \sqrt{4 \times 6}$

$= \sqrt{4} \times \sqrt{6}$ ◀ **Using property 1.**

$= 2\sqrt{6}$

Note the square number, 4.

c $6\sqrt{7} + 2\sqrt{7} = (6 + 2)\sqrt{7}$ ◀ **Using property 3.**

$= 8\sqrt{7}$

d $5\sqrt{3} - \sqrt{27} = 5\sqrt{3} - \sqrt{9 \times 3}$

$= 5\sqrt{3} - (\sqrt{9} \times \sqrt{3})$ ◀ **Using property 1.**

$= 5\sqrt{3} - 3\sqrt{3} = 2\sqrt{3}$ ◀ **Using property 4.**

Notice how 27 can be written as a product involving a square number.

Example 4

Expand and simplify $(\sqrt{8} - \sqrt{3})(\sqrt{8} + \sqrt{3})$.

Solution

$$
\begin{aligned}
(\sqrt{8} - \sqrt{3})(\sqrt{8} + \sqrt{3}) &= \sqrt{8}(\sqrt{8} + \sqrt{3}) - \sqrt{3}(\sqrt{8} + \sqrt{3}) \\
&= (\sqrt{8})^2 + \sqrt{8}\sqrt{3} - \sqrt{3}\sqrt{8} - (\sqrt{3})^2 \\
&= (\sqrt{8})^2 - (\sqrt{3})^2 \\
&= 8 - 3 = 5
\end{aligned}
$$

Remember that $\sqrt{8}\sqrt{3} = \sqrt{3}\sqrt{8}$

Example 4 demonstrates the algebraic result for **difference of two squares:**

$$(a + b)(a - b) = a^2 - b^2$$

◀ **Learn this result.**

For example, $(\sqrt{8} + \sqrt{3})(\sqrt{8} - \sqrt{3}) = (\sqrt{8})^2 - (\sqrt{3})^2$, as demonstrated in Example 4. This technique will be very useful later.

Rationalising the denominator

Division by square roots can appear daunting, but it can be avoided by writing 1 in a surd form and multiplying by it. This allows the following technique to be applied.

Example 5

Rationalise:

a $\dfrac{5}{\sqrt{3}}$ **b** $\dfrac{15}{\sqrt{5}}$ **c** $\dfrac{1}{7 - \sqrt{2}}$

Solution

a $\dfrac{5}{\sqrt{3}} = \dfrac{5}{\sqrt{3}} \times \dfrac{\sqrt{3}}{\sqrt{3}}$

$= \dfrac{5\sqrt{3}}{3}$

Notice how 1 has been written in surd form as $\frac{\sqrt{3}}{\sqrt{3}}$.

b $\dfrac{15}{\sqrt{5}} = \dfrac{15}{\sqrt{5}} \times \dfrac{\sqrt{5}}{\sqrt{5}}$

$= \dfrac{15\sqrt{5}}{5}$

$= 3\sqrt{5}$

Notice how 1 has been written in surd form.

Notice that 5 is a factor of both numerator and denominator.

This process is sometimes called **rationalising** the denominator because the original number is rewritten without the surd occurring in the denominator.

c The choice of surd form for 1 isn't obvious here. However the difference of two squares provides the answer.

$$\frac{1}{7-\sqrt{2}} = \frac{1}{(7-\sqrt{2})} \times \frac{(7+\sqrt{2})}{(7+\sqrt{2})}$$

Notice the form of 1.

$$= \frac{(7+\sqrt{2})}{(7)^2 - (\sqrt{2})^2}$$

The denominator is now the difference of two squares.

$$= \frac{7+\sqrt{2}}{49-2}$$

$$= \frac{7+\sqrt{2}}{47}$$

This choice of multiplier is by no means accidental. When more complicated expressions need rationalising the multiplier is simply the **conjugate** of the original denominator. (Think of the conjugate as having the same components, with one of the signs changed.)

Example 6

Rationalise $\frac{\sqrt{17}-\sqrt{5}}{\sqrt{17}+\sqrt{5}}$.

Solution

$$\frac{\sqrt{17}-\sqrt{5}}{\sqrt{17}+\sqrt{5}} = \frac{\sqrt{17}-\sqrt{5}}{\sqrt{17}+\sqrt{5}} \times \frac{(\sqrt{17}-\sqrt{5})}{(\sqrt{17}-\sqrt{5})}$$

Spot the conjugate.

$$= \frac{(\sqrt{17}-\sqrt{5})(\sqrt{17}-\sqrt{5})}{(\sqrt{17})^2 - (\sqrt{5})^2}$$

Spot the difference of two squares.

$$= \frac{(\sqrt{17})^2 - \sqrt{17}\sqrt{5} - \sqrt{5}\sqrt{17} + (\sqrt{5})^2)}{17-5}$$

Multiply out the numerator.

$$= \frac{17+5-2\sqrt{5}\sqrt{17}}{12}$$

Collect like terms.

$$= \frac{22-2\sqrt{85}}{12}$$

◀ Use surd property 1.

Factorise the numerator.

$$= \frac{2(11-\sqrt{85})}{12}$$

$$= \frac{11-\sqrt{85}}{6}$$

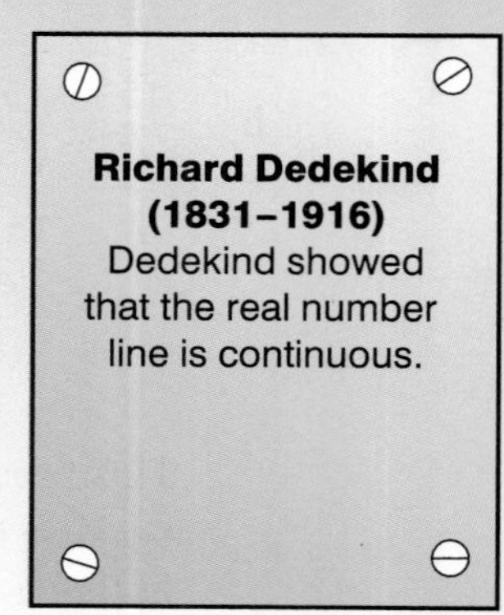

Richard Dedekind (1831–1916)
Dedekind showed that the real number line is continuous.

The real number system

The set of **real numbers** contains all the irrational numbers in addition to all the rational numbers. This set is denoted by $\mathbb{R}$. Real numbers can be represented by points on a line, called the real number line.

1.1 The Number System and Surds

Exercise

Technique

1 Simplify the following:

a $\sqrt{18}$
b $\sqrt{27}$
c $\sqrt{48}$
d $\sqrt{44}$
e $\sqrt{125}$
f $\sqrt{153}$
g $\sqrt{225}$
h $\sqrt{72}$

2 Simplify the following and express each as a single surd:

a $5\sqrt{3} - 2\sqrt{3}$
b $7\sqrt{2} + 2\sqrt{2}$
c $3\sqrt{18} - \sqrt{32}$
d $5\sqrt{32} - \sqrt{200}$
e $2\sqrt{27} + 3\sqrt{3} - \sqrt{12}$
f $2\sqrt{20} - \sqrt{45} + \sqrt{500}$

3 Expand and simplify the following:

a $(\sqrt{3} - \sqrt{2})(\sqrt{3} + \sqrt{2})$
b $(\sqrt{3} - \sqrt{2})(\sqrt{3} - \sqrt{2})$
c $(\sqrt{5} - \sqrt{3})(\sqrt{5} - \sqrt{3})$
d $(\sqrt{5} - \sqrt{3})(\sqrt{5} + \sqrt{3})$
e $(2\sqrt{5} + 1)(\sqrt{5} - 1)$
f $(4\sqrt{5} - 1)(2\sqrt{5} - 1)$
g $(\sqrt{7} - \sqrt{2})(\sqrt{7} + \sqrt{2})$
h $(\sqrt{11} - 3)(\sqrt{11} + 3)$

4 Rationalise the denominator in each of the following fractions:

a $\dfrac{1}{\sqrt{3}}$
b $\dfrac{3}{\sqrt{5}}$
c $\dfrac{1}{1 + \sqrt{5}}$
d $\dfrac{1}{\sqrt{2} - 1}$
e $\dfrac{7}{\sqrt{13} - \sqrt{11}}$
f $\dfrac{6}{2 + \sqrt{7}}$
g $\dfrac{\sqrt{5} - \sqrt{2}}{\sqrt{5} + \sqrt{2}}$
h $\dfrac{\sqrt{11} - \sqrt{7}}{\sqrt{11} + \sqrt{7}}$

4 **b**

1.2 Indices

We can write $2 \times 2 \times 2 \times 2 \times 2$ as 2^5. The '5' is known as the **power** (sometimes called an exponent or index); 'a to the power x' is written as a^x. So a^x is an expression in which a is the **base** and x is the power.

Multiplication and division using powers

Consider multiplying the same number raised to different powers.

$$3^3 \times 3^2 = (3 \times 3 \times 3) \times (3 \times 3) = 3^5$$

$$4^2 \times 4^5 = (4 \times 4) \times (4 \times 4 \times 4 \times 4 \times 4) = 4^7$$

Try some of your own examples. What do you notice about the powers?

$$\boldsymbol{a^p \times a^q = a^{(p+q)}}$$ Property 1 ◀ **Learn this property.**

Notice that when the base is the same, multiplication has the effect of summing the powers.
Now try multiplying a power by itself several times.

$$\begin{aligned}(3^3)^2 &= 3^3 \times 3^3 \\ &= (3 \times 3 \times 3) \times (3 \times 3 \times 3) \\ &= 3^6\end{aligned}$$

$$\begin{aligned}(4^2)^5 &= 4^2 \times 4^2 \times 4^2 \times 4^2 \times 4^2 \\ &= (4 \times 4) \times (4 \times 4) \times (4 \times 4) \times (4 \times 4) \times (4 \times 4) \\ &= 4^{10}\end{aligned}$$

Try some examples of your own. What is happening to the powers?

$$\boldsymbol{(a^p)^q = a^{p \times q} = a^{pq}}$$ Property 2 ◀ **Learn this property.**

Notice that the powers are multiplying.
Now try division using powers. Remember to keep the base the same.

$$\begin{aligned}6^5 \div 6^3 &= \frac{6 \times 6 \times 6 \times 6 \times 6}{6 \times 6 \times 6} \\ &= 6 \times 6 = 6^2\end{aligned}$$

Try some examples of your own. What do you think is happening to the powers?

$$\boldsymbol{a^p \div a^q = \frac{a^p}{a^q} = a^{p-q}}$$ Property 3 ◀ **Learn this property.**

Notice how the powers now subtract.

There are some special cases to consider.

1. Division when powers are equal

$$6^3 \div 6^3 = 6^{3-3}$$
$$1 = 6^0$$

Recall that any number divided by itself gives 1, except zero, which is a special case.

This result leads to another property.

$a^0 = 1$ **provided** $a \neq 0$ Property 4 ◀ **Learn this property.**

Think of this as 'any number raised to the power zero must equal 1'.

2. Division when the second power is larger than the first

$$7^3 \div 7^5 = 7^{3-5}$$
$$\frac{7 \times 7 \times 7}{7 \times 7 \times 7 \times 7 \times 7} = 7^{-2}$$
$$\frac{1}{7 \times 7} = 7^{-2}$$
$$\frac{1}{7^2} = 7^{-2}$$

Try some examples of your own. What does the negative power mean?

$a^{-p} = \frac{1}{a^p}$ Property 5 ◀ **Learn this property.**

A negative power indicates a reciprocal. (Think of a negative power as producing a fraction.)

3. Fractional powers

Property 1 can be used to introduce a meaning for a fractional power. Suppose that $p = q = \frac{1}{2}$ in property 1.

Notice that the left-hand side (LHS) is a number multiplied by itself.

$$a^{\frac{1}{2}} \times a^{\frac{1}{2}} = a^{\frac{1}{2}+\frac{1}{2}}$$
$$(a^{\frac{1}{2}})^2 = a^1 = a$$
$$\Rightarrow \quad a^{\frac{1}{2}} = \sqrt{a}$$

Now take the square root of both sides.

The meaning of power $\frac{1}{3}$ can be established in a similar way.

$$a^{\frac{1}{3}} \times a^{\frac{1}{3}} \times a^{\frac{1}{3}} = a^{(\frac{1}{3}+\frac{1}{3}+\frac{1}{3})}$$
$$(a^{\frac{1}{3}})^3 = a^1 = a$$
$$\Rightarrow \quad a^{\frac{1}{3}} = \sqrt[3]{a}$$

The LHS can be written more concisely using powers.

This means 'power $\frac{1}{3}$' can be thought of as a cube root. Investigate powers $\frac{1}{4}$, $\frac{1}{5}$, and so on in the same way. Notice how the fraction is related to the root.

$a^{\frac{1}{p}} = \sqrt[p]{a}$ Property 6 ◀ **Learn this property.**

Property 6 can also be used to establish a meaning for fractional powers where the numerator isn't 1. For example, $a^{2/3}$ can be written in other forms.

$$a^{\frac{2}{3}} = (a^2)^{\frac{1}{3}} = (a^{\frac{1}{3}})^2$$ ◀ Use property 2.

The first version, $a^{\frac{2}{3}} = (a^2)^{\frac{1}{3}}$, allows the following interpretation.

$$a^{\frac{2}{3}} = (a^2)^{\frac{1}{3}} = \sqrt[3]{a^2}$$

Notice how the fractional power creates a root of a power.

$$\boldsymbol{a^{\frac{p}{q}} = \sqrt[q]{a^p} = (a^{\frac{1}{q}})^p}$$ Property 7 ◀ Learn this property.

These seven properties provide useful techniques for simplifying algebraic expressions.

Example 1

Simplify:

a $\dfrac{3^5 \times 3^6}{3^4}$ **b** $\dfrac{18x^2y^5}{3x^4y}$ **c** $(3x^5)^2$

Solution

a $\dfrac{3^5 \times 3^6}{3^4} = \dfrac{3^{5+6}}{3^4}$ ◀ Use property 1 on the numerator.

$= \dfrac{3^{11}}{3^4}$

$= 3^{11-4}$ ◀ Use property 3.

$= 3^7$

b $\dfrac{18x^2y^5}{3x^4y} = \dfrac{6x^2y^5}{x^4y}$ Divide the whole numbers.

$= 6x^{(2-4)}y^{(5-1)}$ ◀ Use property 3 on x and y separately.

$= 6x^{-2}y^4$

$= \dfrac{6y^4}{x^2}$ ◀ Use property 5.

c $(3x^5)^2 = 3^2 \times (x^5)^2$ Each term inside the bracket must be squared.

$= 9x^{10}$ ◀ Use property 2.

Example 2

Write the following expressions in index form:

a $\frac{2}{x^3}$ **b** $\frac{1}{2x^4}$ **c** $(x^4)^{\frac{1}{2}}$ **d** $\sqrt[3]{\frac{54x^4}{2x}}$

Solution

a $\frac{2}{x^3} = 2x^{-3}$ ◀ Use property 5.

b $\frac{1}{2x^4} = \frac{1}{2}x^{-4}$ ◀ Use property 5.

Notice in part **b** how the variable (x) is put into index form, but the fraction ($\frac{1}{2}$) is left as a multiplier.

c $(x^4)^{\frac{1}{2}} = x^{4\times\frac{1}{2}}$ ◀ Use property 2.

$= x^2$

d $\sqrt[3]{\frac{54x^4}{2x}} = \sqrt[3]{27x^{(4-1)}}$

Divide the number terms, and use property 3 on the variable x.

$= \sqrt[3]{27x^3}$

$= \sqrt[3]{27} \times \sqrt[3]{x^3}$ ◀ Use surd property 1.

$= 3x$

Notice that property 1 is true for cube roots too. This is because $(ab)^{\frac{1}{m}} = a^{\frac{1}{m}}b^{\frac{1}{m}}$

Example 3

Without using a calculator, evaluate:

a $9^{-\frac{3}{2}}$ **b** $(1\frac{11}{25})^{-\frac{1}{2}}$

Solution

a $9^{-\frac{3}{2}} = \frac{1}{9^{\frac{3}{2}}}$ ◀ Use property 5.

$= \frac{1}{(9^{\frac{1}{2}})^3}$ ◀ Use property 2.

Since $9^{\frac{1}{2}} = \sqrt{9} = 3$, by property 6.

$= \frac{1}{3^3} = \frac{1}{27}$

b $(1\frac{11}{25})^{-\frac{1}{2}} = (\frac{36}{25})^{-\frac{1}{2}}$

Remove the mixed number.

$= \frac{1}{(\frac{36}{25})^{\frac{1}{2}}}$ ◀ Use property 5.

$= \frac{1}{\sqrt{\frac{36}{25}}}$ ◀ Use property 6.

$= \frac{1}{(\frac{6}{5})} = \frac{5}{6}$

Remember that division by a fraction means invert the fraction (and multiply).

The properties, or rules, of indices can also be used in equation solving.

Example 4

Find the value of x when:

a $5^x = 125$ **b** $x^{\frac{2}{3}} = 4$

Solution

a $5^x = 125$

This type of problem can sometimes be solved using a trial and improvement approach, as follows, although this may be time consuming for very large numbers, and for non-integer solutions.

$5^1 = 5$

$5^2 = 5 \times 5 = 25$

$5^3 = 5 \times 5 \times 5 = 125$

So $x = 3$

b $x^{\frac{2}{3}} = 4$ ◀ Use property 7.

$\sqrt[3]{x^2} = 4$

$x^2 = 4^3$ Cubing both sides.

$x^2 = 64$

$x = \pm\sqrt{64}$ Taking the square root of both sides.

$x = \pm 8$

1.2 Indices
Exercise
Technique

1 Simplify the following expressions:

a $\dfrac{4^2 \times 4^7}{4^3}$

b $\dfrac{5^3 \times 5^4}{5^2}$

c $\dfrac{5^9}{5^2 \times 5^7}$

d $\dfrac{7^{11}}{7^3 \times 7^4}$

e $\dfrac{8x^3y^2}{4xy}$

f $\dfrac{12x^5y^4}{6x^3y^3}$

2 Simplify the following expressions:

a $(x^3)^4$

b $(x^2)^3$

c $2(x^3)^2$

d $3(x^5)^3$

e $(2x^4)^3$

f $(3x^2)^3$

3 Write the following expressions in index form:

a $\dfrac{3}{x^7}$

b $\dfrac{1}{3x^7}$

c $\dfrac{4^2 \times 4^7}{4^{12}}$

d $\dfrac{5^3 \times 5^5}{5^{10}}$

e $\dfrac{12x^2y^3}{24x^4y^7}$

f $\dfrac{3x^5y^3}{9x^2y^5}$

4 Write the following expressions in their simplest form:

a $\dfrac{(x^4)^{\frac{1}{2}}}{(x^6)^{\frac{1}{3}}}$

b $\dfrac{(x^8)^{\frac{1}{4}}}{x^{-2} \times x^4}$

c $\sqrt{\dfrac{9x^4}{y^2}}$

d $\sqrt{\dfrac{5x^6}{20x^2}}$

e $\sqrt[3]{\dfrac{16x^9}{2x^2 \times x}}$

f $\sqrt[4]{\dfrac{x^9 \times x^3}{(x^2)^2}}$

5 Evaluate the following expressions without using a calculator:

a $16^{\frac{3}{2}}$

b $64^{-\frac{2}{3}}$

c $(-27)^{-\frac{2}{3}}$

d $(-27)^{\frac{2}{3}}$

e $\left(\frac{9}{25}\right)^{-\frac{1}{2}}$

f $\left(\frac{9}{64}\right)^{-\frac{1}{2}}$

g $\left(3\frac{3}{8}\right)^{\frac{1}{3}}$

h $\left(2\frac{1}{4}\right)^{-\frac{3}{2}}$

6 Using trial and improvement, or otherwise, solve (find the value of x for) these equations:

a $2^x = 8$ b $3^x = 9$ c $7^x = \frac{1}{7}$ d $12^x = 1$

e $x^{-3} = \frac{1}{8}$ f $x^{-3} = \frac{27}{64}$ g $x^{-\frac{2}{3}} = \frac{1}{4}$ h $x^3 = 343$

1.3 Polynomials

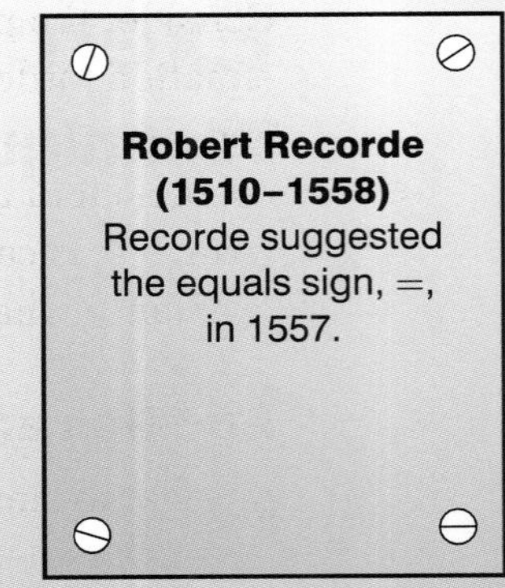

An **expression** is a combination of numbers, variables (usually represented by the letters x and y) and mathematical operations ($+$, $-$, $\times$, $\div$). Some examples of expressions are $3x + 2$, $7x^2 + 3y$, and $x^2 - 5x + 6$. When two expressions are linked by the symbol of equality an equation is formed.

For example, the following are all equations:

$$3x + 2 = 5 \qquad 7x^2 + 3y = x + 2 \qquad x^2 - 5x + 6 = 0$$

The general form of a simple equation can be written in various ways.

$$y = ax + b, \quad y = mx + c \quad \text{and} \quad y = a_1x + a_0$$

a, b, m, c, a_1 and a_0 are constants distinct from x and y, which represent variables.

are all forms of **linear equations**.

Why are these equations linear? Try drawing their graphs for some values of a and b, m and c, or a_1 and a_0. Notice how the graph is always a straight line.

For example, $y = 2x + 1$ is one version of $y = ax + b$, with $a = 2$ and $b = 1$. It is illustrated here.

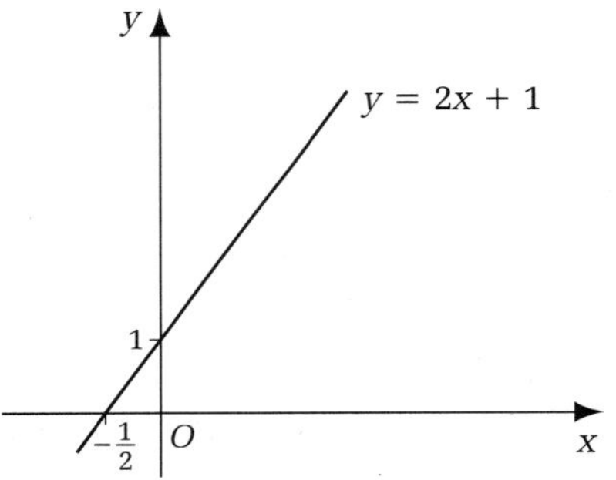

An equation of the form $y = x^n$, where n is a positive integer, is known as a **polynomial**. The general form of this type is written $y = a_nx^n + a_{n-1}x^{n-1} + \ldots + a_2x^2 + a_1x + a_0$, where $a_n \neq 0$. This is called a polynomial equation of degree n.

The word polynomial is Greek, from 'poly' meaning many and 'nomial' meaning terms or names.

$$y = x^2 + 3x - 1$$

is a polynomial of degree 2, because its highest power is 2.

$x^2 + \sqrt{x} - 3$ is not a polynomial. This is because $\sqrt{x} = x^{\frac{1}{2}}$ and $\frac{1}{2}$ isn't a positive integer.

$$y = 2x^5 + 7x^3 - 8x + 4$$

is a polynomial of degree 5, because its highest power is 5.

What about the numbers in the polynomials? Notice how each term of the equation is distinct, separated by the operators $+$ and $-$. The number in front of each **variable** (letter) is called a **coefficient**.

Consider the polynomial $y = 2x^5 + 7x^3 - 8x + 4$. This is a quintic equation (order 5, because the highest power of x is 5). The numbers 2, 7 and -8 are coefficients: 2 is the coefficient of the x^5 term; 7 is the coefficient of the x^3 term; and -8 is the coefficient of the x term. The final term, $+4$, is called a **constant** because it remains the same (its value is constant), whatever the value of x.

Addition and subtraction

In order to simplify polynomials, like terms are collected together. Like terms can then be added or subtracted algebraically. Notice the distinction between like and unlike terms.

Remember like terms contain the same variables (letters) raised to the same powers.

- *Examples of like terms*

  x^2, $-3x^2$, and $2x^2$ are like terms, because they all have the same variable, x^2

  xy and $3yx$ are like terms, because they both have the same variable, xy

- *Examples of unlike terms*

  x and xy are unlike terms, because they contain different variables

  x^2y and y^2x are unlike terms, because they contain different variables

Example 1

Simplify:

a $(3x^2 + 8x - 2) + (5x^2 + 3x + 8)$

b $(6x^2 + 8x - 2) - (5x^2 + 2x - 7)$

Solution

a
$$\begin{aligned}(3x^2 + 8x - 2) + (5x^2 + 3x + 8) &= 3x^2 + 8x - 2 + 5x^2 + 3x + 8 \\ &= 3x^2 + 5x^2 + 8x + 3x - 2 + 8 \\ &= 8x^2 + 11x + 6\end{aligned}$$

Collect together the like terms.

Combine the like terms.

b
$$\begin{aligned}(6x^2 + 8x - 2) - (5x^2 + 2x - 7) &= 6x^2 + 8x - 2 - 5x^2 - 2x + 7 \\ &= 6x^2 - 5x^2 + 8x - 2x - 2 + 7 \\ &= x^2 + 6x + 5\end{aligned}$$

Recall that a minus sign outside the bracket changes the sign of each term inside the bracket, and collect together like terms.

Multiplication

Multiplication of polynomials is achieved by applying the **distributive law**. In algebra this law can be stated,

$$\boldsymbol{a(b + c) = ab + ac}$$

Verify this law for yourself using numbers.

and

$$\boldsymbol{(a + b)(c + d) = a(c + d) + b(c + d) = ac + ad + bc + bd}$$

For example, 23×17 can be written

$$(20 + 3) \times (10 + 7) = 20(10 + 7) + 3(10 + 7)$$
$$= 200 + 140 + 30 + 21 = 391$$

What is the effect of this law? Notice that every term in the second bracket has been multiplied by each of the terms in the first bracket. This is the principle used in polynomial multiplication.

Example 2

Expand and simplify:

a $(2x + 3)(4x^3 + 3x^2 - 2x + 5)$
b $(3x^3 - x^2 + 7)(2x^3 + 2x^2 - 3x + 2)$ **c** $(x + 2)^3$

Solution

a Recall the structure of the distributive law. Each term in the second bracket must be multiplied by each term in the first bracket.

$$(2x + 3)(4x^3 + 3x^2 - 2x + 5)$$
$$= 2x(4x^3 + 3x^2 - 2x + 5) + 3(4x^3 + 3x^2 - 2x + 5)$$

Multiply the second bracket by $2x$ and by 3.

$$= 8x^4 + 6x^3 - 4x^2 + 10x + 12x^3 + 9x^2 - 6x + 15$$
$$= 8x^4 + 6x^3 + 12x^3 - 4x^2 + 9x^2 + 10x - 6x + 15$$

Collect like terms.

$$= 8x^4 + 18x^3 + 5x^2 + 4x + 15$$

b Recall the structure of the distributive law.

$$(3x^3 - x^2 + 7)(2x^3 + 2x^2 - 3x + 2)$$
$$= 3x^3(2x^3 + 2x^2 - 3x + 2) - x^2(2x^3 + 2x^2 - 3x + 2)$$
$$+ 7(2x^3 + 2x^2 - 3x + 2)$$
$$= 6x^6 + 6x^5 - 9x^4 + 6x^3 - 2x^5 - 2x^4 + 3x^3 - 2x^2$$
$$+ 14x^3 + 14x^2 - 21x + 14$$

Notice how the indices combine.

$$= 6x^6 + 6x^5 - 2x^5 - 9x^4 - 2x^4 + 6x^3 + 3x^3 + 14x^3 - 2x^2 + 14x^2$$
$$- 21x + 14$$

Collect like terms.

$$= 6x^6 + 4x^5 - 11x^4 + 23x^3 + 12x^2 - 21x + 14$$

c
$$(x + 2)^3 = (x + 2)(x + 2)(x + 2)$$
$$= (x + 2)[x(x + 2) + 2(x + 2)]$$

◀ **Using the distributive law on the second pair of brackets.**

$$= (x + 2)[x^2 + 2x + 2x + 4]$$

Simplify the expression in square brackets.

$$= (x + 2)(x^2 + 4x + 4)$$
$$= x(x^2 + 4x + 4) + 2(x^2 + 4x + 4)$$
$$= x^3 + 4x^2 + 4x + 2x^2 + 8x + 8$$
$$= x^3 + 6x^2 + 12x + 8$$

Notice how the faint crossing out can help to collect and combine like terms quickly.

Division

Before attempting division of polynomials think back to division with integers (whole numbers). Numerical division can be represented by fractions.

Fractions in the form $\frac{3}{4}$, $\frac{1}{10}$, $\frac{2}{5}$, $\frac{3}{8}$ are known as **proper fractions**. Here the numerator (top number) is less than the denominator (bottom number).

How are **improper fractions** written? Here the reverse is true. The numerator is greater than the denominator. Some examples are $\frac{7}{4}$, $\frac{11}{10}$, $\frac{18}{5}$, and $\frac{19}{8}$. How else could these be written? Improper fractions can also be written as mixed numbers, that is a mixture of an integer (whole number) and a proper fraction.

$$\tfrac{7}{4} = 1\tfrac{3}{4}, \quad \tfrac{11}{10} = 1\tfrac{1}{10}, \quad \tfrac{18}{5} = 3\tfrac{3}{5} \quad \text{and} \quad \tfrac{19}{8} = 2\tfrac{3}{8}.$$

Similarly **algebraic fractions** (fractions involving polynomials) can be both proper and improper.

$$\frac{3}{x+1}, \quad \frac{2}{x-5}, \quad \frac{x+1}{x^2+5x+3} \quad \text{are all proper algebraic fractions.}$$

$$\frac{x+2}{x+5}, \quad \frac{x^2+13}{x-4}, \quad \frac{x^2+5x+6}{x^2-7x+12} \quad \text{are all improper algebraic fractions.}$$

What's the difference between proper and improper algebraic fractions? Look at the degree, or order, of the polynomials in the numerator and denominator. For an algebraic fraction to be proper the order of the numerator must be *less than* the order of the denominator. If not, the fraction is improper.

Example 3

Make the expression $\dfrac{x+3}{x+5}$ a proper algebraic fraction.

Solution

Notice that $\dfrac{x+3}{x+5}$ is improper (the numerator and denominator are both order 1, or linear). There are two techniques that could be used to make this a proper algebraic fraction.

Here the 'x's cannot be cancelled because they are not factors of both numerator and denominator.

Method 1: The division algorithm

Write $\dfrac{x+3}{x+5}$ as a division problem, and try a division by x.

$$x+5\overline{)x+3}\quad 1$$

$$\begin{array}{r} 1 \\ x+5\overline{)x+3} \\ x+5 \\ \hline -2 \end{array}$$

Because x in $(x + 5)$ will divide into the x in $(x + 3)$ once.

Subtract $1 \times (x + 5)$ from $(x + 3)$. The remainder is $3 - 5 = -2$.

So $\dfrac{x+3}{x+5} = 1 - \dfrac{2}{x+5}$

Notice the positions of the remainder and the divisor in the result.

Method 2: Algebraic manipulation
In this technique the numerator is written as a multiple of the denominator and a remainder.

$$\frac{x+3}{x+5} = \frac{(x+5)-2}{x+5}$$

Then the numerator is split into two distinct parts.

$$\frac{x+3}{x+5} = \frac{x+5}{x+5} - \frac{2}{x+5} = 1 - \frac{2}{x+5}$$

Because a number, $(x + 5)$, divided by itself is always 1.

Notice how both techniques give the same result. The fraction in the answer is proper.

Example 4

Write as proper fractions:

a $\dfrac{4x}{1-x}$ **b** $\dfrac{3x+6}{x+3}$

Solution

a Using the division algorithm,

$$\begin{array}{r} -4 \\ 1-x\overline{)4x} \\ 4x-4 \\ \hline 4 \end{array}$$

Because $4x \div -x = -4$. Then $-4 \times (1 - x) = -4 + 4x = 4x - 4$. Finally, $0 - (-4) = 4$.

$$\frac{4x}{1-x} = -4 + \frac{4}{(1-x)}$$

b $\dfrac{3x+6}{x+3} = \dfrac{3(x+3)-3}{x+3}$

$$= \frac{3(x+3)}{x+3} - \frac{3}{x+3}$$

$$= 3 - \frac{3}{x+3}$$

The coefficient of x in the numerator is 3, so $(x + 3)$ is multiplied by 3. Multiplying out the bracket, the constant term in the numerator is 9. We require it to be $+6$, so we subtract 3.

1.3 Polynomials
Exercise
Technique

1 For each of the following polynomials write down (**i**) the order (degree) and (**ii**) the coefficient of x^2:

a $3x^3 + 2x^2 - 1$
b $5x^4 - 2x^2 + x$
c $7x^5 - 3x^4 - 7x^2 + 9$
d $3x^2 - 7$
e $3x^3 - 6x + 9$
f $8x^2 - 2x + 3$

2 Add:

a $3x^2 + 7x - 3$ and $5x^2 - 2x + 8$
b $6x^2 + 6x + 3$ and $6x^2 + 3x - 2$
c $4x^3 + 2x^2 + 3x + 6$ and $3x^3 + 7x - 3$
d $12x^5 + 7x^3 - 3x + 9$ and $-3x^5 + 2x^4 + 7x^2 + 7x$

3 Find $y_1 - y_2$ when:

a $y_1 = 5x^2 + 12x + 3$ and $y_2 = 3x^2 + 7x - 4$
b $y_1 = 7x^2 + 12x - 2$ and $y_2 = 2x^2 - 5x + 7$
c $y_1 = 5x^4 + 3x^3 - 2x^2 + 8x$ and $y_2 = 7x^4 - 2x^3 - 2x^2 + 2x - 5$
d $y_1 = -3x^3 - 2x^2 + 7x + 13$ and $y_2 = 5x^3 - 3x^2 + 6x + 12$

4 Multiply and simplify the following:

a $(2x + 1)$ and $(3x + 2)$
b $(2x + 3)$ and $(2x^2 + 1)$
c $(2x - 1)$ and $(x^2 + 3x + 1)$
d $(3x - 1)$ and $(x^2 - 2x + 1)$
e $(3 - x)$ and $(x^2 + 3x - 2)$
f $(4 - x)$ and $(2x^2 - 5x + 7)$

4 **a**

5 Expand and simplify the following:

a $(2x + 3)(3x^2 - 2x + 8) + (x + 1)(x^2 + 3x + 2)$
b $(5x - 1)(2x^2 + 3x + 2) + (x + 3)(2x^2 + 4x - 3)$
c $(3x - 2)(3 + 2x - x^2) + (x - 5)(x^2 - 2x + 1)$
d $(4x - 3)(2x + 7 - 2x^2) + (x - 1)(x^2 + 5x - 1)$
e $(5x + 1)(x^2 + 2x + 2) - (x + 1)(x^2 + 3x + 1)$
f $(3x - 2)(2x^3 + 7x - 5) - (x - 1)(x^3 - 3x + 2)$

6 Expand and simplify the following:

a $(2x + 3)(2x + 3)$
b $(2x + 3)(2x + 3)^2$
c $(2x + 3)^4$
d $(1 + 2x)^4$
e $(x + 1)^4$
f $(x - 1)^4$

7 Write the following as proper fractions:

a $\dfrac{x + 2}{x + 5}$
b $\dfrac{2x + 2}{x + 5}$
c $\dfrac{4x + 10}{x - 1}$
d $\dfrac{6x + 7}{2x - 1}$
e $\dfrac{3x - 2}{x + 2}$
f $\dfrac{2x + 3}{x - 2}$

1.4 Factorisation

The distributive law $a(b + c) = ab + ac$ has been used to demonstrate multiplication of polynomials. The same law can be used in reverse, so a sum of terms can be written as a product. Doing this often introduces brackets into the algebra. The process is called **factorisation**.

Factorisation can be shown with natural numbers. The integers that divide exactly into 8 are 1, 2, 4 and 8. These are called the **factors** of 8. Notice that 8 can be written as a product of some of these factors.

$$8 = 1 \times 8 \qquad 8 = 2 \times 4$$

Polynomials too can sometimes be factorised. Consider first polynomials of degree 2. These are more commonly known as **quadratics**. One such quadratic expression is $x^2 + 3x - 18$. It can be factorised as follows.

$$x^2 + 3x - 18 = (x + 6)(x - 3)$$

Check this by multiplying out the brackets. We call $(x + 6)$ and $(x - 3)$ the **factors** of the quadratic $x^2 + 3x - 18$.

Quadratics can be factorised using one of three basic techniques:

- extracting a common factor
- trial and improvement
- standard results – difference of two squares.

Extracting a common factor

Example 1

Factorise $4x^3y^2 - 8x^2y^3$.

Factorisation by extracting a common factor is not restricted to quadratics.

Solution

Here it is possible to extract common factors.
4 and 8 have the common factor 4 (4 is the largest factor of both numbers).
x^3 and x^2 have the common factor x^2 (x^2 is the largest factor of both terms).
y^2 and y^3 have the common factor y^2 (y^2 is the largest factor of both terms).
So $4x^3y^2 - 8x^2y^3 = 4x^2y^2 \times$ (some other term).
Notice how the common factors are extracted from both terms in the expression and appear outside the bracket. These form one part of the product. The bracket must contain the terms necessary to combine with the common factor to create the original expression.

$$4x^3y^2 - 8x^2y^3 = 4x^2y^2(x - 2y)$$

Check that $4x^2y^2 \times x = 4x^3y^2$ and that $4x^2y^2 \times (-2y) = -8x^2y^3$.

In order to factorise quadratics, first check the coefficients in the expression.

Consider again the quadratic expression, $x^2 + 3x - 18$. The coefficient of x^2 is 1, the coefficient of x is 3 and the constant term is -18. So the three distinct numbers in this expression are 1, 3 and -18. Now look at the factors of that expression, $(x + 6)$ and $(x - 3)$. These contain the two distinct numbers 6 and -3. How are these two sets of numbers connected? Notice that adding the numbers in the factors and multiplying the numbers in the factors creates the two larger numbers given by the coefficients.

$6 + (-3) = 3$, which is the coefficient of x

$6 \times (-3) = -18$, which is the constant term.

The general rule, for a quadratic expression where the coefficient of x^2 is 1, is that the expression can be factorised if two numbers can be found that add to give the coefficient of x and multiply to give the constant term.

Trial and improvement

Example 2

Factorise:

a $x^2 + 7x + 12$ **b** $x^2 - 8x + 15$

Solution

a The coefficient of x^2 is 1, so we know that we need to find two numbers that add to make 7 and multiply to make 12. Notice that 4 and 3 work.

$x^2 + 7x + 12 = (x + 4)(x + 3)$

Check this by multiplying out the factors.

b The coefficient of x^2 is 1, so we need to find two numbers that add to -8 and multiply to 15. We find that -5 and -3 work

$-5 + (-3) = -8$

$(-5) \times (-3) = 15$

So $x^2 - 8x + 15 = (x - 5)(x - 3)$.

Check this by multiplying out the factors.

By finding the factors of the constant term first, much of the trial and improvement in these examples can be done quickly.

What happens when the coefficient of x^2 is greater than 1? This trial and improvement technique can then be modified. The method, or process, is sometimes known as 'PAFF', the letters P, A, F and F representing the four stages of the process: **P**roduct, **A**ddition, **F**actors and **F**actorise. The idea is to change the algebra into smaller numerical problems leading to some less complicated factorisation.

Follow each stage of the technique in Example 3.

Example 3

Factorise $12x^2 + 17x - 14$.

Solution

Notice that the coefficient of x^2 is 12 so the technique used in Example 2 won't work. Try PAFF, the stages of which are as follows.

1. P – Product
   Multiply the coefficient of x^2 by the constant term.

   Here $P = 12 \times (-14)$

   $P = -168$

2. A – Addition
   This is the coefficient of x, something that factors need to add to.

   Here, $A = 17$

3. F – Factors
   Using the same technique as before, but this time find two numbers that multiply to give P and add to give A.

   In this example -7 and 24 work.

   $(-7) \times 24 = -168$

   $-7 + 24 = 17$

4. F – Factorise
   Use the factors identified in Step 3 to help factorise the expression. These allow the coefficient of x to be split.

   $12x^2 + 17x - 14 = 12x^2 - 7x + 24x - 14$

   Notice how the factors in Step 3 are used to produce a four-term expression from the original three-term quadratic.

   This new expression can now be factorised by extracting common factors. Imagine factorising the first pair of terms and the second pair of terms separately.

   $12x^2 - 7x + 24x - 14 = x(12x - 7) + 2(12x - 7)$

   Notice that $(12x - 7)$ is a new common factor.

   $12x^2 - 7x + 24x - 14 = (12x - 7)(x + 2)$

   So $12x^2 + 17x - 14 = (12x - 7)(x + 2)$

   Check by multiplying out the factors.

This process looks complicated and time consuming, but with practice can be a very effective algorithm for factorising quadratics where the coefficient of x^2 is greater than 1.

Example 4

Factorise $4x^2 - 2x - 30$.

Solution

The coefficient of x^2 is 4, so use PAFF.

P: $4 \times (-30) = -120$

A: the coefficient of x is -2

F: the factors need to multiply to -120, and add to -2. Check that -12 and 10 work.

F: $$\begin{aligned} 4x^2 - 2x - 30 &= 4x^2 - 12x + 10x - 30 \\ &= 4x(x-3) + 10(x-3) \\ &= (x-3)(4x+10) \end{aligned}$$

So $4x^2 - 2x - 30 = (x-3)(4x+10)$

What do you notice about the second factor? The numbers 4 and 10 have 2 as a common factor, so this bracket can be factorised further.

$$4x + 10 = 2(x+5)$$

So the original quadratic expression has three distinct factors.

$$4x^2 - 2x - 30 = 2(x+5)(x-3)$$

An alternative method here would be to extract the common factor first and use PAFF on a simpler equation.

Factorise the first and second pair of terms separately.

Notice that $(x - 3)$ is a new common factor.

Check this by multiplying out the factors.

Difference of two squares

Sometimes the coefficient of x can be zero. In this case the quadratic will contain an x^2 term and a constant term only. Factorisation of these expressions can often be achieved by extracting a common factor or using another standard result: the **difference of two squares**.

Example 5

Factorise $x^2 - 49$.

Solution

Notice that 49 is a square number; that is, $49 = 7^2$. The expression can therefore be rewritten,

$$x^2 - 49 = x^2 - 7^2$$

The right-hand side is now the difference of two squares. This factorises in a particular way.

$$\begin{aligned} x^2 - 49 &= x^2 - 7^2 \\ &= (x+7)(x-7) \end{aligned}$$

The result demonstrated in Example 5 can be generalised as

$$a^2 - b^2 = (a + b)(a - b)$$

This result can be used as an aid to computation. Some 'difficult' problems can be done quickly without using a calculator.

Example 6

a Factorise $12x^2 - 3$.
b Factorise $5\tan^2\theta - 5$.
c Evaluate $101^2 - 100^2$.

Solution

a $12x^2 - 3 = 3(4x^2 - 1)$

$$= 3[(2x)^2 - 1^2]$$

$$= 3(2x + 1)(2x - 1)$$

Extract the common factor 3. The bracketed factor is the difference of two squares.

b $5\tan^2\theta - 5 = 5(\tan^2\theta - 1)$

$$= 5(\tan^2\theta - 1^2)$$

$$= 5(\tan\theta + 1)(\tan\theta - 1)$$

c $101^2 - 100^2 = (101 + 100)(101 - 100)$

$$= 201 \times 1$$

$$= 201$$

Use your calculator to check that $101^2 - 100^2 = 201$.

1.4 Factorisation

Exercise

Technique

1 Factorise the following quadratic expressions:

1 g

a $x^2 + 3x + 2$
b $x^2 + 7x + 10$
c $x^2 - x - 20$
d $x^2 - 7x - 18$
e $x^2 + 3x - 18$
f $x^2 + x - 12$
g $x^2 + 6x - 16$
h $x^2 + x - 6$

2 Factorise the following quadratic expressions using the difference of two squares:

a $x^2 - 16$
b $y^2 - 9$
c $9x^2 - 1$
d $16y^2 - 1$
e $\cos^2 \theta - 1$
f $\sin^2 \theta - 1$
g $4x^2 - 25y^2$
h $81x^2 - 36y^2$

3 Factorise the following expressions completely:

Hint: Remove the common factor first.

a $2x^2 - 32$
b $3y^2 - 27$
c $20x^2 - 5$
d $50y^2 - 200$
e $2t^3 - 450t$
f $2\cos^2 \theta - 2$

4 Factorise the following expressions:

4 b

a $3x^2 + x - 2$
b $2x^2 - 5x + 3$
c $7x^2 + 22x + 3$
d $4x^2 - 12x + 5$
e $10x^2 - 41x - 45$
f $8x^2 - 21x - 9$
g $8x^2 - 17x + 9$
h $6x^2 - 7x - 3$

5 Factorise the following expressions:

a $4x^2 - 10x + 6$
b $x^2 + 2xy - 8y^2$
c $x^2 + 5xy - 36y^2$
d $10x^2 - 18x - 4$
e $36x^2 - 33x + 6$
f $16x^2 - 100x + 150$
g $2x^2y - 7xy + 3y$
h $60x^2y - 55xy - 25y$

1.5 Solving Quadratic Equations

As in a quadratic expression, a quadratic equation in one unknown has the variable occurring at least once raised to the second power. The variable doesn't occur to any higher powers. Some examples of quadratic equations are $x^2 - 4 = 0$, $a^2 + 4a - 5 = 0$, $2t^2 - 16t + 36 = 0$, $p^2 + p = 2$.

Greek mathematicians solved algebraic problems like these using geometry. They could solve all quadratic equations that had real number solutions. See Book X of the 'Elements' of Euclid (450–380 BC).

Quadratic equations often occur in the solution of real-life problems, such as in echo sounding, calculating depths of wells and hardness testing.

Can all quadratic equations be solved? The main techniques used to solve quadratic equations are:

- factorising
- completing the square
- using the quadratic formula
- graphical methods.

Quadratic equations generally have two solutions, which can be distinct or repeated.

Factorising quadratic equations

Example 1

Solve $(x - 5)(x + 2) = 0$.

Solution

Notice that the left-hand side of this equation is a product of two factors. The result of multiplying these factors is zero. *If two quantities multiply to zero then one of them must be zero.*
Since $(x - 5)(x + 2) = 0$, then $(x - 5) = 0$ or $(x + 2) = 0$.
These linear equations can now be solved.

$$x - 5 = 0 \Rightarrow x = 5$$
$$\text{and } x + 2 = 0 \Rightarrow x = -2$$

The symbol $\Rightarrow$ means 'implies'.

Check that these are solutions by substituting them back into the original equation. Notice that both of these values of x are solutions; there are two solutions.

Example 2

Solve:

a $x^2 - 4x - 5 = 0$
b $2x^2 - 32 = 0$
c $x^2 - 3x = 0$

Solution

a First factorise the quadratic expression.

$$x^2 - 4x - 5 = 0$$
$$(x+1)(x-5) = 0$$
So $(x+1) = 0$ or $(x-5) = 0$
$$x = -1 \text{ or } x = 5$$

The coefficient of x^2 is 1. $(+1) + (-5) = -4$, $(+1) \times (-5) = -5$

Substitute both values of x separately into the original equation; $x = -1$ and $x = 5$ are its solutions.

b $2x^2 - 32 = 0$

$$2x^2 - 32 = 2(x^2 - 16)$$
$$= 2(x^2 - 4^2) = 2(x+4)(x-4)$$

So $2x^2 - 32 = 2(x+4)(x-4) = 0$

Recognise that $16 = 4^2$, and then use the difference of two squares.

Now there are three factors multiplying to give a zero result.

Since $2 \neq 0$, $(x+4) = 0$ or $(x-4) = 0$

So $x = -4$ or $x = 4$

Both solutions satisfy $2x^2 - 32 = 0$.

c $x^2 - 3x = x(x-3) = 0$

So $x = 0$ or $(x-3) = 0$

$x = 0$ or $x = 3$

Both solutions satisfy $x^2 - 3x = 0$.

Example 3

Solve the quadratic equation $12x^2 + 17x - 14 = 0$.

Solution

$$12x^2 + 17x - 14 = 0$$

In this example the coefficient of x^2 isn't 1, so try PAFF.

This particular quadratic expression was factorised in Example 3 of Section 1.4.

$$12x^2 + 17x - 14 = (12x - 7)(x + 2) = 0$$
So $(12x - 7) = 0$ or $(x+2) = 0$
$$x = \tfrac{7}{12} \text{ or } x = -2$$

Notice that one of the solutions, $\frac{7}{12}$, isn't an integer (whole number). Its fractional value is exact, but the decimal representation is recurring. Check this using a calculator.

Completing the square

Sometimes the quadratic expression cannot be factorised easily. The equation may then be solved using a technique called **completing the square**.

To complete the square we need to write the quadratic in the form $(x+a)^2 = b$, where a and b are real numbers. Then the value of x can be found by taking the square root of both sides of the equation. Writing the quadratic in this form requires some skill in algebraic manipulation.

Example 4

Solve the equation $x^2 - 6x - 5 = 0$.

Solution

Try factorisation. What happens? Notice that no pair of integers add to give -6 and multiply to give -5. Don't despair: complete the square. First rewrite the equation, separating the variables from the constant term.

We need the LHS to be a perfect square (we want to write it in the form $(x + a)^2$), so add 9 to both sides.

We can now factorise the LHS because $(-3) + (-3) = -6$ and $(-3) \times (-3) = 9$.

$$x^2 - 6x - 5 = 0$$

So $$x^2 - 6x = 5$$

$$x^2 - 6x + 9 = 5 + 9 = 14$$

So $$(x - 3)(x - 3) = 14$$

That is, $$(x - 3)^2 = 14$$

$$x - 3 = \pm\sqrt{14}$$

Recall that any positive square number has a positive square root and a negative square root.

The solutions are therefore $x = 3 \pm \sqrt{14}$.

Notice that the steps in the process of completing the square are:

Step ① Separate the constant term from the variable terms.
Step ② Add a value to each side of the equation to force one side to be a perfect square.

How did you know what value to add? There is a simple rule. Provided the coefficient of x^2 is 1, simply halve the coefficient of x and then square this value.

Example 5

Solve $x^2 - 3x - 5 = 0$.

Solution

First check that factorisation doesn't work easily.

$$x^2 - 3x - 5 = 0 \Rightarrow x^2 - 3x = 5$$ ◀ **① Separate the terms.**

The coefficient of x is -3. Half this is $-\frac{3}{2}$. Squaring that, we have $\frac{9}{4}$. So add $\frac{9}{4}$ to both sides of the equation.

$$x^2 - 3x + \tfrac{9}{4} = 5 + \tfrac{9}{4}$$ ◀ **② Force one side to be a perfect square.**

The left-hand side is now a perfect square, so we can factorise it.

$$(x - \tfrac{3}{2})^2 = 5 + \tfrac{9}{4} = \tfrac{29}{4}$$

Take the square root of both sides.

$$x - \frac{3}{2} = \pm\sqrt{\frac{29}{4}}$$

$$x = \frac{3}{2} \pm \frac{\sqrt{29}}{2} = \frac{3 \pm \sqrt{29}}{2}$$

Recall the properties of surds.

Notice that written in this form (a surd), we have exact solutions and not decimal approximations. The solutions have also been written concisely with a common denominator.

Remember that this technique only works when the coefficient of x^2 is 1. When it isn't, divide each term in the equation by the coefficient of x^2. This often creates equations with fractions as coefficients.

Example 6

Solve $3x^2 + 4x - 5 = 0$.

Solution

The coefficient of x^2 is 3, so divide each term by 3.

$$3x^2 + 4x - 5 = 0 \Rightarrow x^2 + \tfrac{4}{3}x - \tfrac{5}{3} = 0$$

Now the algorithm can be used as before.

$x^2 + \tfrac{4}{3}x = \tfrac{5}{3}$ ◀ ① **Separate the terms.**

Add $\tfrac{4}{9}$ to both sides of the equation (recall that this number is reached by halving the coefficient of x, and then squaring the result).

$x^2 + \tfrac{4}{3}x + \tfrac{4}{9} = \tfrac{5}{3} + \tfrac{4}{9}$ ◀ ② **Force one side to be a perfect square.**

$$(x + \tfrac{2}{3})^2 = \tfrac{19}{9}$$

$$x + \tfrac{2}{3} = \pm\sqrt{\frac{19}{9}} = \pm\frac{\sqrt{19}}{3}$$

$$x = \frac{-2 \pm \sqrt{19}}{3}$$

Check with a calculator that these values satisfy the original equation.

Sometimes the quadratic equation doesn't have to be solved. It may be sufficient to write it in the form of a perfect square. Suppose that $y = ax^2 + bx + c$ can be written in the form $y = a(x + p)^2 + q$, where a, b, c, p and q are all real numbers.

$$\begin{aligned} \text{Then } ax^2 + bx + c &= a(x + p)^2 + q \\ &= a(x^2 + 2px + p^2) + q \\ ax^2 + bx + c &= ax^2 + 2apx + ap^2 + q \end{aligned}$$

By comparing coefficients you should see a relationship between a, b, c and p, q. Compare the coefficients of x; that is, see how many 'x's there are on each side of the equation.

$$b = 2ap$$

Comparing the constant terms in the same way,

$$c = ap^2 + q$$

Since a, b and c are already known (directly from the quadratic) these two results can sometimes be used to establish p and q quickly.

Example 7

Express the following in the form $a(x + p)^2 + q$:

a $x^2 - 3x - 5$ **b** $-5x^2 - 2x + 3$

Solution

a Notice that $a = 1$, $b = -3$ and $c = -5$.
We require $x^2 - 3x - 5 = a(x + p)^2 + q$.
Since $a = 1$, this can be simplified to

$$\begin{aligned} x^2 - 3x - 5 &\equiv (x + p)^2 + q \\ &\equiv (x^2 + 2px + p^2) + q \\ &\equiv x^2 + 2px + p^2 + q \end{aligned}$$

The symbol $\equiv$ is used to show that these expressions are equivalent for all values of x.

Now comparing coefficients of x and constant terms,

$$-3 = 2p \quad \text{and} \quad -5 = p^2 + q$$

Then $p = -\frac{3}{2}$

and $q = -5 - p^2 = -5 - \frac{9}{4} = -\frac{29}{4}$

So $x^2 - 3x - 5 \equiv (x - \frac{3}{2})^2 - \frac{29}{4}$

Notice that when $x = \frac{3}{2}$, $(x - \frac{3}{2})^2 = 0$. This means the quadratic expression has a least value of $-\frac{29}{4}$

b Let $-5x^2 - 2x + 3 \equiv a(x + p)^2 + q$

$$\begin{aligned} &\equiv a(x^2 + 2px + p^2) + q \\ &\equiv ax^2 + 2apx + ap^2 + q \end{aligned}$$

Comparing coefficients of x^2, x and the constant terms,

$$-5 = a, -2 = 2ap \quad \text{and} \quad 3 = ap^2 + q$$

Since $a = -5$, $-2 = 2ap$ becomes $-2 = 2 \times (-5) \times p = -10p$
So $p = \frac{1}{5}$

$-5x^2 - 2x + 3 \equiv -5(x + \frac{1}{5})^2 + q$

Now $3 = ap^2 + q$

So $3 = -5(\frac{1}{5})^2 + q$

$q = 3 + \frac{5}{25} = 3 + \frac{1}{5} = \frac{16}{5}$

So $-5x^2 - 2x + 3 \equiv -5(x + \frac{1}{5})^2 + \frac{16}{5}$

Check this by multiplying out the bracket and collecting like terms.

Verify that $\frac{16}{5}$ is the maximum value of this expression.

The quadratic formula

By completing the square on the general quadratic expression $ax^2 + bx + c$, we can create a formula that can be used to solve quadratic equations simply by substituting values for a, b and c.
Suppose $ax^2 + bx + c \equiv 0$ for some real values of a, b and c.

Then $x^2 + \dfrac{bx}{a} + \dfrac{c}{a} = 0$.

Divide by a to make the coefficient of x^2 equal to 1.

Now complete the square on this expression in the same way as before.

$$x^2 + \frac{bx}{a} = -\frac{c}{a}$$ ◀ ① Separate the terms.

The value to add to both sides of the equation is found, as before, by halving the coefficient of the x term, and then squaring the result.

$$x^2 + \frac{bx}{a} + \left(\frac{b}{2a}\right)^2 = \left(\frac{b}{2a}\right)^2 - \frac{c}{a}$$ ◀ ② Force one side to be a perfect square.

Recall that the LHS is now a perfect square.

$$\left(x + \frac{b}{2a}\right)^2 = \left(\frac{b}{2a}\right)^2 - \frac{c}{a} = \frac{b^2}{4a^2} - \frac{c}{a}$$

$$\left(x + \frac{b}{2a}\right)^2 = \frac{b^2 - 4ac}{4a^2}$$

$$x + \frac{b}{2a} = \pm\frac{\sqrt{b^2 - 4ac}}{2a}$$

$$\boldsymbol{x = \frac{-b \pm \sqrt{b^2 - 4ac}}{2a}}$$ ◀ Learn this result.

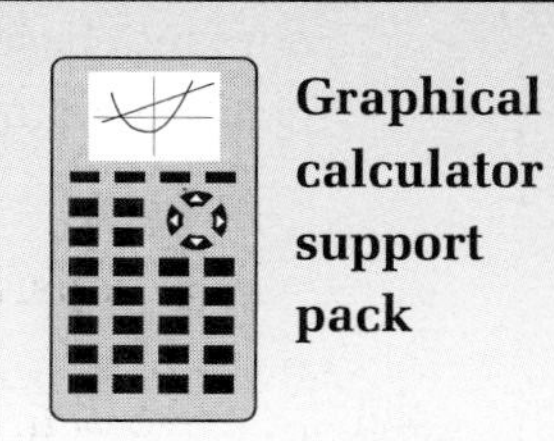

Once a, b and c have been identified, this formula can be used to solve quadratic equations.

Example 8

Solve $x - 7 = \frac{4}{x}$.

Solution

This may not at first appear to be a quadratic equation, but multiplying both sides by x gives $x(x - 7) = 4$. Notice how the denominator has multiplied the whole of the left-hand side of the equation. Now multiply $x(x - 7)$ out to give $x^2 - 7x = 4$. Moving the constant term, the original equation has been rearranged to the form for which the formula works.

$$x^2 - 7x - 4 = 0$$

Now, $a = 1$, $b = -7$ and $c = -4$.

$$x = \frac{-b \pm \sqrt{b^2 - 4ac}}{2a}$$

Always quote the formula.

$$x = \frac{7 \pm \sqrt{49 - 4 \times 1 \times (-4)}}{2 \times 1}$$

$$= \frac{7 \pm \sqrt{49 - (-16)}}{2} = \frac{7 \pm \sqrt{65}}{2}$$

So the equation $x - 7 = \frac{4}{x}$ has two distinct solutions,

$$x = \frac{7 + \sqrt{65}}{2} \quad \text{and} \quad x = \frac{7 - \sqrt{65}}{2}.$$

Evaluate these results using a calculator. What do you notice? Both answers are irrational so the calculator screen should give decimal expansions that do not recur. The numerical values correct to two decimal places are 7.53 and −0.53.

Example 9

It is proposed that a new tunnel be built under the English Channel. This tunnel will be for cars to drive through. The road will be built on a concrete base inside the circular tunnel.

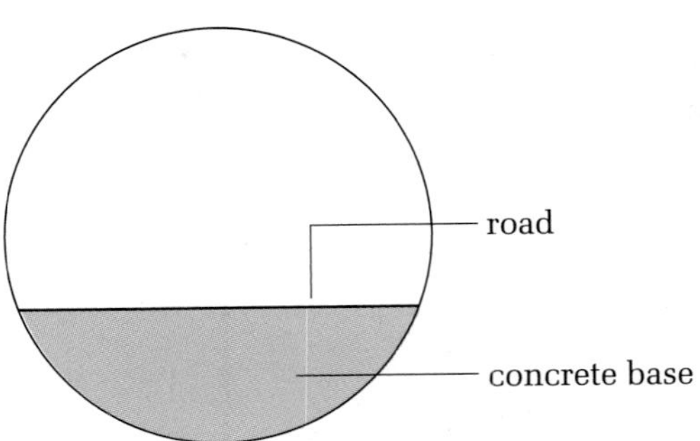

If the radius of the tunnel is 5.2 m and the width of the road surface is to be 9.2 m, what depth of concrete should be used?

Solution

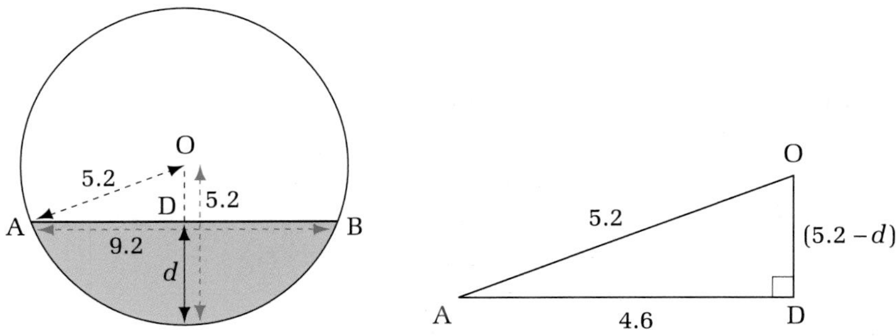

The first step is to redraw the diagram using the given measurements.

Notice that AD is half the width of the road surface, and that OD is $(5.2 - d)$ metres.

Let d metres be the depth of concrete. From the diagram identify the right-angled triangle with the road surface as base.

Using Pythagoras' theorem,

$$OA^2 = AD^2 + OD^2$$

$$5.2^2 = 4.6^2 + (5.2 - d)^2$$

$$5.2^2 = 4.6^2 + (5.2^2 - 10.4d + d^2)$$

$$\text{So } 0 = 4.6^2 - 10.4d + d^2$$

Multiply out the bracketed term.

Notice the 5.2^2 on both sides of the equation.

That is, $d^2 - 10.4d + 21.16 = 0$.

This is a quadratic equation in d where $a = 1$, $b = -10.4$ and $c = 21.16$. Now use the formula.

$$d = \frac{-b \pm \sqrt{b^2 - 4ac}}{2a}$$

$$= \frac{10.4 \pm \sqrt{(-10.4)^2 - 4 \times 1 \times 21.16}}{2}$$

$$= \frac{10.4 \pm \sqrt{23.52}}{2}$$

$$= 5.2 \pm 2.425 \text{ (3 d.p.)}$$

Remember not to reduce working to the required number of decimal places until the final solution is written.

Notice that there are two solutions. The first, 2.78 m, has the road in the lower half of the tunnel. The second, 7.63 m, has the road in the upper half of the tunnel.

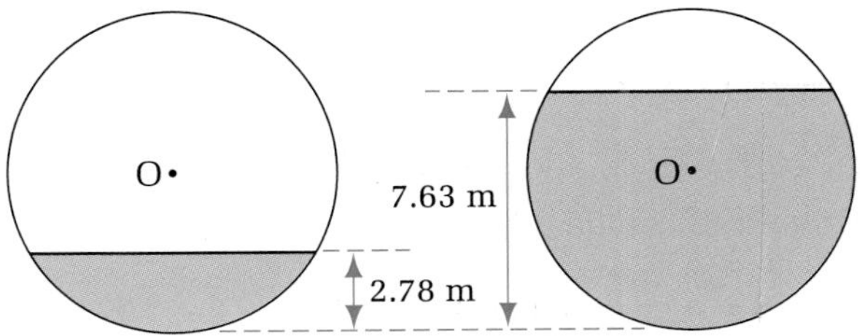

This example illustrates one use of the quadratic formula in a problem solving context.

Remember that although in many applications both solutions can be interpreted in the context of the problem, one solution will usually be preferable. Notice also that this quadratic equation had decimals as coefficients. The quadratic formula has given solutions that have been rounded, to give answers correct to three significant figures.

Graphical methods

A graphical calculator can be used to solve quadratic equations. This is also a good method to use if you simply want to check solutions from factorisation, completing the square or the quadratic formula.

Example 10

Using a graphical calculator, or graph plotting software on a computer, draw the graphs of the following.

a $y = x^2 - 4x - 5$ **b** $y = x^2 - 3x$

c $y = x^2 - 6x - 5$ **d** $y = 3x^2 + 4x - 5$

Using the trace facility, find the coordinates of the points of intersection with the x axis. Now compare these results with the results from Examples 2**a**, 2**c**, 4 and 6. What do you notice? You should find that the calculator gives either an exact answer or a decimal approximation to the solutions calculated by other methods. Remember that the accuracy of these solutions will depend upon your calculator. Many will not state irrational results exactly; instead a decimal is given to 8, 10 or 12 places.

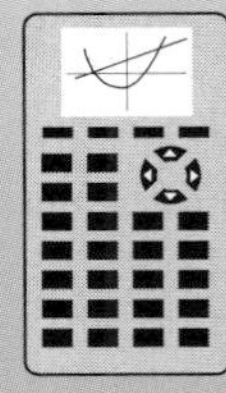

Trace
The TRACE facility on a graphical calculator allows a point to move along the last graph drawn, simultaneously showing either the x-coordinate or the y-coordinate of the point.

Notice that the graphs of these quadratic equations all have the same basic shape. This curve is known as a **parabola**, but can be transformed by changing the values of the coefficients a, b and c in the expression $ax^2 + bx + c$.

Notice also that all the graphs are symmetrical. Is this line of symmetry related to the coefficients a, b and c? Think back to the quadratic formula. This gives the solutions to the equation $ax^2 + bx + c = 0$ in a form that helps answer this question.

The equation $y = ax^2 + bx + c$ crosses the x-axis at $y = 0$.

The points of intersection with the x-axis are written as $(\frac{-b}{2a} \pm$ a square-root term, 0). This suggests that the **line of symmetry** for the quadratic is $x = -\frac{b}{2a}$.

What about the square-root term? What does $\sqrt{b^2 - 4ac}$ represent? The expression $b^2 - 4ac$ is known as the **discriminant**. It can be used to give an indication of how many times the graph will cross the x-axis, as follows.

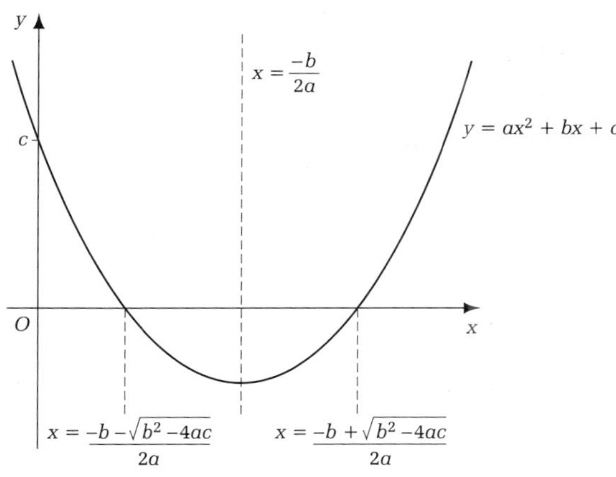

- If $b^2 - 4ac > 0$, it has two real square roots and $ax^2 + bx + c = 0$ has two distinct solutions: the graph will cross the x-axis twice – at $(\frac{-b + \sqrt{b^2-4ac}}{2a}, 0)$ and $(\frac{-b - \sqrt{b^2-4ac}}{2a}, 0)$.
- If $b^2 - 4ac = 0$, $ax^2 + bx + c = 0$ has one (repeated) solution: the graph will touch the x-axis at $(-\frac{b}{2a}, 0)$.
- If $b^2 - 4ac < 0$, $ax^2 + bx + c = 0$ has no (real) solutions: the graph will not cross the x-axis.

Example 11

Write down the equation of the line of symmetry of the graphs of the following quadratics, and predict the number of times the graph will cross the x-axis.

a $y = x^2 + x + 3$ **b** $y = x^2 + 5x + 6$ **c** $y = x^2 + 2x + 1$

Solution

a $y = x^2 + x + 3$

When $y = 0$ (on the x-axis), $x^2 + x + 3 = 0$, and $a = 1$, $b = 1$ and $c = 3$ in the quadratic formula.

The line of symmetry, $x = -\frac{b}{2a}$, is $x = -\frac{1}{2}$.

To check to see if (and how many times) the graph crosses the x-axis, check the discriminant.

$b^2 - 4ac = 1^2 - (4 \times 1 \times 3) = 1 - 12 = -11 < 0$, so the graph doesn't cross the x-axis.

Draw the graph of each quadratic.

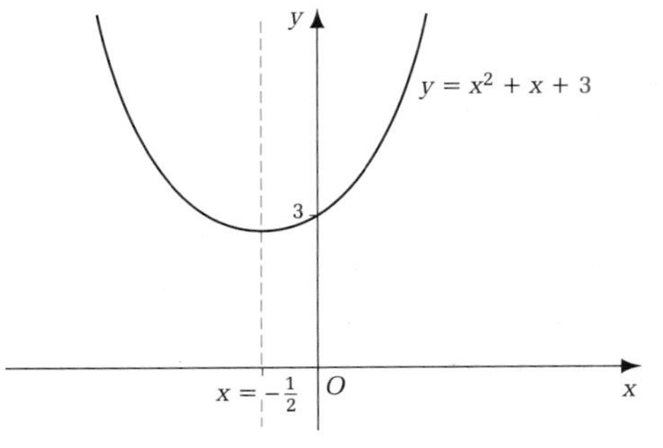

b $y = x^2 + 5x + 6$
When $y = 0$, $a = 1$, $b = 5$ and $c = 6$ in the quadratic formula.
The line of symmetry, $x = -\frac{b}{2a}$, is $x = -\frac{5}{2}$.
The discriminant $b^2 - 4ac = 5^2 - (4 \times 1 \times 6) = 25 - 24 = 1 > 0$, so the graph will cross the x-axis at two places.

Check that the graph cuts the x-axis at $x = -3$ and $x = -2$ using factorisation or the quadratic formula.

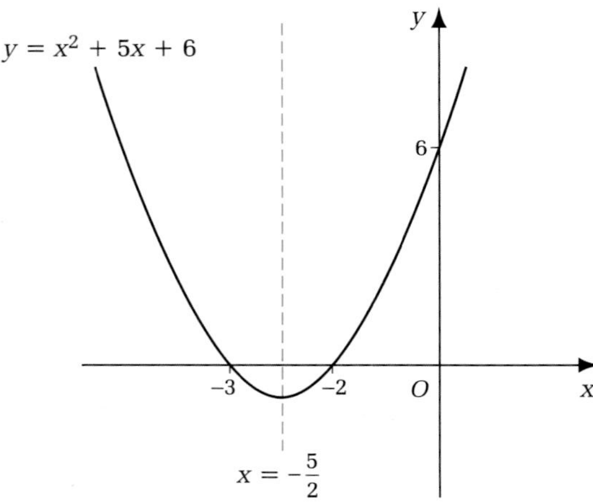

c $y = x^2 + 2x + 1$
Here $a = 1$, $b = 2$ and $c = 1$. The line of symmetry, $x = -\frac{b}{2a}$, is $x = -\frac{2}{2}$. That is, $x = -1$.
The discriminant $b^2 - 4ac = 2^2 - (4 \times 1 \times 1) = 4 - 4 = 0$, so the graph will touch the x-axis at one point. Check that $x^2 + 2x + 1 = 0$ when $x = -1$ by factorisation (so the graph touches at $(-1, 0)$).

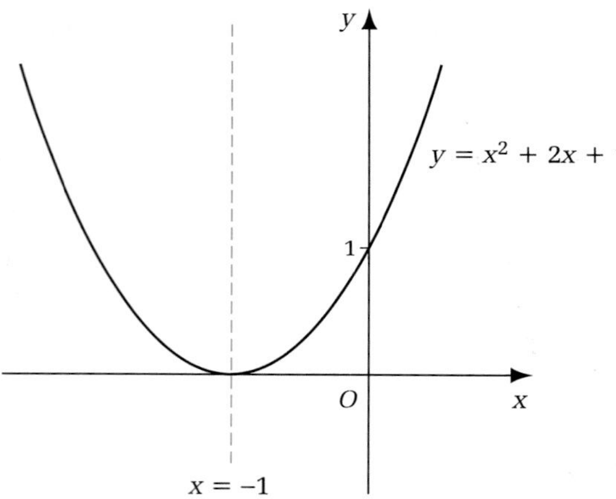

1.5 Solving Quadratic Equations

Exercise

Technique

1 Solve the following:

a $(x-3)(x+2)=0$
b $(x-3)(x-4)=0$
c $(x-1)(x+3)=0$
d $(x+5)(x+1)=0$
e $(2x+5)(2x+5)=0$
f $x(x+2)=0$
g $12(x+3)(2x+1)=0$
h $3(x-7)(3x+4)=0$

2 Solve, by factorising, the following equations:

a $x^2+5x+4=0$
b $x^2+2x-15=0$
c $x^2-6x+5=0$
d $x^2-x-6=0$
e $4x^2-19x+12=0$
f $9x^2+24x+16=0$

3 Solve, by completing the square, the following equations:

a $x^2-6x-16=0$
b $x^2+2x-8=0$
c $x^2-2x-3=0$
d $x^2-6x+1=0$
e $2x^2-2x-1=0$
f $-3x^2+8x+7=0$

4 Solve, using the quadratic formula, the following equations:

a $3x^2-2x-8=0$
b $3x^2+10x-8=0$
c $2x^2+x-4=0$
d $x^2-12x-5=0$
e $2x^2+15x+6=0$
f $3x^2-18x+10=0$

5 Solve the following equations. In each case check the solutions by using a graphical calculator to find the points of intersection between the quadratic and the x-axis:

a $8x^2-24x+6=0$
b $3x(x-4)+5=-6$
c $3(x^2-2)=2(9x-2)$
d $x^2+6x+4=0$
e $2x^2+6x+2=0$
f $\dfrac{x^2+3}{3x}=2$

6 Write the following expressions in the form $a(x+p)^2+q$:

a x^2-2x+3
b x^2+4x+1
c $-x^2+2x+2$
d $-x^2+8x-19$
e $-2x^2+5x-3$
f $2x^2-3x-2$

Contextual

1 The formula $h = ut - \frac{1}{2}gt^2$ gives the height h a body will reach after time t, when it is thrown vertically upwards with velocity u, where g is a constant. Calculate t when $g = 9.8$, $u = 16$ and $h = 6$. Why are there two answers?

2 What is the shaded area of the washer illustrated here, where the diameter of the washer is 4.2 cm and the diameter of the hole is 1.8 cm?

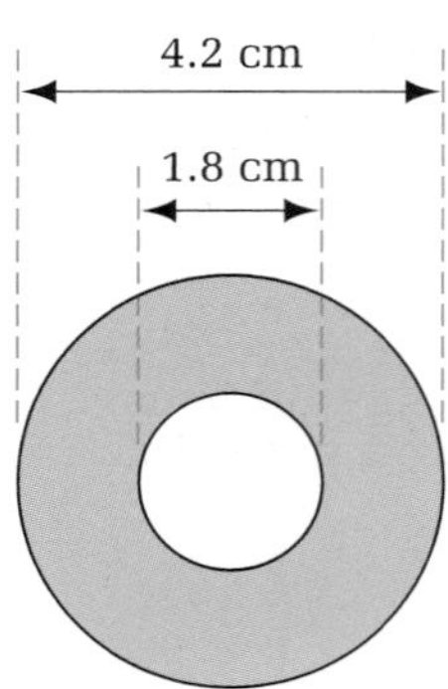

3 The sum of the first n natural numbers $(1 + 2 + 3 + \ldots + n)$ is given by the formula $S = \frac{1}{2}n(n + 1)$. If the sum of the numbers is 78, how many numbers have been added?

4 The formula $\frac{1}{2}n(n - 3)$ defines the number of diagonals in a polygon where n is the number of sides. A chef cuts a cake along its 65 diagonals. How many sides does the cake have?

5 By completing the square, find the minimum value of $3x^2 - 12x + 13$.

6 How deep is the water in this oil drum, given that the radius is 30 cm and AC is 20 cm?

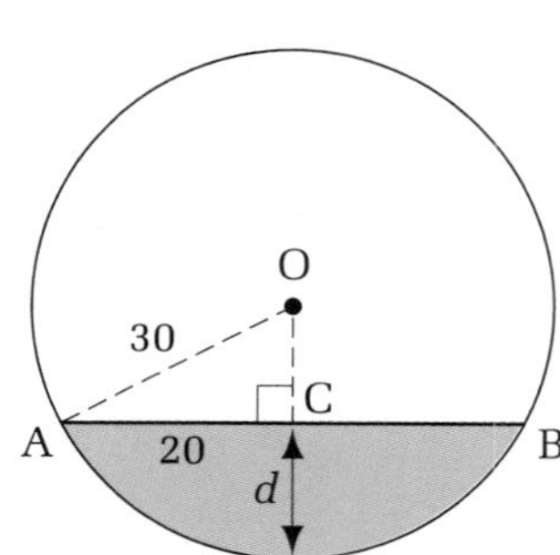

Hint: Use Pythagoras' theorem in triangle OCA, and let $OC = 30 - d$.

1.6 Simultaneous Equations

Polynomial equations can be graphed. If two or more polynomials are graphed on the same axes then the graphs may cross. The coordinates of the point (or points) where the graphs cross satisfy both polynomial equations at the same time; that is, simultaneously.

Simultaneous linear equations

Linear equations may be put in the form $y = a_1x + a_0$ where a_1 and a_0 are real numbers. The highest power of the variable x is 1, so they are of degree 1. When graphed, these equations produce straight lines, which is why they are called linear.

$x + y = 3$ is linear and can be written as $y = -x + 3$.

A system of two linear equations can sometimes be solved simultaneously, using:

- substitution
- elimination
- graphical methods.

Two equations can be solved simultaneously, if a solution (or solutions) can be found that satisfies both equations.

Example 1

Solve the equations $x + 2y = 7$ and $2x + 3y = 10$ simultaneously.

Solution

1. Using the **substitution** technique gives a solution as follows.

$x + 2y = 7$ call this equation [1]

$2x + 3y = 10$ call this equation [2]

Make x the subject of equation [1].

$x = 7 - 2y$

◀ ① **Make one variable (letter) the subject of one of the equations.**

That is, write the equation in the form $x = \ldots$ or $y = \ldots$

Substitute for x in equation [2]. ◀ ② **Substitute.**

$2x + 3y = 10$, so $2(7 - 2y) + 3y = 10$ call this equation [3]

Equation [3] now has only one variable (letter). Solve this (find the variable) by multiplying out the bracket and collecting like terms.

$14 - 4y + 3y = 10$ ◀ ③ **Solve the new equation.**

$14 - y = 10$

$14 - 10 = y$

$4 = y$

Substitute this value of y back into equation [1].

$x = 7 - 2y$

$x = 7 - (2 \times 4) = 7 - 8$

$x = -1$

◀ ④ **Substitute this value into the first equation to find the value of the other variable.**

The values of x and y that simultaneously satisfy both equations are $x = -1$ and $y = 4$. How can we check this? Substitute the values back into the original equations.

$-1 + (2 \times 4) = 7$ and $(2 \times -1) + (3 \times 4) = 10$

◀ ⑤ Check by substituting the values back into the original equations.

Since both of these numeric equations are valid, $x = -1$ and $y = 4$ are the simultaneous solutions to $x + 2y = 7$ and $2x + 3y = 10$.

2. Using the **elimination** technique gives a solution of the following form.

$x + 2y = 7$ call this equation [1]

$2x + 3y = 10$ call this equation [2]

We want to make the coefficient of x the same in each equation. Multiplying equation [1] by 2,

◀ ① Multiply each equation by a value that will make the coefficient of one of the variables the same in both equations.

$2x + 4y = 14$ call this equation [3]

Notice that x now has a coefficient of 2, the same as in equation [2]. We can eliminate the terms in the x variable from equations [2] and [3] by subtracting corresponding terms in these equations.

$2x + 4y = 14$

$2x + 3y = 10$

◀ ② Combine the new equations to eliminate the variable with the same coefficient (usually by subtraction), and solve the resulting equation.

Taking each term separately, $2x - 2x = 0$ (so the new combined equation has no x term), $4y - 3y = y$ (so the new combined equation simply has y on the left-hand side), and $14 - 10 = 4$ (so the new combined equation simply has 4 on the right-hand side).

So $y = 4$.

Why were the equations subtracted? We have made the number of 'x's the same, and any number minus itself always gives zero. So subtracting the equation eliminates the x terms from the calculation.

Now substitute $y = 4$ back into one of the original equations to find x.

◀ ③ Substitute this into one of the original equations to find the value of the other variable.

$$x + (2 \times 4) = 7$$

$$x + 8 = 7$$

$$x = -1$$

As before, $x = -1$ and $y = 4$ are solutions.

◀ ④ Check by substituting both variables in the original equations.

We could have eliminated y instead of x in the first step, but both equations would have required multiplication because the coefficient of y in equation [1] is 2 and the coefficient in equation [2] is 3.

Equation [1] multiplied by 3 gives $3x + 6y = 21$

Equation [2] multiplied by 2 gives $4x + 6y = 20$

The coefficients of y are now the same, so that term could be eliminated by subtracting one equation from the other.

Solve these equations simultaneously and show that you get the same solution.

3. Using a **graphical method**, on the same axes draw the graphs of $x + 2y = 7$ and $2x + 3y = 10$. Notice that the two lines cross. The point where they cross is on both lines, and so satisfies both equations. Using a graphical calculator the 'trace' function can be used to find the coordinates of the point of intersection. In this example it is $(-1, 4)$, as before.

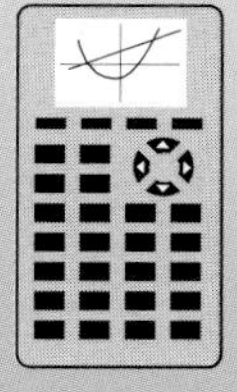

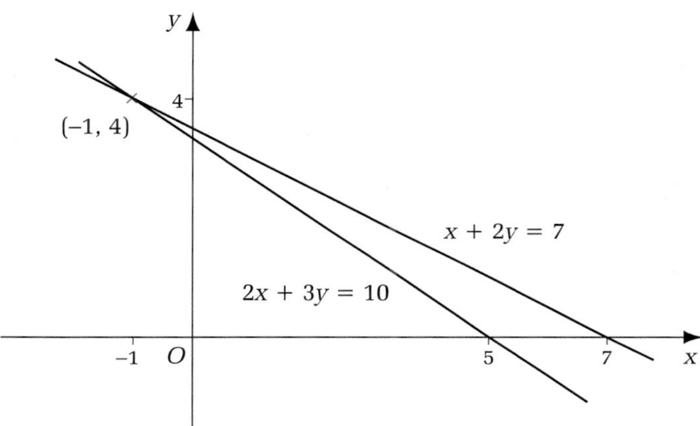

The graphical technique is a useful tool for checking the algebraic methods.

Simultaneous equations: linear and non-linear

A non-linear equation is a polynomial equation of degree 2 or higher. These can be solved using the same techniques as for linear equations. However, there is usually more than one solution.

Example 2

Solve the simultaneous equations $x - y + 3 = 0$ and $x^2 + y^2 = 29$.

Solution

Using the substitution technique, make y the subject in the first equation.

◀ ① Make one variable (letter) the subject of one of the equations.

$$x - y + 3 = 0 \Rightarrow y = x + 3$$

Now substitute for y in the second equation.

$$x^2 + (x + 3)^2 = 29$$
$$x^2 + (x^2 + 6x + 9) = 29$$
$$2x^2 + 6x - 20 = 0$$
$$2(x^2 + 3x - 10) = 0$$

◀ ② **Substitute this result into the second equation.**

Factorising the quadratic,

◀ ③ **Solve the new equation in one variable.**

$2(x + 5)(x - 2) = 0$

Since $2 \neq 0$ then $(x + 5) = 0$ or $(x - 2) = 0$.

Therefore, $x = -5$ or $x = 2$.

Notice that there are two solutions for x. Substitute each of these into the equation where y is the subject.

$y = x + 3$

$y = -5 + 3$ or $y = 2 + 3$

$y = -2$ or $y = 5$

◀ ④ **Substitute the new-found values of x into the first equation.**

So there are two distinct solutions: $x = -5$, $y = -2$ and $x = 2$, $y = 5$. These can be written in coordinate form as $(-5, -2)$ and $(2, 5)$. Check these solutions graphically.

If you are using a graphical calculator it may not draw $x^2 + y^2 = 29$. Instead, rearrange the equation to make y the subject.

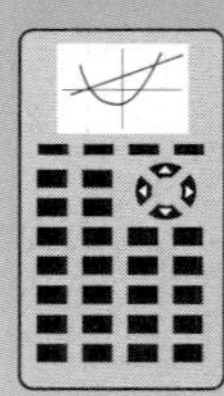

$$x^2 + y^2 = 29 \Rightarrow y^2 = 29 - x^2 \Rightarrow y = \pm\sqrt{29 - x^2}$$

If your calculator produces an ellipse on screen you may need to choose a more appropriate scale to make the shape circular.

If you 'overlap' $y = +\sqrt{29 - x^2}$ and $y = -\sqrt{29 - x^2}$, your calculator should produce a circle, centred on the origin. Set the range as $x_{min} = -6$, $x_{max} = 6$, $y_{min} = -6$ and $y_{max} = 6$, and use the trace function to find the points of intersection with the line $y = x + 3$. What do you notice about the solutions? The straight line crosses the circle at the points $(-5, -2)$ and $(2, 5)$.

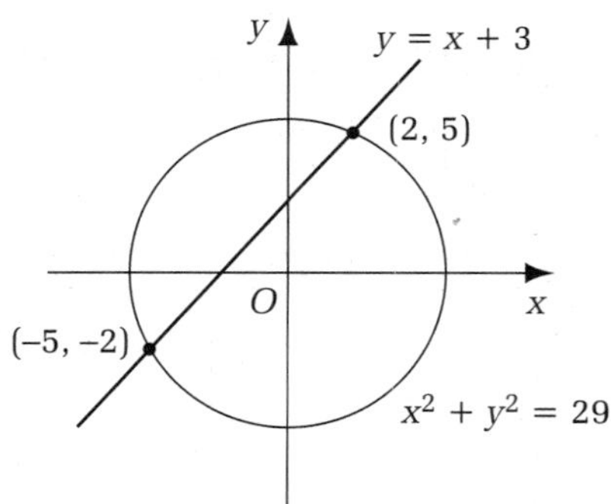

1.6 Simultaneous Equations
Exercise
Technique

1 Solve the following pairs of linear simultaneous equations:

a $2x + y = 8$ and $3x + 2y = 14$
b $x + 3y = 11$ and $5x + y = 13$
c $x + 2y = 13$ and $4x - 5y = -13$
d $3x + y = 11$ and $2y - 5x = 11$
e $2x + 3y = 7$ and $3x - y = -6$
f $4x - y = -0.5$ and $3x + 2y = -4.5$

2 Solve the following pairs of simultaneous equations:

a $y = 2(x - 2)$ and $y = x^2 - 3x + 2$
b $y = x^2 - 2x - 1$ and $y = x - 3$
c $y - 5x = 2$ and $y = x^2 + 5x - 2$
d $y = 15 - x$ and $y = x^2 - 2x + 3$
e $x - y = 2$ and $x^2 + y^2 = 34$
f $x - y = 3$ and $x^2 + xy + 2y^2 = 22$

3 Solve the following pairs of simultaneous equations:

a $70 - T = 7a$ and $T - 40 = 5a$
b $\frac{1}{3}(2x + y) = 4$ and $\frac{1}{5}(13x - 4y) = 3$
c $2y - 2x + 1 = 0$ and $x^2 - xy + 2y^2 = 8$
d $2x = 2y - 9$ and $y = \frac{8}{x}$

Contextual

1 The graph $y = x^2 + 2x - 3$ crosses the line $y = 4x$ at the points A and B. Find the coordinates of the points.

2 For a football match, the attendance was 44,000 people: x people paid £30, y people paid £20 and the total receipts for the game came to £1.2 million. How many people paid for the higher price tickets?

3 Four CDs and three tapes cost £126. Two CDs and five tapes cost £112. Find the individual costs of a CD and a tape.

4 Melanie's straight line passes through the points (2, 7) and (5, 13). Using the general equation for a straight line, $y = mx + c$, find m and c.

5 Three years from now, Callum will be twice as old as Lydia was five years ago. At the moment, half their combined ages is 16. Find their ages.

Consolidation

Exercise A

1 Diane throws a tennis ball vertically upwards. Given the formula

$$h = ut + \tfrac{1}{2}gt^2$$

where h is the height, u is the initial velocity of the ball and g is the gravitational acceleration, calculate the time for the ball to reach a 6 m height when $u = 14\text{ m s}^{-1}$ and $g = -9.8\text{ m s}^{-2}$.

2 The diagram shows the graphs of $y = x^2 - 4x$ and $y + x = 10$, which cross at A and B. Find the coordinates of A and B.

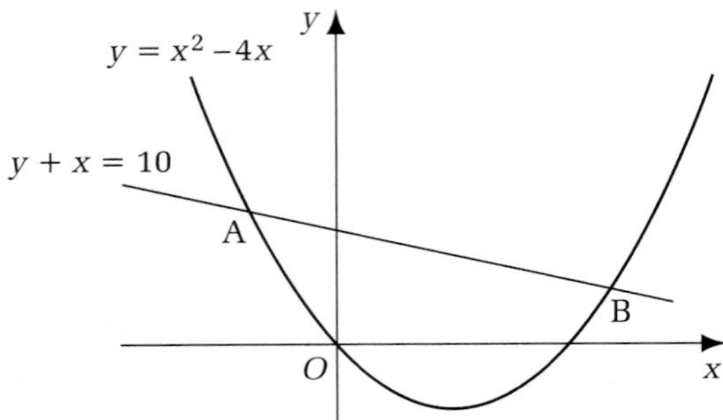

3 An opera is attended by 240 people: x people paid £31, y people paid £16, and the box office took in £5595.

a Form two equations using this information.

b Solve them to find out how many people paid £31.

4 A cement company supplies cement for 1200 m of underground concrete tunnels. Show that the area of the cross-section of the tunnel shown is $\pi(R - r)(R + r)$. If $R = 1$ m and $r = 0.95$ m, find the volume of concrete mix needed to make the tunnel in terms of π.

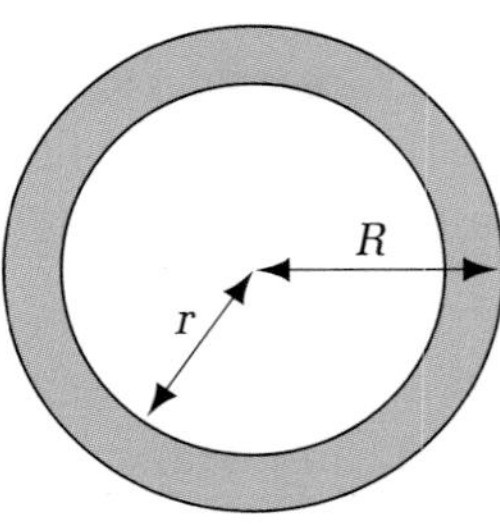

5 A ball is kicked, and just lands on a roof 5 m high. Using some basic knowledge to find the angle it was kicked at, θ, Ahmed correctly comes up with the formula $2 = 4\tan\theta - (1 + \tan^2\theta)$. Solve this equation to find the angle the ball was kicked at.

6 A uniform solid hemisphere is at rest. Kate looks at the forces involved and deduces that $\frac{1}{4}N_1 - N_2 = 0$ and $N_1 + \frac{1}{2}N_2 - 99 = 0$. Use her equations to find N_1 and N_2.

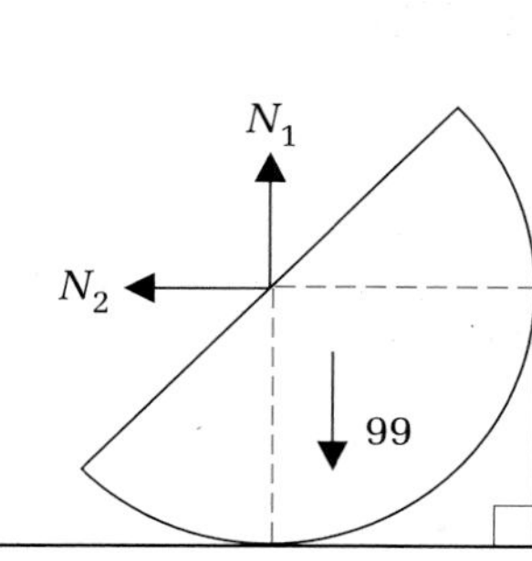

7 Show that the elimination of x from the simultaneous equations $x - 2y = 1$ and $3xy - y^2 = 8$ produces the equation $5y^2 + 3y - 8 = 0$. Solve this quadratic equation and hence find the pairs (x, y) for which the simultaneous equations are satisfied.

(*ULEAC*)

Exercise B

1 Julie throws a cricket ball vertically upwards. Given the formula

$$h = ut + \tfrac{1}{2}gt^2$$

where h is the height, u is the initial velocity of the ball and g is the gravitational acceleration, calculate the time for the ball to reach a height of 13 m when $u = 18\ \text{m s}^{-1}$ and $g = -9.8\ \text{m s}^{-2}$.

2 The graphs $y = x^2 - 2x - 3$ and $y + 3x + 1 = 0$ cross at A and B. Find the coordinates of A and B.

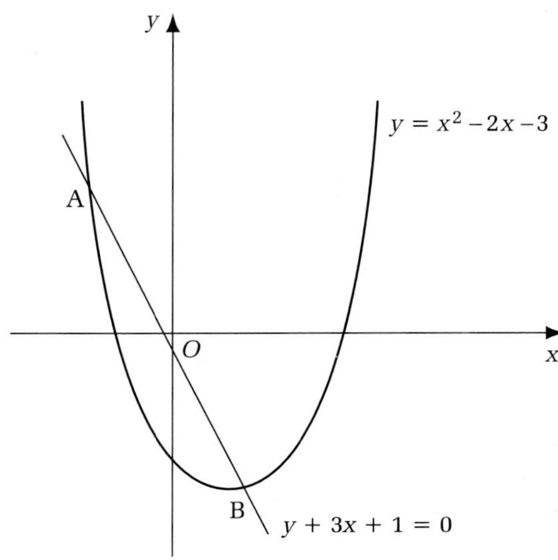

3 A 'Science Fiction mania-day' is attended by 600 people: x people pay £22 at the door, y people pay £17 for tickets in advance, and the organisers took a total of £11,400.

a Form two equations using this information.
b How many paid at the door and how many bought tickets in advance?

4 A plastics company supply 800 m of underground cable tubing. Show that the area of the cross-section is $\pi(R-r)(R+r)$. If $R = 5.2$ cm and $r = 4.8$ cm, find the volume of plastic needed to make the tubing.

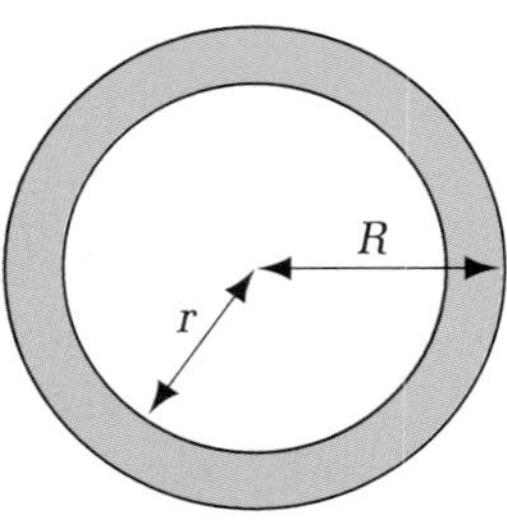

5 Elaine hits a golf ball over a tree. Using some basic knowledge to find the angle at which the ball was initially hit, her caddy correctly comes up with the formula $5 = 5\tan\theta - (1 + \tan^2\theta)$. Solve the equation to find what the angle might be.

6 The sketch shows the curve with equation $y = 2 - 6x - 3x^2$, and its axis of symmetry, $x = -1$.

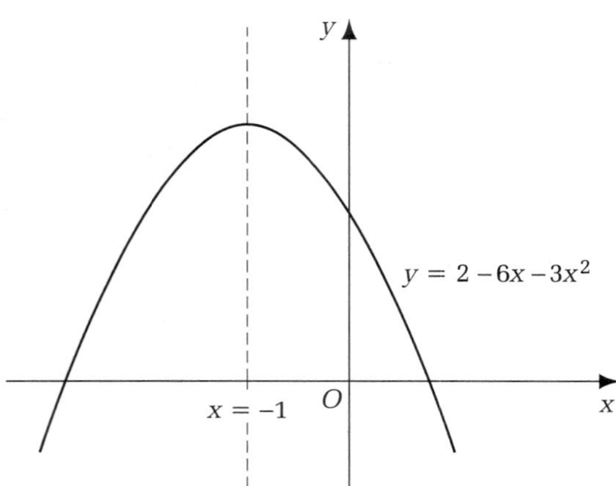

a Give the coordinates of the vertex and the value of y when $x = 0$.
b Find the values of the constants a and b such that $2 - 6x - 3x^2 = a(x+1)^2 + b$.

(OCSEB)

7 Solve the following quadratic equations:

a $x^{\frac{2}{3}} - 5x^{\frac{1}{3}} + 4 = 0$
b $2(2^x)^2 - 3(2^x) + 1 = 0$

Hint: In **a** put $y = x^{\frac{1}{3}}$ and in **b** put $y = 2^x$.

Applications and Activities

1 Complete the square for the following six quadratics:

a $y = x^2 - 6x - 16$

b $y = x^2 + 2x - 8$

c $y = x^2 - 2x - 3$

d $y = 2x^2 - 2x - 1$

e $y = x^2 - 6x + 1$

f $y = -3x^2 + 8x + 7$

2 Now draw their graphs using graph paper or a graphical calculator. Look at the coordinates of the bottom (or top) of your curve. What do you notice when you compare these coordinates to the equation in its 'complete the square' form?

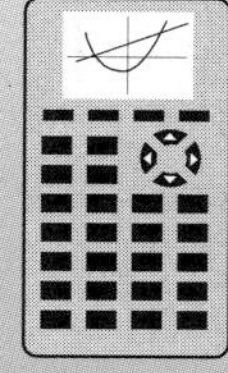

Summary

- Surds are irrational numbers containing a square root, and have the following properties:

$$\sqrt{ab} = \sqrt{a} \times \sqrt{b}$$

$$\sqrt{\frac{a}{b}} = \frac{\sqrt{a}}{\sqrt{b}}$$

$$a\sqrt{b} + c\sqrt{b} = (a + c)\sqrt{b}$$

$$a\sqrt{b} - c\sqrt{b} = (a - c)\sqrt{b}$$

- To rationalise a surd denominator, multiply by the conjugate:

$$\frac{1}{a + \sqrt{b}} = \frac{1}{a + \sqrt{b}} \times \frac{a - \sqrt{b}}{a - \sqrt{b}} = \frac{a - \sqrt{b}}{a^2 - b}$$

- The properties of indices are:

$$a^p \times a^q = a^{p+q}$$

$$(a^p)^q = a^{p \times q}$$

$$a^p \div a^q = a^{p-q}$$

$$a^0 = 1 \text{ provided } a \neq 0$$

$$a^{-p} = \frac{1}{a^p}$$

$$a^{\frac{1}{p}} = \sqrt[p]{a}$$

$$a^{\frac{p}{q}} = \sqrt[q]{a^p} = (a^{\frac{1}{q}})^p$$

- An equation in the form $y = a_n x^n + a_{n-1} x^{n-1} + \ldots + a_1 x + a_0$, is a **polynomial equation**.
- An equation of the form $y = ax + b$ has degree (or order) 1 and is called a **linear equation**.
- A polynomial equation of degree (or order) 2 is called a **quadratic equation** and is of the form $y = ax^2 + bx + c$;
- In $ax^2 + bx + c$, the **coefficient** of x is b, and c is the **constant** term.
- When factorising, common factors are extracted; $ax + bx = x(a + b)$.
- A **difference of two squares** (square minus a square) is factorised according to the rule

$$\boldsymbol{a^2 - b^2 = (a - b)(a + b)}$$

- Complete the square when factorising by adding the square of half the coefficient of x. By comparing coefficients, you can then write a quadratic in the form $a(x + p)^2 + q$.
- The formula for solving $ax^2 + bx + c = 0$ is

$$\boldsymbol{x = \frac{-b \pm \sqrt{b^2 - 4ac}}{2a}}$$

- The **discriminant**, $b^2 - 4ac$, informs you of the behaviour of the graph of the quadratic.
- Simultaneous equations can be solved by substitution, elimination and graphical methods.

2 Coordinate Geometry

What you need to know

- How to change the subject of an equation.
- How to use Pythagoras' theorem; $a^2 + b^2 = c^2$.
- How to expand $(a + b)^2$.
- How to expand $(a - b)^2$.

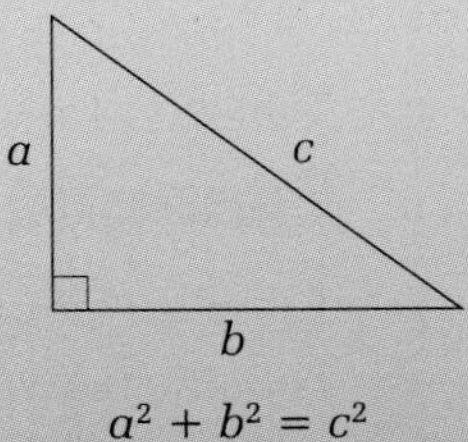

$a^2 + b^2 = c^2$

Review

1 Make y the subject of the following equations:

a $y - x = 7$

b $y + x + 6 = 11$

c $y + 4 = 2(x + 3)$

d $y - 5 = 3(x - 2)$

e $\dfrac{y + 2}{x - 3} = 4$

f $\dfrac{y - 3}{x + 2} = \frac{1}{2}$

2 For each triangle **a–c**, find the length of the lettered side without using a calculator.

a

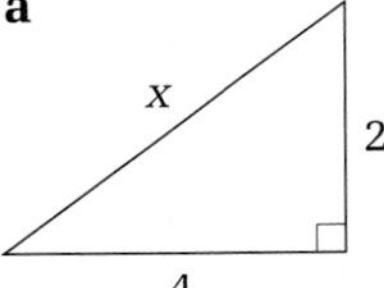

b

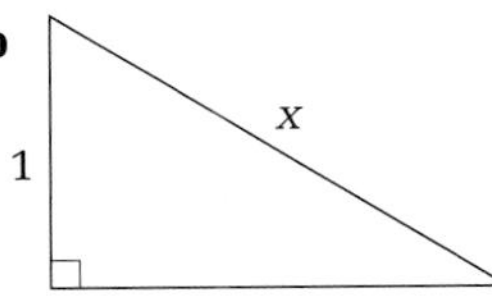

c

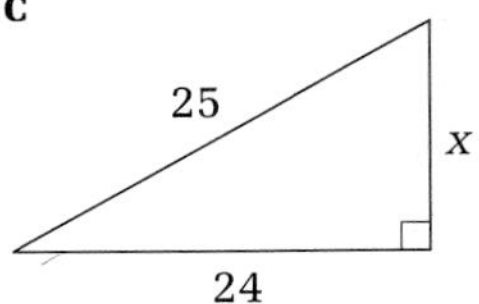

3 Expand the following expressions:

a $(x + 2)^2$

b $(x + 3)^2$

c $(x + 5)^2$

d $(a + b)^2$

e $(2x + 1)^2$

f $(3x + 2)^2$

4 Expand the following expressions:

a $(x - 3)^2$

b $(x - 1)^2$

c $(a - b)^2$

d $(3x - 2)^2$

e $(2x - 3)^2$

f $(5x - 1)^2$

2.1 Coordinate Geometry

Coordinate geometry is the study of straight lines and curves using algebraic methods. The **Cartesian coordinate system** (named after Descartes) is one where axes are drawn perpendicular to each other and the same scale is chosen on each axis. If two points are plotted on this set of axes they can always be joined by a single straight line.

René Descartes (1596–1650)
Descartes linked geometry and algebra. In his work *Discours de la Méthode* (1637) he explained the principles of analytic geometry.

Pierre de Fermat (1601–1665)
Fermat also worked out the method for analytic geometry and published his own work in 1679.

Example 1

If A is the point (1, 2) and B is the point (7, 10) what is the shortest distance between them?

Solution

The shortest distance between the points is the length of the straight line joining them. By drawing this line, and then creating a right-angled triangle, Pythagoras' theorem can be applied.

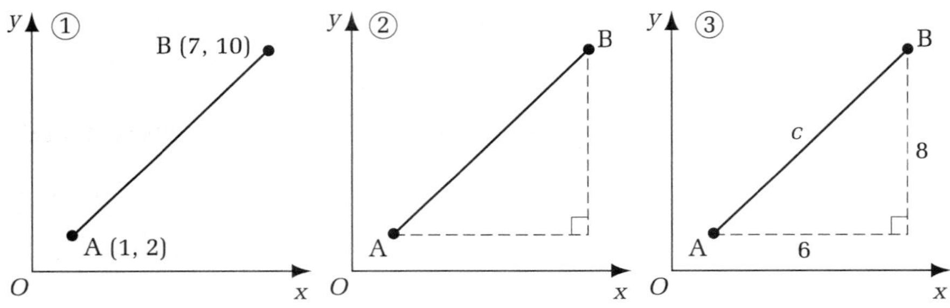

Step ① Join A and B.
Step ② Draw lines parallel to the axes from A and B to create a right-angled triangle.
Step ③ Use the coordinates of A and B to find the lengths of the shorter sides.
Step ④ State Pythagoras' theorem, and use it to find c, the length of the line joining A and B.

$$\begin{aligned} c^2 &= a^2 + b^2 \\ &= 6^2 + 8^2 \\ &= 36 + 64 = 100 \end{aligned}$$

So $c = \sqrt{100}$

$c = 10$

Notice that a crucial step is to find the lengths of the shorter sides from the coordinates of A and B. This is done by finding the difference between the

x-coordinates of A and B, and the difference between the y-coordinates of A and B. So in Example 1, for A (1, 2) and B (7, 10),

$$\begin{aligned}\text{length parallel to } x\text{-axis} &= x\text{-coordinate of B} - x\text{-coordinate of A}\\ &= 7 - 1 = 6\\ \text{length parallel to } y\text{-axis} &= y\text{-coordinate of B} - y\text{-coordinate of A}\\ &= 10 - 2 = 8\end{aligned}$$

So we found the shortest distance between A (1, 2) and B (7, 10) by using

$$c = \sqrt{a^2 + b^2} = \sqrt{(7-1)^2 + (10-2)^2}$$

◀ **Check this using your calculator.**

In general the distance between two points A and B with coordinates (x_1, y_1) and (x_2, y_2) respectively is given by

$$\boldsymbol{AB = \sqrt{(x_2 - x_1)^2 + (y_2 - y_1)^2}}$$

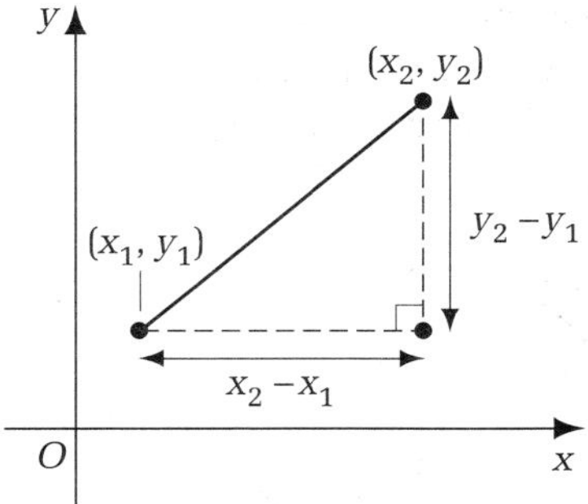

This process is still valid when $x_2 - x_1$ and $y_2 - y_1$ are negative.

◀ Learn this result.

Example 2

Find the distance between the following pairs of points:

a A (2, 7) and B (1, 9)
b C (−3, 7) and D (−2, −1)
c E (1, −2) and F (t, t^2).

Solution

a Distance AB $= \sqrt{(1-2)^2 + (9-7)^2}$
$= \sqrt{(-1)^2 + 2^2} = \sqrt{1+4}$
$= \sqrt{5}$

Remember that you can leave the answer in surd form.

b Distance CD $= \sqrt{[(-2) - (-3)]^2 + [(-1) - 7]^2}$
$= \sqrt{(-2+3)^2 + (-1-7)^2}$
$= \sqrt{1^2 + (-8)^2} = \sqrt{1+64}$
$= \sqrt{65}$

c Distance EF $= \sqrt{(t-1)^2 + [t^2 - (-2)]^2}$

$= \sqrt{(t-1)^2 + (t^2+2)^2}$

$= \sqrt{t^2 - 2t + 1 + t^4 + 4t^2 + 4}$

$= \sqrt{t^4 + 5t^2 - 2t + 5}$

Expand each bracket inside the square root.

Collect like terms.

The formula for the distance between two points can be extended into three dimensions (3D). In the Cartesian system there would now be three axes (x, y and z) and points would have three coordinates, (x, y, z). Consider the points A (x_1, y_1, z_1) and B (x_2, y_2, z_2). Draw a sketch to show these points in 3D space. What is the distance between A and B now?

The x, y and z coordinate axes are also called Ox, Oy and Oz.

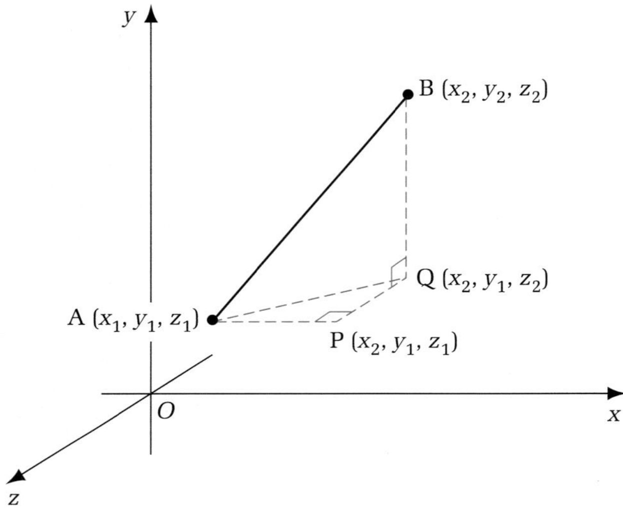

Axes x, y and z are perpendicular. In this view the z-axis is drawn coming 'out of' the page.

In mechanics it is more usual to make the z-axis vertical.

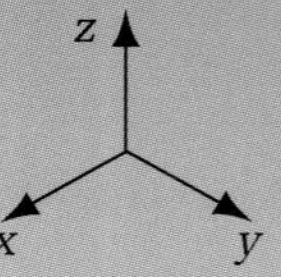

Construct two triangles as indicated.

By Pythagoras' theorem.

In ΔAPQ, $(AQ)^2 = (AP)^2 + (PQ)^2$ call this equation [1]

In ΔAQB, $(AB)^2 = (AQ)^2 + (BQ)^2$ call this equation [2]

Substitute for $(AQ)^2$ from equation [1] into equation [2]

$$(AB)^2 = (AP)^2 + (PQ)^2 + (BQ)^2$$

But $AP = x_2 - x_1$, $BQ = y_2 - y_1$ and $PQ = z_2 - z_1$

so $(AB)^2 = (x_2 - x_1)^2 + (y_2 - y_1)^2 + (z_2 - z_1)^2$

The distance $AB = \sqrt{(x_2 - x_1)^2 + (y_2 - y_1)^2 + (z_2 - z_1)^2}$

This result is still true if $x_2 - x_1$, $y_2 - y_1$ or $z_2 - z_1$ is negative.

Example 3

An infra-red alarm detector placed in the corner of the grand hall, at P (0, 12, 5), has a range of 14 m. Will it be able to detect a burglar entering the room at Q (4, 0, 0)?

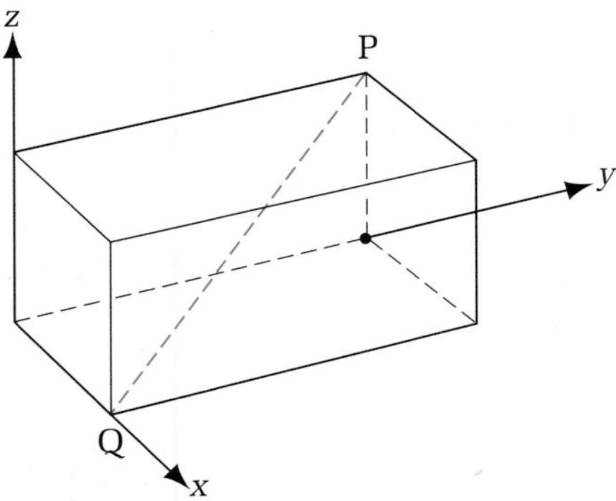

Solution

The detector will be able to detect a burglar if the distance between P and Q is less than 14 m.

$$\text{Distance PQ} = \sqrt{(0-4)^2 + (12-0)^2 + (5-0)^2}$$

$$= \sqrt{(-4)^2 + 12^2 + 5^2}$$

$$= \sqrt{16 + 144 + 25} = \sqrt{185}$$

$$\text{Distance PQ} = 13.6\text{ m}$$

Since this is within the 14 m range the burglar will be detected.

The gradient of a line joining two points

The gradient of a line is a measure of its steepness. It is given by the ratio of the change in the y-coordinate to the change in the x-coordinate. Gradients can be positive, zero or negative.

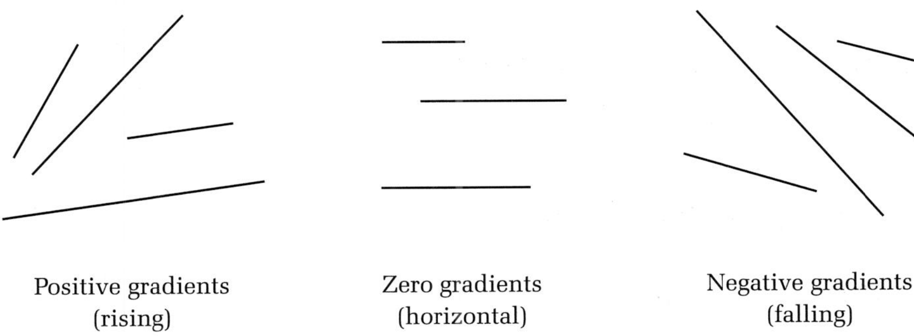

Consider more closely some positive gradients. The gradient of line A is 1. Notice how it makes an angle of 45° with the x-axis. The gradient of lines

B and C are greater than 1. These lines are steeper than line A. The gradients of lines D and E are less than 1, but bigger than 0. Which line has the smallest gradient? The gradient of line E is smallest, because it is closest to the horizontal.

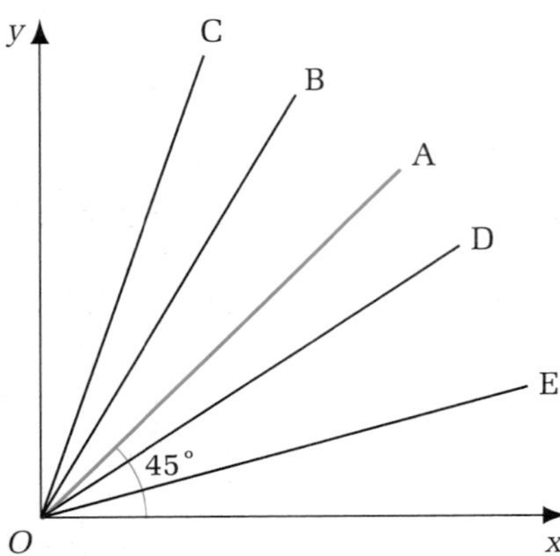

The gradient can be calculated algebraically using the rule

$$\text{gradient} = \frac{\text{change in } y\text{-coordinate}}{\text{change in } x\text{-coordinate}}$$

An alternative is to think of the gradient as the tangent of the angle between the line and the x-axis.

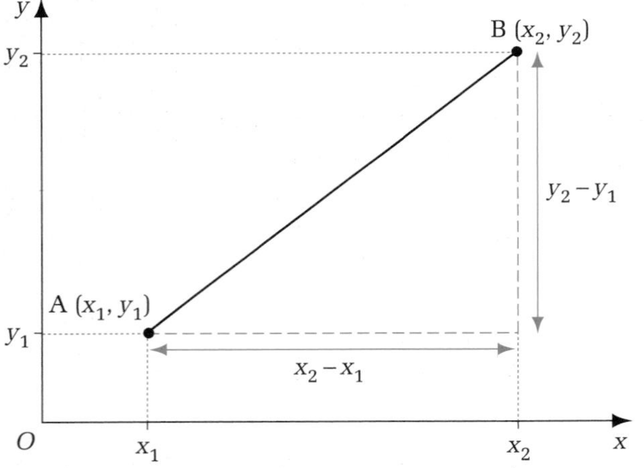

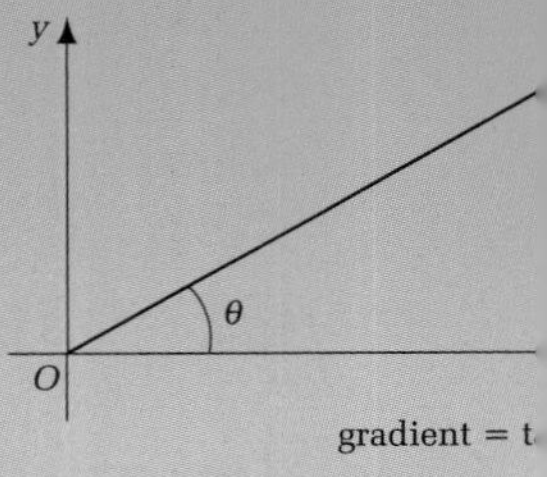

The gradient of the straight line joining A (x_1, y_1) and B (x_2, y_2) is given by gradient $= \dfrac{y_2 - y_1}{x_2 - x_1}$

◀ **Learn this result.**

This result gives both the sign (+/−) and the magnitude (size) of the gradient.

Example 4

a Find the gradient of the straight line joining A (1, 2) and B (7, 10).

b If the gradient of the straight line joining P (a, 3) and Q (2, 8) is 5, find the value of a.

Solution

a gradient $= \frac{10 - 2}{7 - 1} = \frac{8}{6} = \frac{4}{3}$

The gradient is often represented mathematically by the letter m. It could be written here as gradient $m_{AB} = \frac{4}{3}$ or $m = \frac{4}{3}$.

b We know that gradient $m_{PQ} = \frac{y_2 - y_1}{x_2 - x_1}$

So $\quad 5 = \frac{8 - 3}{2 - a}$

Then $\quad 5(2 - a) = 8 - 3 = 5$

So $\quad 2 - a = 1$

$-a = 1 - 2 = -1$

$a = 1$

Multiply both sides by $(2 - a)$.
Divide both sides by 5.

Parallel lines

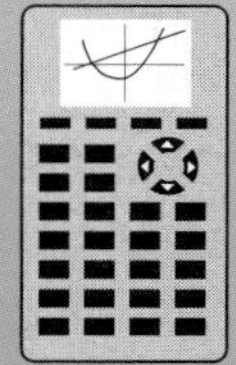

Use a graphical calculator to draw the graphs of $y = 3x$, $y = 3x + 5$ and $y = 3x - 1$. What do you notice? The lines are parallel. Now calculate the gradient of each line. The gradient of each line is 3, the same as the coefficient of x in each equation.

Try drawing some graphs of your own linear equations where the coefficient of x is the same. What happens? If the equation starts $y =$, then when the coefficient of x is the same the equations produce lines that are parallel. These lines never cross and so the equations that represent them cannot be solved simultaneously. Conversely, if two linear equations cannot be solved simultaneously then their graphs must be parallel lines.

Example 5

Show that the following pairs of lines are parallel: $y = 2x + 3$, $y = 2x + 5$.

Solution

$y = 2x + 3$ call this equation [1]

$y = 2x + 5$ call this equation [2]

Recall how to solve two linear equations simultaneously.

$2x + 3 = 2x + 5$ ◀ **Substitute for y from equation [1] in equation [2].**

$2x - 2x = 5 - 3$

$x(2 - 2) = 5 - 3 = 2$

$x = \frac{2}{0}$

Take out the common factor and rearrange the equation.

Division by zero doesn't give a real number; it is undefined. So x cannot be found to satisfy both equations simultaneously. This means the lines do not cross; so they are parallel.

It is often quicker to show that two straight lines are parallel by comparing the coefficients of x. To do this, we sometimes need to rearrange the equations in order to make y the subject.

Example 6

Show that the following pairs of lines are parallel: $y = 2(3x + 1)$, $2y - 12x + 6 = 0$.

Solution

$$y = 2(3x + 1) \Rightarrow y = 6x + 2$$

$$2y - 12x + 6 = 0 \Rightarrow y = 6x - 3$$

The coefficient of x is the same in both equations, 6, so the lines are parallel.

Perpendicular lines

Consider a line OP where P is some point (a, b) and O is the origin. Rotate OP 90° anticlockwise about O (a quarter turn) and call this new line OQ. Now the angle between the lines OP and OQ is 90°. We say that OP is **perpendicular** to OQ; 'perpendicular to' means 'at right angles to'.

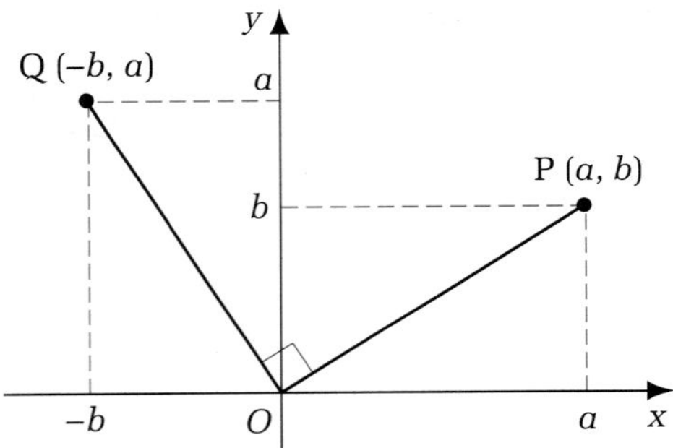

What do you notice about the coordinates of Q? Using the symmetry of the diagram, notice that the coordinates of Q are $(-b, a)$. These have the same numerical values, but there is a change of order and one change of sign in the x-coordinate.
Now consider the gradient of each line.

$$\text{gradient OP} = \frac{b}{a} \qquad \text{gradient OQ} = \frac{-a}{b}$$

Multiply these two gradients together. What happens? Their product is -1. In fact, the product of the gradients of perpendicular lines is always -1. This is a very useful test for whether two straight lines are perpendicular to each other.

The gradient of OQ can be found using the formula with $(x_2, y_2) = (0, 0)$.

$$\text{gradient} = \frac{(0-a)}{[0-(-b)]} = -\frac{a}{b}$$

Example 7

a Find the gradient of the line joining A (0, 7) and B (2, 10).

b Find the gradient of a line perpendicular to AB.

Solution

a Gradient of the line AB, $m_{AB} = \dfrac{10 - 7}{2 - 0} = \frac{3}{2}$

b Gradient of a line perpendicular to AB $= -\frac{2}{3}$, because $\frac{3}{2} \times (-\frac{2}{3}) = -1$.

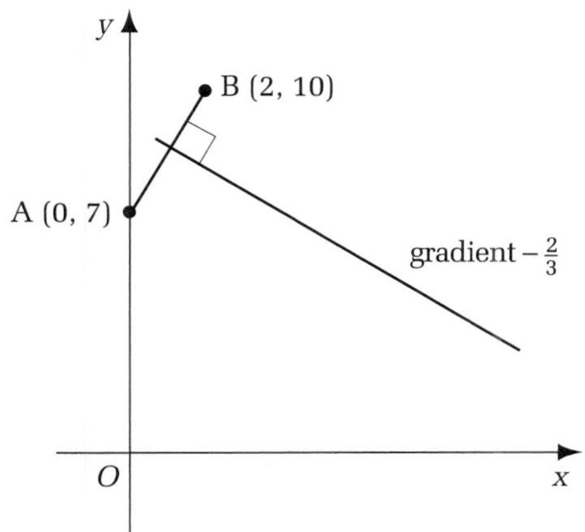

Example 8

If A is the point (3, −2) and B is the point (5, 2), find the gradient of:

a the line AB

b a line perpendicular to AB.

Solution

a Gradient of the line AB, $m_{AB} = \dfrac{2 - (-2)}{5 - 3} = \dfrac{4}{2} = 2$

b Gradient of a line perpendicular to AB is $-\frac{1}{2}$

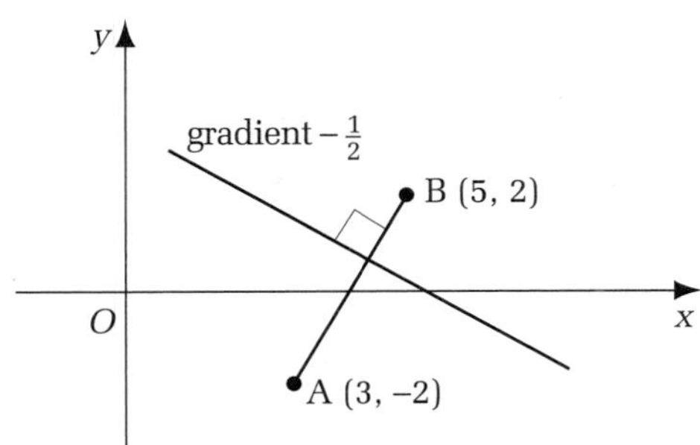

2.1 Coordinate Geometry

Exercise

Technique

1 Find the shortest distance between the following pairs of points:

a (3, 5) and (1, 4)
b (3, 5) and (5, 6)
c (1, 7) and (−2, 3)
d (1, 7) and (0, −1)
e (−2, −3) and (−7, −1)
f (8, −4) and (−7, −4)
g (2, 1, 5) and (5, 13, 9)
h (7, −2, 18) and (−3, 3, 8)

2 Find the length of the straight line joining the following pairs of points:

a A (7, −1) and B (−2, 5)
b A (−1, −2) and B (−2, −5)
c A (3, 2) and B (−1, −5)
d A (−2, −1) and B (0, 3)
e A (4, −8) and B (0, 6)
f A (4, 4) and B (−1, 2)
g A (6, 11, −3) and B (1, 1, 7)
h A (2, 3, 4) and B (4, 6, 10)

3 Find the gradient of the straight line formed by joining the following pairs of points:

a (3, 2) and (5, 12)
b (2, 1) and (4, 9)
c (5, 3) and (7, 1)
d (0, 7) and (−2, 9)
e (−2, −1) and (6, −1)
f (3, 2) and (5, −8)

4 For the following pairs of points, A and B, find:

i the gradient of the line AB
ii the gradient of a line perpendicular to AB.

a A (0, 6) and B (2, 7)
b A (5, 2) and B (−3, −3)
c A (−3, 0) and B (2, −5)
d A (−3, 6) and B (−1, −3)
e A (−3, −2) and B (6, −6)
f A (−2, 0) and B (7, 2)

5 Rearrange the following equations to make y the subject. State whether the pairs of lines are parallel or perpendicular to each other.

a $y = 2x + 3$ and $y = 2x - 7$
b $y = 3x + 7$ and $y = 5 - \frac{1}{3}x$
c $y = 2x - 5$ and $y - 2x = 3$
d $2y + 6x + 8 = 0$ and $3x + y = -7$
e $8x + 2y = 6$ and $4y = 9 + x$
f $3y = 9(x - 1)$ and $6y + 2x = 6$

Contextual

1 Katie moves her position from the point (2, 6) to the point (5, 3) on the park map. The map is drawn to a scale of 1:10 000. Find

a the shortest distance in centimetres that Katie covers on the map

b the actual distance she moves in km.

2 Twins Peter and David radio their respective coordinates to each other. Peter is at position (3, 9) and David is at (−2, −3). How far apart are they?

3 The night before military manoeuvres, an army troop are given starting coordinates, (965, 386), and finishing coordinates, (943, 379). By considering only the final two digits of each coordinate, find the distance on the Ordnance Survey map moved by the troop, in centimetres. If the scale of their map is 1:25 000, find the actual distance covered in kilometres.

4 According to a garden plan, the cottage (7, 9) is the same distance from the ash tree (5, 2) and the beech tree (9, 2). Investigate this statement.

5 A parallelogram is formed by lines joining the points P, Q, R and S. Given the coordinates of points P (−2, 3), Q (3, 4) and R (2, −1):

a Find the coordinates of S.

b Show that PQRS is a rhombus.

6 The diagram shows a sketch of a cuboid. Given the coordinates of A (1, 2, 1) and F (4, 5, 5), find the shortest distance between A and F.

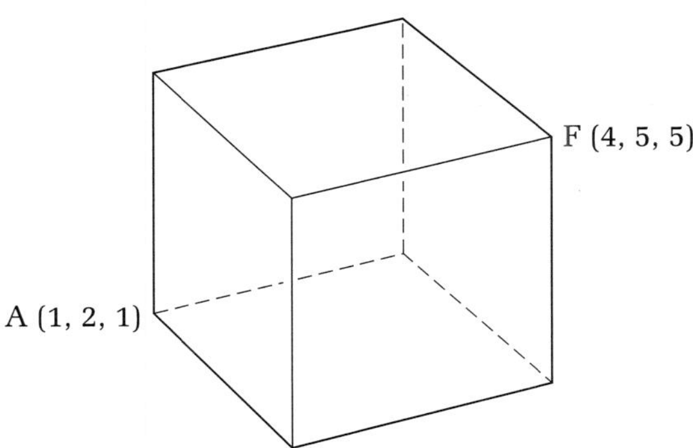

2.2 The Equation of a Straight Line

Linear equations can be written in many forms. The general form is $\mathbf{ax + by + c = 0}$ where a, b and c are real numbers.

Example 1

Rearrange the following equations into the general form $ax + by + c = 0$:

a $y = -3x - 8$

b $y + 2 = -\frac{1}{3}(x - 1)$

Solution

a $3x + y + 8 = 0$

b $y + 2 = -\frac{1}{3}(x - 1)$

$3y + 6 = -(x - 1)$

$3y + 6 = -x + 1$

$x + 3y + 5 = 0$

Multiply throughout by 3 to remove the fraction.

The minus sign outside the bracket changes the sign of each term inside when the bracket is removed.

The general equation can be rearranged to make y the subject. It is then written $\mathbf{y = mx + c}$ When written in this form it instantly highlights two important properties; the gradient of the line and its intercept with the y-axis. Consider the line $y = \frac{1}{2}x - 3$. This is in the form $y = mx + c$, with $m = \frac{1}{2}$ and $c = -3$. Notice that the gradient is $\frac{1}{2}$ and the y-intercept is $(0, -3)$.

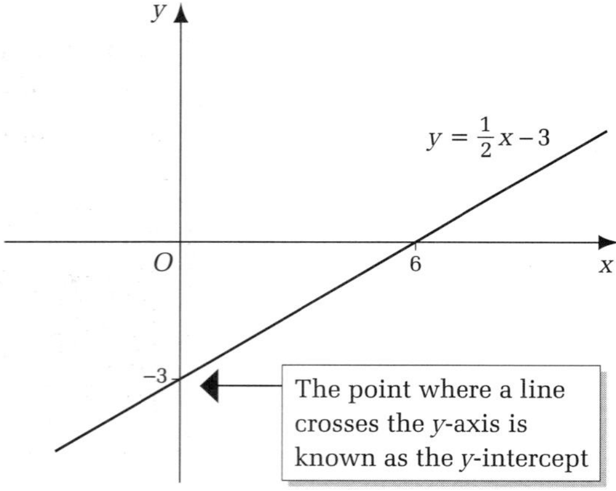

The equation $y = \frac{1}{2}x - 3$ can be written in other forms:

$y = \frac{1}{2}x - 3$

$2y = x - 6$

$x - 2y - 6 = 0$

Multiplying throughout by 2 removes the fraction.

In the last version, the equation is in the more general form $ax + by + c = 0$, with $a = 1$, $b = -2$ and $c = -6$. Notice that $y = \frac{1}{2}x - 3$ and $x - 2y - 6 = 0$ both represent the same straight line.

Example 2

Find the gradient and y-intercept of the straight lines represented by the following equations and sketch their graphs:

a $3x + 3y - 7 = 0$ **b** $2x - 5y + 1 = 0$

Solution

a $3x + 3y - 7 = 0 \Rightarrow 3y = -3x + 7$

$$y = \frac{-3x}{3} + \frac{7}{3} = -x + \frac{7}{3}$$

First express the equation in the form $y = mx + c$.

So the gradient is -1 and the y-intercept is $(0, \frac{7}{3})$.

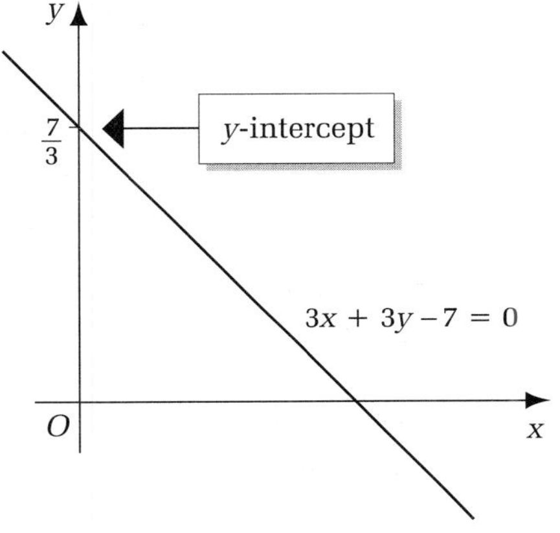

◀ Check this sketch using a graphical calculator.

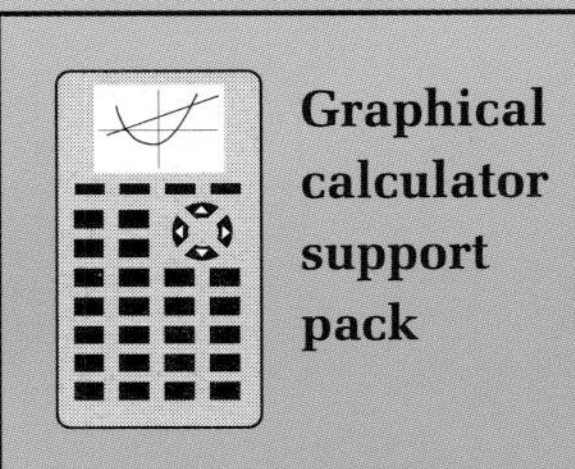

Remember to label the axes and origin on your sketch. Label the line with its equation, and mark the y-intercept.

b $2x - 5y + 1 = 0 \Rightarrow 2x + 1 = 5y$

$$\tfrac{2}{5}x + \tfrac{1}{5} = y$$

Remember to use the $y = mx + c$ form on your calculator.

So the gradient is $\frac{2}{5}$ and the y-intercept is $(0, \frac{1}{5})$.

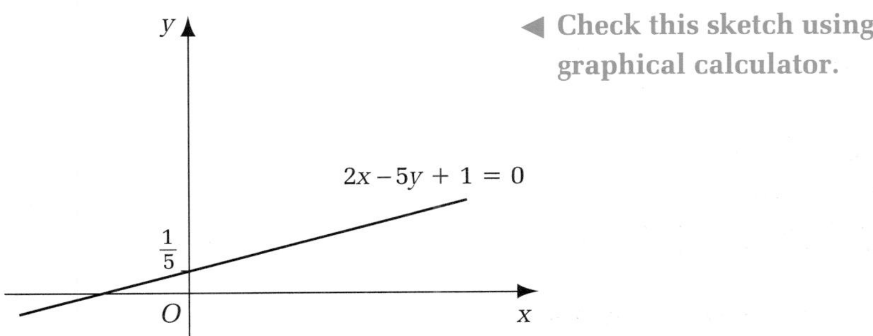

◀ Check this sketch using a graphical calculator.

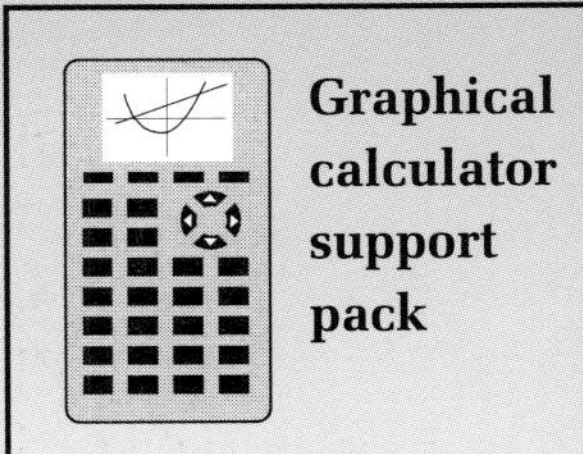

The equations can be entered into the calculator in the form $y = \ldots$.

The technique of rearranging equations into the form $y = mx + c$ is particularly useful when solving simultaneous equations with a graphical method.

Example 3

Solve the simultaneous equations $x + y = 4$ and $2y - 3x = 3$ using a graphical method.

Solution

We could rearrange each equation into the form $y = mx + c$ to identify the gradient and intercept for each graph. However, it is often quicker to draw each graph by calculating where they cross the axes.

To find where the lines cross the y-axis, put $x = 0$ into each equation. To find where the lines cross the x-axis, substitute $y = 0$ instead.

For $x + y = 4$, when $x = 0, y = 4$

and when $y = 0, x = 4$

This line crosses the axes at (0, 4) and (4, 0).

For $2y - 3x = 3$, when $x = 0$, $2y = 3$

$y = \frac{3}{2}$

and when $y = 0$, $-3x = 3$

$x = -1$

This line crosses the axes at $(0, \frac{3}{2})$ and $(-1, 0)$.

The graphical solution of the simultaneous equations is given by the coordinates of the point of intersection of these two lines.

An alternative method is to rearrange each equation into the form $y = mx + c$. Use a graphical calculator to draw these lines and find out where they cross.

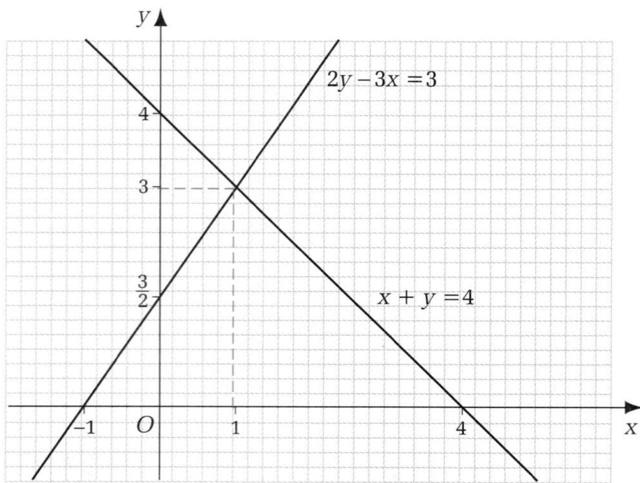

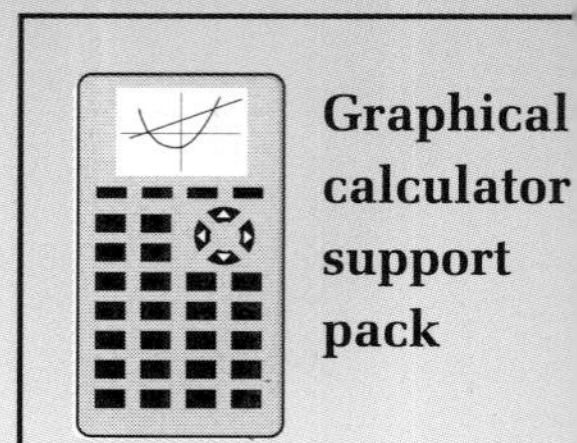

You should find that the coordinates of this point are $x = 1$ and $y = 3$. So the point (1, 3) lies on both lines and $x = 1, y = 3$ is the solution because it satisfies both equations simultaneously.

2.2 The Equation of a Straight Line

Exercise

Technique

1 Rearrange the following equations into the form $y = mx + c$:

a	$3x + y + 7 = 0$	**e**	$x + y + 3 = 0$
b	$4x + y - 3 = 0$	**f**	$2x - y - 5 = 0$
c	$\dfrac{y - 2}{x - 3} = 4$	**g**	$\dfrac{y - 7}{2} = 4x$
d	$\dfrac{y + 2}{x - 5} = 2$	**h**	$\dfrac{3 - y}{2} = x$

2 State the gradient and the y-intercept of the straight-line graphs produced by the following equations:

a	$y = 5x - 3$	**b**	$y = -2x + 3$
c	$y = 7 - 2x$	**d**	$y = \frac{1}{2}x + 5$

3 For the straight lines produced by following equations, find the gradient and the coordinates of the y-intercept:

a	$2x + y + 8 = 0$	**d**	$2x - y + 7 = 4$
b	$-2x + 3y - 2 = 0$	**e**	$-3x + 7y = 14$
c	$5x + 10y - 2 = 8$	**f**	$ax + by + c = 0$

4 The equation of the line shown is given by $3x + y - 6 = 0$. Find the gradient and the coordinates of A and B.

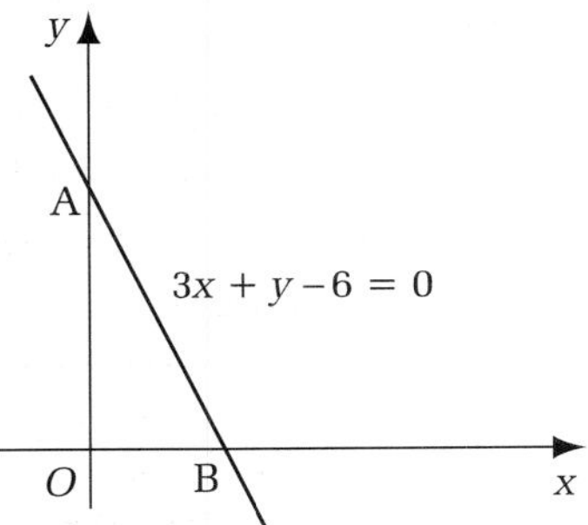

5 Rearrange the equation $\dfrac{y - 5}{x + 4} = \frac{1}{2}$ into the form $y = mx + c$. Now sketch the graph of this equation.

6 Solve the simultaneous equations $x + y = 6$ and $4x - 2y + 6 = 0$ using a graphical method.

2.3 More on the Straight Line

Think about the information needed to describe a particular straight line. How can we write the equation of a line by looking only at the graph of the line? We find that we can write the equation if we know:

- the gradient of the line and the coordinates of a point on it
- the coordinates of two points on the line.

The equation of a line given its gradient and the coordinates of one point on the line

Suppose the gradient m and the coordinates of point P (x_1, y_1) on the line are known. A general point (x, y) on the line can then be used to find the equation of the line. The known gradient, m, can be expressed by the sides of a right-angled triangle drawn on P and the general point (x, y).

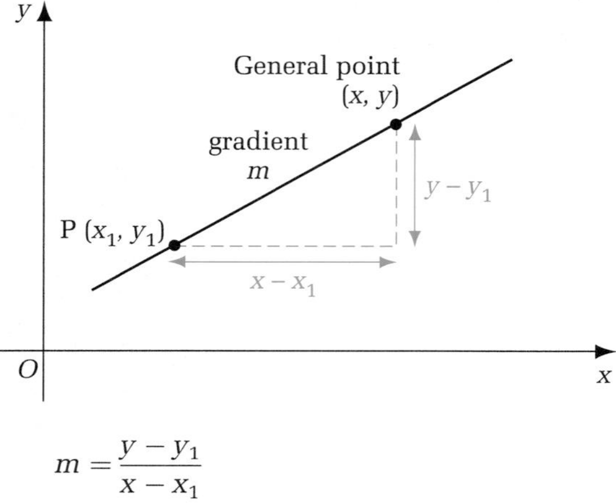

$$m = \frac{y - y_1}{x - x_1}$$

This can be rearranged into the very useful result,

$$\boldsymbol{y - y_1 = m(x - x_1)}$$

◀ **Learn this result.**

Example 1

a Find the equation of the straight line with gradient 2 that passes through the point (3, 4).

b Find the equation of the straight line with gradient $\frac{1}{2}$ that passes through the point (−2, −6).

Solution

a Use $y - y_1 = m(x - x_1)$

Substitute the known values of m, x_1 and y_1.

Then $y - 4 = 2(x - 3)$

$y - 4 = 2x - 6$

This equation can now be rearranged into either form of the equation of a straight line.

$ax + by + c = 0$, or $y = mx + c$.

$2x - y - 2 = 0$ or $y = 2x - 2$

b Use $y - y_1 = m(x - x_1)$

Then $y - (-6) = \frac{1}{2}(x - (-2))$

$y + 6 = \frac{1}{2}(x + 2)$

$y + 6 = \frac{1}{2}x + 1$

$y = \frac{1}{2}x + 1 - 6 = \frac{1}{2}x - 5$

Take care when manipulating the negative signs.

So the equation of the line is $y = \frac{1}{2}x - 5$.

The equation of a straight line passing through two known points

Suppose that two points P (x_1, y_1) and Q (x_2, y_2) are known to lie on the straight line. The gradient of this line can be found by drawing in a right-angled triangle.

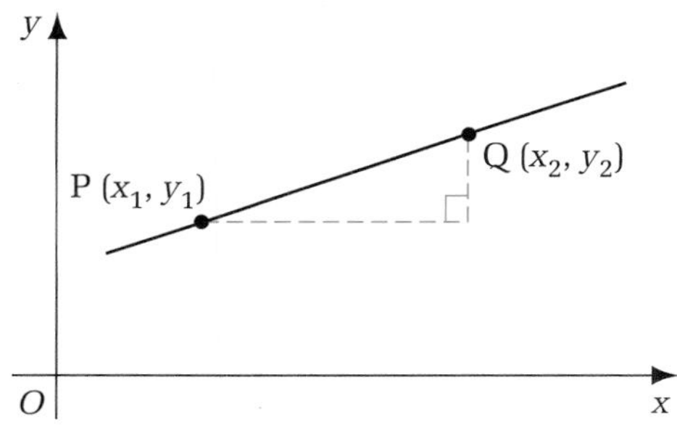

$$m = \frac{y_2 - y_1}{x_2 - x_1}$$

Now that we have the gradient, the problem is simple. We can use the result $y - y_1 = m(x - x_1)$ on either P or Q.

Example 2

Find the equation of the straight line that passes through the points A (2, 3) and B (4, 4).

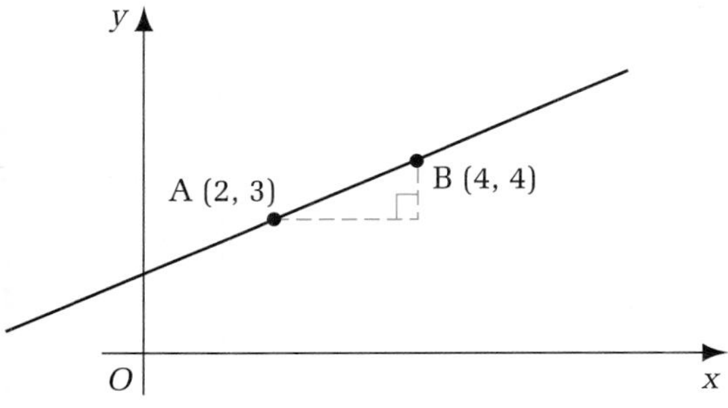

Solution

The gradient of the straight line passing through A (2, 3) and B (4, 4) is

$$m = \frac{4-3}{4-2} = \tfrac{1}{2}$$

Now use $y - y_1 = m(x - x_1)$, with $m = \tfrac{1}{2}$ and B (4, 4) as the known point.

$$\begin{aligned} y - y_1 = m(x - x_1) \Rightarrow \quad y - 4 &= \tfrac{1}{2}(x - 4) \\ y - 4 &= \tfrac{1}{2}x - 2 \\ y &= \tfrac{1}{2}x + 2 \end{aligned}$$

Check that you arrive at the same equation using A (2, 3) instead of B (4, 4).

The expression for the gradient, $m = \dfrac{y_2 - y_1}{x_2 - x_1}$, can be substituted directly into the equation for a straight line, $y - y_1 = m(x - x_1)$. At first the algebra might appear quite daunting, but it provides a very useful result.

$$y - y_1 = \frac{y_2 - y_1}{x_2 - x_1}(x - x_1)$$

This equation can now be rearranged so that the x terms and y terms are separated, producing the equation of the straight line directly once the values of (x_1, y_1) and (x_2, y_2) are known.

$$\frac{y - y_1}{y_2 - y_1} = \frac{x - x_1}{x_2 - x_1}$$

◀ **Learn this result.**

Example 3

Find the equation of the straight line joining P (5, −6) and Q (−3, 2).

Solution

Using the result $\dfrac{y - y_1}{y_2 - y_1} = \dfrac{x - x_1}{x_2 - x_1}$

$$\frac{y - (-6)}{2 - (-6)} = \frac{x - 5}{(-3) - 5}$$

$$\frac{y + 6}{8} = \frac{x - 5}{-8}$$

Simplify the numeric components.

$$y + 6 = \frac{8}{-8}(x - 5)$$

$$y + 6 = -(x - 5) = -x + 5$$

$$y = -x + 5 - 6 = -x - 1$$

Make y the subject.

Check that this equation could also be written $x + y + 1 = 0$.

Finding the mid-point of a line

Given a line joining two known points the mid-point can be established using the mean of the x and y coordinates.

Recall that the mean average is the sum of the numbers divided by how many of them there are. In this case, taking the mean of two coordinates, we would add the coordinates and then divide by 2, to find the point half-way between them.

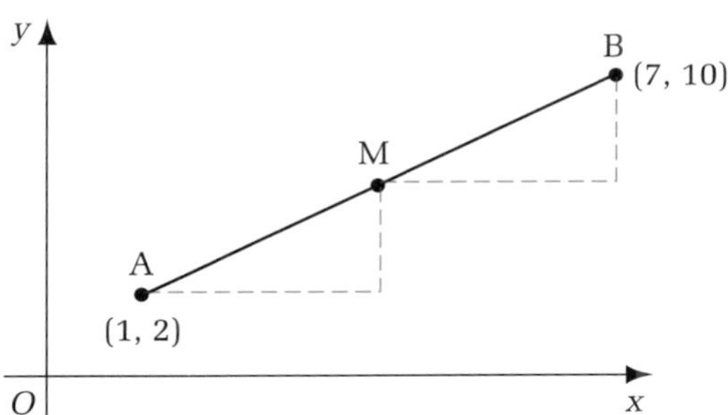

Consider the line joining A (1, 2) and B (7, 10). If M is the mid-point of this line then M is half-way between A and B, both horizontally and vertically. In this case the coordinates of M are $(4, 6)$.

Notice that $(4, 6) = \left(\frac{1+7}{2}, \frac{2+10}{2}\right)$.

The mid-point M of a line joining the points A (x_1, y_1) and B (x_2, y_2) has coordinates $\left(\frac{x_1+x_2}{2}, \frac{y_1+y_2}{2}\right)$.

Example 4

The vertices of an isosceles triangle are A (2, 7), B (5, 8) and C (4, 5).

a State the coordinates of the mid-point of AC.

b Find the equation of the straight line through B and the mid-point of AC.

c Find the equation of the perpendicular bisector of BC.

The perpendicular bisector of a line is another line at right angles to the first, that passes through the mid-point of the original line.

Solution

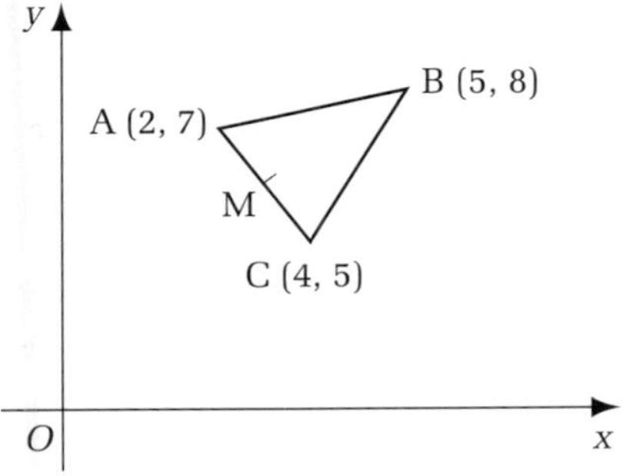

a Let M be the mid-point of AC. Then the coordinates of M are $\left(\frac{2+4}{2}, \frac{7+5}{2}\right) = (3, 6)$.

b We need to find the equation of the straight line through two known points; B (5, 8) and M (3, 6).

Using $\dfrac{y - y_1}{y_2 - y_1} = \dfrac{x - x_1}{x_2 - x_1}$

$$\frac{y-8}{6-8} = \frac{x-5}{3-5}$$

So $$\frac{y-8}{-2} = \frac{x-5}{-2}$$

$$y - 8 = \frac{-2}{-2}(x-5) = x - 5$$

$$y = x - 5 + 8 = x + 3$$

So the equation of the straight line passing through B and the mid-point of AC is $y = x + 3$.

c Let P be the mid-point of BC. Then the coordinates of P are $\left(\dfrac{5+4}{2}, \dfrac{8+5}{2}\right) = \left(\frac{9}{2}, \frac{13}{2}\right)$.

The gradient of the line BC is given by $m = \dfrac{8-5}{5-4} = \frac{3}{1} = 3$.

So the gradient of the line perpendicular to BC is $-\frac{1}{3}$. Now that we know the gradient of the perpendicular bisector, and a point on it (the mid-point of BC), its equation can be found using $y - y_1 = m(x - x_1)$.

Recall that the product of gradients of perpendicular straight lines is -1.

$$y - \tfrac{13}{2} = -\tfrac{1}{3}\left(x - \tfrac{9}{2}\right)$$

$$\Rightarrow \quad 6y - \frac{6 \times 13}{2} = -\tfrac{6}{3}\left(x - \tfrac{9}{2}\right)$$

Multiply by 6 to remove the fractions.

$$\Rightarrow \quad 6y - 39 = -2\left(x - \tfrac{9}{2}\right)$$

$$\Rightarrow \quad 6y - 39 = -2x + 9$$

$$\Rightarrow \quad 2x + 6y - 48 = 0$$

Check that this straight line can also be expressed as $y = 8 - \frac{1}{3}x$.

2.3 More on the Straight Line

Exercise

Technique

1 Find the equation of the straight line with the given gradient passing through the stated point in each of the following:

a gradient 3, point (3, 2)
b gradient 6, point (−1, 2)
c gradient 5, point (3, −2)
d gradient −3, point (0, 4)
e gradient $\frac{1}{2}$, point (2, −3)
f gradient $-\frac{1}{3}$, point (−1, 4)

2 Find the equation of the straight line joining the following pairs of points:

a A (2, 4) and B (3, 6)
b R (−3, 4) and S (1, 2)
c T (−1, 1) and V (0, 6)
d A (0, −2) and B (3, 4)
e P (8, 6) and Q (2, 12)
f R (−1, −1) and S (5, 2)

3 Find the mid-point and the equation of the perpendicular bisector of AB in each of the following cases:

a A (1, −1) and B (3, 7)
b A (4, 1) and B (5, 0)
c A (−2, 5) and B (0, 3)
d A (−1, −2) and B (1, 6)

Contextual

1 A straight line passing through the points A (−1, 1) and B (p, 13), has gradient 2. Determine the value of p and find the equation of the straight line.

2 Consider two points, P (2, 7) and Q (4, 13).

a Find the mid-point of PQ.
b Find the gradient of PQ.
c Write down the gradient of the line perpendicular to the line PQ.
d Find the equation of the perpendicular bisector of PQ. Write it in the form $ax + by + c = 0$.

3 Sketch a diagram to show the points A (0, −1), B (4, 3) and C (4, 5). Let M be the mid-point of AB. Find the coordinates of M and write down the equation of the straight line that passes through M and C.

4 A is the point (6, 6) and B (8, 2) lies on the straight line $x - 2y - 4 = 0$.

a Find the equation of the straight line parallel to $x - 2y - 4 = 0$ that passes through A. Write it in the form $ax + by + c = 0$.
b Show that the straight line joining A and B is perpendicular to the line $x - 2y - 4 = 0$.
c Find the perpendicular distance between the two parallel lines.

2.4 Inequalities

There are four inequality symbols.

$>$ means 'is greater than'
$\geq$ means 'is greater than or equal to'
$<$ means 'is less than'
$\leq$ means 'is less than or equal to'

Learn the mathematical meaning of each of these symbols.

Inequalities produce a range of acceptable answers. They can be represented on number lines using arrows. The base of the arrow is circular, and is shaded when the value is to be included in the range, and clear when the value is not to be included in the range.

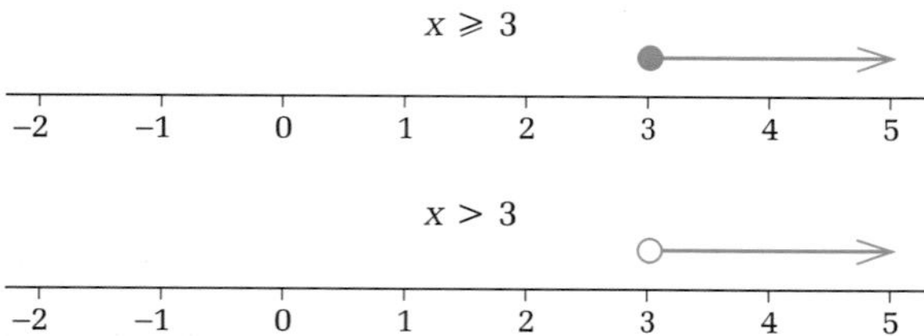

Inequalities can be categorised into two types; those without variables (letters) and those with variables. Inequalities without variables are called **propositions**. Statements such as $2 < 7, \frac{1}{2} > \frac{1}{5}$, and $-3 < -2$ are propositions and are either true or false. Inequalities with variables can be solved using similar techniques to those used when solving equations. However, a solution set is often produced showing a range of acceptable answers.

A solution set is an inequality, or a set of inequalities, showing the range of values that are acceptable as solutions to the problem.

Example 1

Solve the inequalities:

a $2x + 1 \geq 7$ **b** $1 - 2x \geq 7$

c $5x + 2 < 3x + 10$ **d** $\frac{6+x}{3} \geq x + 7$

Solution

a $2x + 1 \geq 7$

$2x \geq 6$ Subtract 1 from both sides of the inequality.

$x \geq 3$ Divide both sides by 2.

b $1 - 2x \geq 7 \Rightarrow -2x \geq 6$

Notice that the coefficient of x is -2. To find x we need to divide both sides of the inequality by -2. When dividing by a negative number the inequality needs to be reversed.

$$-2x \geq 6 \Rightarrow x \leq \frac{6}{-2}$$

$$x \leq -3$$

Check this result by substituting a value of x smaller than -3 in the original inequality. Does the original inequality work?

c The process of solving linear inequalities is similar to solving linear equations. Collect the like terms together, with numbers on one side of the inequality and variables on the other.

$$
\begin{aligned}
& 5x + 2 < 3x + 10 \\
\Rightarrow\ & 5x - 3x < 10 - 2 \\
\Rightarrow\ & 2x < 8 \\
\Rightarrow\ & x < 4
\end{aligned}
$$

Check this result by substituting a value of x smaller than 4 in the original inequality.

d Again use a similar process to that used when solving linear equations. Eliminate the fractions (by multiplying by a common multiple), collect like terms and find a condition on x by using division.

$$
\begin{aligned}
& \frac{6+x}{3} \geq x + 7 \\
\Rightarrow\ & 6 + x \geq 3(x + 7) \\
\Rightarrow\ & 6 + x \geq 3x + 21 \\
\Rightarrow\ & 6 - 21 \geq 3x - x \\
\Rightarrow\ & -15 \geq 2x \\
\Rightarrow\ & -\tfrac{15}{2} \geq x
\end{aligned}
$$

That is, $x \leq -\frac{15}{2}$

This illustrates a useful 'trick'. The variable x is collected on the RHS of the inequality, making the resulting term, $2x$, positive.

Notice how the following rules were used:

- Any term can be added to, or subtracted from, both sides of the inequality and the symbol doesn't change.
- Both sides of an inequality can be multiplied, or divided, by the same positive number and the symbol doesn't change.
- When both sides of an inequality are multiplied, or divided, by the same negative number then the symbol is reversed.

Quadratic inequalities

One example of a quadratic inequality is $x^2 > 4$. It has two sets of solutions. Consider $x^2 = 4$. This has two solutions; $x = 2$ and $x = -2$. Why? Because to solve the equation $x^2 = 4$ we take the square root of both sides of the equation.

$$x^2 = 4 \Rightarrow x = \pm\sqrt{4} = \pm 2$$

So what do we know about x when $x^2 > 4$? We can see that $x > 2$ works. Check this result. What is the other solution? Is there a condition involving -2? We find that $x < -2$ is also a condition that works.

To see why the solutions are $x > 2$ and $x < -2$, think about the proposition $x^2 > 4$. Draw two graphs; $y = x^2$ and $y = 4$. Where is the parabola above the line $y = 4$? This is the same as asking for which values of x the graph of $y = x^2$ is above the line $y = 4$, or for which values $x^2 > 4$. The curve is above the line for $x > 2$ and for $x < -2$.

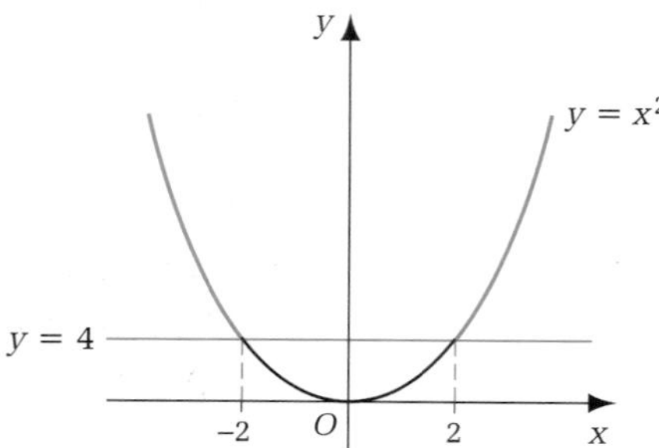

An alternative is to rearrange the original inequality. Then $x^2 > 4$ becomes $x^2 - 4 > 0$. This may not look simpler, but the new statement has a quadratic expression and a zero separated by an inequality symbol. A graph of $y = x^2 - 4$ can now be drawn, and we are looking for the points where $y > 0$ (that is, for points of the curve above the x-axis).

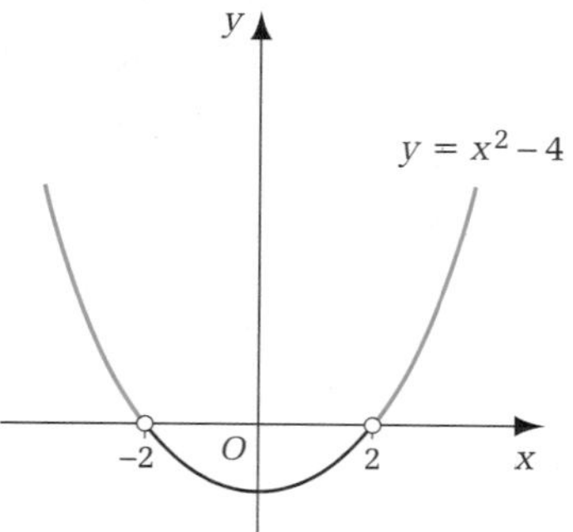

Since 2 and -2 are not part of the solution, the dots here are left unshaded.

Find the points where the curve crosses the x-axis (by solving $x^2 - 4 = 0$, or using your graphical calculator). Notice that the curve is above (greater than) the x-axis ($y = 0$) for $x > 2$ and $x < -2$.

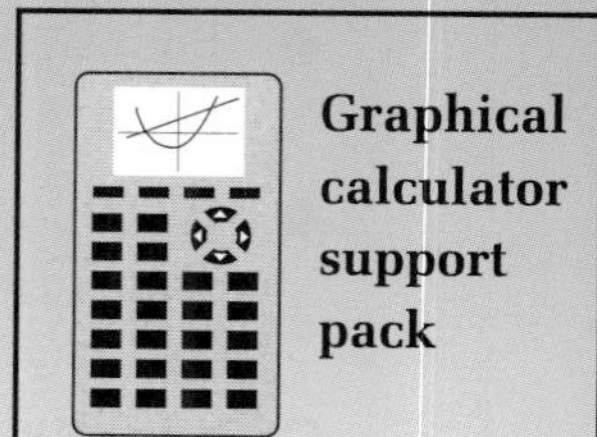

This technique of sketching the graph is a useful way of checking that no solutions have been lost.

Example 2

Solve:

a $x^2 - 7x < -10$ **b** $x^2 - 3x - 5 \geq 0$ **c** $x^2 + x + 1 \leq 0$

Solution

a This is a quadratic inequality. It can be rewritten as a quadratic expression and a zero separated by an inequality symbol.

$$x^2 - 7x < -10 \Rightarrow x^2 - 7x + 10 < 0$$

The quadratic expression can be factorised. Recall 'PAFF' from Chapter 1.

Recall that since the coefficient of x^2 is 1 the expression can be factorised from this step.

P: 10 A: −7 F: −2, −5

Then $x^2 - 7x + 10 < 0$ becomes $(x - 2)(x - 5) < 0$.
What does this expression suggest about x?
If the inequality symbol was an equality (that is, $(x - 2)(x - 5) = 0$) then $x = 2$ or $x = 5$ would be the solution. Since we have an inequality, these **critical values** should be examined more closely.
Begin by sketching the curve $y = x^2 - 7x + 10$. Notice how it crosses the x-axis at $x = 2$ and $x = 5$.

Critical values are points where the quadratic expression changes sign.

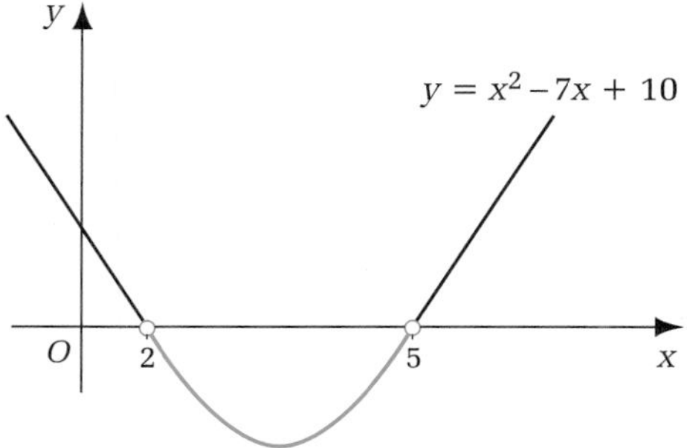

The parabola is below the x-axis for all values of x between $x = 2$ and $x = 5$. This means $x^2 - 7x + 10$ is negative for all these values of x. So $x^2 - 7x + 10 < 0$ when $x > 2$ and $x < 5$.
Another way of writing this set of inequalities is as a 'sandwich': $2 < x < 5$.
Notice how the x appears between the values of 2 and 5 found in the factorisation process.

b Try the technique used in **a**, and see what happens.
Try factorising the quadratic expression $x^2 - 3x - 5$, using PAFF.

P: −5 A: −3 F: ?

Values for F cannot be found easily so this quadratic expression cannot be factorised using PAFF, but the critical values can be identified by solving $x^2 - 3x - 5 = 0$. Since PAFF isn't working, use the quadratic formula with $a = 1$, $b = -3$ and $c = -5$.

$$x = \frac{-b \pm \sqrt{b^2 - 4ac}}{2a}$$

◀ **Remember to quote the formula.**

$$= \frac{3 \pm \sqrt{9 - 4 \times 1 \times (-5)}}{2}$$

$$= \frac{3 \pm \sqrt{9 + 20}}{2} = \frac{3 \pm \sqrt{29}}{2}$$

Notice that these values of x are both irrational due to the $\sqrt{29}$ term. Now sketch the curve of $y = x^2 - 3x - 5$. (Use a graphical calculator if you have one.)

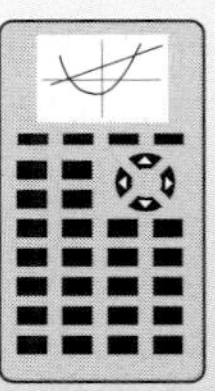

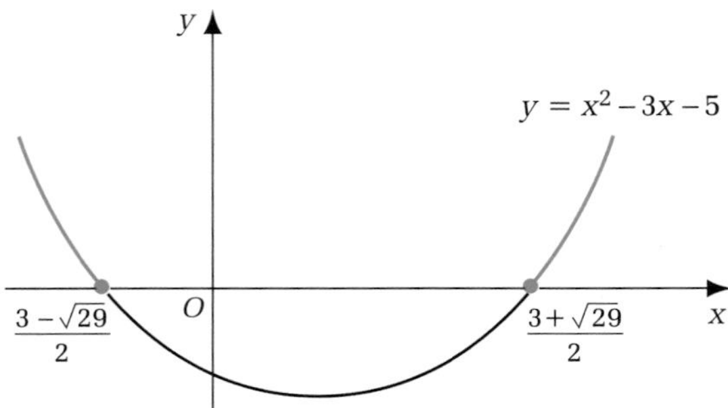

The critical values are part of the solution so the dots on the graph are shaded.

Notice that the curve is on or above the x-axis (that is $y \geq 0$) when $x \leq \frac{1}{2}(3 - \sqrt{29})$ and $x \geq \frac{1}{2}(3 + \sqrt{29})$. These inequalities are separate and cannot be condensed into a 'sandwich'.

This is because x must be smaller than the leas critical value and bigge than the highest critica value.

c Remember that the technique has been to identify critical values. By sketching the graph a set of inequalities has been identified where the graph is above or below the axis.
Sketch the graph of $y = x^2 + x + 1$. What happens?

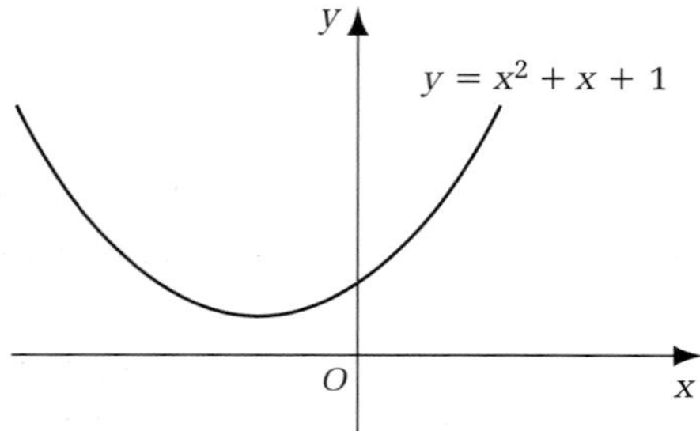

The graph doesn't cross the axis. The expression has no critical values. Check this by trying to factorise $x^2 + x + 1$, or use the quadratic formula. Since the curve is always above the x-axis, $x^2 + x + 1$ is never negative, and $x^2 + x + 1 \leq 0$ has no solutions.

Alternatively we can complete the square.
$x^2 + x + 1 \equiv (x + \frac{1}{2})^2 +$
$\geq \frac{3}{4}$
So there are no real solutions.

In summary the technique for solving quadratic inequalities is as follows:

① Establish zero on one side of the inequality symbol. This means the quadratic expression can then be tested for being positive (>0) or negative (<0).
② Establish the critical values. These are the values of x that make the quadratic expression equal zero.
③ Identify the set of inequality solutions. Often this can be done by sketching a suitable graph.
④ Decide which sides of the critical points form the solution set.

An alternative method is to check the sign of the expression below the smallest critical value, between the critical values and above the largest critical value.

Example 3

Solve $2x^2 - 9x + 9 \geq 0$.

Solution

Notice that the first step has been done. This is a quadratic expression that needs to be positive (≥ 0). Now use PAFF to factorise the expression $2x^2 - 9x + 9$. ◀ ② **Identify the critical values.**

P: $2 \times 9 = 18$ A: -9 F: $-6, -3$

$$\text{F}: \quad 2x^2 - 9x + 9 = 2x^2 - 6x - 3x + 9$$
$$= 2x(x-3) - 3(x-3)$$
$$= (x-3)(2x-3)$$

So the critical values are 3, when $x - 3 = 0$, and $\frac{3}{2}$, when $2x - 3 = 0$.
Notice that the problem has changed from solving $2x^2 - 9x + 9 \geq 0$ to solving $(x-3)(2x-3) \geq 0$.
We will use the method where we check the sign of the expression against the critical values. Look at the sign of $(x-3)(2x-3)$ by comparing the signs of the separate factors.

	$x < \frac{3}{2}$	$\frac{3}{2}$	$\frac{3}{2} < x < 3$	3	$x > 3$
$(x-3)$	$-$		$-$		$+$
$(2x-3)$	$-$		$+$		$+$
$(x-3)(2x-3)$	$(-) \times (-)$ positive		$(-) \times (+)$ negative		$(+) \times (+)$ positive

Using a number line showing the critical values, check the sign of the quadratic for values on either side of each critical value.

So $(x-3)(2x-3)$ is positive when values of x are smaller than the least critical value, and larger than the highest critical value.
The set of solutions for $2x^2 - 9x + 9 \geq 0$ is $x \leq \frac{3}{2}$ and $x \geq 3$. Check this result by sketching the graph of $y = 2x^2 - 9x + 9$.

2.4 Inequalities

Exercise

Technique

1 Solve these linear inequalities: 1 d

a $x + 3 > 8$ **b** $2x + 3 \leq 7$

c $3x + 2 \geq x + 8$ **d** $\dfrac{2 + x}{3} < x + 4$

2 Solve these quadratic inequalities:

a $x^2 > 9$ **b** $x^2 \leq 25$ **c** $x^2 - 49 > 0$ **d** $x^2 - 64 < 0$

3 Solve these quadratic inequalities:

a $x^2 + 8x + 15 > 0$ **b** $x^2 + 5x - 6 \geq 0$ **c** $x^2 + 7x + 10 < 0$

d $x^2 - 2x - 15 < 0$ **e** $x^2 - 5x + 6 \leq 0$ **f** $x^2 + 3x - 4 > 0$

4 Transform these statements into quadratic inequalities involving zero. Solve the inequality in each case.

a $x^2 - 10x \geq 24$ **b** $x^2 + x > 6$ **c** $x^2 \leq 11x - 24$

d $x^2 + 6x > -9$ **e** $x^2 < 4x + 77$ **f** $x^2 + 4 \leq 4x$

5 Solve these quadratic inequalities:

a $3x^2 + 7x + 2 > 0$ **b** $7x^2 + 22x + 3 \leq 0$ **c** $3x^2 + 5x + 2 < 0$

d $3x^2 + 1 > 4x$ **e** $2x^2 \geq 5x + 3$ **f** $3x^2 + x > 2$

Contextual

1 Solve the inequality $x + 3 > x^2$, leaving your answer in the form $a + b\sqrt{c}$ where a, b and c are rational. 1

2 Find an inequality represented by the highlighted section of this graph.

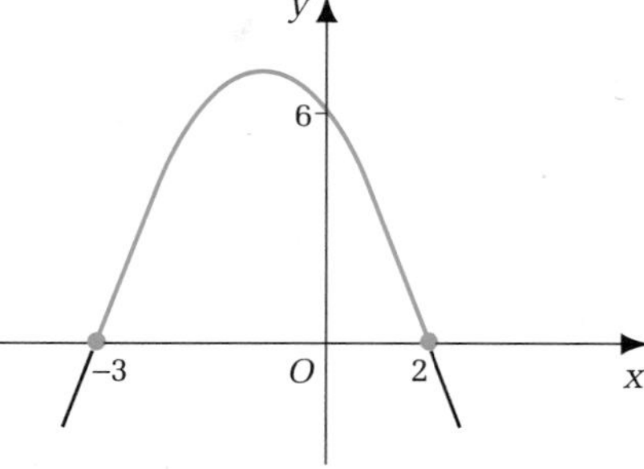

3 Find the set of values of x for which $(3x - 1)^2 < 3x^2 + 13$.

4 Solve the equation $x^2 - 5\sqrt{2}x + 12 = 0$, writing your answer using surds. Hence, or otherwise, solve $x^2 - 5\sqrt{2}x + 12 < 0$.

2.5 The Equation of a Circle

Consider a circle of radius r whose centre is at the origin, and let P (x, y) be any point on the circle. This means the distance OP must always be equal to the radius of the circle.

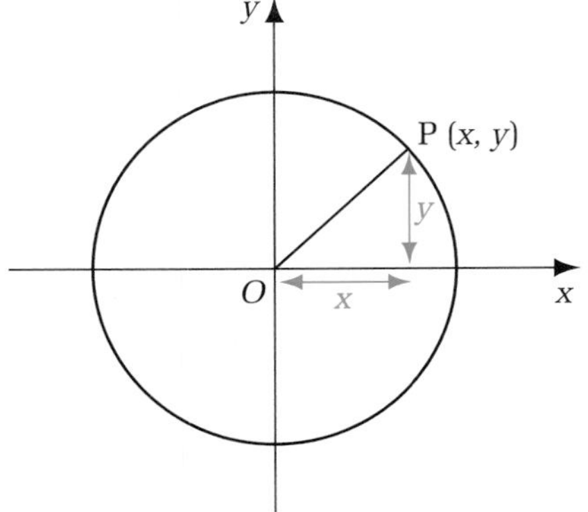

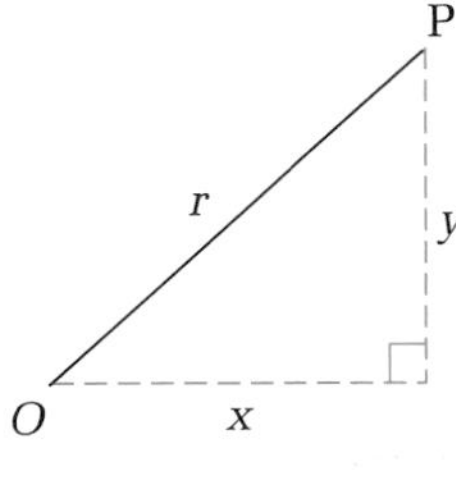

Pythagoras' theorem can be used to find the relationship between x, y and r.

The equation of a circle of radius r whose centre is at the origin (0, 0) is:

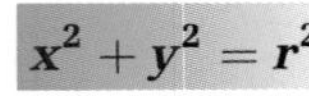

$$x^2 + y^2 = r^2$$

Check that this is true for points on the circle where P has negative coordinates.

What happens if the centre of the circle is moved to a new position Q (a, b)? Again, let P (x, y) be some point on the circumference of the circle. Notice that PQ is a radius of length r. A new right-angled triangle can be drawn on PQ so that the shorter sides are parallel to the x-axis and y-axis respectively.

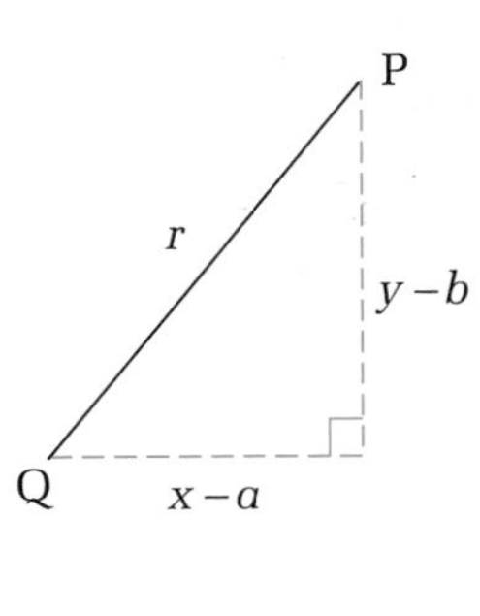

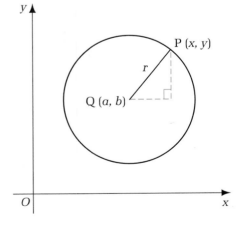

The lengths of these sides are $(x - a)$ and $(y - b)$. Check this from the diagram. Now use Pythagoras' theorem on this triangle. What happens?

$$(x - a)^2 + (y - b)^2 = r^2$$

This is the equation of a circle of radius r whose centre is the point (a, b).

Example 1

State the radius and centre of the following circles:

a $(x-7)^2+(y+2)^2=36$
b $(x+1)^2+(y-5)^2=23$

Solution

a Compare $(x-7)^2+(y+2)^2=36$ with $(x-a)^2+(y-b)^2=r^2$. The equation is in the same form with $a=7$, $b=-2$ and $r=6$.
So $(x-7)^2+(y+2)^2=36$ is the equation of a circle of radius 6, centre $(7,-2)$.

Note that since the radius is a distance it is always taken to be positive.

b $(x+1)^2+(y-5)^2=23$ can be compared with $(x-a)^2+(y-b)^2=r^2$, to give $a=-1$, $b=5$ and $r=\sqrt{23}$.
So $(x+1)^2+(y-5)^2=23$ is the equation of a circle of radius $\sqrt{23}$ whose centre is $(-1,5)$.

Example 2

a The point $(k,2)$ lies on the circle $x^2+y^2=13$. Find the values of k.
b The point $(k,0)$ lies on the circle with centre $(7,2)$ and radius $\sqrt{8}$. Find the possible values of k.

Solution

a Substitute $(k,2)$ into the equation of the circle.

$$\text{Then } x^2+y^2=13 \Rightarrow k^2+2^2=13$$
$$\Rightarrow k^2+4=13$$
$$\Rightarrow k^2=9$$
$$\Rightarrow k=\pm\sqrt{9}=\pm 3$$

So there are two possible values of k. These can be interpreted geometrically by sketching a diagram of the circle.

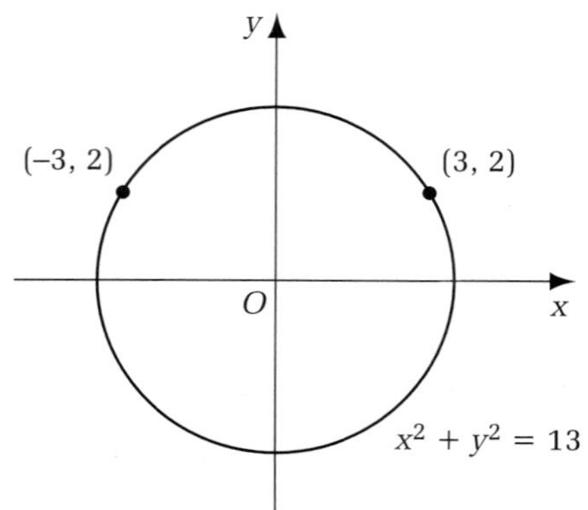

b The equation for a circle of radius $\sqrt{8}$, centre $(7, 2)$ is given by

$$(x-7)^2+(y-2)^2=8$$

Now put $x = k$ when $y = 0$ into this equation.

$$(k-7)^2+(0-2)^2=8$$
$$\Rightarrow \quad (k-7)^2+4=8$$
$$\Rightarrow \quad (k-7)^2=4$$
$$\Rightarrow \quad (k-7)=\pm\sqrt{4}=\pm 2$$
$$\Rightarrow \quad k=7\pm 2$$

So $k = 9$ or $k = 5$.

We have seen that the equation of a circle of radius r and centre (a, b) can be written $(x-a)^2+(y-b)^2=r^2$. It can also be written in another form by multiplying out the bracketed terms and then collecting like terms.

$$(x-a)^2+(y-b)^2=r^2$$
$$\Rightarrow \quad (x^2-2ax+a^2)+(y^2-2by+b^2)=r^2$$
$$\Rightarrow \quad x^2+y^2-2ax-2by+(a^2+b^2-r^2)=0$$

Since a, b and r are all constants this can be 'simplified' to the **general form** of the equation for a circle (by writing $a^2+b^2-r^2=c$).

$$\mathbf{x^2+y^2-2ax-2by+c=0}$$

Notice that in this form:

- The centre (a, b) can be identified from the coefficients of the x and y terms.
- The radius is not as straightforward to identify as it was in the other form.

Example 3

a Find the equation of a circle of radius $\sqrt{7}$ and centre $(3, -2)$ in its general form.

b The equation of a circle is $x^2+y^2-2x+4y-4=0$. Find the centre and radius of the circle.

Solution

a If the centre is $(3, -2)$ and the radius $\sqrt{7}$ then the equation of the circle is

$$(x-3)^2+(y+2)^2=(\sqrt{7})^2$$

Expanding the brackets, $(x^2 - 6x + 9) + (y^2 + 4y + 4) = 7$

$$\Rightarrow \quad x^2 + y^2 - 6x + 4y + (9 + 4 - 7) = 0$$

$$\Rightarrow \quad x^2 + y^2 - 6x + 4y + 6 = 0$$

b Compare $x^2 + y^2 - 2x + 4y - 4 = 0$ to the general form of the equation for a circle, $x^2 + y^2 - 2ax - 2by + c = 0$. Notice that a and b can be found by equating coefficients of x and y.

Equating coefficients of x, $\quad -2 = -2a, \quad$ so $a = 1$.

Equating coefficients of y, $\quad 4 = -2b, \quad$ so $b = -2$.

So the centre of the circle, (a, b), is $(1, -2)$.
Now equating the constant terms in each equation, $c = -4$.
Recall that $c = a^2 + b^2 - r^2$

$$\text{So} \quad a^2 + b^2 - r^2 = -4$$

$$\Rightarrow \quad (1)^2 + (-2)^2 - r^2 = -4$$

$$\Rightarrow \quad 1 + 4 - r^2 = -4$$

$$\Rightarrow \quad r^2 = 1 + 4 + 4$$

$$\Rightarrow \quad r^2 = 9$$

$$\Rightarrow \quad r = 3$$

We only take the positive square root because we are looking at something we know to be a positive value; the radius.

So the centre of the circle is $(1, -2)$ and the radius is 3.

Tangents and normals

A **tangent** to a circle is a straight line that touches the circle at one distinct point. A **normal** is the straight line perpendicular to the tangent that passes through the point of contact between the tangent and the circle. Notice that the normal is an extension of a diameter.

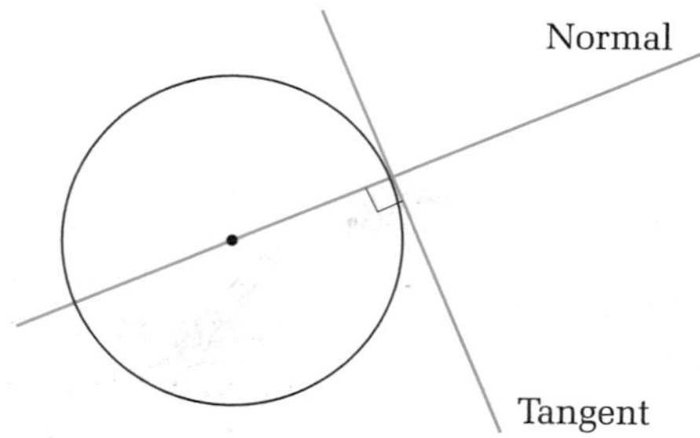

Example 4

Find the equation of the tangent to the circle $x^2 + y^2 - 3x - y - 2 = 0$ at the point (3, 2). Then find the equation of the normal.

Solution

Compare $x^2 + y^2 - 3x - y - 2 = 0$ to the general form $x^2 + y^2 - 2ax - 2by + c = 0$. The values of a and b can be established by equating coefficients.

Both the tangent and the normal pass through (3, 2); we know one point on each line. The normal passes through the centre of the circle, so start by finding the centre, (a, b), of the circle.

Equating coefficients of x, $\quad -3 = -2a, \quad$ so $a = \frac{3}{2}$.

Equating coefficients of y, $\quad -1 = -2b, \quad$ so $b = \frac{1}{2}$.

So the centre of the circle, $(a, b) = (\frac{3}{2}, \frac{1}{2})$.

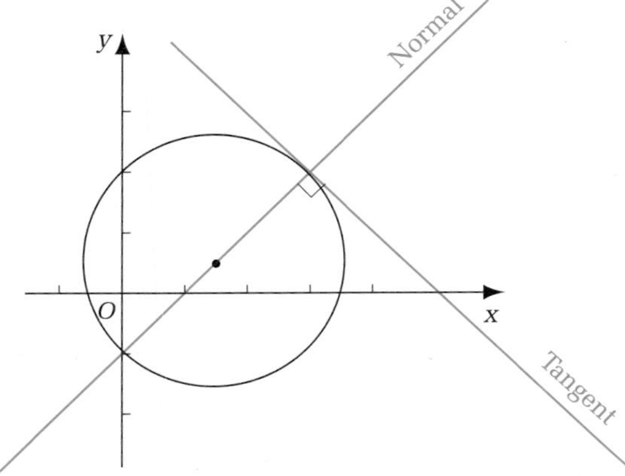

The gradient of the normal can now be found by using the points $(3, 2)$ and $(\frac{3}{2}, \frac{1}{2})$.

$$\text{gradient of normal} = \frac{2 - \frac{1}{2}}{3 - \frac{3}{2}} = \frac{\frac{3}{2}}{\frac{3}{2}} = 1$$

Since the tangent is perpendicular to the normal its gradient must be -1. We now know the gradient of the tangent and the coordinates of a point on the tangent (3, 2), so the equation of the tangent is given by

Recall that the product of the gradients of two perpendicular lines is always -1.

$$y - y_1 = m(x - x_1)$$
$$\Rightarrow \quad y - 2 = -1(x - 3)$$
$$\Rightarrow \quad y - 2 = -x + 3$$
$$\Rightarrow \quad y + x - 5 = 0$$

Similarly, we know the gradient of the normal and the coordinates of a point on the normal, so the equation of the normal is given by

We knew another point on the normal (the centre of the circle), so we could also have used the technique for finding the equation of a straight line knowing two points on that line.

$$y - y_1 = m(x - x_1)$$
$$\Rightarrow \quad y - 2 = 1(x - 3)$$
$$\Rightarrow \quad y - 2 = x - 3$$
$$\Rightarrow \quad y - x + 1 = 0$$

2.5 The Equation of a Circle

Exercise

Technique

1 Find the centre and radius of each of the following circles:

a $(x-5)^2+(y-3)^2=7^2$ **b** $(x+6)^2+(y+1)^2=25$

c $x^2+(y+7)^2=121$ **d** $(x+1)^2+(y-2)^2=11$

2 Write the equations of the circles with the given centres and radii in the form $x^2+y^2-2ax-2by+c=0$:

a centre $(-1,3)$, radius 2 **b** centre $(2,-1)$, radius 3

c centre $(-2,0)$, radius $\sqrt{5}$ **d** centre $(3,-3)$, radius $3\sqrt{2}$

3 Find the centre and radius of the following circles.

a $x^2+y^2-6x-2y+6=0$ **b** $x^2+y^2+2x-4y+1=0$

c $x^2+y^2+2x+8y+8=0$ **d** $x^2+y^2+4y+1=0$

Contextual

1 The point $(3,k)$ lies on the circle $x^2+y^2-6x-4y-51=0$. Find the values of k.

2 The point $(k,0)$ lies on the circle with centre $(4,1)$ and radius $\sqrt{10}$. Find two possible values of k.

3 The point A lies on the circle with centre $(1,3)$ and radius $\sqrt{5}$. Given that A lies on the y-axis, find the possible coordinates of A.

4 Find the equation of the tangent to the circle $x^2+4x+y^2=21$ at the point $(1,4)$. Find also the equation of the normal at this point.

5 A straight line touches the circle $x^2-4x+y^2-10y-71=0$ at the point $(8,-3)$. Find the equation of the line and the equation of any line perpendicular to it passing through the point $(4,3)$.

6 The points A $(-7,7)$ and B $(1,1)$ form the diameter of a circle. Find the equation of the circle.

7 Find the length of the tangent from the point $(9,8)$ to the circle $x^2+y^2-2x-4y=31$.

Consolidation

Exercise A

1 A, B, C are the points with coordinates $(4, 7)$, $(-1, 2)$ and $(6, 1)$ respectively.

a Prove that the triangle ABC is isosceles. State the coordinates of the mid-point, M, of AC and find the area of the triangle.
b Find the equation of the line BM.
c Find the equation of the line through A, perpendicular to BC.
d Find the coordinate of the point H where these two lines meet, and deduce that CH is perpendicular to AB.

(*OCSEB*)

2 The coordinates of the points A and B are $(2, 3)$ and $(4, -3)$ respectively. Find the length of AB and the coordinates of the mid-point of AB.

(*UCLES*)

3 P, Q, R are the points whose coordinates are $(2, 4)$, $(8, -4)$ and $(14, 8)$ respectively.

a Find the equations of the perpendicular bisectors of the lines PQ and PR.
b If the two bisectors meet at C, calculate the coordinates of C and show that $CP^2 = 50$.
c Deduce the equation of the circle through P, Q, and R in the form $x^2 + y^2 + px + qy + r = 0$.

(*OCSEB*)

4 A line through the origin with gradient m cuts the fixed circle in Fig. 1 in two points provided that $2(2m + 1)^2 > 9(m^2 + 1)$. Show that this inequality is equivalent to $m^2 - 8m + 7 < 0$ and find the solution set for m.

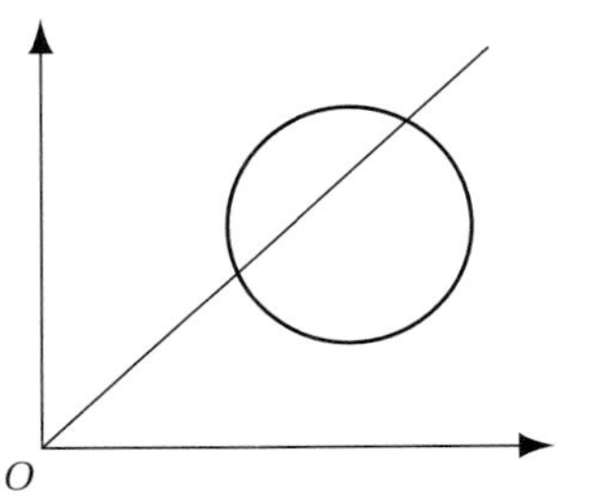

Fig. 1

(*OCSEB*)

5 Find the length of the tangent from the point (6, 2) to the circle $x^2 + y^2 + 2x = 9$.

6 Solve the inequality $(x - 3)(x - 6) > x + 9$.

(*AEB*)

Exercise B

1 The coordinates of the points A and B are (3, 2) and (4, −5) respectively. Find the coordinates of the mid-point of AB, and the gradient of AB. Hence find the equation of the perpendicular bisector of AB, giving your answer in the form $ax + by + c = 0$, where a, b and c are integers.

(*UCLES*)

2 The straight line P passes through the point (10, 1) and is perpendicular to the line R with equation $2x + y = 1$. Find the equation of P. Find also the coordinates of the point of intersection of P and R and deduce the perpendicular distance from the point (10, 1) to the line R.

(*UCLES*)

3 Find the length of the tangent from the point (7, 6) to the circle $x^2 + y^2 - 2x = 15$.

4 Find the equation of the straight line that is parallel to $y + 20x = 90$ and passes through the point (4, −10).

(*NEAB*)

5 Find the set of values for which $\dfrac{x}{x+4} > 2$.

(*ULEAC*)

Hint: Solve $x > 2(x + 4)$ and $x + 4 > 0$.

6 A circle, centre P, passes through A (1, 1), B (−2, 2) and C (−7, −3).

a Find the equation of the perpendicular bisector of AB.

b Find the equation of the perpendicular bisector of BC.

c Using your answers to **a** and **b**, solve the equations simultaneously to find centre P.

d Find the distance *AP*.

e Hence write down the equation of the circle.

Applications and Activities

Constructing a circle through three known points

1 Mark three points anywhere on a piece of paper. Now try to construct a circle that passes through all three. Can it always be done?

2 Mark the three points on a piece of graph paper so that their coordinates can be read. Repeat the problem but this time find:

a the coordinates of the centre of the circle

b the radius of the circle and

c the equation of the circle.

Summary

- The formula for the distance between points A (x_1, y_1) and B (x_2, y_2) is

$$AB = \sqrt{(x_2 - x_1)^2 + (y_2 - y_1)^2}$$

- The **gradient** of a line is a measure of its steepness.
- gradient $= \dfrac{\text{change in } y\text{-coordinate}}{\text{change in } x\text{-coordinate}}$
- **Parallel** straight lines have the same gradient.
- The product of the gradients of **perpendicular** straight lines is -1.
- The equation of a straight line is generally written in the forms $y = mx + c$ $(y = a_1x + a_0)$ and $ax + by + c = 0$.
- The equation of a straight line with gradient m passing through (x_1, y_1) is

$$y - y_1 = m(x - x_1)$$

- The equation of a straight line passing through (x_1, y_1) and (x_2, y_2) is

$$\frac{y - y_1}{y_2 - y_1} = \frac{x - x_1}{x_2 - x_1}$$

- The mid-point M of a line joining the points A (x_1, y_1) and B (x_2, y_2) has coordinates

$$\left(\frac{x_1 + x_2}{2}, \frac{y_1 + y_2}{2}\right)$$

- The symbols $>$, $\leq$, $<$, $\geq$ mean 'greater than', 'less than or equal to', 'less than' and 'greater than or equal to', respectively.

- Linear equalities can be represented on a number line using ○⟶ and ●⟶ as appropriate.
- Quadratic inequalities can be solved by rearranging them as factorised quadratic expressions with zero on one side. Solutions can be checked by drawing graphs.
- The equation of a circle has general forms

$$(x-a)^2+(y-b)^2=r^2$$

and

$$x^2+y^2-2ax-2by+c=0$$

- A circle, $(x-a)^2+(y-b)^2=r^2$, has centre (a, b) and radius r.
- The **normal** to a circle at a given point is perpendicular to the tangent at that point, and passes through the centre of the circle.

3 Trigonometry I

What you need to know

- How to use Pythagoras' theorem.
- Factorisation methods, including factorisation of quadratic equations.
- How to write down the sine, cosine and tangent ratios for acute angles.
- How to find the area of a triangle.
- That the term solving a triangle means finding the lengths of the unknown sides and the sizes of the unknown angles.
- How to calculate bearings.

Review

1 Use Pythagoras' theorem to find the length of side AB in the following triangles:

Pythagoras of Samos (c. 560–c. 480BC)
Pythagoras provided the first logical proof of the theorem $a^2 + b^2 = c^2$ for right-angled triangles, and used letters on geometric figures.

a

B
6
A
8
C

b

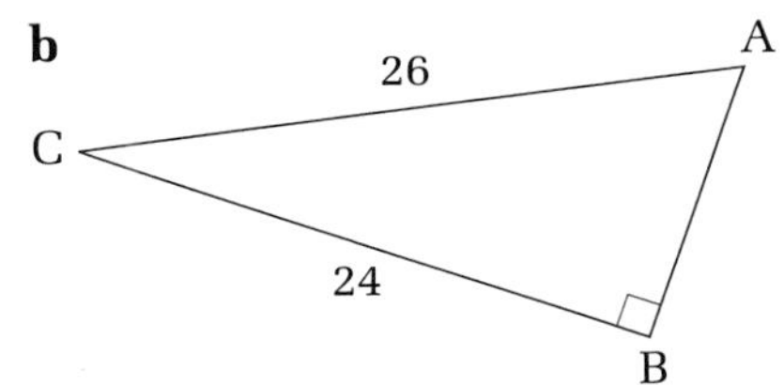

c

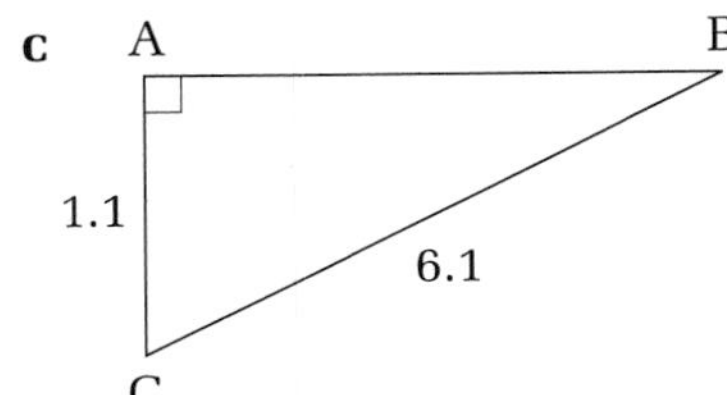

d

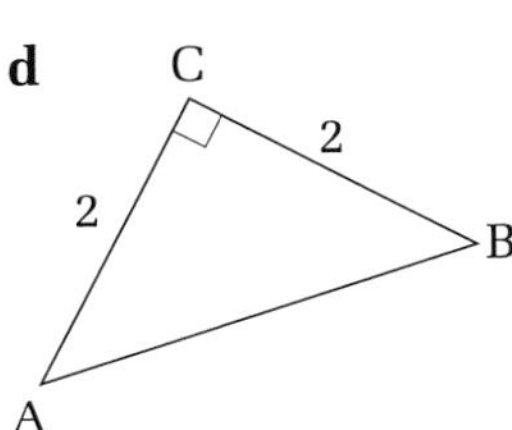

2 Factorise each of the following expressions and solve the equations:

a $a^2 - b^2$

b $c^2 + 3c + 2$

c $h^2 + h - 12$

d $k^2 - 7k + 12$

e $p^2 - 8p + 12 = 0$

f $3p^2 + 14p - 5 = 0$

3 Write down the values of $\sin x$, $\cos x$ and $\tan x$ for the following triangles:

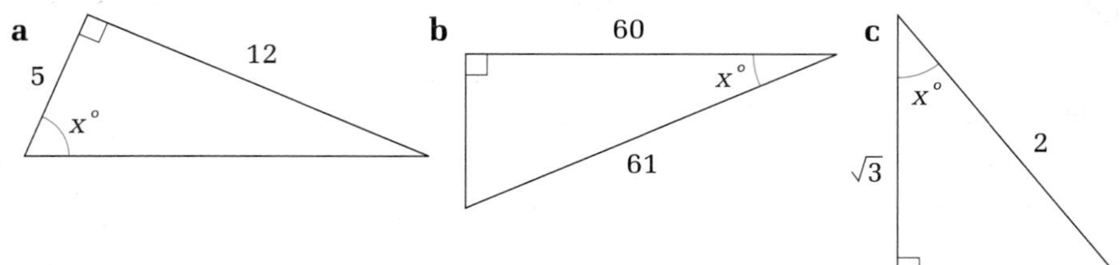

4 Calculate, to three significant figures, the areas of the following triangles:

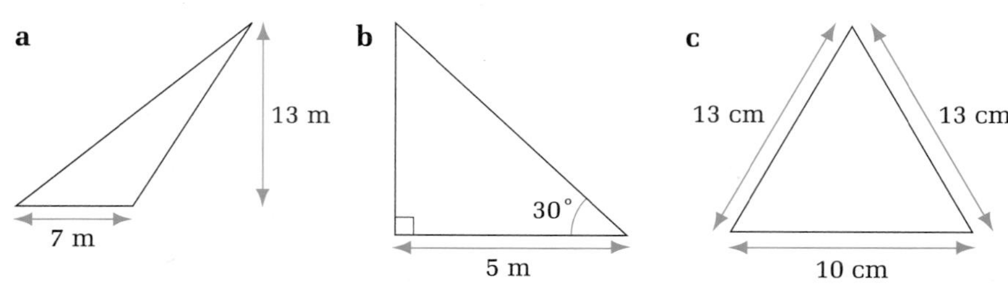

5 Solve the following triangles:

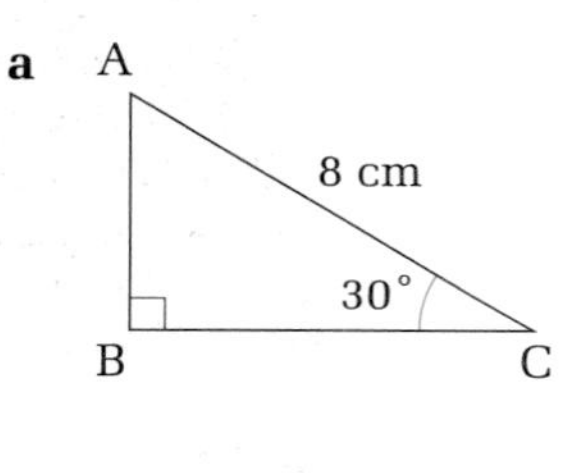

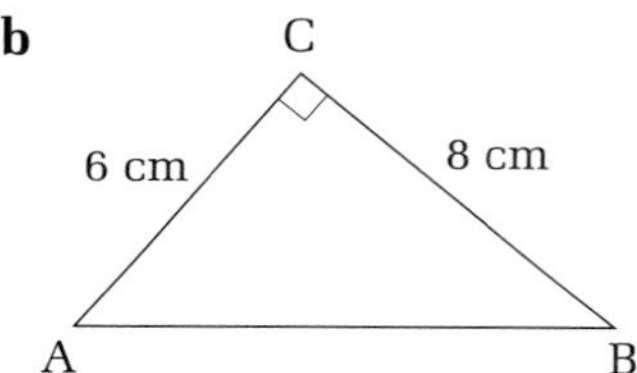

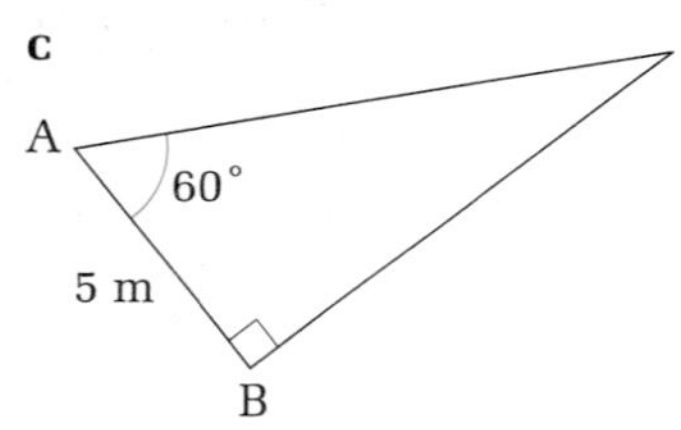

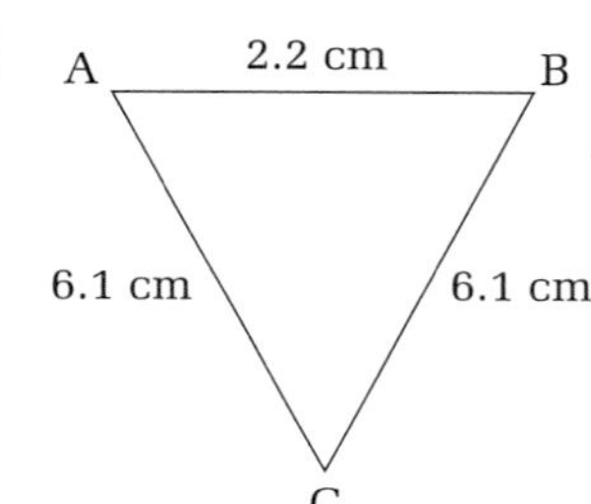

6 For each of the following diagrams write down the bearing of B from A:

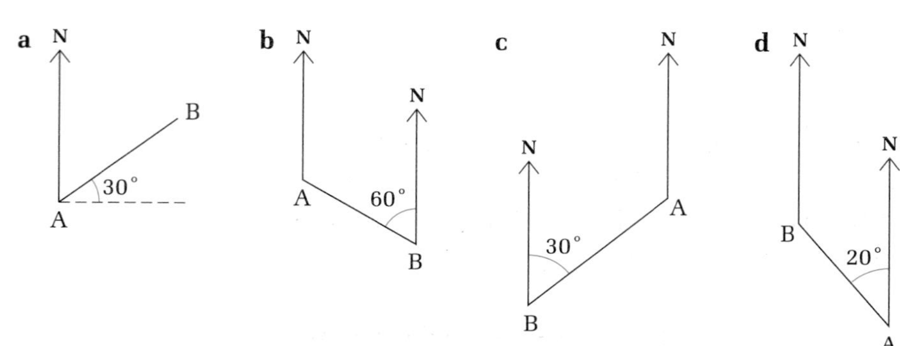

3.1 Trigonometric Functions

Trigonometry is the study of angle measurement, and in particular the study of triangle measurement and calculation. In order to distinguish between angles and lengths of sides the convention of capital letters for vertices and lower case letters for the corresponding opposite side is adopted.

The origins of the development of trigonometry are obscure. It was largely a Hindu invention, a mixture of algebra and geometry, used whenever lengths and angles needed to be calculated.

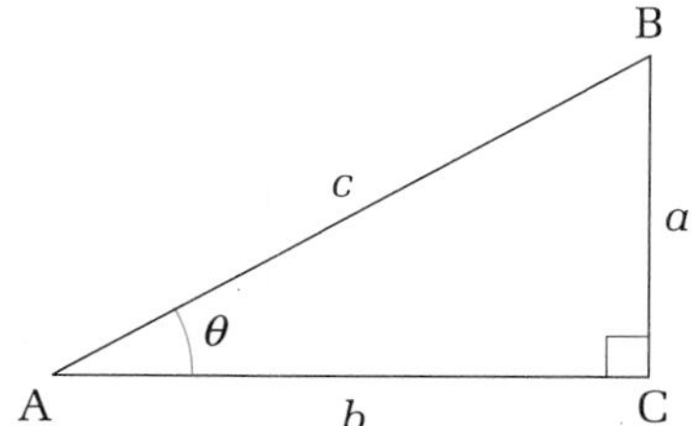

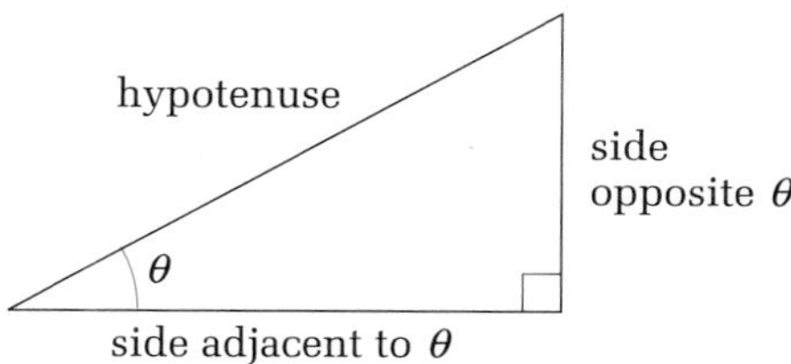

Right-angled triangles are used to define the three basic trigonometric functions for some acute angle θ; sine, cosine and tangent.

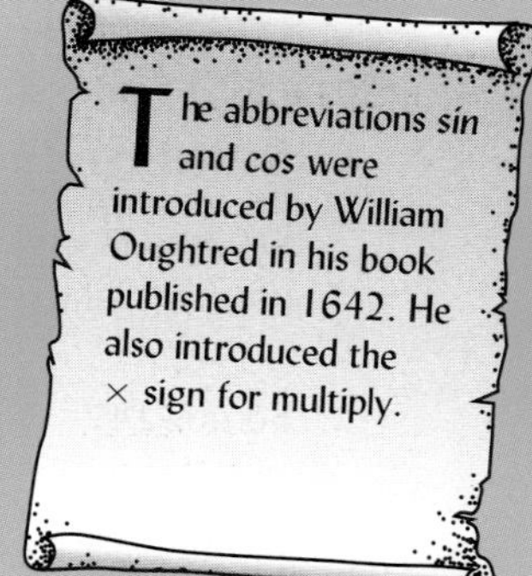

$$\sin\theta = \frac{a}{c} = \frac{\text{side opposite } \theta}{\text{hypotenuse}} \qquad \cos\theta = \frac{b}{c} = \frac{\text{side adjacent to } \theta}{\text{hypotenuse}}$$

$$\tan\theta = \frac{a}{b} = \frac{\text{side opposite } \theta}{\text{side adjacent to } \theta}$$

This principle can be used to define the sine, cosine and tangent of any angle θ.

Draw perpendicular axes Ox and Oy, and a circle centred on the origin, with radius 1 unit. Then θ will fix some point P on the circle.

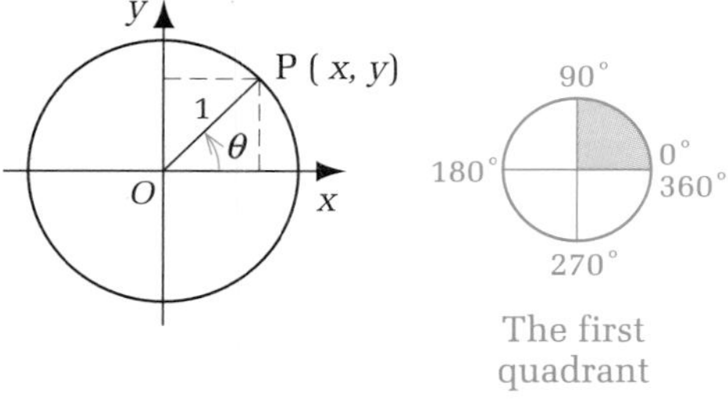

The first quadrant

The coordinates of P (x, y) are then $(\cos\theta, \sin\theta)$. Now adopt the convention that θ is measured anti-clockwise from the positive x-axis. The **quadrant** between the positive x-axis and the positive y-axis is called the **first quadrant**. In this quadrant θ is always acute.

The **second quadrant** is between the positive y-axis and the negative x-axis. In this quadrant θ is always obtuse. When θ is obtuse (greater than

90°) $\sin\theta$ and $\cos\theta$ are equal in magnitude to the sine and cosine ratio of the acute angle $(180° - \theta)$. So in the second quadrant the coordinates of P are still $(\cos\theta, \sin\theta)$, but note that in this quadrant $\sin\theta$ is positive, and $\cos\theta$ is negative. ◀ $\sin(180° - \theta) \equiv \sin\theta$
$\cos(180° - \theta) \equiv -\cos\theta$

The magnitude is the numerical value, or size of the trigonometric ratio, ignoring the sign (positive or negative).

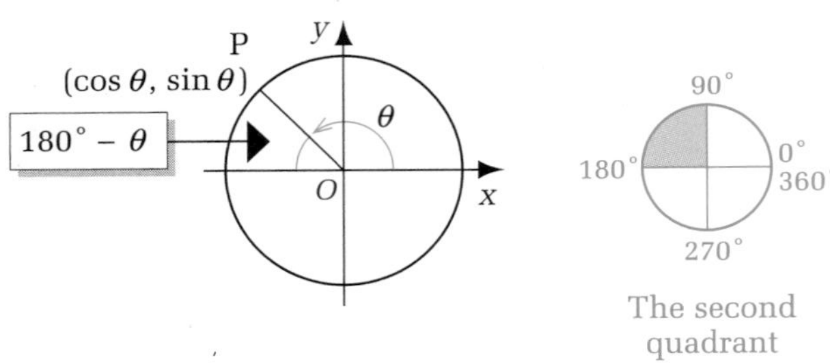

The second quadrant

Example 1

Find $\cos 147°$ as a trigonometric ratio of an acute angle.

Solution

We know that 147° lies in the second quadrant and, for obtuse θ, $\cos\theta = -\cos(180° - \theta)$.

So $\cos 147° = -\cos(180° - 147°) = -\cos 33°$.

Check this result on a calculator.

By making θ a reflex angle, we can extend these results into the third and fourth quadrants. In the third quadrant both $\sin\theta$ and $\cos\theta$ are negative. In the fourth quadrant $\cos\theta$ is positive and $\sin\theta$ is negative. (Think carefully about the coordinates of the point P).

$\sin(\theta - 180°) = -\sin\theta$
$\cos(\theta - 180°) = -\cos\theta$

$\sin(360° - \theta) = -\sin\theta$
$\cos(360° - \theta) = \cos\theta$.

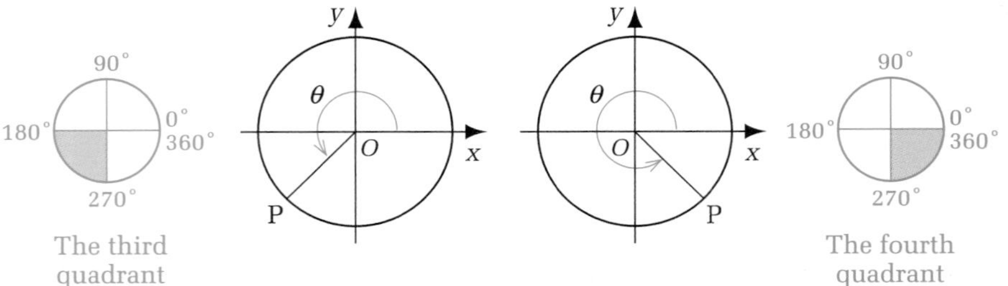

The third quadrant

The fourth quadrant

Remembering the definition of $\cos\theta$ and $\sin\theta$ as the coordinates of P, the gradient of the line OP gives us $\tan\theta$.

$$\tan\theta = \frac{y}{x} = \frac{\sin\theta}{\cos\theta}$$

This allows us to establish the quadrants in which each of the three trigonometric ratios are positive. One way of remembering which trigonometric ratios are positive and which negative in each quadrant is to remember only the positive ones. Think about the coordinates of P $(\cos\theta, \sin\theta)$ and remember that $\tan\theta$ is positive when $\sin\theta$ and $\cos\theta$ have the same sign.

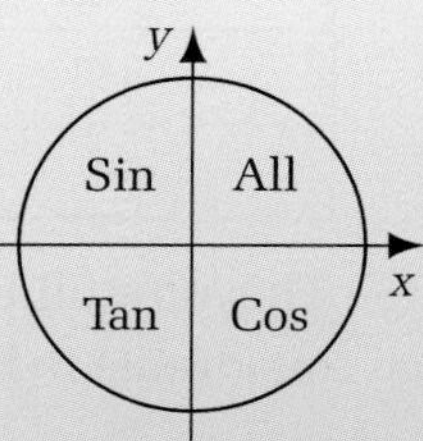

All the trigonometric ratios are positive in the first quadrant, sine is positive in the second, tangent is positive in the third and cosine is positive in the fourth quadrant. There are several good mnemonics (aids to memory), such as **A**ll **S**illy **T**om **C**ats; **A**ll **S**quirrels **T**ake **C**hestnuts; **A**ll **S**ilver **T**ea **C**ups.

Example 2

Write $\tan 227^\circ$ as a trigonometric ratio of an acute angle.

Solution

We know that 227° lies in the third quadrant, and that $\tan\theta$ is positive in the third quadrant. So $\tan 227^\circ = \tan(227^\circ - 180^\circ) = \tan 47^\circ$

Check this result on a calculator.

Special angles

Some acute angles are special because they occur so frequently. Two triangles in particular are very useful for finding the trigonometric ratios of these angles. These triangles have the advantage of giving exact results and not decimal approximations.

- An isosceles right-angled triangle with sides 1 unit.

From Pythagoras' 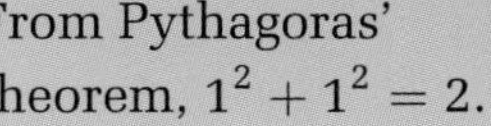
theorem, $1^2 + 1^2 = 2$.

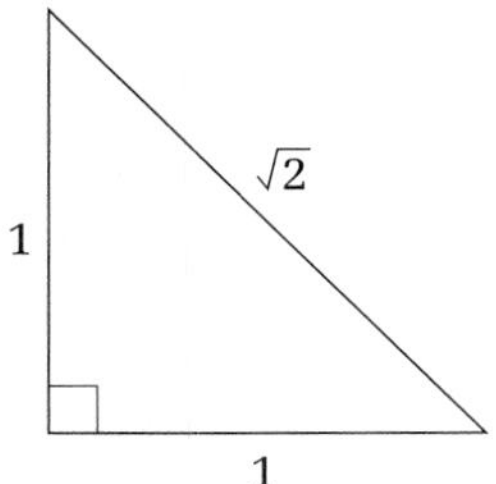

- Half of an equilateral triangle of side 2 units.

From Pythagoras' theorem, $2^2 - 1^2 = 3$.

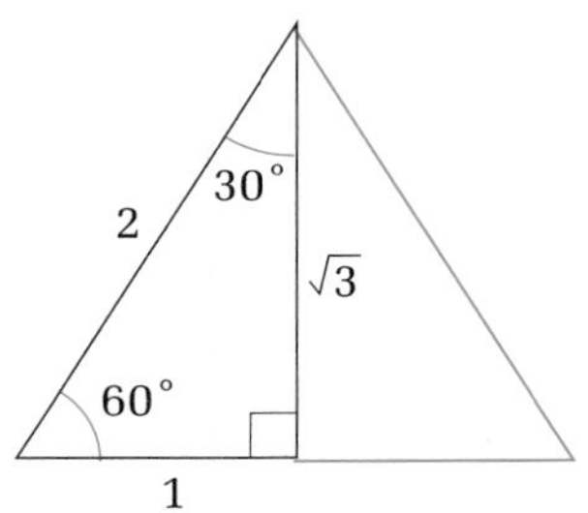

Using these triangles we have the following special results.

Copy and memorise them.

θ	$\sin\theta$	$\cos\theta$	$\tan\theta$
30°	$\frac{1}{2}$	$\frac{\sqrt{3}}{2}$	$\frac{1}{\sqrt{3}}$
45°	$\frac{1}{\sqrt{2}}$	$\frac{1}{\sqrt{2}}$	1
60°	$\frac{\sqrt{3}}{2}$	$\frac{1}{2}$	$\sqrt{3}$

This now allows the ratios of related angles in the second, third and fourth quadrants to be evaluated exactly.

Example 3

a Find $\sin 150°$.

b Find $\cos 330°$.

c Find $\sin 410°$ as a trigonometric ratio of an acute angle.

Solution

a We know that 150° lies in the second quadrant, where sine is positive. So $\sin 150° = \sin(180° - 150°) = \sin 30° = \frac{1}{2}$.

Check this result on a calculator.

b We know that 330° is in the fourth quadrant, and cosine is positive in the fourth quadrant. So $\cos 330° = \cos(360° - 330°) = \cos 30° = \frac{\sqrt{3}}{2}$.

Recall that $\frac{\sqrt{3}}{2}$ is irrational. If you check this result on a calculator your screen will probably show 0.8660 . . .

c Angles outside the range 0°–360° always lie in one of the four quadrants. We find that $410° - 360° = 50°$, so 410° is in the first quadrant, where sine is positive.

So $\sin 410° = \sin(410° - 360°)$

$= \sin 50°$

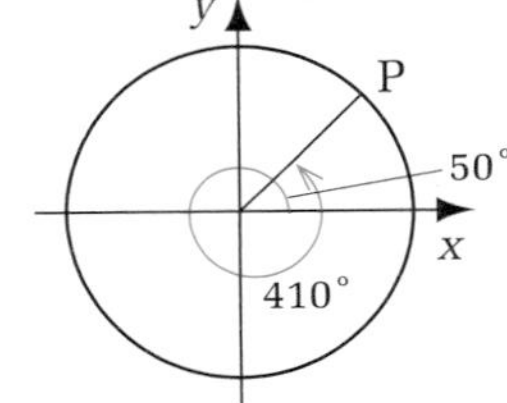

Graphs of the trigonometric functions

Now draw a new pair of axes and plot the angle θ along the x-axis and the y-coordinate of P ($\sin\theta$) along the y-axis. This gives a continuous curve. This curve, or wave, repeats itself every 360°, so the sine curve is said to have a **period** of 360°. The curve has a maximum value of 1 (when $\theta = 90°$) and a minimum of -1 (when $\theta = 270°$). These correspond to P being at the top and bottom of the circle.

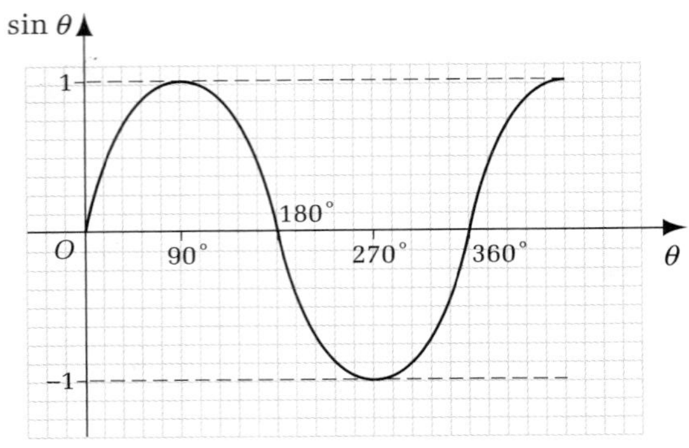

The systematic study of trigonometry is usually attributed to Hipparchus, an Alexandrian astronomer who lived around 150BC. He made a table of sines and used it to find the distance between the Moon and the Earth.

You can draw a similar graph plotting the angle θ along the x-axis and the x-coordinate of P ($\cos\theta$) along the y-axis. The graph of $\cos\theta$ is the same shape as that of $\sin\theta$, but it has been shifted by $90°$. The $90°$ is sometimes referred to as the **phase difference** between the two graphs.

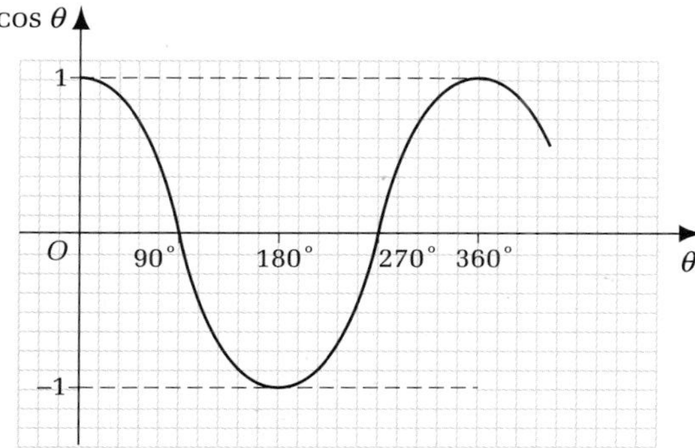

The similarities can be described using the following equations.

$\mathbf{\sin(\theta + 90°) = \cos\theta}$ $\quad$ $\mathbf{\sin(90° - \theta) = \cos\theta}$

$\mathbf{\cos(\theta + 90°) = -\sin\theta}$ $\quad$ $\mathbf{\cos(90° - \theta) = \sin\theta}$

Example 4

Show that $\sin 120° = \cos 30°$.

Solution

$$\begin{aligned}\sin 120° &= \sin(180° - 120°)\\ &= \sin 60°\\ &= \tfrac{\sqrt{3}}{2}\\ &= \cos 30°\end{aligned}$$

120° is in the second quadrant, so sin is positive.

Recall that $\frac{\sqrt{3}}{2}$ is the trigonometric ratio of a special angle.

An alternative method would be to read off $\sin 120°$ and $\cos 30°$ from the graphs for sine and cosine. In both cases there is an answer of 0.8660 ... ($\approx \frac{\sqrt{3}}{2}$), although you are unlikely to be able to read a graph to this level of accuracy.

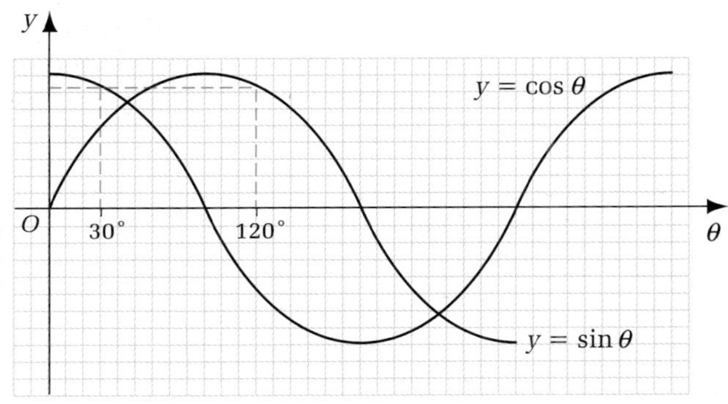

The graph of $\tan\theta$ doesn't look like either of the other two graphs. This is because $\tan\theta$ is defined as

$$\tan\theta = \frac{\sin\theta}{\cos\theta}$$

The denominator, $\cos\theta$, has the value 0 when $\theta = 90°$. This means that the graph of $\tan\theta$ will not be continuous. To show this on the graph we use dotted lines called **asymptotes**. Like $\sin\theta$ and $\cos\theta$, $\tan\theta$ is periodic, but this time the period is 180° instead of 360°.

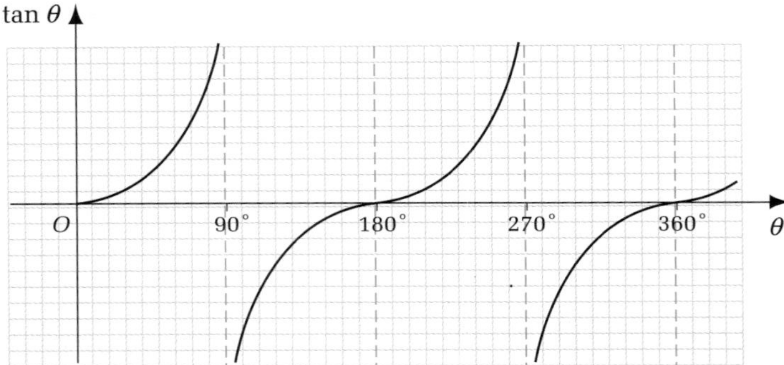

You should memorise the main features of the sine, cosine and tangent graphs. The main features are the general shape, maximum and minimum points, intersections with axes and positions of asymptotes.

Trigonometric equations

A trigonometric equation is one containing a trigonometric function such as sine, cosine or tangent. Solving these equations means finding values of the angle that satisfy the equation. Usually the range of angles that are acceptable as solutions will be restricted. The restriction could be due to the nature of the problem, or imposed by the person setting the question. To find angles within these ranges the trigonometric graphs can be used.

In addition to finding the sine, cosine and tangent of a known angle, a calculator can be used to find an angle with a particular sine, cosine or tangent. The inverse trigonometric functions, written $\sin^{-1}$, $\cos^{-1}$ and $\tan^{-1}$, are used. On a calculator they are usually located above the 'sin', 'cos' and 'tan' function keys. Sometimes an 'inverse', 'shift', '2nd function' or 'arc' key needs to be pressed first.

Alternative notation for inverse trigonometric angles that you may come across is **arcsin**, **arccos** and **arctan** (and sometimes arsin, arcos and artan).

If a calculator is used to find an angle it will give an answer called the **principal value**. Other solutions can then sometimes be found by adding multiples of the period for that function. Alternatively, once the principal value is known, the symmetry of the trigonometric graphs can be used to find solutions.

Example 5

a Find values of θ for which $4\sin\theta = 3$ such that $0° \le \theta \le 360°$.
b Solve the equation $\tan\theta = -2$ for $0° \le \theta \le 360°$.

Solution

a $4\sin\theta = 3 \Rightarrow \sin\theta = \frac{3}{4}$ ◀ **Recall that ⇒ means 'implies'.**

$$\theta = \sin^{-1}(0.75) = 48.6° \text{ (3 s.f.)}$$

First isolate the trigonometric ratio (sine), and notice that $\sin\theta$ is positive, so we expect solutions in the first and second quadrants.

The solution in the first quadrant is 48.6°.
The solution in the second quadrant is $180° - 48.6° = 131.4°$

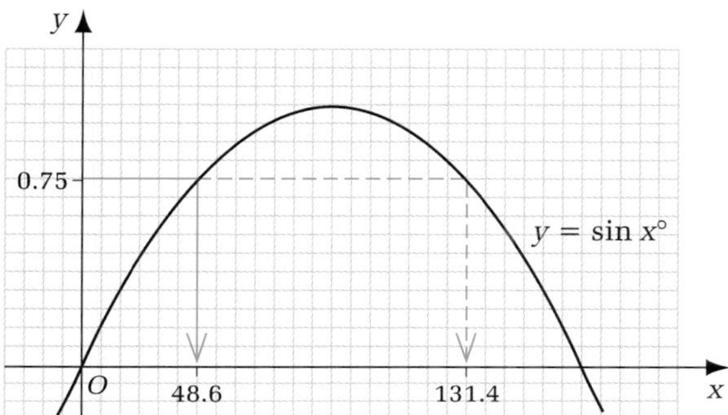

b $\tan\theta = -2 \Rightarrow \theta = \tan^{-1}(-2)$

$$\theta = -63.4° \text{ (3 s.f.)}$$

In this case the calculator gives a principal value outside the acceptable range, and negative.

Add multiples of 180°, the period of $\tan\theta$, to find solutions that lie within the acceptable range.

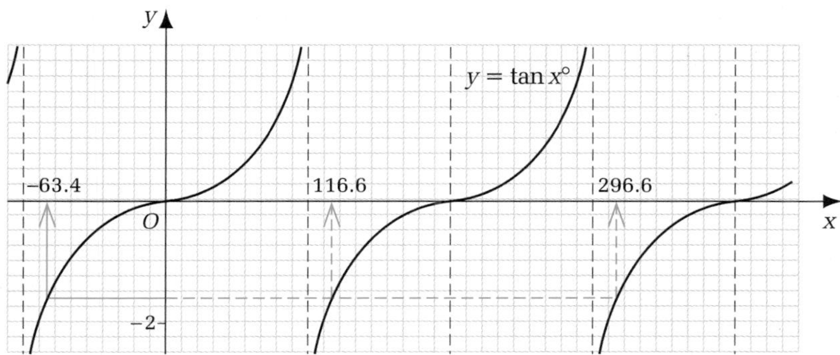

$\theta = -63.4° + 180° = 116.6°$

$\theta = -63.4° + 360° = 296.6°$

$\theta = -63.4° + 540° = 476.6°$, which is outside the acceptable range.

There are two solutions; $\theta = 116.6°$ and $296.6°$. (Notice that they are in the second and fourth quadrants, where $\tan\theta$ is negative.)

Graphical calculator support pack

The reciprocal ratios

There are three other trigonometric ratios, which are known as the **reciprocal ratios**. These are cosecant (cosec), secant (sec) and cotangent (cot).

These ratios are used less frequently but are applied in astronomy, navigation and mechanics, particularly in projectile motion.

$$\operatorname{cosec}\theta = \frac{1}{\sin\theta} \qquad \sec\theta = \frac{1}{\cos\theta} \qquad \cot\theta = \frac{1}{\tan\theta}$$

Example 6

Find:

a $\operatorname{cosec} 30°$ **b** $\cot 60°$ **c** $\sec 42°$

Solution

a $\operatorname{cosec} 30° = \dfrac{1}{\sin 30°}$

$= \dfrac{1}{\frac{1}{2}} = 2$

Recall that 30° is a special angle.

b $\cot 60° = \dfrac{1}{\tan 60°} = \dfrac{1}{\sqrt{3}}$

c $\sec 42° = \dfrac{1}{\cos 42°}$

$= \dfrac{1}{0.7431} = 1.3457$ (4 d.p.)

Work to four decimal places with the trigonometric ratios.

Example 6**c** demonstrates the need to work to an appropriate degree of accuracy when using trigonometric functions on a calculator.

If you use full screen accuracy with cos 42° then sec 42° = 1.3456 (4 d.p.). Note the rounding error.

Example 7

Find one solution to $\operatorname{cosec}\theta = 3$.

Solution

$\operatorname{cosec}\theta = 3 \Rightarrow \dfrac{1}{\sin\theta} = 3$

$\Rightarrow \quad 1 = 3\sin\theta$

$\Rightarrow \sin\theta = \frac{1}{3}$

$\theta = \sin^{-1}(\frac{1}{3}) = 19.5°$ (3 s.f.)

Notice that this solution is the principal value.

From these examples we see that a useful strategy for solving trigonometric equations is as follows.

Step ① Rearrange the equation to make sine, cosine or tangent the subject.
Step ② Use a calculator (if necessary) to find the principal value.
Step ③ Using a graph or by adding multiples of the period find solutions in the acceptable range of angles.

3.1 Trigonometric Functions
Exercise
Technique

1 Write each of the following as trigonometric ratios of positive acute angles:

a $\sin 120°$
b $\cos 165°$
c $\tan 220°$
d $\cos 305°$
e $\tan 400°$
f $\cos(-137°)$
g $\sin(-29°)$
h $\sin(-697°)$

2 Write down the exact value of the following, leaving answers in terms of surds if appropriate:

a $\cos 150°$
b $\sin 225°$
c $\tan 300°$
d $\sin 330°$
e $\cos 120°$
f $\tan 420°$
g $\cos(-300°)$
h $\sin(-420°)$

3 Solve the following trigonometric equations for $0 \leq \theta \leq 360°$. Give your answers correct to one decimal place:

a $\sin \theta = 0.314$
b $\cos \theta = -0.52$
c $\tan \theta = 2.561$
d $3 \tan \theta = \sqrt{2}$
e $\sin \theta = \cos \theta$
f $2 \sin \theta = 3 \cos \theta$

4 Find, correct to four significant figures, the value of:

a $\operatorname{cosec} 39°$
b $\sec 41°$
c $\cot 93°$
d $\sec 129°$
e $\cot 200°$
f $\operatorname{cosec} 307°$
g $\cot 420°$
h $\operatorname{cosec}(-15°)$

5 Find the principal value solutions to the following:

Remember to work to 1 d.p. when finding angles.

a $5 \sin \theta = -3$
b $\tan \theta + 3 = -7$
c $\sec \theta = 4$
d $2 \cot \theta - 3 = 0$
e $4 - 3 \tan \theta = 11$
f $2 \operatorname{cosec} \theta = 3$

6 Construct a table giving values of $\sin \theta$, $\cos \theta$ and $\tan \theta$ for appropriate values of θ in the range $-90° \leq \theta \leq 450°$. On separate pieces of paper, draw the graphs of $\sin \theta$, $\cos \theta$ and $\tan \theta$ for this range of angles. Use the graphs to solve the equations:

a $\sin \theta = -0.5$
b $\cos \theta = 0.8$
c $\tan \theta = 3$

7 Draw the graph of $y = \sin\theta$ for values of θ in the range $-90° \le \theta \le 90°$. Use your graph to find:

a $\sin^{-1}(-0.5)$ **b** $\sin^{-1}(0.71)$

Contextual

1 The depth of water in a harbour, y metres, can be modelled by the equation $y = 5\sin(30t)° + 12$, where t is the time in hours from midnight on a particular day.

a Draw the graph of this function over a period of 24 hours.
b From the graph, find the times of high and low tides.
c Use the graph to find the length of time for which the depth of water in the harbour is greater than 15 metres.

2 The height of a tide can be modelled by a function of the form $h = a\cos bt° + c$, where h is the height in metres of the water and t is the time in hours after midnight. Find the values of a, b and c for the following tide table.

Tide	Time	Height (m)
High	00:00	12
Low	06:00	2
High	12:00	12
Low	18:00	2

3 The hours of daylight over a period of time can be modelled using a trigonometric equation. If n is the number of hours of daylight and x is the number of days from 1 January, then, $n = 12 - 6\cos(x + 10)°$.

a Calculate the length of the daylight on 1 April, which is day 90.
b Use the equation to find the dates of the longest and shortest days.
c Comment on the reliability of the model.
d Suggest an amendment to the model.

3.2 Equations and Identities

Trigonometric equations can increase in complexity and solving them requires combining algebraic techniques and knowledge of the trigonometric functions.

Example 1

Solve $4\sin\theta - 3\cos\theta = 0$ for $0° \leq \theta \leq 360°$.

Solution

$$4\sin\theta - 3\cos\theta = 0 \Rightarrow 4\sin\theta = 3\cos\theta$$

Rearrange the equation using algebra.

$$\Rightarrow \frac{\sin\theta}{\cos\theta} = \frac{3}{4}$$

$$\Rightarrow \tan\theta = 0.75$$

Recall the definition of $\tan\theta$.

$$\theta = \tan^{-1}(0.75) = 36.9°$$

Remember that the calculator gives the principal value.

Tangent is positive in the first and third quadrants. The solution in the first quadrant is 36.9°, and the solution in the third quadrant is 216.9°. ◀ $180° + 36.9° = 216.9°$.

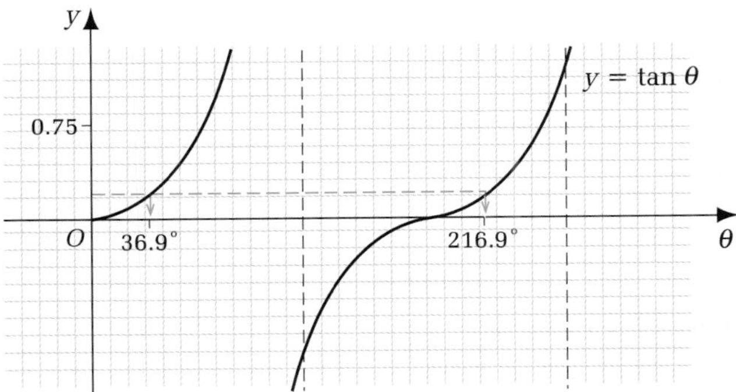

Example 2

Solve $\cos\theta\sin\theta = 2\sin\theta$, for $0° \leq \theta \leq 360°$.

Solution

$$\cos\theta\sin\theta = 2\sin\theta \Rightarrow \cos\theta\sin\theta - 2\sin\theta = 0$$

$$\Rightarrow \sin\theta(\cos\theta - 2) = 0$$ ◀ Factorise.

$$\Rightarrow \sin\theta = 0 \text{ or } (\cos\theta - 2) = 0$$

When rearranging, remember that you can't divide throughout by $\sin\theta$, because $\sin\theta$ may be zero.

When $\sin\theta = 0$, $\theta = 0°, 180°, 360°$.
When $\cos\theta = 2$ there are no solutions.
So the solutions are $\theta = 0°, 180°, 360°$.

Example 3

Solve the equation $2\sin^2\theta + \sin\theta - 1 = 0$, for $0° \le \theta \le 360°$.

The notation $\sin^2\theta$ means $(\sin\theta)^2$.

Solution

The equation $2\sin^2\theta + \sin\theta - 1 = 0$ is a quadratic in $\sin\theta$. It can be solved directly, or by making a substitution for $\sin\theta$ (which can make the process look less complex).

- *Direct solution*

$$2\sin^2\theta + \sin\theta - 1 = 0 \Rightarrow (2\sin\theta - 1)(\sin\theta + 1) = 0$$
$$\Rightarrow 2\sin\theta - 1 = 0 \text{ or } \sin\theta + 1 = 0$$

So $\sin\theta = \frac{1}{2}$ or $\sin\theta = -1$.

- *Substitution*

Let $y = \sin\theta$.

$$2\sin^2\theta + \sin\theta - 1 = 0 \Rightarrow 2y^2 + y - 1 = 0$$
$$\Rightarrow (2y - 1)(y + 1) = 0$$
$$\Rightarrow 2y - 1 = 0 \text{ or } y + 1 = 0$$
$$\Rightarrow y = \tfrac{1}{2} \text{ or } y = -1$$

But $y = \sin\theta$, so $\sin\theta = \frac{1}{2}$ or $\sin\theta = -1$.

Both methods give the same result. What else do you notice? You should notice that these are the trigonometric ratios for 'special angles'. When $\sin\theta = \frac{1}{2}$, $\theta = 30°, 150°$ for $0° \le \theta \le 360°$, and when $\sin\theta = -1$, $\theta = 270°$. So the solutions are $\theta = 30°, 150°, 270°$.

Notice that this quadrati[c] equation in $\sin\theta$ has thr[ee] distinct solutions for the given range of angles. Do[n't] assume that all quadrati[cs] will always give two solutions.

Another type of trigonometric equation is one involving brackets.

Example 4

Solve the equation $\cos(\theta + 30°) = \frac{1}{2}$ for $-180° \le \theta \le 180°$.

Remember that this has many solutions.

Solution

$$\cos(\theta + 30°) = \tfrac{1}{2} \Rightarrow (\theta + 30°) = \cos^{-1}(\tfrac{1}{2})$$
$$\Rightarrow \theta + 30° = \ldots, -60°, 60°, \ldots$$
$$\Rightarrow \theta = -90°, 30° \text{ in the given range}$$

So the solutions are $\theta = -90°, 30°$.
Check that these are solutions by substituting them back into the original equation.

Give solutions in the required range only.

$$\cos(-90° + 30°) = \cos(-60°) = \tfrac{1}{2}$$
$$\cos(30° + 30°) = \cos 60° = \tfrac{1}{2}$$

Example 5

Solve $\tan 2\theta = 1$, for $0° \le \theta \le 360°$.

Solution

If $\tan 2\theta = 1$ then 2θ must be a special angle. Note also the range of values for θ. The equation is in 2θ, so we must solve it for 2θ in the range $0° \le 2\theta \le 720°$.

$$\tan 2\theta = 1 \Rightarrow 2\theta = \tan^{-1}(1)$$

$$2\theta = 45°, 225°, 405°, 585°$$

$$\theta = 22.5°, 112.5°, 202.5°, 292.5°$$

Find all values of 2θ before dividing by 2.

Pythagorean identities

When equations involve more than one trigonometric function, and factorisation does not appear to be an obvious method, other techniques can be used. Often it is possible to substitute an equivalent expression for one already in the equation. Three results in particular are useful for this. They are known as **Pythagorean identities**. An **identity** is an equation that is true for all values of the variable. It is sometimes distinguished by the symbol $\equiv$ instead of $=$.

The Pythagorean identities are:

$\mathbf{\sin^2\theta + \cos^2\theta \equiv 1}$ Identity 1

$\mathbf{\tan^2\theta + 1 \equiv \sec^2\theta}$ Identity 2 ◀ $\sec^2\theta - \tan^2\theta \equiv 1$

$\mathbf{1 + \cot^2\theta \equiv \operatorname{cosec}^2\theta}$ Identity 3 ◀ $\operatorname{cosec}^2\theta - \cot^2\theta \equiv 1$

Identity 1 can be demonstrated by using Pythagoras' theorem.

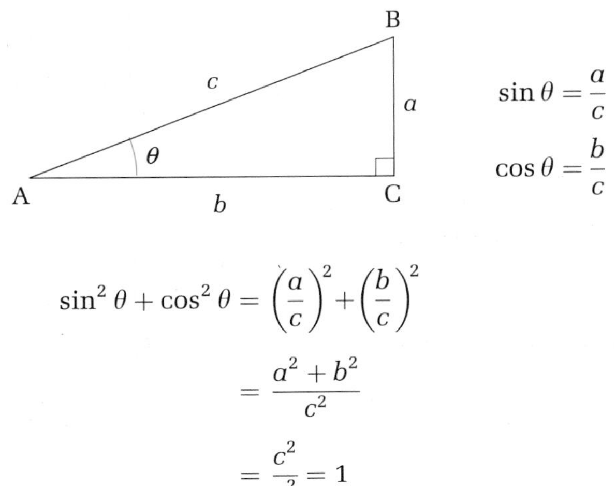

$$\sin\theta = \frac{a}{c}$$

$$\cos\theta = \frac{b}{c}$$

$$\sin^2\theta + \cos^2\theta = \left(\frac{a}{c}\right)^2 + \left(\frac{b}{c}\right)^2$$

$$= \frac{a^2 + b^2}{c^2}$$

$$= \frac{c^2}{c^2} = 1$$

Alternatively we can use the unit circle $x^2 + y^2 = 1$. Now $x = \cos\theta$ and $y = \sin\theta$.

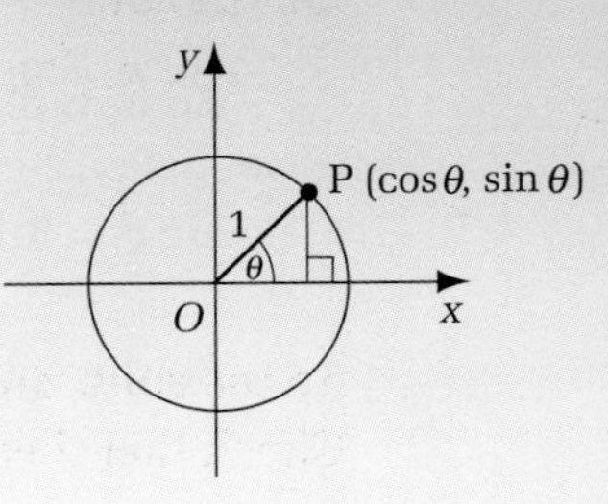

$\sin^2\theta + \cos^2\theta = 1$ works in all four quadrants.

The following examples illustrate how these results can be used to simplify trigonometric equations and establish further identities.

Example 6

Solve the equations:

a $2\sin^2\theta + 5\cos\theta + 1 = 0$ for $-180° \leq \theta \leq 180°$

b $3\cot^2\theta + 5\operatorname{cosec}\theta + 1 = 0$ for $0° \leq \theta \leq 360°$.

Solution

a $2\sin^2\theta + 5\cos\theta + 1 = 0 \Rightarrow 2(1-\cos^2\theta) + 5\cos\theta + 1 = 0$ — Using identity 1.

$\Rightarrow \quad 2 - 2\cos^2\theta + 5\cos\theta + 1 = 0$

$\Rightarrow \quad 2\cos^2\theta - 5\cos\theta - 3 = 0$

Multiply out the bracket, collect like terms and make the highest power term positive.

This is a quadratic in $\cos\theta$ that can be factorised.

$(2\cos\theta + 1)(\cos\theta - 3) = 0$

So $\quad 2\cos\theta + 1 = 0$ or $\cos\theta - 3 = 0$

$\cos\theta = -\frac{1}{2}$ or $\cos\theta = 3$

$\cos\theta = -\frac{1}{2} \Rightarrow \theta = -120°, 120°$

$\cos\theta = 3$ has no solutions

Solutions in the second and third quadrants, where $\cos\theta$ is negative.

So the solutions are $\theta = \pm 120°$.

b $3\cot^2\theta + 5\operatorname{cosec}\theta + 1 = 0 \Rightarrow 3(\operatorname{cosec}^2\theta - 1) + 5\operatorname{cosec}\theta + 1 = 0$ — Using identity 3.

$\Rightarrow \quad 3\operatorname{cosec}^2\theta - 3 + 5\operatorname{cosec}\theta + 1 = 0$

$\Rightarrow \quad 3\operatorname{cosec}^2\theta + 5\operatorname{cosec}\theta - 2 = 0$ — Factorising.

$\Rightarrow \quad (3\operatorname{cosec}\theta - 1)(\operatorname{cosec}\theta + 2) = 0$

$\Rightarrow \quad 3\operatorname{cosec}\theta - 1 = 0$ or $\operatorname{cosec}\theta + 2 = 0$

So $\operatorname{cosec}\theta = \frac{1}{3}$ or $\operatorname{cosec}\theta = -2$.

So now $\sin\theta = 3$ or $\sin\theta = -\frac{1}{2}$. — Using the definition of $\operatorname{cosec}\theta$.

$\sin\theta = 3$ has no solutions and $\sin\theta = -\frac{1}{2} \Rightarrow \theta = 210°, 330°$

So the solutions are $\theta = 210°, 330°$.

Example 7

Prove the identity $\sin\theta\tan\theta \equiv \sec\theta - \cos\theta$.

Solution

$$\sin\theta\tan\theta = \sin\theta\frac{\sin\theta}{\cos\theta}$$

Using the definition of $\tan\theta$.

$$= \frac{\sin^2\theta}{\cos\theta}$$

$$= \frac{1-\cos^2\theta}{\cos\theta}$$ ◀ Using identity 1.

$$= \frac{1}{\cos\theta} - \frac{\cos^2\theta}{\cos\theta}$$

$$= \sec\theta - \cos\theta$$

Remembering the definition of $\sec\theta$.

That is, $\sin\theta\tan\theta \equiv \sec\theta - \cos\theta$.

Example 7 illustrates a useful procedure to adopt when establishing identities. Begin with the left-hand side (LHS) and then perform logical manipulations line by line until the form of the right-hand side (RHS) appears. At first this may appear very difficult, but keep in mind where you are trying to go. The range of equivalent forms mean that tasks like these are difficult for computers and symbol manipulators to do quickly.

Example 8

Prove the identity $\tan\theta + \cot\theta \equiv \sec\theta\,\mathrm{cosec}\,\theta$.

Solution

Beginning with the LHS,

$$\tan\theta + \cot\theta \equiv \frac{\sin\theta}{\cos\theta} + \frac{\cos\theta}{\sin\theta}$$

Writing the LHS in terms of $\sin\theta$ and $\cos\theta$.

$$\equiv \frac{\sin^2\theta + \cos^2\theta}{\sin\theta\cos\theta}$$

$$\equiv \frac{1}{\sin\theta\cos\theta}$$ ◀ Using identity 1.

$$\equiv \frac{1}{\sin\theta} \times \frac{1}{\cos\theta}$$

Recalling how fractions are multiplied.

$$\equiv \sec\theta \times \mathrm{cosec}\,\theta$$

And so we arrive at the RHS.

That is, $\tan\theta + \cot\theta \equiv \sec\theta\,\mathrm{cosec}\,\theta$.

Another useful technique that can help in proving identities is the ability to multiply by 1, with 1 written in a convenient form that allows further algebraic manipulation.

For example, $\frac{\sin\theta}{\sin\theta} \equiv 1$, $\frac{1+\cos\theta}{1+\cos\theta} \equiv 1$, $\frac{1-\tan\theta}{1-\tan\theta} \equiv 1$, and so on.

Example 9

Prove the identity $\dfrac{\cos\theta}{1-\sin\theta} \equiv \sec\theta + \tan\theta$.

Solution

Beginning with the LHS, $\dfrac{\cos\theta}{1-\sin\theta}$ is already written in terms of sine and cosine, so we appear to be stuck. However, multiply by 1, and force the denominator to be the difference of two squares.

$$\begin{aligned}\frac{\cos\theta}{1-\sin\theta} &\equiv \frac{\cos\theta}{1-\sin\theta} \times \frac{1+\sin\theta}{1+\sin\theta} \\ &\equiv \frac{\cos\theta(1+\sin\theta)}{1^2-\sin^2\theta} \\ &\equiv \frac{\cos\theta(1+\sin\theta)}{\cos^2\theta} \qquad \blacktriangleleft \text{ Using identity 1.} \\ &\equiv \frac{1+\sin\theta}{\cos\theta} \\ &\equiv \frac{1}{\cos\theta} + \frac{\sin\theta}{\cos\theta} \\ &\equiv \sec\theta + \tan\theta\end{aligned}$$

Note that $\cos\theta$ is a common factor in the numerator and the denominator.

So we arrive at the RHS, as required. That is,

$$\frac{\cos\theta}{1-\sin\theta} \equiv \sec\theta + \tan\theta$$

3.2 Equations and Identities
Exercise
Technique

1 Solve the following trigonometric equations for $0^\circ \le \theta \le 360^\circ$ (giving angles correct to one decimal place):

a $3\sin\theta - 4\cos\theta = 0$
b $\sin\theta + 2\cos\theta = 0$
c $3\sin\theta + \cos\theta = 0$
d $4\sin\theta = \cos\theta$
e $\cot\theta = \tan\theta$
f $2\sin\theta = \frac{1}{2}\operatorname{cosec}\theta$

1 b

2 Solve these equations completely for $-180^\circ \le \theta \le 180^\circ$:

a $\tan^2\theta - 3\tan\theta + 2 = 0$
b $3\sin^2\theta - 4\sin\theta + 1 = 0$
c $2\cos^2\theta + \cos\theta - 1 = 0$
d $4\cos^2\theta = 3$
e $8\sin^2\theta - 6\sin\theta + 1 = 0$
f $3\tan^2\theta = 1$

3 Solve these equations completely in the range $0^\circ \le \theta \le 360^\circ$ (giving answers correct to one decimal place where necessary):

a $\sin 2\theta = \frac{1}{2}$
b $\tan(\theta - 33^\circ) = 0.4816$
c $\cos(2\theta - 20^\circ) = 0.212$
d $\tan(3\theta - 40^\circ) = 6$
e $\sin(\theta - 90^\circ) = 0.75$
f $\tan 2\theta = 1$

3 a

4 Use Pythagorean identities to solve these equations in the range $-180^\circ \le \theta \le 180^\circ$:

a $6\cos^2\theta + \sin\theta - 5 = 0$
b $2\sin^2\theta + 5\cos\theta + 1 = 0$
c $\sec^2\theta = 3 - \tan\theta$
d $2\sec^2\theta = 5\tan\theta$
e $\operatorname{cosec}^2\theta = 3\cot\theta - 1$
f $\tan^2\theta + \sec^2\theta = 17$

5 Prove the following identities:

a $\sec^2\theta + \operatorname{cosec}^2\theta \equiv \sec^2\theta\operatorname{cosec}^2\theta$
b $\sec\theta + \tan\theta \equiv \dfrac{1 + \sin\theta}{\cos\theta}$
c $\cos^2\theta + 3\sin^2\theta \equiv 3 - 2\cos^2\theta$
d $\cos^4\theta - \sin^4\theta \equiv \cos^2\theta - \sin^2\theta$
e $\cot^2\theta + \cos^2\theta \equiv (\operatorname{cosec}\theta - \sin\theta)(\operatorname{cosec}\theta + \sin\theta)$
f $\dfrac{\sin\theta\tan\theta}{1 - \cos\theta} \equiv 1 + \sec\theta$

Contextual

1 The trajectory of a golf ball struck from a tee can be modelled by the equation

$$y = x\tan\theta - \frac{x^2\sec^2\theta}{80}$$

where θ is the acute angle of projection, x is the horizontal distance of the ball from the tee in metres and y is the vertical height of the ball above the fairway, also measured in metres. If the ball just clears a tree 16.8 m high, whose base is 16 m from the tee, find, to three significant figures, the angle of projection.

2 The equation of the path of a projectile referred to horizontal and upward vertical axes Ox, Oy for a golf ball is

$$y = x\tan\theta - \frac{x^2\sec^2\theta}{50}$$

Show how to reduce this equation to a quadratic equation in $\tan\theta$. Show that there are two distinct values of θ for which the ball can pass through a given point (X, Y), where $X > 0$, provided $200Y < 2500 - 4X^2$. Interpret this result in terms the golfer would understand.

3.3 Compound and Double Angle Formulas

In the trigonometry studied so far all the relationships contain trigonometric functions of a single variable, θ. There are other useful relationships that involve trigonometric functions of two variables and these are known as compound angle formulas. They are also known as the addition theorems since they show how the trigonometric functions of a sum or difference of two angles can be expressed in terms of the trigonometric functions of the individual angles.

$\sin(A+B) \equiv \sin A \cos B + \cos A \sin B$ Identity 1 ◀ **Learn these formulas.**

$\sin(A-B) \equiv \sin A \cos B - \cos A \sin B$ Identity 2

$\cos(A+B) \equiv \cos A \cos B - \sin A \sin B$ Identity 3

$\cos(A-B) \equiv \cos A \cos B + \sin A \sin B$ Identity 4

Notice that they are written as identities. This is because they are true for all values of A and B.

Identity 1 can be proved for the case A and B acute by considering a diagram illustrating the geometry of the angle sum $(A+B)$.

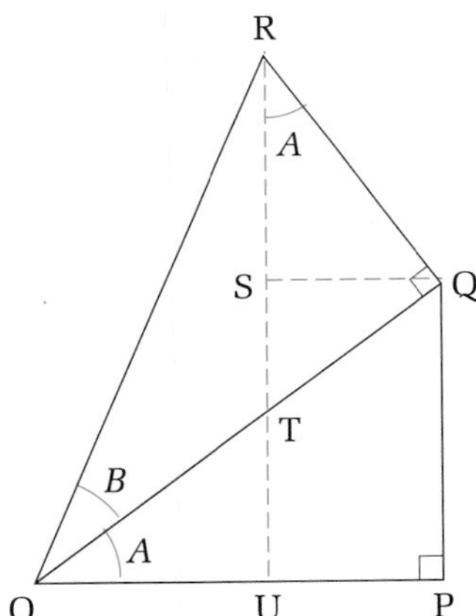

Let OPQ and OQR be right-angled triangles containing angles A and B respectively (as shown in the diagram). Look at triangle OQR.

Use the geometry of figure to show that $\angle SRQ$ must be A; that is triangles OPQ and RSQ are similar.

If $OR = 1$ then $RQ = \sin B$ and $OQ = \cos B$.

Now look at triangle RQT.

$RQ = \sin B$, so $RS = \sin B \cos A$ (call this result [1]).

Now look at triangle OQR.

$QP = OQ \sin A$, and $OQ = \cos B$,

so $QP = \cos B \sin A$ (call this result [2]).

Now look at triangle ORU.

$$OR = 1, \text{ so } RU = \sin(A + B).$$

But $RU = RS + SU = RS + QP$, so from results [1] and [2],

$$\sin(A + B) = \sin B \cos A + \cos B \sin A.$$

That is, $\sin(A + B) = \sin A \cos B + \cos A \sin B$.

It is usual to write these expressions with the angles in alphabetical order.

This demonstrates a proof for A and B acute. The proof of $\cos(A + B)$ is very similar. The results for the differences, $\sin(A - B)$ and $\cos(A - B)$, can be found by replacing B with $-B$ in each of the proven results and using the results $\sin(-B) = -\sin B$ and $\cos(-B) = \cos(B)$. These last results can be seen clearly from the graphs of sine and cosine.

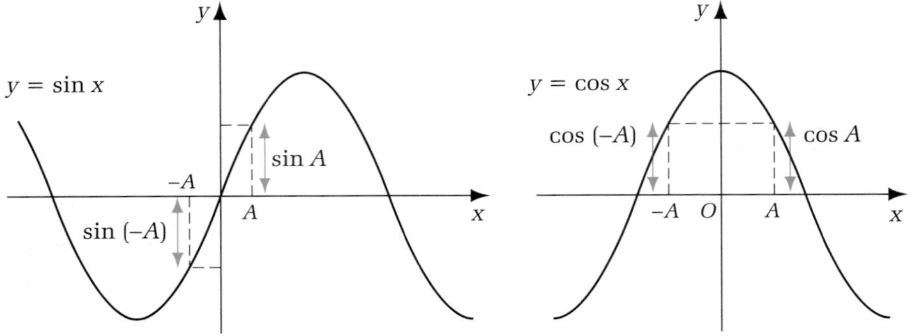

They illustrate the results for negative angles.

$$\mathbf{\sin(-A) = -\sin A \qquad \cos(-A) = \cos A}$$

The compound angle formulas hold for *all* angles.

These compound angle formulas allow us to evaluate more sines and cosines exactly and demonstrate further identities.

Example 1

a Find $\sin 15°$ in surd form.

b Find the exact value of $\cos 75°$.

Solution

a $\sin 15° = \sin(60° - 45°)$

$$= \sin 60° \cos 45° - \cos 60° \sin 45° \quad \text{◀ Using identity 2.}$$

$$= \left(\frac{\sqrt{3}}{2} \times \frac{1}{\sqrt{2}}\right) - \left(\frac{1}{2} \times \frac{1}{\sqrt{2}}\right)$$

$$= \frac{1}{2\sqrt{2}}(\sqrt{3} - 1)$$

$$= \frac{\sqrt{2}}{4}(\sqrt{3} - 1)$$

We know we want an answer in surd form, so try to write the angle as a sum of special angles.

Remember to rationalise the denominator.

b $\cos 75° = \cos(45° + 30°)$

$= \cos 45° \cos 30° - \sin 45° \sin 30°$

$= \left(\frac{1}{\sqrt{2}} \times \frac{\sqrt{3}}{2}\right) - \left(\frac{1}{\sqrt{2}} \times \frac{1}{2}\right)$

$= \frac{1}{2\sqrt{2}}(\sqrt{3} - 1)$

$= \frac{\sqrt{2}}{4}(\sqrt{3} - 1)$

This is consistent with the result from Section 3.1, where $\cos\theta = \sin(90° - \theta)$ when θ is acute.

These compound angle formulas also allow the addition theorems for tangent to be established.

$$\tan(A + B) \equiv \frac{\tan A + \tan B}{1 - \tan A \tan B}$$ Identity 5 ◀ **Learn these results.**

$$\tan(A - B) \equiv \frac{\tan A - \tan B}{1 + \tan A \tan B}$$ Identity 6

Example 2

Prove the identity $\tan(A + B) \equiv \frac{\tan A + \tan B}{1 - \tan A \tan B}$.

Solution

Beginning with the LHS,

$$\tan(A + B) = \frac{\sin(A + B)}{\cos(A + B)}$$

Recalling the definition of tangent.

$$= \frac{\sin A \cos B + \cos A \sin B}{\cos A \cos B - \sin A \sin B}$$ ◀ **Using identities 1 and 3.**

$$= \frac{\frac{\sin A \cos B}{\cos A \cos B} + \frac{\cos A \sin B}{\cos A \cos B}}{\frac{\cos A \cos B}{\cos A \cos B} - \frac{\sin A \sin B}{\cos A \cos B}}$$

Dividing each term in both the numerator and denominator by $\cos A \cos B$, converts sines into tangents.

$$= \frac{\tan A + \tan B}{1 - \tan A \tan B}$$

Eliminate terms; write tangents where possible.

So we arrive at the RHS. The compound angle formula for $\tan(A - B)$ can be derived in the same way.

Example 3

Solve the equation $\sin(\theta + 45°) = 2\cos(\theta + 45°)$ for $0° \le \theta \le 360°$.

Solution

$$\sin(\theta + 45^\circ) = 2\cos(\theta + 45^\circ) \Rightarrow \frac{\sin(\theta + 45^\circ)}{\cos(\theta + 45^\circ)} = 2$$

$$\Rightarrow \quad \tan(\theta + 45^\circ) = 2$$

An alternative method is to solve $\theta + 45^\circ = \tan^{-1}(2)$.

$$\Rightarrow \quad \frac{\tan\theta + \tan 45^\circ}{1 - \tan\theta\tan 45^\circ} = 2$$

◀ Using identity 5.

$$\Rightarrow \quad \frac{\tan\theta + 1}{1 - \tan\theta} = 2$$

Remembering that 45° a special angle.

$$\Rightarrow \quad \tan\theta + 1 = 2 - 2\tan\theta$$

So $3\tan\theta = 1$, and $\tan\theta = \frac{1}{3}$.
The solutions are $\theta = 18.4^\circ, 198.4^\circ$ (1 d.p.).

Double angles

The compound angle formulas provide some more very useful results in the special case where $A = B$. These are known as double angle formulas.

$$\mathbf{\sin 2\theta = 2\sin\theta\cos\theta}$$

◀ Learn these results.

$$\mathbf{\cos 2\theta = \cos^2\theta - \sin^2\theta}$$

$$\mathbf{\tan 2\theta = \frac{2\tan\theta}{1 - \tan^2\theta}}$$

To get these results simply put $A = B = \theta$ in the formulas for $\sin(A + B)$, $\cos(A + B)$ and $\tan(A + B)$. We can also use the Pythagorean identity, $\sin^2\theta + \cos^2\theta = 1$, in the expression for $\cos 2\theta$ to provide two other versions.

$$\mathbf{\cos 2\theta = 2\cos^2\theta - 1}$$

◀ Learn these results.

$$\mathbf{\cos 2\theta = 1 - 2\sin^2\theta}$$

Example 4

Find $\cos 2\theta$ when $\cos\theta = -\frac{1}{2}$.

Solution

Using $\cos 2\theta = 2\cos^2\theta - 1$,

$$\cos 2\theta = 2 \times (-\tfrac{1}{2})^2 - 1$$
$$= 2 \times \tfrac{1}{4} - 1 = -\tfrac{1}{2}$$

The result can be checked by using the methods of Section 3.1. When $\cos\theta = -\frac{1}{2}$, the cosine is negative so θ is in the second or third quadrant.

We know that $\cos 60° = \frac{1}{2}$, because 60° is a special angle. So in the second quadrant, $\cos(180° - 60°) = -\frac{1}{2}$. That is, $\cos 120° = -\frac{1}{2}$. So $\theta = 120°$, and $2\theta = 240°$.

Now $\cos 240° = \cos(180° + 60°)$, and 240° is in the third quadrant, so $\cos 240° = -\cos 60° = -\frac{1}{2}$. So when $\cos\theta = -\frac{1}{2}$, $\cos 2\theta = -\frac{1}{2}$.

Example 5

Find the exact value of $\dfrac{2\tan 67\frac{1}{2}°}{1 - \tan^2 67\frac{1}{2}°}$.

Solution

$$\begin{aligned}\frac{2\tan 67\frac{1}{2}°}{1-\tan^2 67\frac{1}{2}°} &= \tan(2\times 67\tfrac{1}{2}°)\\ &= \tan 135°\\ &= \tan(180° - 45°)\\ &= -\tan 45°\\ &= -1\end{aligned}$$

Recall that $\tan 2\theta = \dfrac{2\tan\theta}{1-\tan^2\theta}$.

In the second quadrant, tangent is negative.

Example 6

Prove the identity $\tan\theta + \cot\theta \equiv 2\operatorname{cosec} 2\theta$.

Solution

Beginning with the LHS,

$$\begin{aligned}\tan\theta + \cot\theta &= \frac{\sin\theta}{\cos\theta} + \frac{\cos\theta}{\sin\theta}\\ &= \frac{\sin^2\theta + \cos^2\theta}{\cos\theta\sin\theta}\\ &= \frac{1}{\sin\theta\cos\theta}\\ &= \frac{2}{2\sin\theta\cos\theta}\\ &= \frac{2}{\sin 2\theta}\\ &= 2\operatorname{cosec} 2\theta\end{aligned}$$

◀ Adding fractions.

◀ Remember the definition of cosec θ.

Remember the definition of cot θ.

$\sin^2\theta + \cos^2\theta = 1$.

Multiply numerator and denominator by 2 to create a double angle formula.

3.3 Compound and Double Angle Formulas

Exercise

Technique

1 Without using a calculator, find the exact value of the following:

Hint: use compound angle formulas

a $\sin 75°$ **b** $\cos 105°$ **c** $\tan 15°$
d $\cos 15°$ **e** $\sin 105°$ **f** $\tan 105°$

2 Write down the exact value of the following expressions:

a $\cos 40° \cos 50° - \sin 40° \sin 50°$
b $\sin 60° \cos 15° - \cos 60° \sin 15°$
c $\dfrac{\tan 47° - \tan 17°}{1 + \tan 47° \tan 17°}$
d $\sin 40° \cos 20° + \cos 40° \sin 20°$
e $\cos 85° \cos 25° + \sin 85° \sin 25°$
f $\dfrac{\tan 90° + \tan 30°}{1 - \tan 90° \tan 30°}$

2 c

3 Solve the following equations for $0° \leq \theta \leq 360°$, giving angles correct to one decimal place:

a $\sin(\theta + 30°) = 2\cos\theta$ **b** $\sin(\theta + 15°) = 3\cos(\theta - 15°)$
c $\cos(\theta - 60°) = \frac{1}{2}\sin\theta$ **d** $\sin(\theta + 45°) = -2\cos\theta$

3 a

4 Prove the following identities:

a $\cos(45° - \theta) - \cos(45° + \theta) \equiv \sqrt{2}\sin\theta$
b $\tan(\theta + 45°) + \tan(\theta - 45°) \equiv 2\tan 2\theta$
c $\sin(A + B) + \sin(A - B) \equiv 2\sin A \cos B$
d $\tan A + \tan B \equiv \dfrac{\sin(A + B)}{\cos A \cos B}$

5 If $\sin A = \frac{3}{5}$, where A is acute, and $\cos B = \frac{5}{13}$, find the exact value of the following:

a $\sin(A + B)$ **e** $\tan(A + B)$ **i** $\tan 2A$
b $\cos(A + B)$ **f** $\tan(A - B)$ **j** $\sin 2B$
c $\sin(A - B)$ **g** $\sin 2A$ **k** $\cos 2B$
d $\cos(A - B)$ **h** $\cos 2A$ **l** $\tan 2B$

6 Prove the following identities:

a $\sec\theta \operatorname{cosec}\theta \equiv 2\operatorname{cosec} 2\theta$
b $\sec 2\theta + \tan 2\theta \equiv \dfrac{\cos\theta + \sin\theta}{\cos\theta - \sin\theta}$
c $\dfrac{\sin 2\theta}{1 - \cos 2\theta} \equiv \cot\theta$
d $\dfrac{\sin 2\theta}{1 + \cos 2\theta} \equiv \tan\theta$

6 d

Contextual

1 **a** A ramp for a wheelchair, as illustrated in the diagram, can be moved by a person lifting on a handle at B and wheeling the ramp on a castor attached at A. The dimensions of the ramp are $AB = 3$ m and $BC = 50$ cm. The base of the ramp is inclined at an angle θ to the ground as shown.

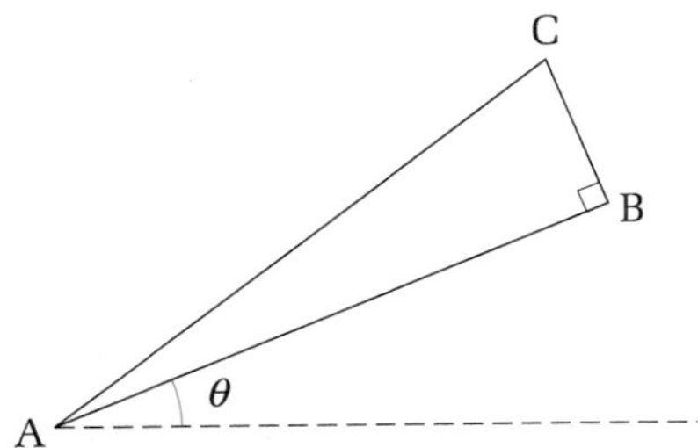

i If the ramp is to be moved through a doorway 2 m high, explain why $\sin(\theta + 9.5^\circ) \leq 0.6576$.

ii Solve this equation for θ.

iii Comment on the practicalities of θ achieving its maximum value.

b A second ramp can similarly be moved by a person lifting on a handle at B. The ramp can be wheeled on a castor at A. The dimensions of this ramp are $AB = 2.5$ m and $BC = 60$ cm.

i Write down the new equation for θ.

ii Solve the equation.

iii Compare the heights to which B has to be lifted.

3.4 The Cosine Rule and the Sine Rule

'Solve a triangle' means find all the angles and the lengths of all the sides of the triangle. Given three of the six quantities (angles or sides) can the remaining three be found?

Pythagoras' theorem applies to right-angled triangles. How do we deal with non-right-angled triangles? One technique is to use the **cosine rule**.

The cosine rule

For any triangle ABC,

$$a^2 = b^2 + c^2 - 2bc \cos A$$

To demonstrate this result, drop a perpendicular from C to meet AB at D. Now look at triangle ACD.

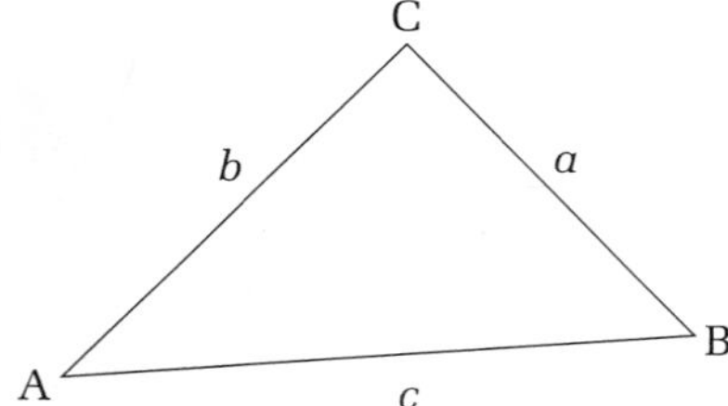

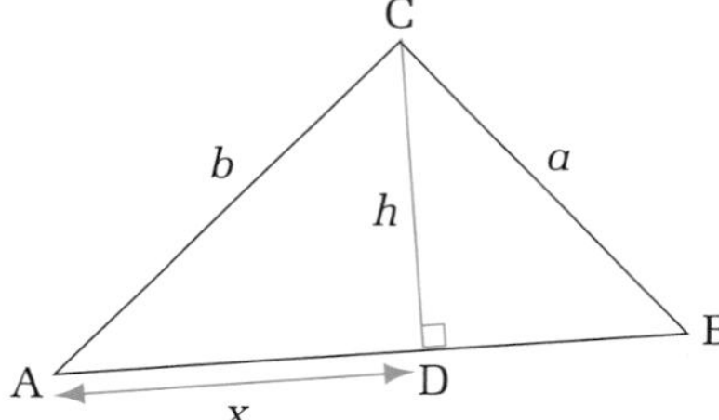

Using Pythagoras' theorem,

$$b^2 = h^2 + x^2$$

So $h^2 = b^2 - x^2$ [1]

Now look at triangle BCD. Using the same technique,

$$a^2 = h^2 + (c - x)^2$$

$h^2 = a^2 - (c - x)^2$ [2]

Eliminating h by equating [1] and [2],

$$b^2 - x^2 = a^2 - (c - x)^2$$

So $b^2 - x^2 = a^2 - (c^2 - 2cx + x^2)$

Multiplying out the bracket.

$$b^2 - x^2 = a^2 - c^2 + 2cx - x^2$$

$$b^2 = a^2 - c^2 + 2cx$$

The x^2 terms cancel each other out.

$$a^2 = b^2 + c^2 - 2cx$$

But from triangle ACD, $\cos A = \frac{x}{b}$, giving $x = b\cos A$.

So now $a^2 = b^2 + c^2 - 2bc\cos A$.

By using a symmetrical argument, the two other equivalent versions can be found (that is, by dropping the perpendicular from any angle, or simply by relabelling the triangle).

$$\boldsymbol{b^2 = a^2 + c^2 - 2ac\cos B}$$

$$\boldsymbol{c^2 = a^2 + b^2 - 2ab\cos C}$$

So the cosine rule can be used to find the length of the third side, when the lengths of two sides in a triangle and the angle between them are known.

Example 1

In triangle ABC, $b = 10$ cm, $c = 8$ cm and $A = 50°$. Find a.

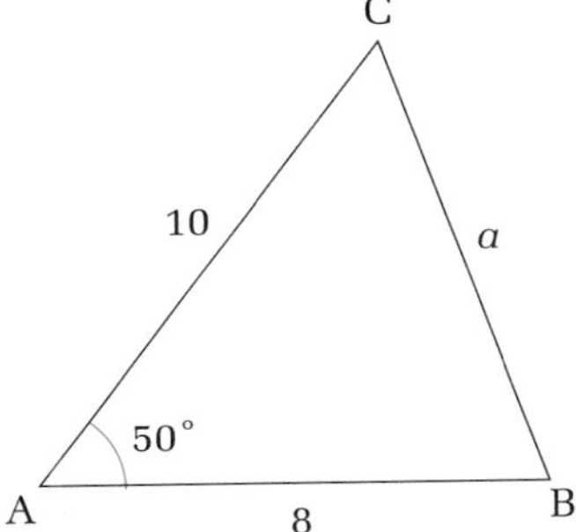

Solution

Using $a^2 = b^2 + c^2 - 2bc\cos A$,

$$\begin{aligned} a^2 &= 10^2 + 8^2 - 2 \times 10 \times 8 \times \cos 50° \\ &= 100 + 64 - 160\cos 50° \\ &= 164 - 102.85 \\ &= 61.15 \end{aligned}$$

$$\begin{aligned} \text{So } a &= \sqrt{61.15} \\ &= 7.82 \text{ cm (3 s.f.)} \end{aligned}$$

Example 2

In triangle ABC, $a = 12$ cm, $c = 17$ cm and $B = 129°$. Find b.

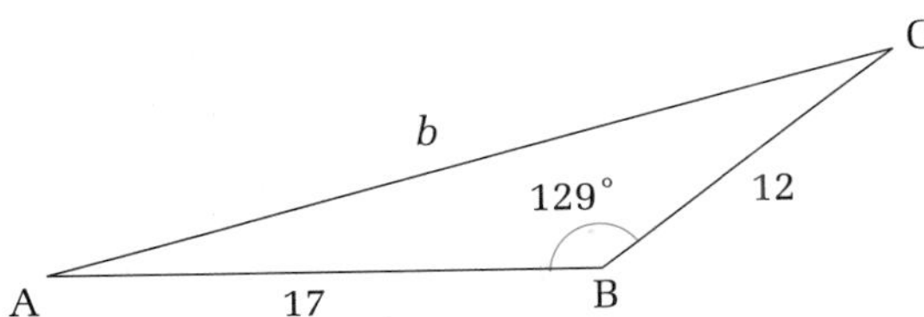

Solution

Although B is obtuse, the rule still applies.
Using $b^2 = a^2 + c^2 - 2ac\cos B$,

$$\begin{aligned} b^2 &= 12^2 + 17^2 - 2 \times 12 \times 17 \times \cos 129^\circ \\ &= 144 + 289 + 256.76 \\ &= 689.76 \end{aligned}$$

There is a change of sig[n] because $\cos 129^\circ$ is negative.

$$\begin{aligned} \text{So} \quad b &= \sqrt{689.76} \\ &= 26.3\ \text{cm (3 s.f.)} \end{aligned}$$

The three cosine rule formulas can be rearranged to give expressions for $\cos A$, $\cos B$ and $\cos C$ in terms of a, b and c.

$$\cos A = \frac{b^2 + c^2 - a^2}{2bc} \qquad \cos B = \frac{a^2 + c^2 - b^2}{2ac} \qquad \cos C = \frac{a^2 + b^2 - c^2}{2ab}$$

Learn these results.

This means that if the lengths of each of the three sides are known then each of the three angles can be found.

Example 3

In triangle ABC if $a = 12$ cm, $b = 20$ cm and $c = 14$ cm, find A, B and C.

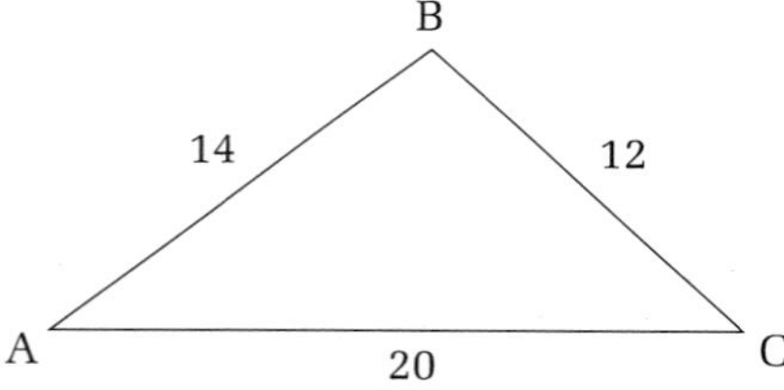

Solution

Using $\cos A = \dfrac{b^2 + c^2 - a^2}{2bc}$,

$$\begin{aligned} \cos A &= \frac{20^2 + 14^2 - 12^2}{2 \times 20 \times 14} \\ &= \frac{400 + 196 - 144}{560} = \frac{452}{560} = 0.8071 \end{aligned}$$

$$\begin{aligned} \text{So} \quad A &= \cos^{-1}(0.8071) \\ A &= 36.2^\circ \text{ (1 d.p.)} \end{aligned}$$

Using $\cos B = \dfrac{a^2 + c^2 - b^2}{2ac}$,

$$\cos B = \frac{12^2 + 14^2 - 20^2}{2 \times 12 \times 14}$$

$$= \frac{144 + 196 - 400}{335} = -\frac{60}{336} = -0.1786$$

The negative cosine implies that the angle is obtuse (second quadrant).

So $B = \cos^{-1}(-0.1786)$

$B = 100.3^\circ$ (1 d.p.)

We know that the angles in a triangle add up to 180°. So now

$$C = 180^\circ - (A + B)$$

$$= 180^\circ - (36.2^\circ + 100.3^\circ)$$

$$= 180^\circ - 136.5^\circ$$

$$= 43.5^\circ \text{ (1 d.p.)}$$

The sine rule

The sine rule is another useful result to help solve triangles. For any triangle ABC,

Unlike the cosine rule this doesn't look at all like Pythagoras' theorem.

$$\frac{a}{\sin A} = \frac{b}{\sin B} = \frac{c}{\sin C}$$

This particular version of the sine rule is useful for finding sides. To find angles the more convenient form to use is

$$\frac{\sin A}{a} = \frac{\sin B}{b} = \frac{\sin C}{c}$$

To demonstrate this result, drop a perpendicular from C to meet AB at D.

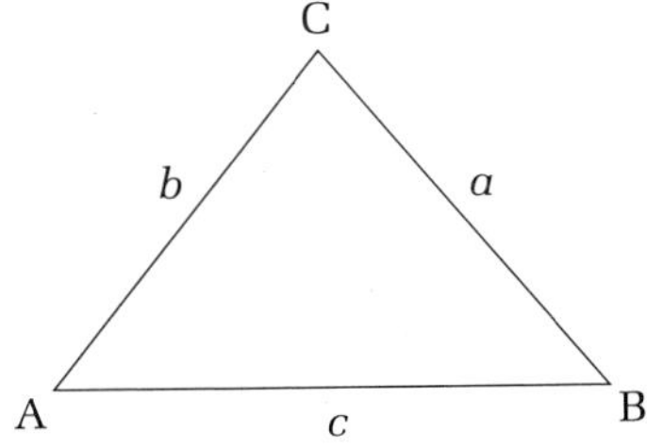

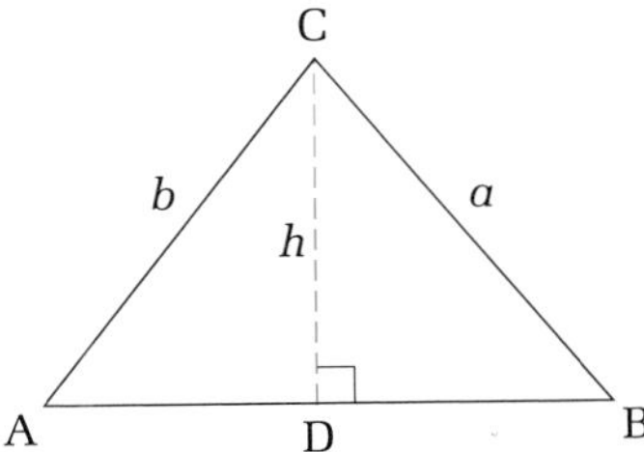

Looking at triangle ACD, $\frac{h}{b} = \sin A$.

So $h = b \sin A$

Looking at triangle BCD, $\frac{h}{a} = \sin B$.

So $h = a \sin B$

Now eliminate h by equating these two results.
Then $a \sin B = b \sin A$.

$$\frac{b}{\sin B} = \frac{a}{\sin A}$$

Use the geometry of the figure or simply relabel to find the equivalent ratio $\frac{c}{\sin C}$.

The sine rule is useful in the following situations:

- two (and hence three) angles and one side are known;
- two sides and one angle (but not the angle between them) are known;
- one angle and its opposite side, and one other piece of information are known.

Example 4

In triangle ABC, $A = 35°$, $a = 17$ cm and $B = 50°$. Find b.

Notice that we could find $C = 95°$ directly from the information given in the question using the angle sum of a triangle.

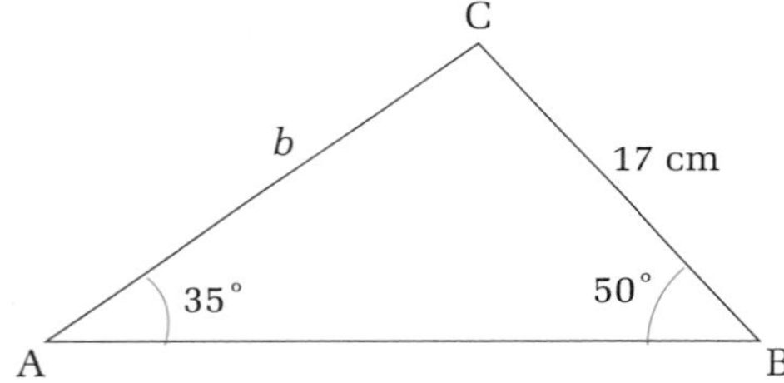

Solution

Using $\frac{a}{\sin A} = \frac{b}{\sin B}$,

$$\frac{17}{\sin 35°} = \frac{b}{\sin 50°}$$

$$\text{So} \quad b = \frac{17 \times \sin 50°}{\sin 35°}$$

$$= \frac{17 \times 0.7660}{0.5736}$$

$$b = 22.7\text{ cm (1 d.p.)}$$

Example 5

In triangle ABC, $A = 60°$, $a = 6$ cm and $b = 5$ cm. Find B.

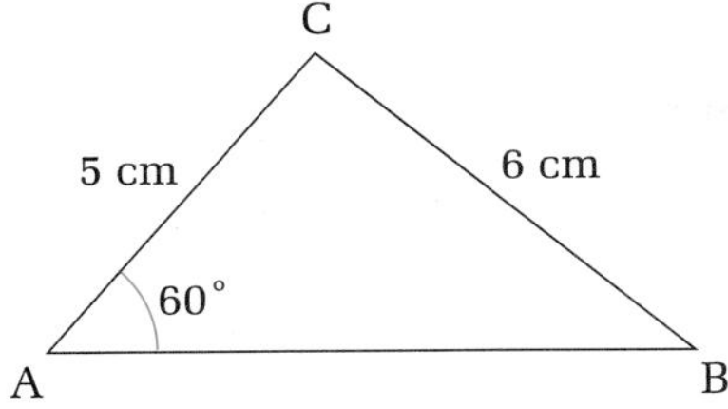

Solution

Using $\dfrac{\sin A}{a} = \dfrac{\sin B}{b}$,

Use this form so that the unknown is in the numerator (hence simplifying the algebra).

$$\frac{\sin 60°}{6} = \frac{\sin B}{5}$$

$$\Rightarrow \sin B = \frac{5 \times 0.8660}{6}$$

$$= 0.7217$$

So $B = \sin^{-1}(0.7217) = 46.2°$

Exercise some caution when using the sine rule to find angles. Sometimes an ambiguity may arise, where two possible angles will solve the trigonometric equation involving sine. The calculator will always give the acute angle but on occasions the obtuse angle gives an equally valid, if different, solution.

Example 6

Solve the triangle for which $A = 30°$, $a = 8$ cm and $c = 10$ cm.

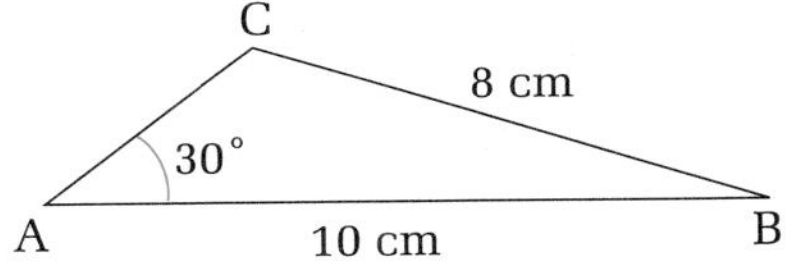

Solution

Using the sine rule to find C,

$$\frac{\sin C}{c} = \frac{\sin A}{a}$$

$$\frac{\sin C}{10} = \frac{\sin 30°}{8}$$

$$\sin C = \frac{0.5 \times 10}{8} = 0.625$$

So $C = 38.7°, 141.3°$ (1 d.p.)

Notice that the obtuse angle (141.3°) is possible here.

Angle B can now be found by using the angle sum of a triangle.

When $C = 38.7°$, $B = 180° - (30° + 38.7°) = 111.3°$.
When $C = 141.3°$, $B = 180° - (30° + 141.3°) = 8.7°$.

Now use the cosine rule (or the sine rule again) to find b for each of the possibilities for B.

Using the cosine rule, when $B = 111.3°$,

$$\begin{aligned} b^2 &= a^2 + c^2 - 2ac\cos B \\ &= 8^2 + 10^2 - 2 \times 8 \times 10 \times \cos 111.3° \\ &= 164 + 58.12 \\ &= 222.12 \end{aligned}$$

So $\quad b = 14.9\,\text{cm}$ (1 d.p.).

Using the cosine rule, when $B = 8.7°$,

$$\begin{aligned} b^2 &= a^2 + c^2 - 2ac\cos B \\ &= 8^2 + 10^2 - 2 \times 8 \times 10 \times \cos 8.7° \\ &= 164 - 158.16 \\ &= 5.84 \end{aligned}$$

So $\quad b = 2.4\,\text{cm}$ (1 d.p.)

This means the triangle ABC has two distinct solutions.

$A = 30°,\ a = 8\,\text{cm}$	$A = 30°,\ a = 8\,\text{cm}$
$B = 111.3°,\ b = 14.9\,\text{cm}$	$B = 8.7°,\ b = 2.4\,\text{cm}$
$C = 38.7°,\ c = 10\,\text{cm}$	$C = 141.3°,\ c = 10\,\text{cm}$

One sketch can be used to illustrate the geometrical interpretation.

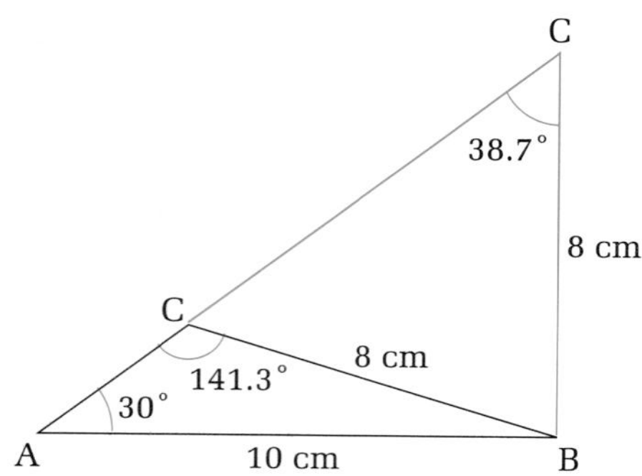

3.4 The Cosine Rule and the Sine Rule

Exercise

Technique

1 Use the cosine rule to find the length of b in the following triangles:

a $B = 70°$, $a = 8$ cm, $c = 12$ cm
b $B = 120°$, $a = 11$ cm, $c = 15$ cm
c $B = 48°$, $a = 14.2$ cm, $c = 8.5$ cm

In this exercise give lengths of sides and sizes of angles correct to 1 d.p.

2 Use the cosine rule to find the angles in the following triangles:

a $a = 6$ cm, $b = 4$ cm, $c = 5$ cm
b $a = 13$ cm, $b = 12$ cm, $c = 19$ cm
c $a = 7$ cm, $b = 8$ cm, $c = 14$ cm.

3 Calculate the length of the lettered side in the following triangles:

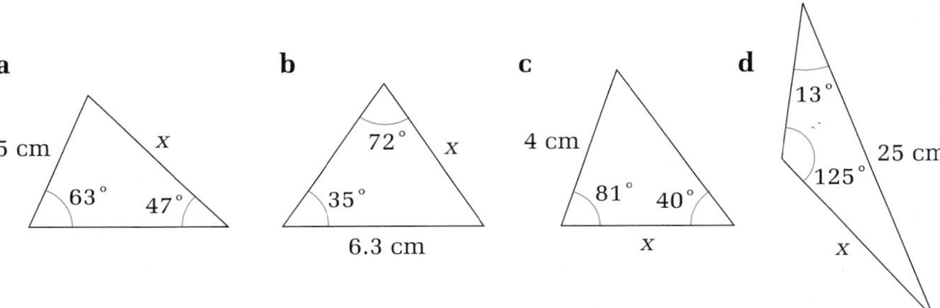

4 Solve the following triangles:

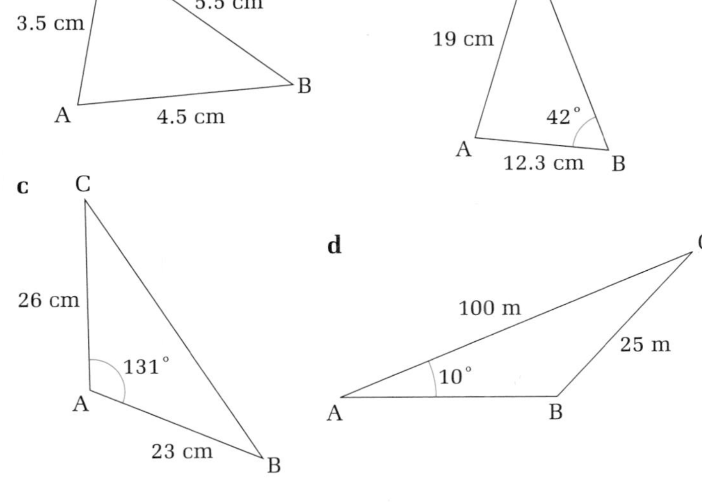

Contextual

1 A ship sails 4 nautical miles from A to B on a bearing of 075°. It then changes to a bearing of 150° and sails 6 nautical miles to C. Calculate the distance AC and the bearing of C from A.

2 Ship A is 12 miles from lighthouse B on a bearing of 050°. A second ship C is 15 miles from the same lighthouse on a bearing of 330°. Find the distance between A and C and the bearing of C from A.

3 A, B and C are three triangulation points used on an Ordnance Survey map. B is 5 km due south of A. C is 4 km from B on a bearing of 300°. Find the distance from A to C and the bearing of C from A.

4 From a point A on the same level as the base of a radio mast, the angle of elevation of the top of the mast is 25°. From a point B, 20 metres closer to the mast, and on the same level, the angle of elevation is 32°. Find the height of the radio mast.

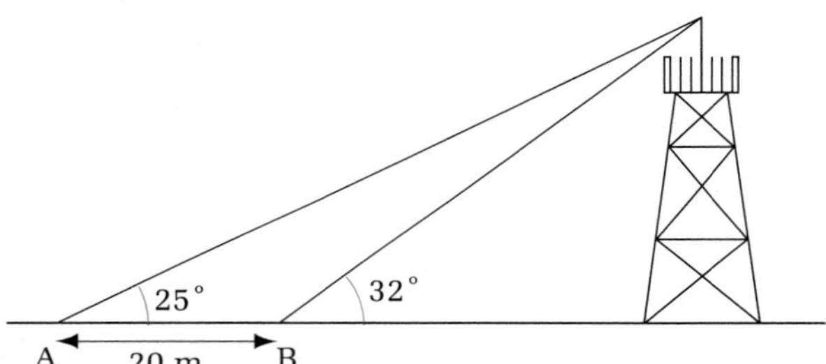

3.5 The Area of a Triangle

You should already be familiar with the rule for the area of a triangle that reads:

$$\text{area} = \tfrac{1}{2} \times \text{base} \times \text{perpendicular height}$$

This formula is only useful if the length of the 'base' and the 'perpendicular height' of the triangle are known. When this is not the case other techniques are required.

A more useful result is one that incorporates lengths of sides and sizes of angles. In general the area of a triangle ABC is given by:

$$\textbf{area} = \tfrac{1}{2}bc\sin A = \tfrac{1}{2}ab\sin C = \tfrac{1}{2}ac\sin B$$ ◀ **Learn these results.**

One way of remembering these formulas is that they include two sides and the angle between them.

Remember the symmetry of this expression.

To demonstrate these results drop a perpendicular from A, B or C to meet a, b or c respectively. Suppose a perpendicular that meets AB at D is drawn, as shown.

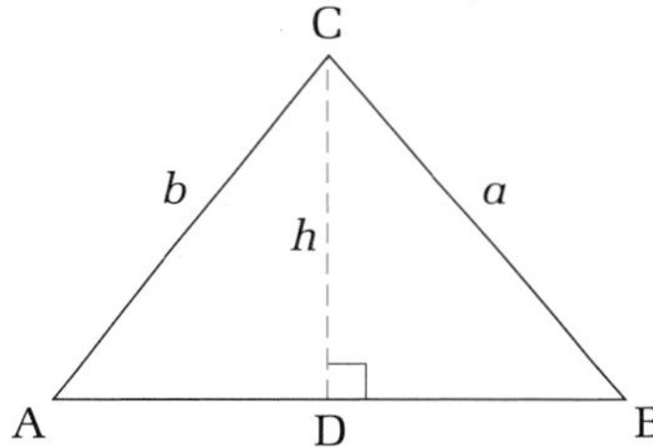

Looking at triangle ACD, $\frac{h}{b} = \sin A$.

$$\begin{aligned}\text{area of triangle ACB} &= \tfrac{1}{2} \times \text{base} \times \text{perpendicular height}\\ &= \tfrac{1}{2} \times c \times h\\ &= \tfrac{1}{2} \times c \times b \times \sin A\\ &= \tfrac{1}{2}bc\sin A\end{aligned}$$

To show one of the other symmetrical versions, simply drop perpendicular lines onto BC or AC.

Example 1

Find the areas of the following triangles:

a

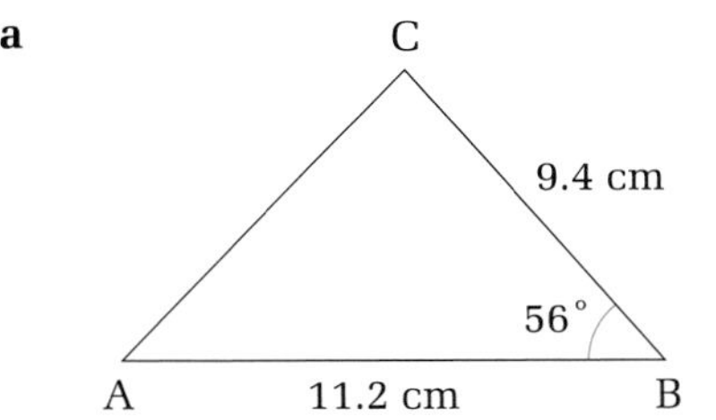

b

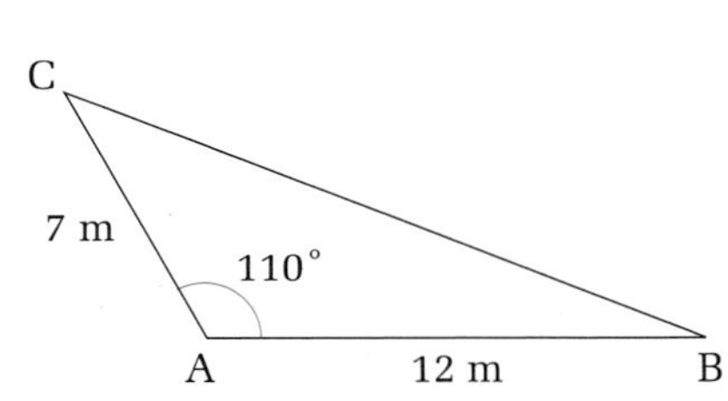

Solution

a Using area $= \frac{1}{2}ac\sin B$,

$$\text{area} = \tfrac{1}{2} \times 9.4 \times 11.2 \times \sin 56^\circ$$

$$= 43.6\,\text{cm}^2 \text{ (3 s.f.)}$$

b Using area $= \frac{1}{2}bc\sin A$,

$$\text{area} = \tfrac{1}{2} \times 7 \times 12 \times \sin 110^\circ$$

$$= 39.5\,\text{m}^2 \text{ (3 s.f.)}$$

Hero's formula

These formulas for area are not really useful if only the lengths of the sides of the triangle are known. The cosine rule could be used to find an angle but often it is much more efficient to use another method called Hero's formula. This is named after Heron of Alexandria (who lived about 75BC). Hero's formula has many practical applications. For example surveyors who know lengths of sides of a three-sided lot can easily compute the area.

In the great city of Alexandria, mathematicians were forced to consider the a of calculation by probler encountered during thei study of astronomy and mechanics. This is an example of where the need to solve problems forced the development c new techniques in mathematics.

Hero's formula states that, for any triangle ABC with sides of length a, b and c:

area $= \sqrt{s(s-a)(s-b)(s-c)}$

where s is the semi-perimeter, $s = \dfrac{a+b+c}{2}$. ◀ **Learn this result.**

Example 2

Which of the following triangles has the larger area?

1

C

25 m 25 m

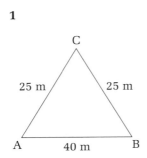

A 40 m B

2

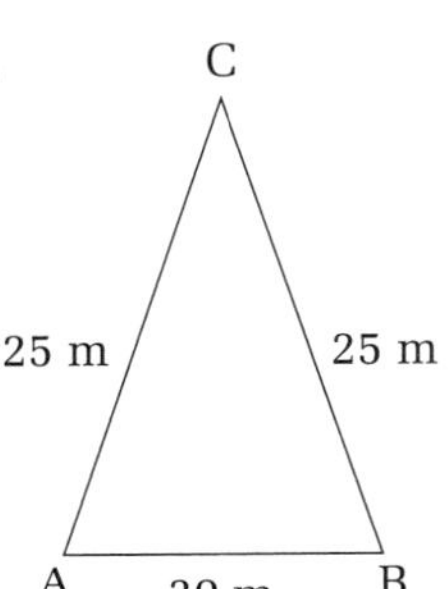

Solution

Looking at triangle **1**,

$$s = \tfrac{1}{2}(25 + 25 + 40) = 45$$

$$\text{So the area of triangle } \mathbf{1} = \sqrt{45(45-25)(45-25)(45-40)}$$
$$= \sqrt{45 \times 20 \times 20 \times 5}$$
$$= \sqrt{90\,000}$$
$$= 300\,\text{m}^2$$

Looking at triangle **2**,

$$s = \tfrac{1}{2}(25 + 25 + 30) = 40$$

$$\text{So the area of triangle } \mathbf{2} = \sqrt{40(40-25)(40-25)(40-30)}$$
$$= \sqrt{40 \times 15 \times 15 \times 10}$$
$$= \sqrt{90\,000}$$
$$= 300\,\text{m}^2$$

Since the area of both triangles **1** and **2** is $300\,\text{m}^2$, neither has a larger area.

3.5 The Area of a Triangle

Exercise

Technique

1 For a right-angled triangle with sides 3 m, 4 m and 5 m find the area using:

a area $= \frac{1}{2}$(base × perpendicular height)
b area $= \frac{1}{2}ab\sin C$
c Hero's formula.

2 Find the areas of the following triangles:

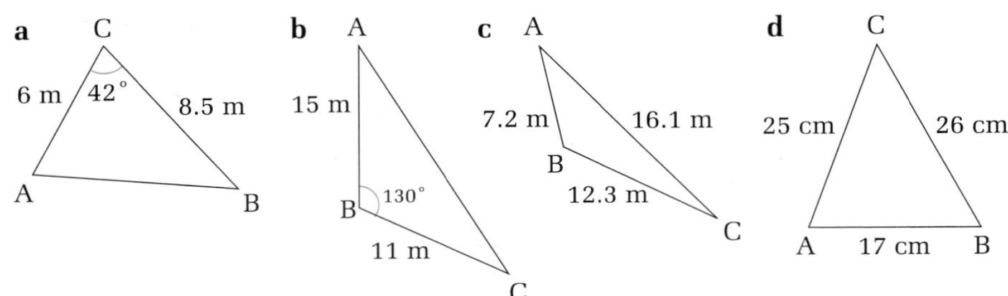

Contextual

1 The area of an acute-angled triangle ABC is 12 cm^2. Given that $a = b = 5$ cm, find c.

2 A surveyor wishes to estimate the area of a triangular patch of woodland. A sketch is made showing the following measurements. Estimate the area of the woodland.

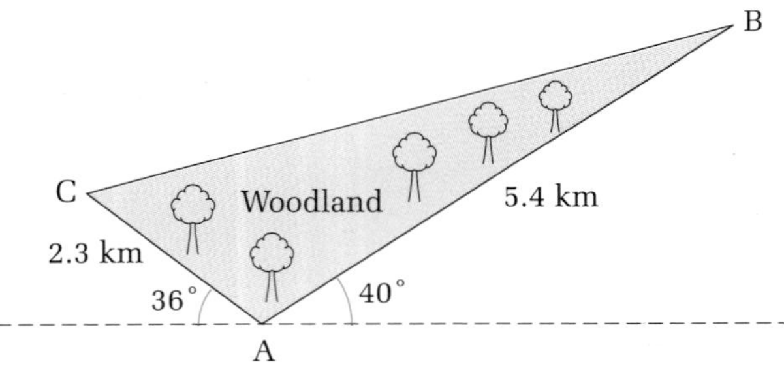

3 Paula, the mathematician, wants to share her square birthday cake equally amongst the seven people at her party. She wants everyone to have the same amount of cake and icing. Her friend, Kevin, suggests dividing the perimeter by 7 and cutting from the centre to the appropriate points on the perimeter. If the cake measures 7 inches down each side and is 3 inches high will Kevin's suggestion work?

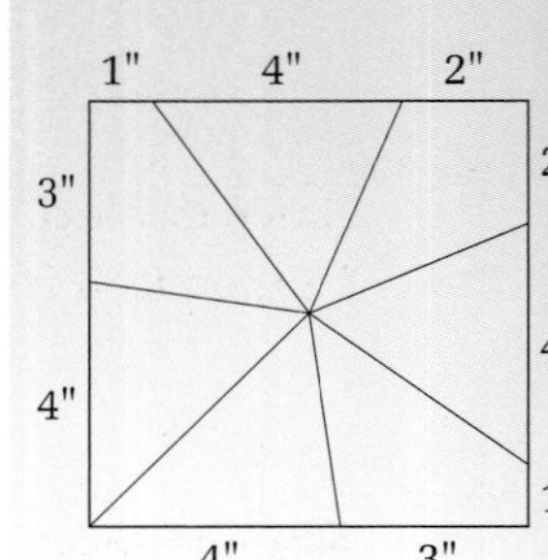

3.6 Radian Measure

All methods of measuring angles are based on division of the circle. We have previously measured angles in degrees, where $360°$ is a full circle. So a degree is simply $\frac{1}{360}$ of a circle. Another way of measuring angles is to compare the length of an arc formed by the angle with the radius of the circle. The unit used in this method is called the **radian**.

In the diagram the radius of the circle is r and the length of the arc PQ is also r. The angle θ is said to be 1 radian.

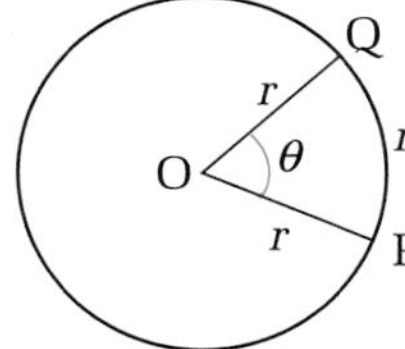

$$\frac{\text{arc length}}{\text{radius}} = \frac{r}{r} = 1$$

An alternative notation for radian measure is the use of a lower case c: $1\,\text{rad} = 1^c$.

The circumference of the circle is $2\pi r$. This means that a complete circle, defined in degrees as $360°$, is 2π in radians.

$$\frac{\text{circumference}}{\text{radius}} = \frac{2\pi r}{r} = 2\pi$$

So $360° = 2\pi$ radians (rad).
Then $180° = \pi\,\text{rad}$, so

Halving both sides.

$$\mathbf{1° = \frac{\pi}{180}\,rad}$$

Similarly, a radian has an equivalence in degrees.
We have $2\pi\,\text{rad} = 360°$, so

$$\mathbf{1\,rad = \frac{360°}{2\pi}}$$

$1\,\text{rad} = \frac{180°}{\pi}$

Using a calculator to evaluate this statement,

$$1\,\text{rad} = 57.29578\ldots°$$
$$= 57.3°\ (3\text{ s.f.})$$

Since this isn't a rational value (because of the involvement of π, which is irrational) it is more usual to express radians as fractions of π.

Example 1

Express the special angles $30°$, $45°$, $60°$ and $90°$ as radians.

Solution

Since $1^\circ = \frac{\pi}{180}$ rad,

$$30^\circ = 30 \times \frac{\pi}{180} = \frac{\pi}{6} \text{ rad} \qquad 60^\circ = 60 \times \frac{\pi}{180} = \frac{\pi}{3} \text{ rad}$$

Learn these results.

$$45^\circ = 45 \times \frac{\pi}{180} = \frac{\pi}{4} \text{ rad} \qquad 90^\circ = 90 \times \frac{\pi}{180} = \frac{\pi}{2} \text{ rad}$$

Example 2

Convert $\frac{5\pi}{6}$ rad to degrees.

Solution

$$1 \text{ rad} = \frac{360^\circ}{2\pi} \Rightarrow \frac{5\pi}{6} \text{ rad} = \frac{5\pi}{6} \times \frac{360^\circ}{2\pi}$$
$$= 150^\circ$$

In multiplying the fractions, π cancels.

Radian measure has several advantages in mathematics and will be used later in curve sketching and integration. This measure allows both axes to be scaled in real numbers and is particularly advantageous when the requirement is to solve a problem by reflecting in the line $y = x$, or finding the intersection of graphs.

Another application of radians is in finding arc lengths and sector areas. If we take a sector of a circle its arc length and area will be a fraction of the whole circle. The formulas for these have a simpler form when the sector angle is measured in radians.

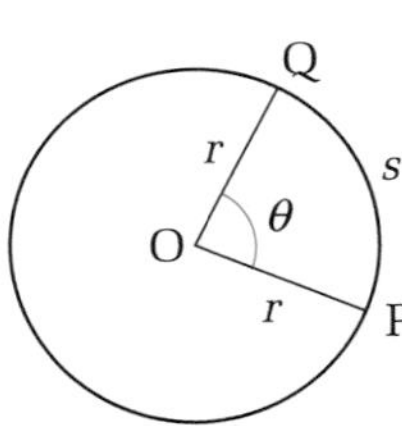

When θ is in radians,

arc length, $s = r\theta$

sector area, $A = \frac{1}{2}r^2\theta$ ◀ **Learn these results.**

Example 3

Find the arc length and area of a sector of radius 4 cm and angle 1.5 rad.

Solution

When θ is measured in radians,

$$\text{arc length } s = r\theta = 4 \times 1.5 = 6 \text{ cm}$$
$$\text{sector area } A = \tfrac{1}{2}r^2\theta = \tfrac{1}{2} \times 4^2 \times 1.5 = 12 \text{ cm}^2$$

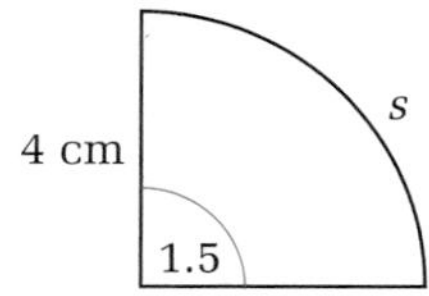

Example 4

A piece of wire 40 cm long is bent into the shape of a sector. If the area of this sector is $100\,\text{cm}^2$ find:

a an expression for the sector angle θ in terms of radius r

b the value of r

c the value of θ.

Solution

a Think carefully about the given information. The three lengths (both radii and the arc length) add up to 40 cm. So arc length $s = 40 - 2r$. Also, $s = r\theta$.

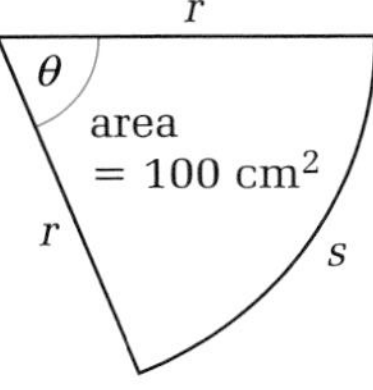

So $r\theta = 40 - 2r$

$$\theta = \frac{40 - 2r}{r}$$

b Now use the information about the area.

$A = \frac{1}{2}r^2\theta$

Substituting for θ from **a**,

$$100 = \tfrac{1}{2} \times r^2 \times \left(\frac{40 - 2r}{r}\right)$$

$$100 = \frac{r}{2} \times (40 - 2r)$$

Eliminating r from the denominator.

$$100 = \frac{r}{2} \times 2(20 - r)$$

Taking out the common factor, 2.

$$100 = 20r - r^2$$

So $r^2 - 20r + 100 = 0$

Form and solve the quadratic equation.

$\Rightarrow (r - 10)(r - 10) = 0$

$(r - 10)^2 = 0$

So $r = 10$. That is, the radius is 10 cm.

c $\theta = \dfrac{40 - 2r}{r} = \dfrac{40 - (2 \times 10)}{10} = 2$

So the sector angle is 2 rad.

3.6 Radian Measure
Exercise
Technique

1 Without using a calculator convert the following angles into radians, leaving the answer in terms of π:

a 15° **c** 75° **e** 225°
b 150° **d** 180° **f** 315°

2 Convert the following to radians, writing your answers correct to three significant figures:

a 20° **c** 129° **e** 269°
b 78° **d** 222° **f** 351°

3 Without using a calculator convert the following angles to degrees:

a π **c** 3π **e** $\frac{\pi}{8}$
b $\frac{3\pi}{4}$ **d** $\frac{4\pi}{15}$ **f** $\frac{7\pi}{8}$

4 Find the arc lengths and sector areas of the following sectors, correct to one decimal place:

a $\theta = 1$ rad, $r = 5$ cm **b** $\theta = 1.5$ rad, $r = 8$ cm
c $\theta = 2$ rad, $r = 11$ cm **d** $\theta = 2.6$ rad, $r = 9$ cm

5 A sector OPQ has arc length 20 cm and sector area 100 cm^2 (as shown). Write down the two equations involving r and θ (the radius and sector angle). Solve these equations to find the value of r and θ.

5

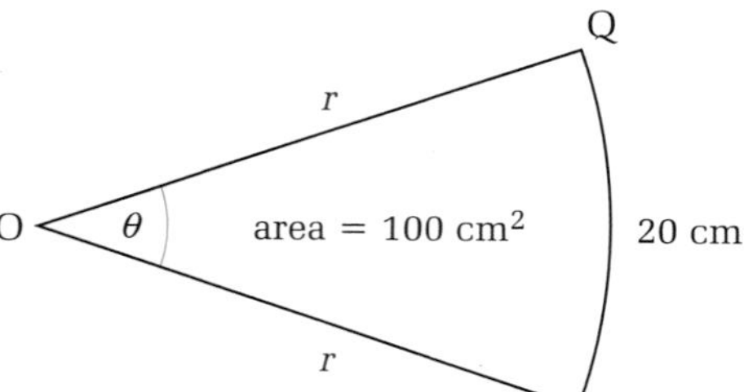

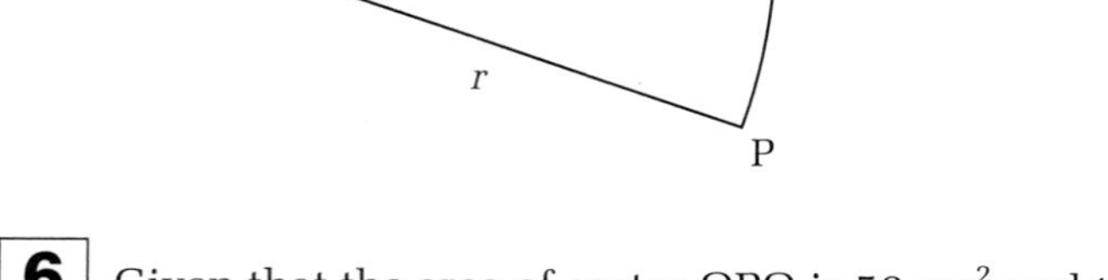

6 Given that the area of sector OPQ is 50 cm^2 and that $\theta = 1.2$ rad, find the radius of the circle.

6

7 Now go back to Exercise 3.2 on page 105 and do questions 1, 2, and 4 using radians.

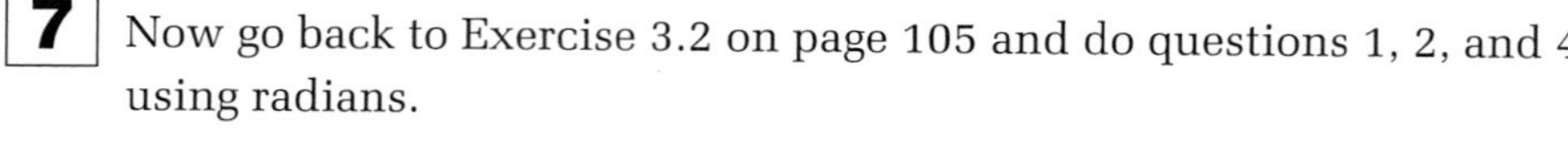

Contextual

1 A wedge of cheese, 0.5 cm thick, has a cross-section that is a sector of a circle. If the radius of the circle is 5 cm and the arc length is 4 cm, find the volume of the cheese.

2 An oil drum of diameter 80 cm is floating, as shown.

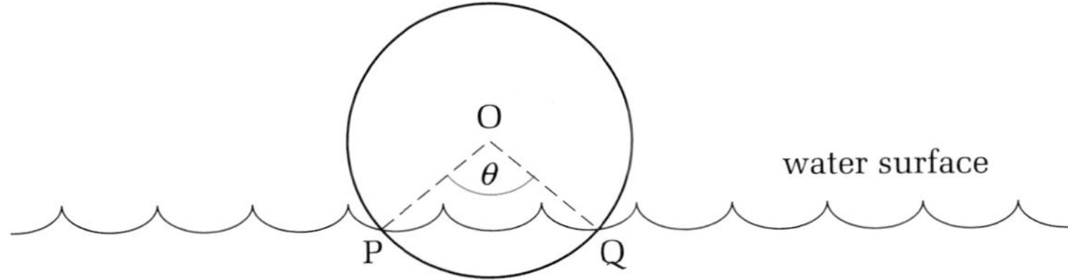

a If the arc length PQ is 90 cm, find θ (in radians).
b Find the area of the minor sector OPQ.
c Use the cosine rule to work out the length of the chord PQ.
d Find the area of the triangle OPQ.
e If the drum is 1.2 m long, find the volume of the drum lying below the water surface level, correct to three significant figures.

Remember to put your calculator in RADIAN mode.

3 A circular cone with base radius r and slant height l is unrolled into a circular sector. Find the angle of this sector in radians. Use your answer to explain why the curved surface area of the cone is πrl.

4 A windscreen wiper clears a region ABCD of a car windscreen (assumed to be flat), where AB and DC are circular arcs centred at O. Given that $OD = 20$ cm, $DA = 50$ cm and $\angle AOB = 2.3$ rad, calculate the area of region ABCD.

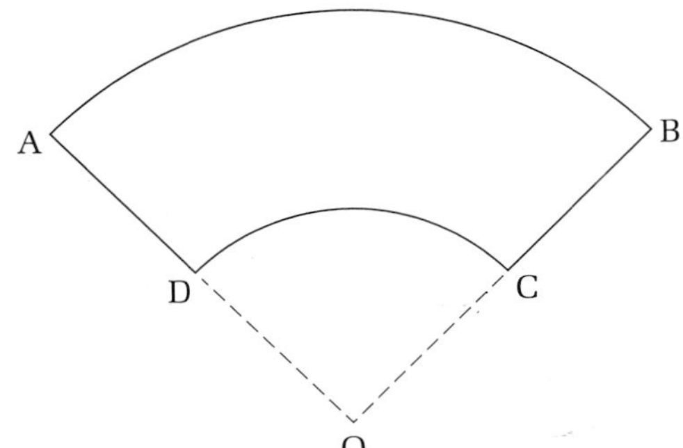

(NEAB)

Consolidation

Exercise A

1 Find the four solutions of the equation $\sin 2\theta = \cos^2 \theta$ in the interval $0° < \theta < 360°$. Give each of these solutions correct to the nearest degree.

(NEAB)

2 The diagram shows a triangle ABC in which angle $C = 30°$, $BC = x$ cm and $AC = (x + 2)$ cm. Given that the area of triangle ABC is $12\ \text{cm}^2$, calculate the value of x.

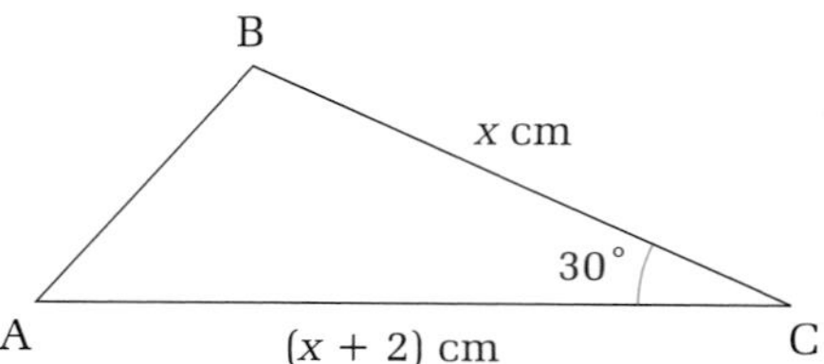

(UCLES)

3 Figure 1 shows the points A and B which two ships have reached after leaving a harbour H. The points A and B are at distance of 8 km and 11 km from H respectively. The bearings of A and B from H are 048° and 120° respectively. Calculate:

a the distance between A and B, giving your answer to 0.1 km;
b the bearing of B and A, giving your answer to the nearest degree.

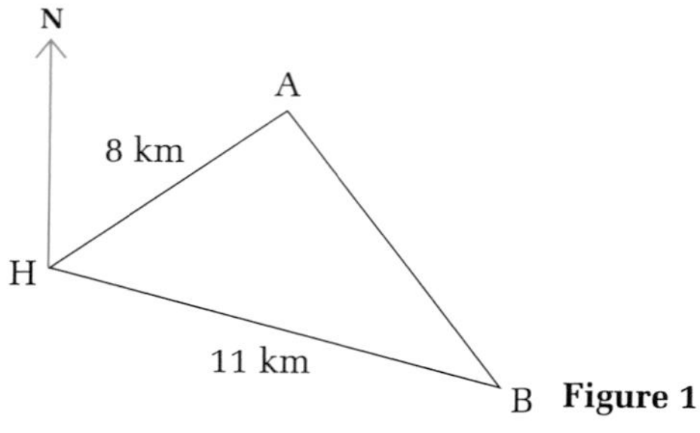

Figure 1

(ULEAC)

4 Solve the equation $4\cot^2 \theta + 12\operatorname{cosec}\theta + 1 = 0$, giving all values of θ to the nearest degree in the interval $0° \leq \theta \leq 360°$.

(AEB)

5 Find, in degrees, the solution of the equation $\tan(2x + 30°) = -\sqrt{3}$, for $0° \leq x \leq 360°$.

(NICCEA)

6 The angles x and y are acute.

a If $\cos 2x$ is negative, explain why you can say that $x > 45°$.
b If $\sin 4y$ is negative and $\cos 4y$ is positive, what value must y exceed?
c If the conditions in **a** and **b** remain true, state, with reasons, whether the following are positive or negative:
i $\tan(x + y)$
ii $\tan 3y$.

(MEI)

7 **a** Use the formula $\tan 3\theta = \dfrac{3\tan\theta - \tan^3\theta}{1 - 3\tan^2\theta}$ to show that $\tan(\pi/12)$ is a root of the cubic equation $x^3 - 3x^2 - 3x + 1 = 0$.
b Solve the equation $\sin 2y = 2 - 2\cos 2y$ $(0 \leq y \leq \pi)$.

(OCSEB)

8 Show that $(\operatorname{cosec} x - 1)(\operatorname{cosec} x + 1)(\sec x - 1)(\sec x + 1) \equiv 1$.

(UCLES)

9 A circle centre O has an arc AB of length 13.44 cm and $\angle$AOB = 1.6 rad.

a Calculate the radius of the circle.
b Find the area of the region enclosed by the arc AB and the chord AB.

(WJEC)

10 **a** Determine, in degrees, the solutions of the equation $\tan x = 5$ for which $0° \leq x \leq 360°$, giving your answers to the nearest tenth of a degree.
b Determine, in radians, the solutions of the equation $3\cos^2 y + 8\sin y = 0$ for which $0 \leq y \leq 2\pi$, giving your answers to two decimal places.

(ULEAC)

Exercise B

1 Solve the following for x, y, z and t, giving all the values from $0°$ to $360°$ inclusive:

a $\sin(x/2) = 0.7$ **b** $\sec 2y = 1.5$
c $3\tan z = 5\sin z$ **d** $\sin^2 t = 1 + \cos t$

(OCSEB)

2 **a** Square both sides of the equation $\sin\theta - \cos\theta = \sin 2\theta$ and rearrange the resulting equation as a quadratic in $\sin 2\theta$.

b Deduce that $\sin 2\theta = \frac{1}{2}(\sqrt{5} - 1)$.

c Find the two solutions of the equation in **b** that lie in the range $0° < \theta < 180°$ and hence find the smallest positive value of θ that satisfies the equation given in **a**.

(WJEC)

3 A tetrahedron is as shown in the sketch ($AB = 12$ m, $DC = 15$ m, $\angle ACB = 40°$, $\angle ADB = 70°$), with AB vertical and the triangle DBC horizontal. Find, correct to two decimal places:

a the length of AC
b the length of AD
c the angle $\angle DAC$.

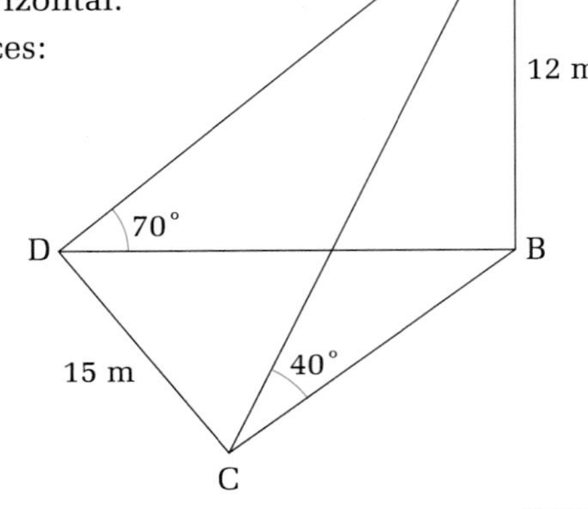

(NICCEA)

4 From a coastguard station at O, three buoys, A, B and C, can be seen out at sea. A, B and C lie on a straight line such that the bearing of both B and C from A is 135°. The bearings of A and B from O are 030° and 100° respectively. The bearing of A is marked in the diagram, $OA = 1$ km, and $BC = 1.2$ km.

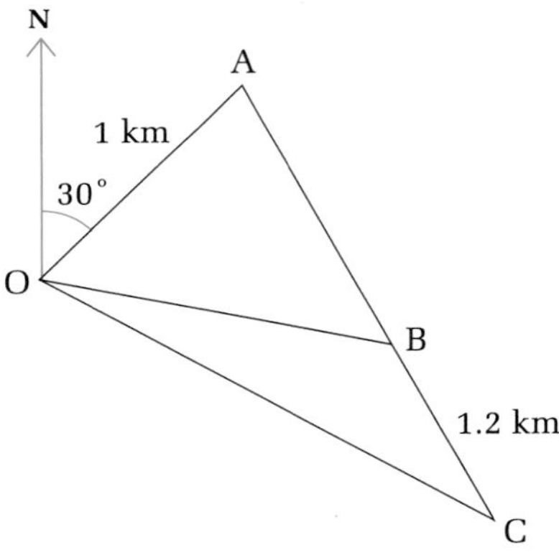

a State the angles of triangle OAB.

b Calculate the distance *OB*, giving your answer in kilometres correct to three significant figures.

c Calculate the distance *OC* and the bearing of C from O.

(OCSEB)

5 Express $\sin 4\theta$ in terms of $\sin 2\theta$ and $\cos 2\theta$, and hence express $\dfrac{\sin 4\theta}{\sin \theta}$ in terms of $\cos \theta$ only.

(UCLES)

6 **a** Show that $4(1 + \cos\theta + \cos 2\theta) - 3(\sin\theta + \sin 2\theta)$ may be written in the form $(1 + 2\cos\theta)(a\cos\theta + b\sin\theta)$, where a and b are integers to be determined.
Hence solve the equation $4(1 + \cos\theta + \cos 2\theta) - 3(\sin\theta + \sin 2\theta) = 0$, giving all solutions between 0° and 360°.

b Given that $\tan(\alpha - \pi/4) = \frac{71}{97}$, find the exact values of $\tan\alpha$ and $\cos\alpha$.
In triangle ABC, $AB = 25$ cm, $AC = 17$ cm and angle BAC $= \alpha$. Find the length of BC.

(WJEC)

7 Figure 2 shows an equilateral triangle ABC whose vertices lie on a circle, centre O, of radius r.

a Show that the length of a side of this triangle is $r\sqrt{3}$.

b Show that the ratio of the area of the shaded region to the area of the triangle is $(4\pi\sqrt{3} - 9) : 9$.

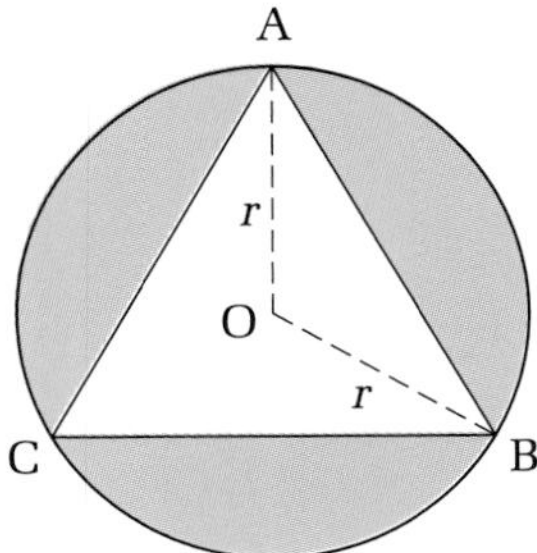

Fig. 2

(ULEAC)

Applications and Activities

All methods of measuring angles are based on division of a circle. Degrees are $\frac{1}{360}$ of a circle and can be subdivided into sixty minutes and then each minute subdivided into sixty seconds. Many calculators have a degree mode (DEG is usually displayed on the screen) and a key $^{\circ}\,'\,''$. The degree mode is usually located close to radian mode (RAD) and one other system of measuring angles; GRAD.

1 Investigate the GRAD system of measuring angles.

2 Find out what GRAD means and draw the graphs of $\sin\theta$, $\cos\theta$ and $\tan\theta$ when θ is measured in 'grads'.

3 What applications are there in everyday life with this scale?

Summary

- The trigonometric ratios are positive for angles in the following quadrants.

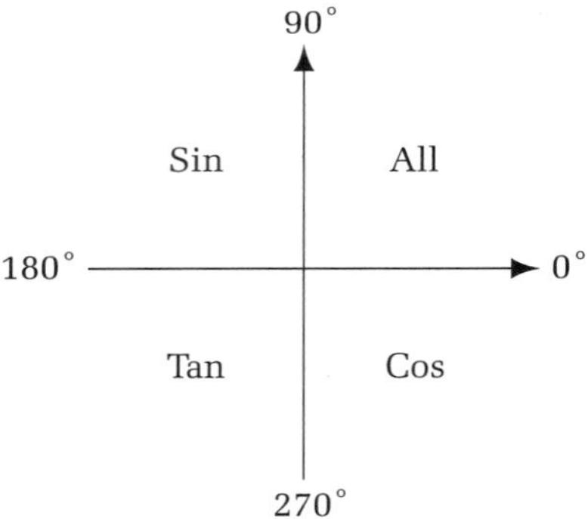

- $\tan\theta = \dfrac{\sin\theta}{\cos\theta}$

- The exact values of the trigonometric ratios of the special angles are:

θ	$\sin\theta$	$\cos\theta$	$\tan\theta$
30°	$\frac{1}{2}$	$\frac{\sqrt{3}}{2}$	$\frac{1}{\sqrt{3}}$
45°	$\frac{1}{\sqrt{2}}$	$\frac{1}{\sqrt{2}}$	1
60°	$\frac{\sqrt{3}}{2}$	$\frac{1}{2}$	$\sqrt{3}$

- The graphs of $y = \sin x$, $y = \cos x$ and $y = \tan x$ have periods 360°, 360° and 180° respectively, and look like:

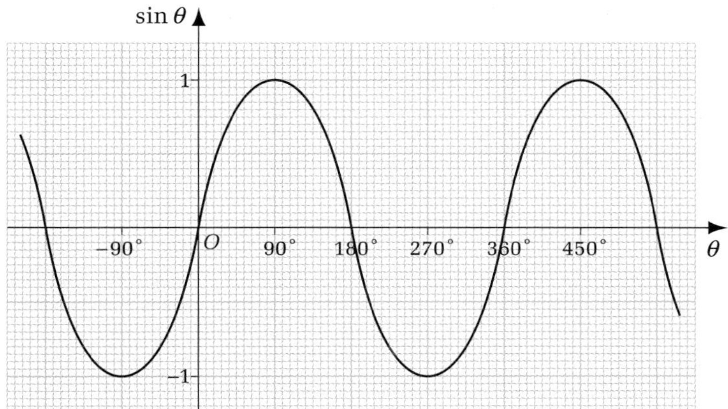

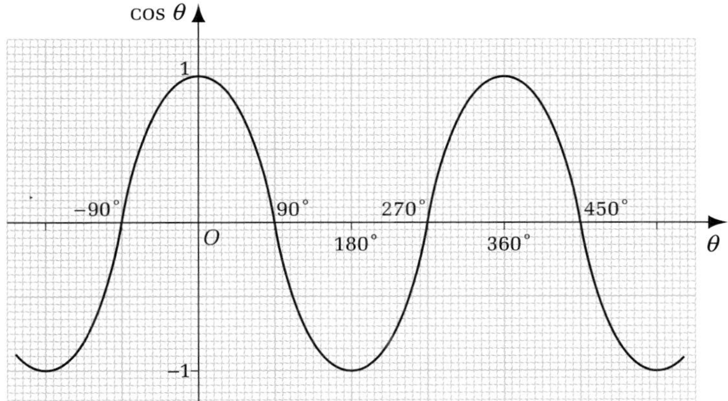

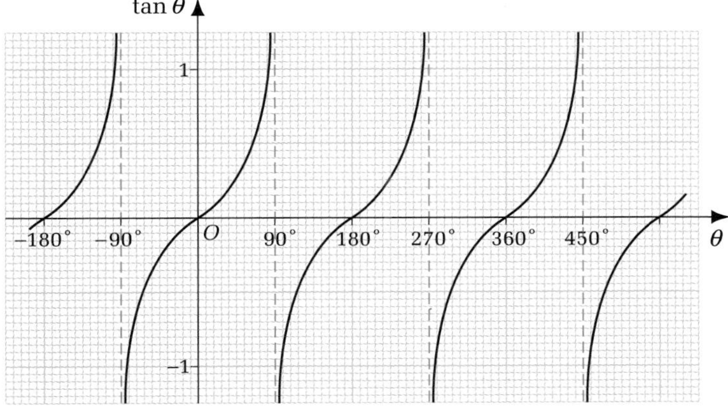

- The reciprocal ratios are:

$$\mathbf{cosec}\,\theta = \frac{1}{\sin\theta} \qquad \mathbf{sec}\,\theta = \frac{1}{\cos\theta} \qquad \mathbf{cot}\,\theta = \frac{1}{\tan\theta}$$

- The Pythagorean identities are:

$$\sin^2\theta + \cos^2\theta \equiv 1$$
$$\tan^2\theta + 1 \equiv \sec^2\theta$$
$$1 + \cot^2\theta \equiv \operatorname{cosec}^2\theta$$

- The compound angle formulas are:

$$\sin(A \pm B) \equiv \sin A\cos B \pm \cos A\sin B$$
$$\cos(A \pm B) \equiv \cos A\cos B \mp \sin A\sin B$$
$$\tan(A \pm B) \equiv \frac{\tan A \pm \tan B}{1 \mp \tan A\tan B}$$

- The double angle formulas are:

$$\sin 2A \equiv 2\sin A\cos B$$
$$\cos 2A \equiv \cos^2 A - \sin^2 A$$
$$\equiv 2\cos^2 A - 1$$
$$\equiv 1 - 2\sin^2 A$$
$$\tan 2A \equiv \frac{2\tan A}{1 - \tan^2 A}$$

- The cosine rule, in its various forms is:

$$a^2 = b^2 + c^2 - 2bc\cos A$$
$$\cos A = \frac{b^2 + c^2 - a^2}{2bc}$$

- The sine rule is:

$$\frac{a}{\sin A} = \frac{b}{\sin B} = \frac{c}{\sin C}$$

- The area of a triangle can be calculated using

$$\text{area} = \tfrac{1}{2} \times \text{base} \times \text{perpendicular height}$$
$$\text{area} = \tfrac{1}{2}ab\sin C$$

Hero(n)'s formula: $\text{area} = \sqrt{s(s-a)(s-b)(s-c)}$

where $s = \tfrac{1}{2}(a + b + c)$.

- $1\text{ radian} = \dfrac{360^\circ}{2\pi}$.

- In radian form, arc length $s = r\theta$ and sector area $A = \tfrac{1}{2}r^2\theta$

4 Functions

What you need to know

- How to change the subject of an equation.
- How to 'complete the square' for a quadratic expression.
- How to solve quadratic equations using either the factorisation method or the quadratic formula.
- How to express simple improper algebraic fractions as mixed fractions.

Review

1 Make x the subject of each of the following equations:

a $5x + 2y = 1$

b $y = 3x^2 - 2$

c $y = 4\sqrt{x - 1}$

d $y = \sqrt[3]{x} + 7$

e $y = 3 - \dfrac{10}{x}$

f $y = \dfrac{2x + 1}{x}$

2 Write each of the following expressions in the form $(x + a)^2 + b$ or $c(x + a)^2 + b$, where a, b and c are constants:

a $x^2 + 8x + 5$

b $x^2 - 4x + 3$

c $x^2 + x + 1$

d $x^2 - 3x - 5$

e $2x^2 + 12x$

f $3x^2 - 6x + 7$

3 Find the exact solutions of the following quadratic equations:

a $x^2 + 5x - 24 = 0$

b $x^2 - 5 = 0$

c $2x^2 - 14x + 20 = 0$

d $x^2 + 4x - 3 = 0$

e $x^2 + 6x - 1 = 0$

f $2x^2 - 6x + 1 = 0$

4 Rearrange each of the following into expressions that eliminate improper algebraic fractions:

a $\dfrac{x + 2}{x + 1}$

b $\dfrac{x + 1}{x + 2}$

c $\dfrac{x + 3}{x - 5}$

d $\dfrac{2x + 7}{x + 3}$

e $\dfrac{4x + 5}{2x - 1}$

f $\dfrac{3x}{1 - x}$

An improper algebraic fraction is one where the highest power in the numerator is the same as or larger than the highest power in the denominator.

4.1 Mappings and Functions

Mappings

A **mapping** is a rule that relates one set of items or numbers to another. For example, the diagram below shows the mapping of seven leading European football clubs to their home cities. The set of inputs for a mapping is called the **domain**, and a set of outputs from the mapping is called the **co-domain**. In this example, the set of clubs is the domain and the set of cities is the co-domain.

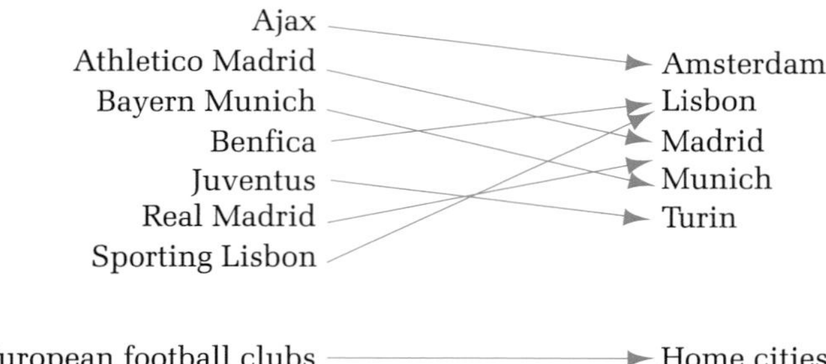

This relationship between the football clubs and their home cities is an example of a **many-to-one mapping**. Although each club obviously has only one home city, more than one club or **element** in the domain may map onto any given city in the co-domain. For example, Benfica and Sporting Lisbon are both based in the Portuguese capital, Lisbon.

If we reverse this relationship, and map the cities to their football clubs we obtain a **one-to-many mapping**, as shown below. This shows that it is possible for an element in the domain to map to more than one element in the co-domain.

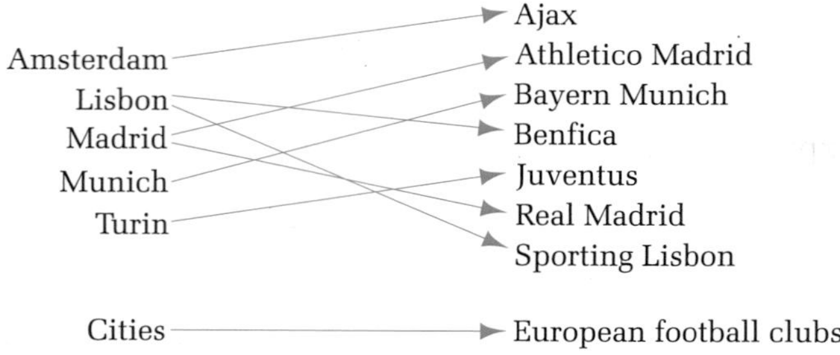

Two other types of mapping exist:

- one-to-one mappings
- many-to-many mappings.

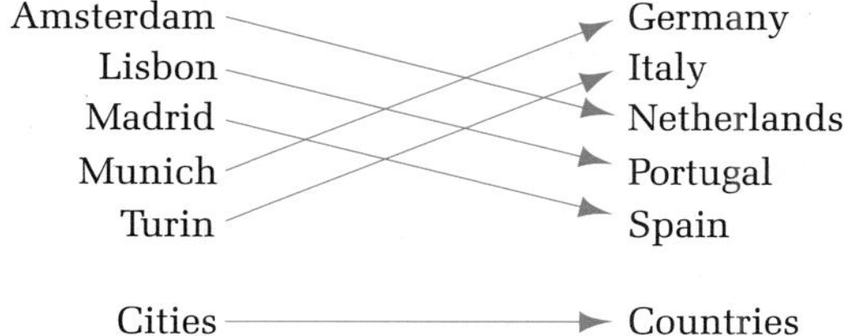

The relationship between these five cities and their countries is a **one-to-one mapping**. Each city in the domain maps to one and only one country in the co-domain.

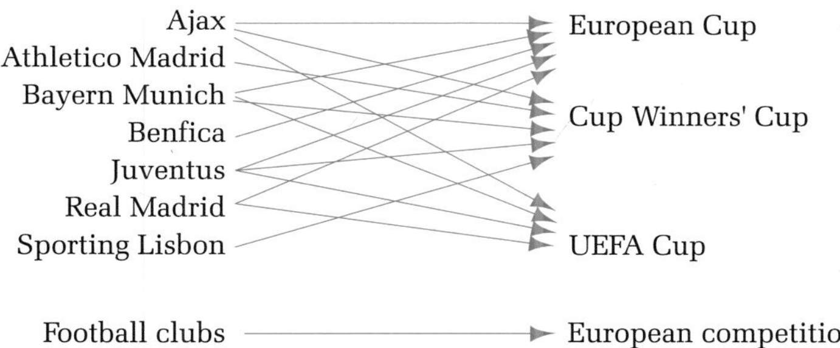

The relationship between the seven football clubs and the major European club competitions is an example of a **many-to-many mapping**. Several of these clubs have won more than one of these competitions.

Functions

Any mathematical mapping that takes any object in the domain and maps it to one, and only one, element in the co-domain is called a **function**. Since there can only be one possible image for each object in the domain, only many-to-one and one-to-one mappings are functions.

Example 1

Which of the following mappings are functions?

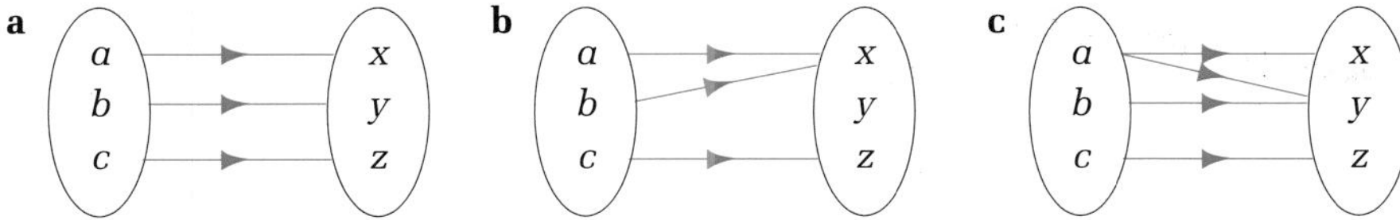

Solution

a This one-to-one mapping is a function. Each object in the domain maps to one, and only one, image.

b This many-to-one mapping is also a function. Note that it is not necessary for every element in the co-domain to be an image of an object in the domain.

c This many-to-many mapping is not a function because the element 'a' in the domain maps to more than one element in the co-domain.

The domain of a function is the set of **objects** or **input values** for which the function is defined. In Example 1 the set $\{a, b, c\}$ is the domain in functions **a** and **b**. The co-domain is a set containing the possible output values of a function. In Example 1 the set $\{x, y, z\}$ is the co-domain in functions **a** and **b**.

The **range** of a function is the set of **images**, or **output values**, to which the objects in the domain map. This can be the entire co-domain, as in the function in Example 1**a**, which has the range $\{x, y, z\}$, or it can be a subset of the co-domain, as in the function in Example 1**b**, which has the range $\{x, z\}$.

The words *onto* and *into* are used to highlight the difference. The domain of the function in Example 1**a** maps *onto* its co-domain, because it uses every element in the co-domain. The domain of the function in Example 1**b** maps *into* its co-domain, because only some of the elements are used.

A number of different but equivalent notations are used to define a function. For example, the function f, which maps values of x in the domain to values of $2x$ in the co-domain, may be written

$$f: x \to 2x$$ ◀ **f maps x to $2x$.**

or $f(x) = 2x$

or $y = 2x$

In this last form of notation, objects x in the domain map to images y in the co-domain. These (x, y) pairs can be used to represent the function graphically.

Example 2

Functions f and g are defined for domain $\{-2, -1, 0, 1, 2\}$ by $f: x \to 2x + 1$ and $g: x \to x^2$. Draw a mapping diagram for each function. State the range of each function and explain which type of mapping is shown.

f maps x to $2x + 1$
g maps x to x^2

Solution

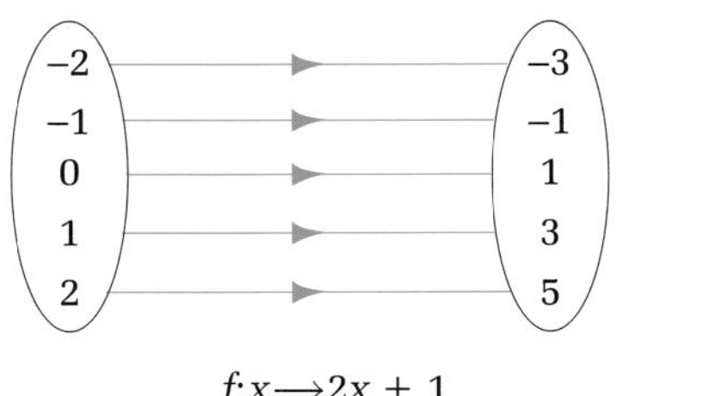

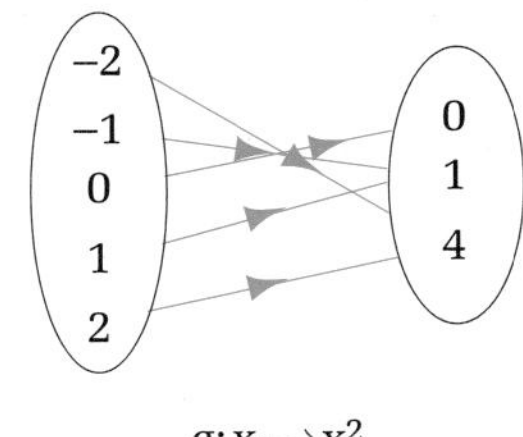

$f: x \longrightarrow 2x + 1$ $\quad$ $g: x \longrightarrow x^2$

The range of function f, for the given domain, is $\{-3, -1, 1, 3, 5\}$.
$f\colon x \to 2x + 1$ is a one-to-one mapping.

The range of function g, for the given domain, is $\{0, 1, 4\}$.
$g\colon x \to x^2$ is a many-to-one mapping.

It has been possible to draw mapping diagrams for each function in Example 2 because the domain is **discrete**. This means the domain consists of separate values of x, and does not contain any values between those stated.

If the domain isn't discrete then it can contain any value within specified limits. In this case the domain is said to be **continuous**. Functions with continuous domains are usually represented graphically.

Example 3

The functions f and g in Example 2 are defined for the continuous domain $\{x \in \mathbb{R}\colon -2 \leq x \leq 2\}$. In each case, sketch the graph of the function, and state the range.

$\{x \in \mathbb{R}\colon -2 \leq x \leq 2\}$ means all the real numbers between -2 and 2 (inclusive).

Solution

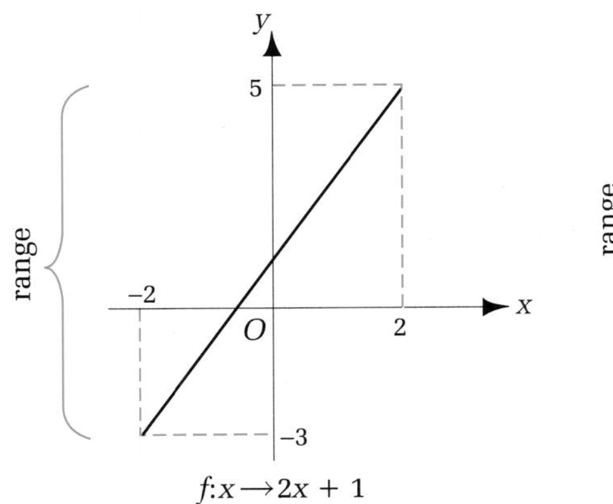

$f: x \longrightarrow 2x + 1$

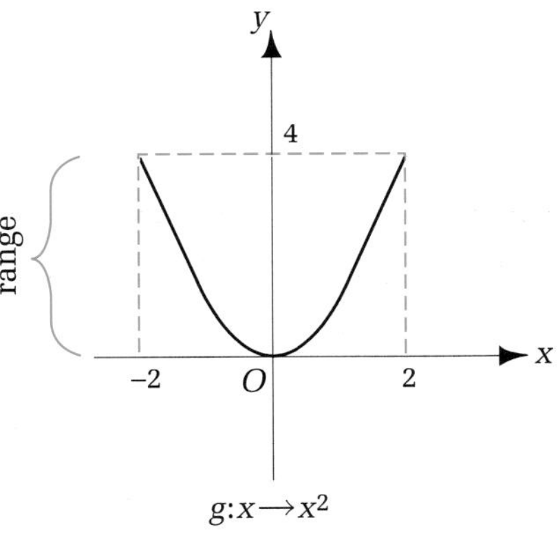

$g: x \longrightarrow x^2$

The range of function f, for the given domain, is $\{y \in \mathbb{R}\colon -3 \leq y \leq 5\}$.

This means that the range of f is all the real numbers between -3 and 5 inclusive.

The range of function g, for the given domain, is $\{y \in \mathbb{R}\colon 0 \leq y \leq 4\}$.

All **linear** functions can be written in the form $f: x \to ax + b$, where a and b are constants. If a and b are both unknown, then they can be calculated using the value of the function at two different values of x.

Example 4

The linear function $f: x \to ax + b$ is such that $f(1) = 8$ and $f(3) = 14$. Find the values of a and b.

Solution

$f(1)$ and $f(3)$ are found by substituting $x = 1$ and $x = 3$ into the function.

$$f(1) = 8 \quad \Rightarrow \quad a + b = 8 \qquad [1]$$

$$f(3) = 14 \Rightarrow 3a + b = 14 \qquad [2]$$

We now have two linea simultaneous equation

Eliminating b by subtracting equation [1] from equation [2],

$$2a = 6$$

$$\Rightarrow \quad a = 3$$

Substituting $a = 3$ into equation [1],

$$3 + b = 8$$

$$\Rightarrow \quad b = 5$$

So $a = 3$, $b = 5$ and the function is $f: x \to 3x + 5$.

All quadratic functions can be written in the general form $f: x \to ax^2 + bx + c$, where $a \neq 0$. If the coefficients a, b and c are all unknown, they can be found in a similar way to that used for linear functions (Example 4). This time use the value of the function f at three different values of x. This creates three linear simultaneous equations involving a, b and c. These can then be solved using either the elimination or substitution methods.

4.1 Mappings and Functions
Exercise
Technique

1 The functions below are defined for the given discrete domains. In each case:

i draw a mapping diagram
ii state the range of the function
iii state the type of mapping.

a $f: x \rightarrow 1 - 2x$ for $\{x: -10, -5, 0, 5, 10\}$
b $f: x \rightarrow 2x^2$ for $\{x: -2, -1, 0, 1, 2\}$
c $f: x \rightarrow +\sqrt{x}$ for $\{x: 0, 1, 4, 9, 16\}$
d $f: x \rightarrow \frac{2}{x}$ for $\{x: 1, 2, 3, 4, 5\}$

2 The functions below are defined for the given continuous domains. In each case:

i sketch the graph of the function
ii state the range of the function
iii state the type of mapping.

a $f: x \rightarrow \frac{1}{2}x + 3$ for $\{x \in \mathbb{R}: \ 2 \leq x \leq 6\}$
b $f: x \rightarrow x^2 - 1$ for $\{x \in \mathbb{R}: -3 \leq x \leq 3\}$
c $f: x \rightarrow x^3$ for $\{x \in \mathbb{R}: -2 \leq x \leq 2\}$
d $f: x \rightarrow \frac{1}{x}$ for $\{x \in \mathbb{R}: \ 0 < x \leq 3\}$

3 State whether or not each of the following graphs represents a function, giving reasons for your answer:

a

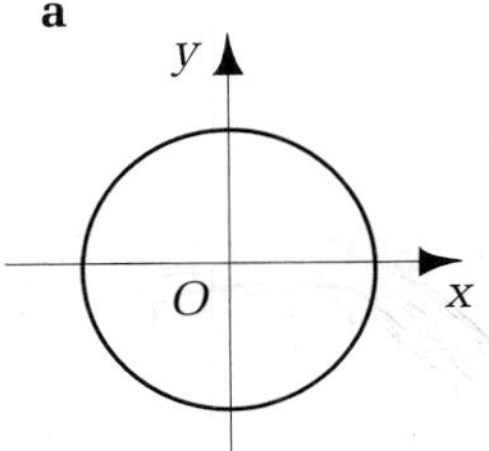

b

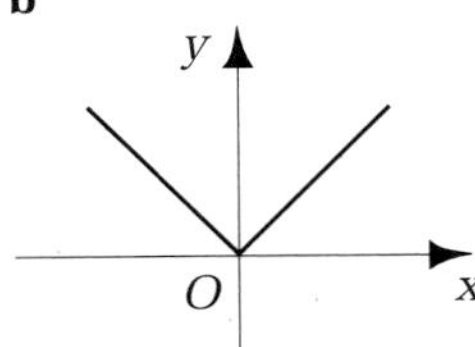

c

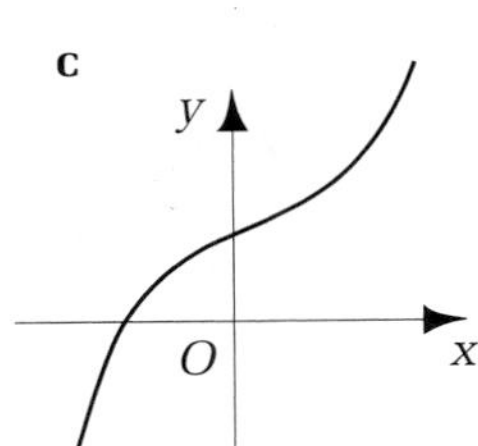

d

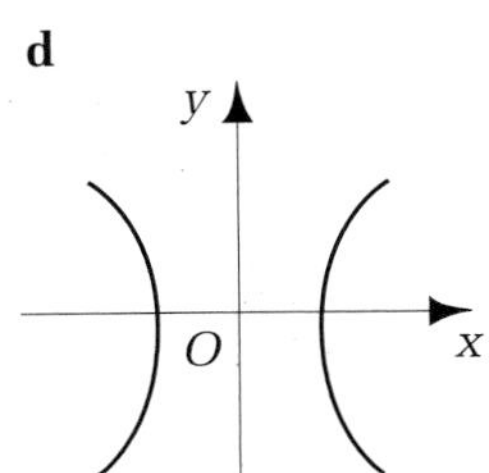

4 The mappings f and g are defined by:

$$f: x \rightarrow \begin{cases} 5 - x & \text{for } x \leq 2 \\ \frac{1}{2}x^3 & \text{for } x \geq 2 \end{cases} \qquad g: x \rightarrow \begin{cases} 12x & \text{for } x \leq 4 \\ 3x^2 & \text{for } x \geq 4 \end{cases}$$

Explain why g is a function, but f is not a function.

5 The functions f and g are such that $f(x) = 13x - 4$ and $g(x) = 4x^2 - 1$.

a Find the value of a for which $f(a) = 35$.
b Find the values of b for which $g(b) = 15$.
c Find the values of c for which $f(c) = g(c)$.

6 The linear function f is defined by $f: x \rightarrow ax + b$, where a and b are constants. Given that $f(2) = 3$ and $f(-3) = 13$, find a and b. Hence, calculate the value of c for which $f(c) = 0$.

7 The quadratic function g is defined by $g: x \rightarrow ax^2 + bx + c$, where a, b and c are constants. Given that $g(0) = -3$, $g(1) = 4$ and $g(2) = 15$, find a, b and c. Hence calculate the values of d for which $g(d) = 0$.

4.2 Inverse Functions

For many mathematical mappings, there is a corresponding mapping that has the opposite or reversing effect. For example, the mapping 'subtract 6', or $x \to x - 6$ is the opposite of the mapping 'add 6', or $x \to x + 6$. For the domain $\{0, 1, 2, 3\}$, this last mapping has the range $\{6, 7, 8, 9\}$.

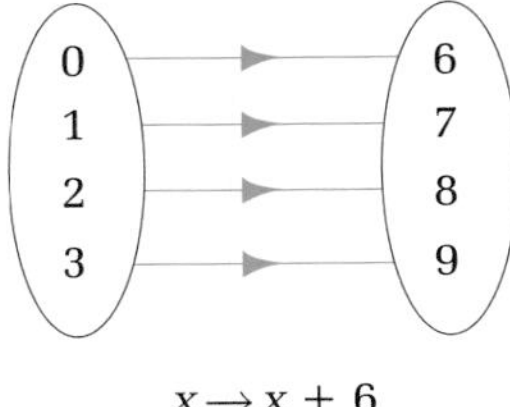

$x \to x + 6$

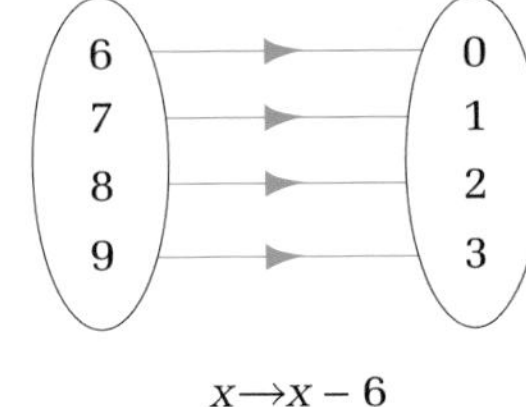

$x \to x - 6$

Taking $\{6, 7, 8, 9\}$ as the domain for the reverse mapping, $x \to x - 6$, this maps back onto the original domain.

So for this particular domain, the mapping $x \to x + 6$ and its inverse $x \to x - 6$ are both one-to-one relationships. They are therefore both functions.

To write this more formally, if the function f is defined such that $f: x \to x + 6$, then its inverse function f^{-1} is defined as $f^{-1}: x \to x - 6$.

When working with functions, f^{-1} means 'the inverse of function f', and not 'the reciprocal of function f'.

Now consider the function $f(x) = x^2$, defined for the domain $\{x \in \mathbb{Z}: -2 \le x \le 2\}$. For this particular domain, the mapping of $x \to x^2$ is 'many-to-one'. Therefore $f(x)$ is a function. However, the reverse mapping is one-to-many. There is no unique relationship between the objects and images of this mapping. So, by definition, it cannot be a function.

Recall that $\mathbb{Z}$ is the set of all integers.

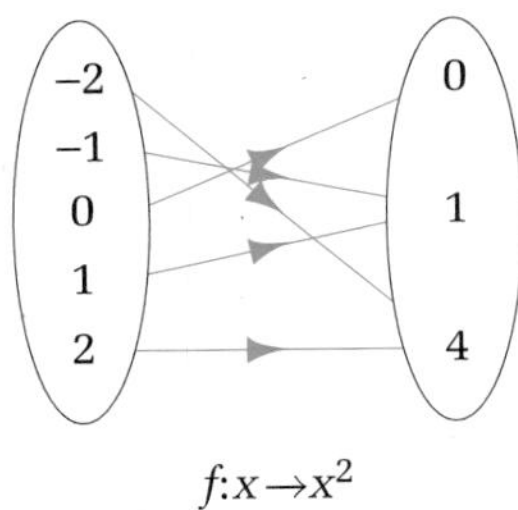

$f: x \to x^2$

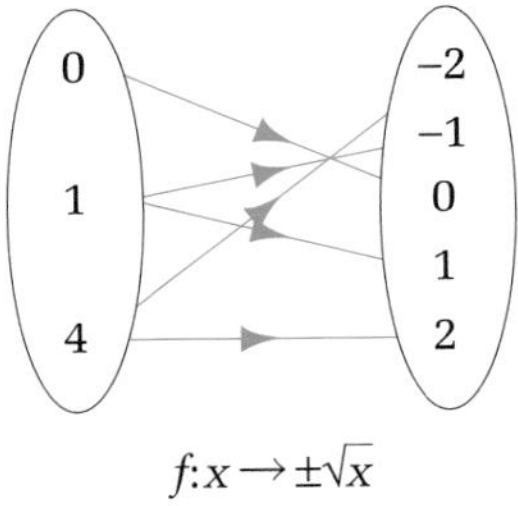

$f: x \to \pm\sqrt{x}$

Only those functions which, for a given domain, are one-to-one mappings, have inverse functions. This point can be illustrated graphically by changing the domain over which the function $f: x \to x^2$ is defined to $\{x \in \mathbb{R}: -2 \le x \le 2\}$. Find $f(-1)$ and $f(1)$. What do you notice? Both $f(-1)$ and $f(1)$ equal 1. So two different values of x in the domain can give the same output value from the function. However, if we reverse the mapping, an input of 1 results in not one, but two distinct outputs, 1 and -1.

Recall that $\mathbb{R}$ is the set of all real numbers.

A one-to-many mapping.

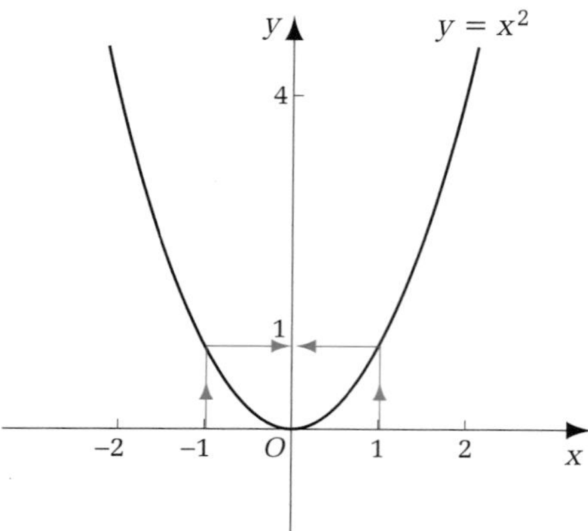

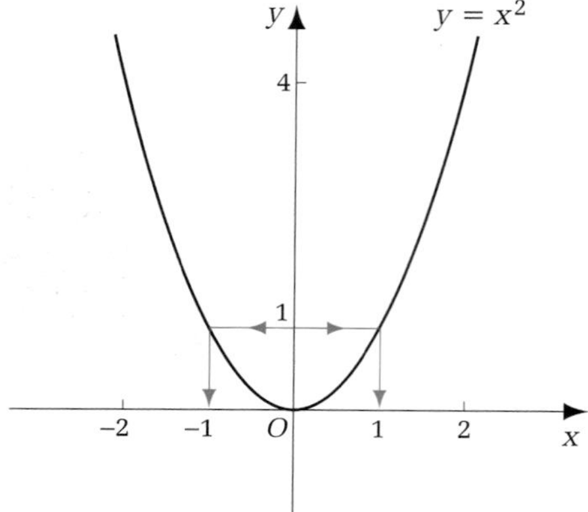

It is, however, possible to define an inverse function if we restrict the domain to values of x for which the mapping is one-to-one. For example, if $f: x \to x^2$ is defined for the restricted domain $\{x \in \mathbb{R}: 0 \leq x \leq 2\}$ then the inverse function $f^{-1}: x \to +\sqrt{x}$ exists.

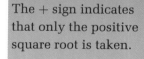

The + sign indicates that only the positive square root is taken.

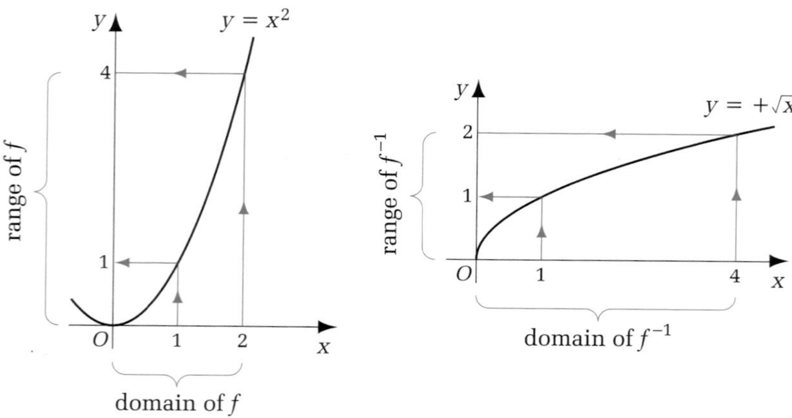

It is important to realise that the inverse function maps values in the range of the original function back onto the domain of the original function.

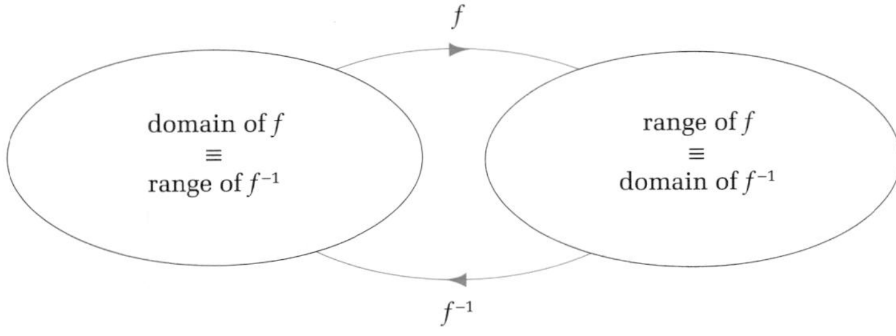

The graphical representation of a function can be used to determine whether it is a one-to-one mapping. If it is a one-to-one mapping then it has an inverse function.

Example 1

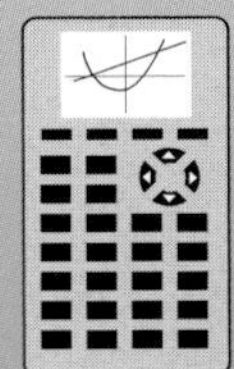

Use a graphical calculator, or alternative method, to sketch the graphs of the following functions:

$f: x \rightarrow x - 3, \ x \in \mathbb{R}$

$g: x \rightarrow x^3, \ x \in \mathbb{R}$

$h: x \rightarrow x^3 - 12x, \ x \in \mathbb{R}.$

Use the graphs to decide which of these functions have inverse functions.

Solution

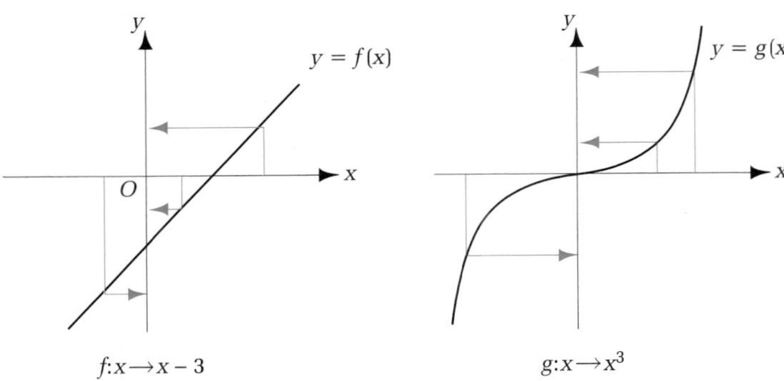

Functions f and g are both one-to-one mappings. Therefore both have inverse functions.

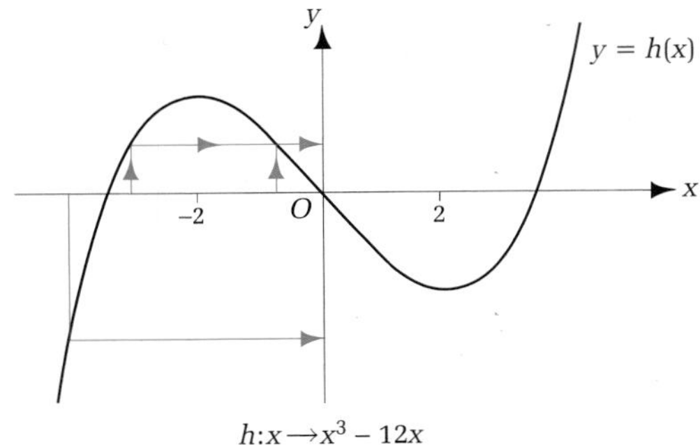

Notice that the graph of $y = h(x)$ has two **turning points**; at $x = -2$ and $x = 2$. It doubles back on itself between these two points. Function h is therefore not a one-to-one mapping and so, for the given domain, h does not have an inverse function.

A turning point is a maximum or minimum point on a graph.

If the domain of function h is restricted to a set of values of x for which the mapping is one-to-one, for example $\{x \in \mathbb{R}: -2 \leq x \leq 2\}$, then the inverse function h^{-1} exists. Since $h(-1) = 11$, it follows that, $h^{-1}(11) = -1$.

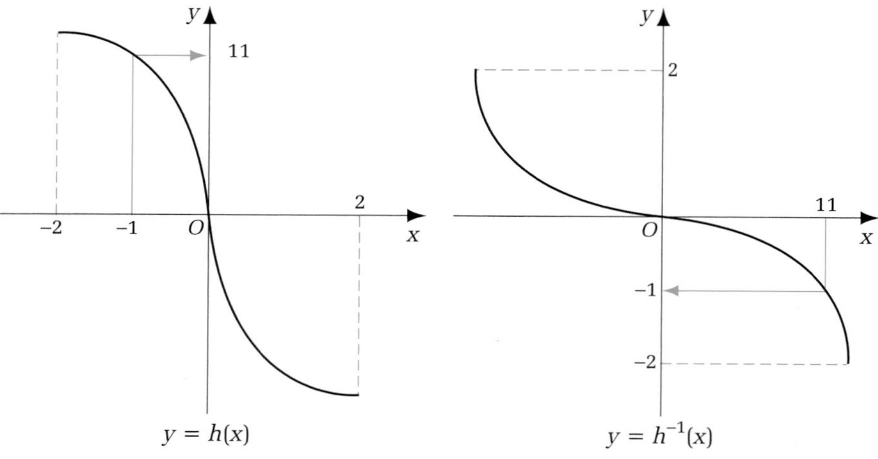

The graph of an inverse function

If a function f maps values of x in its domain to values of y in its range then the inverse function f^{-1} maps values of y back to the corresponding values of x. It follows that for every point (x, y) on the graph of function f there is a corresponding point with coordinates (y, x) on the graph of the inverse function f^{-1}. Geometrically, this interchanging of x and y is equivalent to a reflection in the line $y = x$.

The graph of the inverse function $y = f^{-1}(x)$ can be sketched by simply reflecting the graph of $y = f(x)$ in the line $y = x$.

To carry out this reflection properly, it is important to use the same scale on both axes.

Example 2

Sketch each of the following graphs, and draw in the line $y = x$. Reflect each of the graphs in $y = x$ to obtain the graph of the inverse function.

Remember to use the same scale for both axes.

a $f(x) = 2x + 1$
b $f(x) = 3 - x$
c $f(x) = x^3 + 1$

Solution

a

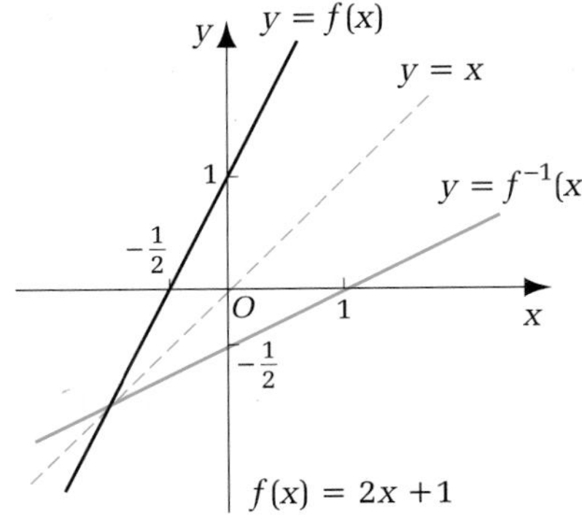

◀ (0, 1) corresponds to (1, 0), and $(-\frac{1}{2}, 0)$ corresponds to $(0, -\frac{1}{2})$

b

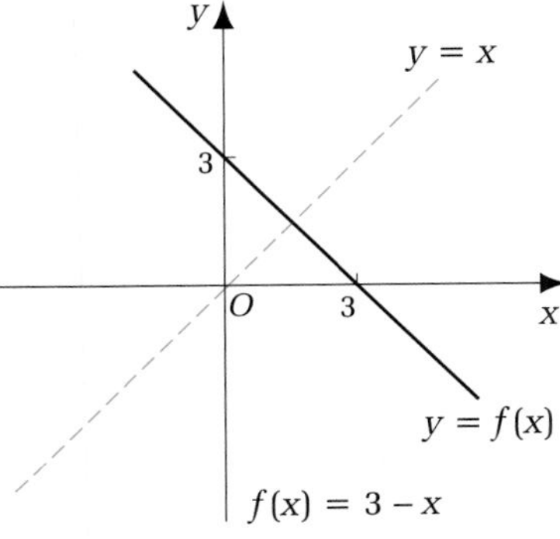

◀ (3, 0) corresponds to (0, 3), and (0, 3) corresponds to (3, 0)

The line $y = 3 - x$ is symmetrical about the line $y = x$. This means that $f(x)$ is its own inverse; **self-inverse**. Therefore $f^{-1}(x) = 3 - x$.

c

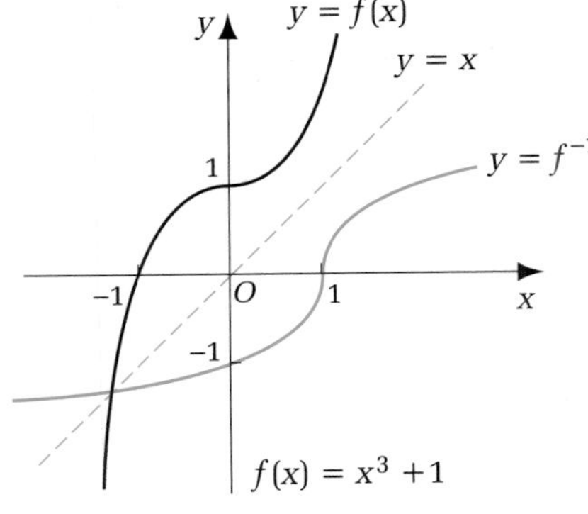

◀ (0, 1) corresponds to (1, 0), and (−1, 0) corresponds to (0, −1)

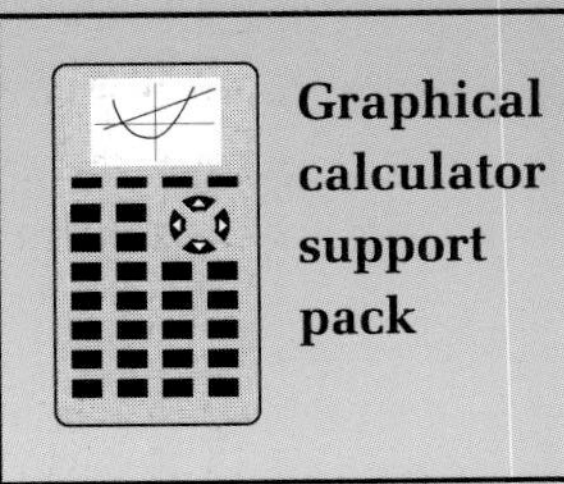

Finding the inverse function

Two different methods can be used to find an algebraic expression for the inverse of a function:

- express the function as a 'flow diagram' or 'function machine', and then reverse the direction,
- express the function in the form $y = f(x)$, interchange x and y, and then rearrange the equation to make y the subject of the equation again.

Example 3

a Find the inverse function of $f(x) = 2x + 5$.

b The function $f: x \to \frac{2}{x}$ is defined for $\{x \in \mathbb{R}: x \neq 0\}$. Find its inverse function.

Solution

a *Method 1:* Express the function as a 'function machine'.

$$x \xrightarrow{\times 2} 2x \xrightarrow{+5} f(x) = 2x + 5$$

The inverse function is found by reversing each of the individual operations and the order in which they are carried out.

$$f^{-1}(x) = \frac{x-5}{2} \xleftarrow{\div 2} x - 5 \xleftarrow{-5} x$$ ◀ **Read from right to left.**

Therefore, the inverse function is $f^{-1}(x) = \frac{1}{2}(x - 5)$.

Try this approach with the functions in Example 2. Notice that this particular method will only work if x appears only once in the function.

Method 2: Expressing the function in the form $y = 2x + 5$, and interchanging x and y,

Interchanging x and y is the algebraic equivalent of reflecting the function in the line $y = x$.

$$x = 2y + 5$$

Now make y the subject of the equation.

$$y = \tfrac{1}{2}(x - 5)$$

So, as before, the inverse function is $f^{-1}(x) = \frac{1}{2}(x - 5)$.
Use a graphical calculator to draw the lines $y = 2x + 5$, $y = \frac{1}{2}(x - 5)$ and $y = x$. Check that the graph of the inverse function is a reflection of the graph of the function in the line $y = x$. Remember to use the same scale on both axes.

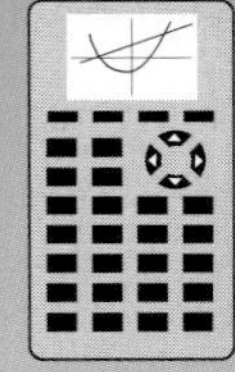

b The function machine for f looks like,

$$x \xrightarrow{\text{invert}} \frac{1}{x} \xrightarrow{\times 2} f(x) = \frac{2}{x}$$

Now reverse the individual operations and the order in which they are applied:

$$f^{-1}(x) = \frac{2}{x} \xleftarrow{\text{invert}} \frac{x}{2} \xleftarrow{\div 2} x$$

Therefore $f^{-1}: x \to \frac{2}{x}$, and function f is another example of a self-inverse. Draw the graph of $y = \frac{2}{x}$. What do you notice? The graph of $y = \frac{2}{x}$ is symmetrical about the line $y = x$.

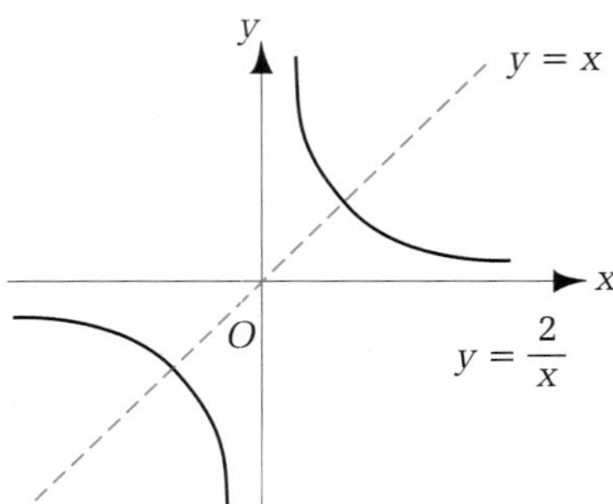

Use a graphical calculator to draw the line $y = x$ and the graphs of functions of the form $f(x) = a - x$ and $f(x) = \frac{a}{x}$ for different values of the real number a. What happens? You should discover that all functions of the form $f(x) = a - x$ and $f(x) = \frac{a}{x}$, where a is a real number, are symmetrical about the line $y = x$. They are all self-inverses.

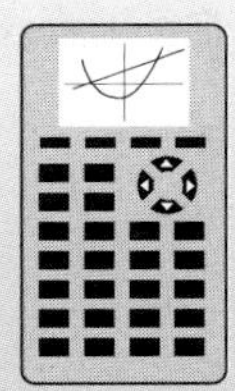

Example 4

The function $g(x) = \dfrac{x+1}{x-3}$ is defined for the domain $\{x \in \mathbb{R}: x \neq 3\}$. Find its inverse function, and state the value of x for which $g^{-1}(x)$ is not defined.

Solution

Writing the function in the form $y = g(x)$, and interchanging x and y gives $x = \dfrac{y+1}{y-3}$.

Rearrange this equation to make y the subject,

$$x(y-3) = y+1$$

$$\Rightarrow \quad xy - 3x = y + 1$$

$$\Rightarrow \quad xy - y = 3x + 1$$

$$\Rightarrow \quad y(x-1) = 3x + 1$$

$$y = \frac{3x+1}{x-1}$$

$$\text{So} \quad g^{-1}(x) = \frac{3x+1}{x-1}$$

Try putting $x = 1$ into the inverse function. What happens? Division by zero causes a problem, creating an answer that is undefined. So this inverse function is defined for all real values of x except $x = 1$.

Example 5

The quadratic function $f(x) = x^2 - 8x + 14$ is defined for the domain $\{x \in \mathbb{R}: x \geq 4\}$.

a By ‘completing the square’, express f in the form $(x + a)^2 + b$, where a and b are integers.

b Hence, or otherwise, find an expression for the inverse function f^{-1}.

c Sketch the graph of $y = f^{-1}(x)$, and state the domain and range of this inverse function.

d Solve the equation $f(x) = f^{-1}(x)$.

Solution

a $$f(x) = x^2 - 8x + 14$$
$$= x^2 - 8x + 16 - 2$$
$$= (x - 4)^2 - 2$$
$$\Rightarrow \quad a = -4 \text{ and } b = -2.$$

Completing the square, and spotting that $16 = 4^2$.

b Writing the function in the form $y = (x - 4)^2 - 2$, and interchanging x and y,

$$x = (y - 4)^2 - 2$$

Rearranging to make y the subject,

$$(y - 4)^2 = x + 2$$
$$\Rightarrow \quad y - 4 = \sqrt{x + 2}$$
$$\Rightarrow \quad y = 4 + \sqrt{x + 2}$$

Take the positive square root.

Therefore, the inverse function is $f^{-1}(x) = 4 + \sqrt{x + 2}$.

c Reflecting the graph of $y = f(x)$ in the line $y = x$ gives the graph of $y = f^{-1}(x)$.
The domain of f^{-1} is $\{x \in \mathbb{R}: x \geq -2\}$.
The range of f^{-1} is $\{y \in \mathbb{R}: y \geq 4\}$.

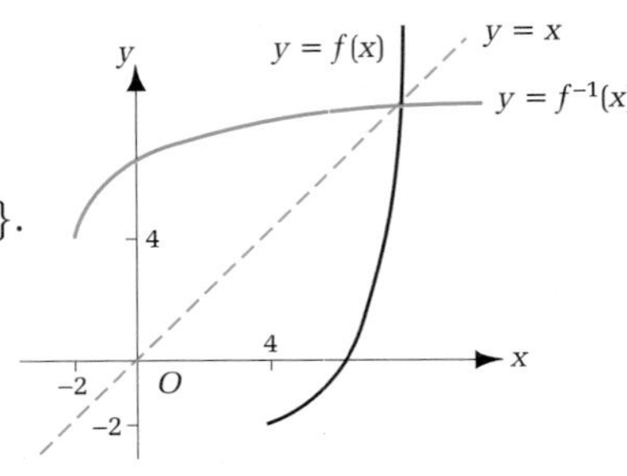

d Equating $f(x) = x^2 - 8x + 14$ with $f^{-1}(x) = 4 + \sqrt{x + 2}$ gives

$$x^2 - 8x + 14 = 4 + \sqrt{x + 2}$$

Although progress can be made with this equation, it will involve cubic (x^3) and quartic (x^4) terms. Look at the graphs. Notice that the point at which $f(x) = f^{-1}(x)$ is also the point of intersection of the line $y = x$ and the curve $y = f(x)$, so solving the simultaneous equations $y = x$ and $y = f(x)$ may be an easier way to find the solution.

$$x = x^2 - 8x + 14$$

If $y = x$ and $y = f(x)$ then $x = f(x)$.

$$\Rightarrow x^2 - 9x + 14 = 0$$ ◀ **Collecting like terms.**

$$\Rightarrow (x - 2)(x - 7) = 0$$ ◀ **Factorising.**

$$\Rightarrow x = 2 \text{ or } x = 7$$

Since function f is only defined for $x \geq 4$, ignore the solution $x = 2$. Therefore, the only solution to the equation $f(x) = f^{-1}(x)$ is $x = 7$.

Sometimes it may be easier to solve the equation $f(x) = f^{-1}(x)$ by finding the intersection of $y = x$ and $y = f^{-1}(x)$. This is the same as solving $x = f^{-1}(x)$.

Inverse trigonometric functions

The sine, cosine and tangent functions are periodic. For the domain of real numbers they are many-to-one mappings, as illustrated.

The coloured sections show the restricted domains where the functions are one-to-one mappings.

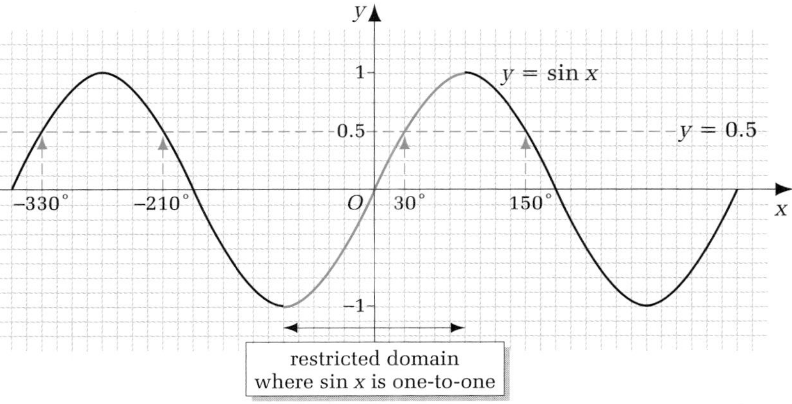

$\sin x = 0.5$ for $x = -330°, -210°, 30°, 150°$, and so on.

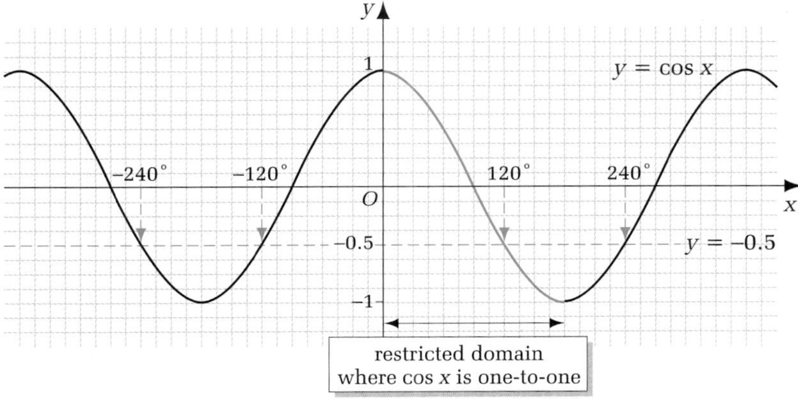

$\cos x = -0.5$ for $x = -240°, -120°, 120°, 240°$, and so on.

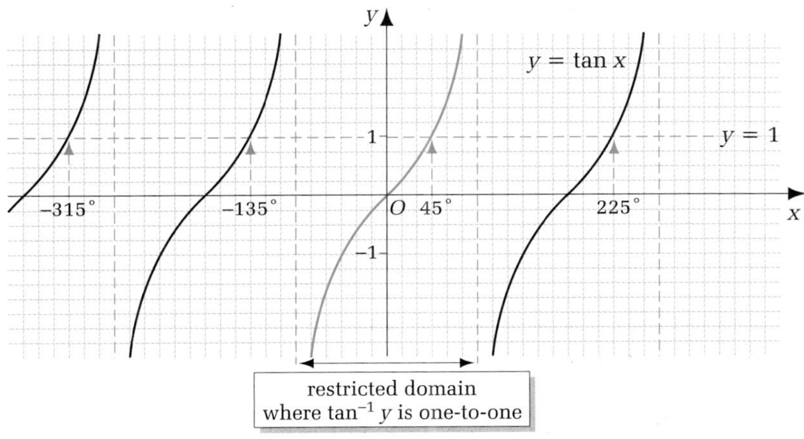

$\tan x = 1$ for $x = -315°, -135°, 45°, 225°$, and so on.

The inverse trigonometric functions $\sin^{-1}$, $\cos^{-1}$ and $\tan^{-1}$ can each be defined for a restricted domain. These domains are the values of x for which the sine, cosine and tangent mappings are one-to-one. The restrictions are different for each of the three trigonometric functions.

Another notation is arcsin, arccos and arctan.

For $f(x) = \sin x$ and $f(x) = \tan x$ to be one-to-one mappings, $-90° \leq x° \leq 90°$, or $-\frac{\pi}{2} \leq x \leq \frac{\pi}{2}$ if x measured in radians. However, for $f(x) = \cos x$ to be a one-to-one mapping, $0° \leq x° \leq 180°$, or $0 \leq x \leq \pi$ if x is measured in radians.

The graphs of $y = \sin^{-1} x$, $y = \cos^{-1} x$ and $y = \tan^{-1} x$ can be sketched by reflecting the graphs of $y = \sin x$, $y = \cos x$ or $y = \tan x$ in the line $y = x$. Remember to use the same scale on both axes and to measure the angles in radians.

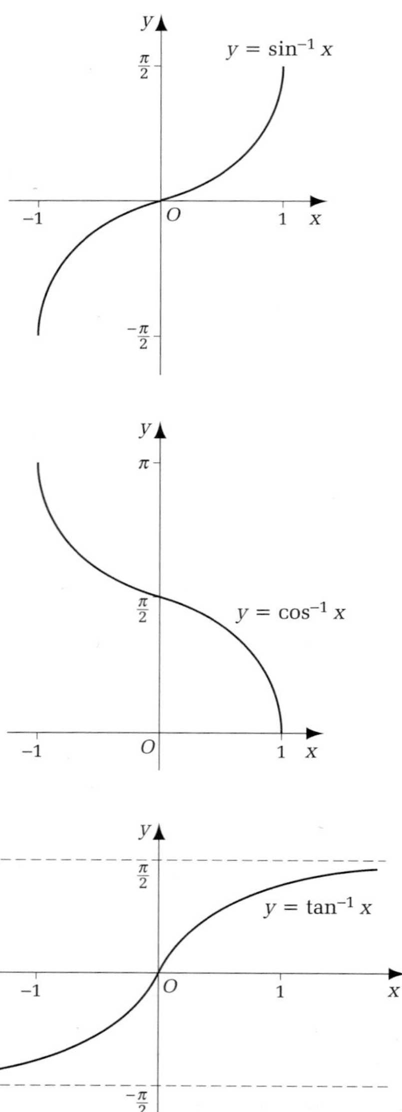

4.2 Inverse Functions
Exercise
Technique

1 For each of the following functions:

i state whether an inverse function exists, giving a reason for your answer

ii sketch the graph of the inverse function if it exists.

a

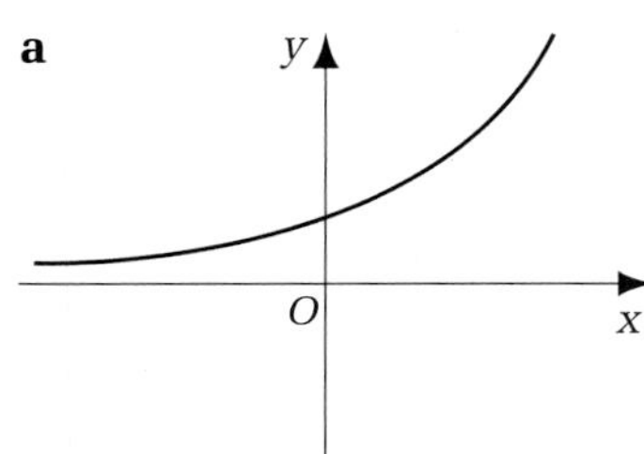

b

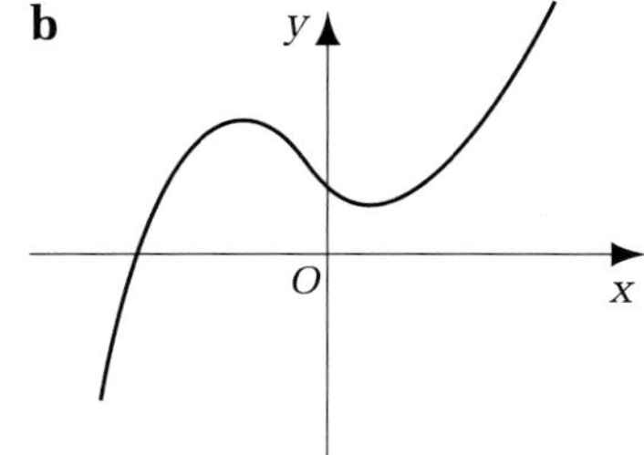

c

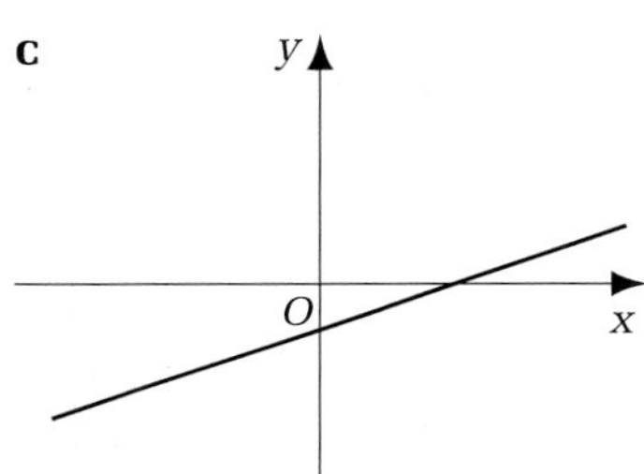

d

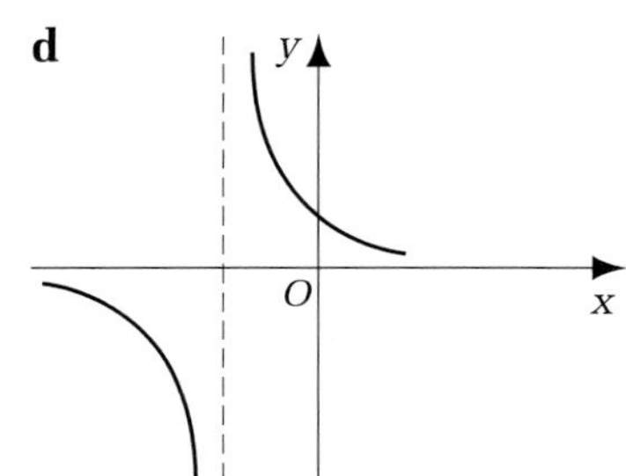

2 Find an expression for f^{-1} for each of the following functions:

2 **a, b, c**

a $f: x \to 3x - 8$

b $f: x \to \dfrac{4}{x+3},\ x \neq -3$

c $f: x \to 2x^2 + 7,\ x \geq 0$

d $f: x \to \frac{1}{2}\sqrt{x^2 + 5},\ x \geq 0$

e $f: x \to \dfrac{2}{x} + 3,\ x \neq 0$

f $f: x \to \dfrac{4}{x^2},\ x > 0$

3 The rational functions f, g and h are defined on the set of real numbers such that:

$$f(x) = \frac{3}{x-4}, \qquad g(x) = \frac{2x}{x+1}, \qquad h(x) = \frac{2x+3}{x-5}$$

a State the values of x for which each of these functions are undefined.

b Find an expression for each of the inverse functions, and state their domains.

4 The functions f and g are defined such that

$$f(x) = \frac{ax + 2}{x - 3}, \qquad g(x) = \frac{5x - 1}{2x + b}$$

where a and b are constants.

a Find expressions for $f^{-1}(x)$ and $g^{-1}(x)$.
b State the values of a and b for which functions f and g are self-inverses.

5 **a** Express $x^2 - 2x - 4$ in the form $(x + a)^2 + b$, where a and b are integers.
b Function $f(x) = x^2 - 2x - 4$ is defined for the domain $x \in \mathbb{R}: x \geq q$. Find the least value of q for which function f is a one-to-one mapping.
c State the range of f.
d Find an expression for the inverse function f^{-1}.
e Solve the equation $f(x) = f^{-1}(x)$.

6 The function f is defined for the domain $0 \leq x \leq \frac{\pi}{9}$ by $f(x) = \cos 3x$.

a Find an expression for f^{-1}. State the domain of f^{-1}.
b Calculate the value of $f^{-1}(\frac{\sqrt{3}}{2})$ in terms of π.

7

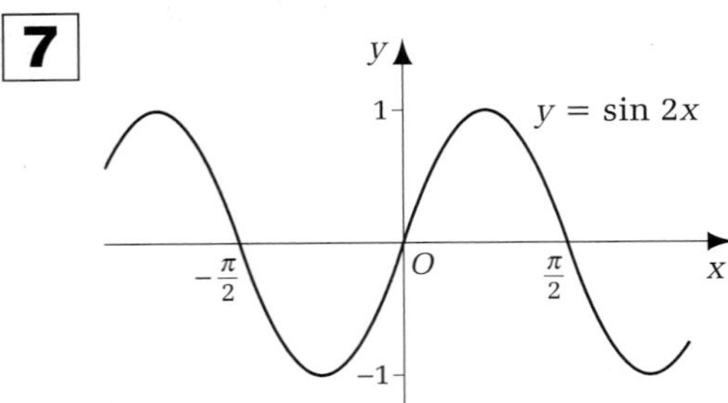

The diagram shows the graph of $y = f(x)$, where $f(x) = \sin 2x$.

a State the restricted domain for which function f is a one-to-one mapping.
b For this restricted domain:
  i find an expression for f^{-1}
  ii state the domain of f^{-1}
  iii sketch the graphs of $y = f(x)$ and $y = f^{-1}(x)$ on one set of axes, using the same scale on both axes.
c State the domain of the function $g(x) = \sin ax$, where a is a positive constant, if the inverse function g^{-1} exists.

4.3 Composite Functions

The output values of two or more functions can be combined using addition, subtraction, multiplication and division. If $f(x) = 3x$ and $g(x) = \sin x$, possible combinations include:

$$f(x) + g(x) = 3x + \sin x$$

$$f(x) - g(x) = 3x - \sin x$$

$$f(x) \times g(x) = 3x \sin x$$

$$f(x) \div g(x) = \frac{3x}{\sin x} \text{ (provided } \sin x \neq 0)$$

It is also possible to take the output values from one function and use them as the input values for another function. Using $f(x) = 3x$ and $g(x) = \sin x$, first evaluate function g for different values of x, and then input the values of $g(x)$ into function f. What happens?

$$x \xrightarrow{g} g(x) = \sin x \xrightarrow{f} f(g(x)) = 3 \sin x$$

The resulting composite function (or 'function of a function') is $f(g(x)) = 3 \sin x$, and is commonly referred to as $fg(x)$. Note that the g is written closest to the x because function g is the first stage of this composite function.

An alternative notation for the composite function $fg(x)$ is $f \circ g(x)$.

Now evaluate function f first and use the corresponding values of $f(x)$ as inputs into function g. What happens?

$$x \xrightarrow{f} f(x) = 3x \xrightarrow{g} g(f(x)) = \sin 3x$$

Notice that the composite function isn't the same. This time the output is $gf(x) = \sin 3x$.

Example 1

The functions f, g and h are defined by $f: x \rightarrow \cos x$, $g: x \rightarrow x^2$, $h: x \rightarrow 2x + 1$. Find expressions for the following composite functions:

a $gf(x)$ **b** $hg(x)$ **c** $gh(x)$

d $hf(x)$ **e** $hgf(x)$ **f** $fhg(x)$

Solution

a $gf(x) = g(f(x))$

$= g(\cos x)$

$= (\cos x)^2$

$= \cos^2 x$

Input $\cos x$ into function g.

Recall the conventional way of writing $(\cos x)^2$.

b $hg(x) = h(g(x))$
$= h(x^2)$
$= 2(x^2) + 1$
$= 2x^2 + 1$

x^2 replaces x in functio h.

c $gh(x) = g(h(x))$
$= g(2x + 1)$
$= (2x + 1)^2$

d $hf(x) = h(f(x))$
$= h(\cos x)$
$= 2(\cos x) + 1$
$= 2 \cos x + 1$

$\cos x$ replaces x in function h.

e $hgf(x) = h(g(f(x)))$
$= h(g(\cos x))$
$= h(\cos^2 x)$
$= 2(\cos^2 x) + 1$
$= 2 \cos^2 x + 1$

Input composite function $gf(x)$ into function h.

f $fhg(x) = f(hg(x))$
$= f(2x^2 + 1)$
$= \cos(2x^2 + 1)$

From **b**, $hg(x) = 2x^2 +$

Example 2

Each of the following functions are composite functions of the form $gf(x)$. In each case find the component functions f and g.

a $p(x) = \dfrac{1}{x + 2}$ **b** $q(x) = 8x^3$ **c** $r(x) = 5 - x$

Solution

Use flow diagrams to decompose each of these functions.

a $p(x): x \xrightarrow{+2} x + 2 \xrightarrow{\text{invert}} \dfrac{1}{x + 2}$

Therefore $p(x) \equiv gf(x)$, where $f(x) = x + 2$ and $g(x) = \frac{1}{x}$.

b $q(x): x \xrightarrow{\text{cube}} x^3 \xrightarrow{\times 8} 8x^3$

Therefore $q(x) \equiv gf(x)$, where $f(x) = x^3$ and $g(x) = 8x$.
There is an alternative way of expressing function q as the composite of two functions.

$q(x): x \xrightarrow{\times 2} 2x \xrightarrow{\text{cube}} 8x^3$

Then $q(x) \equiv gf(x)$, where $f(x) = 2x$ and $g(x) = x^3$.

c $r(x): x \xrightarrow{\times(-1)} -x \xrightarrow{+5} -x + 5 = 5 - x$

Therefore $r(x) \equiv gf(x)$, where $f(x) = -x$ and $g(x) = x + 5$.
Again, there is an alternative.

$r(x): x \xrightarrow{-5} x - 5 \xrightarrow{\times(-1)} -(x - 5) = 5 - x$

Then $r(x) \equiv gf(x)$, where $f(x) = x - 5$ and $g(x) = -x$.

Instead of feeding the output from one particular function into a different function, we could input back into the original function itself. Using $f(x) = 3x$ again, the composite function

$$ff(x) = f(f(x)) = f(3x) = 9x$$

Note that $ff(x)$ is often referred to as $f^2(x)$, indicating that the function is to be carried out twice (*and not that the output from the function is to be squared*). Similarly, for this particular function,

$$f^3(x) \equiv fff(x) = f(f(f(x))) = 3(3(3x)) = 3(9x) = 27x$$

Example 3

The functions f, g and h are defined by

$$f(x) = 2 - x, \qquad g(x) = \frac{3}{x+1} \quad (x \neq -1), \qquad \text{and} \qquad h(x) = 2x - 1$$

a Show that $f^2(x) = x$.
b Find an expression for $g^2(x)$, and state for which two values of x it is undefined.
c Solve the equation $h^3(x) = x$.

Solution

a
$$\begin{aligned} f^2(x) &= f(f(x)) \\ &= f(2 - x) \\ &= 2 - (2 - x) = x \end{aligned}$$

b
$$\begin{aligned} g^2(x) &= g(g(x)) \\ &= g\left(\frac{3}{x+1}\right) \\ &= \frac{3}{\frac{3}{x+1} + 1} \\ &= \frac{3}{\frac{x+4}{x+1}} = \frac{3(x+1)}{x+4} \end{aligned}$$

Making $x + 1$ the common denominator of the fraction in the denominator.

Since $g(x)$ is undefined for $x = -1$, it is not possible to evaluate $g^2(x)$ when $x = -1$. You can see that $g^2(x)$ is also undefined for $x = -4$.

c $h^2(x) = h(h(x))$
$= h(2x - 1)$
$= 2(2x - 1) - 1$
$= 4x - 3$

Now $h^3(x) = h(h^2(x))$
$= h(4x - 3)$
$= 2(4x - 3) - 1$
$= 8x - 7$

So when $h^3(x) = x$,

$$8x - 7 = x$$
$$\Rightarrow \quad 7x = 7$$
$$\Rightarrow \quad x = 1$$

Domain of a composite function

The relationships between the domains and ranges of functions f and g, and the range of composite function gf are illustrated here.

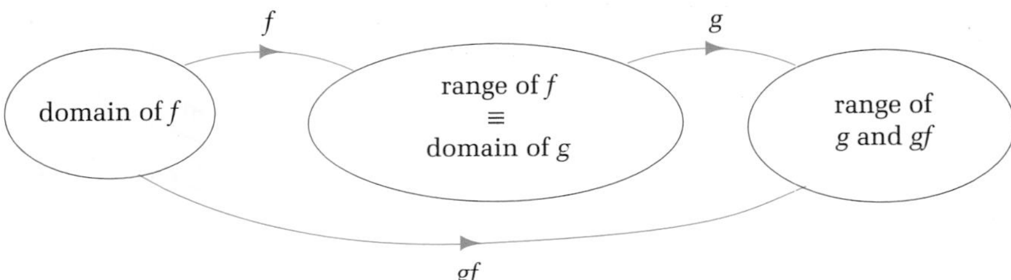

How is the domain of a composite function found? First, establish which values of x in the domain of function f produce values of $f(x)$ that lie in the domain of function g. These can then be fed into $g(x)$. However, depending upon the nature of functions f and g, and the values of x in the domains for which they are defined, the composite function gf may have a restricted domain.

Example 4

The functions f and g are defined by

$$f(x) = 1 + 2x \text{ for } \{x \in \mathbb{R}: x \geq 0\}$$

$$g(x) = \frac{1}{x - 1} \text{ for } \{x \in \mathbb{R}: x > 1\}$$

a State the range of f and g for the given domains.
b Find an expression for $gf(x)$, and determine its domain.
c Find an expression for $fg(x)$, and determine its domain.

Solution

a For the given domain, the least value of $f(x)$ is 1. This is when $x = 0$. Therefore the range of $f(x)$ is $\{y \in \mathbb{R}: y \geq 1\}$.

What about $g(x)$? As x increases, $x - 1$ also increases. This means that as x increases $\frac{1}{x-1}$ decreases. As x becomes very large, $g(x)$ will tend towards zero. Conversely, for values of x close to 1, the denominator is very small and $g(x)$ becomes very large. This means that the range of $g(x)$ is $\{y \in \mathbb{R}: y > 0\}$.

b $gf(x) = g(1 + 2x)$

$$= \frac{1}{(1 + 2x) - 1} = \frac{1}{2x}$$

The domain of the composite function gf is the set of values of x in the domain of function f that give values of $f(x)$ that are in the domain of function g.

What about the domain of g? The domain of function g is $\{x \in \mathbb{R}: x > 1\}$, so we require the values of x in the domain of f for which $f(x) > 1$. Are there values in the domain of f that do not satisfy this? The only value of x in the domain of f that does not satisfy this condition is $x = 0$. This means that the domain of the composite function $gf(x)$ is $\{x \in \mathbb{R}: x > 0\}$.

c $fg(x) = f\left(\frac{1}{x - 1}\right)$

$$= 1 + 2\left(\frac{1}{x - 1}\right)$$

$$= \frac{x - 1 + 2}{x - 1} = \frac{x + 1}{x - 1}$$

The domain of the composite function fg is the set of values of x in the domain of function g which give values of $g(x)$ that are in the domain of function f.

What about the domain of f? The domain of function f is $\{x \in \mathbb{R}: x > 0\}$. This means that we require $g(x) \geq 0$. Are there any values in the domain of g that do not satisfy this? All values of x in the domain of g satisfy the condition $g(x) \geq 0$. So the domain of the composite function $fg(x)$ is $\{x \in \mathbb{R}: x > 1\}$; that is, the entire domain of g.

The inverse of a composite function

The flow diagram shows how the composite function fg is obtained by putting values of x into g, and then putting values of $g(x)$ into f.

$$x \xrightarrow{g} g(x) \xrightarrow{f} fg(x)$$

The inverse of this composite function is $(fg)^{-1}$. This is obtained by reversing each of the individual component functions and the order in which they are applied.

$$g^{-1}f^{-1} \xleftarrow{g^{-1}} f^{-1}(x) \xleftarrow{f^{-1}} x$$

Read from right to left.

So values of x are put into f^{-1}, and then values of $f^{-1}(x)$ are put into g^{-1}. This gives:

$$(fg)^{-1}(x) \equiv g^{-1}f^{-1}(x)$$

Example 5

The functions f and g defined for $x \in \mathbb{R}$ by $f: x \to x^3$ and $g: x \to 2x + 1$. Find:

a f^{-1} and g^{-1} **b** fg and $(fg)^{-1}$ **c** gf and $(gf)^{-1}$

Solution

a $f^{-1}: x \to \sqrt[3]{x}$

$g^{-1}: x \to \dfrac{x-1}{2}$

Check these by substituting values from the function into the inverse function.

b
$$fg(x) = f(2x+1) = (2x+1)^3$$
$$(fg)^{-1}(x) = g^{-1}f^{-1}(x)$$
$$= g^{-1}(\sqrt[3]{x})$$
$$= \frac{\sqrt[3]{x}-1}{2}$$

Check this result by substituting values for x.

c
$$gf(x) = g(x^3) = 2x^3 + 1$$
$$(gf)^{-1}(x) = f^{-1}g^{-1}(x)$$
$$= f^{-1}\left(\frac{x-1}{2}\right)$$
$$= \sqrt[3]{\frac{x-1}{2}}$$

Check this result by substituting values for x.

Note that having found the composite function, the inverse can also be found by writing it in the form $y = fg(x)$ (or $y = gf(x)$), interchanging the x and y, and then making y the subject of the equation.

Applying this technique to Example 5**b**, writing fg as $y = (2x+1)^3$ and then interchanging x and y gives $x = (2y+1)^3$. Making y the subject of this equation, $y = \frac{1}{2}(\sqrt[3]{x} - 1)$. So $(fg)^{-1}(x) = \frac{1}{2}(\sqrt[3]{x} - 1)$.

Applying this technique to Example 5**c**, writing gf as $y = 2x^3 + 1$ and then interchanging x and y gives $x = 2y^3 + 1$. Making y the subject of this equation, $y = \sqrt[3]{\frac{1}{2}(x-1)}$. So $(gf)^{-1}(x) = \sqrt[3]{\frac{1}{2}(x-1)}$, as before.

4.3 Composite Functions

Exercise

Technique

1

1 The functions f, g and h are defined by $f(x) = x^2$, $g(x) = \frac{3}{x}$ and $h(x) = 2 - x$. Find an expression for each of the following composite functions in terms of x.

a	fg	**b**	gf	**c**	fh	**d**	hf	**e**	gh
f	hg	**g**	g^2	**h**	h^2	**i**	ghf	**j**	hgf

2 For each of the following, express function p as a composite of the functions $f: x \to 5x$, $g: x \to x + 3$ and $h: x \to \sin x$:

a $p: x \to 5x + 3$

b $p: x \to \sin(x + 3)$

c $p: x \to \sin x + 3$

d $p: x \to 5 \sin x + 15$

e $p: x \to x + 6$

f $p: x \to \sin(5x + 15)$.

3 Given that $f(x) = x - 3$, $g(x) = 10x$ and $h(x) = \frac{1}{x}$ $(x \neq 0)$:

a find an expression for $fgh(x)$

b solve the equation $fgh(x) = x$

4 Functions f and g are defined by $f(x) = 3x + 5$ and $g(x) = \dfrac{x - 5}{3}$.

a Find expressions for $f^2(x)$ and $g^2(x)$.

b Show that $fg(x) = x$ and $gf(x) = x$.

c Comment on the significance of your results in **b**.

5 The functions f and g are defined by $f: x \to 4 - x^2$ for $\{x \in \mathbb{R}\}$ and $g: x \to \sqrt{x}$ for $\{x \in \mathbb{R}, x \geq 0\}$.

a State the ranges of f and g for the given domains.

b Find an expression for fg, and determine its domain.

c Find an expression for gf, and determine its domain.

6 The functions f and g are defined by $f: x \to \frac{1}{4}x^2$ for $\{x \in \mathbb{R}\}$ and $g: x \to \dfrac{2}{x - 1}$ for $\{x \in \mathbb{R}, x \neq 1\}$. Find expressions for the following, in each case stating any values of x for which the composite functions are undefined:

a $fg(x)$ **b** $gf(x)$ **c** $f^2(x)$ **d** $g^2(x)$

7 Given that $f(x) = x^3$, $g(x) = 1 - 3x$ and $h(x) = \frac{2}{x}$ $(x \neq 0)$, find expressions for:

a f^{-1}, g^{-1} and h^{-1}

b fg, $(fg)^{-1}$ and $g^{-1}f^{-1}$

c hg, $(hg)^{-1}$ and $g^{-1}h^{-1}$

d fh, $(fh)^{-1}$ and $h^{-1}f^{-1}$

4.4 Transformations of Graphs and Functions

Translations

Graphs of the form y = f(x) + a

Graphical calculator support pack

Using a graphical calculator draw the graphs of $y = x^2$, $y = x^2 + 5$ and $y = x^2 - 3$ on the same axes. How are the graphs of $y = x^2 + 5$ and $y = x^2 - 3$ related to the graph of $y = x^2$? Notice that the shape of the curve is the same. The curve has been **translated**, or moved.

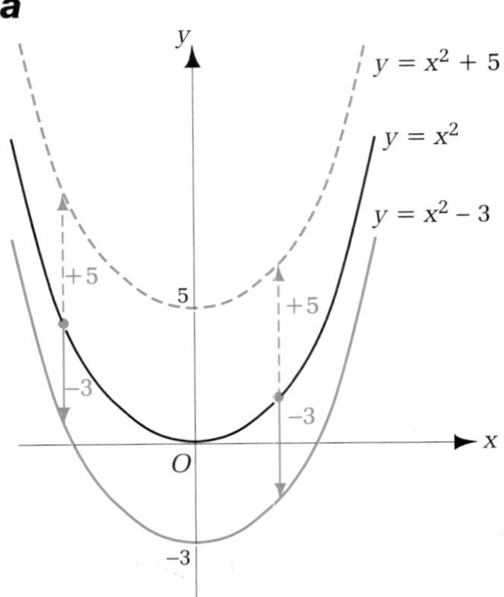

The three curves all have the same shape. Although they appear to be getting closer together, their vertical separation at every value of x is constant; the graph of $y = x^2 + 5$ is 5 units above the graph $y = x^2$, while the graph of $y = x^2 - 3$ is 3 units below $y = x^2$. In fact the curve $y = x^2 + 5$ is obtained by simply **translating** the curve $y = x^2$ by $+5$ units parallel to the y-axis and the curve $y = x^2 - 3$ is obtained by translating the curve $y = x^2$ by -3 units parallel to the y-axis. This can be generalised as follows.

The graph of $y = f(x) + a$ is obtained by translating the graph of $y = f(x)$ through a units parallel to the y-axis.

Graphs of the form y = f(x + a)

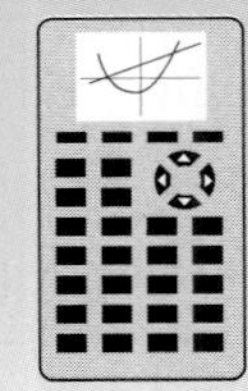

Graphical calculator support pack

Using a graphical calculator, draw the graphs of $y = x^2$, $y = (x + 3)^2$ and $y = (x - 4)^2$ on the same axes. How are the graphs of $y = (x + 3)^2$ and $y = (x - 4)^2$ related to the graph of $y = x^2$?

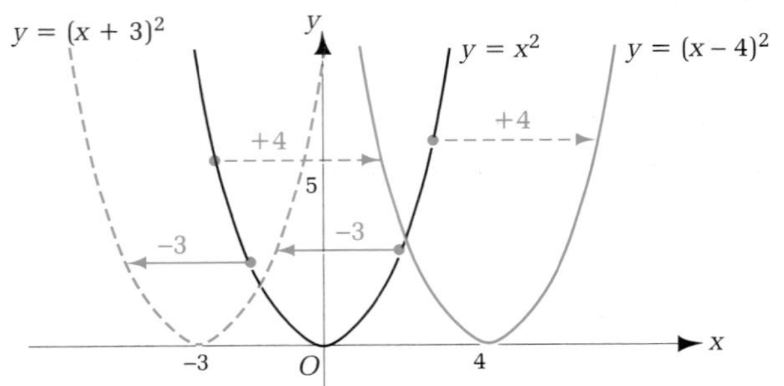

The graphs of $y = x^2$, $y = (x + 3)^2$ and $y = (x - 4)^2$ all have the same shape. The curve $y = (x + 3)^2$ is obtained by translating each point on the curve $y = x^2$ by -3 units parallel to the x-axis. The graphs of $y = x^2$ and $y = (x + 3)^2$ have the same value of y when the x-coordinate on the curve $y = (x + 3)^2$ is 3 units smaller than that on the curve $y = x^2$. The curve $y = (x - 4)^2$ is obtained by translating the curve $y = x^2$ by $+4$ units parallel to the x-axis. These results can be generalised as follows.

The graph of $y = f(x + a)$ is obtained by translating the graph of $y = f(x)$ through $-a$ units parallel to the x-axis.

Example 1

The diagram shows the graph of $y = f(x)$ for $f(x) = x^3 - 3x^2 - 9x + 11$. Functions $g(x)$ and $h(x)$ are related to $f(x)$ with $g(x) = f(x - 1)$ and $h(x) = f(x + 2) - 3$.

a Explain how the graphs of $y = g(x)$ and $y = h(x)$ can be obtained from the graph of $y = f(x)$.

b Sketch both of these graphs, indicating the coordinates of their turning points.

c Show that $g(x) = x^3 - 6x^2 + 16$ and $h(x) = x^3 + 3x^2 - 9x - 14$.

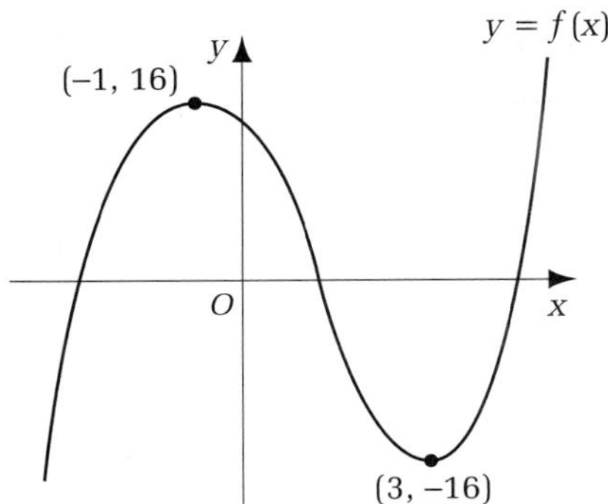

Solution

a The graph of $y = g(x) = f(x - 1)$ is obtained by translating the $y = f(x)$ graph by $+1$ unit parallel to the x-axis.

The graph of $y = h(x) = f(x + 2) - 3$ is obtained by translating the $y = f(x)$ graph by -2 units parallel to the x-axis, and -3 units parallel to the y-axis.

b

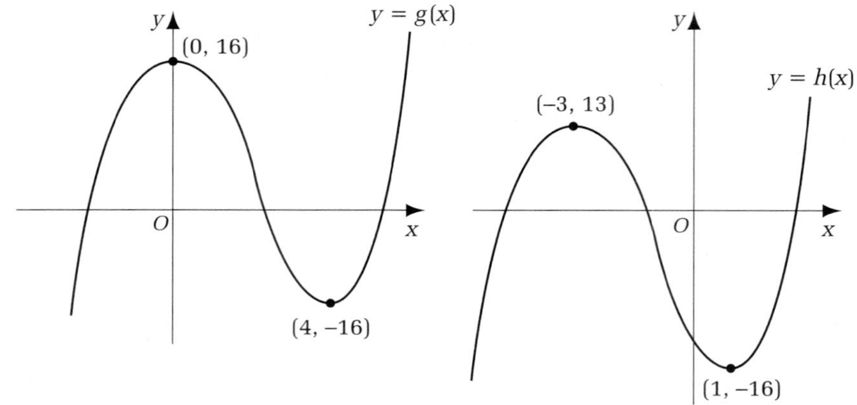

Notice how the coordinates of the turning points have been translated.

c $g(x) = f(x - 1)$

$= (x - 1)^3 - 3(x - 1)^2 - 9(x - 1) + 11$

$= (x^3 - 3x^2 + 3x - 1) - (3x^2 - 6x + 3) - (9x - 9) + 11$

$= x^3 - 6x^2 + 16$, as required

Expand the brackets, collect like terms and simplify.

$h(x) = f(x + 2) - 3$

$= (x + 2)^3 - 3(x + 2)^2 - 9(x + 2) + 11 - 3$

$= (x^3 + 6x^2 + 12x + 8) - (3x^2 + 12x + 12) - (9x + 18) + 8$

$= x^3 + 3x^2 - 9x - 14$, as required

Example 2

The diagram shows the graph of $y = x^3$. The graphs of $y = f(x)$ and $y = g(x)$ have been obtained by translating the curve $y = x^3$.

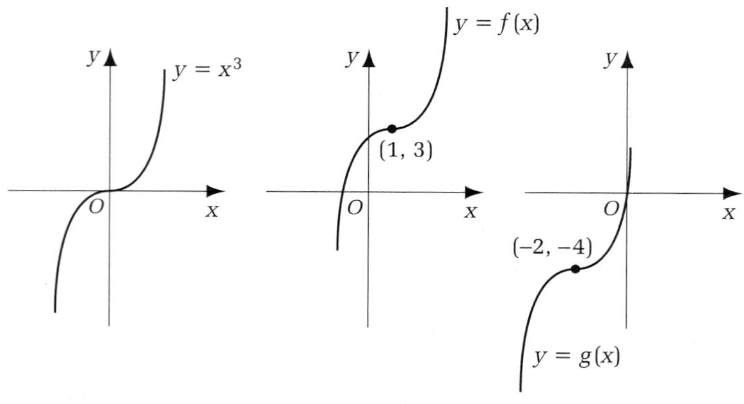

a Describe the transformation by which the graph of $y = x^3$ is mapped to the graphs of $y = f(x)$ and $y = g(x)$.

b Find expressions for $f(x)$ and $g(x)$.

Solution

a The graph of $y = f(x)$ is obtained by translating the curve $y = x^3$ by $+1$ unit parallel to the x-axis, and $+3$ units parallel to the y-axis. The graph of $y = g(x)$ is obtained by translating the curve $y = x^3$ by -2 units parallel to the x-axis, and -4 units parallel to the y-axis.

b $f(x) = (x - 1)^3 + 3$

The x-axis translation is the -1, and the y-axis translation is the $+3$.

Expanding the brackets and collecting like terms,

$f(x) = x^3 - 3x^2 + 3x + 2$

$g(x) = (x + 2)^3 - 4$

The x-axis translation is the $+2$, and the y-axis translation is the -4.

Expanding the brackets and collecting like terms,

$g(x) = x^3 + 6x^2 + 12x + 4$

Stretches

Graphs of the form $y = af(x)$

Using a graphical calculator, draw the graphs of $y = \sin x$, $y = 3\sin x$ and $y = \frac{1}{2}\sin x$ on the same axes. How are the graphs of $y = 3\sin x$ and $y = \frac{1}{2}\sin x$ related to the graph of $y = \sin x$?

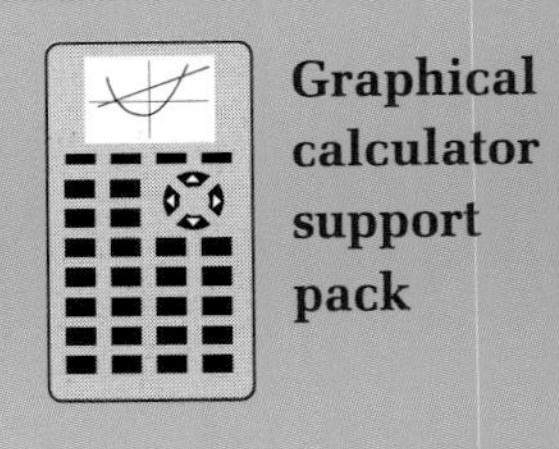

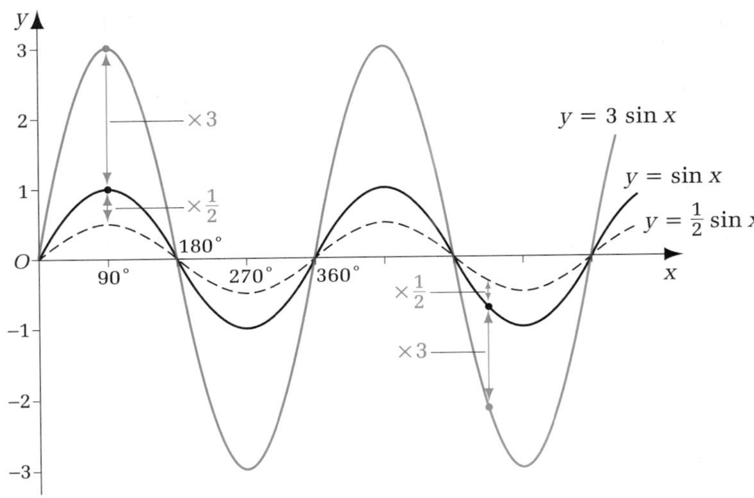

Look at the graphs of $y = \sin x$ and $y = 3\sin x$. Both curves repeat themselves with a period of 360°. This is a characteristic of the sine function. However, the curve $y = 3\sin x$ has an amplitude of 3. This is because its maximum and minimum values are $+3$ and -3 respectively. In fact, the curve $y = 3\sin x$ can be drawn by simply stretching the curve $y = \sin x$ parallel to the y-axis by a factor of 3 (**scale factor** 3).

Amplitude is the greatest height reached by the wave from the x-axis.

The graph $y = \frac{1}{2}\sin x$ also has a period of 360°. Notice that its amplitude is 0.5. It can be obtained by 'stretching' the curve $y = \sin x$ by a scale factor of $\frac{1}{2}$ parallel to the y-axis. Notice also that, a stretch factor between 0 and 1 actually has the effect of compressing the curve (that is making it closer to the x-axis).

This can be generalised as follows:

The graph of $y = af(x)$ is obtained from the graph of $y = f(x)$ by a one-way stretch, of scale factor a, parallel to the y-axis.

Graphs of the form $y = f(ax)$

Using a graphical calculator, draw the graphs of $y = \cos x$, $y = \cos 2x$ and $y = \cos(\frac{x}{2})$ on the same axes. How are the graphs of $y = \cos 2x$ and $y = \cos(\frac{x}{2})$ related to the graph of $y = \cos x$? Explain the transformation required to obtain the graph of $y = f(ax)$ from the graph of $y = f(x)$.

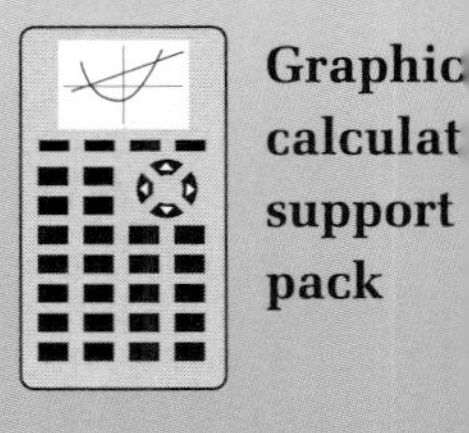

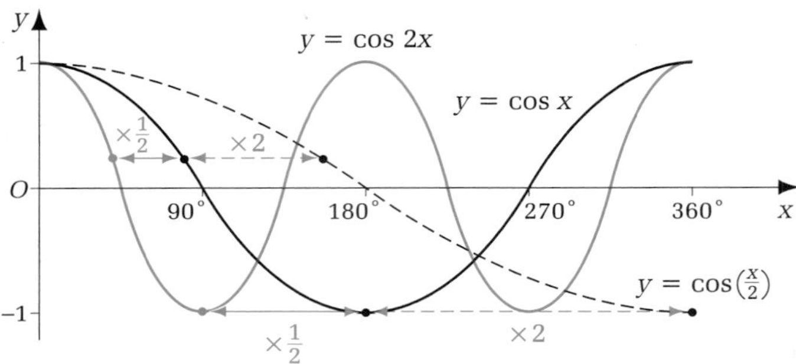

The graph of $y = \cos x$ repeats itself every 360°. The curve $y = \cos 2x$ has a period of only 180°. It completes two full cycles every 360°. In fact, the curve $y = \cos 2x$ has been obtained by 'stretching' the graph of $y = \cos x$ parallel to the x-axis by a *scale factor* of $\frac{1}{2}$. This has the effect of compressing each cycle into half the space. Notice that this is a one-way stretch and that the amplitude of the cosine curve is not altered.

The graph of $y = \cos(\frac{x}{2})$ completes half of a full cycle within 360°. It has a period of 720°. It is obtained from the graph of $y = \cos x$ by a one-way stretch of scale factor 2 parallel to the x-axis.

Stretches like this can be summarised as:

The graph of $y = f(ax)$ is obtained from the graph of $y = f(x)$ by a one-way stretch, scale factor $\frac{1}{a}$, parallel to the x-axis.

Example 3

The diagram shows the graph of $y = f(x)$, where $f(x) = 3 - 2x - x^2$. This graph is mapped to $y = g(x)$ by a stretch of factor 2 parallel to the y-axis.

The graph of $y = g(x)$ is then itself mapped to $y = h(x)$ by a stretch of factor 3 parallel to the x-axis.

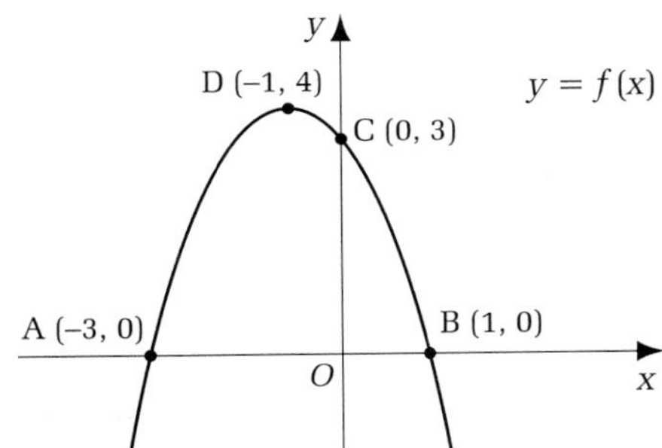

a Sketch the graphs of $y = g(x)$ and $y = h(x)$. Indicate clearly the coordinates of the images of points A, B, C and D.

b Find expressions for $g(x)$ and $h(x)$ in terms of x.

Solution

a

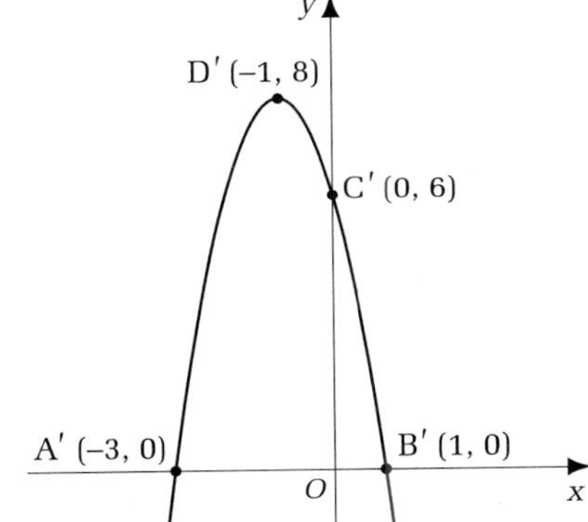

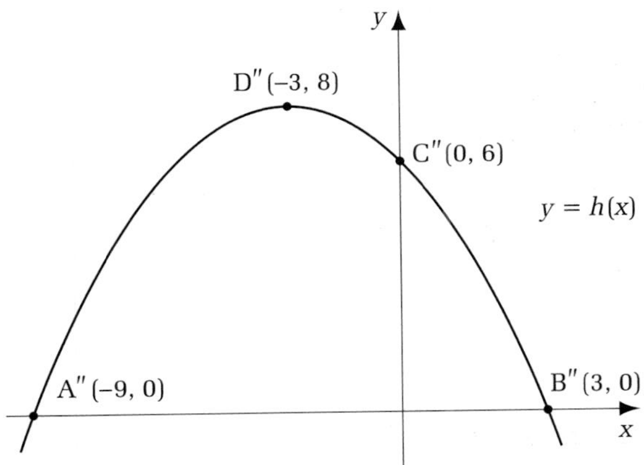

b The graph of $y = g(x)$ is obtained by stretching the graph of $y = f(x)$ by a factor of 2 parallel to the y-axis. So

$$\begin{aligned} g(x) &= 2f(x) \\ &= 2(3 - 2x - x^2) \\ &= 6 - 4x - 2x^2 \end{aligned}$$

The graph of $y = h(x)$ is obtained by stretching the graph of $y = g(x)$ by a factor of 3 parallel to the x-axis. So

$$\begin{aligned} h(x) &= g(\tfrac{1}{3}x) \\ &= 6 - \frac{4x}{3} - 2\left(\frac{x}{3}\right)^2 \\ &= 6 - \frac{4x}{3} - \frac{2x^2}{9} \end{aligned}$$

Reflections

Graphs of the form $y = -f(x)$

Using a graphical calculator, draw the graphs of $y = 2x + 1$ and $y = -(2x + 1)$. How are these two graphs related to each other? Now draw the graphs of $y = x^3 + 1$ and $y = -(x^3 + 1)$. Are these two graphs related in the same way?

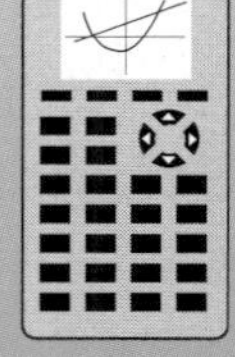

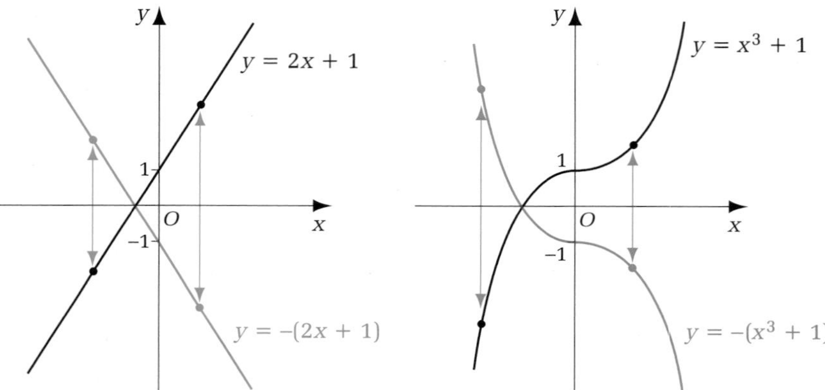

The graphs of $y = 2x + 1$ and $y = -(2x + 1)$ are shown. The latter has been obtained by reflecting the line $y = 2x + 1$ in the x-axis. Positive values of $y = 2x + 1$ become negative values of $y = -(2x + 1)$. The curve $y = -(x^3 + 1)$ is similarly a reflection of the curve $y = x^3 + 1$ in the x-axis.

This can be generalised as follows:

The graph of $y = -f(x)$ is a reflection of the graph of $y = f(x)$ in the x-axis.

Graphs of the form $y = f(-x)$

Use a graphical calculator to draw the graphs of $y = 2x + 1$ and $y = 2(-x) + 1$ on the same axes. Now draw the graphs of $y = x^3 + 1$ and $y = (-x)^3 + 1$. How are these curves related to one another?

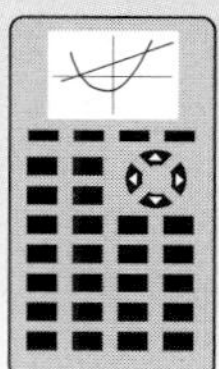

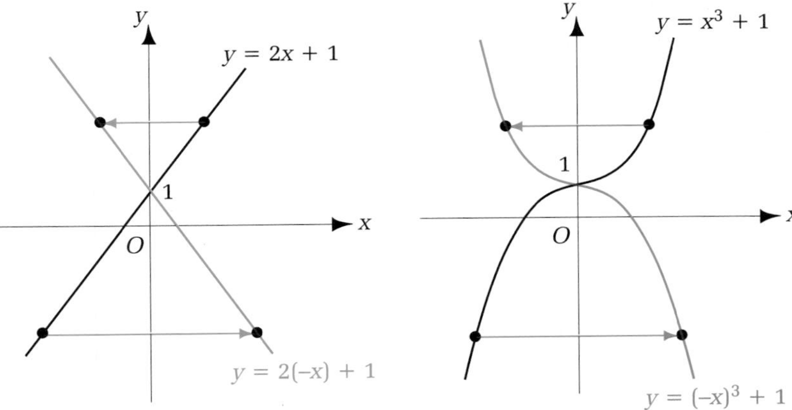

The graphs of $y = f(x)$ and $y = f(-x)$ for $f(x) = 2x + 1$ and $f(x) = x^3 + 1$ respectively are shown. In both examples, the graph of $y = f(-x)$ is obtained by reflecting the graph of $y = f(x)$ in the y-axis.

This transformation can be summarised as:

The graph of $y = f(-x)$ is obtained by reflecting the graph of $y = f(x)$ in the y-axis.

Example 4

The graph of $y = f(x)$ is mapped to the graph of $y = g(x)$ by a reflection in one axis, and a translation. Describe the transformations that have occurred. Clearly state the order in which they were carried out. Find an expression for $g(x)$.

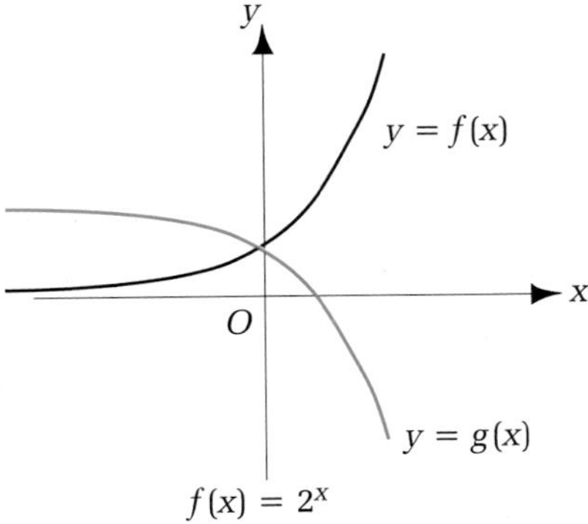

Solution

Notice that there are two ways in which the graph of $y = 2^x$ can be mapped to $y = g(x)$:

- a reflection in the x-axis, followed by a translation of $+2$ units parallel to the y-axis;
- a translation of -2 units parallel to the y-axis, followed by a reflection in the x-axis.

Using the first of these, an expression for $g(x)$ can be found. Therefore $g(x) = -2^x + 2y$

$$y = 2^x$$
$\downarrow$ reflection in x-axis
$$= -2^x$$
$\downarrow$ translation of $+2$ units parallel to y-axis
$$y = -2^x + 2$$

The second combination of transformations gives the same expression.

$$y = 2^x$$
$\downarrow$ translation of -2 units parallel to y-axis
$$y = 2^x - 2$$
$\downarrow$ reflection in x-axis
$$y = -(2^x - 2) = -2^x + 2$$

The general quadratic curve

All quadratic expressions can be written in the form $c[(x+a)^2 + b]$, where a, b and c are constants. Why is this rearrangement useful? The graphs of $y = x^2$ and $y = c[(x+a)^2 + b]$ can be compared. The values of a, b and c then give an indication of the transformations used.

See Applications and Activities, Chapter 1.

Example 5

Express the function $g(x) = 2x^2 + 8x + 6$ in the form $c[(x+a)^2 + b]$, where a, b and c are constants. Describe the transformations by which the curve $y = x^2$ is mapped to the graph of this function. Sketch the graph of $y = g(x)$.

Solution

$$\begin{aligned} g(x) &= 2x^2 + 8x + 6 \\ &= 2(x^2 + 4x + 3) \\ &= 2(x^2 + 4x + 4 - 1) \\ &= 2[(x+2)^2 - 1] \end{aligned}$$

Complete the square.

The graph of $y = x^2$ is mapped to the graph of $y = g(x)$ by translations of -2 units parallel to the x-axis and -1 unit parallel to the y-axis, followed by a stretch of factor 2 parallel to the y-axis.

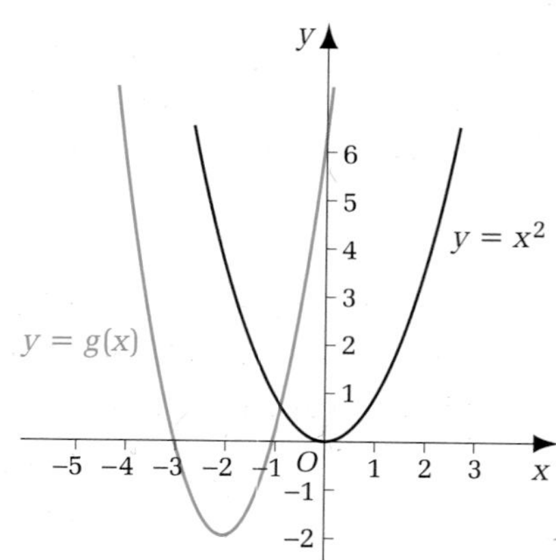

The order in which the translations are applied does not matter, although they *must* be applied before the stretch.

4.4 Transformations of Graphs and Functions

Exercise

Technique

1 The diagram shows the graph of $y = f(x)$, where $f(x) = x^2 - 2x$.

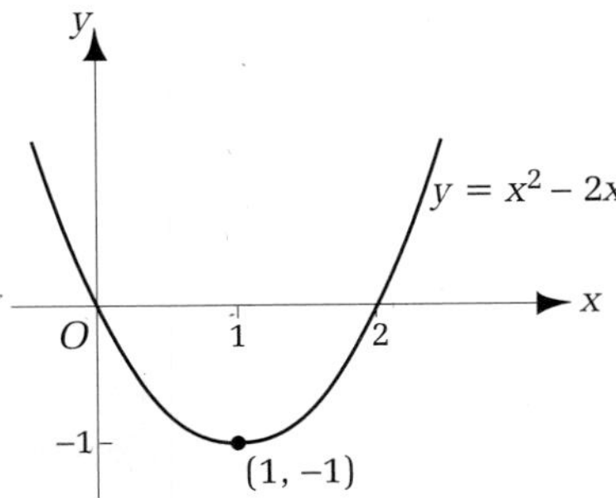

For each of the following transformations of this function:

i describe the transformation(s) geometrically;
ii write down an expression for the new function;
iii sketch the graph of the transformed function, indicating the coordinates of its intersection with the axes and the turning point:

a $y = f(x) + 2$ **b** $y = f(x - 3)$ **c** $y = f(2x)$
d $y = -3f(x)$ **e** $y = f(-\frac{1}{3}x)$ **f** $y = f(x + 1) + 4$

 2

2 The function f is defined by $f(x) = x^2 + 6x + 8$.

a Express f in the form $f(x) = (x + a)^2 + b$, where a and b are integers.
b Describe the transformation by which the graph of $y = x^2$ is mapped to the graph of $y = f(x)$.

3 The function g is defined by $g(x) = 2x^2 - 12x + 19$.

a Express g in the form $g(x) = 2(x + a)^2 + b$, where a and b are integers.
b Describe the transformations by which the graph of $y = x^2$ is mapped to the graph of $y = g(x)$. Clearly state the order in which they must be applied.

4 Each of the following quadratic curves is a transformation of the curve $y = x^2$. In each case, state the transformation(s) that have occurred. State also the order in which they must be applied.

a $y = x^2 + 3$
b $y = 4x^2$
c $y = (x - 2)^2$
d $y = x^2 + 2x + 5$
e $y = \frac{1}{2}x^2 + 1$
f $y = x^2 - 6x + 10$
g $y = x^2 + 4x$
h $y = 2x^2 - 4x + 3$

5 The diagram shows the graph of $y = x^3 - 3x^2$.

i Describe the transformations that map this graph to each of the following graphs. State the order in which they must be applied.

ii Use these transformations to write down the equation of each graph.

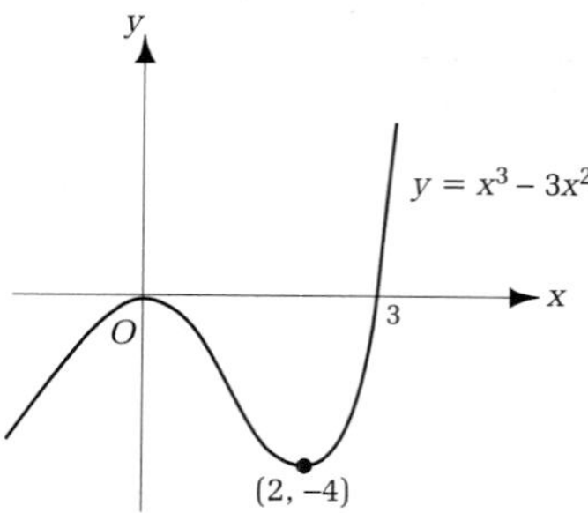

a

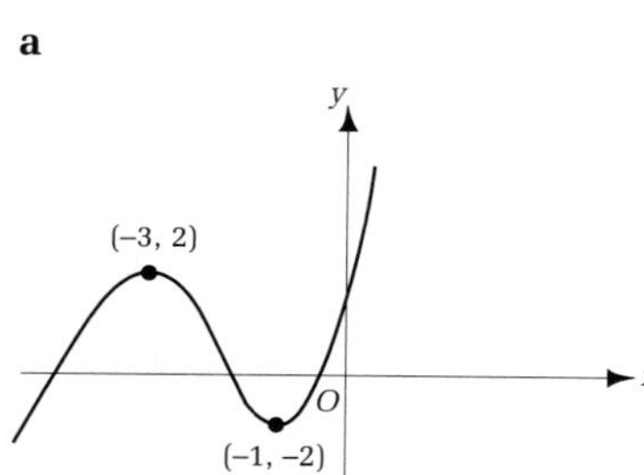

b

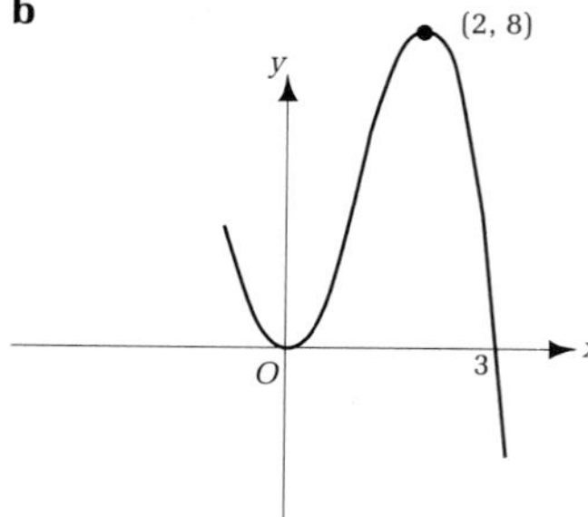

c

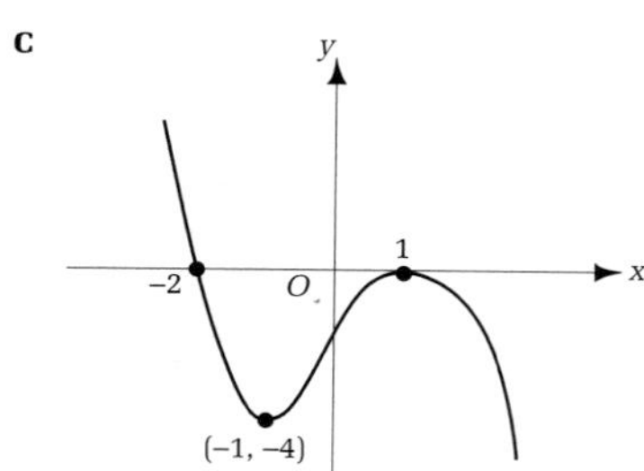

d

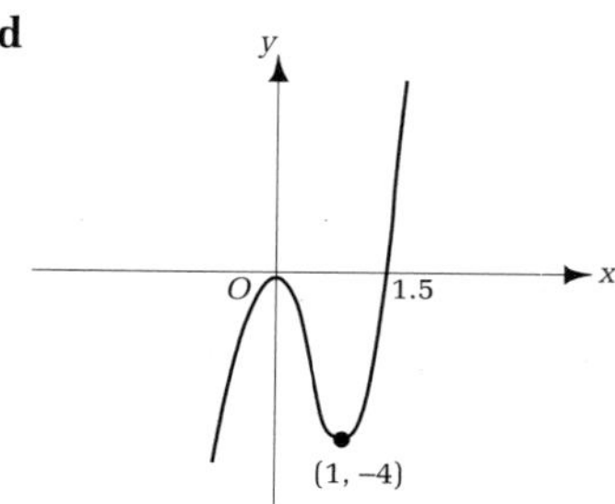

6 **i** Describe the transformations by which the graph of $y = \sin x$ is mapped to each of the curves below.

ii Make a sketch of the graph of each of the transformed functions for $-360° \leq x \leq 360°$.

a $y = \sin(x + 90°)$ **b** $y = \sin(\frac{x}{2})$

c $y = -2\sin x$ **d** $y = 3 + \sin x$

7 The function $f: x \to \frac{1}{x}, x \neq 0$ is transformed to give the function g. For each of the following transformations:

i find an expression for g;

ii state the value of x for which function g is undefined:

a a stretch of factor 3 parallel to the y-axis

b a translation of $+2$ units parallel to the x-axis

c a stretch of factor $\frac{1}{2}$ parallel to the x-axis, followed by a translation of -4 units parallel to the y-axis

d a translation of -5 units parallel to the x-axis, followed by a stretch of factor 12 parallel to the y-axis.

4.5 Even, Odd and Periodic Functions

Several of the functions considered so far have graphs that are symmetrical in some way. We can categorise these functions as even, odd or periodic.

Even functions

The graph of an even function has the y-axis as a line of symmetry. Examples of even functions include $f(x) = x^2$ and $f(x) = \cos x$.

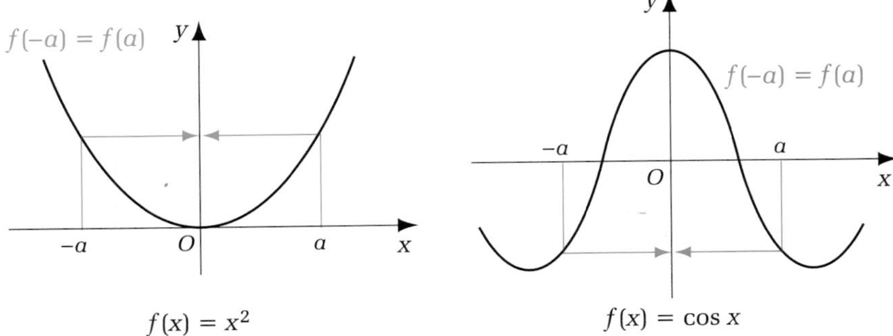

The reflection of the graph of $y = f(x)$ in the y-axis gives the graph of $y = f(-x)$. What does this suggest to you? Even functions satisfy the condition $f(-x) = f(x)$. This condition can be used to check whether or not a function is even.

Odd functions

The graphs of odd functions have rotational symmetry about the origin. Examples of odd functions include $f(x) = x^3$ and $f(x) = \sin x$.

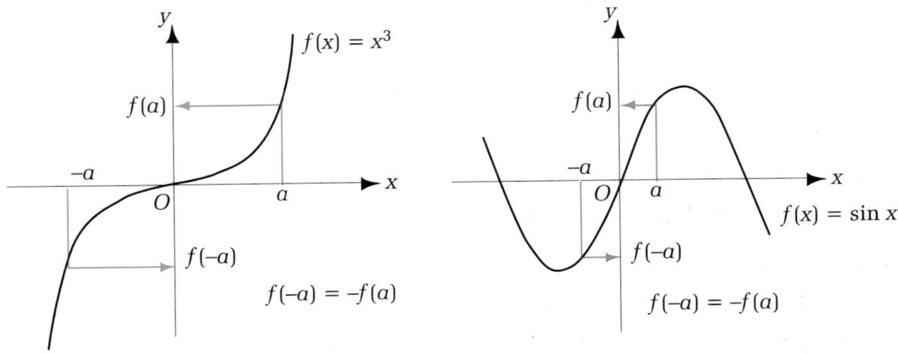

Odd functions satisfy the condition $f(-x) = -f(x)$. This condition can be used to check whether or not a function is odd.

Example 1

State whether the following are graphs of even functions, odd functions, or neither:

a

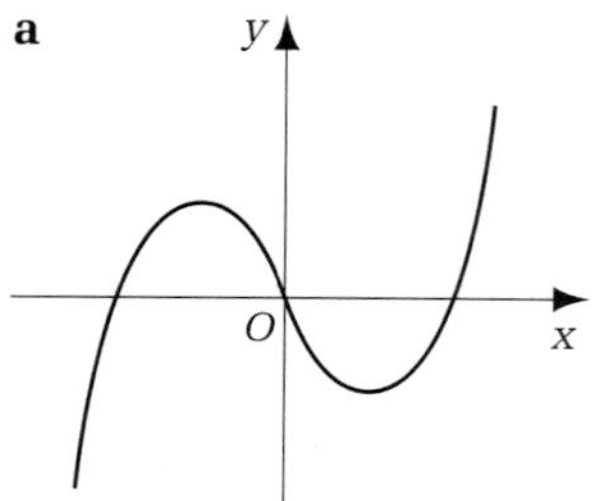

b

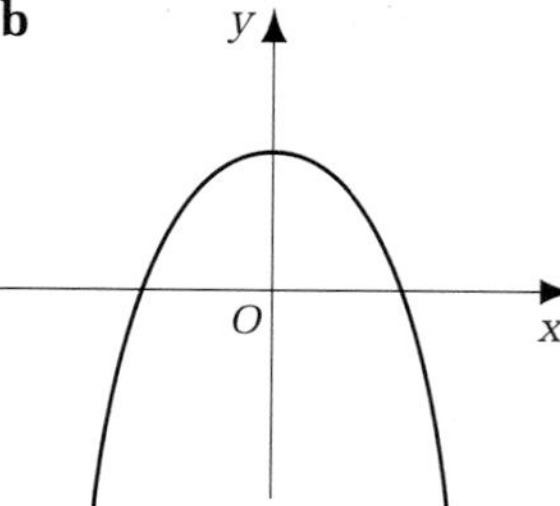

c

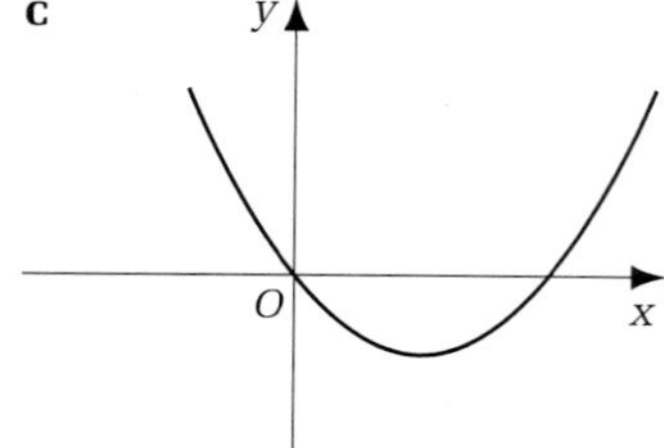

d

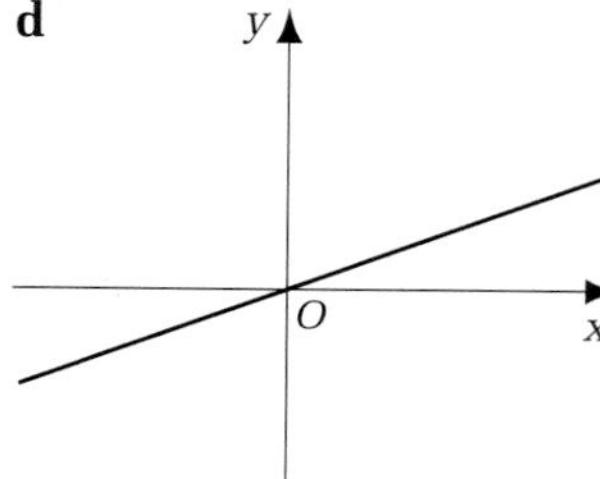

Solution

a The graph has rotational symmetry about the origin. This is the graph of an odd function.

b The graph is symmetrical about the y-axis. This is the graph of an even function.

c This graph has no rotational symmetrical about the origin and no reflective symmetry about the y-axis. The function is neither even nor odd.

d This is a graph of an odd function because it has rotational symmetry about the origin.

Example 2

The functions f, g and h are defined by $f(x) = x^3 - 2x$, $g(x) = 1 + x^2 - 5x^4$ and $h(x) = 3x^2 + 2x$. Determine which of these functions are even or odd.

Solution

Check whether or not a function is even or odd by substituting $-x$ into the function in place of x.

$$f(-x) = (-x)^3 - 2(-x)$$

$$= -x^3 + 2x$$

$$= -(x^3 - 2x)$$

Writing this in terms of the original function.

So $f(-x) = -f(x)$

Therefore $f(x) = x^3 - 2x$ is an odd function.

$$g(-x) = 1 + (-x)^2 - 5(-x)^4$$
$$= 1 + x^2 - 5x^4$$

So $g(-x) = g(x)$

Therefore $g(x) = 1 + x^2 - 5x^4$ is an even function.

$$h(-x) = 3(-x)^2 + 2(-x)$$
$$= 3x^2 - 2x$$

Since $h(-x) \neq h(x)$ and $h(-x) \neq -h(x)$, function h is neither even nor odd.

The modulus function

The modulus function $f(x) = |x|$ reflects negative values into their positive equivalents. It is defined by:

$$f(x) = x, \text{ for } x \geq 0 \qquad \text{and} \qquad f(x) = -x, \text{ for } x < 0$$

Since its graph is symmetrical about the y-axis, the modulus function $f(x) = |x|$ is even.

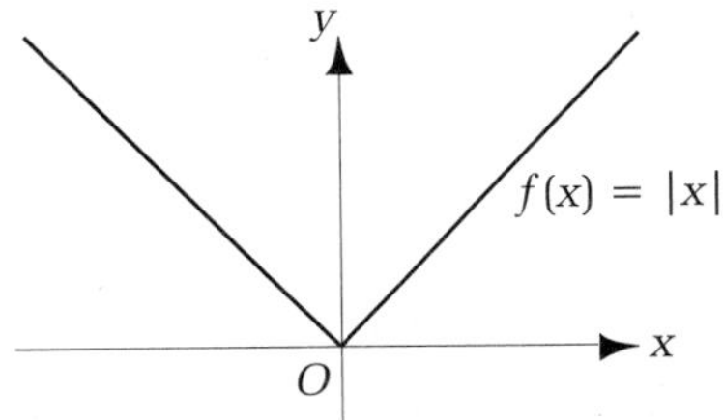

To obtain the graph of $y = |f(x)|$, first sketch the graph of $y = f(x)$. The parts of this graph for which y is positive are kept: the parts for which y is negative are reflected in the x-axis.

Example 3

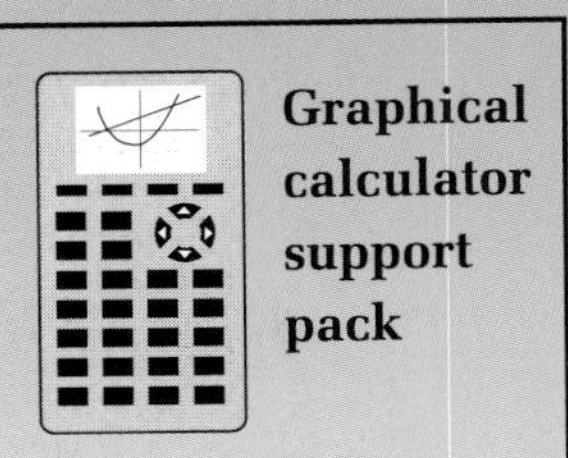

Sketch the graphs of:

a $y = |x^2 - 4|$ **b** $y = |\sin x|$

Solution

a First sketch the graph of $y = x^2 - 4$. Now reflect in the x-axis those parts of this graph that lie below the x-axis.

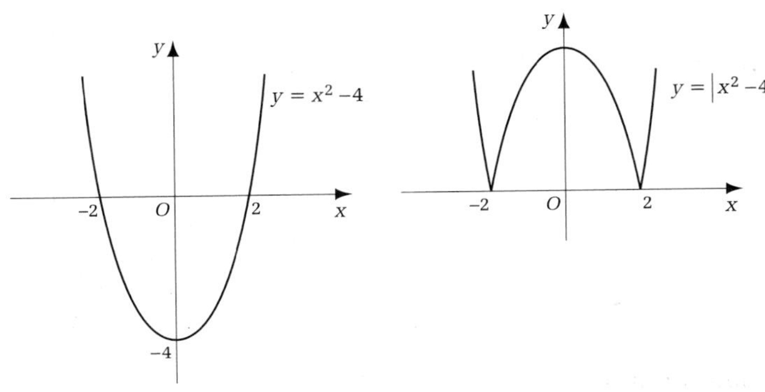

b Sketch the graph of $y = \sin x$ and then reflect in the x-axis those parts that lie below the x-axis.

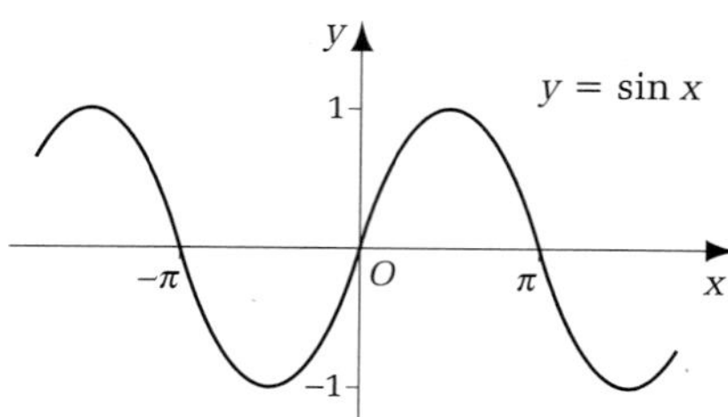

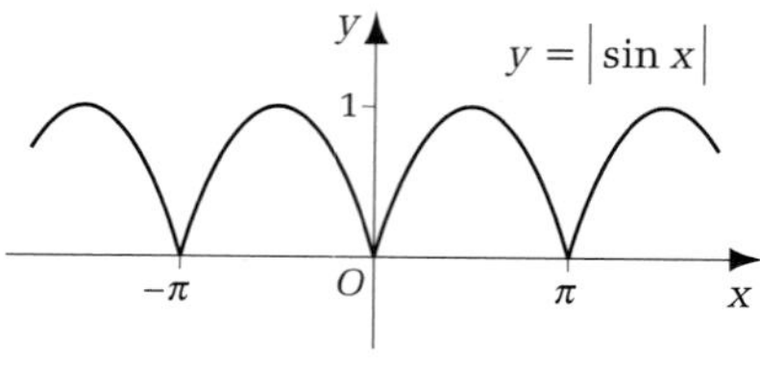

The graphs of functions related to the modulus function can be sketched by applying the appropriate transformations to the graph of $y = |x|$.

Example 4

Sketch the graphs of:

a $y = |x + 3|$ **b** $y = |2x + 1|$.

Solution

a The graph of $y = |x + 3|$ is obtained by translating the graph of $y = |x|$ by -3 units parallel to the x-axis.

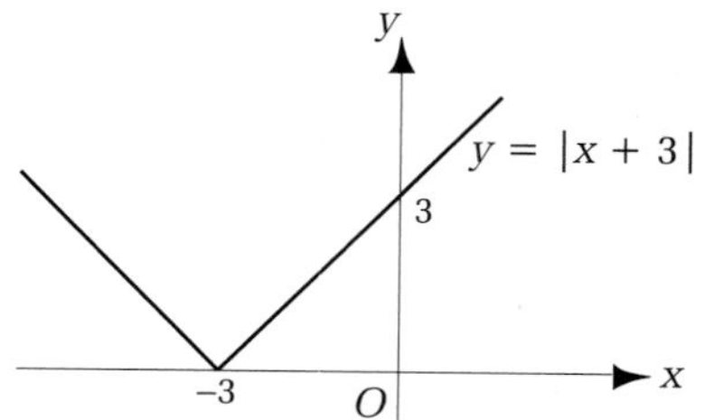

b The graph of $y = |2x + 1|$ is obtained by stretching the graph of $y = |x|$ by a factor of $\frac{1}{2}$ parallel to the x-axis, and a translation of $-\frac{1}{2}$ parallel to the x-axis.

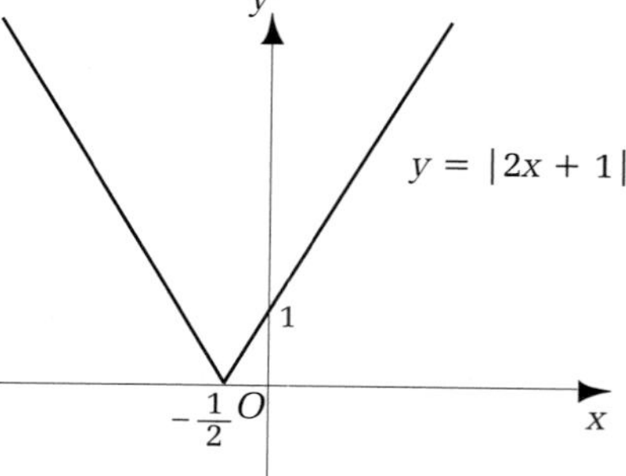

To obtain the graph of $y = f(|x|)$, first sketch the graph of $y = f(x)$ for positive values of x. For negative values of x, the value of $y = f(|x|)$ is found by substituting the equivalent positive value of x into the function. This simply reflects the graph of $y = f(x)$ for positive values of x in the y-axis.

Example 5

Sketch the graphs of:

a $y = |x| - 2$ **b** $y = \sin |x|$.

Solution

a The graph of $y = |x| - 2$ is obtained by first drawing the graph of $y = x - 2$ for positive values of x, and then reflecting this in the y-axis.

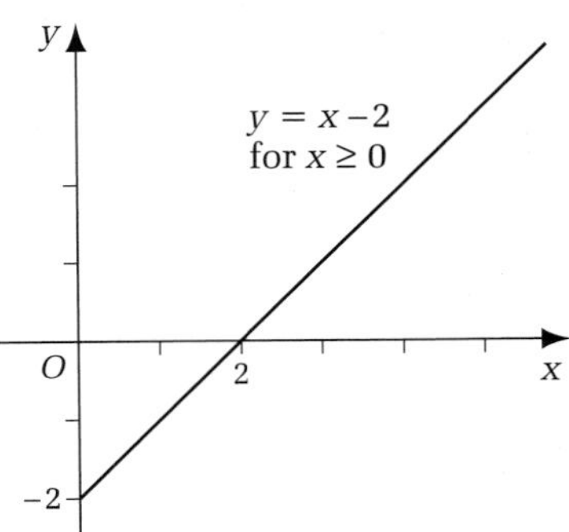

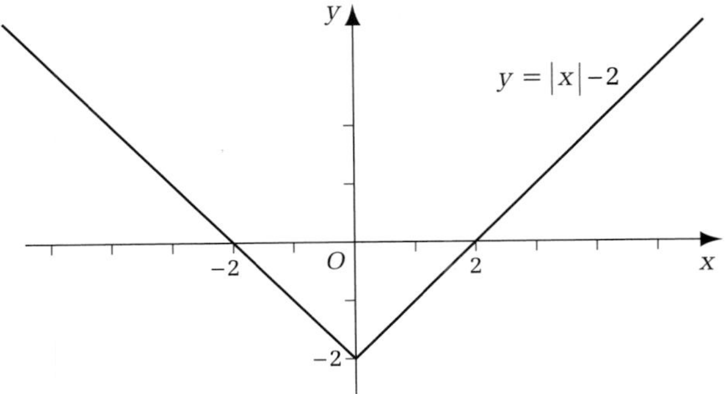

b The graph of $y = \sin|x|$ is obtained by first drawing the graph of $y = \sin x$ for positive values of x, and then reflecting this in the y-axis.

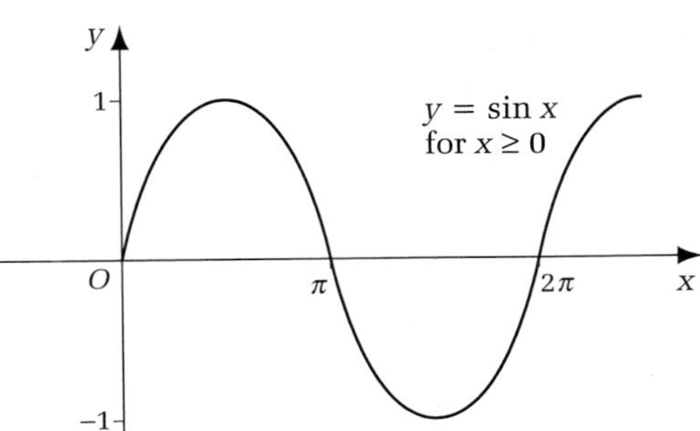

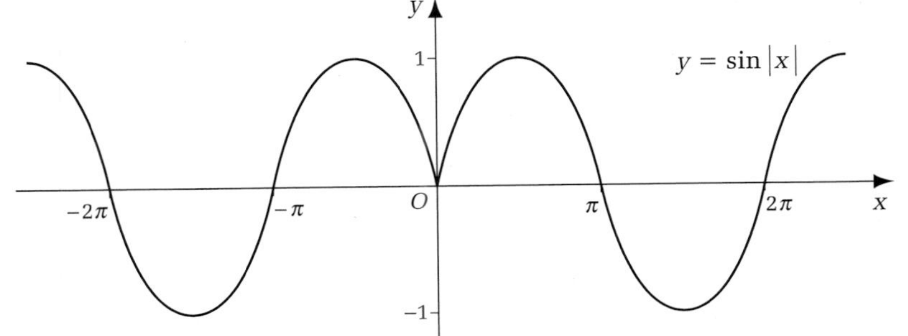

Periodic functions

Periodic functions have graphs that regularly repeat themselves. Examples of periodic functions include the sine, cosine and tangent functions. The graphs of $y = \sin x$ and $y = \cos x$ repeat themselves every 360° or 2π radians. This value is referred to as the **period** of the function. The graph of $y = \tan x$ has a period of only 180° or π radians.

In general, periodic functions $f(x)$ are such that for some constant k, $f(x \pm k) \equiv f(x)$, for all values of x, where k is the period of the function.

k is the smallest distance over which t function repeats itsel

Writing the trigonometric functions in this form

$$\sin(x \pm 360°) \equiv \sin x \qquad \cos(x \pm 360°) \equiv \cos x \qquad \tan(x \pm 180°) \equiv \tan x$$

Once the behaviour over one period is known, the graph of a periodic function can be drawn.

Example 6

The function $f(x)$ is periodic with a period of 4 units. It is defined by

$$f(x) = \tfrac{1}{2}x^3, \qquad 0 \le x \le 2$$

$$f(x) = 8 - 2x, \qquad 2 \le x \le 4$$

a Sketch the graph of $y = f(x)$ for $0 \le x \le 4$. Use its periodic behaviour to extend the graph to $-6 \le x \le 10$.

b Determine the values of $f(5)$ and $f(-1.5)$.

Solution

a Between 0 and 2, the graph is cubic in nature. Between 2 and 4 it is linear with a gradient of -2.

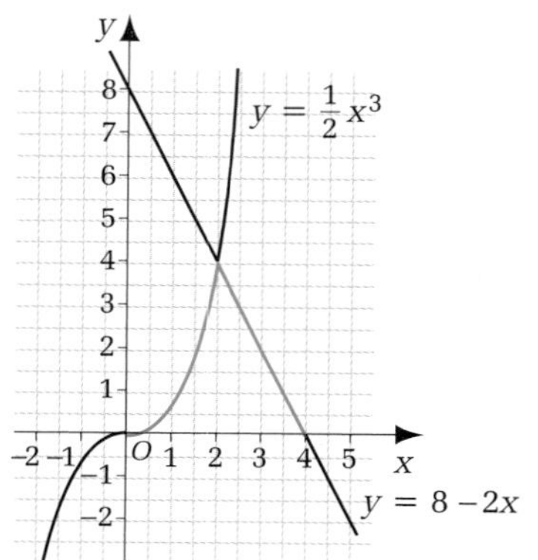

The coloured line sho the shape of the periodic function $f(x)$ for $0 \le x \le 4$.

The function $f(x)$ repeats itself with a period of 4. Now sketch its graph for $-6 \le x \le 10$.

The function repeats itself every 4 units.

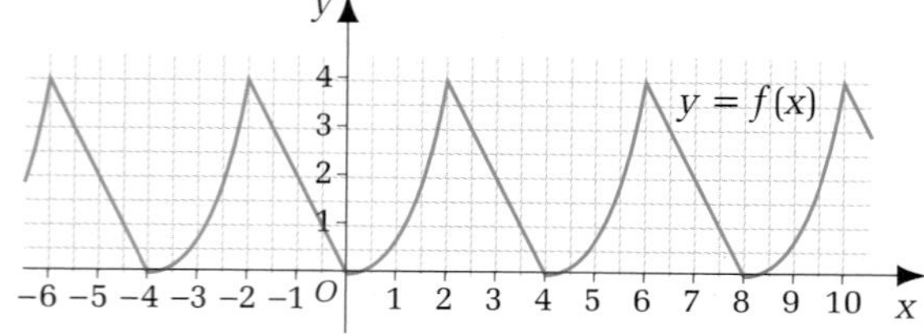

The function is cubic when $x = 1$.

The function is linear when $x = 2.5$.

b

$$f(5) \equiv f(1) \qquad\qquad f(-1.5) \equiv f(2.5)$$

$$= \tfrac{1}{2}(1)^3 \qquad\qquad = 8 - 2(2.5)$$

$$= \tfrac{1}{2} \qquad\qquad = 3$$

4.5 Even, Odd and Periodic Functions

Exercise

Technique

1 Which of the following graphs represents the graph of an even or an odd function?

a

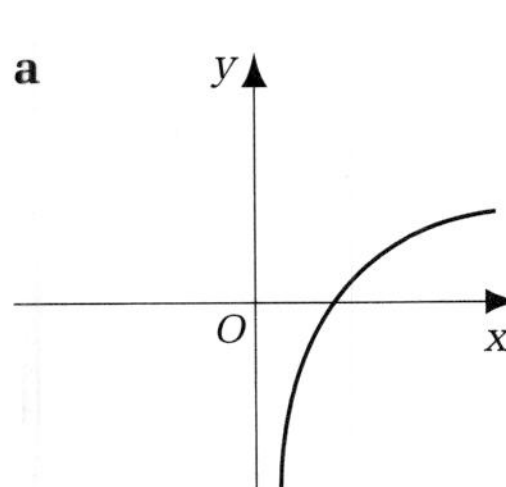

b

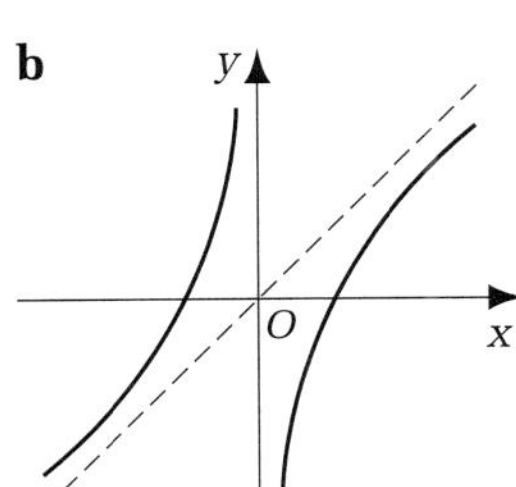

c

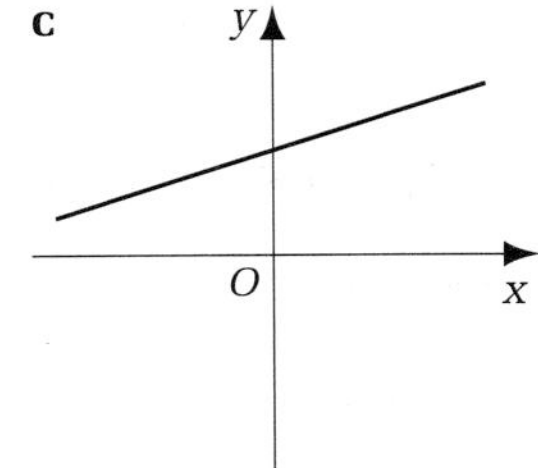

d

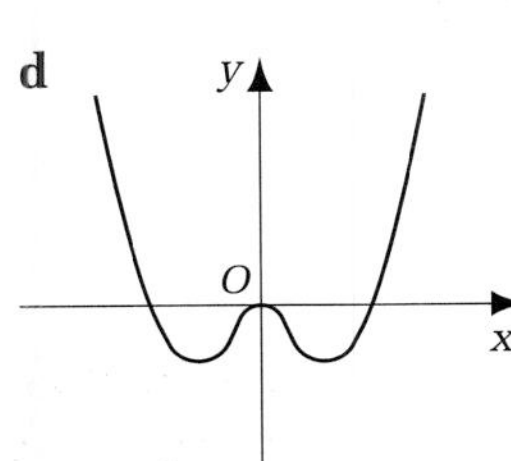

e

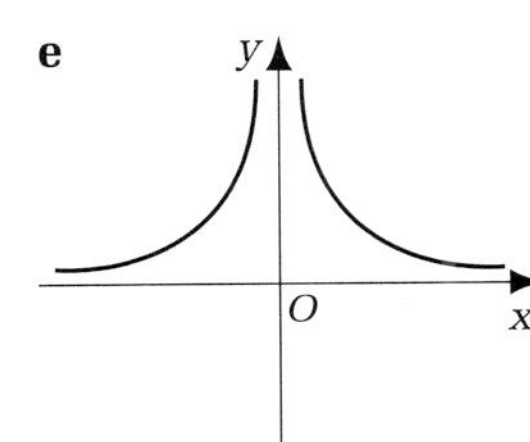

f

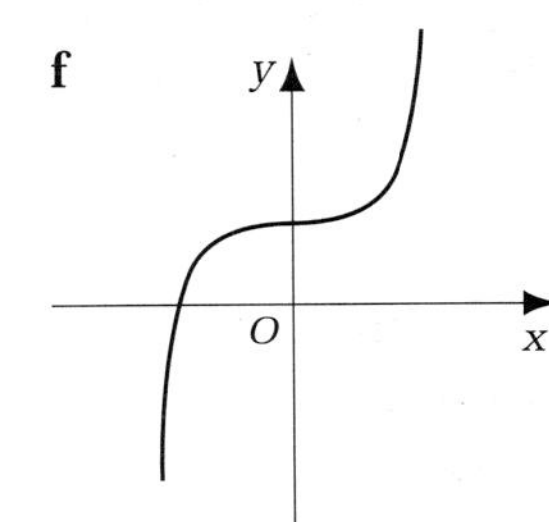

2 Which of the following functions are even, odd or neither even nor odd?

a $f(x) = x - \frac{1}{x}$

b $f(x) = 2x + |x|$

c $f(x) = \sin^2 x$

d $f(x) = (x+1)^2$

e $f(x) = (x+1)^3$

f $f(x) = \dfrac{1}{2x+1}$

g $f(x) = \dfrac{x}{2x+1}$

h $f(x) = (x^2+4)^3$

3 The diagram shows the graph of $y = |f(x)|$ for some cubic function $f(x)$.

a On separate diagrams sketch the two possible graphs of $y = f(x)$.

b Briefly explain how to distinguish between these two possibilities.

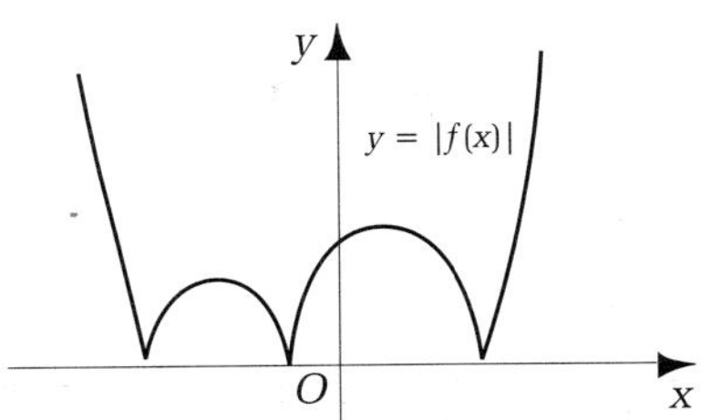

4 The function $f(x)$ is periodic with a period of 4, and is defined by

$$f(x) = x^2 + 1 \text{ for } -1 \leq x \leq 1 \qquad \text{and} \qquad f(x) = 2 \text{ for } 1 \leq x \leq 3$$

a Sketch the graph of $y = f(x)$ for $-5 \leq x \leq 5$.

b Determine the values of $f(4.5)$ and $f(10)$.

Consolidation

Exercise A

a State whether or not each of graphs **i**, **ii** and **iii** represents a function.

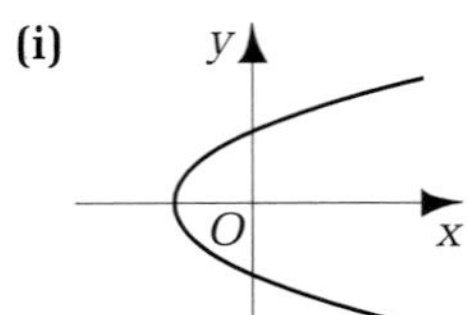

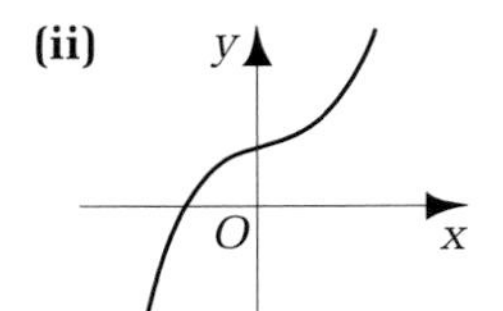

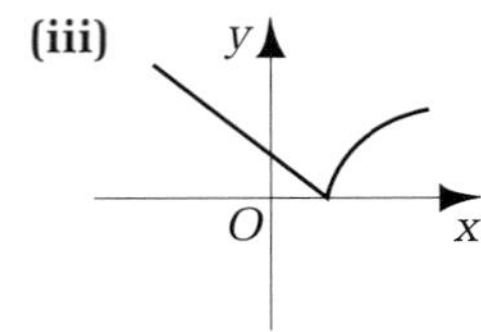

b One of the graphs is such that the function f represented by the graph has an inverse f^{-1}. Assuming equal scales on the axes of the graphs drawn, sketch the graph of f^{-1}.

(AEB)

2 Functions f and g are defined for all real values of x by $f\colon x \to x^2$ and $g\colon x \to 4 - 9x$.

a Express the composite function gf in terms of x.
b Sketch the curve with equation $y = gf(x)$ and label the coordinates of the points at which your curve intersects the x-axis.
c Determine the range of the function gf.
d Find the value of x for which $g(x) = g^{-1}(x)$, where g^{-1} is the inverse function of g.

(ULEAC)

3 The functions f and g are defined by $f\colon x \to 9x^2 - 4$ for $\{x \in \mathbb{R}: x \geq 0\}$ and $g\colon x \to \sqrt{x+1}$, for $\{x \in \mathbb{R}: x \geq 0\}$.

a State the range of f.
b Sketch the graph of f and hence explain why the inverse function f^{-1} exists. Find f^{-1}, stating its domain.
c The composite function $f \circ g$ is defined for $x \geq 0$.
  i Find $f \circ g(x)$.
  ii Determine the exact surd solution to the equation $f(x) = f \circ g(x)$.

(AEB)

$f \circ g$ is alternative notation for the composite function $fg(x)$.

4 The function f has as its domain the set of all non-zero real numbers, and is given by $f(x) = \frac{1}{x}$ for all x in this set. On a single diagram, sketch the following graphs, and indicate the geometrical relationships between them:

a $y = f(x)$ **b** $y = f(x+1)$ **c** $y = f(x+1) + 2$

Deduce, explaining your reasoning, the coordinates of the point about which the graph of $y = \dfrac{2x+3}{x+1}$ is symmetrical.

(UCLES)

5 Function f is defined on the domain $0 \leq x \leq \frac{\pi}{8}$ by $f(x) = \tan 2x$. Find an expression for $f^{-1}(x)$ and state, or obtain, the domain of f^{-1}.

(NEAB)

6 Functions f and g are defined by $f: x \to 4 - x$ for $\{x \in \mathbb{R}\}$ and $g: x \to 3x^2$ for $\{x \in \mathbb{R}\}$.

a Find the range of g.
b Solve $gf(x) = 48$.
c Sketch the graph of $y = |f(x)|$ and hence find the values of x for which $|f(x)| = 2$.

(ULEAC)

7 Functions f and g are defined by $f: x \to 3x - 1$ for $\{x \in \mathbb{R}\}$ and $g: x \to x^2 + 1$ for $\{x \in \mathbb{R}\}$.

a Find the range of g.
b Determine the values of x for which $gf(x) = fg(x)$.
c Determine the values of x for which $|f(x)| = 8$.
d Function $h: x \to x^2 + 3x$ for $\{x \in \mathbb{R}, x \geq q\}$ is one-to-one. Find the least value of q and sketch the graph of this function.

(ULEAC)

8 The diagram shows the curve $y = f(x + a)$, where a is a positive constant. The maximum and minimum points on the curve are $(-a, 3a)$ and $(a, 0)$ respectively.

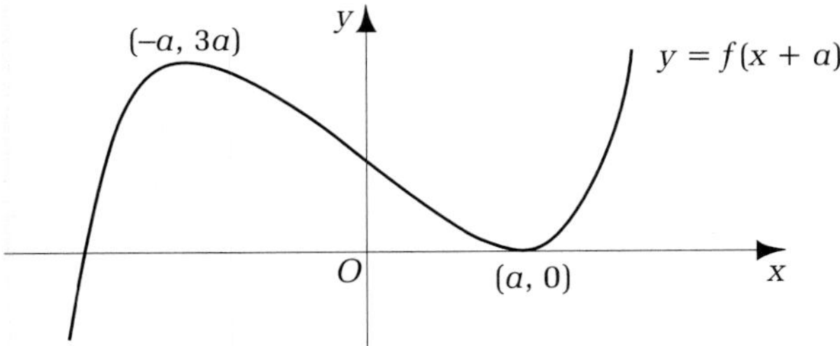

Sketch the following curves, on separate diagrams, in each case stating the coordinates of the maximum and minimum points:

a $y = f(x)$ **b** $y = -2f(x + a)$.

(UCLES)

9 The function f is defined on the domain $x > 0$ by $f(x) = 1 + \frac{2}{x}$.

a **i** Find an expression for $f^{-1}(x)$.
ii State the domain of f^{-1}.

The composite function g is defined by $g = ff$.

b **i** Find an expression for $g(x)$.
ii State the range of g.

(WJEC)

10 Function f is defined on the domain $-1 \leq x \leq 2$ by $f(x) = 4 - 2x - x^2$.

a Determine the values of a and b such that $f(x) = a - (b + x)^2$.

The diagram shows a sketch of the graph of $y = f(x)$.

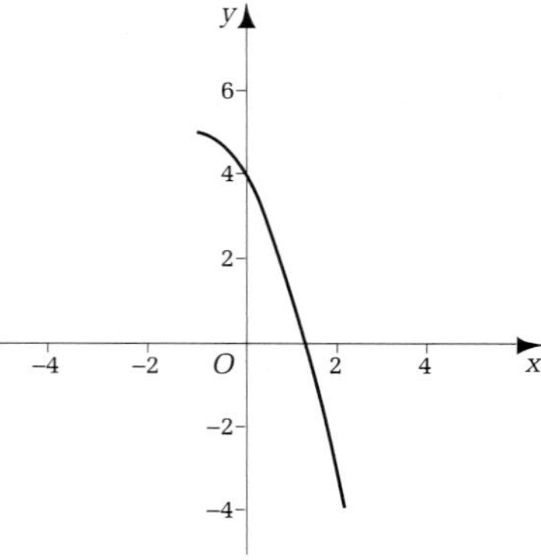

b Describe, as either a single transformation or as two separate transformations, how the graph of $y = f(x)$ may be obtained from part of the graph of $y = -x^2$, $\{x \in \mathbb{R}\}$.

c State the coordinates of the points of $y = -x^2$ which correspond to the end points of $y = f(x)$.

d Sketch the graph of $y = f^{-1}(x)$.

e Calculate the value of x for which $f(x) = f^{-1}(x)$.

(NEAB)

Exercise B

1 The figure shows part of the graph of $y = \sqrt{x}$ (the scales on the two axes being the same). Describe the transformations that map this graph on to the graphs of:

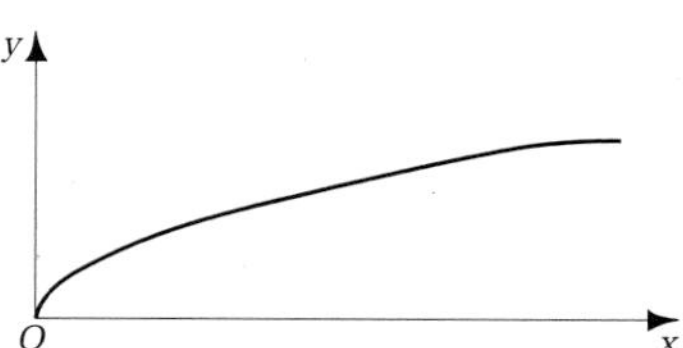

a $y = 50 + \sqrt{x}$ **b** $y = \sqrt{x + 50}$ **c** $y = -\sqrt{x}$

d $x = \sqrt{y}$ **e** $y = 30\sqrt{x}$

(OCSEB)

2 Functions f and g are defined by $f(x) = 1 + x^2$ for $\{x \in \mathbb{R}\}$ and $g(x) = \tan x$ for $\{x \in \mathbb{R}\colon -\frac{\pi}{2} < x < \frac{\pi}{2}\}$.

a Write down $fg(x)$ and state the domain of fg.

b Find $g^{-1}(\sqrt{3})$ in terms of π.

c Explain briefly why f does not have an inverse.

(NEAB)

3 Functions f, g and h are defined for $\{x \in \mathbb{R}\colon x > 0\}$ by $f\colon x \to x^2$, $g\colon x \to \frac{2}{x}$ and $h\colon x \to \sqrt{x}$. Express in terms of x:

a $gh(x)$ **b** $fgh(x)$

State which two of the three functions f, g and h are inverses of each other.

(UCLES)

4 Functions f and g are defined with their respective domains by $f: x \to \frac{3}{(2x-1)}$ for $\{x \in \mathbb{R}, x \neq \frac{1}{2}\}$ and $g: x \to x^2 + 1$ for $\{x \in \mathbb{R}\}$.

a Find the values of x for which $f(x) = x$.
b Find the range of g.
c The domain of the composite function $f \circ g$ is $\mathbb{R}$. Find $f \circ g(x)$ and state the range of $f \circ g$.

(AEB)

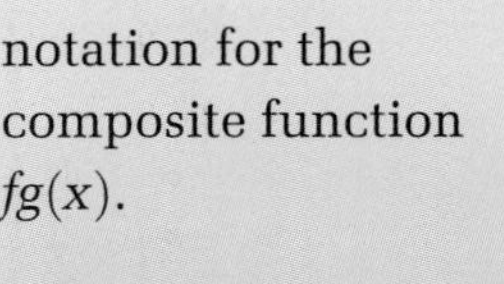

Recall the alternative notation for the composite function $fg(x)$.

5 Function f is defined on the domain $0 \leq x \leq 2$ by $f(x) = x^2$. Function g is defined by translating the graph of $y = f(x)$, with this domain, 3 units in the positive x direction and 5 units in the positive y direction to give the graph of $y = g(x)$.

a Sketch the graphs of $y = f(x)$ and $y = g(x)$.
b State the domain and range of function g.
c Find an expression for $g(x)$.
d Find an expression for $g^{-1}(x)$.
e State the domain and range of the function g^{-1}.

(NEAB)

6 Express $x^2 + 4x$ in the form $(x + a)^2 + b$, stating the numerical values of a and b. Functions f and g are defined as $f: x \to x^2 + 4x$ for $\{x \in \mathbb{R}: x > -2\}$ and $g: x \to x + 6$ for $\{x \in \mathbb{R}\}$.

a Show that the equation $gf(x) = 0$ has no real roots.
b State the domain of f^{-1}.
c Find an expression in terms of x for $f^{-1}(x)$.
d Sketch, on a single diagram, the graphs of $y = f(x)$ and $y = f^{-1}(x)$.

(UCLES)

7 The diagram shows the graph of the function f defined for $x \geq 0$ by $f: x \to 1 + \sqrt{x}$.

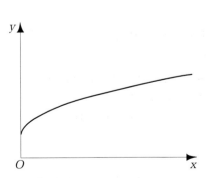

a Copy the sketch, and show on the same diagram the graph of f^{-1}, making clear the relationship between the two graphs.
b Give an expression in terms of x for $f^{-1}(x)$, and state the domain of f^{-1}.
c There is one value of x for which $f(x) = f^{-1}(x)$. By considering your diagram, explain why this value of x satisfies the equation $1 + \sqrt{x} = x$.
d By treating the equation $1 + \sqrt{x} = x$ as a quadratic equation for $\sqrt{x}$, or otherwise, show that the value of x satisfying $f(x) = f^{-1}(x)$ is $x = \frac{1}{2}(3 + \sqrt{5})$.

(UCLES)

Applications and Activities

1 There are four possible functions that map elements in the set $\{a, b\}$ across to elements in the set $\{p, q\}$, as illustrated by the mapping diagrams below.

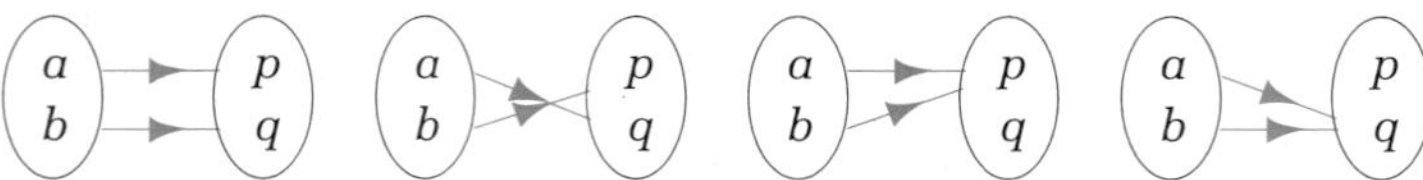

In the first two mappings, $\{a, b\}$ is the domain and $\{p, q\}$ is the range, containing all the output values. However, in the second two mappings, $\{p, q\}$ is the co-domain of the functions, containing the possible output values.

Now consider the functions that could possibly map elements in $\{a, b, c\}$ to elements in $\{p, q\}$.

a How many have $\{p, q\}$ as their range, and how many have $\{p, q\}$ as their co-domain?

b What is the total number of possible functions?

c How many different functions exist in the more general case of m elements in the domain and n elements in the co-domain?

Summary

- A **function** is a many-to-one or one-to-one mapping for which each input value in the **domain** gives only one output value.
- The **range** of a function is the set of output values to which values in its domain map; the range is a subset of the co-domain.
- Only functions which, for a given domain, are one-to-one mappings, have inverse functions.
- The graph of the inverse function $y = f^{-1}(x)$ is obtained by reflecting the graph of $y = f(x)$ in the line $y = x$ for values of x where f is one-to-one.
- An algebraic expression for $f^{-1}(x)$ can be found by interchanging x and y in the equation $y = f(x)$ and then rearranging it to make y the subject of the equation again.
- Functions for which $f^{-1}(x) \equiv f(x)$ are **self-inverses**.
- The inverse trigonometric functions $y = \sin^{-1} x$, $y = \cos^{-1} x$ and $y = \tan^{-1} x$ only exist for the restricted domains in which the sine, cosine and tangent functions are one-to-one.

- The composite function $fg(x)$ (alternative notation $f \circ g(x)$) is obtained by putting values of $g(x)$ into function f.
- The composite function $ff(x)$, or $f^2(x)$, is obtained by putting values of $f(x)$ back into the function f again.
- The graph of $y = f(x)$ can, by a combination of translations, stretches, and reflections, be transformed into the graph of a related function, as shown in this table.

Function	Transformation
$f(x) + a$	translation of $+a$ units parallel to the y-axis
$f(x + a)$	translation of $-a$ units parallel to the x-axis
$af(x)$	one-way stretch, of factor a, parallel to the y-axis
$f(ax)$	one-way stretch, of factor $\frac{1}{a}$, parallel to the x-axis
$-f(x)$	reflection in the x-axis
$f(-x)$	reflection in the y-axis

- **Even** functions are those that satisfy the condition $f(-x) = f(x)$, and are therefore symmetrical about the y-axis.
- **Odd** functions are those that satisfy the condition $f(-x) = -f(x)$, and therefore have rotational symmetry about the origin.
- **Periodic** functions are those for which $f(x \pm k) \equiv f(x)$ for some constant k; such functions repeat themselves every k units along the x-axis, and k is the period of the function.

5 Differentiation I

What you need to know

- How to find the gradient of the straight line joining two points.
- How to find the value of a function.
- How to find the equation of the straight line that passes through a given point, when its gradient is known.
- How to solve simple trigonometric equations.
- How to use negative and fractional indices.

Review

1 Find the gradient of the straight line joining the following pairs of points:

a $(2, 1)$ and $(6, 9)$ **b** $(0, 7)$ and $(3, 1)$
c $(-2, 11)$ and $(1, -7)$ **d** $(-1, -2)$ and $(-4, -11)$

2 Find the value of the following functions at the given value of x:

a $f(x) = x^2 + 5x + 6$, when $x = -4$
b $f(x) = 3x + \frac{1}{x^2}$, when $x = \frac{1}{2}$
c $f(x) = \sin 2x - 2\cos^2 x$, when $x = \frac{\pi}{4}$

3 Find the equation of the straight line that passes through the given point with the gradient indicated, giving your answer in the form $y = mx + c$:

a $(1, 4)$, gradient 6 **b** $(3, -11)$, gradient -3
c $(-5, 2)$, gradient $-\frac{1}{4}$ **d** $(2, 3)$, gradient $\frac{2}{3}$

4 Solve the following trigonometric equations for $0 \leq \theta \leq 2\pi$:

a $\tan 2\theta = \sqrt{3}$ **b** $\sin\theta + \cos\theta = 0$
c $\sin 2\theta = \cos\theta$ **d** $\cos 2\theta + \cos\theta = 0$

5 Write each of the following in index notation:

a $\dfrac{2}{x^3}$ **d** $\dfrac{10}{\sqrt{x}}$
b $\sqrt{x^3}$ **e** $(\sqrt[3]{x})^4$
c $\dfrac{1}{x+5}$

5.1 Finding the Gradient of a Curve

The gradient at each point on the graph of a linear function, such as $y = 2x + 1$, is constant. However, many mathematical functions are not linear, and have curved graphs whose gradients are continuously changing.

Look at the graph of $y = x^2$. Notice that the gradient changes from being negative to positive as the graph crosses the y-axis. It also becomes steeper for larger positive and negative values of x.

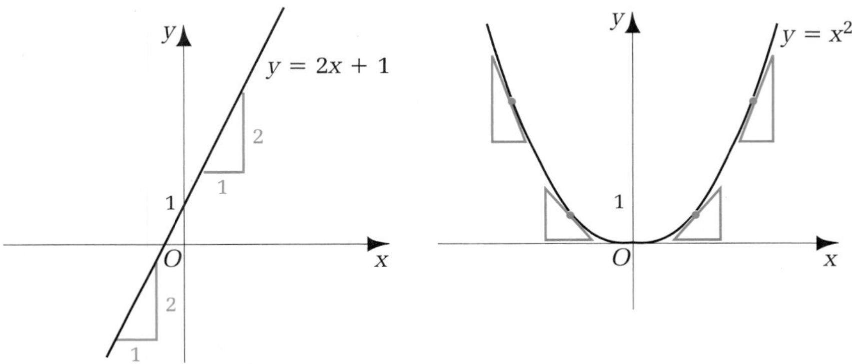

Finding the gradient of the curve is not as straightforward as it is for the linear function. The gradient of the curved graph at any particular point can be found by calculating the gradient of the tangent to the curve at this point. Look at the graph of $y = x^2$ again in more detail.

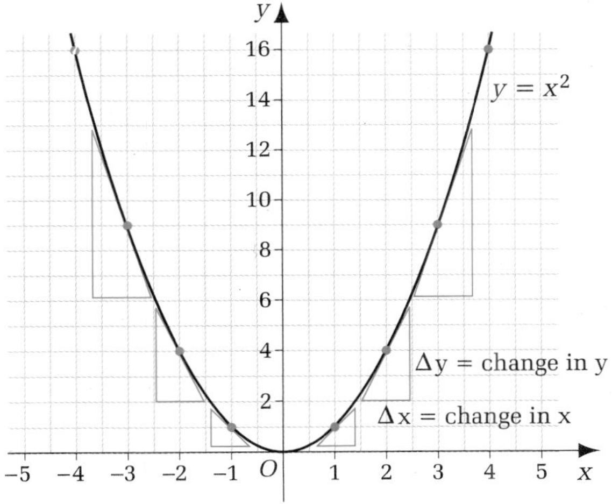

Draw tangents to this graph at the points $x = -3, -2, -1, 0, 1, 2, 3$. Notice that for $x > 0$, the gradient is positive and increases as the tangents become steeper. When $x < 0$, the gradient is negative, and becomes more negative as x decreases. By constructing right-angled triangles and using

$$\text{gradient} = \frac{\text{change in } y}{\text{change in } x} = \frac{\Delta y}{\Delta x}$$

we can estimate the gradient of the curve at these different points.

The Greek letter Δ is used to mean 'a change in'.

x	−3	−2	−1	0	1	2	3
Gradient of the curve $y = x^2$	−6	−4	−2	0	2	4	6

These results suggest that the **gradient function** of the curve $y = x^2$ is $2x$. This means that the gradient at any point on this curve can be calculated by multiplying the x-coordinate by 2. The gradient function describes algebraically how the gradient is changing.

However this method of finding the gradient function, by drawing tangents to the curve at a number of different points and then calculating their gradients, has a number of drawbacks.

- Its accuracy depends on the accuracy with which the graph and the tangents to it are drawn, and on the accuracy of the measurements of Δx and Δy.
- It cannot easily be translated into an algebraic procedure.

How else could the gradient function be found? An alternative method would be to draw a chord from a particular point on a curve to some nearby point. For example, the gradient of the curve $y = x^2$ at $x = 2$ can be estimated by finding the gradient of the chord drawn from $x = 2$ to $x = 3$ on the curve. The gradient of this chord can be calculated using,

$$\begin{aligned}\text{gradient of chord} &= \frac{\text{change in } y}{\text{change in } x} = \frac{\Delta y}{\Delta x}\\ &= \frac{3^2 - 2^2}{3 - 2}\\ &= \frac{9 - 4}{1}\\ &= 5\end{aligned}$$

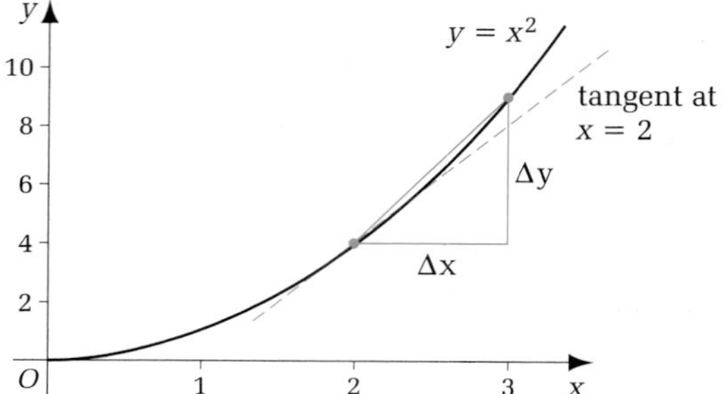

The gradient of this chord is only a rough approximation to the gradient of the tangent, and to the gradient of the curve itself at $x = 2$. A more accurate value can be found using the chord between the points on the graph corresponding to $x = 2$ and $x = 2.5$.

$$\begin{aligned}\text{gradient of chord} &= \frac{\Delta y}{\Delta x}\\ &= \frac{2.5^2 - 2^2}{2.5 - 2}\\ &= \frac{6.25 - 4}{0.5}\\ &= 4.5\end{aligned}$$

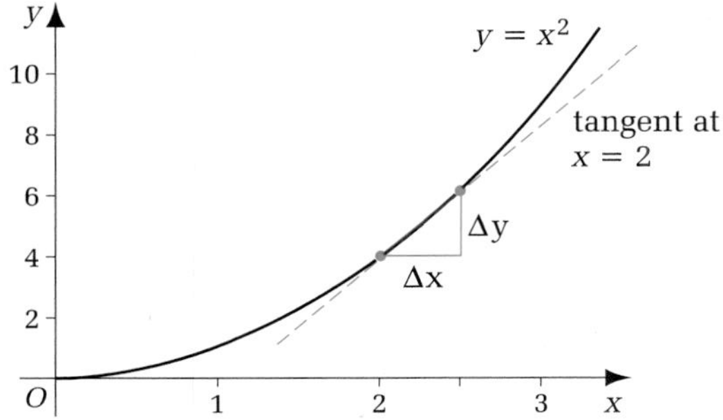

Notice that the smaller the change in x (denoted Δx) over which this chord is drawn, the closer its gradient will approximate that of the tangent to the curve at $x = 2$.

Try using $\Delta x = 0.1$.

$$\begin{aligned}\text{gradient of chord} &= \frac{\Delta y}{\Delta x}\\ &= \frac{2.1^2 - 2^2}{2.1 - 2}\\ &= \frac{4.41 - 4}{0.1}\\ &= 4.1\end{aligned}$$

Repeat this procedure with $\Delta x = 0.01$, and tabulate all your results. What do you notice?

Δx	1	0.5	0.1	0.01
Gradient of chord drawn from $x = 2$	5	4.5	4.1	4.01

From these results, notice that as Δx **tends towards** zero (written '$\Delta x \to 0$'), the gradient of the chord tends towards a value of 4. Try $\Delta x = 0.001$ at $x = 2$. Does your result get closer to the value of 4?

Find the gradient of the curve $y = x^2$ at the points $x = -3, -2, -1, 0, 1,$ and 3 by calculating the gradient of the chords drawn from these points, using $\Delta x = 1, 0.1,$ and 0.01. Notice that as $\Delta x \to 0$, the gradients of these chords converge towards a **limiting value**. These results also suggest that the gradient function of the curve $y = x^2$ is $2x$.

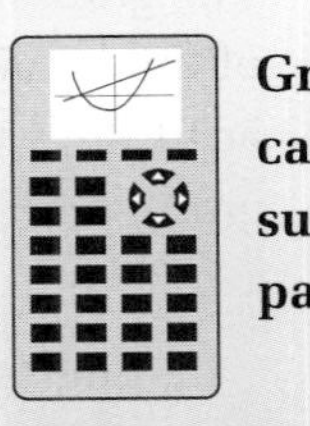

This method of finding the gradient of a curve by drawing chords between two nearby points on it has two major advantages.

- It does not rely on the accurate drawing of a tangent to the curve, and measurement of Δy and Δx because Δy can be calculated for any given value of Δx.
- It can be translated into an algebraic procedure, known as **differentiation from first principles**.

Check to see if your graphical calculator has a derivative function key. This will give the numerical value of the gradient of a curve at a chosen point.

Differentiation from first principles

Consider the point P with coordinates (x, y) on the curve $y = f(x)$. Let the nearby point Q on the curve have coordinates $(x + \delta x, y + \delta y)$, where δx is the *small* change in the value of the x-coordinate between P and Q, and δy is the corresponding *small* change in the value of the y-coordinate.

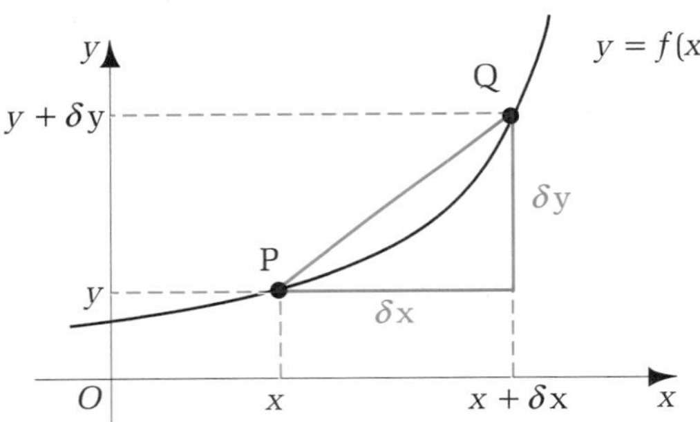

The gradient of the chord PQ is given by

$$\frac{\text{change in } y\text{-coordinate}}{\text{change in } x\text{-coordinate}} = \frac{\delta y}{\delta x} = \frac{(y + \delta y) - y}{(x + \delta x) - x}$$
$$= \frac{f(x + \delta x) - f(x)}{\delta x}$$

If $y = f(x)$ then $y + \delta y = f(x + \delta x)$

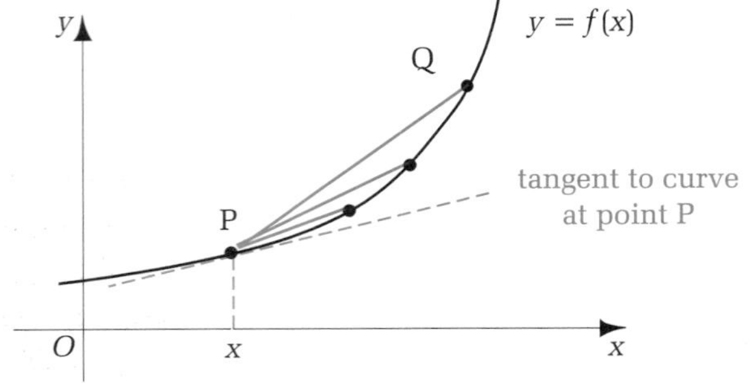

For smaller values of δx, point Q approaches point P. The gradient of the chord PQ becomes closer to the gradient of the tangent to the curve at point P. So, in the limiting case, as $\delta x \to 0$,

$$\text{gradient of the curve at point P} = \underset{\delta x \to 0}{\text{limit}} \left(\frac{\delta y}{\delta x} \right)$$
$$= \underset{\delta x \to 0}{\text{limit}} \left[\frac{f(x + \delta x) - f(x)}{\delta x} \right]$$

This process of finding the gradient of a curve at some point P (x, y) by calculating the gradient of the chord to the point Q $(x + \delta x, y + \delta y)$, as δx tends towards zero, is called differentiation from first principles.

The resulting **gradient function** of the curve is denoted $\frac{dy}{dx}$ or $f'(x)$, and is a function of x.

$$\frac{\mathbf{dy}}{\mathbf{dx}} = \boldsymbol{f'(x)} = \underset{\delta x \to 0}{\textbf{limit}} \left[\frac{\boldsymbol{f(x + \delta x) - f(x)}}{\boldsymbol{\delta x}} \right]$$

Note that $\frac{dy}{dx}$ is *not* a fraction. It refers to the gradient of the graph of $y = f(x)$.

Example 1

Using differentiation from first principles, show that the gradient function of the curve $y = x^2$ is $\frac{dy}{dx} = 2x$.

Solution

Let $y = f(x)$, where $f(x) = x^2$. A small change δx in the x-coordinate of some point on the curve $y = x^2$ will result in a corresponding small change δy in its y-coordinate, such that

$$\delta y = f(x + \delta x) - f(x)$$
$$= (x + \delta x)^2 - x^2$$
$$= x^2 + 2x\,\delta x + (\delta x)^2 - x^2$$
$$= 2x\,\delta x + (\delta x)^2$$

The gradient function of the curve is given by

$$\frac{dy}{dx} = \underset{\delta x \to 0}{\text{limit}} \left(\frac{\delta y}{\delta x} \right)$$
$$= \underset{\delta x \to 0}{\text{limit}} \left[\frac{2x\,\delta x + (\delta x)^2}{\delta x} \right]$$
$$= \underset{\delta x \to 0}{\text{limit}} (2x + \delta x)$$

◀ **As $\delta x \to 0$, $(2x + \delta x) \to 2x$**

$$= 2x$$

So, the gradient at any point on the curve $y = x^2$ can be calculated using the gradient function $\frac{dy}{dx} = 2x$.

Example 2

Find the gradient function for the general quadratic curve $y = ax^2 + bx + c$, where a, b and c are constants.

Solution

Let $y = f(x)$, where $f(x) = ax^2 + bx + c$. The small change δy in the value of y that results from a small change δx in the value of x is given by

$$\begin{aligned}\delta y &= f(x + \delta x) - f(x)\\ &= [a(x + \delta x)^2 + b(x + \delta x) + c] - [ax^2 + bx + c]\\ &= ax^2 + 2ax\,\delta x + a(\delta x)^2 + bx + b\,\delta x + c - ax^2 - bx - c\\ &= 2ax\,\delta x + a(\delta x)^2 + b\,\delta x\end{aligned}$$

The gradient function of the curve is given by

$$\begin{aligned}\frac{dy}{dx} &= \lim_{\delta x \to 0}\left(\frac{\delta y}{\delta x}\right)\\ &= \lim_{\delta x \to 0}\left[\frac{2ax\,\delta x + a(\delta x)^2 + b\,\delta x}{\delta x}\right]\\ &= \lim_{\delta x \to 0}(2ax + a\delta x + b)\\ &= 2ax + b\end{aligned}$$

So, the gradient function at any point o[n] a quadratic curve of the form $y = ax^2 + bx + c$ i[s] given by $\frac{dy}{dx} = 2ax + b$.

Differentiating $y = x^n$

Differentiating from first principles is a way of establishing the gradient function (or **derivative**) of different types of functions, but this process can be tedious. The derivative of functions of the form $y = x^n$, where n is a positive integer, all follow a similar pattern.

Remember that the process of finding the gradient function is known as **differentiation**.

Function	$y = x^1$	$y = x^2$	$y = x^3$	$y = x^4$	$y = x^5$
Derivative	1	$2x$	$3x^2$	$4x^3$	$5x^4$

$y = x$ is a straight line [of] gradient 1.

Can you spot the similarities in the derivatives? Notice that the following algebraic rule explains the similarities.

If $y = x^n$, then $\frac{dy}{dx} = nx^{n-1}$

◀ Learn this result.

Expressed in words, this rule becomes 'multiply by the power, and *then* reduce the power by one'. A more general rule for differentiating powers of x, is:

These rules also hold f[or] fractional and negative powers.

If $y = ax^n$, where a is a constant, then $\frac{dy}{dx} = nax^{n-1}$

◀ Learn this result.

Example 3

Differentiate the following with respect to x:

a $y = x^{10}$ **b** $y = 5x^6$ **c** $y = \sqrt{x}$

d $y = \dfrac{3}{x^2}$ **e** $y = \dfrac{1}{\sqrt[3]{x}}$ **f** $y = 4$

Solution

a $y = x^{10}$

$$\frac{dy}{dx} = 10x^{10-1} = 10x^9$$

Remember, multiply by the power, 10, and then reduce the power by 1, $10 - 1 = 9$.

b $y = 5x^6$

$$\frac{dy}{dx} = 6 \times 5x^{6-1} = 30x^5$$

c $y = \sqrt{x} = x^{\frac{1}{2}}$

$$\frac{dy}{dx} = \frac{1}{2}x^{\frac{1}{2}-1} = \frac{1}{2}x^{-\frac{1}{2}}$$

$$= \frac{1}{2} \times \frac{1}{\sqrt{x}} = \frac{1}{2\sqrt{x}}$$

Express the function in the form $y = ax^n$ before differentiating; that is, convert roots to powers.

Recall, $x^{-n} = \dfrac{1}{x^n}$.

d $y = \dfrac{3}{x^2} = 3x^{-2}$

$$\frac{dy}{dx} = -2 \times 3x^{-2-1}$$

$$= -6x^{-3} = -\frac{6}{x^3}$$

e $y = \dfrac{1}{\sqrt[3]{x}} = \dfrac{1}{x^{\frac{1}{3}}} = x^{-\frac{1}{3}}$

$$\frac{dy}{dx} = -\frac{1}{3}x^{-\frac{1}{3}-1}$$

$$= -\frac{1}{3}x^{-\frac{4}{3}} = -\frac{1}{3x^{\frac{4}{3}}}$$

$-\dfrac{1}{3x^{\frac{4}{3}}}$ can also be written $-\dfrac{1}{3\sqrt[3]{x^4}}$ or $\dfrac{-1}{3(\sqrt[3]{x})^4}$.

f $y = 4$ can be expressed $y = 4x^0$, since $x^0 = 1$

$$\frac{dy}{dx} = 0 \times 4x^{0-1} = 0$$

This is as expected, because the graph of $y = 4$ is horizontal; its gradient is 0.

By differentiating from first principles, it can be shown that the derivative of the sum (or difference) of two or more functions is simply the sum (or difference) of their individual derivatives. That is,

$$\frac{d}{dx}[f(x) \pm g(x)] = \frac{df}{dx} \pm \frac{dg}{dx} = f'(x) \pm g'(x)$$

◀ **Learn this result.**

Example 4

Find the derivatives of the following functions of x:

a $y = x^3 + 4x^2 - 9x - 13$ **b** $y = 5x + \frac{1}{x} - \frac{2}{x^3}$

c $y = (2x - 1)(x + 3)$ **d** $y = \frac{x^3 + 1}{x^2}$

Solution

a $y = x^3 + 4x^2 - 9x - 13$

$$\frac{dy}{dx} = \frac{d}{dx}(x^3) + \frac{d}{dx}(4x^2) - \frac{d}{dx}(9x) - \frac{d}{dx}(13)$$

$$= 3x^2 + 8x - 9 - 0$$

$$= 3x^2 + 8x - 9$$

Differentiating each term separately.

b $y = 5x + \frac{1}{x} - \frac{2}{x^3}$

$$= 5x + x^{-1} - 2x^{-3}$$

$$\frac{dy}{dx} = \frac{d}{dx}(5x) + \frac{d}{dx}(x^{-1}) - \frac{d}{dx}(2x^{-3})$$

$$= 5 + (-1 \times x^{-1-1}) - (-3 \times 2x^{-3-1})$$

$$= 5 - x^{-2} + 6x^{-4}$$

$$= 5 - \frac{1}{x^2} + \frac{6}{x^4}$$

Remember to express each term as a power o x before differentiating

Take care with the sign when multiplying by negative numbers.

c $y = (2x - 1)(x + 3)$

$$= 2x^2 + 5x - 3$$

$$\frac{dy}{dx} = 4x + 5$$

Expand brackets and collect like terms befor differentiating.

d $y = \frac{x^3 + 1}{x^2}$

$$= \frac{x^3}{x^2} + \frac{1}{x^2} = x + x^{-2}$$

$$\frac{dy}{dx} = 1 + (-2x^{-3}) = 1 - 2x^{-3}$$

$$= 1 - \frac{2}{x^3}$$

$$= \frac{x^3 - 2}{x^3}$$

Separate the fraction into two terms.

The last step simply puts the answer in the form of the question, as a single fraction, using the common denominator x^3.

Differentiation has so far been mainly confined to functions of the form $y = f(x)$, where $f(x) = ax^n$. The rules for differentiating can be applied when other letters are used. For example, if $z = g(t)$, where $g(t) = at^n$ and a is a constant, we can differentiate z 'with respect to' t. The derivative $\frac{dz}{dt} = g'(t) = nat^{n-1}$.

Example 5

Find the derivatives of the following functions:

a $s = ut + \frac{1}{2}at^2$, where u and a are constant

b $p = \theta - \dfrac{\theta^3}{6} + \dfrac{\theta^5}{120}$

c $\theta = \dfrac{2A}{r^2}$, where A is constant.

Solution

a $s = ut + \frac{1}{2}at^2$

$$\frac{ds}{dt} = u + (2 \times \tfrac{1}{2}at^{2-1}) = u + at$$

The variable on the RHS is t. Both u and a are constant.

Differentiating s with respect to t.

b $p = \theta - \dfrac{\theta^3}{6} + \dfrac{\theta^5}{120}$

The variable on the RHS is θ.

$$\frac{dp}{d\theta} = 1 - \frac{3\theta^2}{6} + \frac{5\theta^4}{120}$$

$$= 1 - \frac{\theta^2}{2} + \frac{\theta^4}{24}$$

Differentiating p with respect to θ.

c $\theta = \dfrac{2A}{r^2} = 2Ar^{-2}$

The variable is r.

$$\frac{d\theta}{dr} = -4Ar^{-3} = -\frac{4A}{r^3}$$

Differentiating θ with respect to r.

Rates of change

The derivative, $\frac{dy}{dx}$ or $f'(x)$, describes the rate at which the value of y changes with respect to x at different points on the curve. The rate of change at any particular value of x can be found by substituting this value into the expression derived for $\frac{dy}{dx}$. For example, $f'(2)$ is the rate at which the function $y = f(x)$ is changing with respect to x when $x = 2$.

The concept of 'rate of change' can be applied to equations in other variables. Consider the volume of a sphere, given by $V = \frac{4}{3}\pi r^3$. The derivative with respect to variable r, $\frac{dV}{dr} = 4\pi r^2$, gives the rate at which the volume V changes with respect to the radius r at any given value of r.

Example 6

Find the rate of change with respect to the given variable of the following functions at the values indicated:

a $f(x) = x^2 - 7x$, when $x = 3$

b $u(\theta) = (\theta^2 - 1)(\theta + 1)$, when $\theta = \frac{1}{3}$.

Solution

a $f(x) = x^2 - 7x$

$\Rightarrow f'(x) = 2x - 7$

Substituting $x = 3$, $f'(3) = 6 - 7$

$= -1$

b $u(\theta) = (\theta^2 - 1)(\theta + 1)$

$= \theta^3 + \theta^2 - \theta - 1$

Expand brackets first

$\Rightarrow u'(\theta) = 3\theta^2 + 2\theta - 1$

Differentiate u with respect to θ.

Substituting $\theta = \frac{1}{3}$, $u'(\frac{1}{3}) = 3 \times \frac{1}{9} + 2 \times \frac{1}{3} - 1$

$= \frac{3}{9} + \frac{2}{3} - 1 = 0$

Example 7

Find the coordinates of the point(s) on the following curves at which the gradient has the value indicated:

a $y = x^2 + 4x + 1, \quad \frac{dy}{dx} = 8$

b $y = \frac{1}{x} - 2x, \quad \frac{dy}{dx} = -6$

Solution

a $y = x^2 + 4x + 1 \Rightarrow \frac{dy}{dx} = 2x + 4$

If $\frac{dy}{dx} = 8$, then $2x + 4 = 8$

This gives $2x = 4 \Rightarrow x = 2$

$\Rightarrow y = (2)^2 + (4 \times 2) + 1 = 13$

Substituting the value x in the original equation.

So, the gradient of the curve $y = x^2 + 4x + 1$ is 8 at the point (2, 13).

b $y = \frac{1}{x} - 2x = x^{-1} - 2x$

$\Rightarrow \frac{dy}{dx} = -x^{-2} - 2 = -\frac{1}{x^2} - 2$

If $\frac{dy}{dx} = -6$, then $-\frac{1}{x^2} - 2 = -6$

$\Rightarrow \quad \frac{1}{x^2} = 4$

$\Rightarrow \quad x^2 = \frac{1}{4}$

$\Rightarrow \quad x = \frac{1}{2}$ or $x = -\frac{1}{2}$

When $x = \frac{1}{2}$, $y = \dfrac{1}{\left(\frac{1}{2}\right)} - 2 \times \left(\frac{1}{2}\right) = 2 - 1 = 1$

When $x = -\frac{1}{2}$, $y = \dfrac{1}{\left(-\frac{1}{2}\right)} - 2 \times \left(-\frac{1}{2}\right) = -2 + 1 = -1$

So the curve $y = \frac{1}{x} - 2x$ has a gradient of -6 at the points $\left(\frac{1}{2}, 1\right)$ and $\left(-\frac{1}{2}, -1\right)$.

Differentiating with respect to *y*

It can be shown that the rate of change of x with respect to y, $\frac{dx}{dy}$, is the reciprocal of $\frac{dy}{dx}$.

$$\frac{dx}{dy} = \frac{1}{\left(\frac{dy}{dx}\right)}$$

◀ **Learn this result.**

For example, if $y = 3x^2 + 2x$, then $\frac{dy}{dx} = 6x + 2$, and $\frac{dx}{dy} = \dfrac{1}{\left(\frac{dy}{dx}\right)} = \dfrac{1}{6x + 2}$.

This particular method is quicker than having to rearrange $y = 3x^2 + 2x$ to express x in terms of y before differentiating with respect to y.

Higher derivatives

Sometimes it is useful to know the gradient of the gradient function at a particular point on the curve $y = f(x)$. This is called the **second derivative**. It is found by differentiating the first derivative, $\frac{dy}{dx}$, with respect to x to give $\frac{d}{dx}\left(\frac{dy}{dx}\right)$, written $\frac{d^2y}{dx^2}$, or $f''(x)$.

The expression $\frac{d^2y}{dx^2}$ is read 'd-two-y-by-d-x-squared', and shows that the differentiation process has happened twice. It is *not* the same as squaring $\frac{dy}{dx}$.

It is important to remember that $\frac{d^2y}{dx^2} \neq \left(\frac{dy}{dx}\right)^2$.

Differentiating again with respect to x would give the third derivative, $\frac{d^3y}{dx^3}$, or $f'''(x)$.

$\frac{d^3y}{dx^3}$ is read 'd-three-y-by-d-x-cubed'.

Higher derivatives, of the form $\frac{d^ny}{dx^n}$ or $f^{(n)}(x)$, can be obtained by differentiating $y = f(x)$ n times with respect to x.

Example 8

Find the first, second and third derivatives of the following functions:

a $y = x^4 + 5x^3 - 9x^2 + 2x - 7$
b $f(x) = x^3 - \frac{1}{x}$

Solution

a $y = x^4 + 5x^3 - 9x^2 + 2x - 7$

$$\Rightarrow \frac{dy}{dx} = 4x^3 + 15x^2 - 18x + 2$$

$$\begin{aligned}\frac{d^2y}{dx^2} &= \frac{d}{dx}\left(\frac{dy}{dx}\right)\\ &= \frac{d}{dx}(4x^3 + 15x^2 - 18x + 2)\\ &= 12x^2 + 30x - 18\end{aligned}$$

$$\begin{aligned}\frac{d^3y}{dx^3} &= \frac{d}{dx}\left(\frac{d^2y}{dx^2}\right)\\ &= \frac{d}{dx}(12x^2 + 30x - 18)\\ &= 24x + 30\end{aligned}$$

b

$$\begin{aligned}f(x) &= x^3 - \frac{1}{x}\\ &= x^3 - x^{-1}\\ f'(x) &= 3x^2 + x^{-2}\\ &= 3x^2 + \frac{1}{x^2}\\ f''(x) &= 6x - 2x^{-3}\\ &= 6x - \frac{2}{x^3}\\ f'''(x) &= 6 + 6x^{-4}\\ &= 6 + \frac{6}{x^4}\end{aligned}$$

Remember to express each term in the form ax^n before differentiating.

5.1 Finding the Gradient of a Curve

Exercise

Technique

1 Differentiate each of the following from first principles to find $\frac{dy}{dx}$:

a $y = x^3$ **b** $y = 3x^2 - 9x + 5$ **c** $y = \frac{1}{x}$

2 Differentiate each of the following with respect to x:

a $y = x^8$

b $y = 7 + x - 3x^2 - \frac{1}{3}x^3$

c $y = (3x - 5)(2x + 1)$

d $y = \sqrt[4]{x}$

e $y = -\dfrac{4}{x^3}$

f $y = \dfrac{2 - x^3}{x^2}$

g $y = \dfrac{6}{\sqrt{x}}$

h $y = \dfrac{3x^2 - 2x}{\sqrt{x}}$.

2 **b**

3 Find the first derivative of each of the following functions:

a $f(x) = \frac{1}{4}x^2 - \frac{1}{2}x$

b $f(t) = (t + 1)(2 - t)$

c $f(s) = s^3 - 7s^2 - 2s$

d $h(p) = \dfrac{2p^4 - 5p}{p^3}$

e $\theta(t) = 6t^{\frac{1}{3}}$

4 Find the gradient of each of the following curves at the point indicated:

a $y = x^2 + 6x - 3$ at $(2, 13)$

b $y = 2x^3 - 7x - 5$ at $(-1, 0)$

c $y = \frac{4}{x} + \frac{x^2}{4}$ at $(2, 3)$

d $y = (x^2 - 2)(x + 1)$ at $(-3, -14)$

4 **c**

5 Find the coordinates of the points on each of the following curves at which the gradient has the value indicated:

a $y = x^3 - 6x^2 + 7x$, where $\frac{dy}{dx} = -2$

b $y = 3 - 5x + x^3$, where $\frac{dy}{dx} = 7$

c $y = 2x + 1 - \frac{4}{x^2}$, where $\frac{dy}{dx} = 1$

d $y = \frac{1}{x}$, where $\frac{dy}{dx} = -\frac{4}{9}$

5 **c**

6 Find the gradient of each of the following curves at their points of intersection with the x- and y-axes:

a $y = x^2 + 2x - 3$ **b** $y = (2x + 3)(x - 1)$

6 **a**

7 Find the first, second and third derivatives of each of the following:

a $y = 5x^4 + 2x^3 - 7x^2 - 9x + 2$ **b** $f(x) = \frac{4}{x} - \frac{1}{x^2}$

5.2 Stationary Points

Look at the graph below. What do points A, B, C and D have in common?

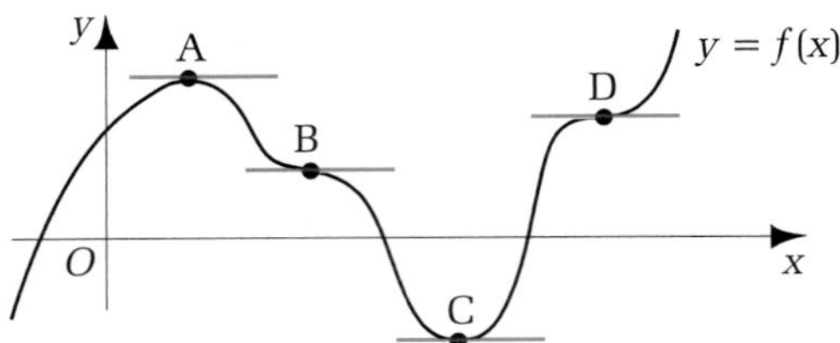

Notice that the gradient of the curve is zero at these four points. This means that $\frac{dy}{dx} = 0$ at A, B, C and D.

Points like A, B, C and D are known as **stationary points**. They correspond to values of x for which the gradient of the curve is zero. This means the function $f(x)$ is momentarily 'stationary', that is neither increasing or decreasing.

Points A and C are known as **turning points** on the graph. Notice that at a turning point $f(x)$ changes from being an increasing function of x to a decreasing function of x, or vice versa. Point A is called a **local maximum point** and point C is a **local minimum point**.

What about points B and D? $f(x)$ is a decreasing function on either side of point B. It is an increasing function on either side of point D, but the gradient is zero at both points. Such points are called **stationary points of inflexion**.

Colin Maclaurin (1698–1746)
Maclaurin was the first present the correct theory for distinguishir between the minimun and maximum values a function.

An alternative spelling of 'inflexion' is 'inflection'.

Distinguishing between stationary points

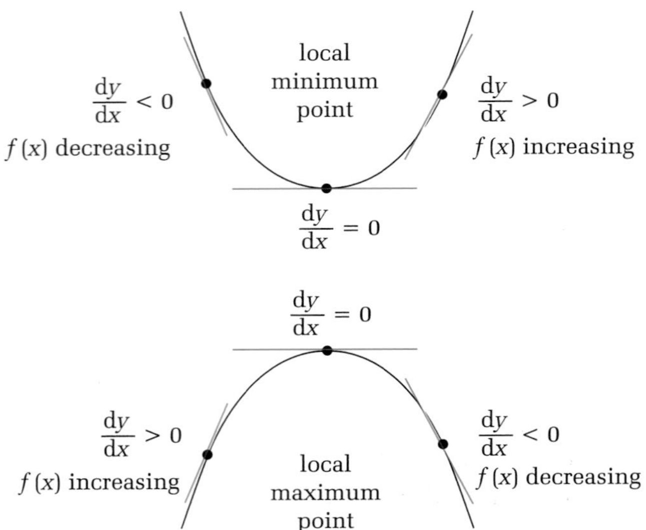

As a graph passes through a local minimum point, its gradient function, $\frac{dy}{dx}$ changes from being negative to positive. It is zero at the minimum point itself. On either side of a local maximum point, there is a corresponding change in the sign of $\frac{dy}{dx}$ from positive to negative.

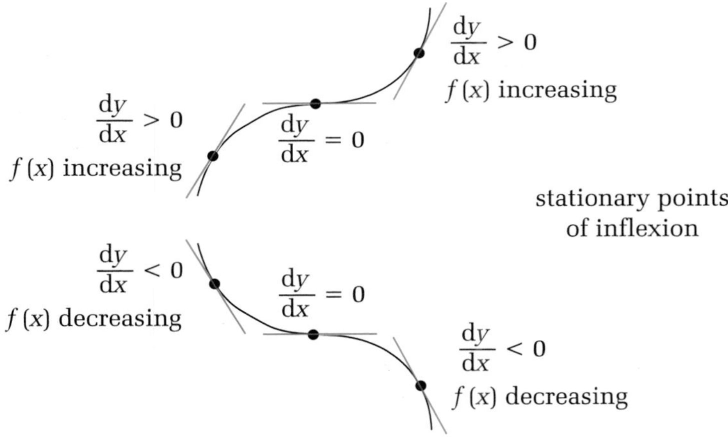

Since the curve is either an increasing or decreasing function of x on *both* sides of a stationary point of inflexion, its gradient $\frac{dy}{dx}$ remains either positive or negative on both sides of the point of inflexion. The gradient is zero at the point of inflexion itself.

So, the stationary points on a curve can be located by solving $\frac{dy}{dx} = 0$. Then their nature can be determined by examining the gradient of the curve on either side of the stationary point. The table below summarises the changes in the sign of $\frac{dy}{dx}$ and the corresponding type of stationary point.

You must find these points and their nature before you can make an accurate sketch of a curve.

Change in $\frac{dy}{dx}$	Type of stationary point
−ve → 0 → +ve	minimum
+ve → 0 → −ve	maximum
+ve → 0 → +ve	point of inflexion
−ve → 0 → −ve	point of inflexion

◀ **Learn these important results.**

Example 1

Find the coordinates of the points where the quadratic curve $y = x^2 - 2x - 15$ crosses the x- and y-axes. Find the coordinates of the stationary point on the curve, and determine its nature. Then, sketch the graph of $y = x^2 - 2x - 15$.

Solution

The graph crosses the x-axis when $y = 0$.

$$\Rightarrow \quad x^2 - 2x - 15 = 0$$
$$\Rightarrow (x + 3)(x - 5) = 0$$
$$\Rightarrow x = -3 \text{ or } x = 5$$

So the graph crosses the x-axis at $(-3, 0)$ and $(5, 0)$.

It crosses the y-axis when $x = 0 \Rightarrow y = -15$. So the graph crosses the y-axis at $(0, -15)$.

The gradient function for the graph of $y = x^2 - 2x - 15$ is given by $\frac{dy}{dx} = 2x - 2$. To find the location of the stationary point on this graph, solve $\frac{dy}{dx} = 0$.

$$\frac{dy}{dx} = 0 \Rightarrow 2x - 2 = 0$$
$$\Rightarrow \quad x = 1$$

Now substitute this value into the equation of the graph to find the y-coordinate.

When $x = 1$, $y = (1)^2 - 2(1) - 15 = -16$.

So, the stationary point is at $(1, -16)$.

Now look at $\frac{dy}{dx}$ on either side of $x = 1$.

When $x = 0$, $\frac{dy}{dx} = -2$. That is, $\frac{dy}{dx} < 0$.

When $x = 2$, $\frac{dy}{dx} = 2$. That is, $\frac{dy}{dx} > 0$.

Since the gradient changes from being negative to positive as the graph passes through $(1, -16)$ this is a local minimum point. The graph of the quadratic can now be sketched by drawing a parabola through the four calculated points.

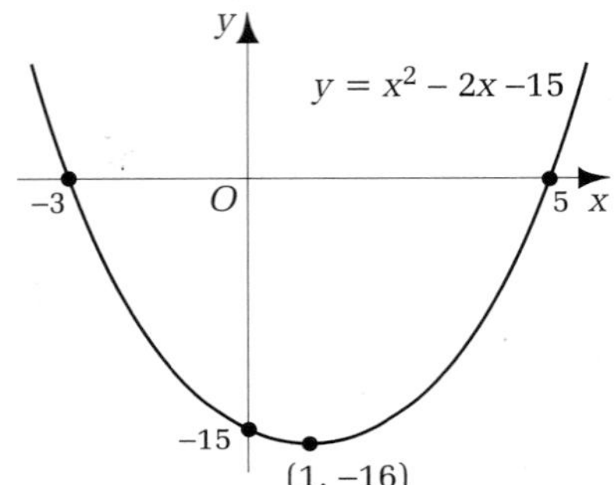

Example 2

For each of the following cubic functions, find the coordinates of any stationary points, and determine their nature. Use a graphical calculator to plot the graphs of these functions. Use the TRACE facility to *check* your results.

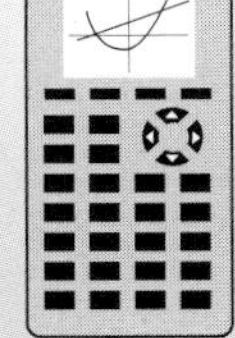

a $y = x^3 - 3x^2 - 9x + 10$ **b** $y = x^3 - 3x^2 + 3x + 1$

Solution

a The gradient function for the graph of $y = x^3 - 3x^2 - 9x + 10$ is given by $\frac{dy}{dx} = 3x^2 - 6x - 9$. To find the location of any stationary points on this graph, solve $\frac{dy}{dx} = 0$.

$$3x^2 - 6x - 9 = 0$$

$$\Rightarrow \quad 3(x^2 - 2x - 3) = 0$$

$$\Rightarrow \quad 3(x + 1)(x - 3) = 0$$

$$\Rightarrow \quad x = -1 \text{ or } x = 3$$

When $x = -1$, $y = (-1)^3 - 3(-1)^2 - 9(-1) + 10$

$= -1 - 3 + 9 + 10 = 15$

When $x = 3$, $y = (3)^3 - 3(3)^2 - 9(3) + 10$

$= 27 - 27 - 27 + 10 = -17$

So, the graph of $y = x^3 - 3x^2 - 9x + 10$ has stationary points at $(-1, 15)$ and $(3, -17)$.

Now look at the sign of $\frac{dy}{dx}$ on both sides of $x = -1$.

When $x = -2$, $\frac{dy}{dx} = 3(-2)^2 - 6(-2) - 9 = 15$. That is, $\frac{dy}{dx} > 0$.

When $x = 0$, $\frac{dy}{dx} = 3(0)^2 - 6(0) - 9 = -9$. That is, $\frac{dy}{dx} < 0$

To the left of the stationary point the function is increasing.

To the right of the stationary point the function is decreasing.

Since the gradient changes from positive to negative as the graph passes through $(-1, 15)$, this is a local maximum point.

Now look at the sign of $\frac{dy}{dx}$ on both sides of $x = 3$.

When $x = 2$, $\frac{dy}{dx} = 3(2)^2 - 6(2) - 9 = -9$. That is, $\frac{dy}{dx} < 0$.

When $x = 4$, $\frac{dy}{dx} = 3(4)^2 - 6(4) - 9 = 15$. That is, $\frac{dy}{dx} > 0$.

Since the gradient changes from negative to positive, $(3, -17)$ is a local minimum point on the curve.

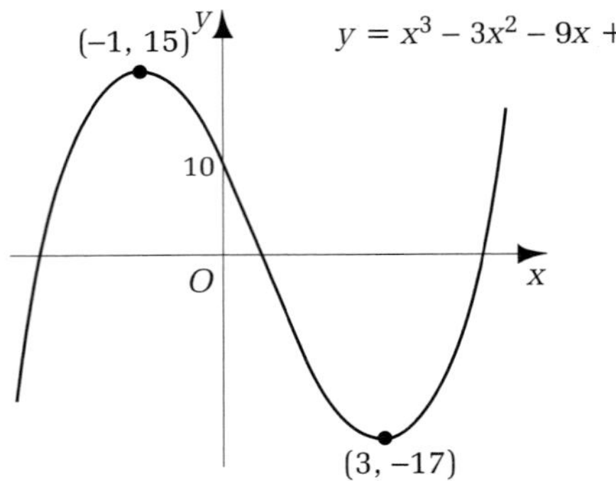

The y-intercept is four by substituting $x = 0$ into the equation of the curve.

b Any stationary points on the graph of $y = x^3 - 3x^2 + 3x + 1$ are found by solving $\frac{dy}{dx} = 0$.

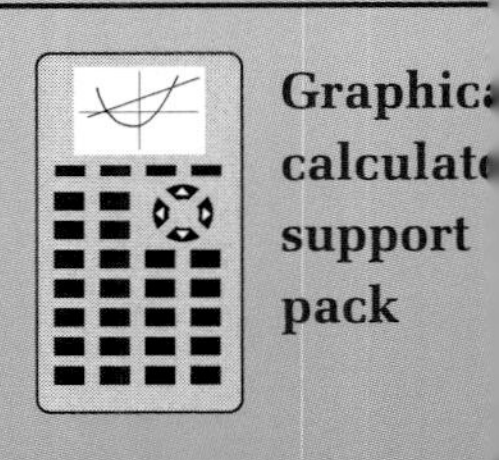

Since $\quad \dfrac{dy}{dx} = 3x^2 - 6x + 3$

then $\quad \dfrac{dy}{dx} = 0 \Rightarrow \quad 3x^2 - 6x + 3 = 0$

$$\Rightarrow 3(x^2 - 2x + 1) = 0$$

$$\Rightarrow \quad 3(x-1)^2 = 0$$

$$\Rightarrow \quad x = 1$$

Note the repeated root

When $x = 1, \quad y = (1)^3 - 3(1)^2 + 3(1) + 1 = 2.$

So the only stationary point on this curve is located at $(1, 2)$.
To determine its nature, look at the sign of $\frac{dy}{dx}$ on either side of $x = 1$.

When $x = 0, \ \dfrac{dy}{dx} = 3. \quad$ That is, $\dfrac{dy}{dx} > 0.$

When $x = 2, \ \dfrac{dy}{dx} = 3. \quad$ That is, $\dfrac{dy}{dx} > 0.$

So the gradient is positive on both sides of $(1, 2)$, which must be a stationary point of inflexion.

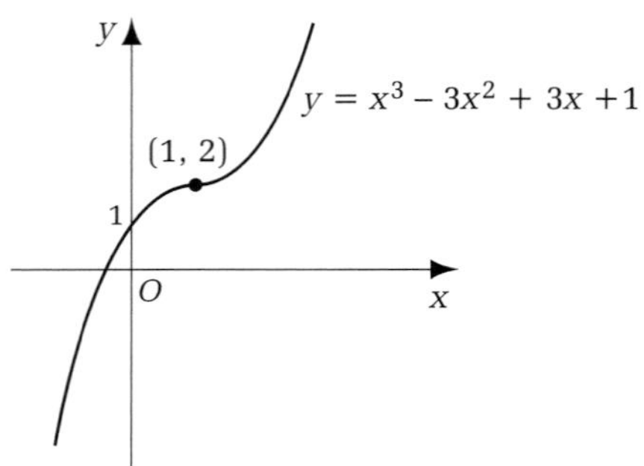

Increasing and decreasing functions

We are sometimes more interested in whether a function is increasing or decreasing at various points along its curve. At points on the graph of $y = f(x)$ where the gradient is not zero, y must be either an increasing or decreasing function of x.

- If $\frac{dy}{dx} > 0$ (a positive gradient), then y is an increasing function of x.
- If $\frac{dy}{dx} < 0$ (a negative gradient), then y is a decreasing function of x.

For continuous functions, sections of increasing and decreasing behaviour are always separated by a stationary point. In order to find out for which values of x a function is increasing or decreasing, its stationary point(s) must first be located.

Example 3

Find the values of x for which the function $y = x^3 - 9x^2 + 15x + 13$ is increasing.

Solution

$$y = x^3 - 9x^2 + 15x + 13$$

$$\Rightarrow \frac{dy}{dx} = 3x^2 - 18x + 15$$

At stationary values of function y, $\frac{dy}{dx} = 0$.

$$\Rightarrow 3x^2 - 18x + 15 = 0$$

$$\Rightarrow 3(x^2 - 6x + 5) = 0$$

$$\Rightarrow 3(x - 1)(x - 5) = 0$$

$$\Rightarrow x = 1 \text{ or } x = 5$$

To determine the nature of these two stationary values, look at the gradient of $\frac{dy}{dx}$ on both sides.

When $x = 0$, $\frac{dy}{dx} = 15$. That is, $\frac{dy}{dx} > 0$.

When $x = 3$, $\frac{dy}{dx} = -12$. That is, $\frac{dy}{dx} < 0$.

When $x = 6$, $\frac{dy}{dx} = 15$. That is, $\frac{dy}{dx} > 0$.

This means that y has a maximum value at $x = 1$ and a minimum value at $x = 5$. It follows that y will be a decreasing function in the interval $1 < x < 5$, and an increasing function of x for $x < 1$ and $x > 5$.

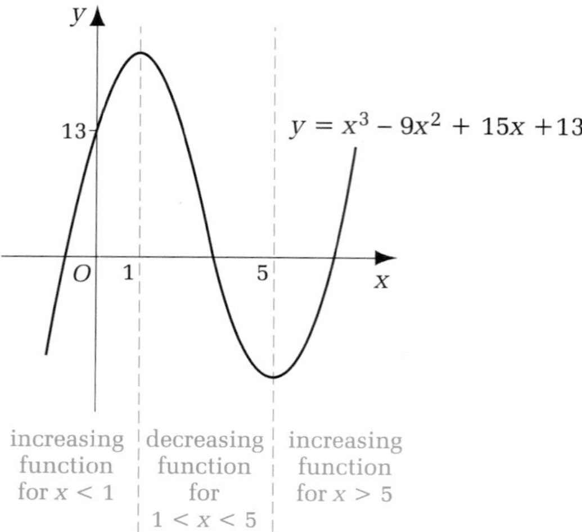

Optimisation

Many practical problems involve finding the maximum or minimum values of a function as it changes with respect to a particular variable. If the problem can be modelled in terms of a *mathematical* function, differentiation can be used to locate and distinguish between any maximum and minimum values.

Example 4

An open-topped gift box is formed by cutting squares of side length x from each corner of a 60 cm × 60 cm square of cardboard, and folding the remaining flaps to make the vertical sides.

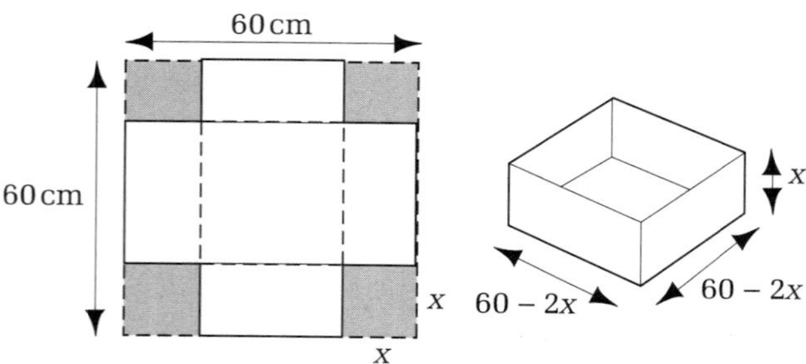

a Find an expression in terms of x for the volume V (in cm^3) of the gift box.

b Use differentiation to find the value of x that corresponds to the maximum possible volume of the gift box.

c Calculate this maximum volume.

Solution

a The volume of the folded box is given by

V = length of box × width of box × height of box

and the dimensions of the box are

length = width = $60 - 2x$ and height = x

So $V = (60 - 2x) \times (60 - 2x) \times x$

$= x(60 - 2x)^2$

$V = 4x^3 - 240x^2 + 3600x$

b Differentiating with respect to x, the gradient of this volume function is given by

$$\frac{dV}{dx} = 12x^2 - 480x + 3600$$

At the maximum and minimum volumes, $\frac{dV}{dx} = 0$

$\Rightarrow \ 12x^2 - 480x + 3600 = 0$

$\Rightarrow \ 12(x^2 - 40x + 300) = 0$

$\Rightarrow \ 12(x - 10)(x - 30) = 0$

$\Rightarrow \ x = 10$ or $x = 30$

Look at the sign of $\frac{dV}{dx}$ on both sides of $x = 10$.

Alternatively, use $\frac{dV}{dx} = 12(x - 10)(x - 30)$.

When $x = 5$, $\frac{dV}{dx} = 12(5)^2 - 480(5) + 3600 = 1500$.

That is, $\frac{dV}{dx} > 0$.

When $x = 15$, $\frac{dV}{dx} = 12(15)^2 - 480(15) + 3600 = -900$.

That is, $\frac{dV}{dx} < 0$.

This means that $x = 10$ corresponds to a maximum value of V.
Look at the sign of $\frac{dV}{dx}$ on both sides of $x = 30$.

When $x = 25$, $\frac{dV}{dx} = 12(25)^2 - 480(25) + 3600 = -900$.

That is, $\frac{dV}{dx} < 0$.

When $x = 35$, $\frac{dV}{dx} = 12(35)^2 - 480(35) + 3600 = 1500$.

That is, $\frac{dV}{dx} > 0$.

This means that $x = 30$ corresponds to a minimum value of x. In fact, the volume of the folded box is zero when $x = 30$ because cutting squares of this size from each corner of the original sheet would leave no cardboard at all to fold into a box.

c From **b**, the maximum volume of the folded box occurs when $x = 10$ cm.

Then $V = 4(10)^3 - 240(10)^2 + 3600(10) = 16\,000\text{ cm}^3$

The optimum dimensi[ons] of the box are length = width = 40 c[m] and height = 10 cm.

In many optimisation problems, the function to be maximised or minimised is dependent on two variables. However, usually one of these variables can be eliminated using additional information given about the situation.

Example 5

A manufacturer wishes to make cylindrical steel cans with a capacity of 500 ml using the smallest quantity of metal possible. (Remember that 1 millilitre $\equiv$ 1 cm^3.)

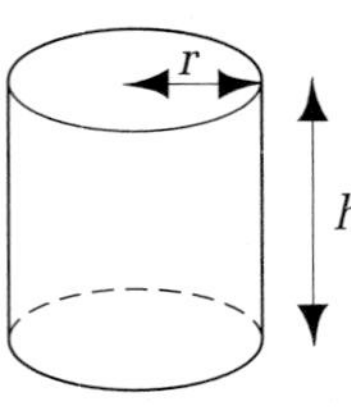

It is assumed that the can has no metal lip around the top or bottom, which would have to be accounted by adding an extra te[rm] to the expression for S.

a Find an expression for the total surface area S cm^2 of a cylindrical can, in terms of its radius r cm only.

b Find, correct to one decimal place, the values of r and h, the can's height, that would give the smallest surface area.

Solution

a The total surface area of the can, S, is given by

$$S = 2\pi r^2 + 2\pi rh \qquad [1]$$

At the moment S is expressed as an equation with two variables, r and h. We are required to express it in terms of r only, so we must eliminate h.

The volume of the cylinder is given by $V = \pi r^2 h$, where h is the height of the can.

For this particular can the volume is 500 cm^3, so

$$\pi r^2 h = 500 \qquad [2]$$

Rearranging equation [2], $h = \dfrac{500}{\pi r^2}$.

Substituting this expression for h into equation [1],

$$S = 2\pi r^2 + 2\pi r\frac{500}{\pi r^2}$$
$$= 2\pi r^2 + \frac{1000}{r}$$

Eliminating πr in the second term.

b $$\frac{dS}{dr} = 4\pi r - 1000r^{-2}$$
$$= 4\pi r - \frac{1000}{r^2}$$

At the maximum and minimum values of surface area, $\frac{dS}{dr} = 0$.

$$\frac{dS}{dr} = 0 \Rightarrow 4\pi r - \frac{1000}{r^2} = 0$$
$$\Rightarrow 4\pi r^3 - 1000 = 0$$
$$\Rightarrow r^3 = \frac{1000}{4\pi} = \frac{250}{\pi}$$
$$\Rightarrow r = \sqrt[3]{\frac{250}{\pi}} = 4.3 \text{ cm (1 d.p.)}$$

Multiply throughout by r^2.

Substituting for r in the rearranged form of equation [2] to find the corresponding height,

$$h = \frac{500}{\pi r^2} = \frac{500}{\pi} \times \frac{1}{\left(\sqrt[3]{\frac{250}{\pi}}\right)^2}$$
$$= \frac{500}{\pi} \times \left(\frac{250}{\pi}\right)^{-2/3}$$
$$= \frac{500}{\pi} \times \left(\frac{\pi}{250}\right)^{2/3}$$
$$= 8.6 \text{ cm (1 d.p.)}$$

Use the surd form of r, to avoid introducing inaccuracies due to rounding.

To decide whether these values for the radius and height correspond to a maximum or minimum value for the surface area, look at the value of $\frac{dS}{dr}$ on either side of $r = 4.3$.

When $r = 4$, $\frac{dS}{dr} = 16\pi - \frac{1000}{16} \approx -12.2$. That is, $\frac{dS}{dr} < 0$.

When $r = 5$, $\frac{dS}{dr} = 20\pi - \frac{1000}{25} \approx 22.8$. That is, $\frac{dS}{dr} > 0$.

This means that the surface area of a 500 ml cylindrical can is minimised when $r = 4.3$ cm and $h = 8.6$ cm.

These values of r and h minimise the surface area. The manufacturer may be more interested in minimising wasted metal when cutting the pieces, and this may give different values of r and h.

5.2 Stationary Points
Exercise
Technique

1 For each of the following quadratic functions:

i find the coordinates of the points where the graph of $y = f(x)$ crosses the axes

ii find the coordinates of the stationary point on the graph, and determine its nature

iii sketch the graph of $y = f(x)$. Check your graph using a graphical calculator.

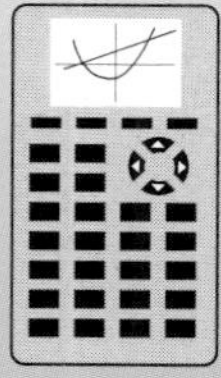

a $f(x) = x^2 - 2x - 8$ **b** $f(x) = 35 + 2x - x^2$
c $f(x) = 4x^2 - 16x - 9$ **d** $f(x) = x^2 + 8x + 28$

2 For each of the following cubic functions, find the coordinates of any stationary points, and determine their nature:

a $y = x^3 + 6x^2 + 12x + 7$ **b** $y = 2x^3 - 12x^2 + 18x - 5$
c $y = x^3 + 7x^2 + 19x + 2$ **d** $y = 3x^3 - 3x^2 + 1$

3 **a** Find the coordinates of the points where the quartic curve $y = x^4 - 12x^3$ crosses the axes.

b Find $\frac{dy}{dx}$. Hence find the location, and determine the nature, of the stationary points on the curve.

c Sketch $y = x^4 - 12x^3$. Check your graph using a graphical calculator.

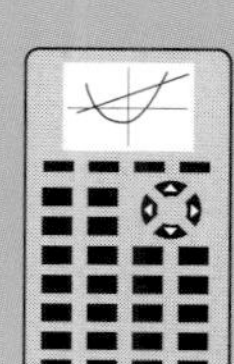

4 For each of the following functions, find an expression for $f'(x)$, and hence locate and determine the nature of any stationary points on the graph of $y = f(x)$:

a $f(x) = x + \dfrac{4}{x}$ **b** $f(x) = \dfrac{50}{x} - \dfrac{x^2}{5}$

c $f(x) = \dfrac{8}{x^2} + \dfrac{x}{4}$ **d** $f(x) = \dfrac{3}{x} - \dfrac{9}{x^2}$

5 Given that $s = 3t^2 - 8t + 3$, find the minimum value of s and the value of t for which this occurs.

5

6 Given that $v = 26 + 11r - r^2$, find the maximum value of v and the value of r for which this occurs.

7 Find the values of x for which $f(x) = 20 + 8x - x^2$ is a decreasing function of x.

7

8 Find the values of t for which $g(t) = t^3 + 3t^2 - 9t + 6$ is an increasing function of t.

Contextual

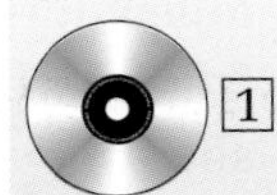

1 An open box is formed from a 120 cm × 70 cm rectangular sheet of cardboard by cutting squares of side length x cm from each corner. The remaining flaps are then folded up to make the vertical sides of the box.

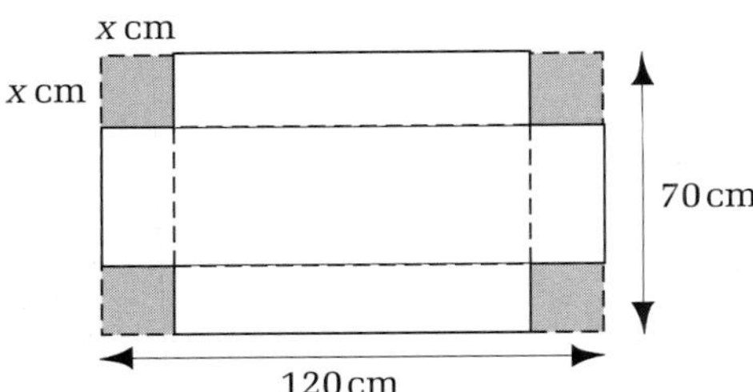

a Find an expression in terms of x for the volume V (in cm^3) of the box.

b Find $\frac{dV}{dx}$ and then solve the equation $\frac{dV}{dx} = 0$.

c Find the maximum possible volume of the box. Justify your answer.

2 A garden centre wishes to use fencing to enclose three equally sized rectangular plots next to each other, as shown in the diagram. The total area A of the three plots is to be 288 m^2.

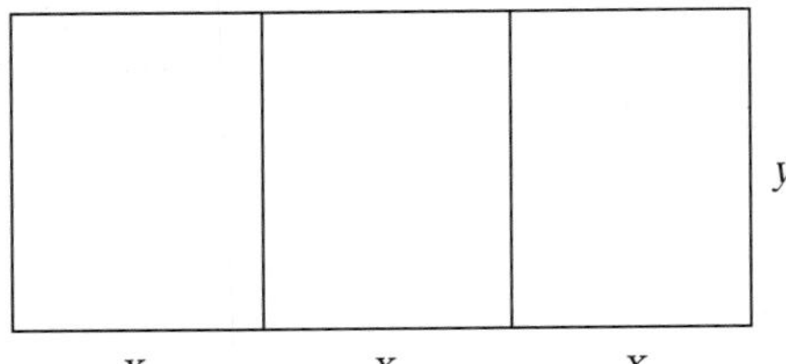

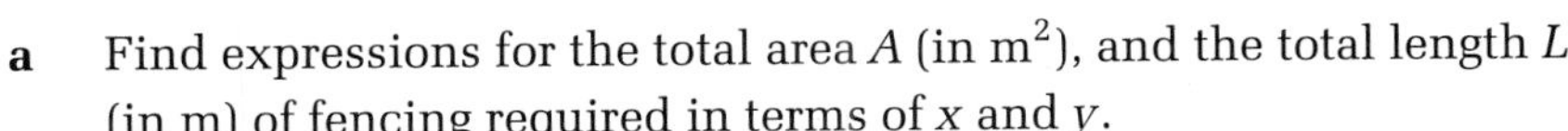

a Find expressions for the total area A (in m^2), and the total length L (in m) of fencing required in terms of x and y.

b Express L in terms of x only.

c Hence, find the dimensions of each rectangular plot if the total length of fencing is to be kept as low as possible. Justify your answer.

d What is the minimum length of fencing required?

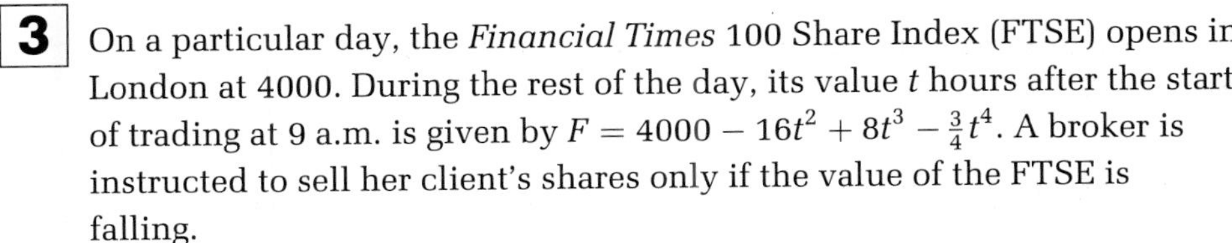

3 On a particular day, the *Financial Times* 100 Share Index (FTSE) opens in London at 4000. During the rest of the day, its value t hours after the start of trading at 9 a.m. is given by $F = 4000 - 16t^2 + 8t^3 - \frac{3}{4}t^4$. A broker is instructed to sell her client's shares only if the value of the FTSE is falling.

a What is the value of the FTSE at noon?

b Calculate the highest value of the index during the day. To the nearest minute, at what time does this occur?

c If trading finishes at 4.30 p.m., by how much has the index risen or fallen during the day?

d During which times of the day could the broker have sold her clients shares?

4 A cuboidal water tank, of height h cm, width x cm and length $2x$ cm, is designed to hold 700 litres when full.

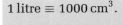

1 litre $\equiv$ 1000 cm^3.

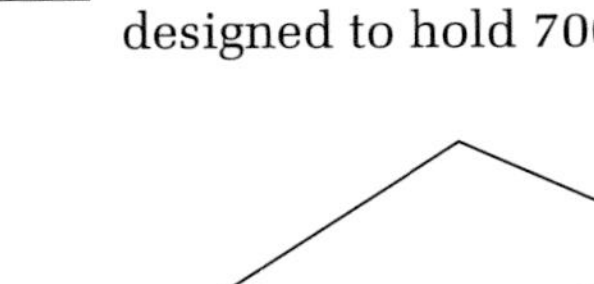

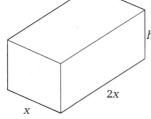

a Show that $h = \frac{350\,000}{x^2}$.

b Find an expression for the total surface area, S m^2, of the six faces of the tank in terms of x only.

c Find the dimensions of the tank that correspond to the least surface area. Justify your answer. (Give your answers to the nearest cm.)

5 A school decides to organise a monthly raffle in order to raise funds. It estimates that 2000 tickets would be bought if the price of each one was 50 pence, and that only 1000 tickets would be bought if they cost £1 each. The cost c of organising the raffle each month is £150 for prizes and 2 pence per ticket for printing.

a The number of tickets sold is modelled by $n = a + bs$, where s pence is the selling price, and a and b are constants. Find a and b.

b Show that $c = (21\,000 - 40s)$ pence.

c Show that, in terms of the selling price s, the monthly profit generated by the raffle is given by $p = 3040s - 21\,000 - 20s^2$, and find the selling price that would maximise the profit. Calculate the maximum profit and the number of tickets sold to achieve it.

5.3 Further Applications of Differentiation

Tangents and normals

The gradient of a tangent drawn to a curve at any particular point is the same as the gradient of the curve at this point. This means that the gradient of a tangent can be found by differentiation. For example, consider the tangent drawn to the curve $y = x^2$ at the point $(1, 1)$.

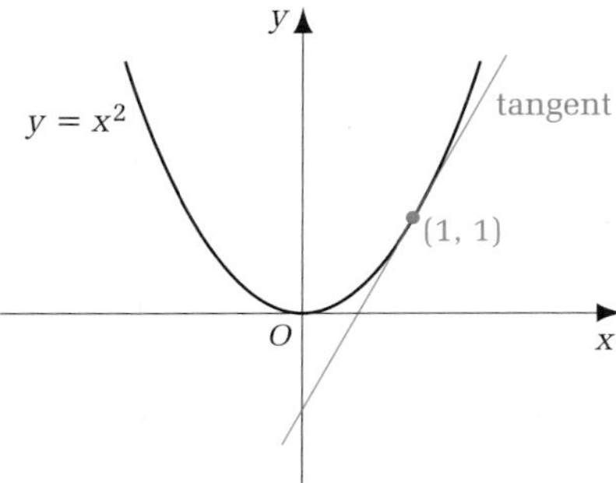

The gradient function of this curve is $\frac{dy}{dx} = 2x$. So the gradient of the curve, and therefore the gradient of the tangent, at the point $(1, 1)$ is 2. Recall from Chapter 2 that the equation of a line with gradient m, that passes through a point with coordinates (x_1, y_1), is given by $\mathbf{y - y_1 = m(x - x_1)}$. So the equation of this particular tangent is given by $y - 1 = 2(x - 1)$ or $y = 2x - 1$.

The normal to a curve at any point is the straight line that passes through the curve at right-angles to the tangent at that point. Because the tangent and normal are perpendicular to each other, their gradients, m_1 and m_2 respectively, satisfy the condition $m_1 m_2 = -1$. So,

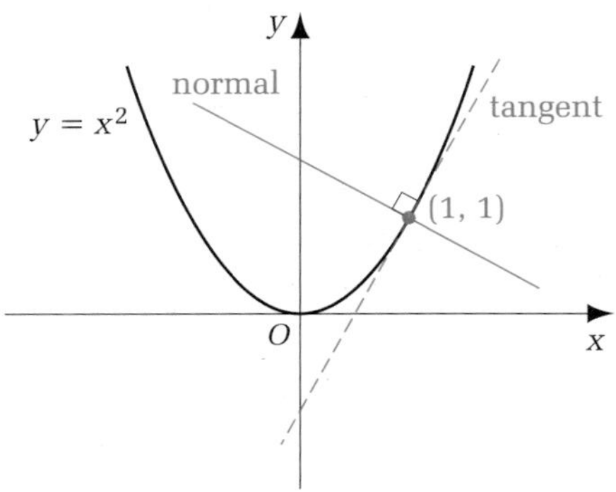

$$\textbf{gradient of normal} = \frac{-1}{\textbf{gradient of tangent}}$$

◀ **Learn this result.**

So the gradient of the normal to the curve $y = x^2$ at $(1, 1)$ is $-\frac{1}{2}$. Now use $y - y_1 = m(x - x_1)$ to find the equation of this normal.

$$y - 1 = -\tfrac{1}{2}(x - 1)$$

$$\Rightarrow y - 1 = -\tfrac{1}{2}x + \tfrac{1}{2}$$

$$\Rightarrow y = -\tfrac{1}{2}x + \tfrac{3}{2}$$

Example 1

Find the gradient of the curve $y = (x + 2)(4 - x)$ at the point where $x = 3$. Hence, find the equations of the tangent and the normal to the curve at this point.

Solution

$$y = (x + 2)(4 - x)$$
$$= 8 + 2x - x^2$$

$$\text{So } \frac{dy}{dx} = 2 - 2x$$

When $x = 3, y = 5$ and $\frac{dy}{dx} = -4$.

So the gradient of the tangent to the curve at $(3, 5)$ is -4.

This means that the gradient of the normal is $\frac{1}{4}$.

Now use $y - y_1 = m(x - x_1)$ to find the equations of both the tangent and the normal to the curve at $(3, 5)$.

The equation of the tangent is $y - 5 = -4(x - 3)$

$$\Rightarrow \quad y - 5 = -4x + 12$$
$$\Rightarrow \quad y = -4x + 17$$

The equation of the normal is $y - 5 = \frac{1}{4}(x - 3)$

$$\Rightarrow \quad y = \frac{1}{4}x + \frac{17}{4}$$
$$\Rightarrow \quad x - 4y + 17 = 0$$

Recall that straight line equations, involving fractions, can be rearranged into the form $ax + by + c = 0$.

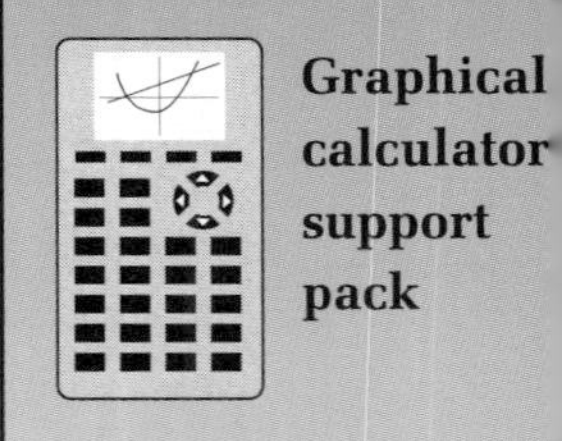
Graphical calculator support pack

Use a graphical calculator or graph plotting software to draw the quadratic curve $y = (x + 2)(4 - x)$. On the same graph plot the lines $y = -4x + 17$ and $y = \frac{1}{4}x + \frac{17}{4}$. Verify that they are the tangent and normal to the curve at the point $x = 3$.

Ensure that you have a 'square' view; that is, one in which the x- and y-axes have the same scale.

Example 2

Find the equation of the normal to the curve $y = x^2 + 4x - 2$ at the point where $x = -3$. Find the coordinates of the other point where this normal intersects $y = x^2 + 4x - 2$.

Solution

$$y = x^2 + 4x - 2$$

$$\text{So } \frac{dy}{dx} = 2x + 4$$

When $x = -3, y = -5$ and $\frac{dy}{dx} = -2$.
Since the gradient of the tangent to the curve at $(-3, -5)$ is -2, the gradient of the normal will be $\frac{1}{2}$.
Use $y - y_1 = m(x - x_1)$ to find the equation of this normal.

$$y - (-5) = \tfrac{1}{2}(x - (-3))$$
$$\Rightarrow \quad y + 5 = \tfrac{1}{2}x + \tfrac{3}{2}$$
$$\Rightarrow \quad y = \tfrac{1}{2}x + \tfrac{3}{2} - 5$$
$$\Rightarrow \quad y = \tfrac{1}{2}x - \tfrac{7}{2}$$

At the points of intersection of this normal and the curve $y = x^2 + 4x - 2$,

$$x^2 + 4x - 2 = \tfrac{1}{2}x - \tfrac{7}{2}$$
$$\Rightarrow \quad 2x^2 + 8x - 4 = x - 7$$
$$\Rightarrow \quad 2x^2 + 7x + 3 = 0$$
$$\Rightarrow \quad (2x + 1)(x + 3) = 0$$
$$\Rightarrow \quad x = -\tfrac{1}{2}, \text{ or } x = -3$$

Recall factorisation using PAFF: $P = 6, A = 7, F = 6, 1$.

This means the x-coordinate of the other point of intersection is $-\frac{1}{2}$. The corresponding y-coordinate can be found by substituting $x = -\frac{1}{2}$ into the equation of the normal. Check that this gives $y = -\frac{15}{4}$. So the normal to the curve at $(-3, -5)$ crosses the curve again at $(-\frac{1}{2}, -\frac{15}{4})$. Check this result using a graphical calculator and the TRACE facility.

The y-coordinate could also be found by substituting this value of x into the equation for the curve.

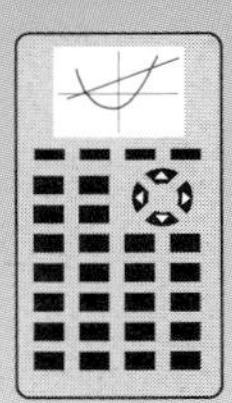

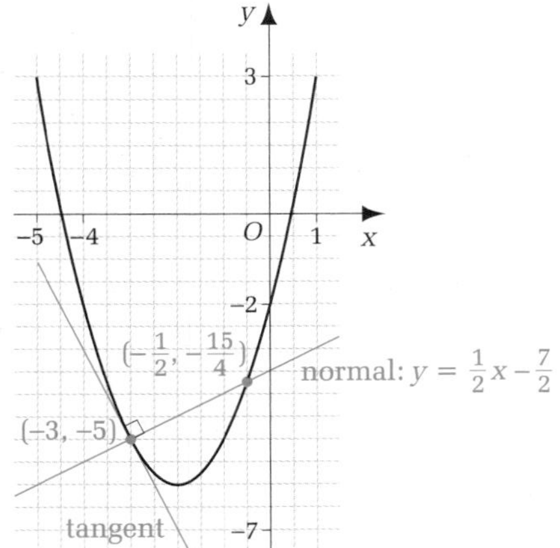

Displacement, velocity and acceleration

The branch of mathematics concerned with the study of moving objects, and in particular their displacement, velocity and acceleration, is called **kinematics**.

The **displacement** s of an object moving in a straight line is the distance it has travelled from a fixed point on the line in a specified direction. In many real-life situations, displacement can be a function of time t.

The **velocity** v of an object is the speed with which it is travelling in the specified direction. By definition, velocity is the rate at which the object's displacement is changing with respect to time. So $v = \frac{ds}{dt}$.

If displacement is measured in metres and time is measured in seconds, then the units of velocity are metres per second (written m/s or $m\,s^{-1}$).

- If $v = 0$ then the object is stationary.
- If $v > 0$ then the object is moving along the line in the specified direction.
- If $v < 0$, then the object is moving in the opposite direction.

The **acceleration** a of a moving object is the rate at which its speed in the specified direction is changing. So acceleration is the rate of change of velocity with respect to time;

$$a = \frac{dv}{dt} = \frac{d}{dt}\left(\frac{ds}{dt}\right) = \frac{d^2s}{dt^2}$$

Notice that acceleration is the first derivative of velocity, and the second derivative of displacement. If velocity is measured in $m\,s^{-1}$ then the units of acceleration are metres per second per second, or 'metres per second squared' (written m/s^2 or $m\,s^{-2}$).

- If $a = 0$ the object is moving with constant velocity (that is at constant speed in a straight line).
- If $a > 0$ the object is **accelerating**; that is its speed in the specified direction is increasing.
- If $a < 0$, then the object is **decelerating**; that is its speed in the specified direction is decreasing.

Example 3

The height h metres at time t seconds of a ball thrown vertically upwards, from a fixed point O, with initial velocity 12 $m\,s^{-1}$, is given by $h = 12t - 5t^2$.

a Find the greatest height reached by the ball.
b Find the acceleration of the ball.
c Find the height of the ball after 0.3 and 1.7 seconds.
d Find the distance travelled by the ball between these two times.
e Find the average speed of the ball during this time interval.

Solution

a Height h takes the place of displacement s in this problem.
The velocity of the ball at any time is given by

$$v = \frac{dh}{dt} = 12 - 10t \quad (\text{m s}^{-1})$$

At its maximum height, the velocity of the ball is zero.

Then $12 - 10t = 0 \Rightarrow t = 1.2$ seconds

When $t = 1.2$, $h = 12(1.2) - 5(1.2)^2 = 7.2$

So, the greatest height reached is 7.2 m.

You must always include a unit in your answer if units are given in the question.

b Acceleration, $a = \frac{dv}{dt} = \frac{d}{dt}(12 - 10t) = -10 \ (\text{m s}^{-2})$

This is the downwards acceleration due to gravity. A more accurate value would be $9.81\,\text{m s}^{-2}$.

c When $t = 0.3$, $h = 12(0.3) - 5(0.3)^2 = 3.15\,\text{m}$

When $t = 1.7$, $h = 12(1.7) - 5(1.7)^2 = 5.95\,\text{m}$

d Consider the graph of h against t.

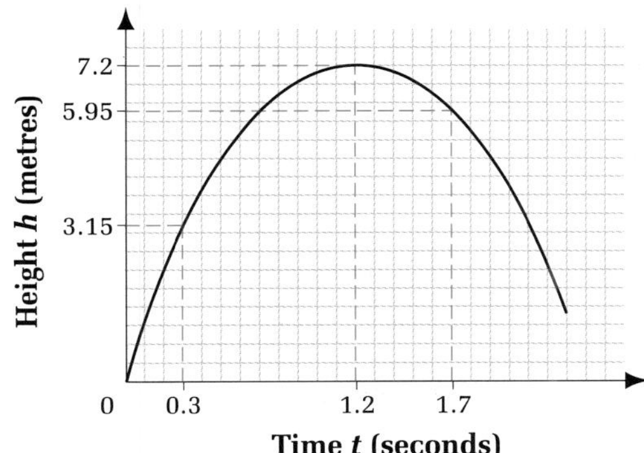

The ball reaches its greatest height and changes direction between $t = 0.3$ seconds and $t = 1.7$ seconds. The distance travelled during this time interval is the sum of the distance the ball rises and the distance the ball then falls.
Between $t = 0.3$ seconds and $t = 1.2$ seconds, the ball rises and travels $(7.2 - 3.15) = 4.05$ metres upwards.
Between $t = 1.2$ seconds and $t = 1.7$ seconds, the ball falls and travels $(7.2 - 5.95) = 1.25$ metres downwards.
So it travels a total distance of $(4.05 + 1.25) = 5.3\,\text{m}$.

e
$$\text{average speed} = \frac{\text{distance travelled}}{\text{time taken}}$$
$$= \frac{5.3\ (\text{m})}{1.4\ (\text{s})}$$
$$= 3.8\,\text{m s}^{-1}\ (1\text{ d.p.})$$

Small changes

If $y = f(x)$, then recall that by definition the gradient of its graph at any particular point is given by

$$\frac{\mathrm{d}y}{\mathrm{d}x} = \lim_{\delta x \to 0} \left(\frac{\delta y}{\delta x}\right)$$

Remember that δy is the small change in the value of the y-coordinate at this point corresponding to a small change, δx, in the x-coordinate. Provided δx is very small,

$$\frac{\delta y}{\delta x} \approx \frac{\mathrm{d}y}{\mathrm{d}x}$$

This means that the ratio $\frac{\delta y}{\delta x}$ gives a good approximation to $\frac{\mathrm{d}y}{\mathrm{d}x}$, the gradient function at that point. Remember that $\frac{\mathrm{d}y}{\mathrm{d}x}$ is the gradient of the curve $y = f(x)$ at the point from which this small change is being made. This approximation allows the change in the value of y resulting from a small change in the value of x (or vice versa) to be calculated quickly.

Example 4

The side length of a 100 cm × 100 cm × 100 cm cube is increased by 2 cm. Find the approximate increase in the cube's surface area.

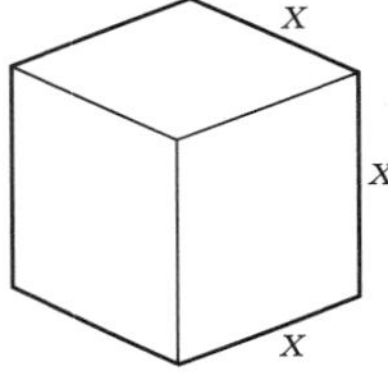

Solution

If the side length of the cube is x, then the surface area $S = 6x^2$.

$$\text{So } \frac{\mathrm{d}S}{\mathrm{d}x} = 12x.$$

Because the change in the side length, δx, is small relative to the original length,

$$\frac{\delta S}{\delta x} \approx \frac{\mathrm{d}S}{\mathrm{d}x}$$

where δS is the corresponding small change in surface area, and $\frac{\mathrm{d}S}{\mathrm{d}x}$ is the value of the gradient function when $x = 100$ cm. Therefore

$$\begin{aligned}\delta S &\approx \frac{\mathrm{d}S}{\mathrm{d}x} \times \delta x \\ &= 12x \times \delta x \\ &= 12(100) \times 2 = 2400\,\text{cm}^2\end{aligned}$$

The approximate increase in the cube's surface area is $2400\,\text{cm}^2$.

To see how accurate this approximation is put $x = 102$ cm in the equation for surface area, $S = 6x^2$. The new surface area is $62\,424\,\text{cm}^2$. The actual increase in surface area is therefore $2424\,\text{cm}^2$ the approximation is good.

The change in a measurement or quantity is often expressed as a percentage of the original value. If $y = f(x)$, then $\pm\frac{\delta x}{x} \times 100$ is the percentage increase (+) or decrease (−) in the value of x, and $\pm\frac{\delta y}{y} \times 100$ is the corresponding percentage increase (+) or decrease (−) in the value of y.

Example 5

The time period T of a simple swinging pendulum is a function of the length L of the pendulum, such that $T = 2\pi\sqrt{L/g}$, where g is a constant. Find the percentage change in the period if the pendulum is shortened by 6%.

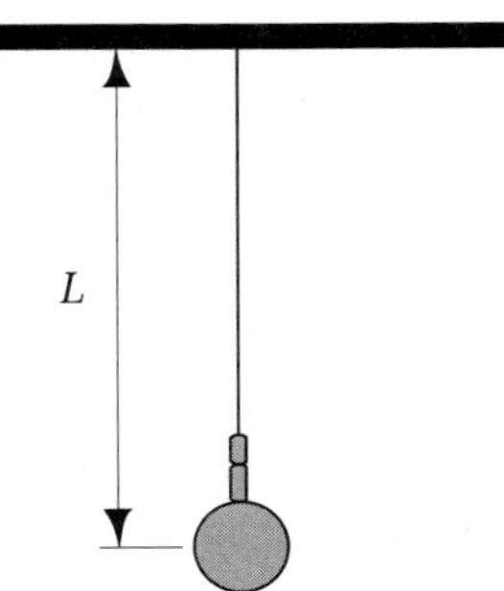

Solution

$$T = 2\pi\sqrt{\frac{L}{g}} = \frac{2\pi}{\sqrt{g}}L^{1/2}$$

So $$\frac{\mathrm{d}T}{\mathrm{d}L} = \frac{2\pi}{\sqrt{g}} \times \frac{1}{2}L^{-1/2} = \frac{\pi}{\sqrt{g}} \times \frac{1}{\sqrt{L}} = \frac{\pi}{\sqrt{gL}}$$

The percentage change in the value of L is −6%, the minus sign indicating a decrease. Therefore

$$\frac{\delta L}{L} = -0.06$$

◀ $6\% \equiv \frac{6}{100} = 0.06$

Because this is a small change

$$\frac{\delta T}{\delta L} \approx \frac{\mathrm{d}T}{\mathrm{d}L}$$

$$\Rightarrow \frac{\delta T}{\delta L} \approx \frac{\pi}{\sqrt{gL}}$$

◀ Using $\frac{\mathrm{d}T}{\mathrm{d}L} = \frac{\pi}{\sqrt{gL}}$.

$$\Rightarrow \delta T \approx \frac{\pi}{\sqrt{gL}}\delta L$$

$$\Rightarrow \frac{\delta T}{T} \approx \frac{\pi}{\sqrt{gL}}\frac{\delta L}{T}$$

$$= \frac{\pi}{\sqrt{gL}} \times \frac{1}{2\pi}\sqrt{\frac{g}{L}} \times \delta L$$

◀ Using $T = 2\pi\sqrt{\frac{L}{g}}$.

That is, $\frac{\delta T}{T} \approx \frac{1}{2} \times \frac{\delta L}{L} = \frac{1}{2} \times -0.06 = -0.03$.

This means, the percentage change in the period of the pendulum, as the length is shortened, is a decrease of 3%.

The minus sign indicates a decrease in the value of T.

5.3 Further Applications of Differentiation

Exercise

Technique

Give your answers in the form $ax + by + c = 0$.

1 Find the equations of the tangent and normal to each of the following curves at the points indicated:

a $y = x^2 - 5x + 1$ at $(6, 7)$
b $y = (2x + 1)(x - 5)$ at $(1, -12)$
c $y = x^3 - 6x^2 + 3x + 1$ at $(3, -17)$
d $y = x + \frac{3}{x}$ at $(2, 3\frac{1}{2})$
e $y = \sqrt{x}$ at $(9, 3)$
f $y = 2x - x^3$ at $(-\frac{1}{2}, -\frac{7}{8})$

2 Find the equations of the tangents to the curve $y = x^2 - 4x + 3$ at the points where it crosses the x-axis. Show that these tangents intersect at the point $(2, -2)$.

3 Show that the equation of the tangent to the curve $y = x^3 - 6x^2 + 3x + 10$ at the point where it crosses the y-axis is $y = 3x + 10$. Find the coordinates of the other point on the curve whose tangent is parallel to $y = 3x + 10$. Find the equation of this second tangent.

4 Find the equation of the normal to the curve $y = x - \frac{6}{x}$ at the point where $x = 3$. Find the coordinates of the other point where this normal intersects $y = x - \frac{6}{x}$.

Contextual

1 The height, h metres, of an object thrown vertically upwards at time t seconds after its release is given by $h = 40t - 5t^2$.

a Calculate how long it takes for the object to return to its point of projection.
b Find the value of t at which the object is momentarily stationary, and hence calculate the maximum height reached by the object.

2 The displacement, s metres, of an object from some fixed point O at time t seconds is given by $s = t^3 - 3t^2 + 4t + 5$.

a Find expressions for the velocity v and acceleration a at time t.
b Show that the object is never stationary.
c Calculate the average speed of the object during the first three seconds.

3 A closed cylinder has a base radius of 8 cm and a height of 20 cm. Calculate the small changes

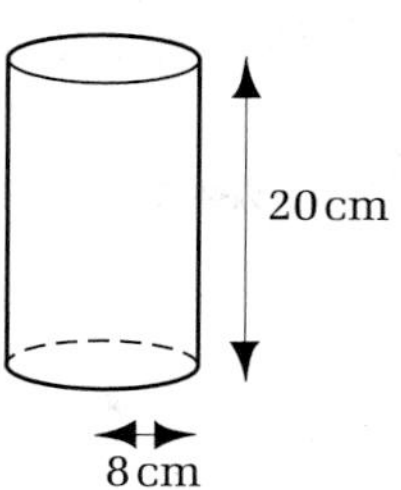

a in its volume and

b in it surface area

that result from a small change of 0.1 cm in its radius. Leave your answers in terms of π and assume height remains constant.

4 A cuboidal box has height x, length $3x$, and width $2x$. Calculate the percentage increase in the value of x if the volume is to increase by 4.5%.

5.4 The Chain Rule and Related Rates of Change

Functions such as $y = (x + 1)^3$ and $y = (2x - 3)^5$ are examples of composite functions. They are also known as 'functions of a function'. Notice that $y = (x + 1)^3$ can be written as $y = u^3$ where $u = x + 1$.

One method of finding derivatives of composite functions is to expand the brackets and then differentiate term-by-term. For example,

$$\begin{aligned} y &= (x+1)^3 \\ &= (x+1)(x+1)(x+1) \\ &= (x^2+2x+1)(x+1) \\ &= x^3+3x^2+3x+1 \end{aligned}$$

$$\begin{aligned} \text{So} \quad \frac{dy}{dx} &= 3x^2+6x+3 \\ &= 3(x^2+2x+1) \\ &= 3(x+1)^2 \end{aligned}$$

Notice that the gradi[ent] function includes th[e] bracket featured in t[he] original function, rai[sed] to a lower power.

Try finding $\frac{d}{dx}(2x - 3)^5$ in the same way. What happens when you differentiate term-by-term? Notice that the algebra gets quite complicated. Factorisation of such expressions, which we would need to do to locate stationary points, can be very tricky. This is a major disadvantage of this 'expansion and term-by-term differentiation' method.

We also need an alternative method of differentiating composite functions such as $y = (4 - x)^{-1}$ and $y = \sqrt{3x + 1}$, which cannot be expanded into a finite number of terms involving powers.

Differentiating composite functions – the chain rule

Suppose $y = f(x)$ is a composite function of x. This means that $y = f(u)$, where $u(x)$ is some intermediate function of x that can be identified in the construction of function f. Any small change in the value of x, δx, gives rise to a small change in the value of u, δu. This then gives rise to a small change in the value of y, δy. Differentiating from first principles,

$$\frac{dy}{dx} = \lim_{\delta x \to 0} \left(\frac{\delta y}{\delta x} \right)$$

but since it is possible to write

$$\frac{\delta y}{\delta x} = \frac{\delta y}{\delta u} \times \frac{\delta u}{\delta x}$$

it follows that

$$\frac{dy}{dx} = \lim_{\delta x \to 0} \left(\frac{\delta y}{\delta u} \times \frac{\delta u}{\delta x} \right)$$

However, $\delta u \to 0$ as $\delta x \to 0$, and therefore

$$\frac{dy}{dx} = \lim_{\delta u \to 0} \left(\frac{\delta y}{\delta u} \right) \times \lim_{\delta x \to 0} \left(\frac{\delta u}{\delta x} \right)$$

This gives

$$\frac{dy}{dx} = \frac{dy}{du} \times \frac{du}{dx}$$

◀ **Learn this important result.**

This method of differentiating composite functions by introducing an intermediate variable u is the **chain rule**.

Example 1

Differentiate the following with respect to x, using the chain rule.

a $y = (x + 1)^3$ **b** $y = (2x - 3)^5$

Solution

a For $y = (x + 1)^3$, let $y = u^3$, where $u = x + 1$.

Therefore $\frac{dy}{du} = 3u^2$ and $\frac{du}{dx} = 1$.

Differentiating y with respect to u and u with respect to x.

Using the chain rule

$$\frac{dy}{dx} = \frac{dy}{du} \times \frac{du}{dx} = 3u^2 \times 1 = 3u^2$$

Substituting $u = x + 1$, $\frac{dy}{dx} = 3(x + 1)^2$

b For $y = (2x - 3)^5$, let $y = u^5$ where $u = 2x - 3$.

$$\frac{dy}{du} = 5u^4 \quad \text{and} \quad \frac{du}{dx} = 2$$

Using the chain rule,

$$\frac{dy}{dx} = \frac{dy}{du} \times \frac{du}{dx} = 5u^4 \times 2 = 10u^4$$

Substituting $u = 2x - 3$, $\frac{dy}{dx} = 10(2x - 3)^4$

Example 2

Use the chain rule to find the gradient function for each of the following:

a $y = \frac{1}{4x - 5}$ **b** $y = \sqrt{3x - 1}$

Solution

a Before using the chain rule, $y = \dfrac{1}{4x - 5}$ must be written as a bracket raised to a power. In this case, $y = \dfrac{1}{4x - 5} = (4x - 5)^{-1}$.
Now let $y = u^{-1}$, where $u = 4x - 5$.

Then $\dfrac{dy}{du} = -u^{-2} = -\dfrac{1}{u^2}$ and $\dfrac{du}{dx} = 4$.

Using the chain rule,

$$\frac{dy}{dx} = \frac{dy}{du} \times \frac{du}{dx} = -\frac{1}{u^2} \times 4 = -\frac{4}{u^2}$$

Substituting $u = 4x - 5$, $\dfrac{dy}{dx} = -\dfrac{4}{(4x - 5)^2}$

b Similarly, write $y = \sqrt{3x - 1}$ as $y = (3x - 1)^{1/2}$.
Now let $y = u^{1/2}$, where $u = 3x - 1$.

Then $\dfrac{dy}{du} = \dfrac{1}{2}u^{-1/2} = \dfrac{1}{2\sqrt{u}}$ and $\dfrac{du}{dx} = 3$

Using the chain rule,

$$\frac{dy}{dx} = \frac{dy}{du} \times \frac{du}{dx} = \frac{1}{2\sqrt{u}} \times 3 = \frac{3}{2\sqrt{u}}$$

Substituting $u = 3x - 1$, $\dfrac{dy}{dx} = \dfrac{3}{2\sqrt{3x - 1}}$

When using the chain rule, the choice of the intermediate function $u(x)$ is very important. It is essential that $u(x)$ can be easily differentiated.

In general, any composite function of the form $y = [f(x)]^n$, involving some function $f(x)$ raised to a rational power n, can be differentiated using the chain rule.

Let $y = u^n$, where $u = f(x)$.

Then $\dfrac{dy}{du} = nu^{n-1}$, and $\dfrac{du}{dx} = f'(x)$.

Using the chain rule,

$$\frac{dy}{dx} = \frac{dy}{du} \times \frac{du}{dx}$$

So $\dfrac{dy}{dx} = nu^{n-1} \times f'(x)$

$$\boldsymbol{\frac{d}{dx}[f(x)]^n = n[f(x)]^{n-1} \times f'(x)}$$

Note that $n[f(x)]^{n-1}$ is the derivative of the bracket ignoring its contents, and $f'(x)$ is derivative of the contents of the bracket

Example 3

The tangent to the curve $y = \dfrac{5}{1 + x^2}$ at $x = 2$ crosses the y-axis at A and the x-axis at B.

a Find the equation of the tangent.

b Find the coordinates of points A and B.

c Show that the area of triangle OAB is $\frac{169}{40}$ square units.

Solution

a In order to find the equation of the tangent to the curve at $x = 2$, first calculate the gradient of the curve at this point.

Use the chain rule to differentiate $y = \dfrac{5}{1 + x^2}$.

Let $y = \dfrac{5}{u} = 5u^{-1}$, where $u = 1 + x^2$.

Then $\dfrac{dy}{du} = -5u^{-2}$, and $\dfrac{du}{dx} = 2x$.

Using the chain rule,

$$\frac{dy}{dx} = \frac{dy}{du} \times \frac{du}{dx} = -\frac{5}{u^2} \times 2x$$

Substituting $u = 1 + x^2$, $\dfrac{dy}{dx} = -\dfrac{10x}{(1 + x^2)^2}$

Now, when $x = 2$,

$$\frac{dy}{dx} = -\frac{10 \times 2}{(1 + 2^2)^2} = -\frac{20}{25} = -\frac{4}{5}$$

The gradient of the curve, and therefore the gradient of the tangent drawn to the curve, at $x = 2$ is $-\frac{4}{5}$.
Use $y - y_1 = m(x - x_1)$ to find the equation of the tangent.

When $x = 2$, $y = \dfrac{5}{1 + 2^2} = 1$

So $\quad y - 1 = -\dfrac{4}{5}(x - 2)$

$$y = -\frac{4}{5}x + \frac{13}{5}$$

or $5y + 4x - 13 = 0$

b At point A, where the tangent crosses the y-axis, $x = 0 \Rightarrow y = \frac{13}{5}$.
The coordinates of A are $(0, \frac{13}{5})$.

At point B, where the tangent crosses the x-axis,

$$y = 0 \Rightarrow -\frac{4}{5}x + \frac{13}{5} = 0$$

$$\Rightarrow \quad x = \frac{13}{4}$$

The coordinates of B are $(\frac{13}{4}, 0)$

c

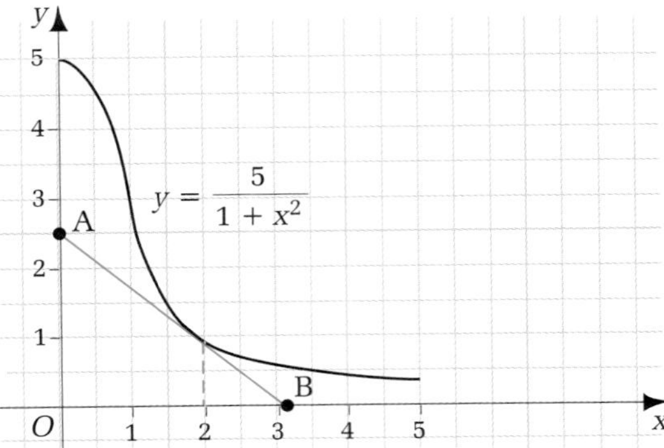

Recall that the area of a triangle is given by
area $= \frac{1}{2}$ base × perpendicular height.
So area of triangle OAB $= \frac{1}{2} \times \frac{13}{4} \times \frac{13}{5} = \frac{169}{40}$ square units.

Related rates of change

Consider how to calculate the rate at which the area of a circular oil slick, of uniform thickness, changes. Using the area of a circle, $A = \pi r^2$, the rate of change of area with respect to the slick's radius r, $\frac{dA}{dr}$ can be found by differentiation. That is, $\frac{dA}{dr} = 2\pi r$.

From aerial observation, or by more detailed mathematical modelling, it may be possible to determine the rate of change of the radius with respect to time, $\frac{dr}{dt}$.

The chain rule can now be used to link these two related rates of change together. The rate of change of the slick's area with respect to time is given by

$$\frac{dA}{dt} = \frac{dA}{dr} \times \frac{dr}{dt}$$

$$= 2\pi r \frac{dr}{dt}$$

It is important to remember that if a particular variable is increasing then its rate of change will be positive, and if it is decreasing, its rate of change will be negative.

Unless specified otherwise, the phrase 'rate of change' refers to the rate at which a variable is changing *with respect to time*.

Example 4

A metallic cube, of side length x cm, is being heated in a furnace. The side lengths are expanding at the rate of 0.1 cm s^{-1}. Find the rates at which the cube's surface area and the cube's volume are changing when $x = 10$ cm.

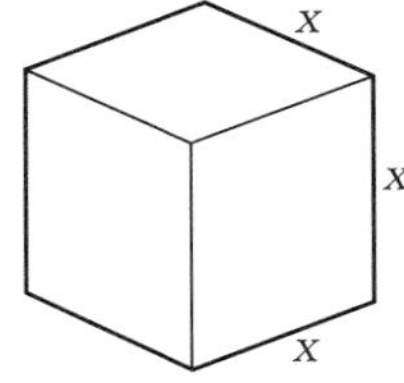

Solution

The surface area of the cube, $S = 6x^2$. Hence $\frac{dS}{dx} = 12x$.

The volume of the cube, $V = x^3$. So $\frac{dV}{dx} = 3x^2$.

Since the side lengths are expanding at the rate of 0.1 cm s^{-1},

$$\frac{dx}{dt} = 0.1$$

Using the chain rule, the rate of change of surface area,

$$\frac{dS}{dt} = \frac{dS}{dx} \times \frac{dx}{dt}$$
$$= 12x \times 0.1 = 1.2x \text{ cm}^2 \text{ s}^{-1}$$

When $x = 10$ cm, $\frac{dS}{dt} = 12 \text{ cm}^2 \text{ s}^{-1}$.

Using the chain rule, the rate of change of volume,

$$\frac{dV}{dt} = \frac{dV}{dx} \times \frac{dx}{dt}$$
$$= 3x^2 \times 0.1 = 0.3x^2 \text{ cm}^3 \text{ s}^{-1}$$

When $x = 10$ cm, $\frac{dV}{dt} = 30 \text{ cm}^3 \text{ s}^{-1}$.

Example 5

Air is being pumped into a spherical balloon at the rate of 300 cm^3 s^{-1}. Find the rate at which the surface area of the balloon is increasing when the radius is 15 cm.

Solution

The rate of change of volume, $\frac{dV}{dt} = 300 \text{ cm}^3 \text{ s}^{-1}$.
Since the surface area of a sphere is $S = 4\pi r^2$, its rate of change with respect to radius r is $\frac{dS}{dr} = 8\pi r$.
But it is not possible to link these two related rates of change together to form an expression for $\frac{dS}{dt}$, the rate at which the surface area is changing with respect to time. Instead, we must involve a third expression.

Using the chain rule,

$$\frac{dS}{dt} = \frac{dS}{dr} \times \frac{dr}{dV} \times \frac{dV}{dt}$$

Since the volume of this spherical balloon is $V = \frac{4}{3}\pi r^3$, then

$$\frac{dV}{dr} = 4\pi r^2$$

and so $\frac{dr}{dV} = \frac{1}{4\pi r^2}$

$$\frac{dr}{dV} = \frac{1}{\left(\frac{dV}{dr}\right)}$$

The rate of change of surface area is then

$$\begin{aligned}\frac{dS}{dt} &= \frac{dS}{dr} \times \frac{dr}{dV} \times \frac{dV}{dt}\\ &= 8\pi r \times \frac{1}{4\pi r^2} \times 300\\ &= \frac{600}{r}\ \text{cm}^2\ \text{s}^{-1}\end{aligned}$$

When $r = 15$ cm, $\frac{dS}{dt} = 40\ \text{cm}^2\ \text{s}^{-1}$.

Example 6

Water is emptying out of a 85 cm × 85 cm square-based cuboidal tank at the rate of 900 millilitres per second. Find, correct to 2 decimal places, the rate at which the height of the water is falling in the tank. Calculate how long it takes for the height to fall by 10 cm.

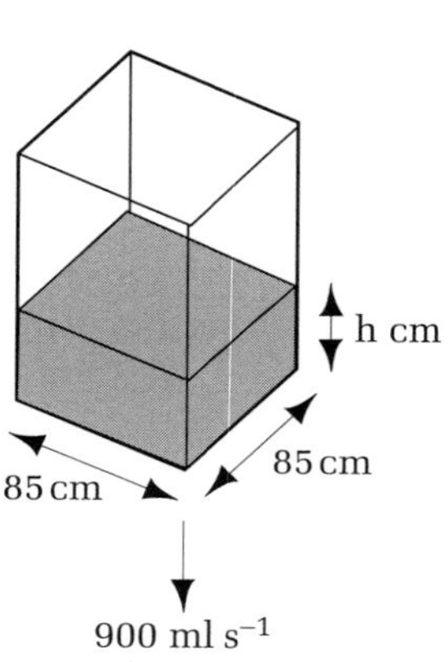

1 millilitre ≡ 1 cm³.

Solution

$$\begin{aligned}\frac{dV}{dt} &= -900\ \text{ml s}^{-1}\\ &= -900\ \text{cm}^3\ \text{s}^{-1}\end{aligned}$$

The minus sign indicates that the volume is decreasing.

The volume of the water left in the tank, when its height is h cm, is given by

$$\begin{aligned}V &= 85 \times 85 \times h\\ &= 7225h\ \text{cm}^3\end{aligned}$$

This means the rate of change of volume V with respect to height h is $\frac{dV}{dh} = 7225$.

Using the chain rule, the rate of change of height,

$$\frac{dh}{dt} = \frac{dh}{dV} \times \frac{dV}{dt}$$
$$= \frac{1}{7225} \times -900$$
$$= -0.125\ \text{cm s}^{-1} \quad (3\ \text{d.p.})$$

$$\frac{dh}{dV} = \frac{1}{\left(\frac{dV}{dh}\right)}$$

This means the height falls by approximately 0.125 cm per second.
The fall in the height of the water in the tank over a period of time can be found using

fall in height of water = fall per second × time taken

The time taken for the height of the water to fall 10 cm is given by

$$\text{time taken} = \frac{\text{fall in height of water}}{\text{fall per second}}$$
$$= \frac{10\ \text{cm}}{0.125\ \text{cm s}^{-1}}$$
$$= 80\ \text{seconds (to nearest second)}$$

5.4 The Chain Rule and Related Rates of Change

Exercise

Technique

1 Use the chain rule to find $\frac{dy}{dx}$ for each of the following:

a $y = (x+2)^4$

b $y = (3-x)^5$

c $y = (4x-5)^3$

d $y = (x^2+1)^6$

e $y = (2x^3 - x + 1)^5$

f $y = \dfrac{1}{5x+9}$

g $y = \sqrt{2x+3}$

h $y = (x^4+2)^{5/2}$

i $y = \dfrac{1}{(7-6x)^2}$

j $y = \dfrac{1}{\sqrt{25-x^2}}$

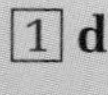

1 d

2 Use the chain rule to find the derivative of each of the following functions:

a $s(t) = (2t+5)^7$

b $h(r) = (9r-4)^{-2}$

c $v(t) = \sqrt{t^2-2}$

d $A(\theta) = \sqrt[3]{6\theta+2}$

e $P(t) = \dfrac{3}{\sqrt{1-t}}$

f $V(x) = \dfrac{12}{x^3+2x}$

g $g(s) = s + \dfrac{1}{s}$

h $l(u) = (1+\sqrt{u})^3$

3 Find the gradient of each of the following curves at the point indicated:

a $y = (x-3)^5$ at $(5, 32)$

b $y = (2x+3)^4$ at $(-1, 1)$

c $y = (13-5x)^3$ at $(3, -8)$

d $y = \dfrac{5}{3x+1}$ at $(-2, -1)$

e $y = \sqrt{4x^2+9}$ at $(2, 5)$.

3 d

4 Find the coordinates of the point(s) on each of the following curves at which the gradient has the value indicated:

a $y = (x+6)^4$ where $\dfrac{dy}{dx} = -4$

b $y = (2x-8)^3$ where $\dfrac{dy}{dx} = 24$

c $y = \sqrt{x-7}$ where $\dfrac{dy}{dx} = \dfrac{1}{6}$

5 Given that $p = s^2 + 3s - 4$ and $s = 5t+1$, find $\frac{dp}{ds}$ and $\frac{ds}{dt}$.
Hence, use the chain rule to find an expression for $\frac{dp}{dt}$ in terms of t only.

6 Given that $V = (3y-2)^4$ and $y = (1+x)^2$, use the chain rule to find an expression for $\frac{dV}{dx}$ in terms of x only.

Contextual

1 The radius of a circular oil slick is increasing at the rate of $\frac{500}{100 + r^2}$ metres per hour. Find the rates at which the slick's perimeter and area are changing when the radius is 20 metres (leave your answers in terms of π).

2 As air is pumped into a spherical balloon, the rate at which its surface area increases remains a constant $16\pi\ \text{cm}^2\ \text{s}^{-1}$.

a Find the rate at which the radius of the balloon is changing when $r = 5$ cm.

b What is the volume of air in the balloon (in litres) when the rate at which the radius is increasing has dropped to $0.1\ \text{cm}\,\text{s}^{-1}$?

Remember, 1 litre $\equiv 1000\ \text{cm}^3$

3 Find the coordinates of the stationary points on the graph of $y = x + \frac{1}{4x+6}$ and determine their nature.

4 A cylindrical metal rod, of radius r cm and length $8r$ cm, is being heated in a furnace. Its volume increases at the constant rate of $48\pi\ \text{cm}^3$ per second.

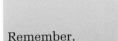

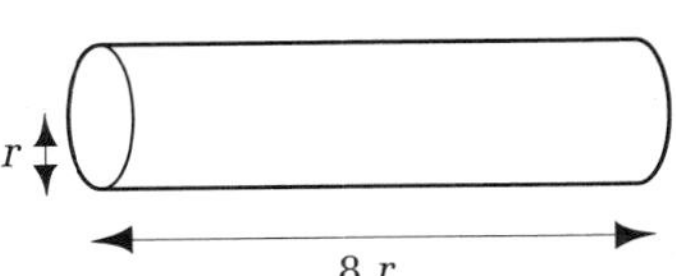

a Express the volume V in terms of r only. Hence, find $\frac{dV}{dr}$.

b Use the chain rule to calculate the rate at which the radius is increasing when $r = 5$ cm.

c Find an expression for the surface area S of the rod in terms of r. Hence, calculate the rate at which it is changing when $r = 5$ cm.

5 A right-circular cone, of height 30 cm and radius 12 cm, is filled with sand. The sand is then allowed to drain from the apex of the cone at the rate of $30\ \text{cm}^3$ per second. At any given time, it can be assumed that the remaining sand forms a right-circular cone of height h and radius r.

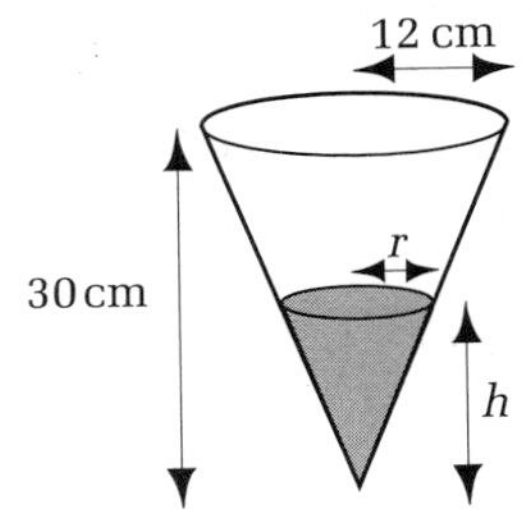

Recall that a right-circular cone is one with its apex directly above or below the centre of the circular base.

a Express the volume V of remaining sand in terms of h only. (Hint: The proportions of this particular cone are such that $h = \frac{5}{2}r$).

b Find an expression for $\frac{dV}{dh}$. Use the chain rule to calculate the rate at which the height of the remaining sand is falling when $h = 15$ cm.

c How long, to the nearest second, does it take for the initially full cone to empty?

5.5 Differentiation of Trigonometric Functions

Small angle approximations

In order to be able to differentiate the sine, cosine and tangent functions from first principles, their behaviour for *small* angles must first be established.

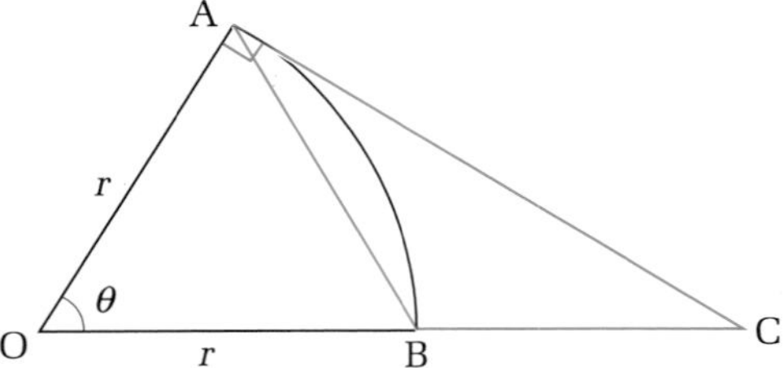

$\triangle$ OAC is right-angle[d] so $\tan\theta = \frac{AC}{OA} = \frac{AC}{r}$.

In the diagram, AB is an arc of radius r which subtends an angle θ at its centre O. The line AC is a tangent to this arc at the point A. This means that triangle OAC is right-angled at A. Since AC $= r\tan\theta$, it follows that

$$\begin{aligned}\text{area of triangle OAC} &= \tfrac{1}{2}\text{ base } \times \text{perpendicular height}\\ &= \tfrac{1}{2}r \times r\tan\theta\\ &= \tfrac{1}{2}r^2\tan\theta\end{aligned}$$

Also, area of triangle OAB $= \frac{1}{2}r^2\sin\theta$.

Recall from Chapter 3 the other formula for [the] area of a triangle, area $= \frac{1}{2}ab\sin C$.

Given that angle θ is measured in radians, area of sector OAB $= \frac{1}{2}r^2\theta$. From the diagram, notice that

Recall from Chapter 3 that sector area $= \frac{1}{2}r^2\theta$ (when θ is measured in radians).

$$\text{area of triangle OAB} < \text{ area of sector OAB} < \text{area of triangle OAC}$$

This means $\frac{1}{2}r^2\sin\theta < \frac{1}{2}r^2\theta < \frac{1}{2}r^2\tan\theta$

So $\sin\theta < \theta < \tan\theta$

Dividing this inequality throughout by $\sin\theta$ gives

$$1 < \frac{\theta}{\sin\theta} < \frac{1}{\cos\theta}$$

Recall that for small angles, $\cos\theta \approx 1$. This means that for small θ,

$$\frac{\theta}{\sin\theta} \approx 1$$

So if θ is small and measured in radians, $\sin\theta \approx \theta$.

Alternatively, dividing $\sin\theta < \theta < \tan\theta$ throughout by $\tan\theta$ gives

$$\frac{\sin\theta}{\tan\theta} < \frac{\theta}{\tan\theta} < 1$$

$$\cos\theta < \frac{\theta}{\tan\theta} < 1$$

Again, since $\cos\theta \approx 1$ for very small values of θ in radians, it follows that

$$\frac{\theta}{\tan\theta} \approx 1$$

This means that $\tan\theta \approx \theta$ for small angles measured in radians.

The behaviour of the cosine function for small angles can be established using the Pythagorean identity:

$$\sin^2\theta + \cos^2\theta = 1$$

$$\Rightarrow \quad \cos^2\theta = 1 - \sin^2\theta$$

$$\Rightarrow \quad \cos\theta = (1 - \sin^2\theta)^{\frac{1}{2}}$$

For small values of θ, $\sin\theta \approx \theta$, so

$$\cos\theta \approx (1 - \theta^2)^{\frac{1}{2}}$$

The expression $(1 - \theta^2)^{\frac{1}{2}}$ can be expanded using the binomial expansion (see Chapter 8), to give

$$\cos\theta \approx 1 - \tfrac{1}{2}\theta^2$$

In summary, the behaviour of sine, cosine and tangent functions for small angles measured in radians are:

$\mathbf{sin}\,\theta \approx \theta$

$\mathbf{cos}\,\theta \approx 1 - \frac{1}{2}\theta^2$

$\mathbf{tan}\,\theta \approx \theta$

◀ **Learn these important results.**

Differentiation of sine and cosine

The diagram shows the graphs of $y = \sin x$ and its gradient function for the interval $0 \le x \le 2\pi$. By considering the gradient of the sine curve at several values of x, it is possible to gain some insight into the nature of its gradient function.

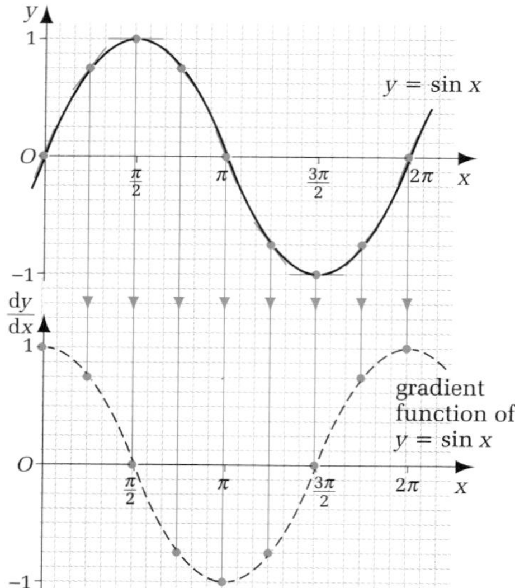

For example, at $x = \frac{\pi}{2}$ and $x = \frac{3\pi}{2}$, the gradient is zero. Between these two values, $\sin x$ is a decreasing function of x, and the gradient of the sine curve is therefore negative. The gradient is at its most negative when $x = \pi$, and this corresponds to a minimum point on the graph of the gradient function.

For $0 \leq x \leq \frac{\pi}{2}$ and $\frac{3\pi}{2} < x < 2\pi$, $\sin x$ is an increasing function of x. The sine curve has a positive gradient in these intervals. The gradient function therefore reaches a maximum at $x = 0$ and $x = 2\pi$.

What do you notice about the graph of the gradient function? The outline graph of the gradient function obtained appears to resemble the curve $y = \cos x$. Its exact nature can be found algebraically by differentiating the sine function from first principles.

Consider the chord drawn from the point P (x, y) to the point Q $(x + \delta x, y + \delta y)$ on the curve $y = \sin x$.

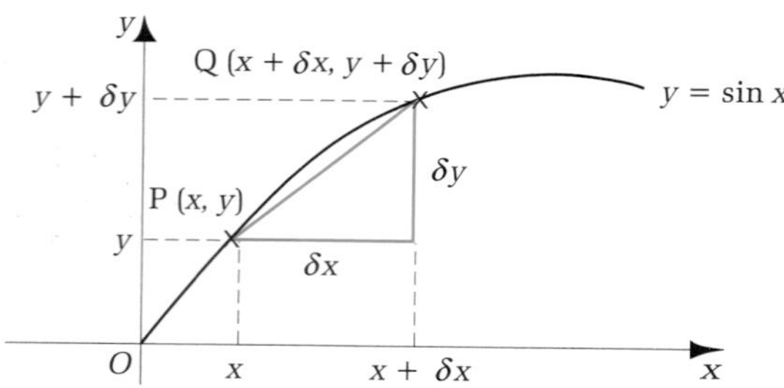

$$\text{gradient of the chord PQ} = \frac{\text{change in } y\text{-coordinate}}{\text{change in } x\text{-coordinate}} = \frac{\delta y}{\delta x}$$

$$= \frac{(y + \delta y) - y}{\delta x}$$

$$= \frac{\sin(x + \delta x) - \sin x}{\delta x}$$

Recall that if $y = \sin x$, then $y + \delta y = \sin(x + \delta x)$.

Now use the compound angle formula,

$$\sin(A+B) = \sin A\cos B + \cos A\sin B$$

to give $\sin(x+\delta x) = \sin x\cos\delta x + \cos x\sin\delta x$.
This means

$$\frac{\delta y}{\delta x} = \left(\frac{\sin x\cos\delta x + \cos x\sin\delta x - \sin x}{\delta x}\right)$$

Differentiating from first principles, the gradient function for the curve $y = \sin x$ can be found by finding the limiting value of $\frac{\delta y}{\delta x}$ as $\delta x \to 0$.

$$\begin{aligned}\frac{dy}{dx} &= \underset{\delta x\to 0}{\text{limit}}\left(\frac{\delta y}{\delta x}\right)\\ &= \underset{\delta x\to 0}{\text{limit}}\left(\frac{\sin x\cos\delta x + \cos x\sin\delta x - \sin x}{\delta x}\right)\end{aligned}$$

Now, use the small angle approximations $\sin\theta \approx \theta$ and $\cos\theta \approx 1 - \frac{1}{2}\theta^2$.

For small values of δx, $\sin\delta x \approx \delta x$ and $\cos\delta x \approx 1 - \frac{1}{2}(\delta x)^2$.

Using these approximations,

$$\begin{aligned}\frac{dy}{dx} &= \underset{\delta x\to 0}{\text{limit}}\left(\frac{[1-\frac{1}{2}(\delta x)^2]\sin x + \delta x\cos x - \sin x}{\delta x}\right)\\ &= \underset{\delta x\to 0}{\text{limit}}\left(\frac{\sin x - \frac{1}{2}(\delta x)^2\sin x + \delta x\cos x - \sin x}{\delta x}\right)\\ &= \underset{\delta x\to 0}{\text{limit}}\left(\cos x - \tfrac{1}{2}(\delta x)\sin x\right)\\ &= \cos x\end{aligned}$$

If $y = \sin x$ then $\frac{dy}{dx} = \cos x$ ◀ **Learn this result.**

Remember that this result is dependent on x being in radians.

We can also find the gradient function of the cosine function by differentiating from first principles.

If $y = \cos x$, then

$$\begin{aligned}\frac{dy}{dx} &= \underset{\delta x\to 0}{\text{limit}}\left(\frac{\delta y}{\delta x}\right)\\ &= \underset{\delta x\to 0}{\text{limit}}\left(\frac{\cos(x+\delta x) - \cos x}{\delta x}\right)\end{aligned}$$

Use the compound angle formula

$$\cos(A+B) = \cos A \cos B - \sin A \sin B$$

to give $\cos(x+\delta x) = \cos x \cos \delta x - \sin x \sin \delta x$. Then

$$\frac{dy}{dx} = \lim_{\delta x \to 0} \left(\frac{\cos x \cos \delta x - \sin x \sin \delta x - \cos x}{\delta x} \right)$$

Use the small angle approximations, $\sin \delta x \to \delta x$ and $\cos \delta x \to 1 - \frac{1}{2}(\delta x)^2$ as $\delta x \to 0$,

$$\begin{aligned}
\frac{dy}{dx} &= \lim_{\delta x \to 0} \left(\frac{[1 - \frac{1}{2}(\delta x)^2] \cos x - \delta x \sin x - \cos x}{\delta x} \right) \\
&= \lim_{\delta x \to 0} \left(\frac{\cos x - \frac{1}{2}(\delta x)^2 \cos x - \delta x \sin x - \cos x}{\delta x} \right) \\
&= \lim_{\delta x \to 0} \left(-\tfrac{1}{2}(\delta x) \cos x - \sin x \right) \\
&= -\sin x
\end{aligned}$$

If $y = \cos x$, then $\frac{dy}{dx} = -\sin x$ ◀ **Learn this result.**

It is important to note that trigonometric functions can only be differentiated if angles are measured in radians. This is because the derivation of their gradient functions from first principles relies upon small angle approximations for $\sin\theta$ and $\cos\theta$. These are only valid for angles measured in radians.

The chain rule can be used to differentiate composite functions of sine or cosine involving double or multiple angles.

Example 1

Differentiate the following with respect to x:

a $y = \sin 2x$

b $y = 4\cos 3x$

c $y = \sin(ax+b)$ where a and b are constants

d $y = \cos(x^2 + \pi)$.

Solution

a Let $y = \sin u$, where $u = 2x$.

Then $\frac{dy}{du} = \cos u$ and $\frac{du}{dx} = 2$

Using the chain rule,

$$\frac{dy}{dx} = \frac{dy}{du} \times \frac{du}{dx} = \cos u \times 2$$

Substituting $u = 2x$, $\frac{dy}{dx} = 2\cos 2x$

b Let $y = 4\cos u$, where $u = 3x$.

Then $\frac{dy}{du} = -4\sin u$ and $\frac{du}{dx} = 3$

Using the chain rule,

$$\frac{dy}{dx} = \frac{dy}{du} \times \frac{du}{dx} = -4\sin u \times 3$$

Substituting $u = 3x$, $\frac{dy}{dx} = -12\sin 3x$

c Let $y = \sin u$, where $u = ax + b$.

Then $\frac{dy}{du} = \cos u$ and $\frac{du}{dx} = a$

Using the chain rule,

$$\frac{dy}{dx} = \frac{dy}{du} \times \frac{du}{dx} = \cos u \times a$$

Substituting $u = ax + b$, $\frac{dy}{dx} = a\cos(ax + b)$

d Let $y = \cos u$, where $u = x^2 + \pi$.

Then $\frac{dy}{du} = -\sin u$ and $\frac{du}{dx} = 2x$

Using the chain rule, $\frac{dy}{dx} = \frac{dy}{du} \times \frac{du}{dx} = -\sin u \times 2x$

Substituting $u = x^2 + \pi$, $\frac{dy}{dx} = -2x\sin(x^2 + \pi)$

The chain rule can also be used to differentiate functions involving powers of sine and cosine.

Example 2

Differentiate the following with respect to θ.

a $x = \sin^2\theta$ **b** $y = \cos^3 4\theta$

Solution

a For $x = \sin^2 \theta = (\sin \theta)^2$, let $x = u^2$, where $u = \sin \theta$.

Then $\dfrac{dx}{du} = 2u$ and $\dfrac{du}{d\theta} = \cos \theta$

Using the chain rule,

$$\frac{dx}{d\theta} = \frac{dx}{du} \times \frac{du}{d\theta} = 2u \cos \theta$$

Substituting $u = \sin \theta$, $\dfrac{dx}{d\theta} = 2 \sin \theta \cos \theta = \sin 2\theta$

b For $y = \cos^3 4\theta = (\cos 4\theta)^3$, let $y = u^3$, where $u = \cos 4\theta$.

Then $\dfrac{dy}{du} = 3u^2$ and $\dfrac{du}{d\theta} = -4 \sin 4\theta$

Use the chain rule again to find $\frac{dy}{d\theta}$.

Using the chain rule,

$$\frac{dy}{d\theta} = \frac{dy}{du} \times \frac{du}{d\theta} = 3u^2 \times -4 \sin 4\theta$$

Substituting $u = \cos 4\theta$, $\dfrac{dy}{d\theta} = -12(\cos 4\theta)^2 \sin 4\theta = -12 \cos^2 4\theta \sin 4\theta$

Example 3

Find the equations of the tangent and normal to the curve $y = \cos 2x$ at the point where $x = \frac{\pi}{6}$.

Solution

If $y = \cos 2x$, then $\frac{dy}{dx} = -2 \sin 2x$

When $x = \dfrac{\pi}{6}$, $y = \cos \dfrac{\pi}{3} = \dfrac{1}{2}$ and $\dfrac{dy}{dx} = -2 \sin \dfrac{\pi}{3} = -\sqrt{3}$

So the gradient of the tangent to the curve at $x = \frac{\pi}{6}$ is $-\sqrt{3}$, and the gradient of the normal is $\frac{1}{\sqrt{3}}$.
Using $y - y_1 = m(x - x_1)$ to find the equations of the tangent and the normal at the point $(\frac{\pi}{6}, \frac{1}{2})$:

The equation of the tangent is $y - \dfrac{1}{2} = -\sqrt{3}\left(x - \dfrac{\pi}{6}\right)$

$$\Rightarrow \quad y = -\sqrt{3}x + \frac{1}{2} + \frac{\pi\sqrt{3}}{6}$$

The equation of the normal is $y - \dfrac{1}{2} = \dfrac{1}{\sqrt{3}}\left(x - \dfrac{\pi}{6}\right)$

$$\Rightarrow \quad y = \frac{x}{\sqrt{3}} + \frac{1}{2} - \frac{\pi}{6\sqrt{3}}$$

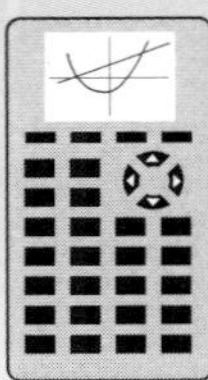

Check that your calculator is in 'radian' mode, with a 'square view'.

Use a graphical calculator to verify that they are the tangent and normal to the curve at $(\frac{\pi}{6}, \frac{1}{2})$.

Example 4

Find the coordinates of the stationary points on the graph of $y = \sin x + \cos x$ in the interval $0 \leq x \leq 2\pi$. Determine their nature. Hence sketch the graph of $y = \sin x + \cos x$.

Solution

If $y = \sin x + \cos x$, then $\frac{dy}{dx} = \cos x - \sin x$.
At stationary points on the graph, $\frac{dy}{dx} = 0$.

$$\text{So } \cos x - \sin x = 0$$
$$\Rightarrow \quad \cos x = \sin x$$
$$\Rightarrow \quad \tan x = 1$$
$$x = \tan^{-1}(1)$$

Remember that this equation has more than one solution in the interval $0 \leq x \leq 2\pi$. The solutions are $x = \frac{\pi}{4}$ and $x = \frac{5\pi}{4}$.
When $x = \frac{\pi}{4}$,

$$y = \sin\left(\frac{\pi}{4}\right) + \cos\left(\frac{\pi}{4}\right)$$
$$= \frac{1}{\sqrt{2}} + \frac{1}{\sqrt{2}}$$
$$= \frac{2}{\sqrt{2}} = \sqrt{2}$$

When $x = \frac{5\pi}{4}$,

$$y = \sin\left(\frac{5\pi}{4}\right) + \cos\left(\frac{5\pi}{4}\right)$$
$$= -\frac{1}{\sqrt{2}} - \frac{1}{\sqrt{2}}$$
$$= -\frac{2}{\sqrt{2}} = -\sqrt{2}$$

To determine the nature of the stationary points at $\left(\frac{\pi}{4}, \sqrt{2}\right)$ and $\left(\frac{5\pi}{4}, -\sqrt{2}\right)$ consider the sign of the gradient of the curve at points on each side of them.
Considering the point $\left(\frac{\pi}{4}, \sqrt{2}\right)$:

$$\text{When } x = \frac{\pi}{6}, \ \frac{dy}{dx} = \cos\left(\frac{\pi}{6}\right) - \sin\left(\frac{\pi}{6}\right) = \frac{\sqrt{3}}{2} - \frac{1}{2}$$

That is, $\frac{dy}{dx} > 0$. ◀ **The function is increasing.**

$$\text{When } x = \frac{\pi}{3}, \ \frac{dy}{dx} = \cos\left(\frac{\pi}{3}\right) - \sin\left(\frac{\pi}{3}\right) = \frac{1}{2} - \frac{\sqrt{3}}{2}$$

That is, $\frac{dy}{dx} < 0$ ◀ **The function is decreasing.**

This means $\left(\frac{\pi}{4}, \sqrt{2}\right)$ is a maximum point on the curve.

Considering the point $(\frac{5\pi}{4}, -\sqrt{2})$:

When $x = \pi$, $\dfrac{dy}{dx} = \cos\pi - \sin\pi = -1 - 0$

That is, $\dfrac{dy}{dx} < 0$. ◀ The function is decreasing.

When $x = \dfrac{3\pi}{2}$, $\dfrac{dy}{dx} = \cos\left(\dfrac{3\pi}{2}\right) - \sin\left(\dfrac{3\pi}{2}\right) = 0 - (-1)$

That is, $\dfrac{dy}{dx} > 0$. ◀ The function is increasing.

This means $(\frac{5\pi}{4}, -\sqrt{2})$ is a minimum point on the curve.

The graph crosses the x-axis when $y = \sin x + \cos x = 0$

$\Rightarrow \tan x = -1$

$\Rightarrow x = \dfrac{3\pi}{4}$ and $x = \dfrac{7\pi}{4}$ (in the stated range).

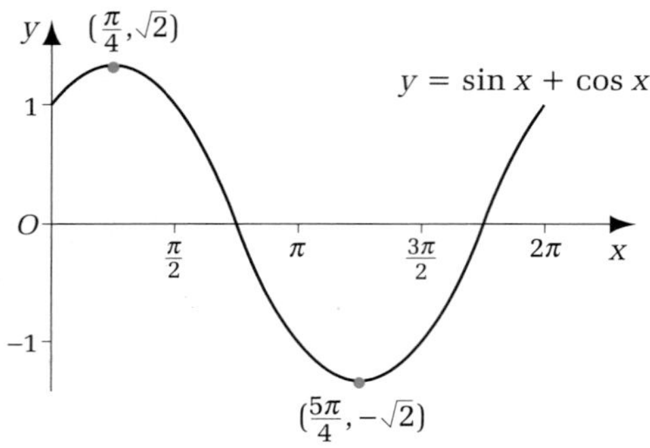

Check this result using a graphical calculator.

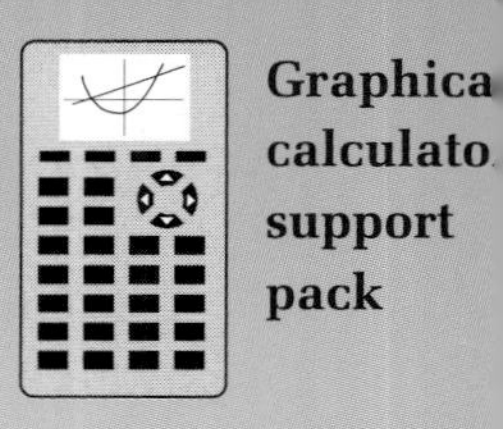

Example 5

A Ferris wheel at an amusement park, with a radius of 10 m, is centred 11 m above the ground. It completes a revolution every 20 s. The height of a particular chair on the wheel varies according to

$$h = 11 + 8\sin\left(\frac{\pi t}{10}\right) + 6\cos\left(\frac{\pi t}{10}\right).$$

Find, to the nearest second, the times during the first revolution that this chair is rising, and the times during which it is falling.

Solution

When the chair is rising, height h is an increasing function of time t. This means that we need to find the times when $\frac{dh}{dt} > 0$. When the chair is falling, h is a decreasing function of time t. This means that we need to find the times when $\frac{dh}{dt} < 0$.

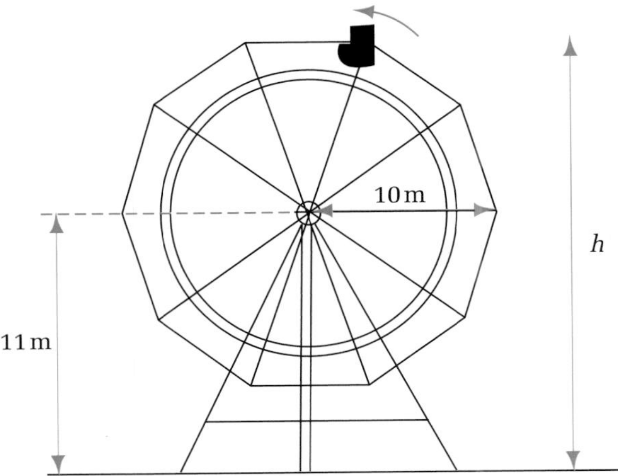

In order to decide when the chair is rising and falling, first locate and determine the nature of the stationary points on the height–time curve. Using the chain rule to differentiate the sine and cosine terms,

$$\begin{aligned}\frac{\mathrm{d}h}{\mathrm{d}t} &= 8\cos\left(\frac{\pi t}{10}\right) \times \frac{\pi}{10} - 6\sin\left(\frac{\pi t}{10}\right) \times \frac{\pi}{10} \\ &= \frac{4\pi}{5}\cos\left(\frac{\pi t}{10}\right) - \frac{3\pi}{5}\sin\left(\frac{\pi t}{10}\right)\end{aligned}$$

At stationary points on the height–time curve

$$\begin{aligned}\frac{\mathrm{d}h}{\mathrm{d}t} = 0 \Rightarrow \frac{4\pi}{5}\cos\left(\frac{\pi t}{10}\right) - \frac{3\pi}{5}\sin\left(\frac{\pi t}{10}\right) &= 0 \\ \Rightarrow \qquad \frac{4\pi}{5}\cos\left(\frac{\pi t}{10}\right) &= \frac{3\pi}{5}\sin\left(\frac{\pi t}{10}\right) \\ \Rightarrow \qquad \frac{\sin\left(\frac{\pi t}{10}\right)}{\cos\left(\frac{\pi t}{10}\right)} &= \frac{\left(\frac{4\pi}{5}\right)}{\left(\frac{3\pi}{5}\right)} \\ \Rightarrow \qquad \tan\left(\frac{\pi t}{10}\right) &= \frac{4}{3} \\ \Rightarrow \qquad \frac{\pi t}{10} &= \tan^{-1}\left(\frac{4}{3}\right)\end{aligned}$$

So $\frac{\pi t}{10} = 0.927, 4.069, 7.210, \ldots$
and $t = 2.95, 12.95, 22.95, \ldots$ (2 d.p.)
So during the first 20-second revolution, there are stationary points after 2.95 and 12.95 seconds. To find the nature of these stationary points, look at values of the gradient function on each side.

Considering the stationary point at $t = 2.95$ s:

When $t = 2$, $\frac{dh}{dt} = \frac{4\pi}{5}\cos\left(\frac{\pi}{5}\right) - \frac{3\pi}{5}\sin\left(\frac{\pi}{5}\right)$

That is, $\frac{dh}{dt} > 0$. ◀ **The function is increasing.**

When $t = 4$, $\frac{dh}{dt} = \frac{4\pi}{5}\cos\left(\frac{2\pi}{5}\right) - \frac{3\pi}{5}\sin\left(\frac{2\pi}{5}\right)$

That is, $\frac{dh}{dt} < 0$. ◀ **The function is decreasing.**

So $t = 2.95$ s is the location of a maximum point on the height–time curve.

Considering $t = 12.95$ s:

When $t = 12$, $\frac{dh}{dt} = \frac{4\pi}{5}\cos\left(\frac{6\pi}{5}\right) - \frac{3\pi}{5}\sin\left(\frac{6\pi}{5}\right)$

That is, $\frac{dh}{dt} < 0$. ◀ **The function is decreasing.**

When $t = 14$, $\frac{dh}{dt} = \frac{4\pi}{5}\cos\left(\frac{7\pi}{5}\right) - \frac{3\pi}{5}\sin\left(\frac{7\pi}{5}\right)$

That is, $\frac{dh}{dt} > 0$. ◀ **The function is increasing.**

Hence, there is a minimum point when $t = 12.95$ s. Given that the wheel is centred 11 metres above the ground, and has a radius of 10 metres, the maximum and minimum heights of the chair (at these stationary points) are 21 m and 1 m respectively.

When $t = 0$, $h = 11 + 8\sin(0) + 6\cos(0) = 17$ m. Since the wheel completes a revolution every 20 seconds, the height of the chair will be 17 metres when $t = 20$.

Use this information to sketch the height-time graph. From the graph notice that, to the nearest second, the chair is rising between 0 and 3 seconds, and between 13 and 20 seconds during its first revolution. This means it is falling between $t = 3$ and $t = 13$ seconds.

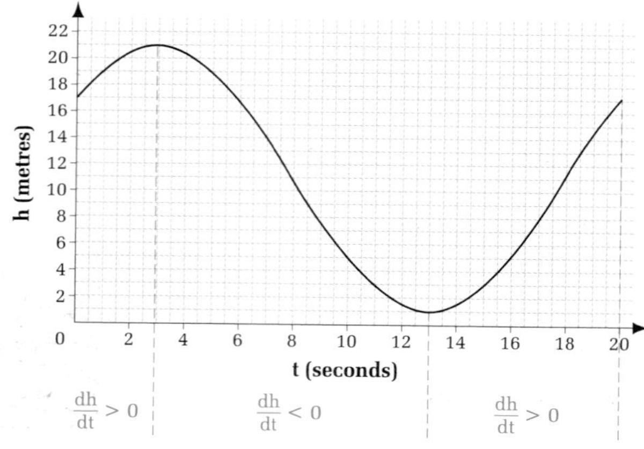

5.5 Differentiation of Trigonometric Functions

Exercise

Technique

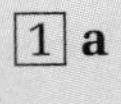

1 Differentiate each of the following with respect to x:

a $y = \cos^2 x$
b $y = \sin 4x + \sin 2x$
c $y = \cos \frac{3}{4}x$
d $y = 5 \sin 2x$
e $y = \cos(5 - x)$
f $y = \sin^3 x$
g $y = \cos^2(3x)$
h $y = \sin(x^2 + 5)$
i $y = 4 \cos^2 \frac{x}{2}$
j $y = a \sin(px) + b \cos(qx)$, where a, b, p and q are constants

2 Find the gradient of each of the following curves at the point indicated:

a $y = 3 \cos x$, where $x = \frac{\pi}{2}$
b $y = \sin^2 x$, where $x = \frac{\pi}{4}$
c $y = 6 \cos \frac{x}{2}$, where $x = 3\pi$
d $y = x^2 - \cos x$, where $x = \frac{\pi}{2}$

3 Find the coordinates of the points on each of the following curves at which the gradient has the value indicated:

a $y = 6 \sin x$, for $0 \leq x \leq 2\pi$, where $\frac{dy}{dx} = 6$
b $y = \cos^2 x$, for $0 \leq x \leq \pi$, where $\frac{dy}{dx} = 1$
c $y = 1 - 2 \cos \frac{x}{2}$, for $0 \leq x \leq 2\pi$, where $\frac{dy}{dx} = \frac{1}{2}$
d $y = \sin 2x$, for $0 \leq x \leq \pi$, where $\frac{dy}{dx} = \sqrt{2}$

4 For each of the following trigonometric functions, find an expression for $f'(x)$. Hence locate, and determine, the nature of any stationary points on the graph of $y = f(x)$ in the interval $0 \leq x \leq 2\pi$.

a $f(x) = \sin \frac{3x}{2}$ **b** $f(x) = \frac{1}{2}x - \cos x$ **c** $f(x) = 2x + \sin 2x - 5$

5 For each of the following trigonometric functions, in the interval $0 \leq x \leq 2\pi$:

i Find the coordinates of the points where the graph of $y = f(x)$ crosses the axes.
ii Find the coordinates of the stationary points on the graph, and determine their nature.
iii Sketch the graph of $y = f(x)$.
Check your results using a graphical calculator.

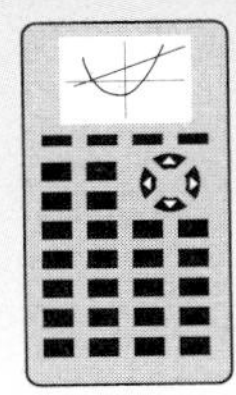

a $f(x) = \cos x - \sin x$
b $f(x) = \sin x + \sqrt{3} \cos x$
c $f(x) = 3 \sin x - \cos x$

6 Find the equations of the tangent and normal to the curve $y = 2\cos x - 3\sin x$ at the point where:

a $x = 0$ **b** $x = \pi$

Contextual

1 The hours of daylight h in York during a calendar year can be modelled by

$$h = 12 + 2.5\cos\left[\frac{2\pi(t-172)}{365}\right],$$

where t is the number of days after the start of the year. So, $t = 1$ on 1 January and $t = 365$ on 31 December (leap years are ignored).

a Find the number of hours daylight predicted by the model on 1 June and 26 August.
b Find an expression for $\frac{dh}{dt}$.
c On which days does this model predict that the summer solstice (day with the most daylight hours) and winter solstice (day with the least daylight hours) will happen?
d Find the rate at which h is either increasing or decreasing on 28 January and on 2 November.

2 An object is attached to a spring, and is oscillating such that its distance x cm below some fixed point O, t seconds after its release, is given by

$$x = 20 + 8\cos(\pi t) - 5\sin(\pi t)$$

a Find an expression for $\frac{dx}{dt}$. Hence calculate the initial velocity of the object, indicating in which direction the object is moving.
b Calculate the times at which the object is momentarily at rest during its first oscillation.
c Calculate the velocity with which the object is moving the first time it moves through the midpoint of its oscillation (again indicate the direction).

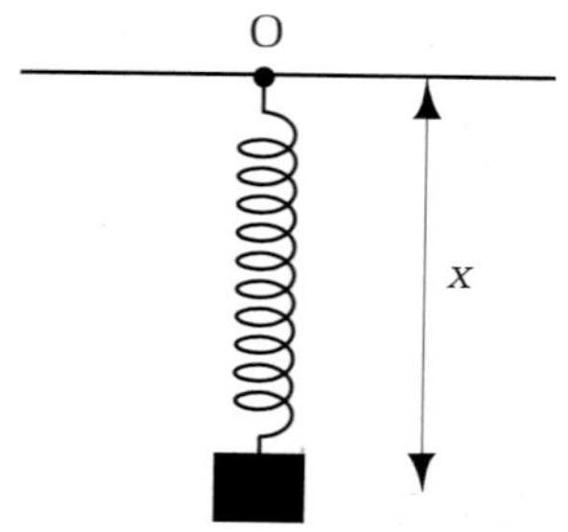

Consolidation

Exercise A

1 A curve has the equation $y = 2x^3 - 3x^2 - 36x + 120$.

- **a** Calculate the values of y when x is 3 and when x is -2.
- **b** Find $\frac{dy}{dx}$.
- **c** Use your expression for $\frac{dy}{dx}$ to find the coordinates of the two stationary points on the curve.
- **d** By considering the values of $\frac{dy}{dx}$ near the stationary points, decide which type of stationary point each is.
- **e** Sketch the curve. Deduce the range of values of h for which the equation $2x^3 - 3x^2 - 36x + 120 = h$ has three real roots.

(OCSEB)

2 A drinks machine delivers water into a cup at constant rate of $20\,\text{cm}^3\,s^{-1}$. When the height of water in the cup is h cm, the volume of water contained in the cup is $\frac{1}{30}\pi h^3\,\text{cm}^3$. Calculate the rate, in $\text{cm}\,\text{s}^{-1}$, at which the height is increasing when $h = 5$, giving your answer correct to two decimal places.

(UCLES)

3 The equation of a curve is $y = (3 - x^2)^6$. Find:

- **a** $\frac{dy}{dx}$
- **b** the equation of the normal at the point on the curve where $x = 2$.

(UCLES)

4 On its journey from station A to station B, a rapid transit train T passes a certain landmark C at noon. The train's journey from A to B may be modelled by the equation

$$x = \frac{1}{20}(24t - 9t^2 - 2t^3)$$

where x km denotes the displacement of T from C at t minutes past noon.

- **a** Find the velocity of the train at t minutes past noon.
- **b** Find the time of departure of the train from A and its time of arrival at B.
- **c** Find the distance between the stations.
- **d** Calculate the average speed of the train for the journey from A to B.
- **e** Determine the greatest speed of the train during its journey.

(WJEC)

5 A curve is defined for $0 \le x \le 2\pi$ by the equation $y = 4\cos x + 2\cos^2 x$.

a Calculate the exact value of the gradient of the curve at the point where $x = \frac{\pi}{3}$.

b Determine the equation of the tangent to the curve at the point where $x = \frac{\pi}{3}$.

(AEB)

6 The two variables x and y are related by the equation $y = 3x - \frac{4}{x}$.

a Obtain an expression for $\frac{dy}{dx}$ in terms of x.

b Hence find the approximate increase in y as x increases from 2 to $2 + p$, where p is small.

(UCLES)

7 A cylindrical biscuit tin has a close-fitting lid which overlaps the tin by 1 cm, as shown. The radii of the tin and the lid are both x cm. The tin and the lid are made from a thin sheet of metal of area $80\pi\,\text{cm}^2$ and there is no wastage. The volume of the tin is $V\,\text{cm}^3$.

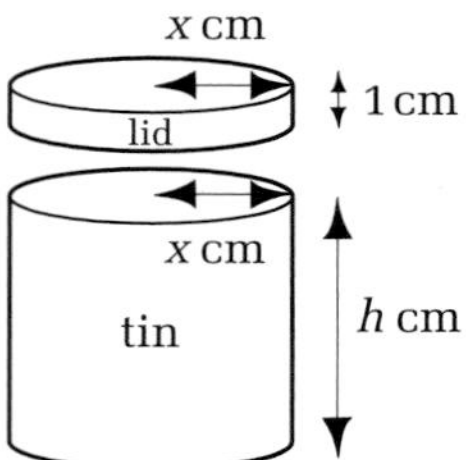

a Show that $V = \pi(40x - x^2 - x^3)$.

Given that x can vary:

b use differentiation to find the positive value of x for which V is stationary

c prove that this value of x gives a maximum value of V.

d Find the maximum value of V.

e Determine the percentage of the sheet metal used in the lid when V is a maximum.

(ULEAC)

8 A curve is defined by $y = x^3 - 6x^2 + 8$.

a Find an expression for $\frac{dy}{dx}$.

b Find the equation of the tangent at the point $(2, -8)$.

c Find the equation of the normal at the point where $x = 3$.

(MEI)

9 A train has to travel a distance of 60 km at a constant speed. When the train has a speed of $v\,\text{km}\,\text{h}^{-1}$ the running cost of the train is

$$£\left(v^2 + \frac{32\,000}{v}\right) \text{ per hour.}$$

a Find the time taken for the journey of 60 km at a constant speed of $v\,\text{km}\,\text{h}^{-1}$.

b Show that the total cost of the whole journey is £$(60v + \frac{1920\,000}{v^2})$.

c Find the speed at which the train should travel so that the cost of the journey is a minimum.

d Explain, briefly, why the total distance travelled does not affect the speed found in **c**.

(NICCEA)

10 An importer and distributor of computers has found an exclusive source of laptop micro-computers. They will cost her £250 per machine. In addition she will incur a cost of £5000 to adapt her distribution system to sell them, no matter how many machines she buys. The total cost of adapting her distribution system and buying n machines is £c.

a Express c in terms of n.

b Experience suggests that the number, n, of machines sold is related to the selling price per machine, s, by the equation $n = a + bs$, where a and b are constants. The importer has been informed by her market research department that if she fixes the selling price at £400 per machine she is likely to sell about 5500 machines, and if she fixes it at £500 this will fall to about 3500 machines. Find a and b based on the information supplied by the market research department.

c Show that the profit, £p, the importer will make from selling all these machines is given by $p = 18\,500s - 20s^2 - 3380\,000$.

d Find the selling price per machine which will maximise the importer's total profit and hence find the number of machines she should purchase and her total profit on selling all the machines.

(NEAB)

Exercise B

1 Find the equation of the tangent to the curve $y = (4x + 3)^5$ at the point $(-\frac{1}{2}, 1)$, giving your answer in the form $y = mx + c$.

(UCLES)

2 A storm has damaged an oil rig and caused a circular oil slick with a uniform thickness of 2 inches. The oil is spilling at a rate of 112 cubic feet per minute. Calculate the rate at which the radius of the oil slick is increasing when its radius is 50 feet. (The volume V of a cylinder of radius r and height h is given by $V = \pi r^2 h$.)

(WJEC)

3 A large tank in the shape of a cuboid is to be made from 54 m^2 of sheet metal. The tank has a horizontal rectangular base and no top. The height of the tank is x metres. Two of the opposite vertical faces are squares.

a Show that the volume, V m^3, of the tank is given by $V = 18x - \frac{2}{3}x^3$.

b Given that x can vary, use differentiation to find the maximum value of V.

c Justify that the value of V you have found is a maximum.

(ULEAC)

4 Prove that the equation of the tangent to the curve $y = x^3 - 3x^2 - 7$ at $P(3, -7)$ is $y = 9x - 34$. Find the coordinates of the other point on the curve at which the tangent is parallel to the tangent at P.

(MEI)

5 A particle moves in a straight line so that, t seconds after leaving a fixed point O, its displacement, s metres, is given by $s = \frac{1}{3}t^3 - 2t^2 + 3t$. Given that the particle returns to O when $t = T$, find the value of T. Using this value of T, find:

a the maximum displacement from O of the particle during the interval $0 \le t \le T$.

b the acceleration of the particle at time T seconds.

(UCLES)

6 A manufacturer wishes to make cylindrical containers to hold a dry powder. Each container has to hold $72\ \text{cm}^3$ of dry powder and has a base radius of x cm and a height of h cm.

a Write down an equation, in terms of x and h, for the volume of a container. State what assumptions you have made.

b Write down an expression, in terms of x and h, for the curved surface area of a container. Now write this expression in terms of x only.

The top is to be made of plastic and the sides and base are to be made of cardboard.

c If plastic costs 0.2 pence for $1\ \text{cm}^2$ and cardboard costs 0.1 pence for $1\ \text{cm}^2$, show that the total cost, in pence, of a container is

$$c = 0.3\pi x^2 + \frac{14.4}{x}$$

d Find the dimensions of a container so that the cost of the materials is a minimum.

(NICCEA)

7 **a** When the height of liquid in a tub is x metres the volume of liquid is $V\ \text{m}^3$, where $V = 0.05[(3x + 2)^3 - 8]$.

i Find an expression for $\frac{dV}{dx}$.

ii The liquid enters the tub at a constant rate of $0.081\ \text{m}^3\ \text{s}^{-1}$. Find the rate which the height of liquid is increasing when $V = 0.95$.

b Given that $y = \frac{8}{x^3}$ use differentiation to determine, in terms of p, where p is small, the approximate change:

i in y as x increases from 4 to $4 + p$,

ii in x as y decreases from 1 to $1 - p$.

(UCLES)

Applications and Activities

1

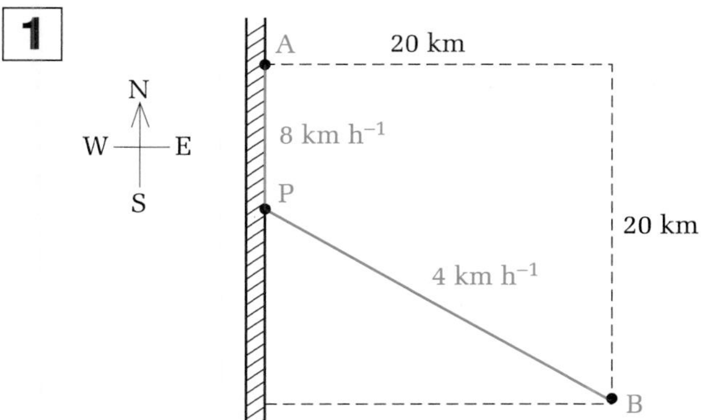

As part of a training exercise, a group of soldiers have to walk from point A to point B, which lie at opposite corners of a 20 *km* × 20 *km* square. They start off by travelling south along a track that runs along the western edge of the square. Their average speed is 8 km h^{-1}. Upon reaching some point P, they turn off the track and head directly towards B. Due to the difficult nature of the terrain they are crossing, the soldiers can only average a speed of 4 km h^{-1} inside the square.

a Find an expression for the total time taken for this two stage journey.

b Find the position of point P, that minimises the total time taken. What is this minimum time, to the nearest minute?

Summary

- The **gradient function**, or **derivative**, of $y = f(x)$ is denoted by $\frac{dy}{dx}$ or $f'(x)$.
- **Differentiation from first principles** uses

$$\frac{dy}{dx} = \lim_{\delta x \to 0} \left(\frac{f(x + \delta x) - f(x)}{\delta x} \right)$$

- 'Multiply by the power and then reduce the power by one' to differentiate powers of x.
- Differentiate the first derivative again to find the **second derivative**, the gradient of the gradient function.
- A **stationary point** is a point where $\frac{dy}{dx} = 0$.
- A **local maximum point** is a stationary point where the gradient function changes from being positive to negative.
- A **local minimum point** is a stationary point where the gradient function changes from being negative to positive.
- The gradient function on both sides of a **stationary point of inflexion** remains either positive or negative.
- Local maximum and minimum points are called **turning points**.
- If the gradient function is positive then the function is **increasing**; if it is negative the function is **decreasing**.
- The equations of the tangent and the normal to a curve $y = f(x)$ at some point (x_1, y_1) are found using $\frac{dy}{dx}$ and the result $y - y_1 = m(x - x_1)$.
- A composite function can be differentiated using the **chain rule**,

$$\frac{dy}{dx} = \frac{dy}{du} \times \frac{du}{dx}$$

- For a small change δy in the value of the y-coordinate corresponding to a small change δx in the x-coordinate,

$$\frac{\delta y}{\delta y} \approx \frac{dy}{dx}$$

- When the angle θ is small and measured in radians,

$$\sin\theta \approx \theta, \quad \cos\theta \approx 1 - \frac{\theta^2}{2}, \quad \text{and} \quad \tan\theta \approx \theta$$

- Trigonometric functions can be differentiated using

$$\frac{d}{dx}(\sin x) = \cos x \quad \text{and} \quad \frac{d}{dx}(\cos x) = -\sin x.$$

Remember that x mu be measured in radia

6 Algebra II

What you need to know

- How to use the long division algorithm (method).
- How to add and subtract proper fractions.
- How to express simple improper algebraic fractions as mixed fractions.
- The characteristics of the graphs of linear, quadratic, cubic and simple rational functions.

Review

1 Use the long division algorithm (method) to find the following, leaving any remainders as fractions:

a $4251 \div 7$ **b** $92144 \div 5$ **c** $31541 \div 12$ **d** $65235 \div 13$

2 Write each of the following in its simplest form:

a $\frac{1}{4} + \frac{1}{5}$ **b** $\frac{1}{3} + \frac{2}{9}$ **c** $\frac{3}{7} + \frac{1}{5}$ **d** $\frac{1}{4} - \frac{2}{9}$

3 Express each of the following as a mixed fraction (that is, a number and a proper algebraic fraction):

Hint: First rewrite the numerator in terms of the denominator.

a $\dfrac{x+3}{x-4}$ **b** $\dfrac{x+4}{x+1}$ **c** $\dfrac{2x+3}{x+2}$ **d** $\dfrac{4x}{1-x}$

4 Match each of the following equations to the graphs:

a $y = x^2$ **b** $y = x^3$ **c** $y = x^2 + 1$
d $y = \frac{1}{x}$ **e** $y = (x+2)^2 + 1$

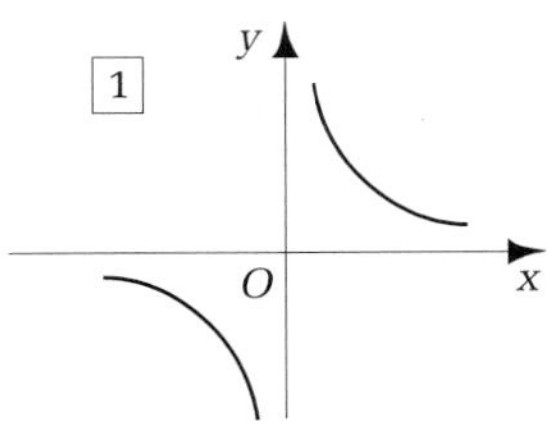

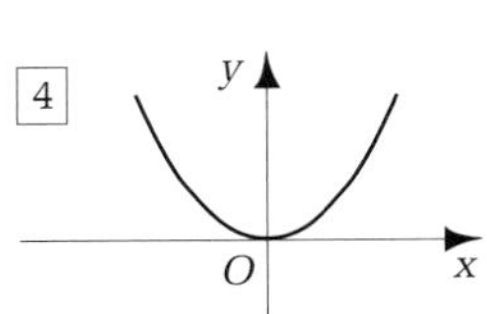

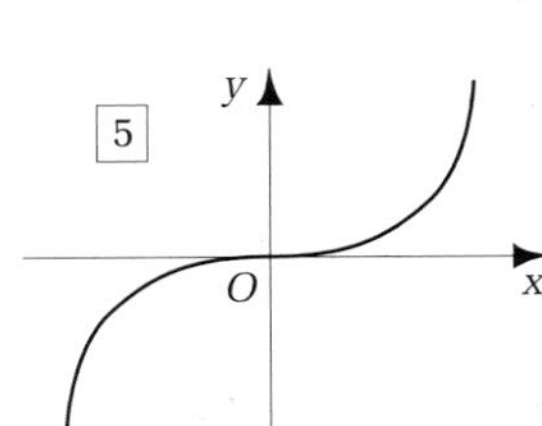

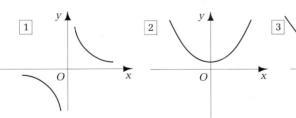

6.1 Polynomial Division

Without using a calculator work out $1452 \div 11$. There are many ways of doing this calculation but using the **long division algorithm** the solution takes the following form.

$11\overline{)1452}$ Rewrite the problem in the standard form.

$$\begin{array}{r} 1 \\ 11\overline{)1452} \end{array}$$

Find the number of 11s in 14, and subtract this result.

$$\begin{array}{r} 13 \\ 11\overline{)1452} \\ \underline{11\downarrow} \\ 35 \\ \underline{-33} \end{array}$$

Bring the next figure, 5, down to the result of the subtraction, 3. Find the number of 11s in 35 and repeat the process.

$$\begin{array}{r} 132 \\ 11\overline{)1452} \\ \underline{-11\downarrow} \\ 35 \\ \underline{-33\downarrow} \\ 22 \\ \underline{-22} \\ 0 \end{array}$$

The completed solution shows an exact answer of 132.

Use another method to check this solution.
The process for polynomial division is very similar, but instead of keeping figures in columns the powers of x are kept in columns.

Example 1

Find $\dfrac{x^3 + 4x^2 + 5x + 2}{x + 1}$.

Solution

$x + 1\overline{)x^3 + 4x^2 + 5x + 2}$

First rewrite the problem using the standard format for the long-division algorithm, as above.

$$\begin{array}{r} x^2 \qquad\qquad\quad \\ x + 1\overline{)x^3 + 4x^2 + 5x + 2} \\ \underline{-(x^3 + \ x^2)} \qquad\quad \end{array}$$

Next divide x^3 by x, and subtract the result, multiplied by $(x + 1)$, from the polynomial.

x goes into x^3 exactly x^2 times, and $x^2(x + 1) = x^3 + x^2$.

$$\begin{array}{r} x^2 + 3x \qquad \\ x + 1\overline{)x^3 + 4x^2 + 5x + 2} \\ \underline{-(x^3 + \ x^2) \quad \downarrow} \quad \\ 3x^2 + 5x \quad \end{array}$$

Notice how the powers of x are kept under each other in straight columns. Now the subtraction takes place and the next term in the polynomial, $5x$, is brought down.

$$\begin{array}{r} x^2 + 3x \phantom{{}+2} \\ x+1\overline{)x^3 + 4x^2 + 5x + 2} \\ \underline{-(x^3 + x^2)} \downarrow \phantom{{}+2} \\ 3x^2 + 5x \phantom{{}+2} \\ \underline{-(3x^2 + 3x)} \phantom{{}+2} \end{array}$$

Now repeat the process, dividing $3x^2$ by x.

x goes into $3x^2$ exactly $3x$ times, and $3x(x+1) = 3x^2 + 3x$.

$$\begin{array}{r} x^2 + 3x + 2 \\ x+1\overline{)x^3 + 4x^2 + 5x + 2} \\ \underline{-(x^3 + x^2)} \downarrow \phantom{{}+2} \\ 3x^2 + 5x \phantom{{}+2} \\ \underline{-(3x^2 + 3x)} \downarrow \\ (2x + 2) \\ \underline{-(2x + 2)} \\ 0 \end{array}$$

Repeating the process again gives the full solution.

x goes into $2x$ exactly twice, and $2(x+1) = 2x + 2$.

This means that $\dfrac{x^3 + 4x^2 + 5x + 2}{x + 1} = x^2 + 3x + 2$.

Notice that this result can be checked in several ways.

1. Show that $(x + 1)(x^2 + 3x + 2) = x^3 + 4x^2 + 5x + 2$.
2. Check that $\dfrac{x^3 + 4x^2 + 5x + 2}{x^2 + 3x + 2} = x + 1$.
3. Since the division is true for all values of x put $x = 10$ into each expression. What happens now? Notice how the polynomial division has produced $1452 \div 11$ again, with a result of 132. Try other values of x and see what happens.

You can also use your calculator to graph $y = \frac{x^3+4x^2+5x+2}{x+1}$ and $y = x^2 + 3x + 2$.

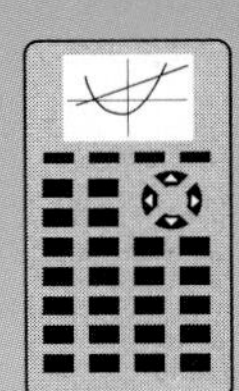

Example 2

Divide $x^3 + 4x - 2$ by $x - 1$.

Solution

Notice that the cubic polynomial has no x^2 term. This means the coefficient of x^2 in this polynomial must be zero.
$x^3 + 4x - 2$ can be re-written as $x^3 + 0x^2 + 4x - 2$
In this way the distinct columns for the powers of x are retained.

$$x-1\overline{)x^3 + 0x^2 + 4x - 2}$$

Rewrite the problem using the standard format.

$$\begin{array}{r} x^2 \phantom{{}+4x-2} \\ x-1\overline{)x^3 + 0x^2 + 4x - 2} \\ \underline{-(x^3 - x^2)} \phantom{{}+4x-2} \end{array}$$

x into x^3 goes x^2 times and $x^2(x - 1) = x^3 - x^2$

$$\begin{array}{r} x^2 + x \phantom{{}-2} \\ x-1\overline{)x^3 + 0x^2 + 4x - 2} \\ \underline{-(x^3 - x^2)} \downarrow \phantom{{}-2} \\ x^2 + 4x \phantom{{}-2} \\ \underline{-(x^2 - x)} \phantom{{}-2} \end{array}$$

Subtract. Bring down the $4x$ term. x into x^2 goes x times. $x(x - 1) = x^2 - x$

$0x^2 - (-x^2) = +x^2$

$$\begin{array}{r l}
& x^2 + x + 5 \\
x - 1 & \overline{)x^3 + 0x^2 + 4x - 2} \\
& -(x^3 - x^2) \quad \downarrow \\
& \qquad x^2 + 4x \\
& \qquad -(x^2 - x) \downarrow \\
& \qquad\qquad 5x - 2 \\
& \qquad\qquad -(5x - 5) \\
& \qquad\qquad\qquad 3
\end{array}$$

Repeat the process. Notice that the final subtraction does not give a zero result.

Since the result of the final subtraction is 3 the original division problem must have a remainder of 3.

$$\frac{x^3 + 4x - 2}{x - 1} = (x^2 + x + 5) \text{ with remainder } 3$$

which can be rewritten

$$\frac{x^3 + 4x - 2}{x - 1} = (x^2 + x + 5) + \frac{3}{x - 1}$$

Notice how the remainder term has the same divisor as the original problem.

Check this result by:

1. Multiplying $(x^2 + x + 5)$ by $(x - 1)$ and then adding the remainder of 3. The result should be $x^3 + 4x - 2$
2. Substituting $x = 10$ and showing that $1398 \div 9$ has a remainder of 3.

Example 3 demonstrates that polynomial division can create an answer with two distinct components:

- a polynomial, whose degree, or order, is less that the degree of the polynomial in the problem – this term is called the **quotient**
- an algebraic fraction, whose denominator is the divisor of the original problem and whose numerator is called the **remainder**.

So $\dfrac{x^3 + 4x - 2}{x - 1}$ has a quotient of $(x^2 + x + 5)$ and a remainder of 3.

Example 3

Find the quotient and remainder for $(4x^3 + 2x^2 - 8x + 6)$ divided by $(2x - 3)$.

Solution

These can be found by using the long division algorithm (method) for $\dfrac{4x^3 + 2x^2 - 8x + 6}{2x - 3}$.

$$
\begin{array}{r}
2x^2 + \;\; 4x + 2 \\
2x - 3 \overline{\big) 4x^3 + 2x^2 - \;\; 8x + 6} \\
\underline{4x^3 - 6x^2} \quad \downarrow \;\; \\
8x^2 - \;\; 8x \quad \\
\underline{8x^2 - 12x} \quad \downarrow \\
4x + 6 \\
\underline{4x - 6} \\
12
\end{array}
$$

Since

$$\frac{4x^3 + 2x^2 - 8x + 6}{2x - 3} = (2x^2 + 4x + 2) + \frac{12}{(2x - 3)}$$

the quotient is $(2x^2 + 4x + 2)$ and the remainder is 12.

Check this result by substituting $x = 10$ to show $4126 \div 17$ has a remainder of 12.

The remainder theorem

When a polynomial $P(x)$ is divided by a linear factor $(x - a)$ then the remainder is $P(a)$.

Learn this important result and follow the argument used in its proof.

This is a useful result if information about the remainder is needed from polynomial division.

Proof of the remainder theorem

Let $P(x)$ be a polynomial of degree n where $n \geq 2$. Then
$P(x) \equiv (x - a)Q(x) + R$, where $Q(x)$ is the quotient and R is the remainder.
This identity is true for all x, and so it is true for $x = a$.
When $x = a$, this becomes $P(a) = (a - a)Q(a) + R$.
Since $(a - a) = 0$, the remainder $R = P(a)$.

Recall that '$\equiv$' represents an identity.

Example 4

Use the remainder theorem to find the remainders when:

a $3x^2 + 2x - 5$ is divided by $x - 4$
b $x^3 - 2x^2 - 3x + 1$ is divided by $2x + 1$.

Solution

a Let $P(x) = 3x^2 + 2x - 5$.
The remainder when $P(x)$ is divided by $(x - 4)$ is $P(4)$.

$$R = P(4) = 3(4)^2 + 2(4) - 5$$
$$= 48 + 8 - 5 = 51$$

b Let $P(x) = x^3 - 2x^2 - 3x + 1$.
The remainder when $P(x)$ is divided by $(2x + 1)$ is $P(-\frac{1}{2})$.

$$R = P(-\tfrac{1}{2}) = (-\tfrac{1}{2})^3 - 2(-\tfrac{1}{2})^2 - 3(-\tfrac{1}{2}) + 1$$
$$= -\tfrac{1}{8} - \tfrac{2}{4} + \tfrac{3}{2} + 1 = \tfrac{15}{8}$$

Check these results using the long division algorithm (method).

Example 5

When $5x^2 + x - 8k$ is divided by $(x - 1)$ the remainder is 2. Find k.

Solution

Let $P(x) = 5x^2 + x - 8k$.

$$P(1) = 5 + 1 - 8k = 6 - 8k$$

But $P(1) = R$, where R is the remainder when $P(x)$ is divided by $(x - 1)$. Since $R = 2$, it follows that $6 - 8k = 2$

By the remainder theorem.

$$\Rightarrow \quad 8k = 4$$

$$\Rightarrow \quad k = \tfrac{1}{2}$$

The factor theorem

The remainder theorem can also be used to provide a useful result for analysing higher order polynomials. If the remainder from dividing the polynomial $P(x)$ by $(x - a)$ is zero, then the linear term $(x - a)$ must be a factor of the polynomial $P(x)$.

If $P(a) = 0$ then $(x - a)$ is a factor of $P(x)$.

Example 6

Factorise $x^3 + 2x^2 - 5x - 6$.

Solution

Let $P(x) = x^3 + 2x^2 - 5x - 6$, a cubic polynomial of order 3. To find the linear factors of $P(x)$, if any exist, substitute values of x until $P(x) = 0$. Adopt a trial and error approach, substituting factors of the constant term, -6, in $P(x)$.

$P(x)$ could have no factors, one linear and one quadratic or three linear factors.

$$P(1) = 1^3 + 2(1)^2 - 5(1) - 6 \neq 0$$
$$P(2) = 2^3 + 2(2)^2 - 5(2) - 6 = 8 + 8 - 10 - 6 = 0$$

Since $P(2) = 0$, $(x - 2)$ is a factor of $P(x)$.

$$P(3) = 3^3 + 2(3)^2 - 5(3) - 6 \neq 0$$
$$P(6) = 6^3 + 2(6)^2 - 5(6) - 6 \neq 0$$

$$P(-1) = (-1)^3 + 2(-1)^2 - 5(-1) - 6 = -1 + 2 + 5 - 6 = 0$$

Since $P(-1) = 0$, $(x + 1)$ is a factor of $P(x)$.

$$P(-2) = (-2)^3 + 2(-2)^2 - 5(-2) - 6 \neq 0$$
$$P(-3) = (-3)^3 + 2(-3)^2 - 5(-3) - 6 = -27 + 18 + 15 - 6 = 0$$

Since $P(-3) = 0$, $(x + 3)$ is also a factor of $P(x)$.

So $P(x) = (x - 2)(x + 1)(x + 3)$

◀ **Check that $(x - 2)(x + 1)(x + 3) = x^3 + 2x^2 - 5x - 6$.**

It may not be necessary to keep substituting values of x until all the factors have been found. Once one factor has been found the polynomial $P(x)$ can be rewritten as $P(x) = (x - a)Q(x)$, and the resulting quotient $Q(x)$ may then be easier to factorise.

Example 7

Factorise $3x^3 + 2x^2 - 19x + 6$.

Solution

Let $P(x) = 3x^3 + 2x^2 - 19x + 6$.

$$P(1) = 3(1)^3 + 2(1)^2 - 19(1) + 6 \neq 0$$

$$P(2) = 3(2)^3 + 2(2)^2 - 19(2) + 6 = 24 + 8 - 38 + 6 = 0$$

Try substituting factors of the constant term, 6, into P(x) until P(x)= 0 and a linear factor can be identified.

Since $P(2) = 0$, $(x - 2)$ is a factor of $P(x)$.

So $P(x) = (x - 2)Q(x)$

The quotient $Q(x)$ could be found by using the long division algorithm or by using a technique known as **algebraic juggling** and then equating coefficients. The juggling method uses both terms of the linear factor to find the quotient by comparing coefficients of the polynomials on each side of the equals sign as follows.

$$P(x) = (x - 2)Q(x)$$

$$\Rightarrow 3x^3 + 2x^2 - 19x + 6 = (x - 2)(ax^2 + bx + c)$$

$$= ax^3 + bx^2 + cx - 2ax^2 - 2bx - 2c$$

$$= ax^3 + (b - 2a)x^2 + (c - 2b)x - 2c$$

Comparing coefficients of x^3, $a = 3$.
Comparing coefficients of x^2, $b - (2 \times 3) = b - 6 = 2$. So $b = 8$.
Comparing constant terms, $-2c = 6$. So $c = -3$.

So $3x^3 + 2x^2 - 19x + 6 = (x - 2)(3x^2 + 8x - 3)$

Check this by expanding the RHS.

The quotient can now be factorised by using either the factor theorem again or by another appropriate method. Since $Q(x)$ is a quadratic it can be factorised using PAFF.

$$Q(x) = 3x^2 + 8x - 3$$

P: $3 \times (-3) = -9$ A: $+8$ F: $9, -1$

$$Q(x) = 3x^2 + 8x - 3 = 3x^2 + 9x - x - 3$$

$$= 3x(x + 3) - 1(x + 3)$$

$$= (x + 3)(3x - 1)$$

P is the constant term multiplied by the coefficient of x^2, A is the number of 'x's and F values add to A and multiply to P.

Having factorised $Q(x)$ the original polynomial $P(x)$ can be written in a factorised form as

$$\begin{aligned} P(x) &= 3x^3 + 2x^2 - 19x + 6 \\ &= (x-2)Q(x) \\ &= (x-2)(x+3)(3x-1) \end{aligned}$$

Writing cubic polynomials in their factorised form is particularly useful if the graph needs to be sketched or related inequalities solved.

Example 8

Sketch the graph of $y = x^3 - 2x^2 - 13x - 10$. Hence, or otherwise, state the range of values of x for which $y \geq 0$.

Solution

Use the factor theorem first to show that,
$y = x^3 - 2x^2 - 13x - 10 = (x+2)(x+1)(x-5)$.
So $y = 0$ when $x = -2, -1, 5$; the graph cuts the x-axis at $(-2, 0)$, $(-1, 0)$ and $(5, 0)$.
The graph cuts the y-axis when $x = 0$ at the point $(0, -10)$.
Given the general shape of the cubic graph and the four points through which it must pass a sketch can be made.

◀ **Check this result using a graphical calculator.**

The values of x for which $y \geq 0$ can be read from the graph; $y \geq 0$ when $-2 \leq x \leq -1$ and $x \geq 5$.

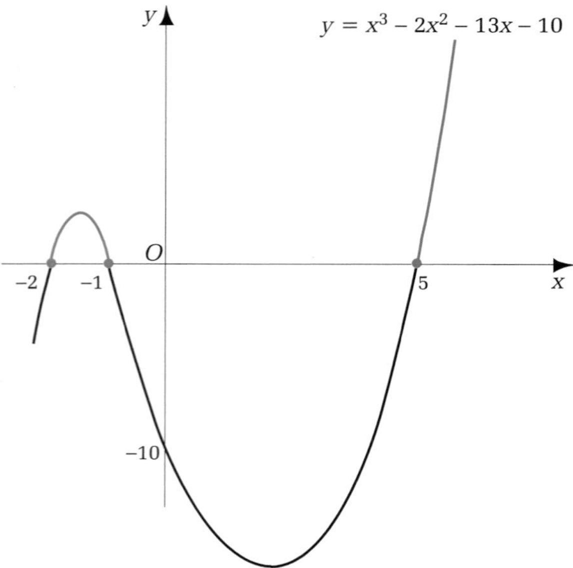

Remember that this is sketch, and the axes a not scaled accurately.

The remainder and factor theorems can also be used to find the value of unknown coefficients in a polynomial. This often creates simultaneous equations.

Example 9

The polynomial $2x^3 + ax^2 + bx + 8$ has $(x - 1)$ as a factor and gives a remainder of 50 when divided by $(x - 3)$. Find a and b.

Solution

Let $P(x) = 2x^3 + ax^2 + bx + 8$
Since $(x - 1)$ is a factor, $P(1) = 0$.

$$P(1) = 2 + a + b + 8 = 0$$

$$a + b = -10 \qquad [1]$$

When $P(x)$ is divided by $(x - 3)$ there is a remainder of 50. This means $P(3) = 50$.

$$P(3) = 2.3^3 + a.3^2 + b.3 + 8 = 50$$

$$54 + 9a + 3b + 8 = 50$$

$$9a + 3b = -12 \qquad [2]$$

Equations [1] and [2] are simultaneous equations. Using the elimination technique we can find a.

From equation [2], $\quad 9a + 3b = -12$

$3 \times$ equation [1] $\quad 3a + 3b = -30$

Subtracting, $\quad 6a = 18$

$\Rightarrow \quad a = 3$

Put $a = 3$ in equation [1] $\quad 3 + b = -10$

$\Rightarrow \quad b = -13$

So $P(x) = 2x^3 + 3x^2 - 13x + 8$, with $a = 3$ and $b = -13$.

6.1 Polynomial Division

Exercise

Technique

1 Use the long division algorithm to find:

a $\dfrac{x^3 + 3x^2 + 5x + 3}{x + 1}$　　b $\dfrac{x^3 + x^2 - x - 10}{x - 2}$

c $\dfrac{x^3 - x^2 - 9x - 6}{x + 2}$　　d $\dfrac{2x^3 - x^2 + 4x + 15}{2x + 3}$

2 Use the remainder theorem to find the remainder in the following:

2 a

a $\dfrac{x^2 + 2x - 5}{x - 2}$　　b $\dfrac{3x^2 + 2x + 2}{x + 1}$

c $\dfrac{2x^2 + 3x - 3}{2x + 1}$　　d $\dfrac{4x^2 + 2x - 1}{2x - 3}$

3 Factorise completely the following polynomials:

Hint: Use the factor theorem first.

3 b

a $x^3 - x^2 - 4x + 4$　　d $x^3 + 5x^2 - 8x - 12$

b $x^3 - 6x^2 + 11x - 6$　　e $2x^3 + 13x^2 + 22x + 8$

c $x^3 - 4x^2 - x + 4$　　f $2x^3 + 5x^2 + x - 2$

4 Solve the following inequalities:

4 e

a $x^3 - 12x^2 + 39x - 28 > 0$　　d $x^3 - x^2 - 30x \geq 0$

b $x^3 - 10x^2 + 11x + 70 < 0$　　e $x^3 + x^2 - 12x < 0$

c $x^3 - 6x^2 - 13x + 42 \leq 0$　　f $2x^3 - 7x^2 - 46x - 21 > 0$

Contextual

1 Let $f(x) = x^4 - 2x^3 - 12x^2 + 40x - 32$.

a Factorise $f(x)$ completely.　　b When is $f(x) > 0$?

2 $(x + 1)$ and $(x - 2)$ are both factors of $x^3 + ax^2 + bx - 6$. Find a, b and the third linear factor.

3 Find the coordinates of the points where $y = x^3 - 3x^2 - 16x - 12$ crosses the x-axis.

4 When $x^3 + ax^2 + bx - 1$ is divided by $(x - 2)$ and $(x + 2)$ the remainders are 27 and 3 respectively. Find a and b.

5 Solve the equation $6x^3 - 7x^2 - 9x - 2 = 0$.

Hint: First write the expression as the product of three linear factors.

6 If $f(x) = 4x^3 - 19x^2 + 19x + 6$, find the range of values of x for which $f(x) \leq 0$.

6.2 Algebraic Fractions

An algebraic fraction is a fraction that contains an algebraic term. Some examples are

$$\frac{x}{3}, \quad \frac{2}{y}, \quad \frac{3}{4x+1}, \quad \frac{6t+7}{t^2+3t-1}$$

Algebraic fractions can be combined in the same way as numerical fractions, and obey the same rules for addition, subtraction, multiplication and division.

Addition and subtraction

Find $\frac{1}{3}+\frac{2}{5}$. Check that you get a result of $\frac{11}{15}$. How did you arrive at this result? When adding fractions the first step is to find a common denominator. This is usually the least (or lowest) common multiple (LCM) of the denominators of the fractions being added. Having found a common denominator each fraction is then written in an equivalent form using this new denominator. The numerators can then be added to give the solution to the problem.

Here the LCM of 3 and 5 is 15 but 15, 30, 45, ... would serve equally well as denominators.

$$\tfrac{1}{3}+\tfrac{2}{5}=\tfrac{5}{15}+\tfrac{6}{15}=\tfrac{11}{15}$$

Common denominator of 15 – the LCM of 3 and 5. Notice the new equivalent fractions.

The same technique can be used to add and subtract algebraic fractions.

Example 1

a Find $\dfrac{2}{(x-3)}+\dfrac{3}{(x+5)}$. **b** Find $\dfrac{10}{(2x-1)}-\dfrac{5}{(x+3)}$.

Solution

a The common denominator will be $(x-3)(x+5)$. Notice that this is the LCM of $(x-3)$ and $(x+5)$.

Rewrite the fractions using the common denominator.

Expand the brackets and collect like terms.

$$\begin{aligned}\frac{2}{(x-3)}+\frac{3}{(x+5)} &= \frac{2(x+5)}{(x-3)(x+5)}+\frac{3(x-3)}{(x-3)(x+5)}\\ &= \frac{2x+10+3x-9}{(x-3)(x+5)}\\ &= \frac{5x+1}{(x-3)(x+5)}\end{aligned}$$

b The common denominator will be $(2x-1)(x+3)$.

$$\begin{aligned}\frac{10}{(2x-1)}-\frac{5}{(x+3)} &= \frac{10(x+3)-5(2x-1)}{(2x-1)(x+3)}\\ &= \frac{10x+30-10x+5}{(2x-1)(x+3)}\\ &= \frac{35}{(2x-1)(x+3)}\end{aligned}$$

Example 2

Express as a single fraction, $\dfrac{3}{(x+2)} + \dfrac{2x-1}{(x^2+4x+1)}$.

Solution

Again notice that both algebraic fractions are proper. Notice also that the quadratic expression in the denominator will not factorise. The same technique can be used, even though one of the denominators is quadratic and not linear.

The order (degree) of th[e] polynomial in the numerator is less than [the] order (degree) of the polynomial in the denominator.

$$\begin{aligned}\frac{3}{(x+2)} + \frac{2x-1}{(x^2+4x+1)} &= \frac{3(x^2+4x+1)+(2x-1)(x+2)}{(x+2)(x^2+4x+1)} \\ &= \frac{(3x^2+12x+3)+(2x^2+4x-x-2)}{(x+2)(x^2+4x+1)} \\ &= \frac{5x^2+15x+1}{(x+2)(x^2+4x+1)}\end{aligned}$$

Check this result by substituting $x = 10$.

Example 3

Express $\dfrac{3}{x+2} - \dfrac{1}{(x+2)^2}$ as a single fraction.

Solution

Notice that the term $(x+2)$ appears in both denominators and that the LCM of $(x+2)$ and $(x+2)^2$ is $(x+2)^2$. This means the common denominator will also be $(x+2)^2$.

$$\begin{aligned}\frac{3}{x+2} - \frac{1}{(x+2)^2} &= \frac{3(x+2)}{(x+2)^2} - \frac{1}{(x+2)^2} \\ &= \frac{3(x+2)-1}{(x+2)^2} \\ &= \frac{3x+6-1}{(x+2)^2} = \frac{3x+5}{(x+2)^2}\end{aligned}$$

Multiplication and division

Find $\frac{2}{3} \times \frac{6}{7}$. Check that you can get a result of $\frac{4}{7}$. How did you arrive at this result? When multiplying fractions the first step is to find if there is a common factor in the numerator and the denominator. If a common factor does exist, it can be 'cancelled down'. Then multiply the numerators and denominators separately to give the numerator and denominator of the result.

$$\frac{2}{3} \times \frac{6}{7} = \frac{2}{{}_1\cancel{3}} \times \frac{\cancel{6}^{\,2}}{7} = \frac{2 \times 2}{1 \times 7} = \frac{4}{7}$$

6 and 3 have a commo[n] factor 3, so it can be 'cancelled'.

The same technique can be used to multiply algebraic fractions.

Example 4

a Simplify $\frac{3(x+5)}{7} \times \frac{1}{6x}$.

b Express as a single fraction, $\frac{2(x+3)}{5} \times \frac{1}{(x^2-9)}$.

c Simplify $\frac{3x-12}{10} \times \frac{5x}{2x-8}$.

Solution

a $\frac{3(x+5)}{7} \times \frac{1}{6x} = \frac{{}^{1}\cancel{3}(x+5)}{7} \times \frac{1}{{}_{2}\cancel{6}x}$

$= \frac{x+5}{14x}$

The numerator and the denominator have the common factor 3.

b $\frac{2(x+3)}{5} \times \frac{1}{(x^2-9)} = \frac{2(x+3)}{5} \times \frac{1}{(x-3)(x+3)}$ ◀ **Difference of two squares.**

$= \frac{2\cancel{(x+3)}^{1}}{5} \times \frac{1}{(x-3)\cancel{(x+3)}_{1}}$

$= \frac{2}{5(x-3)}$

Factorise the quadratic expression
The common factor is $(x + 3)$.

c $\frac{3x-12}{10} \times \frac{5x}{2x-8} = \frac{3(x-4)}{10} \times \frac{5x}{2(x-4)}$

$= \frac{3\cancel{(x-4)}^{1}}{{}_{2}\cancel{10}} \times \frac{{}^{1}\cancel{5}x}{2\cancel{(x-4)}_{1}}$

$= \frac{3x}{4}$

Factorise the terms in the fractions first.

There are two common factors; $(x - 4)$ and 5.

The division of fractions can be tackled by reducing the problem to multiplication. Remember that to divide fractions, invert the second fraction and change the sign from division to multiplication. For example, $\frac{2}{3} \div \frac{7}{6} = \frac{2}{3} \times \frac{6}{7} = \frac{4}{7}$. The same technique can be applied to algebraic fractions.

Check this result using a calculator with fraction keys.

Example 5

a Simplify $\frac{5x}{3} \div \frac{11x}{6}$.

b Express as a single fraction $\frac{3x-6}{8x} \div \frac{5x^2-5x-10}{6x}$.

Solution

a $\frac{5x}{3} \div \frac{11x}{6} = \frac{5x}{3} \times \frac{6}{11x}$

$= \frac{5\cancel{x}^1}{{}_1\cancel{3}} \times \frac{\cancel{6}^2}{11\cancel{x}_1}$

$= \frac{10}{11}$

b $\frac{3x-6}{8x} \div \frac{5x^2-5x-10}{6x} = \frac{3(x-2)}{8x} \div \frac{5(x-2)(x+1)}{6x}$ ◀ **Factorising.**

$= \frac{3(x-2)}{8x} \times \frac{6x}{5(x-2)(x+1)}$

Inverting the second fraction and multiplying.

$= \frac{3\cancel{(x-2)}}{{}_4\cancel{8x}} \times \frac{{}^3\cancel{6x}}{5\cancel{(x-2)}(x+1)}$

$= \frac{9}{20(x+1)}$

6.2 Algebraic Fractions

Exercise

Technique

1 Find:

a $\dfrac{3}{x-1}+\dfrac{5}{x+2}$

b $\dfrac{4}{x-2}+\dfrac{6}{x+2}$

c $\dfrac{6}{x-2}-\dfrac{6}{x+3}$

d $\dfrac{3}{x-1}-\dfrac{2}{x+1}$

e $\dfrac{7}{x+1}-\dfrac{3}{x-1}$

f $\dfrac{1}{x+1}+\dfrac{4}{x+2}$

2 Express each of the following as single fractions:

a $\dfrac{2}{3-2x}-\dfrac{3}{2x+1}$

b $\dfrac{2}{x-1}+\dfrac{5}{4x+3}$

c $\dfrac{4}{2x+1}-\dfrac{2}{x-2}$

d $\dfrac{3}{x-2}+\dfrac{2}{7x+1}$

e $\dfrac{2}{3x-2}+\dfrac{1}{x-1}$

f $\dfrac{3}{3x-2}-\dfrac{2}{1-2x}$

3 Identify the LCM of these denominators and use it to write each of the following as a single algebraic fraction:

3 d

a $\dfrac{2x+1}{x^2+x-12}+\dfrac{2x+3}{(x+4)(x-2)}$

b $\dfrac{x}{2x^2+3x-2}-\dfrac{3}{x+1}$

c $\dfrac{1}{x+1}+\dfrac{3}{x^2+2x+1}$

d $\dfrac{3}{x^2-9}-\dfrac{2}{x-3}$

e $\dfrac{3}{x^2+x-2}-\dfrac{2}{3x-1}$

f $\dfrac{2}{3(x+2)}+\dfrac{2}{(x+2)^2}$

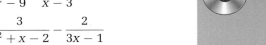

4 Express each of the following as a single fraction:

a $\dfrac{3x}{8}\times\dfrac{2}{x}$

b $\dfrac{5(x-1)}{3}\times\dfrac{2}{15x}$

c $\dfrac{3(x-7)}{6}\times\dfrac{1}{(x^2-49)}$

d $\dfrac{2x-6}{7}\times\dfrac{2x}{4(x^2-9)}$

e $\dfrac{(x+1)}{14}\times\dfrac{2}{(x^2-2x-3)}$

f $\dfrac{3}{x+2}\times\dfrac{x^2+4x+4}{6x}$

5 Simplify:

a $\dfrac{2}{5x}\div\dfrac{8}{x}$

b $\dfrac{2x}{9}\div\dfrac{8(x+1)}{3}$

c $\dfrac{x-1}{15}\div\dfrac{x^2-1}{3}$

d $\dfrac{3x-6}{2}\div\dfrac{6(x^2-4)}{x}$

e $\dfrac{x+3}{9}\div\dfrac{x^2+2x-3}{3}$

f $\dfrac{2x}{x-7}\div\dfrac{4}{x^2-8x+7}$

6.3 Partial Fractions

Two or more proper fractions can be combined to give a single fraction. For example $\frac{1}{3}+\frac{2}{5}=\frac{11}{15}$. Equally, a fraction can be expressed as a sum or difference of two or more proper fractions, known as **partial fractions**.

We can usually apply this technique to algebraic fractions, and it is sometimes quite advantageous to write an algebraic fraction as a sum or difference of simpler algebraic fractions (see Chapter 12). The key to this process lies in the factorisation of the denominator. We will consider three categories of denominators:

- linear factors in the denominator
- quadratic factors in the denominator
- repeated factors in the denominator.

Linear factors in the denominator

Look at the fraction $\dfrac{5x+1}{(x-3)(x+5)}$.

The denominator has been factorised into two linear factors, $(x-3)$ and $(x+5)$. This suggests that this algebraic fraction could be rewritten as

$$\frac{5x+1}{(x-3)(x+5)} \equiv \frac{A}{(x-3)} + \frac{B}{(x+5)},$$

where A and B are constants. Checking back to Section 6.2, Example 1**a**, you will find that $A = 2$ and $B = 3$ provide the solution.

$$\frac{5x+1}{(x-3)(x+5)} \equiv \frac{2}{(x-3)} + \frac{3}{(x+5)}$$

Two techniques can be used to find the constants that form the numerators of the partial fractions. The first uses the following steps:

Step ① Identify the linear factors in the denominator.

Step ② Write each linear factor as a new denominator with a constant term numerator.

Step ③ Add the algebraic fractions together and then equate the two numerators.

Step ④ Substitute values of x that make the coefficients of A and B zero, in turn, and solve the resulting equation.

Example 1

Write $\dfrac{5x+7}{(x+3)(x-1)}$ in partial fractions.

Solution

Notice that the denominator has been factorised into two linear factors, $(x+3)$ and $(x-1)$. This suggests that

$$\frac{5x+7}{(x+3)(x-1)} \equiv \frac{A}{(x+3)} + \frac{B}{(x-1)}$$

◀ ② **Write each linear factor as a new fraction.**

Now add together the algebraic fractions on the RHS of the identity.

Recall that RHS means right-hand side.

$$\frac{5x+7}{(x+3)(x-1)} \equiv \frac{A(x-1)+B(x+3)}{(x+3)(x-1)}$$

◀ ③ **Add the fractions.**

Since the denominators on both sides are equal it follows that the two numerators must be equivalent to each other.

So $\quad 5x+7 \equiv A(x-1)+B(x+3)$ ◀ ③ **Equate the numerators.**

This statement is true for all values of x, so A can be found by substituting values of x that reduce the coefficient of B to zero, and vice versa.

When $x = 1$, $\quad 5+7 = A(0)+B(4)$ ◀ ④ **Substitute values of x.**

$$\Rightarrow \quad 12 = 4B$$

$$\Rightarrow \quad B = 3$$

When $x = -3$, $\quad -15+7 = A(-3-1)+B(0)$

$$\Rightarrow \quad -8 = -4A$$

$$\Rightarrow \quad A = 2$$

So $\dfrac{5x+7}{(x+3)(x-1)} \equiv \dfrac{2}{(x+3)} + \dfrac{3}{(x-1)}$

Check this result by adding these two algebraic partial fractions together.

Example 2

Express $\dfrac{3}{x^2-x-2}$ in partial fractions.

Solution

The denominator of this fraction is a quadratic. Since it has not been written as a product of linear factors the first step is to factorise the denominator.
Check that $x^2-x-2 = (x+1)(x-2)$. ◀ ① **Identify the linear factors.**

So $\dfrac{3}{x^2-x-2} \equiv \dfrac{3}{(x+1)(x-2)}$

Now the denominator contains two distinct linear factors.

$$\frac{3}{(x+1)(x-2)} \equiv \frac{A}{(x+1)} + \frac{B}{(x-2)}$$

◀ ② **Use each linear factor to write down a new fraction.**

Adding together the algebraic partial fractions,

$$\frac{3}{(x+1)(x-2)} \equiv \frac{A(x-2)+B(x+1)}{(x+1)(x-2)}$$ ◀ ③ **Add the fractions.**

Equating the numerators,

$$3 \equiv A(x-2)+B(x+1)$$ ◀ ③ **Equate the numerators.**

When $x=2$, $\quad 3 = A(0)+B(3)$ ◀ ④ **Substitute values of x.**

$$\Rightarrow 3 = 3B$$

$$\Rightarrow B = 1$$

When $x=-1$, $\quad 3 = A(-1-2)+B(0)$

$$\Rightarrow 3 = -3A$$

$$\Rightarrow A = -1$$

So $\dfrac{3}{x^2-x-2} \equiv -\dfrac{1}{(x+1)} + \dfrac{1}{(x-2)}$

Check this result by combining the terms on the RHS of the equivalence.

Step ④ provides the second method of finding partial fractions. It is known as the **'cover-up' rule**. The cover-up rule uses the fact that some values of x create a zero in the denominator. From above, we have seen that these values are also the ones that allow us to calculate the required numerators in the partial fractions. By covering-up these factors the whole process can be speeded up, and can often be calculated mentally.

Example 3

Use the cover-up rule to express $\dfrac{5x+7}{(x+3)(x-1)}$ in partial fractions.

Solution

Look at the fraction $\dfrac{5x+7}{(x+3)(x-1)}$.

Notice that this is another way of tackling Example 1.

Notice that $(x+3)=0$ when $x=-3$.
Cover up $(x+3)$ and substitute $x=-3$ in the parts of the fraction you can still see.

$$\frac{5x+7}{(\quad)(x-1)} = \frac{-15+7}{-4} = \frac{-8}{-4} = 2$$

The solution 2 is found when $(x+3)$ is covered up.

Also notice that $(x-1)=0$ when $x=1$.
Cover up $(x-1)$ and substitute $x=1$ in the parts of the fraction you can still see.

$$\frac{5x+7}{(x+3)(\quad)} = \frac{5+7}{4} = \frac{12}{4} = 3$$

The solution 3 is found when $(x-1)$ is covered up.

So $\dfrac{5x+7}{(x+3)(x-1)} \equiv \dfrac{2}{(x+3)} + \dfrac{3}{(x-1)}$

Notice how the number found when 'covering-up' becomes the numerator above that 'covered' linear factor.

This means the cover-up rule can only be used with linear denominators.

Example 4

Express $\dfrac{5x^2+3x-14}{(x-2)(x-1)(x+4)}$ in partial fractions.

Solution

Notice that the denominator has three linear factors. Using the cover-up rule this can be put into partial fractions in three steps.
Covering up $(x-2)$ and substituting $x=2$,

$$\frac{5x^2+3x-14}{(\quad)(x-1)(x+1)} = \frac{20+6-14}{1\times 3} = \frac{12}{3} = 4$$

Covering up $(x-1)$ and substituting $x=1$,

$$\frac{5x^2+3x-14}{(x-2)(\quad)(x+1)} = \frac{5+3-14}{-1\times 2} = \frac{-6}{-2} = 3$$

Covering up $(x+1)$ and substituting $x=-1$,

$$\frac{5x^2+3x-14}{(x-2)(x-1)(\quad)} = \frac{5-3-14}{-3\times -2} = \frac{-12}{6} = -2$$

So $\dfrac{5x^2+3x-14}{(x-2)(x-1)(x+4)} \equiv \dfrac{4}{(x-2)} + \dfrac{3}{(x-1)} - \dfrac{2}{(x+1)}$

Check this result by adding the algebraic fractions.

Quadratic factors in the denominators

Some algebraic fractions have denominators that contain a quadratic factor that doesn't factorise; for example, $\dfrac{3x^2+5x+6}{(x+1)(x^2+3)}$.

Notice that the denominator has a linear factor $(x+1)$, and a quadratic factor (x^2+3), which doesn't factorise.
What happens when fractions of this type are written in partial fractions?
The linear factor has a constant numerator, A, and the quadratic factor has a linear numerator of the form $(Bx+C)$.

Example 5

Express $\dfrac{3x^2+5x+6}{(x+1)(x^2+3)}$ in partial fractions.

Solution

This fraction can be written as the sum of two distinct fractions; one with $(x + 1)$ as its denominator and the other with $(x^2 + 3)$ as its denominator. The latter fraction has a linear numerator.

$$\frac{3x^2 + 5x + 6}{(x + 1)(x^2 + 3)} \equiv \frac{A}{(x + 1)} + \frac{Bx + C}{(x^2 + 3)}$$

Now add together the algebraic fractions on the RHS.

$$\frac{3x^2 + 5x + 6}{(x + 1)(x^2 + 3)} \equiv \frac{A(x^2 + 3) + (Bx + C)(x + 1)}{(x + 1)(x^2 + 3)}$$

Since the denominators on both sides are equal the two numerators must be equivalent.

$$3x^2 + 5x + 6 \equiv A(x^2 + 3) + (Bx + C)(x + 1)$$

A, B and C can now be found from a combination of:

- substituting suitable values of x
- equating coefficients of powers of x.

Let $x = -1$

Then $3(-1)^2 + 5(-1) + 6 = A[(-1)^2 + 3] + (-B + C)(0)$

$\Rightarrow \quad 3 - 5 + 6 = 4A + 0$

$\Rightarrow \quad 4 = 4A$

$\Rightarrow \quad A = 1$

Then $x + 1 = 0$, and we eliminate the term $(Bx + C)$.

Let $x = 0$

Then $3(0)^2 + 5(0) + 6 = A(0^2 + 3) + C(0 + 1)$

$\Rightarrow \quad 6 = 3A + C$

This eliminates the term Bx.

Substituting $A = 1$, $6 = 3 + C$

$\Rightarrow \quad C = 3$

Returning to the equivalence between the numerators,

$$\begin{aligned} 3x^2 + 5x + 6 &\equiv A(x^2 + 3) + (Bx + C)(x + 1) \\ &= Ax^2 + 3A + Bx^2 + Bx + Cx + C \\ &= (A + B)x^2 + (B + C)x + (3A + C) \end{aligned}$$

Equating the coefficients of the different powers of x:

$$x^2: \quad 3 = A + B \qquad [1]$$

$$x: \quad 5 = B + C \qquad [2]$$

$$\text{constant terms:} \quad 6 = 3A + C \qquad [3]$$

We know that $A = 1$ and $C = 3$, so the value of B can be established from equation [1] and checked in equation [2], or vice versa.
From [1], $3 = 1 + B \Rightarrow B = 2$
In [2], $5 = B + C = 2 + 3 = 5$
Having found $A = 1$, $B = 2$ and $C = 3$, the original fraction can be rewritten in terms of partial fractions as:

$$\frac{3x^2 + 5x + 6}{(x+1)(x^2+3)} \equiv \frac{1}{(x+1)} + \frac{2x+3}{(x^2+3)}$$

Check this result by:
(i) adding the two algebraic fractions;
(ii) substituting $x = 10$.

Example 6

Express $\dfrac{3x^2 + 2x + 3}{(x+1)(x^2+3)}$ in partial fractions.

Solution

$$\frac{3x^2 + 2x + 3}{(x+1)(x^2+3)} \equiv \frac{A}{(x+1)} + \frac{Bx + C}{(x^2+3)}$$

$$\equiv \frac{A(x^2+3) + (Bx+C)(x+1)}{(x+1)(x^2+3)}$$

Equating the numerators,

$$3x^2 + 2x + 3 \equiv A(x^2 + 3) + (Bx + C)(x + 1)$$

When $x = -1$, ◀ **Substitute suitable values of x.**

So $(x + 1) = 0$ and we eliminate the term $(Bx + C)$.

$$3(-1)^2 + 2(-1) + 3 = A[(-1)^2 + 3]$$

$$\Rightarrow 3 - 2 + 3 = 4A$$

$$\Rightarrow 4 = 4A$$

$$\Rightarrow A = 1$$

When $x = 0$,

This eliminates the term Bx.

$$3(0)^2 + 2(0) + 3 = A(0^2 + 3) + C(0 + 1)$$

$$\Rightarrow 3 = 3A + C$$ ◀ **From above working, $A = 1$.**

$$\Rightarrow 3 = 3 + C$$

$$\Rightarrow C = 0$$

Equating the coefficients of the powers of x:

$$x^2: \quad 3 = A + B \qquad [1]$$

$$x: \quad 2 = B + C \qquad [2]$$

$$\text{constants:} \quad 3 = 3A + C \qquad [3]$$

We know $A = 1$ and $C = 0$, so equation [1] or [2] can be used to find B. From [1],

$$3 = A + B$$

$$3 = 1 + B$$

$$B = 2$$

◀ **Check using equation [2].**

So $\dfrac{3x^2 + 2x + 3}{(x+1)(x^2+3)} = \dfrac{1}{(x+1)} + \dfrac{2x}{(x^2+3)}$.

◀ **Check this result.**

Repeated factors in the denominator

Some algebraic fractions have denominators that contain repeated factors; for example, $\dfrac{3x+5}{(x+2)^2}$ and $\dfrac{5x+15}{(x-1)(x+4)^2}$.

What happens when fractions of this type are written in partial fractions?

Example 7

Express $\dfrac{3x+5}{(x+2)^2}$ in partial fractions.

Solution

$$\frac{3x+5}{(x+2)^2} \equiv \frac{A}{(x+2)} + \frac{B}{(x+2)^2}$$

Notice that the partial fractions have denominators $(x+2)$ and $(x+2)^2$. The two numerators are assumed to be constants. Adding the algebraic fractions gives

$$\frac{3x+5}{(x+2)^2} \equiv \frac{A(x+2)+B}{(x+2)^2}$$

The two numerators can now be equated since the denominators of these two fractions are equivalent.

$$3x + 5 \equiv A(x+2) + B$$

Since this statement is true for all values of x substitutions can be made.

Alternatively, equate coefficients of x and th[e] constants.

x: $3 = A$

constants: $5 = 2A + B$ [

Check that this gives th[e] same solution.

When $x = -2$, $3(-2) + 5 = B$

$\Rightarrow \quad -6 + 5 = B$

$B = -1$

When $x = 0$, $3(0) + 5 = A(0 + 2) + B$

$\Rightarrow \quad 5 = 2A + B$

$5 = 2A - 1$

$2A = 6$

$A = 3$

So $$\frac{3x + 5}{(x + 2)^2} \equiv \frac{3}{(x + 2)} + \frac{-1}{(x + 2)^2} \equiv \frac{3}{(x + 2)} - \frac{1}{(x + 2)^2}$$

Check this by:
(i) adding together the algebraic fractions;
(ii) putting $x = 10$.

Example 8

Express $\dfrac{5x + 15}{(x - 1)(x + 4)^2}$ in partial fractions.

Solution

Notice that the denominator has a linear factor $(x - 1)$ and a repeated factor $(x + 4)$. This means the fraction will split into three partial fractions, with denominators $(x - 1)$, $(x + 4)$ and $(x + 4)^2$.

$$\frac{5x + 15}{(x - 1)(x + 4)^2} \equiv \frac{A}{(x - 1)} + \frac{B}{(x + 4)} + \frac{C}{(x + 4)^2}$$

Adding together the algebraic fractions with a common denominator of $(x - 1)(x + 4)^2$,

$$\frac{5x + 15}{(x - 1)(x + 4)^2} \equiv \frac{A(x + 4)^2 + B(x - 1)(x + 4) + C(x - 1)}{(x - 1)(x + 4)^2}$$

Equating the numerators,

$$5x + 15 \equiv A(x + 4)^2 + B(x - 1)(x + 4) + C(x - 1)$$

When $x = 1$, $5(1) + 15 = A(1 + 4)^2$ ◀ **Substitute suitable values of x.**

$\Rightarrow \quad 5 + 15 = 25A$

$\Rightarrow \quad A = \dfrac{20}{25}$

$\Rightarrow \quad A = \dfrac{4}{5}$

When $x = -4$, $5(-4) + 15 = C(-4 - 1)$

$\Rightarrow \quad -20 + 15 = -5C$

$\Rightarrow \quad -5 = -5C$

$\Rightarrow \quad C = 1$

To determine B, either substitute another value of x or equate coefficients of some power of x. Equating coefficients is usually the quicker method. So, equating coefficients of x^2,

$$x^2: \quad 0 = A + B$$

Try equating coefficients of x or constant terms and check whether you get the same result.

We know $A = \frac{4}{5}$, so $B = -\frac{4}{5}$.

$$\text{So} \quad \frac{5x+15}{(x-1)(x+4)^2} \equiv \frac{\frac{4}{5}}{(x-1)} - \frac{\frac{4}{5}}{(x+4)} + \frac{1}{(x+4)^2}$$

$$\equiv \frac{4}{5(x-1)} - \frac{4}{5(x+4)} + \frac{1}{(x+4)^2}$$

Check this result by adding the algebraic fractions.

Improper fractions

These techniques can be extended to improper algebraic fractions. Remember that fractions are improper when the numerator is of a degree equal to, or higher than, the denominator. In these cases polynomial long division must be used first.

Example 9

Write the improper fraction $\dfrac{5x^3+15}{(x-2)(x+3)}$ in partial fractions.

Solution

Notice that the numerator is a polynomial of degree 3 and the denominator is a quadratic in factorised form; the fraction is improper.

$$(x-2)(x+3) = x^2 + x - 6$$

Now rewrite the problem in the usual long division format. The long division algorithm gives

Remember to include $0x^2$ and $0x$ to retain the column structure.

$$\begin{array}{r@{}l} & 5x - 5 \\ x^2+x-6 \,\big) & 5x^3 + 0x^2 + 0x + 15 \\ & \underline{5x^3 + 5x^2 - 30x} \quad \downarrow \\ & -5x^2 + 30x + 15 \\ & \underline{-5x^2 - 5x + 30} \\ & 35x - 15 \end{array}$$

$$\text{So} \quad \frac{5x^3+15}{(x-2)(x+3)} = 5x - 5 + \frac{35x-15}{(x-2)(x+3)}$$

The quotient is $(5x-5)$ and the remainder is $35x-15$.

We can now write the proper algebraic fraction in terms of partial fractions, in the same way as before.

$$\frac{35x-15}{(x-2)(x+3)} \equiv \frac{A}{(x-2)} + \frac{B}{(x+3)}$$

Since the denominators are all linear we can use the cover-up rule. Covering up $(x - 2)$ and putting $x = 2$,

$$\frac{35x - 15}{(\quad)(x + 3)} = \frac{70 - 15}{5} = 11$$

Covering up $(x + 3)$ and putting $x = -3$,

$$\frac{35x - 15}{(x - 2)(\quad)} = \frac{-105 - 15}{-5} = 24$$

So $A = 11$ and $B = 24$.

So $\dfrac{5x^3 + 15}{(x - 2)(x + 3)} \equiv 5x - 5 + \dfrac{11}{(x - 2)} + \dfrac{24}{(x + 3)}$

Check this result by substitution, using $x = 10$.

The partial fractions techniques can be summarised as follows:

Factors of the denominator	**Example**	**Partial fractions**
Linear	$\frac{5x+7}{(x+3)(x-1)}$	$\frac{A}{x+3} + \frac{B}{x-1}$
	$\frac{2x-3}{(x+4)(x+1)(x-5)}$	$\frac{A}{x+4} + \frac{B}{x+1} + \frac{C}{x-5}$
Quadratic that does not factorise	$\frac{3x^2+5x+6}{(x+1)(x^2+3)}$	$\frac{A}{x+1} + \frac{Bx+C}{x^2+3}$
Repeated	$\frac{5x+15}{(x-1)(x+4)^2}$	$\frac{A}{x-1} + \frac{B}{x+4} + \frac{C}{(x+4)^2}$

A useful rule to remember is that the number of constants $(A, B, C, \ldots)$ needed when first writing down the partial fractions is equal to the order of the denominator of the original proper fraction. For example, $(x - 1)(x + 4)^2$ is of order 3, so three constants, A, B and C, are needed.

6.3 Partial Fractions
Exercise
Technique

1 Express the following in partial fractions (denominators with linear factors):

a $\dfrac{6}{(x-5)(x+1)}$

b $\dfrac{2x}{(x-1)(x+3)}$

c $\dfrac{5x+29}{(x-4)(x+3)}$

d $\dfrac{2(3x+5)}{(x-1)(x+3)}$

e $\dfrac{7x-12}{x^2-3x+2}$

f $\dfrac{5x-17}{x^2-7x+12}$

1 b

2 Express the following in partial fractions (denominators with quadratic factors):

a $\dfrac{3x^2-2x+7}{(x-2)(x^2+1)}$

b $\dfrac{5x^2-2x+15}{x(x^2+3)}$

c $\dfrac{2(x^2+2x-4)}{(x-3)(x^2+2)}$

d $\dfrac{4x^2+5x+9}{(x+1)(x^2+x+4)}$

e $\dfrac{3x^2+20x+3}{(x-2)(x^2+3x+1)}$

f $\dfrac{3x^2+5x+14}{(x+1)(x^2+x+4)}$

2 b

3 Express the following in partial fractions (denominators with a repeated factor):

a $\dfrac{x+2}{(x+4)^2}$

b $\dfrac{x+1}{(x-2)^2}$

c $\dfrac{2x+5}{(x+5)^2}$

d $\dfrac{2(2x+3)}{(x+3)^2}$

e $\dfrac{4x-1}{(x-1)^3}$

f $\dfrac{18x-9}{(x+2)(x-1)^2}$

3 f

4 Express these improper algebraic fractions as partial fractions:

a $\dfrac{2x^3-x^2-18x-22}{(x-4)(x+2)}$

b $\dfrac{5x^3+15}{(x-2)(x+3)}$

c $\dfrac{3x^3+12}{(x-1)(x^2+2)}$

d $\dfrac{10x^3+20}{(x-3)(x^2+1)}$

e $\dfrac{x^3-4x}{(x-2)(x+1)^2}$

f $\dfrac{2x^3+4x^2+5x-5}{(x+1)^2}$

5 Express the following in partial fractions:

a $\dfrac{3x^2+2x-41}{(x+1)(x-3)(x-4)}$

b $\dfrac{8x^2-34x+32}{(x-3)(x-2)(x-1)}$

c $\dfrac{4x^2+16x-60}{(x+1)(x^2-25)}$

d $\dfrac{3x^2+5x+6}{(x+1)(x^2+3)}$

e $\dfrac{x^2+11x+4}{(x-1)(x+1)^2}$

f $\dfrac{4x^2+x-2}{(x-2)(x^2+x+2)}$

6.4 Curve Sketching

'Curve-sketching' means producing an outline graph that shows the general behaviour of a function or polynomial. It is not necessary to draw a table of values and plot points accurately. The sketch should show the main features.

Step ① Find where the graph crosses or intercepts the axes.
Step ② Identify any stationary points (local maxima, minima or stationary points of inflexion).
Step ③ Find out what happens for large positive and negative values of the variable (the behaviour as x tends to $+\infty$ and $-\infty$).
Step ④ Identify any values for which the function is undefined (or discontinuous).

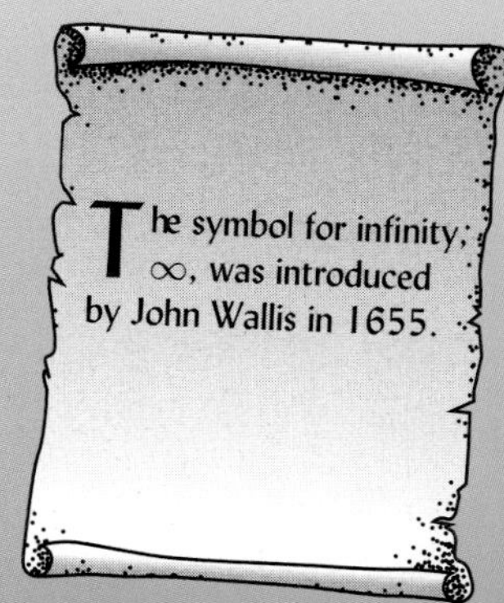

The symbol for infinity, ∞, was introduced by John Wallis in 1655.

Example 1

Sketch the curve $y = 2x^2 + 8x + 6$.

Solution

The main features of this curve are identified separately and then a sketch is produced combining them all.

- The graph crosses the y-axis when $x = 0$. ◀ **① Intercepts.**

  $x = 0 \Rightarrow y = 2(0)^2 + 8(0) + 6 = 6$

  So the graph passes through $(0, 6)$.

  The graph crosses the x-axis when $y = 0$.

  $$\begin{aligned} y = 0 \Rightarrow\ & 0 = 2x^2 + 8x + 6 \\ \Rightarrow\ & 2(x^2 + 4x + 3) = 0 \\ \Rightarrow\ & 2(x + 3)(x + 1) = 0 \\ \Rightarrow\ & (x + 3) = 0 \quad \text{or} \quad (x + 1) = 0 \\ \Rightarrow\ & x = -3 \quad \text{or} \quad x = -1 \end{aligned}$$

  Use factorisation to solve this quadratic equation.

  So the graph passes through $(-3, 0)$ and $(-1, 0)$.

- Stationary points occur when $\frac{dy}{dx} = 0$. ◀ **② Stationary points.**

  $$y = 2x^2 + 8x + 6 \Rightarrow \frac{dy}{dx} = 4x + 8$$

  $$\frac{dy}{dx} = 0 \Rightarrow 4x + 8 = 0 \Rightarrow x = -2$$

  When $x = -2$, $y = 2(-2)^2 + 8(-2) + 6 = -2$

So there is a stationary point at $(-2, -2)$.
Using the techniques from Chapter 5, verify that it is a minimum point.

Remember to look at t gradient of the curve c either side of $x = -2$.

- As x gets large $(x \to +\infty)$, y also gets large $(y \to +\infty)$. ◀ ③ **Large x.**
  Similarly as $x \to -\infty$, $y \to +\infty$ because of the x^2 term.
- The function is defined for all values of x, so the graph should be a continuous curve. ◀ ④ **Continuity.**

Now combine all four findings into one graph. Verify that the graph of $y = 2x^2 + 8x + 6$ has this form using a graphical calculator.

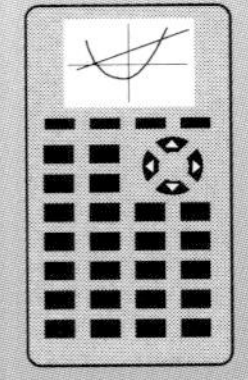

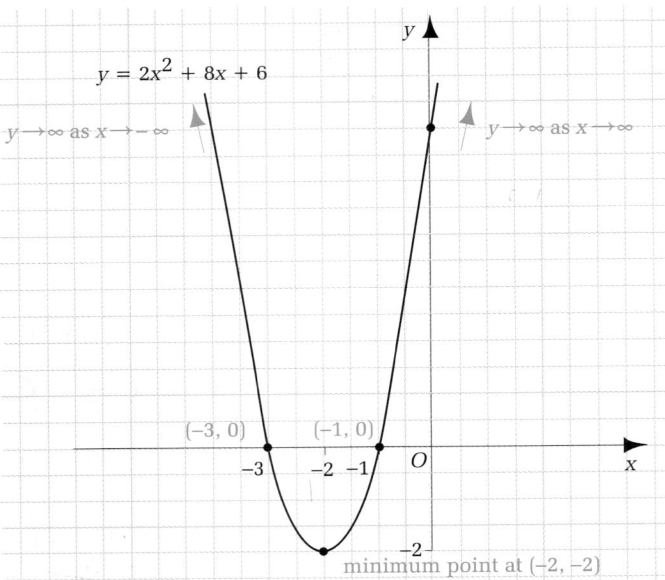

Example 2

Sketch the curve $y = x^3 + 2x^2 - x - 2$.

Solution

The graph crosses the y-axis when $x = 0$.

- $x = 0 \Rightarrow y = (0)^3 + 2(0)^2 - (0) - 2 = -2$ ◀ ① **Intercepts.**

  The graph passes through $(0, -2)$.

  The graph crosses the x-axis when $y = 0$.

  $y = 0 \Rightarrow x^3 + 2x^2 - x - 2 = 0$

  This cubic equation can be solved using the factor theorem.

  Let $P(x) = x^3 + 2x^2 - x - 2$
  Check that $P(-2)$, $P(-1)$ and $P(1)$ are all zero.
  This means $(x + 2)$, $(x + 1)$ and $(x - 1)$ are all factors of $P(x)$.
  This means the graph crosses the x-axis at three distinct points: $(-2, 0)$, $(-1, 0)$ and $(1, 0)$.

Check that $P(x) = (x + 2)(x + 1)(x$

- Stationary points can be found from $\frac{dy}{dx} = 0$. ◀ ② **Stationary points.**

  If $y = x^3 + 2x^2 - x - 2$ then $\frac{dy}{dx} = 3x^2 + 4x - 1$

  So $\frac{dy}{dx} = 0 \Rightarrow 3x^2 + 4x - 1 = 0$

  This particular quadratic equation cannot be solved by factorising, so use 'completing the square' or the 'quadratic formula' instead.

  Verify that the solutions are $x = \frac{1}{3}(-2 \pm \sqrt{7})$.

  This means there are two turning points. The approximate coordinates are $(-1.55, 0.63)$ and $(0.22, -2.11)$. Check that these turning points are a maximum and a minimum point, respectively, by looking at the values of $\frac{dy}{dx}$ on either side of each point.

- As $x \to \infty$, $y \to \infty$ because of the behaviour of the x^3 term. Similarly, as $x \to -\infty$, $y \to -\infty$. ◀ ③ **Large x.**

- The graph will be defined for all values as this polynomial can be evaluated for all values of x. ◀ ④ **Continuity.**

  Combine all four findings into one graph.

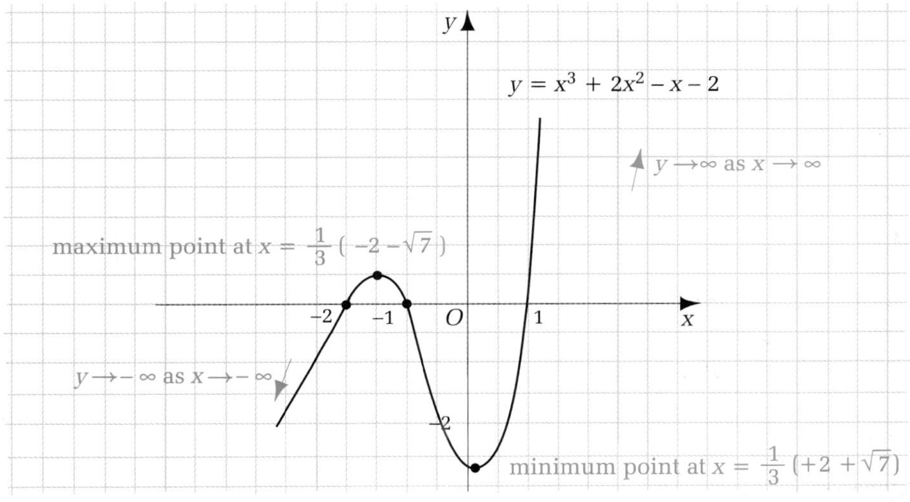

Check this graph using a graphical calculator.

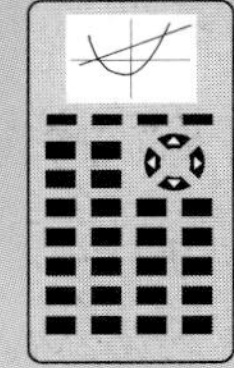

Graphs of discontinuous functions

Discontinuous functions have graphs that get closer and closer to some straight line and yet never cross it. This straight line is called an **asymptote**. This type of graph has been met already.

Look at the graph of $y = \tan\theta$ in Chapter 3.

Recall that $\tan\theta$ is undefined for a sequence of values of θ.

$$\ldots -\frac{3\pi}{2}, -\frac{\pi}{2}, \frac{\pi}{2}, \frac{3\pi}{2}, \frac{5\pi}{2}, \ldots$$

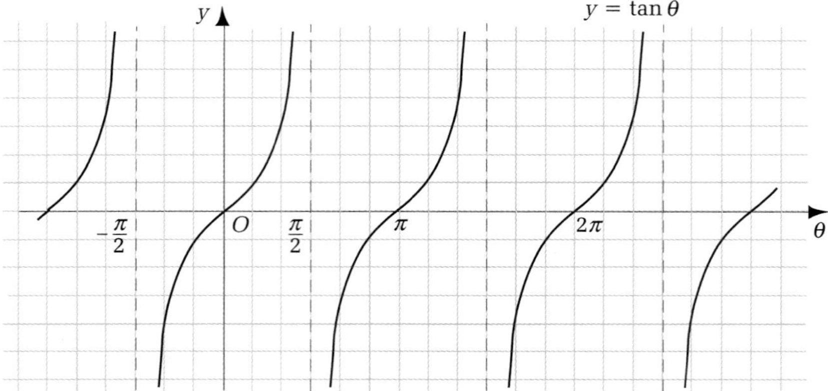

What is special about these values of θ?

Recall that $\tan\theta = \dfrac{\sin\theta}{\cos\theta}$.

For these values of θ, $\cos\theta = 0$. The rational function that then defines $\tan\theta$ has a denominator of zero.

This observation indicates a useful technique to adopt when sketching rational functions. Identify those values that produce a zero denominator. Vertical asymptotes will be located at those values.

Example 3

Sketch the graph of $y = \dfrac{3}{(x-2)}$.

Solution

- $x = 0 \Rightarrow y = \dfrac{3}{-2} = -\dfrac{3}{2}$ ◀ ① **Intercepts.**

  The graph crosses the y-axis at $(0, -\frac{3}{2})$.

  $y = 0 \Rightarrow 0 = \dfrac{3}{(x-2)}$

  Since there is no value of x for which $y = 0$ the graph does not cross the x-axis. So the line $y = 0$ (the x-axis) must be an asymptote.

- $y = \dfrac{3}{(x-2)} \Rightarrow \dfrac{dy}{dx} = -\dfrac{3}{(x-2)^2}$ ◀ ② **Stationary points.**

  Since $\frac{dy}{dx} \neq 0$ for all values of x there are no stationary points.

- As $x \to +\infty$, $y \to 0^+$ ◀ ③ **Large x.**

  As $x \to -\infty$, $y \to 0^-$

- The function $\frac{3}{(x-2)}$ is undefined when $x - 2 = 0$ ◀ ④ **Continuity.**

  So the graph is discontinuous when $x = 2$.

  Since $x = 2$ is an asymptote the behaviour of y either side of this value should be checked.

  As $x \to 2^+$ (from above), $x - 2 \to 0^+$, so $y = \dfrac{3}{(x-2)} \to +\infty$.

  As $x \to 2^-$ (from below), $x - 2 \to 0^-$, so $y \to -\infty$.

0^+ means $x \to 0$ from above (positive) and 0^- means $x \to 0$ from below (negative).

All of these features can now be combined to give the graph of $y = \dfrac{3}{(x-2)}$.

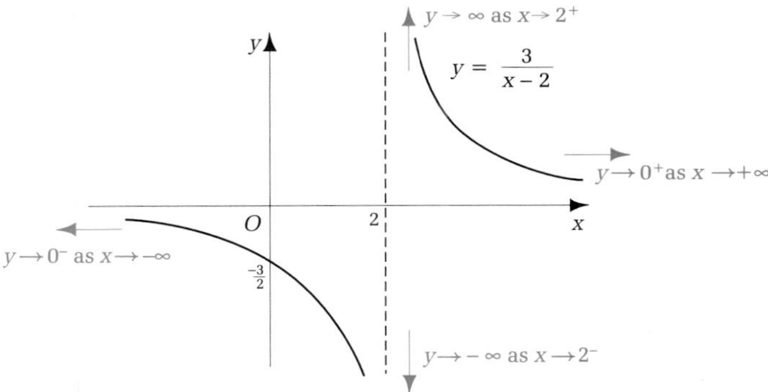

Check this result using a graphical calculator.

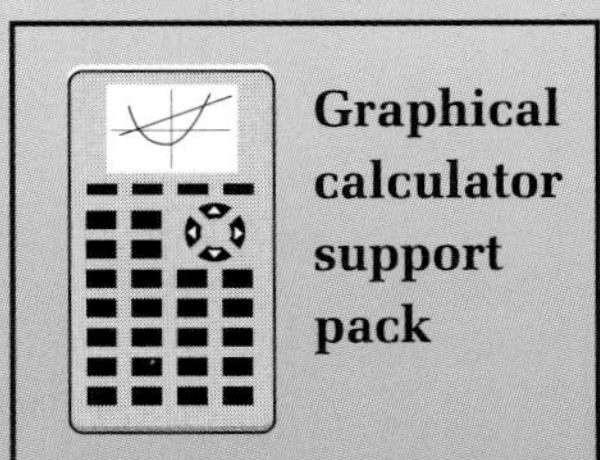

Example 4

Sketch the graph of $y = \dfrac{x+1}{x+5}$.

Solution

Look closely at the algebraic fraction. Spot that it is improper and rewrite it in quotient/remainder form.

Verify that $y = \dfrac{x+1}{x+5}$ can be written as $y = 1 - \dfrac{4}{x+5}$.

- Putting $x = 0$ gives $y = \frac{1}{5}$. So $(0, \frac{1}{5})$ is the intercept on the y-axis. Putting $y = 0$ gives $x = -1$. So the graph crosses the x-axis at $(-1, 0)$. ① Intercepts.
- Verify that $\dfrac{dy}{dx} = \dfrac{4}{(x+5)^2}$. Since $\dfrac{dy}{dx} \neq 0$ for all values of x, there are no stationary points. ② Stationary points.
- As $x \to \pm\infty$, $y \to 1$, so $y = 1$ is a horizontal asymptote. ③ Large x.
- The graph is not defined for $x = -5$. When $x = -5$ the denominator is zero. So $x = -5$ is a vertical asymptote. ④ Continuity.

These can now be combined to give the graph.

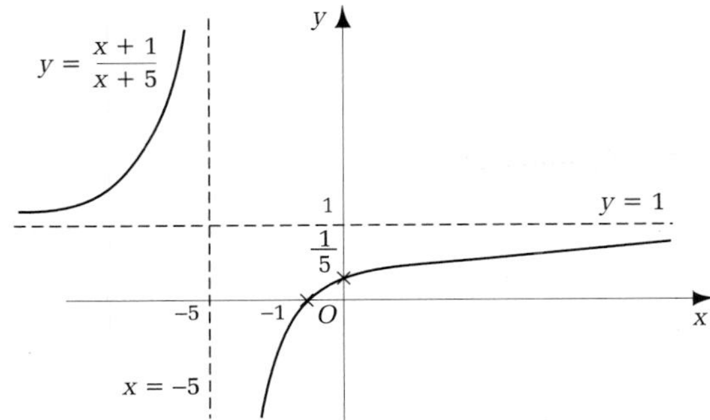

Check this result using a graphical calculator or by transforming the graph of $y = \frac{1}{x}$ using the techniques from Chapter 4.

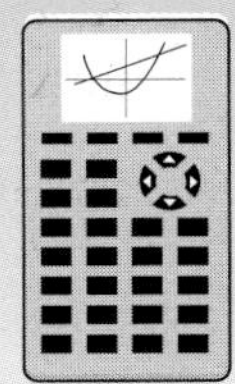

Example 5

Sketch the graph of $y = \dfrac{x^2+2}{x-1}$.

Solution

Look closely at the algebraic fraction. Spot that it is improper.

Writing the equation in different forms allows you to gather relevant information more easily.

Check that $y = \dfrac{x^2+2}{x-1}$ can be written as $y = x + 1 + \dfrac{3}{x-1}$.

The quotient is now $(x + 1)$ and contains the variable x.

- The graph crosses the y-axis when $x = 0$ at $(0, -2)$. ◀ ① Intercepts.

  Confirm this result.

  The graph does not cross the x-axis. Why? If $y = 0$ then the numerator $x^2 + 2 = 0$, and this equation has no real solutions.

- If $y = x + 1 + \dfrac{3}{x-1}$, then $\dfrac{dy}{dx} = 1 - \dfrac{3}{(x-1)^2}$ ◀ ② Stationary points.

  For stationary values, $\frac{dy}{dx} = 0$.

  $$1 - \frac{3}{(x-1)^2} = 0 \Rightarrow (x-1)^2 = 3$$
  $$\Rightarrow \quad x - 1 = \pm\sqrt{3}$$
  $$\Rightarrow \quad x = 1 \pm \sqrt{3}$$

  Check that the stationary point at $x = 1 + \sqrt{3}$ is a minimum point and that the stationary point at $x = 1 - \sqrt{3}$ is a maximum point by looking at the value of the gradient of the curve on either side.

- As x becomes very large (both positive and negative), $\dfrac{3}{x-1}$ becomes very small, and tends towards zero. Therefore $y \to x + 1$ as $x \to \pm\infty$. So $y = x + 1$ is a skew, or slant asymptote. ③ Large x.

- The graph is not defined for $x = 1$. When $x = 1$ the original denominator is zero. So $x = 1$ is a vertical asymptote. ④ Continuity.

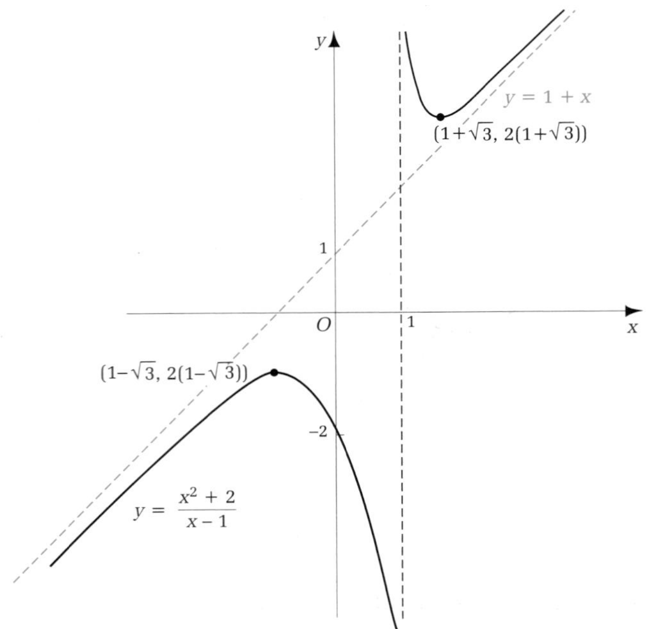

Modulus graphs

The modulus of a function, $|f(x)|$, was defined in Chapter 4. To sketch graphs of the modulus of a function, first sketch the graph of the function $f(x)$, and then reflect in the x-axis all parts of the graph for which the y-coordinate is negative.

Example 6

Sketch the graphs of:

a $y = \left|\dfrac{3}{x-2}\right|$ **b** $y = \left|\dfrac{x+1}{x+5}\right|$ **c** $y = \left|\dfrac{x^2+2}{x-1}\right|$.

Solution

Compare these with the graphs of the functions found in Examples 3–5. All that is required now is to reflect the parts of the graph that are below the x-axis (where y-coordinates are zero) in the x-axis.

a

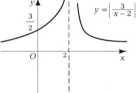

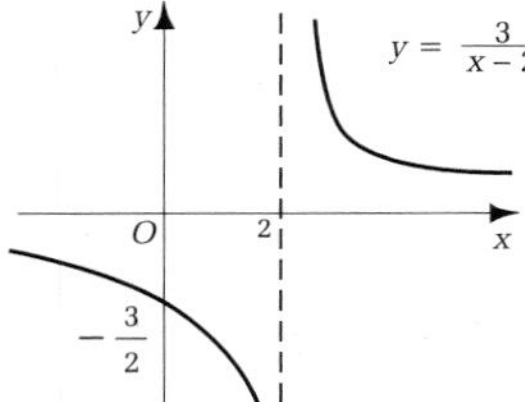

b

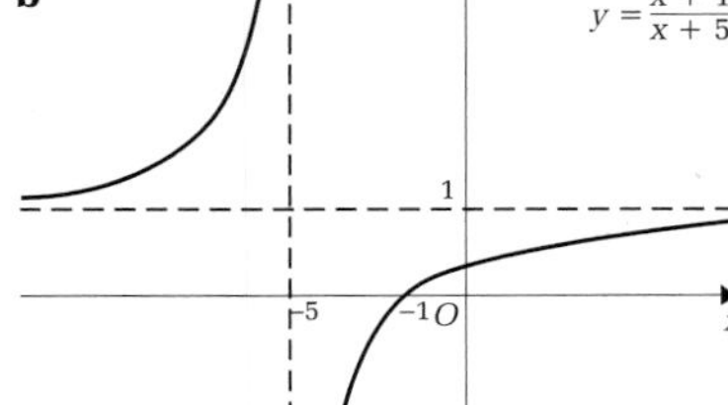

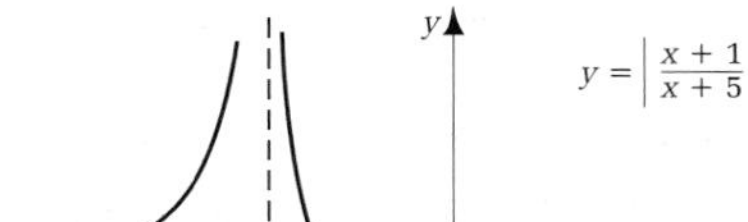

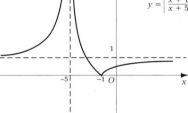

c

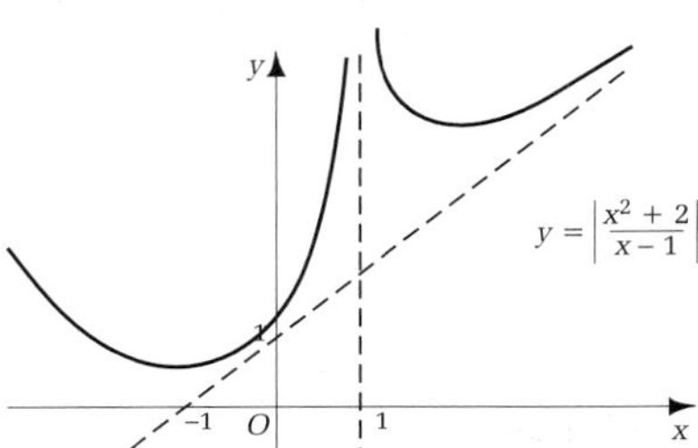

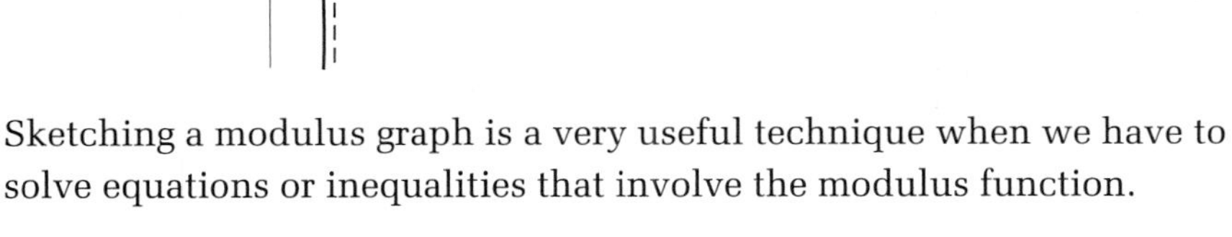

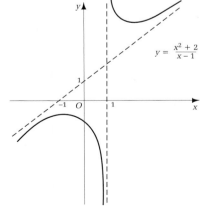

Sketching a modulus graph is a very useful technique when we have to solve equations or inequalities that involve the modulus function.

Check these results using a graphical calculator.

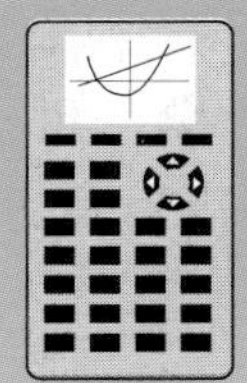

Example 7

Solve the equation $|x| = |8x - 24|$. Hence, or otherwise, solve $|x| \leq |8x - 24|$.

Solution

To solve the equation first sketch the graphs of $y = |x|$ and $y = |8x - 24|$ on the same axes.
Notice that we get two distinct V-shaped graphs. The graph of $y = |8x - 24|$ is steeper and touches the x-axis at $x = 3$.

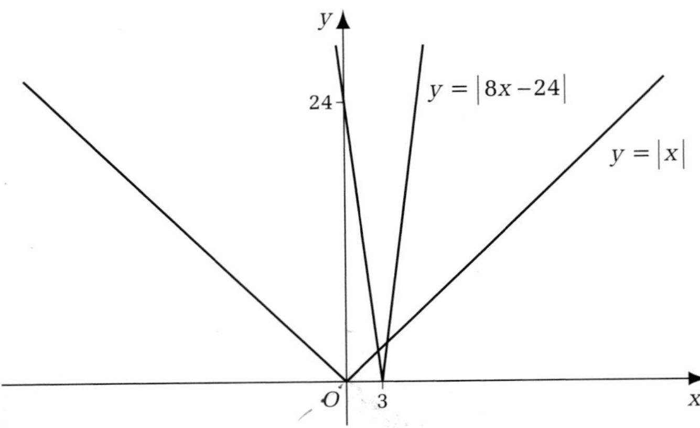

The points of intersection of the two graphs are the solutions to $|x| = |8x - 24|$. These can be found algebraically by solving two sets of equations:

$$x = 8x - 24$$

and $$x = -(8x - 24)$$

The first equation corresponds to the point where $y = x$ intersects $y = 8x - 24$. The second equation gives the solution created by the reflection in the x-axis. This corresponds to the point where $y = x$ intersects $y = -(8x - 24)$.
Solving these equations gives

Check that this is equivalent to $y = -x$ intersecting with $y = 8x - 24$.

$$x = 8x - 24 \quad \Rightarrow \quad 7x = 24$$
$$x = \tfrac{24}{7}$$
$$x = -(8x - 24) \quad \Rightarrow \quad 9x = 24$$
$$x = \tfrac{24}{9}$$

Check that $x = \frac{24}{7}$ and $x = \frac{24}{9}$ satisfy the equation $|x| = |8x - 24|$.

To solve the inequality $|x| \leq |8x - 24|$, use the graph. Notice that the graph of $y = |x|$ is below the graph of $y = |8x - 24|$ when $x \leq \frac{24}{9}$ or $x \geq \frac{24}{7}$. So $|x| \leq |8x - 24|$ when $x \leq \frac{24}{9}$ and $x \geq \frac{24}{7}$.
When we need to solve inequalities that involve the modulus function it is often useful to check the graphs. We can usually identify where the required condition is, geometrically, by finding where a graph is either above or below another graph or axis.

Verify this result on a graphical calculator.

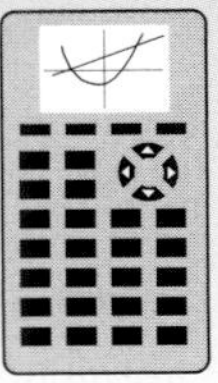

6.4 Curve Sketching
Exercise
Technique

1 Sketch the graphs of the following continuous functions:

a $f(x) = 2x^3 + 7x^2 - 5x - 4$ **b** $h(x) = |x^2 - 6x - 7|$
c $g(x) = x^3 - 19x + 30$ **d** $h(x) = |2x^3 + 15x^2 + 31x + 12|$

2 Sketch the graphs of the following rational functions:

a $g(x) = \frac{3}{x - 4}$ **b** $f(x) = \frac{2}{1 - x}$
c $g(x) = \frac{1}{3 - 4x}$ **d** $h(x) = \left|\frac{1}{2x + 3}\right|$

3 Sketch the graphs of the following rational functions:

a $f(x) = \frac{x + 1}{x - 3}$ **b** $g(x) = \frac{x + 3}{x + 4}$
c $h(x) = \frac{x - 3}{x - 2}$ **d** $h(x) = \left|\frac{5x + 1}{3x - 2}\right|$

4 Solve the following:
a $|x| = |5x - 40|$ **b** $|x| = |12 - 3x|$ **c** $|x - 2| = |6 - 2x|$
d $|x| \leq |8x - 40|$ **e** $|x| \geq |1 - 5x|$ **f** $|2x + 1| \geq |5 - 3x|$

Contextual

1 Given that $f(x) = 3x^3 - 7x^2 - 7x + 3$:

a factorise $f(x)$ and then sketch its graph
b on a separate diagram sketch the graph of $|f(x)|$.

2 Given that $f(x) = 2x + 1$ and $g(x) = x + 2$, find the range of values of x for which:

a $f(x) > 0$ **b** $g(x) > 0$ **c** $\frac{f(x)}{g(x)} > 0$

Hint: Sketch the appropriate graphs first.

3 Sketch the graph of $y = \frac{4x + 1}{2x - 5}$. Hence or otherwise find the range of values of x for which $y < 0$

4 On separate diagrams sketch the graphs of:

a $y = \frac{2x - 6}{x + 8}$ **b** $y = \left|\frac{2x - 6}{x + 8}\right|$

Consolidation

Exercise A

1 Use the factor theorem to find a linear factor of $x^3 - x - 6$. Hence express $x^3 - x - 6$ as the product of a linear factor and a quadratic factor.

(OCSEB)

2 It is given that $g(x) = (2x - 1)(x + 2)(x - 3)$.

a Express $g(x)$ in the form $Ax^3 + Bx^2 + Cx + D$, giving the values of the constants A, B, C and D.

b Find the value of the constant a, given that $(x + 3)$ is a factor of $g(x) + ax$.

c Express $\dfrac{x-3}{g(x)}$ in partial fractions.

d Solve the inequality $g(x) > 3x(x + 2)(x - 3)$.

(UCLES)

3 **a** When divided by $(x - 3)$ the expression $x^3 + ax^2 - (a^2 - 3a + 17)x$ gives a remainder of 3. Find the value of a.

b Find the three linear factors of $3x^3 - x^2 - 75x + 25$.

4 The polynomial $p(x) = x^3 + cx^2 + 7x + d$ has a factor of $(x + 2)$, and leaves a remainder of 3 when divided by $(x - 1)$.

a Determine the value of each of the constants c and d.

b Find the exact values of the three roots of the equation $p(x) = 0$.

(AEB)

5 Given that $\dfrac{(x-1)^3}{x^2} = Ax + B + \dfrac{C}{x} + \dfrac{D}{x^2}$, $x \neq 0$, find the values of A, B, C and D.

(OCSEB)

6 Given that $y = \dfrac{2x+1}{x(2x-1)^2}$, express y in the form $\dfrac{A}{x} + \dfrac{B}{(2x-1)} + \dfrac{C}{(2x-1)^2}$.

(NEAB)

7 The cubic polynomial $x^3 - 2x^2 - x - 6$ is denoted by $f(x)$. Show that $(x - 3)$ is a factor of $f(x)$. Factorise $f(x)$. Hence find the number of real roots of the equation $f(x) = 0$, justifying your answer.

Hence write down the number of points of intersection of the graphs with equations $y = x^2 - 2x - 1$ and $y = \frac{6}{x}$, justifying your answer.

(UCLES)

8 If $p(x) = 2x^3 - 5x^2 - 28x + 15$:

a factorise $p(x)$ **b** solve $p(x) = 0$
c sketch the graph of $p(x)$ **d** solve $p(x) \geq 0$.

9 Sketch the curve $y = \dfrac{x+3}{x-5}$. Now find the values of x for which $y > 0$.

10 Given $f(x) = \dfrac{2x+1}{x+2}$:

a sketch the graph of $f(x)$
b on a separate diagram sketch the graph of $|f(x)|$.

Exercise B

1 **a** When the cubic expression $x^3 + ax^2 - (2a^2 + 12)x + (7a + 10)$ is divided by $(x - 1)$ the remainder is 7. Find a.
b Find the three linear factors of $x^3 + 2x^2 - 20x + 24$. *(WJEC)*

2 A polynomial $f(x)$ can be expressed in the form $p(x + 2)^4 + q$ where p and q are constants. When $f(x)$ is divided by $(x - 1)$ the remainder is 40 and when $f(x)$ is divided by $(x + 3)$ the remainder is zero. Find the values of p and q. *(NEAB)*

3 Given $f(x) = (3x - 2)(x - 1)(x + 1)$:

a express $f(x)$ in the form $Ax^3 + Bx^2 + Cx + D$
b express $\dfrac{x+1}{f(x)}$ in partial fractions
c solve the inequality $f(x) \geq 2x(x - 1)(x + 1)$.

4 The cubic polynomial $f(x) = 5x^3 + px^2 - 11x + q$ has a remainder of -12 when divided by $(x - 1)$ and also has an exact factor $(x - 3)$.

a Find the values of p and q.
b Express the cubic polynomial as the product of three linear factors.
c With the aid of a sketch, solve $f(x) < 0$.

5 A curve has equation $y = \dfrac{3x+4}{(x-2)(2x+1)}$.

a Express $\dfrac{3x+4}{(x-2)(2x+1)}$ in partial fractions.
b Show that $\dfrac{dy}{dx} = \dfrac{2}{(2x+1)^2} - \dfrac{2}{(x-2)^2}$ and hence, or otherwise, show that the curve has a turning point when $x = -3$. Determine the value of x at the other stationary point of the curve. *(AEB)*

Applications and Activities

Parametric equations

Sometimes, instead of having an equation relating x and y directly, $y = f(x)$, x and y are written in terms of a third variable, called a **parameter**. Then x and y are represented by two separate functions, $x = g(t)$ and $y = h(t)$, called **parametric equations**. Eliminating the parameter, or variable, reduces the two parametric equations into a Cartesian form with two variables.

Parametric equations are a useful technique to use with graphical calculators, when it is difficult to write y as a function of x. Use a graphical calculator in the parametric mode to help you with the following activities.

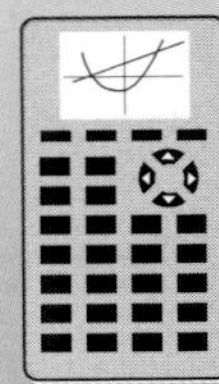

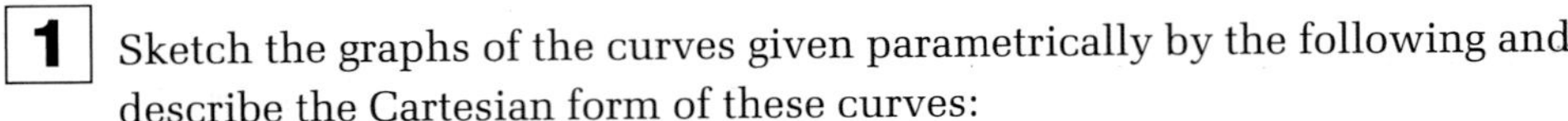

1 Sketch the graphs of the curves given parametrically by the following and describe the Cartesian form of these curves:

a $x = \cos\theta$ and $y = \sin\theta$
b $x = 3 + \cos\theta$ and $y = 4 + \sin\theta$
c $x = -3 + \cos\theta$ and $y = 4 + \sin\theta$
d $x = -3 + \cos\theta$ and $y = -4 + \sin\theta$
e $x = 3 + \cos\theta$ and $y = -4 + \sin\theta$

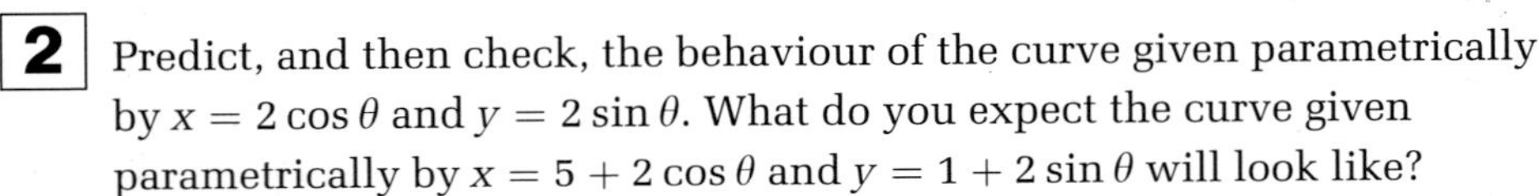

2 Predict, and then check, the behaviour of the curve given parametrically by $x = 2\cos\theta$ and $y = 2\sin\theta$. What do you expect the curve given parametrically by $x = 5 + 2\cos\theta$ and $y = 1 + 2\sin\theta$ will look like?

3 Investigate other parametric coordinates.

Summary

- A polynomial can be divided by a linear factor and the result is checked using either multiplication or substitution.
- The **remainder theorem** says that when a polynomial $P(x)$ is divided by a linear factor $(x - a)$ then the remainder is $P(a)$.
- The **factor theorem** says that if $P(a) = 0$ then $(x - a)$ is a factor of $P(x)$.
- The **factor theorem** can be used to factorise cubic and higher order polynomial expressions.
- **Partial fractions** can be classified into three categories: those with linear factors in their denominators; those with quadratic factors in the denominator; and those with repeated factors in the denominator.
- The **cover-up rule** uses the fact that some values of x create a zero in the denominator to calculate the required numerators in the partial fractions.
- To sketch the graphs of continuous and discontinuous functions, check:

  ① where the graph crosses the axes
  ② the location and nature of any stationary points
  ③ the behaviour as $x \to \pm\infty$
  ④ where the function is undefined.

- The graph can be discontinuous at a point. This is shown by a line called an **asymptote**.
  - A *vertical* asymptote can be found when the denominator of a rational function is zero.
  - A *horizontal* asymptote can be found when the function tends towards a fixed value for large positive and negative values of x.
  - A *skew* asymptote can be found by writing an improper algebraic fraction in its quotient–remainder form.
- Produce a sketch of the modulus of a function, $|f(x)|$, by reflecting in the x-axis all parts of the graph for which the function is negative.

7 Exponentials and Logarithms

What you need to know

- How to write numbers in standard index form.
- The laws of indices.
- How to evaluate negative and fractional indices.
- How to use the $x^{1/y}$ or $\sqrt[x]{\ }$ function key on your calculator.

Review

1 Write the following numbers in standard (index) form:

a 93 000 000   **b** 0.006 25
c ten million   **d** three hundredths

2 Simplify the following:

a $a^7 \times a^5$ **b** $a^6 \div a^2$ **c** $(m^6)^3$
d m^0, where $m \neq 0$ **e** $a^m \times a^n$ **f** $\dfrac{a^m}{a^n}$

3 Without using a calculator, work out:

a $16^{\frac{1}{2}}$ **b** $27^{\frac{1}{3}}$ **c** 4^{-3}
d $(\frac{1}{4})^{\frac{1}{2}}$ **e** $64^{\frac{2}{3}}$ **f** $125^{-\frac{1}{3}}$

4 Use your calculator to find the values of the following, correct to three significant figures:

a $10^{\frac{1}{3}}$ **b** $(0.03)^{\frac{2}{5}}$
c $(1.2)^{-3}$ **d** $(-200)^{-\frac{1}{3}}$

7.1 The Exponential Function

Any function of the form a^x, where a is a positive constant, is known as an **exponential** (or power) **function**. The variable of the function is x. Examples of exponential functions include 2^x, 3^{5x}, 5^x and 10^{x+3}. The graphs of these functions all have the same basic shape.

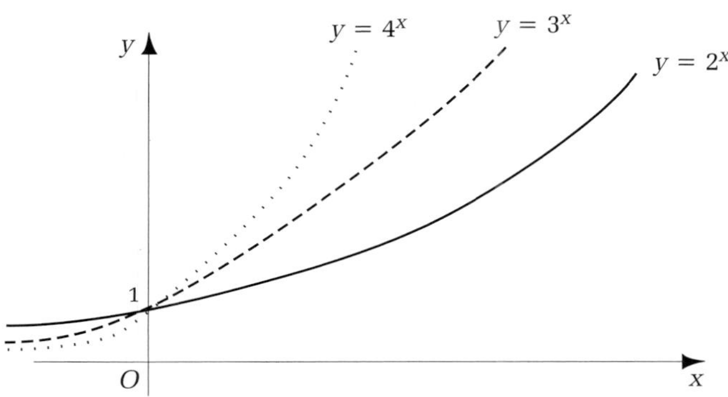

Since $a^0 = 1$, all graphs of the form $y = a^x$ cross the y-axis at $(0, 1)$.

- The graphs are defined for all values of x.
- The graphs are always above the x-axis.
- The x-axis (the line $y = 0$) is an asymptote, and each graph tends to infinity quickly as x gets large.

Exponential functions are always positive.

Exponential functions can be used to model growth and decay. To model decay we find that the exponent needs to be negative. Graphs of exponential functions with negative exponents are the same shape as those with positive exponents, but reflected in the line $x = 0$ (or the y-axis).
Exponential functions are used to predict population growth, describe radioactive decay and determine compound interest.

Population growth

The world's human population is growing by about 3% each year. Given that the population at the end of 1989 was estimated at 4.5 billion (4.5×10^9), we can predict population figures for future years using an exponential graph.

Year end	1989	1990	1991	1992	1993
Population in billions	4.5	4.5×1.03	$4.5 \times (1.03)^2$	$4.5 \times (1.03)^3$	$4.5 \times (1.03)^4$

Multiplying by 1.03 increases by 3%.

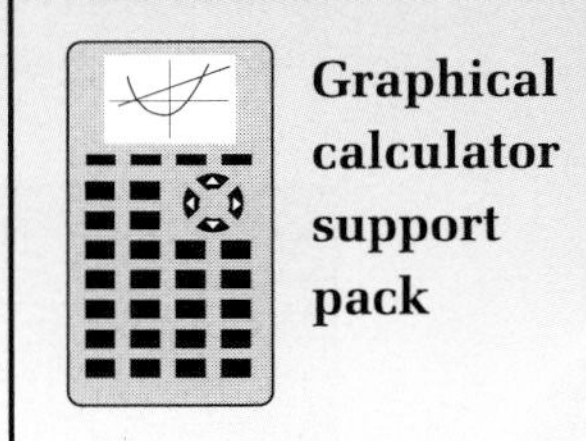

Complete a table of values or use a graphical calculator to draw the graph of $y = 4.5 \times 1.03^x$. Notice that the curve crosses the y-axis at 4.5 (representing 4.5 billion in 1989, our initial year). Using a trace and zoom function we can find when the population doubles ($y = 2 \times 4.5 = 9$).

We find that $y = 9.0$ when $x = 23.449\,772$. So $x \approx 24$.

This means we can predict that the world's human population will have doubled in size from its 1989 estimate by the end of the year 2013 (1989 + 24 years).

Trace and zoom
The 'Trace' facility on a graphical calculator was described on p. 34. The 'Zoom' facility enables you to zoom in on a region, or section, of a plotted graph. Most calculators will zoom in on the graph at the point traced along to, and then redraw the graph with a preset scale factor.

Radioactive decay

Radioactive substances have 'half-lives' that are determined by the time it takes the radioactivity to halve. Radon-219, an isotope of the element radon, has a half-life of approximately four seconds. This means that if at some time $t = 0$ we have 10 000 Radon-219 nuclei, then four seconds later ($t = 4$) there will be only 5000.
The exponential model for radioactive decay will have a negative exponent (power). To find it, first tabulate some values.

Time after sample is identified	0	4	8	12	16
Number of nuclei remaining	10 000	$10\,000 \times (\frac{1}{2})$ $= 5000$	$10\,000 \times (\frac{1}{2})^2$ $= 2500$	$10\,000 \times (\frac{1}{2})^3$ $= 1250$	$10\,000 \times (\frac{1}{2})^4$ $= 625$

Remember the laws of indices.

Notice that every four seconds the power increases by 1. If $N(t)$ is the number of atoms at time t, then

$$\begin{aligned} N(t) &= 10\,000 \times (\tfrac{1}{2})^{\frac{t}{4}} \\ &= 10\,000 \times (2^{-1})^{\frac{t}{4}} \\ &= 10\,000 \times 2^{-\frac{t}{4}} \end{aligned}$$

This model now allows us to calculate the number of nuclei of Radon-219 present in the sample at any time after timing commenced ($t = 0$).

Compound interest

Banks and building societies add the interest to certain accounts at the end of a year. In the following year interest is also calculated on this interest. This method of calculation is known as 'compound interest'. Consider investing £500. What would give the best return, 10% per year or 1% every $\frac{1}{10}$ year? Compare the balance at the start of each year.

Year	1	2	3	4	5
10% per year (£)	500	550	605	665.50	732.05
1% every $\frac{1}{10}$ year (£)	500	552.31	610.10	673.92	744.43

Clearly the second option gives a better return. But how can these figures be calculated quickly?
In the first account £500 can be multiplied by $(1.1)^n$ where n is the number of interest paying years. In the second account £500 can be multiplied by $(1.01)^n$ where n is the number of $\frac{1}{10}$ years for which interest is paid. Thus £500 $\times$ $(1.01)^{10} =$ £552.31.
The idea of reducing the interest rate but increasing the number of times it is paid is nothing new. Today interest can be paid daily (so in a year, n would be 365) but the rate will be only a fraction of 1%.
Now look at the following pattern:

$$(1 + 0.1)^{10} = 2.593\,742\,46$$
$$(1 + 0.01)^{100} = 2.704\,813\,829$$
$$(1 + 0.001)^{1000} = 2.716\,923\,932$$
$$(1 + 0.0001)^{10\,000} = 2.718\,145\,927$$

The left-hand column is generating the pattern $(1 + \frac{1}{n})^n$ for powers of 10. The figures on the RHS are converging to a limit that begins 2.718 .... This number is known as '**e**' and is the **limit** of this **sequence**.

This can be written mathematically as $\mathrm{e} = \underset{n\to\infty}{\text{limit}} \left(1 + \frac{1}{n}\right)^n$ or more usually as $\mathrm{e} = \lim\limits_{n\to\infty} \left(1 + \frac{1}{n}\right)^n$.

The exponential function as a series

The number e can also be defined as $\mathrm{e} = 1 + \frac{1}{1!} + \frac{1}{2!} + \frac{1}{3!} + \cdots$.

The function e^x is often referred to as *the* **exponential function**. It can be defined, in a similar way to e, as:

$$\mathbf{e^x = 1 + \frac{x}{1!} + \frac{x^2}{2!} + \frac{x^3}{3!} + \cdots}$$

Alternative notation you may come across for e^x is exp x or exp (x). Do not confuse this with the EXP key on a scientific calculator.

If we differentiate this infinite power series term by term we get a remarkable result.

$$\frac{\mathrm{d}}{\mathrm{d}x}(\mathrm{e}^x) = 1 + \frac{x}{1!} + \frac{x^2}{2!} + \frac{x^3}{3!} + \cdots = \mathrm{e}^x$$

That is, the gradient function equals the function itself for all real values. It is this result that makes the exponential function, e^x, unique.

7.1 The Exponential Function

Exercise

Technique

1 Using a calculator find, correct to three significant figures, the values of:

a e^2 **b** e^{-1} **c** $e^{-1} - e^{-3}$ **d** $e^{\frac{1}{2}}$

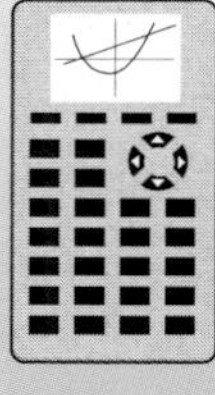

2 Use a graphical calculator to sketch the graphs of the following. In each case describe the transformation that maps $y = e^x$ onto each of these functions:

a $y = e^{(x+1)}$ **b** $y = e^x + 1$ **c** $y = e^{(x-2)}$ **d** $y = e^x - 2$

2 **a, d**

3 Draw the graph of $y = 2^x$. From your graph find, as accurately as you can, the value of:

a $2^{1.5}$ **b** $2^{0.3}$ **c** $2^{-0.5}$ **d** $2^{-3.5}$

4 Using a calculator, sketch the graph of $y = e^x$. Use the trace and zoom functions to find values of x correct to three significant figures for which:

a $e^x = 6$ **b** $e^x = 8.12$ **c** $e^x = 0.5$ **d** $e^x = \pi$

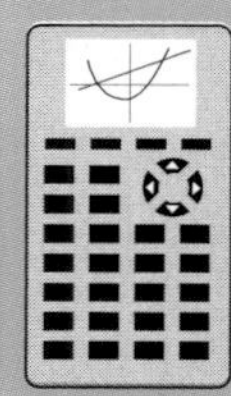

Contextual

1 The mass of a colony of bacteria, measured in grams, doubles each day and is given by the formula $M(t) = 7.0 \times 2^t$. Find the initial mass of the bacteria and the number of days needed for the total mass of the bacteria to exceed 500 g.

2 The decay of a radioactive isotope can be modelled by $M(t) = M_0\,e^{-kt}$, where $M(t)$ is the remaining mass after t days. If a given isotope has a half-life of 10 days and after this time 60 g remain, find:

a how much isotope was present initially (the value of M_0).
b the value of the decay constant k.
c how much isotope has remained after 30 days.
d the number of days required for 80% of the isotope to have decayed.

3 Engine oil, at temperature T°C cools down according to the model $T = 60\,e^{-kt} + 10$, where t is the time in minutes from the moment the engine was switched off.

a What is the initial temperature of the oil when the engine is first switched off?
b If the oil cools to 32°C after three minutes find the value of k.
c How long will it take for the oil to cool to a temperature of 15°C?

4 The cost of living is increasing by 4% per year. By how much does the cost of living increase in:

a a month **b** six months **c** five years?

How long will it take for the cost of living to double from its present value?

5 A car bought for £12 000 depreciates at 20% per year. After t years it is worth £x.

a Sketch a graph of x against t.

b Use your graph to calculate:

i when the car is worth half its original value;

ii when its value first falls below £1000.

7.2 Logarithms

When comparing numbers written in standard form, first look at the index, (exponent or power) of the number ten. This gives an indication of the magnitude of the number.
For example, if the index is 6 then the number will be in the millions because

$$10^6 = 1\,000\,000 = 1 \text{ million}$$

Now consider numbers between 10 and 100. Since $10 = 10^1$ and $100 = 10^2$ we would expect the index for these numbers to be between 1 and 2. What about 1.5? What number is equivalent to $10^{1.5}$? The answer is not 50. Using the 'x^y' function key on a calculator you should find that $10^{1.5} = 31.622\,777$ (6 d.p.).
The number 1.5 is called the **logarithm** of 31.622 777 in base 10. If you now try the 'log' function key on the calculator notice that $\log(31.622\,777) = 1.5$

Although invented in Europe by John Napier in the sixteenth century, there is plenty of evidence to show that logarithms were known to Asian mathematicians in the period around the eighth century. The Japanese may have developed the idea of logs without using them for any practical purpose.

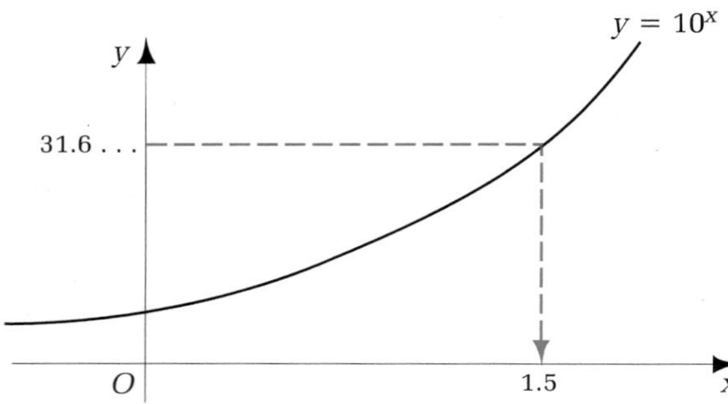

Mathematicians generalise this relationship as follows,

If $y = a^x$ then $x = \log_a y$

and x is known as the logarithm of y in base a.

$$\text{Since } 31.622\,777 = 10^{1.5} \text{ then } 1.5 = \log_{10} 31.622\,777$$

Logarithms can be in bases other than 10.

Henry Briggs (1561–1630)
Logarithms to base 10 are known as 'common logs' or 'Briggs logs' in honour of Briggs, who calculated the first table of common logarithms.

Example

For each of the following, write down an expression for a logarithm in a suitable base:

a $81 = 3^4$ **b** $8 = 2^3$

c $100 = 10^2$ **d** $\dfrac{1}{32} = \dfrac{1}{2^5}$

Solution

a $81 = 3^4$, so $4 = \log_3 81$

b $8 = 2^3$, so $3 = \log_2 8$

c $100 = 10^2$, so $2 = \log_{10} 100$

d $\frac{1}{32} = \frac{1}{2^5} = 2^{-5}$, so $-5 = \log_2(\frac{1}{32})$

Recall that $a^{-n} = \dfrac{1}{a^n}$.

The logarithm of a number is the power to which the base must be raised in order to equal that number. So $\log_{10} 100$ is 2 because the base, 10, must be raised to power 2 to equal 100.

The most common bases used for logarithms are 10 and e. In value, $e \approx 2.718\,2818$ and logarithms taken to this base are called **natural logarithms**.

This value can be found as your calculator by evaluating e^1.

To distinguish between these types of logarithms the following notation is used.

$\log_{10} x$ is written $\log x$ or $\lg x$

$\log_e x$ is written $\ln x$

Calculators have two different function keys for logarithms, 'LN' and 'LOG', with inverse functions e^x and 10^x respectively.
The relationship between e^x and $\ln x$ is very important.

Check that $\ln(e^x) = x$ and $e^{\ln x} = x$.

If $y = e^x$ then $x = \ln y$.

The use of e as a base for logarithms is by no means accidental. The number e has many applications in mathematics.

Transcendental numbers

A number that cannot satisfy an algebraic equation with integer coefficients is called a **transcendental number**. Many irrationals are not transcendental. For example, $\sqrt{2}$ satisfies $x^2 = 2$ or $x^2 - 2 = 0$, which are equations with integer coefficients. Both e and π are transcendental.

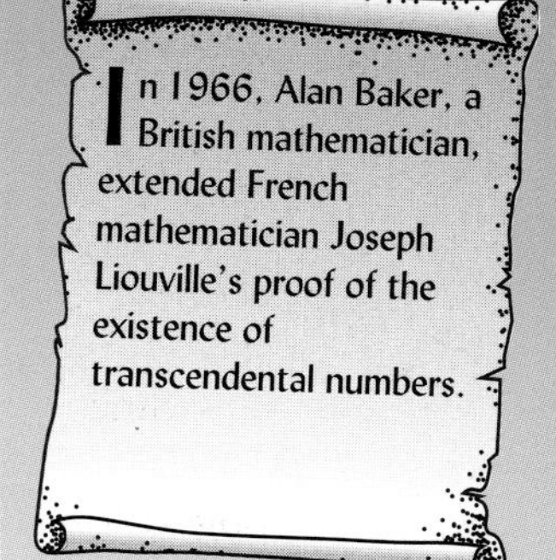

In 1966, Alan Baker, a British mathematician, extended French mathematician Joseph Liouville's proof of the existence of transcendental numbers.

7.2 Logarithms
Exercise
Technique

1 Without using a calculator, find the values of:

a $\log 1000$ **b** $\log 0.01$
c $\log 10\,000\,000$ **d** $\log 0.0001$

2 Find the values of the following, to three significant figures:

a $\log 50$ **b** $\log 2$
c $\log(\frac{1}{3})$ **d** $\log(\frac{2}{3})$

3 Without using a calculator find the exact values of x in:

a $x = \log_2 64$ **b** $x = \log_3 27$
c $x = \log_2(\frac{1}{2})$ **d** $x = \log_3(\frac{1}{81})$

4 Find the value of the base, a, of the following logarithms:

a $3 = \log_a 125$ **b** $\frac{1}{2} = \log_a 6$
c $-2 = \log_a(\frac{1}{25})$ **d** $\frac{1}{2} = \log_a 25$

5 Find the values of the following, to three significant figures:

a $\ln 2$ **b** $\ln 50$
c $\ln 100$ **d** $\ln 25$

6 Evaluate the following without using a calculator:

a $\ln e^2$ **b** $\ln \sqrt{e}$
c $\ln\left(\frac{1}{\sqrt[3]{e}}\right)$ **d** $\ln\left(\frac{1}{\sqrt{e^3}}\right)$

7 Copy and complete the following table:

Exponent form	Logarithmic form
$2^4 = 16$	$\log_2 16 = 4$
$2^{-1} = \frac{1}{2}$	$\log_2(\frac{1}{2}) = -1$
$2^5 = 32$	
	$\log_2 64 = 6$
$3^2 = 9$	
$3^{-2} = \frac{1}{9}$	
$4^{\frac{1}{2}} = 2$	

Contextual

1 The Richter scale measures the magnitude of earthquakes using logarithms. The Richter value is only part of the number describing an earthquake's strength. If it has a Richter value of 6, the magnitude of the earthquake is 10^6. Many people believe an earthquake with a Richter value of 8 is twice as strong as one with a value of 4. How do the two actually compare in intensity?

2 The human ear responds to the ratio of the powers, measured in watts, when the power of sound increases. This ratio is measured in bels (B) but in practice the bel is too large and the decibel (dB) is used. This is calculated using the rule

$$\text{change in dB} = 10\log_{10}\left(\frac{\text{new power}}{\text{old power}}\right)$$

a Explain why an increase in power output from 100 W to 200 W is only 3 dB.

b Approximately how many times will the power level emitted by a source of sound have increased if the sound level increases by 10 dB?

c If the volume control on a personal stereo is turned down so that the power output from the loudspeaker changes from 500 mW (milliwatts) to 100 mW, what is the corresponding fall in sound level in dB?

3 In chemistry the acidity or alkalinity of a solution is measured by its pH factor, defined by $\text{pH} = -\log_{10}[\text{H}^+]$. In this rule $[\text{H}^+]$ is a measure of the quantity of hydrogen ions present in the solution. A pH value of 7 indicates a neutral solution for which $[\text{H}^+] = 10^{-7}$ moles per litre. If the pH value is greater than 7 the solution is alkaline. If the pH value is less than 7 the solution is acidic.

a Calculate the pH value for a hair shampoo of strength 2.5×10^{-9} moles per litre.

b An acid X, has a pH of 5.0, and an acid, Y, a pH of 2.5. How many times more concentrated than acid X is acid Y?

7.3 Laws of Logarithms

If $y = a^x$ then $x = \log_a y$.

Remember that these two mathematical statements are identical and interchangeable. Now suppose that there are positive numbers c and d such that $c = m^p$ and $d = m^q$ for some $m > 0$.

Then $p = \log_m c$ and $q = \log_m d$

and $c \times d = m^p \times m^q = m^{(p+q)}$

Remember the laws of indices.

In logarithm form this can be written,

$$\log_m(c \times d) = p + q = \log_m c + \log_m d$$

This result is true for any two positive numbers c and d and for any suitable base m. Since it is true for any base,

$\log ab = \log a + \log b$ **Property 1** ◀ **Learn this result.**

John Napier (1550–1617)
Napier introduced the use of logarithms as a breakthrough in simplifying computation. It reduced multiplication and division to addition and subtraction. This was the principle on which the slide rule, forerunner to the calculator was based.

Example 1

Given $\log 2 = 0.301$ and $\log 6 = 0.778$ find $\log 12$.

Solution

$$\begin{aligned} \log 12 &= \log(2 \times 6) \\ &= \log 2 + \log 6 \\ &= 0.301 + 0.778 \\ &= 1.079 \end{aligned}$$

Check this using your calculator.

Now return to property 1 and put $a = b$. This gives the following result:

$$\log a^2 = \log a + \log a = 2 \log a$$

This can be generalised to

$\log a^n = n \log a$ **Property 2** ◀ **Learn this result.**

This is valid for all values of n, and not just integers.

Example 2

Given $\log 6 = 0.778$ find $\log 36$.

Solution

$$\log 36 = \log 6^2$$
$$= 2\log 6$$
$$= 2 \times 0.778 = 1.556$$

Check this using your calculator.

Now return to $c = m^p$ and $d = m^q$ with $m > 0$ and try division instead of multiplication.

$$\frac{c}{d} = \frac{m^p}{m^q} = m^{p-q}$$

Remember the laws of indices.

In logarithm form this can be written,

$$\log_m\left(\frac{c}{d}\right) = p - q = \log_m c - \log_m d$$

This can be generalised to

$$\log\left(\frac{a}{b}\right) = \log a - \log b$$ **Property 3** ◀ **Learn this result.**

Example 3

Using the results from Examples 1 and 2, evaluate log 3.

Solution

$$\log 3 = \log\left(\frac{36}{12}\right)$$
$$= \log 36 - \log 12$$
$$= 1.556 - 1.079 = 0.477$$

Check also that
$\log 3 = \log(\frac{6}{2})$
$= \log 6 - \log 2$

There are two other logarithm properties worth noting, based on the indices statements $a^0 = 1$ and $a^1 = a$.

$\log_a 1 = 0$ **Property 4**

◀ **Learn these results.**

$\log_a a = 1$ **Property 5**

These five properties can be used to simplify expressions containing logarithms and to solve logarithmic equations.

The slide rule, a calculating device commonly used right up to the development of the electronic calculator, was invented by William Oughtred in 1622. The slide rule used a logarithmic scale.

Example 4

Write the following as single logarithms:

a $\log 8 - \log 6 + \log 9$ **b** $2\log a + 3\log b - \log c$

Solution

a $\log 8 - \log 6 + \log 9 = \log(\frac{8}{6}) + \log 9$ — Using property 3.

$$= \log\left(\frac{8 \times 9}{6}\right)$$ Using property 1.

$$= \log 12$$

b $2\log a + 3\log b - \log c = \log a^2 + \log b^3 - \log c$ — Using property 2.

$$= \log(a^2b^3) - \log c$$ Using property 1.

$$= \log\left(\frac{a^2b^3}{c}\right)$$ Using property 3.

Some logarithmic equations are a mixture of logarithms and ordinary numbers. When that is the case, try collecting together the logarithmic terms so that the logarithm properties can be used to combine them into a single logarithmic term.

Example 5

Given that $1 + \log_a(7x - 2a) = 2\log_a x + \log_a 3$, find, in terms of a, the possible values of x.

Solution

$$1 + \log_a(7x - 2a) = 2\log_a x + \log_a 3$$

$$\Rightarrow \quad 1 = 2\log_a x + \log_a 3 - \log_a(7x - 2a)$$

$$\Rightarrow \quad 1 = \log_a x^2 + \log_a 3 - \log_a(7x - 2a)$$ Using property 2.

$$\Rightarrow \quad 1 = \log_a(3x^2) - \log_a(7x - 2a)$$ Using property 1.

$$\Rightarrow \quad 1 = \log_a \frac{3x^2}{7x - 2a}$$ Using property 3.

But $\log_a a = 1$, so — By property 5.

$$\frac{3x^2}{7x - 2a} = a$$

$$\Rightarrow \quad 3x^2 = a(7x - 2a)$$

$$\Rightarrow \quad 3x^2 = 7ax - 2a^2$$

$$\Rightarrow 3x^2 - 7ax + 2a^2 = 0$$

Using PAFF:

P: $3 \times 2a^2 = 6a^2$

A: coefficient of $x = -7a$

F: $-6a$ and $-a$.

F: Replace $-7ax$ with $-6ax - ax$, and factorise.

Factorising,

$$(3x - a)(x - 2a) = 0$$

So $x = \frac{a}{3}$ or $x = 2a$

7.3 Laws of Logarithms
Exercise
Technique

1 Write the following as single logarithms:

a $\ln 7 + \ln 2$
b $\log 2 + \log 3 + \log 4$
c $2 \ln 3$
d $\log 12 - \log 6$
e $\ln 6 + \ln 10 - \ln 5$
f $\log 1 - \log 3$

2 Given that $\log 2 = 0.301$ and $\log 3 = 0.477$ find, without using a calculator:

a $\log 4$
b $\log 27$
c $\log 18$
d $\log 36$
e $\log 144$
f $\log 1\frac{1}{2}$

3 Simplify:

a $\log x + 2 \log y + \log z$
b $3 \ln x - 2 \ln y$
c $\log a - 2 \log b - 3 \log c$
d $\ln x^2 - \frac{1}{2} \ln x$
e $3 \log x + 2 \log z$
f $\ln x - 2 \ln y + \ln z$

4 Express, in terms of $\ln x$, $\ln y$ and $\ln z$:

a $\ln(xyz)$
b $\ln\left(\frac{x^3y^2}{z}\right)$
c $\ln \frac{x\sqrt{y}}{z}$
d $\ln \sqrt[3]{xy}$
e $\ln \sqrt{\frac{xy}{z}}$
f $\ln x\sqrt{yz^3}$

5 Solve the following logarithmic equations:

a $\log_x 9 = \frac{1}{2}$
b $\log_x 16 = -4$
c $\ln x^3 - \ln x + \ln \sqrt{x} = 3$
d $\log_x 24 + \log_x 9 + 3 = 3 \log_x 4$

Contextual

1 Explain why $xy = 100$ and $\log_{10} x + \log_{10} y = 2$ are equivalent, interchangeable statements.

2 On the same axes sketch the graphs of $y = \ln x$ and $y = \ln(\frac{1}{x})$. Using the laws of logarithms suggest a possible transformation for these graphs. Describe an inverse function for $y = \ln(\frac{1}{x})$.

3 **a** Show that $\log_2 12 = \log_4 144$
b Evaluate $\log_2 12 - \log_4 9$ without using a calculator.

4 By taking natural logarithms, or otherwise, find $g(x)$ such that $x^x = e^{xg(x)}$ for all values of x.

5 Given that $\log_2 x + 2 \log_4 y = 4$, explain why $xy = 16$.

7.4 Solving $a^x = b$

Consider the equation $3^x = 20$. This can be solved by trial and improvement using the **power function** key 'x^y' on any scientific calculator, although this method can be quite time consuming. A more concise way of solving **exponential equations** like these is to use the properties of logarithms. The method is based on the principle that if two sides of an equation are equal then the logarithm of one side must be equal to the logarithm of the other.

Example 1

Solve $3^x = 20$.

Solution

Taking natural logarithms of both sides,

Either $\log_{10}$ or ln can b used; both bases will give the same answer.

$$\ln 3^x = \ln 20$$

$$x \ln 3 = \ln 20$$ ◀ **Using property 2.**

$$x = \frac{\ln 20}{\ln 3}$$

$$= \frac{2.996}{1.099} = 2.73 \text{ (3 s.f.)}$$

Check that $\log_{10}$ also gives $x = 2.73$.

The same principle can be used when the powers become more complicated.

Example 2

Solve $4^{(3x+1)} = 79$.

Solution

Taking logarithms of both sides,

Use either $\log_{10}$ or ln.

$$\log_{10} 4^{(3x+1)} = \log_{10} 79$$

$$(3x+1)\log_{10} 4 = \log_{10} 79$$

$$3x + 1 = \frac{\log_{10} 79}{\log_{10} 4}$$

$$x = \frac{1}{3}\left(\frac{\log_{10} 79}{\log_{10} 4} - 1\right)$$

$$= \frac{1}{3}\left(\frac{1.8976}{0.6021} - 1\right) = 0.717 \text{ (3 s.f.)}$$

Check that $4^{(3 \times 0.717 + 1)}$ is close to 79. Notice th rounding error.

This technique provides a useful tool for solving more complicated exponential equations where one power is a multiple of another.

Example 3

Solve the equation $e^{4x}+e^{2x}-6=0$.

Solution

Notice that $4x=2(2x)$, so this equation could be written

$$(e^{2x})^2+e^{2x}-6=0$$

Remember the laws of indices.

Now substitute $y=e^{2x}$. This transforms the exponential equation into a quadratic equation.

$$y^2+y-6=0$$

$$\Rightarrow \quad (y+3)(y-2)=0$$

Factorising.

$$\Rightarrow \quad y=-3 \text{ or } y=2$$

$$\text{So } e^{2x}=-3 \text{ or } e^{2x}=2.$$

Remember that $y=e^{2x}$.

These two statements can be analysed using logarithmic functions.

$e^{2x}=-3$ has no solutions since $e^{2x}>0$ for all values of x.

Exponential functions are always positive.

$$\text{If } e^{2x}=2 \text{ then } \ln(e^{2x})=\ln 2$$

$$2x\ln e=\ln 2$$

By property 5, $\ln e=1$.

$$2x=\ln 2$$

$$x=\tfrac{1}{2}\ln 2$$

$$=0.347 \text{ (3 s.f.)}$$

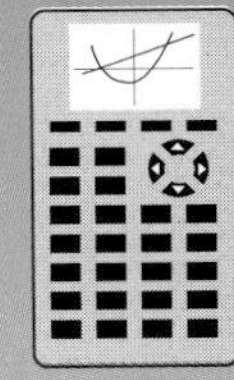

So the equation $e^{4x}+e^{2x}-6=0$ has only one solution; $x=0.347$ (3 s.f.).

Check this result on your calculator.

Logarithms can also be used to solve problems involving exponential functions and inequalities.

Example 4

a Find the smallest integer p such that 2.5^p exceeds one million.
b Find the largest integer x such that $(0.7)^x>5$.

This means solve $2.5^p>1\,000\,000$.

Solution

a Taking logarithms of both sides,

$$\log_{10}2.5^p>\log_{10}1\,000\,000$$

$$\Rightarrow p\log_{10}2.5>6$$

Note that $\log_{10}$ is preferable here because $1\,000\,000$ is a power of 10.

$$\Rightarrow \quad p>\frac{6}{\log_{10}2.5}$$

$$\Rightarrow \quad p>15.077$$

Since p has to be an integer, $p=16$.

Check that $2.5^{16}>1\times10^6$ and $2.5^{15}<1\times10^6$.

b Taking logarithms of both sides,

$$\log_{10}(0.7^x) > \log_{10} 5$$
$$\Rightarrow x\log_{10} 0.7 > \log_{10} 5$$
$$\Rightarrow x < \frac{\log_{10} 5}{\log_{10} 0.7}$$
$$\Rightarrow x < -4.512$$

Remember to reverse the inequality becaus $\log_{10} 0.7$ is negative.

Since x must be an integer, $x = -5$.

Check that the negative result is sensible. This can be done graphically by considering the intersection of $y = 0.7^x$ and $y = 5$. Check this result on a graphical calculator.

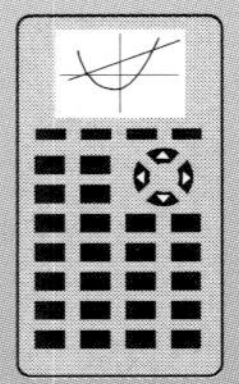

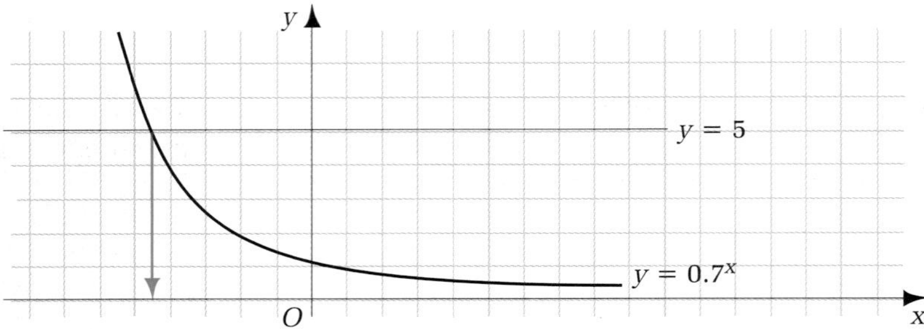

Sometimes x can appear as a power on both sides of an equation. To solve this logarithms can still be used.

Example 5

Find a value of x such that $5^x = 7^{(x-2)}$.

Solution

Start by taking logarithms of both sides:

$$\ln 5^x = \ln 7^{(x-2)}$$
$$\Rightarrow x\ln 5 = x\ln 7 - 2\ln 7$$
$$\Rightarrow x\ln 5 - x\ln 7 = -2\ln 7$$
$$\Rightarrow x(\ln 5 - \ln 7) = -2\ln 7$$
$$\Rightarrow x = -\frac{2\ln 7}{\ln 5 - \ln 7} = \frac{2\ln 7}{\ln 7 - \ln 5}$$
$$\Rightarrow x = 11.6 \text{ (3 s.f.)}$$

Using property 2.

Collecting like terms and factorising.

Compare $5^{11.6}$ and 7^9 on your calculator.

Graphical applications

We have looked at techniques of solving problems of the form $a^x = b$. These techniques also have a graphical application. If an exponential relationship exists between two sets of data, then logarithms can be used to simplify their exponential graph into a straight line. This technique is called **reduction to linear form**. There are two basic cases to consider:

- the exponent is variable
- the exponent is constant.

'Exponent', 'index' and 'power' all mean the same.

The exponent is variable

This means that the relationship between x and y is such that $y = a \times b^x = ab^x$ where a and b are constants. By using the logarithm techniques:

$$\log y = \log ab^x$$

$$\log y = \log a + \log b^x \quad \blacktriangleleft \text{ By property 1.}$$

$$\log y = \log a + x\log b \quad \blacktriangleleft \text{ By property 2.}$$

Look carefully at this result. What do you notice? It has the form $Y = mX + c$ where $Y = \log y$, $X = x$, $m = \log b$ and $c = \log a$. So plotting $\log y$ vertically against x horizontally should give a straight line of gradient $\log b$ with a vertical intercept of $\log a$.

Which is the form of a *linear* equation.

Example 6

The relationship between the values of x and y in the following table is $y = ab^x$, where a and b are positive integers. Find a and b.

x	0	1	2	3	4
y	5	10	20	40	80

Solution

Plotting the data on a graph gives an exponential style curve.

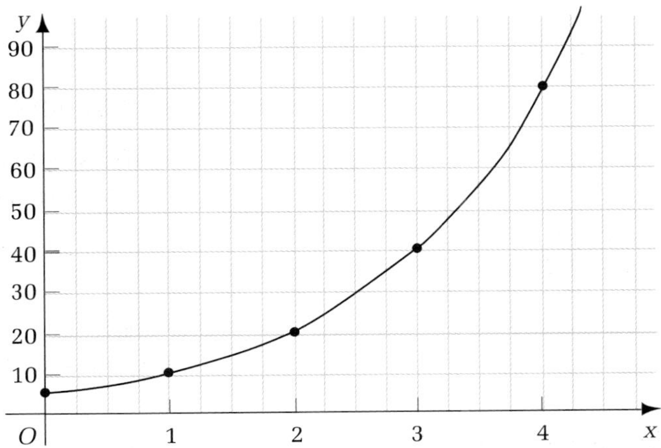

However, when $\log y$ is plotted against x a straight line is obtained.

x	0	1	2	3	4
$\log y$	0.699	1.000	1.301	1.602	1.903

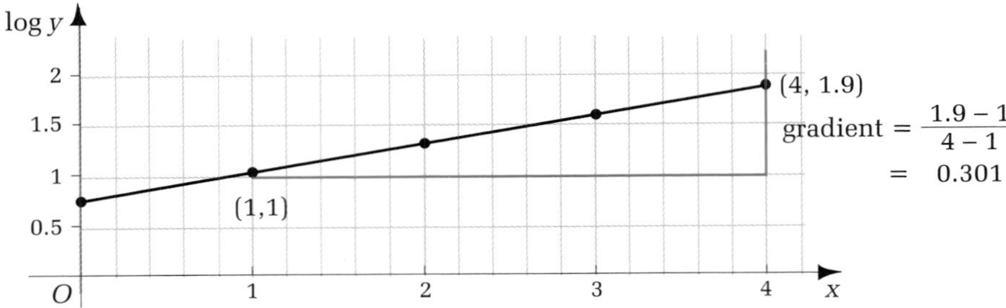

From the straight-line graph notice that the intercept with the 'y-axis' is approximately 0.7 and the gradient is about 0.301. We have already seen that an exponential equation in the form $y = ab^x$ can be written in the linear form $\log y = \log a + x \log b$, where $\log b$ is the gradient of the line $\log y = \log a + x \log b$, and $\log a$ is the intercept with the vertical axis.
From the graph, $\log a \approx 0.7$ and $\log b \approx 0.301$.
So $a = 5$ and $b = 2$
So the equation that fits the data is $y = 5 \times 2^x$.

Check this model against the original d

The exponent is constant

This means that the relationship between x and y is such that $y = a \times x^b = ax^b$, where a and b are constants. This is really a power function and not an exponential function. Using the logarithm properties,

$$\log y = \log(ax^b)$$

$$\log y = \log a + \log x^b \quad \blacktriangleleft \text{ By property 1.}$$

$$\log y = \log a + b \log x \quad \blacktriangleleft \text{ By property 2.}$$

What do you notice about this result? This also has the linear form $Y = mX + c$ if $\log y$ is plotted vertically as Y and $\log x$ is plotted horizontally as X. The resulting straight line will have a gradient of b and a vertical intercept of $\log a$.

In the early ninetee century, Charles Babbage and fellow Cambridge student J Herschel recalculated corrected logarithm t which at that stage w notoriously inaccurate This was laborious, tedious work and dem a high degree of accu Babbage once made seemed to be a passin comment, 'It is a pity can't be done by stean later went on to develo number of machines, including the first calcu which he called his 'analytical engine'.

Example 7

The relationship between x and y in the following table of values is $y = ax^b$ where a and b are positive integers. Use a graphical method to find a and b.

x	0	1	2	3	4
y	0	2	16	54	128

Solution

The data plotted on a graph gives a curve.

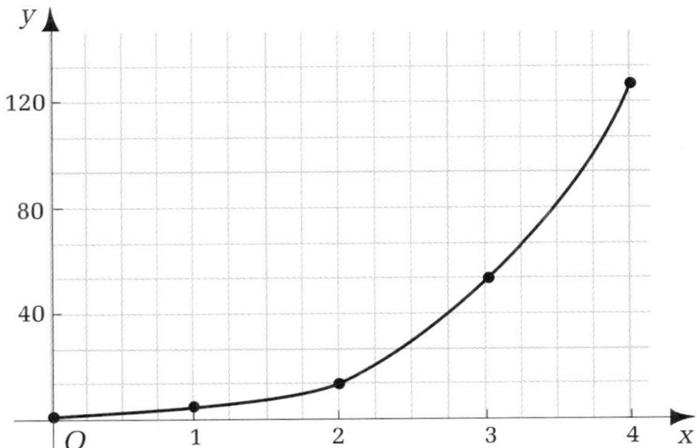

Now take logarithms and retabulate the data.

Note that the point $x = 0, y = 0$ cannot be used.

$\log x$	0	0.301	0.477	0.602
$\log y$	0.301	1.204	1.732	2.107

Plotting $\log y$ against $\log x$ gives a straight-line graph.

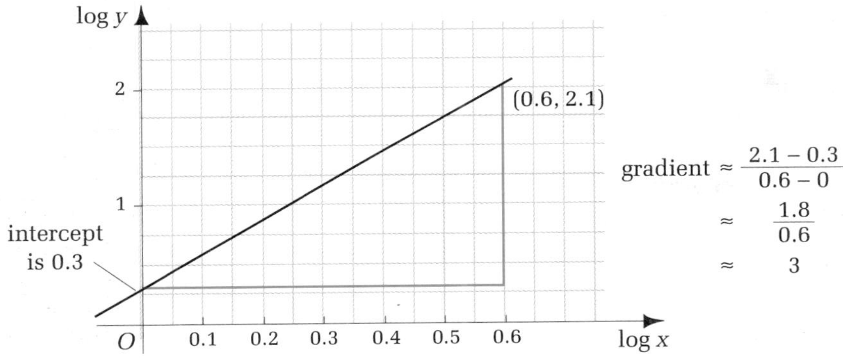

From the graph notice that the vertical intercept is 0.3 and the gradient is 3. From the linear equation in $\log x$ and $\log y$, $\log y = \log a + b \log x$, this means $\log a \approx 0.3$ and $b \approx 3$.

Remember that a and b are integers.

So $a = 2$ and $b = 3$.

Thus the equation that fits this data is $y = 2x^3$.

Check this model against the original data.

When you get sets of data like these a decision has to be made. Which model should be used? If either of the graphs gives a straight line then an exponential or power form would be the expected equation. One way of saving time is to look at the original data and determine if it goes through the origin. If it does, then suspect that the exponent is constant.

7.4 Solving $a^x = b$

Exercise

Technique

1 Solve the following equations:

a $2^x = 4000$ **b** $5^x = 500$
c $11^x = 151$ **d** $4^x = 17$

2 Solve the equations:

a $3^{x+1} = 25$ **b** $4^{x-3} = 30$
c $5^{2x+3} = 51$ **d** $3^{2x-1} = 29$

3 Find the value of x in the following:

3 **a**

a $5^{3x} = 7^{x-2}$ **b** $2^{x+1} = 3^x$
c $7^{x+3} = 3^{x-2}$ **d** $2^{3x+1} = 3^{2x-3}$

4 Solve the following exponential equations:

a $e^{2x} - 5e^x + 6 = 0$ **b** $2e^{2x} - 9e^x + 4 = 0$
c $e^{2x} + e^x - 6 = 0$ **d** $6e^{4x} - 13e^{2x} - 5 = 0$

5 Find the smallest integer p such that:

a $2^p > 1000$ **b** $3^p > 2000$
c $(0.9)^p < 0.0001$ **d** $(0.5)^p < 0.001$

6 Find equations for the following sets of data:

a

x	0	1	2	3	4
y	3	15	75	375	1875

b

x	0	1	2	3	4
y	0	3	96	729	3072

c

x	0	0.5	1.0	1.5	2.0
y	2	3.46	6	10.4	18

d

x	0	0.5	1.0	1.5	2.0
y	3	1.10	0.406	0.149	0.0549

Hint: Use ln in part d

Hint: Let $y = 10^x$.

7 Solve the following equations:

7 **a**

a $100^x - 10^{x+1} + 16 = 0$ **b** $10^{2x} - 10^{x+1} + 21 = 0$
c $10^{2x} - 10.10^x + 24 = 0$ **d** $10^{2x} - 100 = 0$

Contextual

1 The population, P thousands, of a new town is calculated every t years after 1979. The results are summarised in the table below.

t	1	2	3	4	5
P	12.1	18.4	28.0	42.5	64.6

It is believed that P and t are connected by an exponential relationship of the form $P = ab^t$, where a and b are constants. Verify this graphically and find the values of a and b. When is the population expected to exceed half a million?

2 Show that the equation $e^{2x} - 7e^x - 8 = 0$ has one real solution. Why does the second solution of the related quadratic not produce a solution to the exponential equation?

3 Before Newton's theory of gravitation, the best mathematical model to describe planetary motion was formulated by Kepler (1571–1630). Kepler stated three laws, the third of which gave a relationship between the distance of the planet from the sun, R (millions of km), and the period of its orbit, T (years). Kepler had data for the following six planets.

Planet	Distance from the Sun (millions of km)	Period of orbit (years)
Mercury	57.9	0.241
Venus	108.2	0.616
Earth	149.6	1.0
Mars	227.9	1.881
Jupiter	778.3	11.852
Saturn	1427.0	29.440

Using the model $T = aR^b$, where a and b are constants, find Kepler's third law. Check this model on the following data for planets not known to Kepler:

Planet	Distance (R)	Period of orbit (T)
Uranus	2870	83.943
Neptune	4497	164.681
Pluto	5907	248.241

How accurate is the model?

4 Find the real value of k for which $10^x = e^{kx}$ for all values of x.

Consolidation

Exercise A

1 Without using a calculator show that $\dfrac{\log 9\sqrt{3} - \log 4\sqrt{2}}{\log 3 - \log 2} = \dfrac{5}{2}$.

2 Solve the following inequalities:

a $\ln(x + 2) < 3$ **b** $(0.7)^x > 3$

3 The value of a car (in £) can be modelled by the equation $V = 8500e^{-\lambda t}$, where t is the age of the car in years and λ is a constant.

a State the value of the car when it was new.
b After two years the value of the car was £6580. Use this information to calculate the value of λ.
c Estimate the value of the car after three years.
d How long would it take for the value of the car to be half its original value?

4 **a** If $A_0 = 100$ and $A_{n+1} = 1.07A_n$ find a formula for A_n in terms of n.
b If n represents the number of years a sum of money is left in an account and A_0 represents an initial investment of £100, what does 1.07 represent?
c How many years would it take for the investment to double?

5 Given that $y = 10^x$, show that:

a $y^2 = 100^x$
b $\frac{y}{10} = 10^{x-1}$
c Using the results from **a** and **b** write the equation $100^x - 10\,001(10^{x-1}) + 100 = 0$ as an equation in y.
d By first solving the equation in y, find the values of x which satisfy the given equation in x.

(ULEAC)

6 The population of Portugal t years after 1990 can be modelled by the equation $P = P_0e^{kt}$.

a In 1990 the population was estimated to be 10.5 million. Write down the value of P_0.
b The growth rate was expected to be 0.5% per annum. Explain why the population projection for 1991 is $1.05 \times 10^7 \times (1.005)$.
c Use the result from **b** to find the value of k correct to three significant figures.
d Use the result from **c** to predict the population for 2000.

7 Given that $y = \log_b 45 + \log_b 25 - 2\log_b 75$, express y as a single logarithm in base b. In the case when $b = 5$, state the value of y.

(AEB)

8 For certain planets, the approximate mean distance x, in millions of kilometres from the centre of the Sun, and the orbit T, in Earth years, are recorded.

x	57.9	108.2	227.9	778.3
T	0.24	0.62	1.88	11.86

Assuming a law of the form $T = Ax^n$, draw a graph of $\ln T$ against $\ln x$. Estimate the values of A and n, giving your answers to two significant figures. Use your graph to estimate the approximate mean distance in millions of kilometres of the Earth from the Sun.

(AEB)

9 The graph shows the function $f(x) = e^{-x^2/2}$ for $x > 0$. By writing $y = e^{-x^2/2}$ find an expression for x in terms of y. Hence write down $f^{-1}(x)$.

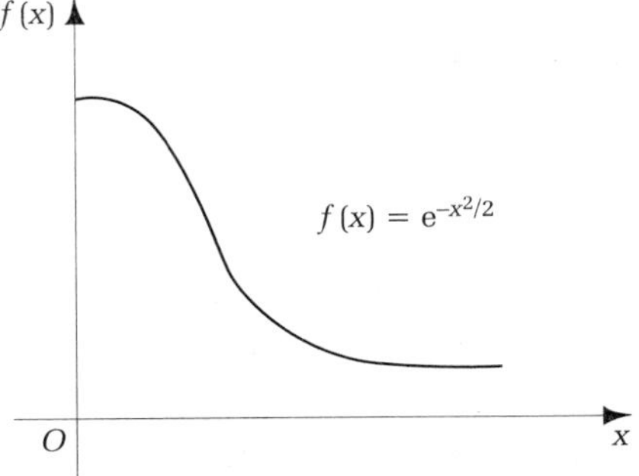

10 A slide into a ball pool at a children's play centre can be modelled by the curve $y = 3 \times 10^{-x/2}$ where x and y are measured in metres. The slide has three supports, fixed to the ground at positions A, B and C as shown in the diagram.

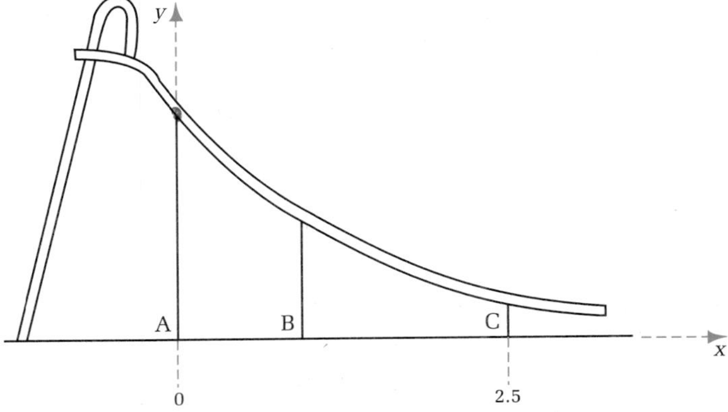

a Calculate the height of the supports at A and C.

b The support at B is half the height of the support at A. How far along the ground is support B from support A.

Exercise B

1 Without using a calculator express as a single logarithm,

$$2\log\left(\frac{5}{\sqrt{2}}\right) + \log 3 + 2\log 2$$

2 Solve the following inequalities:

a $\ln(2x) < 5$ **b** $(0.95)^{x+1} > 8$

3 The value V of a particular car, in pounds, at age t months from new can be modelled by the equation $V = 12000e^{-kt} + 2000$, where k is a constant.

a Use this model to write down the value of the car when new.

b The value of the car is expected to be £8000 after 24 months. On this basis, calculate the value of k.

(AEB)

4 An employee joins a large firm on 1 January of a particular year. In order to provide a sum of money for the employee's retirement, £1500 is paid into a special account on 1 January each year for the previous year's work. In addition, on each 1 January, interest is added to the account, the interest being 6% of the total amount in the account immediately prior to the annual payment of £1500.

a Show that for an employee, who retires on 1 January after serving n years with the firm, the sum of money in the special account is equal to £25 000$(1.06^n - 1)$.

b Find the least number of years required for the sum to exceed £100 000.

(WJEC)

5 By treating the following equation as a quadratic in e^x, find the two values of x satisfying $e^{2x} - 5e^x + 6 = 0$.

(WJEC)

6 The population of Iceland t years after 1990 can be modelled by the equation $P = 0.251e^{\lambda t}$, where P is measured in millions.

a If the growth rate is estimated to be 0.8% per annum, estimate the value of λ.

b In what year would the population reach half a million?

7 Given than $\ln(3x - 5) - \ln 4 = 2\ln y$:

a find the value of y when $x = 2$

b express x in terms of y in a form not involving logarithms.

(AEB)

Applications and Activities

1 *Fibonacci numbers*

This sequence of numbers owes its name to the Italian mathematician Leonardo da Pisa (1170–1230). Each term of the sequence is the sum of the two previous terms. Since $1 + 1 = 2$, $1 + 2 = 3$, $2 + 3 = 5$ and so on the sequence becomes 1, 1, 2, 3, 5, 8, 13, ...
If these numbers are tabulated,

x	1	2	3	4	5	6	7
y	1	1	2	3	5	8	13

and then plotted graphically, a curve is formed.
Find the equation for the curve generated by the Fibonacci numbers.

Hint: Try $y = ab^x$.

2 *The logarithmic spiral*

This spiral intersects all radii at a fixed angle and the distances from its pole increase in a geometric sequence. To sketch a logarithmic spiral quickly use European DIN paper size A0. Fold the A0 size sheet of paper in descending 'A' size order and draw a line from one corner to the opposite corner of each section in a clockwise or anticlockwise order.

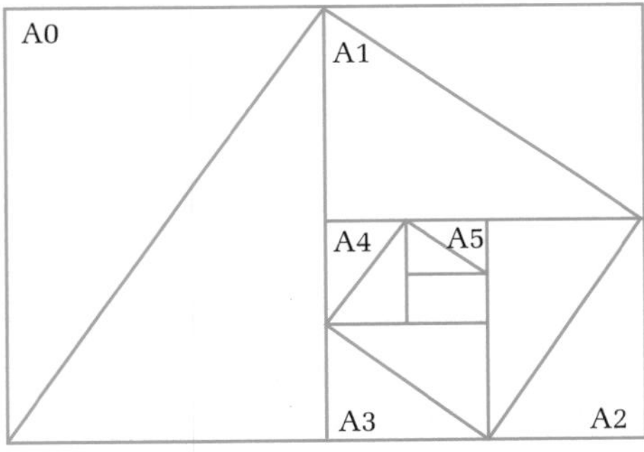

Descartes (1596–1650)
The logarithmic spiral was first recognised by Descartes and found so fascinating by Jacob Bernoulli (1654–1705) that he arranged to have it engraved on his tombstone.

Logarithmic spirals occur often in nature. Investigate!

Summary

- If $y = a^x$ then $x = \log_a y$.
- **Common logarithms** have base 10, and are written as $\log_{10}$ or log.
- **Natural logarithms** have base e, and are written as $\log_e$ or ln.
- The five basic properties of logarithms for all bases are:

$$\log ab = \log a + \log b$$

$$\log a^n = n \log a$$

$$\log \frac{a}{b} = \log a - \log b$$

$$\log 1 = 0$$

$$\log_a a = 1$$

- e^x is the **exponential function** and is used to model growth and decay.
- Relationships of the form $y = ab^x$ can be transformed from an exponential curve to a straight line by plotting $\log y$ vertically against x horizontally. The gradient of the straight line is $\log b$ and the y-intercept is $\log a$.
- Relationships of the form $y = ax^b$ can be transformed from an exponential curve to a straight line by plotting $\log y$ vertically against $\log x$ horizontally. The gradient of the straight line is b and the y-intercept is $\log a$.

8 Sequences and Series

What you need to know

- How to collect 'like terms'.
- How to expand brackets.
- How to substitute values into expressions.
- How to express an algebraic fraction in terms of its partial fractions.

Review

1 By collecting together like terms, simplify the following expressions:

a $a + a + 2d$ **b** $a + a + (n-1)d$

c $a + ar + ar$ **d** $1 + x^2 + x^3 - \frac{1}{2}(x^2 + x^3)$

2 Expand the following:

a $(n+3)(n+4)$ **b** $(r+2)(r-1)$

c $r(r+1)$ **d** $(1+x)^2$

3 Evaluate:

a $2n + 3$, when $n = 3$

b $3n - 1$, when $n = 5$

c $n^2 - 1$, when $n = 4$

d $\frac{1}{2}n(n-1)(n-2)$, when $n = 3$

e ar^4, when $a = \frac{1}{2}$, $r = 2$

f $\dfrac{a(1-r^n)}{(1-r)}$, when $a = 10$, $r = \frac{1}{2}$, $n = 4$.

4 Express each of the following in terms of their partial fractions:

a $\dfrac{5}{r(r+1)}$ **b** $\dfrac{6}{(r+1)(r+2)}$

c $\dfrac{7}{(n+1)(n+2)}$ **d** $\dfrac{12}{n(n+1)}$

8.1 Sequences and Series

Sequences

A **sequence** is a set of numbers occurring in order. Some examples of sequences are:

$2, 4, 6, 8, \ldots$	the sequence of even numbers
$1, 4, 9, 16, \ldots$	the sequence of perfect squares
$1, 3, 6, 10, \ldots$	the sequence of triangular numbers.

The terms of a sequence are often represented by ordered lower-case letters. Thus u_1 denotes the first term and u_2 denotes the second, and the sequence becomes:

$$u_1, u_2, u_3, \ldots$$

For the sequence of even numbers, $u_1 = 2$, $u_2 = 4$, $u_3 = 6$, and so on. A sequence can be described in several different ways. One method is to give an algebraic expression for **the *n*th term**. The nth term for the sequence of even numbers is $2n$. This can be written:

$$u_n = 2n$$

Check that $u_n = n^2$ and $u_n = \frac{1}{2}n(n+1)$ generate the sequence of perfect squares and the sequence of triangular numbers respectively.

Example 1

Find the first five terms of the sequence whose nth term is given by

$$u_n = \frac{n(n-1)(n-2)}{6}$$

Solution

To find the first five terms put $n = 1, 2, 3, 4$ and 5 respectively into the expression for u_n.

$$u_1 = \frac{1(1-1)(1-2)}{6} = 0$$

$$u_2 = \frac{2(2-1)(2-2)}{6} = 0$$

$$u_3 = \frac{3(3-1)(3-2)}{6} = 1$$

$$u_4 = \frac{4(4-1)(4-2)}{6} = 4$$

$$u_5 = \frac{5(5-1)(5-2)}{6} = 10$$

So the first five terms are 0, 0, 1, 4, 10.

There are other types of sequences where the sign oscillates between positive and negative.

Example 2

Find the nth term of the sequence $-1, 3, -5, 7 \ldots$

Solution

Notice that without the change of sign this sequence is the sequence of odd numbers. For odd numbers, $u_n = 2n - 1$.
The change of sign in the sequence can be generated by using powers of -1.

$(-1)^1 = -1$ ◀ Odd powers give negative results.

$(-1)^2 = +1$ ◀ Even powers give positive results.

$(-1)^3 = -1$

$(-1)^4 = +1$

So the nth term of the sequence $-1, 3, -5, 7$ is given by

$$u_n = (-1)^n(2n - 1)$$

Verify this result for $n = 1, 2, 3$ and 4.

Sometimes the rule for defining a sequence can be given in the form of a **recurrence relation**. This means the nth term u_n can be calculated only when the preceding terms are known.

Example 3

The **Fibonacci sequence**, $1, 1, 2, 3, 5, 8, 13, 21, \ldots$ can be defined by a recurrence relation. Find this rule.

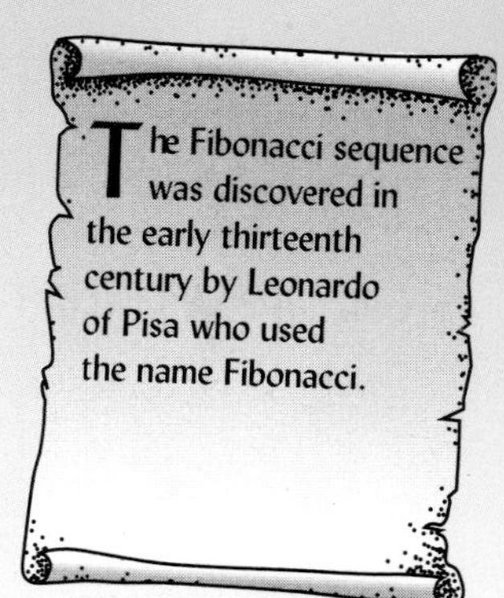

The Fibonacci sequence was discovered in the early thirteenth century by Leonardo of Pisa who used the name Fibonacci.

Solution

To find the recurrence relation look at how the terms of the sequence are related to each other.

$u_1 = 1$

$u_2 = 1$

$u_3 = 2 = u_2 + u_1$

$u_4 = 3 = u_3 + u_2$

$u_5 = 5 = u_4 + u_3$

$u_6 = 8 = u_5 + u_4$

So $u_n = u_{n-1} + u_{n-2}$

The nth term in the Fibonacci sequence can only be found if the previous two terms, u_{n-1} and u_{n-2}, are known.

Example 4

a Find the first four terms of the sequence defined by the recurrence relation $u_n = u_{n-1} + 2$ with $u_1 = 3$.

b Find the first five terms of the sequence defined by $u_n = 3u_{n-1} - u_{n-2}$, with $u_1 = 1$ and $u_2 = 2$.

Solution

a Given u_1, find u_2 using the given recurrence relation. Then calculate u_3 and u_4 using the same technique.

$u_1 = 3$

$u_2 = u_1 + 2 = 5$

$u_3 = u_2 + 2 = 7$

$u_4 = u_3 + 2 = 9$

So the first four terms of the sequence are 3, 5, 7, 9.

b Use the values of u_1 and u_2 to find u_3. Then generate u_4 and u_5 using the same recurrence relation.

$u_1 = 1$

$u_2 = 2$

$u_3 = 3u_2 - u_1 = 6 - 1 = 5$

Remember to put $n =$3 in the recurrence relation.

$u_4 = 3u_3 - u_2 = 15 - 2 = 13$

$u_5 = 3u_4 - u_3 = 39 - 5 = 34$

So the first five terms of the sequence are 1, 2, 5, 13, 34.

Series

When the terms of a sequence are added together, a **series** is formed.

$2 + 4 + 6 + 8$ is a finite series

$1 + 4 + 9 + 16 + \cdots$ is an infinite series

If a sequence has five terms, u_1, u_2, u_3, u_4 and u_5, then the series based on this sequence would be

$$u_1 + u_2 + u_3 + u_4 + u_5$$

This series can be written in a more concise form. Instead of appearing as a string of terms added together, the series is written using **sigma notation**.

$$u_1 + u_2 + u_3 + u_4 + u_5 = \sum_{r=1}^{5} u_r$$

Σ is the Greek letter, sigma. It is used in mathematics to represent a summation. The letter r is a **dummy variable**. The $r = 1$ at the foot of the sigma indicates the term with which the summation should start, and the 5 at the top indicates the term with which the summation should finish. Thus $\sum_{r=4}^{7} u_r$ means start with the fourth term, u_4 and sum to the seventh term, u_7.

Example 5

If $u_r = 2r - 1$, find $\sum_{r=1}^{5} u_r$.

Solution

To sum this series, first substitute the values of r from 1 to 5 into the expression for the rth term of the sequence and then sum the results.

$$\begin{aligned}\sum_{r=1}^{5} u_r &= \sum_{r=1}^{5} (2r - 1) \\ &= (2 - 1) + (4 - 1) + (6 - 1) + (8 - 1) + (10 - 1) \\ &= 1 + 3 + 5 + 7 + 9 \\ &= 25\end{aligned}$$

Sigma notation is particularly useful when the series is infinite. In these cases there is no last term, so writing the series as a summation string would be impossible. In sigma notation, however, we can write:

$$\sum_{r=1}^{\infty} u_r = u_1 + u_2 + u_3 + \cdots$$

So the sum of the even numbers can be written:

$$2 + 4 + 6 + 8 + \cdots = \sum_{r=1}^{\infty} 2r$$

Writing a series in sigma notation is dependant upon an algebraic expression for the nth term being known.

Example 6

Express:

a $1 + 3 + 6 + 10 + 15$ in sigma notation

b $7 + 10 + 13 + 16$ in the form $\sum_{r=3}^{n} f(r)$

Solution

a The terms in this series are from the sequence of triangular numbers. The nth term, $u_n = \frac{1}{2}n(n+1)$. Since $1 + 3 + 6 + 10 + 15$ begins with the first term and ends with the fifth term,

$$1 + 3 + 6 + 10 + 15 = \sum_{r=1}^{5} \frac{r(r+1)}{2}$$

Recall that r is a dumm variable.

b The first step is to find an expression for the nth term. Notice that the sequence 7, 10, 13, 16 increases in equal steps of 3. This suggests the expression for the nth term should contain a 3. Rewrite the sequence using this factor of 3. Note that $r = 3$ for the first term.

$u_3 = 7$ $\qquad$ $u_4 = 10$ $\qquad$ $u_5 = 13$

$= 3 \times 3 - 2$ $\qquad$ $= 4 \times 3 - 2$ $\qquad$ $= 5 \times 3 - 2$

This suggests that we can write the nth term as

$$u_n = n \times 3 - 2 = 3n - 2$$

The series is finite with last term 16.

Hence $3n - 2 = 16$

$3n = 18$

$n = 6$

Therefore $7 + 10 + 13 + 16 = \sum_{r=3}^{6} (3r - 2)$

8.1 Sequences and Series
Exercise
Technique

1 Find the first four terms of the sequences with the following nth terms:

a $u_n = 3n + 4$ **b** $u_n = 4n - 1$ **c** $u_n = 6n - 1$
d $u_n = (n+3)(n+4)$ **e** $u_n = 2^{n-1}$ **f** $u_n = n^3 + 1$

2 Find u_n, the nth term, for the following sequences:

a $6, 8, 10, 12, \ldots$ **d** $12, 10, 8, 6, \ldots$ **g** $\frac{2}{3}, \frac{3}{4}, \frac{4}{5}, \frac{5}{6}, \frac{6}{7}, \ldots$
b $14, 17, 20, 23, \ldots$ **e** $-3, -5, -7, -9, \ldots$ **h** $0, \frac{1}{4}, \frac{2}{9}, \frac{3}{16}, \ldots$
c $1, 6, 11, 16, 21, \ldots$ **f** $0, 3, 8, 15, 24, \ldots$

3 Use the following recurrence relations to find the next four terms of each sequence:

a $u_n = u_{n-1} + 3,\ u_1 = 1$ **d** $u_n = 2u_{n-1} - u_{n-2},\ u_2 = 2,\ u_1 = 1$
b $u_n = 2u_{n-1} + 1,\ u_1 = 1$ **e** $u_n = 2u_{n-1} + u_{n-2},\ u_2 = 2,\ u_1 = 1$
c $u_n = 3u_{n-1} - 1,\ u_1 = 2$ **f** $u_n = \frac{1}{2}(u_{n-1}) + 1,\ u_1 = 4$

3 c

4 Express the following series in sigma notation:

a $1 + 4 + 9 + 16$ **d** $3 + 5 + 7 + 9 + 11 + 13$
b $3 + 6 + 11 + 18$ **e** $0 + 2 + 6 + 12 + 20 + 30 + 42$
c $4 + 5 + 6 + 7 + 8 + 9$ **f** $2 + 6 + 12 + 20 + 30 + 42 + 56$

5 Evaluate:

a $\sum_{r=1}^{3} r^3$ **b** $\sum_{r=2}^{4} (r^2 + 1)$ **c** $\sum_{r=3}^{5} r^3$
d $\sum_{r=4}^{6} (5r - 2)$ **e** $\sum_{r=3}^{6} r(r+1)$ **f** $\sum_{r=3}^{5} (r+1)(r+2)$

6 Express the following series in the given form of sigma notation:

a $5 + 8 + 11 + 14,\quad \sum_{r=3}^{n} f(r)$

b $5 + 8 + 11 + 14 + 17 + 20,\quad \sum_{r=3}^{n} f(r)$

c $9 + 11 + 13 + 15,\quad \sum_{r=2}^{n} f(r)$

d $9 + 15 + 21 + 27,\quad \sum_{r=4}^{n} f(r)$

e $7 + 10 + 13 + 16 + 19,\quad \sum_{r=2}^{n} f(r)$

f $6 + 8 + 10 + 12 + 14 + 16 + 18,\quad \sum_{r=3}^{n} f(r)$

8.2 Arithmetic Progression

An **arithmetic progression** is a sequence in which each term is produced by adding a fixed number. For example $2, 5, 8, 11, \ldots$ is an arithmetic progression and $10, 7, 4, 1, -2, \ldots$ is also an arithmetic progression. Notice that the number that is added throughout the sequence can be positive or negative. It is called the **common difference**.
The phrase 'arithmetic progression' is often abbreviated to AP. The first term is usually denoted by a and the common difference by d.
Consider the AP $2, 5, 8, 11, \ldots$. Here $a = 2$ and $d = 3$. This sequence can now be rewritten as

$$2, \quad 2+3, \quad 2+(2\times 3), \quad 2+(3\times 3), \quad 2+(4\times 3), \ldots$$

The nth term would be $2 + (n-1)\times 3$.

In general the nth term of an AP is
$\boldsymbol{u_n = a + (n-1)d}$

◀ **Learn this important result.**

Example 1

Find an expression for the nth term of the AP $10, 7, 4, 1, -2, \ldots$.

Solution

For this AP, $a = 10$ and $d = -3$.

$$\begin{aligned} u_n &= a + (n-1)d \\ &= 10 + (n-1)\times(-3) \\ &= 10 - 3n + 3 \\ &= 13 - 3n \end{aligned}$$

Check this expression for u_n for values of n from 1 to 5.

The terms of an AP can be added to form an **arithmetic series**.

$$a + (a+d) + (a+2d) + (a+3d) + \cdots + (a+(n-1)d) + \cdots$$

If this series is finite then it has a last term and it is possible to find an expression for the sum of the series.

Example 2

Find the sum of the first 100 natural numbers.

Solution

The first 100 natural numbers form an AP, with $a = 1$ and $d = 1$. The sum of this AP is a finite arithmetic series:

$$1 + 2 + 3 + 4 + \cdots + 100$$

How can this total be calculated?

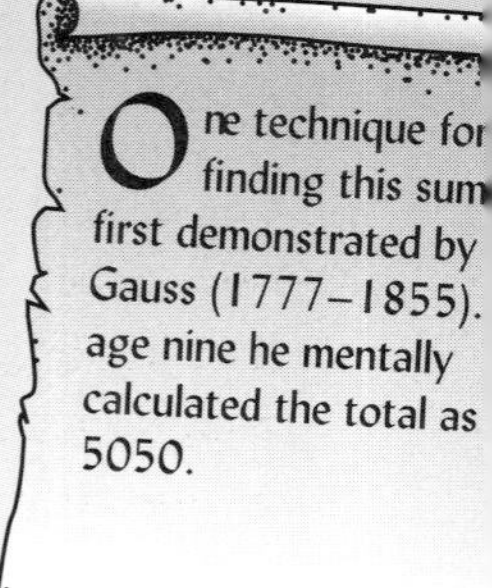

One technique for finding this sum first demonstrated by Gauss (1777–1855). age nine he mentally calculated the total as 5050.

Let S_{100} be the sum of the first 100 terms.

$$S_{100} = 1 + 2 + 3 + \cdots + 99 + 100 \qquad [1]$$

Now write the sum again in reverse.

$$S_{100} = 100 + 99 + 98 + \cdots + 2 + 1 \qquad [2]$$

Adding [1] and [2], term by term,

$$2 \times S_{100} = 101 + 101 + 101 + \cdots + 101 + 101$$

We know that there are 100 terms on the RHS, so

$$2 \times S_{100} = 100 \times 101$$

$$\Rightarrow \quad S_{100} = \tfrac{1}{2}(100 \times 101) = 5050$$

The same idea can be applied to every finite arithmetic series.

$$S_n = a + (a + d) + (a + 2d) + \cdots + (a + (n - 1)d)$$

$$S_n = [a + (n - 1)d] + \cdots + (a + 2d) + (a + d) + a$$

$$2S_n = [2a + (n - 1)d] + \cdots + [2a + (n - 1)d]$$

There are n terms on the RHS, so

$$S_n = \frac{n}{2}[2a + (n - 1)d]$$

◀ **Learn this important result.**

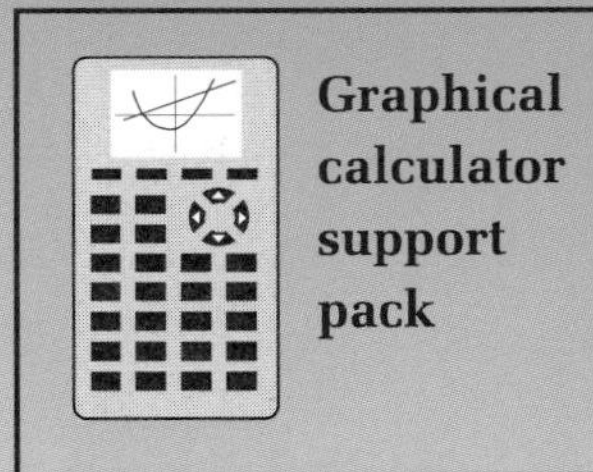

The sum to n terms of an arithmetic series can be written in another equivalent form:

$$S_n = \frac{n(a + l)}{2}$$

$a =$ first term
$l =$ last term

Example 3

For the AP $5, 9, 13, 17, \ldots$, find:

a the sixth term, u_6

b the sum of the first five terms, S_5.

Solution

First identify the first term and the common difference. The standard results for nth term and the sum to n terms can then be applied.
For the AP $5, 9, 13, 17, \ldots$, $a = 5$ and $d = 4$

a $\quad u_n = a + (n - 1)d$

$$\Rightarrow \quad u_6 = 5 + (6 - 1) \times 4 = 5 + (5 \times 4) = 25$$

b $S_n = \frac{n}{2}[2a + (n-1)d]$

$$S_5 = \frac{5}{2} \times [(2 \times 5) + (5-1) \times 4] = \frac{5}{2} \times (10 + 16) = 65$$

Example 4

Find the sums of the following arithmetic series:

a $2 + 5 + 8 + 11 + \cdots + 47$ **b** $47 + 41 + 35 + \cdots + (-43)$

Solution

a Here $a = 2$ and $d = 3$.
The number of terms in the series, n, can be found by making the last term, 47, the nth term.

Remember to check that the sequences are APs. Identify the first terms and common differences *before* using any other formula.

$$u_n = a + (n-1)d$$

$$\Rightarrow 47 = 2 + (n-1) \times 3 = 3n - 1$$

So $3n = 47 + 1 \Rightarrow n = 16$

The sum to 16 terms of the series can be found by using one of the formulas for S_{16}.

$$S_{16} = \frac{n(a+l)}{2} = \frac{16(2+47)}{2} = 392$$

b Here $a = 47$ and $d = -6$. Making -43 the nth term,

$$u_n = a + (n-1)d$$

$$\Rightarrow -43 = 47 + (n-1)(-6)$$

$$\Rightarrow -43 = 47 - 6n + 6 = 53 - 6n$$

So $6n = 53 + 43 \Rightarrow n = 16$

This arithmetic series also has 16 terms.

$$S_{16} = \frac{n(a+l)}{2} = \frac{16[47 + (-43)]}{2} = 32$$

Why is this total so low? Recall that many of the terms were negative.

$$S_{16} = 47 + 41 + 35 + \cdots - 25 - 31 - 37 - 43$$

This technique of identifying the first term, a, and common difference, d, for the AP is particularly useful when the information given relates to other terms in the series.

Example 5

The fifth term of an AP is twice the second term. The two terms differ by 9. Find the sum of the first 10 terms of the AP.

Solution

The information given is that

$$u_5 = 2u_2 \quad \text{and} \quad u_5 - u_2 = 9$$

Using the fact that the nth term of an AP is given by $u_n = a + (n-1)d$, these two equations can be rewritten as simultaneous equations in a and d.

$$\begin{aligned}
u_5 = 2u_2 \Rightarrow \quad & u_5 - 2u_2 = 0 \\
\Rightarrow \quad & (a+4d) - 2(a+d) = 0 \\
\Rightarrow \quad & a + 4d - 2a - 2d = 0 \\
\Rightarrow \quad & 2d - a = 0 \qquad [1] \\
u_5 - u_2 = 9 \Rightarrow \quad & (a+4d) - (a+d) = 9 \\
\Rightarrow \quad & a + 4d - a - d = 9 \\
\Rightarrow \quad & 3d = 9 \\
\Rightarrow \quad & d = 3 \qquad [2]
\end{aligned}$$

Notice that equation [2] gives the value of d. Substituting this value of d into equation [1] gives

$$(2 \times 3) - a = 0 \Rightarrow a = 6$$

The sum of the first 10 terms can now be found. Use these values of a and d with $n = 10$ in the formula for the sum to n terms.

$$\begin{aligned}
S_n &= \tfrac{1}{2}n(2a + (n-1)d) \\
\text{So } S_{10} &= \tfrac{10}{2}(12 + (9 \times 3)) \\
&= 5(12 + 27) = 195
\end{aligned}$$

Example 6

Evaluate $\sum_{r=3}^{16} (2r+1)$.

Recall how the sigma notation works; r is a dummy variable.

Solution

$$\begin{aligned}
\sum_{r=3}^{16} (2r+1) &= (6+1) + (8+1) + \cdots + (32+1) \\
&= 7 + 9 + \cdots + 33
\end{aligned}$$

This arithmetic series is generated by an AP where $a = 7$ and $d = 2$. Check that there are 14 terms in the series. The sum of the series can now be calculated.

Hint: Reduce $r = 3$ to $r = 1$ in the dummy variable.

$$S_n = \tfrac{1}{2}n[2a + (n-1)d]$$

So $$S_{14} = \tfrac{14}{2}[(2 \times 7) + (13 \times 2)]$$
$$= 7(14 + 26) = 280$$

So $\displaystyle\sum_{r=3}^{16}(2r+1) = 280$

Example 7

Pat saves £10 in the first month, £12 in the second month and increases the monthly savings by £2 each month. How long will it take Pat to save £500?

Solution

Notice that the monthly savings form an AP in which $a = 10$ and $d = 2$. Suppose Pat saves £500 in n months. This means the sum of the first n terms of the AP is 500.

So $S_n = 500$

$\Rightarrow \tfrac{1}{2}n(20 + 2(n-1)) = 500$ ◀ **Recall that $a = 10$ and $d = 2$.**

$\Rightarrow n(20 + 2n - 2) = 1000$

$\Rightarrow 18n + 2n^2 = 1000$

$\Rightarrow 2n^2 + 18n - 1000 = 0$

This is a quadratic equation in n. Solve it using the quadratic formula.

$n = \dfrac{-b \pm \sqrt{b^2 - 4ac}}{2a}$

$$n = \frac{-18 \pm \sqrt{18^2 - 4 \times 2 \times (-1000)}}{2 \times 2}$$
$$= 18.3 \quad \text{or} \quad -27.3 \text{ (3 s.f.)}$$

The negative answer can be ignored because the number of months cannot be negative.
So £500 is saved in 18.3 months. Given that Pat saves monthly, the savings exceed £500 after 19 months.

The number of mont[h]s must be an integer.

8.2 Arithmetic Progression
Exercise
Technique

1 Find (**i**) the next two terms and (**ii**) the nth term u_n, of each of the following arithmetic progressions:

a $13, 15, 17, 19, \dots$ **b** $8, 14, 20, 26, \dots$
c $34, 31, 28, 25, \dots$ **d** $-2, -5, -8, -11, \dots$

2 Given the arithmetic progressions $3, 7, 11, 15, \dots, u_n$; $6, 11, 16, 21, \dots, v_n$; and $70, 66, 62, 58, \dots, w_n$, find:

a u_6 **b** u_{30} **c** v_{11}
d v_{100} **e** w_9 **f** w_{30}

3 Find the sums of the following arithmetic series:

a $1 + 5 + 9 + 13 + \cdots + 41$ **b** $2 + 8 + 14 + 20 + \cdots + 38$
c $4 + 7 + 10 + 13 + \cdots + 25$ **d** $22 + 27 + 32 + \cdots + 47$

4 Use the method of Gauss (Example 2) to calculate:

a $16 + 14 + 12 + \ldots + 2$ **d** $28 + 27 + 26 + \ldots + 17$
b $27 + 24 + 21 + \ldots + 9$ **e** $22 + 17 + 12 + \ldots - 18$
c $56 + 52 + 48 + \ldots + 32$ **f** $-3 - 5 - 7 - 9 \ldots - 21$

5 Evaluate:

a $\sum_{r=1}^{10} (3r + 2)$ **b** $\sum_{r=2}^{14} (2r - 1)$
c $\sum_{r=5}^{20} (2r + 5)$ **d** $\sum_{r=6}^{16} (3r - 10)$

 5 c

Contextual

1 The number of beams in a bridge structure form a sequence $3, 5, 7, 9, \dots$. What is the nth term of this sequence?

2 Calculate the 20th term of the sequence $-8, -2, +4, +10, \dots$.

3 Find the sum of the arithmetic series $15 + 18 + 21 + \cdots + 60$. Check the result using the method of Gauss (Example 2).

4 Find the sum of the first 16 terms of the arithmetic progression $11 + 18 + 25 + 32 + \dots$.

5 The ninth term of an arithmetic series is three times the second term and the difference between the sixth term and twice the first term is 10. Find:

a the first term
b the common difference of the AP.

6 The sum of the first five terms of an AP is 72. The sum of the first ten terms is 189. Find the sum of the first fifteen terms.

7 When x is added to 6, 12, and 14 respectively and the results are squared, the new sequence is an arithmetic progression. Find x.

8 Luke's piggy bank deposits increase by 5p each week. His initial deposit is 10p. How long will it be before Luke's savings are at least:

a £10 **b** £100?

In the week his savings exceeded £100, how much did Luke deposit?

9 An AP has three consecutive terms with a sum of 33 and a product of 935. Find the terms.

10 An AP has first term 10 and common difference 0.8. If the sum of the first n terms is to exceed 250, find the value of n.

8.3 Geometric Progression

A **geometric progression** is a sequence in which each term is produced from the preceding term by multiplying by a fixed number. For example $3, 6, 12, 24, \ldots$ is a geometric progression, and so is $1, -\frac{1}{2}, \frac{1}{4}, -\frac{1}{8}, \frac{1}{16}$. Notice that the multiplier throughout the sequence can be positive or negative. It is known as the **common ratio**.

In general the phrase 'geometric progression' is abbreviated to GP. The first term is denoted by a and the common ratio by r.

A GP can then be written as

$$a, ar, ar^2, ar^3, ar^4, \ldots$$

The common ratio can be found by comparing successive terms in the sequence.

$$\frac{u_2}{u_1} = \frac{u_3}{u_2} = \frac{u_4}{u_3} = \frac{u_5}{u_4} = r$$

In general, the nth term of a GP is $u_n = ar^{n-1}$

◀ Learn this important result.

Example 1

Find an expression for the nth term of the GP $3, 6, 12, 24, \ldots$.

Solution

Look closely at the sequence.

$$u_1 = 3,\ u_2 = 6,\ u_3 = 12,\ u_4 = 24$$

So $\frac{u_2}{u_1} = 2$, $\frac{u_3}{u_2} = 2$, and $\frac{u_4}{u_3} = 2$.

This GP has first term 3 and common ratio 2.

$$u_1 = 3,\ u_2 = 3 \times 2,\ u_3 = 3 \times 2^2,\ u_4 = 3 \times 2^3,\ \ldots,\ u_n = 3 \times 2^{n-1}$$

So the nth term is $3 \times 2^{n-1}$

Example 2

Find an expression for the nth term of the GP $1, -\frac{1}{2}, \frac{1}{4}, -\frac{1}{8}, \frac{1}{16}, \ldots$.

Solution

Notice that for this GP, $a = 1$ and $r = -\frac{1}{2}$.

$$\begin{aligned} u_n &= ar^{n-1} \\ &= 1 \times (-\tfrac{1}{2})^{n-1} \\ &= (-\tfrac{1}{2})^{n-1} \end{aligned}$$

Check this result by substituting values $n = 1, 2, 3, 4$ and 5

The terms in a GP can be added to form a **geometric series**. For example, the GP 3, 6, 12, 24 could be used to create the finite geometric series $3 + 6 + 12 + 24$. It is also possible to find a rule to sum a geometric series. The first term, a, and the common ratio, r, of the GP need to be known.
Let $S = 3 + 6 + 12 + 24$
Since this GP has $a = 3$ and $r = 2$ this can be written as

$$S = 3 + (3 \times 2) + (3 \times 2^2) + (3 \times 2^3) \qquad [1]$$

Notice the use here of $u_n = ar^{n-1}$.

Now multiply each term by the common ratio

$$2S = (3 \times 2) + (3 \times 2^2) + (3 \times 2^3) + (3 \times 2^4) \qquad [2]$$

Subtracting equation [1] from equation [2].

This eliminates many the terms on the RHS.

$$2S - S = (3 \times 2^4) - 3$$

$$S(2 - 1) = 3(2^4 - 1)$$

$$S = \frac{3(2^4 - 1)}{(2 - 1)} = 45$$

Check this result against the sum of the four terms of the geometric series.
This procedure can be generalised to find the sum of any *finite* geometric series.

$$\text{Let } S_n = a + ar + ar^2 + \cdots + ar^{n-1} \qquad [1]$$

$$\text{Then } rS_n = ar + ar^2 + ar^3 + \cdots + ar^n \qquad [2]$$

Subtracting [2] from [1],

$$S_n - rS_n = a - ar^n$$

$$S_n(1 - r) = a(1 - r^n)$$

$$\boldsymbol{S_n = \frac{a(1 - r^n)}{1 - r}}$$

◀ **Learn this important result.**

Example 3

For the sequence $3, 6, 12, 24, \ldots$, find:

a the next two terms
b the nth term
c the sum of the first five terms.

Solution

The sequence 3, 6, 12, 24 is a GP with $a = 3$ and $r = 2$.

a The next two terms are u_5 and u_6. Using $u_n = ar^{n-1}$,

$$u_5 = 3 \times 2^4 = 3 \times 16 = 48$$

$$u_6 = 3 \times 2^5 = 3 \times 32 = 96$$

b The nth term is u_n.

$$u_n = ar^{n-1} = 3 \times 2^{n-1}$$

c The sum of the first five terms is S_5.

$$\begin{aligned} S_5 &= \frac{a(1-r^5)}{1-r} \\ &= \frac{3(1-2^5)}{1-2} \\ &= \frac{3(1-32)}{-1} \\ &= \frac{3(-31)}{-1} \\ &= 93 \end{aligned}$$

Notice that in Example 3**c** the formula for S_5 created a negative numerator and denominator. This was because the common ratio, r, was greater than 1. In order to reduce problems with negative results an alternative form of the sum to n terms can be used.

If $r > 1$, then use $S_n = \dfrac{a(r^n - 1)}{r - 1}$

If $r < 1$, then use $S_n = \dfrac{a(1 - r^n)}{1 - r}$

◀ **Learn these results.**

These results are equivalent. Choosing the appropriate one reduces negative signs in calculations.

Example 4

A geometric series has first term 8 and common ratio 1.4. Find the sum of the first 10 terms.

Solution

Since $r > 1$, use the alternative form for the sum of a GP.

$$\begin{aligned} S_{10} &= \frac{a(r^{10} - 1)}{r - 1} = \frac{8(1.4^{10} - 1)}{1.4 - 1} \\ &= 558.51 \text{ (2 d.p.)} \end{aligned}$$

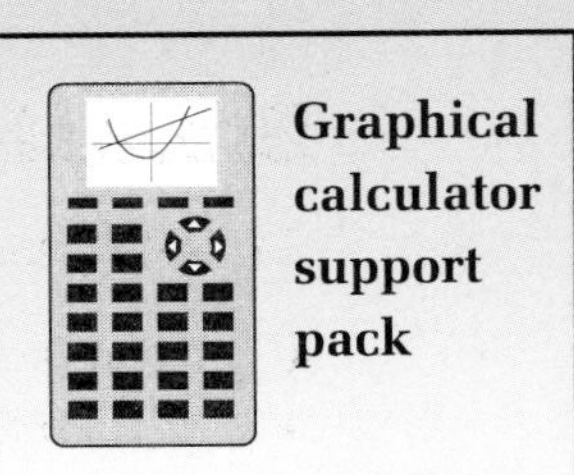

Finding the number of terms in a geometric series involves solving an exponential equation. Recall from Chapter 7 that this can be done using logarithms.

Example 5

Find the number of terms in the geometric series $4 + 6 + 9 + \cdots + 30.375$.

Solution

Since the series is geometric the ratio of successive terms will give the common ratio.

$$r = \frac{u_3}{u_2} = \frac{9}{6} = 1.5$$

This means $a = 4$ and $r = 1.5$.

Now examine the last, or nth, term.

$$\begin{aligned} u_n &= ar^{n-1} \\ \Rightarrow \quad 30.375 &= 4 \times 1.5^{n-1} \\ \Rightarrow \quad \tfrac{1}{4} \times 30.375 &= 1.5^{n-1} \\ \Rightarrow \quad 7.593\,75 &= 1.5^{n-1} \end{aligned}$$

Notice that the variable n now appears as a power.
Taking logarithms of both sides of the equation,

$$\begin{aligned} \log(7.593\,75) &= \log(1.5^{n-1}) \\ &= (n-1)\log(1.5) \end{aligned}$$

Recall that $\log a^n = n \log a$.

$$\text{So} \qquad n - 1 = \frac{\log(7.593\,75)}{\log(1.5)} = 5$$

That is, $n = 6$
So the series $4 + 6 + 9 + \cdots + 30.375$ has six terms.

8.3 Geometric Progression
Exercise
Technique

1 Find (**i**) the next two terms and (**ii**) the nth term of the following geometric progressions:

a $1, 2, 4, 8, \ldots$ **b** $2, 6, 18, 54, \ldots$
c $4, 6, 9, 13\frac{1}{2}, \ldots$ **d** $0.1, 0.3, 0.9, 2.7, \ldots$

2 Given the geometric progressions $2, 10, 50, \ldots, u_n$, $48, 24, 12, \ldots, v_n$, and $1, 3, 9, 27, \ldots, w_n$, find:

a u_5 **b** u_8 **c** v_7
d v_{10} **e** w_6 **f** w_9

3 Given the first term and common ratio of a geometric series, find the sum of the terms indicated:

a $a = 2, r = 2$: S_6 **b** $a = 10, r = -3$: S_7
c $a = 8, r = \frac{1}{2}$: S_6 **d** $a = -10, r = -\frac{4}{5}$: S_8 3 c

4 Find the sums of the following geometric series:

a $2 + 4 + 8 + \cdots + 256$ **d** $2 - 6 + 18 - 54 + \cdots - 39\,366$
b $2 - 6 + 18 - 54 + \cdots + 13\,122$ **e** $20 - 30 + 45 - \cdots - 341.72$
c $16 + 24 + 36 + \cdots + 182.25$ **f** $0.1 + 0.5 + 2.5 + \cdots + 312.5$

Contextual

1 Find the ninth term of the geometric series $12 + 8 + 5\frac{1}{3} + 3\frac{5}{9} + \cdots$, correct to three significant figures.

2 Find the common ratio of a geometric series given that the third term is 6 and the seventh term is 486. 2

3 Find the sum of the first ten terms of a geometric series with common ratio 2 and first term $1\frac{1}{2}$.

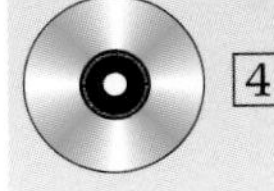

4 Write down the first three terms of $\sum_{n=1}^{10} 25(\frac{4}{5})^n$. State clearly: 4

a the first term of the GP
b the common ratio
c the sum of this series.

5 Evaluate:

a $\sum_{n=1}^{5} 200(1.1)^n$ **b** $\sum_{n=2}^{6} 80(\frac{7}{8})^n$

8.4 Convergence, Divergence and Oscillation

Consider the following sequences.

$3, 5, 7, 9, 11, \ldots, u_n, \ldots$

$1, 2, 1, 2, 1, \ldots, v_n, \ldots$

$\frac{1}{2}, \frac{1}{5}, \frac{1}{8}, \frac{1}{11}, \frac{1}{14}, \ldots, w_n, \ldots$

As n increases, what happens to u_n, v_n and w_n?

Notice that the first sequence is an AP with $a = 3$ and $d = 2$. The nth term, $u_n = 2n + 1$. As n gets large ($n \to \infty$) u_n gets large ($u_n \to \infty$). This sequence is said to **diverge**.

The second sequence simply oscillates between 1, when n is odd, and 2, when n is even. This sequence is said to be **oscillating**. A sequence that repeats itself in a regular pattern is **periodic**.

The third sequence is not an AP or GP. Check this by trying to find a common difference or common ratio. The sequence has nth term $w_n = \dfrac{1}{3n - 1}$. As n gets large ($n \to \infty$), w_n gets small ($w_n \to 0$). This sequence is said to **converge**. The terms of the sequence get closer and closer to a limit of zero.

Verify this by considering the sequence formed by the denominators only. Show that this is an AP with $a = 2$ and $d = 3$.

A graph can provide a good illustration of the behaviour of the sequence as n increases.

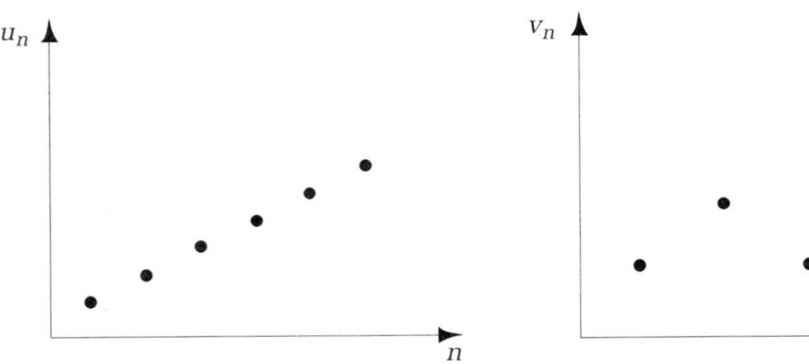

The sequence diverges to infinity. The values grow in size as n increases.

The sequence oscillates.

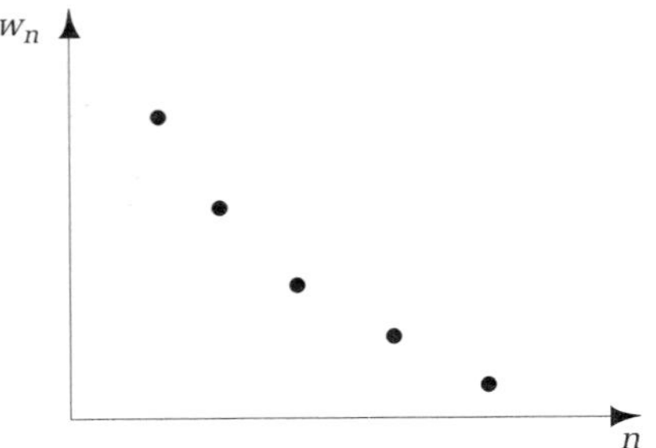

The sequence converges to a fixed value. In this case, $w_n \to 0$ as n increases.

Example 1

A sequence is defined by the recurrence relation $u_{n+1} = |6 - u_n|$. If $u_1 = 2$, describe the behaviour of the sequence.

Solution

Start by finding the first few terms of the sequence.

$$u_1 = 2$$

$$u_2 = |6 - u_1| = |6 - 2| = 4$$

$$u_3 = |6 - u_2| = |6 - 4| = 2$$

$$u_4 = |6 - u_3| = |6 - 2| = 4$$

The sequence is oscillating between 2 and 4. So $u_n = 2$ for odd n, and $u_n = 4$ for even n.

Example 2

Describe the behaviour of the GP $20, -10, 5, -2.5, 1.25, \ldots$.

Solution

This GP has $a = 20$ and $r = -\frac{1}{2}$. The nth term $u_n = 20 \times (-\frac{1}{2})^{n-1}$. As n gets large, $u_n \to 0$. This sequence converges and oscillates. The behaviour of this GP can be illustrated on a graph.

The behaviour of a sequence can be very important if the terms are being combined to form a series. This can determine if the series will diverge or converge as a large number of terms are added together. Adding an infinite number of terms of a series is known as a **sum to infinity**.

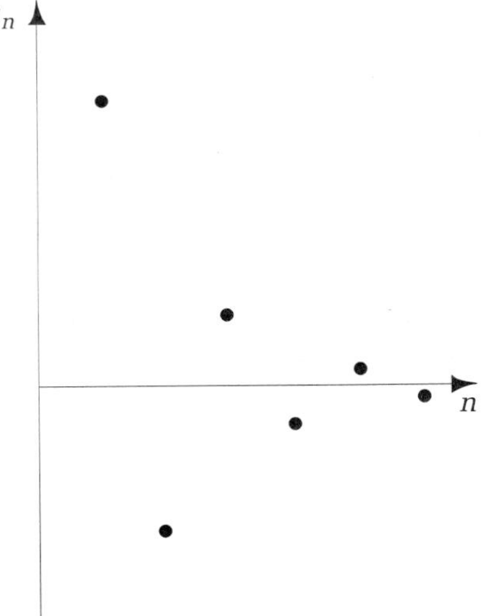

Example 3

Find the sum to infinity of the series $1 - \frac{1}{4} + \frac{1}{16} - \frac{1}{64} + \ldots$.

Solution

Notice that this series is created from a GP with $a = 1$ and $r = -\frac{1}{4}$. The nth term $u_n = 1 \times (-\frac{1}{4})^{n-1}$.

As n gets large, $u_n \to 0$. This means that the series increases by smaller numbers that oscillate between positive and negative.

To find the sum to infinity of the series write down the sum of the first n terms.

$$S_n = \frac{a(1-r^n)}{1-r} = \frac{1(1-(-\frac{1}{4})^n)}{1+\frac{1}{4}} = \frac{4}{5}(1-(-\tfrac{1}{4})^n)$$

As $n \to \infty$, $(-\frac{1}{4})^n \to 0$.

This means that $S_{n\to\infty} = \frac{4}{5}$.

So $1 - \frac{1}{4} + \frac{1}{16} - \frac{1}{64} + \cdots = \frac{4}{5}$.

This result can be generalised for any GP in which the common ratio r is such that $-1 < r < 1$.

This is often written i[n] mathematical shortha[nd] as $|r| < 1$.

The sum to infinity of a GP

GPs with common ratio r such that $|r| < 1$ generate convergent infinite series where $S_n \to S_\infty$ as $n \to \infty$, and

$$S_\infty = \frac{a}{1-r}$$

◀ **Learn this important result.**

Example 4

a A GP has first term 500 and common ratio $\frac{2}{5}$. What is the sum to infinity of the GP?

b The sum to infinity of a GP is 90. If the common ratio is $\frac{3}{5}$, what is the first term?

Solution

a $S_\infty = \dfrac{a}{1-r} = \dfrac{500}{1-\frac{2}{5}} = \dfrac{500}{\frac{3}{5}} = 833\frac{1}{3}$

b $S_\infty = \dfrac{a}{1-r} \Rightarrow 90 = \dfrac{a}{1-\frac{3}{5}} = \dfrac{a}{\frac{2}{5}}$

$$a = 90 \times \tfrac{2}{5} = 36$$

Series other than those generated by GPs can have a sum to infinity. These are often expressed using sigma notation and require the use of partial fractions (see Chapter 6).

Example 5

Find $\displaystyle\sum_{r=1}^{\infty} \frac{3}{(r+1)(r+2)}$

Solution

Substituting values of r in the sigma notation generates the following series.

$$\sum_{r=1}^{\infty} \frac{3}{(r+1)(r+2)} = \frac{3}{2 \times 3} + \frac{3}{3 \times 4} + \frac{3}{4 \times 5} + \cdots$$
$$= \frac{3}{6} + \frac{3}{12} + \frac{3}{20} + \cdots$$
$$= \frac{1}{2} + \frac{1}{4} + \frac{3}{20} + \cdots$$

Notice that the generated sequence, $\frac{1}{2}, \frac{1}{4}, \frac{3}{20}, \ldots$, is neither an AP nor a GP. To sum this series, consider the expression for the nth term found from the sigma notation.

$$u_n = \frac{3}{(n+1)(n+2)}$$

This rational expression can be rewritten in partial fractions.

Recall from Chapter 6 that since the denominators are all linear factors the cover-up rule can be used.

$$u_n = \frac{3}{(n+1)(n+2)} \equiv \frac{3}{(n+1)} - \frac{3}{(n+2)}$$

Now return to the original series.

$$\sum_{r=1}^{\infty} \frac{3}{(r+1)(r+2)} \equiv \sum_{r=1}^{\infty} \left[\frac{3}{(r+1)} - \frac{3}{(r+2)} \right]$$

Substituting values of r from 1 to n, where n is a large number,

$$\sum_{r=1}^{n} \left[\frac{3}{(r+1)} - \frac{3}{(r+2)} \right] = \left(\frac{3}{2} - \frac{3}{3} \right) + \left(\frac{3}{3} - \frac{3}{4} \right) + \left(\frac{3}{4} - \frac{3}{5} \right) + \cdots$$
$$+ \left(\frac{3}{n} - \frac{3}{n+1} \right) + \left(\frac{3}{n+1} - \frac{3}{n+2} \right)$$

Notice that, except for the first and last terms, all terms are repeated with one positive and one negative. These will cancel each other out.

So $$\sum_{r=1}^{n} \left[\frac{3}{(r+1)} - \frac{3}{(r+2)} \right] = \frac{3}{2} - \frac{3}{n+2}$$

Check this by summing successive terms of the series using a calculator. You should find that the sum of the series never exceeds $\frac{3}{2}$.

As $n \to \infty$, $\frac{3}{n+2} \to 0$. So the series converges to the value $\frac{3}{2}$.

$$\sum_{r=1}^{\infty} \frac{3}{(r+1)(r+2)} = \frac{3}{2}$$

8.4 Convergence, Divergence and Oscillation

Exercise

Technique

1 Find the sum to infinity for a geometric progression with:

a $a = 200, r = \frac{1}{2}$
b $a = 64, r = \frac{1}{8}$
c $a = 600, r = 0.6$
d $a = 30, r = \frac{4}{3}$
e $a = 200, r = 0.88$
f $a = 1000, r = 0.1$

2 Describe the behaviour of the following sequences:

a $u_{n+1} = |8 - u_n|$ where $u_1 = 10$
b $\cos(30n)$
c $\ln 8, (\ln 8)^2, (\ln 8)^3,$
d $\ln 1.8, (\ln 1.8)^2, (\ln 1.8)^3, \ldots$
e $u_n = \dfrac{5}{(n+2)(n+3)}$
f $u_n = \dfrac{10}{n(n+1)}$

3 Find the sums to infinity of the following geometric series:

a $243 + 81 + 27 + \ldots$
b $243 - 81 + 27 - \ldots$
c $12 + 4 + \frac{4}{3} + \ldots$
d $100 + 80 + 64 + \ldots$
e $20 - 8 + 3.2 - \ldots$
f $20 - 18 + 16.2 - \ldots$

4 For the following geometric progressions find the values of the unknown terms:

a $r = \frac{1}{4}, S_\infty = 40, a = ?$
b $a = 3, S_\infty = 8, r = ?$
c $r = \frac{3}{5}, S_\infty = 45, a = ?$
d $a = 10, S_\infty = 30, r = ?$
e $a = 45, S_\infty = 50, r = ?$
f $r = -\frac{7}{8}, S_\infty = 16, a = ?$

Contextual

1 Find the sum to infinity of the geometric series with first term 15 and common ratio $\frac{3}{4}$.

2 The first term of a geometric series is 24 and the common ratio is $-\frac{1}{2}$. Find the sum to infinity.

3 The sum to infinity of a GP is 80 and the first term is 16. Find the common ratio.

4 Given that the common ratio of a geometric series is $\frac{3}{8}$ and the sum to infinity is 32, find the first term.

5 The sum to infinity of a geometric progression is ten times the first term. Find the common ratio.

6 The sum to infinity of a GP is 81 and the sum of the first four terms is 65. Find the first term and the common ratio.

7 Gerry says, 'The sum to infinity of a GP with first term 12 and common ratio $\frac{4}{3}$ is 48'. John immediately says that it must be wrong.

a Explain why John is correct.

b Given that the sum to infinity and the first term are correct, find the common ratio.

8.5 The Binomial Theorem and Power Series

What does 'binomial' mean? 'Bi' is Latin, meaning 'double' so a binomial is an expression with two terms. Some examples of binomials are $(a+b)^2$, $(3+x)^4$, and $(5-y)^{\frac{1}{2}}$.
The binomial $(a+b)^2$ can be rewritten as a sum of algebraic terms.

Recall from Chapter 1 that 'polynomial' is Greek for 'many terms'

$$(a+b)^2 = a^2 + 2ab + b^2$$

There are also algebraic expressions for binomials with powers greater than 2

$$\begin{aligned}(a+b)^3 &= a^3 + 3a^2b + 3ab^2 + b^3\\ (a+b)^4 &= (a+b)(a+b)^3\\ &= (a+b)(a^3 + 3a^2b + 3ab^2 + b^3)\\ &= a(a^3 + 3a^2b + 3ab^2 + b^3) + b(a^3 + 3a^2b + 3ab^2 + b^3)\\ &= a^4 + 3a^3b + 3a^2b^2 + ab^3 + ba^3 + 3a^2b^2 + 3ab^3 + b^4\\ &= a^4 + 4a^3b + 6a^2b^2 + 4ab^3 + b^4\end{aligned}$$

Consider the following structure:

$$(a+b)^1 = a + b$$

$$(a+b)^2 = a^2 + 2ab + b^2$$

$$(a+b)^3 = a^3 + 3a^2b + 3ab^2 + b^3$$

$$(a+b)^4 = a^4 + 4a^3b + 6a^2b^2 + 4ab^3 + b^4$$

Now write down the coefficients only of the terms in these expansions. As they are written down arrange them in a triangular form under each other.

$$\begin{array}{ccccccccc} & & & 1 & & 1 & & & \\ & & 1 & & 2 & & 1 & & \\ & 1 & & 3 & & 3 & & 1 & \\ 1 & & 4 & & 6 & & 4 & & 1 \end{array}$$

Blaise Pascal (1623–1662)
Pascal, a French mathematician, is credited with a pattern formed by the coefficients in these expansions. It is usually called Pascal's triangle.

Write down the next row in this triangle. Check that each figure is created by adding the numbers directly above it.

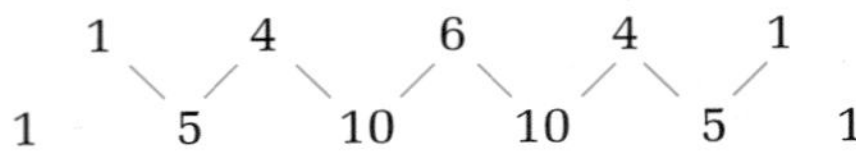

So $(a+b)^5 = a^5 + 5a^4b + 10a^3b^2 + 10a^2b^3 + 5ab^4 + b^5$
Notice:

- the position of the coefficients from **Pascal's triangle**
- that the powers of a decrease from 5 to 0 and the powers of b increase from 0 to 5
- that adding the powers of a and b in any term gives 5, which is the power on the original binomial.

It is useful to remember these points when expanding a binomial.

Example 1

Expand:

a $(2+x)^4$ **b** $(3-x)^5$

Solution

a Notice that the index, or power, here is 4. The fourth line of Pascal's triangle is

1 4 6 4 1

These will be the coefficients of the terms in the expansion. Build up the expansion in two steps.
Insert powers of the first term, '2'.

$1 \times 2^4 \quad 4 \times 2^3 \quad 6 \times 2^2 \quad 4 \times 2^1 \quad 1 \times 2^0$

Insert powers of the second term, 'x'.

$1 \times 2^4 \times x^0 \quad 4 \times 2^3 \times x^1 \quad 6 \times 2^2 \times x^2 \quad 4 \times 2^1 \times x^3 \quad 1 \times 2^0 \times x^4$

Now evaluate any numbers raised to a power, recalling that $a^0 = 1$ for all values of a. The expansion now becomes

$(2+x)^4 = 16 + 32x + 24x^2 + 8x^3 + x^4$

b The power here is 5. The fifth line of Pascal's triangle is required.

1 5 10 10 5 1

Insert powers of the first term, '3'.

$1 \times 3^5 \quad 5 \times 3^4 \quad 10 \times 3^3 \quad 10 \times 3^2 \quad 5 \times 3^1 \quad 1 \times 3^0$

Insert powers of the second term, '$-x$'.

Remember to include the negative sign.

$1 \times 3^5 \times (-x)^0 \quad 5 \times 3^4 \times (-x)^1 \quad 10 \times 3^3 \times (-x)^2$

$10 \times 3^2 \times (-x)^3 \quad 5 \times 3^1 \times (-x)^4 \quad 1 \times 3^0 \times (-x)^5$

Even powers of $(-x)$ are positive and odd powers of $(-x)$ are negative, so

$$(3 - x)^5 = 243 - 405x + 270x^2 - 90x^3 + 15x^4 - x^5$$

This technique can be used to expand $(a + x)^n$ or $(a - x)^n$ for any positive integer n. The problem then becomes finding the values of the coefficients in the nth row of Pascal's triangle.

Factorial notation

A **factorial** is a product of consecutive natural numbers, starting at 1.
So 3 factorial, written $3! = 3 \times 2 \times 1$ and $6! = 6 \times 5 \times 4 \times 3 \times 2 \times 1$
A table of factorial totals shows how concise this notation can be.

$1! = 1$	$3! = 6$	$5! = 120$	$7! = 5040$	$9! = 362\,880$
$2! = 2$	$4! = 24$	$6! = 720$	$8! = 40\,320$	$10! = 3\,628\,800$

How do factorials fit with the coefficients in Pascal's triangle? The terms of Pascal's triangle are known also as **binomial coefficients**. The third coefficient on the fourth row can be written using factorials as

$$\binom{4}{3} = \frac{4!}{3!(4-3)!} = \frac{24}{6 \times 1} = 4$$

Check this result in Pascal's triangle.

In a similar way the rth coefficient on the nth row of Pascal's triangle can be written as

$$\binom{n}{r} = \frac{n!}{r!(n-r)!}$$

◀ **Learn this important result.**

Remember that r starts at 0, not 1, and that $0! = 1$ by definition.

The general result for the expansion of $(a + x)^n$ is:

$$(a + x)^n = a^n + \binom{n}{1}a^{n-1}x + \binom{n}{2}a^{n-2}x^2 + \cdots + \binom{n}{r}a^{n-r}x^r + \cdots + x^n$$

◀ **Learn this result.**

Check how the powers of a and x relate to the terms inside the binomial coefficient.

Example 2

Find the values of:

a $\binom{6}{4}$ **b** $\binom{7}{2}$

Solution

a $\binom{6}{4} = \frac{6!}{4!(6-4)!} = \frac{6!}{4!2!} = \frac{720}{24 \times 2} = 15$

b $\binom{7}{2} = \frac{7!}{2!(7-2)!} = \frac{7!}{2!5!} = \frac{5040}{2 \times 120} = 21$

To calculate the value of binomial coefficients not all factorials need be remembered. The fraction can be cancelled down quickly since each factorial is a product of numbers beginning at 1.

Example 3

Without using a calculator, find $\binom{8}{3}$.

Solution

$$\binom{8}{3} = \frac{8!}{3!(8-3)!} = \frac{8!}{3!5!} = \frac{8 \times 7 \times 6 \times 5 \times 4 \times 3 \times 2 \times 1}{(3 \times 2 \times 1) \times (5 \times 4 \times 3 \times 2 \times 1)}$$

Notice that 5! is a common factor of both the denominator and the numerator. This means it can be cancelled.

$$\binom{8}{3} = \frac{8 \times 7 \times 6}{3 \times 2 \times 1}$$

Now look for other common factors.

The 3×2 in the denominator eliminates the 6 in the numerator.

$$\binom{8}{3} = \frac{8 \times 7}{1} = 56$$

One advantage of using factorial notation is that particular terms in an expansion can be found without finding the whole series.

Example 4

Find the term involving x^9 in the expansion of $(1 + 2x)^{12}$.

Solution

Recall the general result for expanding $(a + x)^n$,

$$(a + x)^n = a^n + \cdots + \binom{n}{r} a^{n-r} x^r + \cdots + x^n$$

So the term involving x^9 in this expansion will be

$$\binom{12}{9} 1^3 (2x)^9$$

Notice that $n = 12$, $r = 9$ and $a = 1$, and x has a multiplier (coefficient) of 2

$$\binom{12}{9} = \frac{12 \times 11 \times 10}{3 \times 2 \times 1} = 220$$

So the term in x^9 is then $220 \times 1^3 \times 2^9 x^9 = 112\,640x^9$

Notice that this provides a quick method of identifying terms in the series.

The expansion of binomials using factorial notation for the binomial coefficients is often stated as a mathematical theorem.

The binomial theorem

$$(a+b)^n = \sum_{r=0}^{n} \binom{n}{r} a^{n-r} b^r$$
$$= \binom{n}{0} a^n + \binom{n}{1} a^{n-1} b$$
$$+ \cdots + \binom{n}{n-1} ab^{n-1} + \binom{n}{n} b^n$$

◀ Learn this result.

Notice that $\binom{n}{0}$ and $\binom{n}{n}$ both involve 0!.

The expansion of the brackets can be written as a series using sigma notation. The binomial coefficients relate clearly to the powers of the terms a and b. The case where $a = 1$ and b is the variable x is particularly interesting.

This series was discovered by Ne in 1676 and correctly derived by Euler abou 100 years later.

$$(1+x)^n = 1 + \binom{n}{1}x + \binom{n}{2}x^2 + \binom{n}{3}x^3 + \cdots$$

This can be used to find the approximate value of powers of numbers close to 1.

Example 5

a Find an approximation correct to four decimal places of $(1.01)^6$.

b Find $(0.99)^4$ without using a calculator.

Solution

a This approximation can be made by using the binomial series for $(1+x)^6$

$$(1+x)^6 = 1 + \binom{6}{1}x + \binom{6}{2}x^2 + \binom{6}{3}x^3 + \cdots$$
$$= 1 + 6x + 15x^2 + 20x^3 + \cdots$$

Now write 1.01 as $(1 + 0.01)$. This is better expressed as $(1 + \frac{1}{100})$. Substitute $x = \frac{1}{100}$ into the series expansion.

$$(1.01)^6 = 1 + \frac{6}{100} + \frac{15}{100^2} + \frac{20}{100^3} + \cdots$$
$$= 1 + 0.06 + 0.0015 + 0.000\,02 + \cdots$$
$$= 1.061\,52$$

Notice that successi terms are so small th they will not influen the first four decima places.

So, to four decimal places, an approximation for $(1.01)^6$ is 1.0615.

b Since $0.99 = 1 - 0.01$, $(0.99)^4$ can be rewritten as $(1 - 0.01)^4$. Use the binomial series for $(1-x)^4$ with $x = \frac{1}{100}$

$$(1-x)^4 = 1 + \binom{4}{1}(-x) + \binom{4}{2}(-x)^2 + \binom{4}{3}(-x)^3 + (-x)^4$$
$$= 1 - 4x + 6x^2 - 4x^3 + x^4$$

$$\left(1-\frac{1}{100}\right)^4 = 1-\frac{4}{100}+\frac{6}{100^2}-\frac{4}{100^3}+\frac{1}{100^4}$$
$$= 1 - 0.04 + 0.0006 - 0.000\,004 + 0.000\,000\,01$$
$$= 0.960\,596\,01$$

Power series

A power series is a polynomial. The terms of the series are powers of a variable, usually x , multiplied by a coefficient.

$$a_0 + a_1x + a_2x^2 + \cdots = \sum_{r=1}^{n} a_r x^r$$

Power series can be **divergent** or **convergent**. When the series is convergent there is usually a restriction on the range of values of the variable x.
A power series can be created from a binomial expansion where the power is fractional and not an integer. The expansion is now written slightly differently to how it was before, because the binomial coefficient, $\binom{n}{r}$, is nonsensical when n is a fraction.

When n is negative or fractional, the binomial series for $(1+x)^n$ is given by

$$(1+x)^n = 1 + nx + \frac{n(n-1)x^2}{2!} + \frac{n(n-1)(n-2)x^3}{3!} + \cdots$$

◀ Learn this result.

Notice that this series will be infinite if n is negative or fractional because the numerator will never contain the factor $(n-n)$.
This power series will converge provided $-1 < x < 1$. This condition is particularly important because it means that the series is not valid for all values of x.

Example 6

Find the first five terms in the binomial expansion of $\frac{1}{1-x}$ and state the range of values for which it is valid.

Solution

Applying the law of indices, $\frac{1}{1-x} = (1-x)^{-1}$. This is a binomial with power -1. The series can be found by substituting $n = -1$ into the binomial expansion (carefully checking the sign of x).

Recall that $\frac{1}{a} = a^{-1}$.

$$(1+x)^n = 1 + nx + \frac{n(n-1)x^2}{2!} + \frac{n(n-1)(n-2)x^3}{3!} + \cdots$$

$$\text{So } (1-x)^{-1} = 1 + (-1)(-x) + \frac{(-1)(-2)(-x)^2}{2!} + \frac{(-1)(-2)(-3)(-x)^3}{3!}$$
$$+ \frac{(-1)(-2)(-3)(-4)(-x)^4}{4!} + \cdots$$

$$= 1 + x + \frac{2x^2}{2} + \frac{6x^3}{6} + \frac{24x^4}{24} + \cdots$$
$$= 1 + x + x^2 + x^3 + x^4 + \cdots$$

This series is valid for $-1 < x < 1$; that is, $|x| < 1$.

Check what happens when $x = \frac{1}{2}$ and $x = 2$. Notice the need for the restriction $|x| < 1$.

Example 7

Find the first four terms of the binomial series for $\sqrt{1+x}$. State the range of values of x for which the series converges.

Solution

$\sqrt{1+x} = (1+x)^{\frac{1}{2}}$. This is a binomial, with power $\frac{1}{2}$.

$$(1+x)^n = 1 + nx + \frac{n(n-1)x^2}{2!} + \frac{n(n-1)(n-2)x^3}{3!} + \cdots$$

$$\text{So } (1+x)^{\frac{1}{2}} = 1 + \tfrac{1}{2}x + \frac{\frac{1}{2}(-\frac{1}{2})x^2}{2!} + \frac{\frac{1}{2}(-\frac{1}{2})(-\frac{3}{2})x^3}{3!} + \cdots$$
$$= 1 + \tfrac{1}{2}x - \tfrac{1}{8}x^2 + \tfrac{3}{48}x^3 - \cdots$$
$$= 1 + \tfrac{1}{2}x - \tfrac{1}{8}x^2 + \tfrac{1}{16}x^3 - \cdots$$

This series is valid for $|x| < 1$.

The binomial series can be used to provide a power series expansion for rational functions.

Example 8

Write $\dfrac{1-x}{(1+2x)^4}$ as a series of ascending powers of x, up to and including the term in x^3. State the range of values of x for which the series is valid.

Solution

Once the rational function is written as a product the application of the binomial theorem can be seen.
Expand $(1+2x)^{-4}$ as a power series, then multiply this result by $(1-x)$.

Check that $(1+2x)^{-4} = 1 - 8x + 40x^2 - 160x^3 + \cdots$

Then $(1-x)(1+2x)^{-4} = (1-x)(1 - 8x + 40x^2 - 160x^3 + \cdots)$

$$= 1 - 9x + 48x^2 - 200x^3 + \cdots$$

This series is valid for $-1 < 2x < 1$; that is $|x| < \frac{1}{2}$.

8.5 The Binomial Theorem and Power Series

Exercise

Technique

1 Find the expansion of the following binomials using Pascal's triangle:

a $(1+x)^6$ **b** $(3-x)^4$ **c** $(5-x)^4$ **d** $(2+x)^5$

1 d

2 Find the values of the following binomial coefficients:

a $\binom{4}{2}$ **b** $\binom{7}{4}$ **c** $\binom{5}{3}$ **d** $\binom{20}{18}$

3 Expand the following using the binomial theorem:

a $(1+x)^7$ **b** $(4-x)^4$ **c** $(2-3x)^6$ **d** $(x-\frac{3}{x})^4$

4 Write the following as series of ascending powers of x, up to and including the term in x^3:

a $(1-x)^{20}$ **b** $(3-x)^5$ **c** $(y+x)^7$ **d** $(2-3x)^5$

5 Find the range of values of x for which the series expansions of the following are valid:

a $(1+x)^{\frac{1}{2}}$ **b** $(3-2x)^{\frac{1}{3}}$ **c** $\sqrt[3]{1+\frac{1}{5}x}$ **d** $(4-3x)^{-10}$

6 Find the first four terms of the binomial series for the following functions:

a $(1+x)^{-8}$ **b** $\sqrt[3]{1+2x}$ **c** $\sqrt{1-2x}$ **d** $\dfrac{1+x^2}{(1-x)^4}$

6 c

Contextual

1 Find the binomial expansion of $(4+x)^6$. When is this expansion valid?

2 Find the term involving x^9 in the expansion of $(1+2x)^{11}$.

3 Find the coefficient of the x^7 term in the expansion of $(1-3x)^{15}$.

4 The expansion of $(x-\frac{3}{x})^{12}$ has a term that does not contain x. State the value of this term.

5 Find the value of $(1.01)^7$ to four decimal places using the binomial expansion of $(1+x)^n$.

6 Expand $\sqrt{1-4x}$ as a series of ascending powers of x, up to and including the term in x^3. State the range of values of x for which the expansion is valid.

Consolidation

Exercise A

1 Find the sum of the arithmetic series $2 + 5 + 8 + \cdots + 398$.

(NEAB)

2 The tenth term of the arithmetic progression is zero and the sum of the first 10 terms is 15.

a Find the first term and the common difference.

b How many more terms must be added for the sum of the arithmetic progression to be zero?

(OCSEB)

3 A geometric series has third term 27 and sixth term 8.

a Show that the common ratio of the series is $\frac{2}{3}$.

b Find the first term of the series.

c Find the sum to infinity of the series.

d Find, to three significant figures, the difference between the sum of the first 10 terms of the series and the sum to infinity of the series.

(ULEAC)

4 Find the sum of the series with first term 11 and last term 40, in which each term, after the first, exceeds the previous term by $\frac{1}{2}$.

(UCLES)

5 The nth term of a sequence is u_n, where $u_n = 95(\frac{4}{5})^n$, $n = 1, 2, 3, \ldots$.

a Find the values of u_1 and u_2.

Giving your answers to three significant figures, calculate:

b the value of u_{21}

c $\displaystyle\sum_{n=1}^{15} u_n$

d Find the sum to infinity of the series whose first term is u_1 and whose nth term is u_n.

(ULEAC)

6 Find, in the simplest form, the first three terms in the expansion of $(1 + 3t)^{\frac{2}{3}}$, in ascending powers of t, where $|t| < \frac{1}{3}$.

(NEAB)

7 Two sequences $u_1, u_2, u_3, \ldots$ are defined as follows:

Sequence A: $u_1 = 2 \quad u_{n+1} = 3 - u_n$

Sequence B: $u_1 = 2 \quad u_{n+1} = u_n + \dfrac{1}{2^n}$

a For each of the two sequences, find the values of u_2, u_3, u_4, and u_5.
b State for each sequence whether it is convergent, divergent or oscillating.

(NEAB)

8 Given that $|x| < \frac{1}{2}$, expand $\sqrt{1 + 2x}$ as a series of ascending powers of x, up to and including the term in x^3, simplifying the coefficients.

(UCLES)

9 Find the term in x^{12} in the binomial expansion of $(x + 2x^2)^{10}$.

(OCSEB)

10 **a** Use the binomial theorem to give the expansion of $(x + y)^4$.
b Hence obtain the expansion of $(x + \frac{2}{x})^4$, expressing each term in a simplified form.
c Find the coefficient of x^2 in the expansion of $(1 + x^2)(x + \frac{2}{x})^4$.

(NEAB)

Exercise B

1 Find the sum of the arithmetic series $3 + 7 + 11 + \cdots + 79$.

2 Helen's father gives her a loan of £10 800 to buy a car. The loan is to be repaid by 12 unequal monthly instalments, starting with an initial payment of £A in the first month. There are no interest charges on the remaining debt but the instalments increase by £60 per month so that the second monthly payment is £$(A + 60)$, the third monthly payment is £$(A + 120)$ and so on.

a Show that $A = 570$.
b Find an expression in terms of n for the remaining debt immediately after Helen makes her nth payment. Give your answer in a fully factorised form.

(NEAB)

3 **a** **i** Express $\dfrac{8}{(2r - 1)(2r + 3)}$ in partial fractions.

ii Hence find the sum of n terms of the series

$$\frac{8}{1 \times 5} + \frac{8}{3 \times 7} + \frac{8}{5 \times 9} + \ldots$$

b A sequence of integers u_1, u_2, u_3 is defined by $u_1 = 5$ and $u_{n+1} = 3u_n - 2^n$ for $n \geq 1$. Use this definition to find u_2 and u_3.

(OCSEB)

4 **a** The sixth term of a geometric progression is 6.075; the fifth term is 4.05. Calculate:

i the common ratio

ii the first term

iii the 30th term (correct to three significant figures).

b State, with a reason, whether the geometric series

$$\ln 3 + (\ln 3)^2 + (\ln 3)^3 + \cdots$$

is divergent or convergent.

c The series S is given by

$$\ln 3 + \ln(3^2) + \ln(3^3) + \cdots + \ln(3^{30}) = \sum_{r=1}^{30} \ln(3^r)$$

Show that S is an arithmetic series whose sum is approximately 511.

d Show that $\sum_{r=1}^{n} \ln(3r) = n \ln 3 + \ln(n!)$.

(OCSEB)

5 **a** The first term of an arithmetic progression is 9 and the seventh term is three times the second term. Find the common difference and the sum of the first 32 terms of the arithmetic progression.

b The first term of a geometric progression is 81 and the fourth term is 24. Find the common ratio and the sum to infinity of the geometric progression.

(WJEC)

6 A sequence is defined inductively as follows:

$$u_1 = 2$$

$$u_{n+1} = \text{units digit of } 2u_n \text{ (that is, the remainder when } 2u_n \text{ is divided by 10)}$$

a Write down the values of u_i for $i = 1, 2, 3, 4, 5$ and show that $u_6 = 4$.

b State whether or not this sequence is periodic or convergent

c Find the units digit of 2^{222}, explaining how you obtain your answer.

(OCSEB)

7 The nth term, u_n, of four sequences is defined below. For each sequence decide whether it is convergent, divergent to $+\infty$, divergent to $-\infty$ or oscillating. For each convergent sequence, state the limit to which it tends as $n \to \infty$.

a $u_n = 2 + \sqrt{n}$

b $u_n = 5 - \dfrac{1}{n^2}$

c $u_n = \sin(\frac{1}{2}n\pi)$

d $u_n = \dfrac{3n}{1+n}$

(AEB)

Applications and Activities

Loan repayments

The sum of a geometric series can be used to find:

- the time taken to repay a loan given a debt, interest rate and repayment instalments;
- the repayment instalment given a debt, interest rate and repayment term.

1 You borrow £1000 at 14% APR and pay back £300 per year. How long will it take to repay the debt?

APR is the Annual Percentage Rate and must, by law, be quoted on all credit arrangements.

2 You borrow £1000 at 14% APR and want to repay the debt in three years. What should your monthly instalment be?

3 Investigate credit terms for finance companies and check the repayment tables for the quoted APR.

Summary

- A **sequence** is a set of numbers occurring in order. When the terms of a sequence are added together, a **series** is formed.
- A sequence can be described using an algebraic term for u_n or by a **recurrence relation**.
- A series can be written using **sigma notation**, which uses the Greek letter Σ to represent summation over a number of terms.
- The nth term of an AP is $\boldsymbol{a + (n-1)d}$, where a is the first term, and d is the **common difference**.
- The **sum to** n **terms** of an arithmetic series can be written in equivalent forms

$$S_n = \frac{n}{2}[2a + (n-1)d]$$

$$S_n = \frac{n(a+l)}{2}$$ where l is the last term.

- The nth term of a GP is ar^{n-1} where a is the first term and r is the **common ratio**.

- The sum to n terms of a geometric series with first term a and **common ratio** r is given by

$$S_n = \frac{a(1-r^n)}{1-r}$$

- A sequence is said to **diverge** if $u_n \to \infty$ as $n \to \infty$, **converge** if $u_n \to$ a limit as $n \to \infty$, and be **periodic** if it repeats itself in a regular pattern.
- GPs with a common ratio r such that $|r| < 1$ create convergent infinite series where $S_n \to S_\infty$ as $n \to \infty$, and

$$S_\infty = \frac{a}{1-r}$$

- The coefficients in a binomial expansion, $(a+b)^n$, can be written down using Pascal's triangle.
- A **factorial** is a product of consecutive natural numbers; so $3! = 3 \times 2 \times 1$ and $0! = 1$ by definition.
- The binomial theorem states that, for positive integral values of n ($n \in \mathbb{Z}^+$) says:

$$\begin{aligned}(a+b)^n &= \sum_{r=0}^{n} \binom{n}{r} a^{n-r} b^r \\ &= \binom{n}{0} a^n + \binom{n}{1} a^{n-1} b \\ &\quad + \cdots + \binom{n}{n-1} ab^{n-1} + \binom{n}{n} b^n\end{aligned}$$

- The binomial theorem can be used to write a binomial series for integer, negative and rational powers. This power series will have a condition on the values for which it is convergent.

9 Integration I

What you need to know

- How to differentiate standard functions.
- How to use the laws of indices.
- How to find the value of an algebraic expression.
- How to sketch graphs.
- How to use sigma notation.

Review

1 Find:

a $\frac{d}{dx}(x^2 + 1)$

b $\frac{d}{dx}(\frac{1}{2}x^2 - 6x + 2)$

c $\frac{d}{dx}\left(x^{\frac{1}{2}} - \frac{1}{x}\right)$

d $\frac{d}{dx}(\cos x)$

e $\frac{d}{dx}(\sin 2x)$

f $\frac{d}{dx}(2 - x^2 + 3\cos 5x)$

2 Write each of the following expressions as Ax^n or $(Ax^n + Bx^m)$, where A and B are constants.

a $\frac{1}{x^2}$ **b** $\frac{3x^2}{x^5}$ **c** $\frac{7x - x^2}{x^5}$

d $\frac{2x}{x^{\frac{1}{2}}}$ **e** $\frac{5}{\sqrt{x}}$ **f** $\sqrt{x}(1 + \sqrt{x})$

3 Find the value of each of the following expressions for the given value of x:

a $3x^3 + 5x^2 + x$, when $x = 2$

b $\frac{1}{4}x^4 - x^3 - x$, when $x = -2$

c $2x^{\frac{1}{2}} - x^{-\frac{1}{2}} + 1$, when $x = 9$

d $x^{\frac{2}{3}}$, when $x = 8$

4 Sketch the graphs of:

a $y = 1$ **b** $y = x^2$ **c** $y = x^3$

d $y = \sin x$ **e** $y = 1 + \sin x$ **f** $y = 2\cos x$

5 Simplify the following using sigma notation:

a $1 + 2 + 3$

b $1 + 4 + 9 + 16 + 25$

c $2 + 4 + 6 + 8$

d $4 + 7 + 10 + 13$

9.1 Indefinite Integration

Integration can be described as a reverse operation. Consider some familiar reverse operations.

Operation	Reverse operation	Example
Add	Subtract	7 → +3 → 10; 10 → −3 → 7
Multiply	Divide	12 → ×3 → 36; 36 → ÷3 → 12
Cube	Cube-root	2 → cube → 8; 8 → cube root → 2

Mathematicians studying what we now call differentiation and integration realised that these processes were closely related. Leibniz (1646–1716) and Isaac Newton (1643–1727) independently discovered that integration is the reverse of differentiation. This fact is called the **fundamental theorem of calculus.**

The notation used f[or] differentiation and integration is based on notation developed by Leibniz. He was a seventeenth century mathematician, philosop[her] and statesman. He published his work on calculus in 1684.

Operation	Reverse operation	Example
Differentiation	Integration	x^n → differentiate: multiply by n, reduce power by 1 → nx^{n-1}; nx^{n-1} → integrate: add 1 to the power, divide by this number → x^n

The principle of the reverse process will be used to integrate powers of x by increasing the power by 1 and then dividing the new term by this number – the reverse of differentiation.

$$\int x^2\,dx = \tfrac{1}{3}x^3$$ ◀ Differentiating $\frac{1}{3}x^3$ gives x^2.

Check this by differentiating the answer; it should reverse the integration process.

But note that $\frac{d}{dx}\left(\frac{1}{3}x^3 + 1\right) = 3 \times \frac{1}{3}x^2 + 0 = x^2$

and $\frac{d}{dx}\left(\frac{1}{3}x^3 + 2\right) = 3 \times \frac{1}{3}x^2 + 0 = x^2$

and so on.

Notation

$\int$ is the symbol for 'integrate'

The term that is being integrated is the **integrand**.

'dx' means integrate 'with respect to' the variable x

So $\int f(x)\,dx$ means integrate the integran[d] $f(x)$ with respect to x.

This means that any of the expressions $\frac{1}{3}x^3, \frac{1}{3}x^3+1, \frac{1}{3}x^3+2, \ldots$ could be the answer to $\int x^2 dx$. Differentiation of each of these expressions gives x^2. Since there is no definite answer the expression $\int x^2 dx$ is called an **indefinite integral**. The complete answer is

$$\int x^2 dx = \frac{1}{3}x^3 + c, \text{ where } c \text{ is a constant.}$$

If the variable was t, not x, we would 'integrate t^2 with respect to t'; $\int t^2\, dt = \frac{1}{3}t^3 + c$.

All indefinite integrals have '$+c$' at the end where c is a constant. The following table illustrates the basic principles of integration.

$\int f(x)dx$	$g(x)$	Check $g'(x) = f(x)$	In general:
$\int dx = \int 1\, dx$ $\int 5dx$	$x + c$ $5x + c$	$\frac{d}{dx}(x + c) = 1 + 0 = 1$ $\frac{d}{dx}(5x + c) = 5 + 0 = 5$	$\int k\, dx = kx + c$, where k is any number
$\int x\, dx$ $\int 7x\, dx$	$\frac{1}{2}x^2 + c$ $\frac{7}{2}x^2 + c$	$\frac{d}{dx}(\frac{1}{2}x^2 + c) = \frac{1}{2} \times 2x + 0 = x$ $\frac{d}{dx}(\frac{7}{2}x^2 + c) = \frac{7}{2} \times 2x + 0 = 7x$	$\int kf(x)\, dx = k\int f(x)\, dx$, where k is any constant
$\int x^2\, dx$ $\int x^3\, dx$ $\int x^{\frac{1}{2}}dx$	$\frac{1}{3}x^3 + c$ $\frac{1}{4}x^4 + c$ $\frac{2}{3}x^{3/2} + c$	$\frac{d}{dx}(\frac{1}{3}x^3 + c) = \frac{1}{3} \times 3x^2 + 0 = x^2$ $\frac{d}{dx}(\frac{1}{4}x^4 + c) = \frac{1}{4} \times 4x^3 + 0 = x^3$ $\frac{d}{dx}(\frac{2}{3}x^{3/2} + c) = \frac{2}{3} \times \frac{3}{2}x^{1/2} + 0 = x^{1/2}$	$\int x^n\, dx = \frac{x^{n+1}}{n+1} + c$ ◀ True for all n, except for the special case $n = -1$ (see Chapter 12).
$\int (2x^2 - x + 6)\, dx$	$\frac{2}{3}x^3 - \frac{1}{2}x^2 + 6x + c$	$\frac{d}{dx}(\frac{2}{3}x^3 - \frac{1}{2}x^2 + 6x + c) =$ $\frac{2}{3} \times 3x^2 - \frac{1}{2} \times 2x + 6 + 0 =$ $2x^2 - x + 6$	$\int (f(x) + g(x))\, dx =$ $\int f(x)\, dx + \int g(x)\, dx$

Recall that $g'(x)$ is alternative notation for $\frac{d}{dx}g(x)$.

The constant can be 'pulled outside' the integral sign.

$\int x^{1/2}\, dx = \frac{1}{\frac{3}{2}}x^{3/2} + c$; to divide by a fraction, invert it and multiply, to give $\frac{2}{3}x^{3/2} + c$.

Integrate each term separately.

Summary of the basic principles

- $\int k\, dx = kx + c$, where k is any number
- $\int kf(x)\, dx = k\int f(x)dx$, where k is any number
- $\int x^n\, dx = \frac{x^{n+1}}{n+1} + c$, where n is any number except -1
- $\int (f(x) + g(x))\, dx = \int f(x)\, dx + \int g(x)dx$

Example 1

Find:

a $\int x(x-3)dx$ **b** $\int (1 - 3\sqrt{x})dx$ **c** $\int \left(\frac{3x^2 - 1}{x^2}\right)dx$

Solution

a The technique here is to expand the brackets first, and then integrate each term separately.

$$\int x(x-3)\, dx = \int (x^2 - 3x)\, dx$$

Use $\int x^n\, dx = \frac{x^{n+1}}{n+1} + c$.

$$= \frac{1}{3}x^3 - 3 \times \frac{1}{2}x^2 + c$$

◀ Always add a constant for an indefinite integral.

$$= \frac{1}{3}x^3 - \frac{3}{2}x^2 + c$$

b To integrate the square root, first express it in powers of x.

$$\int (1 - 3\sqrt{x})\,dx = \int (1 - 3x^{\frac{1}{2}})\,dx$$

$$= x - 3 \times \frac{1}{\frac{3}{2}} x^{\frac{3}{2}} + c$$

$$= x - 2x^{\frac{3}{2}} + c$$

◀ Check the answer by differentiation.

Recall that $\sqrt{x} = x^{\frac{1}{2}}$.

Use $\int x^n\,dx = \frac{x^{n+1}}{n+1} +$

To divide by a fractio invert and multiply.

c First express the integrand as powers of x.

$$\int \left(\frac{3x^2 - 1}{x^2}\right) dx = \int \left(\frac{3x^2}{x^2} - \frac{1}{x^2}\right) dx$$

$$= \int \left(3 - \frac{1}{x^2}\right) dx$$

$$= \int (3 - x^{-2})\,dx$$

$$= 3x - \frac{x^{-1}}{-1} + c$$

$$= 3x + \frac{1}{x} + c$$

◀ Remember to add a constant for an indefinite integral.

Note the common denominator.

Use $\int x^n\,dx = \frac{x^{n+1}}{n+1} +$

Example 2

The gradient of a curve $y = f(x)$ is given by $\frac{dy}{dx} = (2 - x)(2 - 3x)$. Find the equation of the curve, given that it passes through the point $(3, 2)$.

Solution

To find y from $\frac{dy}{dx}$, reverse the differentiation by using integration.

$$y = \int (2 - x)(2 - 3x)dx$$

$$= \int (4 - 8x + 3x^2)dx$$

$$= 4x - \frac{8x^2}{2} + \frac{3x^3}{3} + c$$

$$y = 4x - 4x^2 + x^3 + c$$

To integrate, expand brackets and integrat each term separately.

This equation represents a whole family of curves. The graphs can be drawn on a graphical calculator using different values of c. The graphs show that there are many functions with a gradient of $(2 - x)(2 - 3x)$. However, there is only one graph that passes through the point $(3, 2)$. Check that the value of c must be -1.

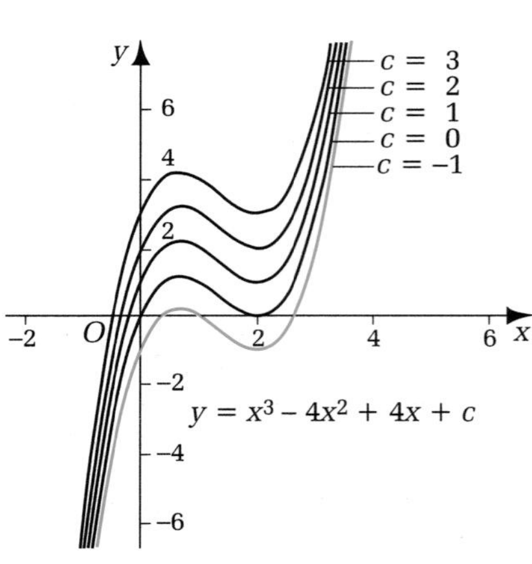

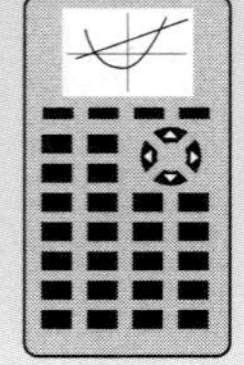

An alternative to the graphical method is to use algebra to find, or check, the value of c. Substituting the values of $x = 3$ and $y = 2$ into the expression for y,

$$y = 4x - 4x^2 + x^3 + c$$

$$\Rightarrow \quad 2 = 4 \times 3 - 4 \times 9 + 27 + c$$

$$\Rightarrow \quad 2 = 12 - 36 + 27 + c$$

$$\Rightarrow \quad -1 = c$$

So the equation of the curve is $y = x^3 - 4x^2 + 4x - 1$.

Integration and mechanics

In Chapter 5, mechanics was used as a context for differentiation. Recall that if s = distance travelled in time t then the velocity is given by $v = \frac{ds}{dt}$, and the acceleration is given by $a = \frac{dv}{dt}$. Using integration as the reverse process to differentiation it is now possible to work backwards. This means that we can find v if we know a, and can find s if we know v. The new equations become:

$$v = \int a\,dt \quad \text{and} \quad s = \int v\,dt.$$

Example 3

An aircraft taxies at a constant speed of $7.5\ \text{m s}^{-1}$ to the start of a straight runway. It then begins to accelerate. Its acceleration after t seconds is given by $a = 2t - \frac{1}{5}t^2$.

a Find an expression for the velocity at time t seconds.

b An observer estimates that 10 seconds after leaving the start of the runway the plane takes off. What distance has it travelled along the runway in that time?

Solution

Draw a diagram to illustrate the situation.

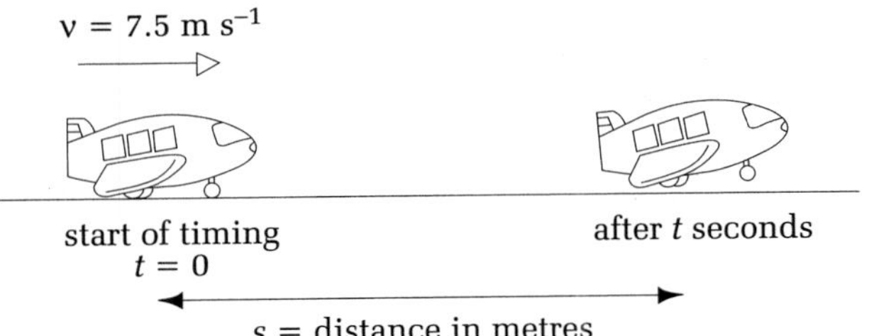

a $a = \frac{dv}{dt} = 2t - \frac{1}{5}t^2$

We know that $v = \int a\,dt$, so we integrate the acceleration to find the velocity.

The variable is t.

$\int t^n\,dt = \frac{t^{n+1}}{n+1} + c$

$$\begin{aligned} v &= \int a\,dt \\ &= \int (2t - \tfrac{1}{5}t^2)\,dt \\ &= 2 \times \tfrac{1}{2}t^2 - \tfrac{1}{5} \times \tfrac{1}{3}t^3 + c \\ &= t^2 - \tfrac{1}{15}t^3 + c \end{aligned}$$

There is enough information in the question to calculate c. At the start of the straight runway the speed of the aircraft is $7.5\,\mathrm{m\,s^{-1}}$. So when $t = 0$, $v = 7.5$. Substitute these values into the expression for v.

$$7.5 = 0 - 0 + c$$

$$\tfrac{15}{2} = c$$

$$v = t^2 - \tfrac{1}{15}t^3 + \tfrac{15}{2}$$

b $v = \frac{ds}{dt} = t^2 - \frac{1}{15}t^3 + \frac{15}{2}$

So $s = \int v\,dt$

$$\begin{aligned} s &= \int (t^2 - \tfrac{1}{15}t^3 + \tfrac{15}{2})\,dt \\ &= \tfrac{1}{3}t^3 - \tfrac{1}{15} \times \tfrac{1}{4}t^4 + \tfrac{15}{2}t + c \\ &= \tfrac{1}{3}t^3 - \tfrac{1}{60}t^4 + \tfrac{15}{2}t + c \end{aligned}$$

The distance is measured from the start of the runway. So when $t = 0$, $s = 0$. Substitute these into the expression for s.

$$0 = 0 - 0 + 0 + c$$

$$0 = c$$

$$s = \tfrac{1}{3}t^3 - \tfrac{1}{60}t^4 + \tfrac{15}{2}t$$

To find the distance covered in the first 10 seconds substitute $t = 10$ into this expression for s.

$$\begin{aligned} s &= \tfrac{1}{3} \times 10^3 - \tfrac{1}{60} \times 10^4 + \tfrac{15}{2} \times 10 \\ &= \frac{1000}{3} - \frac{10\,000}{60} + \frac{150}{2} \\ &= \frac{1000}{3} - \frac{1000}{6} + \frac{150}{2} \\ &= \frac{2000}{6} - \frac{1000}{6} + \frac{450}{6} \\ &= \frac{1450}{6} = \frac{725}{3} \end{aligned}$$

So $s = 241\tfrac{2}{3}$ m ◀ **Always include the appropriate unit.**

Note the exact answer.

9.1 Indefinite Integration
Exercise
Technique

1 Use integration notation to describe each of the following statements:

a integrate $2x^2 - 3x + 1$ with respect to x
b integrate e^{2t} with respect to t
c integrate $\cos\theta$ with respect to θ.

2 Integrate each of the following with respect to x:

a 3 **b** $2x - 5$ **c** $x^2 + x - 7$
d $x(2 - 3x)$ **e** $(x - 3)(x + 5)$ **f** $(x + 1)^2$

2 e

3 Find:

a $\int dx$ **e** $\int \frac{1}{t^2}\,dt$ **i** $\int 100x^{1.2}\,dx$
b $\int 10\,dr$ **f** $\int x^{\frac{2}{3}}\,dx$ **j** $\int \frac{1}{\sqrt{r}}\,dr$
c $\int (t^3 + 1)\,dt$ **g** $\int 5r^9\,dr$ **k** $\int 3x^{-\frac{4}{3}}\,dx$
d $\int \sqrt{x}\,dx$ **h** $\int \frac{2}{t^3}\,dt$

4 Find:

a $\int (x^2 - 3x + 2)\,dx$ **b** $\int (2t - 5)^2\,dt$ **c** $\int x(2 + x)\,dx$
d $\int t(1 - t^2)^2\,dt$ **e** $\int (x + 1)(x - 3)\,dx$ **f** $\int 14x^{\frac{5}{2}}\,dx$

5 Find:

a $\int \left(\frac{x^4 + 2}{x^3}\right) dx$ **b** $\int \left(\frac{x + 3}{\sqrt{x}}\right) dx$ **c** $\int \left(\frac{1}{t^3} + \frac{2}{t^2} + 3t\right) dt$
d $\int (\sqrt{x} - 1)^2\,dx$ **e** $\int \left(\frac{1 - 3x^2}{\sqrt{x}}\right) dx$ **f** $\int (6 + x)\sqrt{x}\,dx$

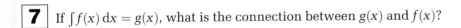

5 c, e

6 If $f'(x) = 8x$, and $f(1) = 4$, find $f(x)$.

7 If $\int f(x)\,dx = g(x)$, what is the connection between $g(x)$ and $f(x)$?

Contextual

1 The velocity of a particle, at time t, is given by $v = t + 3$. Find an expression for the distance, s, travelled by the particle at time t, given that $s = 0$ when $t = 0$.

2 Copy and complete the following, where each '•' represents a missing term:

- **a** $\int(2x^3 - 10x^2 - \bullet + \bullet)\,dx = \bullet - \frac{10}{3}x^3 - \frac{1}{2}x^2 + 3x + c$
- **b** $\int(\bullet - 15t)\,dt = \bullet\int(2 - 3t)\,dt = \bullet(\bullet - \bullet) + \bullet$
- **c** $\int dy = \bullet + \bullet$
- **d** $\int \bullet = \theta + c$
- **e** $\int(\bullet - \bullet + 1)\,dx = \frac{4}{3}x^{\frac{3}{2}} - \frac{1}{2}x^2 + \bullet + \bullet$
- **f** $\int(\bullet - \bullet + t^5)\bullet = \frac{5}{2}t^2 - t^3 + \bullet + \bullet$
- **g** $\int(\bullet - 3)\bullet = u^2 - \bullet + \bullet$

3 If $g(x) = \int 6x(x+1)\,dx$:

- **a** write down $g'(x)$ and solve $g'(x) = 0$
- **b** find $g(x)$ given that $g(-1) = 5$.

4 The gradient of a curve at any point is given by $\frac{dy}{dx} = 4 - 2x$.

- **a** Explain why the curve has a maximum value when $x = 2$.
- **b** If the maximum value of the curve is 1 find the equation of the curve.

5 If $g'(x) = 1 - 4x^3$, and $(2, -13)$ is a point on the curve $g(x)$, find $g(x)$.

6 The gradient at any point (x, y) on a curve is given by $\frac{dy}{dx} = -\frac{4}{x^3}$. If the curve passes through the point $(2, 3\frac{1}{2})$, find the equation of the curve.

7 A train starts from rest at station A and $2\frac{1}{2}$ minutes later stops at station B. Its velocity, t seconds after starting, is given by $v = 0.6t - 0.004t^2$ m s^{-1}.

Model only applies during the time for the journey from A to B.

- **a** Find an expression for the distance travelled from A.
- **b** Find the distance between the two stations.

8 A particle leaves a fixed point O with a velocity of 20 m s^{-1}. It travels in a straight line and its acceleration after t seconds is given by $a = (14 - 8t)$ m s^{-2}.

- **a** Find an expression for the velocity in terms of t.
- **b** Find an expression for the displacement of the particle after leaving O.

9.2 The Area Under a Graph

Integration is used for summation; usually of lengths, areas or volumes. The S-shaped symbol was devised by Leibniz because integration represents a sum. It was perceived as the sum of the areas of an infinite number of rectangles of height $f(x)$ and infinitesimally small width δx. So each rectangle would be thinner than a pencil line and its area would be $f(x)\,\delta x$.

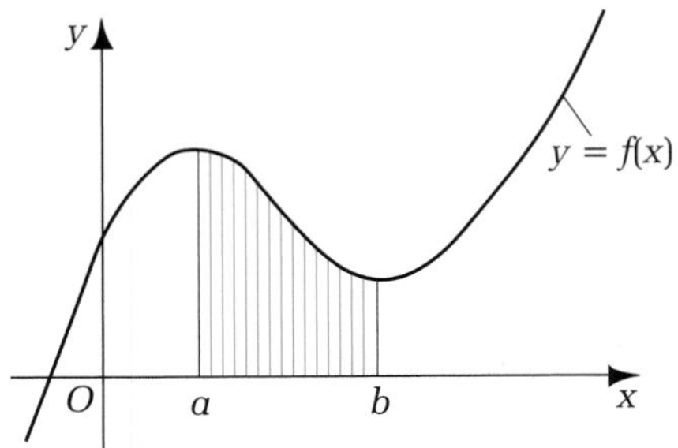

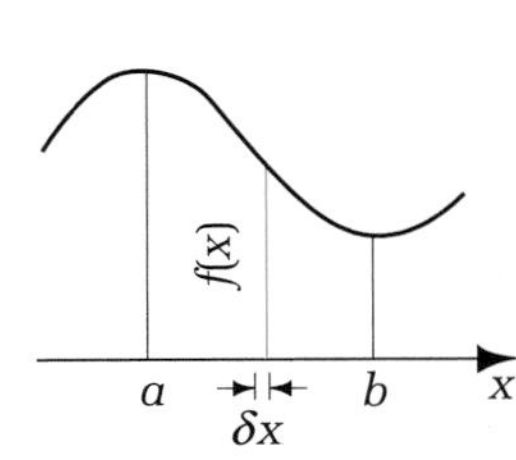

Height of pencil line is from the x-axis up to the graph.

We can find the area under the curve $y = x^2$, between $x = 2$ and $x = 3$, using Leibniz's idea that $\int_a^b f(x)\,dx$ is the sum of the areas of many thin rectangles.

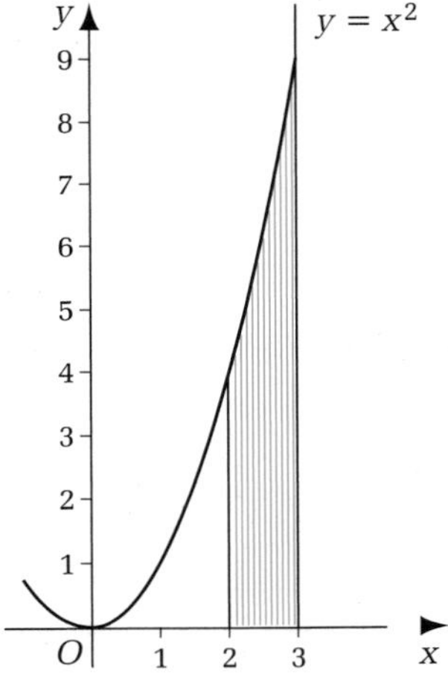

Consider splitting the area into a series of thin rectangles.

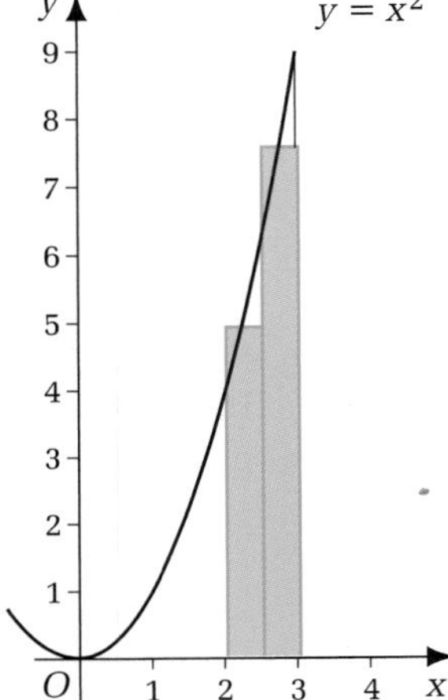

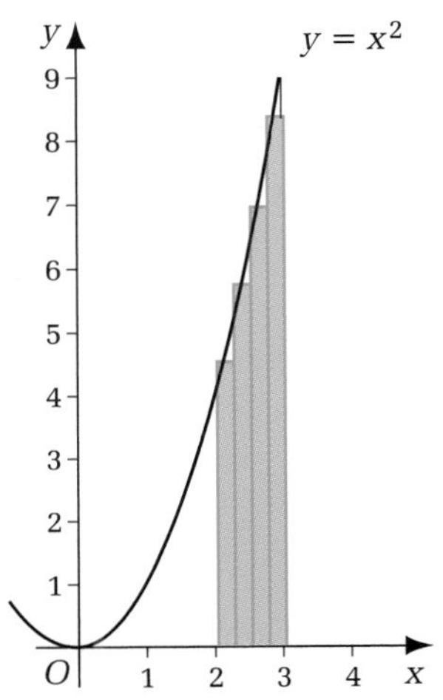

When the area is split into two rectangles the width of each is 0.5. The height of the first rectangle is $f(2.25)$ and the height of the second rectangle as $f(2.75)$. The two distinct areas are then $0.5 \times f(2.25)$ and $0.5 \times f(2.75)$. Calculate these two values:

$$0.5 \times f(2.25) = 0.5 \times 5.0625 = 2.531\,25$$
$$0.5 \times f(2.75) = 0.5 \times 7.5625 = 3.781\,25$$

The total area under the curve is estimated to be

$$2.531\,25 + 3.781\,25 = 6.3125$$

Repeat the process, this time splitting the area into four rectangles. The width of each rectangle is then 0.25, and their heights are $f(2.125)$, $f(2.375)$, $f(2.625)$ and $f(2.875)$. Check that the total area is now 6.328 125. This process could be repeated many times. In each case the width of each rectangle gets much smaller. As the width becomes infinitesimally small (as $\delta x \to 0$), the heights become $f(x)$ for all values of x between $x = 2$ and $x = 3$. The total area of all the rectangles then becomes a better approximation to the exact area under the curve. The area can be calculated as

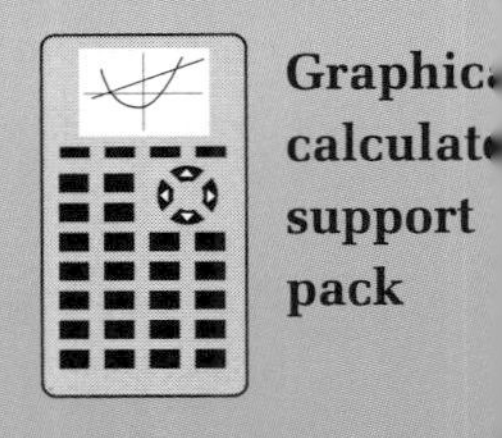

$$\sum_{x=2}^{3} f(x)\,\delta x$$

You could investigate the sum of the rectang areas further using the program option on a graphical calculator.

where this expression represents the sum of the areas of each rectangle with height $f(x)$ and width δx, between $x = 2$ and $x = 3$.

The limit as $\delta x \to 0$ of $\sum_{x=2}^{3} f(x)\,\delta x$ is $\int_2^3 f(x)\,dx$.

In general, adding the areas of all these rectangles gives the area under the graph between $x = a$ and $x = b$ as

area of the shaded region $= \int_a^b f(x)\,dx$ ◀ Learn this result.

The constant term doe not have to be written down for a definite integral.

We call 'b' the **upper limit** of the integral and 'a' the **lower limit** of the integral. An integral with limits is a **definite integral**.
The shaded area under the curve $y = x^2$ is given by $\int_2^3 x^2\,dx$.

$$\int_2^3 x^2\,dx = \left[\tfrac{1}{3}x^3\right]_2^3$$ ◀ Square brackets are used to separate the limits from the integrated expression.

$$= \left(\tfrac{27}{3}\right) - \left(\tfrac{8}{3}\right)$$
$$= \tfrac{19}{3} = 6\tfrac{1}{3}$$

Putting $x = 3$ and $x =$ gives the area under t graph between $x = 0$ a $x = 3$, and $x = 0$ and x respectively. Subtract the second from the fi gives the area under t graph between $x = 2$ a $x = 3$.

So the area under the curve is $6\frac{1}{3}$ square units. Compare this to the result for four rectangles.

Example 1

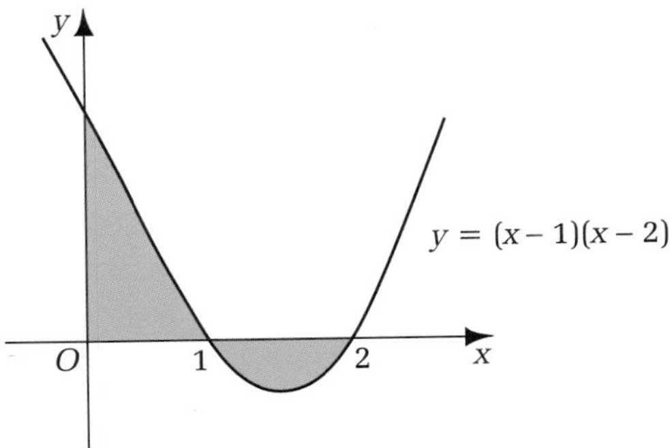

The graph shows the curve $y = (x - 1)(x - 2)$.

a Find $\int_0^1 (x-1)(x-2)\,dx$ and $\int_1^2 (x-1)(x-2)\,dx$. Comment on your answer.

b What would you expect $\int_0^2 (x-1)(x-2)\,dx$ to equal?

c Find the area of the shaded region.

Solution

a To use integration first express y as a polynomial in x.

$$y = (x-1)(x-2) = x^2 - 3x + 2$$

$$\int_0^1 (x-1)(x-2)\,dx = \int_0^1 (x^2 - 3x + 2)\,dx$$

Integrating each term separately.

$$= \left[\tfrac{1}{3}x^3 - \tfrac{3}{2}x^2 + 2x\right]_0^1$$
$$= \left(\tfrac{1}{3} - \tfrac{3}{2} + 2\right) - (0 - 0 + 0)$$
$$= \tfrac{2}{6} - \tfrac{9}{6} + \tfrac{12}{6}$$
$$= \tfrac{5}{6}$$

The area between the curve $y = (x-1)(x-2)$ and the x-axis between $x = 0$ and $x = 1$ is $\frac{5}{6}$ square units.

$$\int_1^2 (x-1)(x-2)\,dx = \left[\tfrac{1}{3}x^3 - \tfrac{3}{2}x^2 + 2x\right]_1^2$$

From the first part of the question.

$$= \left(\tfrac{1}{3} \times 8 - \tfrac{3}{2} \times 4 + 2 \times 2\right) - \left(\tfrac{1}{3} - \tfrac{3}{2} + 2\right)$$
$$= \tfrac{16}{6} - \tfrac{36}{6} + \tfrac{24}{6} - \tfrac{2}{6} + \tfrac{9}{6} - \tfrac{12}{6}$$
$$= -\tfrac{1}{6}$$

The value of the integral between $x = 1$ and $x = 2$ is $-\frac{1}{6}$. This is interpreted as an area of $\frac{1}{6}$ square units below the x-axis.

The value of the integral between $x = 1$ and $x = 2$ is negative. This is because the region bounded by the curve, $x = 1$, $x = 2$ and the x-axis lies below the x-axis.

b Since integration is a summation process we might expect that

$$\int_0^2 (x-1)(x-2)\,dx = \int_0^1 (x-1)(x-2)\,dx + \int_1^2 (x-1)(x-2)\,dx$$
$$= \tfrac{5}{6} + \left(-\tfrac{1}{6}\right) = \tfrac{4}{6} = \tfrac{2}{3}$$

c Looking at the sketch of the function, we can avoid adding the areas algebraically. The graph shows that part of the curve is below the x-axis, and for this region the integral is negative. Adding the integrals, as in **b**, would give too small a result for the area. Therefore,

total shaded area $= \frac{5}{6} + \frac{1}{6} = \frac{6}{6} = 1$ square unit.

A sketch of the curve will always give you a indication of whether the curve crosses the x-axis. If it does, you must calculate the are of the regions above a below the axis separately, and then a them together to find t total area.

Example 2

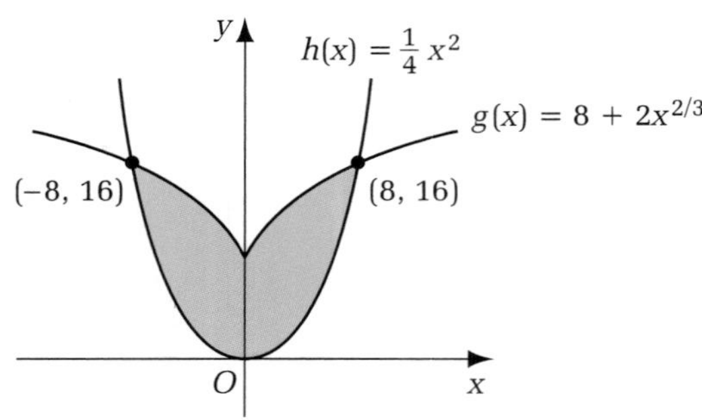

Find the area of shaded region enclosed between $g(x) = 8 + 2x^{\frac{2}{3}}$ and $h(x) = \frac{1}{4}x^2$.

Solution

The area is symmetrical, with the y-axis as the line of symmetry. So we can find the area of the whole shaded region by doubling the area of the part of the region lying in the first quadrant. Call the area under the curve $g(x)$ area A, and the area under the curve $h(x)$ area B.

The first quadrant is th part of the curve wher and y coordinates are both positive; above th x-axis and to the right the y-axis.

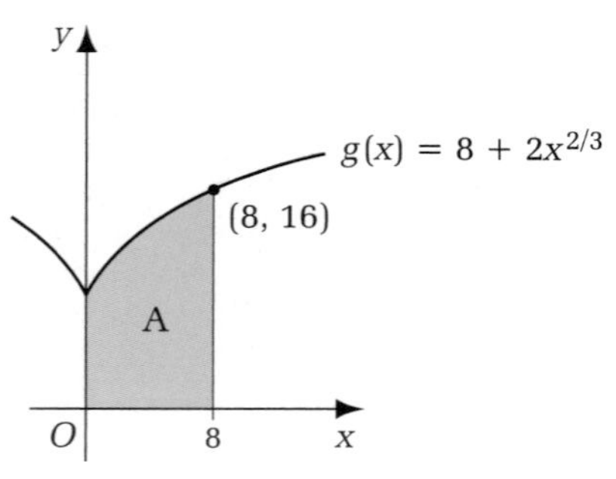

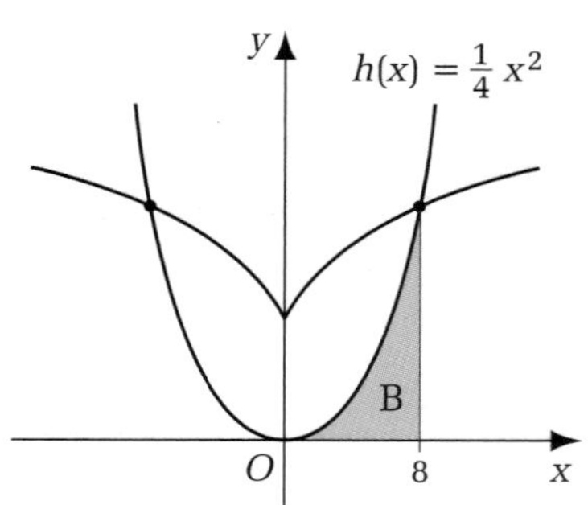

On the diagram, notice the coordinates of the point where $g(x)$ and $h(x)$ cross. The x-coordinate is 8, so w require the area betwe $x = 0$ and $x = 8$.

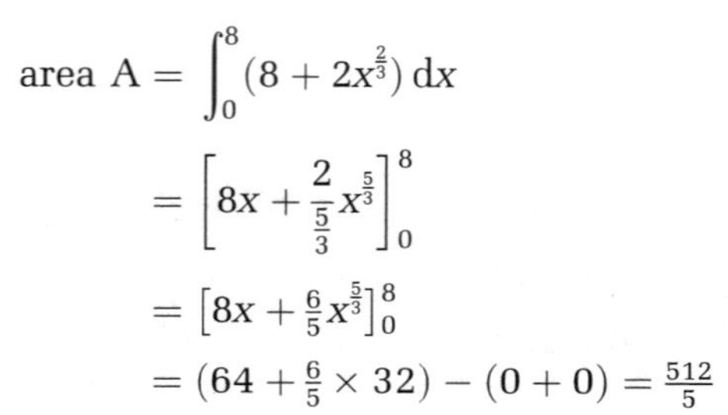

$$\text{area A} = \int_0^8 (8 + 2x^{\frac{2}{3}})\,dx$$
$$= \left[8x + \frac{2}{\frac{5}{3}}x^{\frac{5}{3}}\right]_0^8$$
$$= \left[8x + \tfrac{6}{5}x^{\frac{5}{3}}\right]_0^8$$
$$= (64 + \tfrac{6}{5} \times 32) - (0 + 0) = \tfrac{512}{5}$$

$$\text{area B} = \int_0^8 \tfrac{1}{4}x^2\,dx = \tfrac{1}{4}\int_0^8 x^2\,dx$$
$$= \tfrac{1}{4}\left[\tfrac{1}{3}x^3\right]_0^8$$
$$= \tfrac{1}{4}[(\tfrac{1}{3} \times 512) - 0]$$
$$= \tfrac{512}{12} = \tfrac{128}{3}$$

Recall that $\int kf(x)\,dx = k\int f(x)\,dx$.

So the area of the shaded region $= 2 \times (\text{area A} - \text{area B})$

$$= 2 \times \left(\tfrac{512}{5} - \tfrac{128}{3}\right) = \tfrac{1792}{15}$$

Area of the shaded region $= 119.47$ square units (2 d.p.).

Example 3

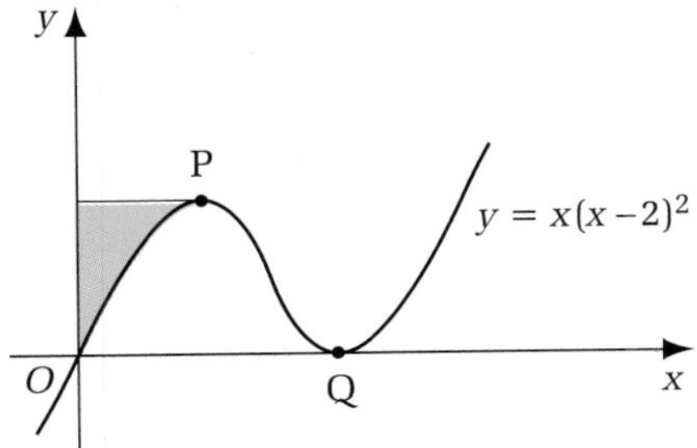

The graph shows a sketch of the curve $y = x(x-2)^2$.

a Find the coordinates of P.

b Find the shaded area.

Solution

a
$$y = x(x-2)^2$$
$$= x(x^2 - 4x + 4)$$
$$= x^3 - 4x^2 + 4x$$
$$\Rightarrow \frac{dy}{dx} = 3x^2 - 8x + 4$$

P is a local maximum point, so $\frac{dy}{dx} = 0$ at P. That is, $3x^2 - 8x + 4 = 0$.

This is a quadratic equation. The coefficient of x^2 is larger than 1, so factorise and solve it using PAFF:

P: $3 \times 4 = 12$
A: -8
F: $-2, -6$

$$3x^2 - 8x + 4 = 3x^2 - 2x - 6x + 4$$
$$= x(3x-2) - 2(3x-2)$$
$$= (3x-2)(x-2)$$

When $3x^2 - 8x + 4 = 0$, $(3x-2)(x-2) = 0$.
So $x = \frac{2}{3}$ or $x = 2$.

Substituting each of these coordinates into the original equation, we find that the coordinates of P are $\left(\frac{2}{3}, \frac{32}{27}\right)$ and the coordinates of Q are $(2, 0)$.

Check these against the sketch of the graph.

b The area of the shaded region can be found by subtracting the area of the region below the graph between $x = 0$ and $x = \frac{2}{3}$ from the area of the rectangle with corners $(0, 0)$, $(0, \frac{32}{27})$, P $(\frac{2}{3}, \frac{32}{27})$ and $(\frac{2}{3}, 0)$.

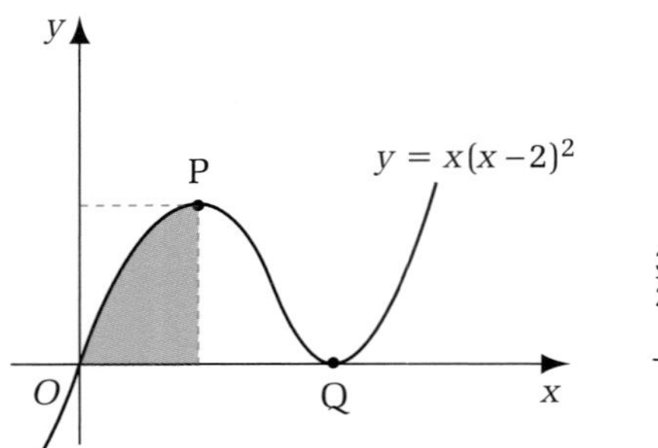

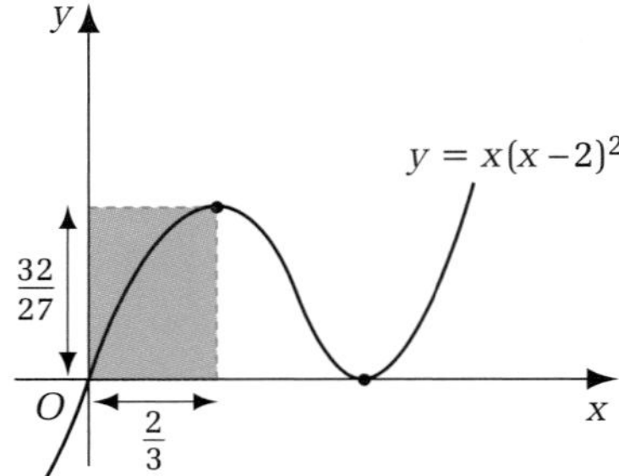

The area of the rectangle is $\frac{2}{3} \times \frac{32}{27} = \frac{64}{81}$

The area under the graph $y = x(x-2)^2$ between $x = 0$ and $x = \frac{2}{3}$ is given by

$$\begin{aligned}
\text{area} &= \int_0^{\frac{2}{3}} (x^3 - 4x^2 + 4x)\,dx \\
&= \left[\tfrac{1}{4}x^4 - \tfrac{4}{3}x^3 + 2x^2\right]_0^{\frac{2}{3}} \\
&= \left(\tfrac{1}{4} \times \tfrac{16}{81} - \tfrac{4}{3} \times \tfrac{8}{27} + 2 \times \tfrac{4}{9}\right) - (0 - 0 + 0) \\
&= \tfrac{4}{81} - \tfrac{32}{81} + \tfrac{72}{81} \\
&= \tfrac{44}{81}
\end{aligned}$$

So the area of the original shaded region $= \frac{64}{81} - \frac{44}{81} = \frac{20}{81}$ square units.

9.2 The Area Under a Graph

Exercise

Technique

1 Copy and complete the following:

a $\int_a^b (x+3)\,dx = [\,\bullet\,]_a^b$

b $\int_a^b (t^3 + 2t^2 - 1)\,dt = [\,\bullet\,]_a^b$

c $\int_a^b dx = [\,\bullet\,]_a^b$

d $\int_a^b dr = [\,\bullet\,]_a^b$

e $\int_a^b 10\,dr = [\,\bullet\,]_a^b$

f $\int_a^b (\bullet)\,dx = [\frac{1}{3}x^3 - 3x^2 + 9x]_a^b$

2 Use the notation for integration to describe the areas of the shaded regions in the following:

 2

a

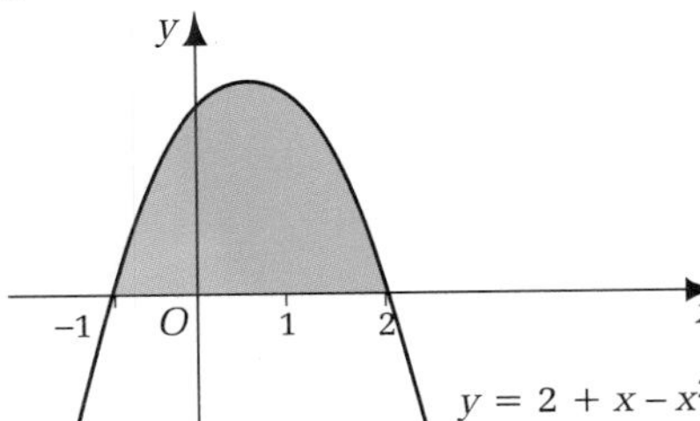

b

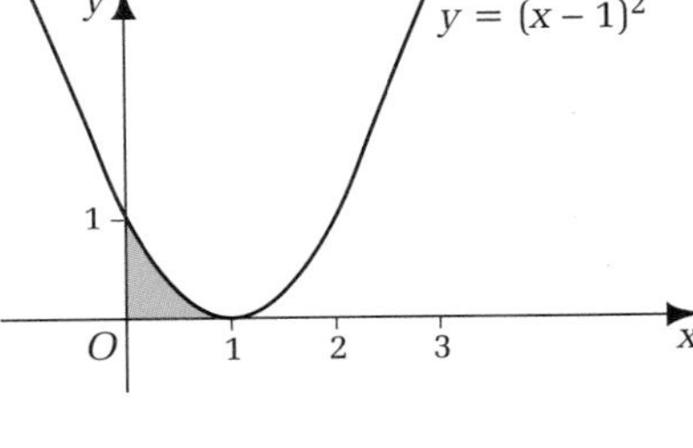

3 Peter is finding the area of the region under the curve $y = x^2 - 2x + 4$ between $x = 0$ and $x = 2$. His working is shown here. Complete his integration.

y

0

2

x

$$\text{area} = \int_0^2 (x^2 - 2x + 4)\,dx$$

$$= \left[\tfrac{1}{3}x^3 - x^2 + 4x\right]_0^2$$

$$=$$

4 Use integration to find the area of the shaded region in each of the following:

a

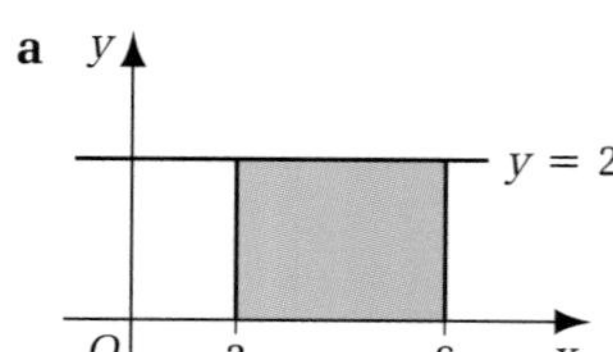

b

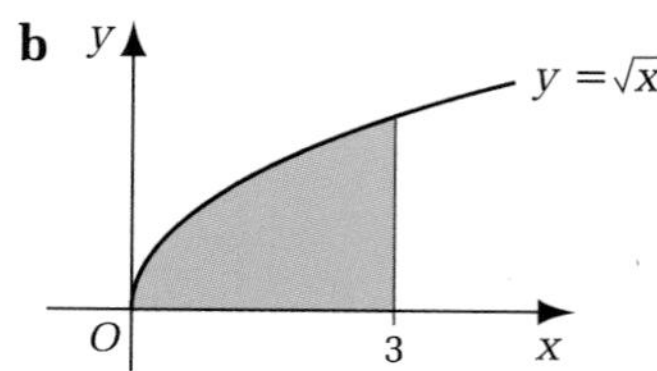

c

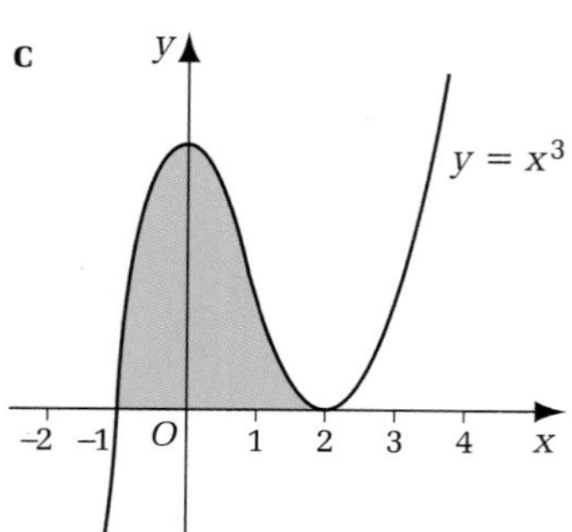

d

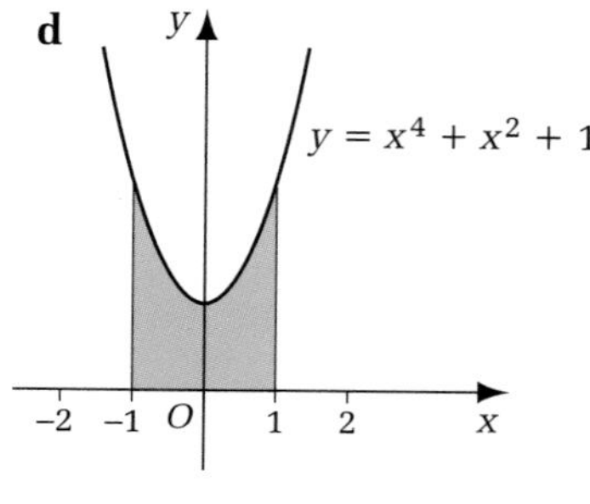

5 Evaluate the following definite integrals:

a $\int_1^2 (5x^4 - 6x^3 + x + 1)\,dx$ **b** $\int_{-2}^3 (x^2 - x - 6)\,dx$

c $\int_{-3}^1 (10 - 2x + 6x^2)\,dx$ **d** $\int_{-2}^1 (1 - 10x^4)\,dx$

6 The graph shows a sketch of the curve $y = (2 - x)(x - 4)$.

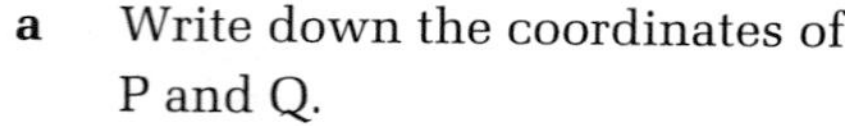

a Write down the coordinates of P and Q.

b Explain why it is necessary to evaluate two separate integrals in order to calculate the area of the shaded region.

c Calculate the area of the shaded region.

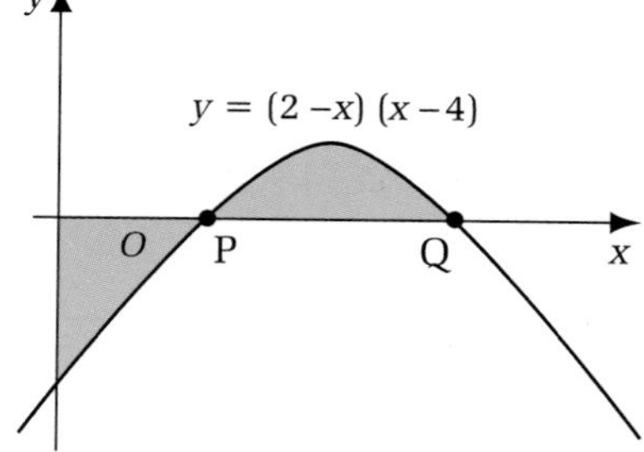

7 This diagram shows the curve $y = x^2 - 3x + 3$ and the line $y = 2x - 1$.

a Find the value of $\int_1^4 (x^2 - 3x + 3)\,dx$.

b Find the value of $\int_1^4 (2x - 1)\,dx$.

c Hence find the area of the shaded region.

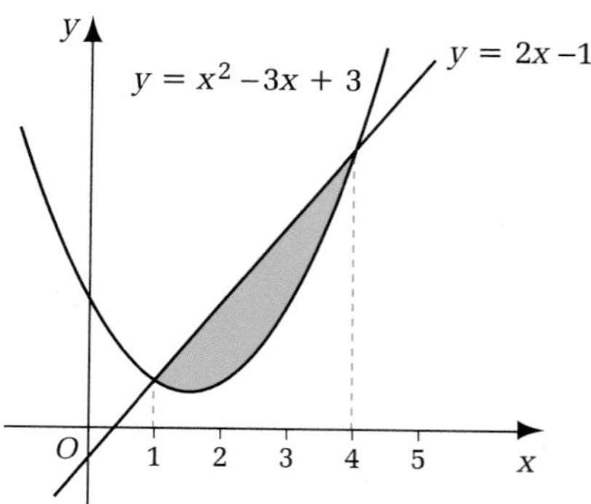

8 **a** Find the area of this shaded region.

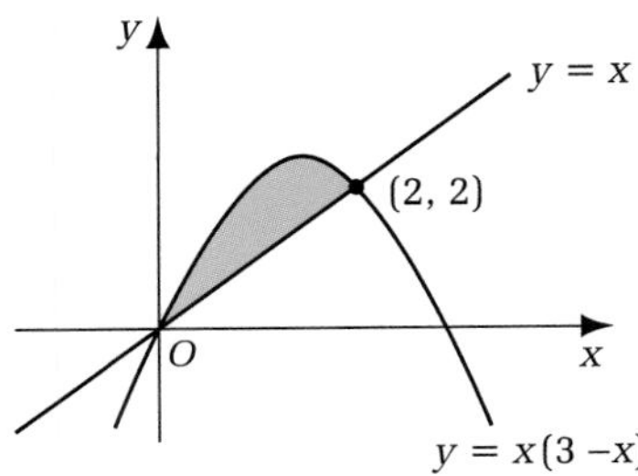

b Now find the area of this pattern.

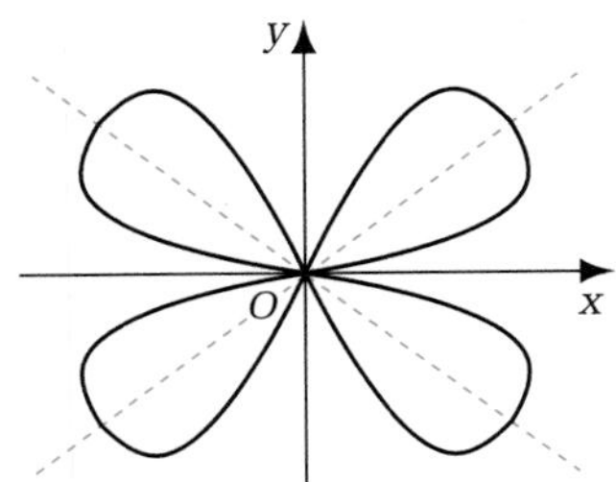

9 Evaluate the following integrals:

a $\int_1^4 \frac{2}{\sqrt{x}}\,dx$

b $\int_0^{16} (\sqrt{x} - 1)\,dx$

c $\int_2^6 \frac{4}{x^3}\,dx$

d $\int_1^4 5x^{\frac{3}{2}}\,dx$

Contextual

1 Find the area of the shaded region in each of the following:

a

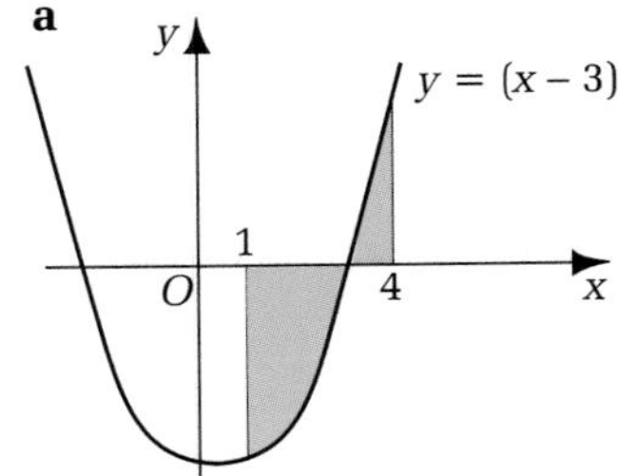

b

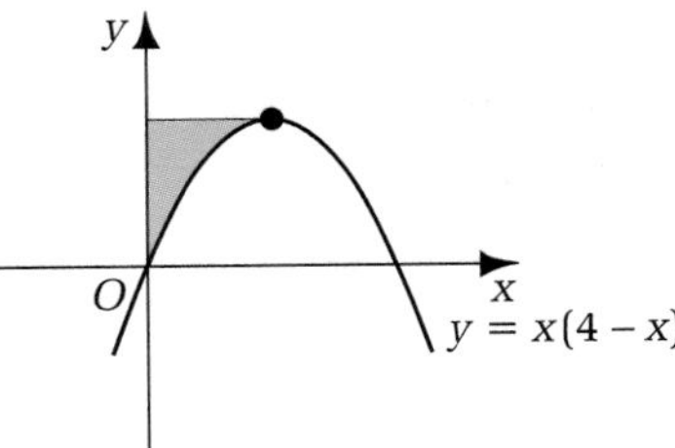

2 The diagram shows the vertical section through a tunnel 14 m long. The roof is an arc modelled by the equation $y = 6 - 0.08x^2 - 0.0006x^4$.

a Find the area of the cross-section.

b Find the volume of the tunnel.

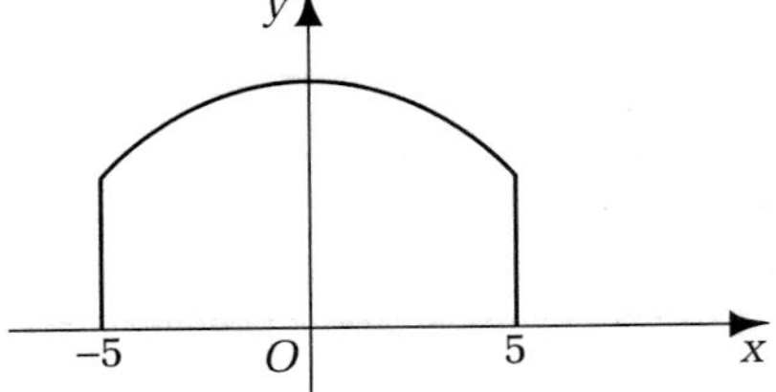

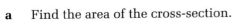

3

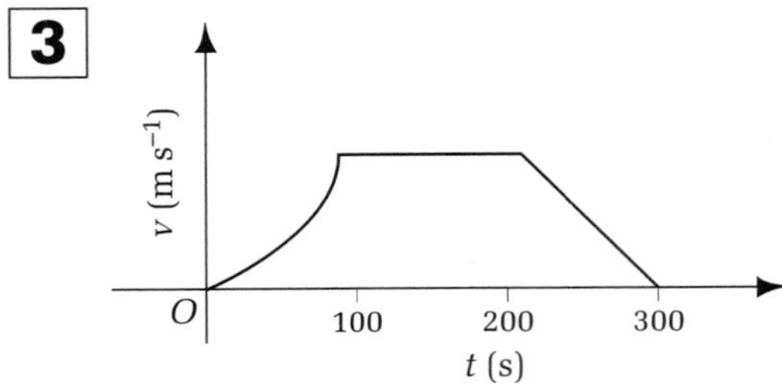

The graph shows the velocity of a tram as it travels from one station to another. In the first $1\frac{1}{2}$ minutes its velocity is given by $v = 0.0025t^2$. For the next two minutes it travels at a constant speed of 20.25 m s^{-1}. It then slows down at a uniform rate, during which time the velocity is given by $v = 67.5 - 0.225t$. The area under a velocity–time graph represents displacement. Find the distance between the two stations by calculating this area.

4 The work done by a gas as its volume increases from 1 cm^3 to 3 cm^3 is given by $\int_1^3 p \, dv$, where $pv^{1.2} = 1000$.

a Express p in terms of v.
b Calculate the work done.

5

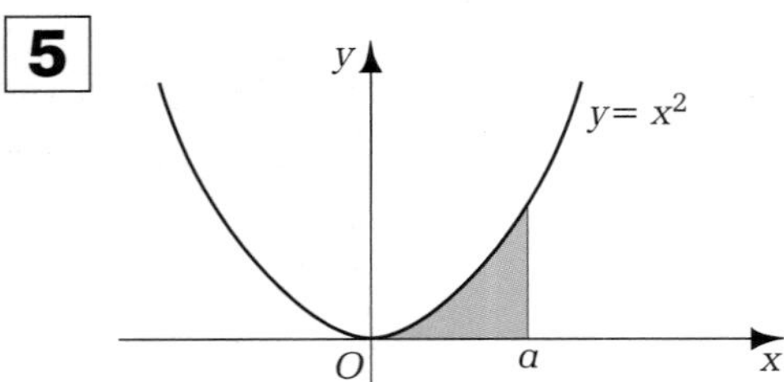

Find a if the area of the shaded region is 2 square units.

Hint: Find the area of shaded region in tern of a, and then equate this with 2.

9.3 The Area Between the Vertical Axis and a Curve

In the previous section we used integration to find the sum of the areas of an infinite number of vertical rectangles. This gave the area under the curve between limits $x = a$ and $x = b$. Integration can also be used to sum the areas of an infinite number of horizontal rectangles. This time it gives the area of the region between the curve and the y-axis. The limits are now $y = a$ and $y = b$.

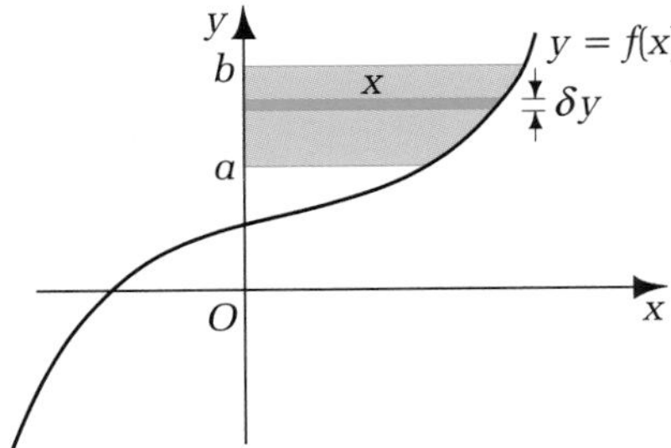

The area of the shaded region is the sum of the areas of an infinite number of horizontal rectangles. The length of each rectangle is x and the width is δy, where δy is infinitesimally small.

Area of the shaded region $= \sum_{y=a}^{b} x\,\delta y \quad$ as $\delta y \to 0$.

How else can this be written?

Recall that integration can be used to find $\sum_{y=a}^{b} x\,\delta y$ as $\delta y \to 0$.

area of the shaded region $= \int_a^b x\,\mathrm{d}y$ ◀ **Learn this result.**

The 'dy' indicates that the variable that may be integrated is y. The equation of the curve $y = f(x)$ will need to be rearranged to make x the subject; that is x should be written in terms of y.

Example 1

Find the areas of each of the following shaded regions:

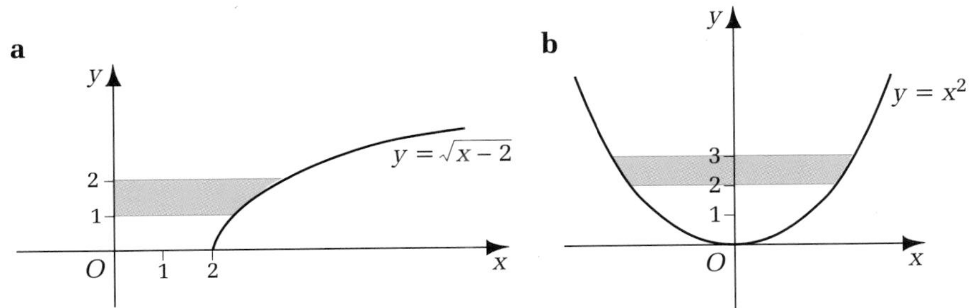

Solution

a Notice that the shaded area is between the curve and the y-axis.

So, area $= \int_1^2 x\,dy$

We need to rearrange $y = \sqrt{x-2}$ to make x the subject.

$$y = \sqrt{x-2}$$
$$\Rightarrow \quad y^2 = x - 2$$
$$\Rightarrow \quad x = y^2 + 2$$

Now the shaded area $= \int_1^2 (y^2 + 2)\,dy$

$$= \left[\tfrac{1}{3}y^3 + 2y\right]_1^2$$
$$= \left(\tfrac{8}{3} + 4\right) - \left(\tfrac{1}{3} + 2\right)$$
$$= \tfrac{7}{3} + 2 = \tfrac{13}{3}$$

The area of the shaded region is $\frac{13}{3}$ square units.

b Notice that the y-axis is a line of symmetry. This means we can calculate the required area by simply doubling the area of the region enclosed by the curve on one side of the y-axis as shown.

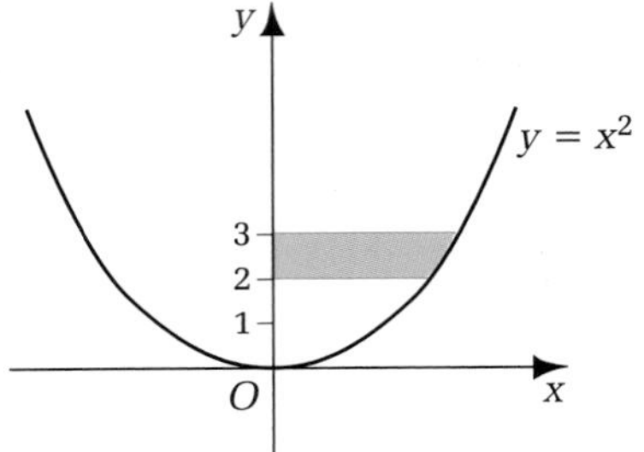

If $y = x^2$, $x = \pm\sqrt{y}$; us the positive square ro

$$\text{area} = 2\int_2^3 x\,dy$$
$$= 2\int_2^3 \sqrt{y}\,dy$$
$$= 2\int_2^3 y^{\frac{1}{2}}\,dy$$
$$= 2 \times \left[\frac{1}{\frac{3}{2}}\,y^{\frac{3}{2}}\right]_2^3$$
$$= 2 \times \left[\tfrac{2}{3}\,y^{\frac{3}{2}}\right]_2^3$$
$$= 2 \times \left(\tfrac{2}{3} \times 3^{\frac{3}{2}} - \tfrac{2}{3} \times 2^{\frac{3}{2}}\right)$$
$$= 2 \times \left(\tfrac{2}{3} \times 3\sqrt{3} - \tfrac{2}{3} \times 2\sqrt{2}\right)$$
$$= \tfrac{4}{3}\left(3\sqrt{3} - 2\sqrt{2}\right)$$

9.3 The Area Between the Vertical Axis and a Curve

Exercise

Technique

1 The graph shows the line $y = x + 1$.

a Find x in terms of y.

b Use integration to find the sum of an infinite number of horizontal rectangles that describe the shaded area.

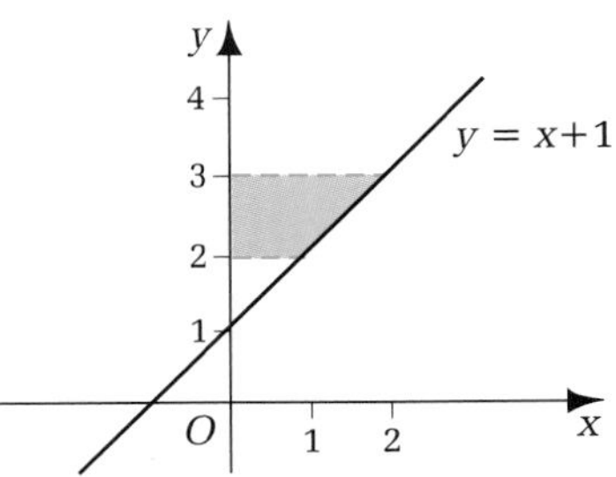

Check your answer for **b** by finding the shaded area as the area of a trapezium.

2

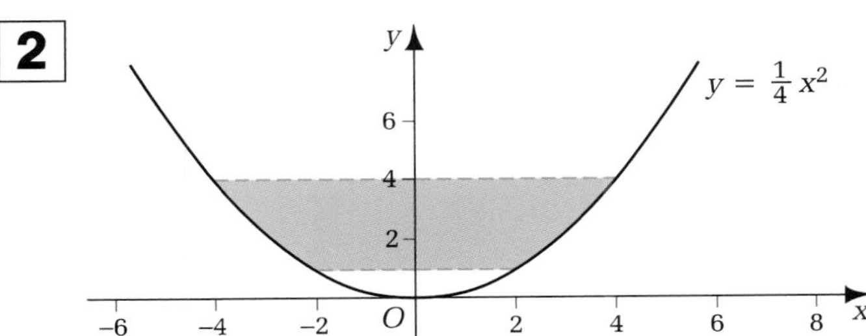

The graph shows the curve $y = \frac{1}{4}x^2$. Express x in terms of y and then calculate the area of the shaded region.

3 The graph shows the curve $y = x^3$. Express x in terms of y. Hence calculate the area of the shaded region, correct to two decimal places.

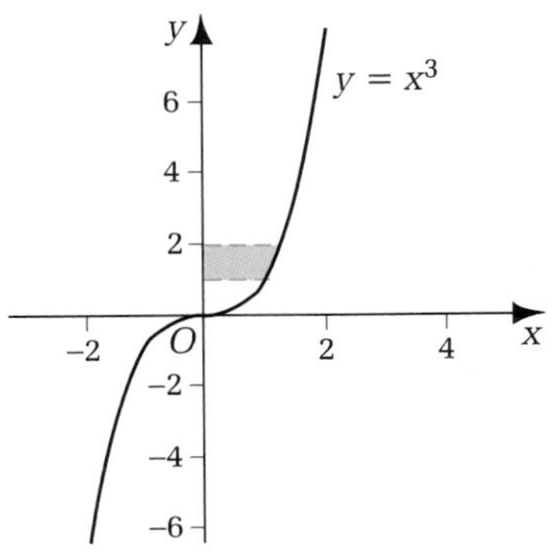

4 The curve shows the graph of $y = \sqrt[3]{(x-1)}$. Express x in terms of y. Hence calculate the exact area of the shaded region.

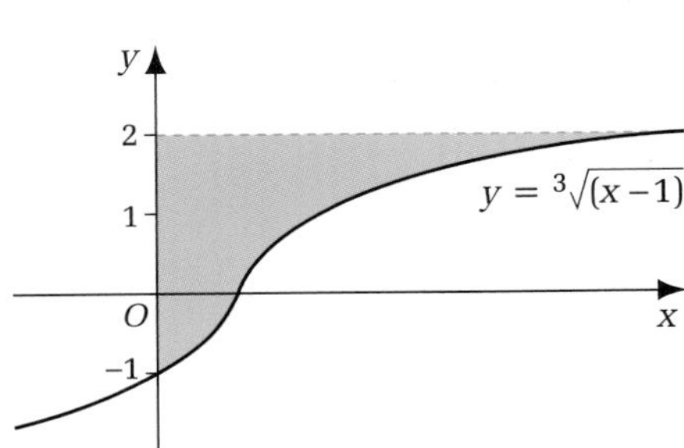

9.4 The Area Between Two Curves

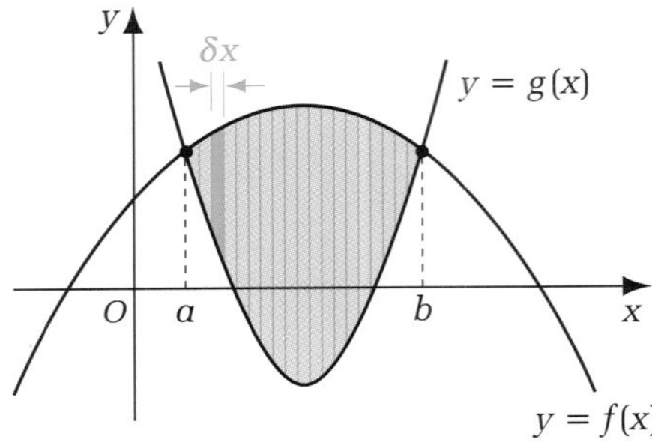

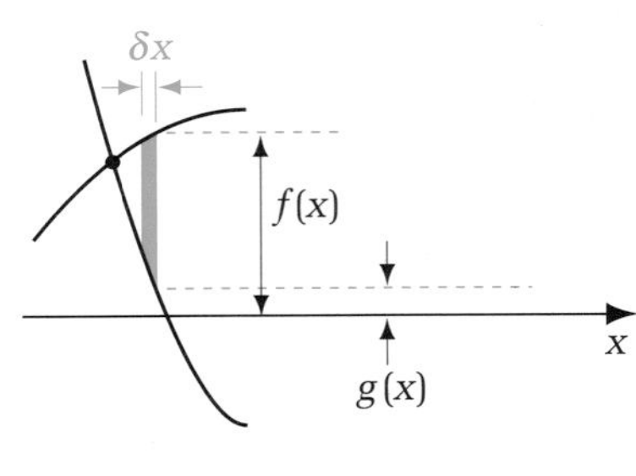

The shaded region is enclosed between the graphs of $y = f(x)$ and $y = g(x)$. Divide the area into vertical strips. Notice that when $f(x) > g(x)$ the length of each strip is $f(x) - g(x)$. This is the case for all values of x between $x = a$ and $x = b$. Adding together the areas of all the thin rectangular strips gives the area of the shaded region.

The area of each strip $(f(x) - g(x)) \times \delta x$.

The area between the two curves is $\sum_{x=a}^{b} (f(x) - g(x))\,\delta x$.

As $\delta x \to 0$ and the width of each strip becomes extremely small, the area can be calculated by integration.

The area between the two curves is $\int_a^b (f(x) - g(x))\,dx$.

This method is very useful if one of the curves lies below the x-axis.

Example 1

Find the area enclosed between the curves $y = x^3 + 2$ and $y = 3x^2 - 2$.

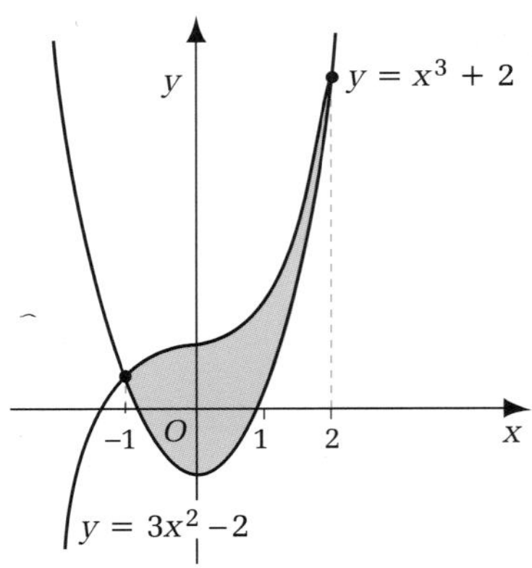

Solution

Since $y = x^3 + 2$ is greater than $y = 3x^2 - 2$ between $x = -1$ and $x = 2$, use

$$\text{area} = \int_a^b (f(x) - g(x))\,dx$$

where $f(x) = x^3 + 2$ and $g(x) = 3x^2 - 2$.

$$\text{So shaded area} = \int_{-1}^{2} [(x^3 + 2) - (3x^2 - 2)]\,dx$$
$$= \int_{-1}^{2} (x^3 - 3x^2 + 4)\,dx = \left[\tfrac{1}{4}x^4 - x^3 + 4x\right]_{-1}^{2}$$
$$= (\tfrac{1}{4} \times 16 - 8 + 8) - (\tfrac{1}{4} \times 1 + 1 - 4)$$
$$= 4 - (-2\tfrac{3}{4}) = 6\tfrac{3}{4}$$
$$= 6\tfrac{3}{4} \text{ square units}$$

Example 2

Find the area bounded by the line $y = x - 1$ and the curve $y = x^2 - 3x - 6$.

Solution

Draw a sketch of the line and the curve on the same axes.

- $y = x^2 - 3x - 6$ is a U-shaped quadratic; passing through $(0, -6)$.
- $y = x - 1$ is a straight line with gradient $+1$, passing through $(0, -1)$.
- To find the area between the graphs we need to locate the points of intersection. At the points of intersection,

  $x - 1 = x^2 - 3x - 6 \Rightarrow 0 = x^2 - 4x - 5$

  Factorising, $(x + 1)(x - 5) = 0$
  So $x = -1$ or $x = 5$.
  When $x = -1, y = -2$ and when $x = 5, y = 4$.
  The points of intersection are $(-1, -2)$ and $(5, 4)$.

Put $x = -1$ and $x = 5$ into $y = x - 1$ to find y.

Check the sketch using a graphical calculator.

This information allows us to sketch the required area. Notice that $y = x - 1$ is greater than $y = x^2 - 3x - 6$ between $x = -1$ and $x = 5$. So the area of the shaded region (the area bounded by the line and the curve) can be found using:

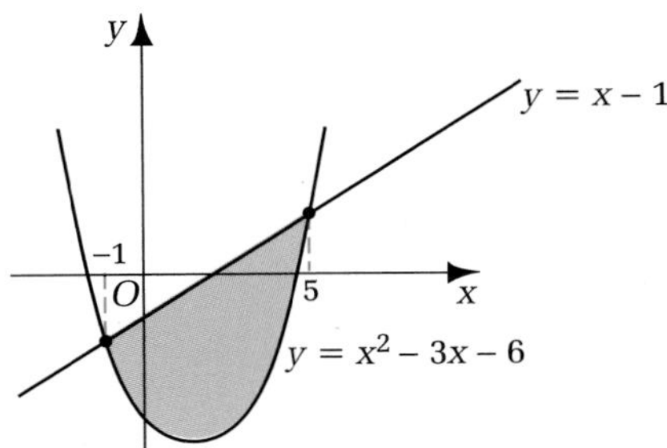

$$\text{area} = \int_{-1}^{5} [(x - 1) - (x^2 - 3x - 6)]\,dx$$
$$= \int_{-1}^{5} (-x^2 + 4x + 5)\,dx = \left[-\tfrac{1}{3}x^3 + 2x^2 + 5x\right]_{-1}^{5}$$
$$= (-\tfrac{1}{3} \times 125 + 2 \times 25 + 25) - (-\tfrac{1}{3} \times -1 + 2 - 5)$$
$$= -\tfrac{125}{3} + 50 + 25 - \tfrac{1}{3} - 2 + 5 = 36$$

required area = 36 square units

This result can be checked on some graphical calculators.

9.4 The Area Between Two Curves

Exercise

Technique

1 Find the area between the curves $y = x^2 - 2x$ and $y = 4 - x^2$.

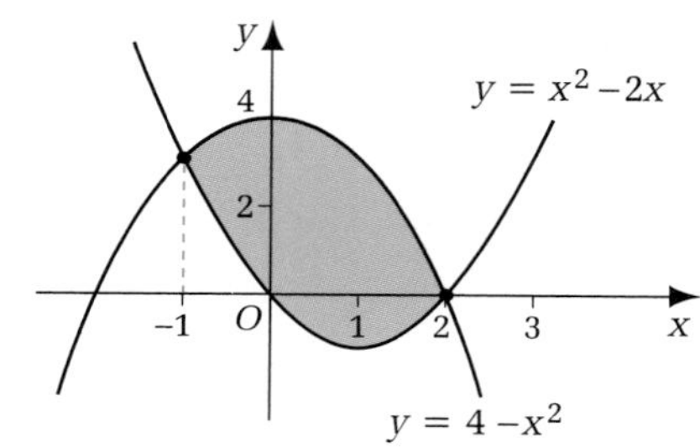

2 Find the area between the curves $y = x^2 - x$ and $y = 7x - x^2$.

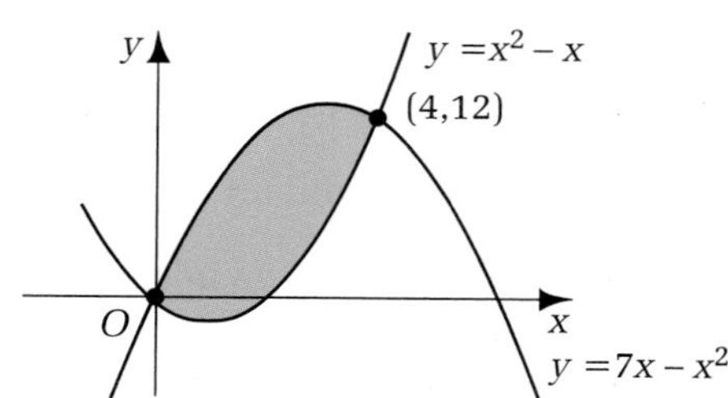

3 Find the area between the curves $y = \sqrt{x}$ and $y = x^3$.

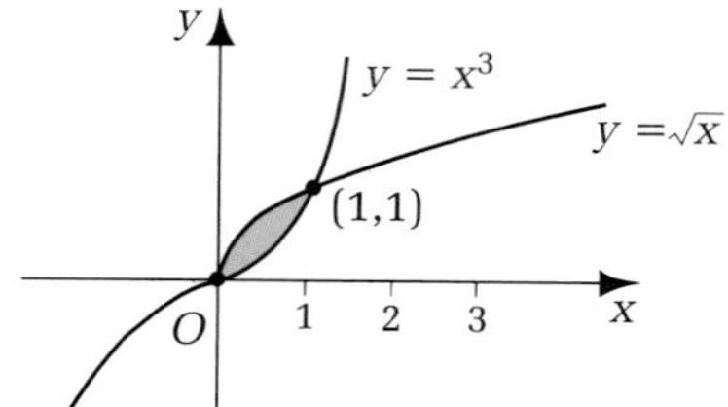

Contextual

1

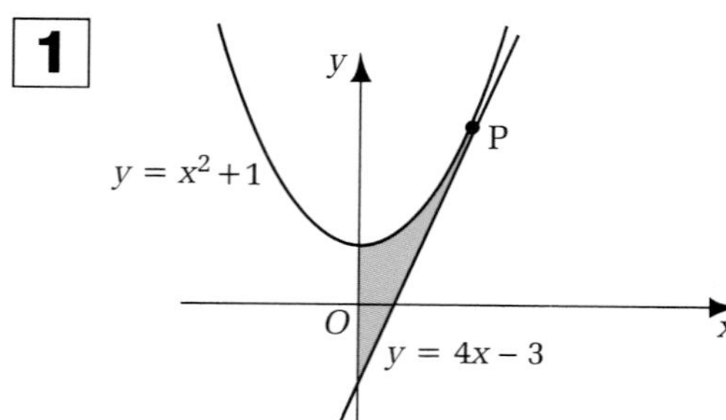

The graph shows the tangent $y = 4x - 3$ to the curve $y = x^2 + 1$.

a Find the coordinates of P.

b Find the area of the shaded region.

2

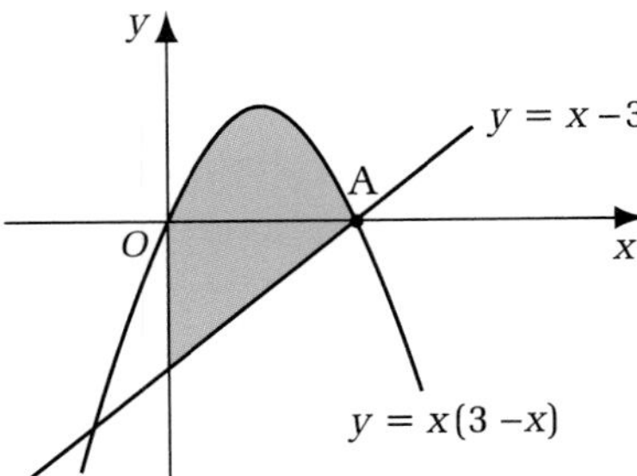

The graph shows the line $y = x - 3$ and the parabola $y = x(3 - x)$.

a Find the coordinates of A, the point where the graphs cross the x-axis.
b Calculate the area of the shaded region.

3

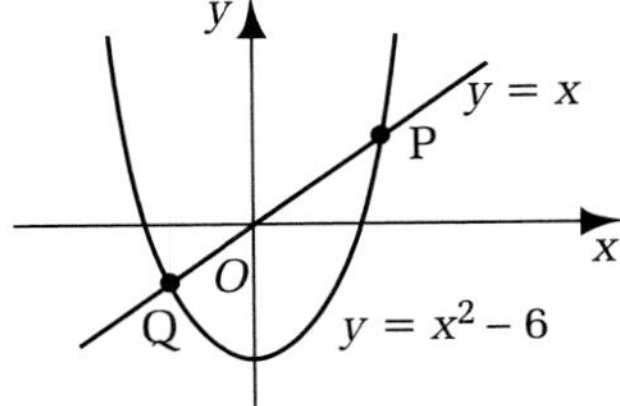

The graph shows the line $y = x$ and the quadratic $y = x^2 - 6$.

a Find the coordinates of P and Q.
b Use your result from **a** to find the area between the line and the quadratic.

4 Find the area between the curves $y = x^2$ and $y = 2x^2 - 9$.

5 Find the area between the following curves:

a $y = 2x$ and $y = \sqrt{x^3}$
b $y = x$ and $y^2 = 4x$

9.5 Volumes of Revolution

What happens when a line is rotated about an axis? Think about the motion of a skipping rope. What kind of shape is formed?
A line rotated about an axis forms the surface of a solid. This is called a **solid of revolution** or a **solid of rotation**. Integration can be used to calculate the volume of solids formed by rotating a curve or plane area about the x-axis or about the y-axis.

Rotating a line about axis creates a hollow object. Rotating an ar creates a solid object.

Rotation about the *x*-axis

Find the volume generated when the shaded area is rotated about the x-axis through 360°.

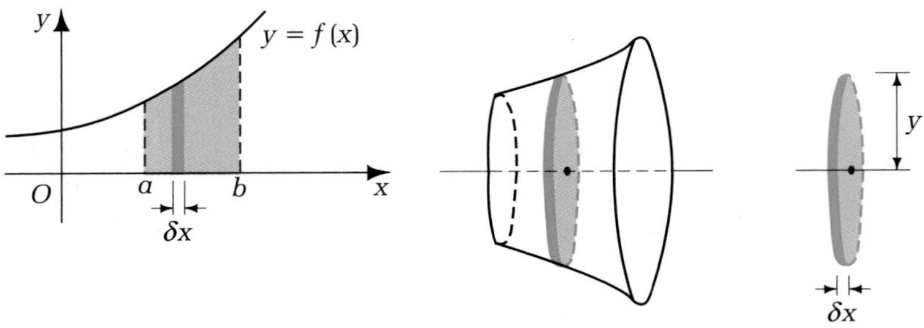

Rotating the shaded area around the x-axis forms a solid of revolution. The approximate thin rectangle becomes a thin disc of radius y and thickness δx.
Volume of the thin disc $= \pi y^2\, \delta x$.
The volume of the solid of revolution is found by adding together the volumes of all the discs.
Volume of revolution $= \sum_{x=a}^{b} \pi y^2\, \delta x$,
where δx is infinitesimally small. This sum can be evaluated accurately using integration.

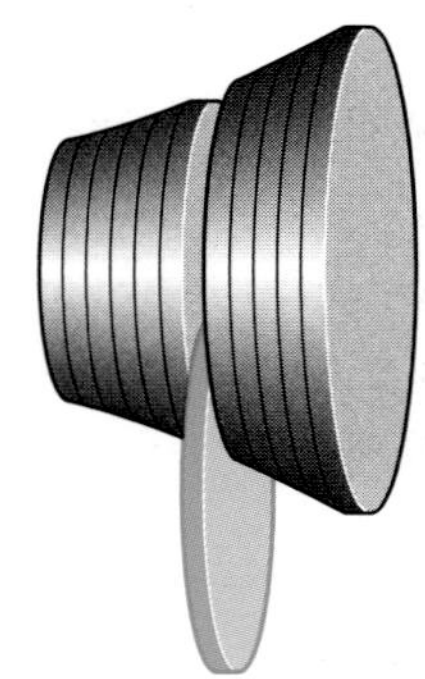

A disc is just an extremely thin cylinc recall that the volum a cylinder of radius r height/length h is πr^2

volume of revolution about the *x*-axis	$= \int_a^b \pi y^2\, dx$ **or** $\int_a^b \pi(f(x))^2\, dx$

where $y = f(x)$ is the equation of the graph of the curved edge of the area.

Example 1

Find the volume generated by rotating the area bounded by the curve $y = x^2 + 1$, the x-axis, and the lines $x = -1$ and $x = 1$ about the x-axis.

Solution

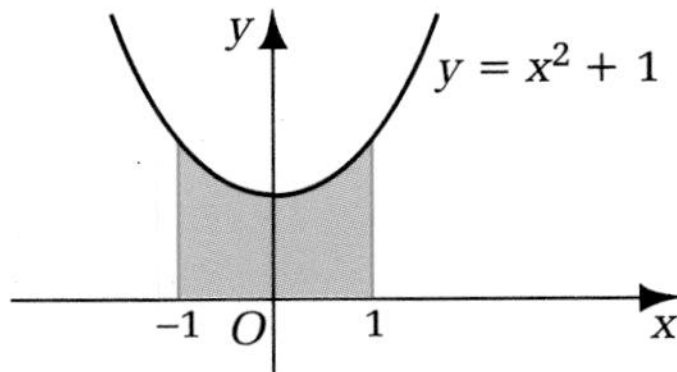

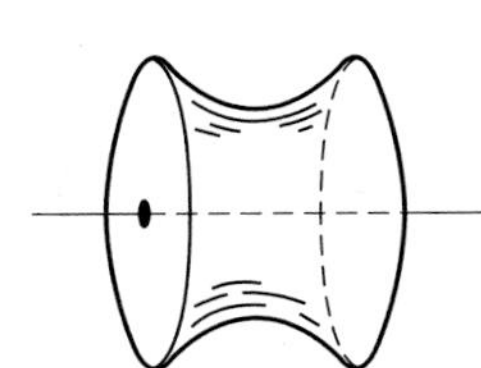

The solid formed by the rotation

$$\text{volume} = \int_a^b \pi y^2 \, dx$$

Recall that the dx indicates that the integration is carried out with respect to x.

First find an expression for y^2 in terms of x.

$$y = x^2 + 1$$

$$\Rightarrow y^2 = (x^2 + 1)^2 = x^4 + 2x^2 + 1$$

$$\text{So volume of revolution} = \int_{-1}^{1} \pi(x^4 + 2x^2 + 1)\, dx$$

$$= \pi \int_{-1}^{1} (x^4 + 2x^2 + 1)\, dx$$

$$= \pi\left[\tfrac{1}{5}x^5 + \tfrac{2}{3}x^3 + x\right]_{-1}^{1}$$

$$= \pi\{(\tfrac{1}{5} + \tfrac{2}{3} + 1) - (-\tfrac{1}{5} - \tfrac{2}{3} - 1)\}$$

$$= \pi(\tfrac{28}{15} + \tfrac{28}{15}) = \tfrac{56\pi}{15}$$

The limits, $a = -1$ and $b = 1$, are read from the sketch.

Notice that this exact result can be approximated to 11.7 cubic units (3 s.f.).

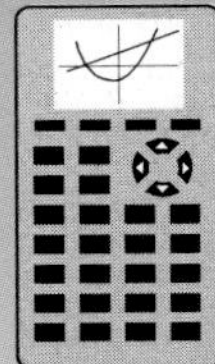

Check this result using a graphical calculator.

Rotation about the *y*-axis

Find the volume generated when the shaded area bounded by $y = f(x)$ and the y-axis, from $y = a$ to $y = b$, is rotated about the y-axis.
The width of the approximate rectangle, δy, is a small measurement along the y-axis.
Rotating the shaded area about the y-axis forms a solid.
The rectangle becomes a thin horizontal disc, of depth δy and radius x.

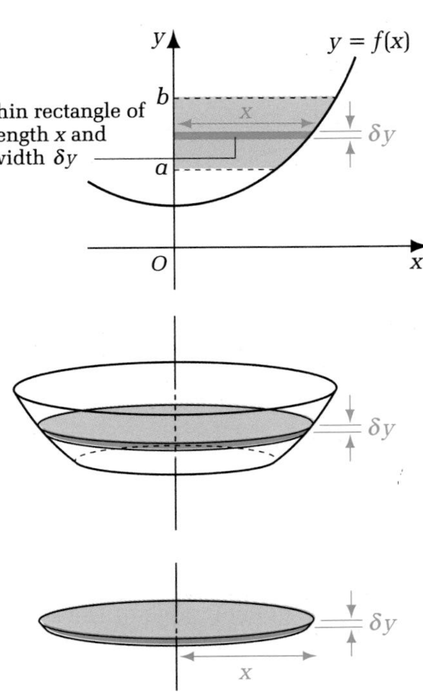

The volume of the thin disc is $\pi x^2 \delta y$.

The volume of the solid of revolution is found by adding together the volumes of all the discs.

Volume of solid of revolution $= \sum_{y=a}^{b} \pi x^2 \, \delta y$, where δy is infinitesimally small.

We use integration to sum the volumes of the discs.

volume of revolution about the y-axis $= \int_a^b \pi x^2 \, dy$

Compare this result with the formula for rotation about the x-axis. In particular notice the $y^2 dx$ and $x^2 dy$ terms.

Recall that dy means integrate 'with respec to' y.

Example 2

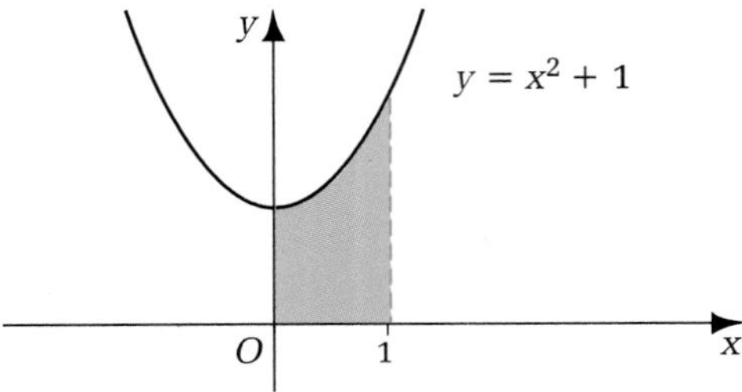

Find the volume of the solid generated by rotating the shaded region about the y-axis.

Solution

Make a sketch of the solid.

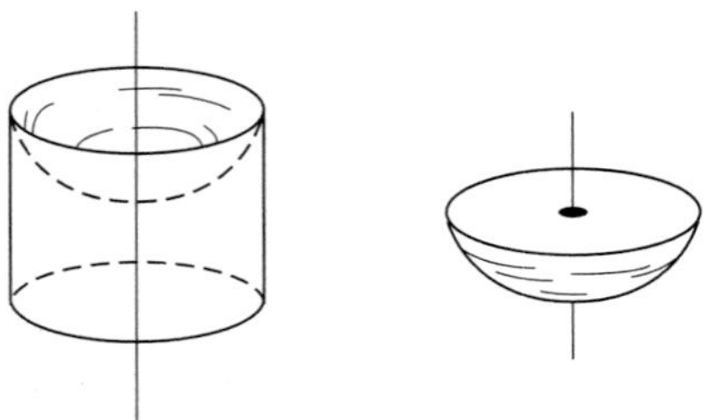

Given $y = x^2 + 1$, wh $x = 1, y = 1^2 + 1 = 2$ the height of the soli 2 units.

cross-section

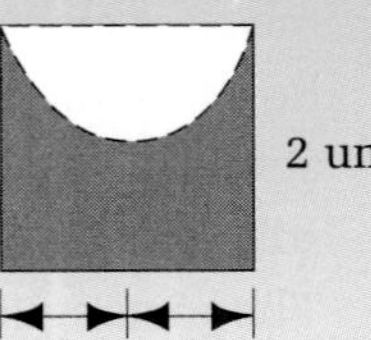

It is a cylinder with a bowl shape removed, so we can find its volume by subtracting the volume of the bowl shape from the volume of the cylinder.

$$\begin{aligned} \text{volume of cylinder} &= \pi r^2 h \\ &= \pi \times 1^2 \times 2 \\ &= 2\pi \text{ cubic units} \end{aligned}$$

The coordinates of the curve at each edge of the shaded region are $(0, 1)$ and $(1, 2)$, so the bowl shaped solid is obtained by rotating the region between the y-axis and the curve between $y = 1$ and $y = 2$ through 360°.

To use the equation that we know for volumes of revolution around the y-axis, we need to find the equation of the curve in terms of x^2.

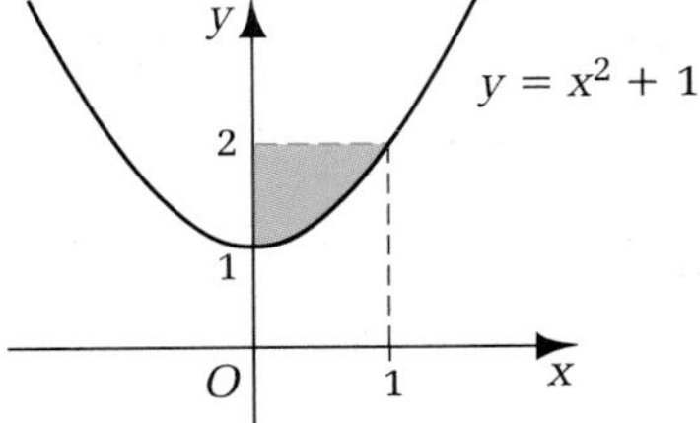

$$y = x^2 + 1 \quad \Rightarrow \quad y - 1 = x^2$$

$$\begin{aligned}\text{volume} &= \int_1^2 \pi x^2 \, dy \\ &= \int_1^2 \pi(y-1) \, dy \\ &= \pi\left[\tfrac{1}{2}y^2 - y\right]_1^2 \\ &= \pi[(\tfrac{1}{2} \times 4 - 2) - (\tfrac{1}{2} \times 1 - 1)] \\ &= \tfrac{1}{2}\pi \text{ cubic units}\end{aligned}$$

So the required volume $= 2\pi - \frac{1}{2}\pi = \frac{3}{2}\pi$ cubic units.

Volume = 4.71 cubic units (3 s.f.)

Example 3

Find the volume generated when the region bounded by the curve $y = x^3$, the y-axis, and the lines $y = 1$ and $y = 3$ is rotated through four right angles about the y-axis.

Solution

First, sketch the curve and the solid of revolution formed by the rotation about the y-axis.

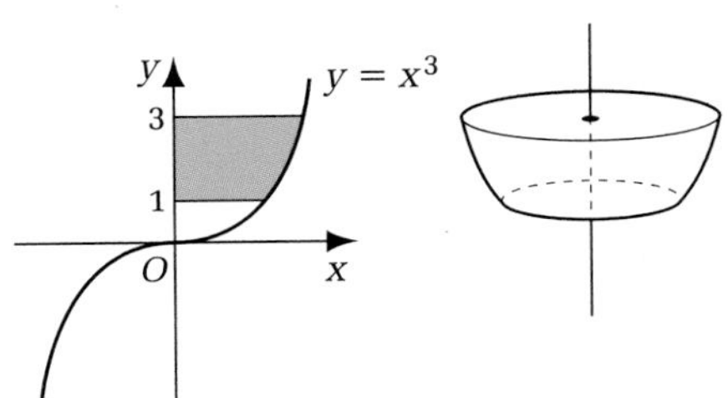

$$\begin{aligned}\text{volume of revolution} &= \int_a^b \pi x^2 \, dy \\ &= \pi \int_1^3 x^2 \, dy \\ &= \pi \int_1^3 y^{\frac{2}{3}} \, dy \\ &= \pi \left[\frac{1}{\frac{5}{3}} y^{\frac{5}{3}}\right]_1^3 \\ &= \pi\left[\tfrac{3}{5}y^{\frac{5}{3}}\right]_1^3 \\ &= \pi[(\tfrac{3}{5} \times 3^{\frac{5}{3}}) - (\tfrac{3}{5} \times 1)] \\ &= \frac{3\pi}{5}(3^{\frac{5}{3}} - 1) \\ &= 9.88 \text{ cubic units (3 s.f.)}\end{aligned}$$

$y = x^3 \Rightarrow y^{\frac{1}{3}} = x$

Then $\quad x^2 = (y^{\frac{1}{3}})^2$

$\qquad\qquad = y^{\frac{2}{3}}$

9.5 Volumes of Revolution
Exercise
Technique

1 Find the volume of each of the solids formed by rotating the following areas about the x-axis, showing clearly the necessary integration:

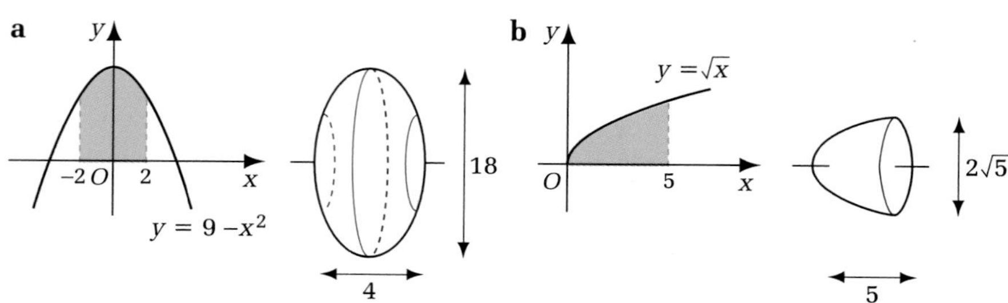

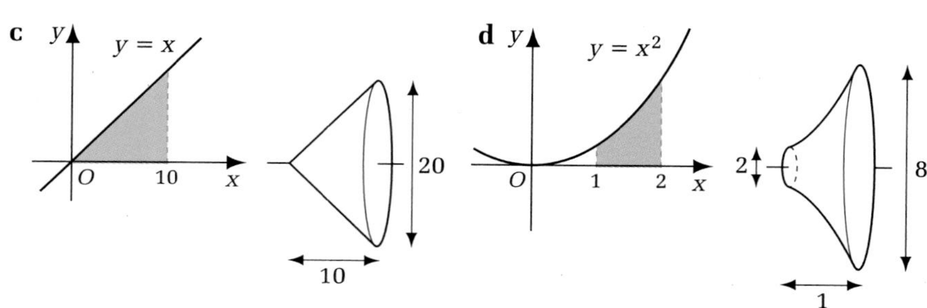

2

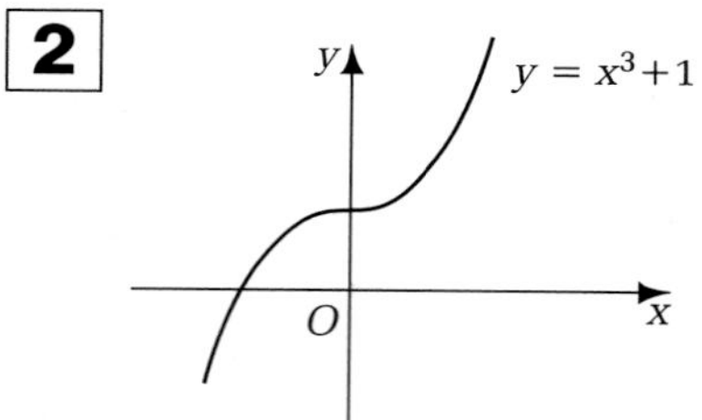

Sketch the solid formed when the area under the curve $y = x^3 + 1$, from $x = -1$ to $x = 2$, is rotated through four right angles about the x-axis. Calculate the volume of this solid.

3

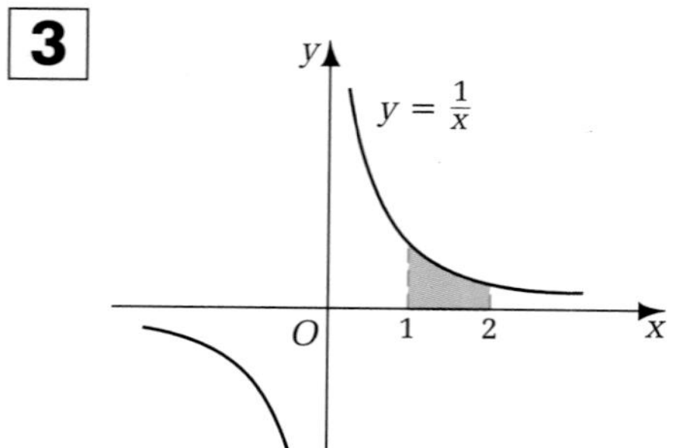

 3

Find the volume of the solid formed when the shaded area is rotated about the x-axis.

Contextual

1 A ball has a diameter of 6 cm. Its volume can be calculated using integration. The equation of a circle of radius 3 is $x^2 + y^2 = 9$. Find the volume of the hemisphere formed when the area under the curve between $x = 0$ and $x = 3$ is rotated through one complete turn about the x-axis. Hence find the volume of the ball. Check this result using the formula for volume of a sphere.

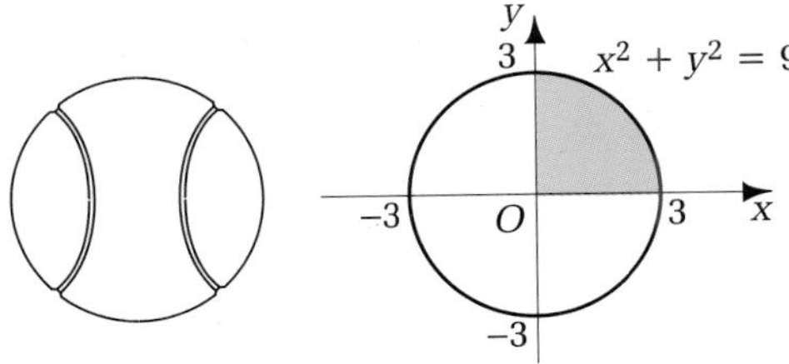

2

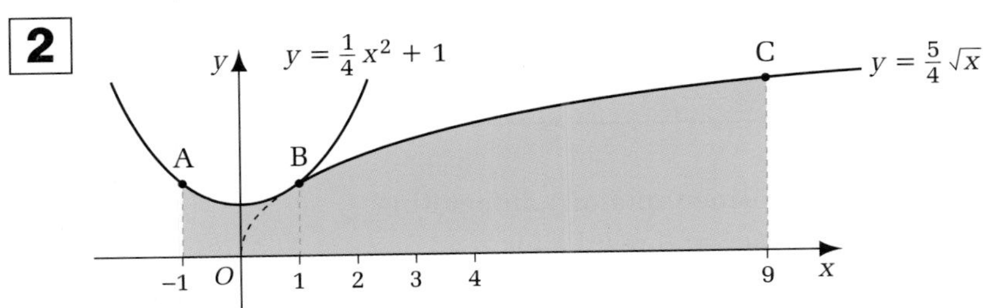

A small vase is formed when the shaded region is rotated through one complete turn about the x-axis. The arc AB is the part of the curve $y = \frac{1}{4}x^2 + 1$ between $x = -1$ and $x = 1$. The arc BC is the part of the curve $y = \frac{5}{4}\sqrt{x}$ between $x = 1$ and $x = 9$. Find the volume of the vase.

3

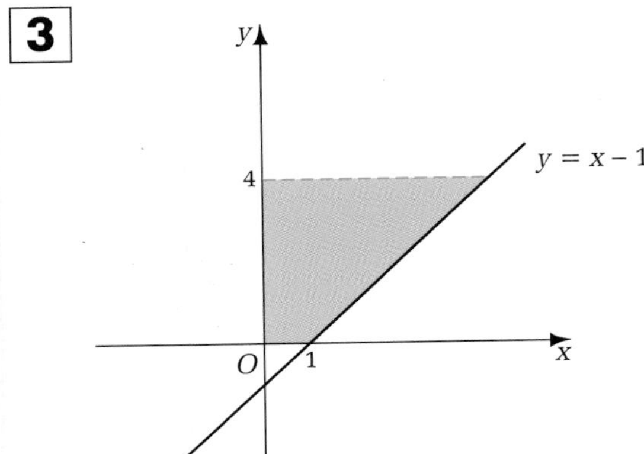

A funnel is formed when the shaded region, bounded by the line $y = x - 1$, the y-axis, and the lines $y = 0$ and $y = 4$, is rotated through one complete turn about the y-axis. Find the volume of the funnel.

9.6 Integration of Sine and Cosine

We have defined integration as the reverse of differentiation, and can use this to integrate trigonometrical functions.

Differentiation	Integration
$\frac{d}{dx}(\sin x) = \cos x$	$\int \cos x dx = \sin x + c$
$\frac{d}{dx}(\sin 3x) = 3\cos 3x$ $\frac{d}{dx}(\frac{1}{3}\sin 3x) = \frac{1}{3} \times 3\cos 3x = \cos 3x$	$\int \cos 3x dx = \frac{1}{3}\sin 3x + c$
$\frac{d}{dx}(\cos x) = -\sin x$ $\frac{d}{dx}(-\cos x) = -(-\sin x) = \sin x$	$\int \sin x dx = -\cos x + c$
$\frac{d}{dx}(\cos 2x) = -2\sin 2x$ $\frac{d}{dx}(-\frac{1}{2}\cos 2x) = -\frac{1}{2} \times -2\sin 2x = \sin 2x$	$\int \sin 2x dx = -\frac{1}{2}\cos 2x + c$

Remember to add a constant for indefinite integration.

Remember also to work in radians.

Integrating the sine function gives negative cosine functions. Integrating the cosine function gives sine functions. The general results for integration of trigonometric functions are:

$$\int \cos x \, dx = \sin x + c \qquad \int \cos mx \, dx = \frac{1}{m}\sin mx + c$$

$$\int \sin x \, dx = -\cos x + c \qquad \int \sin mx \, dx = -\frac{1}{m}\cos mx + c$$

◀ Learn these results.

Where m is a real number.

Example 1

Find:

a $\int \sin 5\theta \, d\theta$ **b** $\int (1 + \cos x - 2\sin x) \, dx$

c $\int \cos(ax + b) \, dx$ **d** $\int \sin^2 x \, dx$

Solution

a The variable is θ.

$$\int \sin 5\theta \, d\theta = -\tfrac{1}{5}\cos 5\theta + c$$

b
$$\int (1 + \cos x - 2\sin x) \, dx = x + \sin x - 2 \times (-\cos x) + c$$
$$= x + \sin x + 2\cos x + c$$

Check these by differentiating the resul

c Recall that $\frac{d}{dx}(\sin(ax+b)) = a\cos(ax+b)$
This means $\int \cos(ax+b)\,dx = \frac{1}{a}\sin(ax+b) + c$

d $\int \sin^2 x\,dx$ is not one of the standard integrals. Use the double angle formula from Chapter 3 to rewrite $\sin^2 x$ in terms of a multiple angle.

$$\cos 2x = 1 - 2\sin^2 x$$

$$\Rightarrow\ 2\sin^2 x = 1 - \cos 2x$$

$$\Rightarrow\ \sin^2 x = \tfrac{1}{2} - \tfrac{1}{2}\cos 2x$$

$$\text{Now}\quad \int \sin^2 x\,dx = \int\left(\tfrac{1}{2} - \tfrac{1}{2}\cos 2x\right)dx$$

$$= \tfrac{1}{2}\int(1 - \cos 2x)\,dx$$

$$= \tfrac{1}{2}\left(x - \tfrac{1}{2}\sin 2x\right) + c$$

$$= \tfrac{1}{2}x - \tfrac{1}{4}\sin 2x + c$$

Since we could just write a new constant of integration equal to $\frac{1}{2}c$, there is no need to include c in the part of the integral multiplied by $\frac{1}{2}$.

Example 2

Find the area enclosed by the x-axis, y-axis and the curve $y = 1 + \sin x$.

Solution

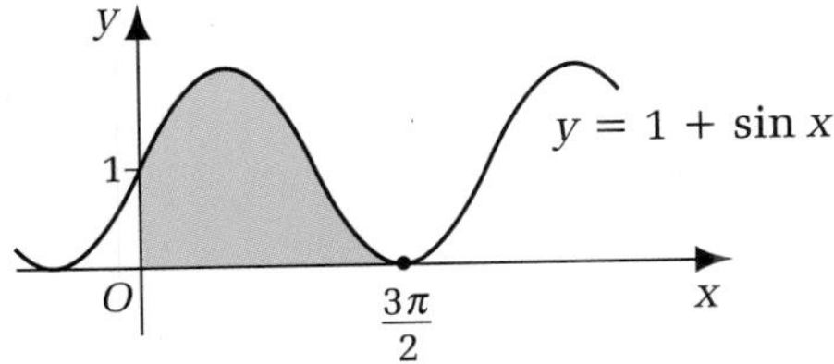

Sketch the curve to establish the limits.

Notice the translation of the sine curve.

$$\text{area} = \int_0^{3\pi/2}(1 + \sin x)\,dx$$

$$= \left[x - \cos x\right]_0^{3\pi/2}$$

$$= \left[\frac{3\pi}{2} - \cos\left(\frac{3\pi}{2}\right)\right] - (0 - \cos 0)$$

Recall the special angles in radian form; $\cos(\frac{3\pi}{2}) = 0$.

$$= \frac{3\pi}{2} - 0 - 0 + 1$$

$$= \frac{3\pi}{2} + 1$$

Example 3

Evaluate $\int_0^{\pi/12} (\cos 4x - 6\sin 2x)\,dx$.

Solution

$$\int_0^{\pi/12} (\cos 4x - 6\sin 2x)\,dx = \left[\tfrac{1}{4}\sin 4x - 6\times\tfrac{1}{2}(-\cos 2x)\right]_0^{\pi/12}$$

Take care with the sign changes.

$$= \left[\tfrac{1}{4}\sin 4x + 3\cos 2x\right]_0^{\pi/12}$$

$$= \left[\frac{1}{4}\sin\left(\frac{\pi}{3}\right) + 3\cos\left(\frac{\pi}{6}\right)\right] - \left[\frac{1}{4}\sin 0 + 3\cos 0\right]$$

Special angles:

$\sin\frac{\pi}{3} = \frac{\sqrt{3}}{2}$

$\cos\frac{\pi}{6} = \frac{\sqrt{3}}{2}$

$$= \left(\frac{1}{4}\times\frac{\sqrt{3}}{2}\right) + \left(3\times\frac{\sqrt{3}}{2}\right) - 0 - 3$$

$$= \frac{\sqrt{3}}{8} + \frac{3\sqrt{3}}{2} - 3$$

Add the fractions.

$$= \frac{13\sqrt{3}}{8} - 3$$

Example 4

Find the volume of the solid formed when the shaded region is rotated through 360° about the x-axis.

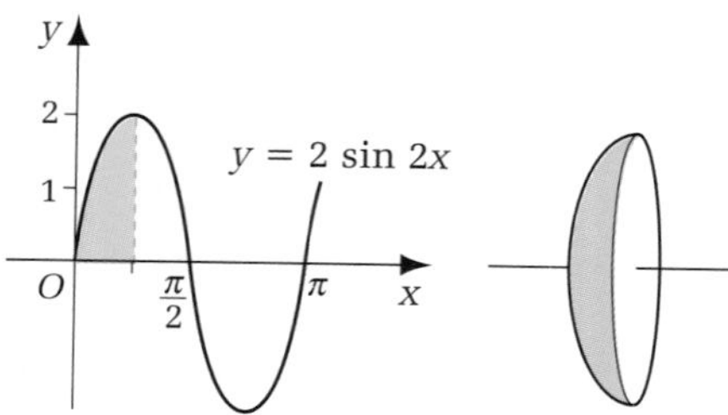

Solution

Since the solid has been formed by a rotation about the x-axis, use

$$\text{volume} = \int_a^b \pi y^2\,dx$$

We know that $y = 2\sin 2x$, so $y^2 = 4\sin^2 2x$.
From the graph, the limits are $a = 0$ and $b = \frac{1}{4}\pi$.

$$\text{volume} = \int_0^{\pi/4} \pi(4\sin^2 2x)\,dx$$

$$= 4\pi\int_0^{\pi/4} \sin^2 2x\,dx$$

Taking the constant multipliers out of the integrand.

The integrand contains $\sin^2 2x$, which we can't integrate directly. We must use the multiple angle formula to write it in terms of double angles.

$$\cos 2A = 1 - 2\sin^2 A \Rightarrow \sin^2 A = \tfrac{1}{2} - \tfrac{1}{2}\cos 2A$$

Putting $A = 2x$ gives $\sin^2 2x = \tfrac{1}{2} - \tfrac{1}{2}\cos 4x$

$$\begin{aligned}
\text{volume} &= 4\pi \int_0^{\pi/4} \sin^2 2x \,\mathrm{d}x \\
&= 4\pi \int_0^{\pi/4} \left(\tfrac{1}{2} - \tfrac{1}{2}\cos 4x\right) \mathrm{d}x \\
&= 2\pi \int_0^{\pi/4} (1 - \cos 4x)\,\mathrm{d}x \\
&= 2\pi \left[x - \tfrac{1}{4}\sin 4x\right]_0^{\pi/4} \\
&= 2\pi\left[\left(\tfrac{\pi}{4} - \tfrac{1}{4}\sin \pi\right) - \left(0 - \tfrac{1}{4}\sin 0\right)\right] \\
&= 2\pi \times \left(\tfrac{\pi}{4} - 0 - 0 + 0\right) \\
&= \tfrac{1}{2}\pi^2 \text{ cubic units}
\end{aligned}$$

Take a factor of $\tfrac{1}{2}$ outside the integral.

9.6 Integration of Sine and Cosine

Exercise

Technique

1 Copy and complete each of the following statements, in which • represents a missing term.

a $\int \sin x \mathrm{d}x = \bullet + c$ and $\int \cos x \mathrm{d}x = \bullet + c$

b $\int (1 + \cos x + 2 \sin x)\mathrm{d}x = x + \bullet + 2\bullet + c = x + \bullet - \bullet + c$

c $\int (t - 5 - 7 \sin t - 2 \cos t)\bullet = \frac{1}{2}t^2 - 5t - 7\bullet - 2\bullet + c$
$= \frac{1}{2}t^2 - 5t + \bullet - \bullet + c$

2 Integrate the following:

a $2 \sin x$ **b** $-3 \sin x$ **c** $5 \cos x$ **d** $-2 \cos x$

3 Find:

a $\int (1 + 3 \cos \theta)\, \mathrm{d}\theta$

b $\int (1 - \cos t + 3 \sin t)\, \mathrm{d}t$

c $\int (\frac{1}{2}\theta + a \cos \theta - b \sin \theta)\, \mathrm{d}\theta$, where a and b are constants.

d $\int (10 - 3t^2 + 2 \cos t - \frac{1}{2} \sin t)\, \mathrm{d}t$

4 Find a solution for these integrals, using differentiation to check your answers:

a $\int \sin 2x\, \mathrm{d}x$

b $\int \cos 4x\, \mathrm{d}x$

c $\int (1 + \cos 3x)\, \mathrm{d}x$

d $\int 15 \sin 3x\, \mathrm{d}x$

e $\int (3 + 4 \cos 2x)\, \mathrm{d}x$

f $\int (10 - 3 \cos x - 8 \sin 4x)\, \mathrm{d}x$

5 Evaluate:

a $\int_0^{\pi/2} \sin \frac{1}{2}x\, \mathrm{d}x$ **b** $\int_0^{\pi/2} \cos \frac{1}{2}x\, \mathrm{d}x$

6

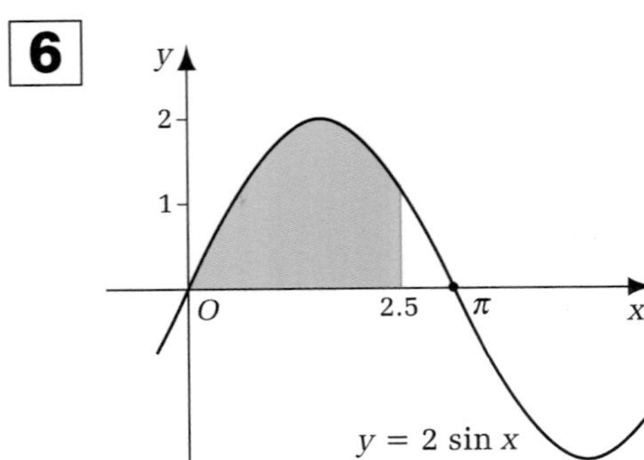

Find the area of the shaded region correct to two decimal places.

7 Find the areas of the following shaded regions:

a

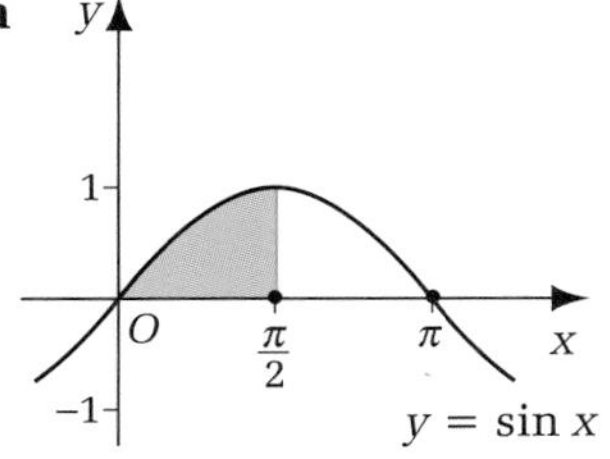

b

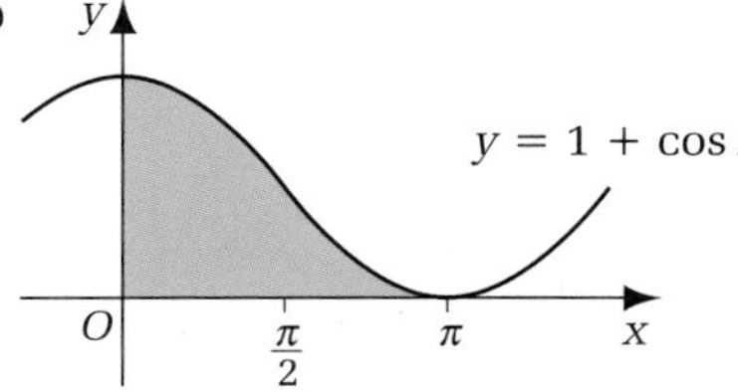

c

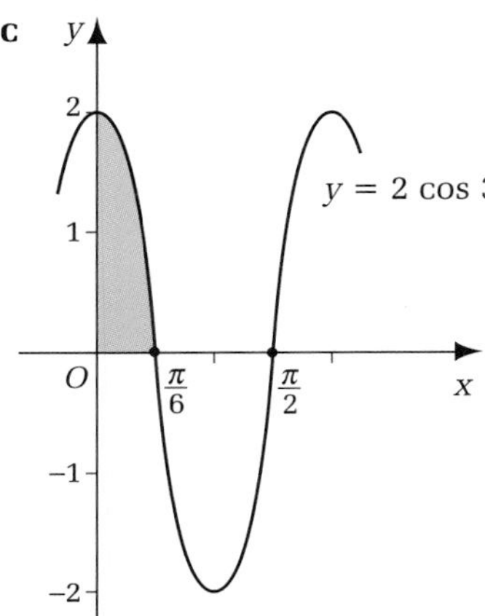

d

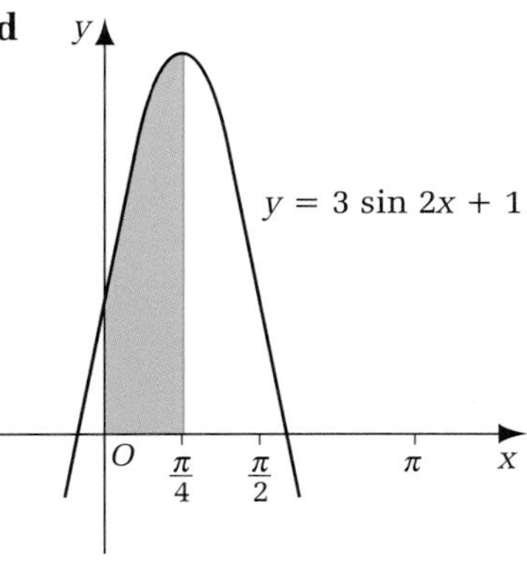

8 Find:

a $\int \sin^2 x \, dx$

b $\int \cos^2 x \, dx$

Contextual

1

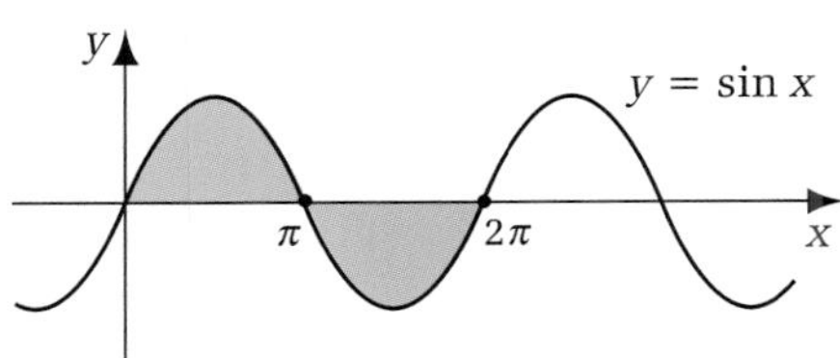

The graph shows $y = \sin x$.

a Explain why $\int_0^{2\pi} \sin x \, dx = 0$.

b What area is represented by $\int_0^{\pi/2} \sin x \, dx$? Evaluate this integral.

c Use your answer to **b** to calculate the area of the shaded region.

2 A particle moves in a straight line. Its velocity at time t is given by $v = 12 \cos 3t$. Find an expression for the displacement, s, after t seconds, if $s = 0$ when $t = 0$.

3 Identify the transformation of the sine or cosine function in these graphs. Use your results to find the areas of the shaded regions:

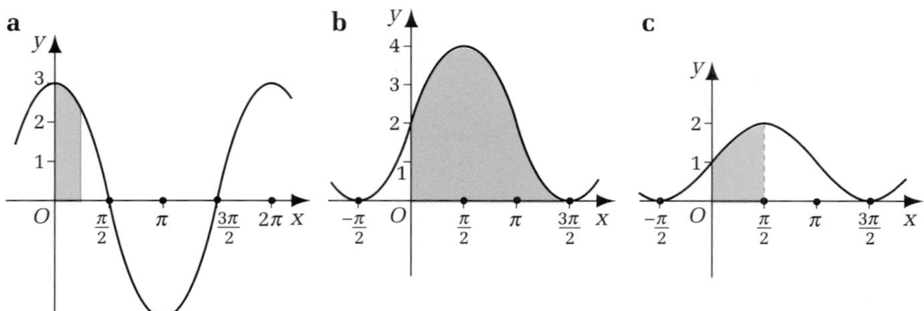

4 The diagram shows part of the curve $y = \sin x + \sin 2x$.

a Verify that the x-coordinate of A is $\frac{2}{3}\pi$.

b Find the area of the shaded region.

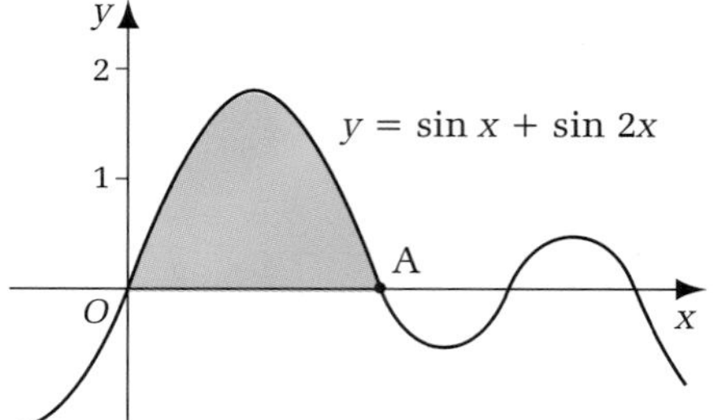

5 The diagram shows part of the curve $y = \cos x + \cos 2x$.

a Verify that the x-coordinate of P is $\frac{\pi}{3}$.

b Evaluate

$$\int_0^{\pi/3} (\cos x + \cos 2x)\,dx.$$

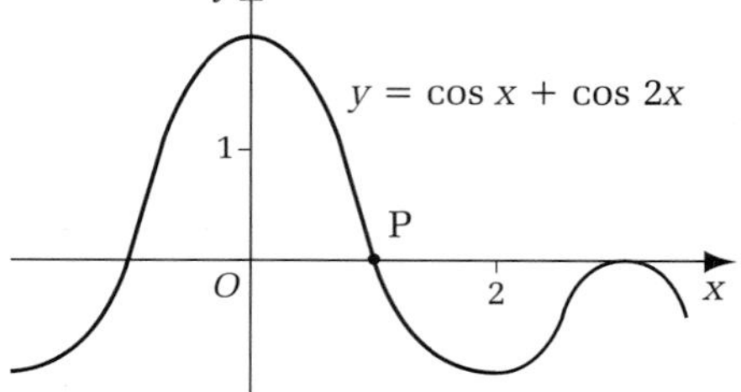

6 The diagram shows part of the curve $y = 2\cos x$. The shaded region is rotated through 360° about the x-axis. Calculate the volume of the solid created.

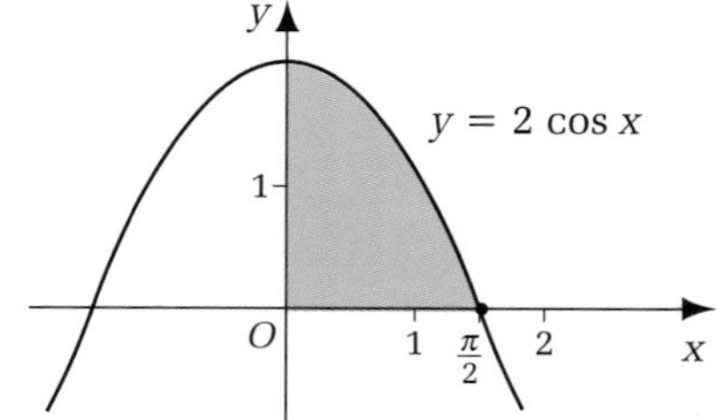

7 The graph shows part of the curve $y = \sin x + \cos x$.

a Show that $(\sin x + \cos x)^2 = 1 + \sin 2x$.

b Find the volume generated when the shaded region is rotated through 360° about the x-axis.

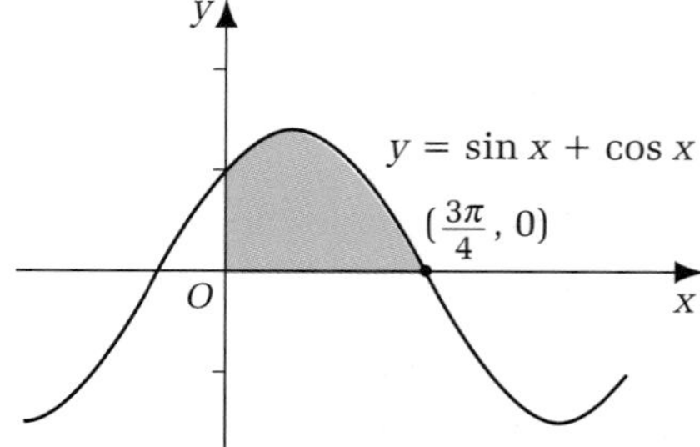

Consolidation

Exercise A

1 Find:

a $\int (2x - 3)^2 \, dx$

b the equation for a curve, $y = f(x)$, for which $\frac{dy}{dx} = 6x - 1$ and which passes through the point $(1, 9)$.

2 The sketch shows the graph of $y = x(3 - x)$.

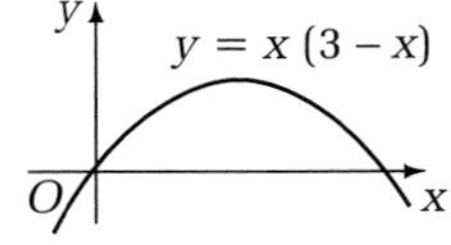

a Find $\int x(3 - x)\, dx$.

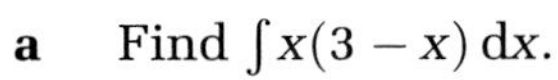

b Hence calculate the area between the curve and the x-axis.

(SMP)

3 The sketch shows a graph of the curve $y = 5x^4 - x^5$.

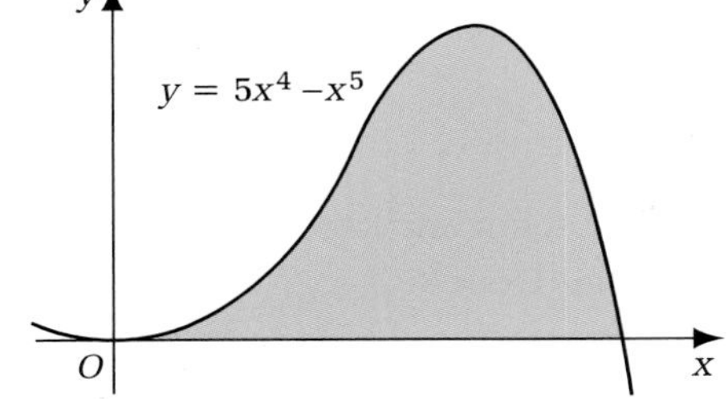

a Find $\frac{dy}{dx}$ and calculate the coordinates of the stationary points.

b Calculate the area of the shaded region enclosed between the curve and the x-axis.

c Evaluate $\int_0^6 x^4(5 - x)\, dx$, and comment on your result.

(MEI)

4

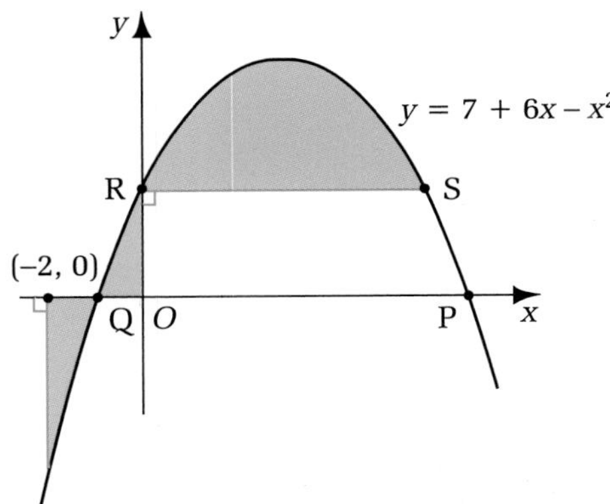

The diagram shows part of the curve $y = 7 + 6x - x^2$. Find:

a the coordinates of the points P, Q, R and S.

b the area of each shaded region.

(UCLES)

5

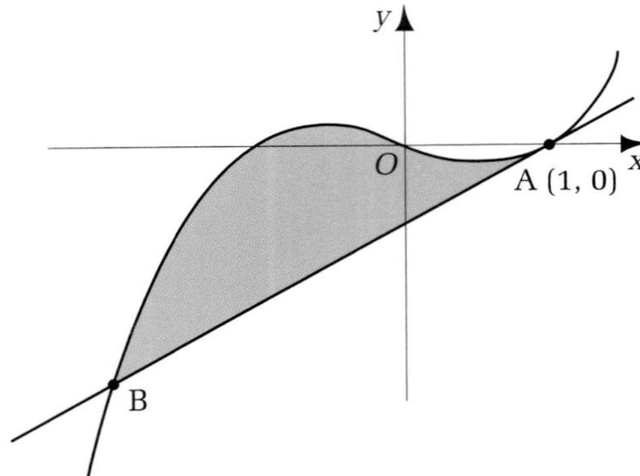

The sketch shows the graph of $y = x^3 - x$ together with the tangent to the curve at the point A $(1, 0)$.

a Use differentiation to find the equation of the tangent to the curve at A and verify that the point B where the tangent cuts the curve again has coordinates $(-2, -6)$.

b Use integration to find the area of the region bounded by the curve and the tangent (shaded in the diagram), giving your answer as a fraction in its lowest terms.

(UCLES)

6 **a** Find the area of the region enclosed by the curve $y = \frac{12}{x^2}$, the x-axis and the lines $x = 1$ and $x = 3$.

b The area of the region enclosed by $y = \frac{12}{x^2}$, the x-axis and the lines $x = 2$ and $x = a$, where $a > 2$, is 3.6 units squared. Find the value of a.

(UCLES)

7

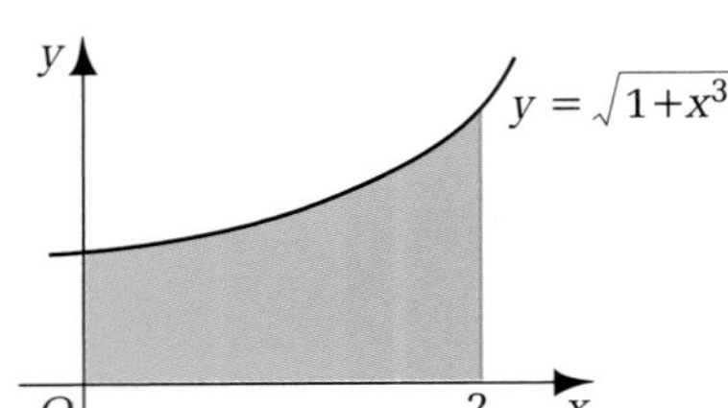

The diagram shows part of the curve $y = \sqrt{1 + x^3}$. Calculate the volume formed when the shaded region is rotated through $360°$ about the x-axis.

8 **a** Find $\int (2\cos x - 3\sin x)\,dx$.

b Find $\int (1 - 6\sin 3x)\,dx$.

c Evaluate $\displaystyle\int_0^{\pi/2} 2\cos 2t\,dt$.

d Sketch the curve $y = 1 + \cos x$. Find the area enclosed between the axes and curve from $x = 0$ to $x = \pi$.

9

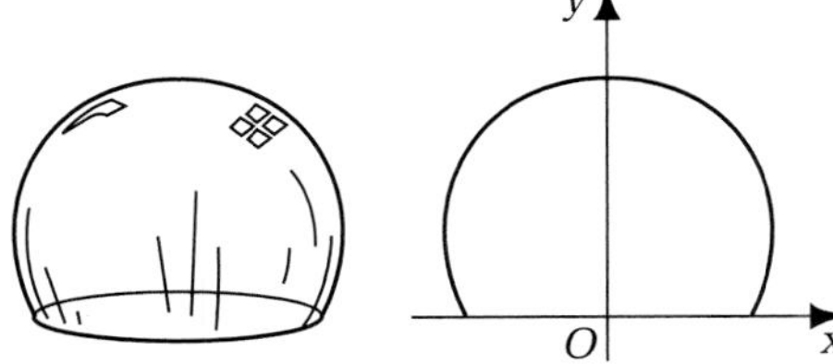

The shape of a glass paperweight is that of the solid formed by rotating about the y-axis the part of the curve $3x^2 + 2y^2 - 12y = 32$ for which $y \geq 0$ (in centimetres).

a Verify that the paperweight is 8 cm high.

b Calculate the volume of the paperweight. You may leave π in your answer.

(SMP)

10 **a** Show that $(\cos x - \sin x)^2 = 1 - \sin 2x$.

b

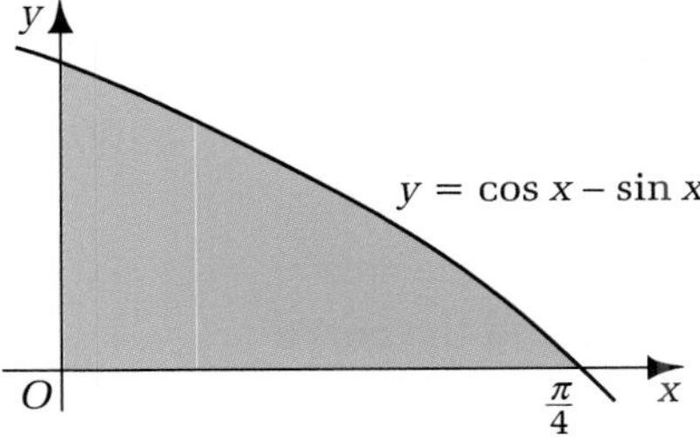

The diagram shows part of the curve $y = \cos x - \sin x$. Find the volume generated when the shaded region is rotated through a complete revolution about the x-axis.

(UCLES)

Exercise B

1 **a** Find $\int \left(\sqrt{x} + \frac{12}{x^2}\right) dx$.

b Hence evaluate $\int_4^9 \left(\sqrt{x} + \frac{12}{x^2}\right) dx$.

(NEAB)

2 **a** A curve satisfies $\frac{dy}{dx} = (3x - 1)^2$. Given that the curve passes through $(1, 4)$, find its equation.

b A particle moves in a straight line so that t seconds after leaving a fixed point A, its velocity v (m s^{-1}) is given by $v = t^2 - 4t + 3$. Find the displacement, s metres, for the particle at t seconds, if $s = 0$ when $t = 0$.

3 The sketch shows the curve $y = x^3$. Find a if the area of the shaded region is 1 square unit.

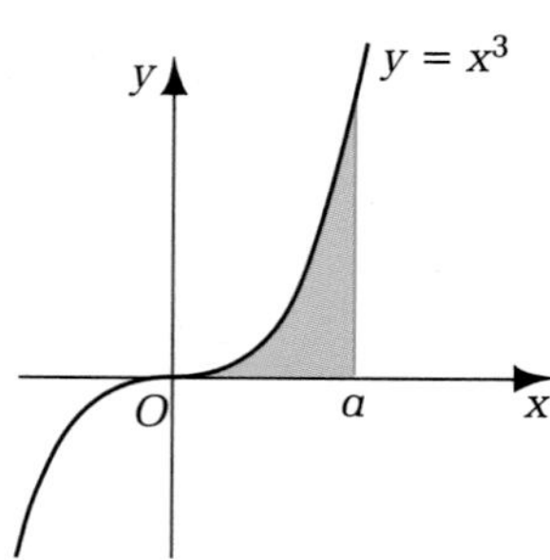

4 The diagram shows the curve $y = x^2$, and the lines $x = 4$ and $y = 8 - 2x$.

a Find the coordinates of A.

b Find the area of the shaded region.

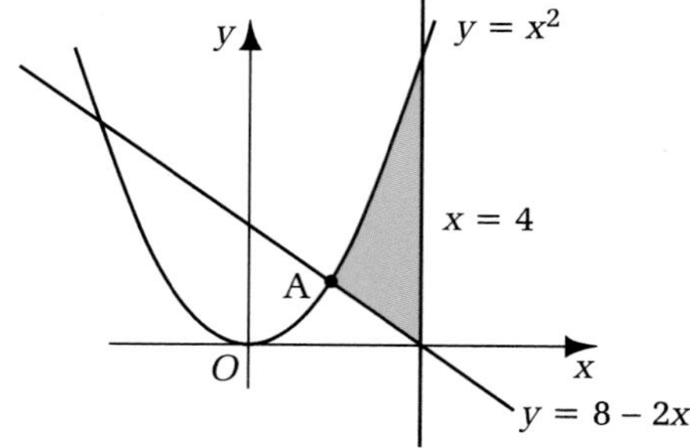

5 **a** On the same graph, sketch the line with equation $y = x + 1$ and the curve with equation $y = 5x - x^2 + 6$. Values of x should be taken from $x = -2$ to $x = +8$. Shade in the region between the line and the curve.

b Calculate the points of intersection of the line $y = x + 1$ and the curve $y = 5x - x^2 + 6$.

c Use integration to calculate the area of the region that you shaded in **a**.

(MEI)

6 A cup has the shape made by rotating the graph of $y = 3x^2$, for $0 \leq x \leq 1$, through four right angles about the y-axis. Find the volume of the cup, giving your answer in terms of π.

(UCLES)

7 The graph shows part of the curve $y = 3\cos x$. The shaded region is rotated about the x-axis through four right angles. Calculate the volume formed.

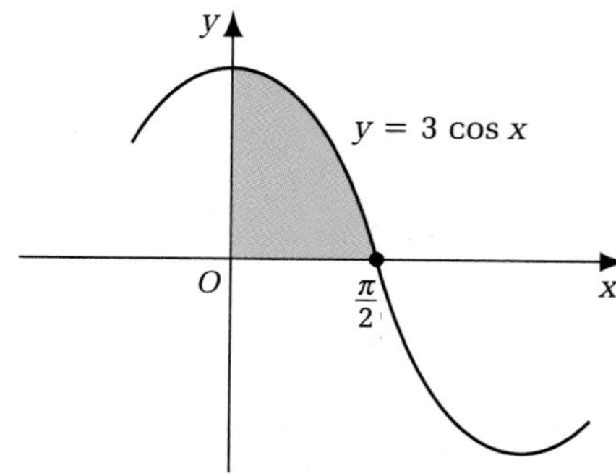

Applications and Activities

1 Volume of a pyramid

It has been documented that the Greek Democritus (460–361 BC) may have calculated the volume of a pyramid by considering it as an infinite number of thin cross-sections. Let A(z) be the area of the horizontal cross-section z cm from the top, and δz be the thickness of the cross-section.

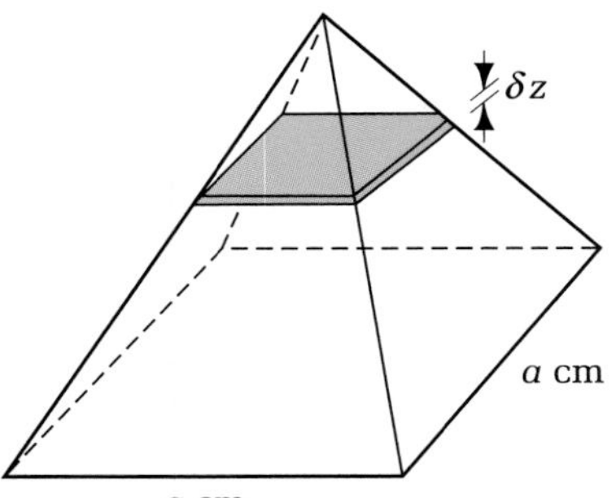

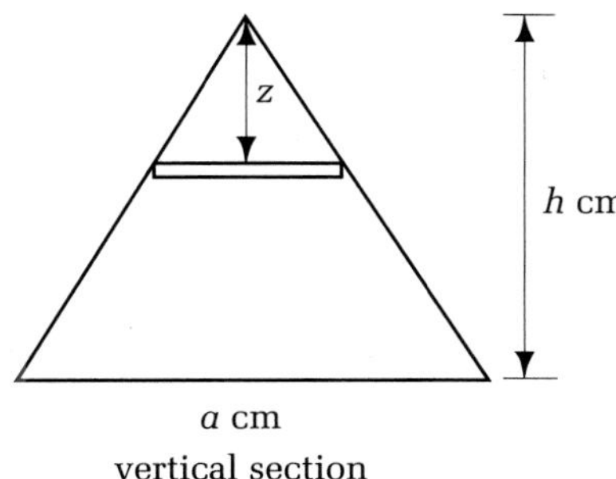

vertical section

a Find A(z) in terms of z, a and h.

b Investigate how to calculate $\sum_{z=0}^{h} A(z)\,\delta z$.

c Find the volume of the pyramid.

2 Area under a curve

The area under the curve $y = x^2$ between $x = 0$ and $x = 1$ is divided up into h rectangles of equal width.

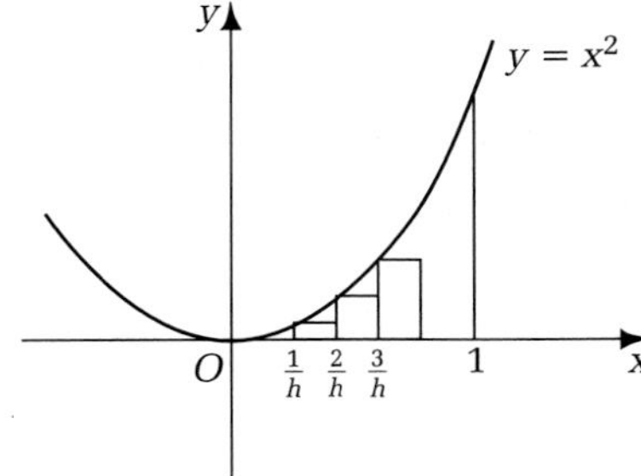

a Using $\sum_{r=1}^{n} r^2 = \frac{1}{6}n(n+1)(2n+1)$, show that the area of all the rectangles can be written $\frac{1}{6h^2}(h-1)(2h-1)$.

b Investigate the total area under the curve $y = x^2$ between $x = 0$ and $x = 1$ for different values of h.

c Explain why $\int_0^1 x^2\,dx > \frac{1}{6h^2}(h-1)(2h-1)$.

d By writing $\frac{1}{6h^2}(h-1)(2h-1)$ in a different form, deduce its value as $h \to \infty$. Comment on your answer.

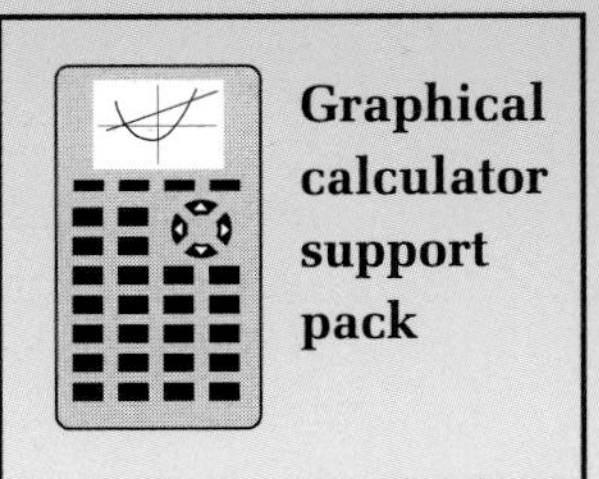

This can be investigated using a graphical calculator or spreadsheet.

Summary

- If $\int f(x)\,dx = g(x)$, then $g'(x) = f(x)$.
- An **indefinite integral** is one in which no limits appear on the integration symbol.
- For all n except $n = -1$, $\displaystyle\int x^n\,dx = \frac{x^{n+1}}{n+1} + c$.
- A **definite integral** is one with two stated limits, and often represents the area under a curve between these two values.
- Integration is a **summation** process, and as $\delta x \to 0$

$$\sum_{x=a}^{b} f(x)\,\delta x = \int_a^b f(x)\,dx.$$

- $\int_a^b y\,dx$ gives the area between the curve $y = f(x)$ and the x-axis between $x = a$ and $x = b$.
- $\int_a^b x\,dy$ gives the area between the curve $y = f(x)$ and the y-axis between $y = a$ and $y = b$.
- $\int_a^b \pi y^2\,dx$ gives the volume of the solid generated when the area enclosed by the x-axis, the curve $y = f(x)$ and the lines $x = a$ and $x = b$ is rotated by $360°$ about the x-axis.
- $\int_a^b \pi x^2\,dy$ gives the volume of the solid generated when the area enclosed by the y-axis, the curve $y = f(x)$ and the lines $y = a$ and $y = b$ is rotated by $360°$ about the y-axis.
- $\int \sin x\,dx = -\cos x + c$ and $\int \sin mx\,dx = -\frac{1}{m}\cos mx + c$.
- $\int \cos x\,dx = \sin x + c$ and $\int \cos mx\,dx = \frac{1}{m}\sin mx + c$.
- $\sin^2 x$ or $\cos^2 x$ need to be written in double angle form before they can be integrated.

10 Trigonometry II

What you need to know

- The compound and double angle formulas.
- How to convert angle measurements between degrees and radians.
- The trigonometric ratios for the 'special angles'.

Review

1 Write down the compound angle expansions for the following:

a $\sin(A + B)$
b $\cos(A - B)$
c $\tan 2A$
d $\cos(x + 60°)$
e $\sin(x - 30°)$
f $\tan(x - 45°)$

2 **a** Convert the following angles into radians, leaving the answers in terms of π:

i 45°
ii 120°
iii 315°
iv 220°
v 400°
vi −40°

b Convert the following angles into degrees:

i $\frac{\pi}{6}$
ii $\frac{\pi}{2}$
iii $\frac{5\pi}{4}$
iv $\frac{\pi}{20}$
v $\frac{11\pi}{9}$
vi $-\frac{7\pi}{10}$

3 Without using a calculator, write down the exact value of the following:

a $\sin 60°$
b $\tan \frac{\pi}{6}$
c $\cos 90°$
d $\sin \frac{2\pi}{3}$
e $\tan \pi$
f $\cos 120°$

10.1 The Factor Formulas

In Chapter 3 we established the concept of an identity as an equation that is true for all values of the variable. One set of trigonometric identities is known as the **factor formulas**. They convert expressions like $\sin A + \sin B$ into a product; similar to factorising the expression. Another common name for these identities is **sum and product formulas**.

$$\sin C + \sin D \equiv 2\sin\left(\frac{C+D}{2}\right)\cos\left(\frac{C-D}{2}\right) \quad [1]$$

$$\sin C - \sin D \equiv 2\cos\left(\frac{C+D}{2}\right)\sin\left(\frac{C-D}{2}\right) \quad [2]$$

$$\cos C + \cos D \equiv 2\cos\left(\frac{C+D}{2}\right)\cos\left(\frac{C-D}{2}\right) \quad [3]$$

$$\cos C - \cos D \equiv -2\sin\left(\frac{C+D}{2}\right)\sin\left(\frac{C-D}{2}\right) \quad [4]$$

These four identities have a straightforward derivation from the compound angle formulas encountered in Chapter 3. To derive identity [1], recall the formulas:

$$\sin(A+B) = \sin A\cos B + \cos A\sin B$$

$$\sin(A-B) = \sin A\cos B - \cos A\sin B$$

Adding these two equations,

$$\sin(A+B) + \sin(A-B) = 2\sin A\cos B$$

Now let $C = A + B$ and $D = A - B$.
The LHS becomes $\sin C + \sin D$, and we have
$C + D = (A+B) + (A-B) = 2A$ and
$C - D = (A+B) - (A-B) = A + B - A + B = 2B$

So $A = \frac{1}{2}(C+D)$ and $B = \frac{1}{2}(C-D)$

The RHS of the equation becomes $2\sin[\frac{1}{2}(C+D)]\cos[\frac{1}{2}(C-D)]$

So $\sin C + \sin D = 2\sin\left(\frac{C+D}{2}\right)\cos\left(\frac{C-D}{2}\right)$

Use the same technique to derive identity [2].

Subtract the result for $\sin(A-B)$ from $\sin(A+B)$.

To derive identities [3] and [4] we need to use the compound angle formulas for cosine.

$$\cos(A+B) = \cos A \cos B - \sin A \sin B$$

$$\cos(A-B) = \cos A \cos B + \sin A \sin B$$

Identity [3] can be derived by adding these results.

$$\cos(A+B) + \cos(A-B) = 2\cos A \cos B$$

Now let $C = (A+B)$ and $D = (A-B)$ as before. We find that:

$$\cos C + \cos D = 2\cos\left(\frac{C+D}{2}\right)\cos\left(\frac{C-D}{2}\right)$$

Derive identity [4], by subtracting the cosine results instead of adding them.

Note carefully the symmetries and patterns in the four factor formulas. They can often be more easily remembered if you say the words as well as write the symbols, for example:

'sine plus sine equals twice the sine of half the sum,

cos of half the difference'.

Alternatively, 'sine plus sine equals twice the sine the semi sum, cos the semi difference'. Write down a phrase you will remember for the other formulas, taking care to spot the negative signs.

The factor formulas provide a powerful mathematical tool for dealing with trigonometric functions. They can be used to solve equations, simplify expressions and prove more identities.

Example 1

Find $\sin 105° - \sin 15°$, without using a calculator.

Solution

$$\begin{aligned}\sin 105° - \sin 15° &= 2\cos\tfrac{1}{2}(105° + 15°)\sin\tfrac{1}{2}(105° - 15°)\\ &= 2\cos 60° \sin 45°\\ &= 2 \times \tfrac{1}{2} \times \tfrac{\sqrt{2}}{2} = \tfrac{\sqrt{2}}{2}\end{aligned}$$

Using the factor formula for the difference of two sines and recalling special angles.

Example 2

Prove the following identities:

a $\cos 2\theta + \cos 3\theta + \cos 4\theta \equiv \cos 3\theta(1 + 2\cos\theta)$

b $\dfrac{\sin 3\theta + \sin\theta}{\cos 3\theta + \cos\theta} \equiv \tan 2\theta$

Solution

a Notice that the LHS has three terms, one of which is $\cos 3\theta$. This also appears on the RHS so it would be sensible to apply one of the factor formulas on the other two terms.

$$\begin{aligned}\text{LHS} &= \cos 2\theta + \cos 3\theta + \cos 4\theta \\ &= \cos 4\theta + \cos 2\theta + \cos 3\theta \\ &= 2\cos 3\theta \cos \theta + \cos 3\theta \\ &= \cos 3\theta(2\cos\theta + 1) \\ &= \text{RHS}\end{aligned}$$

$$\cos 2\theta + \cos 3\theta + \cos 4\theta \equiv \cos 3\theta(1 + 2\cos\theta)$$

Reorder so that the factor formula for the sum of two cosines is straightforward to apply.

Factorising.

b

$$\begin{aligned}\text{LHS} &= \frac{\sin 3\theta + \sin\theta}{\cos 3\theta + \cos\theta} \\ &= \frac{2\sin 2\theta\cos\theta}{\cos 3\theta + \cos\theta} \\ &= \frac{2\sin 2\theta\cos\theta}{2\cos 2\theta\cos\theta} \\ &= \frac{\sin 2\theta}{\cos 2\theta} \\ &= \tan 2\theta = \text{RHS}\end{aligned}$$

$$\frac{\sin 3\theta + \sin\theta}{\cos 3\theta + \cos\theta} \equiv \tan 2\theta$$

Apply the factor formulas separately to the numerator and denominator.

Example 3

Use the factor formulas to express the following as a sum or difference of two trigonometrical functions:

a $2\sin 2A\cos A$ **b** $-2\sin 4A\sin 2A$

Solution

a Notice that $2\sin 2A\cos A$ is a product of two trigonometric terms. Since it contains one sine and one cosine term, it must be the result of summing two sine terms. Compare it with the factor formulas.

If $\sin x + \sin y = 2\sin 2A\cos A$, then

$$x + y = 4A$$
and $$x - y = 2A$$

'Half the sum' must be $2A$ and 'half the difference' must be A.

The solutions of these simultaneous equations are $x = 3A$ and $y = A$.

So $2\sin 2A\cos A = \sin 3A + \sin A$

b $-2\sin 4A\sin 2A$ contains two sine terms and a negative sign. The factor formulas suggest that this is a difference of two cosines.

If $-2 \sin 4A \sin 2A = \cos x - \cos y$, then

$$x + y = 8A$$

and $\quad x - y = 4A$

These simultaneous equations have solutions $x = 6A$ and $y = 2A$.

So $\;-2 \sin 4A \sin 2A = \cos 6A - \cos 2A$.

Example 4

Without using a calculator, evaluate $2 \cos 75^\circ \cos 15^\circ$.

Solution

Notice the two cosine terms. The factor formulas suggest that this is created from the sum of two cosines.

If $2 \cos 75^\circ \cos 15^\circ = \cos x + \cos y$, then ◀ **Identity 3.**

$$x + y = 150^\circ$$

and $\quad x - y = 30^\circ$

These simultaneous equations have solutions $x = 90^\circ$ and $y = 60^\circ$.

So $2 \cos 75^\circ \cos 15^\circ = \cos 90^\circ + \cos 60^\circ = 0 + \frac{1}{2} = \frac{1}{2}$

When $C < D$ the factor formulas will produce negative angles. Sometimes the ratios could simply be reversed as in Example 5; $\sin x + \sin 5x = \sin 5x + \sin x$. In the cases where this is not easily achieved, however, use the following useful results, which can be seen from the graphs for sine and cosine.

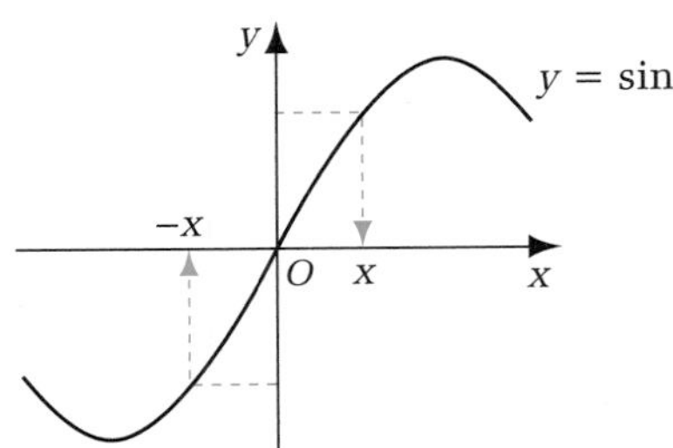

Note the rotational symmetry

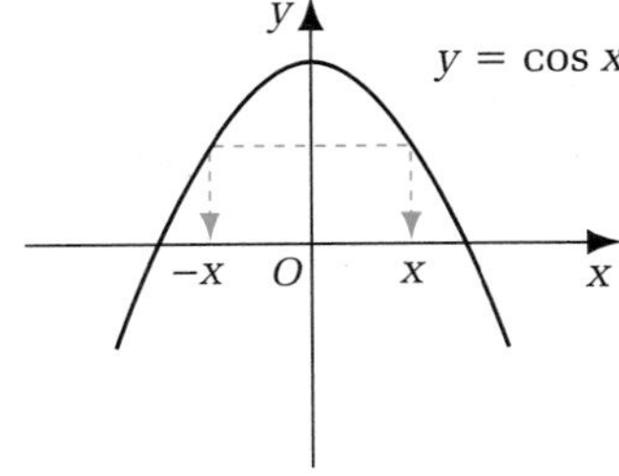

Note the reflection in the y-axis

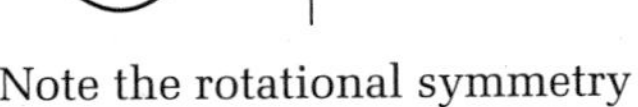

$\mathbf{\sin(-x) = -\sin x}$ ◀ **Learn these results.**

$\mathbf{\cos(-x) = \cos x}$

These results for negative angles can 'simplify' the factor formulas including negative angles.

Example 5

Solve:

a $\sin x + \sin 5x = \sin 3x$ for $0 \le x \le \pi$

b $\sin 3x - \sin 5x = \sin x$ for $0 \le x \le 180°$.

Solution

a Notice the three distinct angles, x, $3x$ and $5x$. The factor formula will help reduce this to a problem with fewer angles. The equation is easier to manipulate if rewritten as

$$\sin 5x + \sin x = \sin 3x$$

Then

$$2\sin\tfrac{1}{2}(5x + x)\cos\tfrac{1}{2}(5x - x) = \sin 3x$$

Use the factor formul[a] for the sum of two si[nes]

$$\Rightarrow \quad 2\sin 3x\cos 2x = \sin 3x$$

Do not divide throughout by $\sin 3x$; you will lose solutio[ns]

$$\Rightarrow \quad 2\sin 3x\cos 2x - \sin 3x = 0$$

$$\Rightarrow \quad \sin 3x(2\cos 2x - 1) = 0$$

Factorising.

So $\sin 3x = 0$ or $2\cos 2x - 1 = 0$

$\sin 3x = 0$ or $\cos 2x = \frac{1}{2}$

$$\sin 3x = 0 \Rightarrow 3x = 0, \pi, 2\pi, 3\pi, \ldots$$

$$\Rightarrow x = 0, \tfrac{\pi}{3}, \tfrac{2\pi}{3}, \pi, \ldots$$

$$\cos 2x = \tfrac{1}{2} \Rightarrow 2x = \tfrac{\pi}{3}, \tfrac{5\pi}{3}, \tfrac{7\pi}{3}, \tfrac{11\pi}{3}, \ldots$$

$$\Rightarrow x = \tfrac{\pi}{6}, \tfrac{5\pi}{6}, \tfrac{7\pi}{6}, \tfrac{11\pi}{6}, \ldots$$

Remember to use the range in the question

The values of x within the given range are: $0, \frac{\pi}{6}, \frac{\pi}{3}, \frac{2\pi}{3}, \frac{5\pi}{6}, \pi$.

b Instead of rearranging $\sin 3x - \sin 5x = \sin x$ to make all terms positive (giving the equation $\sin 3x = \sin 5x + \sin x$, which we solved in **a**), we can apply the factor formulas to the original equation, and create a negative angle.

$$\sin 3x - \sin 5x = \sin x$$

$$\Rightarrow 2\cos 4x\sin(-x) = \sin x$$

Using the result $\sin(-x) = -\sin x$, gives

$$-2\cos 4x\sin x = \sin x$$

$$\Rightarrow 2\cos 4x\sin x + \sin x = 0$$

$$\Rightarrow \quad \sin x(2\cos 4x + 1) = 0$$

Then $\sin x = 0$ or $2\cos 4x + 1 = 0$

So $\sin x = 0$ or $\cos 4x = -\frac{1}{2}$

$$\sin x = 0 \quad \Rightarrow \quad x = 0°, 180°, 360°, \ldots$$
$$\cos 4x = -\tfrac{1}{2} \Rightarrow 4x = 120°, 240°, 480°, 600°, \ldots$$
$$\Rightarrow \quad x = 30°, 60°, 120°, 150°, \ldots$$

So the solutions to $\sin 3x - \sin 5x = \sin x$, for $0° \le x \le 180°$ are:

$x = 0°, 30°, 60°, 120°, 150°, 180°$

Check that these are the same values as those in **a**.

This can be checked graphically by identifying the points of intersection of the graphs of $\sin x$ and $\sin 3x - \sin 5x$ over this range.

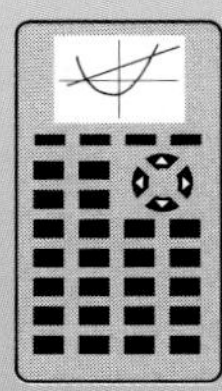

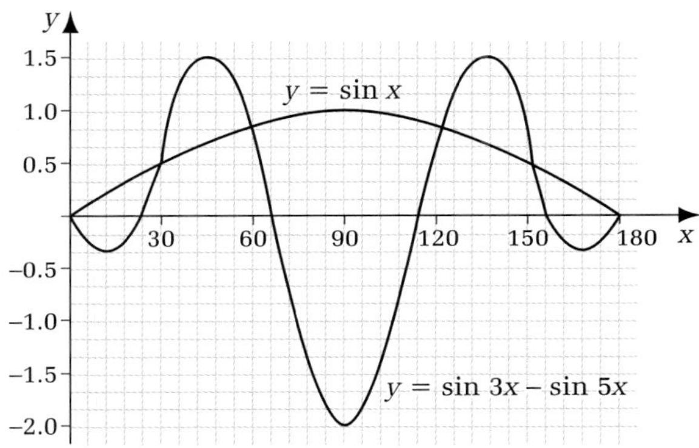

10.1 The Factor Formulas
Exercise
Technique

1 Solve the following equations for $0° \le x \le 360°$:

a $\sin x + \sin 2x + \sin 3x = 0$
b $\sin 5x - \sin x = 0$
c $\cos x + \cos 3x + \cos 5x = 0$
d $\sin 3x - \sin x = \cos 2x$

2 Solve the following equations for $0 \le x \le \pi$:

a $\sin x + \sin 2x - \sin 3x = 0$
b $\sin x + \sin 3x = 2 \sin 2x$
c $\cos 4x - \cos 2x + \sin 3x = 0$
d $\cos 5x - \cos x = 0$

3 Prove the following identities:

a $\sin \theta + \sin 2\theta + \sin 3\theta \equiv \sin 2\theta(1 + 2\cos \theta)$
b $\dfrac{\sin 3\theta + \sin 5\theta}{\sin 4\theta + \sin 6\theta} \equiv \dfrac{\sin 4\theta}{\sin 5\theta}$
c $\sin 3\theta + \sin \theta \equiv 4 \sin \theta - 4 \sin^3 \theta$
d $\dfrac{\sin \theta + \sin 2\theta + \sin 3\theta}{\cos \theta + \cos 2\theta + \cos 3\theta} \equiv \tan 2\theta$
e $\dfrac{\cos 3\theta - \cos 5\theta}{\sin 4\theta} \equiv 2 \sin \theta$

4 Write each of the following as the sum or difference of two trigonometrical functions:

a $2 \sin 4\theta \cos 2\theta$
b $2 \cos 5\theta \sin \theta$
c $2 \cos 4\theta \cos 3\theta$
d $-2 \sin 4\theta \sin 3\theta$
e $2 \sin 4\theta \sin 2\theta$
f $2 \sin 3\theta \sin 6\theta$

5 Without using a calculator find the exact value of the following:

a $\cos 105° - \cos 15°$
b $\sin 75° + \sin 15°$
c $2 \sin 37\frac{1}{2}° \sin 7\frac{1}{2}°$
d $\sin 37\frac{1}{2}° \cos 7\frac{1}{2}°$

10.2 Functions of the form $f(x) = a \sin x + b \cos x$

Using a graphical calculator and making sure you are working in degree mode, set the range as follows.

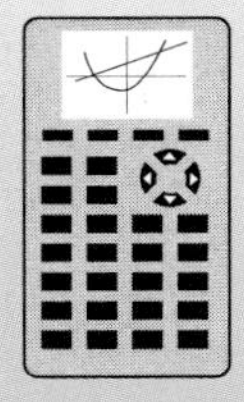

$x_{\text{MIN}} = -360 \qquad x_{\text{MAX}} = 360 \qquad x_{\text{SCL}} = 60$

$y_{\text{MIN}} = -10 \qquad y_{\text{MAX}} = 10 \qquad y_{\text{SCL}} = 1$

Draw graphs of $y = a \sin x + b \cos x$ for various values of a and b. Try $a = 1, b = 2$ ($y = \sin x + 2 \cos x$) or $a = 3, b = -1$ ($y = 3 \sin x - \cos x$). What happens? The resulting graph in each case is a 'sine wave' or 'cosine wave'.

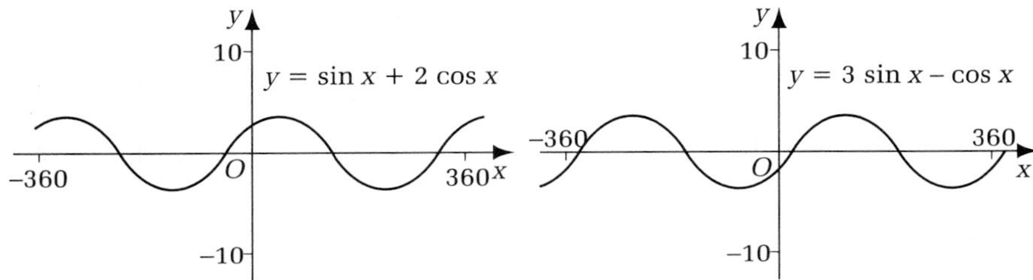

Each can be obtained from the graphs of $y = \sin x$ or $y = \cos x$ by performing two transformations:

- a translation parallel to the x-axis by some value (called the **phase angle**)
- a stretch parallel to the y-axis by some scale factor (called the **amplitude**).

These results suggest that functions of the form $f(x) = a \sin x + b \sin x$ can be written in the following forms:

$$R \sin(x \pm \alpha) \text{ or } R \cos(x \pm \alpha),$$

By convention we always assume $R > 0$.

where α is the phase angle and R is the amplitude. The values of α and R depend on the values of a and b. This can be interpreted algebraically using the necessary compound angle formulas.

Suppose $\qquad f(x) \equiv R \sin(x + \alpha)$

Then $\qquad a \sin x + b \cos x \equiv R \sin(x + \alpha)$

So $\qquad a \sin x + b \cos x \equiv R \sin x \cos \alpha + R \cos x \sin \alpha$

Now compare the coefficients of $\sin x$ and $\cos x$ on each side of this identity.

Recall the formula for $\sin(x + \alpha)$.

$\sin x: \quad a = R \cos \alpha \qquad [1]$

$\cos x: \quad b = R \sin \alpha \qquad [2]$

Since the values of a and b are known, the simultaneous equations [1] and [2] can be solved. Dividing equation [2] by equation [1] gives

$$\frac{b}{a} = \frac{R\sin\alpha}{R\cos\alpha}$$

$$\Rightarrow \quad \frac{b}{a} = \tan\alpha$$

Notice that R will cancel.

So the phase angle $\boldsymbol{\alpha = \tan^{-1}\left(\frac{b}{a}\right)}$ ◀ Recall the alternative notation $\arctan\left(\frac{b}{a}\right)$.

The principal value of can be found using a calculator.

We can also find R. Squaring equations [1] and [2] and then adding them together gives,

$$\begin{aligned} a^2 + b^2 &= R^2\cos^2\alpha + R^2\sin^2\alpha \\ &= R^2(\sin^2\alpha + \cos^2\alpha) \\ &= R^2 \end{aligned}$$

By the Pythagorean identity, $\sin^2\theta + \cos^2\theta \equiv 1$.

So the amplitude $\boldsymbol{R = \sqrt{a^2 + b^2}}$

Note the positive root; $R > 0$.

Example 1

Write $f(x) = 3\sin x + 4\cos x$ in the form $R\sin(x + \alpha)$ with $0° \leq \alpha \leq 90°$. Hence sketch the graph of $y = f(x)$ for $0° \leq x \leq 360°$.

Solution

Let $\quad 3\sin x + 4\cos x = R\sin(x + \alpha)$.

Then $\; 3\sin x + 4\cos x = R\sin x\cos\alpha + R\cos x\sin\alpha$

Equating coefficients of $\sin x$ and $\cos x$,

$$\sin x: \quad 3 = R\cos\alpha \qquad [1]$$

$$\cos x: \quad 4 = R\sin\alpha \qquad [2]$$

Dividing equation [2] by equation [1],

$$\tfrac{4}{3} = \tan\alpha$$

So $\alpha = \tan^{-1}\left(\frac{4}{3}\right) = 53.1°$ (1 d.p.)

Find R by squaring and adding equations [1] and [2]:

$$\begin{aligned} 3^2 + 4^2 &= R^2\cos^2\alpha + R^2\sin^2\alpha \\ \Rightarrow \quad 9 + 16 &= R^2(\sin^2\alpha + \cos^2\alpha) \\ \Rightarrow \quad 25 &= R^2 \\ \Rightarrow \quad R &= \sqrt{25} = 5 \end{aligned}$$

Recall that $R > 0$, so we ignore -5 as a solution.

$f(x)$ can now be written in the required form.

$$f(x) = 3\sin x + 4\cos x = 5\sin(x + 53.1°)$$

This result shows us that $f(x)$ has an amplitude of 5 and a phase angle of 53.1°, which means that the graph of $y = \sin x$ has been translated by 53.1° parallel to the x-axis and then stretched parallel to the y-axis by a scale factor 5. This enables us to sketch the graph of the function.

Recall that amplitude is the stretch factor parallel to the y-axis.

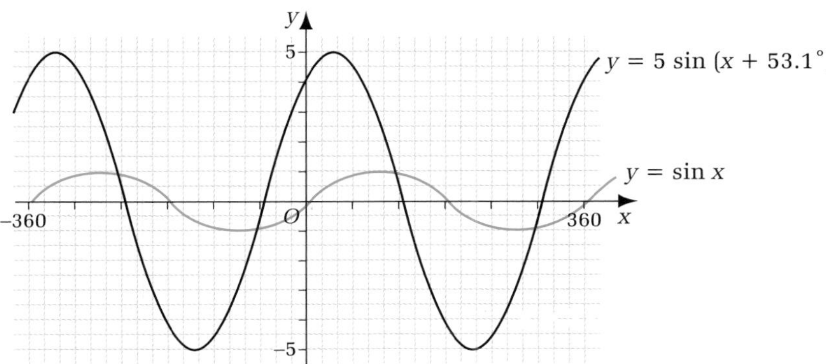

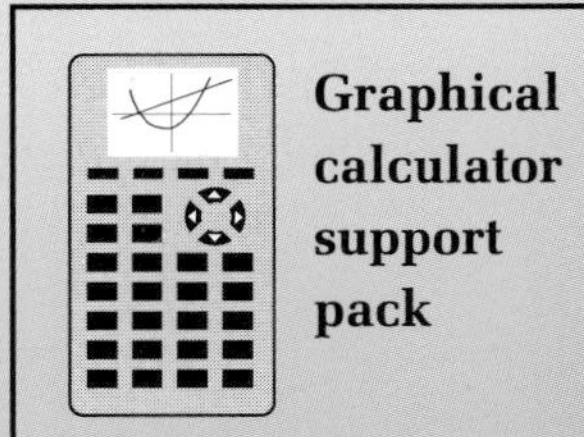

Example 2

Write $f(x) = 24\cos x - 7\sin x$ in the form $R\cos(x + \alpha)$ with $0° \leq \alpha \leq 90°$. Use the result to state the maximum and minimum values of $f(x)$.

Solution

Let $24\cos x - 7\sin x = R\cos(x + \alpha)$.

Then $24\cos x - 7\sin x = R\cos x\cos\alpha - R\sin x\sin\alpha$

Notice that both coefficients of $\sin x$ are negative.

Equating coefficients of $\sin x$ and $\cos x$,

$$\sin x: \quad 7 = R\sin\alpha \qquad [1]$$

$$\cos x: \quad 24 = R\cos\alpha \qquad [2]$$

When choosing the form in which to express $f(x)$ it is important to match the signs of the terms. Then $\sin\alpha$ and $\cos\alpha$ are positive, ensuring that α is acute.

Dividing equation [1] by equation [2],

$$\tfrac{7}{24} = \tan\alpha$$

So $\alpha = \tan^{-1}(\tfrac{7}{24}) = 16.3°$ (3 s.f.)

Find R by squaring and adding equations [1] and [2]:

$$7^2 + 24^2 = R^2\sin^2\alpha + R^2\cos^2\alpha$$

$$\Rightarrow 49 + 576 = R^2(\sin^2\alpha + \cos^2\alpha) = R^2$$

$$\Rightarrow \quad R = \sqrt{625} = 25$$

Recall that $R > 0$.

So $f(x) = 24\cos x - 7\sin x = 25\cos(x + 16.3°)$

We would usually differentiate $f(x)$ to find its maximum and minimum values, but in this case they can be found without differentiating. Consider the behaviour of the cosine function. It oscillates between a maximum value of $+1$ and a minimum value of -1. So $\cos(x + 16.3°)$ has a maximum value of $+1$ and a minimum value of -1, and since we have a stretch factor of 25, $f(x)$ has a maximum value of 25 and a minimum value of -25.

Remember to use radians when differentiating.

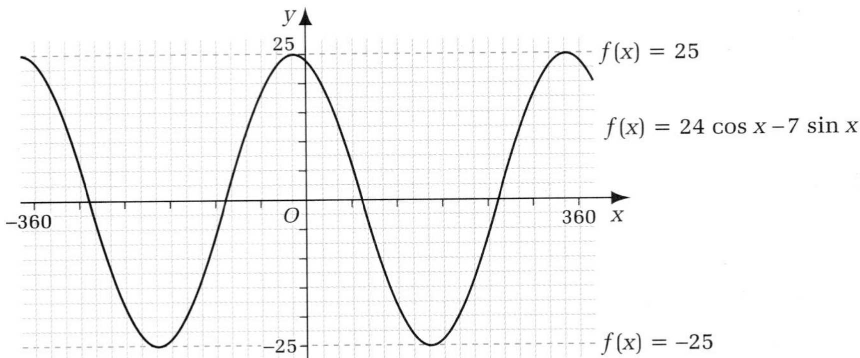

The equation $a \sin x + b \cos x = c$

Equations of the form $a \sin x + b \cos x = c$, where a, b and c are real numbers can be solved by first expressing the trigonometric terms as one function (either sine or cosine). The techniques discussed in Chapter 3 can then be applied and appropriate solutions to the equation identified within a given range of values for x.

Example 3

Express $12 \cos x + 5 \sin x$ in the form $R \cos(x - \alpha)$. Hence solve the equation $12 \cos x + 5 \sin x = 10$ for $0 \leq x \leq \pi$.

Solution

Let $\quad 12 \cos x + 5 \sin x = R \cos(x - \alpha)$.

Then $\; 12 \cos x + 5 \sin x = R \cos x \cos \alpha + R \sin x \sin \alpha$

Equating coefficients of $\sin x$ and $\cos x$,

$$\sin x: \quad 5 = R \sin \alpha \qquad [1]$$

$$\cos x: \quad 12 = R \cos \alpha \qquad [2]$$

Dividing equation [1] by equation [2],

In this example we are working in radians, since they are used to specify the required range in the question.

$$\tfrac{5}{12} = \tan \alpha$$

$$\Rightarrow \alpha = \tan^{-1}\left(\tfrac{5}{12}\right) = 0.395 \text{ (3 s.f.)}$$

Find R by squaring and adding equations [1] and [2]:

$$5^2 + 12^2 = R^2 \sin^2 \alpha + R^2 \cos^2 \alpha$$

$$\Rightarrow \quad 25 + 144 = R^2(\sin^2 \alpha + \cos^2 \alpha)$$

$$\Rightarrow \quad 169 = R^2$$

So $\quad R = \sqrt{169} = 13$

So $12 \cos x + 5 \sin x = 13 \cos(x - 0.395)$.

We know that $12 \cos x + 5 \sin x = 10$. Substituting the new expression we have just found,

$$13 \cos(x - 0.395) = 10$$

$$\cos(x - 0.395) = \tfrac{10}{13}$$

One possibility for x is given by

$$x - 0.395 = \cos^{-1}(\tfrac{10}{13}) = 0.693$$

So $\quad x = 0.693 + 0.395 = 1.088$

$$x = 1.09 \text{ (3 s.f.)}$$

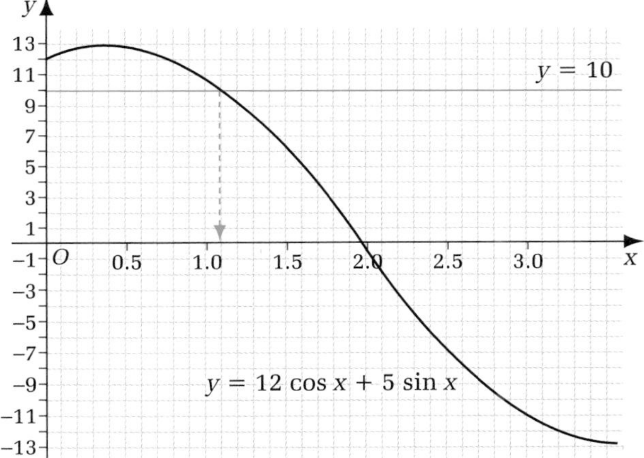

Check that there is only one solution: $\cos(x - 0.395) = (\tfrac{10}{13})$ has other solutions, including -0.693 and 6.976, but they are outside the given range.

Maximising and minimising rational functions

Sometimes the denominator of a rational function contains terms involving $\sin x$ and $\cos x$. The technique of expressing these two terms as one trigonometric ratio can be useful in identifying the maximum and minimum values of the original function.

Example 4

Find the maximum and minimum values of $\dfrac{1}{15 \cos x - 8 \sin x + 23}$.

Solution

Notice that the denominator contains $15\cos x - 8\sin x$. This can be expressed in the form $R\cos(x+\alpha)$.

$$15\cos x - 8\sin x = R\cos(x+\alpha)$$
$$= R\cos x\cos\alpha - R\sin x\sin\alpha$$

Equating coefficients of $\cos x$ and $\sin x$,

$$\cos x: \quad 15 = R\cos\alpha \qquad [1]$$

$$\sin x: \quad 8 = R\sin\alpha \qquad [2]$$

Dividing equation [2] by equation [1],

$$\tfrac{8}{15} = \tan\alpha$$

So $\alpha = \tan^{-1}(\tfrac{8}{15}) = 0.49$ (2 d.p.) ◀ In radians.

Squaring and adding equations [1] and [2],

$$15^2 + 8^2 = R^2\cos^2\alpha + R^2\sin^2\alpha$$
$$\Rightarrow 225 + 64 = R^2(\sin^2\alpha + \cos^2\alpha)$$
$$289 = R^2$$
$$R = \sqrt{289} = 17$$

So $15\cos x - 8\sin x = 17\cos(x + 0.49)$

The original rational function can now be simplified and analysed.

$$\frac{1}{15\cos x - 8\sin x + 23} = \frac{1}{17\cos(x+0.49)+23}$$

Recall how the cosine function varies between +1 and −1. This means the trigonometric term in the denominator will vary between +17 and −17, allowing the maximum and minimum values of the rational function to be identified.

The smallest value o[f] $17\cos(x+0.49)+2$[3] will give the maxim[um] and the largest value will give the minim[um]

The maximum value is $\dfrac{1}{(-17+23)} = \dfrac{1}{6}$

The minimum value is $\dfrac{1}{(17+23)} = \dfrac{1}{40}$

Notice that:

- the trigonometric term $\cos(x + 0.49)$ could be used to identify values of x at which these limits occur.
- the rational function is defined for all values of x since the denominator can never be zero.

The maximum occurs when $\cos(x + 0.49) = -1$.

Periodic motion

Periodic motion is any motion that repeats itself in equal intervals of time. Equations used to model this type of motion contain trigonometric terms, because the sine and cosine functions are periodic. Examples of this type of motion include:

- a mass oscillating on the end of a spring;
- a buoy moving up and down on the waves on the surface of the water in a harbour;
- the tip of a sewing machine needle moving up and down.

A special case of this type of motion is known as '**simple harmonic motion**'.

Example 5

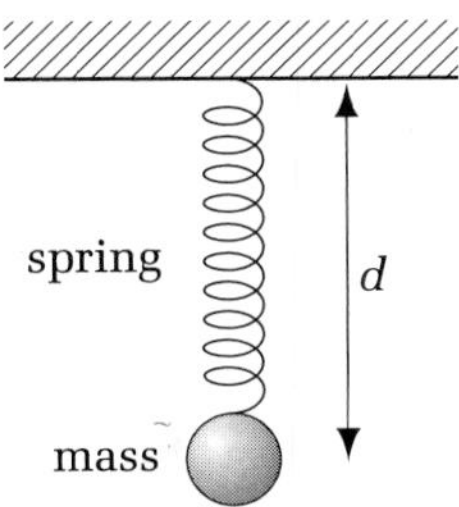

A mass is suspended from the end of a spring as shown in the diagram. The mass is oscillating. The distance d cm between the fixture point and the mass is given by

$$d = 17 + 12\sin 2t - 5\cos 2t,$$

where t seconds is the time after release. Find:

a the maximum and minimum distances from the fixture point reached by the mass

b the time at which the mass is first at its lowest point.

Notice that the angle is measured in radians; there is no degree symbol.

Solution

a Notice that the expression for d contains two trigonometric terms. $12\sin 2t - 5\cos 2t$ can be rewritten in the form $R\sin(2t - \alpha)$, where $0 \le \alpha \le \frac{\pi}{2}$.

$$12\sin 2t - 5\cos 2t \equiv R\sin(2t - \alpha)$$
$$\equiv R\sin 2t\cos\alpha - R\cos 2t\sin\alpha$$

Equating coefficients of $\sin 2t$ and $\cos 2t$,

$\sin 2t$: $\quad R\cos\alpha = 12 \qquad [1]$

$\cos 2t$: $\quad R\sin\alpha = 5 \qquad [2]$

Dividing equation [2] by equation [1],

$$\tan\alpha = \frac{5}{12}$$

So $\qquad \alpha = \tan^{-1}(\frac{5}{12}) = 0.395$ (3 s.f.)

Squaring and adding equations [1] and [2],

$$R^2\cos^2\alpha + R^2\sin^2\alpha = 12^2 + 5^2$$

$$\Rightarrow \quad R^2 = 169$$

$$\Rightarrow \quad R = \sqrt{169} = 13$$

So $d = 17 + 13\sin(2t - 0.395)$

Since the sine function varies between $+1$ and -1, d will vary between $17 + 13$ and $17 - 13$.

Maximum value of d is 30 cm.

Minimum value of d is 4 cm.

The lowest point is reached at the maximum value of si[n] which is 1.

b Notice that the lowest part is reached when $\sin(2t - 0.395) = 1$.

$2t - 0.395 = \frac{\pi}{2}, \frac{5\pi}{2}, \ldots$

◀ **Recall that there is more than one solution.**

The smallest solution is given by

$$2t = 1.571 + 0.395$$

$$2t = 1.966$$

$$t = 0.983$$

So the mass reaches the lowest point for the first time after 0.983 seconds (3 s.f.).

10.2 Functions of the form $f(x) = a \sin x + b \cos x$

Exercise

Technique

1 Express each of the following in the form $R\sin(x+\alpha)$, with $0° \leq \alpha \leq 90°$:

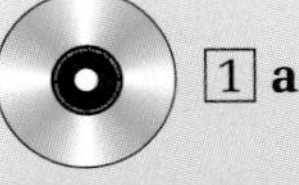

a $5\sin x + 12\cos x$ **b** $7\sin x + 24\cos x$
c $11\sin x + 60\cos x$ **d** $2\sin x + 5\cos x$

2 Express each of the following in the form $R\sin(x-\alpha)$ with $0 \leq \alpha \leq \frac{\pi}{2}$:

a $\sqrt{3}\sin x - \cos x$ **b** $2\sin x - 2\cos x$
c $\sin x - \sqrt{3}\cos x$ **d** $\sin x + \cos x$

3 Express each of the following in the form $R\cos(x+\alpha)$ with $0° \leq \alpha \leq 90°$:

a $8\cos x - 6\sin x$ **b** $3\cos x - 4\sin x$
c $3\cos x - 2\sin x$ **d** $7\cos x - 5\sin x$

4 Express each of the following in the form $R\cos(x-\alpha)$ with $0 \leq \alpha \leq \frac{\pi}{2}$:

a $12\cos x + 5\sin x$ **b** $8\cos x + 6\sin x$
c $\cos x + \sqrt{3}\sin x$ **d** $6\cos x + 5\sin x$

5 Find the maximum and minimum values of the following expressions, in each case giving the value of x at which this is achieved for $0° \leq x \leq 360°$:

a $\sin x + \cos x$ **b** $60\sin x - 11\cos x$
c $24\cos x - 7\sin x$ **d** $5\cos x + 3\sin x$

6 Solve the following equations for $0° \leq x \leq 360°$:

a $\sin x - \cos x = 1$ **b** $\sqrt{3}\sin x + \cos x = \sqrt{3}$
c $\sin x + \cos x = -\sqrt{\frac{3}{2}}$ **d** $\sin x + \sqrt{3}\cos x = 1$

7 Solve the following equations for $-\pi \leq x \leq \pi$:

a $\sin x + \cos x = 1$ **b** $\sqrt{3}\cos x - \sin x = 1$
c $5\sin x - 3\cos x = 2$ **d** $4\cos x - 3\sin x = 2$

8 Find the maximum and minimum values of the following functions:

a $\dfrac{1}{15\sin x + 8\cos x + 18}$ **b** $\dfrac{5}{63\cos x - 16\sin x + 70}$

c $\dfrac{3}{5\sin x - 12\cos x + 26}$ **d** $\dfrac{5}{24\sin x + 7\cos x + 30}$

Contextual

1 The depth of water in a leaking storage tank is d cm at time t hours after midnight on Sunday. The value of d is given by $d = 10 - 2\sqrt{3}\cos 4t^\circ - 2\sin 4t^\circ$. Find:

a the least and greatest depth of water possible with this model

b the time at which the depth first reaches these values.

2 A mass is suspended vertically from the end of a spring. It is allowed to oscillate so that the distance of the mass from the fixture point, d cm, is given by $d = 23 - 5\sqrt{3}\sin 3t - 5\cos 3t$, where t seconds is the time after release. Find:

a the minimum and maximum distances from the fixture point reached by the mass

b the times at which these points are first reached by the mass.

10.3 General Solutions of Trigonometric Equations

Solve the equation $\cos\theta = \frac{1}{2}$. Now check what you have written. A calculator in degree mode gives an answer of 60°, but recall that this is only the principal solution. Check that $\theta = 300°$, $\theta = 420°$ and $\theta = -60°$ also work. The equation $\cos\theta = \frac{1}{2}$ had no restriction on the range of values of θ that are acceptable as solutions. A check of this equation graphically demonstrates that there is an infinite number of solutions.

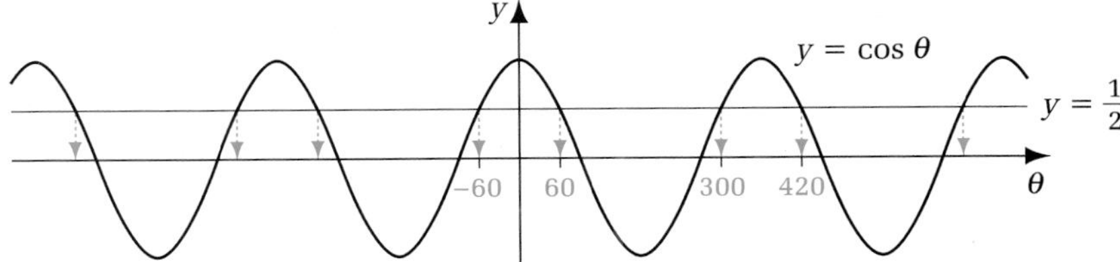

These solutions can, however, be written concisely in one algebraic statement. Notice that all of the solutions can be found by adding multiples of 360° to either 60° or −60°. This means that

$$\theta = 360°n \pm 60°, \quad \text{where } n \in \mathbb{Z}$$

$\mathbb{Z}$ is the set of all integers (both positive and negative).

describes all of the possible solutions. The statement $\theta = 360°n \pm 60°$ is the **general solution** to the equation $\cos\theta = \frac{1}{2}$. Substitute appropriate values of n into the general equation to verify that $\theta = 300°$, $\theta = 420°$ and $\theta = -60°$ can be derived from it.

Look again at the structure of the general solution. Notice that it has two distinct parts.

- $360°n$ multiples of 360° ($n \in \mathbb{Z}$)
- $\pm 60°$ the principal solution.

This means that the general solution to the equation $\cos\theta = k$ where $-1 \le k \le 1$ can be found by

- finding the principal solution by evaluating $\cos^{-1} k$; and
- adding a term to include multiples of 360° or 2π radians.

Example 1

Find the general solution, in degrees, of the equation $\cos\theta = 0.3$.

Solution

The principal solution is $\theta = \cos^{-1}(0.3) = 72.5°$

The general solution is $\theta = 360°n \pm 72.5°$, where $n \in \mathbb{Z}$

Example 2

Find the general solution of the equation $\cos\theta = \frac{\sqrt{3}}{2}$.

Since degrees aren't mentioned, work in radians.

Solution

The principal solution is $\theta = \cos^{-1}(\frac{\sqrt{3}}{2}) = \frac{\pi}{6}$

Special angle.

The general solution is $\theta = 2\pi n \pm \frac{\pi}{6}$, where $n \in \mathbb{Z}$.

There are also general solution results for the equations $\sin\theta = k$ where $-1 \le k \le 1$ and $\tan\theta = k$ where $k \in \mathbb{R}$.

Consider the equation $\sin\theta = k$, where $-1 \le k \le 1$. Notice that for this curve all the solutions can be found by adding multiples of $360°$ (or 2π) to either the principal solution α, or the second solution, $180 - \alpha$ (or $\pi - \alpha$).

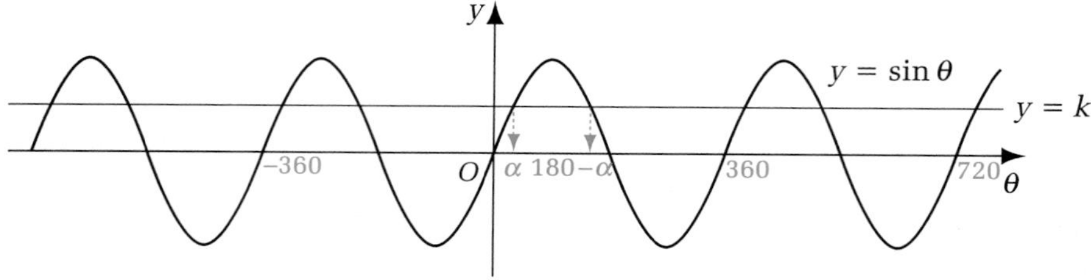

The general solution to $\sin\theta = k$ where $-1 \le k \le 1$ now has two distinct parts.

$$\theta = 360°n + \alpha; \quad \text{where } n \in \mathbb{Z}$$

$$\text{and} \quad \theta = 360°n + (180° - \alpha); \quad \text{where } n \in \mathbb{Z}$$

Example 3

Find the general solution, in degrees, of the equation $\sin\theta = \frac{1}{2}$.

Check that for $n = 0$, $\theta = 30°$; $n = 1$, $\theta = 150°$ and $n = 2$, $\theta = 390°$.

Solution

The principal solution is $\theta = \sin^{-1}(\frac{1}{2}) = 30°$

The second solution is $\theta = (180° - 30°) = 150°$

The general solution is $\theta = 360°n + 30°$ and $\theta = 360°n + 150°$, where $n \in \mathbb{Z}$.

This solution can be rewritten in the more concise form

$$\theta = 180°n + (-1)^n 30°, \quad \text{where } n \in \mathbb{Z}$$

Verify that these statements are equivalent by substituting different values for n.

Now consider the equation $\tan\theta = k$ where $k \in \mathbb{R}$. Notice that all of the solutions can be found by adding on multiples of 180° (or π) to the principal solution α. This means that the general solution to $\tan\theta = k$, where $k \in \mathbb{R}$, has the form $\theta = 180°n + \alpha$.

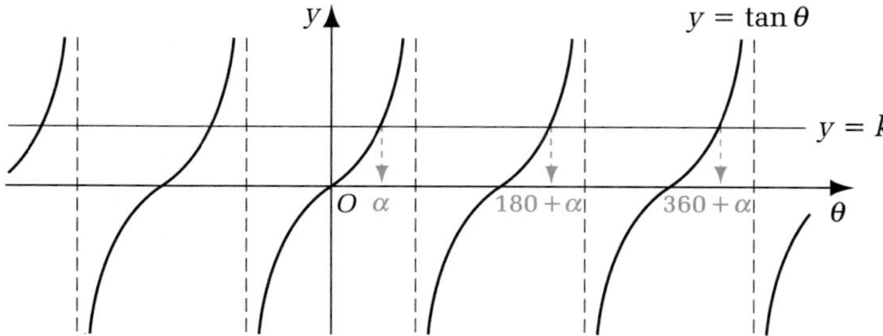

Example 4

Find the general solution, in degrees, of the equation $\tan\theta = -3$.

Solution

The principal solution is $\theta = \tan^{-1}(-3) = -71.6°$.
The general solution is $\theta = 180°n - 71.6°$, where $n \in \mathbb{Z}$.
Check this solution graphically.

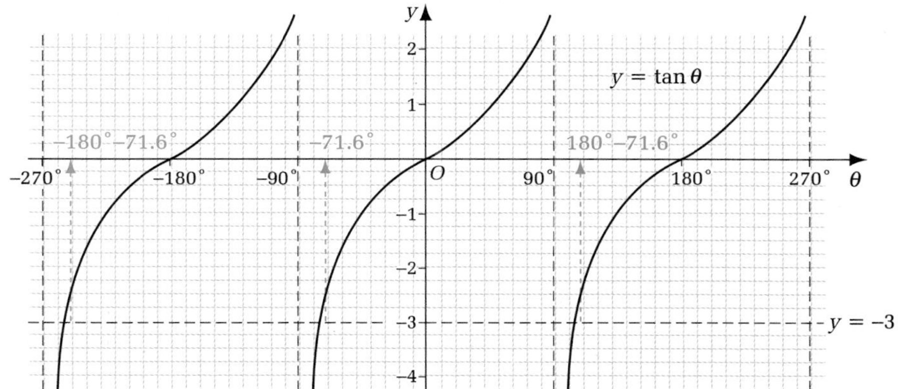

General solutions can also be found in equations involving double angles, multiple angles and both the sine and cosine functions.

Example 5

Find the general solution to the equation $\cos\theta = \cos 2\theta$.

Solution

One way of solving this would be to expand the double angle using $\cos 2\theta = 2\cos^2\theta - 1$. This creates a quadratic in $\cos\theta$ that can be solved.

Check this by expanding $\cos 2\theta$ and solving the resulting quadratic.

An alternative method is to allow the expression 2θ to be the principal solution.

If $\quad \cos\theta = \cos 2\theta$

then $\quad \theta = 2\pi n \pm 2\theta; n \in \mathbb{Z}$

Notice that the second set of solutions, $\theta = -2\pi n$, is included in the first set because multiples of $\frac{2}{3}\pi$ include the multiples of 2π.

Adding and subtracting 2θ on both sides,

$$3\theta = 2\pi n \quad \text{or} \quad -\theta = 2\pi n$$

$$\theta = \frac{2\pi n}{3} \quad \text{or} \quad \theta = -2\pi n$$

So the general solution is $\theta = \frac{2}{3}\pi n$, where $n \in \mathbb{Z}$.

Example 6

Find the general solution of the equation $3\cos\theta + 4\sin\theta = 1$.

Solution

Notice that this equation is of the form $a\cos\theta + b\sin\theta = c$. The LHS of the equation can be rewritten using an expression of the form $R\cos(\theta - \alpha)$. Check that

$$3\cos\theta + 4\sin\theta = 5\cos(\theta - 53.1^\circ)$$

Now $3\cos\theta + 4\sin\theta = 1 \Rightarrow 5\cos(\theta - 53.1^\circ) = 1$

So $\cos(\theta - 53.1^\circ) = \frac{1}{5}$

The principal solution is given by $\theta - 53.1^\circ = \cos^{-1}(\frac{1}{5}) = 78.5^\circ$.
So $\theta - 53.1^\circ = 360^\circ n \pm 78.5^\circ$, $n \in \mathbb{Z}$.
The general solution for θ is in two parts.

$$\theta = 360^\circ n + 78.5^\circ + 53.1^\circ$$

$$\Rightarrow \quad \theta = 360^\circ n + 131.6^\circ$$

$$\text{and} \quad \theta = 360^\circ n - 78.5^\circ + 53.1^\circ$$

$$\Rightarrow \quad \theta = 360^\circ n - 25.4^\circ, \quad \text{where } n \in \mathbb{Z}$$

10.3 General Solutions of Trigonometric Equations

Exercise

Technique

1 Find the general solutions, in degrees, of the following equations:

a $\cos\theta = 0.9$
b $\cos\theta = -0.25$
c $\sin\theta = 0.2$
d $\sin\theta = -0.6$
e $\tan\theta = 0.5$
f $\tan\theta = -1.5$

2 Find the general solutions of the following equations:

a $\cos\theta = \frac{1}{2}$
b $\cos\theta = -\frac{\sqrt{3}}{2}$
c $\sin\theta = \frac{\sqrt{3}}{2}$
d $\sin\theta = -1$
e $\tan\theta = 1$
f $\tan\theta = 0$

3 Find the general solutions of the following equations:

a $\sin 2\theta = \frac{1}{2}$
b $\cos\theta = \cos 3\theta$
c $\sin\theta = \sin 3\theta$
d $\cos 4\theta = -\frac{1}{2}$

4 Find the general solution, in degrees, of the equation $\cos\theta + 3\sin\theta = 2$.

5 Find the general solution of the equation $\cos\theta + \cos 3\theta + \cos 5\theta = 0$.

6 Find the general solution of the equation $\sin(x + 30°) = \cos(x + 45°)$.

Consolidation

Exercise A

1 Solve the equation $\cos\theta + \cos 5\theta = 2\cos 2\theta$ for $0 \le \theta \le 2\pi$.

2 Express $63\sin x + 16\cos x$ in the form $R\sin(x + \alpha)$, where R is positive and α is acute. Find:

a the acute angle x for which $63\sin x + 16\cos x = 50$

b the obtuse angle x for which $63\sin x + 16\cos x = 0$.

(UCLES)

3 Express $4\sin\theta - 3\cos\theta$ in the form $R\sin(\theta - \alpha)$, where R is positive and α is an acute angle. Hence, or otherwise, find the greatest and least values of the expression

$$\frac{1}{(10 - 3\cos\theta + 4\sin\theta)}.$$

(NICCEA)

4 Prove the identity $\cos 2\theta - \cos 4\theta \equiv 2\cos^2\theta - 2\cos^2 2\theta$. By substituting $\theta = 36°$, show, without using a calculator, that $\cos 36° - \cos 72° = \frac{1}{2}$. Hence find the value of $\cos 36°$ in the form $a + b\sqrt{5}$, where a and b are to be found.

(WJEC)

5 Express $3\sin\theta - 4\cos\theta$ in the form $R\sin(\theta - \alpha)$ where $R > 0$ and $0 \le \alpha \le \frac{\pi}{2}$. Give the value of α in radians to three decimal places. Determine the greatest and least values of the following:

a $(3\sin\theta - 4\cos\theta)^2$

b $\dfrac{1}{(3\sin\theta - 4\cos\theta)^2 + 1}$

State a value of θ in radians for which the least value of the expression in **b** occurs.

(AEB)

6 **a** Express the function $3\cos x° + 4\sin x°$ in the form $R\sin(x + \alpha)°$, stating the values of R and α.

b Write down the maximum value of $3\cos x° + 4\sin x°$.

c Solve the equation $3\cos x° + 4\sin x° = 0$ for $0° \le x \le 360°$.

(NEAB)

7 Express $\sqrt{3}\sin\theta - \cos\theta$ in the form $R\sin(\theta - \alpha)$, where $R > 0$ and $0° < \alpha < 90°$. Hence, or otherwise, find all values of θ, for $0° \le \theta \le 360°$, which satisfy the equation $\sqrt{3}\sin\theta - \cos\theta = \sqrt{2}$.

(UCLES)

8 Prove the identity $(\cos A + \cos B)^2 + (\sin A + \sin B)^2 \equiv 2 + 2\cos(A - B)$. Solve the equation $(\cos 4\theta + \cos\theta)^2 + (\sin 4\theta + \sin\theta)^2 = 2\sqrt{3}\sin 3\theta$, giving the general solution in degrees.

(AEB)

9 **a** Rewrite $2\cos x - \sin x$ in the form $R\cos(x + \alpha)$, where R is real and α is acute.

b Hence find the general solution of the equation $2\cos x - \sin x = 1$.

(NICCEA)

Exercise B

1 Solve the equation $\sin 8\theta - \sin 2\theta = 0$ for $0 \le \theta \le \frac{\pi}{2}$.

2 Find all values of θ lying between $0°$ and $360°$ satisfying the equation $4\sin\theta + 3\cos\theta = 1$. Give your answers correct to the nearest degree.

(WJEC)

3 Given that $4\cos\theta + 3\sin\theta \equiv R\cos(\theta - \alpha)$, find the value of R and the value of α where $R > 0$ and $0° < \alpha < 90°$.

a Hence find all values of θ between $0°$ and $360°$ satisfying the equations:

i $4\cos\theta + 3\sin\theta = 2$

ii $4\cos 2\theta + 3\sin 2\theta = 5\cos\theta$.

b Find the greatest and least values of the expression $\dfrac{1}{(4\cos\theta + 3\sin\theta + 6)}$, and give the corresponding values of θ between $0°$ and $360°$.

(WJEC)

4 The function f is defined for all real values of x by $f(x) = (\cos x - \sin x)(17\cos x - 7\sin x)$.

a By first multiplying out the brackets, show that $f(x)$ may be expressed in the form $5\cos 2x - 12\sin 2x + k$, where k is a constant. State the value of k.

b Given that $5\cos 2x - 12\sin 2x \equiv R\cos(2x + \alpha)$, where $R > 0$ and $0 < a < \frac{\pi}{2}$, state the value of R and find the value of α in radians to three decimal places.

c Determine the greatest and least values of $\dfrac{39}{f(x) + 14}$, and state a value of x at which the greatest value occurs.

(AEB)

5 Express $2\cos\theta + 2\sin\theta$ in the form $R\cos(\theta - \alpha)$, where $R > 0$ and $0 < \alpha < \frac{1}{2}\pi$, giving the values of R and α in exact form. Hence, or otherwise, show that one of the acute angles θ satisfying the equation $2\cos\theta + 2\sin\theta = \sqrt{6}$ is $\frac{5\pi}{12}$, and find the other acute angle.

(UCLES)

6 [In this question, give your answers correct to the nearest 0.1°, where appropriate.]

a Find the general solution, in degrees, of the equation $5\cos 2\theta = 3$.

b Solve each of the following equations, for $0 < \theta < 180^\circ$:

i $5\cos\theta + 2\sin^2\theta = 4$

ii $5\sin\theta + 3\cos\theta = 5$

(UCLES)

7 By squaring both sides of the identity $\sin^2\theta + \cos^2\theta \equiv 1$, prove that $4(\sin^4\theta + \cos^4\theta) \equiv 3 + \cos 4\theta$. Find the general solution in radians of the equation $4(\sin^4\theta + \cos^4\theta) = 2 - \cos 2\theta$.

(AEB)

Applications and Activities

1 *The mathematical representation of a wave*

The general equation for a wave represents every point x on the wave at every time t,

$$y = A\sin(kx - \omega t),$$

where A is the amplitude of the wave, k is the wave number and ω is the angular frequency (velocity). Then k is the number of waves contained in the interval of 2π.
Now consider sound as an example of a wave. If two waves y_1 and y_2 given by

$$y_1 = A_1 \sin(k_1 x - \omega_1 t) \quad \text{and} \quad y_2 = A_2 \sin(k_2 x - \omega_2 t)$$

act at the same time, the resultant sound (from the **principle of superposition**) is given by $y_1 + y_2$. Investigate the behaviour of $y_1 + y_2$, and particularly the analysis of the resultant wave in the real world. How is this interpreted?

2 *Simple harmonic motion (SHM)*

SHM is motion in which the acceleration of a body is directly proportional to its displacement from the equilibrium position but in the opposite direction. Investigate SHM when the displacement of the object performing the motion is written in the form

$$x = A\cos\omega t + B\sin\omega t,$$

where ω is the angular velocity, t is time and A and B are constants to be determined. What is an advantage of writing displacement in this form?

Summary

- The factor formulas, used to convert sums and differences of sines and cosines into products, are:

$$\sin C + \sin D \equiv 2\sin\left(\frac{C+D}{2}\right)\cos\left(\frac{C-D}{2}\right)$$

$$\sin C - \sin D \equiv 2\cos\left(\frac{C+D}{2}\right)\sin\left(\frac{C-D}{2}\right)$$

$$\cos C + \cos D \equiv 2\cos\left(\frac{C+D}{2}\right)\cos\left(\frac{C-D}{2}\right)$$

$$\cos C - \cos D \equiv -2\sin\left(\frac{C+D}{2}\right)\sin\left(\frac{C-D}{2}\right)$$

- The function $a\sin x + b\cos x$ can be expressed as:

  $R\sin(x+\alpha)$ $R\sin(x-\alpha)$ $R\cos(x+\alpha)$ $R\cos(x-\alpha)$

  depending on the sign values of a and b. R and α can be found by first expanding using the appropriate compound angle formula, and then equating coefficients to produce two simultaneous equations. Squaring and adding them gives $R = \sqrt{a^2+b^2}$ and dividing them gives an equation for $\tan\alpha$.
  This technique is useful for

  1. solving equations of the form $a\sin x + b\cos x = c$;
  2. finding maximum and minimum values of rational functions with trigonometric denominators;
  3. analysing periodic motion.

- Trigonometric equations of the form:

  $\sin\theta = k$ and $\cos\theta = k$, where $-1 \le k \le 1$ and $\tan\theta = k$, where $k \in \mathbb{R}$

  can be solved to give both a principal solution and a general solution. The principal solution can be found using a calculator. The general solution formula can then be used to generate other valid solutions as required. Remember that the general solution can be written in both degree and radian form.

  1. If $\cos\theta = k$, then $\theta = 360°n \pm \alpha$ or $\theta = 2\pi n \pm \alpha$.
  2. If $\sin\theta = k$, then $\theta = 180°n + (-1)^n\alpha$ or $\theta = \pi n + (-1)^n\alpha$.
  3. If $\tan\theta = k$ then $\theta = 180°n + \alpha$ or $\theta = \pi n + \alpha$.

11 Differentiation II

What you need to know

- How to differentiate rational powers of x, and sine and cosine functions.
- How to use the chain rule to differentiate composite functions.
- How to locate stationary points on a curve and determine their nature by looking at the sign of $\frac{dy}{dx}$ on either side of the stationary point.
- How to find the equation of the tangent and the normal to a curve at a given point.
- How to solve equations involving e^x and $\ln x$.
- How to write down the Cartesian equation of a circle.
- How to use the binomial theorem to express $(1 + ax)^n$ as a series of ascending powers of x, where n is rational.

Review

1 Differentiate each of the following with respect to x:

a $y = x^2 - 9x + 11$
b $y = 10\sqrt{x}$
c $y = x^{\frac{7}{2}} - x^{\frac{5}{2}}$
d $y = 3x + \frac{1}{2x}$
e $y = \sin 4x$
f $y = 3\sin^2 x$
g $y = \cos(\frac{1}{2}x + \frac{1}{4}\pi)$
h $y = 2x - \cos 2x$

2 Use the chain rule to find $\frac{dy}{dx}$ for each of the following:

a $y = (x + 11)^4$
b $y = (4x - 1)^8$
c $y = \sqrt{x + 5}$
d $y = \sqrt{2 - x^2}$
e $y = \frac{6}{3x+1}$
f $y = \frac{4}{\sqrt{x+2}}$

3 Find the coordinates of the stationary points on the graph of $y = \frac{1}{4}x^4 - x^3 - 3x^2 + 8x + 3$ and determine their nature.

Hint: Use the factor theorem to factorise $\frac{dy}{dx}$.

4 Find the equations of the tangent and the normal to the curve $y = \frac{4}{x}$ at the point where $x = 2$.

5 Find the exact solutions of the following exponential and logarithmic equations:

a $e^{x-3} = 4$
b $\ln(5x) = -3$
c $e^{4x} = 10$
d $\ln(x - 1) = 6$

6 Write down the Cartesian equation for each of the following circles:

a radius 4, centre (0, 0)
b radius 6, centre (0, 3)
c radius 7, centre (4, −2)
d radius $\sqrt{3}$, centre (−1, 6)

7 Use the binomial theorem to express each of the following as a series of ascending powers of x, up to and including the x^3 term:

a $(1+x)^{-2}$
b $(1-x)^{\frac{1}{3}}$
c $\dfrac{1}{1-3x}$
d $\sqrt{1+4x}$

11.1 Differentiating Products and Quotients

In Chapter 5, the techniques for differentiating polynomials, functions involving rational powers of x, and sine and cosine functions were developed. Many other mathematical functions are formed by multiplying or dividing two or more of these types of functions. Some of these products and quotients can be differentiated by first expressing the function as a polynomial, and then differentiating term by term.

However, there are many products and quotients, such as $y = (2x + 3)(x - 1)^4$ and $y = \frac{(3x+1)}{(x-2)}$, where it is either difficult or impossible to express the overall function as a polynomial. Functions of this type can be differentiated using two standard results, or algorithms, which are known as the **product** and **quotient rules**.

The product rule

Suppose $y = u(x)v(x)$ is the product of two separate functions of x; u and v. Any small change, δx, in the value of x will give rise to corresponding small changes, δu and δv, in the values of functions u and v respectively. These in turn result in a small change, δy, in the value of y, such that

$$\begin{aligned}\delta y &= (y + \delta y) - y \\ &= u(x + \delta x)v(x + \delta x) - u(x)v(x)\end{aligned}$$

Since $y + \delta y = u(x + \delta x)v(x + \delta x)$ is the value of the function corresponding to $x + \delta x$.

It is possible to rewrite this expression for δy in the form

$$\delta y = u(x + \delta x)v(x + \delta x) - u(x + \delta x)v(x) + v(x)u(x + \delta x) - u(x)v(x)$$

Adding the terms $-u(x + \delta x)v(x)$ and $v(x)u(x + \delta x)$. Notice that these terms cancel.

It follows then that

$$\delta y = u(x + \delta x)[v(x + \delta x) - v(x)] + v(x)[u(x + \delta x) - u(x)]$$

Differentiating from first principles,

$$\begin{aligned}\frac{dy}{dx} &= \lim_{\delta x \to 0}\left(\frac{\delta y}{\delta x}\right) \\ &= \lim_{\delta x \to 0}\left[u(x + \delta x)\left(\frac{v(x + \delta x) - v(x)}{\delta x}\right)\right] \\ &\quad + \lim_{\delta x \to 0}\left[v(x)\left(\frac{u(x + \delta x) - u(x)}{\delta x}\right)\right] \\ &= \lim_{\delta x \to 0}[u(x + \delta x)] \times \lim_{\delta x \to 0}\left[\frac{v(x + \delta x) - v(x)}{\delta x}\right] \\ &\quad + v(x) \times \lim_{\delta x \to 0}\left[\frac{u(x + \delta x) - u(x)}{\delta x}\right] \\ &= u(x) \times \frac{dv}{dx} + v(x) \times \frac{du}{dx}\end{aligned}$$

As $\delta x \to 0$,

$$u(x + \delta x) \to u(x)$$

$$\frac{v(x + \delta x) - v(x)}{\delta x} \to \frac{dv}{dx}$$

$$\frac{u(x + \delta x) - u(x)}{\delta x} \to \frac{du}{dx}$$

The **product rule** for differentiating functions of the form $y = u(x)v(x)$ can be stated as

$$\textbf{If } y = uv, \textbf{ then } \frac{dy}{dx} = u\frac{dv}{dx} + v\frac{du}{dx}.$$

Using the abbreviations u' and v' for $\frac{du}{dx}$ and $\frac{dv}{dx}$ respectively, the product rule is more commonly stated as

$$\textbf{If } y = uv, \textbf{ then } \frac{dy}{dx} = uv' + vu'$$

◀ **Learn this important result.**

Example 1

Using the product rule, differentiate $y = (2x + 3)(x - 1)^4$ with respect to x.

Solution

Let $y = uv$ where $u = (2x + 3)$ and $v = (x - 1)^4$. Then $u' = 2$ and $v' = 4(x - 1)^3$.

Remember to use the chain rule to find v'.

Using the product rule,

$$\begin{aligned}\frac{dy}{dx} &= uv' + vu' \\ &= (2x+3) \times 4(x-1)^3 + (x-1)^4 \times 2 \\ &= 4(2x+3)(x-1)^3 + 2(x-1)^4 \\ &= 2(x-1)^3[2(2x+3) + (x-1)] \\ &= 2(x-1)^3(5x+5) \\ &= 10(x+1)(x-1)^3\end{aligned}$$

Spot the common factor $2(x - 1)^3$.

Factorise the expression as much as possible.

An advantage of the product rule is that it is usually possible to get a factorised expression for $\frac{dy}{dx}$. This is particularly useful when trying to locate and determine the nature of any stationary points.

Example 2

Find the gradient of the curve $y = x^2 \cos x$ when $x = \pi$.

Solution

Let $y = uv$ where $u = x^2$ and $v = \cos x$. Then $u' = 2x$ and $v' = -\sin x$.

Using the product rule,

$$\begin{aligned}\frac{dy}{dx} &= uv' + vu' \\ &= x^2 \times (-\sin x) + \cos x \times 2x \\ &= -x^2 \sin x + 2x \cos x \\ &= x(2\cos x - x\sin x)\end{aligned}$$

When $x = \pi$, the gradient of the curve $y = x^2 \cos x$ is

$$\frac{dy}{dx} = \pi(2\cos\pi - \pi\sin\pi)$$
$$= -2\pi$$

Recall the special angles: $\cos\pi = -1$ and $\sin\pi = 0$.

The quotient rule

Suppose $y = \frac{u(x)}{v(x)}$ is the quotient of two separate functions of x; u and v. This can be rewritten as the product of u and $\frac{1}{v}$, such that

$$y = \frac{u}{v} = u \times \frac{1}{v}$$

Using the product rule to differentiate $y = u \times \frac{1}{v}$ gives

$$\frac{dy}{dx} = u\frac{d}{dx}\left(\frac{1}{v}\right) + \frac{1}{v}\frac{du}{dx}$$
$$= u \times -\frac{1}{v^2}\frac{dv}{dx} + \frac{1}{v}\frac{du}{dx}$$
$$= -\frac{u}{v^2}\frac{dv}{dx} + \frac{v}{v^2}\frac{du}{dx}$$
$$= \frac{1}{v^2}\left[-u\frac{dv}{dx} + v\frac{du}{dx}\right]$$

Using the chain rule,

$$\frac{d}{dx}\left(\frac{1}{v}\right) = \frac{d}{dv}\left(\frac{1}{v}\right) \times \frac{dv}{dx}$$
$$= -\frac{1}{v^2}\frac{dv}{dx}$$

The common denominator is v^2.

So we have the **quotient rule** for differentiating functions of the form $y = \frac{u(x)}{v(x)}$.

If $y = \frac{u}{v}$, then $\frac{dy}{dx} = \frac{1}{v^2}\left[v\frac{du}{dx} - u\frac{dv}{dx}\right]$

This is more commonly written as

If $y = \frac{u}{v}$, then $\frac{dy}{dx} = \frac{vu' - uv'}{v^2}$

◀ **Learn this important result.**

Example 3

Use the quotient rule to differentiate the following functions with respect to x:

a $y = \frac{3x+1}{x-2}$ **b** $y = \frac{\sqrt{x}}{2x+5}$ **c** $y = \frac{\sin 2x}{x^2}$

Solution

a Let $y = \frac{u}{v}$, where $u = 3x + 1$ and $v = x - 2$. Then $u' = 3$ and $v' = 1$.

Using the quotient rule,

$$\frac{dy}{dx} = \frac{vu' - uv'}{v^2}$$

$$= \frac{(x-2) \times 3 - (3x+1) \times 1}{(x-2)^2}$$

$$= \frac{3x - 6 - 3x - 1}{(x-2)^2}$$

$$= \frac{-7}{(x-2)^2}$$

b Let $y = \frac{u}{v}$ where $u = \sqrt{x}$ and $v = 2x + 5$. Then $u' = \frac{1}{2\sqrt{x}}$ and $v' = 2$.

Using the quotient rule,

$$\frac{dy}{dx} = \frac{vu' - uv'}{v^2}$$

$$= \frac{(2x+5) \times \dfrac{1}{2\sqrt{x}} - \sqrt{x} \times 2}{(2x+5)^2}$$

$$= \frac{1}{(2x+5)^2} \times \left[\frac{(2x+5)}{2\sqrt{x}} - 2\sqrt{x}\right]$$

$$= \frac{1}{(2x+5)^2} \times \left[\frac{(2x+5) - (2\sqrt{x})(2\sqrt{x})}{2\sqrt{x}}\right]$$

Common denominator is $2\sqrt{x}$.

$$= \frac{2x + 5 - 4x}{2\sqrt{x}(2x+5)^2}$$

$$= \frac{5 - 2x}{2\sqrt{x}(2x+5)^2}$$

c Let $y = \frac{u}{v}$ where $u = \sin 2x$ and $v = x^2$. Then $u' = 2\cos 2x$ and $v' = 2x$.

Using the quotient rule,

$$\frac{dy}{dx} = \frac{vu' - uv'}{v^2}$$

$$= \frac{x^2 \times 2\cos 2x - \sin 2x \times 2x}{(x^2)^2}$$

$$= \frac{2x^2 \cos 2x - 2x \sin 2x}{x^4}$$

$$= \frac{2x(x\cos 2x - \sin 2x)}{x^4}$$

$$= \frac{2(x\cos 2x - \sin 2x)}{x^3}$$

11.1 Differentiating Products and Quotients

Exercise

Technique

1 Use the product and quotient rules to differentiate each of the following with respect to x:

a $y = x(x+4)^6$

b $y = (4x+3)(x+1)^4$

c $y = (x-6)\sqrt{x-1}$

d $y = x^3 \sin 2x$

e $y = \frac{2x+1}{x-3}$

f $y = \frac{3x}{(x-2)^2}$

g $y = \frac{\sin x}{2x}$

h $y = \frac{\sin 3x}{\cos 2x}$

1 c, d

2 Find the gradient of each of the following curves at the points indicated:

a $y = 3x(x-4)^3$ at $(5, 15)$

b $y = (x-3)(x+2)^4$ at $(-3, -6)$

c $y = \frac{x+5}{2x+7}$ at $(1, \frac{2}{3})$

d $y = \frac{x^3}{x-2}$ at $(-2, 2)$

e $y = (2x-3)\sin x$ at $(\frac{\pi}{2}, \pi - 3)$

f $y = (1-2x)\sqrt{x}$ at $(4, -14)$

Contextual

1 Find the equations of the tangent and the normal to the following curves at the points indicated:

a $y = \frac{x+2}{2x-5}$ at $(2, -4)$

b $y = (x-2)(x+4)^3$ at $(-3, -5)$

c $y = x^2 \cos x$ at $(\pi, -\pi^2)$

d $y = \frac{x^2}{x^2+3}$ at $(-1, \frac{1}{4})$

11.2 Differentiating Exponentials and Logarithms

Exponential functions

In Chapter 7, exponential functions were used to model growth and depreciation. Real-life applications include population changes, radioactive decay, temperature cooling and compound interest calculations. You need to be able to differentiate these functions in order to calculate their rates of change at particular points.

Suppose $y = a^x$ where a is some positive constant. Any small change, δx, in the value of x gives rise to a small change, δy, in the value of y, such that

$$\begin{aligned}\delta y &= (y + \delta y) - y \\ &= a^{x+\delta x} - a^x \\ &= a^x a^{\delta x} - a^x \\ &= a^x(a^{\delta x} - 1)\end{aligned}$$

Recall that $a^{m+n} = a^{m}$

Differentiating from first principles,

$$\begin{aligned}\frac{\mathrm{d}y}{\mathrm{d}x} &= \lim_{\delta x \to 0}\left(\frac{\delta y}{\delta x}\right) \\ &= \lim_{\delta x \to 0}\left[\frac{a^x(a^{\delta x} - 1)}{\delta x}\right] \\ &= a^x \lim_{\delta x \to 0}\left(\frac{a^{\delta x} - 1}{\delta x}\right)\end{aligned}$$

This means the derivative of any exponential function $y = a^x$ is the product of a^x itself and a factor $\lim_{\delta x \to 0}\left(\frac{a^{\delta x}-1}{\delta x}\right)$ to be determined. Notice that this factor is dependent on the value of a.

Use a calculator to find values of $\frac{(a^{\delta x}-1)}{\delta x}$ for $a = 2$, 3 and 4 when $\delta x = 0.1$, 0.01, 0.001, 0.0001 and 0.000 01. Investigate what happens as $\delta x \to 0$. Tabulate the results as follows:

	$a = 2$	$a = 2.5$	$a = 2.7$	$a = 2.8$	$a = 3$	$a = 4$
$\delta x = 0.1$	0.717 73				1.161 23	1.486 98
$\delta x = 0.01$	0.695 56				1.104 67	1.395 95
$\delta x = 0.001$	0.693 39				1.099 22	1.387 26
$\delta x = 0.0001$	0.693 17				1.098 67	1.386 39
$\delta x = 0.000\,01$	0.693 15				1.098 62	1.386 30
limit as $\delta x \to 0$	0.693 15				1.098 61	1.386 29

Notice that as $\delta x \to 0$, the factor $\frac{a^{\delta x}-1}{\delta x}$ converges to a limiting value, which is different for each value of a. For example,

$$\frac{\mathrm{d}}{\mathrm{d}x}(2^x) \approx 0.69315 \times 2^x$$

$$\frac{\mathrm{d}}{\mathrm{d}x}(3^x) \approx 1.09861 \times 3^x$$

This suggests that there is a value of a between 2 and 3 for which $\lim_{\delta x \to 0}\left(\frac{a^{\delta x}-1}{\delta x}\right) = 1$. For this particular value of a, it follows that $\frac{\mathrm{d}}{\mathrm{d}x}(a^x) = a^x$.

Use a calculator to complete the above table of values of $\frac{a^{\delta x}-1}{\delta x}$ for $a = 2.5$, 2.7 and 2.8. By further trial and improvement, find the value of a, correct to three decimal places, for which $\lim_{\delta x \to 0}\left(\frac{a^{\delta x}-1}{\delta x}\right) = 1$.

This value of a is an irrational number. Its value is $\mathrm{e} = 2.718\,281\,8$, correct to seven decimal places. It follows that

$$\lim_{\delta x \to 0}\left(\frac{\mathrm{e}^{\delta x}-1}{\delta x}\right) = 1.$$

This means that the derivative of *the* exponential function $y = \mathrm{e}^x$ is

$$\frac{\mathrm{d}}{\mathrm{d}x}(\mathrm{e}^x) = \mathrm{e}^x$$

◀ **Learn this important result.**

The exponential function is the only function that remains unaltered when differentiated.

An alternative way of establishing this result is to use the series expansion of e^x introduced in Chapter 7:

$$\mathrm{e}^x = 1 + \frac{x}{1!} + \frac{x^2}{2!} + \frac{x^3}{3!} + \frac{x^4}{4!} + \ldots$$

Differentiating this infinite power series term by term,

$$\frac{\mathrm{d}}{\mathrm{d}x}(\mathrm{e}^x) = 0 + \frac{1}{1!} + \frac{2x}{2!} + \frac{3x^2}{3!} + \frac{4x^3}{4!} + \dots$$
$$= 1 + \frac{x}{1!} + \frac{x^2}{2!} + \frac{x^3}{3!} + \dots$$
$$= \mathrm{e}^x$$

It can also be shown that the derivative of any exponential function of the form $y = a^x$ is

$$\frac{\mathrm{d}}{\mathrm{d}x}(a^x) = a^x \ln a$$

◀ **Learn this important result.**

This confirms that $\frac{\mathrm{d}}{\mathrm{d}x}(\mathrm{e}^x) = \mathrm{e}^x$, because $\ln e = 1$.

This means that $\lim_{\delta x \to 0}\left(\frac{a^{\delta x} - 1}{\delta x}\right) = \ln a$.

The chain rule can be used to differentiate exponential functions of the form $y = e^{f(x)}$, where $f(x)$ is some function of x.
Let $y = \mathrm{e}^u$, where $u = f(x)$. Then $\frac{\mathrm{d}y}{\mathrm{d}u} = \mathrm{e}^u$ and $\frac{\mathrm{d}u}{\mathrm{d}x} = f'(x)$

Using the chain rule,

$$\frac{\mathrm{d}y}{\mathrm{d}x} = \frac{\mathrm{d}y}{\mathrm{d}u} \times \frac{\mathrm{d}u}{\mathrm{d}x}$$
$$= e^u \times f'(x)$$
$$= f'(x)\mathrm{e}^{f(x)}$$

◀ **Derivative of the power × original exponential function**

Example 1

Differentiate each of the following with respect to x:

a $y = \mathrm{e}^{3x+1}$
b $y = \mathrm{e}^{\sin x}$
c $y = 3^{2x}$

Solution

a Let $y = \mathrm{e}^u$ where $u = 3x + 1$. Then $\frac{\mathrm{d}y}{\mathrm{d}u} = \mathrm{e}^u$ and $\frac{\mathrm{d}u}{\mathrm{d}x} = 3$.

Using the chain rule,

$$\frac{\mathrm{d}y}{\mathrm{d}x} = \frac{\mathrm{d}y}{\mathrm{d}u} \times \frac{\mathrm{d}u}{\mathrm{d}x}$$
$$= \mathrm{e}^u \times 3$$
$$= 3\mathrm{e}^{3x+1}$$

b Let $y = e^u$ where $u = \sin x$. Then $\frac{dy}{du} = e^u$ and $\frac{du}{dx} = \cos x$.

Using the chain rule,

$$\frac{dy}{dx} = \frac{dy}{du} \times \frac{du}{dx}$$

$$= e^u \cos x$$

$$= \cos x \times e^{\sin x}$$

Check these results using the general result for differentiating a^x on p. 440.

c Let $y = 3^u$ where $u = 2x$. Then $\frac{dy}{du} = 3^u \ln 3$ and $\frac{du}{dx} = 2$.

Using the chain rule,

$$\frac{dy}{dx} = \frac{dy}{du} \times \frac{du}{dx}$$

$$= 3^u \ln 3 \times 2$$

$$= 3^{2x} \times 2 \ln 3$$

Recall the laws of logarithms: $n \ln a = \ln a^n$

We can use the product and quotient rules to differentiate functions involving the multiplication, or division, of an exponential function with a polynomial or trigonometric function.

Example 2

Find the derivatives of the following functions:

a $y = xe^x$
b $y = \frac{(3x+2)}{e^x}$
c $x = e^{2t} \cos 3t$

Solution

a Let $y = uv$, where $u = x$ and $v = e^x$. Then $u' = 1$ and $v' = e^x$.

Using the product rule,

$$\frac{dy}{dx} = uv' + vu'$$

$$= xe^x + e^x$$

$$= (x + 1)e^x$$

b Let $y = \frac{u}{v}$ where $u = (3x + 2)$ and $v = e^x$. Then $u' = 3$ and $v' = e^x$.

Using the quotient rule,

$$\begin{aligned}\frac{dy}{dx} &= \frac{vu' - uv'}{v^2}\\ &= \frac{3e^x - (3x+2)e^x}{(e^x)^2}\\ &= \frac{(1-3x)e^x}{(e^x)^2}\\ &= \frac{1-3x}{e^x}\end{aligned}$$

c Let $x = uv$, where $u = e^{2t}$ and $v = \cos 3t$. Then $u' = \frac{du}{dt} = 2e^{2t}$ and $v' = \frac{dv}{dt} = -3\sin 3t$.

Using the product rule,

$$\begin{aligned}\frac{dx}{dt} &= uv' + vu'\\ &= -3e^{2t}\sin 3t + 2e^{2t}\cos 3t\\ &= e^{2t}(2\cos 3t - 3\sin 3t)\end{aligned}$$

Common factor of e^{2t}

Example 3

As a result of a slump in the housing market, a property initially valued at £60 000 on 1 January depreciates. Its value t weeks later can be modelled by $V = 60\,000e^{kt}$ where its value is £V and k is a constant to be determined. Exactly one year later, the property remains unsold and is valued at only £50 000.

a Find an expression for k.

b Find the market value of the property after 26 weeks to the nearest pound.

c Find an expression for $\frac{dV}{dt}$. Then find the rate at which the property's value is depreciating at the start and end of the year to the nearest pound.

Solution

a After one year, when $t = 52$, $V = 50\,000$.
Substituting into the expression for V gives

$$50\,000 = 60\,000e^{52k}$$

$$\Rightarrow \quad e^{52k} = \tfrac{5}{6}$$

$$\Rightarrow \quad 52k = \ln\left(\tfrac{5}{6}\right)$$

$$\Rightarrow \quad k = \tfrac{1}{52}\ln\left(\tfrac{5}{6}\right)$$

Take logarithms of both sides.

$k \approx -0.0035$; a negative value is expected for depreciation.

b When $t = 26$

$$\begin{aligned}V &= 60\,000e^{26k}\\ &= 60\,000e^{\frac{1}{2}\ln\left(\frac{5}{6}\right)}\\ &= £54\,772\end{aligned}$$

c Given that $V = 60\,000e^{kt}$, where $k = \frac{1}{52}\ln(\frac{5}{6})$, differentiate V with respect to t.

$$\frac{dV}{dt} = 60\,000ke^{kt}$$

$$= \tfrac{60\,000}{52}\ln(\tfrac{5}{6})e^{\frac{t}{52}\ln(\frac{5}{6})}$$

At the start of the year, $t = 0$. The rate at which the property's value is depreciating is found by putting $t = 0$ into this expression.
Check that

$$\frac{dV}{dt} = \tfrac{60\,000}{52}\ln(\tfrac{5}{6})e^{0}$$

$$= -210.37$$

To the nearest pound, the rate of depreciation is £210 per week.
Carry out a similar calculation by substituting $t = 52$. Verify that after one year, the rate of depreciation is £175 per week

Logarithmic functions

To differentiate the natural logarithmic function $y = \ln x$ from first principles, consider the small change, δy, in the value of this function that results from a small change, δx, in the value of x.

$$\text{Since}\quad \delta y = (y + \delta y) - y$$

$$= \ln(x + \delta x) - \ln x,$$

where $y + \delta y = \ln(x + \delta x)$ is the value of the function corresponding to $x + \delta x$, it follows that

$$\frac{dy}{dx} = \lim_{\delta x \to 0}\left(\frac{\delta y}{\delta x}\right)$$

$$= \lim_{\delta x \to 0}\left[\frac{\ln(x + \delta x) - \ln x}{\delta x}\right]$$

Unfortunately there is no easy way of expanding the $\ln(x + \delta x)$ term in this expression. An alternative approach must be taken in order to find $\frac{dy}{dx}$.
Recall that the natural logarithmic function $y = \ln x$ is the inverse of the exponential function $y = e^x$.
If $y = \ln x$, then $x = e^y$.
Differentiating both sides with respect to y,

$$\frac{dx}{dy} = e^y$$

This means that

$$\frac{dy}{dx} = \frac{1}{e^y} \quad \blacktriangleleft \text{ Using } \frac{dy}{dx} = \frac{1}{\left(\frac{dx}{dy}\right)}$$

$$= \frac{1}{x}$$

Using $x = e^y$

The derivative of the natural logarithmic function $y = \ln x$ is

$$\frac{d}{dx}(\ln x) = \frac{1}{x}$$

◀ **Learn this important result.**

Natural logarithmic functions of the form $y = \ln(f(x))$, where $f(x)$ is some function of x, can be differentiated using the chain rule.

Let $y = \ln u$, where $u = f(x)$. Then $\frac{dy}{du} = \frac{1}{u}$ and $\frac{du}{dx} = f'(x)$.
Using the chain rule,

$$\frac{dy}{dx} = \frac{dy}{du} \times \frac{du}{dx}$$

$$= \frac{1}{u} \times f'(x)$$

$$= \frac{f'(x)}{f(x)}$$

Derivative of function ÷ original function

Therefore

$$\frac{d}{dx}[\ln f(x)] = \frac{f'(x)}{f(x)}$$

◀ **Learn this important result.**

We will use this result in Chapter 12 to integrate some quotient functions.

The function $\ln x$ is widely used in mathematics. Logarithmic functions that use other bases, such as $\log_{10} x$ with base 10, can also be differentiated.

Suppose $y = \log_a x$

Then $x = a^y$

Base a.

Differentiating both sides with respect to y gives

$$\frac{dx}{dy} = a^y \ln a$$

Note the natural logarithm.

So $$\frac{dy}{dx} = \frac{1}{a^y \ln a}$$

$$= \frac{1}{x \ln a}$$

Using $x = a^y$.

So, for example,

$$\frac{d}{dx}(\log_{10} x) = \frac{1}{x \ln 10}$$

◀ **Learn this result.**

Example 4

Differentiate the following with respect to x:

a $y = \ln(x^2 + 3x - 2)$

b $y = \ln(\cos x)$

c $y = x \ln x$

d $y = \frac{(\ln x)}{e^x}$

e $y = \log_{10}(x^2 + 1)$

Solution

Use $\frac{d}{dx}[\ln f(x)] = \frac{f'(x)}{f(x)}$.

a $y = \ln(x^2 + 3x - 2) \Rightarrow \frac{dy}{dx} = \frac{2x+3}{x^2+3x-2}$

b $y = \ln(\cos x) \Rightarrow \frac{dy}{dx} = \frac{-\sin x}{\cos x} = -\tan x$

c Let $y = uv$, where $u = x$ and $v = \ln x$. Then $u' = 1$ and $v' = \frac{1}{x}$.

Using the product rule, $\frac{dy}{dx} = uv' + vu'$

$$= x\left(\frac{1}{x}\right) + \ln x$$

$$= 1 + \ln x$$

d Let $y = \frac{u}{v}$ where $u = \ln x$ and $v = e^x$. Then $u' = \frac{1}{x}$ and $v' = e^x$.

Using the quotient rule, $\frac{dy}{dx} = \frac{vu' - uv'}{v^2}$

$$= \frac{1}{(e^x)^2}\left[e^x\left(\frac{1}{x}\right) - e^x \ln x\right]$$

Common factor e^x.

$$= \frac{1}{e^x}\left(\frac{1}{x} - \ln x\right)$$

Take out factor $\frac{1}{x}$.

$$= \frac{1}{e^x} \times \frac{1}{x}(1 - x\ln x)$$

$$= \frac{(1 - x\ln x)}{xe^x}$$

e Let $y = \log_{10} u$, where $u = (x^2 + 1)$. Then $\frac{dy}{du} = \frac{1}{u \ln 10}$ and $\frac{du}{dx} = 2x$.

Using the chain rule, $\frac{dy}{dx} = \frac{dy}{du} \times \frac{du}{dx}$

$$= \frac{1}{u \ln 10} \times 2x$$

$$= \frac{2x}{(x^2 + 1)\ln 10}$$

11.2 Differentiation of Exponentials and Logarithms

Exercise

Technique

1 Differentiate each of the following with respect to x:

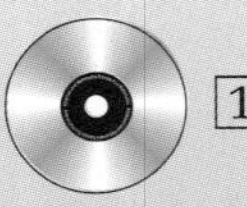
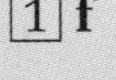

1f

a $y = e^{2x-3}$
b $y = e^{x^3}$
c $y = e^{1-5x}$
d $y = e^{\cos x}$
e $y = 4^{-x}$
f $y = x^2 e^{-x}$
g $y = e^{-x/2} \sin x$
h $y = \frac{e^x + 1}{x^2}$
i $y = e^x \sin 2x$
j $y = \frac{\cos^2 x}{e^x}$

2 Differentiate each of the following with respect to x:

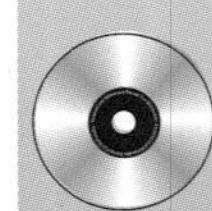

2 f, h

a $y = \ln(4x)$
b $y = \ln(x^4)$
c $y = \ln(x^5)$
d $y = \ln(4x + 1)$
e $y = \ln(x^4 + 1)$
f $y = \ln(\sin x)$
g $y = x^2 \ln x$
h $y = \frac{\ln x}{x^2}$
i $y = \ln(1 + x) - \ln(1 - x)$
j $y = \log_{10}(3x - 4)$

3 For each of the following curves:

i find expressions for $\frac{dy}{dx}$ and $\frac{d^2y}{dx^2}$
ii locate and determine the nature of any stationary points.

a $y = (2x + 1)e^x$
b $y = \ln(x + 2) + \frac{1}{(x + 2)}$
c $y = e^x \sin x \ (-\pi \le x \le \pi)$
d $y = (x + 1)^3 e^{-x}$

Contextual

1 Find the equations of the tangent and the normal to the following curves at the points indicated:

a $y = \ln(3x + 1)$ at $x = 1$
b $y = 3e^{2x+3}$ at $x = -1$
c $y = x^2 \ln x$ at $x = e$
d $y = (x + 1)e^{-x}$ at $x = 2$

2 The population, P, of a new town development grows exponentially for the first 25 years such that $P = 1000 + 200e^{0.13t}$, where t is the number of years since its establishment.

a What is the initial population of the town?
b What is its population after 10 and 20 years?
c Find an expression for the rate at which the population increases at any time t. Use this to calculate the rate of increase after 10 and 20 years.

d Calculate, to the nearest month, how long after its establishment it is before the rate of increase in the population reaches 200 people per year.

3 A ball-bearing is released from rest from the surface of a large tank of oil into which it drops. After t seconds it has reached a depth d centimetres, where $d = 6t - 4e^{-1.5t} + 4$.

a Calculate the depth of the ball-bearing to the nearest millimetre, after 1, 2 and 3 seconds.

b Find expressions for the velocity, v, and acceleration, a, of the ball-bearing after t seconds

c Calculate its velocity and acceleration after 0.5 seconds

d Explain what happens to the acceleration and velocity as t becomes large.

4 The price £P of a particular laptop computer t weeks after its release is given by $P = 1100 + 3t - 30\ln(t + 2)$.

a After how many weeks does the price reach its lowest value? What is the minimum price?

b How much is the laptop after six months and what is the rate at which P is changing at this time?

11.3 Further Trigonometric Differentiation

Differentiating tan and cot

It is possible to find the derivative of the tangent function from first principles, but now that we know the quotient rule we can also express $\tan x$ as $\frac{\sin x}{\cos x}$ to differentiate it.

Suppose $y = \frac{u}{v}$ where $u = \sin x$ and $v = \cos x$. Then $u' = \cos x$ and $v' = -\sin x$.

Using the quotient rule,

$$\begin{aligned}\frac{dy}{dx} &= \frac{vu' - uv'}{v^2}\\ &= \frac{(\cos x)(\cos x) - (\sin x)(-\sin x)}{\cos^2 x}\\ &= \frac{\cos^2 x + \sin^2 x}{\cos^2 x}\\ &= \frac{1}{\cos^2 x}\\ &= \sec^2 x\end{aligned}$$

$\sin^2 x + \cos^2 x \equiv 1$

So the derivative of the tangent function,

$$\frac{d}{dx}(\tan x) = \sec^2 x$$

◀ **Learn this result.**

The derivative of the cotangent function, $\cot x$, can also be found this way. Write $\cot x$ as $\frac{\cos x}{\sin x}$ and use the quotient rule. Since $\cot x = \frac{1}{\tan x}$, it is also possible to use the chain rule. Verify that:

$$\frac{d}{dx}(\cot x) = -\text{cosec}^2 x$$

Verify this result using the quotient rule.

The chain rule can also be used to differentiate composite functions involving $\tan x$ and $\cot x$.

Example 1

Differentiate each of the following with respect to x:

a $y = \tan 2x$
b $y = \cot(x^3 + 2)$
c $y = 2\tan^3 x$

Solution

a Let $y = \tan u$, where $u = 2x$. Then $\frac{dy}{du} = \sec^2 u$ and $\frac{du}{dx} = 2$.

Using the chain rule, $\frac{dy}{dx} = \frac{dy}{du} \times \frac{du}{dx}$

$$= 2\sec^2 u$$

$$= 2\sec^2 2x$$

b Let $y = \cot u$, where $u = (x^3 + 2)$. Then $\frac{dy}{du} = -\text{cosec}^2 u$ and $\frac{du}{dx} = 3x^2$.

Using the chain rule, $\frac{dy}{dx} = \frac{dy}{du} \times \frac{du}{dx}$

$$= -\text{cosec}^2 u \times 3x^2$$

$$= -3x^2 \text{cosec}^2 (x^3 + 2)$$

c Let $y = 2u^3$, where $u = \tan x$. Then $\frac{dy}{du} = 6u^2$ and $\frac{du}{dx} = \sec^2 x$.

Using the chain rule, $\frac{dy}{dx} = \frac{dy}{du} \times \frac{du}{dx}$

$$= 6u^2 \times \sec^2 x$$

$$= 6\tan^2 x \sec^2 x$$

Differentiating cosec and sec

The derivatives of the two other reciprocal trigonometric functions, $\text{cosec}\, x = \frac{1}{\sin x}$ and $\sec x = \frac{1}{\cos x}$, can also be found using the chain rule.

Let $y = \frac{1}{u}$, where $u = \sin x$. Then $\frac{dy}{du} = -\frac{1}{u^2}$ and $\frac{du}{dx} = \cos x$.

Using the chain rule, $\frac{dy}{dx} = \frac{dy}{du} \times \frac{du}{dx}$

$$= -\frac{1}{u^2} \times \cos x$$

$$= -\frac{\cos x}{\sin^2 x}$$

$$= -\frac{1}{\sin x} \times \frac{\cos x}{\sin x}$$

$$= -\text{cosec}\, x \cot x$$

So $\mathbf{\frac{d}{dx}(\text{cosec}\, x) = -\text{cosec}\, x \cot x}$ ◀ **Learn this result.**

Now find the derivative of $\sec x$.

Let $y = \frac{1}{u}$, where $u = \cos x$. Then $\frac{dy}{du} = -\frac{1}{u^2}$ and $\frac{du}{dx} = -\sin x$

Using the chain rule, $\frac{dy}{dx} = \frac{dy}{du} \times \frac{du}{dx}$

$$= -\frac{1}{u^2} \times -\sin x$$

$$= \frac{\sin x}{\cos^2 x}$$

$$= \frac{1}{\cos x} \times \frac{\sin x}{\cos x}$$

$$= \sec x \tan x$$

So $\boldsymbol{\frac{d}{dx}(\sec x) = \sec x \tan x}$ ◀ **Learn this result.**

These results allow the chain rule to be used to differentiate composite functions involving cosec and sec.

Example 2

Differentiate each of the following with respect to x:

a $y = \text{cosec}\, 4x$ **b** $y = \sec(x^2)$ **c** $y = \sec^3(5x)$

Solution

a Let $y = \text{cosec}\, u$, where $u = 4x$. Then $\frac{dy}{du} = -\text{cosec}\, u \cot u$ and $\frac{du}{dx} = 4$.

Using the chain rule, $\frac{dy}{dx} = \frac{dy}{du} \times \frac{du}{dx}$

$$= -4\text{cosec}\, u \cot u$$

$$= -4\text{cosec}\, 4x \cot 4x$$

b Let $y = \sec u$, where $u = x^2$. Then $\frac{dy}{du} = \sec u \tan u$ and $\frac{du}{dx} = 2x$.

Using the chain rule, $\frac{dy}{dx} = \frac{dy}{du} \times \frac{du}{dx}$

$$= \sec u \tan u \times 2x$$

$$= 2x \sec(x^2) \tan(x^2)$$

c Let $y = u^3$, where $u = \sec 5x$. Then $\frac{dy}{du} = 3u^2$ and $\frac{du}{dx} = 5 \sec 5x \tan 5x$

Using the chain rule to differentiate sec $5x$.

Using the chain rule, $\frac{dy}{dx} = \frac{dy}{du} \times \frac{du}{dx}$

$$= 3u^2 \times 5 \sec 5x \tan 5x$$

$$= 15 \sec^3 5x \tan 5x$$

The product and quotient rules can be used to differentiate any function involving the multiplication, or division, of one of these trigonometric function with some other 'standard function'.

Example 3

Find the derivatives of each of the following functions:

a $y = 2x\tan x$ **b** $y = \frac{\operatorname{cosec} x}{x}$ **c** $y = \tan 3x \sec x$

Solution

a Let $y = uv$, where $u = 2x$ and $v = \tan x$. Then $u' = 2$ and $v' = \sec^2 x$.

Using the product rule,
$$\begin{aligned}\frac{dy}{dx} &= uv' + vu' \\ &= 2x\sec^2 x + 2\tan x \\ &= 2(x\sec^2 x + \tan x)\end{aligned}$$

b Let $y = \frac{u}{v}$ where $u = \operatorname{cosec} x$ and $v = x$. Then $u' = -\operatorname{cosec} x \cot x$ and $v' = 1$.

Using the quotient rule,
$$\begin{aligned}\frac{dy}{dx} &= \frac{vu' - uv'}{v^2} \\ &= \frac{-x\operatorname{cosec} x\cot x - \operatorname{cosec} x}{x^2} \\ &= \frac{-\operatorname{cosec} x(x\cot x + 1)}{x^2}\end{aligned}$$

c Let $y = uv$, where $u = \tan 3x$ and $v = \sec x$. Then $u' = 3\sec^2 3x$ and $v' = \sec x\tan x$.

Using the chain rule to differentiate $\tan 3x$.

Using the product rule,
$$\begin{aligned}\frac{dy}{dx} &= uv' + vu' \\ &= \tan 3x\sec x\tan x + 3\sec^2 3x\sec x \\ &= \sec x(\tan 3x\tan x + 3\sec^2 3x)\end{aligned}$$

Differentiating inverse trigonometric functions

If $y = \sin^{-1} x$, then $x = \sin y$. Differentiating both sides of this equation *with respect to y* gives

$$\frac{dx}{dy} = \cos y \Rightarrow \frac{dy}{dx} = \frac{1}{\cos y}$$

◀ Using $\frac{dy}{dx} = \frac{1}{\left(\frac{dx}{dy}\right)}$.

Now, $\cos^2 y + \sin^2 y \equiv 1$

$$\begin{aligned}\Rightarrow \quad \cos^2 y &= 1 - \sin^2 y \\ &= 1 - x^2\end{aligned}$$

That is, $\cos y = \sqrt{1 - x^2}$

Notice that only the positive root is taken. This is because $-\frac{\pi}{2} \le \sin^{-1} x \le \frac{\pi}{2}$, so $-\frac{\pi}{2} \le y \le \frac{\pi}{2}$, giving $\cos y \ge 0$.

So $\mathbf{\frac{d}{dx}(\sin^{-1} x) = \frac{1}{\sqrt{1 - x^2}}}$ ◀ **Learn this result.**

Differentiating $y = \cos^{-1} x$ in the same way,

$$\frac{\mathrm{d}}{\mathrm{d}x}(\cos^{-1} x) = -\frac{1}{\sqrt{1-x^2}}$$ ◀ Learn this result.

Verify this for yoursel using the same technique as for $y = \sin^{-1} x$.

If $y = \tan^{-1} x$, then $x = \tan y$. Differentiating both sides with respect to y gives

$$\frac{\mathrm{d}x}{\mathrm{d}y} = \sec^2 y \Rightarrow \frac{\mathrm{d}y}{\mathrm{d}x} = \frac{1}{\sec^2 y}$$

Since $\tan^2 y + 1 \equiv \sec^2 y$

$$\sec^2 y = 1 + x^2$$

Recall that $x = \tan y$.

So $$\frac{\mathrm{d}}{\mathrm{d}x}(\tan^{-1} x) = \frac{1}{1+x^2}$$ ◀ Learn this result.

This last result has applications in integration (see Chapter 12).

Example 4

Differentiate each of the following with respect to x:

a $y = \sin^{-1}(5x)$ **b** $y = \tan^{-1}(x^2)$
c $y = \sin^{-1}(\frac{x}{a})$ **d** $y = \tan^{-1}(\frac{x}{a})$

Solution

a Let $y = \sin^{-1} u$, where $u = 5x$. Then $\frac{\mathrm{d}y}{\mathrm{d}u} = \frac{1}{\sqrt{1-u^2}}$ and $\frac{\mathrm{d}u}{\mathrm{d}x} = 5$.

Using the chain rule, $$\frac{\mathrm{d}y}{\mathrm{d}x} = \frac{\mathrm{d}y}{\mathrm{d}u} \times \frac{\mathrm{d}u}{\mathrm{d}x} = \frac{1}{\sqrt{1-u^2}} \times 5 = \frac{5}{\sqrt{1-25x^2}}$$

Recall that $u = 5x$.

b Let $y = \tan^{-1} u$, where $u = x^2$. Then $\frac{\mathrm{d}y}{\mathrm{d}u} = \frac{1}{1+u^2}$ and $\frac{\mathrm{d}u}{\mathrm{d}x} = 2x$.

Using the chain rule, $$\frac{\mathrm{d}y}{\mathrm{d}x} = \frac{\mathrm{d}y}{\mathrm{d}u} \times \frac{\mathrm{d}u}{\mathrm{d}x} = \frac{1}{1+u^2} \times 2x = \frac{2x}{1+x^4}$$

c Let $y = \sin^{-1} u$, where $u = \frac{x}{a}$. Then $\frac{\mathrm{d}y}{\mathrm{d}u} = \frac{1}{\sqrt{1-u^2}}$ and $\frac{\mathrm{d}u}{\mathrm{d}x} = \frac{1}{a}$.

Using the chain rule, $$\frac{\mathrm{d}y}{\mathrm{d}x} = \frac{\mathrm{d}y}{\mathrm{d}u} \times \frac{\mathrm{d}u}{\mathrm{d}x} = \frac{1}{\sqrt{1-u^2}} \times \frac{1}{a} = \frac{1}{a\sqrt{1-\frac{x^2}{a^2}}} = \frac{1}{\sqrt{a^2-x^2}}$$

d Let $y = \tan^{-1} u$, where $u = \frac{x}{a}$. Then $\frac{dy}{du} = \frac{1}{1+u^2}$ and $\frac{du}{dx} = \frac{1}{a}$.

Using the chain rule,
$$\frac{dy}{dx} = \frac{dy}{du} \times \frac{du}{dx} = \frac{1}{1+u^2} \times \frac{1}{a}$$
$$= \frac{1}{a\left(1 + \frac{x^2}{a^2}\right)}$$
$$= \frac{a}{a^2 + x^2}$$

Multiply top and bottom by a.

Example 5

Use the product and quotient rules to differentiate each of the following:

a $y = x \sin^{-1} x$ **b** $y = \frac{\tan^{-1} x}{1+x^2}$

Solution

a Let $y = uv$, where $u = x$ and $v = \sin^{-1} x$. Then $u' = 1$ and $v' = \frac{1}{\sqrt{1-x^2}}$.

Using the product rule
$$\frac{dy}{dx} = uv' + vu'$$
$$= \frac{x}{\sqrt{1-x^2}} + \sin^{-1} x$$

b Let $y = \frac{u}{v}$, where $u = \tan^{-1} x$ and $v = 1 + x^2$. Then $u' = \frac{1}{1+x^2}$ and $v' = 2x$.

Using the quotient rule,
$$\frac{dy}{dx} = \frac{vu' - uv'}{v^2}$$
$$= \frac{\left(\frac{1+x^2}{1+x^2}\right) - 2x \tan^{-1} x}{(1+x^2)^2}$$
$$= \frac{1 - 2x \tan^{-1} x}{(1+x^2)^2}$$

11.3 Further Trigonometric Differentiation

Exercise

Technique

1 Differentiate each of the following with respect to x:

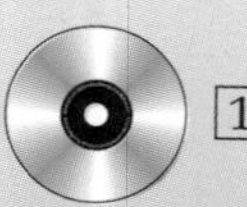

a $y = \tan 7x$

b $y = \sec 3x$

c $y = \cot(x^2)$

d $y = \operatorname{cosec}^2 5x$

e $y = \cos^{-1} 9x$

f $y = \sin^{-1}(1 - x)$

g $y = \tan^{-1} x^2$

h $y = \tan^{-1}(2x + 3)$

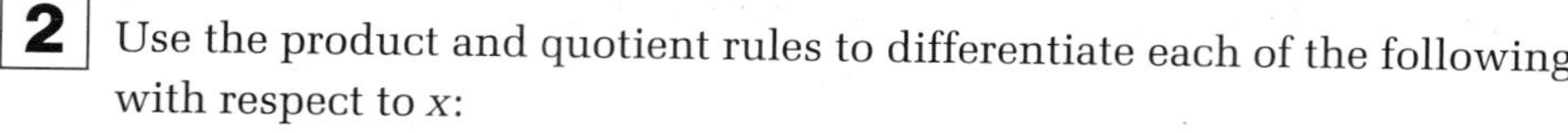

2 Use the product and quotient rules to differentiate each of the following with respect to x:

a $y = x^2 \tan x$

b $y = 5x \sec x$

c $y = 2x \sin^{-1} x$

d $y = x^3 \tan^{-1} x$

Contextual

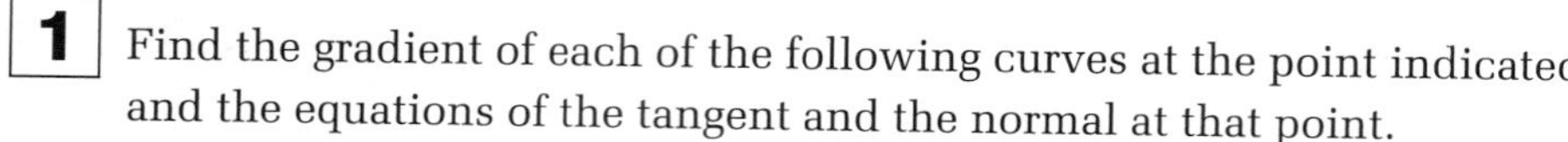

1 Find the gradient of each of the following curves at the point indicated and the equations of the tangent and the normal at that point.

a $y = \tan(\frac{x}{3})$ at $(\pi, \sqrt{3})$

b $y = \sin^{-1}(1 - x)$ at $(\frac{1}{2}, \frac{\pi}{6})$

c $y = x \sec x$ at $(\pi, -\pi)$

11.4 Using the Second Derivative

Stationary points

Recall from Chapter 5 that the stationary points on a graph can be located by solving the equation $\frac{dy}{dx} = 0$. Their nature can be determined by looking at the gradient of the graph on either side of each stationary point. It is also possible to use the second derivative to help decide whether a particular stationary point is a maximum or a minimum point.

The gradient of a curved graph is itself a function of x. By drawing the graphs of $y = f(x)$ and its gradient function $y = f'(x)$, it is possible to relate features that appear on the two graphs.

For example, sketch the graphs of the function $f(x) = x^3 - 3x^2 - 9x + 10$ and its derivative $f'(x) = 3x^2 - 6x - 9$. Check the nature of the stationary points as you draw the graphs. Check your results using a graphical calculator.

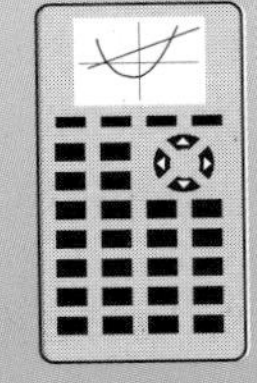

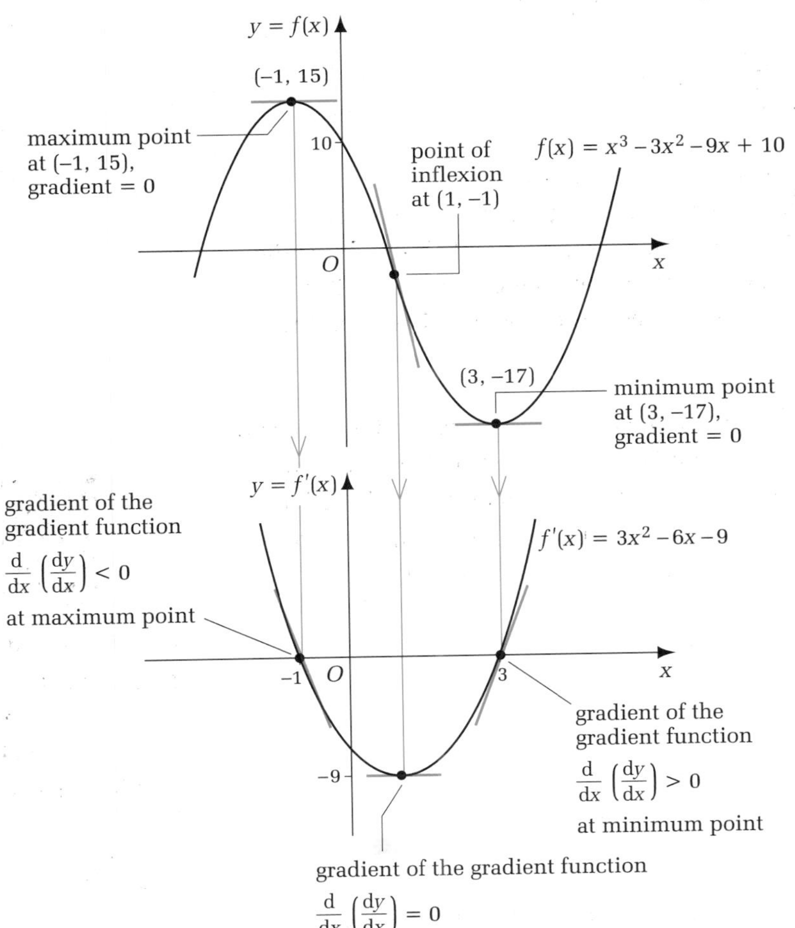

Notice that at the maximum point on the curve $y = x^3 - 3x^2 - 9x + 10$, the function changes from being an increasing function of x to a decreasing function of x. This 'negative' change in the gradient, from positive through zero to negative, as the curve passes through $(-1, 15)$, means that the 'gradient of the gradient function', or **second derivative**, is negative at the maximum point.

So at the maximum point on the curve, $\frac{d}{dx}\left(\frac{dy}{dx}\right) < 0$.

At a maximum point, $\frac{d^2y}{dx^2} < 0$ ◄ **Remember this important result.**

At the minimum point on the curve $y = x^3 - 3x^2 - 9x + 10$, the function changes from being a decreasing function of x to an increasing function of x. The corresponding change in the gradient is from negative through zero to positive as the curve passes through $(3, -17)$. This indicates that the 'gradient of the gradient function', or second derivative, is positive at the minimum point.

So at the minimum point on the curve, $\frac{d}{dx}\left(\frac{dy}{dx}\right) > 0$.

At a minimum point, $\frac{d^2y}{dx^2} > 0$ ◄ **Remember this important result.**

There is also a point of inflexion at $(1, -1)$ on the curve $y = x^3 - 3x^2 - 9x + 10$. This is where the tangent to the curve crosses from one side to another. This is not a stationary point. Instead it is the point at which the gradient of the curve is at its most negative. The 'gradient of the gradient function', or second derivative, is zero at this point of inflexion.

In fact $\frac{d^2y}{dx^2} = 0$ at all points of inflexion, whether they are stationary or not. It is possible, however, for the second derivative to equal zero at points that *are not* points of inflexion. Consider the graph of $y = x^4$. This has a stationary point at $x = 0$. Its second derivative $\frac{d^2y}{dx^2} = 12x^2$ equals zero when $x = 0$, but this stationary point is clearly a minimum.

Check this with a graphical calculator. Check also the graph c $y = -x^4$. This is a maximum at $x = 0$ where $\frac{d^2y}{dx^2} = 0$.

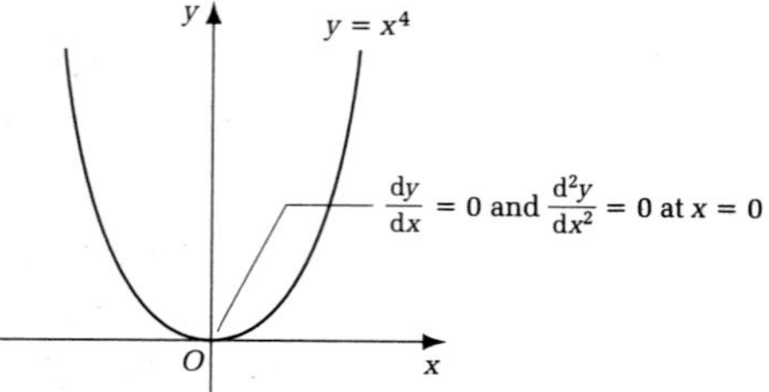

The only reliable way of determining the nature of a stationary point at which $\frac{d^2y}{dx^2} = 0$ is to look at the gradient, $\frac{dy}{dx}$, on either side of the point.

Summary

- $\frac{dy}{dx} = 0$ and $\frac{d^2y}{dx^2} < 0$ at maximum points
- $\frac{dy}{dx} = 0$ and $\frac{d^2y}{dx^2} > 0$ at minimum points
- if $\frac{dy}{dx} = 0$ and $\frac{d^2y}{dx^2} = 0$, the sign of the gradient, $\frac{dy}{dx}$, on either side of the stationary point must then be found to determine its nature – **do not assume that it is a stationary point of inflexion.**

Example 1

Find the coordinates of the stationary points on the curve $y = (x + 3)(x - 2)^4$. Use the second derivative to determine their nature. Sketch the curve.

Solution

Let $y = uv$ where $u = (x + 3)$ and $v = (x - 2)^4$. Then $u' = 1$ and $v' = 4(x - 2)^3$.

Use the chain rule to differentiate $(x - 2)^4$.

Using the product rule,
$$\begin{aligned}\frac{dy}{dx} &= uv' + vu' \\ &= (x + 3) \times 4(x - 2)^3 + (x - 2)^4 \times 1 \\ &= 4(x + 3)(x - 2)^3 + (x - 2)^4 \\ &= (x - 2)^3[4(x + 3) + (x - 2)] \\ &= (x - 2)^3(5x + 10) \\ &= 5(x + 2)(x - 2)^3\end{aligned}$$

At stationary points on the curve, $\frac{dy}{dx} = 0$.

$$5(x + 2)(x - 2)^3 = 0$$
$$\Rightarrow \quad x = -2 \text{ or } x = 2$$

Verify that when $x = -2$, $y = 256$ and that when $x = 2$, $y = 0$.
The stationary points are located at $(-2, 256)$ and $(2, 0)$. Their nature can be determined by evaluating the second derivative at $x = -2$ and $x = 2$ respectively.

Use the product rule again to find $\frac{d^2y}{dx^2}$.
Let $\frac{dy}{dx} = fg$, where $f = 5(x + 2)$ and $g = (x - 2)^3$. Then $f' = 5$ and $g' = 3(x - 2)^2$.
It follows that

Use the chain rule to differentiate $(x - 2)^3$.

$$\begin{aligned}\frac{d^2y}{dx^2} &= fg' + gf' \\ &= 15(x + 2)(x - 2)^2 + 5(x - 2)^3 \\ &= 5(x - 2)^2[3(x + 2) + (x - 2)] \\ &= 20(x - 2)^2(x + 1)\end{aligned}$$

f and *g* have been used here instead of *u* and *v* to avoid confusion with the earlier working.

When $x = -2$, $\frac{d^2y}{dx^2} = 20(-4)^2(-1) = -320 < 0$.
So $(-2, 256)$ is a maximum point.

When $x = 2$, $\frac{d^2y}{dx^2} = 20(0)^2(3) = 0$.
Looking at the gradient of the curve on either side of $x = 2$:

- when $x = 1$, $\frac{dy}{dx} = 5(3)(-1)^3 = -15$
- when $x = 3$, $\frac{dy}{dx} = 5(5)(1)^3 = 25$

The gradient changes from negative to positive as the curve passes through $x = 2$, so (2, 0) is a minimum point.

This information can now be used to sketch the curve.

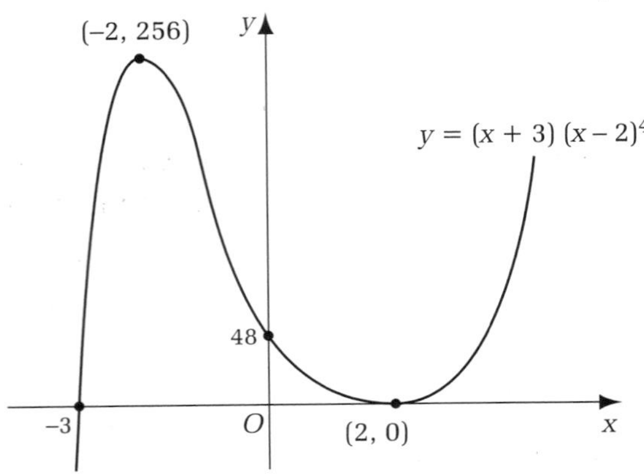

◀ **Check this result using a graphical calculator.**

Check that the curve crosses or touches the axes at (−3, 0), (2, 0) and (0, 48).

General points of inflexion

Stationary points of inflexion have two forms. The gradient of the curve can be positive on both sides of a stationary point of inflexion or negative on both sides, as shown in the diagram. Check that a tangent drawn to the curve at a stationary point of inflexion crosses from one side to the other.

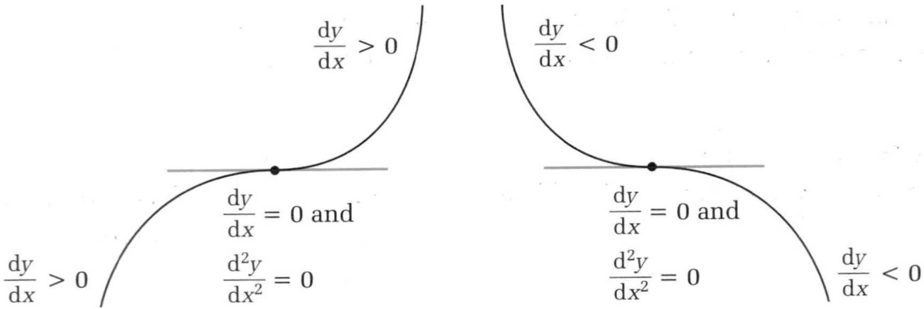

However stationary points of inflexion are special cases. The gradient of a curve does not have to be zero at a point of inflexion. In fact, there must be at least one non-stationary point of inflexion on any smooth continuous curve between two stationary points. This situation can best be described graphically.

The tangent drawn to the curve at the minimum point P is below the curve. The tangent drawn at the maximum point Q is above the curve. So there must be a point R on the curve, between P and Q, where the tangent crosses the curve. This is a non-stationary point of inflexion. In this particular example, it corresponds to the point where the gradient of the curve has its maximum value between P and Q.

It is also the point at which the curvature of the curve changes.

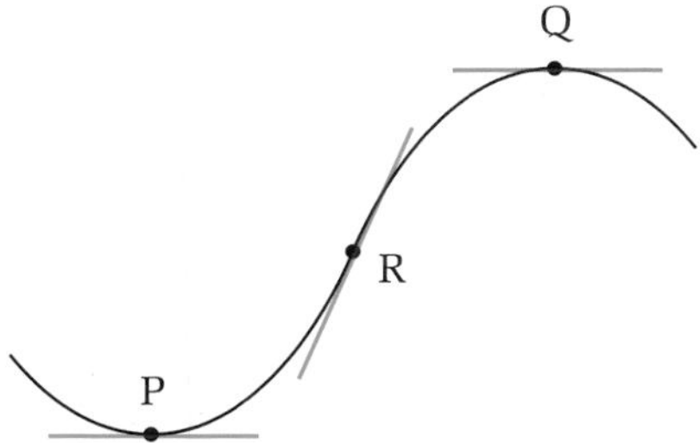

There are four different types of non-stationary points of inflexion. At two of them the gradient of the curve is positive. At the other two the gradient of the curve is negative. These are illustrated in the following diagrams.

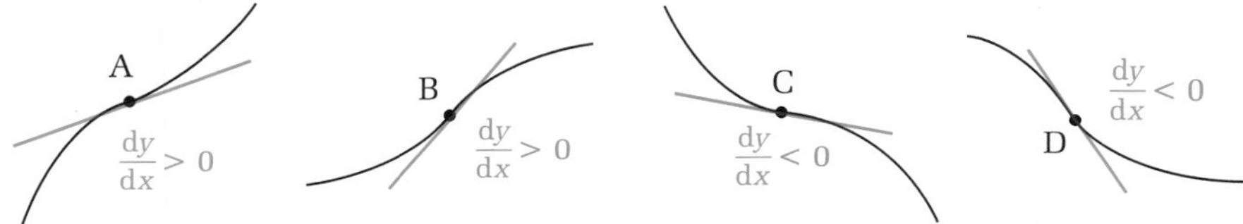

Consider each of these possibilities. Draw the curve near the point of inflexion, with its gradient function underneath.

The gradient $\frac{dy}{dx}$ reaches a minimum value at A. The second derivative, $\frac{d^2y}{dx^2} = 0$ at A. The gradient of the gradient function, $\frac{d^2y}{dx^2}$, is changing from being negative to positive on the graph of $y = f'(x)$ as it passes through A. From what we have already seen of the first and second derivatives, this means that the third derivative $\frac{d^3y}{dx^3} > 0$ at A.

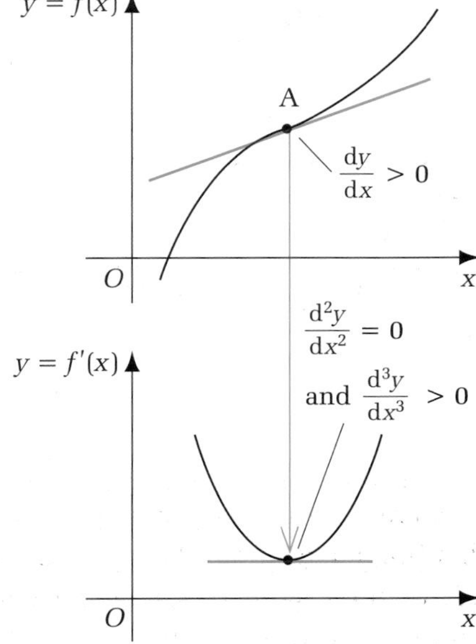

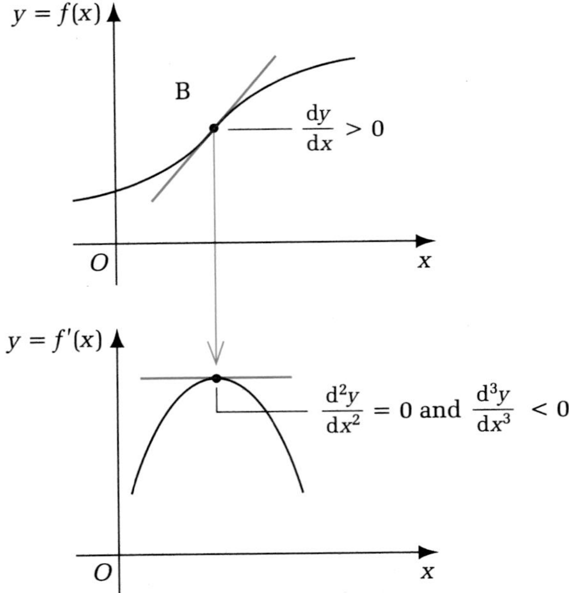

The gradient reaches a maximum value at point B. This means $\frac{d^2y}{dx^2} = 0$. Since the gradient of the gradient function is changing from positive to negative as it passes through B, $\frac{d^3y}{dx^3} < 0$ at B.

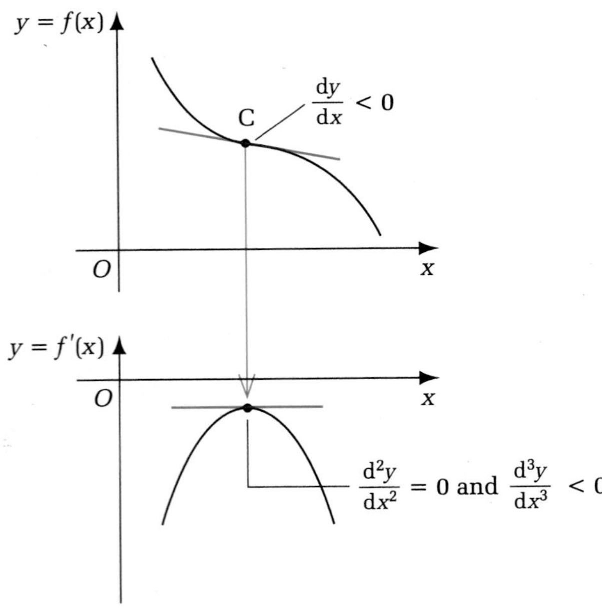

The gradient of the curve is negative on either side of the point C. Its value is least negative (that is at its maximum) at point C. This means $\frac{d^2y}{dx^2} = 0$ at this point. The gradient of the gradient function is changing from positive to negative, so the third derivative $\frac{d^3y}{dx^3} < 0$.

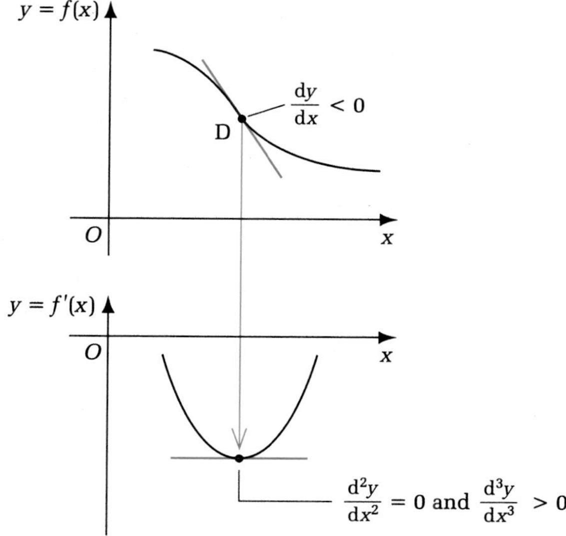

The gradient of the curve reaches its most negative (its minimum) value at point D. This means that $\frac{d^2y}{dx^2} = 0$. Since the gradient of the gradient function is changing from negative to positive, $\frac{d^3y}{dx^3} > 0$ at D.

Summary

- At non-stationary points of inflexion, $\frac{dy}{dx} \neq 0$ and $\frac{d^2y}{dx^2} = 0$.
- The sign of the first derivative $\frac{dy}{dx}$ and the third derivative $\frac{d^3y}{dx^3}$ can be used to distinguish between the four possible types of non-stationary point of inflexion.
- If $\frac{d^3y}{dx^3} < 0$ the gradient of the curve reaches a maximum value at the point of inflexion; if $\frac{d^3y}{dx^3} > 0$ then the gradient of the curve reaches a minimum value at this point.

$\frac{dy}{dx}$	$\frac{d^2y}{dx^2}$	$\frac{d^3y}{dx^3}$	Type of inflexion
+ve	0	+ve	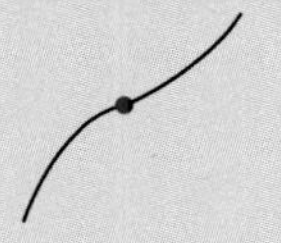
+ve	0	−ve	
−ve	0	−ve	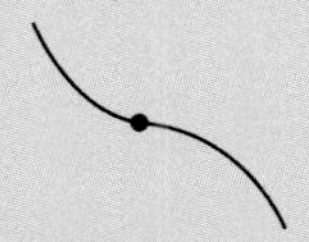
−ve	0	+ve	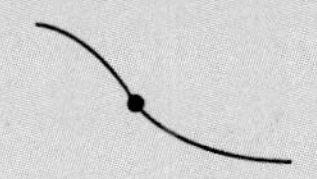

◀ **Learn these results.**

Example 2

Find the coordinates of the points of inflexion on the curve $y = (x + 1)(x - 3)^3$. Use the first and third derivatives to determine their nature.

Solution

Using the product rule for differentiation, verify that

$$\frac{dy}{dx} = 4x(x - 3)^2, \quad \frac{d^2y}{dx^2} = 12x^2 - 48x + 36 \quad \text{and} \quad \frac{d^3y}{dx^3} = 24x - 48$$

Check these results carefully.

At points of inflexion on the curve, $\frac{d^2y}{dx^2} = 0$.

$$\text{So} \quad 12x^2 - 48x + 36 = 0$$
$$\Rightarrow \quad 12(x - 1)(x - 3) = 0$$
$$\Rightarrow \quad x = 1 \text{ or } x = 3$$

When $x = 1$, $y = -16$ and $\frac{dy}{dx} = 16$.
When $x = 3$, $y = 0$ and $\frac{dy}{dx} = 0$.

Check that the gradient of the curve on each side of (3, 0) is positive. Then (3, 0) is a stationary point of inflexion. We also know that there is a non-stationary point of inflexion at (1, −16). Use the first and third derivatives to determine the nature of these points of inflexion:

- When $x = 1$, $\frac{dy}{dx} = 16 > 0$ and $\frac{d^3y}{dx^3} = -24 < 0$

  The gradient of the curve is positive, and reaches a maximum value at (1, −16)

- When $x = 3$, $\frac{dy}{dx} = 0$ and $\frac{d^3y}{dx^3} = 24 > 0$

  The gradient of the curve is zero at (3, 0). This is the minimum value for the gradient in this particular part of the curve.

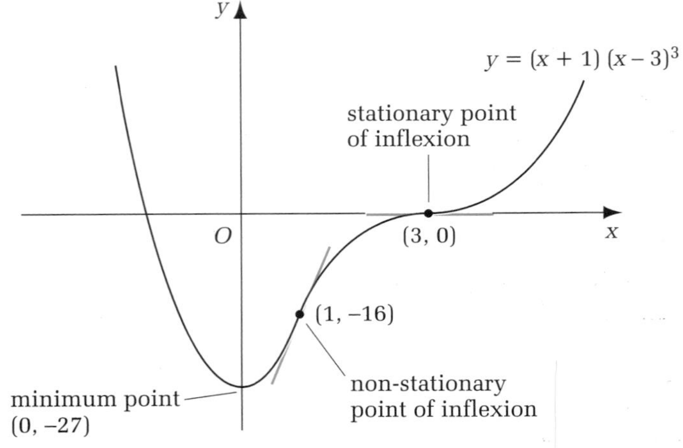

11.4 Using the Second Derivative

Exercise

Technique

1 For each of the following cubic functions:

i find expressions for $f'(x)$ and $f''(x)$

ii find the coordinates of any stationary points on the graph of $y = f(x)$ and use the second derivative to determine their nature

iii sketch the graph of $y = f(x)$.

a $f(x) = x^3 - 12x^2 + 45x - 40$

b $f(x) = 7 - 12x + 6x^2 - x^3$

c $f(x) = 2x^3 - 9x^2 - 108x + 40$

2 a State the coordinates of the points where the curve $y = (x - 5)(x + 3)^3$ crosses the axes.

b Locate and determine the nature of the stationary points on the curve $y = (x - 5)(x + 3)^3$.

Hint: Use the product rule to differentiate.

c Find the coordinates of the non-stationary point of inflexion on this curve. Use the first and third derivatives to determine its nature.

d Sketch $y = (x - 5)(x + 3)^3$.

3 Locate and determine the nature of the maximum and minimum points on the graph $y = x^4 - 24x^2 + 32$. Show that there are two non-stationary points of inflexion on this curve, at $x = -a$ and $x = a$, where a is a positive integer to be determined.

4 a Find the coordinates of the stationary points on the curve $y = x + 2\cos x$ in the interval $-2\pi \leq x \leq 2\pi$. Use the second derivative to determine their nature.

b Find the coordinates of the points of inflexion on the curve in this interval.

c Sketch $y = x + 2\cos x$ for $-2\pi \leq x \leq 2\pi$.

5 For each of the following curves:

i write down the coordinates of the points where the curve crosses the axes

ii write down the equation of any vertical asymptotes

iii find an expression for $\frac{dy}{dx}$

iv locate and determine the nature of any stationary points

v sketch the curve.

a $y = x(x - 1)^4$

b $y = (x + 4)^2(x - 2)^2$

c $y = \frac{x^2}{(2x+6)}$

6 For each of the following curves:

i find expressions for $\frac{dy}{dx}$ and $\frac{d^2y}{dx^2}$;

ii locate and determine the nature of any stationary points.

a $y = (2x + 1)e^x$

b $y = \ln(x + 2) + \dfrac{1}{(x + 2)}$

c $y = e^x \sin x$ (for $-\pi \leq x \leq \pi$)

d $y = (x + 1)^3 e^{-x}$

Contextual

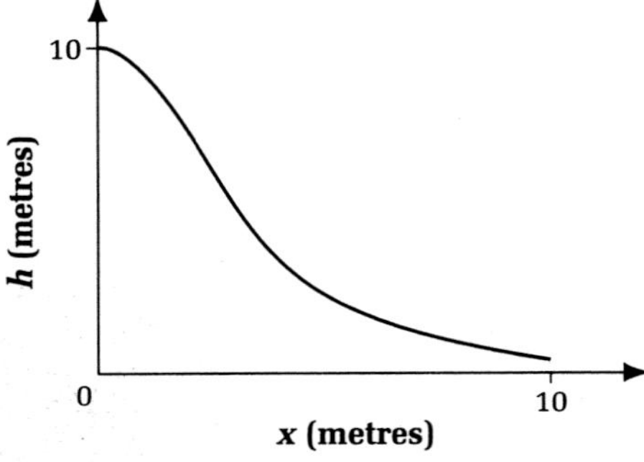

The height h metres above the ground of part of a funfair ride, shown above, can be modelled using $h = 5(x + 2)e^{-x/2}$.

a Find expressions for $\frac{dh}{dx}$ and $\frac{d^2h}{dx^2}$.

b Calculate the value of x at which this section of the ride is steepest, and the height above the ground at this point.

c Calculate this maximum gradient. At what angle, to the nearest degree, is the track to the ground at this point?

11.5 Implicit Differentiation

All of the functions that have been differentiated so far have been expressed in the form $y = f(x)$. However there are curves in the x–y plane, with equations linking x and y, that cannot be written in this way. Some examples are circles, ellipses and hyperbolae. The equations for these curves are called **implicit functions**. The method used to find the gradient at any point on their curves is called **implicit differentiation**.

For example, the Cartesian equation of a circle of radius 3, centred at the origin, is $x^2 + y^2 = 9$.

Rearranging the equation,

$$y^2 = 9 - x^2$$

$$y = \pm\sqrt{9 - x^2}$$

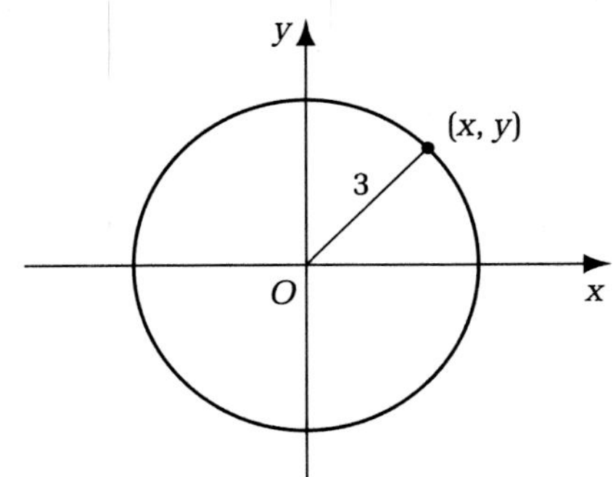

Notice that two explicit functions $y = +\sqrt{9 - x^2}$ and $y = -\sqrt{9 - x^2}$ are needed to completely define this circle. Using a graphical calculator, plot $y = +\sqrt{9 - x^2}$ and $y = -\sqrt{9 - x^2}$. Check that this draws a circle, centred at the origin of radius 3.

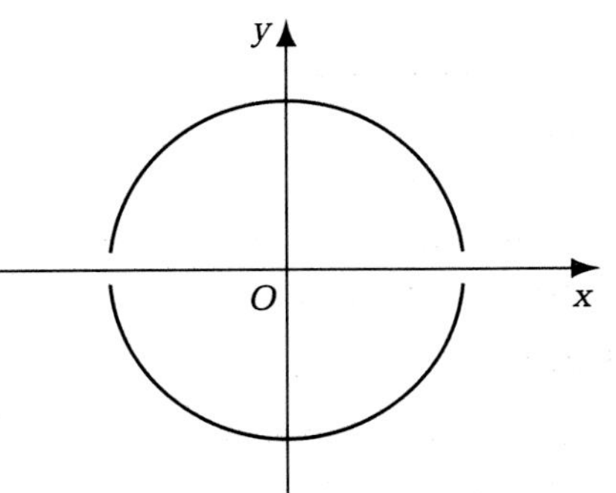

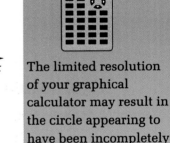

The limited resolution of your graphical calculator may result in the circle appearing to have been incompletely drawn.

Both of these explicit functions can be differentiated using the chain rule. Implicit differentiation allows us to find an expression for $\frac{dy}{dx}$ from the original equation.
Differentiating each term in the equation $x^2 + y^2 = 9$ with respect to x,

$$\frac{d}{dx}(x^2) + \frac{d}{dx}(y^2) = \frac{d}{dx}(9) \qquad [1]$$

We know that $\frac{d}{dx}(x^2) = 2x$, and $\frac{d}{dx}(9) = 0$.
Use the chain rule to change the variable with which the y^2 term is differentiated:

$$\frac{d}{dx}(y^2) = \frac{d}{dy}(y^2) \times \frac{dy}{dx}$$

$$\Rightarrow \frac{d}{dx}(y^2) = 2y\frac{dy}{dx}$$

◀ **Learn this important result.**

From equation [1], these results give

$$2x + 2y\frac{dy}{dx} = 0$$

$$\Rightarrow \quad 2y\frac{dy}{dx} = -2x$$

$$\Rightarrow \quad \frac{dy}{dx} = -\frac{x}{y}$$

This result is true for all circles centred at the origin, because the radius squared term in the equation of the circle is zero when differentiated. This can be confirmed by considering the radial line from the centre O to some point (x, y) on the circumference of the circle.

Notice that the gradient of this line is $\frac{y}{x}$. Because it also intercepts the circle at right angles, it is the normal to the circle at this point. This means that the gradient of the tangent to the circle at this point is $-\frac{x}{y}$.

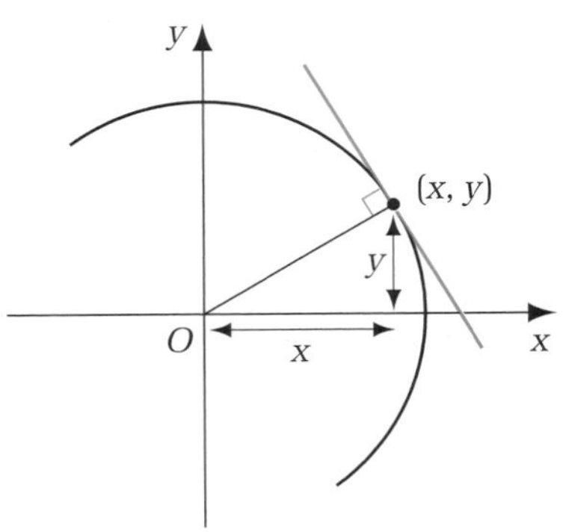

Remember that the gradient of the tangen[t] is also the gradient of the curve (circle) itsel[f] at this point.

Example 1

A circle C is centred at (6, −2) and has a radius of 5 units.

a Write down the Cartesian equation of this circle

b Find an expression for $\frac{dy}{dx}$.

c Find the gradient of the circle at the two points where $x = 9$.

Solution

a Recall that, for a circle of radius r, centred at (a, b),

$$(x - a)^2 + (y - b)^2 = r^2$$

The Cartesian equation of this circle is therefore

$$(x - 6)^2 + (y + 2)^2 = 25$$

Verify that the equivalent form is $x^2 + y^2 - 12x + 4y + 15$

b Differentiating both sides of the equation with respect to x,

$$\frac{d}{dx}(x - 6)^2 + \frac{d}{dx}(y + 2)^2 = \frac{d}{dx}(25)$$

Alternatively, differenti[ate] $x^2 + y^2 - 12x + 4y + 15$ term by term, using t[he] chain rule for the ter[m] in y.

Using the chain rule, $\dfrac{d}{dx}(x-6)^2 = 2(x-6)$

and $$\frac{d}{dx}(y+2)^2 = \frac{d}{dy}(y+2)^2 \times \frac{dy}{dx}$$

$$= 2(y+2)\frac{dy}{dx}$$

So $$2(x-6) + 2(y+2)\frac{dy}{dx} = 0$$

Then $$2(y+2)\frac{dy}{dx} = -2(x-6)$$

$$\Rightarrow \frac{dy}{dx} = \frac{(6-x)}{(y+2)}$$

c Substitute $x = 9$ into $(x-6)^2 + (y+2)^2 = 25$.

This gives $$3^2 + (y+2)^2 = 25$$

$$9 + y^2 + 4y + 4 = 25$$

$$y^2 + 4y - 12 = 0$$

$$(y+6)(y-2) = 0$$

$$\Rightarrow y = -6 \text{ or } y = 2.$$

At $(9, -6)$, $\dfrac{dy}{dx} = \dfrac{6-9}{-6+2} = \dfrac{-3}{-4} = \dfrac{3}{4}$

At $(9, 2)$, $\dfrac{dy}{dx} = \dfrac{6-9}{2+2} = -\dfrac{3}{4}$

Notice that in this example, $\frac{dy}{dx} = \frac{6-x}{y+2}$ is undefined when $y = -2$. This corresponds to the two points on the circle where the tangents are parallel to the y-axis.

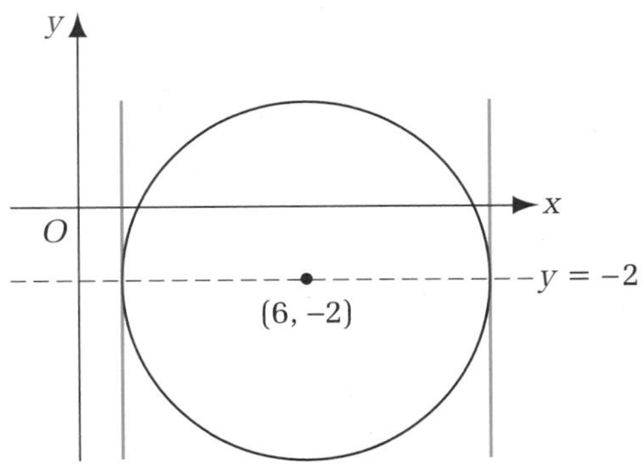

The denominator in $\frac{6-x}{y+2}$ is zero when $y = -2$.

Unlike the equation of a circle, many implicit functions have equations that include product terms. These are expressions such as xy, xy^2 and x^2y. These terms can still be differentiated implicitly but require the use of the product rule.

Example 2

For each of the following, find an expression for $\frac{dy}{dx}$ in terms of x and y.

a $x^2 + 3xy - 4x = 9$ **b** $x^2y^2 + 4x^2 - y^2 = 0$

Solution

a Differentiate both sides of the equation with respect to x.

$$\frac{d}{dx}(x^2) + \frac{d}{dx}(3xy) - \frac{d}{dx}(4x) = \frac{d}{dx}(9)$$

Use the product rule to differentiate the second term. Let $u = 3x$ and $v = y$. Then $u' = 3$ and $v' = \frac{dy}{dx}$.

Now $\frac{d}{dx}(3xy) = uv' + vu' = 3x\frac{dy}{dx} + 3y$

It follows that differentiation of both sides of the equation gives

$$2x + 3x\frac{dy}{dx} + 3y - 4 = 0$$

Rearranging to find $\frac{dy}{dx}$,

$$3x\frac{dy}{dx} = 4 - 2x - 3y$$

$$\Rightarrow \quad \frac{dy}{dx} = \frac{4 - 2x - 3y}{3x}$$

b Differentiate both sides of the equation with respect to x.

$$\frac{d}{dx}(x^2y^2) + 8x - \frac{d}{dx}(y^2) = 0$$

Using the product rule, $\frac{d}{dx}(x^2y^2) = 2x^2y\frac{dy}{dx} + 2xy^2$

and using the chain rule $\frac{d}{dx}(y^2) = 2y\frac{dy}{dx}$

So $2x^2y\frac{dy}{dx} + 2xy^2 + 8x - 2y\frac{dy}{dx} = 0$

$$\Rightarrow \quad (2x^2y - 2y)\frac{dy}{dx} = -(2xy^2 + 8x)$$

$$\Rightarrow \quad 2y(x^2 - 1)\frac{dy}{dx} = -2x(y^2 + 4)$$

Eliminate the common factor 2.

$$\Rightarrow \quad y(1 - x^2)\frac{dy}{dx} = x(y^2 + 4)$$

$$\Rightarrow \quad \frac{dy}{dx} = \frac{x(y^2 + 4)}{y(1 - x^2)}$$

Stationary points and the second derivative

The location of any stationary points on an implicitly defined curve are still found by solving $\frac{dy}{dx} = 0$. Their nature can still be determined by evaluating the second derivative for the relevant values of x and y. An expression for $\frac{d^2y}{dx^2}$ can be found by differentiating the equation in which $\frac{dy}{dx}$ first appears. It may be necessary to substitute for $\frac{dy}{dx}$ to get this expression for the second derivative in terms of x and y only.

Example 3

Find an expression for $\frac{dy}{dx}$ in terms of x and y for the implicitly defined curve $x^2 - 4xy + 4y + 8 = 0$. Locate the stationary points on this curve and use the second derivative to determine their nature.

Solution

Differentiating both sides of the equation with respect to x,

$$2x - 4y - 4x\frac{dy}{dx} + 4\frac{dy}{dx} + 0 = 0$$

So $$(4 - 4x)\frac{dy}{dx} = 4y - 2x$$

$$\frac{dy}{dx} = \frac{2y - x}{2 - 2x}$$

Notice that the common factor 2 has been eliminated.

At stationary points on the curve, $\frac{dy}{dx} = 0$

$$\Rightarrow \quad \frac{2y - x}{2 - 2x} = 0$$

$$\Rightarrow \quad x = 2y$$

Solve this equation by equating the numerator to zero.

Substituting $x = 2y$ into the equation of the curve,

$$(2y)^2 - 4(2y)y + 4y + 8 = 0$$

$$4y^2 - 8y^2 + 4y + 8 = 0$$

$$\Rightarrow \quad 4y^2 - 4y - 8 = 0$$

$$\Rightarrow \quad 4(y + 1)(y - 2) = 0$$

$$\Rightarrow \quad y = -1 \text{ or } y = 2$$

Notice that the common factor 4 has been eliminated.

When $y = -1, x = -2$ and when $y = 2, x = 4$ ◀ Using $x = 2y$

So the stationary points on the curve are located at $(-2, -1)$ and $(4, 2)$.

To find the second derivative for this curve, differentiate each of the terms in the equation $2x - 4y - 4x\frac{dy}{dx} + 4\frac{dy}{dx} = 0$ with respect to x. Check that this gives

$$2 - 4\frac{dy}{dx} - 4\frac{dy}{dx} - 4x\frac{d^2y}{dx^2} + 4\frac{d^2y}{dx^2} = 0$$

Using the product rule, $\frac{d}{dx}\left(4x\frac{dy}{dx}\right) = 4\frac{dy}{dx} + 4x\frac{d^2y}{dx^2}$.

Now factorise and simplify the equation.

$$2 - 8\frac{dy}{dx} + (4 - 4x)\frac{d^2y}{dx^2} = 0$$

$$2 - 8\left(\frac{2y - x}{2 - 2x}\right) + (4 - 4x)\frac{d^2y}{dx^2} = 0$$

Verify that this equation can be rearranged to give

$$4(1 - x)\frac{d^2y}{dx^2} = \frac{16y - 4x - 4}{2(1 - x)}$$

$$\frac{d^2y}{dx^2} = \frac{4y - x - 1}{2(1 - x)^2}$$

When $x = -2$ and $y = -1$, $\frac{d^2y}{dx^2} = -\frac{3}{18} = -\frac{1}{6} < 0$

So $(-2, -1)$ is a maximum point on the curve.

When $x = 4$ and $y = 2$, $\frac{d^2y}{dx^2} = \frac{3}{18} = \frac{1}{6} > 0$

So $(4, 2)$ is a minimum point on the curve.

Notice that the equation of the curve in this example can be rearranged into the form $y = f(x)$. Show that $y = \frac{x^2+8}{4(x-1)}$. Its first and second derivatives can then be found using the quotient rule.
Use a graphical calculator to draw the graph of $y = \frac{x^2+8}{4(x-1)}$. Confirm that the curve has a maximum point at $(-2, -1)$ and a minimum point at $(4, 2)$.

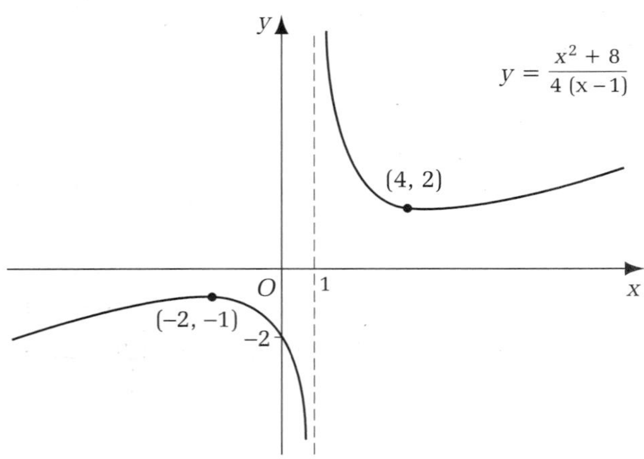

11.5 Implicit Differentiation

Exercise

Technique

1 For each of the following circles:

i write down its Cartesian equation
ii find an expression for $\frac{dy}{dx}$ in terms of x and y
iii calculate the gradient of the circle at the point P, whose coordinates are indicated:

a radius 5, centre (1, 2); P (5, 5)
b radius 13, centre (3, −4); P(−2, 8)
c radius $\sqrt{39}$, centre (5, 0); P $(-1, \sqrt{3})$

2 Find an expression for $\frac{dy}{dx}$ in terms of x and y for each of the following:

a $3x^2 - 2y^2 + xy = 0$
b $x^3 + 4y - 3xy = 0$
c $6x^2 + 2y^2 - y + 4 = 0$
d $4y^3 - 5x + 2xy + 6 = 0$
e $2x + 7y - 3x^2y - 4 = 0$
f $5x - 3y^2 + 2xy^2 + 1 = 0$

3 Find the gradient of each of the following curves at the point indicated:

a $y^3 - 2x^3 - 4xy + 24 = 0$ at $(2, 2)$
b $4y - 3x^2 - y^2 + 17 = 0$ at $(2, 5)$
c $3y^2 - 3x - x^2y - 47 = 0$ at $(-1, 4)$

4 For each of the following curves:

i find an expression for $\frac{dy}{dx}$ in terms of x and y
ii find the coordinates of the stationary points(s) on the curve
iii find an expression for $\frac{d^2y}{dx^2}$ in terms of x, y and $\frac{dy}{dx}$
iv determine the nature of the stationary point(s):

a $3x^2 + y^2 - 3xy - 9 = 0$
b $5x^2 + 2y^2 - 2y - 12 = 0$
c $x + 12y + x^2y + 2 = 0$

5 Find the equations of the tangent and the normal to each of the following curves at the points indicated:

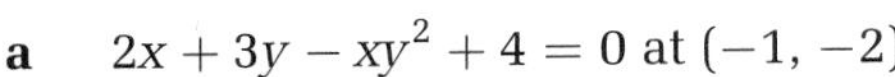
a $2x + 3y - xy^2 + 4 = 0$ at $(-1, -2)$
b $x + 2y^2 + 4xy^2 - 12 = 0$ at $(2, 1)$
c $y^3 + 10x + xy - 15 = 0$ at $(6, -3)$

11.6 Parametric Differentiation

For many curves, it is possible to express both x and y in terms of a third variable. This is usually called a **parameter**. Depending on the relationship between x and y, this parametric form can be more convenient than using the Cartesian equation.

In mechanics, the position of a projectile can be given in terms time, t. Eliminating th parameter t gives the trajectory formula.

In the Applications and Activities section of Chapter 6 (Algebra II) we used parametric equations to find the Cartesian equation of a curve by eliminating the parameter algebraically.

Example 1

Eliminate the parameter from the following parametric equations to find the form of the Cartesian equation.

a $x = 2t, y = t^2, t > 0$
b $x = 3\cos\theta, y = 2\sin\theta, 0 < \theta < 2\pi$

Solution

a Here the parameter is t. Rearranging $x = 2t$ gives

$$t = \frac{x}{2}$$

Substitute this into the equation for y,

$$y = \left(\frac{x}{2}\right)^2 \quad \Rightarrow \quad y = \frac{x^2}{4}$$

So the Cartesian equation of the curve is $y = \frac{x^2}{4}$.

This is the equation o parabola.

b Here the parameter is θ. Since the parameter appears in both sine and cosine functions in the parametric equations, it can be eliminated by squaring and adding.

$$x = 3\cos\theta \quad \Rightarrow \quad \cos\theta = \frac{x}{3}$$

$$y = 2\sin\theta \quad \Rightarrow \quad \sin\theta = \frac{y}{2}$$

Using $\cos^2\theta + \sin^2\theta \equiv 1$, we get

$$\left(\frac{x}{3}\right)^2 + \left(\frac{y}{2}\right)^2 = 1$$

$$\frac{x^2}{9} + \frac{y^2}{4} = 1$$

So the Cartesian equation of the curve is $\frac{x^2}{9} + \frac{y^2}{4} = 1$

This is the equation o an ellipse.

Example 1**b** is particularly important. The parametric equations of an ellipse centred at the origin are $x = a\cos\theta$, $y = b\sin\theta$. Eliminating the parameter θ gives the Cartesian equation for the ellipse as $\frac{x^2}{a^2} + \frac{y^2}{b^2} = 1$.

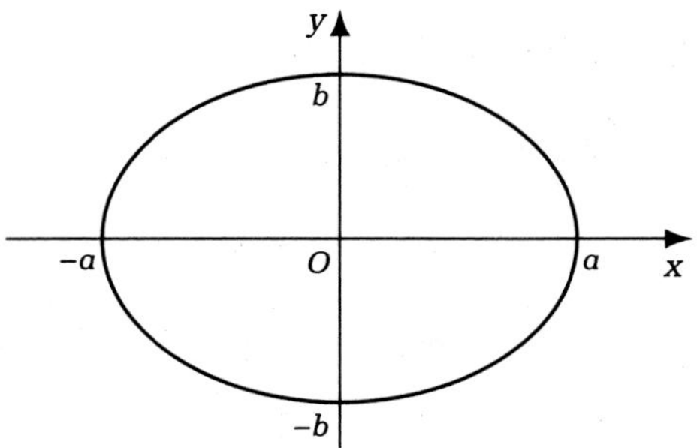

The Cartesian equation of a curve can usually be obtained from parametric equations. Eliminate the parameter, t, from the two parametric equations, $x = f(t)$ and $y = g(t)$. How is the gradient of such a parametrically defined curve found? First differentiate both x and y with respect to the parameter t, to find $\frac{dx}{dt}$ and $\frac{dy}{dt}$ respectively. Then, using the chain rule

$$\frac{dy}{dx} = \frac{dy}{dt} \times \frac{dt}{dx}, \text{ which can be rewritten as}$$

Recall that $\frac{dx}{dt} = \frac{1}{\left(\frac{dt}{dx}\right)}$

$$\frac{dy}{dx} = \left(\frac{dy}{dt}\right) \Big/ \left(\frac{dx}{dt}\right)$$

◀ **Learn this result.**

For example, check that the parametric equations that define the circle of radius 3, centred at the origin, are $x = 3\cos t$ and $y = 3\sin t$. The parameter, t, is the angle, in radians, measured anticlockwise about the origin from the x-axis.

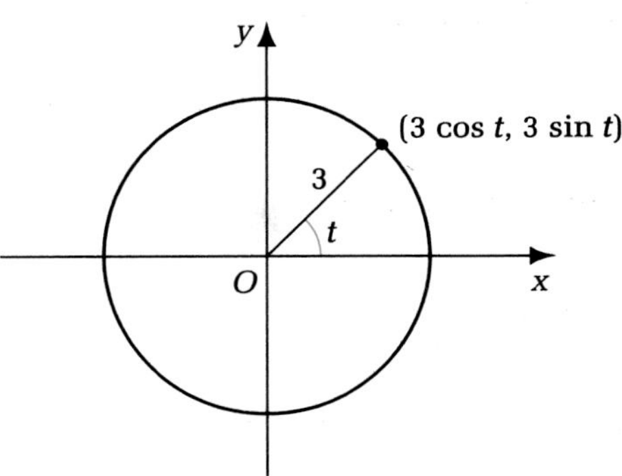

This parameter can be eliminated by squaring and adding the equations for x and y. Check that

$$\begin{aligned} x^2 + y^2 &= (3\cos t)^2 + (3\sin t)^2 \\ &= 9\cos^2 t + 9\sin^2 t \\ &= 9(\cos^2 t + \sin^2 t) \\ &= 9 \end{aligned}$$

◀ $\cos^2\theta + \sin^2\theta \equiv 1$

Thus $x^2 + y^2 = 9$, which is the Cartesian equation of this circle.

Differentiating the two parametric equations $x = 3\cos t$ and $y = 3\sin t$ with respect to t gives

$$\frac{dx}{dt} = -3\sin t \quad \text{and} \quad \frac{dy}{dt} = 3\cos t.$$

Using the chain rule, $\frac{dy}{dx} = \frac{dy}{dt} \times \frac{dt}{dx}$

$$= \left(\frac{dy}{dt}\right) \Big/ \left(\frac{dx}{dt}\right)$$

$$= \frac{3\cos t}{-3\sin t} = -\frac{1}{\tan t}$$

$$\frac{dt}{dx} = \frac{1}{\left(\frac{dx}{dt}\right)}$$

Notice that since $x = 3\cos t$ and $y = 3\sin t$,

$$\frac{dy}{dx} = \frac{3\cos t}{-3\sin t} = -\frac{x}{y}$$

This was the result obtained by implicitly differentiating the Cartesian equation of this circle in the previous section.

Example 2

Find an expression for $\frac{dy}{dx}$ for each of the following parametrically defined curves:

a $x = 4t^2 + 1$
$y = t^3 + t$

b $x = 3\sin\theta$
$y = \cos 2\theta$

Solution

a $\frac{dx}{dt} = 8t$ and $\frac{dy}{dt} = 3t^2 + 1$

So $\frac{dy}{dx} = \left(\frac{dy}{dt}\right) \Big/ \left(\frac{dx}{dt}\right) = \frac{3t^2 + 1}{8t}$

b $\frac{dx}{d\theta} = 3\cos\theta$ and $\frac{dy}{d\theta} = -2\sin 2\theta$

So $\frac{dy}{dx} = \left(\frac{dy}{d\theta}\right) \Big/ \left(\frac{dx}{d\theta}\right)$

$$= -\frac{2\sin 2\theta}{3\cos\theta}$$ ◀ **$\sin 2\theta = 2\sin\theta\cos\theta$**

$$= -\frac{4\sin\theta\cos\theta}{3\cos\theta} = -\tfrac{4}{3}\sin\theta$$

Example 3

Find the coordinates of the point(s) on the following parametrically defined curves where the gradient has the value indicated.

a $x = \frac{4}{t}, y = \frac{8}{t^2}, \frac{dy}{dx} = \frac{2}{3}$

b $x = \sin\theta, y = 2\cos^3\theta, \frac{dy}{dx} = -3$

Solution

a $\frac{dx}{dt} = \frac{-4}{t^2}$ and $\frac{dy}{dt} = \frac{-16}{t^3}$

So $\frac{dy}{dx} = \left(\frac{dy}{dt}\right) \Big/ \left(\frac{dx}{dt}\right) = \left(\frac{-16}{t^3}\right) \Big/ \left(\frac{-4}{t^2}\right) = \left(\frac{-16}{t^3}\right) \times \left(\frac{-t^2}{4}\right) = \frac{4}{t}$

If $\frac{dy}{dx} = \frac{2}{3}$, then $\frac{4}{t} = \frac{2}{3} \Rightarrow t = 6$

When $t = 6$, $x = \frac{4}{6} = \frac{2}{3}$ and $y = \frac{8}{36} = \frac{2}{9}$
So $\frac{dy}{dx} = \frac{2}{3}$ at $(\frac{2}{3}, \frac{2}{9})$

b $\frac{dx}{d\theta} = \cos\theta$ and $\frac{dy}{d\theta} = -6\cos^2\theta\sin\theta$

So $$\frac{dy}{dx} = \left(\frac{dy}{d\theta}\right) \Big/ \left(\frac{dx}{d\theta}\right) = \frac{-6\cos^2\theta\sin\theta}{\cos\theta} = -6\cos\theta\sin\theta = -3\sin 2\theta$$

$\sin 2\theta = 2\sin\theta\cos\theta$

If $\frac{dy}{dx} = -3$, then $-3\sin 2\theta = -3$

So $\sin 2\theta = 1$

Then $2\theta = \frac{\pi}{2}, \frac{5\pi}{2}, \frac{9\pi}{2}, \frac{13\pi}{2}, \ldots$

and $\theta = \frac{\pi}{4}, \frac{5\pi}{4}, \frac{9\pi}{4}, \frac{13\pi}{4}, \ldots$

When $\theta = \frac{\pi}{4}$, $x = \frac{1}{\sqrt{2}}$ and $y = 2(\frac{1}{\sqrt{2}})^3 = \frac{1}{\sqrt{2}}$.

When $\theta = \frac{5\pi}{4}$, $x = -\frac{1}{\sqrt{2}}$ and $y = 2(-\frac{1}{\sqrt{2}})^3 = -\frac{1}{\sqrt{2}}$.

$\theta = \frac{9\pi}{4}$ will repeat coordinates

So $\frac{dy}{dx} = -3$ at $(\frac{1}{\sqrt{2}}, \frac{1}{\sqrt{2}})$, and $(-\frac{1}{\sqrt{2}}, -\frac{1}{\sqrt{2}})$.

It is possible to find a general equation for the tangent, or the normal, at some general point $(x = f(t), y = g(t))$ on a parametric curve. The equation of the tangent, or normal, at a specific point on the curve can then be found by substituting an appropriate value of the parameter t.

Example 4

The curve C has parametric equations $x = t^3$ and $y = 6t$. Find a general equation for both the tangent and the normal at some point $(t^3, 6t)$ on the curve. Write down the equation of the tangent to the curve at (8, 12) and the equation of the normal to the curve at $(-1, -6)$.

Solution

$$\frac{dx}{dt} = 3t^2 \text{ and } \frac{dy}{dt} = 6$$

So $$\frac{dy}{dx} = \left(\frac{dy}{dt}\right) \Big/ \left(\frac{dx}{dt}\right) = \frac{6}{3t^2} = \frac{2}{t^2}$$

The gradient of the tangent, and the normal, to the curve at some general point $(t^3, 6t)$ are $\frac{2}{t^2}$ and $-\frac{1}{2}t^2$, respectively. Use $y - y_1 = m(x - x_1)$ to find the equations of these lines.

The equation of the tangent is

$$y - 6t = \frac{2}{t^2}(x - t^3)$$

Multiply both sides by t^2

$$\Rightarrow\ t^2y - 6t^3 = 2x - 2t^3$$

$$\Rightarrow\ t^2y - 2x = 4t^3 \quad \text{or} \quad t^2y - 2x - 4t^3 = 0$$

The equation of the normal is

Multiply both sides b

$$y - 6t = -\tfrac{1}{2}t^2(x - t^3)$$

$$\Rightarrow \quad 2y - 12t = -t^2x + t^5$$

$$\Rightarrow \quad 2y + t^2x = t^5 + 12t \quad \text{or} \quad 2y + t^2x - t^5 - 12t = 0$$

At the point (8, 12), $t = 2$. The equation of the tangent at this point, found by substituting $t = 2$ into $t^2y - 2x = 4t^3$, is

$$4y - 2x = 32 \quad \text{or} \quad 2y - x - 16 = 0$$

At the point (−1, −6), $t = -1$. Substituting $t = -1$ into the general equation for a normal to the curve $2y + t^2x = t^5 + 12t$, gives

$$2y + x = -13 \quad \text{or} \quad 2y + x + 13 = 0$$

Stationary points and second derivatives

The second derivative $\frac{d^2y}{dx^2}$ of a parametrically defined curve is found by differentiating the first derivative $\frac{dy}{dx}$ with respect to x (that is, $\frac{d}{dx}\left(\frac{dy}{dx}\right)$). But, for most parameter curves, $\frac{dy}{dx}$ will be a function of the parameter, t, and *not* x. This means the chain rule must be used to change the variable by which $\frac{dy}{dx}$ is being differentiated, so that

$$\frac{d^2y}{dx^2} = \frac{d}{dt}\left(\frac{dy}{dx}\right) \times \frac{dt}{dx}$$

Having found an expression for $\frac{d^2y}{dx^2}$, it can be used to determine the nature of any stationary points on the parameter curve.

Example 5

Find an expression for $\frac{dy}{dx}$ and $\frac{d^2y}{dx^2}$ for each of the following parametrically defined curves:

a $x = 2t + 3$, $y = \frac{5}{t}$

b $x = 4\cos\theta$, $y = \sin^2\theta$

Solution

a $\frac{dx}{dt} = 2$ and $\frac{dy}{dt} = \frac{-5}{t^2}$

$$\text{So} \quad \frac{dy}{dx} = \left(\frac{dy}{dt}\right) \Big/ \left(\frac{dx}{dt}\right) = \frac{-5}{2t^2}$$

Now $\dfrac{d^2y}{dx^2} = \dfrac{d}{dt}\left(\dfrac{dy}{dx}\right) \times \dfrac{dt}{dx}$

$= \dfrac{d}{dt}\left(\dfrac{-5}{2t^2}\right) \times \dfrac{dt}{dx}$

$= \dfrac{5}{t^3} \times \dfrac{1}{2}$

$= \dfrac{5}{2t^3}$

Remember that $\frac{dt}{dx} = \frac{1}{\left(\frac{dx}{dt}\right)} = \frac{1}{2}$ in this case.

b $\frac{dx}{d\theta} = -4\sin\theta$ and $\frac{dy}{d\theta} = 2\sin\theta\cos\theta$

So $\dfrac{dy}{dx} = \left(\dfrac{dy}{d\theta}\right) \Big/ \left(\dfrac{dx}{d\theta}\right)$

$= \dfrac{2\sin\theta\cos\theta}{-4\sin\theta}$

$= -\frac{1}{2}\cos\theta$

Now $\dfrac{d^2y}{dx^2} = \dfrac{d}{d\theta}\left(\dfrac{dy}{dx}\right) \times \dfrac{d\theta}{dx}$

$= \dfrac{d}{d\theta}(-\frac{1}{2}\cos\theta) \times \dfrac{d\theta}{dx}$

$= \frac{1}{2}\sin\theta \times \dfrac{1}{(-4\sin\theta)}$

$= -\frac{1}{8}$

Example 6

Find the coordinates of the stationary points on the curve defined in terms of a parameter t by $x = t^2 + 1$ and $y = t^3 - 12t$. Use the second derivative to determine the nature of these points.

Solution

$\frac{dx}{dt} = 2t$ and $\frac{dy}{dt} = 3t^2 - 12$

$\dfrac{dy}{dx} = \left(\dfrac{dy}{dt}\right) \Big/ \left(\dfrac{dx}{dt}\right)$

$= \dfrac{3t^2 - 12}{2t}$

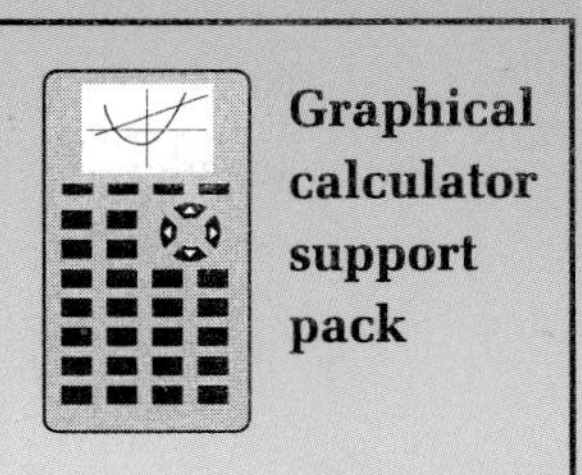

At stationary points on the curve $\frac{dy}{dx} = 0$.

So $\dfrac{3t^2 - 12}{2t} = 0$

$\Rightarrow \quad 3t^2 = 12$

$\Rightarrow \quad t^2 = 4$

$\Rightarrow \quad t = 2$ or $t = -2$

Solve this equation by equating the numerator to zero.

When $t = -2$,

$$x = t^2 + 1 = (-2)^2 + 1 = 5$$

$$y = t^3 - 12t = (-2)^3 - 12(-2) = 16$$

When $t = 2$,

$$x = (2)^2 + 1 = 5$$

$$y = (2)^3 - 12(2) = -16$$

So there are stationary points at (5, 16) and (5, −16) on this curve. Their nature can be determined by evaluating the second derivative at $t = -2$ and $t = 2$ respectively.

$$\frac{d^2y}{dx^2} = \frac{d}{dt}\left(\frac{dy}{dx}\right) \times \frac{dt}{dx}$$

$$= \frac{d}{dt}\left(\frac{3t^2 - 12}{2t}\right) \times \frac{dt}{dx}$$

$$= \frac{6t^2 + 24}{4t^2} \times \frac{1}{2t}$$

$$= \frac{6t^2 + 24}{8t^3}$$

Use the quotient rule.

When $t = -2$,

$$\frac{d^2y}{dx^2} = \frac{6(-2)^2 + 24}{8(-2)^3}$$

$$= -\tfrac{3}{4} < 0$$

So (5, 16) is a maximum point on the curve.

When $t = 2$,

$$\frac{d^2y}{dx^2} = \frac{6(2)^2 + 24}{8(2)^3}$$

$$= \tfrac{3}{4} > 0$$

So (5, −16) is a minimum point on the curve.

Example 7

A curve has parametric equations $x = t^2 + 1$, $y = 1 + 4t - t^2$, $1 \le t \le 5$. Find the coordinates of the stationary point and determine its nature. Sketch the curve.

Solution

$\frac{dx}{dt} = 2t$ and $\frac{dy}{dt} = 4 - 2t$

$$\frac{dy}{dx} = \frac{dy}{dt} \times \frac{dt}{dx}$$
$$= \frac{4 - 2t}{2t}$$

At stationary points on the curve, $\frac{dy}{dx} = 0$.

$$\frac{4 - 2t}{2t} = 0 \quad \Rightarrow \quad 4 - 2t = 0$$
$$t = 2$$

So the stationary point occurs at (5, 5).
To determine its nature we need to evaluate the second derivative.

$$\frac{d^2y}{dx^2} = \frac{d}{dt}\left(\frac{dy}{dx}\right) \times \frac{dt}{dx}$$
$$= \frac{d}{dt}\left(\frac{4 - 2t}{2t}\right) \times \frac{dt}{dx}$$
$$= -\frac{8}{4t^2} \times \frac{1}{2t}$$
$$= -\frac{1}{t^3}$$

When $t = 2$, $\frac{d^2y}{dx^2} < 0$, so (5, 5) is a maximum point.
To sketch the curve we can evaluate x- and y-coordinates for different values of the parameter.

t	1	2	3	4	5
x	2	5	10	17	26
y	4	5	4	1	−4

Together with what we know about the stationary points, we can produce a sketch of the curve:

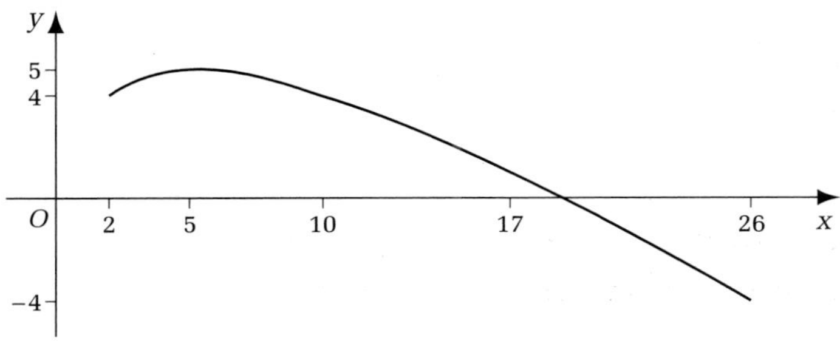

11.6 Parametric Differentiation

Exercise

Technique

1 Eliminate the parameter to find the Cartesian equations of the following curves:

1 a

a $x = 3t,\ y = t^2$

b $x = 2t,\ y = t^3 + 1$

c $x = 5\cos t,\ y = 5\sin t$

d $x = 4\cos\theta,\ y = 3\sin\theta$

e $x = 1 + 2\cos\theta,\ y = 3 + 4\cos\theta$

f $x = a\cos\theta,\ y = b\sin\theta$

2 Find an expression for $\frac{dy}{dx}$ for each of the following parametrically defined curves:

a $x = 1 - t^2$, $y = 6t + 5$

b $x = \cos^2\theta$, $y = 1 - \sin\theta$

c $x = \frac{1}{t+1}$, $y = \frac{1}{t-1}$

3 Find the coordinates of the points on each of the following curves where the gradient has the value indicated:

a $x = t^3 - 3t$, $y = 2t + 1$, $\frac{dy}{dx} = \frac{2}{9}$

b $x = \frac{6}{t}$, $y = t^2$, $\frac{dy}{dx} = -9$

c $x = \tan\theta$, $y = 2 + \sin\theta$, $\frac{dy}{dx} = \frac{1}{8}$

4 Find the equations of the tangent and the normal to the curve with parametric equations $x = e^t,\ y = 1 + e^{2t}$, at the point where $t = 1$.

4

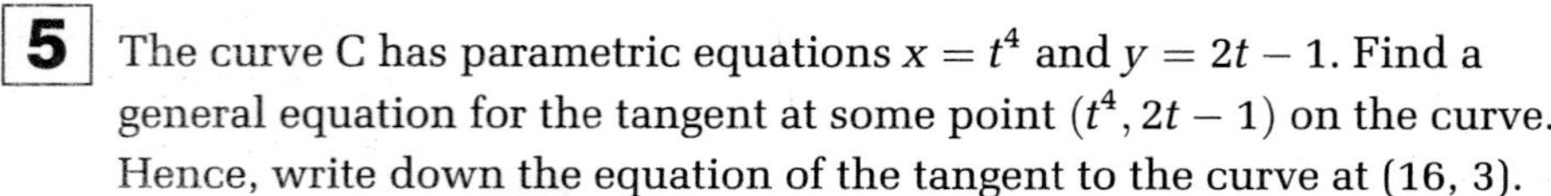

5 The curve C has parametric equations $x = t^4$ and $y = 2t - 1$. Find a general equation for the tangent at some point $(t^4, 2t - 1)$ on the curve. Hence, write down the equation of the tangent to the curve at (16, 3).

6 Find the coordinates of the stationary points on each of the following parametrically defined curves. Find also an expression for the second derivative and use it to determine the nature of these stationary points. Hence, or otherwise, sketch the curve.

a $x = 3t + 1$, $y = t^3 - 6t^2$

b $x = t^3 + 1$, $y = t^2 + t$

11.7 Maclaurin Series

We can express functions such as $\frac{1}{1+3x}$ and $\sqrt{1+2x}$ as a series of ascending powers of x using the binomial theorem (see Chapter 8).

For example,
$$\frac{1}{1+3x} = (1+3x)^{-1}$$
$$= 1 - 3x + 9x^2 - 27x^3 + \ldots \text{ for } |x| < \tfrac{1}{3}$$

and
$$\sqrt{1+2x} = (1+2x)^{\frac{1}{2}}$$
$$= 1 + x - \tfrac{1}{2}x^2 + \tfrac{1}{3}x^3 - \tfrac{5}{8}x^4 + \ldots \text{ for } |x| < \tfrac{1}{2}$$

Recall that the conditions $|x| < \frac{1}{3}$ and $|x| < \frac{1}{2}$ in these expansions ensure that these infinite series will converge. For values outside of these ranges, the series will diverge.

There are several advantages in expressing a function as a power series like this. For small values of x, a linear or quadratic approximation to the function can be made. This can then be used to evaluate the function at a particular value of x, or to find an approximate value for a definite integral involving the function.

Example 1

Use the linear approximation for $\sqrt{1+2x}$ to find the approximate value of the definite integral $\int_0^{0.2} \sqrt{1+2x}\,dx$.

Solution

The binomial expansion for $\sqrt{1+2x}$ is valid for the values of x between the limits of this definite integral. The first two terms of this expansion can be used as a linear approximation to this function.

If the limits of the definite integral had extended beyond $|x| < \frac{1}{2}$ then this linear approximation could not be made.

So
$$\sqrt{1+2x} \approx 1 + x$$

Then
$$\int_0^{0.2} \sqrt{1+2x}\,dx \approx \int_0^{0.2} (1+x)\,dx$$
$$= \left[x + \tfrac{1}{2}x^2\right]_0^{0.2}$$
$$= (0.2 + \tfrac{1}{2} \times 0.2^2) - 0$$
$$= 0.22$$

However, in this particular example the definite integral can be evaluated exactly as follows.

$$\int_0^{0.2} \sqrt{1+2x}\,dx = \left[\tfrac{1}{3}(1+2x)^{\frac{3}{2}}\right]_0^{0.2}$$
$$= \tfrac{1}{3}\left[(1.4)^{\frac{3}{2}} - 1\right]$$
$$= 0.218\,834 \text{ (6 d.p.)}$$

Check the integration using differentiation.

So the linear approximation to the function gives a value for the definite integral that is correct to two decimal places. This approach is particularly useful when evaluating integrals that are difficult to evaluate exactly.

The binomial theorem can only be used to find the series expansions of functions of the form $(a+x)^n$, where n is a rational power. Functions such as $\sin x$, $\cos x$, e^x and $\ln x$ can also be expressed as a series of ascending powers of x using the Maclaurin series.

The Maclaurin series

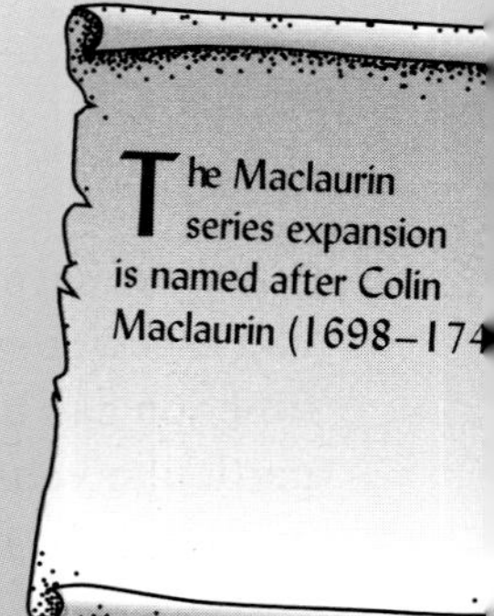

The Maclaurin series expansion is named after Colin Maclaurin (1698–174

Suppose $f(x)$ is some function of x that can be written as a series of ascending powers of x, such that

$$f(x) = a_0 + a_1x + a_2x^2 + a_3x^3 + \ldots + a_rx^r + \ldots$$

where a_r is the coefficient of the x^r term. Assume that $f(x)$ is a function that can be continuously differentiated to find $f'(x)$, $f''(x)$ and its higher derivatives. It follows that

$$f'(x) = a_1 + 2a_2x + 3a_3x^2 + 4a_4x^3 + \ldots$$
$$f''(x) = 2a_2 + 6a_3x + 12a_4x^2 + 20a_5x^3 + \ldots$$
$$f'''(x) = 6a_3 + 24a_4x + 60a_5x^2 + 120a_6x^3 + \ldots$$
$$f^{(4)}(x) = 24a_4 + 120a_5x + 360a_6x^2 + 840a_7x^3 + \ldots \text{ and so on.}$$

$f^{(4)}(x)$ denotes the fourth derivative of $f(x$

Substituting $x = 0$ into these expansions,

$$f(0) = a_0 \qquad \Rightarrow \quad a_0 = f(0)$$
$$f'(0) = a_1 \qquad \Rightarrow \quad a_1 = f'(0)$$
$$f''(0) = 2a_2 = 2! \times a_2 \quad \Rightarrow \quad a_2 = \frac{f''(0)}{2!}$$
$$f'''(0) = 6a_3 = 3! \times a_3 \quad \Rightarrow \quad a_3 = \frac{f'''(0)}{3!}$$
$$f^{(4)}(0) = 24a_4 = 4! \times a_4 \Rightarrow \quad a_4 = \frac{f^{(4)}(0)}{4!}$$

More generally, $$a_r = \frac{f^{(r)}(0)}{r!}$$

where $f^{(r)}(0)$ is the value of the rth derivative of $f(x)$ at $x = 0$. Substituting these values for the coefficients $a_0, a_1, a_2, a_3, a_4, \ldots, a_r, \ldots$ into the series for $f(x)$ gives

$$\mathbf{f(x) = f(0) + xf'(0) + x^2\frac{f''(0)}{2!} + x^3\frac{f'''(0)}{3!} + \ldots + x^r\frac{f^{(r)}(0)}{r!} + \ldots}$$

◀ **Learn this result.**

This is the **Maclaurin series expansion**. It assumes that $f(x)$ is a function that can be expressed as a series of ascending powers of x, and that $f(x)$ and its derivatives are defined at $x = 0$.

Example 2

Find the Maclaurin series expansions for

a e^x **b** $\sin x$

c $\cos x$ **d** $(1+x)^n$, where n is rational.

Solution

a $f(x) = e^x \Rightarrow f(0) = e^0 = 1$

$f'(x) = e^x \Rightarrow f'(0) = e^0 = 1$

$f''(x) = e^x \Rightarrow f''(0) = e^0 = 1$, and so on.

So $f^{(r)}(0) = 1$ for all values of r. Thus the Maclaurin series for e^x is

$$e^x = 1 + x + \frac{x^2}{2!} + \frac{x^3}{3!} + \ldots + \frac{x^r}{r!}$$

◀ **Learn this important result.**

It can be shown that this series converges and is therefore valid for all values of x.

b $f(x) = \sin x \Rightarrow f(0) = \sin 0 = 0$

$f'(x) = \cos x \Rightarrow f'(0) = \cos 0 = 1$

$f''(x) = -\sin x \Rightarrow f''(0) = -\sin 0 = 0$

$f'''(x) = -\cos x \Rightarrow f'''(0) = -\cos 0 = -1$

$f^{(4)}(x) = \sin x \Rightarrow f^{(4)}(0) = \sin 0 = 0$, and so on

So the Maclaurin series for $\sin x$ is

$$\sin x = x - \frac{x^3}{3!} + \frac{x^5}{5!} - \frac{x^7}{7!} + \ldots$$

◀ **Learn this important result.**

This expansion is only valid when the angle is measured in radians.

This series is also valid for all values of x.

c $f(x) = \cos x \Rightarrow f(0) = \cos 0 = 1$

$f'(x) = -\sin x \Rightarrow f'(0) = -\sin 0 = 0$

$f''(x) = -\cos x \Rightarrow f''(0) = -\cos 0 = -1$

$f'''(x) = \sin x \Rightarrow f'''(0) = \sin 0 = 0$

$f^{(4)}(x) = \cos x \Rightarrow f^{(4)}(0) = \cos 0 = 1$, and so on

So the Maclaurin series for $\cos x$ is

$$\cos x = 1 - \frac{x^2}{2!} + \frac{x^4}{4!} - \frac{x^6}{6!} + \dots$$

◀ **Learn this important result.**

This expansion is only valid when the angle is measured in radians.

This series is valid for all values of x.

d
$f(x) = (1+x)^n \Rightarrow f(0) = 1$

$f'(x) = n(1+x)^{n-1} \Rightarrow f'(0) = n$

$f''(x) = n(n-1)(1+x)^{n-2} \Rightarrow f''(0) = n(n-1)$

$f'''(x) = n(n-1)(n-2)(1+x)^{n-3} \Rightarrow f'''(0) = n(n-1)(n-2)$

So the Maclaurin expansion for $(1+x)^n$ is

$$(1+x)^n = 1 + nx + \frac{n(n-1)}{2!}x^2 + \frac{n(n-1)(n-2)}{3!}x^3 + \dots$$

◀ **Learn this important result.**

Notice that the Maclaurin series expansion for $(1+x)^n$ is the same as that obtained using the binomial theorem.

This expansion is valid only if $|x| < 1$.

Example 3

Use the results of Example 2 to find the first three non-zero terms in the Maclaurin series expansions of

a $\sin(\frac{2}{3}x)$ **b** xe^{-4x}

Solution

a Replacing x with $\frac{2}{3}x$ in the Maclaurin series for $\sin x$ gives

$$\begin{aligned}\sin(\tfrac{2}{3}x) &= \tfrac{2}{3}x - \tfrac{1}{3!}(\tfrac{2}{3}x)^3 + \tfrac{1}{5!}(\tfrac{2}{3}x)^5 - \dots\\ &= \tfrac{2}{3}x - \tfrac{1}{6}(\tfrac{8}{27}x^3) + \tfrac{1}{120}(\tfrac{32}{243}x^5) - \dots\\ &= \tfrac{2}{3}x - \tfrac{4}{81}x^3 + \tfrac{4}{3645}x^5 - \dots\end{aligned}$$

This is valid for all x.

b Replacing x with $(-4x)$ in the Maclaurin series for e^x gives

$$\begin{aligned}e^{-4x} &= 1 + (-4x) + \frac{(-4x)^2}{2!} + \dots\\ &= 1 - 4x + \frac{16x^2}{2} + \dots\\ &= 1 - 4x + 8x^2 + \dots\end{aligned}$$

Thus the Maclaurin series for xe^{-4x} is

$$\begin{aligned}xe^{-4x} &= x(1 - 4x + 8x^2 - \dots)\\ &= x - 4x^2 + 8x^3 - \dots\end{aligned}$$

This is valid for all x.

Example 4

Use the quadratic approximation for $\cos x$ to solve the equation $2x = \cos x$, correct to two decimal places.

Solution

Using the Maclaurin expansion derived earlier, the quadratic approximation for $\cos x$ is

$$\cos x \approx 1 - \tfrac{1}{2}x^2$$

So an approximate solution to the equation $2x = \cos x$ can be found by solving

$$2x = 1 - \tfrac{1}{2}x^2$$

$$4x = 2 - x^2$$

Multiply by 2.

$$\Rightarrow\ x^2 + 4x - 2 = 0$$

Check that this quadratic equation has solutions $x = -2 \pm \sqrt{6}$. That is, $x = 0.4495$ or $x = -4.4495$.
The negative root can be ignored because the corresponding value of $2x$ (≈ -8.90) is outside the range of possible values for $\cos x$. This means the approximate solution of the equation $2x = \cos x$ is 0.45 (2 d.p.).

Use a graphical calculator to draw the graphs of $y = \cos x$, $y = 1 - \frac{1}{2}x^2$ and $y = 2x$.

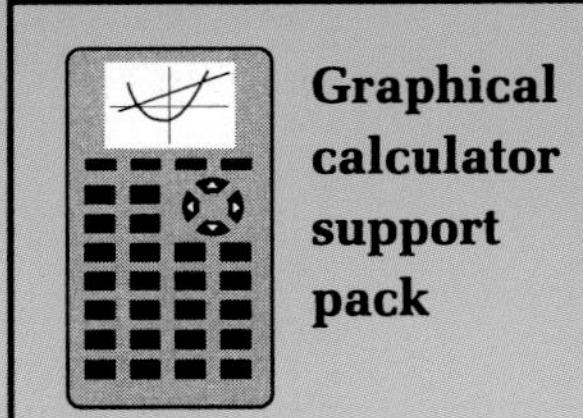

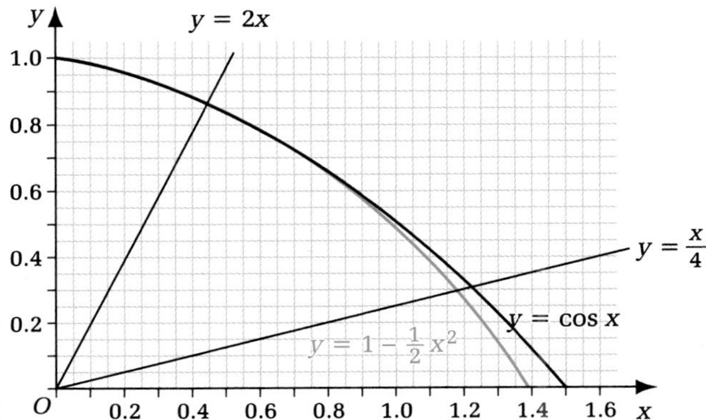

This diagram illustrates that $y = 1 - \frac{1}{2}x^2$ is an extremely good approximation for $\cos x$ for values of x close to 0.45. However, this approximation is not as good for larger values of x close to 1.25, where, for example, the solution of another equation, $\frac{x}{4} = \cos x$, lies.

So it is important to appreciate that this method of solving equations by approximating a function by the first few terms of its series expansion is only valid if the approximation remains good for values of x close to the solution of the equation.

Example 5

Use the Maclaurin series expansion to find the cubic approximation of $\ln(1+x)$. Hence find the approximate value of $\ln(1.1)$.

Solution

$$f(x) = \ln(1+x) \Rightarrow f(0) = \ln 1 = 0$$
$$f'(x) = (1+x)^{-1} \Rightarrow f'(0) = 1$$
$$f''(x) = -(1+x)^{-2} \Rightarrow f''(0) = -1$$
$$f'''(x) = 2(1+x)^{-3} \Rightarrow f'''(0) = 2, \text{ and so on.}$$

Recall that $f'(x) = \frac{1}{(1+x)} = (1+x)$

The Maclaurin series for $\ln(1+x)$ is therefore

$$\ln(1+x) = x - \frac{x^2}{2!} + \frac{2x^3}{3!} - \ldots$$

and the cubic approximation is

$$\ln(1+x) \approx x - \tfrac{1}{2}x^2 + \tfrac{1}{3}x^3$$

Substituting $x = 0.1$ gives

$$\ln(1.1) \approx 0.1 - \tfrac{1}{2}(0.1)^2 + \tfrac{1}{3}(0.1)^3$$
$$\approx 0.1 - 0.005 + 0.000\,3\dot{3}$$
$$\approx 0.0953 \text{ (4 d.p.)}$$

Check this result usi calculator.

By evaluating the higher derivatives of $\ln(1+x)$ when $x = 0$, it is possible to show that the Maclaurin series for $\ln(1+x)$ is

$$\mathbf{\ln(1+x) = x - \tfrac{1}{2}x^2 + \tfrac{1}{3}x^3 - \tfrac{1}{4}x^4 + \tfrac{1}{5}x^5 - \ldots}$$

This expansion is only valid for $-1 < x \leq 1$.

Notice the condition the inequalities.

Replacing x with $-x$ in this series gives

$$\mathbf{\ln(1-x) = -x - \tfrac{1}{2}x^2 - \tfrac{1}{3}x^3 - \tfrac{1}{4}x^4 - \tfrac{1}{5}x^5 - \ldots}$$

This expansion is only valid for $-1 \leq x < 1$.

The Maclaurin expansion cannot be used to find a power series for $\ln x$ because the function and its derivatives $f'(x) = \frac{1}{x}$, $f''(x) = -\frac{1}{x^2}$, $f'''(x) = \frac{2}{x^3}$, and so on, are not defined for $x = 0$.

11.7 Maclaurin Series
Exercise
Technique

1 Find the first three non-zero terms in the Maclaurin series expansions for:

a $\cos\frac{1}{4}x$ **b** x^2e^{5x} **c** $\ln(1+3x)$
d $\tan x$ **e** $\tan^{-1}x$ **f** $e^x\cos x$

2 Use the quadratic approximation for $\cos 2x$ obtained from its Maclaurin series to solve the equation $\cos 2x = 3x$, correct to two decimal places.

3 Find the first three non-zero terms in the Maclaurin series expansion of $\ln(1+2x)$ and $\ln(1-2x)$. Hence, write down a cubic approximation for $\ln\left(\frac{1+2x}{1-2x}\right)$ and, by substituting $x = 0.1$ into it, find the approximate value of $\ln 1.5$ to three decimal places.

Consolidation

Exercise A

1 Given that $y = xe^{-3x}$, find $\frac{dy}{dx}$. Hence find the coordinates of the stationary point on the curve $y = xe^{-3x}$.

(UCLES)

2 A curve is defined by the parametric equations $x = t^2 + 3t$ and $y = 2t - t^2$.

a Find $\frac{dy}{dx}$ in terms of t.

b The normal to the curve at the point P has gradient $\frac{3}{8}$. Determine the coordinates of P.

(AEB)

3

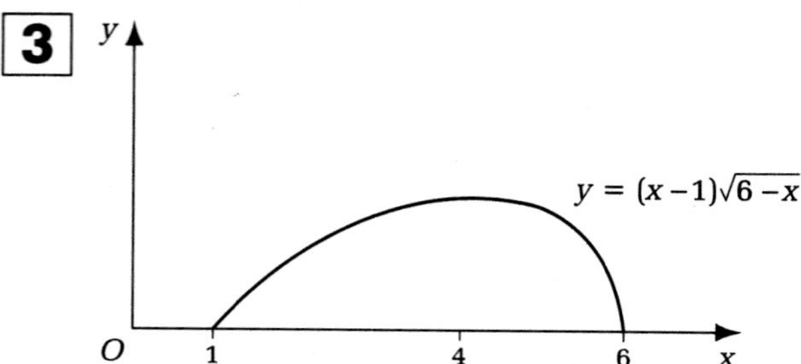

The diagram shows a rough sketch of the graph of $y = (x - 1)\sqrt{6 - x}$.

a Find an expression for $\frac{dy}{dx}$.

b By considering the gradient of the curve at the point where $x = 4$, determine whether the x-coordinate of the maximum point on the graph is less than or greater than 4.

(NEAB)

4 A curve C is given by the equations $x = 2\cos t + \sin 2t$, $y = \cos t - 2\sin 2t$, $0 \le t \le \pi$, where t is a parameter.

a Find $\frac{dx}{dt}$ and $\frac{dy}{dt}$ in terms of t.

b Find the value of $\frac{dy}{dx}$ at the point P on C, where $t = \frac{\pi}{4}$.

c Find an equation of the normal to the curve at P.

(ULEAC)

5 Use Maclaurin's theorem to show that for sufficiently small values of x,

$$(1 + x^2)\tan^{-1} x \approx x + \tfrac{2}{3}x^3 - \tfrac{2}{15}x^5$$

(NICCEA)

6 A curve is defined implicitly by the equation $x^2y + y^2 - 3x - 3 = 0$. Point A has coordinates $(1, 2)$ and point B is where the curve crosses the x-axis.

a Show that point A lies on the curve.
b Find the coordinates of point B.
c Calculate the gradient of the curve at point A.
d Find the equation of the normal to the curve at point A.

(AEB)

7 The parametric equations of a curve are $x = e^{2t} - 5t$ and $y = e^{2t} - 2t$. Find $\frac{dy}{dx}$ in terms of t. Find the exact value of t at the point on the curve where the gradient is 2.

(UCLES)

8 The sketch shows the curve with equation $y = \frac{3x-9}{x^2-x-2}$.

a Write down the equations of the vertical asymptotes.
b Find $\frac{dy}{dx}$ in terms of x and hence determine the coordinates of the maximum and minimum points, A and B, on the curve.

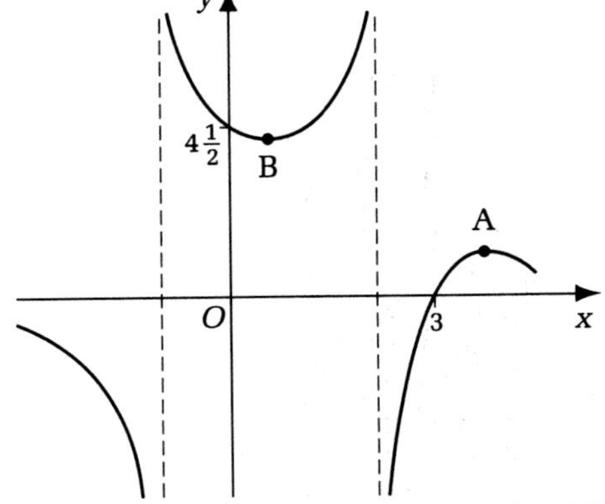

(AEB)

9 It is given that $y = \frac{1}{1+\sin 2x}$. Show that when $x = 0$, $\frac{d^2y}{dx^2} = 8$. Find the first three terms in Maclaurin's series for y.

a Use the series to obtain an approximate value for $\int_{-0.1}^{0.1} y\,dx$, giving your answer correct to four decimal places.
b Find the first two terms of Maclaurin's series for $\frac{dy}{dx}$.

(OCSEB)

10 An oil rig, O, is situated out at sea at a perpendicular distance of 10 km from a straight coastline. The point on the coast nearest to O is P. A refinery, R, is situated on the coast 10 km from P. A project is being planned to bring the oil ashore by means of pipelines running from O directly to a point Q on the coastline and then along the coast to R. The project will cost £5 million per kilometre under the sea and £3 million per kilometre along the coast. Show that if Q is x km from P, the cost of the project will be £C million, where $C = 5\sqrt{100 + x^2} + 30 - 3x$. Show that $\frac{dC}{dx} = 0$ when $x = 7.5$. Find $\frac{d^2C}{dx^2}$ and hence, or otherwise, determine whether C is a maximum or minimum when $x = 7.5$.

(NEAB)

Exercise B

1 A curve has equation $y = x^2 - \frac{54}{x}$. Find $\frac{dy}{dx}$ and $\frac{d^2y}{dx^2}$ in terms of x. Calculate the coordinates of the stationary point of the curve and determine whether it is a maximum or minimum point.

(AEB)

2
a Use Maclaurin's theorem to derive the series expansion for $\cos x$, giving the first three non-zero terms.
b Hence obtain the first three non-zero terms of the series expansions for

i $\cos 2x$ **ii** $\cos^2 x$

(NICCEA)

3 A curve C is defined by the parametric equations $x = 4t + \frac{4}{t}$ and $y = 4t - \frac{4}{t}$.

a Express $\frac{dy}{dx}$ in terms of t, simplifying your answer.
b At the point on the curve C where $t = 2$:

i show that $\frac{dy}{dx} = \frac{5}{3}$
ii find the equation of the normal to the curve.

(NEAB)

4 The number of bacteria present in a culture at time t hours after the beginning of an experiment is denoted by N. The relation between N and t is modelled by $N = 100e^{3t/2}$.

a After how many hours will the number of bacteria be 9000?
b At what rate per hour will the number of bacteria be increasing when $t = 6$?

(UCLES)

5 A curve is given parametrically by the equations $x = 2\theta + \sin 2\theta$, $y = 2\cos^2\theta$, $0 \leq \theta \leq \frac{\pi}{2}$. Show that $\frac{dy}{dx} = -\tan\theta$ (given $\theta \neq \frac{\pi}{2}$). Find the equation of the tangent to the curve at the point where $\theta = \frac{\pi}{4}$.

(AEB)

6 Given that $f(x) = \frac{4x+3a}{x^2+a^2}$, show that $f'(2) = \frac{4(a^2-3a-4)}{(4+a^2)^2}$. Find the two values of the constant a for which $f(x)$ has a stationary value when $x = 2$.

(OCSEB)

7 A curve has equation $x^3 + y^3 + 2x + 5y = 9$. Find an expression for $\frac{dy}{dx}$ in terms of x and y. Hence show that the gradient of the curve is never positive.

(OCSEB)

Applications and Activities

1 *Making a cone*

Cut a sector of angle θ from a circular piece of card of radius 20 cm and attach the two straight edges together to make a right-circular cone of height h cm and base radius r cm.

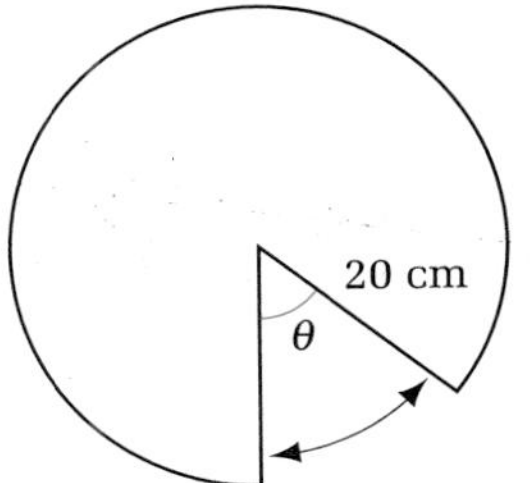

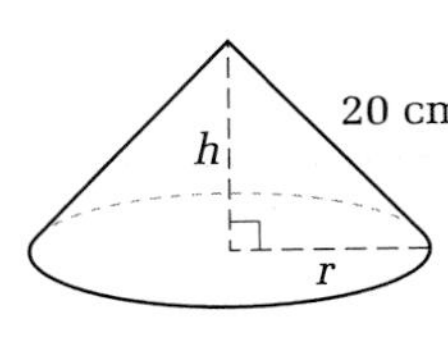

a Find an expression for the perpendicular height, h, of the cone in terms of its base radius, r.

b Use this to find an expression for the volume, V, of the cone in terms of r only.

c Use the product rule to differentiate V with respect to r. Find the exact value of r for which $\frac{dV}{dr} = 0$, and the corresponding value of V. Show that this is the maximum possible volume for a cone made from this particular piece of card.

d Find an expression, in terms of θ, for the length of the circular edge of the piece of card from which the cone is made. Equating this to the circumference of the base of the cone, find the value of θ that corresponds to the maximum possible volume of the cone.

e Repeat these calculations for a cone made from a circular piece of card of radius R cm. In what way is the angle θ that corresponds to the maximum possible volume of the cone dependent on the radius R?

Summary

- The second derivative $\frac{d^2y}{dx^2}$ is used to determine the nature of stationary points:

$$\frac{dy}{dx} = 0 \quad \text{and} \quad \frac{d^2y}{dx^2} > 0 \Rightarrow \text{minimum point}$$

$$\frac{dy}{dx} = 0 \quad \text{and} \quad \frac{d^2y}{dx^2} < 0 \Rightarrow \text{maximum point}$$

- When $\frac{dy}{dx} = 0$ and $\frac{d^2y}{dx^2} = 0$, the gradient must be considered on either side of the stationary point to determine whether it is a maximum point, a minimum point or a point of inflexion.

- A **non-stationary point of inflexion** is a point where the gradient of the curve is at its maximum or minimum value locally. The tangent to the curve at these points crosses from one side of the curve to the other.

- Types of inflexion can be determined by considering the first and third derivatives:

$\frac{dy}{dx}$	$\frac{d^2y}{dx^2}$	$\frac{d^3y}{dx^3}$	Type of inflexion
+ve	0	+ve	
+ve	0	−ve	
−ve	0	−ve	
−ve	0	+ve	

- The **product rule** for differentiation is:

$$\text{If } y = uv, \text{ then } \frac{dy}{dx} = u\frac{dv}{dx} + v\frac{du}{dx} = uv' + vu'$$

- The **quotient rule** for differentiation is:

$$\text{If } y = \frac{u}{v}, \text{ then } \frac{dy}{dx} = \frac{\left(v\frac{du}{dx} - u\frac{dv}{dx}\right)}{v^2} = \frac{(vu' - uv')}{v^2}$$

- $\frac{d}{dx}(e^x) = e^x$ $\quad$ $\frac{d}{dx}(a^x) = a^x \ln a$

- $\frac{d}{dx}(\ln x) = \frac{1}{x}$ $\quad$ $\frac{d}{dx}[\ln f(x)] = \frac{f'(x)}{f(x)}$

- $\frac{d}{dx}(\tan x) = \sec^2 x$ $\quad$ $\frac{d}{dx}(\cot x) = \operatorname{cosec}^2 x$

  $\frac{d}{dx}(\operatorname{cosec} x) = -\operatorname{cosec} x \cot x$ $\quad$ $\frac{d}{dx}(\sec x) = \sec x \tan x$

- $\frac{d}{dx}(\sin^{-1} x) = \frac{1}{\sqrt{1 - x^2}}$ $\quad$ $\frac{d}{dx}(\cos^{-1} x) = -\frac{1}{\sqrt{1 - x^2}}$

  $\frac{d}{dx}(\tan^{-1} x) = \frac{1}{1 + x^2}$

- A function in x and y that cannot be written in the form $y = f(x)$ is an **implicitly defined function**. The method used to find the gradient of an implicit function is **implicit differentiation**, and relies on the chain rule. The product rule and/or the quotient rule may also be needed.

- The first and second derivatives, $\frac{dy}{dx}$ and $\frac{d^2y}{dx^2}$, can be found for parametrically defined curves using the chain rule.

- Maclaurin's theorem can be used to find series expansions for standard functions. For values of x close to 0:

$$f(x) = f(0) + xf'(0) + \frac{x^2 f''(0)}{2!} + \ldots + \frac{x^r f^{(r)}(0)}{r!} + \ldots$$

where $f^{(r)}(0)$ is the rth derivative of $f(x)$ evaluated at $x = 0$.

12 Integration II

What you need to know

- How to integrate polynomials and basic trigonometrical functions by reversing differentiation.
- How to use integration to calculate areas and volumes.
- How to differentiate standard functions and use the product rule.
- How to manipulate algebraic fractions.
- How to express rational functions as partial fractions.
- How to differentiate implicit functions.

Review

1 Integrate the following with respect to x:

Remember that integration is the rev[erse] of differentiation.

a	$x^3 + 5x^2 - x + 10$	**b**	$(x-4)^2$	**c**	$\sin x$
d	$\cos 3x$	**e**	x^n	**f**	$\sin kx$

2 Sketch the curve $y = x^2 + 1$.

a Find the area under the curve between $x = 0$ and $x = 1$.

b Find the volume generated when this area is rotated about the x-axis through one complete turn.

3 Differentiate the following functions with respect to x:

a	$\sin(4x+1)$	**e**	$\ln x$	**h**	$\ln(x^2+7)$
b	e^x	**f**	$\ln 3x$	**i**	xe^x
c	e^{kx}	**g**	$\ln(2x+13)$	**j**	$x \sin 2x$
d	e^{1+3x}				

4 Express each of the following as a proper fraction:

a $\dfrac{x+1}{x-1}$ **b** $\dfrac{x}{x+1}$

5 Express each of the following as partial fractions:

a $\dfrac{x-7}{(x+1)(x+3)}$ **b** $\dfrac{3x-1}{(x+1)(x^2+1)}$ **c** $\dfrac{2x^2-7x-18}{x^2-7x+10}$

6 Find $\frac{dy}{dx}$ for each of the following using implicit differentiation:

a $y^2 = x+1$ **b** $y^2 = x^2 + 2x - 3$

12.1 Standard Integrals

There are many **standard integrals** that can be written down as the direct result of reversing differentiation. In Chapter 9 (Integration I) the following standard integrals were established.

$$\int x^n \, dx = \frac{x^{n+1}}{n+1} + c$$

$$\int \cos kx \, dx = \frac{1}{k} \sin kx + c$$

$$\int \sin kx \, dx = -\frac{1}{k} \cos kx + c, \text{ where } k \text{ is a constant}$$

The use of these standard integrals enables more complicated integration to be carried out far more easily.

Recall that when these standard forms are used to find an indefinite integral, a constant of integration, c, is added at the end. Thus,

$$\int (x^2 + \cos 2x) \, dx = \tfrac{1}{3}x^3 + \tfrac{1}{2}\sin 2x + c$$

Recall the fundamental theorem of calculus from Chapter 9.

This list can be extended by reversing the differentiation of other trigonometrical functions. For example,

$$\frac{d}{dx}(\tan x) = \sec^2 x \Rightarrow \int \sec^2 x \, dx = \tan x + c$$

The chain rule can be used for the more general case.

$$\frac{d}{dx}(\tan kx) = k \sec^2 kx \Rightarrow \int \sec^2 kx \, dx = \frac{1}{k} \tan kx + c$$

Check this result by differentiating $\frac{1}{k}\tan kx$.

What happens if the angle is a function of x?

Try differentiating $\sin(3x - 1)$ and $\cos(3x - 1)$.

Use the chain rule.

$$\frac{d}{dx}[\sin(3x - 1)] = 3\cos(3x - 1)$$

$$\Rightarrow \int \cos(3x - 1) \, dx = \tfrac{1}{3}\sin(3x - 1) + c$$

$$\frac{d}{dx}[\cos(3x - 1)] = -3\sin(3x - 1)$$

$$\Rightarrow \int \sin(3x - 1) \, dx = -\tfrac{1}{3}\cos(3x - 1) + c$$

Look closely at these results. Notice that the angle remains unchanged by both the differentiation and the integration processes.

Example 1

Find:

a $\int \sin 5x\,dx$ **b** $\int \sin(4-2x)\,dx$
c $\int_0^1 \cos(3-x)\,dx$ **d** $\int_0^{\pi/8} \sec^2 2x\,dx$

Solution

a $\displaystyle\int \sin 5x\,dx = -\tfrac{1}{5}\cos 5x + c$ ◀ $\displaystyle\int \sin kx\,dx = -\frac{1}{k}\cos kx + c$

Check that differentiation reverses the integration process.

b $$\int \sin(4-2x)\,dx = -\frac{1}{(-2)}\cos(4-2x)+c$$
$$= \frac{1}{2}\cos(4-2x)+c$$

c $$\int_0^1 \cos(3-x)\,dx = \left[\frac{1}{-1}\sin(3-x)\right]_0^1$$
$$= (-\sin 2) - (-\sin 3)$$
$$= -\sin 2 + \sin 3$$
$$= -0.768 \quad (3\text{ d.p.})$$

Use radians when integrating.

Use a calculator to check that $-\sin 2 + \sin 3 = -0.7$

d $$\int_0^{\pi/8} \sec^2 2x\,dx = \left[\tfrac{1}{2}\tan 2x\right]_0^{\pi/8}$$
$$= \left(\tfrac{1}{2}\tan\tfrac{\pi}{4}\right) - \left(\tfrac{1}{2}\tan 0\right)$$
$$= \left(\tfrac{1}{2}\times 1\right) - \left(\tfrac{1}{2}\times 0\right) = \tfrac{1}{2}$$

$\frac{d}{dx}(\tan kx) = k\sec^2 kx$
$\int \sec^2 kx\,dx = \frac{1}{k}\tan kx$

Remember to use double angle formulas when integrating $\sin^2 x$ or $\cos^2 x$ (see Chapter 9). Sometimes the compound angle formulas can be used to transform an integral into a 'simpler form'.

$$\sin(A+B) = \sin A\cos B + \cos A\sin B \qquad [1]$$

$$\sin(A-B) = \sin A\cos B - \cos A\sin B \qquad [2]$$

$$\cos(A+B) = \cos A\cos B - \sin A\sin B \qquad [3]$$

$$\cos(A-B) = \cos A\cos B + \sin A\sin B \qquad [4]$$

Example 2

Find:

a $\int \sin 5x\cos 2x\,dx$
b $\int_0^{\pi/4} \sin x\sin 3x\,dx$

Solution

a Adding formulas [1] and [2],

$$\sin(A+B)+\sin(A-B)=2\sin A\cos B$$

Now let $A=5x$ and $B=2x$

$$\begin{aligned}\text{Then}\quad \sin(5x+2x)+\sin(5x-2x)&=2\sin 5x\cos 2x\\ \Rightarrow\quad \sin 7x+\sin 3x&=2\sin 5x\cos 2x\\ \Rightarrow\quad \tfrac{1}{2}(\sin 7x+\sin 3x)&=\sin 5x\cos 2x\end{aligned}$$

The product $\sin 5x\cos 2x$ has now been transformed into the sum of two trigonometrical functions, which can be integrated.

$$\begin{aligned}\int \sin 5x\cos 2x\,dx&=\int \tfrac{1}{2}(\sin 7x+\sin 3x)\,dx\\ &=\tfrac{1}{2}\int(\sin 7x+\sin 3x)\,dx\\ &=\tfrac{1}{2}[-\tfrac{1}{7}\cos 7x-\tfrac{1}{3}\cos 3x]+c\\ &=-\tfrac{1}{14}\cos 7x-\tfrac{1}{6}\cos 3x+c\end{aligned}$$

A constant multiplier can be moved outside the integration symbol.

b Subtracting formula [4] from formula [3],

$$\cos(A+B)-\cos(A-B)=-2\sin A\sin B$$

Let $A=x$ and $B=3x$. Then

$$\begin{aligned}\cos(x+3x)-\cos(x-3x)&=-2\sin x\sin 3x\\ -\tfrac{1}{2}[\cos 4x-\cos(-2x)]&=\sin x\sin 3x\end{aligned}$$

Recall that cosine is an even function, so that $\cos(-2x)=\cos 2x$.

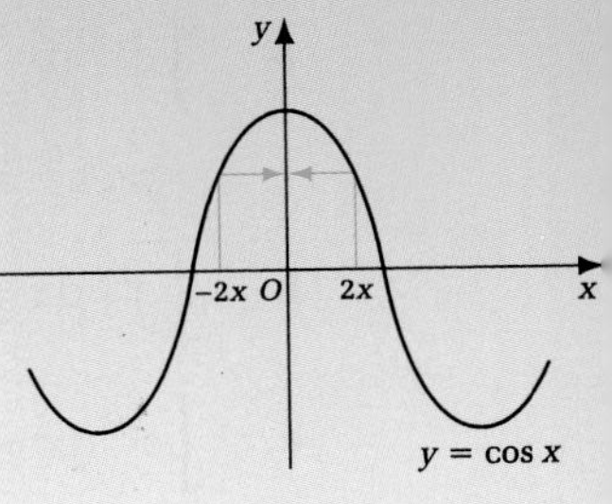

So $\quad \sin x\sin 3x=-\tfrac{1}{2}(\cos 4x-\cos 2x)$

$$\begin{aligned}\text{Now}\quad \int_0^{\pi/4}\sin x\sin 3x\,dx&=\int_0^{\pi/4}-\tfrac{1}{2}(\cos 4x-\cos 2x)\,dx\\ &=-\tfrac{1}{2}\int_0^{\pi/4}(\cos 4x-\cos 2x)\,dx\\ &=-\tfrac{1}{2}\left[\tfrac{1}{4}\sin 4x-\tfrac{1}{2}\sin 2x\right]_0^{\pi/4}\\ &=-\tfrac{1}{2}\left[\left(\tfrac{1}{4}\sin\pi-\tfrac{1}{2}\sin\tfrac{\pi}{2}\right)-\left(\tfrac{1}{4}\sin 0-\tfrac{1}{2}\sin 0\right)\right]\\ &=-\tfrac{1}{2}\left(\tfrac{1}{4}\times 0-\tfrac{1}{2}\times 1-0+0\right)\\ &=-\tfrac{1}{2}\left(-\tfrac{1}{2}\right)=\tfrac{1}{4}\end{aligned}$$

The exponential function

Remember that one important feature of the exponential function is that its gradient function is equal to the function itself. By applying the chain rule to the exponential function, derivatives can be found as follows, and by thinking of integration as the reverse of differentiation we can write down another set of standard integrals.

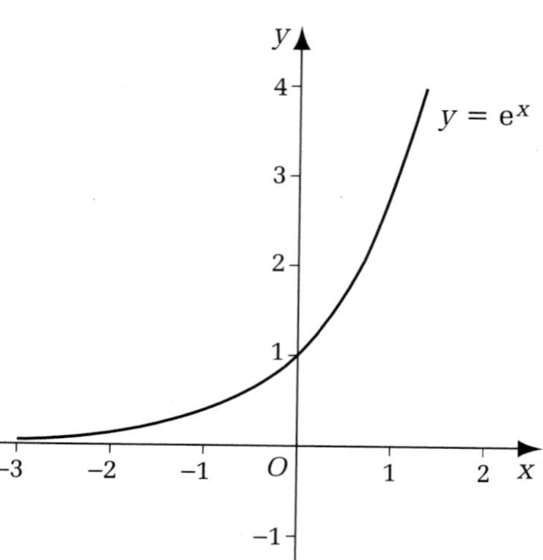

$$\frac{d}{dx}(e^x) = e^x \quad \Rightarrow \quad \int e^x\,dx = e^x + c \qquad [1]$$

◀ Learn these important results.

$$\frac{d}{dx}(e^{ax}) = ae^{ax} \quad \Rightarrow \quad \int e^{ax}\,dx = \frac{1}{a}e^{ax} + c \qquad [2]$$

$$\frac{d}{dx}(e^{ax+b}) = ae^{ax+b} \quad \Rightarrow \quad \int e^{ax+b}\,dx = \frac{1}{a}e^{ax+b} + c \qquad [3]$$

Example 3

Find:

a $\int e^{-x}\,dx$ **b** $\int e^{2x}\,dx$ **c** $\int e^{\frac{1}{2}x}\,dx$ **d** $\int_0^1 e^{2-5x}\,dx$

Solution

a $\int e^{-x}\,dx = \frac{1}{-1}e^{-x} + c$ ◀ Using result [2], with $a = -1$.

$= -e^{-x} + c$

b $\int e^{2x}\,dx = \frac{1}{2}e^{2x} + c$ ◀ Using result [2], with $a = 2$.

c $\int e^{\frac{1}{2}x}\,dx = \frac{1}{\left(\frac{1}{2}\right)}e^{\frac{1}{2}x} + c = 2e^{\frac{1}{2}x} + c$

d $\int_0^1 e^{2-5x}\,dx = \left[-\frac{1}{5}e^{2-5x}\right]_0^1$

$= \left(-\frac{1}{5}e^{2-5}\right) - \left(-\frac{1}{5}e^{2-0}\right)$

$= -\frac{1}{5}e^{-3} + \frac{1}{5}e^2$

$= \frac{1}{5}(e^2 - e^{-3}) = 1.468$ (3 d.p.)

It is always useful to check your integration by mentally differentiating your answer. In **b**, $\frac{d}{dx}\left(\frac{1}{2}e^{2x} + c\right) = \frac{1}{2} \times 2e^{2x}$

Recall that $\frac{1}{\left(\frac{1}{2}\right)} = 2$.

Logarithmic functions

A further set of important integrals can be found by reversing the differentiation of logarithmic functions. Recall from Chapter 11 that

$$\frac{d}{dx}(\ln x) = \frac{1}{x} \quad \Rightarrow \quad \int \frac{1}{x}\,dx = \ln x + c$$

◀ Learn these important results.

True when $x > 0$, since logarithms are defined for positive numbers.

$$\frac{d}{dx}[\ln f(x)] = \frac{f'(x)}{f(x)} \quad \Rightarrow \quad \int \frac{f'(x)}{f(x)}\,dx = \ln[f(x)] + c$$

Example 4

Find:

a $\int \frac{3}{x}\,dx$ **b** $\int \frac{6}{1+3x}\,dx$ **c** $\int \frac{1}{1-x}\,dx$

d $\int \frac{2x}{3x^2+1}\,dx$ **e** $\int \tan x\,dx$

Solution

a $\int \frac{3}{x}\,dx = 3\int \frac{1}{x}\,dx$

$= 3\ln x + c$

Take out the factor 3 then use the standard result.

b $\int \frac{6}{1+3x}\,dx = 2\int \frac{3}{1+3x}\,dx$

$= 2\ln(1+3x) + c$

By extracting a factor of 2, an integrand of the form $\frac{f'(x)}{f(x)}$ is formed.

c $\int \frac{1}{1-x}\,dx = -1\int \frac{-1}{1-x}\,dx$

$= -1 \times \ln(1-x) + c$

$= -\ln(1-x) + c$

Take out the factor -1 to use the standard result.

d $\int \frac{2x}{3x^2+1}\,dx = \frac{1}{3}\int \frac{6x}{3x^2+1}\,dx$

$= \frac{1}{3}\ln(3x^2+1) + c$

$f(x) = 3x^2 + 1$ and $f'(x) = 6x$. Notice how $2x$ is written as $\frac{1}{3} \times 6x = \frac{1}{3} \times f'(x)$.

e $\int \tan x\,dx = \int \frac{\sin x}{\cos x}\,dx$

$= -1\int \frac{-\sin x}{\cos x}\,dx$

$= -\ln(\cos x) + c$

$= \ln(\cos x)^{-1} + c$ ◀ $n\ln x = \ln x^n$

$= \ln(\sec x) + c$

Recall that $(\cos x)^{-1} = \frac{1}{\cos x} = \sec x$.

Definite integrals involving logarithms

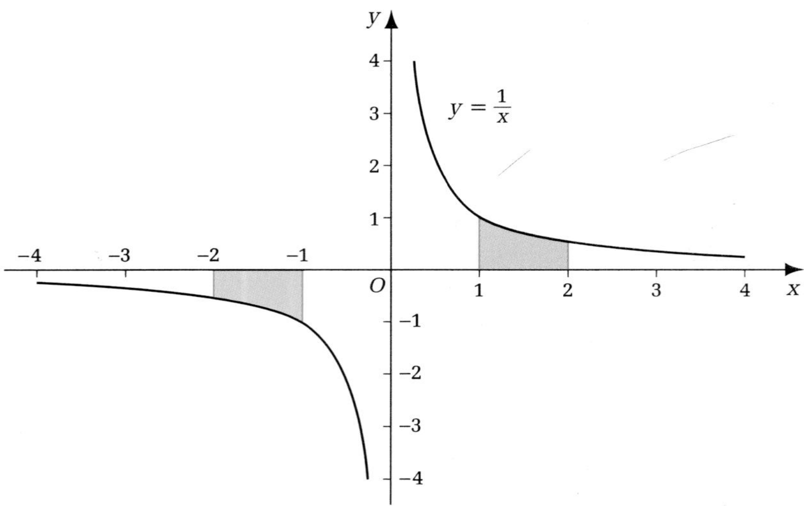

The diagram shows the graph of $y = \frac{1}{x}$. The areas of the shaded regions are equal. Since we find the area under the curve by integrating between limits, we would expect $\int_1^2 \frac{1}{x}\,dx = -\int_{-2}^{-1} \frac{1}{x}\,dx$.

The minus sign indic[ates] that the area is below [the] x-axis.

$$\int_1^2 \frac{1}{x}\,dx = [\ln x]_1^2$$
$$= \ln 2 - \ln 1$$
$$= \ln 2$$

$$\int_{-2}^{-1} \frac{1}{x}\,dx = [\ln x]_{-2}^{-1}$$
$$= \ln(-1) - \ln(-2)$$

But we get stuck here because we cannot find the logarithm of a negative number on a calculator; the logarithmic function is only defined for positive values of x. To avoid unnecessary complications with logarithms of negative numbers, we use the modulus function when integrating with the logarithmic function.
In this example,

$$\int_{-2}^{-1} \frac{1}{x}\,dx = [\ln|x|]_{-2}^{-1}$$
$$= \ln|-1| - \ln|-2|$$
$$= \ln 1 - \ln 2$$
$$= -\ln 2$$

Remember that the modulus function tell[s] us to take the absolut[e] value.

In general:

$$\int_a^b \frac{f'(x)}{f(x)}\,dx = [\ln|f(x)|]_a^b \quad \text{and} \quad \int \frac{f'(x)}{f(x)}\,dx = \ln|f(x)| + c$$

Check Example 4. No[te] that the modulus function is needed fo[r] parts but **d**, because it['s] possible for $f(x) < 0$.

Example 5

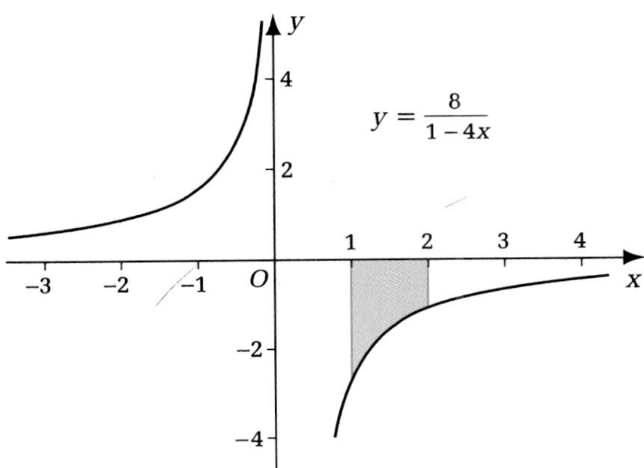

The diagram shows part of the curve $y = \frac{8}{1-4x}$. Find the area of the shaded region.

Solution

Remember to take the limits from the diagram.

$$\text{shaded area} = \int_1^2 \frac{8}{1-4x}\,dx$$

$$= -2\int_1^2 \frac{-4}{1-4x}\,dx$$

$$= -2[\ln|1-4x|]_1^2$$

$$= -2[\ln|-7| - \ln|-3|]$$

$$= -2[\ln 7 - \ln 3]$$

$$= -2\ln\left(\tfrac{7}{3}\right)$$

Use the modulus form because $1 - 4x$ is negative for $x > \frac{1}{4}$.

The minus sign signifies that the area is below the x-axis, so the shaded area is $2\ln\left(\frac{7}{3}\right)$.

Inverse trigonometric functions

Another set of important integrals can be found by studying the results of differentiating inverse trigonometrical functions. Begin with $\sin^{-1}\left(\frac{x}{a}\right)$ and $\tan^{-1}\left(\frac{x}{a}\right)$, where a is a constant. Using general functions like these will allow us to establish another set of general integrals.

Recall the alternative notation $\arcsin\left(\frac{x}{a}\right)$ and $\arctan\left(\frac{x}{a}\right)$.

Let $\qquad y = \sin^{-1}\left(\dfrac{x}{a}\right)$

Then $\qquad \sin y = \dfrac{x}{a}$

Recall from Chapter 11 how to differentiate $\sin y$ implicitly with respect to x.

Differentiating with respect to x,

$$\cos y\frac{dy}{dx} = \frac{1}{a}$$

So $\qquad \dfrac{dy}{dx} = \dfrac{1}{a\cos y}$

Notice that the expression for $\frac{dy}{dx}$ contains a $\cos y$ term. This can be eliminated by using the Pythagorean identity $\sin^2\theta + \cos^2\theta \equiv 1$, as follows.

If $\quad \sin^2 y + \cos^2 y \equiv 1$

Then
$$\cos^2 y = 1 - \sin^2 y$$
$$= 1 - \frac{x^2}{a^2} \quad \blacktriangleleft \text{ Using } \sin y = \frac{x}{a}.$$
$$= \frac{a^2 - x^2}{a^2}$$
$$\cos y = \sqrt{\frac{a^2 - x^2}{a^2}}$$
$$= \frac{\sqrt{a^2 - x^2}}{a}$$

Notice that we only use the positive root, because $-\frac{\pi}{2} \le y \le \frac{\pi}{2}$.

Substituting this result into the expression for $\frac{dy}{dx}$,

$$\frac{dy}{dx} = \frac{1}{a\cos y} = \frac{1}{a\left(\frac{\sqrt{a^2 - x^2}}{a}\right)} = \frac{1}{\sqrt{a^2 - x^2}}$$

Reversing the differentiation we obtain the following important result:

$$\int \frac{1}{\sqrt{a^2 - x^2}}\,dx = \sin^{-1}\left(\frac{x}{a}\right) + c$$

◀ **Learn this result.**

Compare this to the result on page 451 (Ch. 11).

where c is the constant of integration.
The same technique can be used with $\tan^{-1}(\frac{x}{a})$.

Let $\quad y = \tan^{-1}\left(\frac{x}{a}\right)$

Then $\quad \tan y = \frac{x}{a}$

Differentiating with respect to x,

Implicitly differentiate $\tan y$ with respect to x.

$$\sec^2 y \frac{dy}{dx} = \frac{1}{a}$$

So
$$\frac{dy}{dx} = \frac{1}{a\sec^2 y}$$

This time use the Pythagorean identity $1 + \tan^2\theta \equiv \sec^2\theta$ to find $\frac{dy}{dx}$ in terms of x only.

If $\quad \sec^2 y = 1 + \tan^2 y$

Then $\quad \sec^2 y = 1 + \frac{x^2}{a^2} = \frac{a^2 + x^2}{a^2}$

$$\frac{dy}{dx} = \frac{1}{a \times \left(\frac{a^2 + x^2}{a^2}\right)}$$

$$= \frac{1}{\left(\frac{a^2 + x^2}{a}\right)} = \frac{a}{a^2 + x^2}$$

So $\displaystyle \int \frac{a}{a^2 + x^2}\,dx = \tan^{-1}\left(\frac{x}{a}\right) + c$ ◀ **Learn this result.**

and $\displaystyle \int \frac{1}{a^2 + x^2}\,dx = \frac{1}{a}\tan^{-1}\left(\frac{x}{a}\right) + c$

Remember that the constant a can be taken outside the integration symbol.

Example 6

Find:

a $\displaystyle \int \frac{1}{\sqrt{1 - x^2}}\,dx$ **b** $\displaystyle \int \frac{1}{2 + x^2}\,dx$

Solution

a Using the standard result $\displaystyle \int \frac{1}{\sqrt{a^2 - x^2}}\,dx = \sin^{-1}\left(\frac{x}{a}\right) + c$, with $a = 1$

$$\int \frac{1}{\sqrt{1 - x^2}}\,dx = \sin^{-1}\left(\frac{x}{1}\right) + c = \sin^{-1} x + c$$

b Using the standard result $\displaystyle \int \frac{1}{a^2 + x^2}\,dx = \frac{1}{a}\tan^{-1}\left(\frac{x}{a}\right) + c$, with $a = \sqrt{2}$

$$\int \frac{1}{2 + x^2}\,dx = \int \frac{1}{(\sqrt{2})^2 + x^2}\,dx = \frac{1}{\sqrt{2}}\tan^{-1}\left(\frac{x}{\sqrt{2}}\right) + c$$

Example 7

Evaluate $\displaystyle \int_0^1 \frac{3}{\sqrt{4 - x^2}}\,dx$.

Solution

Rearrange the integral in standard form by extracting a factor of 3 outside the integral sign and changing the 4 to 2^2.

$$\int_0^1 \frac{3}{\sqrt{4 - x^2}}\,dx = 3\int_0^1 \frac{1}{\sqrt{2^2 - x^2}}\,dx$$

$$= 3\left[\sin^{-1}\left(\frac{x}{2}\right)\right]_0^1$$

$$= 3[\sin^{-1}(\tfrac{1}{2}) - \sin^{-1}(0)]$$

$$= 3\left[\frac{\pi}{6} - 0\right] = \frac{\pi}{2}$$

Remember to work in radians.

Recall the special angles.

12.1 Standard Integrals Exercise

Technique

1 Find:

a $\int \sin 3x\,dx$ **b** $\int \cos 4x\,dx$ **c** $\int \sin(2x-1)\,dx$

d $\int \cos(1+2x)\,dx$ **e** $\int \sec^2 3x\,dx$ **f** $\int (1+\sec^2 2x)\,dx$

1 a

2 Evaluate:

a $\int_0^{\pi/4} \sin 2\theta\,d\theta$ **b** $\int_0^{3/2} \cos(1+2\theta)\,d\theta$

c $\int_0^{\pi/4} \sec^2 x\,dx$ **d** $\int_0^{\pi/6} \sec^2 2x\,dx$

3 Find:

a $\int \sin 2x \cos x\,dx$ **b** $\int \cos 2x \cos x\,dx$

c $\int_0^{\pi/2} \sin 3x \sin x\,dx$ **d** $\int_0^{\pi} \sin x \cos 2x\,dx$

4 Find:

a $\int e^{5x}\,dx$ **d** $\int e^{\frac{1}{3}x}\,dx$ **g** $\int 2e^{2x}\,dx$

b $\int e^{-x}\,dx$ **e** $\int e^{\frac{2}{3}x}\,dx$ **h** $\int \frac{1}{2}e^{-6x}\,dx$

c $\int \frac{1}{e^{3x}}\,dx$ **f** $\int e^{-\frac{1}{4}x}\,dx$ **i** $\int 3e^{-0.1x}\,dx$

4 f

5 Find:

a $\int (2x+3e^{2x})\,dx$ **d** $\int (1-e^{1-2x})\,dx$ **f** $\int_0^2 (x-3e^{-x})\,dx$

b $\int (1-e^{-x})\,dx$ **e** $\int_0^1 2e^{4x}\,dx$ **g** $\int_0^{1/2} e^{1+2x}\,dx$

c $\int (1+e^x)^2\,dx$

6 Find:

a $\int \frac{4}{x}\,dx$ **b** $\int \frac{1}{2x}\,dx$ **c** $\int \frac{x+1}{x}\,dx$ **d** $\int \frac{1}{x+2}\,dx$

e $\int \frac{4}{2x+1}\,dx$ **f** $\int \frac{3}{7+6x}\,dx$ **g** $\int \frac{5}{2-3x}\,dx$ **h** $\int \frac{1}{1-7x}\,dx$

6 b

7 Find:

a $\int \frac{2x}{1+x^2}\,dx$ **b** $\int \frac{x}{4+3x^2}\,dx$ **c** $\int \frac{2x+1}{x^2+x}\,dx$

d $\int \frac{x}{1-x^2}\,dx$ **e** $\int_1^2 \frac{1}{2x-1}\,dx$ **f** $\int_0^1 \frac{x}{1+x^2}\,dx$

7 b

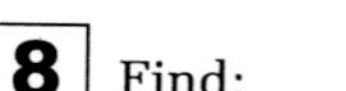

8 Find:

a $\int \cot x\,dx$ **b** $\int \frac{\sin x}{1+\cos x}\,dx$ **c** $\int \frac{\cos x}{1+\sin x}\,dx$

9 Find:

a $\int \frac{1}{\sqrt{1-x^2}}\,dx$ **b** $\int \frac{1}{\sqrt{9-x^2}}\,dx$ **c** $\int \frac{1}{9+x^2}\,dx$

d $\int \frac{2}{3+x^2}\,dx$ **e** $\int \frac{4}{\sqrt{2-x^2}}\,dx$ **f** $\int \frac{1}{7+x^2}\,dx$

9 a

Contextual

1 Sketch the curve $y = 1 + \sin 2x$ for $0 \leq x \leq \pi$. Find the area bound by the curve, the y-axis and the positive x-axis, leaving your answer in terms of π.

2

The graph shows the curve $y = \sin(1 - x)$

a Verify that the x-coordinate of P is 1.

b Calculate the area of the shaded region, giving your answer correct to two decimal places.

3

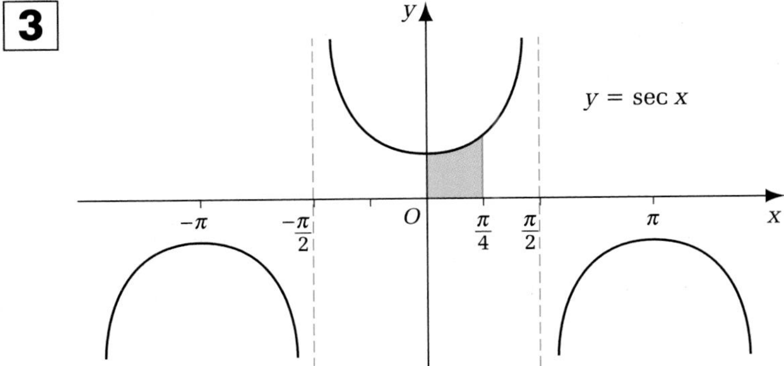

The diagram shows part of the graph of $y = \sec x$. Find the volume generated when the shaded area is rotated about the x-axis through four right-angles.

4 **a** Use $1 + \tan^2 A \equiv \sec^2 A$ to express $\tan^2 2x$ in terms of $\sec^2 2x$.

b Find $\int \tan^2 2x \, dx$.

5 If $g'(x) = 12\cos(1 + 2x)$ and $g(-\frac{1}{2}) = 1$, find $g(x)$.

6 The diagram shows the graph of $y = e^{1-\frac{1}{2}x}$. Calculate the area of the shaded region, leaving your answer in terms of e.

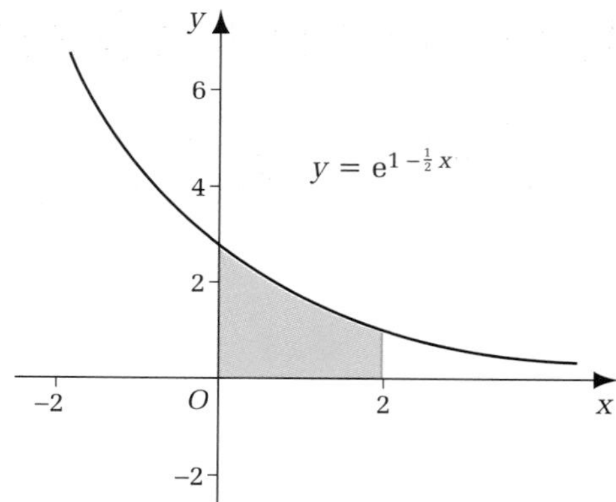

7 Sketch the graph of $y = \frac{1}{2}e^{2x}$. Find the volume generated when the area under the curve between $x = 0$ and $x = 1$ is rotated about the x-axis through one complete revolution.

8 If $2^x = e^m$ find an expression for m in terms of x. Hence evaluate $\int_0^1 2^x \, dx$.

9 Sketch the graph of $y = \frac{2}{x}$. Calculate the area under the graph between $x = 1$ and $x = 4$.

10 **a**

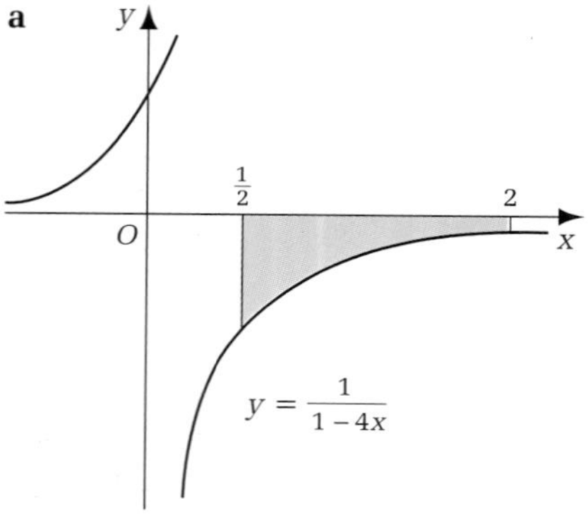

b

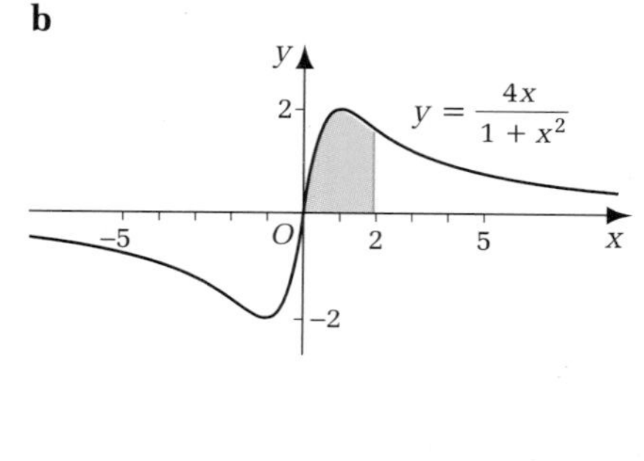

Calculate the areas of the shaded regions.

11 **a**

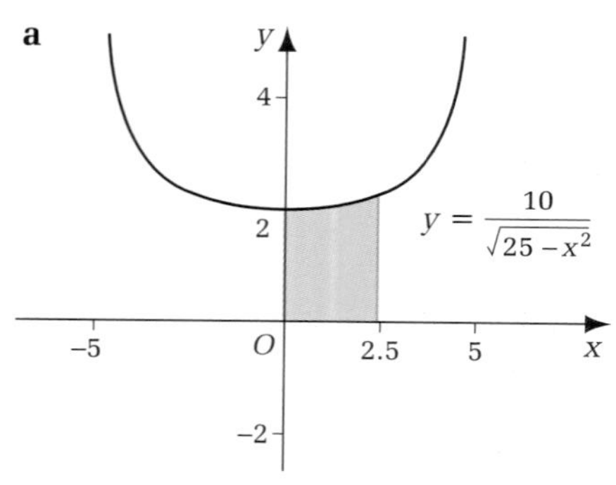

b

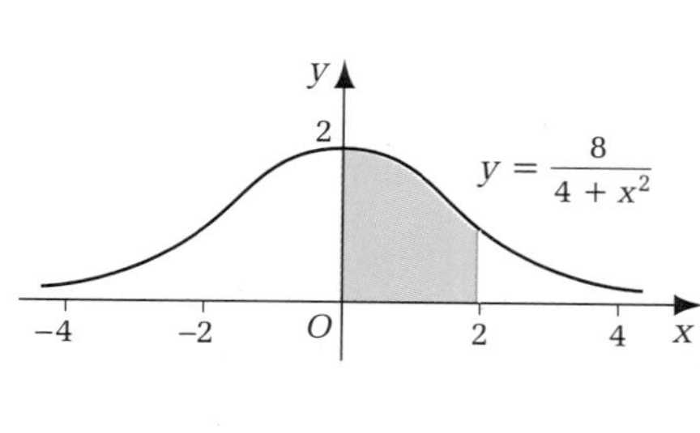

Calculate the areas of the shaded regions.

12.2 Rational Functions

A **rational function** is a fraction where both numerator and denominator are polynomials (the numerator can be a constant). Some examples are:

$$\frac{x}{1+x^2} \quad \frac{x-1}{x+1} \quad \frac{x^2}{1+x} \quad \frac{2x-1}{(x+1)(x-2)}$$

Recall that when the degree of the numerator is less than the degree of the denominator it is called a **proper fraction**. When the degree of the numerator is equal to or greater than the degree of the denominator, it is called an **improper fraction**.

When integrating rational functions, first check to see whether the fraction is proper or improper. For example, $\frac{x}{1+x^2}$ is a proper fraction and can be written in the form $\frac{kf'(x)}{f(x)}$, where k is a constant.

So $$\int \frac{x}{1+x^2}\,dx = \frac{1}{2}\int \frac{2x}{1+x^2}\,dx \quad \blacktriangleleft \text{ Recall } \int \frac{f'(x)}{f(x)}\,dx = \ln[f(x)] + c.$$
$$= \frac{1}{2}\ln(1+x^2) + c$$

The modulus function isn't required because $1 + x^2 > 0$ for all x.

Improper fractions cannot be written in the form $\frac{kf'(x)}{f(x)}$, where k is a constant. To integrate an improper fraction first write it as the sum or difference of proper algebraic fractions. Then try to use the list of standard integrals.

Simple improper fractions

All improper fractions can be expressed as the sum or difference of a polynomial and a proper fraction.

One way of doing this is to write the numerator in terms of the denominator.

Example 1

Find:

a $\displaystyle\int \frac{x}{1-x}\,dx$ **b** $\displaystyle\int \frac{x+1}{x-1}\,dx$ **c** $\displaystyle\int \frac{x^3}{7+x^2}\,dx$

Solution

a First express $\frac{x}{1-x}$ as the sum of a polynomial and a proper fraction. Do this by writing the numerator in terms of the denominator

$$\frac{x}{1-x} = \frac{-(1-x)+1}{1-x} = \frac{-(1-x)}{1-x} + \frac{1}{1-x}$$
$$= -1 + \frac{1}{1-x}$$

Now $\int \frac{x}{1-x}\,dx = \int \left(-1 + \frac{1}{1-x}\right) dx$

$= -x + \int \frac{1}{1-x}\,dx$

$= -x - \int \frac{-1}{1-x}\,dx$ ◀ Use $\int \frac{f'(x)}{f(x)}\,dx = \ln|f(x)| + c$.

$= -x - \ln|1-x| + c$

The integral is now in the standard form $\frac{f'(x)}{f(x)}$ where $f(x) = 1 - x$.

Check this result by differentiation.

b First write $\frac{x+1}{x-1}$ as a sum involving a proper fraction.

$\frac{x+1}{x-1} = \frac{(x-1)+2}{x-1}$

$= \frac{x-1}{x-1} + \frac{2}{x-1}$

$= 1 + \frac{2}{x-1}$

Check that $x - 1 + 2 = x + 1$.

Now $\int \frac{x+1}{x-1}\,dx = \int \left(1 + \frac{2}{x-1}\right) dx$

$= x + 2\int \frac{1}{x-1}\,dx$ ◀ The form $\int \frac{f'(x)}{f(x)}\,dx$.

$= x + 2\ln|x-1| + c$

Integrate each term separately.

Check this result by differentiation.

c $\frac{x^3}{7+x^2} = \frac{7x + x^3 - 7x}{7+x^2} = \frac{x(7+x^2) - 7x}{7+x^2}$

$= \frac{x(7+x^2)}{7+x^2} - \frac{7x}{7+x^2}$

$= x - \frac{7x}{7+x^2}$

Write as a proper algebraic fraction first.

Now $\int \frac{x^3}{7+x^2}\,dx = \int \left(x - \frac{7x}{7+x^2}\right) dx$

$= \frac{1}{2}x^2 - 7\int \frac{x}{7+x^2}\,dx$

$= \frac{1}{2}x^2 - \frac{7}{2}\int \frac{2x}{7+x^2}\,dx$ ◀ The form $\int \frac{f'(x)}{f(x)}\,dx$.

$= \frac{1}{2}x^2 - \frac{7}{2}\ln(7+x^2) + c$

Integrate each term separately.

Check this result by differentiation.

Partial fractions

If the denominator can be factorised, partial fractions can be used to simplify the rational function (see Chapter 6).

Example 2

Use partial fractions to find:

a $\displaystyle\int \frac{x}{x^2 - 4x - 5}\,dx$ **b** $\displaystyle\int \frac{2}{x(1-x)}\,dx$ **c** $\displaystyle\int \frac{1}{x^3 + x^2}\,dx$

Solution

a Recall from Chapter 6 the technique of writing partial fractions.

$$\frac{x}{x^2 - 4x - 5} \equiv \frac{x}{(x+1)(x-5)}$$

Factorising the denominator.

$$\frac{x}{(x+1)(x-5)} \equiv \frac{A}{x+1} + \frac{B}{x-5}$$

$$\equiv \frac{A(x-5) + B(x+1)}{(x+1)(x-5)}$$

Equating the numerators on both sides,

$$x \equiv A(x-5) + B(x+1)$$

Since this is true for all x, it is true for $x = 5$ and $x = -1$.

When $x = 5$, $5 = 6B \Rightarrow B = \frac{5}{6}$

When $x = -1$, $-1 = -6A \Rightarrow A = \frac{1}{6}$

So $\displaystyle\frac{x}{x^2 - 4x - 5} \equiv \frac{1}{6(x+1)} + \frac{5}{6(x-5)}$

Then $\displaystyle\int \frac{x}{x^2 - 4x - 5}\,dx = \int \left[\frac{1}{6(x+1)} + \frac{5}{6(x-5)}\right] dx$

Integrate each term separately.

$\displaystyle= \frac{1}{6}\int \frac{1}{x+1}\,dx + \frac{5}{6}\int \frac{1}{x-5}\,dx$ ◀ **The form** $\displaystyle\int \frac{f'(x)}{f(x)}\,dx$.

Take the constants outside the integration.

$= \frac{1}{6}\ln|x+1| + \frac{5}{6}\ln|x-5| + c$

$= \frac{1}{6}[\ln|x+1| + \ln|x-5|^5] + c$ ◀ $n\ln x = \ln x^n$

$= \frac{1}{6}\ln|(x+1)(x-5)^5| + c$ ◀ $\ln x + \ln y = \ln xy$

b Express $\frac{2}{x(1-x)}$ in partial fractions.

Use $\frac{2}{x(1-x)} \equiv \frac{A}{x} + \frac{B}{1-x}$.

Check that $\displaystyle\frac{2}{x(1-x)} \equiv \frac{2}{x} + \frac{2}{1-x}$

$$\int \frac{2}{x(1-x)}\,dx = \int \left(\frac{2}{x} + \frac{2}{1-x}\right) dx$$

$\displaystyle= 2\int \frac{1}{x}\,dx - 2\int \frac{-1}{1-x}\,dx$ ◀ **The form** $\displaystyle\int \frac{f'(x)}{f(x)}\,dx$.

$= 2\ln|x| - 2\ln|1-x| + c$

$\displaystyle= 2\ln\left|\frac{x}{1-x}\right| + c$

Recall that $\ln x - \ln y = \ln(\frac{x}{y})$.

c Express $\frac{1}{x^3+x^2}$ in partial fractions.

First factorise; $x^3+x^2=x^2(x+1)$. Th[en] use $\frac{1}{x^2(x+1)} \equiv \frac{A}{x^2}+\frac{B}{x}+\frac{C}{x+[1]}$

Check that $\dfrac{1}{x^3+x^2}=\dfrac{1}{x^2}-\dfrac{1}{x}+\dfrac{1}{x+1}$

$$\int \frac{1}{x^3+x^2}\,dx = \int\left(\frac{1}{x^2}-\frac{1}{x}+\frac{1}{x+1}\right)dx$$

$$= \int x^{-2}\,dx - \int \frac{1}{x}\,dx + \int \frac{1}{x+1}\,dx$$

◀ The form $\int \frac{f'(x)}{f(x)}\,dx$.

$$= \frac{x^{-1}}{-1} - \ln|x| + \ln|x+1| + c$$

$$= \ln\left|\frac{x+1}{x}\right| - \frac{1}{x} + c$$

Example 3

a Find the values of a and b if $\displaystyle\int_{-1}^{1}\frac{1}{4-x^2}\,dx = \frac{1}{a}\ln b$.

b Evaluate $\displaystyle\int_0^4 \frac{26x^2+5x+31}{(1+3x)(x^2+16)}\,dx$.

Solution

a Notice that the denominator is the difference of two squares. That is, $4-x^2=(2+x)(2-x)$. Use this to write partial fractions.

Check that $\dfrac{1}{4-x^2}=\dfrac{1}{4(2+x)}+\dfrac{1}{4(2-x)}$

Use $\frac{1}{4-x^2}\equiv\frac{A}{2+x}+\frac{B}{2-x}$.

Now $\displaystyle\int_{-1}^{1}\frac{1}{4-x^2}\,dx = \int_{-1}^{1}\left[\frac{1}{4(2+x)}+\frac{1}{4(2-x)}\right]dx$

$$= \tfrac{1}{4}\int_{-1}^{1}\frac{1}{2+x}\,dx + \tfrac{1}{4}\int_{-1}^{1}\frac{1}{2-x}\,dx$$

Take the factor $\frac{1}{4}$ outsi[de] the integral sign.

$$= \tfrac{1}{4}\int_{-1}^{1}\frac{1}{2+x}\,dx - \tfrac{1}{4}\int_{-1}^{1}\frac{-1}{2-x}\,dx$$

◀ The form $\int \frac{f'(x)}{f(x)}\,dx$.

Use $\int \frac{f'(x)}{f(x)}\,dx = \ln|f(x[)|]$

$$= \tfrac{1}{4}[\ln|2+x|]_{-1}^{1} - \tfrac{1}{4}[\ln|2-x|]_{-1}^{1}$$

$$= \tfrac{1}{4}(\ln 3 - \ln 1) - \tfrac{1}{4}(\ln 1 - \ln 3)$$

$$= \tfrac{1}{4}\ln 3 - 0 - 0 + \tfrac{1}{4}\ln 3$$ ◀ $\ln 1 = 0$

$$= \tfrac{1}{2}\ln 3$$

Now $\tfrac{1}{2}\ln 3 \equiv \tfrac{1}{a}\ln b$, so $a=2$ and $b=3$.

b Express the integrand in partial fractions.

Note the quadratic fac[tor] in the denominator ar[nd] use $\frac{26x^2+5x+31}{(1+3x)(x^2+16)} = \frac{A}{1+3x}+\frac{Bx[+C]}{x^2[+16]}$

Check that $\dfrac{26x^2+5x+31}{(1+3x)(x^2+16)}=\dfrac{2}{1+3x}+\dfrac{8x-1}{x^2+16}$

Now $\displaystyle\int_0^4 \frac{26x^2+5x+31}{(1+3x)(x^2+16)}\,dx$

$$= \int_0^4 \left(\frac{2}{1+3x} + \frac{8x-1}{x^2+16}\right) dx$$

$$= 2\int_0^4 \frac{1}{1+3x}\,dx + \int_0^4 \frac{8x}{x^2+16}\,dx - \int_0^4 \frac{1}{x^2+16}\,dx$$

Separate the integrals.

$$= \tfrac{2}{3}\int_0^4 \frac{3}{1+3x}\,dx + 4\int_0^4 \frac{2x}{x^2+16}\,dx - \int_0^4 \frac{1}{x^2+16}\,dx$$

Write each integral in standard form.

$$= \tfrac{2}{3}[\ln(1+3x)]_0^4 + 4[\ln(x^2+16)]_0^4 - [\tfrac{1}{4}\tan^{-1}(\tfrac{x}{4})]_0^4$$

$$= \tfrac{2}{3}(\ln 13 - \ln 1) + 4(\ln 32 - \ln 16) - [\tfrac{1}{4}\tan^{-1}(1) - \tfrac{1}{4}\tan^{-1}(0)]$$

$$= \tfrac{2}{3}\ln 13 + 4\ln(\tfrac{32}{16}) - \tfrac{1}{4}\times\tfrac{\pi}{4}$$

$$= \tfrac{2}{3}\ln 13 + 4\ln 2 - \tfrac{\pi}{16} = \tfrac{2}{3}\ln 832 - \tfrac{\pi}{16}$$

For $0 \le x \le 4$, both $1+3x$ and x^2+16 are positive, so the modulus function is not required.

Example 4

Evaluate $\displaystyle\int_1^2 \frac{6x^2+3x-1}{(x+1)(2x-1)}\,dx.$

Solution

The integrand is an improper fraction, which must be expressed as the sum of a polynomial and a proper fraction before we can integrate it. First write the numerator in terms of the denominator, and then express the proper fractions as partial fractions.

$$\frac{6x^2+3x-1}{(x+1)(2x-1)} = \frac{3(2x^2+x-1)}{(2x^2+x-1)} + \frac{2}{(2x^2+x-1)}$$

$$= 3 + \frac{2}{(2x^2+x-1)}$$

$$= 3 + \frac{2}{(x+1)(2x-1)}$$

$$= 3 + \frac{4}{3(2x-1)} - \frac{2}{3(x+1)}$$

Use $\frac{2}{(x+1)(2x-1)} \equiv \frac{A}{x+1} + \frac{B}{2x-1}$.

Now the problem can be restated as

$$\int_1^2 \frac{6x^2+3x-1}{(x+1)(2x-1)}\,dx = \int_1^2 \left[3 + \frac{4}{3(2x-1)} - \frac{2}{3(x+1)}\right] dx$$

$$= \int_1^2 3\,dx + \tfrac{2}{3}\int_1^2 \frac{2}{(2x-1)}\,dx - \tfrac{2}{3}\int_1^2 \frac{1}{(x+1)}\,dx$$

Use the cover-up rule to do this quickly.

$$= [3x]_1^2 + \tfrac{2}{3}[\ln(2x-1)]_1^2 - \tfrac{2}{3}[\ln(x+1)]_1^2$$

$$= (6-3) + \tfrac{2}{3}(\ln 3 - \ln 1) - \tfrac{2}{3}(\ln 3 - \ln 2)$$

$$= 3 + \tfrac{2}{3}(\ln 3 - 0 - \ln 3 + \ln 2)$$

$$= 3 + \tfrac{2}{3}\ln 2$$

12.2 Rational Functions
Exercise
Technique

1 Integrate the following, first expressing each as a sum involving a proper fraction:

a $\dfrac{x}{x+1}$ **b** $\dfrac{x-1}{x+1}$ **c** $\dfrac{x}{2x-1}$ **d** $\dfrac{x^2}{x-1}$

2 Find the exact value of:

a $\displaystyle\int_0^{1/2} \frac{12x-1}{6x+1}\,dx$ **b** $\displaystyle\int_0^1 \frac{x^2-1}{x^2+1}\,dx$

3 Evaluate the following integrals, giving your answers correct to two decimal places:

a $\displaystyle\int_1^2 \frac{4x}{1+2x}\,dx$ **b** $\displaystyle\int_2^7 \frac{x}{3+x}\,dx$

4 Use partial fractions to find:

4 **a**

a $\displaystyle\int \frac{4x+7}{x^2+3x+2}\,dx$ **b** $\displaystyle\int \frac{5-11x}{x-2x^2}\,dx$

c $\displaystyle\int \frac{x+5}{x^2-1}\,dx$ **d** $\displaystyle\int \frac{4x-5}{(x+1)(x-2)}\,dx$

5 Find the exact value of:

a $\displaystyle\int_2^3 \frac{1}{x(x-1)}\,dx$ **d** $\displaystyle\int_3^4 \frac{9-3x}{(x-2)(5-x)}\,dx$

b $\displaystyle\int_2^6 \frac{6x}{(1+2x)(1-x)}\,dx$ **e** $\displaystyle\int_2^3 \frac{3}{(x-4)(x-1)}\,dx$

c $\displaystyle\int_2^4 \frac{x}{1-x^2}\,dx$ **f** $\displaystyle\int_3^4 \frac{5}{x(5-2x)}\,dx$

6 Find:

a $\displaystyle\int \frac{1-3x}{x(1+x^2)}\,dx$ **b** $\displaystyle\int \frac{3x^2+2x+4}{(x+1)(4+x^2)}\,dx$

7 Find the exact value of $\displaystyle\int_0^5 \frac{x^2-2x+24}{(1+2x)(25+x^2)}\,dx$.

8 Express the integrand as a sum involving a proper fraction before finding the exact value of $\displaystyle\int_0^1 \frac{2x^2+x-4}{x^2-x-2}\,dx$.

9 $f(x) = \dfrac{8}{(x+1)(x^2+3)}$, $x \neq 1$

a Express $f(x)$ in the form $\dfrac{A}{x+1} + \dfrac{Bx+C}{x^2+3}$.

b Find the value of a such that $\displaystyle\int_0^1 f(x)\,dx = \ln a + \frac{\pi\sqrt{3}}{a^2}$.

Contextual

1

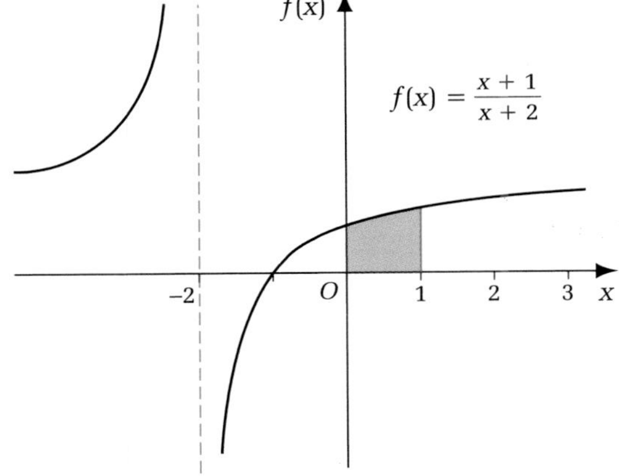

The graph shows the curve $f(x) = \dfrac{x+1}{x+2}$.

a Express $f(x)$ in the form $A + \dfrac{B}{x+2}$.

b Calculate the area of the shaded region.

2

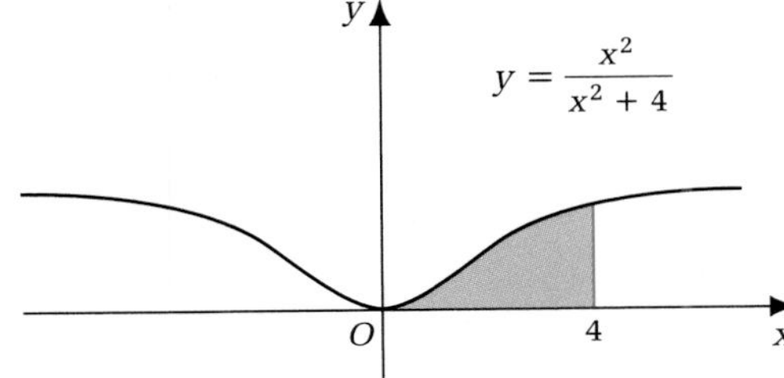

The graph shows the curve $y = \dfrac{x^2}{x^2+4}$.

a Find the values of A and B if $y \equiv A + \dfrac{B}{x^2+4}$.

b Calculate the area of the shaded region.

3

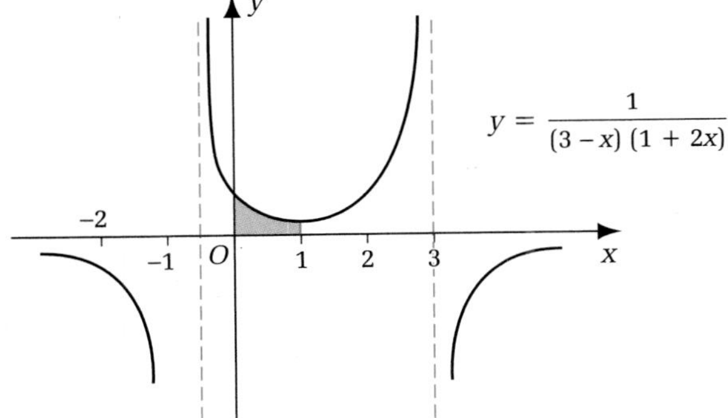

The graph shows the curve $y = \dfrac{1}{(3-x)(1+2x)}$. Find the shaded area.

4 Given that $f(x) = \frac{x+1}{x(2x+1)}$, express $f(x)$ in the form $\frac{A}{x} + \frac{B}{2x+1}$.

Hence evaluate $\int_1^4 f(x)\,dx$.

5 Show that $\int_1^2 \frac{3x-10}{(2-3x)(x+2)}\,dx = 2\ln(\tfrac{3}{2})$.

6 Find the values of a and b if $\int_1^8 \frac{5}{(2x-1)(x+2)}\,dx = \ln\left(\frac{a}{b}\right)$.

7 Express $\frac{2+5x}{x^2(1+4x)}$ in the form $\frac{A}{x^2} + \frac{B}{x} + \frac{C}{1+4x}$.

Hence evaluate $\int_1^2 \frac{2+5x}{x^2(1+4x)}\,dx$ correct to two decimal places.

8 Express $f(x) = \frac{x^2+8x+9}{x^2+3x+2}$ in the form $A + \frac{B}{x+1} + \frac{C}{x+2}$.

Hence find $\int_1^4 f(x)\,dx$.

9 Find $\int \frac{6}{x(x+1)(x+3)}\,dx$.

10 Evaluate $\int_{-1}^0 \frac{x^2+1}{(x-1)(x+2)(x-3)}\,dx$.

12.3 Integration by Parts

What happens if we have a product of two functions?
Write down the product rule for differentiation,

$$\frac{\mathrm{d}}{\mathrm{d}x}(uv) = u\frac{\mathrm{d}v}{\mathrm{d}x} + v\frac{\mathrm{d}u}{\mathrm{d}x}$$

Now try integrating this result.
Integrating both sides with respect to x gives

$$\begin{aligned} uv &= \int \left(u\frac{\mathrm{d}v}{\mathrm{d}x} + v\frac{\mathrm{d}u}{\mathrm{d}x} \right) \mathrm{d}x \\ &= \int u\frac{\mathrm{d}v}{\mathrm{d}x}\,\mathrm{d}x + \int v\frac{\mathrm{d}u}{\mathrm{d}x}\,\mathrm{d}x \end{aligned}$$

Integrate each term separately.

This can be rearranged to give

$$\int u\frac{\mathrm{d}v}{\mathrm{d}x}\,\mathrm{d}x = uv - \int v\frac{\mathrm{d}u}{\mathrm{d}x}\,\mathrm{d}x \quad \text{or} \quad \int uv'\,\mathrm{d}x = uv - \int vu'\,\mathrm{d}x$$

This formula is very useful for integrating the product of two functions.
This method is called **integration by parts**.

For example, try integrating $x\cos x$ with respect to x. One part of the integrand can be labelled u and the other labelled $\frac{\mathrm{d}v}{\mathrm{d}x}$. Then $\frac{\mathrm{d}u}{\mathrm{d}x}$ can be found by differentiating u, and v can be found by integrating $\frac{\mathrm{d}v}{\mathrm{d}x}$, before substituting them into the formula.

In $\int x\cos x\,\mathrm{d}x$, let $u = x$ and $\frac{\mathrm{d}v}{\mathrm{d}x} = \cos x$.

Now, $\dfrac{\mathrm{d}u}{\mathrm{d}x} = \dfrac{\mathrm{d}}{\mathrm{d}x}(x) = 1$ and $v = \displaystyle\int \cos x\,\mathrm{d}x = \sin x$

Don't worry about adding a constant until the final integration is complete, because if it were integrated it would generate a function of x.

Substituting in $\int u\frac{\mathrm{d}v}{\mathrm{d}x}\,\mathrm{d}x = uv - \int v\frac{\mathrm{d}u}{\mathrm{d}x}\,\mathrm{d}x$ ◀ Always state the formula.

$$\begin{aligned} \int x\cos x\,\mathrm{d}x &= x \times \sin x - \int (\sin x \times 1)\,\mathrm{d}x \\ &= x\sin x - \int \sin x\,\mathrm{d}x \\ &= x\sin x - (-\cos x) + c \\ &= x\sin x + \cos x + c \end{aligned}$$

Note that the constant of integration is added here.

The idea is to choose u and v so that $\int v\frac{\mathrm{d}u}{\mathrm{d}x}\,\mathrm{d}x$ is simpler than the original integral, meaning integration by parts can be completed successfully.

Example 1

Find:

a $\int xe^{3x}\,dx$ **b** $\int x^2 \ln x\,dx$

Solution

a Let $u = x$ and $v' = e^{3x}$. Then $u' = 1$ and $v = \int e^{3x}\,dx = \frac{1}{3}e^{3x}$.

Choose which part of t integrand is u and whi is $\frac{dv}{dx}$ so that $\int v\frac{du}{dx}\,dx$ is simpler integral than t original. See what wou happen if we had chos $u = e^{3x}$ and $\frac{dv}{dx} = x$ in t case.

Now, $$\int uv'\,dx = uv - \int vu'\,dx$$

$$\int xe^{3x}\,dx = x \times \tfrac{1}{3}e^{3x} - \int(\tfrac{1}{3}e^{3x} \times 1)\,dx$$

$$= \tfrac{1}{3}xe^{3x} - \tfrac{1}{3}\int e^{3x}\,dx$$

$$= \tfrac{1}{3}xe^{3x} - \tfrac{1}{3} \times \tfrac{1}{3}e^{3x} + c$$ ◀ **Factorise.**

$$= \tfrac{1}{9}e^{3x}(3x - 1) + c$$

Notice that the second integral is much simpl than the original.

b In this example the choice of u and v' are obvious because $\ln x$ cannot be integrated directly. However, it can be differentiated.
So let $u = \ln x$ and let $v' = x^2$. Then $u' = \frac{1}{x}$ and $v = \int x^2\,dx = \frac{1}{3}x^3$

Now, $$\int uv'\,dx = uv - \int vu'\,dx$$

So $$\int x^2 \ln x\,dx = \ln x \times \tfrac{1}{3}x^3 - \int(\tfrac{1}{3}x^3 \times \tfrac{1}{x})\,dx$$

$$= \tfrac{1}{3}x^3 \ln x - \tfrac{1}{3}\int x^2\,dx$$

$$= \tfrac{1}{3}x^3 \ln x - \tfrac{1}{3} \times \tfrac{1}{3}x^3 + c$$

$$= \tfrac{1}{3}x^3 \ln x - \tfrac{1}{9}x^3 + c$$

$$= \tfrac{1}{9}x^3(3\ln x - 1) + c$$

Example 2

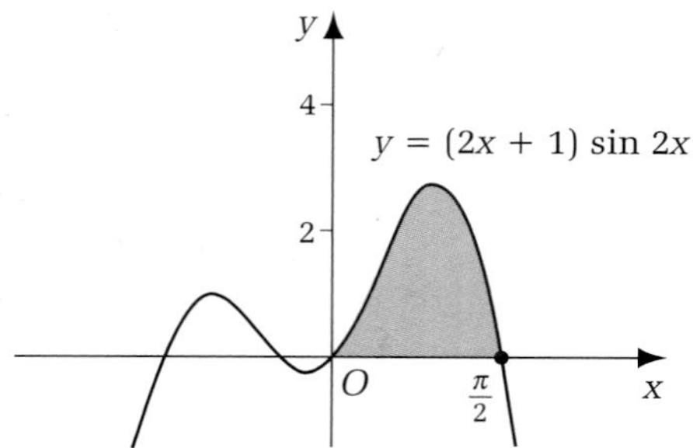

The graph shows part of the curve $y = (2x + 1)\sin 2x$. Find the area under the curve between $x = 0$ and $x = \frac{\pi}{2}$.

Solution

$$\text{shaded area} = \int_0^{\pi/2} (2x+1)\sin 2x\,dx$$

Notice the product of $(2x+1)$ and $\sin 2x$.

Let $u = 2x + 1$ and $v' = \sin 2x$.
Then $u' = 2$ and $v = \int \sin 2x\,dx = -\frac{1}{2}\cos 2x$.

$$\int_a^b uv'\,dx = [uv]_a^b - \int_a^b vu'\,dx$$

$$\begin{aligned}
\text{Shaded area} &= \int_0^{\pi/2} (2x+1)\sin 2x\,dx \\
&= \left[(2x+1)\times -\tfrac{1}{2}\cos 2x\right]_0^{\pi/2} - \int_0^{\pi/2} \left(-\tfrac{1}{2}\cos 2x \times 2\right) dx \\
&= \left[-\tfrac{1}{2}(2x+1)\cos 2x\right]_0^{\pi/2} + \int_0^{\pi/2} \cos 2x\,dx \\
&= \left[-\tfrac{1}{2}(\pi+1)\cos\pi - \left(-\tfrac{1}{2}\times 1\times\cos 0\right)\right] + \left[\tfrac{1}{2}\sin 2x\right]_0^{\pi/2} \\
&= \left[\tfrac{1}{2}(\pi+1) - 1\left(-\tfrac{1}{2}\right)\right] + \left(\tfrac{1}{2}\sin\pi - \tfrac{1}{2}\sin 0\right) \\
&= \tfrac{1}{2}(\pi+1) + \tfrac{1}{2} + (0-0) \\
&= \tfrac{1}{2}(\pi+2) \text{ square units}
\end{aligned}$$

An alternative method when integrating by parts in the definite case is to complete the integraion first and put in the limits at the end. Check that $[-\frac{1}{2}(2x+1)\cos 2x + \frac{1}{2}\sin 2x]_0^{\pi/2}$ gives the same result.

Integration by parts can be used to integrate functions that don't necessarily appear to be a product. The 'trick' is to write the function as a product of 1 and itself.

Example 3

Find $\int \ln x\,dx$ using integration by parts.

Solution

To use integration by parts the integrand should be expressed as a product.

That is, the product $u \times v'$.

$$\int \ln x\,dx = \int 1 \times \ln x\,dx$$

Let $u = \ln x$ and let $v' = 1$. Then $u' = \frac{1}{x}$ and $v = \int 1\,dx = x$.

Let $u = \ln x$ because $\ln x$ can be differentiated.

$$\int uv'\,dx = uv - \int vu'\,dx$$

$$\begin{aligned}
\int \ln x\,dx &= \ln x \times x - \int x \times \frac{1}{x}\,dx \\
&= x\ln x - \int 1\,dx = x\ln x - x + c
\end{aligned}$$

Check this result by differentiation.

Sometimes integration by parts has to be used more than once in the same problem. Try finding $\int x^2 \sin x \, dx$. Integration by parts gives

$$\int x^2 \sin x \, dx = -x^2 \cos x + 2\int x \cos x \, dx$$

Notice that the second integrand is a simpler product than the original one, but still cannot be integrated directly. However, it can be successfully integrated using integration by parts a second time giving:

$$\int x^2 \sin x \, dx = -x^2 \cos x + 2x \sin x + 2 \cos x + c$$

Check this result by differentiation.

The following example is an unusual demonstration of how integration by parts is used twice. When integration by parts is used for a second time the original integral appears again.

Example 4

Find $\int e^{2t} \sin t \, dt$.

Solution

$$\int u \frac{dv}{dt} dt = uv - \int v \frac{du}{dt} dt$$

Note the change of variable from x to t.

Let $u = e^{2t}$ and $\frac{dv}{dt} = \sin t$. Then $\frac{du}{dt} = 2e^{2t}$ and $v = \int \sin t \, dt = -\cos t$.

$$\text{Now} \quad \int e^{2t} \sin t \, dt = e^{2t} \times -\cos t - \int -\cos t \times 2e^{2t} \, dt$$

$$= -e^{2t} \cos t + 2\int e^{2t} \cos t \, dt$$

Using integration by parts again to integrate the second integral, let $u_2 = e^{2t}$ and $\frac{dv_2}{dt} = \cos t$. So $\frac{du_2}{dt} = 2e^{2t}$ and $v_2 = \int \cos t \, dt = \sin t$.

Use u_2 and v_2 so as n[ot] to confuse these functions with u and

$$\text{Now} \quad \int e^{2t} \sin t \, dt = -e^{2t} \cos t + 2\left(e^{2t} \sin t - \int \sin t \times 2e^{2t} \, dt\right)$$

$$\int e^{2t} \sin t \, dt = -e^{2t} \cos t + 2e^{2t} \sin t - 4\int e^{2t} \sin t \, dt$$

Notice that the integral now appears twice. The equation can be rearranged by treating this integral as a distinct term. Adding $4\int e^{2t} \sin t \, dt$ to both sides,

$$5\int e^{2t} \sin t \, dt = -e^{2t} \cos t + 2e^{2t} \sin t$$

$$\Rightarrow \quad \int e^{2t} \sin t \, dt = \tfrac{1}{5} e^{2t}(2 \sin t - \cos t) + c$$

Remember to add a constant of integratio[n]

Check this answer using the product rule. Differentiating $\frac{1}{5} e^{2t}(2 \sin t - \cos t)$ should give the original integrand, $e^{2t} \sin t$.

12.3 Integration by parts

Exercise

Technique

1 Use integration by parts to find:

a $\int xe^{2x}\,dx$ b $\int x^3 \ln x\,dx$

c $\int x \sin x\,dx$ d $\int xe^{-x}\,dx$

2 Find:

a $\int (2x-1)\cos x\,dx$ d $\int x(\sin x + \cos x)\,dx$

b $\int x \sec^2 x\,dx$ e $\int x \ln 3x\,dx$

c $\int 4x \cos 2x\,dx$ f $\int 2xe^{-4x}\,dx$

3 Find:

a $\int (2t+1)e^{-t}\,dt$ b $\int \sqrt{t}\ln t\,dt$

4 Evaluate:

a $\int_0^{\pi/3} x\cos x\,dx$ b $\int_0^2 xe^{-2x}\,dx$ c $\int_1^2 (1-x^2)\ln x\,dx$

5 Use integration by parts twice to find:

a $\int x^2 e^x\,dx$ b $\int x^2 \sin 2x\,dx$ c $\int e^x \sin 2x\,dx$

Contextual

1 Alex is finding $\int xe^{-6x}\,dx$ using integration by parts. She comes to a stop after a few lines of working. The last line of her working is shown here

$$= \frac{1}{2}x^2e^{-6x} + 3\int x^2e^{-6x}\,dx$$

$=$

a How did she arrive at the line of working shown on her page?

b What suggestion would you make to Alex?

c If Alex took your advice what answer would she get?

2 Find the values of a and b if $\int_1^2 x \ln x \, dx = \ln a - \frac{b}{a}$.

3

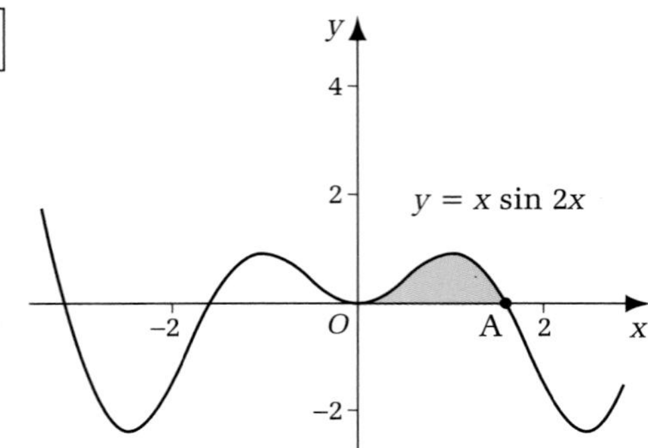

The graph show part of the curve $y = x \sin 2x$.

a Find the coordinates of A.

b Calculate the area of the shaded region.

4

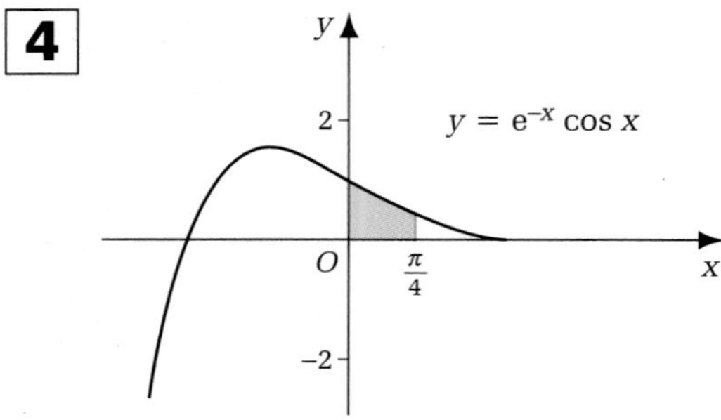

a Find $\int e^{-x} \cos x \, dx$.

b The diagram shows part of the curve $y = e^{-x} \cos x$. Calculate the area of the shaded region.

12.4 Integration by Substitution

Integration by substitution is a technique used to transform difficult integrals into simpler ones in which the standard integrals can be used. How could $\int(1+3x)^6\,dx$ be found quickly? We could expand $(1+3x)^6$ using the binomial expansion and integrate the resulting polynomial term by term. An alternative is to make the substitution $t = 1 + 3x$.

Use that technique to find $\int(1+3x)^6 dx$.

$$\text{Then} \quad \int (1+3x)^6\,dx \quad \text{becomes} \quad \int t^6\,dx.$$

Although the integral has been simplified we cannot integrate t^6 with respect to x. We need a dt rather than a dx after the integrand.

$$\text{Let} \qquad I = \int t^6\,dx, \quad \text{then} \quad \frac{dI}{dx} = t^6 \qquad [1]$$

Recall the fundamental theorem of calculus from Ch. 9.

The chain rule gives

$$\frac{dI}{dt} = \frac{dI}{dx} \times \frac{dx}{dt} = t^6\,\frac{dx}{dt}$$

Integrating both sides with respect to t gives,

$$I = \int t^6\,\frac{dx}{dt}\,dt$$

Comparing this to equation [1], we see that dx is effectively replaced by $\frac{dx}{dt}\,dt$.

Since $t = 1 + 3x$ in this case, $\frac{dt}{dx} = 3$. So $\frac{dx}{dt} = \frac{1}{3}$, and dx is replaced by $\frac{1}{3}\,dt$.

$$\begin{aligned} \text{So} \quad \int (1+3x)^6\,dx &= \int t^6 \times \tfrac{1}{3}\,dt \\ &= \tfrac{1}{3}\int t^6\,dt \\ &= \tfrac{1}{3} \times \tfrac{1}{7}t^7 + c \\ &= \tfrac{1}{21}(1+3x)^7 + c \end{aligned}$$

This can now be integrated.

Substitute $t = 1 + 3x$.

Notice that the substitution makes the integrand simpler. The difficult part is changing the variable with respect to which the integration is carried out from x to t.

Example 1

Use the substitution $t = 5x + 1$ to find $\int \sqrt{5x+1}\,dx$.

Solution

Since $t = 5x + 1$, $\frac{dt}{dx} = 5$ and $\frac{dx}{dt} = \frac{1}{5}$.

Now $$\int \sqrt{5x+1}\,dx = \int \sqrt{t} \times \tfrac{1}{5}\,dt$$
$$= \tfrac{1}{5}\int t^{\frac{1}{2}}\,dt$$
$$= \tfrac{1}{5} \times \tfrac{2}{3}t^{\frac{3}{2}} + c$$
$$= \tfrac{2}{15}t^{\frac{3}{2}} + c$$
$$= \tfrac{2}{15}(5x+1)^{\frac{3}{2}} + c$$

Replace dx with $\frac{dx}{dt}dt$, s
here replace dx with $\frac{1}{5}$ (

Check this result by differentiation.

Example 2

Find $\int \frac{1}{(3-4x)^4}\,dx$, using the substitution $u = 3 - 4x$.

Solution

Since $u = 3 - 4x$, $\frac{du}{dx} = -4$ and $\frac{dx}{du} = -\frac{1}{4}$.

Now $$\int \frac{1}{(3-4x)^4}\,dx = \int \frac{1}{u^4} \times -\tfrac{1}{4}\,du$$
$$= -\tfrac{1}{4}\int u^{-4}\,du$$
$$= -\tfrac{1}{4} \times -\tfrac{1}{3}u^{-3} + c$$
$$= \tfrac{1}{12}u^{-3} + c$$
$$= \tfrac{1}{12}(3-4x)^{-3} + c$$
$$= \frac{1}{12(3-4x)^3} + c$$

Replace dx with $\frac{dx}{du}du$, here replace dx with $-\frac{1}{4}\,du$.

Check this result by differentiation.

Notice that when using a substitution, the variable can be represented by any letter other than the original x.

Substitution can also be used to evaluate definite integrals. However, the limits must also be changed.

Example 3

Evaluate $\int_1^2 (1-x)^3\,dx$.

Solution

Use the substitution $t = 1 - x$. Then $\frac{dt}{dx} = -1$ and $\frac{dx}{dt} = -1$.

Find the values of the new limits:

- when $x = 1$, $t = 1 - 1 = 0$
- when $x = 2$, $t = 1 - 2 = -1$

Do not worry that the upper limit is now less than the lower limit.

So $\int_1^2 (1-x)^3\,dx = \int_0^{-1} t^3 \times (-1)\,dt$

$$= -\int_0^{-1} t^3\,dt$$

$$= -[\tfrac{1}{4}t^4]_0^{-1}$$

$$= -[\tfrac{1}{4} - 0]$$

$$= -\tfrac{1}{4}$$

Replace dx with $\frac{dx}{dt}\,dt$, so here replace dx with $-\,dt$.

Integration by substitution can be used to establish other standard integrals. For example to find $\int (ax+b)^n\,dx$, where a, b and n are real numbers, use the substitution $t = ax + b$. Then $\frac{dt}{dx} = a$, and $\frac{dx}{dt} = \frac{1}{a}$.

Now $\int (ax+b)^n\,dx = \int t^n \times \frac{1}{a}\,dt$

$$= \frac{1}{a}\int t^n\,dt$$

$$= \frac{1}{a} \times \frac{t^{n+1}}{n+1} + c$$

Replace dx with $\frac{1}{a}$ dt.

Therefore

$$\int (\boldsymbol{ax+b})^{\boldsymbol{n}}\,\mathbf{dx} = \frac{\mathbf{1}}{\boldsymbol{a}} \times \frac{(\boldsymbol{ax+b})^{\boldsymbol{n+1}}}{\boldsymbol{n+1}} + \boldsymbol{c}$$

◀ **Learn this result.**

Look back again at Example 1 where $(ax+b)^n = (5x+1)^{\frac{1}{2}}$. Here $a = 5$, $b = 1$ and $n = \frac{1}{2}$.

So $\int (5x+1)^{\frac{1}{2}}\,dx = \frac{1}{5}\frac{(5x+1)^{\frac{3}{2}}}{(\frac{1}{2}+1)} + c$

$$= \tfrac{2}{15}(5x+1)^{\frac{3}{2}} + c$$

Check the integrals in Examples 2 and 3 using this result.

More complex integrals require a higher level of algebraic skill to make sure that the integral has been expressed entirely in terms of the new variable only.

Example 4

Evaluate $\int_{-1}^{0} x\sqrt{1+x}\,dx$.

Solution

Let $t = 1 + x$. Then $\frac{dt}{dx} = 1$ and $\frac{dx}{dt} = 1$.

When $x = -1$, $t = 0$ and when $x = 0$, $t = 1$.

$$\text{Now} \quad \int_{-1}^{0} x\sqrt{1+x}\,dx = \int_{0}^{1} (t-1)\sqrt{t} \times 1\,dt$$

$$= \int_{0}^{1} (t^{3/2} - t^{1/2})\,dt$$

$$= [\tfrac{2}{5}t^{5/2} - \tfrac{2}{3}t^{3/2}]_0^1$$

$$= (\tfrac{2}{5} \times 1 - \tfrac{2}{3} \times 1) - (0 - 0)$$

$$= \tfrac{2}{5} - \tfrac{2}{3}$$

$$= -\tfrac{4}{15}$$

Replace dx with dt.

Notice that the integra[nd] $x\sqrt{1+x}$ is written in terms of t only; $x\sqrt{1+x} = (t-1)\sqrt{t}$.

Example 5

Use the substitution $u^2 = 5 - x$ to find $\int_1^5 (x+1)(5-x)^{\frac{1}{2}}\,dx$.

Solution

Let $u^2 = 5 - x$, and differentiate implicitly with respect to x.
Then $2u\frac{du}{dx} = -1$ and so $\frac{dx}{du} = -2u$.

When $x = 1$, $u^2 = 5 - 1 = 4 \Rightarrow u = 2$
When $x = 5$, $u^2 = 5 - 5 = 0 \Rightarrow u = 0$

Also, $x = 5 - u^2 \Rightarrow x + 1 = 6 - u^2$

$$\text{Now} \quad \int_{1}^{5} (x+1)(5-x)^{\frac{1}{2}}\,dx = \int_{2}^{0} (6-u^2)(u^2)^{\frac{1}{2}} \times -2u\,du$$

$$= -2\int_{2}^{0} (6-u^2)u^2\,du$$

$$= -2\int_{2}^{0} (6u^2 - u^4)\,du$$

$$= -2[2u^3 - \tfrac{1}{5}u^5]_2^0$$

$$= -2[(0-0) - (2 \times 2^3 - \tfrac{1}{5} \times 2^5)]$$

$$= -2(-16 + \tfrac{32}{5})$$

$$= -2(-\tfrac{48}{5})$$

$$= \tfrac{96}{5}$$

$$= 19\tfrac{1}{5}$$

Replace dx with $-2u$ d[u].

An alternative method [is] to use the result $\int_a^b f(x)\,dx = -\int_b^a f(x)$ d[x]. In this case we would evaluate $2\int_0^2 (6u^2 - u^4$ [...]

Choosing suitable substitutions

Try finding $\int xe^{x^2}\,dx$. Using a systematic approach, integration by parts may be your first choice, but the second integral is too difficult to integrate. A good strategy is then to try a substitution.

Spotting the substitution $t = g(x)$, where $g(x)$ is some function of x, often depends on recognising a common factor that appears in the integrand and in $g'(x)$.

Step ① Let t be some function of x so that a factor is created that will cancel or simplify the integrand.

Let $\quad t = x^2$ ◀ **Differentiating $t = x^2$ wrt x gives a factor of x, which appears in the integrand.**

Step ② Write dx in terms of dt.

At this stage some algebra may be necessary to write the integrand in terms of the new variable t.

$$\frac{dt}{dx} = 2x \Rightarrow dx = \frac{1}{2x}dt$$

Now $\displaystyle\int xe^{x^2}\,dx = \int xe^t \times \frac{1}{2x}dt$ ◀ **Notice that the x will cancel.**

$$= \tfrac{1}{2}\int e^t\,dt$$

Step ③ Integrate with respect to t.

$$\int xe^{x^2}\,dx = \tfrac{1}{2}\int e^t\,dt$$

$$= \tfrac{1}{2}e^t + c$$

Step ④ Substitute for t throughout to express the integral in terms of the original variable, x.

$$\int xe^{x^2}\,dx = \tfrac{1}{2}e^{x^2} + c$$

Check this result using differentiation.

Other useful hints

- For integrals containing e^x, try $t = e^x$.
- For integrals containing $\sqrt{a^2 - x^2}$, try $x = a\sin\theta$. For example, with $\sqrt{4 - x^2}$, use $x = 2\sin\theta$.
- For integrals containing $\sqrt{a^2 + x^2}$, try $x = a\tan\theta$. For example, with $\sqrt{9 + x^2}$, use $x = 3\tan\theta$.

Example 6

Find:

a $\displaystyle\int \sin^2\theta\cos\theta\,d\theta$ **b** $\displaystyle\int \frac{e^x + e^{2x}}{1 + e^{2x}}\,dx$

Solution

a Let $t = \sin\theta$. ◀ **① Differentiating $t = \sin\theta$ gives us a factor of $\cos\theta$.**
Then $\frac{dt}{d\theta} = \cos\theta \Rightarrow d\theta = \frac{1}{\cos\theta}dt$. ◀ **② Write d$\theta$ in terms of dt.**

Now $\int \sin^2\theta\cos\theta\,d\theta = \int t^2 \times \cos\theta \times \frac{1}{\cos\theta}\,dt$

$= \int t^2\,dt$

$= \frac{1}{3}t^3 + c$ ◀ ③ Integrate wrt t.

$= \frac{1}{3}\sin^3\theta + c$ ◀ ④ Substitute for t.

Notice that the $\cos\theta$ terms cancel.

b Let $p = e^x$. ◀ ① Exponential functions in the integrand can be simplified.

Then $\frac{dp}{dx} = e^x \Rightarrow dx = \frac{1}{e^x}\,dp$ ◀ ② Write dx in terms of dp.

e^x and e^{2x} can then be replaced by p and p^2.

Now, $\int \frac{e^x + e^{2x}}{1 + e^{2x}}\,dx = \int \frac{p + p^2}{1 + p^2} \times \frac{1}{e^x}\,dp$

$= \int \frac{p + p^2}{1 + p^2} \times \frac{1}{p}\,dp$

$= \int \frac{1 + p}{1 + p^2}\,dp$

$= \int \frac{1}{1 + p^2}\,dp + \int \frac{p}{1 + p^2}\,dp$ ◀ ③ Integrate wrt p.

$= \int \frac{1}{1 + p^2}\,dp + \frac{1}{2}\int \frac{2p}{1 + p^2}\,dp$

$= \tan^{-1}(p) + \frac{1}{2}\ln(1 + p^2) + c$ ◀ ④ Substitute for p.

$= \tan^{-1}(e^x) + \frac{1}{2}\ln(1 + e^{2x}) + c$

The $\frac{1}{p}$ term cancels wi[th] the common factor of [p] in the numerator.

Use $\int \frac{f'(x)}{f(x)}\,dx = \ln|f(x)| + c$. Remember that $1 + p^2 > 0$ for all p

Example 7

Evaluate:

a $\int_0^2 \frac{x}{\sqrt{2x^2 + 1}}\,dx$ **b** $\int_0^{\frac{3}{2}} \sqrt{3 - x^2}\,dx$

Solution

a Let $u = 2x^2 + 1$. ◀ ① Differentiating $u = 2x^2 + 1$ gives us a factor of x.

Then $\frac{du}{dx} = 4x \Rightarrow dx = \frac{1}{4x}\,du$ ◀ ② Write dx in terms of du.

When $x = 0$, $u = 1$ and when $x = 2$, $u = 9$

Find the limits in ter[ms] of u.

Now, $\int_0^2 \frac{x}{\sqrt{2x^2 + 1}}\,dx = \int_1^9 \frac{x}{\sqrt{u}} \times \frac{1}{4x}\,du$

$= \frac{1}{4}\int_1^9 u^{-1/2}\,du$ ◀ ③ Integrate wrt u.

$= \frac{1}{4}[2u^{1/2}]_1^9$

$= \frac{1}{4}(2\sqrt{9} - 2\sqrt{1})$

$= \frac{1}{2}(3 - 1)$

$= 1$

Notice that the x term[s] cancel.

b Let $x = \sqrt{3}\sin\theta$. ◀ ① **This gives a factor of $1 - \sin^2\theta = \cos^2\theta$, which eliminates the square root in the integrand.**

Then $\frac{dx}{d\theta} = \sqrt{3}\cos\theta \Rightarrow dx = \sqrt{3}\cos\theta\,d\theta$ ◀ ② **Write dx in terms of $d\theta$.**

When $x = 0$, $0 = \sqrt{3}\sin\theta \Rightarrow \theta = 0$
When $x = \frac{3}{2}$, $\frac{3}{2} = \sqrt{3}\sin\theta \Rightarrow \theta = \sin^{-1}(\frac{\sqrt{3}}{2}) = \frac{\pi}{3}$

Find the limits in terms of θ, in radians.
Recall special angles.

$$\text{Now} \quad \int_0^{\frac{3}{2}} \sqrt{3 - x^2}\,dx = \int_0^{\frac{\pi}{3}} \sqrt{3 - 3\sin^2\theta} \times \sqrt{3}\cos\theta\,d\theta$$
$$= \sqrt{3}\int_0^{\frac{\pi}{3}} \sqrt{3(1 - \sin^2\theta)}\cos\theta\,d\theta$$
$$= 3\int_0^{\frac{\pi}{3}} \sqrt{\cos^2\theta}\cos\theta\,d\theta$$
$$= 3\int_0^{\frac{\pi}{3}} \cos^2\theta\,d\theta$$

◀ ③ **Integrate wrt θ.**

Notice that another $\sqrt{3}$ has been taken out of the integrand.

To integrate $\cos^2\theta$, express it in terms of double angles.

Recall that
$\cos 2A \equiv 2\cos^2 A - 1$.
So $\cos^2 A = \frac{1}{2}(\cos 2A + 1)$

$$\text{Now} \quad \int_0^{\frac{3}{2}} \sqrt{3 - x^2}\,dx = 3\int_0^{\frac{\pi}{3}} \tfrac{1}{2}(\cos 2\theta + 1)\,d\theta$$
$$= \frac{3}{2}\int_0^{\frac{\pi}{3}} (\cos 2\theta + 1)\,d\theta$$
$$= \frac{3}{2}\left[\tfrac{1}{2}\sin 2\theta + \theta\right]_0^{\frac{\pi}{3}}$$
$$= \frac{3}{2}\left[\tfrac{1}{2}\sin\frac{2\pi}{3} + \frac{\pi}{3} - (\tfrac{1}{2}\sin 0 + 0)\right]$$
$$= \frac{3}{2}\left(\frac{1}{2} \times \frac{\sqrt{3}}{2} + \frac{\pi}{3} - 0\right)$$
$$= \frac{3\sqrt{3}}{8} + \frac{\pi}{2}$$

12.4 Integration by Substitution

Exercise

Technique

1 Use substitution to find:

a $\int (1 + 2x)^2 \, dx$ **b** $\int (3 + 4x)^3 \, dx$ **c** $\int \sqrt{(2x + 1)} \, dx$

d $\int \frac{6}{(1 + 4x)^2} \, dx$ **e** $\int (1 + 3x)^{-\frac{3}{2}} \, dx$ **f** $\int \sqrt[3]{6x - 1} \, dx$

2 By making suitable substitutions evaluate:

a $\int_{\frac{1}{2}}^{1} (1 - 4x)^3 \, dx$ **b** $\int_0^2 \sqrt{4 - 2x} \, dx$

3 Use the substitution $t = ax + b$ to show that

$$\int (ax + b)^n \, dx = \frac{1}{a} \times \frac{(ax + b)^{n+1}}{(n + 1)} + c.$$

Hence use the formula to:

a evaluate $\int_{-\frac{1}{3}}^{0} (1 + 3x)^4 \, dx$ **b** find $\int \frac{2}{\sqrt{5 + 4x}} \, dx$

c find $\int \frac{1}{(3 + 8x)^2} \, dx$.

4 Use the suggested substitutions to find or evaluate:

Hint: Partial fractions will also be needed in

4 f

a $\int_{\frac{1}{2}}^{1} x(2x - 1)^3 \, dx; \quad t = 2x - 1$

b $\int \frac{x}{2 - x} \, dx; \quad t = 2 - x$

c $\int_0^1 \frac{x}{\sqrt{3x + 1}} \, dx; \quad p^2 = 3x + 1$

d $\int x(4 + x)^{-\frac{3}{2}} \, dx; \quad t^2 = 4 + x$

e $\int_1^2 \frac{4x}{(x^2 + 1)^2} \, dx; \quad u = x^2 + 1$

f $\int x^2 e^{2x^3} \, dx; \quad u = 2x^3$

g $\int \cos\theta (1 + \sin^2\theta) \, d\theta; \quad t = \sin\theta$

h $\int \frac{dx}{1 + e^x}; \quad u = e^x$

i $\int \frac{x}{1 + x^4} \, dx; \quad u = x^2$

5 Use a suitable substitution to integrate the following:

a $\int_0^{\frac{\pi}{2}} \cos^3\theta \sin\theta \, d\theta$

b $\int x e^{-\frac{1}{2}x^2} \, dx$

c $\int_0^1 x(1 - x^2)^{\frac{1}{3}} \, dx$

d $\int_0^1 \sqrt{1 - x^2} \, dx$

e $\int \frac{e^x - 2}{e^x + 2} \, dx$

f $\int \frac{1}{(8 + 3x)^{\frac{1}{2}}} \, dx$

g $\int x\sqrt{2 + x} \, dx$

h $\int \frac{x}{\sqrt{x^2 - 1}} \, dx$

i $\int \frac{x^2}{\sqrt{1 + x^3}} \, dx$

Contextual

1 The graph shows part of the curve $y = \frac{3}{6-2x}$. Calculate the volume generated when the shaded area is rotated through one complete turn about the x-axis.

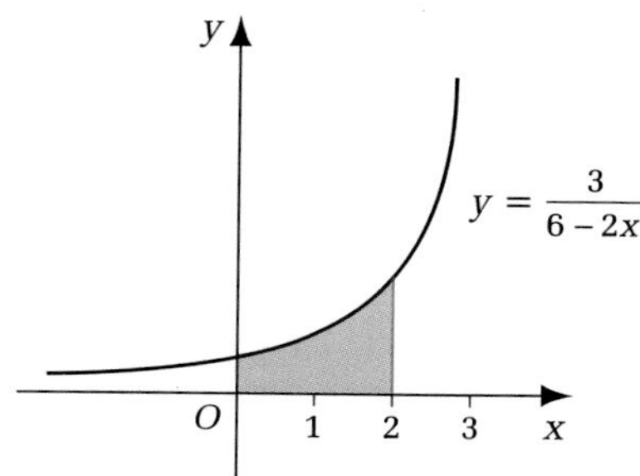

2 **a** Express $\dfrac{2}{x(1+x)^2}$ in the form $\dfrac{A}{x} + \dfrac{B}{(1+x)} + \dfrac{C}{(1+x)^2}$, where A, B and C are constants to be determined.

b Hence find $\displaystyle\int_1^3 \frac{2}{x(1+x)^2}\,dx$.

3 Use the substitution $t = e^x$ to find $\displaystyle\int \frac{e^x}{1+e^{2x}}\,dx$.

4 **a** Show that $\sec^2 x = 1 + \tan^2 x$.

b Use the substitution $u = \cos x$ to show that $\displaystyle\int \frac{\sin x}{\cos^3 x}\,dx = \frac{1}{2}\tan^2 x + c$. Comment on the use of the constant.

5 **a** Use the substitution $u = \ln x$ to find $\displaystyle\int \frac{\ln x}{x}\,dx$.

b

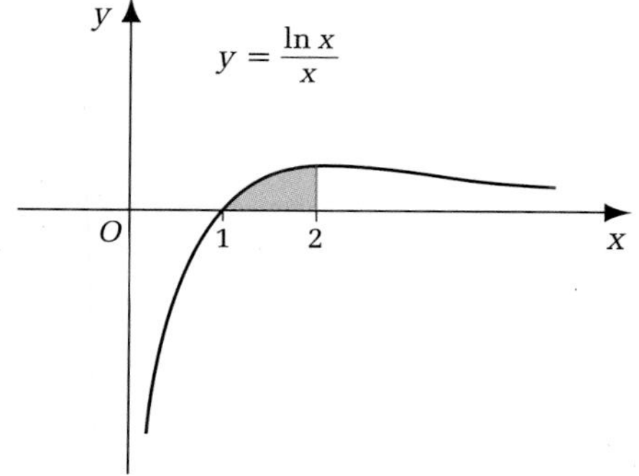

The graph shows the curve $y = \frac{1}{x}\ln x$. Use your answer in **a** to find the area of the shaded region.

6 Use the substitution $u = e^x$ to find $\displaystyle\int \frac{1}{1+e^x}\,dx$.

7 Use the substitution $x = 2\sin\theta$ to evaluate $\displaystyle\int_0^2 \sqrt{4-x^2}\,dx$.

8 Express $\dfrac{25}{(x+2)(2x-1)^2}$ in partial fractions.

Hence evaluate $\displaystyle\int_1^2 \frac{25}{(x+2)(2x-1)^2}\,dx$.

12.5 The Area Under a Parametrically Defined Curve

In Chapter 9 we developed a technique for finding the area under a curve. The equation of the curve was expressed in Cartesian form as $y = f(x)$ and the area calculated as the integral $\int_a^b f(x)\,dx$. The limits $x = a$ and $x = b$ define the boundaries of the area along the x-axis.

What happens when the curve is expressed in parametric form? Instead of $y = f(x)$ we have $y = g(t)$ for some parameter t. Since the integrand is now a function of the parameter t, we cannot use the operator dx. Instead we have to make a substitution and replace dx by $\frac{dx}{dt}\,dt$. Also, since the integrand and operator are expressed in terms of the parameter, so are the limits.

Example 1

A circle can be described by the parametric equations

$$x = 3\cos\theta \qquad y = 3\sin\theta \qquad 0 \le \theta \le 2\pi$$

a Find the area of the first quadrant.

b Verify the answer to **a** using the result

$$\text{area} = \int_{t_1}^{t_2} y(t)\,\frac{d}{dt}(x)\,dt$$

Solution

a $x = 3\cos\theta$, $y = 3\sin\theta$, $0 \le \theta \le 2\pi$ are the parametric equations of a circle, centre the origin and radius 3 (see p. 473).

$$\begin{aligned}\text{area of quadrant} &= \tfrac{1}{4} \times \pi r^2\\ &= \tfrac{1}{4} \times \pi \times 3^2\\ &= \frac{9\pi}{4}\end{aligned}$$

b To verify this result, notice that the first quadrant is described by parametric equations for $0 \le \theta \le \frac{\pi}{2}$.

$$\text{area} = \int_{t_1}^{t_2} y(t)\,\frac{d}{dt}(x)\,dt$$

To find the values of t_1 and t_2, the lower and upper limits on the integral in terms of the parameter t, we first need to consider the corresponding values of x. The first quadrant of the circle is bounded by $x = 0$ and $x = 3$. When $x = 0$, $t = \frac{\pi}{2}$ and when $x = 3$, $t = 0$. This means that $t_1 = \frac{\pi}{2}$ and $t_2 = 0$.

$$\text{Area} = \int_{\frac{\pi}{2}}^{0} 3\sin\theta \frac{\mathrm{d}}{\mathrm{d}\theta}(3\cos\theta)\,\mathrm{d}\theta$$
$$= \int_{\frac{\pi}{2}}^{0} 3\sin\theta(-3\sin\theta)\,\mathrm{d}\theta$$
$$= -9\int_{\frac{\pi}{2}}^{0} \sin^2\theta\,\mathrm{d}\theta$$

To integrate $\sin^2\theta$, recall that we can use the double angle formula from Chapter 3. This gives

$$\int \sin^2 x\,\mathrm{d}x = \tfrac{1}{2}x - \tfrac{1}{4}\sin 2x + c$$

See p. 391.

So

$$\text{area} = -9\left[\tfrac{1}{2}\theta - \tfrac{1}{4}\sin 2\theta\right]_{\frac{\pi}{2}}^{0}$$
$$= -9\left[0 - \left(\frac{\pi}{4} - \tfrac{1}{4}\sin\pi\right)\right]$$
$$= \frac{9\pi}{4}$$

Recall special angles: $\sin\pi = 0$.

Example 2

An ellipse can be described by the parametric equations

$$x = 3\cos\theta \qquad y = 2\sin\theta \qquad 0 \le \theta \le 2\pi$$

Calculate the area of the ellipse that is above the x-axis.

Solution

The parametric equations $x = 3\cos\theta$, $y = 2\sin\theta$, $0 \le \theta \le 2\pi$, define an ellipse centred on the origin. The ellipse crosses the x-axis at $x = -3$ and $x = +3$, and crosses the y-axis at $y = -2$ and $y = 2$.

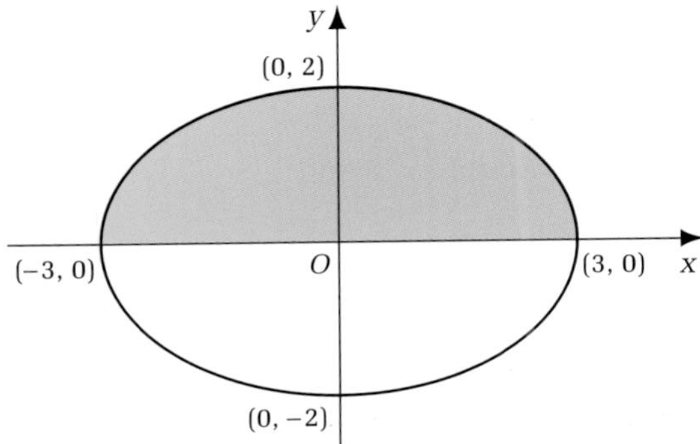

$$\text{area} = \int_{t_1}^{t_2} y(t)\frac{\mathrm{d}}{\mathrm{d}t}(x)\,\mathrm{d}t$$

Look at the boundary of the area in terms of x-coordinates first. These are $x = -3$ and $x = +3$. Notice that the corresponding values of the parameter are $\theta = \pi$ and $\theta = 0$, respectively. These are the new lower and upper limits.

$$\text{Area} = \int_{\pi}^{0} 2\sin\theta \frac{\mathrm{d}}{d\theta}(3\cos\theta)\,\mathrm{d}\theta$$

$$= \int_{\pi}^{0} 2\sin\theta(-3\sin\theta)\,\mathrm{d}\theta$$

$$= -6\int_{\pi}^{0} \sin^2\theta\,\mathrm{d}\theta$$

$$= -6\left[\frac{\theta}{2} - \tfrac{1}{4}\sin 2\theta\right]_{\pi}^{0}$$

$$= -6\left[0 - \left(\frac{\pi}{2} - \tfrac{1}{4}\sin 2\pi\right)\right]$$

$$= 3\pi$$

Check this result by finding the area of a semicircle of radius 2 and stretching it by a scale factor of $\frac{3}{2}$ in the horizontal direction only.

When the parametric equations are polynomials the limits are usually given in terms of the parameter. This makes the integration more straightforward.

Example 3

A curve is defined parametrically by $x = t^2 + 1$, $y = t - 1$, $1 \leq t \leq 5$. Find the area under the curve between $t = 2$ and $t = 3$.

Solution

Before quoting the formula and substituting the relevant figures and expressions, we need to check that the curve does not cross the x-axis between $t = 2$ and $t = 3$. Otherwise part of the area will lie below the x-axis and will contribute a negative component to the calculation.
If the curve crosses the x-axis, then $y = 0$.

$$\Rightarrow \quad t - 1 = 0$$

$$t = 1$$

Since this curve doesn't cross the x-axis between the limits $t = 2$ and $t = 3$, we can now calculate the area very quickly.

$$\text{Area} = \int_{t_1}^{t_2} y(t)\frac{\mathrm{d}}{\mathrm{d}t}(x)\,\mathrm{d}t$$

$$= \int_{2}^{3} (t-1)\frac{\mathrm{d}}{\mathrm{d}t}(t^2+1)\,\mathrm{d}t$$

$$= \int_{2}^{3} (t-1)2t\,\mathrm{d}t$$

$$= \int_2^3 (2t^2 - 2t)\,dt$$

$$= \left[\frac{2t^3}{3} - t^2\right]_2^3$$

$$= (18 - 9) - (\tfrac{16}{3} - 4)$$

$$= 7\tfrac{2}{3}$$

The area under a parametrically defined curve can also be rotated about an axis to form a solid of revolution. The analysis of these is similar to the techniques developed in Chapter 9.

Example 4

The curve has parametric equations $x = 4t$, $y = \frac{4}{t}$, $1 \leq t \leq 5$.

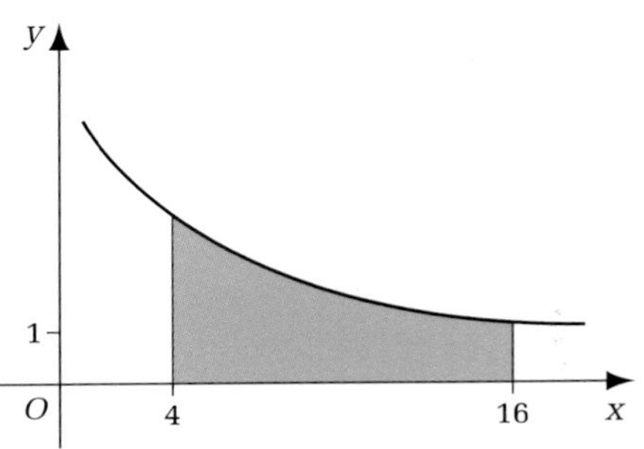

a Find the area of the shaded region, bounded by the curve, the x-axis and the lines $x = 4$ and $x = 16$.

b This region is then rotated through 2π about the x-axis. Find the volume of the solid of revolution formed.

Solution

a First we need to establish the integral for the area in terms of the parameter t. When $x = 4$, $t = 1$ and when $x = 16$, $t = 4$.

$$\text{Area} = \int_{t_1}^{t_2} y(t)\,\frac{d}{dt}(x)\,dt$$

$$= \int_1^4 \frac{4}{t}\,\frac{d}{dt}(4t)\,dt$$

$$= \int_1^4 \frac{16}{t}\,dt$$

$$= 16[\ln|t|]_1^4$$

$$= 16\ln|4| - 16\ln|1|$$

$$= 16\ln|4|$$

Recall that $\int \frac{1}{x}\,dx = \ln|x| + c$.

Recall that $\ln 1 = 0$.

An alternative answer is $32\ln 2$.

b The formula we used for the volume of a solid of revolution was

$$V = \int_{x=a}^{x=b} \pi y^2\,dx$$

In parametric form this integral becomes

$$V = \int_{t_1}^{t_2} \pi(y(t))^2 \frac{d}{dt}(x)\,dt$$

So

$$\begin{aligned}
\text{Volume} &= \int_1^4 \pi\left(\frac{4}{t}\right)^2 \frac{d}{dt}(4t)\,dt \\
&= \int_1^4 \pi\frac{16}{t^2} \times 4\,dt \\
&= 64\pi\int_1^4 \frac{1}{t^2}\,dt \\
&= 64\pi\left[-\frac{1}{t}\right]_1^4 \\
&= 64\pi(-\tfrac{1}{4} + 1) \\
&= 48\pi
\end{aligned}$$

12.5 The Area Under a Parametrically Defined Curve

Exercise

Technique

1 An ellipse is defined parametrically as $x = 3\cos\theta$, $y = 4\sin\theta$, $0 \le \theta \le 2\pi$. Calculate the area of the ellipse above the x-axis.

2 The diagram shows an ellipse centred on the origin.

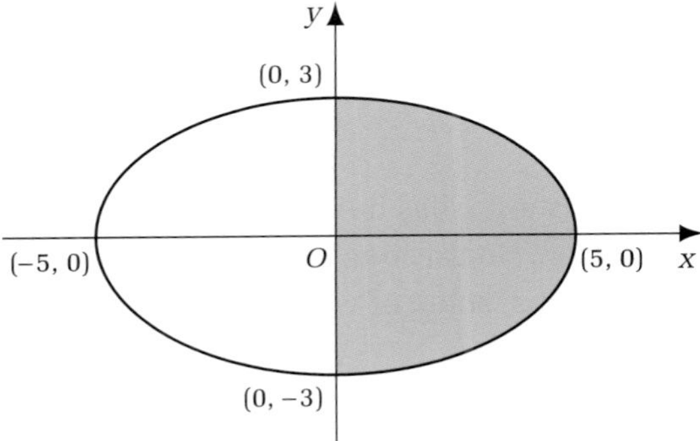

Find the area of the shaded region.

3
- **a** Find the area of a region R bounded by a curve with parametric equations $x = t^2 + 3$, $y = t + 1$, the lines $x = 4$ and $x = 7$ and the x-axis.
- **b** Calculate the volume generated when R is rotated completely about the x-axis.

4 The diagram shows a sketch of the curve $x = t^3 + 1$, $y = \frac{2}{t}$, where t is a parameter and $t > 0$.

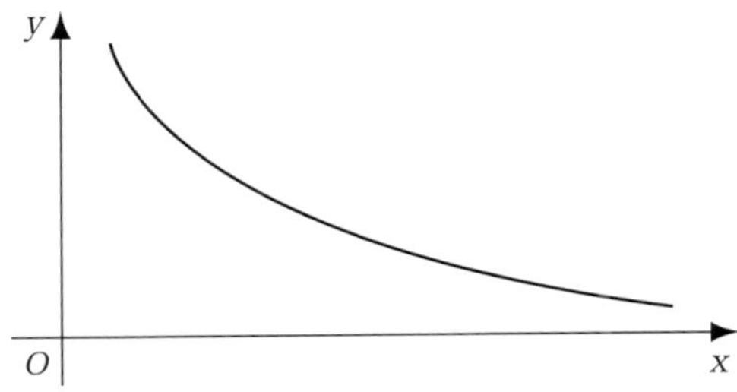

- **a** Find the area bounded by the curve, the lines $x = 2$ and $x = 9$ and the x-axis.
- **b** Calculate the volume of a solid of revolution formed when this area is rotated through 2π about the x-axis.

12.6 Differential Equations

An equation involving the variables x and y and the first derivative $\frac{dy}{dx}$ only is called a **first order differential equation**. If the equation has a term containing the second derivative $\frac{d^2y}{dx^2}$ it is called a **second order differential equation**.

A simple first order differential equation is one in which $\frac{dy}{dx}$ can be expressed in terms of the variable x only. Consider $\frac{dy}{dx} = x$. This differential equation has many solutions.

Integrating both sides with respect to x, $\frac{dy}{dx} = x$ becomes

$$y = \int x \, dx$$

$$y = \tfrac{1}{2}x^2 + c$$

This is called the **general solution**, because the constant c has not been determined. Each value of c will give a valid solution. So this one differential equation has an infinite family of solutions, some of which are illustrated below.

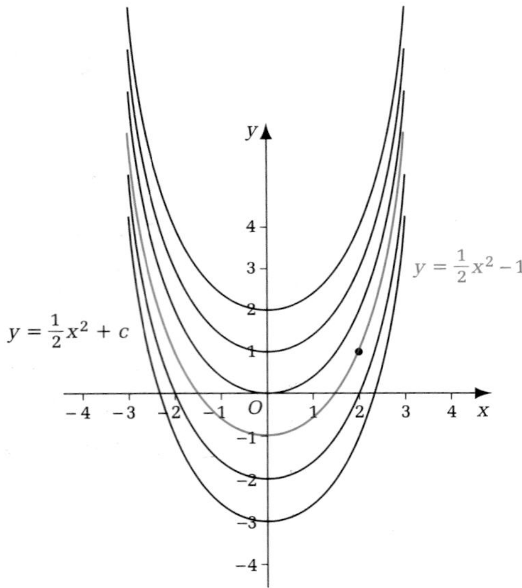

If additional information is given, such as $y = 1$ when $x = 2$, a **particular solution** can be found. Substituting these values of x and y into $y = \frac{1}{2}x^2 + c$,

$$1 = \tfrac{4}{2} + c \;\Rightarrow\; -1 = c$$

So $\quad y = \tfrac{1}{2}x^2 - 1$

This is called a **particular solution** to the differential equation. It is the only curve for which $\frac{dy}{dx} = x$ that passes through $(2, 1)$. This particular solution is illustrated in colour on the diagram above.

Now consider the first order differential equation $\frac{dy}{dx} = xy$. The algebraic solution cannot be found by simply integrating both sides with respect to x. Instead we must first separate the variables so that all the y terms appear on the same side of the equation as $\frac{dy}{dx}$, and all the x terms appear on the other side.

Step ① Separate the variables.

$$\text{Since} \quad \frac{dy}{dx} = xy, \quad \frac{1}{y}\frac{dy}{dx} = x$$

Step ② Integrate both sides with respect to x.

Recall that $\frac{dy}{dx}$ dx can be replaced with dy.

$$\int \frac{1}{y}\frac{dy}{dx}\,dx = \int x\,dx$$

$$\int \frac{1}{y}\,dy = \int x\,dx$$

Notice that the terms have been separated so that all the x terms will be integrated with respect to x and all the y terms with respect to y.

$$\text{Thus} \quad \ln|y| = \tfrac{1}{2}x^2 + c, \quad \text{giving } |y| = e^{\frac{1}{2}x^2 + c}$$

$$\text{Therefore} \quad y = \pm e^{\frac{1}{2}x^2 + c} \quad \text{or} \quad y = \pm e^{\frac{1}{2}x^2} \times e^c$$

Use law of indices $a^{m+n} = a^m \times a^n$.

Step ③ Simplify the constant (or find it if enough information is given in the question).

Since if c is a constant then e^c is also a constant, we can write $A = \pm e^c$.

Then $y = Ae^{\frac{1}{2}x^2}$.

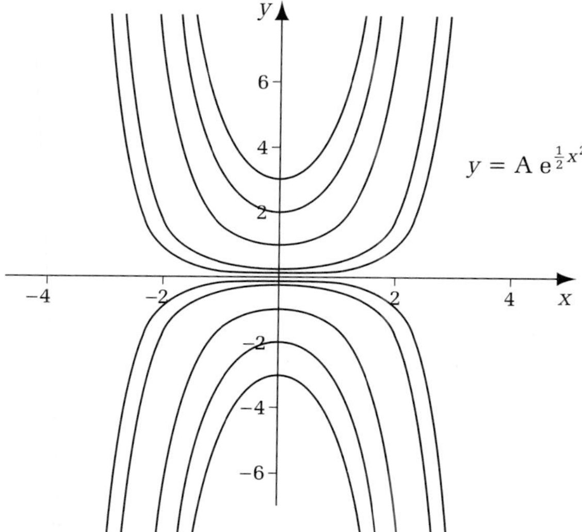

If $A > 0$ the curves above the x-axis are generated. If $A < 0$ the curves below the x-axis are generated.

A particular solution can be found if more information is given. This is called the **variable separable** method of solving first order differential equations.

Example 1

Find the general solutions to:

a $\frac{dy}{dx} = xy^2$ **b** $\frac{dy}{dx} - 2y = 1$

Solution

a

$$\frac{1}{y^2}\frac{dy}{dx} = x$$ ◀ ① Separate the variables.

$$\int \frac{1}{y^2}\frac{dy}{dx}\,dx = \int x\,dx$$ ◀ ② Integrate both sides wrt x.

$\frac{dy}{dx}$ dx is replaced with dy.

$$\int y^{-2}dy = \int x\,dx$$

$$\frac{y^{-1}}{-1} = \tfrac{1}{2}x^2 + c$$

Only one constant of integration is needed.

$$-\frac{1}{y} = \tfrac{1}{2}(x^2 + 2c) = \frac{x^2 + 2c}{2}$$

If c is a constant then is $2c$; let $k = 2c$.

$$y = -\frac{2}{x^2 + k}$$ ◀ ③ Simplify the constant.

This is the general solution.

The general solution will be in the form '$y =$ '.

b

$$\frac{dy}{dx} = 2y + 1$$

$$\Rightarrow \quad \frac{1}{2y+1}\frac{dy}{dx} = 1$$ ◀ ① Separate the variables.

$\frac{dy}{dx}$ dx is replaced with dy.

$$\int \frac{1}{2y+1}\frac{dy}{dx}\,dx = \int dx$$ ◀ ② Integrate both sides wrt x.

$$\tfrac{1}{2}\int \frac{2}{2y+1}\,dy = \int dx$$ ◀ The form $\int \frac{f'(x)}{f(x)}\,dx$.

$$\tfrac{1}{2}\ln|2y+1| = x + c$$

$$\ln|2y+1| = 2x + 2c$$

Let $k = 2c$.

$$\Rightarrow \quad |2y+1| = e^{2x+k}$$

$$2y + 1 = \pm e^{2x} \times e^{k}$$

$$\Rightarrow \quad 2y = Ae^{2x} - 1$$

Let $A = \pm e^k$.

$$y = \tfrac{1}{2}Ae^{2x} - \tfrac{1}{2}$$ ◀ ③ Simplify the constant.

So the general solution is $y = Be^{2x} - \frac{1}{2}$, where B is a constant.

Example 2

Find the solution of the differential equation $(1 + x)\frac{dy}{dx} = 1 - \sin^2 y$, for which $y = \frac{\pi}{4}$ when $x = 0$.

(OCSEB)

Solution

$$\frac{1}{1-\sin^2 y}\frac{dy}{dx} = \frac{1}{1+x}$$ ◀ ① Separate the variables.

$$\int \frac{1}{1-\sin^2 y}\frac{dy}{dx}\,dx = \int \frac{1}{1+x}\,dx$$ ◀ ② Integrate both sides wrt x.

$$\int \frac{1}{\cos^2 y}\,dy = \int \frac{1}{1+x}\,dx$$

$$\int \sec^2 y\,dy = \int \frac{1}{1+x}\,dx$$

$$\tan y = \ln|1+x| + c$$

Use the Pythagorean identity. $\sin^2 y + \cos^2 y = 1$.

When $x = 0, y = \frac{\pi}{4}$.

Thus $\tan\frac{\pi}{4} = \ln 1 + c$ ◀ ③ Find the constant.

$1 = 0 + c$

$\Rightarrow 1 = c$

So $\tan y = \ln|1+x| + 1$

$y = \tan^{-1}(\ln|1+x| + 1)$

Modelling with differential equations

When there is sufficient information to describe how one variable changes with respect to another, the situation can often be modelled by a differential equation.

Newton's law of cooling

This states that the rate of change in temperature of an object is proportional to the *difference* between its temperature and that of its surroundings. Newton's law can be modelled by a differential equation.

For hot water cooling, let θ be the temperature of the water at time t minutes, and the surrounding temperature be 18°C. The difference between them is then $\theta - 18$. Then Newton's law gives

To model a real situation some assumptions have to be made. In this case it is assumed that the temperature of the surroundings is constant.

$$\frac{d\theta}{dt} \propto (\theta - 18)$$

Writing this as an equation,

$$\frac{d\theta}{dt} = -k(\theta - 18), \quad \text{where} \quad k \in \mathbb{R}.$$

The negative sign indicates that θ is decreasing. If it were to be omitted the constant k would work out to be negative.

Population growth

Scientists have crudely suggested that the populations of certain organisms grow at a rate that is proportional to the size of the population. Let N be the population at time t. Then

$$\frac{dN}{dt} \propto N$$

Writing this as an equation,

$$\frac{dN}{dt} = kN, \quad \text{where} \quad k \in \mathbb{R}.$$

Here it is assumed th the environment rem constant. The model probably more realist over a short period of time.

Example 3

According to Newton's Law, the rate of cooling of an object is proportional to the temperature difference between the object and its surroundings. Warm water is poured into a basin, and cools from 41.1°C to 40.0°C in 5 minutes. The temperature of the room is a constant 17°C.

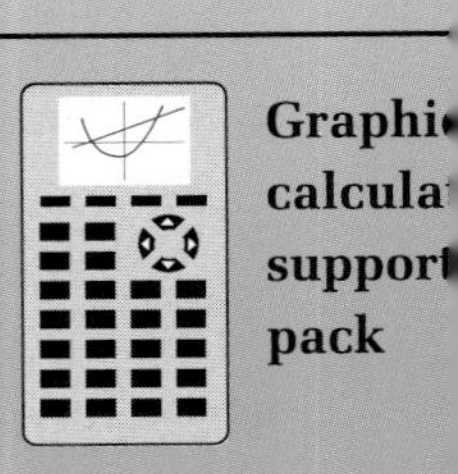

a Write down a differential equation to model the temperature of the water.

b Solve the differential equation, and find the temperature of the water after 10 minutes.

c Find the time taken for the water to cool to 37°C.

Solution

a Let θ be the temperature in degrees Celsius of the water at time t. Then according to Newton's Law the rate of change of θ with respect to time is proportional to $\theta - 17$.

$$\frac{d\theta}{dt} \propto (\theta - 17)$$

$$\frac{d\theta}{dt} = -k(\theta - 17), \text{ where } k \text{ is a constant}$$

Remember that the negative sign indicat cooling.

b $$\frac{1}{\theta - 17}\frac{d\theta}{dt} = -k$$ ◀ ① Separate the variables.

$$\int \frac{1}{\theta - 17}\, d\theta = \int -k\, dt$$ ◀ ② Integrate both sides wrt t.

Since $\theta > 17$ the modulus function is required.

$$\ln(\theta - 17) = -kt + c$$

$$\theta - 17 = e^{-kt+c}$$

$$\theta - 17 = e^{-kt} \times e^{c}$$

$$\theta - 17 = Ae^{-kt}, \text{ where } A \text{ is a constant}$$

$$\theta = 17 + Ae^{-kt}$$

To find the constants A and k use the **initial conditions**.

◀ ③ **Find the constants.**

When $t = 0$, $\theta = 41.1°C$

So $41.1 = 17 + Ae^0$

$41.1 - 17 = A$

$A = 24.1$

When $t = 5$, $\theta = 40°C$

From $\theta = 17 + 24.1e^{-kt}$

$40 = 17 + 24.1e^{-5k}$

Substituting $A = 24.1°C$.

$$\frac{40-17}{24.1} = e^{-5k}$$

$$\ln\left(\frac{40-17}{24.1}\right) = \ln e^{-5k}$$

Take natural logs of both sides.

$$\ln\left(\frac{40-17}{24.1}\right) = -5k\ln e$$ ◀ **ln e = 1**

Using $\ln a^n = n \ln a$.

$$-\tfrac{1}{5}\ln\left(\frac{40-17}{24.1}\right) = k$$

So $k = 0.009\,34$ (3 s.f.)

Now $\theta = 17 + 24.1e^{-0.009\,34t}$

The temperature after 10 minutes can be found by putting $t = 10$ into this equation.

$\theta = 17 + 24.1e^{-0.009\,34 \times 10}$

$= 17 + 24.1e^{-0.0934}$

$\theta = 17 + 22.0$ (1 d.p.)

$= 39.0°C$ (1 d.p.)

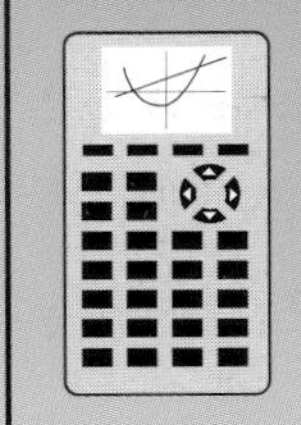

Graphical calculator support pack

c Substitute $\theta = 37$ and find t

$\theta = 17 + 24.1e^{-0.009\,34t}$

$37 = 17 + 24.1e^{-0.009\,34t}$

$20 = 24.1e^{-0.009\,34t}$

$\frac{20}{24.1} = e^{-0.009\,34t}$

$\ln(\frac{20}{24.1}) = \ln e^{-0.009\,34t}$

Take natural logs of both sides.

$\ln(\frac{20}{24.1}) = -0.009\,34t\ln e$

Remember, $\ln e = 1$.

$-\frac{1}{0.009\,34}\ln(\frac{20}{24.1}) = t$

$t = 19.966$

So it will take about 20 minutes for the water to cool to 37°C.

Example 4

Radioactive material decays at a rate proportional to the amount of material present at that time. Let x represent the quantity of radioactive material present at time t, and x_0 be the initial quantity of radioactive material.

a Write down a differential equation that models this situation. Solve it to find x in terms of t and x_0.

b After $1\frac{1}{2}$ hours, one tenth of the material has decayed. Calculate the half-life of this substance, correct to one decimal place.

c A container contains 5 grams of this substance. Determine what mass remains after one day.

Half-life is the time taken for the material decay to half its origin quantity.

Solution

a x is the quantity of radioactive material at time t, and $\frac{dx}{dt}$ is the rate of change of x with respect to t

So $\quad \dfrac{dx}{dt} \propto x$

$\dfrac{dx}{dt} = -\lambda x$, where λ is a constant ◀ ① Separate the variables.

The minus sign indica that x is decreasing.

$\dfrac{1}{x}\dfrac{dx}{dt} = -\lambda$

$\displaystyle\int \frac{1}{x}\,dx = \int -\lambda\,dt$ ◀ ② Integrate both sides wrt t.

$\frac{dx}{dt}$ dt is replaced with dx.

$x > 0$ so modulus function not required

$\ln x = -\lambda t + c$

$x = e^{-\lambda t + c} = e^{-\lambda t} \times e^{c}$

So $\quad x = Ae^{-\lambda t}$, where A is a constant

When $t = 0$, $x = x_0$ ◀ ③ Find the constant.

So $\quad x_0 = Ae^0 = A \quad$ and $\quad x = x_0 e^{-\lambda t}$

b To find the half-life, first find the value of λ. Use the information given in the question.
When $t = 1.5$ hours, $\frac{1}{10}x_0$ has decayed, so $x = \frac{9}{10}x_0$.
Substituting these values into $x = x_0 e^{-\lambda t}$

$\frac{9}{10}x_0 = x_0 e^{-\lambda \times 1.5}$

x_0 cancels

$\frac{9}{10} = e^{-1.5\lambda}$

So $\quad \ln\frac{9}{10} = \ln e^{-1.5\lambda}$, taking natural logs of both sides.

$\ln\frac{9}{10} = -1.5\lambda \ln e$

and $\quad -\frac{1}{1.5}\ln\frac{9}{10} = \lambda$

$\lambda = 0.07$ (2 d.p.)

Final answer is requi to 1 d.p., so use great accuracy at this stage

Therefore $\quad x = x_0 e^{-0.07t}$

The time for half-life occurs when $x = \frac{1}{2}x_0$.

So
$$\frac{1}{2}x_0 = x_0 e^{-0.07t}$$
$$\frac{1}{2} = e^{-0.07t}$$
$$\ln(\tfrac{1}{2}) = \ln e^{-0.07t}$$
$$\ln(\tfrac{1}{2}) = -0.07t \ln e$$
$$-\frac{1}{0.07}\ln(\tfrac{1}{2}) = t$$
$$t = 9.9 \text{ (1 d.p.)}$$

So the half-life of the substance is 9.9 hours.

c If $x_0 = 5$ g, then $x = 5e^{-0.07t}$
After 1 day, $t = 24$ (since t is measured in hours), so

$$x = 5e^{-0.07 \times 24}$$
$$= 0.93$$

Therefore after 1 day, 0.93 g of the substance remains.

12.6 Differential Equations

Exercise

Technique

1 Find the general solution to the following differential equations:

a $\frac{dy}{dx} = 3x^2 + \frac{1}{x}$ **d** $\frac{dy}{dx} = \sqrt{x} + 2e^x$ **g** $2 + x = x^2 \frac{dy}{dx}$

b $\frac{dy}{dx} = x - \frac{1}{x} + e^x$ **e** $\frac{dy}{dx} = x^{\frac{1}{3}} + \sin x$ **h** $\frac{1}{2}e^x + 3\frac{dy}{dx} = 1$

c $\frac{dy}{dx} = x + e^x$ **f** $x\frac{dy}{dx} = 1 - xe^x$ **i** $10\frac{dy}{dx} = x^{\frac{3}{4}} + \frac{20}{x}$

2 Find the general solution to the following differential equations.

a $\frac{dy}{dx} = 12x^2$ **e** $\frac{dy}{dx} = 2y$ **i** $\frac{dy}{dx} - y = 1$

b $\sec x \frac{dy}{dx} = 1$ **f** $\frac{dy}{dx} = 6x^2 y$ **j** $(x+1)\frac{dy}{dx} - 2y = 0$

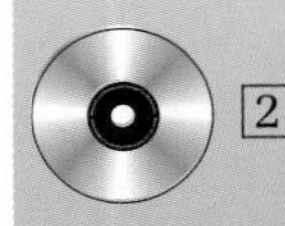
2 f

c $\frac{dy}{dx} = \frac{x+1}{y}$ **g** $\frac{dy}{dx} = y^{\frac{2}{3}}$ **k** $\frac{dy}{dx} = \frac{x^2}{y}$

d $\frac{dy}{dx} = \frac{1}{y}$ **h** $\frac{dy}{dx} = xe^{-y}$ **l** $\frac{dy}{dx} = \frac{xy}{1+x^2}$

3 **a** Find $\int xe^x \, dx$.

b Use your result to **a** to find the general solution to $e^{-x}\frac{dy}{dx} = \frac{x}{y}$.

4 The variables x and y satisfy the differential equation $\frac{dy}{dx} + y\tan x = 0$.

a Find the general solution.

b Find a particular solution where $y = 1$ when $x = \frac{\pi}{3}$.

5

5 **a** Find the general solution to $\frac{dy}{dx} = \frac{2(y-1)}{x}$.

b Find a particular solution where $y = 4$ when $x = 1$.

Contextual

1 An object cools from 100°C to 70°C in 34 minutes. Assume Newton's law of cooling applies. The surrounding air temperature is 20°C.

a State Newton's Law of cooling.

b If T is the temperature of the body at time t minutes, write down a differential equation that describes how the body cools.

c Solve the differential equation to find T in terms of t and use it to find the temperature after 45 minutes.

d How long will the body take to cool to 50°C?

2 The rate of increase of the number of bacteria present in a culture is proportional to the number present at that time.

a If N represents the number of bacteria after t hours write down a differential equation connecting N and t.

b If N_0 represents the number of bacteria present initially show that $N = N_0 e^{kt}$, where k is a positive constant.

c If it takes four hours for the number of bacteria to double find the value of k correct to two decimal places.

d How long will it take for the number of bacteria to triple?

3

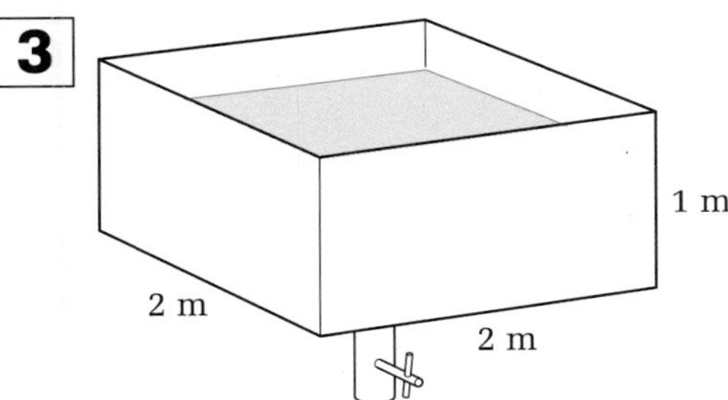

The dimensions of a tank, as shown in the diagram, are 2 m × 2 m × 1 m. The tank is emptied by opening a tap. Water then flows out of the hole in the base of the tank at a rate that is proportional to the square root of the depth of the water at that time.

a If h metres is the depth of the water and V is the volume of the water at time t, write down a differential equation involving $\frac{dV}{dt}$ and h.

b Explain why $V = 4h\,\text{m}^3$ at time t. Hence write down a differential equation involving $\frac{dh}{dt}$ and h.

c Initially the tank is full and when the tap is opened that water level drops by 19 cm in 2 minutes. Solve the differential equation and find the time for the tank to empty.

4 The radioactive isotope, radium 224, has a half-life of 3.64 days. This isotope decays at a rate that is proportional to the quantity present at any particular time. If x is the quantity present at time t and x_0 is the initial quantity of radium, write down and solve a differential equation. Hence find the time required for the radium to decay to one third of the initial amount.

5 The gradient of a curve at any point (x, y) is inversely proportional to the y-coordinate.

a Write down a differential equation to model this situation.

b Solve the differential equation to find the equation of the curve if it passes through $(0, 3)$ and $(1, 2)$.

Two variable quantities are inversely proportional if their product is constant.

Consolidation

Exercise A

1 Integrate the following with respect to x:

a $\frac{1}{x^2}$

b $4\cos(2x+7)$

c $\sin 2x + \cos\frac{1}{2}x$

d $\sec^2 4x$

e $\sin 5x \sin x$

f $1 + e^{3x}$

g $\frac{1}{e^{5x}}$

h $\frac{4x+6}{x^2+3x}$

i $\cot 3x$

j $\frac{1}{25+x^2}$

k $\frac{1}{\sqrt{25-x^2}}$

l $\frac{x}{x+3}$

2 Use integration by parts to find the indefinite integral $\int x^4 \ln x \, dx$. *(SMP)*

3 Evaluate $\int_0^1 xe^{3x}\, dx$. *(ULEAC)*

4 Show that $\displaystyle\int_0^1 \frac{1}{(x+1)(2x+1)}\, dx = \ln a$, where a is a rational number to be determined. *(JMB)*

5 Find the values of a and b if $\displaystyle\int_0^2 \frac{3}{x^2-9}\, dx = -\frac{1}{a}\ln b$.

6 Use the substitution $u = 1 + 3\sin\theta$ to evaluate $\displaystyle\int_0^{\frac{\pi}{2}} \frac{\cos\theta}{\sqrt{1+3\sin\theta}}\, d\theta$. *(SMP)*

7 Find the value of $\int_3^4 x(x-3)^{17}\, dx$. *(ULEAC)*

8 Find y in terms of x given that $\frac{dy}{dx} = ye^x$ and that $y = 1$ when $x = 0$. *(ULEAC)*

9 A balloon is expanding and at time t seconds its surface area is $s\,\text{cm}^2$. The expansion is such that the rate of increase of s is proportional to $\frac{1}{\sqrt{s}}$. When the surface area is $900\,\text{cm}^2$, it is increasing at a rate of $60\,\text{cm}^2\,\text{s}^{-1}$.

a Show that $\frac{ds}{dt} = \frac{1800}{\sqrt{s}}$.

b Solve this differential equation given that $s = 400$ when $t = 0$.

c Find to the nearest second the time at which $s = 900$ cm.

(NEAB)

10 At time t hours the rate of decay of the mass of a radioactive substance is proportional to the mass x kg of the substance at that time. At time $t = 0$ the mass of the substance is A kg.

a By forming and integrating a differential equation, show that $x = Ae^{-kt}$, where k is a constant.

b It is observed that $x = \frac{1}{3}A$ at time $t = 10$. Find the value of t when $x = \frac{1}{2}A$, giving your answer to two decimal places. *(ULEAC)*

Exercise B

1 The curve shown has parametric equations $x = 4\cos\theta$, $y = 5\sin\theta$, $0 \le \theta \le 2\pi$.

The straight line PR is a tangent to the ellipse at P, where $\theta = \frac{\pi}{3}$. Find the area of the shaded region, bound by the curve, the x-axis and the tangent PR.

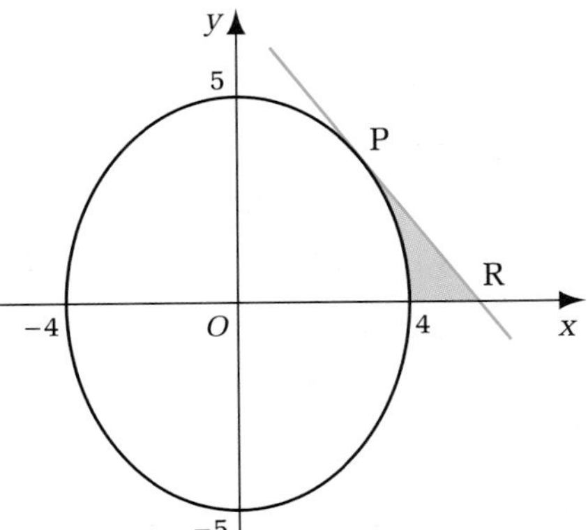

2 Evaluate the following integrals exactly:

a $\int_0^{\frac{\pi}{2}} \sin x \cos 3x \, dx$ **b** $\int_0^{\frac{1}{2}} \frac{1}{\sqrt{1-x^2}} \, dx$

3 **a** Use integration by parts to find $\int xe^{-x} \, dx$.

b

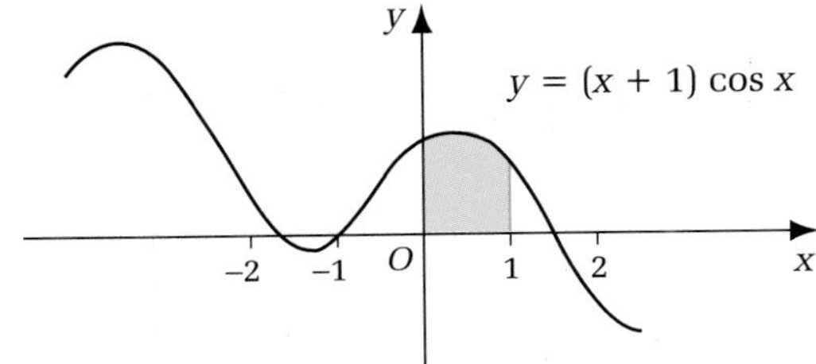

The graph shows part of the curve $y = (x+1)\cos x$. Calculate, correct to two decimal places, the area of the shaded region.

4 **a** Express $\frac{4x^2+2x+1}{(x+1)(2x-1)}$ in the form $A + \frac{B}{(x+1)(2x-1)}$. Use this to find $\int \frac{4x^2+2x+1}{(x+1)(2x-1)} dx$.

b Express $\frac{3x^2+3x+4}{x(x^2+4)}$ in the form $\frac{A}{x} + \frac{Bx+C}{x^2+4}$. Then find $\int \frac{3x^2+3x+4}{x(x^2+4)} dx$.

c Evaluate $\int_0^2 \frac{x(13-3x)}{(x+1)(x-3)^2} dx$.

5 **a** By means of the substitution $u = 6 - x$ or otherwise, show that $\int \frac{1}{6-x} \, dx = -\ln|6-x| + c$.

b As a mathematical model for my regular 6 km morning jog, I assume that my speed is proportional to the distance that I still have to go to reach the end.

  i If I start off at a speed of 8 km h^{-1}, and after t hours have travelled x km, explain why $\frac{dx}{dt} = k(6 - x)$, where k is a constant.

  ii Show that $k = \frac{4}{3}$.

c By solving the differential equation $\frac{dt}{dx} = \frac{3}{4(6-x)}$, find the time taken for me to complete 4 km of the jog, and state my predicted speed at the time.

d By considering the predicted time taken for me to complete the jog, comment on the suitability of the model.

(SMP)

6 Water flows out of a tank through a pipe at the bottom, and at a time t minutes the depth of water in the tank is x metres. At time $t = 0$ the depth of water in the tank is 2 m. After 10 minutes the depth is 1.5 m. It is desired to find the time T, correct to the nearest minute, at which the depth is 1 m.

a In a simple model the rate at which the depth of water in the tank decreases is taken to be constant. Find T using this model.

b In a more refined model the rate at which the depth of water remaining in the tank is decreasing at any instant is proportional to the square root of the depth at that instant.

  i Explain how the more refined model leads to the differential equation $-\frac{dx}{dt} = k\sqrt{x}$, where k is a positive constant.

  ii Find the general solution of the differential equation in **i**.

  iii Find T using the more refined model.

(UCLES)

7 A mathematical model for the population growth of a certain country assumes that the country has a constant birth rate of 22 per thousand and a constant death rate of 7 per thousand. The population of the country at the end of 1995 was 4.80 million and the population of the country at time t years later is denoted by x.

a Show that $\frac{dx}{dt} = 0.015x$.

b Find x in terms of t.

Use the mathematical model to estimate:

c the population of the country at the end of 1998

d the year in which the population of the country will exceed 6 million.

(WJEC)

Applications and Activities

1 *Cooling*

Fill a container with hot water. Note the room temperature and place a thermometer in the hot water and wait until it has adapted to the temperature of the water. At this point begin to note the water temperature every $2\frac{1}{2}$ minutes. Record your results in a table similar to the one below.

Time (t)	0	2.5	5	7.5	10	12.5	15	17.5	20	22.5	25	27.5
Temp. (θ°C)												

a Write down Newton's law of cooling

b Write down a differential equation that will model the temperature of the water.

c Solve the differential equation and use the first and third entries in the table to find θ in terms of t.

d Investigate how well your differential equation models this situation.

e Investigate Newton's law of cooling for different shaped containers.

2 *Integration spotting*

The fundamental theorem of calculus states that differentiation is the reverse of integration. In this activity an integral in the form $\int f(x)g(x)\,dx$ must be made by selecting two function from the box below.

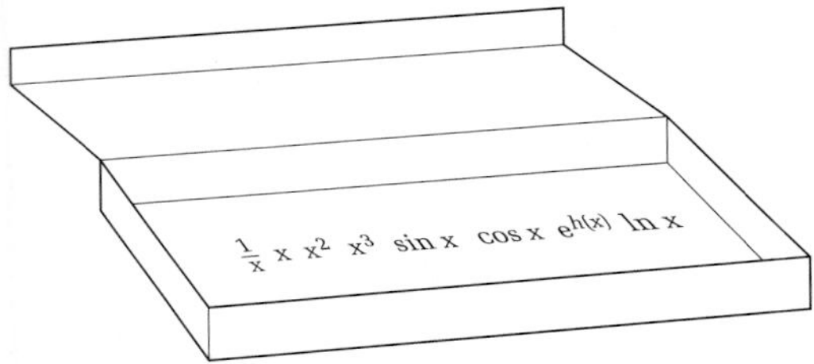

The answer must contain a combination of terms from the second box, below.

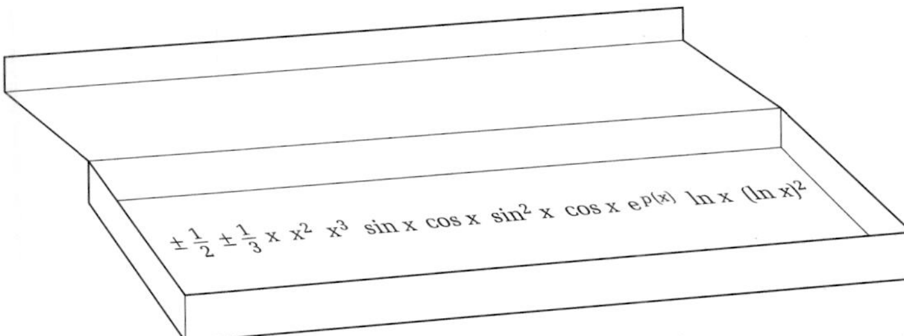

One example is $\int \frac{1}{x} \times x^2\,dx = \frac{1}{2}x^2 + c$.
A more complex example is $\int xe^{x^2}\,dx = \frac{1}{2}e^{x^2} + c$, because $\frac{d}{dx}(e^{x^2} + c) = 2xe^{x^2}$.
How many different integrals complete with answers can you spot?

Summary

- Standard integrals that are the reverse of differentiating standard functions are:

$$\int x^n \, dx = \frac{x^{n+1}}{n+1} + c, \; n \neq -1$$

$$\int e^{ax+b} \, dx = \frac{1}{a} e^{ax+b} + c$$

$$\int \cos kx \, dx = \frac{1}{k} \sin kx + c$$

$$\int \frac{1}{x} \, dx = \ln x + c$$

$$\int \sin kx \, dx = -\frac{1}{k} \cos kx + c$$

$$\int \frac{f'(x)}{f(x)} \, dx = \ln |f(x)| + c$$

$$\int \sec^2 x \, dx = \tan x + c$$

$$\int \frac{1}{\sqrt{a^2 - x^2}} \, dx = \sin^{-1}\left(\frac{x}{a}\right) + c$$

$$\int \sec^2 kx \, dx = \frac{1}{k} \tan kx + c$$

$$\int \frac{a}{a^2 + x^2} \, dx = \tan^{-1}\left(\frac{x}{a}\right) + c$$

- If the integrand has $\cos^2 x$ or $\sin^2 x$ terms, use the double angle formulas before integrating.
- If the integrand is a product of trigonometrical functions, use the compound angle formulas to transform the integrand into a sum of trigonometrical functions.
- Integrate rational functions by first expressing them in proper fraction form and then use partial fractions if required.
- Use integration by parts to integrate a product of functions:

$$\int u \frac{dv}{dx} \, dx = uv - \int v \frac{du}{dx} \, dx$$

- Substitute suitable functions to simplify the integrand.
- The area under a parametrically defined curve is given by $\int_{t_1}^{t_2} y(t) \frac{d}{dt}(x) \, dt$, where t_1 and t_2 are the values of the parameter t corresponding to the lower and upper values of x.
- Solve a differential equation by separating the variables to find either a general solution or a particular solution.
- Newton's law of cooling and rate of change of population are both modelled by differential equations.

13 Numerical Methods

What you need to know

- How to rearrange equations into the form $f(x) = 0$.
- How to rearrange equations into the form $x = g(x)$.
- How to differentiate polynomials and trigonometric, exponential, logarithmic and other 'standard' mathematical functions.
- How to find the exact values of definite integrals, including the use of integration by parts.

Review

1 Rearrange each of the following equations into the form $f(x) = 0$.

a $e^x = x^2 + 2$ **b** $\frac{7}{x-3} = x$ **c** $\sqrt{x+5} = x$

2 Show how the equation $x^3 - 4x - 5 = 0$ can be rearranged into each of the following forms.

a $x = \sqrt[3]{4x+5}$ **b** $x = \frac{1}{4}(x^3 - 5)$ **c** $x = \frac{5}{x^2-4}$

d $x = \frac{4x+5}{x^2}$ **e** $x = \sqrt{\frac{4x+5}{x}}$ **f** $x = \frac{4}{x} + \frac{5}{x^2}$

3 Rearrange each of the following equations into the form $x = g(x)$.

a $e^x + 2x - 1 = 0$ **b** $x - 5 + \ln x = 0$ **c** $x^2 - 4x - 7 = 0$

4 Find $f'(x)$ for each of the following functions:

a $f(x) = x^3 + 2\cos x + 3$ **b** $f(x) = 5x^2 + e^{-x}$

c $f(x) = \ln(x+1) - \frac{4}{x}$ **d** $f(x) = x\sin x - 1$

5 Find the exact value of each of the following definite integrals.

a $\int_1^3 (x^3 + 6x)\,dx$ **b** $\int_0^{\pi/3} x\sin x\,dx$ **c** $\int_0^1 x^2 e^x\,dx$

13.1 Approximate Solutions of Equations

Try solving the equations $2\cos x - x + 1$ and $e^x = x + 3$. If you tried to solve them using algebraic techniques the temptation is to give up and say the equations cannot be solved. However, graphical, or **iterative** methods can be used to find an approximate value for the solution to these equations. These techniques generate numerical values of increasing accuracy. They are based on repeating a procedure or **algorithm** until sufficient accuracy has been achieved.

Graphical methods

The root(s) of any equation of the form $f(x) = 0$ can be found by drawing the graph of $y = f(x)$ and reading off the approximate values of x for which $y = 0$.

$f(x) = 0$ where the gra crosses the x-axis.

Example 1

Construct a table of values for $y = 2x^2 - 12x + 11$ with $0 \leq x \leq 6$. Draw the graph of $y = 2x^2 - 12x + 11$ in that range, and use it to find approximate solutions of the equation $2x^2 - 12x + 11 = 0$, to one decimal place.

Solution

x	0	1	2	3	4	5	6
y	11	1	−5	−7	−5	1	11

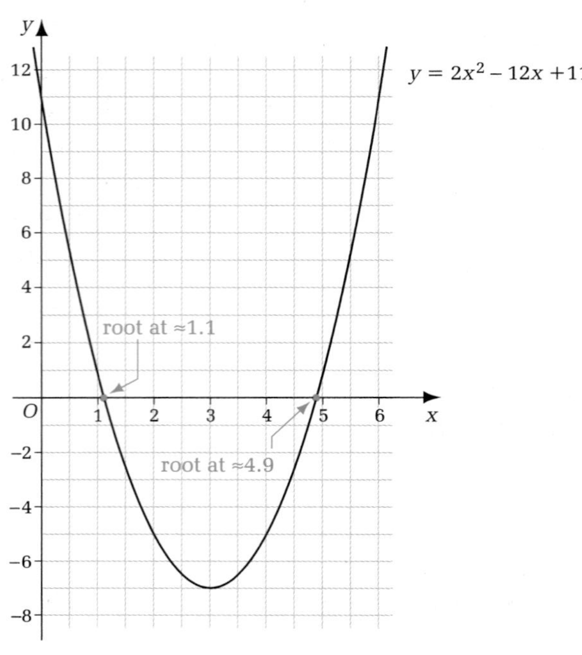

Look for the points of intersection of the graph of $y = 2x^2 - 12x + 11$ and the x-axis. Notice that the approximate values of the roots of the equation $2x^2 - 12x + 11 = 0$ are 1.1 and 4.9, correct to one decimal place.

The exact values of the roots in Example 1 can be found using the quadratic formula,

$$x = \frac{-b \pm \sqrt{b^2 - 4ac}}{2a}$$

$$= \frac{12 \pm \sqrt{144 - 88}}{4}$$

$$= \frac{12 \pm \sqrt{56}}{4} \quad \blacktriangleleft \sqrt{56} = \sqrt{4} \times \sqrt{14} = 2 \times \sqrt{14}$$

$$= \tfrac{1}{2}(6 \pm \sqrt{14})$$

So the exact values of the roots of this equation are $\frac{1}{2}(6 - \sqrt{14})$ and $\frac{1}{2}(6 + \sqrt{14})$. Compare these to the decimal approximations found from the graph. Notice that they agree correct to the first decimal place.

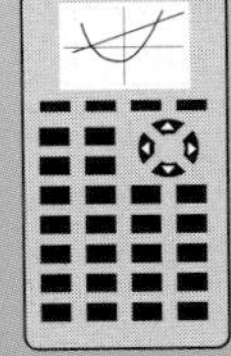

If your calculator has a SOLVE or ROOT function it will solve the equation numerically for you, using an algorithm that has been programmed into it.

Now use a graphical calculator to plot the graph of $y = 2x^2 - 12x + 11$. Use the TRACE function. Verify that the approximate numerical values for the roots of the equation $2x^2 - 12x + 11 = 0$ are 1.1 and 4.9 by finding where your graph crosses the x-axis. Use the ZOOM function to find an answer correct to two or more decimal places.

So graphical methods give a reasonable approximation to a solution of an equation. Many equations are more conveniently solved graphically by first rearranging them into the form $g(x) = h(x)$, where g and h are functions whose graphs are easily sketched. The approximate value of the root(s) of such equations can then be found by reading off the x-coordinate of the point(s) of intersection of the $y = g(x)$ and $y = h(x)$ graphs.

In Example 1 the solutions of $2x^2 - 12x + 11 = 0$ are the intersections of $y = 0$ and $y = 2x^2 - 12x + 11$.

Example 2

Solve the equation $2\cos x - x + 1 = 0$ by a graphical method, correct to one decimal place. Explain why the equation has only one solution.

Solution

This equation can be rearranged into the form $2\cos x = x - 1$. Sketch the graphs of $y = 2\cos x$ and $y = x - 1$ on the same axes, with $-\pi \leq x \leq \pi$ and $-2 \leq y \leq 2$.

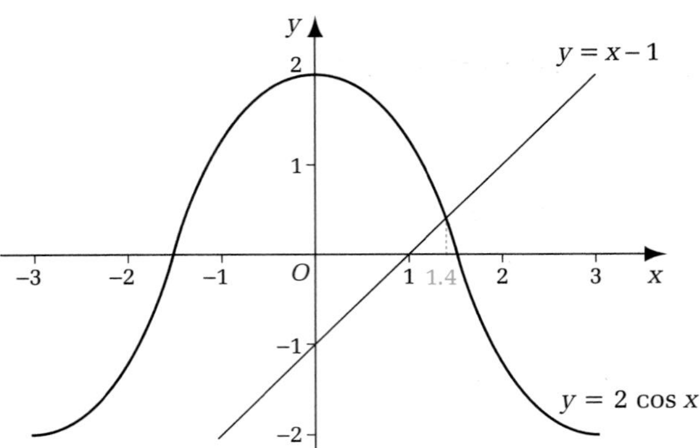

The graph of $y = 2\cos$ is periodic, oscillating between maximum an minimum values of 2 and -2 respectively. T graph of $y = x - 1$ is a straight line.

There is only one point of intersection. Since the graphs of $y = 2\cos x$ and $y = x - 1$ do not intersect anywhere else, the equation $2\cos x - x + 1 = 0$ has only one solution. The x-coordinate at the point of intersection is about 1.4, so the approximate value of the root to this equation is $x = 1.4$ (1 d.p.).

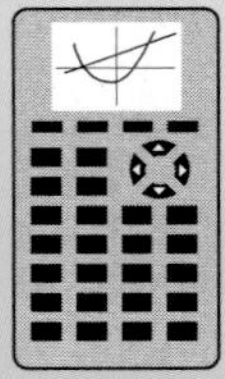

Use a graphical calculator to plot the graphs of $y = 2\cos x$ and $y = x - 1$ on the same axes, and use the TRACE function to confirm that $x = 1.4$ is the approximate solution of the equation $2\cos x = x - 1$. Remember to work in radians.

Investigate whether y calculator has an INTERSECT function that will find values o at which the two grap cross.

Locating roots by a 'change of sign'

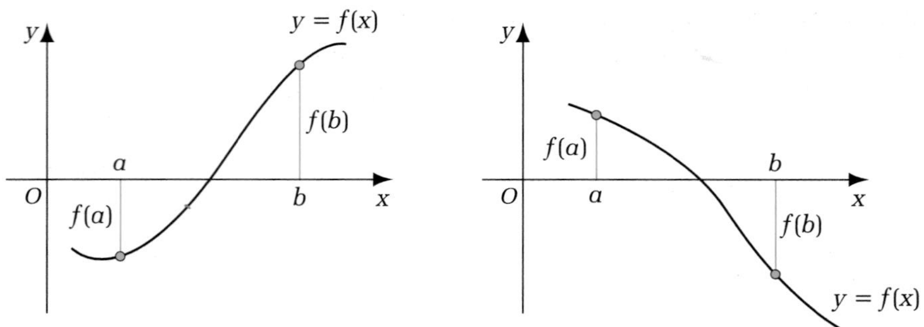

Suppose $f(x)$ is a continuous function, defined for all points between $x = a$ and $x = b$. If $f(a)$ and $f(b)$, the values of the function at $x = a$ and $x = b$, respectively, are opposite in sign to each other, then $f(a) < 0$ and $f(b) > 0$, or vice versa. This is illustrated in the diagrams above. Since the graph changes from negative to positive, or from positive to negative, somewhere between a and b, there must be a solution to the equation $f(x) = 0$ in the interval $a < x < b$.

So by looking for a change of sign in the value of $f(x)$ between nearby values of x, the approximate location of the roots of the equation $f(x) = 0$ can be found.

Example 3

Find the integer values of x between which the equation $e^x = x + 3$ has solutions.

Solution

Since the 'change of sign' method only works for equations of the form $f(x) = 0$, rearrange $e^x = x + 3$ into this form. Check that you get $e^x - x - 3 = 0$.

Let $f(x) = e^x - x - 3$. The value of $f(x)$ at different integer values of x can now be calculated.

x	−5	−4	−3	−2	−1	0	1	2	3	4
$f(x)$	2.01	1.02	0.05	−0.86	−1.63	−2.00	−1.28	2.39	14.09	47.60

Notice the changes of sign between $x = -3$ and $x = -2$, and between $x = 1$ and $x = 2$.

So the equation $e^x = x + 3$ has solutions in the intervals $-3 < x < -2$ and $1 < x < 2$.

In this table, the values of $f(x)$ are only given to two decimal places. This is because all we are looking for is a change in the sign of $f(x)$.
This 'change of sign' method is usually used to find the approximate location of the roots of an equation.

Interval bisection

Suppose the equation $f(x) = 0$ has a root α between $x = a$ and $x = b$. Better approximations for this root can be found by reducing the interval in which it is known to lie. One way of doing this is to use the mid-point of the interval $a < x < b$. Let the mid-point of the interval be at $x = m$.

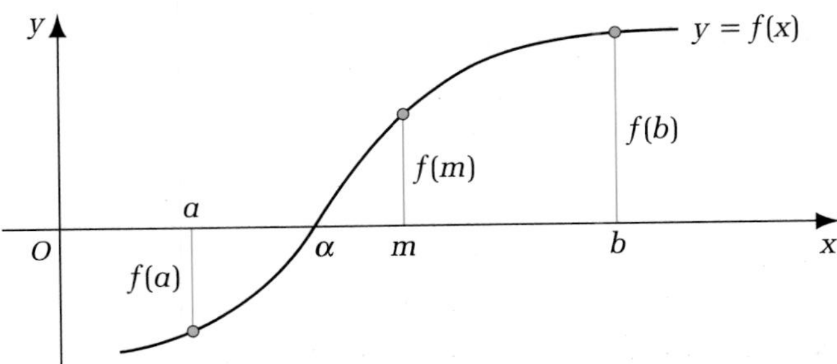

If there is a change of sign in the value of the function $f(x)$ between $x = a$ and $x = m$, then the root α lies in the interval $a < x < m$. If the change of sign in function $f(x)$ occurs between $x = m$ and $x = b$, then α lies between these two values, in the interval $m < x < b$.
This process can be repeated several times until a value for the root is found to the required accuracy. Each new interval containing α is bisected. A change of sign in the value of the function is looked for between the new mid-point and the two end-points.

For each new interval, $a < x < b$, the mid-point m can be calculated quickly using $m = \frac{1}{2}(a + b)$.

Example 4

In Example 3, one of the roots of the equation $e^x - x - 3 = 0$ was found to lie in the interval $1 < x < 2$. Use the interval bisection method to find the value of this root correct to one decimal place.

Solution

The mid-point of the interval $1 < x < 2$ is at $x = \frac{1}{2}(1 + 2) = 1.5$

$$f(x) = e^x - x - 3$$

So $\quad f(1) = -1.28$

$$f(2) = 2.39$$

and $\quad f(1.5) = -0.02$

There is a change of sign in the value of $f(x)$ between $x = 1.5$ and $x = 2$, so the root lies in the interval $1.5 < x < 2$. The mid-point of this new interval is at $x = \frac{1}{2}(1.5 + 2) = 1.75$.

Now $\quad f(1.5) = -0.02$

$$f(2) = 2.39$$

and $\quad f(1.75) = 1.00$

There is a change of sign between $x = 1.5$ and $x = 1.75$. So the root of the equation lies in the interval $1.5 < x < 1.75$. Bisecting this interval again gives a new mid-point value of $x = \frac{1}{2}(1.5 + 1.75) = 1.625$.

Now $\quad f(1.5) = -0.02$

$$f(1.75) = 1.00$$

and $\quad f(1.625) = 0.45$

The root lies in the interval $1.5 < x < 1.625$. The process can be continued to give the results in the following table.

$f(x)$ at mid-point	interval within which root lies	mid-point of interval
	$1 < x < 2$	$x = 1.5$
$f(1.5) = -0.02$	$1.5 < x < 2$	$x = 1.75$
$f(1.75) = 1.00$	$1.5 < x < 1.75$	$x = 1.625$
$f(1.625) = 0.45$	$1.5 < x < 1.625$	$x = 1.5625$
$f(1.5625) = 0.21$	$1.5 < x < 1.5625$	$x = 1.531\,25$
$f(1.531\,25) = 0.09$	$1.5 < x < 1.531\,25$	

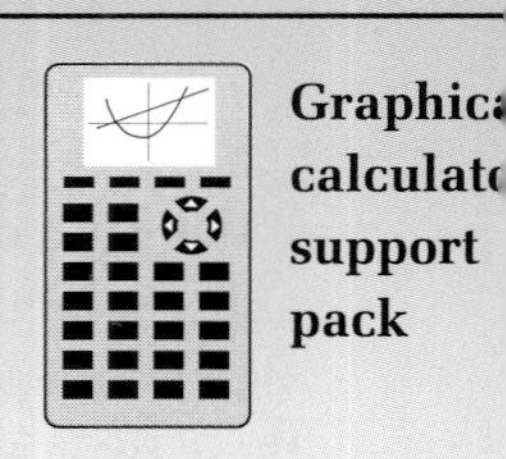

The last interval is smaller than 0.05 so it is possible to conclude that the value of the root of the equation $e^x - x - 3 = 0$ as $x = 1.5$ (1 d.p.).

Notice that five bisections were needed to find the root in Example 4, correct to just one decimal place. In general, the interval bisection method converges to the root of an equation rather slowly. Other iterative procedures can achieve much greater degrees of accuracy in the same number or even fewer steps.

Linear interpolation

The interval bisection method simply uses the mid-point of the interval in which the root of an equation is known to lie. The linear interpolation method divides this interval up in a proportion determined by the value of the function at the end-points of the interval.

Replace the graph of $y = f(x)$ between $x = a$ and $x = b$ with a straight line. The point where this line crosses the x-axis gives a better approximation to the root α of the equation $f(x) = 0$. The sign of the function at this new point will determine whether the root lies in the interval $a < \alpha < x_1$ or $x_1 < \alpha < b$. This process is then repeated, with x_1 replaced by a new b or a, respectively, and the new point where the line crosses the x-axis, x_2, will be closer to α. The process can be repeated until the required level of accuracy is achieved.

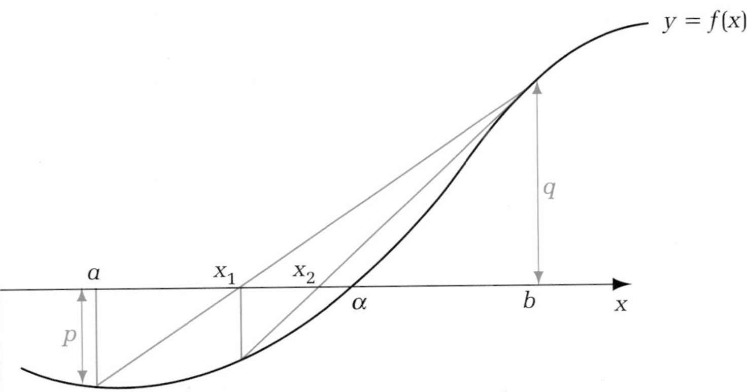

To use this method, we need to find the point where the straight line crosses the x-axis each time it is constructed. Let the equation $f(x) = 0$ have a root α in the interval $a < x < b$. The linear interpolation technique then creates two triangles. Check that these triangles are similar.

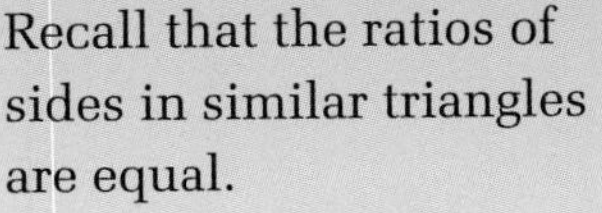
Recall that the ratios of sides in similar triangles are equal.

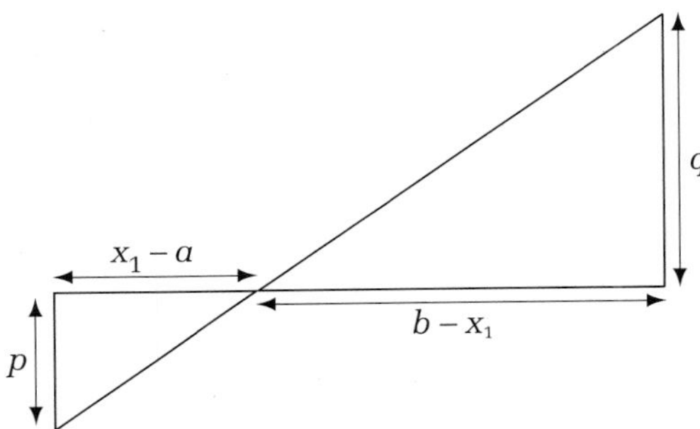

This means that

$$\frac{x_1 - a}{p} = \frac{b - x_1}{q}$$

where p and q are the absolute values of $f(a)$ and $f(b)$, and x_1 is the approximation to the root α. This equation can now be rearranged to make x_1 the subject.

$$(x_1 - a)q = (b - x_1)p$$

$$x_1q - aq = bp - x_1p$$

$$x_1p + x_1q = aq + bp$$

$$x_1(p + q) = aq + bp$$

$$\boldsymbol{x_1 = \frac{aq + bp}{p + q}}$$

◀ **Learn this important result.**

This formula can now be used to find the first and subsequent approximation to the root of the equation.

Example 5

The equation $x^3 + x - 7 = 0$ has a root in the interval $1 < x < 2$. Use linear interpolation to find the approximate value of this root, correct to two decimal places.

Solution

Let $f(x) = x^3 + x - 7$. Check that $f(1) = -5$ and $f(2) = 3$.

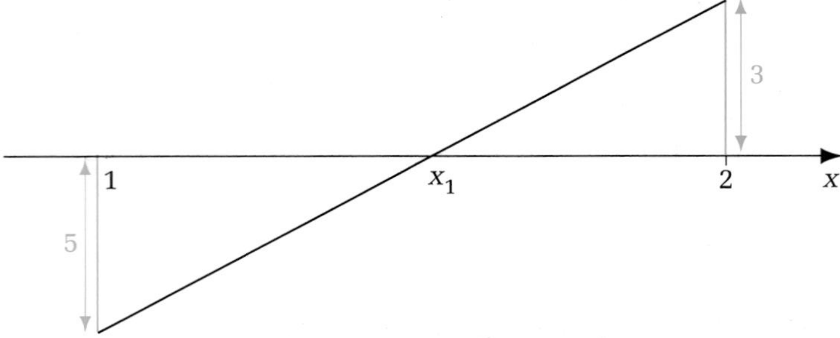

The curve has not be drawn here. We only need to know the absolute values of $f(1)$ and $f(2)$.

Now use the formula $x_1 = \frac{aq+bp}{p+q}$ with $a = 1$, $b = 2$, $p = 5$ and $q = 3$. This will calculate the value of x_1 at which the interval $1 < x < 2$ is divided in linear proportion,

$$x_1 = \frac{(1 \times 3) + (2 \times 5)}{5 + 3}$$
$$= \tfrac{13}{8}$$
$$= 1.625$$

Now $f(1.625) = -1.0840$ (4 d.p.)

Notice that there is a change of sign in the value of $f(x)$ between $x = 1.625$ and $x = 2$. This means that the root lies in the interval $1.625 < x < 2$, so now repeat the process using the same formula, with $a = 1.625$, $b = 2$, $p = 1.0840$ and $q = 3$.

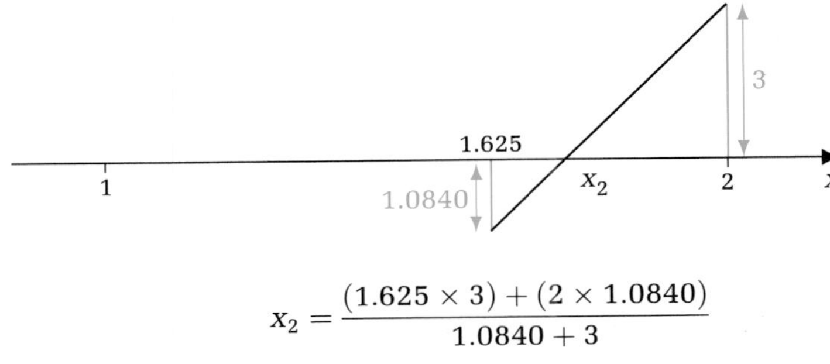

$$x_2 = \frac{(1.625 \times 3) + (2 \times 1.0840)}{1.0840 + 3}$$
$$= 1.7245 \text{ (4 d.p.)}$$

Now $f(1.7245) = -0.1470$ (4 d.p.)

There is a change of sign in the value of the function $f(x)$ between $x = 1.7245$ and $x = 2$ so the root lies in the interval $1.7245 < x < 2$. Repeat the process again, using the formula, with $a = 1.7245$, $b = 2$, $p = 0.1470$ and $q = 3$.

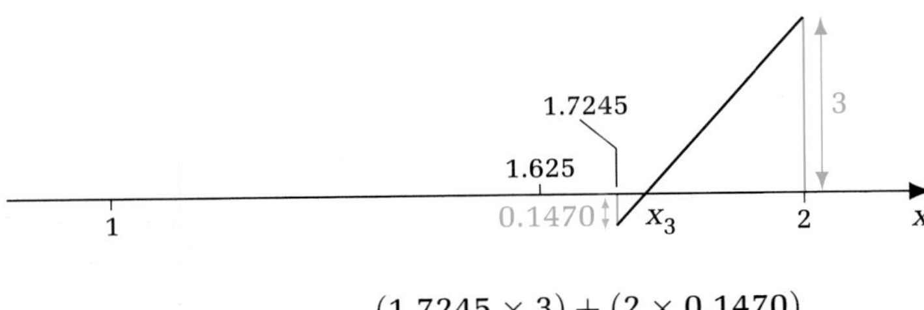

$$x_3 = \frac{(1.7245 \times 3) + (2 \times 0.1470)}{0.1470 + 3}$$
$$= 1.7374 \text{ (4 d.p.)}$$

Now $f(1.7374) = -0.0182$ (4 d.p.)

There is a change of sign in the value of function $f(x)$ between $x = 1.7374$ and $x = 2$, so the root lies in the interval $1.7374 < x < 2$.
The table overleaf shows how the repeated use of the linear interpolation algorithm narrows the interval within which the root can lie. Recall that $f(1)$ is negative and $f(2)$ is positive.

interval within which the root lies	approximate value of the root, x_n	$f(x_n)$
$1 < x < 2$	$x_1 = 1.625$	$f(1.625) = -1.0840$
$1.625 < x < 2$	$x_2 = 1.7245$	$f(1.7245) = -0.1470$
$1.7245 < x < 2$	$x_3 = 1.7374$	$f(1.7374) = -0.0182$
$1.7374 < x < 2$		

Graphical calculator support pack

The value of $f(x)$ at $x = 1.7374$ is very close to zero. So the root is probably very near to $x = 1.74$. Verify that $f(1.745) = 0.0586$ (4 d.p.). This indicates that there is a change of sign between $x = 1.7374$ and $x = 1.745$, so the root must lie in the interval $1.7374 < x < 1.745$. It can be taken to be 1.74 (2 d.p.).

Example 6

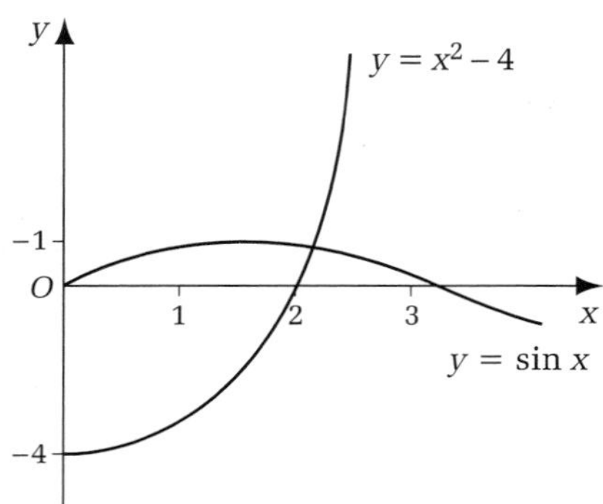

The graphs of $y = \sin x$ and $y = x^2 - 4$ intersect at the point where $x = \alpha$. Given that $2 < \alpha < 2.5$, use linear interpolation to find the value of α correct to two decimal places.

Solution

The point of intersection of these two graphs is found by solving the equation $\sin x = x^2 - 4$. Rearrange this equation into the form $f(x) = 0$.

$$\sin x - x^2 + 4 = 0$$

Now linear interpolation can be used to find α.

Let $\quad f(x) = \sin x - x^2 + 4$

Then $\quad f(2) = 0.9093$ and $f(2.5) = -1.6515$.

Use the formula $x_1 = \frac{aq+bp}{p+q}$ with $a = 2$, $b = 2.5$, $p = 0.9093$ and $q = 1.6515$. Check that this gives $x_1 = 2.1775$.

Work to four decimal places.

Now check that $f(2.1775) = 0.0800$ (4 d.p.). There is a change of sign in the value of $f(x)$ between $x = 2.1775$ and $x = 2.5$, so the root lies in the interval $2.1775 < x < 2.5$. Repeating the process and tabulating the results gives us the following table.

interval within which the root lies	approximate value of the root, x_n	$f(x_n)$
$2 < x < 2.5$	$x_1 = 2.1175$	$f(2.1175) = 0.0800$
$2.1775 < x < 2.5$	$x_2 = 2.1924$	$f(2.1924) = 0.0063$
$2.1924 < x < 2.5$	$x_3 = 2.1936$	$f(2.1936) = 0.0004$
$2.1936 < x < 2.5$		

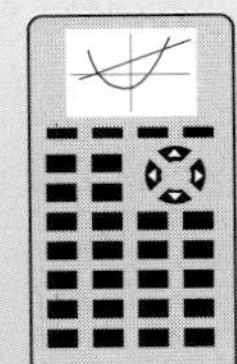

Check this figure using the ZOOM and TRACE functions on a graphical calculator; remember to use radian mode to evaluate the sine ratio.

Since the value of $f(x)$ at $x = 2.1936$ is so close to zero, the root is probably very close to $x = 2.19$. In fact, $f(2.195) = -0.0066$, so there is a change of sign in the value of $f(x)$ between $x = 2.1936$ and $x = 2.195$. This means the root must lie in the interval $2.1936 < x < 2.195$, and can be taken to be 2.19 (2 d.p.). The graphs of $y = \sin x$ and $y = x^2 - 4$ therefore intersect at $x = 2.19$ (2 d.p.).

The Newton–Raphson method

The Newton–Raphson method is often simply called Newton's method. It usually rapidly converges to the root of an equation of the form $f(x) = 0$. It is quicker than both the interval bisection method and linear interpolation. Suppose $x = x_0$ is a first approximation to the root α of the equation $f(x) = 0$. A tangent drawn to the curve $y = f(x)$ at the point where $x = x_0$ can be extended to meet the x-axis at the point where $x = x_1$.

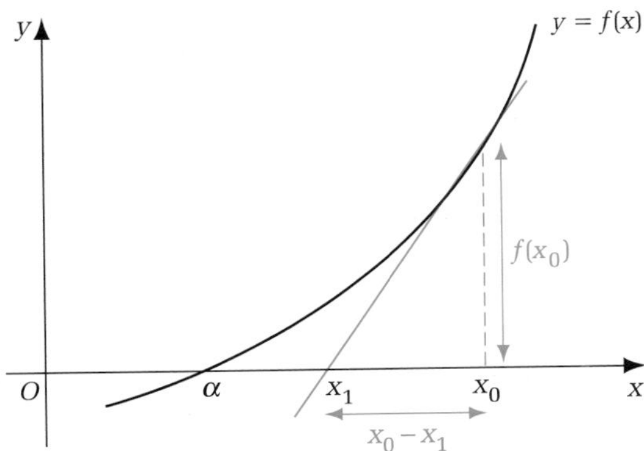

Spot the right-angled triangle formed by the tangent, the x-axis and the line $x = x_0$.

In most cases, x_1 will be a better approximation to the root α than x_0. By considering the gradient of this tangent, it follows that

$$f'(x_0) = \frac{f(x_0)}{x_0 - x_1}$$

Now rearrange to make x_1 the subject of this equation.

$$x_0 - x_1 = \frac{f(x_0)}{f'(x_0)}$$

$$x_1 = x_0 - \frac{f(x_0)}{f'(x_0)}$$

The process can be repeated, with a tangent drawn from the point on the curve where $x = x_1$. The tangent meets the x-axis at $x = x_2$. This is usually an even better approximation to the root α. By considering the gradient of this tangent, we find that

$$x_2 = x_1 - \frac{f(x_1)}{f'(x_1)}$$

This process can be repeated as often as required.

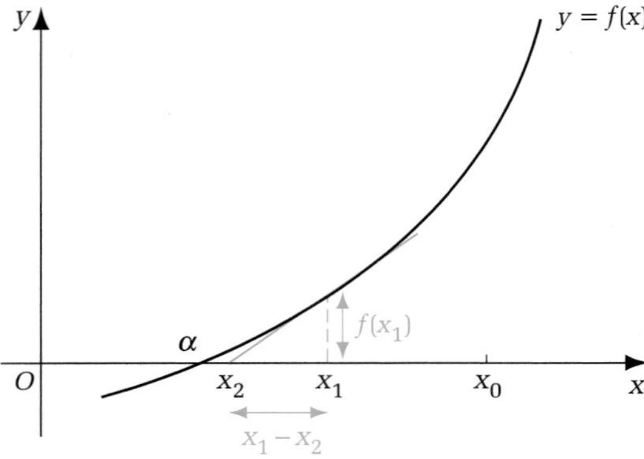

In general, if x_n is a good approximation to the root of an equation of the form $f(x) = 0$, then a better approximation, x_{n+1}, can be found using the iterative formula

An iterative formula i[s] one in which the outp[ut] of one step of a calculation is used as input for the next ste[p]

$$\mathbf{x_{n+1} = x_n - \frac{f(x_n)}{f'(x_n)}}$$

◀ **Learn this important result.**

Here $f(x_n)$ and $f'(x_n)$ are the values of the function $f(x)$ and its derivative $f'(x)$ at $x = x_n$.
The Newton–Raphson method makes repeated use of this iterative formula until the required level of accuracy is achieved.

Example 7

Use Newton's method to find, correct to four decimal places, the root of the equation $e^x - x - 3 = 0$ that lies between $x = 1$ and $x = 2$.

Solution

In order to avoid rounding errors in the calculations, working should be done to at least two more decimal places than are required in the final answer. So in this example, working should be carried out to six decimal places.

Let $\quad f(x) = e^x - x - 3$

Then $\quad f'(x) = e^x - 1$

Take $x_0 = 1$ as a first approximation to the root.
Using Newton's method,

$$x_1 = x_0 - \frac{f(x_0)}{f'(x_0)}$$

$$= 1 - \frac{e^1 - 1 - 3}{e^1 - 1}$$

$$= 1.745\,930 \text{ (6 d.p.)}$$

Then $$x_2 = x_1 - \frac{f(x_1)}{f'(x_1)}$$

$$= 1.745\,930 - \frac{e^{1.745\,930} - 1.745\,930 - 3}{e^{1.745\,930} - 1}$$

$$= 1.537\,676 \text{ (6 d.p.)}$$

and $$x_3 = x_2 - \frac{f(x_2)}{f'(x_2)}$$

$$= 1.537\,676 - \frac{e^{1.537\,676} - 1.537\,676 - 3}{e^{1.537\,676} - 1}$$

$$= 1.505\,904 \text{ (6 d.p.)}$$

Check that $x_4 = 1.505\,242$ (6 d.p.)

and that $x_5 = 1.505\,241$ (6 d.p.)

Notice that the value of x_n has only changed in the sixth decimal place during this last iteration. So the value of the root of the equation $e^x - x - 3 = 0$ must be $x = 1.5052$ (4 d.p.).
We could have taken $x_0 = 2$ as a first approximation to the root. Verify, using Newton's method, that the results of subsequent iterations are:

$x_1 = 1.626\,071$ $\quad x_2 = 1.513\,974$ $\quad x_3 = 1.505\,290$

$x_4 = 1.505\,241$ $\quad x_5 = 1.505\,241$

All are obtained using six decimal places of working.

Again the conclusion is that the root of the equation is $x = 1.5052$ (4 d.p.).

It is possible to generate successive iterations quickly using the **last answer** (ANS) facility on a graphical calculator. For Newton's method, you would first enter the value of the first approximation x_0. The value of x_1 can then be found using the expression:

$$\text{ANS} - \frac{e^{\text{ANS}} - \text{ANS} - 3}{e^{\text{ANS}} - 1}$$

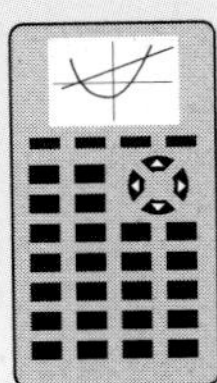

Using the **last entry** facility on the calculator, this expression can be entered again automatically, this time using the value of x_1 to produce x_2, and any further approximations that are required can be generated in the same way. Pressing the EXE or ENTER key gives the successive values $x_2, x_3, x_4, \ldots$ This method has the advantage of using the maximum number of decimal places available on the calculator in working out successive iterations of Newton's method.

Notice that ANS replaces x_0 in the Newton–Raphson iterative formula.

We have solved the same equation in Examples 4 and 7. Using the interval bisection method it took five bisections to find the value of the root correct to just one decimal place. After five iterations, Newton's method produced a value correct to at least four decimal places. This illustrates how quickly the Newton–Raphson method usually converges to the root of an equation.

Occasionally, the Newton–Raphson method 'fails' and instead produces a series of values $x_0, x_1, x_2, \ldots$ that either diverge, or converge to a different root of the equation to that expected. These two different types of behaviour are illustrated in the following diagrams.

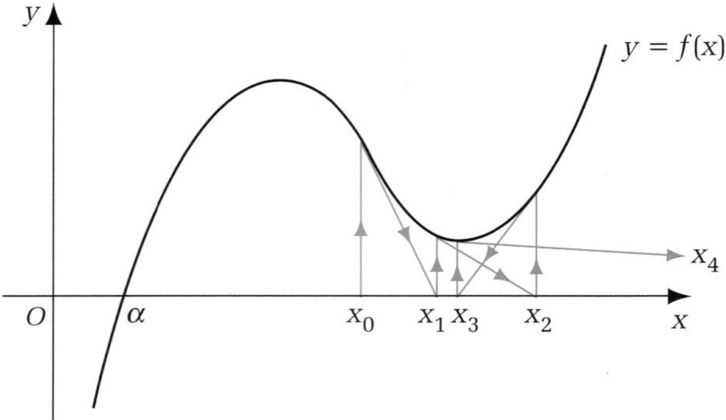

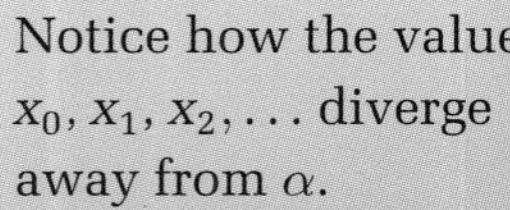

Notice how the value $x_0, x_1, x_2, \ldots$ diverge away from α.

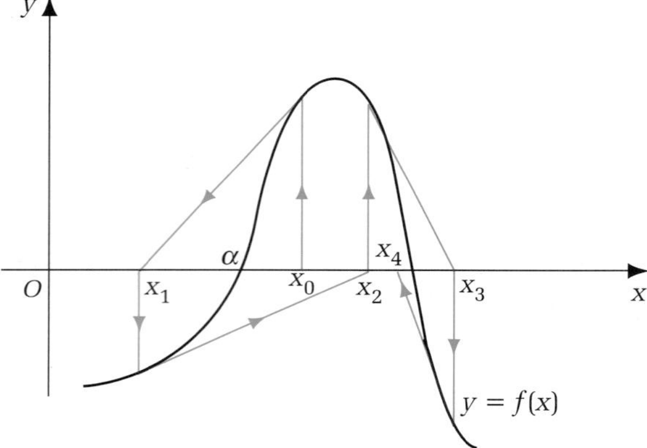

Notice how the value $x_0, x_1, x_2, \ldots$ generate by the Newton–Raph iterative formula converge towards a different root of the equation.

The main reason for these failures of the Newton–Raphson method is that the value of x_0 chosen as the first approximation is not close enough to the root for convergence to occur. Fortunately there are other iterative methods that can be used if a different choice of x_0 still proves unsuccessful.

Notice that the same iterative formula can used to locate differe roots *provided* that suitable starting poin are used.

Fixed point iterative methods

It is usually possible to express an equation $f(x) = 0$ in the form $x = g(x)$. The root α of this type of equation can be found graphically by reading off the x-coordinate at the point of intersection of the $y = x$ and $y = g(x)$ graphs.

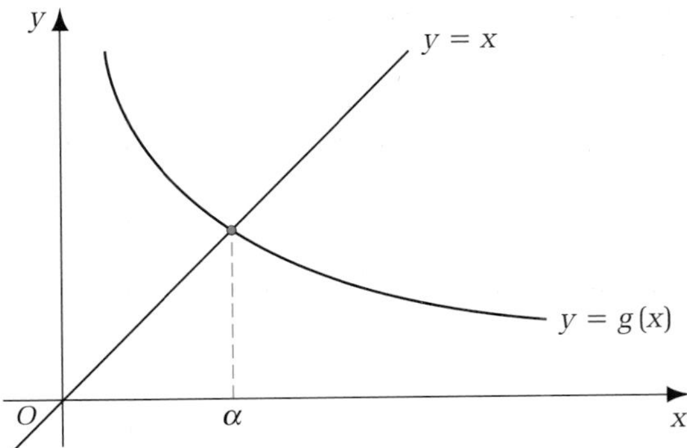

Notice that the absolute value of the gradient of the curve $y = g(x)$ is less than 1 close to $x = \alpha$.

Like the Newton–Raphson method, the fixed point iterative method requires the choice of a first approximation x_0 that is close to the root itself. Provided also that the absolute value of the gradient of the $y = g(x)$ graph is less than 1 close to the root, that is $|g'(\alpha)| < 1$, then a better approximation to the root is given by $x_1 = g(x_0)$. This is shown in the following diagram.

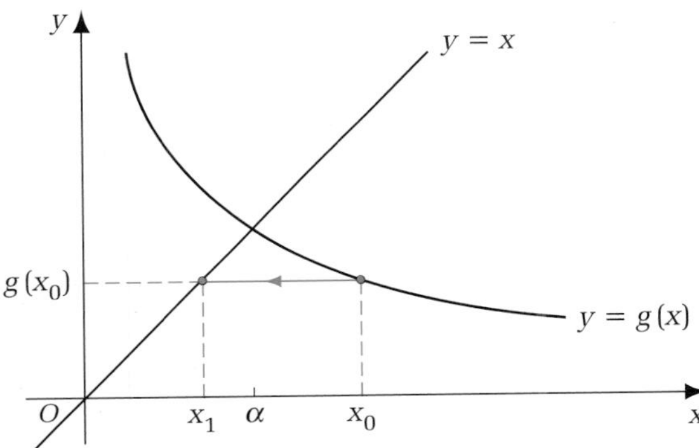

Repeating this process, an even better approximation is given by $x_2 = g(x_1)$, which can be further improved upon by calculating the next approximation x_3, given by $x_3 = g(x_2)$.

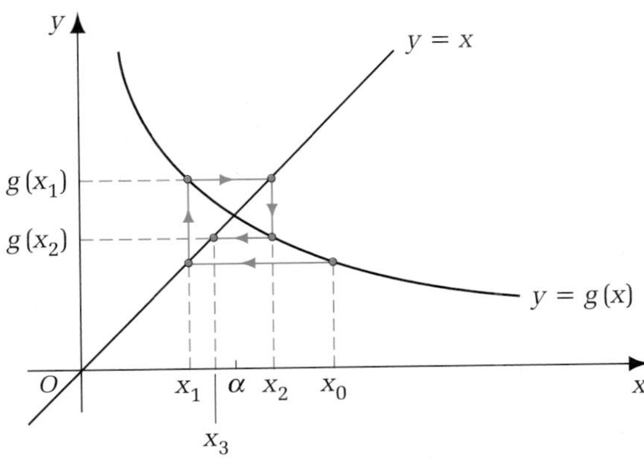

The values of $x_1, x_2, x_3, \ldots$ generated by this iterative procedure are converging towards the root α. The diagram shows a 'cobweb' of lines spiralling towards the point where $x = g(x)$. Such diagrams are often called **cobweb diagrams**.

If $g(x)$ is an *increasing* function of x close to α, then the values of x_n generated by the iterative procedure will converge towards α from one side only, as shown in the following diagram.

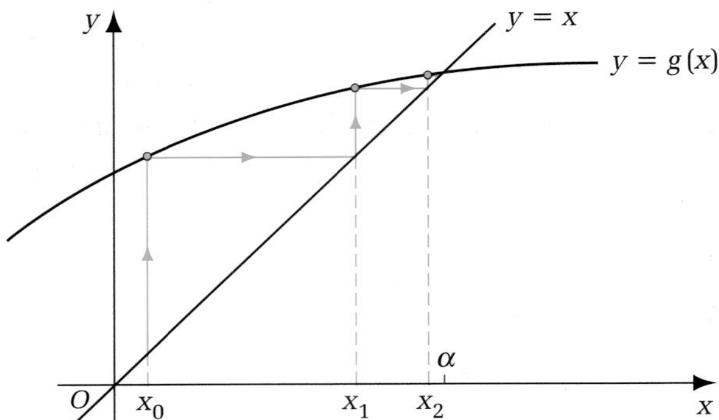

Notice that $|g'(x)| < 1$ values of x close to α, allowing convergence occur.

Such diagrams are often called **staircase diagrams** because of the pattern of the lines converging towards the root α.

Equations with multi roots usually require different rearrangeme to converge to the different roots.

In general, if x_n is an approximation to the root of an equation of the form $x = g(x)$, then, provided $|g'(x)| < 1$ close to the root, a better approximation x_{n+1} can be found using the iterative formula:

$$\mathbf{x_{n+1} = g(x_n)}$$

This formula is used repeatedly until the required level of accuracy is achieved.

Example 8

Show that the equation $x^3 - 4x - 5 = 0$ has a root α in the interval $2 < x < 3$ and use the iterative formula $x_{n+1} = \sqrt[3]{4x_n + 5}$ with a suitable first approximation x_0, to find the value of α correct to four decimal places.

Solution

Let $\quad f(x) = x^3 - 4x - 5$

When $x = 2$, $\quad f(x) = f(2) = -5$

When $x = 3$, $\quad f(x) = f(3) = 10$

This change of sign in the value of $f(x)$ indicates that the equation $x^3 - 4x - 5 = 0$ has a root in the interval $2 < x < 3$.
Rearranging $x^3 - 4x - 5 = 0$ into the form $x = g(x)$,

$$x^3 = 4x + 5$$

$$\Rightarrow \quad x = \sqrt[3]{4x + 5}$$

So the iterative formula $x_{n+1} = \sqrt[3]{4x_n + 5}$ should converge to the root if x_0 is chosen near enough to α. Since the root exists in the interval $2 < x < 3$, take $x_0 = 2$ as a first approximation.

Check that $f'(2) < 1$. We should get a convergent sequence.

$$\text{Now}\quad x_1 = \sqrt[3]{4x_0 + 5}$$
$$= \sqrt[3]{4 \times 2 + 5}$$
$$= 2.351335$$

Remember to work to six decimal places to avoid rounding errors in a four decimal places answer.

The iteration can now continue. Substitute each answer back inside the cube root term.

$$x_2 = \sqrt[3]{4x_1 + 5} = 2.433\,181 \qquad x_6 = \sqrt[3]{4x_5 + 5} = 2.456\,622$$
$$x_3 = \sqrt[3]{4x_2 + 5} = 2.451\,476 \qquad x_7 = \sqrt[3]{4x_6 + 5} = 2.456\,666$$
$$x_4 = \sqrt[3]{4x_3 + 5} = 2.455\,528 \qquad x_8 = \sqrt[3]{4x_7 + 5} = 2.456\,676$$
$$x_5 = \sqrt[3]{4x_4 + 5} = 2.456\,424 \qquad x_9 = \sqrt[3]{4x_8 + 5} = 2.456\,678$$

Notice that the value of x_n has only changed in the sixth decimal place during this last iteration. So the root of the equation $x^3 - 4x - 5 = 0$ must be $x = 2.4567$ (4 d.p.). The convergence towards this value is shown in the following staircase diagram.

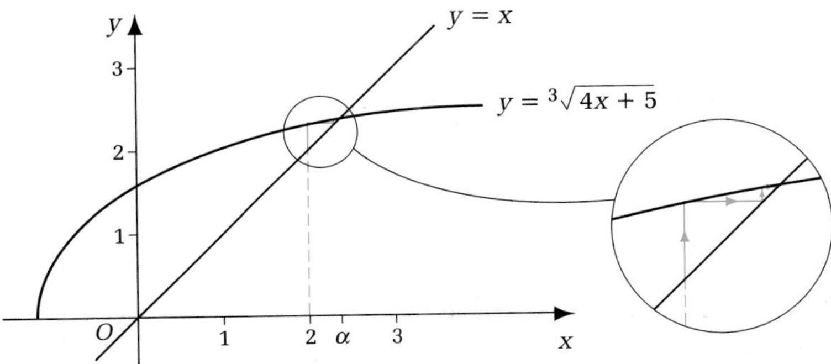

As with the Newton–Raphson method, fixed-point iteration calculations can be carried out on a graphical calculator, using the last answer (ANS) and last entry facilities. First enter the value of the first approximation x_0. The value of the next approximation x_1 can be found by entering the expression $\sqrt[3]{4(\text{ANS}) + 5}$, with ANS replacing x_0 in the iterative formula. Using the last entry facility on the calculator, this expression can be entered again automatically. This time the value of x_1 is used to produce x_2. Further approximations can be generated in the same way, by continuing to press the EXE or ENTER key.

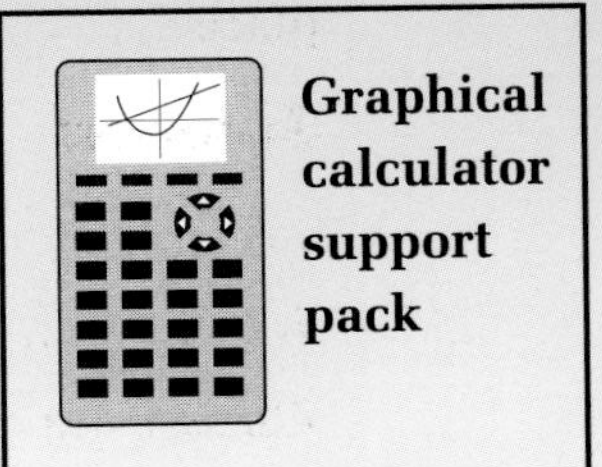

Graphical calculator support pack

Remember that there are several other ways of rearranging the equation $x^3 - 4x - 5 = 0$ into the form $x = g(x)$. Some of these produce the following iterative formulas:

$$x_{n+1} = \tfrac{1}{4}(x_n^3 - 5)$$

$$x_{n+1} = \frac{5}{x_n^2 - 4}$$

$$x_{n+1} = \frac{4x_n + 5}{x_n^2}$$

However, $|g'(\alpha)| > 1$ in each of these cases, so the results of successive iterations starting with $x_0 = 2$ or $x_0 = 3$ do not converge. Instead they diverge. Check this using a graphical calculator.

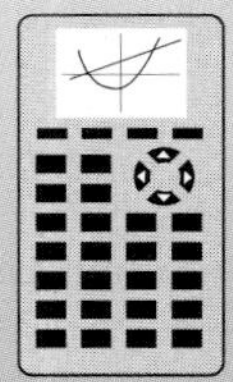

13.1 Approximate Solutions of Equations

Exercise

Technique

1 **a** Show that the equation $x^3 - 3x - 5 = 0$ has a root in the interval $2 < x < 3$.

b Use linear interpolation to find a first approximation for this root and state the interval that contains the root. Give a reason for your answer.

2 **a** Find the consecutive integer values of x between which the equation $x^5 - 3x^2 + 10 = 0$ has a root.

b Use the interval bisection method to find the value of this root, correct to one decimal place.

c Taking a suitable value for the first approximation x_0, use the Newton–Raphson method to find the value of this root correct to four decimal places.

3

3 The sequence of values generated by the iterative formula $x_{n+1} = \sqrt[3]{9x_n + 11}$, with $x_0 = 3$, converges to a value α. Use this formula to find the value of α correct to three decimal places. State an equation satisfied by α.

4 **a** If $f(x) = xe^x - 5x - 6$, find an expression for $f'(x)$.

b Show that the equation $xe^x = 5x + 6$ has two roots. Show that one is in the interval $-2 < x < -1$. The other is in the interval $a < x < b$, where a and b are consecutive positive integers. Find a and b.

c Taking $x_0 = -2$ as an initial approximation, use Newton's method to find the value of the negative root. Write your answer correct to four decimal places.

d Use linear interpolation to find a first approximation for the value of the root that lies in the interval $a < x < b$. Give your answer to two decimal places.

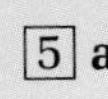
5 a

5 **a** Show that the equation $2x^3 - 3x + 17 = 0$ has a root in the interval $-3 < x < -2$.

b Decide which two of the following iterative formulas could be used to find the root of this equation:

$$x_{n+1} = \frac{17}{2x_n^2 + 3} \qquad x_{n+1} = \frac{17}{3 - 2x_n^2}$$

$$x_{n+1} = \sqrt[3]{\tfrac{1}{2}(3x_n - 17)} \qquad x_{n+1} = \sqrt[3]{\frac{2x_n + 17}{3}}$$

c Taking $x_0 = -2$ as an initial approximation, determine which of these two iterative formulas converges towards a value for the root. Find this value correct to three decimal places.

Contextual

1 a Show that the equation $\ln x - x + 3 = 0$ has a root in the interval $4 < x < 5$.

b Taking $x_0 = 4$ as an initial approximation:

i use the iterative formula $x_{n+1} = \ln(x_n) + 3$ to find the value of this root, correct to two decimal places

ii use the Newton–Raphson method to calculate its value, correct to four decimal places.

c Comment on the differences in the efficiency of these two methods.

2 The diagram shows the graph of $y = x^3 - 2x + 3\cos x$.

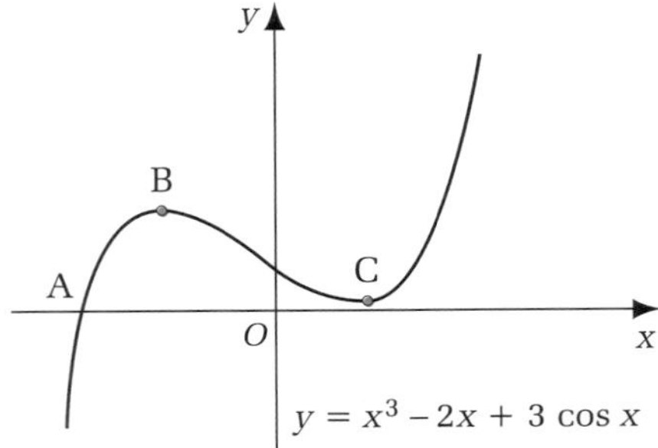

a Show that point A is located between $x = -2$ and $x = -1$.

b Using the Newton–Raphson method, calculate the x-coordinate of A, correct to three decimal places.

c Explain why the x-coordinates of B and C satisfy the equation $3x^2 - 2 - 3\sin x = 0$. By taking $x_0 = -1$ as a first approximation, use the Newton–Raphson method to solve this equation. Find the coordinates of B correct to three decimal places.

d Show that $3x^2 - 2 - 3\sin x = 0$ can also be solved numerically using the iterative formula $x_{n+1} = \sqrt{\frac{2}{3} + \sin x_n}$. Taking $x_0 = 1$ as a first approximation, find the coordinates of C correct to three decimal places.

3 The depth, D metres, of water in a harbour t hours after midday, is given by $D = 5 + \sin(0.48t) - 2\cos(0.48t)$.

a Show that when $D = 6.5$ metres, time t must satisfy the equation $\sin(0.48t) - 2\cos(0.48t) - 1.5 = 0$.

b Show that the water first reaches a depth of 6.5 metres between 3 and 4 o'clock in the afternoon.

c Use Newton's method to find this time to the nearest minute.

13.2 Numerical Integration

What happens when a mathematical function cannot be integrated? In these cases a numerical method can be used to find an approximate value for the definite integral.

Definite integrals were used in Chapters 9 and 12.

These numerical methods can also be used to evaluate the area under a graph drawn by connecting a series of known points. This data could be obtained experimentally and the details of the mathematical function that models the points are not known.

The mid-ordinate rule

Suppose A is the area bounded by the graph of $y = f(x)$, the x-axis and the lines $x = a$ and $x = b$. An approximate value for A can be found by dividing this area up into n rectangular strips. Each strip has width $h = \frac{b-a}{n}$, and the height of each of these rectangles is determined by the value of the function, $f(x)$, at the mid-point of each strip.

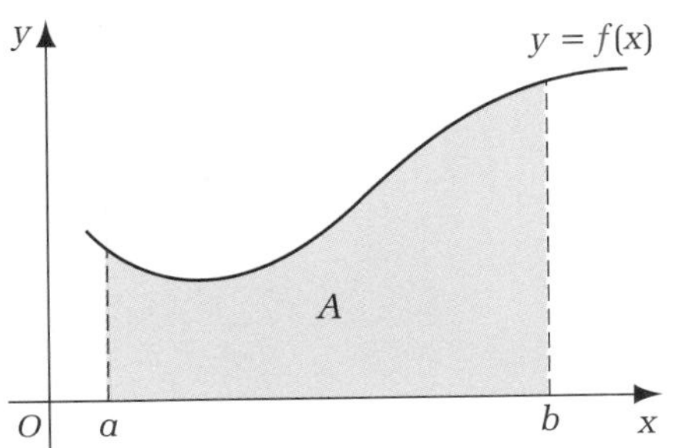

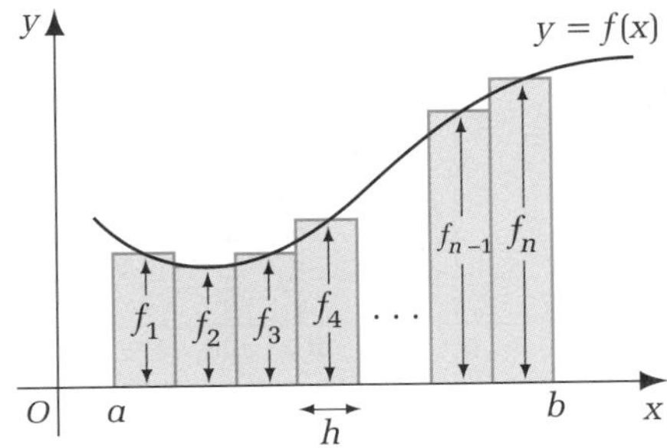

The area of the first of these rectangles is $h \times f_1$ or hf_1. By adding the areas of all of these rectangles together, an approximate value of A is given by

$$\begin{aligned} A &\approx A_1 + A_2 + A_3 + \cdots + A_{n-1} + A_n \\ &\approx hf_1 + hf_2 + hf_3 + \cdots + hf_{n-1} + hf_n \\ &\approx h(f_1 + f_2 + f_3 + \cdots + f_{n-1} + f_n) \end{aligned}$$

This result can be written as:

$$\int_a^b f(x)\,dx \approx h(f_1 + f_2 + f_3 + \cdots + f_{n-1} + f_n)$$

◀ **Learn this important result.**

where $h = \frac{b-a}{n}$ and f_r is the value of $f(x)$ at the mid-point of the rth rectangular strip. This is known as the **mid-ordinate rule**.

Example 1

Use the mid-ordinate rule with:

a 5 strips **b** 10 strips

to find the area under the curve $y = e^{x^2}$, between $x = 0$ and $x = 1$. Give your answers correct to three decimal places.

Solution

Begin by sketching the graph of $y = e^{x^2}$ and identifying the area to be approximated.

a Divide this area up into five rectangular strips. Each will have a width of 0.2. Check that the mid-points are located at $x = 0.1, 0.3, 0.5, 0.7$ and 0.9.

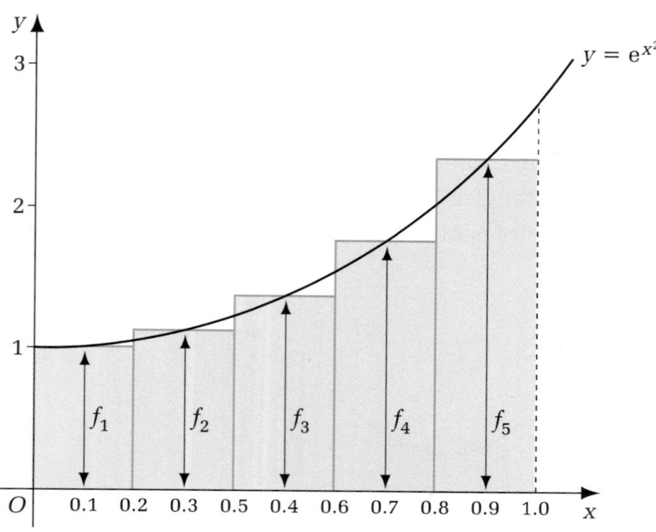

This means that the heights of these rectangles are:

$f_1 = f(0.1) = e^{0.1^2} \approx 1.010\,05$ $\quad f_4 = f(0.7) = e^{0.7^2} \approx 1.632\,32$

$f_2 = f(0.3) = e^{0.3^2} \approx 1.094\,17$ $\quad f_5 = f(0.9) = e^{0.9^2} \approx 2.247\,91$

$f_3 = f(0.5) = e^{0.5^2} \approx 1.284\,03$

Work to at least two more decimal places than required in the fi[nal] answer; working here [is] to five decimal places.

Using the mid-ordinate rule with five strips gives

$$\int_0^1 e^{x^2}\,dx \approx h(f_1 + f_2 + f_3 + f_4 + f_5)$$
$$\approx 0.2(1.010\,05 + 1.094\,17 + 1.284\,03 + 1.632\,32 + 2.247\,91)$$
$$\approx 1.453\,70$$
$$\approx 1.454 \text{ (3 d.p.)}$$

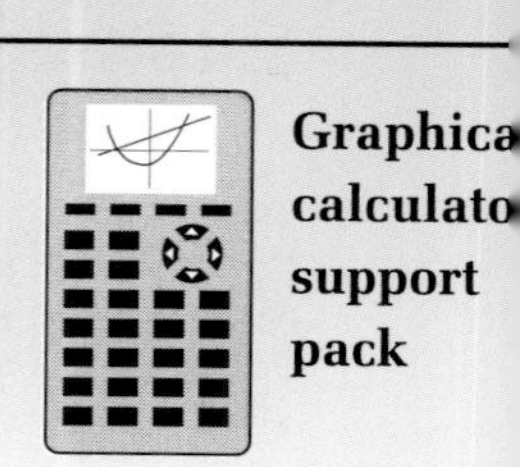

b Divide the area up into 10 rectangular strips. Each will have a width of 0.1. Check that the mid-points are located at $x = 0.05, 0.15, 0.25, 0.35, 0.45, 0.55, 0.65, 0.75, 0.85$ and 0.95.

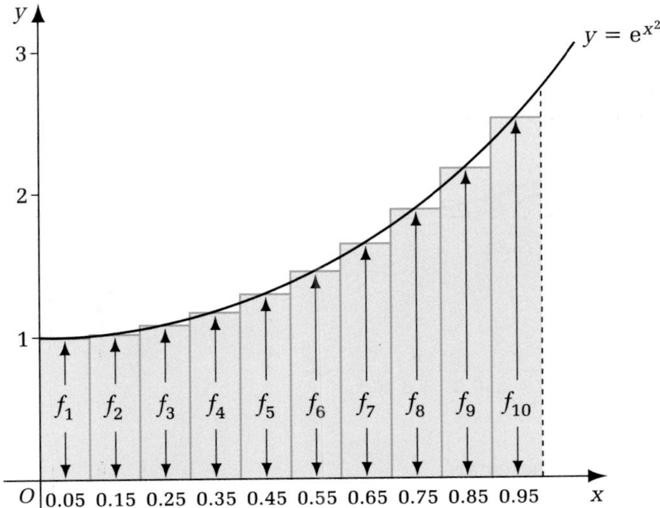

Using the same technique as in **a**, the heights of these rectangles are:

$f_1 = 1.002\,50$

$f_2 = 1.022\,76$

$f_3 = 1.064\,49$

$f_4 = 1.130\,32$

$f_5 = 1.224\,46$

$f_6 = 1.353\,24$

$f_7 = 1.525\,77$

$f_8 = 1.755\,05$

$f_9 = 2.059\,58$

$f_{10} = 2.465\,76$

Using the mid-ordinate rule with 10 strips gives

$$\begin{aligned}\int_0^1 e^{x^2}\,dx &= h(f_1 + f_2 + f_3 + f_4 + f_5 + f_6 + f_7 + f_8 + f_9 + f_{10})\\ &\approx 0.1(1.002\,50 + 1.022\,76 + 1.064\,49 + 1.130\,32 + 1.224\,46\\ &\qquad + 1.353\,24 + 1.525\,77 + 1.755\,05 + 2.059\,58 + 2.465\,76)\\ &\approx 1.460\,39\\ &\approx 1.460 \text{ (3 d.p.)}\end{aligned}$$

Example 2

Use the mid-ordinate rule with eight strips to evaluate $\int_1^3 \frac{1}{1+x}\,dx$ correct to three decimal places.

Solution

Begin with a sketch of the graph and identify the area to be approximated.

Divide the area under the curve $y = \frac{1}{1+x}$ between $x = 1$ and $x = 3$ into eight strips. Each strip will have a width of $\frac{3-1}{8} = 0.25$. Check that the mid-points are located at $x = 1.125$, 1.375, 1.625, 1.875, 2.125, 2.375, 2.625 and 2.875.

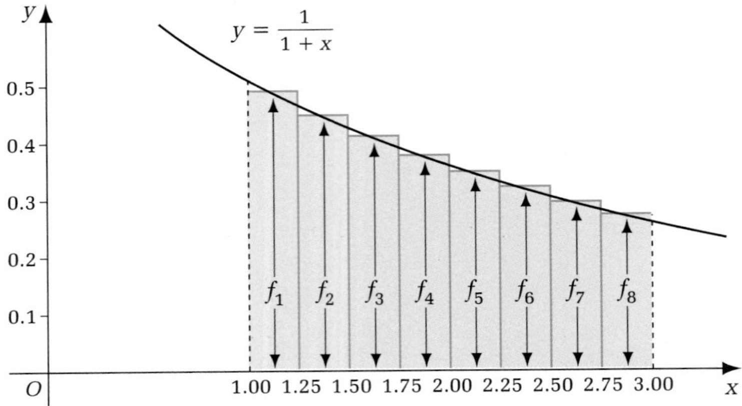

This means that the heights of these rectangles are

$$f_1 = \frac{1}{1+1.125} \approx 0.470\,59 \qquad f_5 = \frac{1}{1+2.125} \approx 0.320\,00$$

$$f_2 = \frac{1}{1+1.375} \approx 0.421\,05 \qquad f_6 = \frac{1}{1+2.375} \approx 0.296\,30$$

$$f_3 = \frac{1}{1+1.625} \approx 0.380\,95 \qquad f_7 = \frac{1}{1+2.625} \approx 0.275\,86$$

$$f_4 = \frac{1}{1+1.875} \approx 0.347\,83 \qquad f_8 = \frac{1}{1+2.875} \approx 0.258\,06$$

Again, working is to fi[ve] decimal places.

Using the mid-ordinate rule with eight strips, each of width $h = 0.25$,

$$\begin{aligned}\int_1^3 \frac{1}{1+x}\,dx &\approx h(f_1+f_2+f_3+f_4+f_5+f_6+f_7+f_8)\\ &\approx 0.25(0.470\,59+0.421\,05+0.380\,95+0.347\,83+0.32\\ &\qquad +0.296\,30+0.275\,86+0.258\,06)\\ &\approx 0.692\,66\\ &\approx 0.693 \text{ (3 d.p.)}\end{aligned}$$

Compare this result w[ith] the exact result

$$\begin{aligned}\int_1^3 \frac{1}{1+x}\,dx &= [\ln|1+ \\ &= \ln 4 - \\ &= 0.693\,1\end{aligned}$$

This technique of splitting up the area to be evaluated can be done with shapes other than rectangles. By changing the shape from a rectangle to a trapezium a better approximation can be made. The process is then known as the **trapezium rule**.

The trapezium rule

The area A under the curve $y = f(x)$ is divided up into n vertical strips. The width of each strip is h. The curve is modelled by a series of straight lines; one across the top of each strip. The area under the curve can then be approximated by adding together the areas of the resulting n trapezia.

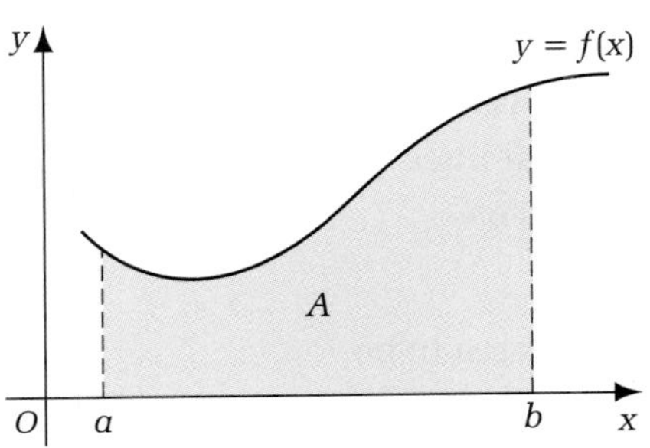

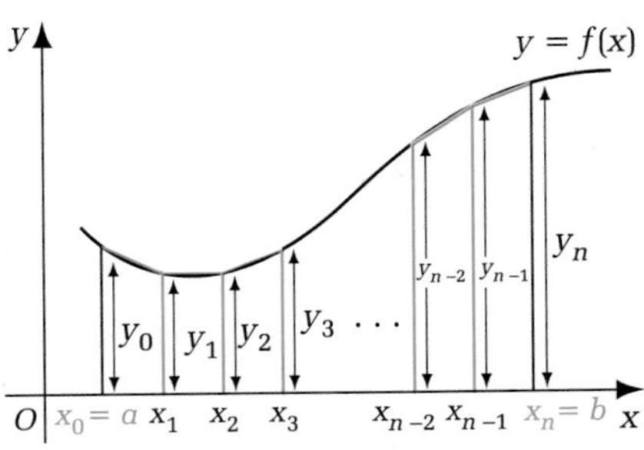

Let $y_0, y_1, y_2, \ldots, y_n$ be values of the function $f(x)$. These correspond to the $(n+1)$ ordinates $x_0, x_1, x_2, \ldots, x_n$ respectively. Using

$$\text{area of trapezium} = \tfrac{1}{2}(\text{width} \times \text{sum of parallel sides})$$

the area of the first trapezium is

$$A_1 = \tfrac{1}{2}h(y_0 + y_1)$$

The areas of the second and third trapezia are then

$$A_2 = \tfrac{1}{2}h(y_1 + y_2)$$
$$A_3 = \tfrac{1}{2}h(y_2 + y_3)$$

Verify that if this process is continued then

$$A_{n-1} = \tfrac{1}{2}h(y_{n-2} + y_{n-1})$$
$$\text{and} \quad A_n = \tfrac{1}{2}h(y_{n-1} + y_n)$$

Now add all of these separate areas together. The approximate value of A is given by

$$\begin{aligned} A &\approx A_1 + A_2 + A_3 + \cdots + A_{n-1} + A_n \\ &\approx \tfrac{1}{2}h(y_0 + y_1) + \tfrac{1}{2}h(y_1 + y_2) + \tfrac{1}{2}h(y_2 + y_3) + \cdots + \tfrac{1}{2}h(y_{n-2} + y_{n-1}) \\ &\qquad + \tfrac{1}{2}h(y_{n-1} + y_n) \\ &\approx \tfrac{1}{2}h(y_0 + 2y_1 + 2y_2 + 2y_3 + \cdots + 2y_{n-1} + y_n) \end{aligned}$$

This method of approximating the area under a curve by n trapezia of equal width h is called the trapezium rule, and the result can be summarised as:

$$\boldsymbol{\int_a^b f(x)\,dx \approx \tfrac{1}{2}h[y_0 + 2(y_1 + y_2 + \cdots + y_{n-1}) + y_n]}$$

◀ **Learn this important result.**

where $h = \frac{b-a}{n}$ and $y_r = f(x_r)$.

Example 3

Use the trapezium rule, with four strips to find an approximate value for the area between the curve $y = x \sin x$, the x-axis and the vertical lines $x = 1$ and $x = 3$. Give your answers correct to three decimal places.

Solution

Begin with a sketch of the graph of $y = x \sin x$, and identify the area to be approximated. Divide this area up into four vertical strips. Notice that each strip has a width of $\frac{1}{2}$ unit.

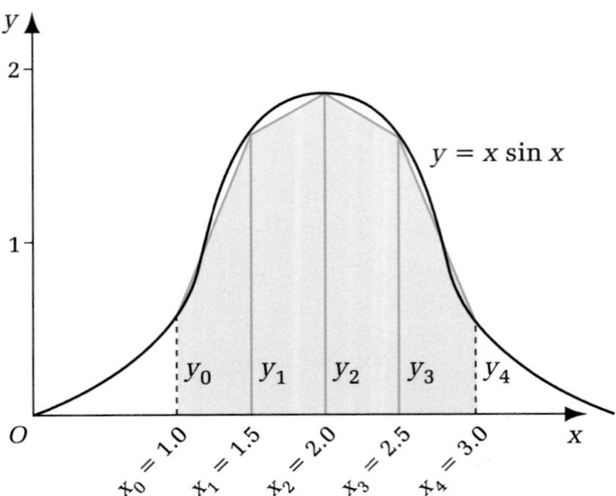

Check that substituting the five ordinates $x_0 = 1, x_1 = 1.5, x_2 = 2, x_3 = 2.5$ and $x_4 = 3$ into $y = x \sin x$ gives

$$y_0 = 0.841\,47 \qquad y_1 = 1.496\,24 \qquad y_2 = 1.818\,59$$

$$y_3 = 1.496\,18 \qquad y_4 = 0.423\,36$$

The trapezium rule now gives

$$\begin{aligned}\int_1^3 x \sin x \, dx &\approx \tfrac{1}{2}h[y_0 + 2(y_1 + y_2 + y_3) + y_4], \text{ where } h = 0.5 \\ &\approx \tfrac{1}{2} \times 0.5[0.841\,47 + 2(1.496\,24 + 1.818\,59 + 1.496\,18) \\ &\qquad + 0.423\,36] \\ &\approx 2.721\,71 \\ &\approx 2.722 \text{ (3 d.p.)}\end{aligned}$$

It is possible to check the accuracy of these calculations. This particular definite integral can be evaluated exactly. Integrate $x \sin x$ using integration by parts (see Chapter 12). Verify that the area under the curve $y = x \sin x$ between $x = 1$ and $x = 3$ is 2.810 (3 d.p.).
In general, the more strips (or ordinates) used, the more accurate the result from the trapezium rule. This greater accuracy obviously involves more calculations.

Example 4

At a certain point in its course, a river is 10 metres wide. Its depth, d metres, is measured at intervals of 1 metre from its left bank at this point. The results are shown in the table below (x metres is the distance from the left bank).

x	0	1	2	3	4	5	6	7	8	9	10
d	0	0.93	1.26	2.81	3.64	3.87	4.09	3.92	3.64	2.36	1.68

Use the trapezium rule to find an approximate value for the cross-sectional area of the river at this point.

Solution

Begin by drawing a graph to show this information. Plot the points, and draw a smooth curve through them to model the cross-section of the river bed. Now divide this cross-sectional area up into 10 vertical strips. Each has a width of 1 metre.

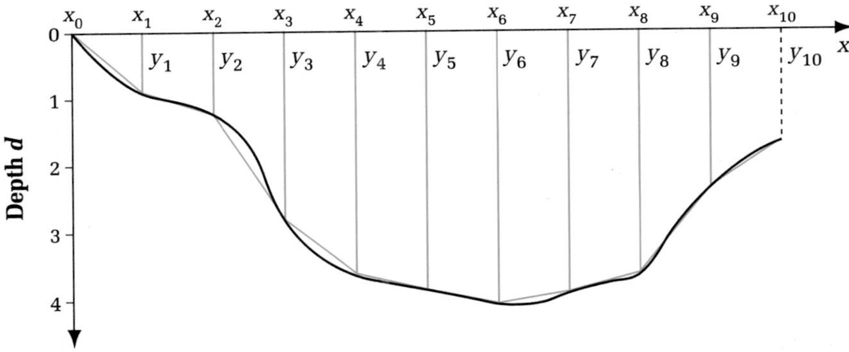

Using the trapezium rule, the cross-sectional area

$$A \approx \tfrac{1}{2}h[y_0 + 2(y_1 + y_2 + y_3 + \cdots + y_9) + y_{10}],$$

where strip width $h = 1\,\text{m}$

$$\approx \tfrac{1}{2} \times 1[0 + 2(0.93 + 1.26 + 2.81 + 3.64 + 3.87 + 4.09 + 3.92 + 3.64 + 2.36) + 1.68]$$

$$\approx 27.36\,\text{m}^2$$

Simpson's rule

A more accurate value for the area under a curve can be obtained by dividing the area into a series of vertical strips, and then approximating the top of each strip by a quadratic curve rather than a straight line.

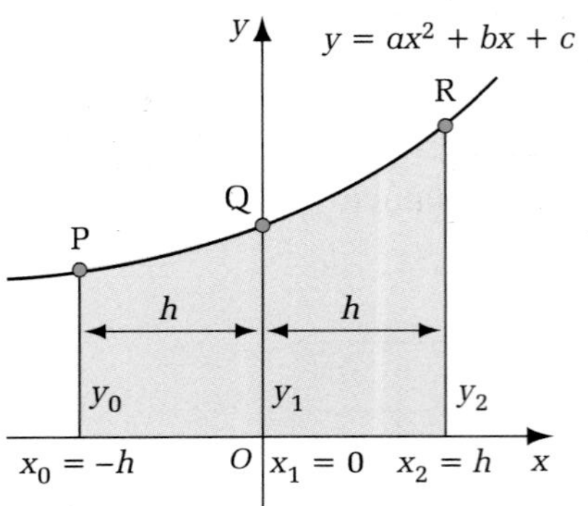

If the quadratic curve $y = ax^2 + bx + c$ passes through the three points P $(-h, y_0)$, Q $(0, y_1)$ and R (h, y_2), then

$$y_0 = ah^2 - bh + c \quad [1]$$

$$y_1 = c \quad [2]$$

$$y_2 = ah^2 + bh + c \quad [3]$$

Substituting the x- an[d] y-coordinates of P, Q [and] R respectively into $y = ax^2 + bx + c$.

The area enclosed by this quadratic curve and the x-axis between $x = -h$ and $x = h$ is given by

$$\begin{aligned}
\text{area} &= \int_{-h}^{h} (ax^2 + bx + c)\,dx \\
&= [\tfrac{1}{3}ax^3 + \tfrac{1}{2}bx^2 + cx]_{-h}^{h} \\
&= (\tfrac{1}{3}ah^3 + \tfrac{1}{2}bh^2 + ch) - (-\tfrac{1}{3}ah^3 + \tfrac{1}{2}bh^2 - ch) \\
&= \tfrac{2}{3}ah^3 + 2ch \\
&= \tfrac{1}{3}h(2ah^2 + 6c)
\end{aligned}$$

Returning to equations [1], [2] and [3],

$$y_0 + y_2 = 2ah^2 + 2c$$

$$\text{so} \quad y_0 + y_2 + 4y_1 = 2ah^2 + 6c$$ ◀ $y_1 = c$, so $4y_1 = 4c$

This means that the area under this quadratic curve can be written as

$$\begin{aligned}
\text{area} &= \tfrac{1}{3}h(2ah^2 + 6c) \\
&= \tfrac{1}{3}h(y_0 + 4y_1 + y_2)
\end{aligned}$$

This result has been established using two vertical strips of width h either side of the y-axis. By translating the coordinate axes system, it can be shown that it holds for two adjacent strips located anywhere along the x-axis.

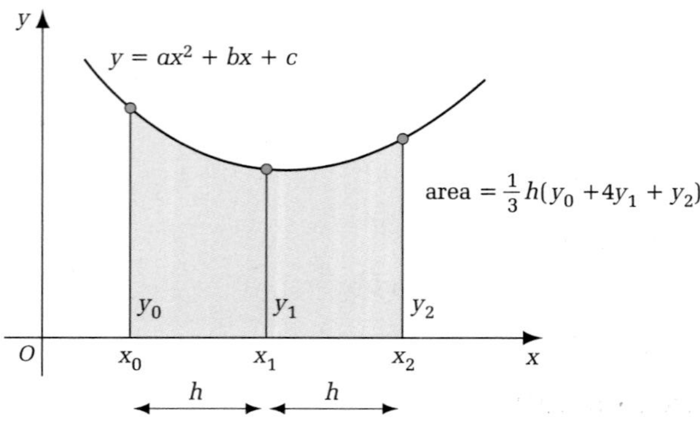

This result can now be used to find an approximation for $\int_a^b f(x)\,dx$. Recall that this integral is the area between the curve $y = f(x)$, the lines $x = a$ and $x = b$ and the x-axis. Unlike in the trapezium rule, this area must be divided up into an even number of vertical strips, because the tops of the first and each subsequent pair of adjacent strips will be approximated by a quadratic curve. So there will be an odd number of ordinates. Each strip is of width h.

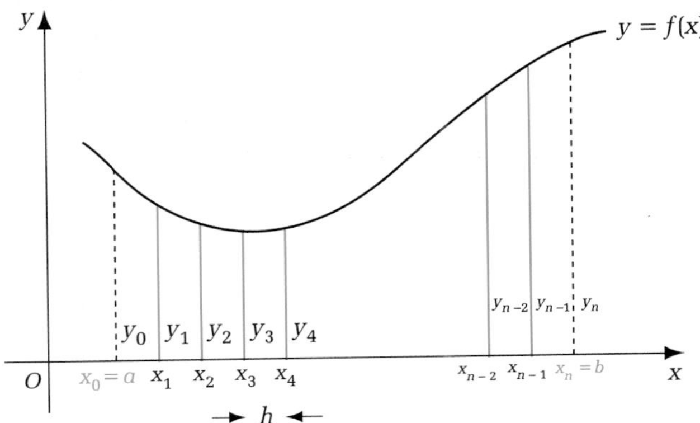

The area of the first pair of vertical strips will be

$$\tfrac{1}{3}h(y_0 + 4y_1 + y_2)$$

The areas of the second, and third, pairs of vertical strips will be

$$\tfrac{1}{3}h(y_2 + 4y_3 + y_4)$$

and $\quad \tfrac{1}{3}h(y_4 + 4y_5 + y_6)$

This pattern continues until finally the last ordinate is reached. The area of the last pair of vertical strips will be

$$\tfrac{1}{3}h(y_{n-2} + 4y_{n-1} + y_n)$$

Adding all of these separate areas together, the approximate value of A is

$$A \approx \tfrac{1}{3}h(y_0 + 4y_1 + y_2) + \tfrac{1}{3}h(y_2 + 4y_3 + y_4) + \tfrac{1}{3}h(y_4 + 4y_5 + y_6) + \cdots + \tfrac{1}{3}h(y_{n-2} + 4y_{n-1} + y_n)$$

This result can be summarised as:

$$\int_a^b f(x)\,dx \approx \tfrac{1}{3}h(y_0 + 4y_1 + 2y_2 + 4y_3 + 2y_4 + \cdots + 2y_{n-2} + 4y_{n-1} + y_n)$$

$$\approx \tfrac{h}{3}[y_0 + y_n + 4(y_1 + y_3 + y_5 + \cdots + y_{n-1}) + 2(y_2 + y_4 + y_6 + \cdots + y_{n-2})]$$

where $h = \dfrac{b-a}{n}$ **and** $y_r = f(x_r)$.

◀ **Learn this important result.**

This method of numerical integration is **Simpson's rule.**

Example 5

Use Simpson's rule, with five ordinates, to find the value of $\int_0^1 \frac{4}{1+x^2}\,dx$. Give your final answer correct to four decimal places.

Solution

Using five ordinates means that the area under the curve will be divided into four strips. Each strip has width $h = \frac{1-0}{4} = 0.25$. Sketch a graph of $y = \frac{4}{1+x^2}$ and identify the area represented by the integral.

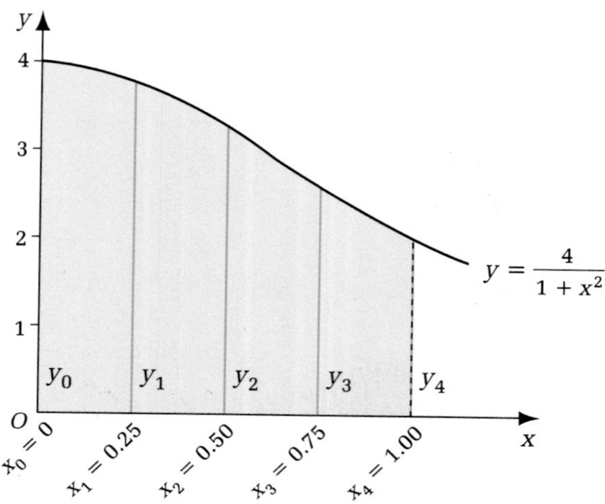

Verify that substituting the five ordinates $x_0 = 0$, $x_1 = 0.25$, $x_2 = 0.5$, $x_3 = 0.75$ and $x_4 = 1$ into $y = \frac{4}{1+x^2}$ gives the following values:

$y_0 = 4$	$y_1 = 3.764\,706$	$y_2 = 3.2$
$y_3 = 2.56$	$y_4 = 2$	

Use Simpson's rule and substitute the calculated values.

$$\begin{aligned}\int_0^1 \frac{4}{1+x^2}\,dx &\approx \tfrac{1}{3}h[y_0 + y_4 + 4(y_1 + y_3) + 2y_2] \\ &\approx \tfrac{1}{3} \times 0.25[4 + 2 + 4(3.764\,706 + 2.56) + 2 \times 3.2] \\ &\approx 3.1416 \text{ (4 d.p.)}\end{aligned}$$

Check this result using the standard integral list established in Chapter 12.

$$\int_0^1 \frac{4}{1+x^2}\,dx = \pi$$

Simpson's rule, with five ordinates, gives an approximation that is correct to four decimal places. A more accurate value of π can be found by repeating this Simpson's rule calculation with a larger number of ordinates.

13.2 Numerical Integration
Exercise
Technique

1 Using the mid-ordinate rule with

a 5 strips **b** 10 strips

calculate the value of $\int_1^2 \sqrt{\ln x}\,dx$ correct to three decimal places. Remember to show five decimal places of working.

2 Find, giving your answers correct to two decimal places, the area under the curve $y = \sqrt{1 + x^2}$ between $x = 0$ and $x = 5$ using:

a the mid-ordinate rule with five strips
b the trapezium rule with five strips.

3 Find, giving your answers correct to four decimal places, the approximate value of $\int_0^1 \cos(x^2)\,dx$ using:

a the trapezium rule with 11 ordinates
b Simpson's rule with 11 ordinates.

4 Given that $\frac{\tan x}{x} = 1$ when $x = 0$, use the trapezium rule with

a 5 strips **b** 10 strips

to calculate the area under the graph of $y = \frac{\tan x}{x}$, between $x = 0$ and $x = 1$, correct to two decimal places.

5 Use Simpson's rule with:

a four strips **b** eight strips

to evaluate $\int_1^5 x^3\,e^{-x}\,dx$, giving your answers correct to four decimal places.

6 Find, correct to four decimal places, the value of $\int_0^3 e^x \sin x\,dx$, using:

a integration by parts
b Simpson's rule with seven ordinates.
c Calculate the percentage error of the result using Simpson's rule.

Contextual

1 A vase has a base radius of 3 cm and a perpendicular height of 20 cm. It can be modelled by rotating area A through 360° about the x-axis, as shown below, where A is the area bounded by the x-axis and the curve $y = 3 + \ln(x + 1)$ between $x = 0$ and $x = 20$.

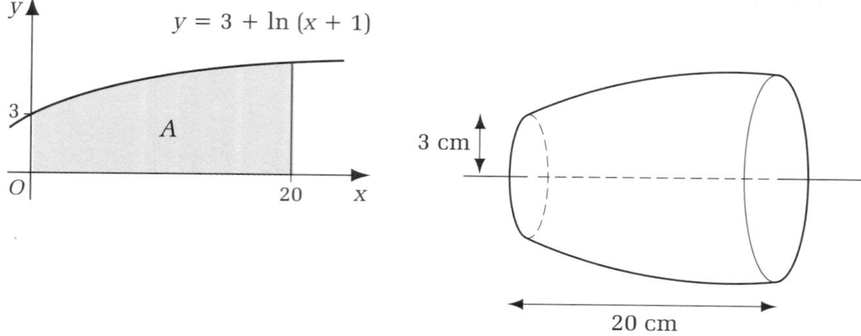

Use Simpson's rule with 10 strips to calculate the volume of the vase. Write your answer correct to one decimal place.

2 The rate R, at which water is leaking from a burst water main is measured at 10 minute intervals. Over a period of two hours, the results are tabulated as follows.

t (min)	0	10	20	30	40	50	60	70	80	90	100	110	120
R (l min^{-1})	520	530	569	591	633	652	629	546	468	401	325	276	254

a Plot time t horizontally against the rate of leakage R vertically.

b The total volume of water wasted during this two-hour period can be estimated by calculating the area under this graph. Use the trapezium rule with 12 strips to find an estimate for the total leakage.

3 A variable force F Newtons is applied to a moving object over a distance of 8 metres. The results are shown in the table below.

Distance d (m)	0	1	2	3	4	5	6	7	8
Force F (N)	350	317	289	300	276	216	153	120	95

a Plot distance d horizontally against force F vertically.

b The total work done W (or energy used) measured in Joules (J) in applying this force can be estimated by calculating the area under this graph. Estimate the value of W using:

i the trapezium rule with eight strips

ii Simpson's rule with eight strips.

Consolidation

Exercise A

1 The equation $\sin x - 2\cos x - 1 = 0$ has a root near $x = 1.5$, where x is measured in radians. Starting with this value, use two iterations of the Newton–Raphson method to find an approximation for this root correct to two decimal places.

(NICCEA)

2

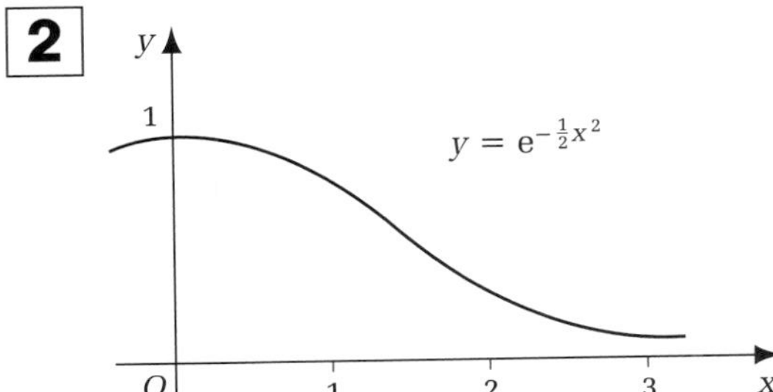

The graph of $y = e^{-\frac{1}{2}x^2}$ is sketched above. Use the trapezium rule, with three strips, to estimate the area under the curve between $x = 0$ and $x = 3$. Give your answer to three decimal places.

(SMP)

3 On a single diagram, sketch the graphs of $y = x^4$ and $y = x^3 + 3$. Hence state the number of roots of the equation $x^4 = x^3 + 3$. This equation may be solved numerically using the iteration $x_{n+1} = \frac{1}{10}(9x_n + \frac{3}{x_n^3} + 1)$. Use this iteration, starting with the value of -1, to find the negative root of the equation $x^4 = x^3 + 3$ correct to two decimal places, showing the result of each iteration.

(UCLES)

4 Use Simpson's rule with five ordinates to find an approximate value of $\int_0^1 x \sec x \, dx$, giving your final answer to three decimal places. The region bounded by the curve with equation $y = \sqrt{x \sec x}$, the x-axis from $x = 0$ to $x = 1$, and the line with equation $x = 1$, is rotated completely about the x-axis. Use your answer from the Simpson's rule approximation to find an *estimate* of the volume of the solid formed, giving your answer to two significant figures.

(AEB)

5 Sketch the curve with equation $y = e^x$, and on the same axes draw an appropriate line to show that the equation $e^x + x - 3 = 0$ has exactly one root, α.

a Prove that α lies between 0.7 and 0.8.

b Using 0.8 as a first approximation to α, use the Newton–Raphson method once to obtain a second approximation to α, giving your answer to three decimal places.

c Show that the equation $e^x + x - 3 = 0$ can be arranged in the form $x = \ln(f(x))$. Use an iteration of the form $x_{n+1} = g(x_n)$ based on this rearrangement with $x_0 = 0.8$ to find the values of x_1 and x_2, giving your answers to three decimal places.

(AEB)

6 A river is 18 metres wide in a certain region and its depth, d metres, at a point x metres from one side is given by the formula $d = \frac{1}{18}\sqrt{x(18-x)(18+x)}$.

a Produce a table showing the depths (correct to three decimal places where necessary) at $x = 0, 3, 6, 9, 12, 15$ and 18.

b Using the trapezium rule, find an estimate for the area of the cross-section of the river in this region.

c Given that, in this region, the river is flowing at a uniform speed of 100 metres per minute, estimate the number of cubic metres of water passing per minute.

(UCLES)

7 Show that the equation $x^5 - 5x - 6 = 0$ has a root in the interval $(1, 2)$. Stating the values of the constants p, q and r, use an iteration of the form $x_{n+1} = (px_n + q)^{1/r}$ the appropriate number of times to calculate this root of the equation $x^5 - 5x - 6 = 0$ correct to three decimal places. Show sufficient working to justify your final answer.

(ULEAC)

8 Show that the equation $x^3 - 9x^2 + 5x - 7 = 0$ has a root between $x = 8$ and $x = 9$. Take $x = 9$ as a first approximation to that root and use the Newton–Raphson method once to find a second approximation. Give your answer to one decimal place.

(AEB)

9

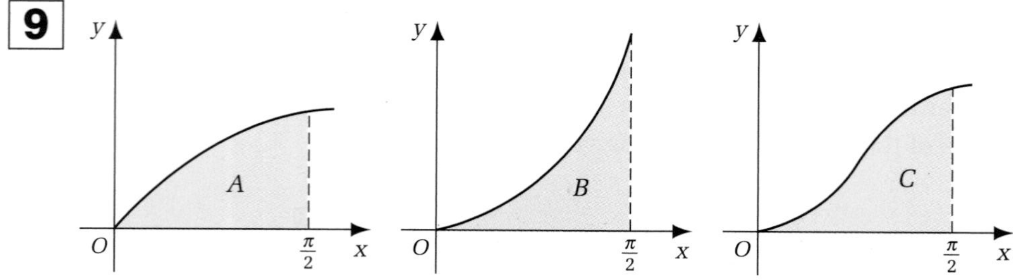

The figures show the graphs of $\sin x$, $x\sin x$ and $\sqrt{x}\sin x$ respectively, over the interval $0 \le x \le \frac{\pi}{2}$. The areas under these graphs are denoted by A, B and C.

a Write the area A as a definite integral, and evaluate it.

b Use the method of integration by parts to find the area B.

c The area C cannot be found exactly, but several approximate methods are possible. Carry out both of the following calculations, giving your answers correct to three decimal places.

i Replace $\sin x$ in the integral for C by its Taylor approximation, $\sin x \approx x - \frac{1}{6}x^3$, and evaluate this alternative integral.

ii Use Simpson's rule with two intervals (three ordinates).

The answers to **i** and **ii** are not very close to each other, so it is desirable to improve the accuracy of these approximations. Without doing any more calculations, suggest, for each method, one way in which this could be done.

(OCSEB)

10

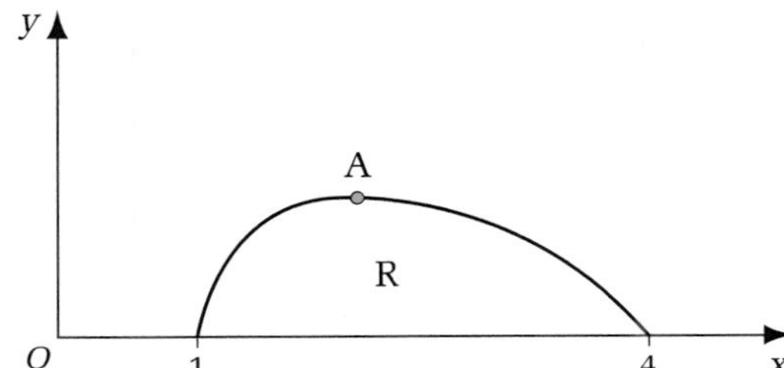

The figure shows a sketch of the curve $y = (4 - x)\ln x$ for $1 \leq x \leq 4$. The point A is a maximum and R denotes the region enclosed between the curve and the x-axis.

a **i** Show that m, the x-coordinate of A satisfies the equation $1 + \ln x - \frac{4}{x} = 0$.

ii Show that m lies between 2.2 and 2.3.

iii The value of m can be found using the iterative formula $x_{n+1} = \frac{4}{1+\ln x_n}$. Taking $x_0 = 2.2$, use this formula as many times as necessary to find the value of m correct to two decimal places, writing down your values of $x_1, x_2, \ldots$ as accurately as your calculator allows.

b Show that the area of R is $8\ln 4 - \frac{33}{4}$.

(WJEC)

Exercise B

1 Use the trapezium rule, with six ordinates, to evaluate, correct to two decimal places, the definite integral $\int_0^1 \frac{1}{1+x^2}\,dx$.

(NICCEA)

2 **a** Show that the equation $x^3 - 3x - 20 = 0$ has a root α that lies between 3 and 4.

b Use the iterative formula $x_{n+1} = \sqrt[3]{3x_n + 20}$ with $x_0 = 3.0$ to find the values of x_1, x_2, x_3 and x_4. Give your answers as accurately as your calculator will allow.

c Without further calculation, state, with a reason, whether it is possible to write down with certainty the value of α correct to four decimal places.

d Prove that the value of α correct to three decimal places is 3.081.

(WJEC)

3 Showing all relevant working, use Simpson's rule with five equally spaced ordinates to find an estimate for $\int_1^9 \ln(1 + x^3)\,dx$, giving your answer to two decimal places.

(ULEAC)

4 Use the trapezium rule, with ordinates at $u = 0, \frac{1}{4}, \frac{1}{2}$ to find an approximate value for

$$\int_0^{\frac{1}{2}} \frac{3u}{1+u^3}\,du$$

giving your answer correct to two decimal places.

(UCLES)

5 Show that the equation $x^3 - 5x^2 - 6 = 0$ has a root between 5 and 6. Use the Newton–Raphson method to find an approximation for this root to one decimal place.

(NICCEA)

6 **a** By sketching the curves with equations $y = 4 - x^2$ and $y = e^x$ show that the equation $x^2 + e^x - 4 = 0$ has one negative root and one positive root.

b Use the iterative formula $x_{n+1} = -(4 - e^{x_n})^{\frac{1}{2}}$ with $x_0 = -2$ to find in turn x_1, x_2, x_3 and x_4, and hence write down an approximation to the negative root of the equation, giving your answer to four decimal places.

c An attempt to evaluate the positive root of the equation is made using the iteration formula $x_{n+1} = (4 - e^{x_n})^{\frac{1}{2}}$ with $x_0 = 1.3$. Describe the result of such an attempt.

(ULEAC)

7 Show that the equation $x = \frac{1}{2+\sqrt{x}}$ has a root α between 0 and 1. By using an iterative formula of the form $x_{n+1} = f(x_n)$, find α correct to two decimal places. You should show clearly your sequence of approximations.

(UCLES)

Applications and Activities

Both the trapezium rule and Simpson's rule for numerical integration divide the area under the curve $y = f(x)$ into n vertical strips, each with width h. The Trapezium rule uses straight lines to approximate the tops of these strips. It makes them into a series of trapezia. Simpson's rule approximates the tops of each adjacent pair of strips by a *quadratic* curve. The number of strips into which the area is divided must be even. Continuing with this process, a new rule for numerical integration can be found by approximating the tops of three adjacent strips by a *cubic* curve. Now the number of strips into which the area is divided is divisible by 3. The derivation is similar to that used to establish Simpson's rule (see p. 573).

1

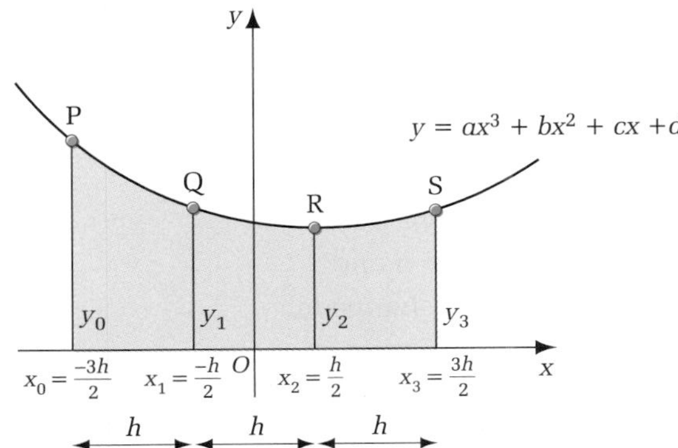

Consider the cubic curve $y = ax^3 + bx^2 + cx + d$ that passes through the four points P $(-\frac{3h}{2}, y_0)$, Q $(-\frac{h}{2}, y_1)$, R $(\frac{h}{2}, y_2)$ and S $(\frac{3h}{2}, y_3)$ as shown in the diagram.

a Find expressions for y_0, y_1, y_2 and y_3 in terms of a, b, c, d and h.

b Then find expressions for $(y_0 + y_3)$ and $(y_1 + y_2)$ in terms of b, d and h only.

c Find an expression for the area under the curve $y = ax^3 + bx^2 + cx + d$ between $x = -\frac{3h}{2}$ and $x = \frac{3h}{2}$ in terms of b, d and h only.

d By eliminating b and d using your expressions for $(y_0 + y_3)$ and $(y_1 + y_2)$, find an expression for this area in terms of y_0, y_1, y_2, y_3 and h.

2

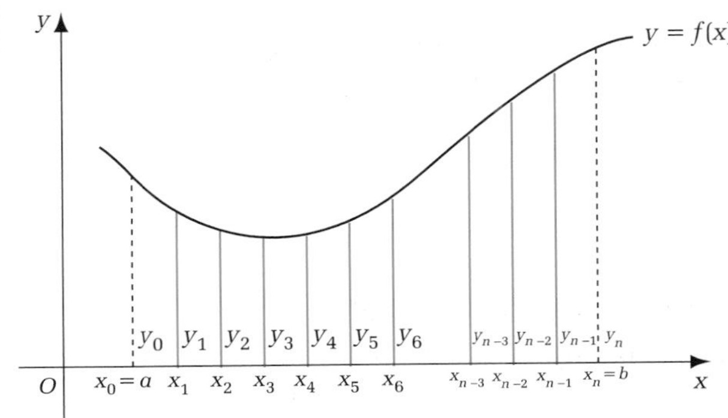

Given that the result in [1] holds for any three adjacent strips of width h located anywhere along the x-axis, find the sum of the areas of all such sets of three strips. Write down the rule of numerical integration based on approximating the curve $y = f(x)$ by a series of cubic curves.

Summary

- Equations of the form $f(x) = 0$ can be solved graphically by finding where the curve $y = f(x)$ crosses the x-axis.
- Use the point of intersection of two graphs to solve equations of the form $g(x) = h(x)$.
- Roots of a continuous function lie between values of x for which the function has different signs.
- If $f(x) = 0$ has a root α between $x = a$ and $x = b$, a better approximation for this root can be found by considering the sign of the function at the mid-point $x = m$ between a and b. If there is a change of sign in the value of the function $f(x)$ between $x = a$ and $x = m$, then the root α lies in the interval $a < x < m$. If the change of sign in function $f(x)$ occurs between $x = m$ and $x = b$, then α lies in the interval $m < x < b$. The mid-point is

  $$\boldsymbol{m = \tfrac{1}{2}(a + b)}.$$

  This is the **bisection** method.
- **Linear interpolation** uses a similar technique to the bisection method, but instead of the mid-point, a better approximation is x_1, where

  $$\boldsymbol{x_1 = \frac{aq + bp}{p + q}}$$

  and p and q are the absolute values of the function $f(x)$ at $x = a$ and $x = b$, respectively.
- The **Newton–Raphson iterative formula**

  $$\boldsymbol{x_{n+1} = x_n - \frac{f(x_n)}{f'(x_n)}}$$

  gives progressively better approximations to the root of the equation $f(x) = 0$.
- The iterative formula $x_{n+1} = g(x_n)$ converges to the root of the equation $x = g(x)$ provided $|g'(x)| < 1$ for values of x close to this root. This is the **fixed point iterative method.**

- **Cobweb** and **staircase** diagrams illustrate convergence towards the root of an equation if a suitable first approximation x_0 is chosen for the fixed point iterative method.
- The **mid-ordinate rule** says that

$$\int_a^b f(x)\,dx \approx h(f_1 + f_2 + f_3 + \cdots + f_{n-1} + f_n)$$

where $h = \frac{b-a}{n}$ and f_r is the value of $f(x)$ at the midpoint of the rth rectangular strip.

- The **trapezium rule** says that

$$\int_a^b f(x)\,dx \approx \tfrac{1}{2}h[y_0 + 2(y_1 + y_2 + \cdots + y_{n-1}) + y_n]$$

where $h = \frac{b-a}{n}$ and $y_r = f(x_r)$.

- **Simpson's rule** says

$$\int_a^b f(x)\,dx \approx \tfrac{1}{3}h[y_0 + y_n + 4(y_1 + y_3 + y_5 + \cdots + y_{n-1}) + 2(y_2 + y_4 + y_6 + \cdots + y_{n-2})]$$

where $h = \frac{b-a}{n}$ and $y_r = f(x_r)$.

14 Vectors

What you need to know

- How to use coordinates in two and three dimensions.
- How to use the cosine rule.
- How to find the area of a triangle using the formula area $= \frac{1}{2}ab \sin C$.

Review

1

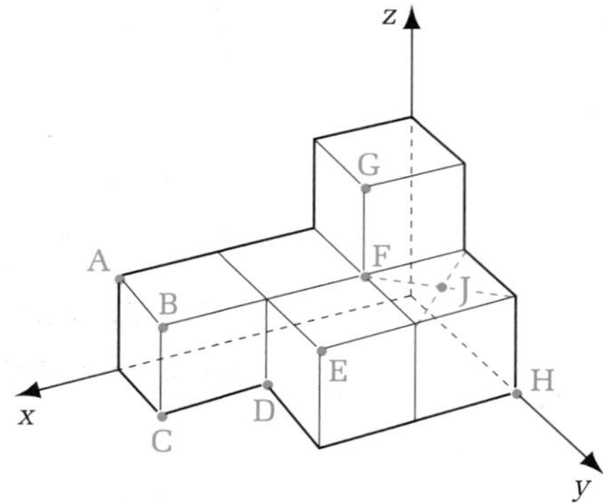

Given that each square block has sides of length 1 unit, write down the coordinates of the points A, B, C, D, E, F, G, H, and J.

2 Use the cosine rule to find θ in the following triangles:

a

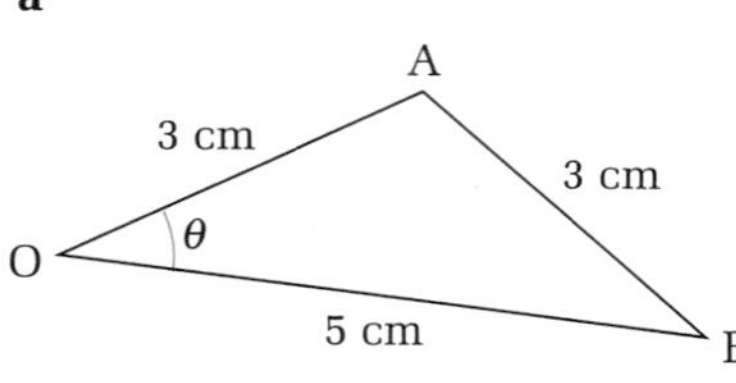

b

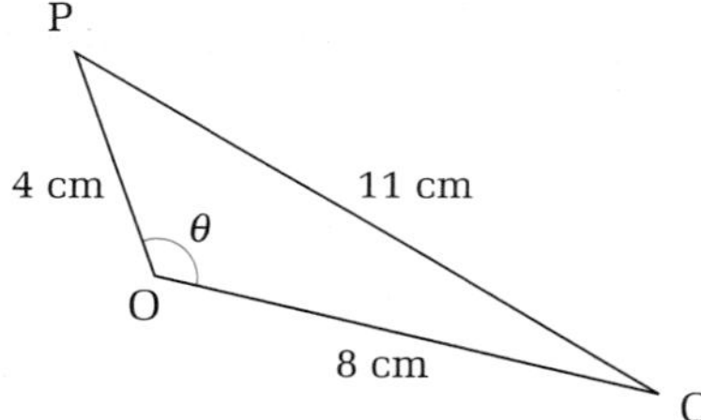

3 Use the formula area $= \frac{1}{2}ab \sin C$ to find the area of the following triangles:

a

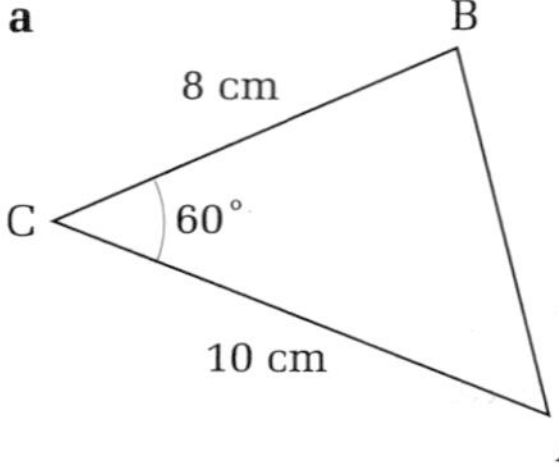

b

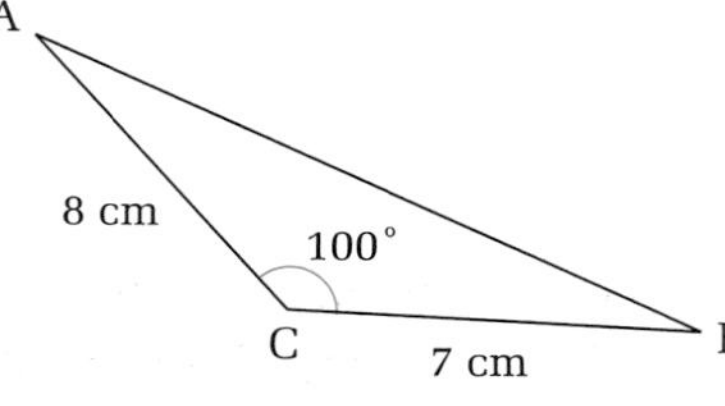

14.1 Vector Geometry

Some quantities like mass, temperature and volume can be described by using a single number to indicate their size. These are called **scalar** quantities. **Vectors** are used to model quantities which have a *direction* as well as size. This chapter is primarily concerned with the geometry and algebra of vectors rather then focusing on examples, such as those in mechanics where vectors are used to model situations.

Vector notation

A vector can be represented by a directed line segment. The arrow indicates the direction of the vector while the length indicates its **magnitude** (or size).

The arrow can be placed in the centre of the line.

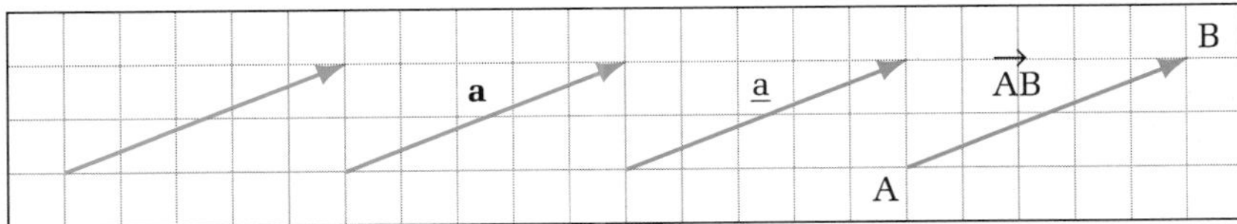

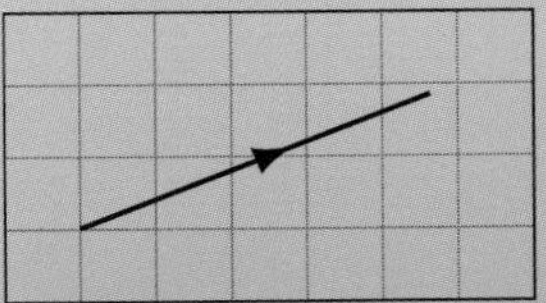

The vector can be denoted in three ways.

You should be familiar with all three.

- In books and examination papers a vector is commonly shown as a bold, lower case letter; **a**. The magnitude, or length of the vector, is indicated by a or $|\mathbf{a}|$.
- When handwritten the same vector is more commonly denoted by $\underline{a}$; the same lower case letter but with a line underneath indicating that it represents a vector. The magnitude of $\underline{a}$ is $|\underline{a}|$ or a.
- The third way is to label its initial point and its terminal point by two capital letters. For example, the vector from some point A to some point B can be denoted by $\overrightarrow{AB}$. The magnitude of the vector is denoted by AB or $|\overrightarrow{AB}|$.

Magnitude

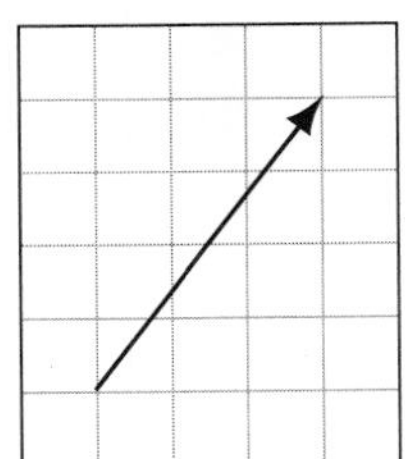

Scale: 1 cm = 1 unit

The magnitude of **b** is 2.5. This can be checked by using a ruler. Therefore $b = 2.5$ (or $|\mathbf{b}| = 2.5$ in the alternative notation). The units of magnitude depend on the quantity that the vector is modelling.

Equal vectors

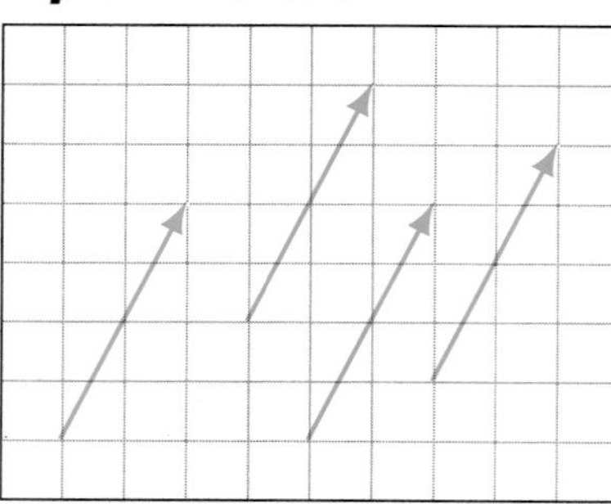

These vectors are equal, even though they start from different positions. Vectors are **equal** if they have the *same magnitude (length) and direction.*

Negative vectors

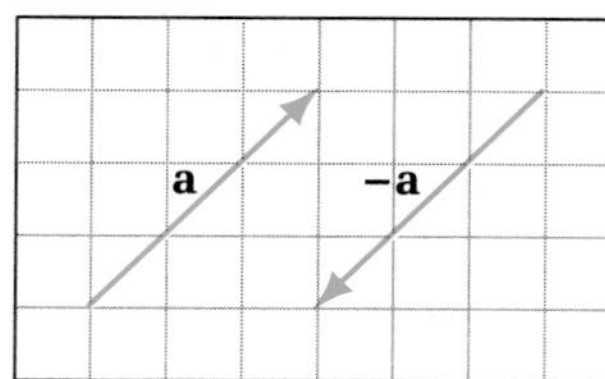

This diagram shows vectors **a** and −**a**. They have the same magnitude (length) but lie in opposite directions.

Multiplying a vector by a scalar

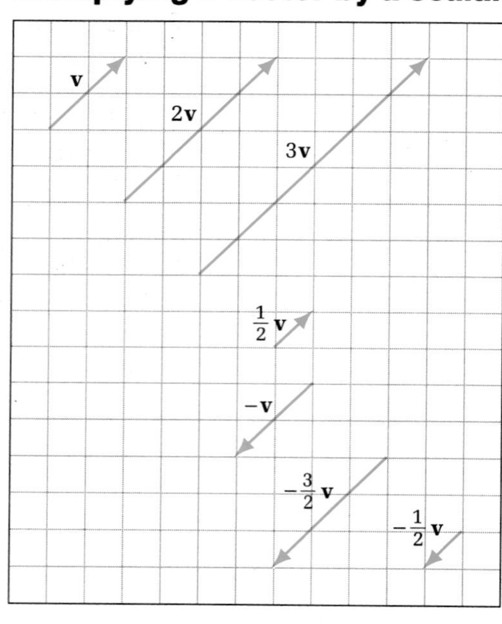

The diagram shows vectors **v**, 2**v**, 3**v**, $\frac{1}{2}$**v**, −**v**, $-\frac{3}{2}$**v** and $-\frac{1}{2}$**v**.

Recall that a scalar quantity is simply a number.

- Multiplying a vector by a scalar greater than one increases its magnitude (length).
- Multiplying a vector by a scalar between 0 and 1 decreases its size.
- Multiplying a vector by a negative scalar also changes the direction of the vector.

For example, $\frac{1}{2}$**v** is a vector in the same direction as **v** but only has half its magnitude. The vector $-\frac{1}{2}$**v** is also half the size of **v** but points in the opposite direction.

Addition of vectors

If **v** and **w** are two vectors then their sum, **v** + **w**, is also a vector, which can be found as follows:

Step ① Draw **v**.
Step ② Draw **w** starting at the end of **v**, as shown below.
Step ③ The directed line segment that goes from the start of **v** to the end of **w** is the new vector **v** + **w**.

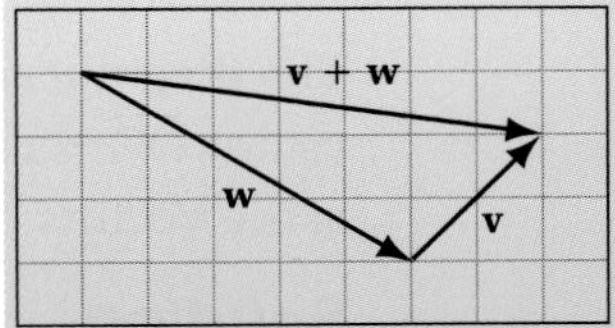

Vector addition is **commutative**; that is $\mathbf{v} + \mathbf{w} = \mathbf{w} + \mathbf{v}$.
The vector **v** + **w** is sometimes referred to as the **resultant** of the vectors **v** and **w**.

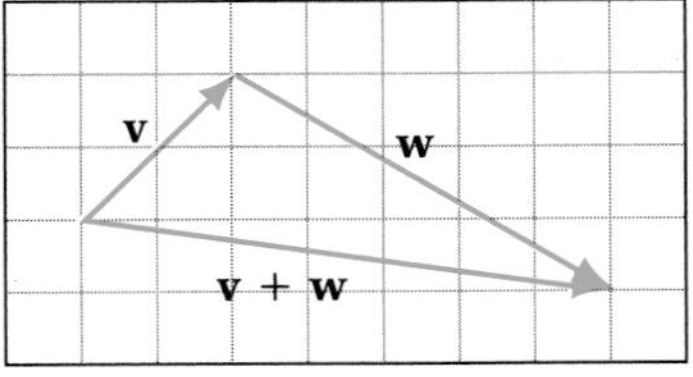

Subtraction of vectors

To find the difference of the two vectors **v** and **w**, that is **v** − **w**, it is useful to write:

$$\mathbf{v} - \mathbf{w} = \mathbf{v} + (-\mathbf{w})$$

So to find **v** − **w**, add the vector −**w** to the end of **v**.
Since vector addition is commutative, the resultant vector **v** − **w** can also be written:

$$\mathbf{v} - \mathbf{w} = -\mathbf{w} + \mathbf{v}$$

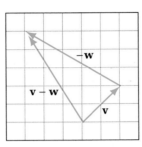

Recall that −**a** is a vector of the same magnitude as **a**, but the opposite direction.

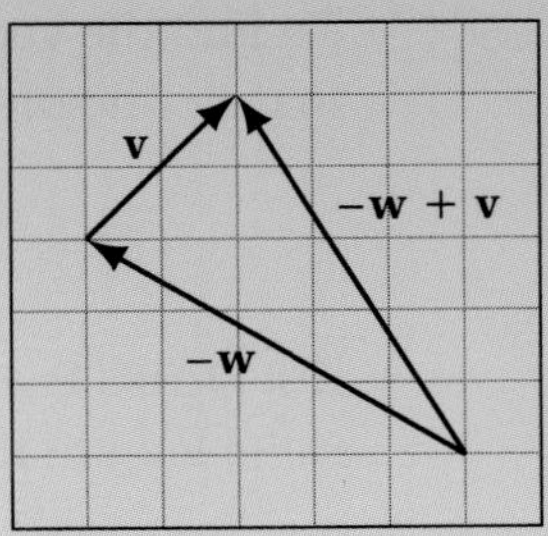

Polygon of vectors

The **polygon of vectors** is used when adding or subtracting more than two vectors.

In the diagram the vectors, **a**, $-\frac{1}{2}\mathbf{b}$ and 3**c** have been added together. Their resultant $\mathbf{a} - \frac{1}{2}\mathbf{b} + 3\mathbf{c}$ forms the side of a polygon.

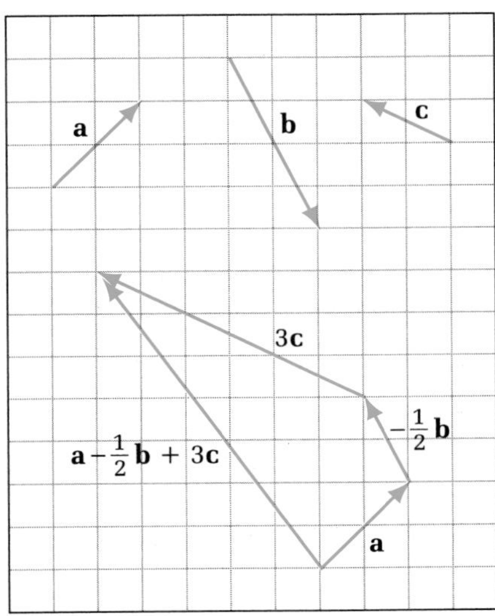

These principles of vector algebra are illustrated in the following examples.

Example 1

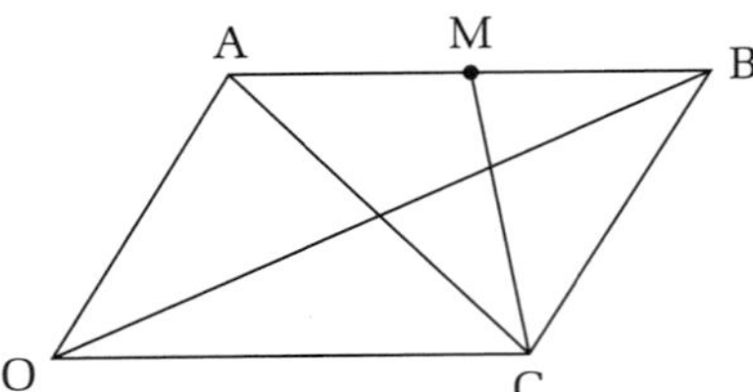

The diagram shows a parallelogram OABC. The vector $\overrightarrow{OA} = \mathbf{a}$ and the vector $\overrightarrow{OC} = \mathbf{c}$. M is the mid-point of the side AB. Find, in terms of $\mathbf{a}$ and $\mathbf{c}$, the vectors $\overrightarrow{OB}$, $\overrightarrow{AC}$ and $\overrightarrow{MC}$.

Solution

Redraw the diagram, adding any more information given in the question.

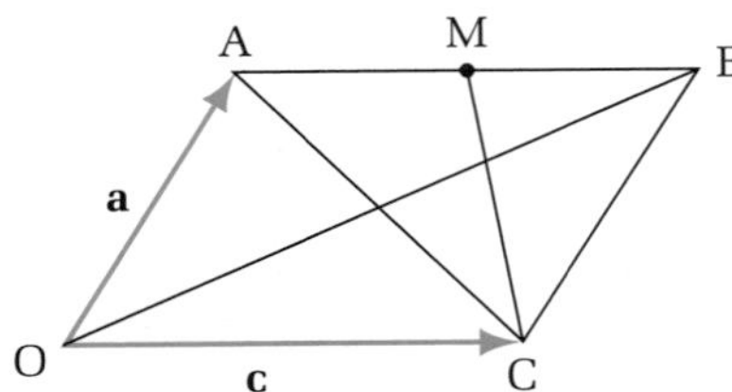

To find the vector $\overrightarrow{OB}$, write down a route from O to B using capital letters to describe the vectors.

$$\overrightarrow{OB} = \overrightarrow{OA} + \overrightarrow{AB}$$

But OABC is a parallelogram, so the side AB is parallel to OC and has the same length; therefore $\overrightarrow{AB}$ and $\overrightarrow{OC}$ are equal vectors.

$\overrightarrow{AB} = \overrightarrow{OC} = \mathbf{c}$.

Now $\quad \overrightarrow{OB} = \overrightarrow{OA} + \overrightarrow{OC}$

Substituting vectors $\mathbf{a}$ and $\mathbf{c}$,

$$\overrightarrow{OB} = \mathbf{a} + \mathbf{c}$$

To find the vector $\overrightarrow{AC}$ in terms of $\mathbf{a}$ and $\mathbf{c}$ use a similar method.

$$\begin{aligned}\overrightarrow{AC} &= \overrightarrow{AO} + \overrightarrow{OC} \\ &= -\mathbf{a} + \mathbf{c}\end{aligned}$$

If $\overrightarrow{OA} = \mathbf{a}$, then $\overrightarrow{AO} = -\mathbf{a}$.

Finally $\quad \begin{aligned}\overrightarrow{MC} &= \overrightarrow{MA} + \overrightarrow{AC} \\ &= \tfrac{1}{2}\overrightarrow{BA} + \overrightarrow{AC} \\ &= -\tfrac{1}{2}\mathbf{c} + (-\mathbf{a} + \mathbf{c}) \\ &= \tfrac{1}{2}\mathbf{c} - \mathbf{a}\end{aligned}$

Recall that M is the mid-point of AB.

Check that you get the same answer if you choose the route $\overrightarrow{MC} = \overrightarrow{MB} + \overrightarrow{BC}$.

Example 2

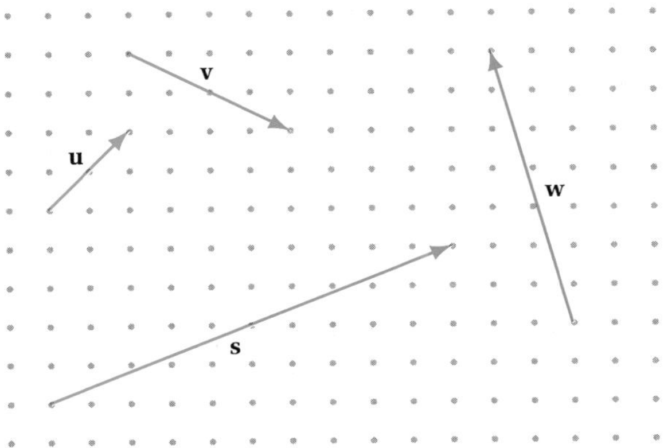

The grid shows the vectors **v**, **u**, **w** and **s**. Find, by drawing:

a vector **w** in terms of **v** and **u**.

b vector **s** in terms of **v** and **u**.

Solution

a Draw the vector **w**. We need to find a route, in terms of **u** and **v**, that begins at the start of **w** and finishes at the end of **w**. Add multiples of **u** to the start of **w**. The direction needs to change so that the path finishes at the end of **w**. Work backwards from the end of **w** with vectors **v** (or −**v** in this case) to meet the line of vector **u**'s.

By vector addition,

$$\mathbf{w} = 2\mathbf{u} + \left(-\tfrac{3}{2}\mathbf{v}\right)$$

$$\mathbf{w} = 2\mathbf{u} - \tfrac{3}{2}\mathbf{v}$$

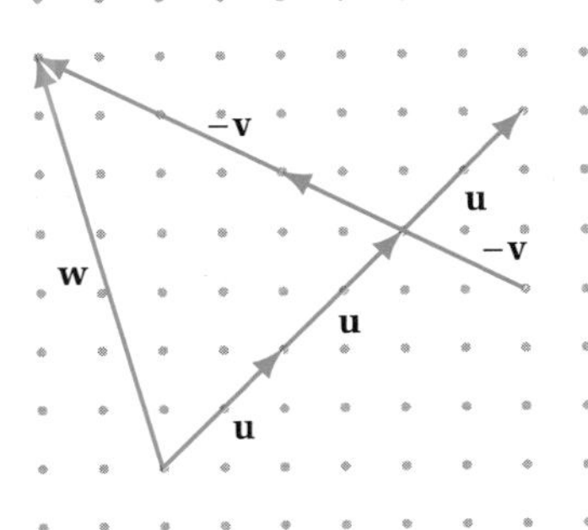

b Use a similar technique. Move along the line of **u**'s and then move along the line of **v**'s.

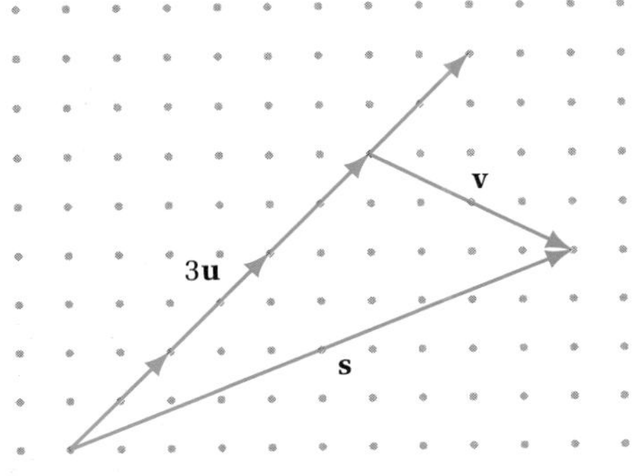

By vector addition

$$\mathbf{s} = 3\mathbf{u} + \mathbf{v}$$

Example 3

In triangle OAB, R, S, and T are the mid-points of OA, OB, and AB respectively, $\overrightarrow{OA} = \mathbf{a}$ and $\overrightarrow{OB} = \mathbf{b}$.

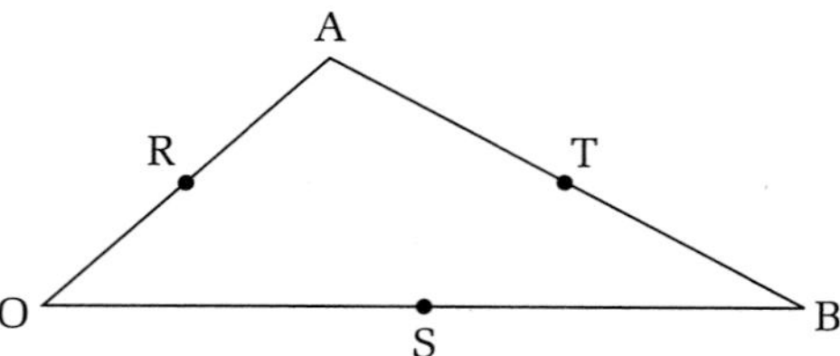

a Find expressions for $\overrightarrow{OR}$, $\overrightarrow{OS}$, $\overrightarrow{AB}$, $\overrightarrow{OT}$ and $\overrightarrow{TO}$ in terms of **a** and **b**.

b Find an expression for $\overrightarrow{RS}$ in terms of **a** and **b**. What is the relationship between the line AB and the line RS?

c P is a point not shown on the diagram such that $\overrightarrow{OP} = \overrightarrow{OA} + \frac{2}{3}\overrightarrow{AS}$. Find an expression for OP. Comment on your answer.

Solution

a Redraw the diagram adding the information given in the question.

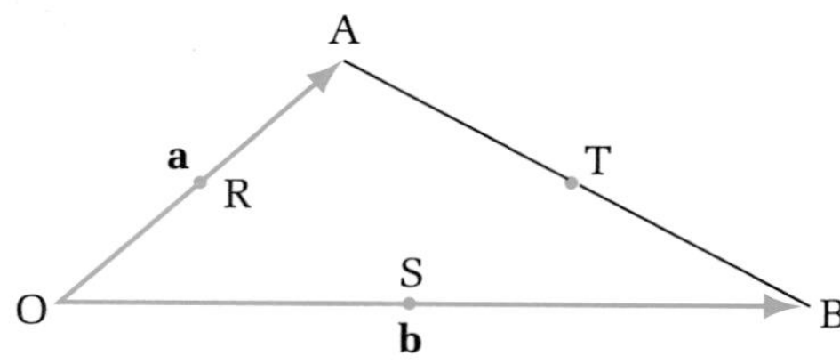

$\overrightarrow{OR} = \frac{1}{2}\overrightarrow{OA} = \frac{1}{2}\mathbf{a}$ and $\overrightarrow{OS} = \frac{1}{2}\overrightarrow{OB} = \frac{1}{2}\mathbf{b}$

Using vector addition, $\overrightarrow{AB} = \overrightarrow{AO} + \overrightarrow{OB}$

$= -\mathbf{a} + \mathbf{b}$

$= \mathbf{b} - \mathbf{a}$

Recall that if $\overrightarrow{OA} = \mathbf{a}$ then $\overrightarrow{AO} = -\mathbf{a}$.

Similarly $\overrightarrow{OT} = \overrightarrow{OA} + \overrightarrow{AT}$

$= \mathbf{a} + \frac{1}{2}\overrightarrow{AB}$

$= \mathbf{a} + \frac{1}{2}(\mathbf{b} - \mathbf{a})$

$= \mathbf{a} + \frac{1}{2}\mathbf{b} - \frac{1}{2}\mathbf{a}$

$= \frac{1}{2}\mathbf{a} + \frac{1}{2}\mathbf{b}$

$= \frac{1}{2}(\mathbf{a} + \mathbf{b})$

$\overrightarrow{TO}$ has the same magnitude as $\overrightarrow{OT}$ but points in the opposite direction.

Therefore $\overrightarrow{TO} = -\overrightarrow{OT}$

$= -\frac{1}{2}(\mathbf{a} + \mathbf{b})$

b Using vector addition

$$\overrightarrow{RS} = \overrightarrow{RO} + \overrightarrow{OS}$$
$$= -\tfrac{1}{2}\mathbf{a} + \tfrac{1}{2}\mathbf{b}$$
$$= \tfrac{1}{2}(\mathbf{b} - \mathbf{a})$$

Since $\overrightarrow{AB} = \mathbf{b} - \mathbf{a}$ and $\overrightarrow{RS} = \tfrac{1}{2}(\mathbf{b} - \mathbf{a})$ we conclude that the line RS is half the length of the line AB and both lines are in the direction of the vector $(\mathbf{b} - \mathbf{a})$. The line RS is therefore parallel to the line AB.

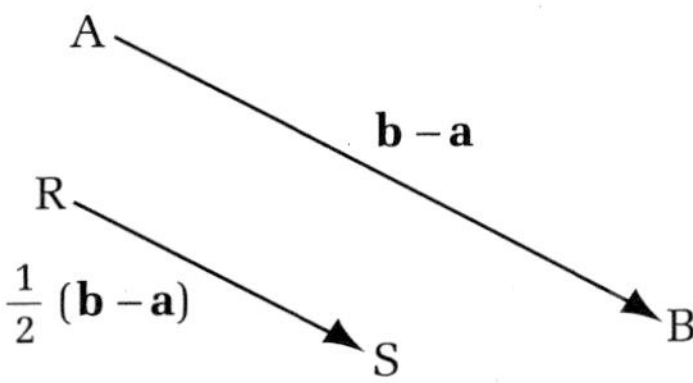

c $\overrightarrow{OP} = \overrightarrow{OA} + \tfrac{2}{3}\overrightarrow{AS}$

$$= \mathbf{a} + \tfrac{2}{3}(\overrightarrow{AO} + \overrightarrow{OS})$$
$$= \mathbf{a} + \tfrac{2}{3}(-\mathbf{a} + \tfrac{1}{2}\mathbf{b})$$
$$= \mathbf{a} - \tfrac{2}{3}\mathbf{a} + \tfrac{1}{3}\mathbf{b}$$
$$= \tfrac{1}{3}\mathbf{a} + \tfrac{1}{3}\mathbf{b}$$
$$= \tfrac{1}{3}(\mathbf{a} + \mathbf{b})$$

Use vector addition to find $\overrightarrow{AS}$.

Now $\overrightarrow{OP} = \tfrac{1}{3}(\mathbf{a} + \mathbf{b})$ and we know that $\overrightarrow{OT} = \tfrac{1}{2}(\mathbf{a} + \mathbf{b})$

$$\tfrac{2}{3} \times \overrightarrow{OT} = \tfrac{2}{3} \times \tfrac{1}{2}(\mathbf{a} + \mathbf{b})$$
$$= \tfrac{1}{3}(\mathbf{a} + \mathbf{b})$$
$$= \overrightarrow{OP}$$

That is, $\overrightarrow{OP} = \tfrac{2}{3}\overrightarrow{OT}$.
This means that P lies $\tfrac{2}{3}$ of the way along the line OT.

14.1 Vector Geometry
Exercise
Technique

1 The figure RSTUVW is a regular hexagon with centre O. Given $\overrightarrow{OV} = \mathbf{v}$ and $\overrightarrow{OW} = \mathbf{w}$, express each of the following vectors in terms of $\mathbf{v}$ and $\mathbf{w}$:

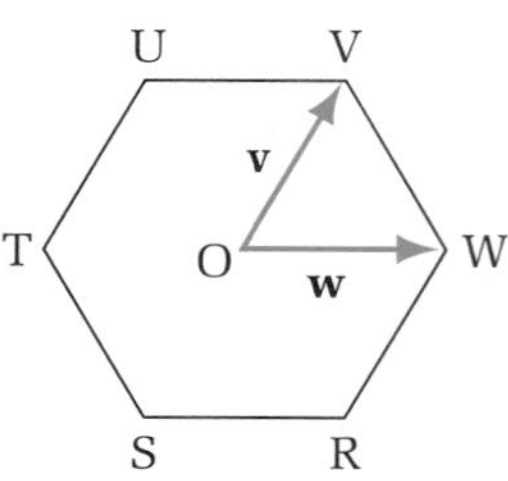

a	$\overrightarrow{UV}$	**d**	$\overrightarrow{VW}$	**g**	$\overrightarrow{WR}$	**j**	$\overrightarrow{TV}$
b	$\overrightarrow{VU}$	**e**	$\overrightarrow{TW}$	**h**	$\overrightarrow{UR}$		
c	$\overrightarrow{TU}$	**f**	$\overrightarrow{VS}$	**i**	$\overrightarrow{TR}$		

2

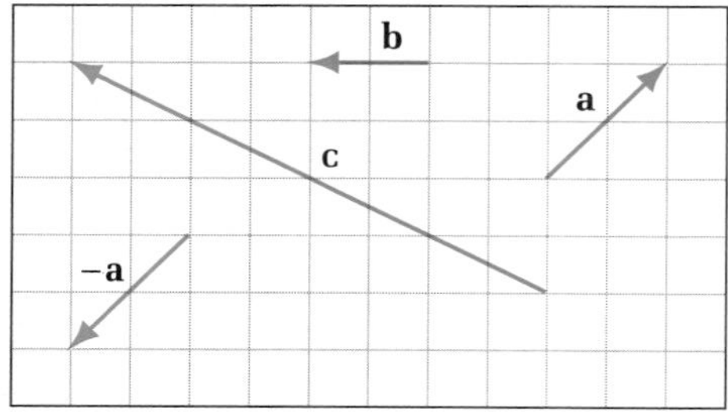

a Copy the diagram showing the vectors $\mathbf{a}$, $\mathbf{b}$, $\mathbf{c}$ and $-\mathbf{a}$. Complete a vector polygon to form the vector $-\mathbf{a} + 2\mathbf{b} - \frac{1}{2}\mathbf{c}$.

b Write the vector $\mathbf{c}$ in terms of $\mathbf{a}$ and $\mathbf{b}$.

3 What is the difference between AB and $\overrightarrow{AB}$?

4 ABCD is a parallelogram where $\overrightarrow{AD} = \mathbf{a}$ and $\overrightarrow{AB} = \mathbf{b}$. Express the vectors $\overrightarrow{BC}$, $\overrightarrow{DC}$, $\overrightarrow{AC}$ and $\overrightarrow{CA}$ in terms of $\mathbf{a}$ and $\mathbf{b}$.

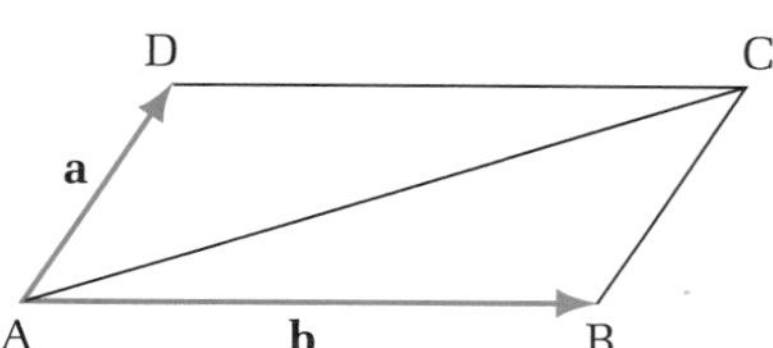

5

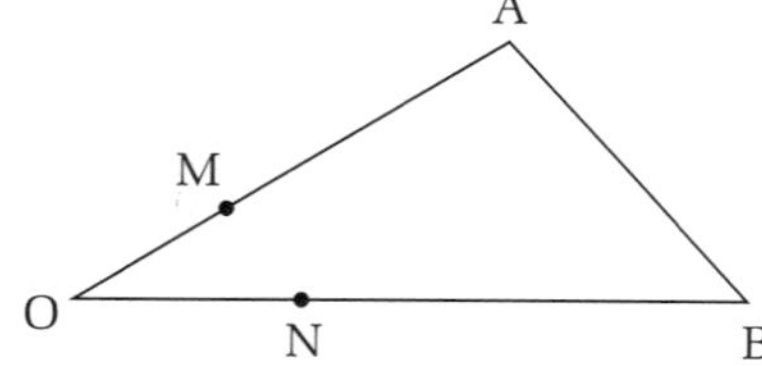

OAB is a triangle in which $\overrightarrow{OA} = \mathbf{a}$ and $\overrightarrow{OB} = \mathbf{b}$. The points M and N lie on OA and OB respectively such that $OM = \frac{1}{3}OA$ and $ON = \frac{1}{3}OB$. Write the vectors $\overrightarrow{OM}$, $\overrightarrow{ON}$, $\overrightarrow{AB}$ and $\overrightarrow{MN}$ in terms of $\mathbf{a}$ and $\mathbf{b}$. What can you say about $\overrightarrow{AB}$ and $\overrightarrow{MN}$?

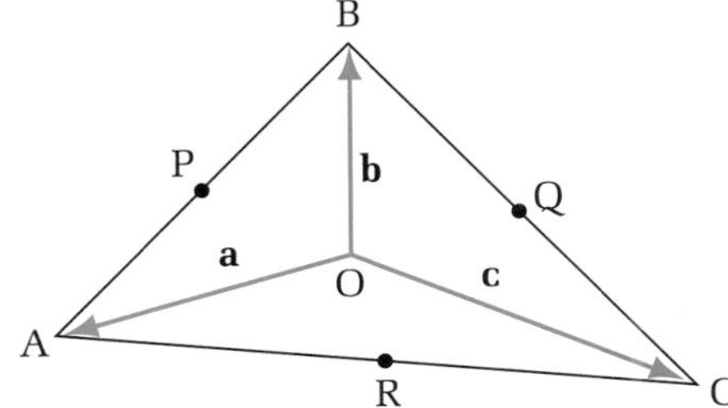

The diagram shows the triangle ABC. P, Q and R are the mid-points of AB, BC and AC respectively.

a Write expressions for the vectors $\overrightarrow{OP}$, $\overrightarrow{OQ}$ and $\overrightarrow{OR}$ in terms of **a**, **b** and **c**.

b Write down an expression for $\overrightarrow{OP} + \overrightarrow{OQ} + \overrightarrow{OR}$.

14.2 Vectors in Two and Three Dimensions

The Cartesian system uses x- and y-axes in two dimensions. In three dimensions there are three perpendicular axes; the x-, y- and z-axes. Vectors that are parallel to coordinate axes and that have a magnitude of 1 are called **base vectors**.

$\mathbf{i}$	is the base vector in the positive x direction
$\mathbf{j}$	is the base vector in the positive y direction
$\mathbf{k}$	is the base vector in the positive z direction

The base vectors **i**, **j** a k are also called **orthogonal** vectors because they are mutually perpendicu

All vectors can be written in terms of one or more of these base vectors **i**, **j** and **k**. The base vectors, like the axes, are mutually perpendicular. The starting point of the base vector is not important. They all have a magnitude of 1.

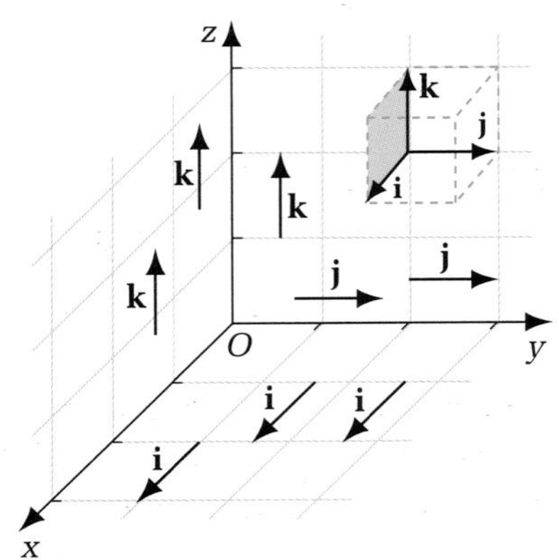

Components of a vector

The diagram shows a vector in two dimensions. The vector **v** can be described as the sum of two perpendicular vectors. The first of these is 2 units long in the direction to the base vector **i** followed by a second vector 1 unit long in the same direction as the base vector **j**.

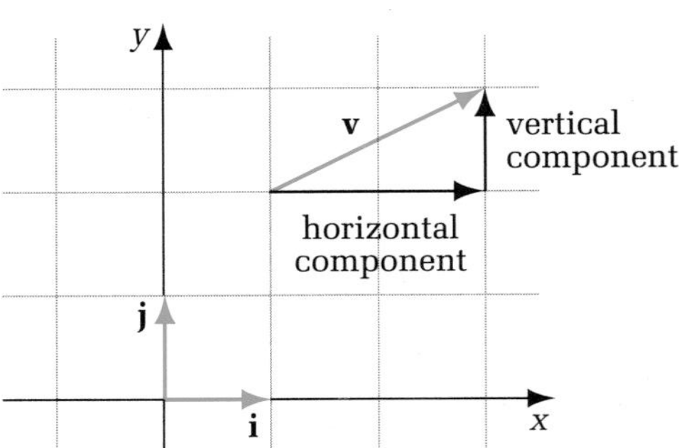

Using vector addition, the vector **v** can be written as $\mathbf{v} = 2\mathbf{i} + \mathbf{j}$. Another way of describing this vector is to use a column matrix. The top number indicates the component of the vector in the x direction and the bottom number indicates the component in the y direction. Therefore $\mathbf{v} = \binom{2}{1}$.

All vectors in two dimensions can be described by these equivalent forms:

$$\mathbf{v} = 2\mathbf{i} + \mathbf{j} = \begin{pmatrix} 2 \\ 1 \end{pmatrix}$$

Example 1

Express the vectors **a**, **b**, **c**, **d**, **t** and **u** in terms of the base vectors **i** and **j**.

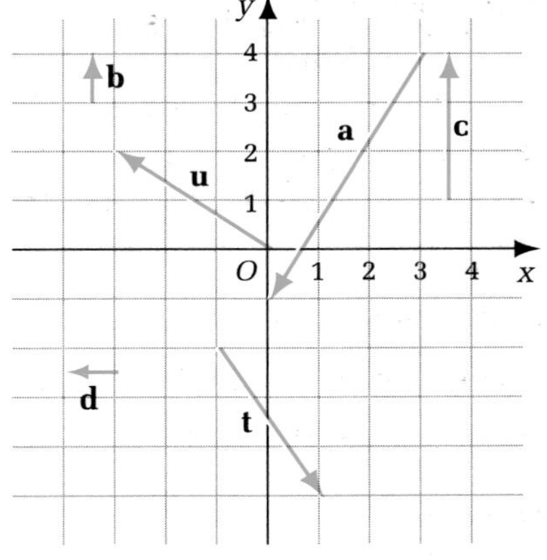

Solution

$\mathbf{a} = -3\mathbf{i} + (-5\mathbf{j}) = -3\mathbf{i} - 5\mathbf{j}$　　　$\mathbf{d} = -\mathbf{i}$

$\mathbf{b} = \mathbf{j}$　　　$\mathbf{t} = 2\mathbf{i} - 3\mathbf{j}$

$\mathbf{c} = 3\mathbf{j}$　　　$\mathbf{u} = -3\mathbf{i} + 2\mathbf{j}$

In column vector form:

$\mathbf{a} = \begin{pmatrix} -3 \\ -5 \end{pmatrix}$ $\mathbf{d} = \begin{pmatrix} -1 \\ 0 \end{pmatrix}$

$\mathbf{b} = \begin{pmatrix} 0 \\ 1 \end{pmatrix}$ $\mathbf{t} = \begin{pmatrix} 2 \\ -3 \end{pmatrix}$

$\mathbf{c} = \begin{pmatrix} 0 \\ 3 \end{pmatrix}$ $\mathbf{u} = \begin{pmatrix} -3 \\ 2 \end{pmatrix}$

Vectors in 3D space can also be expressed in terms of one or more of the base vectors. The vector **w** has a component of 2**i** in the x direction, a component of 4**j** in the y direction and a component of 3**k** in the z direction.

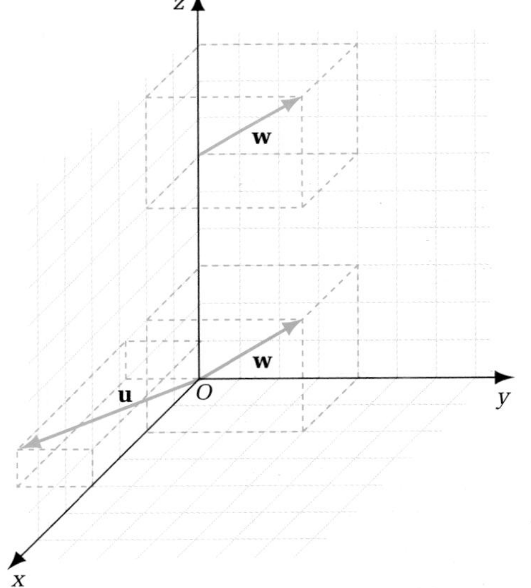

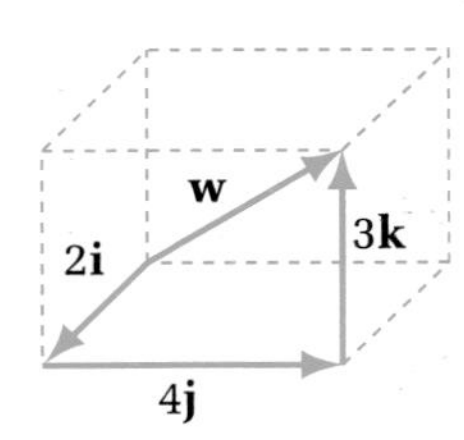

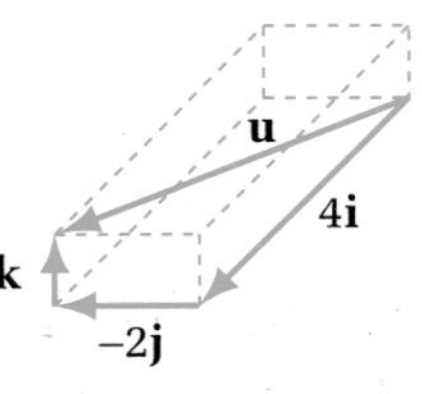

Two line segments in the diagram, one starting at the origin, the other at point (0, 0, 6) describe vector **w**. A different starting point does not make vectors with the same components different.

Using vector addition **w** can be expressed as the sum of these components.

$$\mathbf{w} = 2\mathbf{i} + 4\mathbf{j} + 3\mathbf{k}$$

Similarly, **u** has components 4**i**, −2**j** and **k** in the x, y and z directions, respectively

$$\mathbf{u} = 4\mathbf{i} - 2\mathbf{j} + \mathbf{k}$$

In column vector form the results can be summarised as

$$\mathbf{w} = \begin{pmatrix} 2 \\ 4 \\ 3 \end{pmatrix} \quad \text{and} \quad \mathbf{u} = \begin{pmatrix} 4 \\ -2 \\ 1 \end{pmatrix}$$

Example 2

The diagram shows four vectors in 3D space. Express the following vectors in terms of their **i**, **j**, and **k** components:

a $\overrightarrow{OP}$ **d** **u**
b $\overrightarrow{PQ}$ **e** **t**
c **r** **f** **s**

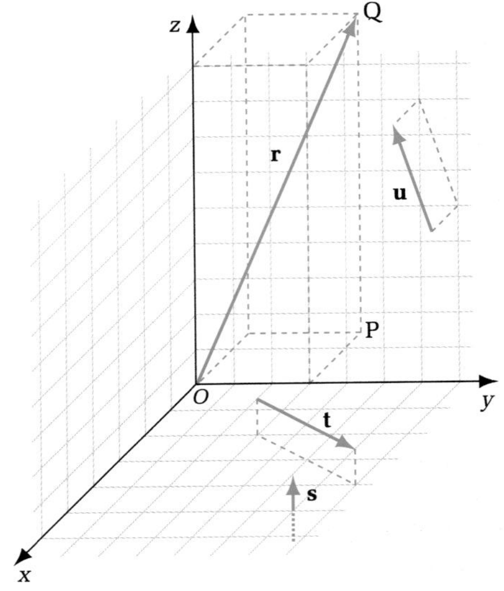

Solution

a $\overrightarrow{OP} = \begin{pmatrix} -2 \\ 3 \\ 0 \end{pmatrix} = -2\mathbf{i} + 3\mathbf{j}$

b $\overrightarrow{PQ} = \begin{pmatrix} 0 \\ 0 \\ 9 \end{pmatrix} = 9\mathbf{k}$

c $\mathbf{r} = \begin{pmatrix} -2 \\ 3 \\ 9 \end{pmatrix} = -2\mathbf{i} + 3\mathbf{j} + 9\mathbf{k}$

d $\mathbf{u} = \begin{pmatrix} 0 \\ -1 \\ 3 \end{pmatrix} = -\mathbf{j} + 3\mathbf{k}$

e $\mathbf{t} = \begin{pmatrix} 2 \\ 4 \\ 0 \end{pmatrix} = 2\mathbf{i} + 4\mathbf{j}$

f $\mathbf{s} = \begin{pmatrix} 0 \\ 0 \\ 2 \end{pmatrix} = 2\mathbf{k}$

Position vectors

A vector that starts at the origin is called a **position vector** because the tip of the vector describes the position of a point P. *All position vectors start from the origin*. So the position vector of B is the vector that starts from the origin and ends at B; $\mathbf{b} = \overrightarrow{OB} = \binom{1}{3}$. The position vectors of A, C, D, E, F and G are: $\binom{4}{0}$, $\binom{-2}{1}$, $\binom{-5}{0}$, $\binom{-3}{-1}$, $\binom{0}{-3}$, and $\binom{3}{-2}$, respectively.

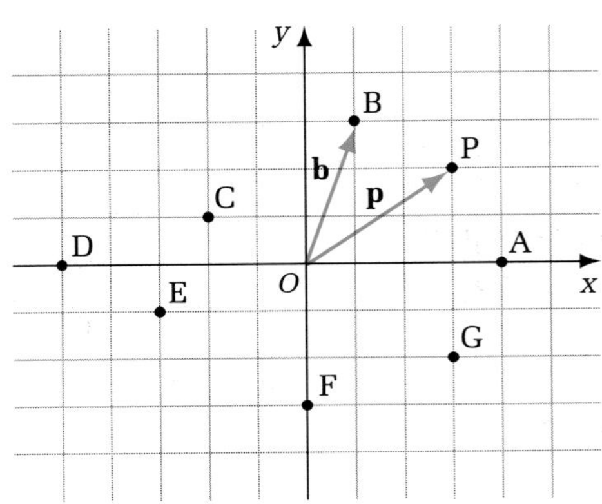

In three dimensions, position vectors also begin at the origin. The diagram shows two vectors both equal to $-2\mathbf{i} + 5\mathbf{j} + 4\mathbf{k}$.

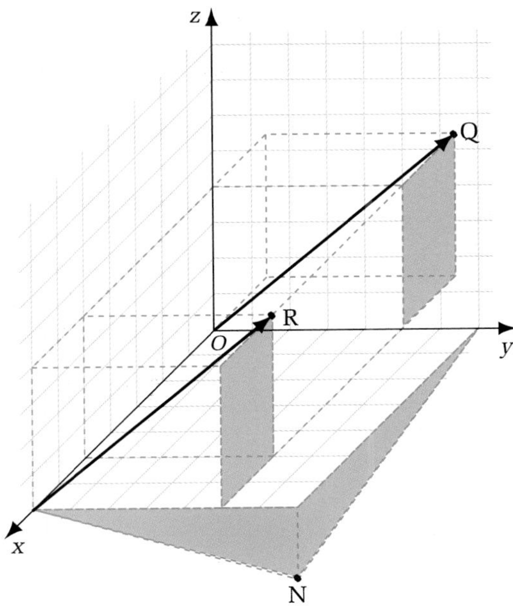

The position vector of Q is again given by the vector that starts at the origin and finishes at Q.

$$\overrightarrow{OQ} = \begin{pmatrix} -2 \\ 5 \\ 4 \end{pmatrix} = -2\mathbf{i} + 5\mathbf{j} + 4\mathbf{k}$$

Check that the position vectors of the points R and N are $5\mathbf{i} + 5\mathbf{j} + 4\mathbf{k}$ and $7\mathbf{i} + 7\mathbf{j} - 2\mathbf{k}$ respectively.

$\overrightarrow{OR} = \begin{pmatrix} 5 \\ 5 \\ 4 \end{pmatrix}$ and $\overrightarrow{ON} = \begin{pmatrix} 7 \\ 7 \\ -2 \end{pmatrix}$.

Magnitude of a vector

The **magnitude** (or size) of a vector is represented by the length of the directed line segment.

The diagram shows vectors $\mathbf{s} = 3\mathbf{i}$, $\mathbf{t} = -2\mathbf{j}$, $\mathbf{u} = \mathbf{i} + 2\mathbf{j}$ and $\mathbf{v} = -3\mathbf{i} - 4\mathbf{j}$. The magnitudes of vectors **s** and **t** can be written down straightaway using modulus notation.

$|\mathbf{s}| = 3 \qquad |\mathbf{t}| = 2$

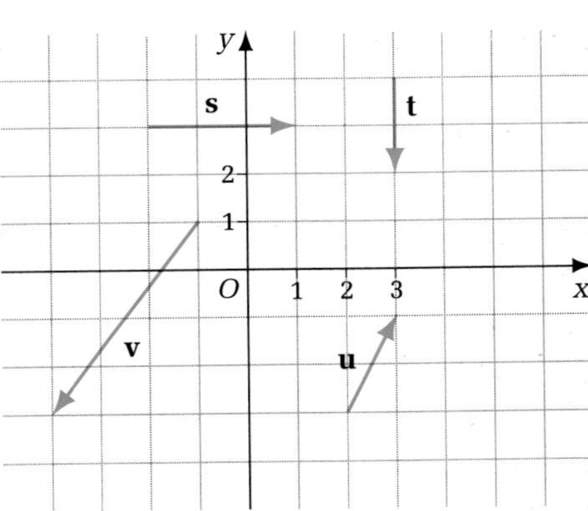

Using column vectors,

$\mathbf{s} = \binom{3}{0} \quad \mathbf{t} = \binom{0}{-2}$

$\mathbf{u} = \binom{1}{2} \quad \mathbf{v} = \binom{-3}{-4}$

When the vector is in the form $\mathbf{a} = a_1\mathbf{i} + a_2\mathbf{j}$ or $\binom{a_1}{a_2}$, we use Pythagoras' theorem to find the magnitude of $\mathbf{a}$ in terms of its rectangular components a_1 and a_2.

By Pythagoras' theorem

$$a^2 = a_1^2 + a_2^2$$

$$\Rightarrow \quad a = \sqrt{a_1^2 + a_2^2}$$

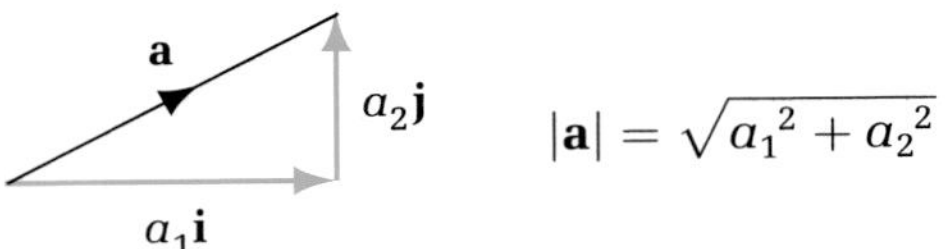

$$|\mathbf{a}| = \sqrt{a_1^2 + a_2^2}$$

We can find $|\mathbf{u}|$ and $|\mathbf{v}|$ using this result.

$$|\mathbf{u}| = \sqrt{1^2 + 2^2} = \sqrt{5} \qquad |\mathbf{v}| = \sqrt{(-3)^2 + (-4)^2} = \sqrt{25} = 5$$

If the vector is a 3D vector then $\mathbf{a} = a_1\mathbf{i} + a_2\mathbf{j} + a_3\mathbf{k}$.

Using Pythagoras' theorem twice,

$$NM^2 = NP^2 + PM^2$$
$$= NP^2 + a_3^2$$
$$= a_1^2 + a_2^2 + a_3^2$$

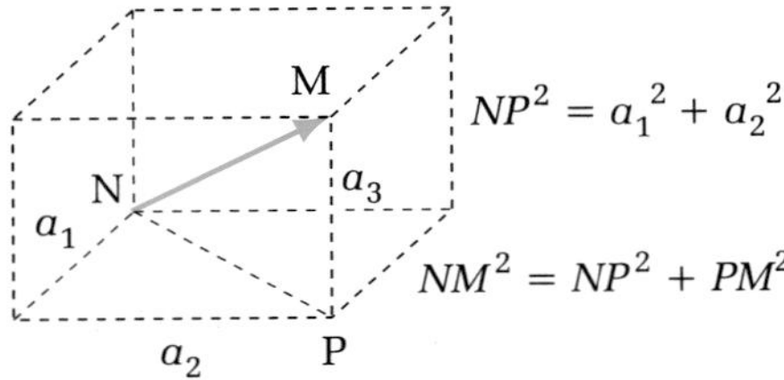

The magnitude of $\mathbf{a}$ is given by

$$|\mathbf{a}| = \sqrt{a_1^2 + a_2^2 + a_3^2}$$

◀ **Learn this result.**

Unit vectors

A **unit vector** is exactly one unit long. The base vectors **i**, **j** and **k**, are examples of unit vectors, but there are unit vectors in many other directions.

This diagram shows the vector $\mathbf{w} = \binom{3}{-4}$. The magnitude of $\mathbf{w}$ is

$$|\mathbf{w}| = \sqrt{3^2 + (-4)^2} = \sqrt{25} = 5$$

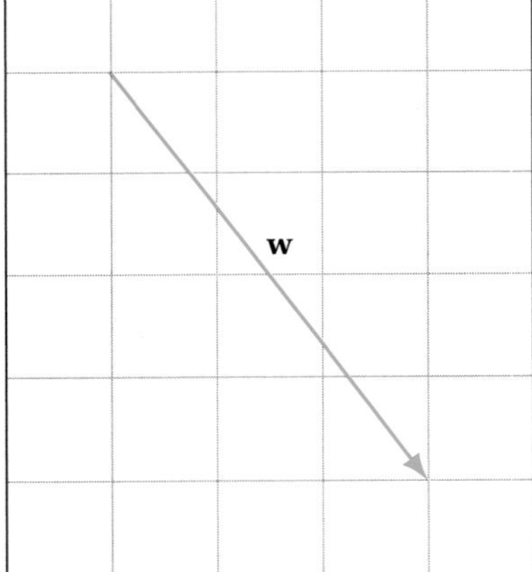

This means that a vector in the same direction as $\mathbf{w}$ but having $\frac{1}{5}$ of its magnitude will be a unit vector. This unit vector in the direction of $\mathbf{w}$, denoted by $\hat{\mathbf{w}}$, is given by.

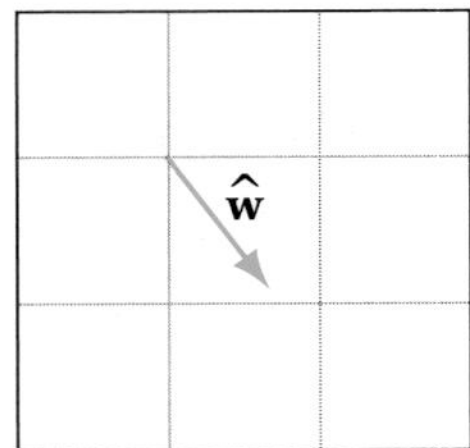

$$\hat{\mathbf{w}} = \frac{1}{5}\begin{pmatrix} 3 \\ -4 \end{pmatrix} = \begin{pmatrix} 0.6 \\ -0.8 \end{pmatrix}$$

This can be generalised so that if each component of a vector is divided by the magnitude of that vector, then the result is a unit vector parallel to the original vector. Algebraically,

$$\hat{\mathbf{a}} = \frac{\mathbf{a}}{|\mathbf{a}|}$$

Example 3

Find the unit vector in the same direction as the vector $\mathbf{a} = \begin{pmatrix} -2 \\ 2 \\ 3 \end{pmatrix}$.

Solution

The magnitude of **a** is

$$|\mathbf{a}| = \sqrt{(-2)^2 + 2^2 + 3^2} = \sqrt{17}$$

So the unit vector in the same direction as **a** is

$$\hat{\mathbf{a}} = \frac{1}{\sqrt{17}}\begin{pmatrix} -2 \\ 2 \\ 3 \end{pmatrix}$$

$$\hat{\mathbf{a}} = \begin{pmatrix} \frac{-2}{\sqrt{17}} \\ \frac{2}{\sqrt{17}} \\ \frac{3}{\sqrt{17}} \end{pmatrix}$$

Vector algebra

Multiplying a vector by a scalar

The diagram shows the vector $\mathbf{v} = -3\mathbf{i} + 2\mathbf{j}$, and vectors $2\mathbf{v}$, $\frac{1}{2}\mathbf{v}$ and $-\mathbf{v}$.

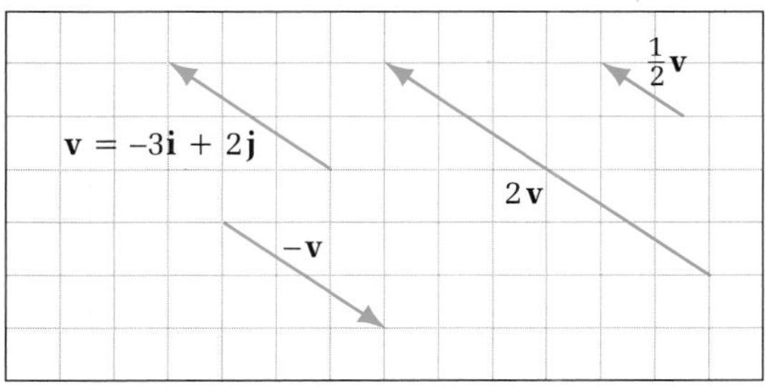

We can see that

$$2\mathbf{v} = 2\begin{pmatrix} -3 \\ 2 \end{pmatrix} = \begin{pmatrix} -6 \\ 4 \end{pmatrix}$$

Alternatively

$$\begin{aligned} 2\mathbf{v} &= 2 \times (-3\mathbf{i} + 2\mathbf{j}) \\ &= (2 \times -3)\mathbf{i} + (2 \times 2)\mathbf{j} \\ &= -6\mathbf{i} + 4\mathbf{j} \end{aligned}$$

If each component of **v** is multiplied by $\frac{1}{2}$, the vector $-1.5\mathbf{i} + \mathbf{j}$ would be obtained. This is the vector $\frac{1}{2}\mathbf{v}$. If each component was multiplied by -1, the vector $3\mathbf{i} - 2\mathbf{j}$ would be obtained. This is the vector $-\mathbf{v}$.

Check that $\frac{1}{2}\mathbf{v} = \begin{pmatrix} -1.5 \\ 2 \end{pmatrix}$ and $-\mathbf{v} = \begin{pmatrix} 3 \\ -2 \end{pmatrix}$.

This principle is also true for vectors in three dimensions. If $\mathbf{a} = a_1\mathbf{i} + a_2\mathbf{j} + a_3\mathbf{k}$ and λ is a scalar (real number), then

$$\text{or} \quad \lambda\mathbf{a} = \lambda\begin{pmatrix} a_1 \\ a_2 \\ a_3 \end{pmatrix} = \begin{pmatrix} \lambda a_1 \\ \lambda a_2 \\ \lambda a_3 \end{pmatrix}$$

Addition and subtraction of vectors in component form

The diagram below shows vectors $\mathbf{v} = -3\mathbf{i} + 2\mathbf{j}$ and $\mathbf{w} = 4\mathbf{i} + \mathbf{j}$, and the geometric construction of their sum and difference.

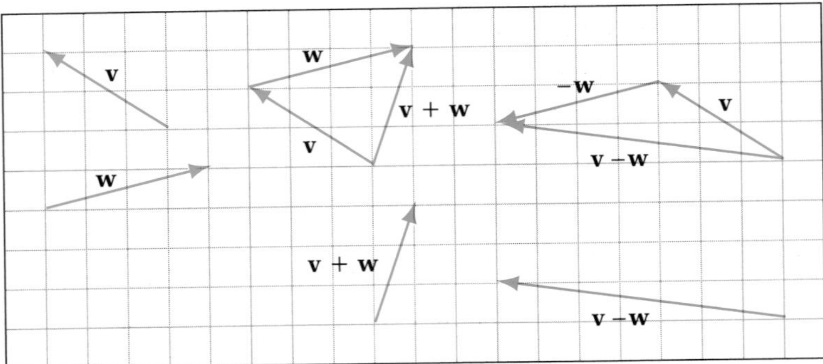

Check that the sum of two vectors can easily be obtained by adding the corresponding **i** and **j** components together and the difference can be obtained by subtracting the corresponding **i** and **j** components.

Verify that $\mathbf{v} + \mathbf{w} = \mathbf{i} + 3\mathbf{j}$ and $\mathbf{v} - \mathbf{w} = -7\mathbf{i} + \mathbf{j}$.

Again this principle of addition and subtraction of vectors is repeated for vectors in 3D.

If $\mathbf{a} = \begin{pmatrix} a_1 \\ a_2 \\ a_3 \end{pmatrix}$ and $\mathbf{b} = \begin{pmatrix} b_1 \\ b_2 \\ b_3 \end{pmatrix}$

then $\mathbf{a} + \mathbf{b} = \begin{pmatrix} a_1 \\ a_2 \\ a_3 \end{pmatrix} + \begin{pmatrix} b_1 \\ b_2 \\ b_3 \end{pmatrix} = \begin{pmatrix} a_1 + b_1 \\ a_2 + b_2 \\ a_3 + b_3 \end{pmatrix}$

and $\mathbf{a} - \mathbf{b} = \begin{pmatrix} a_1 \\ a_2 \\ a_3 \end{pmatrix} - \begin{pmatrix} b_1 \\ b_2 \\ b_3 \end{pmatrix} = \begin{pmatrix} a_1 - b_1 \\ a_2 - b_2 \\ a_3 - b_3 \end{pmatrix}$

Example 4

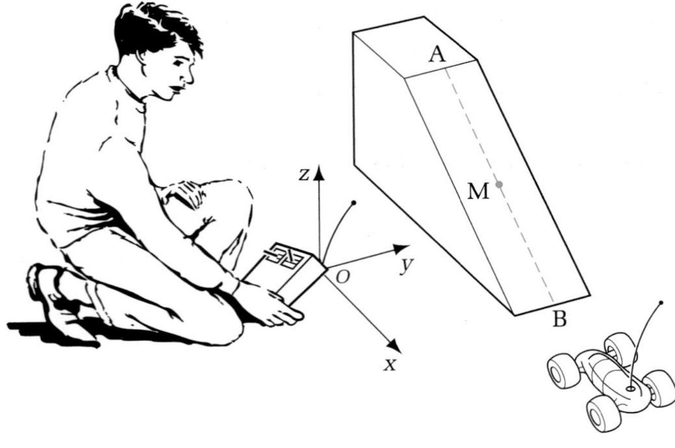

Part of a course for a remote control car is to steer the car up the middle of a ramp marked by a dotted line. A child has the remote control transmitter and is positioned at the point $(0, 0, 0)$. The coordinates of A are $(-2, 5, 4)$ and the coordinates of B are $(2, 4, 0)$ measured in metres.

a Write down the position vectors of the points A and B.

b Find the position vector of the point M half way up the ramp.

c When the car is half way up the ramp, how high is it above the ground? What distance is the car from the transmitter at this point?

Solution

a The position vectors of A and B are $\overrightarrow{OA} = \begin{pmatrix} -2 \\ 5 \\ 4 \end{pmatrix}$ and $\overrightarrow{OB} = \begin{pmatrix} 2 \\ 4 \\ 0 \end{pmatrix}$.

$\overrightarrow{OA} = -2\mathbf{i} + 5\mathbf{j} + 4\mathbf{k}$

$\overrightarrow{OB} = -2\mathbf{i} + 4\mathbf{j}$

b A diagram will help us to find $\overrightarrow{OM}$. The position vector of M is

$$\overrightarrow{OM} = \overrightarrow{OA} + \overrightarrow{AM}$$

$$= \overrightarrow{OA} + \tfrac{1}{2}\overrightarrow{AB} \quad \text{and} \quad \overrightarrow{AB} = \overrightarrow{AO} + \overrightarrow{OB}$$

$$\overrightarrow{AB} = -\begin{pmatrix} -2 \\ 5 \\ 4 \end{pmatrix} + \begin{pmatrix} 2 \\ 4 \\ 0 \end{pmatrix} = \begin{pmatrix} 4 \\ -1 \\ -4 \end{pmatrix}$$

Now $\overrightarrow{OM} = \overrightarrow{OA} + \tfrac{1}{2}\overrightarrow{AB}$

$$\overrightarrow{OM} = \begin{pmatrix} -2 \\ 5 \\ 4 \end{pmatrix} + \tfrac{1}{2}\begin{pmatrix} 4 \\ -1 \\ -4 \end{pmatrix} = \begin{pmatrix} 0 \\ 4\frac{1}{2} \\ 2 \end{pmatrix}$$

Alternatively,
$$\overrightarrow{OM} = \tfrac{1}{2}(\overrightarrow{OA} + \overrightarrow{OB}) = \tfrac{1}{2}\begin{pmatrix} 0 \\ 9 \\ 4 \end{pmatrix} = \begin{pmatrix} 0 \\ 4\frac{1}{2} \\ 2 \end{pmatrix}$$

c The component in the $\mathbf{k}$ direction (parallel to the z-axis) will indicate how high the car is above the ground. This is because O is at ground level. Since $\overrightarrow{OM} = 4\frac{1}{2}\mathbf{j} + 2\mathbf{k}$ the $\mathbf{k}$ component is 2. So the car is 2 m from the ground.
The distance from the transmitter is OM, the magnitude of the vector $\overrightarrow{OM}$.

$$OM = |\overrightarrow{OM}|$$

$$= \sqrt{0^2 + 4.5^2 + 2^2}$$

$$= \sqrt{24.25}$$

$$= 4.9 \text{ (2 s.f.)}$$

So when the car is at point M it is 4.9 m from the transmitter.

Example 5

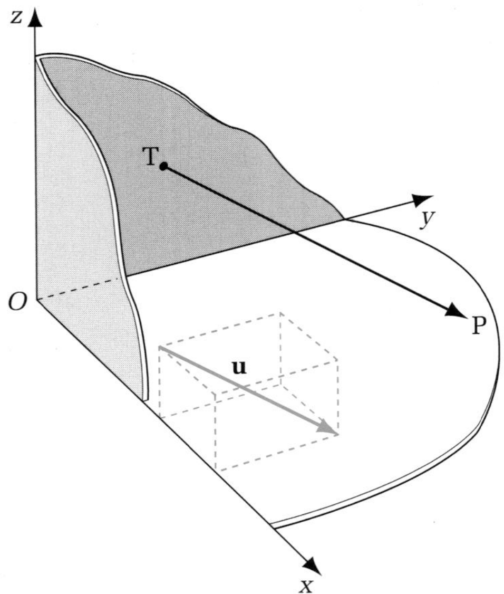

The diagram shows the vector $\mathbf{u} = 3\mathbf{i} + 4\mathbf{j} - 2\mathbf{k}$. Another vector, which is parallel to $\mathbf{u}$, starts at T $(0, 5, 6)$ and cuts the x–y plane at P. Find the coordinates of P.

$\mathbf{u} = \begin{pmatrix} 3 \\ 4 \\ -2 \end{pmatrix}$

Solution

To find the coordinates of P it is necessary to find the position vector of P. Using vector addition,

$$\overrightarrow{OP} = \overrightarrow{OT} + \overrightarrow{TP}$$

$$\overrightarrow{OP} = 5\mathbf{j} + 6\mathbf{k} + \overrightarrow{TP}$$

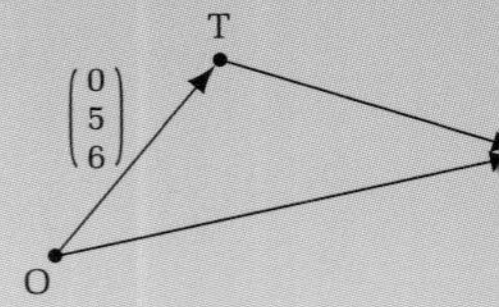

Since $\overrightarrow{TP}$ is parallel to $\mathbf{u}$, $\overrightarrow{TP}$ must be a multiple of $\mathbf{u}$. So let $\overrightarrow{TP} = \lambda\mathbf{u}$ where λ is a number.

$$\text{Then} \quad \overrightarrow{OP} = (5\mathbf{j} + 6\mathbf{k}) + \lambda(3\mathbf{i} + 4\mathbf{j} - 2\mathbf{k})$$
$$= (5\mathbf{j} + 6\mathbf{k}) + (3\lambda\mathbf{i} + 4\lambda\mathbf{j} - 2\lambda\mathbf{k})$$
$$= 3\lambda\mathbf{i} + (5 + 4\lambda)\mathbf{j} + (6 - 2\lambda)\mathbf{k}$$

$\overrightarrow{OP} = \begin{pmatrix} 0 \\ 5 \\ 6 \end{pmatrix} + \lambda\begin{pmatrix} 3 \\ 4 \\ -2 \end{pmatrix}$

$= \begin{pmatrix} 3\lambda \\ 5 + 4\lambda \\ 6 - 2\lambda \end{pmatrix}$

We know that P lies on the x–y plane, so the z-coordinate of P is zero. Equating the z-coordinates,

$$6 - 2\lambda = 0 \quad \Rightarrow \quad \lambda = 3$$

Substitute $\lambda = 3$ into the expression for $\overrightarrow{OP}$.
Now $\overrightarrow{OP} = 9\mathbf{i} + 17\mathbf{j}$ and the coordinates of P are $(9, 17, 0)$.

$\overrightarrow{OP} = \begin{pmatrix} 9 \\ 17 \\ 0 \end{pmatrix}$

Example 6

The right pyramid ABCDV shown in the diagram has a rectangular base ABCD which makes an angle of 45° with the plane $z = 0$. The coordinates of the points A and D are $(0, 3, 3)$ and $(0, 6, 3)$ respectively. The height of the pyramid is $2\sqrt{2}$ units and is denoted by MV where M is the mid-point of the base.

Recall that the vertex of a right pyramid is directly above the centre of the base.

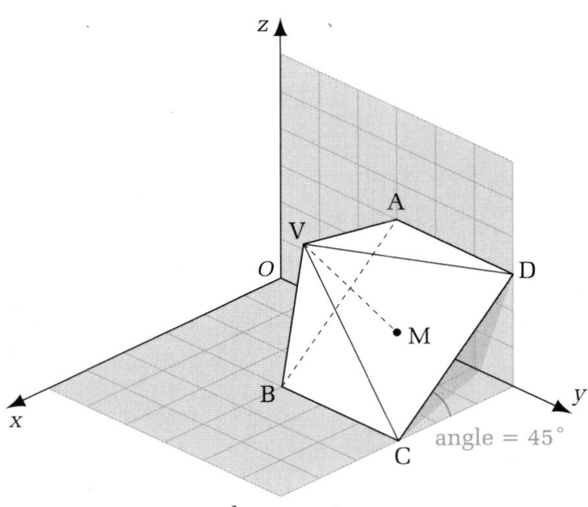

a Find the position vectors of the points A, B, C, D and M.

b Write down a vector that is perpendicular to the base and hence find $\hat{\mathbf{n}}$, the unit vector in this direction.

c Find the vector $\overrightarrow{MV}$. Then find the position vector of the vertex V.

d Find the magnitude of the vector $\overrightarrow{AB}$. Then state the volume of the pyramid.

Solution

a

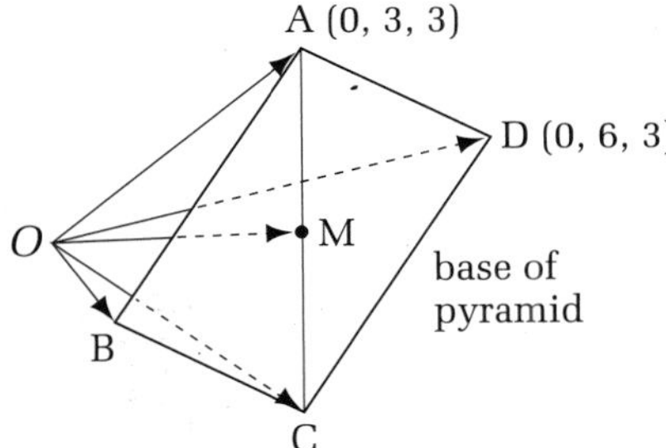

The position vectors of points A, B, C, D and M are the vectors $\overrightarrow{OA}$, $\overrightarrow{OB}$, $\overrightarrow{OC}$, $\overrightarrow{OD}$ and $\overrightarrow{OM}$, respectively.

From the coordinates of A $(0, 3, 3)$, $\overrightarrow{OA} = 3\mathbf{j} + 3\mathbf{k}$

$\overrightarrow{OA} = \begin{pmatrix} 0 \\ 3 \\ 3 \end{pmatrix}$

From the coordinates of D $(0, 6, 3)$, $\overrightarrow{OD} = 6\mathbf{j} + 3\mathbf{k}$

$\overrightarrow{OD} = \begin{pmatrix} 0 \\ 6 \\ 3 \end{pmatrix}$

By symmetry (looking at the diagram and knowing that the angle that the base of the pyramid makes with the x–y plane is 45°), the coordinates of B are $(3, 3, 0)$.

$\overrightarrow{OB} = 3\mathbf{i} + 3\mathbf{j}$

$\overrightarrow{OB} = \begin{pmatrix} 3 \\ 3 \\ 0 \end{pmatrix}$

The position vector of C is $\overrightarrow{OC}$. The base of the pyramid is a rectangle, so $\overrightarrow{AD} = \overrightarrow{BC}$.

$$\begin{aligned}\overrightarrow{AD} = \overrightarrow{AO} + \overrightarrow{OD} &= -\overrightarrow{OA} + \overrightarrow{OD}\\ &= -(3\mathbf{j} + 3\mathbf{k}) + (6\mathbf{j} + 3\mathbf{k})\\ &= 3\mathbf{j}\end{aligned}$$

$$\begin{aligned}\text{Now}\quad \overrightarrow{OC} &= \overrightarrow{OB} + \overrightarrow{BC}\\ &= (3\mathbf{i} + 3\mathbf{j}) + (3\mathbf{j})\\ &= 3\mathbf{i} + 6\mathbf{j}\end{aligned}$$

$$\overrightarrow{OC} = \begin{pmatrix}3\\6\\0\end{pmatrix}$$

M is the centre of the base ABCD, so $\overrightarrow{AM} = \frac{1}{2}\overrightarrow{AC}$.

$$\begin{aligned}\overrightarrow{AC} = \overrightarrow{AO} + \overrightarrow{OC} &= -\overrightarrow{OA} + \overrightarrow{OC}\\ &= -(3\mathbf{j} + 3\mathbf{k}) + (3\mathbf{i} + 6\mathbf{j})\\ &= 3\mathbf{i} + 3\mathbf{j} - 3\mathbf{k}\end{aligned}$$

$$\begin{aligned}\text{Now}\quad \overrightarrow{OM} &= \overrightarrow{OA} + \overrightarrow{AM}\\ &= (3\mathbf{j} + 3\mathbf{k}) + \tfrac{1}{2}\overrightarrow{AC}\\ &= (3\mathbf{j} + 3\mathbf{k}) + \tfrac{1}{2}(3\mathbf{i} + 3\mathbf{j} - 3\mathbf{k})\\ &= 3\mathbf{j} + 3\mathbf{k} + \tfrac{3}{2}\mathbf{i} + \tfrac{3}{2}\mathbf{j} - \tfrac{3}{2}\mathbf{k}\\ &= \tfrac{3}{2}\mathbf{i} + \tfrac{9}{2}\mathbf{j} + \tfrac{3}{2}\mathbf{k}\\ &= \tfrac{1}{2}(3\mathbf{i} + 9\mathbf{j} + 3\mathbf{k})\\ &= \tfrac{3}{2}(\mathbf{i} + 3\mathbf{j} + \mathbf{k})\end{aligned}$$

Alternatively,

$$\begin{aligned}\overrightarrow{OM} &= \tfrac{1}{2}(\overrightarrow{OA} + \overrightarrow{OC})\\ &= \tfrac{1}{2}\left[\begin{pmatrix}0\\3\\3\end{pmatrix} + \begin{pmatrix}3\\6\\0\end{pmatrix}\right]\\ &= \tfrac{1}{2}\begin{pmatrix}3\\9\\3\end{pmatrix}\\ \overrightarrow{OM} &= \tfrac{1}{2}\begin{pmatrix}3\\9\\3\end{pmatrix} = \tfrac{3}{2}\begin{pmatrix}1\\3\\1\end{pmatrix}\end{aligned}$$

b Vectors that are perpendicular to the base will be in a plane parallel to the x–z plane. By drawing a side-on view of the base of the pyramid in the x–z plane ($y = 0$), we can see that $\mathbf{i} + \mathbf{k}$ and $2\mathbf{i} + 2\mathbf{k}$ are two examples.

The magnitude of $\mathbf{i} + \mathbf{k}$ is

$$\begin{aligned}|\mathbf{i} + \mathbf{k}| &= \sqrt{(1)^2 + (0)^2 + (1)^2}\\ &= \sqrt{1 + 0 + 1}\\ &= \sqrt{2}\end{aligned}$$

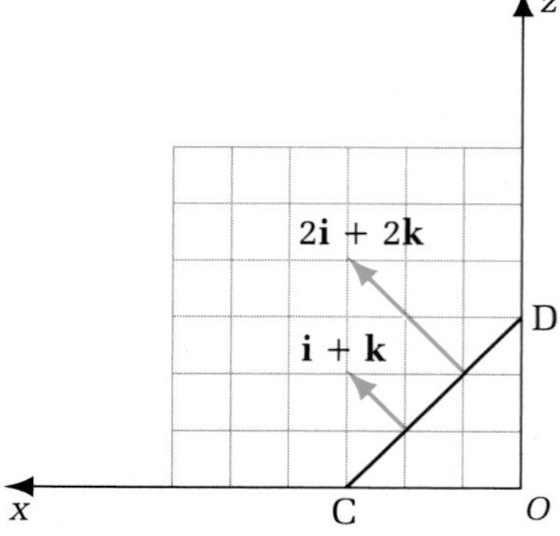

Component in the y direction is zero; $\mathbf{i} + \mathbf{k} = \mathbf{i} + 0\mathbf{j} + \mathbf{k}$

So the unit vector in this direction is $\hat{\mathbf{n}}$ where

$$\hat{\mathbf{n}} = \frac{1}{\sqrt{2}}(\mathbf{i} + \mathbf{k}) = \frac{1}{\sqrt{2}}\mathbf{i} + \frac{1}{\sqrt{2}}\mathbf{k}$$

c The vector $\overrightarrow{MV}$ is in the direction of the unit vector but is $2\sqrt{2}$ units long.

$$\overrightarrow{MV} = 2\sqrt{2}\left(\frac{1}{\sqrt{2}}\mathbf{i} + \frac{1}{\sqrt{2}}\mathbf{k}\right)$$
$$= 2\mathbf{i} + 2\mathbf{k}$$

The position vector of the vertex V is $\overrightarrow{OV}$.

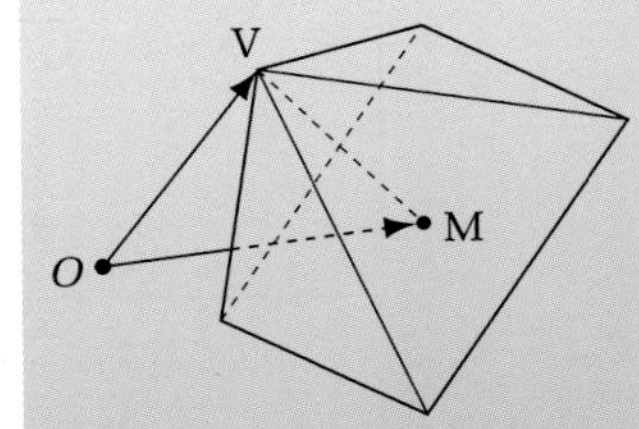

$$\overrightarrow{OV} = \overrightarrow{OM} + \overrightarrow{MV}$$
$$= \tfrac{1}{2}(3\mathbf{i} + 9\mathbf{j} + 3\mathbf{k}) + (2\mathbf{i} + 2\mathbf{k})$$
$$= \tfrac{1}{2}(7\mathbf{i} + 9\mathbf{j} + 7\mathbf{k})$$

d
$$\overrightarrow{AB} = \overrightarrow{AO} + \overrightarrow{OB}$$
$$= -\overrightarrow{OA} + \overrightarrow{OB}$$
$$= -(3\mathbf{j} + 3\mathbf{k}) + (3\mathbf{i} + 3\mathbf{j})$$
$$= -3\mathbf{j} - 3\mathbf{k} + 3\mathbf{i} + 3\mathbf{j}$$
$$= 3\mathbf{i} - 3\mathbf{k}$$

The magnitude of $\overrightarrow{AB}$ is therefore

$$|\overrightarrow{AB}| = \sqrt{(3)^2 + (0)^2 + (-3)^2}$$
$$= \sqrt{9 + 0 + 9}$$
$$= \sqrt{18}$$
$$= 3\sqrt{2} \text{ units}$$

The volume can be calculated because both the area of the base and the perpendicular height can be established.

$$\text{volume} = \tfrac{1}{3}(\text{area of base}) \times \text{height}$$
$$= \tfrac{1}{3}(3 \times 3\sqrt{2}) \times 2\sqrt{2}$$
$$= 12 \text{ cubic units.}$$

14.2 Vectors in Two and Three Dimensions

Exercise

Technique

1

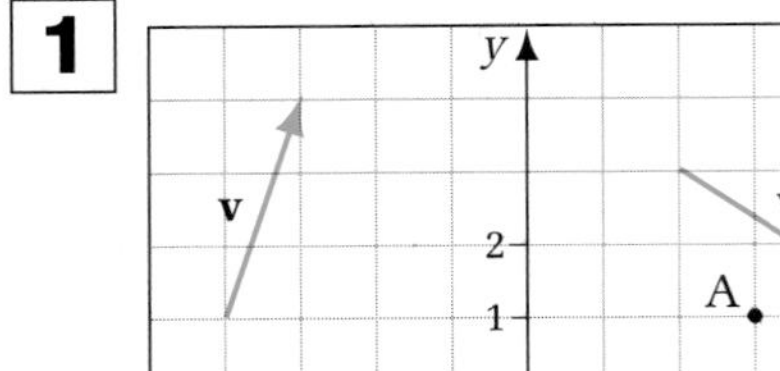

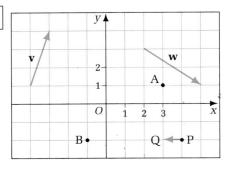

The diagram shows the x–y plane.

a Describe the vectors $\mathbf{v}$, $\mathbf{w}$ and $\overrightarrow{PQ}$ using the base vectors $\mathbf{i}$ and $\mathbf{j}$.

b Write the vectors $\mathbf{v}$, $\mathbf{w}$ and $\overrightarrow{PQ}$ as column vectors.

c Write down the position vectors of points A and B.

d Find $|\mathbf{v}|$.

e Find the unit vector in the direction of $\mathbf{w}$.

f Find, in column vector form, the vectors $2\mathbf{v}$, $\mathbf{v}+\mathbf{w}$, $\mathbf{v}-\mathbf{w}$ and $\frac{1}{2}\mathbf{w}$.

2

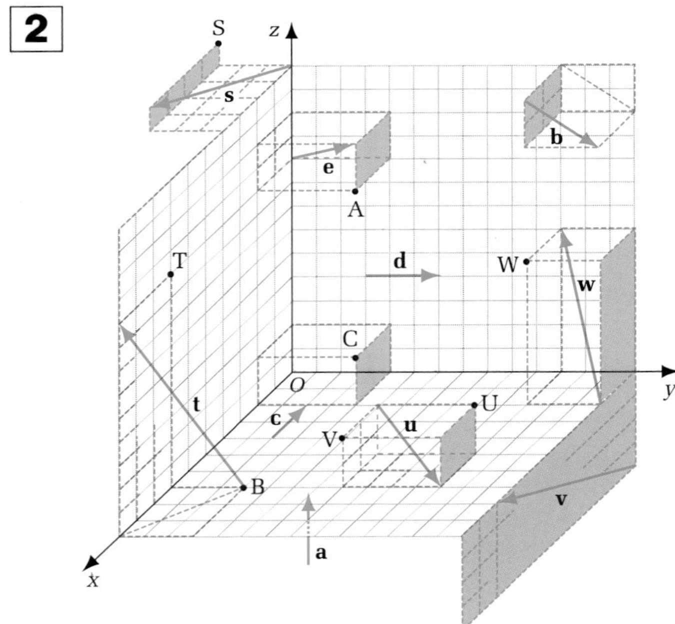

The diagram shows vectors and points in 3D.

a Write down the vectors, $\mathbf{a}$, $\mathbf{b}$, $\mathbf{c}$, $\mathbf{d}$, $\mathbf{e}$, $\mathbf{s}$, $\mathbf{t}$, $\mathbf{u}$ and $\mathbf{v}$ as column vectors.

b Write down the position vectors of points A, B, C, D, S, and T, using column vectors.

c Write down the coordinates of points S, T, U, V and W. What is the connection between the coordinates of a point and its position vector?

d Find the magnitude of vectors **a**, **b**, **c**, **d** and **t**.

e Find a unit vector in the direction of **w**.

f Using your answers to part **b** find the position vector of the mid-point of the line TB.

3

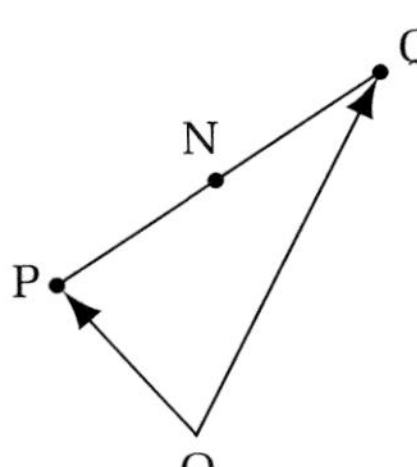

Points P and Q have position vectors $\begin{pmatrix} 9 \\ 0 \\ 4 \end{pmatrix}$ and $\begin{pmatrix} -5 \\ 4 \\ -6 \end{pmatrix}$ respectively. Point N is the mid-point of PQ as shown in the diagram.

a Write down vector $\overrightarrow{PQ}$ in column vector form.

b Find the position vector of N.

c How far is N from the origin?

4 Points A and B have coordinates $(-5, 3, 0)$and $(-7, 6, 6)$.

a Draw a sketch labelling the origin as O.

b Use vector algebra to find the vector $\overrightarrow{AB}$.

c Find a vector that is in the same direction as $\overrightarrow{AB}$ but is exactly 2 units long.

d If M is the mid-point of AB, find the coordinates of M.

5 Point R has position vector $\mathbf{i} - 4\mathbf{j} + 5\mathbf{k}$ and point S has position vector $4\mathbf{i} + 2\mathbf{j} - 4\mathbf{k}$. Point N divides the line RS in the ratio $1:2$.

a Draw a sketch of this situation which includes the points R, S, N and the origin O.

b Find the position vector of N.

6 Points A, B, and C, have coordinates $(2, -7, 3)$, $(1, -4, 7)$ and $(3, -7, -2)$ respectively. They form a triangle ABC.

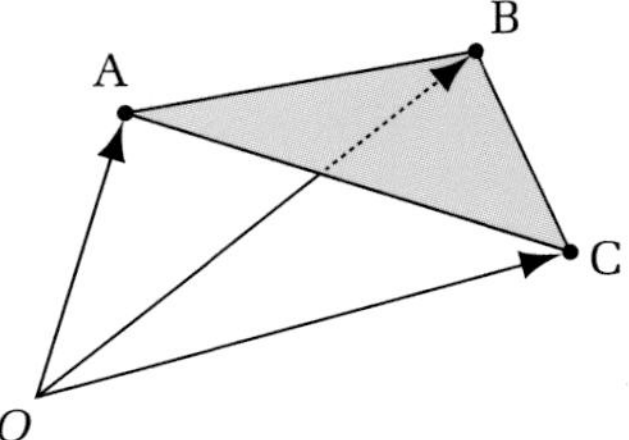

a Write down the vectors $\overrightarrow{OA}$, $\overrightarrow{OB}$ and $\overrightarrow{OC}$.

b Find the vectors $\overrightarrow{AB}$, $\overrightarrow{AC}$, and $\overrightarrow{BC}$.

c Find $|\overrightarrow{AB}|$, $|\overrightarrow{AC}|$ and $|\overrightarrow{BC}|$.

d What sort of triangle is ABC?

14.3 The Scalar Product

We have seen that given two vectors **a** and **b**, expressions can be found for $\mathbf{a}+\mathbf{b}$ and $\mathbf{a}-\mathbf{b}$. These can also be represented on diagrams using directed line segments. But can these two vectors be multiplied together?
It is possible to multiply their two magnitudes $|\mathbf{a}|$ and $|\mathbf{b}|$ together since these are just numbers. However, the 'multiplication' of their directions requires more careful consideration.
If **a** and **b** are any two vectors and θ is the angle between these two vectors, then the size of the angle θ can range from 0 to π. This is illustrated in the diagram below.

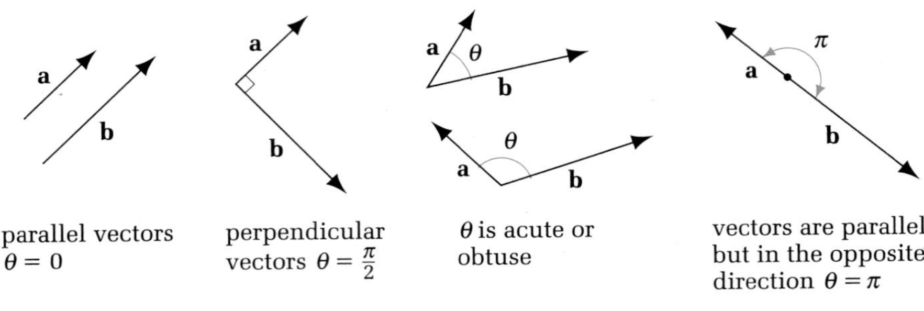

parallel vectors $\theta = 0$ | perpendicular vectors $\theta = \frac{\pi}{2}$ | θ is acute or obtuse | vectors are parallel but in the opposite direction $\theta = \pi$

The **scalar product** (or **dot product**) of the two vectors **a** and **b** is denoted by **a.b** (pronounced **a** dot **b**). The definition of the scalar product of the two vectors **a** and **b** is

$$\mathbf{a}.\mathbf{b} = ab\cos\theta$$

◀ **Learn this important result.**

where a is the magnitude of vector **a**, b is the magnitude of vector **b**, and θ is the angle between the two vectors ($0 \le \theta \le \pi$).
The product of the vectors in this definition is a *scalar*. It has no direction even though the vectors **a** and **b** do.

The diagram below shows three vectors **a**, **b** and **c** where $\mathbf{a} = -3\mathbf{k}$, $\mathbf{b} = 4\mathbf{i} - 4\mathbf{k}$ and $\mathbf{c} = 2\mathbf{i} - 3\mathbf{j} + 6\mathbf{k}$.

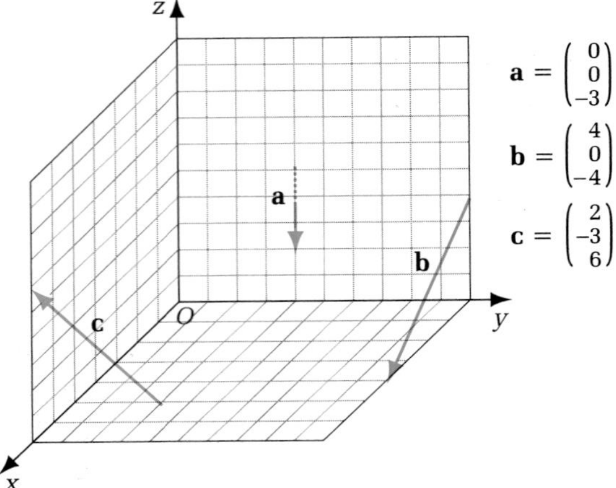

To find **a.b** we need to know the angle between **a** and **b**. Notice that **a** is parallel to the z-axis and that **b** is inclined at 45° to the x–y plane. So the angle between the vectors **a** and **b** is 45° or $\frac{\pi}{4}$.

$$\text{Now}\quad \mathbf{a.b} = ab\cos\theta$$

$$\mathbf{a.b} = \sqrt{0^2 + 0^2 + (-3)^2} \times \sqrt{4^2 + 0^2 + (-4)^2} \times \cos\left(\frac{\pi}{4}\right)$$

Recall special angles.

$$\mathbf{a.b} = \sqrt{9} \times \sqrt{32} \times \frac{1}{\sqrt{2}}$$

$$\mathbf{a.b} = 3 \times 4\sqrt{2} \times \frac{1}{\sqrt{2}}$$

$$\mathbf{a.b} = 12$$

Remember that **a.b** always creates a scalar (numerical) answer.

It isn't always so easy to find the angle between vectors. Without knowing the angle between **a** and **c** and between **b** and **c**, how can **a.c** or **b.c** be found? Return to the definition of scalar product but think about it in component form.
Let $\mathbf{a} = a_1\mathbf{i} + a_2\mathbf{j} + a_3\mathbf{k}$ and $\mathbf{b} = b_1\mathbf{i} + b_2\mathbf{j} + b_3\mathbf{k}$ and let the angle between these two vectors be θ. Vector addition can be used to form a triangle PQR where $\overrightarrow{PQ} = \mathbf{a}$ and $\overrightarrow{PR} = \mathbf{b}$.

$\mathbf{a} = \begin{pmatrix} a_1 \\ a_2 \\ a_3 \end{pmatrix}$ and $\mathbf{b} = \begin{pmatrix} b_1 \\ b_2 \\ b_3 \end{pmatrix}$.

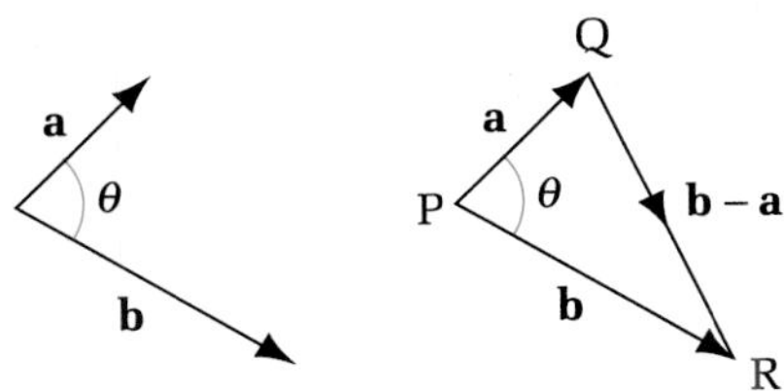

$$\text{Then}\quad \overrightarrow{QR} = \overrightarrow{QP} + \overrightarrow{PR}$$
$$= -\mathbf{a} + \mathbf{b}$$
$$= \mathbf{b} - \mathbf{a}$$

By subtraction of vectors,

$$\mathbf{b} - \mathbf{a} = (b_1 - a_1)\mathbf{i} + (b_2 - a_2)\mathbf{j} + (b_3 - a_3)\mathbf{k} = \begin{pmatrix} b_1 - a_1 \\ b_2 - a_2 \\ b_3 - a_3 \end{pmatrix}$$

Now apply the cosine rule to triangle PQR, since it relates the cosine of an angle to the lengths of the sides of the triangle.

$$(QR)^2 = a^2 + b^2 - 2ab\cos\theta$$

Recall that lower case letters represent sides opposite the angles represented by capital letters.

Since $\mathbf{a.b} = ab\cos\theta$,

$$(QR)^2 = a^2 + b^2 - 2\mathbf{a.b} \qquad [1]$$

But $a = \sqrt{a_1^2 + a_2^2 + a_3^2} \Rightarrow a^2 = a_1^2 + a_2^2 + a_3^2$

and $b = \sqrt{b_1^2 + b_2^2 + b_3^2} \Rightarrow b^2 = b_1^2 + b_2^2 + b_3^2$

Similarly,
$$\begin{aligned}|\overrightarrow{\mathrm{QR}}| &= |\mathbf{b} - \mathbf{a}| \\ &= |(b_1 - a_1)\mathbf{i} + (b_2 - a_2)\mathbf{j} + (b_3 - a_3)\mathbf{k}| \\ &= \sqrt{(b_1 - a_1)^2 + (b_2 - a_2)^2 + (b_3 - a_3)^2}\end{aligned}$$

So
$$\begin{aligned}(QR)^2 &= (b_1 - a_1)^2 + (b_2 - a_2)^2 + (b_3 - a_3)^2 \\ &= b_1^2 - 2a_1b_1 + a_1^2 + b_2^2 - 2a_2b_2 + a_2^2 + b_3^2 - 2a_3b_3 + a_3^2 \\ &= a_1^2 + a_2^2 + a_3^2 + b_1^2 + b_2^2 + b_3^2 - 2(a_1b_1 + a_2b_2 + a_3b_3)\end{aligned}$$

Substituting for a, b and QR in equation [1],

$$\begin{aligned}&a_1^2 + a_2^2 + a_3^2 + b_1^2 + b_2^2 + b_3^2 - 2(a_1b_1 + a_2b_2 + a_3b_3) \\ &\quad = a_1^2 + a_2^2 + a_3^2 + b_1^2 + b_2^2 + b_3^2 - 2\mathbf{a}.\mathbf{b}\end{aligned}$$

Cancelling like terms from both sides of the equation,

$$-2(a_1b_1 + a_2b_2 + a_3b_3) = -2\mathbf{a}.\mathbf{b}$$

This simplified form gives the following important result:

$$\mathbf{a}.\mathbf{b} = a_1b_1 + a_2b_2 + a_3b_3 = ab\cos\theta$$

◀ **Learn this important result.**

So an alternative way of finding **a.b** when the components of each vector are known is to multiply the **i**, **j** and **k** components together separately and then add the results.
We can now find **a.c** and **b.c** using this technique.

Recall that $\mathbf{a} = -3\mathbf{k}$, $\mathbf{b} = 4\mathbf{i} - 4\mathbf{k}$ and $\mathbf{c} = 2\mathbf{i} - 3\mathbf{j} + 6\mathbf{k}$

You may find it easier to see which components to multiply together if you write the vectors in column form.

$$\begin{aligned}\mathbf{a}.\mathbf{c} &= \begin{pmatrix}0\\0\\-3\end{pmatrix}.\begin{pmatrix}2\\-3\\6\end{pmatrix} \\ &= (0 \times 2) + (0 \times -3) + (-3 \times 6) \\ &= 0 + 0 + -18 \\ &= -18\end{aligned}$$

$$\begin{aligned}\mathbf{b}.\mathbf{c} &= \begin{pmatrix}4\\0\\-4\end{pmatrix}.\begin{pmatrix}2\\-3\\6\end{pmatrix} \\ &= (4 \times 2) + (0 \times -3) + (-4 \times 6) \\ &= 8 + 0 - 24 \\ &= -16\end{aligned}$$

The properties of the scalar product

The following properties of the scalar product of two vectors **a** and **b**, can be established:

- **a.b** *is a number that can be positive, zero or negative*

  The magnitude of each vector, denoted by a and b, is always positive, but the $\cos\theta$ term is positive if θ, the angle between the vectors, is acute, zero if the vectors are perpendicular and negative if the angle between the vectors is obtuse.

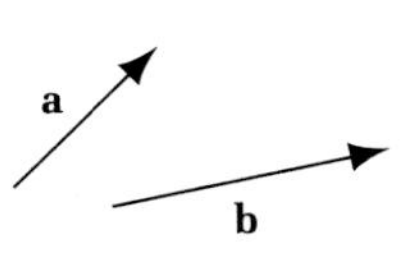

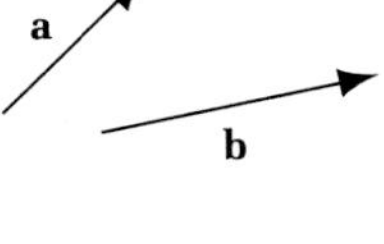

θ is acute
a.b is a positive number

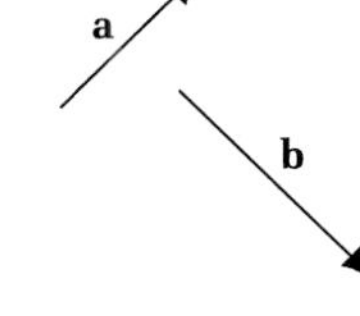

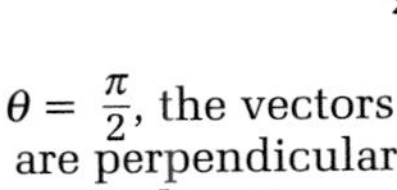

$\theta = \frac{\pi}{2}$, the vectors are perpendicular
a.b $= 0$

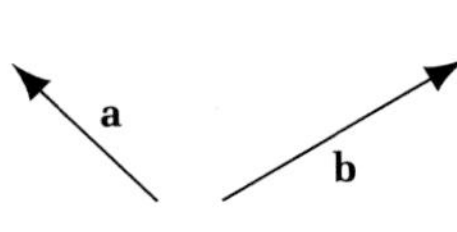

θ is obtuse
a.b is a negative number

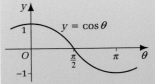

If two vectors are perpendicular then the scalar product is zero.

- *The dot product of two vectors is commutative*

  $\mathbf{a}.\mathbf{b} = ab\cos\theta$

  $\mathbf{b}.\mathbf{a} = ba\cos\theta = ab\cos\theta$

  $\Rightarrow \mathbf{a}.\mathbf{b} = \mathbf{b}.\mathbf{a}$

- *A scalar factor can be taken outside of the dot product*

  Let λ be any real number. Then

$$
\begin{aligned}
(\lambda\mathbf{a}).\mathbf{b} &= (\lambda a)b\cos\theta \\
&= \lambda(ab\cos\theta) \\
&= a(\lambda b)\cos\theta
\end{aligned}
$$

  $\Rightarrow (\lambda\mathbf{a}).\mathbf{b} = \lambda(\mathbf{a}.\mathbf{b}) = \mathbf{a}.(\lambda\mathbf{b})$

If $|\mathbf{a}| = a$, then $|\lambda\mathbf{a}| = \lambda a$.

- *The scalar product follows the distributive law*

  $\mathbf{a}.(\mathbf{b}+\mathbf{c}) = \mathbf{a}.\mathbf{b} + \mathbf{a}.\mathbf{c}$

Example 1

State whether the angle between the following pairs of vectors is acute, obtuse or a right angle:

a $\mathbf{j} + 2\mathbf{k}$ and $\mathbf{i} - 2\mathbf{j} + 5\mathbf{k}$

b $\mathbf{u} = \begin{pmatrix} 2 \\ -3 \\ 7 \end{pmatrix}$ and $\mathbf{v} = \begin{pmatrix} -1 \\ 4 \\ 2 \end{pmatrix}$

c $\mathbf{k}$ and $\mathbf{i} - 2\mathbf{j} - 5\mathbf{k}$

Solution

a $(\mathbf{j}+2\mathbf{k}).(\mathbf{i}-2\mathbf{j}+5\mathbf{k}) = 0+(1\times -2)+(2\times 5)$

$$= 0-2+10$$

$$= 8$$

Notice that the first vector has no compo[nent] in the **i** direction.

The scalar product is positive, so the angle between the vectors is acute.

b $\mathbf{u}.\mathbf{v} = \begin{pmatrix}2\\-3\\7\end{pmatrix}.\begin{pmatrix}-1\\4\\2\end{pmatrix}$

$$= (2\times -1)+(-3\times 4)+(7\times 2)$$

$$= -2+-12+14$$

$$= 0$$

Therefore the vectors **u** and **v** are perpendicular.

Two vectors that are perpendicular are als[o] said to be orthogonal.

c $\mathbf{k}.(\mathbf{i}-2\mathbf{j}-5\mathbf{k}) = (0\times 1)+(0\times -2)+(1\times -5)$

$$= 0+0-5$$

$$= -5$$

Notice that the first vector has no **i** or **j** component.

The scalar product is negative so the angle between these two vectors is obtuse.

Example 2

Find the angle between the vectors $\begin{pmatrix}2\\-1\\3\end{pmatrix}$ and $\begin{pmatrix}1\\0\\-2\end{pmatrix}$.

Solution

Let θ be the angle between the vectors.

Then $\mathbf{a}.\mathbf{b} = ab\cos\theta$

This equation can now be rearranged to make $\cos\theta$ the subject.

$$\cos\theta = \frac{\mathbf{a}.\mathbf{b}}{ab}$$

But $\mathbf{a}.\mathbf{b} = \begin{pmatrix}2\\-1\\3\end{pmatrix}.\begin{pmatrix}1\\0\\-2\end{pmatrix}$

$$= (2\times 1)+(-1\times 0)+(3\times -2)$$

$$= 2+0+-6$$

$$= -4$$

and $a = \sqrt{2^2+(-1)^2+3^2} = \sqrt{14}$ $\quad b = \sqrt{1^2+0^2+(-2)^2} = \sqrt{5}$

So $\cos\theta = \dfrac{-4}{\sqrt{14} \times \sqrt{5}}$

$= -0.478\,09$

$\theta = \cos^{-1}(-0.478\,09)$

$= 2.07 \text{ rad}$

Check that 2.07 radians is about 118.6°.

Cos θ is negative, so we expect an obtuse angle.

Example 3

Find the value of p if the vectors $2\mathbf{i} + p\mathbf{j} - 3\mathbf{k}$ and $\mathbf{i} - 2\mathbf{j} + 4\mathbf{k}$ are perpendicular.

Solution

Recall that two vectors are perpendicular if $\mathbf{a}.\mathbf{b} = 0$.

So $(2\mathbf{i} + p\mathbf{j} - 3\mathbf{k}).(\mathbf{i} - 2\mathbf{j} + 4\mathbf{k}) = 0$

$\Rightarrow \quad (2 \times 1) + (p \times -2) + (-3 \times 4) = 0$

$\Rightarrow \quad 2 - 2p - 12 = 0$

$\Rightarrow \quad -2p = 10$

$\Rightarrow \quad p = -5$

Example 4

Points A, B and C form a triangle. Their position vectors are $\begin{pmatrix} 2 \\ -1 \\ 8 \end{pmatrix}$, $\begin{pmatrix} -1 \\ 4 \\ 4 \end{pmatrix}$ and $\begin{pmatrix} 0 \\ -1 \\ 12 \end{pmatrix}$ respectively. Find:

a the lengths of the sides AB and AC

b the exact value of the cosine of the angle BAC

c the exact area of the triangle.

Solution

a

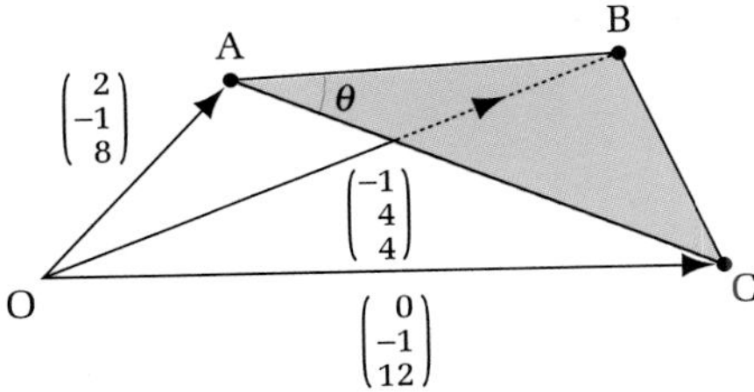

AB and AC are the magnitudes of the vectors $\overrightarrow{AB}$ and $\overrightarrow{AC}$.
Using vector addition,

$\overrightarrow{AB} = \overrightarrow{AO} + \overrightarrow{OB} = -\overrightarrow{OA} + \overrightarrow{OB}$

$= -\begin{pmatrix} 2 \\ -1 \\ 8 \end{pmatrix} + \begin{pmatrix} -1 \\ 4 \\ 4 \end{pmatrix} = \begin{pmatrix} -3 \\ 5 \\ -4 \end{pmatrix}$

$\overrightarrow{OA} = \begin{pmatrix} 2 \\ -1 \\ 8 \end{pmatrix}$ so

$\overrightarrow{AO} = -\overrightarrow{OA} = -\begin{pmatrix} 2 \\ -1 \\ 8 \end{pmatrix}$

$$\overrightarrow{AC} = \overrightarrow{AO} + \overrightarrow{OC} = -\overrightarrow{OA} + \overrightarrow{OC}$$

$$= -\begin{pmatrix} 2 \\ -1 \\ 8 \end{pmatrix} + \begin{pmatrix} 0 \\ -1 \\ 12 \end{pmatrix} = \begin{pmatrix} -2 \\ 0 \\ 4 \end{pmatrix}$$

So $AB = |\overrightarrow{AB}|$

$$= \sqrt{(-3)^2 + 5^2 + (-4)^2}$$

$$= \sqrt{50}$$

$$= 5\sqrt{2}$$

Use surds to simplify [cut off] answers.

$AC = |\overrightarrow{AC}|$

$$= \sqrt{(-2)^2 + 0^2 + 4^2}$$

$$= \sqrt{20}$$

$$= 2\sqrt{5}$$

b To find the angle BAC (denoted by θ on the diagram) use the scalar product.

Angle BAC is the angl[cut off] between $\overrightarrow{AB}$ and $\overrightarrow{AC}$.

$$\overrightarrow{AB} . \overrightarrow{AC} = \begin{pmatrix} -3 \\ 5 \\ -4 \end{pmatrix} . \begin{pmatrix} -2 \\ 0 \\ 4 \end{pmatrix} = -10$$

However, using the alternative definition of the scalar product,

$$\overrightarrow{AB} . \overrightarrow{AC} = AB \times AC \times \cos\theta$$

$$= 5\sqrt{2} \times 2\sqrt{5} \times \cos\theta$$ ◀ From a.

$$= 10\sqrt{10}\cos\theta$$

Therefore,

$$-10 = 10\sqrt{10}\cos\theta$$

$$\Rightarrow \quad \cos\theta = \frac{-1}{\sqrt{10}} = \frac{-\sqrt{10}}{10}$$

Remember to rationali[cut off] the denominator.

The minus sign indicates that the angle θ is obtuse.

c To find the area of a triangle where two sides and the angle between them is known, use the formula

Recall that this result i[cut off] true for all angles, including obtuse angle[cut off]

area $= \frac{1}{2}bc\sin A$

Since the lengths of AB and AC are known we need to find $\sin\theta$ before applying the formula. Notice that the identity $\cos^2\theta + \sin^2\theta \equiv 1$ can be used, since $\cos\theta$ has been calculated in the previous part.

$$\cos^2\theta + \sin^2\theta = 1$$

$$\Rightarrow \qquad \sin^2\theta = 1 - \cos^2\theta$$

$$= 1 - \left(\frac{-\sqrt{10}}{10}\right)^2$$

$$= 1 - \frac{10}{100}$$

$$= \frac{90}{100} = \frac{9}{10}$$

$$\Rightarrow \qquad \sin\theta = \pm\frac{3}{\sqrt{10}}$$

We have already established that θ is obtuse. The sine of an obtuse angle is positive, so

$$\sin\theta = \frac{3}{\sqrt{10}} = \frac{3\sqrt{10}}{10}$$

Now $\quad \text{area} = \frac{1}{2} \times AC \times AB \times \sin\theta$

$$= \frac{1}{2} \times 2\sqrt{5} \times 5\sqrt{2} \times \frac{3\sqrt{10}}{10}$$

$$= 15 \text{ square units}$$

Example 5

Find a vector that is perpendicular to both vectors $2\mathbf{i} - \mathbf{j} + \mathbf{k}$ and $\mathbf{i} - 3\mathbf{j} + 5\mathbf{k}$.

Solution

Let the vector that is perpendicular to both of these vectors be $\mathbf{v} = v_1\mathbf{i} + v_2\mathbf{j} + v_3\mathbf{k}$. The problem is now to find v_1, v_2 and v_3. Finding the scalar product of $\mathbf{v}$ with the original two vectors is going to give us *two* equations, so it would be more useful to have *two* unknowns rather than three.

Take a factor of v_3 out of the vector $\mathbf{v}$. Assuming $v_3 \neq 0$,

$$\mathbf{v} = v_3\left(\frac{v_1}{v_3}\mathbf{i} + \frac{v_2}{v_3}\mathbf{j} + \mathbf{k}\right)$$

Let $\frac{v_1}{v_3} = w_1$ and let $\frac{v_2}{v_3} = w_2$.

Then $\quad \mathbf{v} = v_3(w_1\mathbf{i} + w_2\mathbf{j} + \mathbf{k})$

Since v_3 is a scalar, $\mathbf{w} = w_1\mathbf{i} + w_2\mathbf{j} + \mathbf{k}$ is parallel to $\mathbf{v}$ so $\mathbf{w}$ is also perpendicular to both of the original vectors.

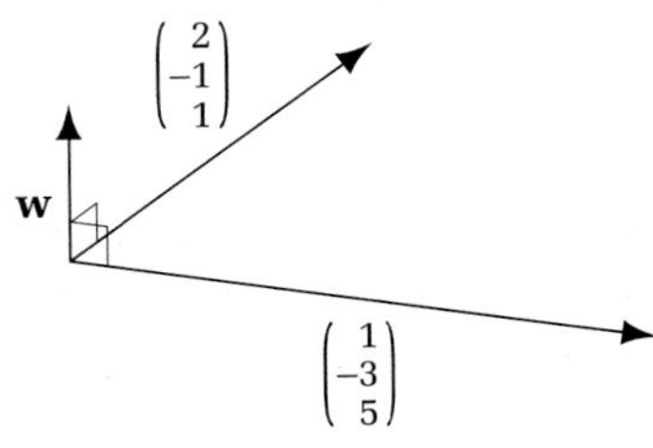

$$\text{So} \quad (w_1\mathbf{i} + w_2\mathbf{j} + \mathbf{k}).(2\mathbf{i} - \mathbf{j} + \mathbf{k}) = 0$$

$$\Rightarrow \quad 2w_1 - w_2 + 1 = 0$$

$$2w_1 - w_2 = -1 \qquad [1]$$

$$\text{and} \quad (w_1\mathbf{i} + w_2\mathbf{j} + \mathbf{k}).(\mathbf{i} - 3\mathbf{j} + 5\mathbf{k}) = 0$$

$$\Rightarrow \quad w_1 - 3w_2 + 5 = 0$$

$$w_1 - 3w_2 = -5 \qquad [2]$$

Equations [1] and [2] are simultaneous equations, which can be solved using the elimination technique (see Chapter 1).
From equation [2],

$$2w_1 - 6w_2 = -10$$

Subtracting this from equation [1],

$$2w_1 - 2w_1 - w_2 + 6w_2 = 9$$

$$5w_2 = 9$$

$$w_2 = \tfrac{9}{5}$$

Substituting for w_2 in equation [2],

$$w_1 - 3 \times \tfrac{9}{5} = -5$$

$$w_1 = -5 + \tfrac{27}{5}$$

$$w_1 = \tfrac{2}{5}$$

So vector $\mathbf{w} = \frac{2}{5}\mathbf{i} + \frac{9}{5}\mathbf{j} + \mathbf{k}$ is perpendicular to both vectors. Since any scalar multiple of $\mathbf{w}$ is parallel to $\mathbf{w}$ and so must also be perpendicular to both vectors, $5\mathbf{w} = 2\mathbf{i} + 9\mathbf{j} + 5\mathbf{k}$ is also perpendicular to both vectors.
So the vector $2\mathbf{i} + 9\mathbf{j} + 5\mathbf{k}$ is perpendicular to $2\mathbf{i} - \mathbf{j} + \mathbf{k}$ and $\mathbf{i} - 3\mathbf{j} + 5\mathbf{k}$.
We can quickly check this.

$$\begin{pmatrix} 2 \\ 9 \\ 5 \end{pmatrix} . \begin{pmatrix} 2 \\ -1 \\ 1 \end{pmatrix} = 4 - 9 + 5 = 0$$

$$\begin{pmatrix} 2 \\ 9 \\ 5 \end{pmatrix} . \begin{pmatrix} 1 \\ -3 \\ 5 \end{pmatrix} = 2 - 27 + 25 = 0$$

14.3 The Scalar Product
Exercise
Technique

1 The diagram shows the vectors $\mathbf{u} = \begin{pmatrix} 0 \\ -2 \\ 2 \end{pmatrix}$ and $\mathbf{v} = \begin{pmatrix} 0 \\ 0 \\ -3 \end{pmatrix}$.

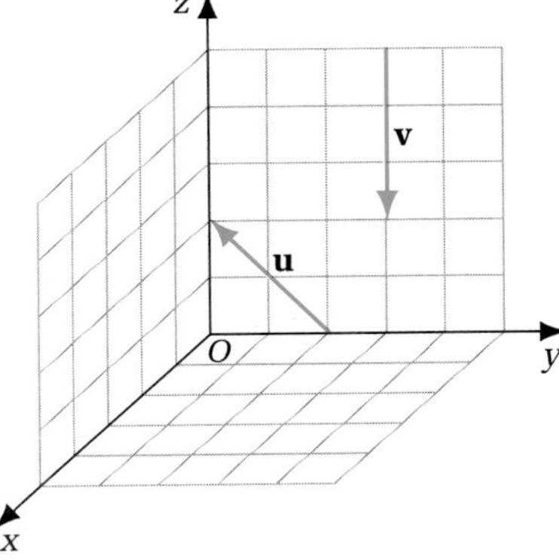

a Write down the angle between these two vectors.
b Find $|\mathbf{u}|$ and $|\mathbf{v}|$.
c Find $\mathbf{u}.\mathbf{v}$ by using the general definition $\mathbf{a}.\mathbf{b} = ab\cos\theta$.
d Find $\mathbf{u}.\mathbf{v}$ by using the components of the vectors.

2 If $\mathbf{r} = \begin{pmatrix} 2 \\ -3 \\ 4 \end{pmatrix}$, $\mathbf{s} = \begin{pmatrix} 1 \\ -7 \\ 2 \end{pmatrix}$ and $\mathbf{t} = \begin{pmatrix} 5 \\ 0 \\ -1 \end{pmatrix}$, find:

a $\mathbf{s} + \mathbf{t}$ b $\mathbf{r}.\mathbf{s}$ c $\mathbf{r}.\mathbf{t}$
d $\mathbf{r}.(\mathbf{s} + \mathbf{t})$ e $\mathbf{r}.\mathbf{s} + \mathbf{r}.\mathbf{t}$

Comment on your answers to parts **d** and **e**.

3 If $\mathbf{u} = 2\mathbf{i} + \mathbf{j} - \mathbf{k}$ and $\mathbf{v} = \mathbf{i} + 2\mathbf{j} + 10\mathbf{k}$, find:

a $\mathbf{u}.\mathbf{u}$ b $\mathbf{u}.\mathbf{v}$ c $\mathbf{v}.\mathbf{u}$ d $\mathbf{u}.(\mathbf{u} + \mathbf{v})$

4 Use the dot product to determine whether the angles between the following pairs of vectors are acute, obtuse or right angles:

a $\begin{pmatrix} 0 \\ -3 \\ 1 \end{pmatrix}$ and $\begin{pmatrix} 1 \\ 1 \\ 2 \end{pmatrix}$
b $\mathbf{i} - \mathbf{j} + 2\mathbf{k}$ and $-4\mathbf{i} + 2\mathbf{j} + 3\mathbf{k}$
c $\begin{pmatrix} 2 \\ -1 \\ 5 \end{pmatrix}$ and $\begin{pmatrix} -1 \\ -7 \\ 1 \end{pmatrix}$

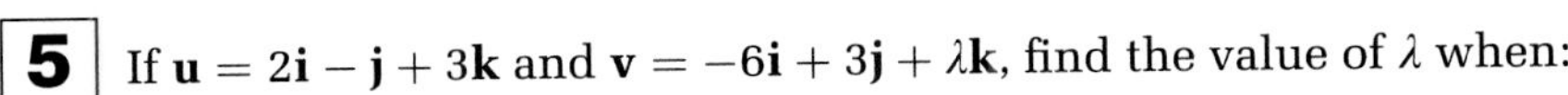

5 If $\mathbf{u} = 2\mathbf{i} - \mathbf{j} + 3\mathbf{k}$ and $\mathbf{v} = -6\mathbf{i} + 3\mathbf{j} + \lambda\mathbf{k}$, find the value of λ when:

a $\mathbf{u}$ and $\mathbf{v}$ are parallel
b $\mathbf{u}$ and $\mathbf{v}$ are perpendicular.

6 Find the angle between the vectors:

a $\mathbf{r} = \begin{pmatrix} -1 \\ 2 \\ 2 \end{pmatrix}$ and $\mathbf{s} = \begin{pmatrix} 2 \\ -3 \\ 6 \end{pmatrix}$

b $\mathbf{u} = \begin{pmatrix} 2 \\ 3 \\ 1 \end{pmatrix}$ and $\mathbf{v} = \begin{pmatrix} 4 \\ -2 \\ -2 \end{pmatrix}$

c $2\mathbf{i} - 7\mathbf{j} + \mathbf{k}$ and $\mathbf{i} + \mathbf{j} - \mathbf{k}$

7 Find the angle between the vector $\begin{pmatrix} 1 \\ 1 \\ 1 \end{pmatrix}$ and the z-axis.

8 Find the values of λ if $\lambda\mathbf{i} + 2\mathbf{j} + 3\mathbf{k}$ and $\lambda\mathbf{i} + \lambda\mathbf{j} - \mathbf{k}$ are perpendicular vectors.

9 The diagram shows the triangle OAB, where O is the origin and A and B have position vectors $\begin{pmatrix} 2 \\ -4 \\ 5 \end{pmatrix}$ and $\begin{pmatrix} 1 \\ 2 \\ 2 \end{pmatrix}$ respectively.

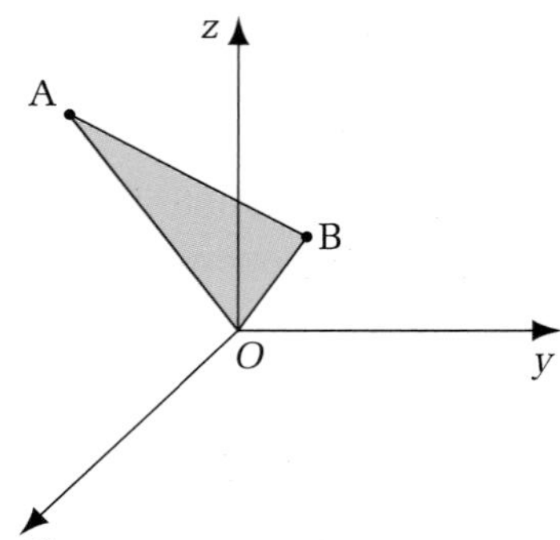

a Find angle AOB.

b Find the area of the triangle OAB.

10 The three points A $(1, 3, 4)$, B $(-5, 3, 12)$ and C $(3, 6, 10)$ form a triangle ABC. Find:

a the exact lengths of AB and AC

b the exact value of the cosine of the angle BAC

c the exact area of the triangle ABC.

11 The angle between the vectors $p\mathbf{i} + \mathbf{j} + \mathbf{k}$ and $\mathbf{j} + \mathbf{k}$ is $\frac{\pi}{3}$. Find the two possible values of p.

12 Find a vector that is perpendicular to both the vectors $2\mathbf{i} - \mathbf{j} + 3\mathbf{k}$ and $3\mathbf{i} + 2\mathbf{j} - 5\mathbf{k}$.

Contextual

1

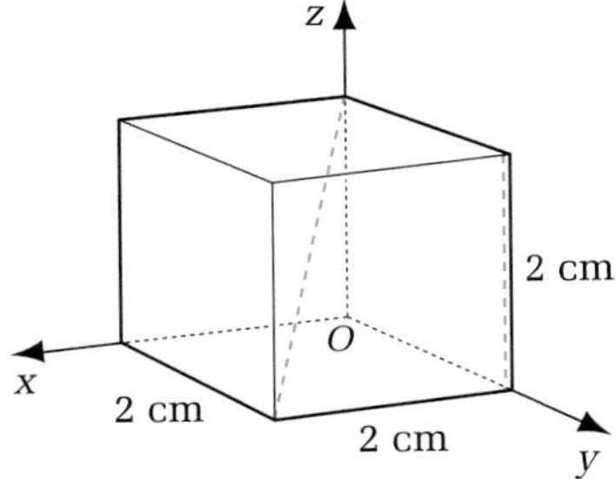

The diagram shows a cube with side 2 cm. One corner is positioned at the origin of a 3D coordinate system. Use vectors to find the angle between a diagonal of the cube and one edge that does not intersect the diagonal.

2

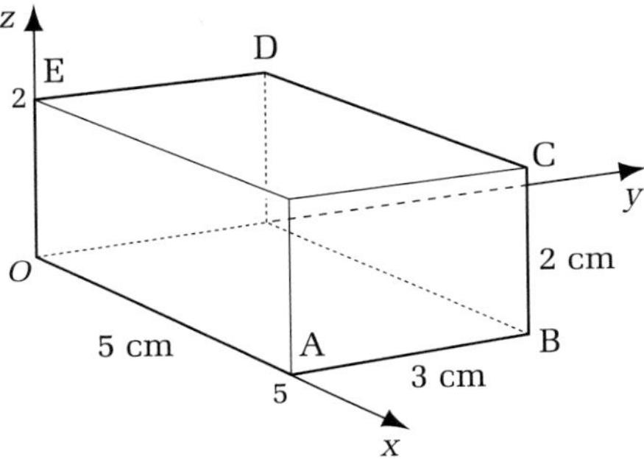

The diagram shows a cuboid 5 cm × 3 cm × 2 cm. It is positioned at the origin of a 3D coordinate system. Use vectors to find the angle between the two diagonals OC and AD of the cuboid.

14.4 The Vector Equation of a Straight Line

The diagram shows a vector $\mathbf{b} = \mathbf{i} + 2\mathbf{j} - 2\mathbf{k}$, two points A $(2, 6, 4)$ and Q $(1, 11, 0)$ and two straight lines L_1 and L_2. Both lines pass through A, and L_1 is parallel to $\mathbf{b}$.

The position vector of A (2, 6, 4) is $\overrightarrow{OA} = 2\mathbf{i} + 6\mathbf{j} + 4\mathbf{k}$ or $\overrightarrow{OA} = \begin{pmatrix} 2 \\ 6 \\ 4 \end{pmatrix}$.

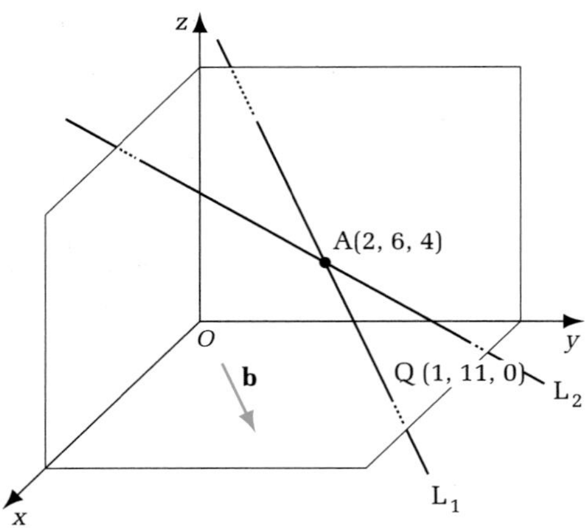

The line L_1 could be described as: 'the straight line that passes through the point $(2, 6, 4)$ and that is parallel to vector $\mathbf{b}$'. The line L_2 could be described as: 'the straight line that passes through the points A $(2, 6, 4)$ and Q $(1, 11, 0)$'. But notice that vector $\overrightarrow{AQ}$ is parallel to the line L_2. Therefore, L_2 could also be described as the line passing through the point $(2, 6, 4)$ that is parallel to $\overrightarrow{AQ}$.
Any straight line can be completely described by identifying a point that the line passes through and a vector that is parallel to the line.

The **vector equation of a line** is the position vector of a general point on the line.

The vector equation of the line L_1 can be denoted by $\mathbf{r}$. If P is a general point on the line, then:

$$\mathbf{r} = \overrightarrow{OP}$$

$$= \overrightarrow{OA} + \overrightarrow{AP}$$ ◀ By vector addition.

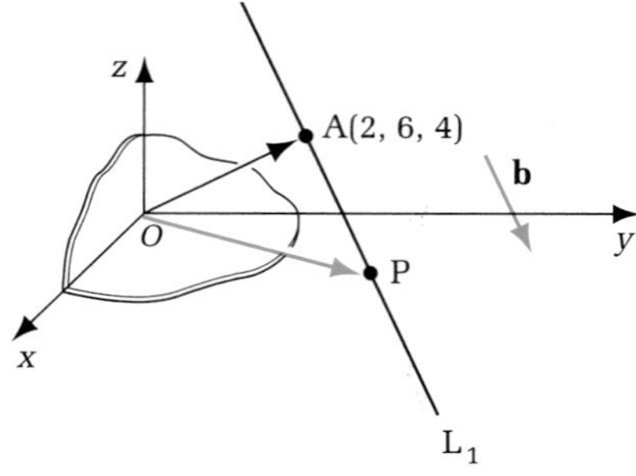

We know that $\overrightarrow{AP}$ is parallel to $\mathbf{b}$, so $\overrightarrow{AP} = \lambda\mathbf{b}$, where λ is a scalar.

Different values of λ correspond to different points along the line.

$$\text{So}\quad \mathbf{r} = \overrightarrow{OA} + \lambda\mathbf{b}$$
$$= (2\mathbf{i} + 6\mathbf{j} + 4\mathbf{k}) + \lambda(\mathbf{i} + 2\mathbf{j} - 2\mathbf{k})$$

This is the vector equation of the line L_1.

The vector equation of the line can also be written as

$$\begin{pmatrix} x \\ y \\ z \end{pmatrix} = \begin{pmatrix} 2 \\ 6 \\ 4 \end{pmatrix} + \lambda\begin{pmatrix} 1 \\ 2 \\ -2 \end{pmatrix} \text{ or}$$

$$\mathbf{r}(\lambda) = \begin{pmatrix} 2 \\ 6 \\ 4 \end{pmatrix} + \lambda\begin{pmatrix} 1 \\ 2 \\ -2 \end{pmatrix}$$

The vector equation of a line, which is usually denoted by $\mathbf{r}$, starts from the origin and ends at any point on the line. The diagram below shows how $\mathbf{r}$ changes for different values of λ.

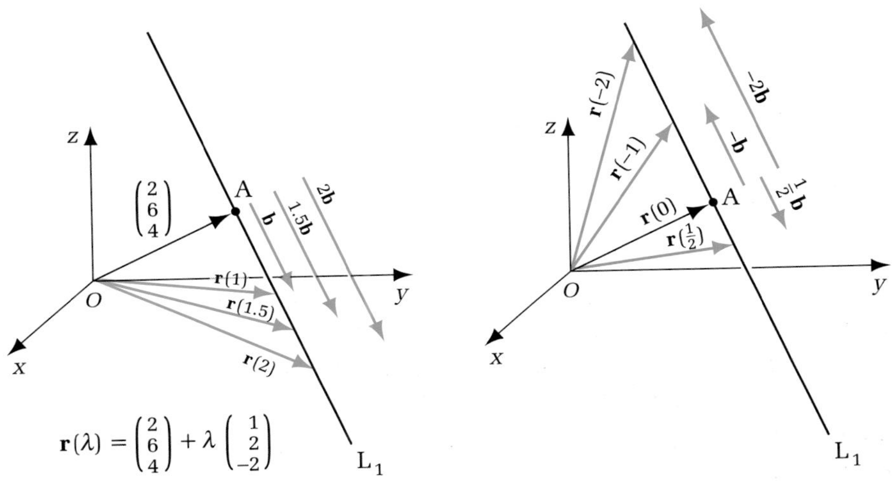

When $\lambda = 0$, $\mathbf{r} = \overrightarrow{OA}$, which is the position vector of the point A.

When $\lambda = 1$, $\mathbf{r}$ is the position vector for the point on L_1 arrived at by travelling along the vector $\mathbf{b}$ from A. Points defined by $0 < \lambda < 1$ are on L_1 closer to A, and points defined by $\lambda > 1$ are further away from A than this point.

When $\lambda = -1$, $\mathbf{r}$ is the position vector for the point on L_1 arrived at by travelling along the vector $-\mathbf{b}$ from A. Points defined by $-1 < \lambda < 0$ are closer to A, and points defined by $\lambda < -1$ are further away from A than this point.

The value of λ tells us how many multiples of $\mathbf{b}$ to move away from A.

The vector equation of a line can be found if we know:

- the position vector of a point on the line
- a vector parallel to the line.

Then $\mathbf{r} = \overrightarrow{OP} = \overrightarrow{OA} + \overrightarrow{AP}$

$$\mathbf{r} = \mathbf{a} + \lambda\mathbf{b}$$

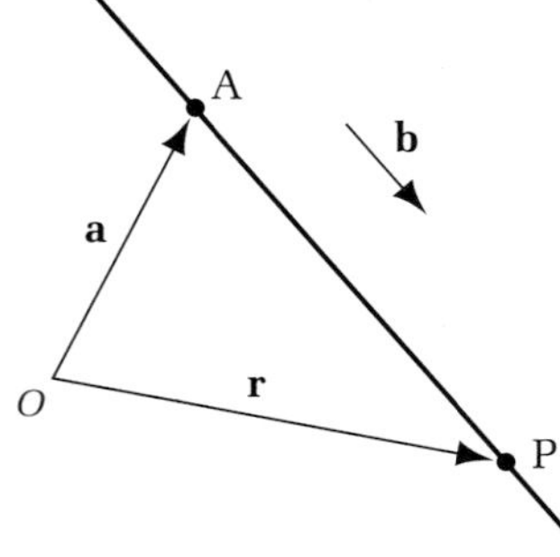

This can also be written as

$$\mathbf{r}(\lambda) = \mathbf{a} + \lambda\mathbf{b}$$ ◀ **Learn this important result.**

This is also known as a vector function for the line.

Returning to our original problem, we have already written the vector equation of the line L_1 in the form $\mathbf{r} = \mathbf{a} + \lambda\mathbf{b}$:

$$\mathbf{r} = (2\mathbf{i} + 6\mathbf{j} + 4\mathbf{k}) + \lambda(\mathbf{i} + 2\mathbf{j} - 2\mathbf{k}) \quad \text{or} \quad \mathbf{r} = \begin{pmatrix} 2 \\ 6 \\ 4 \end{pmatrix} + \lambda \begin{pmatrix} 1 \\ 2 \\ -2 \end{pmatrix}$$

We now need to do the same for L_2.

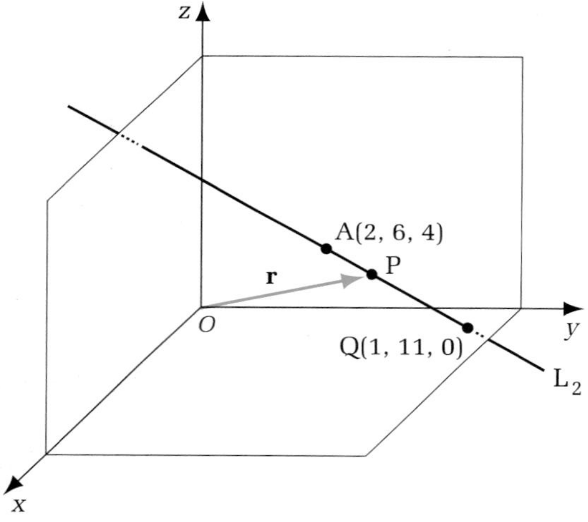

Let P be an arbitrary point on the line L_2. The position vector of P is $\overrightarrow{OP}$. Writing $\mathbf{r} = \overrightarrow{OP}$ we have

An arbitrary point on the line means it could be anywhere on the line.

$$\mathbf{r} = \overrightarrow{OA} + \overrightarrow{AP}$$

where $\overrightarrow{AP}$ is a vector along L_2. The vector $\overrightarrow{AQ}$ is also parallel to the straight line L_2.

The vectors could also be expressed in terms of column vectors.

$$\begin{aligned} \text{Now,} \quad \overrightarrow{AQ} &= \overrightarrow{AO} + \overrightarrow{OQ} \\ &= -(2\mathbf{i} + 6\mathbf{j} + 4\mathbf{k}) + (\mathbf{i} + 11\mathbf{j}) \\ &= -\mathbf{i} + 5\mathbf{j} - 4\mathbf{k} \end{aligned}$$

$\overrightarrow{AQ} = \begin{pmatrix} -1 \\ 5 \\ -4 \end{pmatrix}$.

Since $\overrightarrow{AP}$ is parallel to $\overrightarrow{AQ}$, $\overrightarrow{AP}$ is always a scalar multiple of $\overrightarrow{AQ}$ (for any point P on L_2). Let the scalar multiplier be μ.

$$\mathbf{r} = \overrightarrow{OA} + \mu\overrightarrow{AQ}$$
$$= (2\mathbf{i} + 6\mathbf{j} + 4\mathbf{k}) + \mu(-\mathbf{i} + 5\mathbf{j} - 4\mathbf{k})$$

The vector equation of the line L_2 is

$$\mathbf{r}(\mu) = (2\mathbf{i} + 6\mathbf{j} + 4\mathbf{k}) + \mu(-\mathbf{i} + 5\mathbf{j} - 4\mathbf{k})$$

$$\mathbf{r}(\mu) = \begin{pmatrix} 2 \\ 6 \\ 4 \end{pmatrix} + \mu\begin{pmatrix} -1 \\ 5 \\ -4 \end{pmatrix}$$

We could have used point Q for the fixed vector.

$$\overrightarrow{OQ} = \mathbf{i} + 11\mathbf{j}$$

Check that this then gives the equation for the line as

$$\mathbf{r}(t) = \mathbf{i} + 11\mathbf{j} + t(-\mathbf{i} + 5\mathbf{j} - 4\mathbf{k})$$

$$\mathbf{r}(t) = \begin{pmatrix} 1 \\ 11 \\ 0 \end{pmatrix} + t\begin{pmatrix} -1 \\ 5 \\ -4 \end{pmatrix}$$

This is a different equation from the one found when we used A as the fixed point. Both are equally valid equations for the line. The vector equation for a line can be expressed in many different ways.
Note that we could also write the equation of the line in the following form by adding the corresponding components.

$$\mathbf{r}(t) = (1 - t)\mathbf{i} + (11 + 5t)\mathbf{j} - 4t\mathbf{k}$$

$$\mathbf{r}(t) = \begin{pmatrix} 1-t \\ 11+5t \\ -4t \end{pmatrix}$$

This is not as useful as the standard form, $\mathbf{r}(\lambda) = \mathbf{a} + \lambda\mathbf{b}$, because the more usual form tells us, at a glance, the position vector of a point on the line, and a vector parallel to the line.
The scalar variable λ is called a **parameter**. Each value of the parameter determines a unique point on the line.

If you are talking about more than one line, it is usual to use different parameters, λ, μ, s, t, for each to avoid confusing them.

Example 1

A straight line passes though the point A $(15, -3, 10)$ and is parallel to the vector $\begin{pmatrix} 3 \\ -1 \\ 2 \end{pmatrix}$.

a Find the vector equation of this line.

b Which of the points B $(12, -1, 6)$ and C $(-3, 3, -2)$ also lie on the line?

c Where does the line meet the y–z plane?

Solution

a

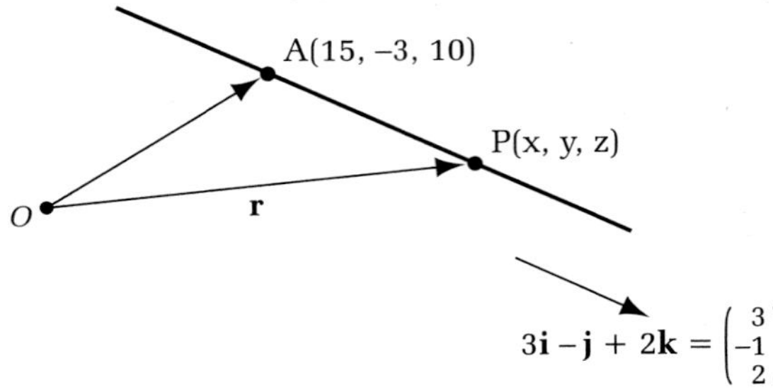

Recall that to write a vector equation for the line we need to know the position vector of a point on the line and a vector parallel to the line.
Point A is on the line

The position vector of A is $\begin{pmatrix} 15 \\ -3 \\ 10 \end{pmatrix}$.

A vector parallel to the line is $\begin{pmatrix} 3 \\ -1 \\ 2 \end{pmatrix}$.

$\mathbf{r} = \overrightarrow{OA} + \overrightarrow{AP}$

$$\mathbf{r} = \begin{pmatrix} 15 \\ -3 \\ 10 \end{pmatrix} + \lambda \begin{pmatrix} 3 \\ -1 \\ 2 \end{pmatrix}$$

This could also be written as $\mathbf{r} = \begin{pmatrix} 15 + 3\lambda \\ -3 - \lambda \\ 10 + 2\lambda \end{pmatrix}$

b Point B lies on the line if there is a value of λ such that

$$\begin{pmatrix} 15 \\ -3 \\ 10 \end{pmatrix} + \lambda \begin{pmatrix} 3 \\ -1 \\ 2 \end{pmatrix} = \begin{pmatrix} 12 \\ -1 \\ 6 \end{pmatrix}$$

Equating components in each direction,

i: $15 + 3\lambda = 12 \Rightarrow 3\lambda = -3 \Rightarrow \lambda = -1$

j: $-3 - \lambda = -1 \Rightarrow -\lambda = 2 \Rightarrow \lambda = -2$

k: $10 + 2\lambda = 6 \Rightarrow 2\lambda = -4 \Rightarrow \lambda = -2$

So there is no single value of λ such that $\mathbf{r} = \begin{pmatrix} 12 \\ -1 \\ 6 \end{pmatrix}$. This means that B does not lie on the line.
Similarly, C lies on the line if a parameter can be found such that

$$\begin{pmatrix} 15 \\ -3 \\ 10 \end{pmatrix} + \lambda \begin{pmatrix} 3 \\ -1 \\ 2 \end{pmatrix} = \begin{pmatrix} -3 \\ 3 \\ -2 \end{pmatrix}$$

Equating components again,

i: $15 + 3\lambda = -3 \Rightarrow 3\lambda = -18 \Rightarrow \lambda = -6$

j: $-3 - \lambda = 3 \Rightarrow -\lambda = 6 \Rightarrow \lambda = -6$

k: $10 + 2\lambda = -2 \Rightarrow 2\lambda = -12 \Rightarrow \lambda = -6$

Since there is a single value of λ such that $\mathbf{r} = \begin{pmatrix} -3 \\ 3 \\ -2 \end{pmatrix}$, C lies on the line.

c All points on the y–z plane have an x-coordinate of 0.

$$\mathbf{r}(\lambda) = \begin{pmatrix} 15 \\ -3 \\ 10 \end{pmatrix} + \lambda \begin{pmatrix} 3 \\ -1 \\ 2 \end{pmatrix} = \begin{pmatrix} 15 + 3\lambda \\ -3 - \lambda \\ 10 + 2\lambda \end{pmatrix}$$

The **i** component must be 0 for this to be the position vector of a point in the y–z plane.

$15 + 3\lambda = 0 \;\Rightarrow\; \lambda = -5$

So the position vector of the point where the line meets the y–z plane is $\mathbf{r}(-5)$. So we can replace λ with -5.

$$\mathbf{r}(-5) = \begin{pmatrix} 15 \\ -3 \\ 10 \end{pmatrix} - 5 \begin{pmatrix} 3 \\ -1 \\ 2 \end{pmatrix} = \begin{pmatrix} 0 \\ 2 \\ 0 \end{pmatrix}$$

The coordinates of the point where the line meets the y–z plane are $(0, 2, 0)$.

Example 2

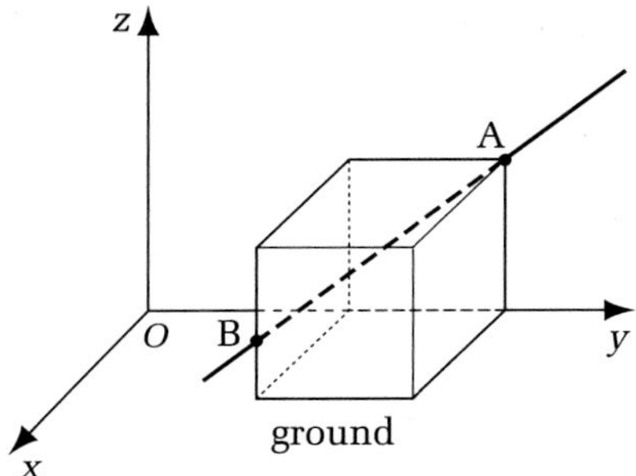

Notice that the ground is represented by the x–y plane; that is, the plane $z = 0$.

A rod is pushed through two holes in a box. It enters the box at A $(0, 9, 4)$ and leaves it at B $(3, 5, 2)$. Find the coordinates of the point where the rod touches the ground.

Solution

Notice that the tip of the rod will move along the straight line passing through the points A $(0, 9, 4)$ and B $(3, 5, 2)$. The vector equation of this line can be used to determine where the rod touches the ground.

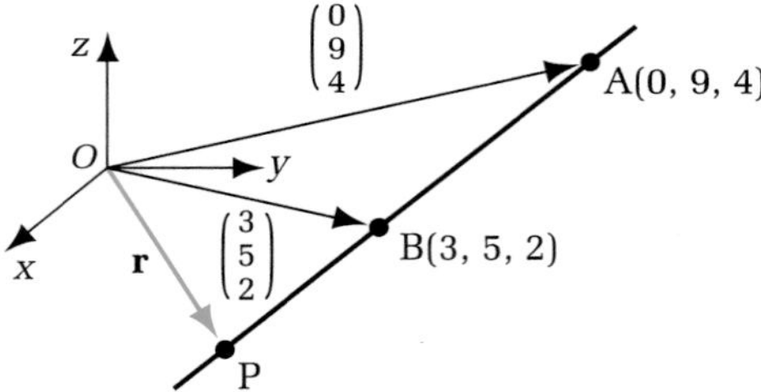

A vector parallel to the line is $\overrightarrow{AB}$.

$$\begin{aligned}\overrightarrow{AB} &= \overrightarrow{AO} + \overrightarrow{OB}\\ &= -(9\mathbf{j} + 4\mathbf{k}) + (3\mathbf{i} + 5\mathbf{j} + 2\mathbf{k})\\ &= 3\mathbf{i} - 4\mathbf{j} - 2\mathbf{k}\end{aligned}$$

$$\overrightarrow{AB} = \begin{pmatrix} 3 \\ -4 \\ -2 \end{pmatrix}$$

The vector equation of the line is therefore

$$\begin{aligned}\mathbf{r} &= \overrightarrow{OP}\\ &= \overrightarrow{OA} + \overrightarrow{AP}\\ &= \overrightarrow{OA} + \lambda\overrightarrow{AB}\\ &= (9\mathbf{j} + 4\mathbf{k}) + \lambda(3\mathbf{i} - 4\mathbf{j} - 2\mathbf{k})\end{aligned}$$

$$\mathbf{r}(\lambda) = \begin{pmatrix} 0 \\ 9 \\ 4 \end{pmatrix} + \lambda\begin{pmatrix} 3 \\ -4 \\ -2 \end{pmatrix} = \begin{pmatrix} 3\lambda \\ 9 - 4\lambda \\ 4 - 2\lambda \end{pmatrix}$$

Recall that each value of λ gives the position vector of a unique point on the line.The z-coordinate of the point where the rod touches the ground must be zero, because the ground is shown as the x–y plane. This means that the **k** component of the position vector of that point must be zero, so equate the **k** component of the straight line equation to zero.

$$\begin{aligned} 4 - 2\lambda &= 0\\ \Rightarrow \qquad \lambda &= 2\end{aligned}$$

Substituting $\lambda = 2$ into the equation of the straight line to find the position vector of the point where it cuts the ground,

$$\begin{aligned}\mathbf{r}(2) &= (9\mathbf{j} + 4\mathbf{k}) + 2(3\mathbf{i} - 4\mathbf{j} - 2\mathbf{k})\\ &= 6\mathbf{i} + \mathbf{j}\end{aligned}$$

$$\mathbf{r}(2) = \begin{pmatrix} 0 \\ 9 \\ 4 \end{pmatrix} + 2\begin{pmatrix} 3 \\ -4 \\ -2 \end{pmatrix} =$$

So the coordinates of the required point are $(6, 1, 0)$.

The angle between two straight lines

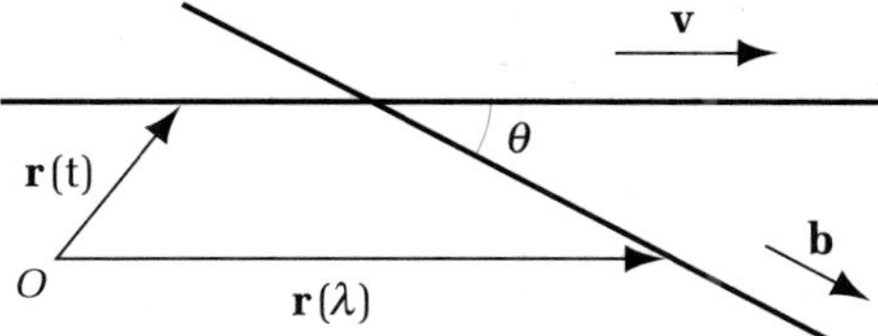

The diagram shows the lines $\mathbf{r}(\lambda) = \mathbf{a} + \lambda\mathbf{b}$ and $\mathbf{r}(t) = \mathbf{u} + t\mathbf{v}$. The vector parallel to $\mathbf{r}(\lambda) = \mathbf{a} + \lambda\mathbf{b}$ is $\mathbf{b}$. Vector $\mathbf{v}$ is parallel to the line $\mathbf{r}(t) = \mathbf{u} + t\mathbf{v}$. The angle between these two lines is the same as the angle between the two vectors parallel to the lines. Recall that this angle can be found using the scalar or dot product.

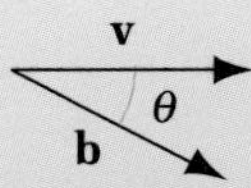

Example 3

The straight line L_1 is defined as $\mathbf{r} = (2 - \lambda)\mathbf{i} + \lambda\mathbf{j} + (1 + 3\lambda)\mathbf{k}$, and the straight line L_2 is defined as

$$\begin{pmatrix} x \\ y \\ z \end{pmatrix} = \begin{pmatrix} 2 \\ 1 - t \\ 5 - 4t \end{pmatrix}$$

Find the angle between these lines.

Solution

Both lines need to be expressed in the form $\mathbf{r} = \mathbf{a} + \lambda\mathbf{b}$ so that the vector parallel to the line can be identified quickly. Using column vectors,

$$\text{for } L_1 \quad \mathbf{r}(\lambda) = \begin{pmatrix} 2 - \lambda \\ \lambda \\ 1 + 3\lambda \end{pmatrix} = \begin{pmatrix} 2 \\ 0 \\ 1 \end{pmatrix} + \lambda \begin{pmatrix} -1 \\ 1 \\ 3 \end{pmatrix}$$

Notice that the terms involving the parameter λ have been collected together.

So a vector parallel to L_1 is $-\mathbf{i} + \mathbf{j} + 3\mathbf{k}$.

Writing the equation for L_2 in the same form,

$$\mathbf{r}(t) = \begin{pmatrix} 2 \\ 1 - t \\ 5 - 4t \end{pmatrix} = \begin{pmatrix} 2 \\ 1 \\ 5 \end{pmatrix} + t \begin{pmatrix} 0 \\ -1 \\ -4 \end{pmatrix}$$

So a vector parallel to L_2 is $-\mathbf{j} - 4\mathbf{k}$.

Now the angle between the two lines is equal to the angle between the vectors $-\mathbf{i} + \mathbf{j} + 3\mathbf{k}$ and $-\mathbf{j} - 4\mathbf{k}$, which we can find using the scalar product.

$$(-\mathbf{i}+\mathbf{j}+3\mathbf{k}).(-\mathbf{j}-4\mathbf{k}) = |-\mathbf{i}+\mathbf{j}+3\mathbf{k}| \times |-\mathbf{j}-4\mathbf{k}| \times \cos\theta$$

$$(-1\times 0)+(1\times -1)+(3\times -4) = \sqrt{(-1)^2+1^2+3^2} \times \sqrt{(-1)^2+(-4)^2} \times \cos\theta$$

$$0-1-12 = \sqrt{11}\times\sqrt{17}\times\cos\theta$$

$$\frac{-13}{\sqrt{187}} = \cos\theta$$

So
$$\theta = \cos^{-1}(-0.9507)$$
$$= 2.83\,\text{rad (2 d.p.)}$$

$\mathbf{a}.\mathbf{b} = ab\cos\theta$

Obtuse angle because the scalar product is negative.

Verify that the angle between the straight lines is 161.9°.

The acute angle betw[een] the lines is $180^\circ - 161.9^\circ = 18.1^\circ$

Intersecting lines

If two straight lines are defined by $\mathbf{r}(\lambda) = \mathbf{a} + \lambda\mathbf{b}$ and $\mathbf{r}(\mu) = \mathbf{c} + \mu\mathbf{d}$, then these lines:

- 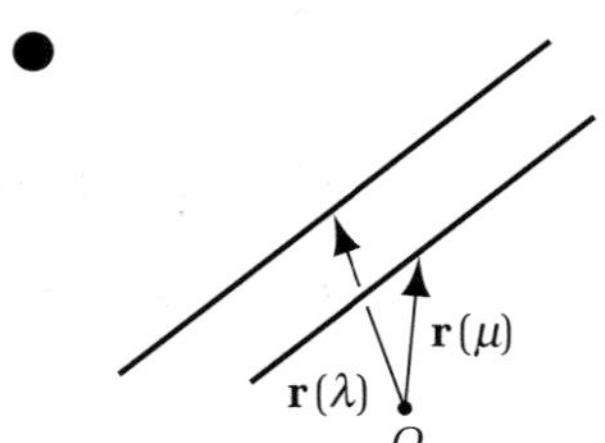

will be **parallel** if $\mathbf{b} = m\mathbf{d}$ where m is a scaler; in this case the lines do not intersect;

- 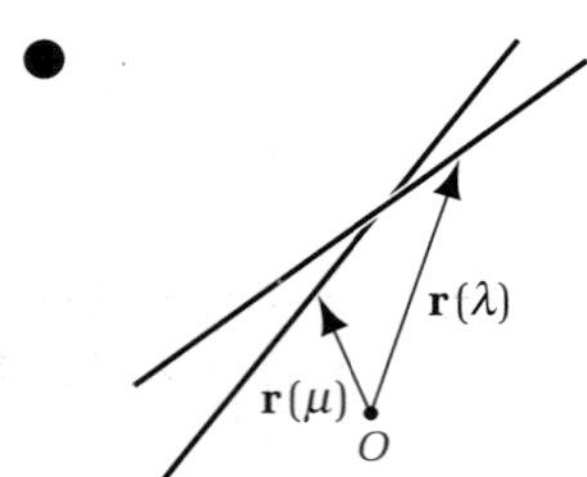

may be skew; two lines are said to be **skew** if they are not parallel and do not intersect; **b** is not parallel to **d** and there are no values for λ and μ that make $\mathbf{r}(\lambda) = \mathbf{r}(\mu)$;

- 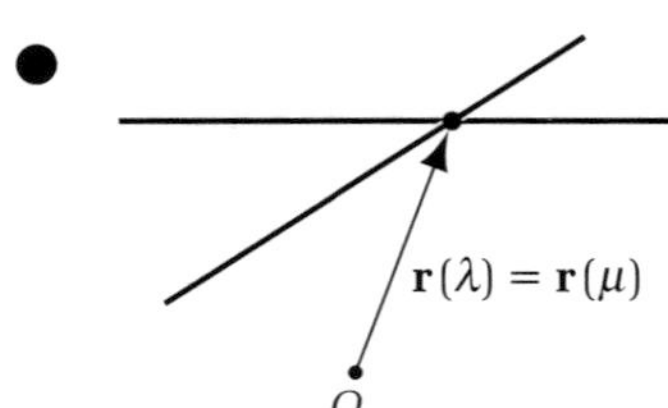

may **intersect** at one point if they are not parallel; **b** is not parallel to **d** but there is a value of λ and a value of μ that make $\mathbf{r}(\lambda) = \mathbf{r}(\mu)$.

Example 4

The straight line L has vector equation

$$\begin{pmatrix} x \\ y \\ z \end{pmatrix} = \begin{pmatrix} -2 \\ 10 \\ 4 \end{pmatrix} + t\begin{pmatrix} -1 \\ 3 \\ 2 \end{pmatrix}$$

The straight line M passes through the points A $(0, 8, 1)$ and B $(-2, 6, 3)$.

a Find the vector equation of the line M.

b Show that M and L intersect and find the coordinates of the point of intersection.

Solution

a

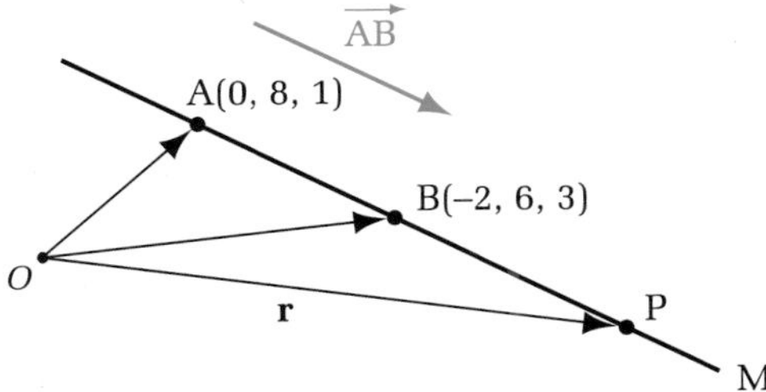

The position vector of A, which is on M, is $\overrightarrow{OA} = \begin{pmatrix} 0 \\ 8 \\ 1 \end{pmatrix}$
A vector parallel to M is $\overrightarrow{AB}$.

$$\overrightarrow{AB} = \overrightarrow{AO} + \overrightarrow{OB}$$

$$= -\begin{pmatrix} 0 \\ 8 \\ 1 \end{pmatrix} + \begin{pmatrix} -2 \\ 6 \\ 3 \end{pmatrix} = \begin{pmatrix} 0 \\ -8 \\ -1 \end{pmatrix} + \begin{pmatrix} -2 \\ 6 \\ 3 \end{pmatrix} = \begin{pmatrix} -2 \\ -2 \\ 2 \end{pmatrix}$$

$$= 2\begin{pmatrix} -1 \\ -1 \\ 1 \end{pmatrix}$$

Since $\begin{pmatrix} -2 \\ -2 \\ 2 \end{pmatrix}$ is parallel to M, $\begin{pmatrix} -1 \\ -1 \\ 1 \end{pmatrix}$ must also be parallel to M.

The vector equation of the line M can now be written as

$$\mathbf{r} = \overrightarrow{OA} + \overrightarrow{AP} = \begin{pmatrix} 0 \\ 8 \\ 1 \end{pmatrix} + s\begin{pmatrix} -1 \\ -1 \\ 1 \end{pmatrix}, \text{ where s is a parameter.}$$

b L and M intersect at Q if we can find a value of t and a value of s such that $\mathbf{r}(t) = \mathbf{r}(s)$.

$\mathbf{r}(t)$ describes line L and $\mathbf{r}(s)$ describes line M.

$$\begin{pmatrix} -2 \\ 10 \\ 4 \end{pmatrix} + t\begin{pmatrix} -1 \\ 3 \\ 2 \end{pmatrix} = \begin{pmatrix} 0 \\ 8 \\ 1 \end{pmatrix} + s\begin{pmatrix} -1 \\ -1 \\ 1 \end{pmatrix}$$

Recall that two vectors are equal if their corresponding components are equal.

$\mathbf{i}$: $-2 - t = 0 - s \Rightarrow \quad s - t = 2$ [1]

$\mathbf{j}$: $10 + 3t = 8 - s \Rightarrow \quad s + 3t = -2$ [2]

$\mathbf{k}$: $4 + 2t = 1 + s \Rightarrow \quad -s + 2t = -3$ [3]

These are simultaneous equations in s and t. There are three equations in two unknowns. Solve equations [1] and [2] by eliminating s.

Subtracting equation [2] from equation [1],

$$-t - 3t = 2 + 2$$
$$-4t = 4$$
$$\text{So} \quad t = -1$$

Substituting $t = -1$ into equation [1] to find s,

$$s - (-1) = 2$$
$$s + 1 = 2$$
$$s = 1$$

Check that these values satisfy equation [3].

Since distinct values for the parameters exist that satisfy all three equations, the lines L and M do intersect.

$$\mathbf{r}(t) = \begin{pmatrix} -2 \\ 10 \\ 4 \end{pmatrix} + t\begin{pmatrix} -1 \\ 3 \\ 2 \end{pmatrix} \Rightarrow \mathbf{r}(-1) = \begin{pmatrix} -2 \\ 10 \\ 4 \end{pmatrix} - \begin{pmatrix} -1 \\ 3 \\ 2 \end{pmatrix} = \begin{pmatrix} -1 \\ 7 \\ 2 \end{pmatrix}$$

$$\mathbf{r}(s) = \begin{pmatrix} 0 \\ 8 \\ 1 \end{pmatrix} + s\begin{pmatrix} -1 \\ -1 \\ 1 \end{pmatrix} \Rightarrow \mathbf{r}(1) = \begin{pmatrix} 0 \\ 8 \\ 1 \end{pmatrix} + \begin{pmatrix} -1 \\ -1 \\ 1 \end{pmatrix} = \begin{pmatrix} -1 \\ 7 \\ 2 \end{pmatrix}$$

The position vector of Q, the point of intersection, is $\begin{pmatrix} -1 \\ 7 \\ 2 \end{pmatrix}$.

The coordinates of Q are $(-1, 7, 2)$.

Example 5

Show that the two straight lines $\mathbf{r}(t) = (3\mathbf{i} + 5\mathbf{k}) + t(-\mathbf{i} + \mathbf{j} + 2\mathbf{k})$ and $\mathbf{r}(s) = (\mathbf{i} + 4\mathbf{j}) + s(\mathbf{i} + \mathbf{j} + \mathbf{k})$ are skew.

$$\mathbf{r}(t) = \begin{pmatrix} 3 \\ 0 \\ 5 \end{pmatrix} + t\begin{pmatrix} -1 \\ 1 \\ 2 \end{pmatrix}$$

$$\mathbf{r}(s) = \begin{pmatrix} 1 \\ 4 \\ 0 \end{pmatrix} + s\begin{pmatrix} 1 \\ 1 \\ 1 \end{pmatrix}$$

Solution

Two lines are skew if they are not parallel and do not intersect. To check that $\mathbf{r}(s)$ and $\mathbf{r}(t)$ are not parallel, check that $(-\mathbf{i} + \mathbf{j} + 2\mathbf{k})$ is not a multiple of $(\mathbf{i} + \mathbf{j} + \mathbf{k})$. These vectors are parallel to the lines $\mathbf{r}(s)$ and $\mathbf{r}(t)$, so if they are not parallel, $\mathbf{r}(s)$ and $\mathbf{r}(t)$ cannot be parallel.

Now check to see if the lines intersect. They will intersect if t and s can be found such that $\mathbf{r}(t) = \mathbf{r}(s)$.

$$(3\mathbf{i} + 5\mathbf{k}) + t(-\mathbf{i} + \mathbf{j} + 2\mathbf{k}) = (\mathbf{i} + 4\mathbf{j}) + s(\mathbf{i} + \mathbf{j} + \mathbf{k})$$

$$\begin{pmatrix} 3 \\ 0 \\ 5 \end{pmatrix} + t\begin{pmatrix} -1 \\ 1 \\ 2 \end{pmatrix} = \begin{pmatrix} 1 \\ 4 \\ 0 \end{pmatrix} + s($$

Equating the corresponding components of **i**, **j** and **k**,

$$\mathbf{i}: \quad 3 - t = 1 + s \Rightarrow s + t = 2 \qquad [1]$$
$$\mathbf{j}: \quad t = 4 + s \Rightarrow t - s = 4 \qquad [2]$$
$$\mathbf{k}: \quad 5 + 2t = s \Rightarrow s - 2t = 5 \qquad [3]$$

Adding equations [1] and [2] in order to eliminate s,

$$2t = 6 \Rightarrow t = 3$$

Substituting for t in equation [1],

$$t + s = 2 \Rightarrow 3 + s = 2$$
$$\Rightarrow \quad s = -1$$

Check that these values work in all three equations. You find that $t = 3$ and $s = -1$ does not satisfy equation [3] so the lines do not intersect. Since they are not parallel they must be skew.

There are no values of t and s that make the position vectors of points on the two lines equal.

The shortest distance between a point and a straight line

Consider a line L with vector equation $\mathbf{r} = \mathbf{a} + \lambda\mathbf{b}$, and a point Q with position vector $\mathbf{q}$, where Q is not on L. The shortest distance between Q and the line L is the perpendicular distance of Q from the line. This is denoted in the diagram by the dotted line.

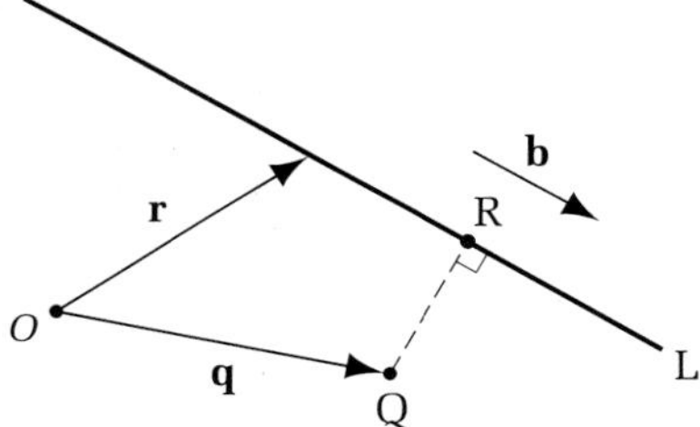

To calculate this distance the position vector of R needs to be found. There will be a value of λ that makes $\mathbf{r}$ point to R. Since $\overrightarrow{QR}$ is perpendicular to $\mathbf{b}$, the vector parallel to line L, we can use the fact that the scalar product of perpendicular vectors is zero.

$$\overrightarrow{QR}.\mathbf{b} = 0$$

By vector addition

$$\overrightarrow{QR} = \overrightarrow{QO} + \overrightarrow{OR}$$
$$= -\mathbf{q} + \mathbf{r}$$

So $\quad (\mathbf{r} - \mathbf{q}).\mathbf{b} = 0 \quad$ [1]

This equation can be solved to find the value of λ that will make $\mathbf{r}$ the position vector of R. The vector $\overrightarrow{QR}$ can then be found in component form and the shortest distance of Q from L calculated.

Example 6

The straight line M has vector equation
$\mathbf{r}(t) = (9\mathbf{i} - 9\mathbf{j} - 16\mathbf{k}) + t(-\mathbf{i} + 2\mathbf{j} + 6\mathbf{k})$.

$\mathbf{r}(t) = \begin{pmatrix} 9 \\ -9 \\ -16 \end{pmatrix} + t\begin{pmatrix} -1 \\ 2 \\ 6 \end{pmatrix}$

a Find the shortest distance between the origin and the line M.
b Show that point T $(10, 1, 15)$ does not lie on the line M.
c Calculate the shortest distance between the point T and the line M.

Solution

a There will be a point Q on M such that $\overrightarrow{OQ}$ is perpendicular to M.

Then $\overrightarrow{OQ}.(-\mathbf{i} + 2\mathbf{j} + 6\mathbf{k}) = 0$

$\mathbf{a}.\mathbf{b} = 0$ when vectors **a** and **b** are perpendicular.

Because Q is a point on the line, $\overrightarrow{OQ} = \mathbf{r}(t)$ for some value of t.

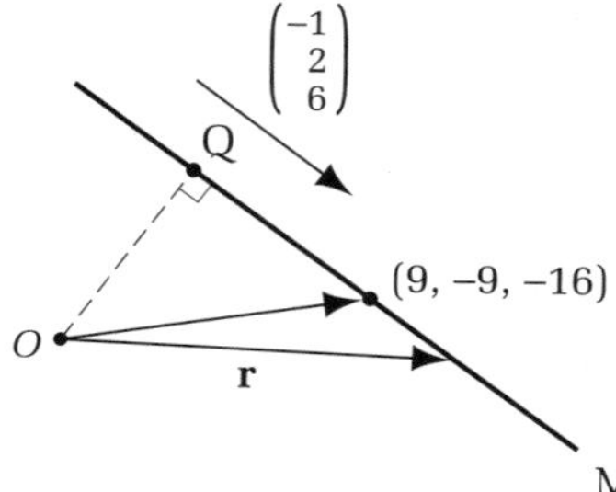

This means that $\overrightarrow{OQ} = (9\mathbf{i} - 9\mathbf{j} - 16\mathbf{k}) + t(-\mathbf{i} + 2\mathbf{j} + 6\mathbf{k})$
$= (9 - t)\mathbf{i} + (-9 + 2t)\mathbf{j} + (-16 + 6t)\mathbf{k}$

$\overrightarrow{OQ} = \begin{pmatrix} 9 \\ -9 \\ -16 \end{pmatrix} + t\begin{pmatrix} -1 \\ 2 \\ 6 \end{pmatrix} = \begin{pmatrix} 9-t \\ -9+2t \\ -16+6t \end{pmatrix}$

The scalar product can now be formed and evaluated.

$$[(9 - t)\mathbf{i} + (-9 + 2t)\mathbf{j} + (-16 + 6t)\mathbf{k}].(-\mathbf{i} + 2\mathbf{j} + 6\mathbf{k}) = 0$$
$$\Rightarrow \quad [(9 - t) \times -1] + [(-9 + 2t) \times 2] + [(-16 + 6t) \times 6] = 0$$
$$\Rightarrow \quad t - 9 - 18 + 4t - 96 + 36t = 0$$
$$\Rightarrow \quad 41t - 123 = 0$$
$$\Rightarrow \quad t = 3$$

$\overrightarrow{OQ}$ is perpendicular to M so

$\begin{pmatrix} 9-t \\ -9+2t \\ -16+6t \end{pmatrix}.\begin{pmatrix} -1 \\ 2 \\ 6 \end{pmatrix} = 0.$

So to find the position vector of Q substitute $t = 3$ into the vector equation of the straight line.
When $t = 3$, $\overrightarrow{OQ} = 6\mathbf{i} - 3\mathbf{j} + 2\mathbf{k}$
The shortest distance from the origin to the point Q is $|\overrightarrow{OQ}|$.

$\overrightarrow{OQ} = \begin{pmatrix} 6 \\ -3 \\ 2 \end{pmatrix}$ when $t = 3$.

$$|\overrightarrow{OQ}| = \sqrt{6^2 + (-3)^2 + 2^2}$$
$$= \sqrt{49}$$
$$= 7 \text{ units}$$

b The point T $(10, 1, 15)$ lies on the line if $\mathbf{r}(t) = 10\mathbf{i} + \mathbf{j} + 15\mathbf{k}$, for some value of t.
Substitute this into the vector equation of the straight line

$$(9\mathbf{i} - 9\mathbf{j} - 16\mathbf{k}) + t(-\mathbf{i} + 2\mathbf{j} + 6\mathbf{k}) = 10\mathbf{i} + \mathbf{j} + 15\mathbf{k}$$
So $(9 - t)\mathbf{i} + (-9 + 2t)\mathbf{j} + (-16 + 6t)\mathbf{k} = 10\mathbf{i} + \mathbf{j} + 15\mathbf{k}$

$\begin{pmatrix} 9 \\ -9 \\ -16 \end{pmatrix} + t\begin{pmatrix} -1 \\ 2 \\ 6 \end{pmatrix} = \begin{pmatrix} 10 \\ 1 \\ 15 \end{pmatrix}$

Equating corresponding components,

$$\mathbf{i}: \quad 9 - t = 10 \Rightarrow t = -1$$

$$\mathbf{j}: \quad -9 + 2t = 1 \Rightarrow t = 5$$

$$\mathbf{k}: \quad -16 + 6t = 15 \Rightarrow t = \tfrac{31}{6}$$

So there is no single value of t that satisfies all three equations. Therefore T does not lie on M.

c

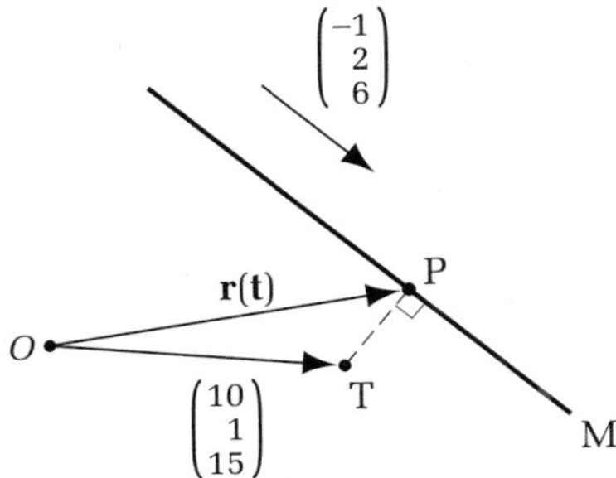

There is a value of t that will make **r** point to P, a point on the line M, where *TP* is the shortest distance between T and M. The vector $\overrightarrow{TP}$ is then perpendicular to M.

$$\overrightarrow{TP} = \overrightarrow{TO} + \overrightarrow{OP}$$

$$= -\begin{pmatrix}10\\1\\15\end{pmatrix} + \begin{pmatrix}9-t\\-9+2t\\-16+6t\end{pmatrix} = \begin{pmatrix}-1-t\\-10+2t\\-31+6t\end{pmatrix}$$

Using the scalar product at P, $\overrightarrow{TP}$ is perpendicular to the line

Remember that if $\mathbf{a}.\mathbf{b} = 0$ then **a** and **b** are perpendicular.

$$\begin{pmatrix}-1-t\\-10+2t\\-31+6t\end{pmatrix} \cdot \begin{pmatrix}-1\\2\\6\end{pmatrix} = 0$$

$$\Rightarrow \quad (-1-t) \times -1 + (-10+2t) \times 2 + (-31+6t) \times 6 = 0$$

$$\Rightarrow \quad 1 + t - 20 + 4t - 186 + 36t = 0$$

$$\Rightarrow \quad t = 5$$

Substituting this value into the expression for $\overrightarrow{TP}$ gives

$$\overrightarrow{TP} = \begin{pmatrix}-6\\0\\-1\end{pmatrix}$$

So the shortest distance from T to M is given by

$$|\overrightarrow{TP}| = \sqrt{(-6)^2 + 0^2 + (-1)^2}$$

$$= \sqrt{37}$$

14.4 The Vector Equation of a Straight Line

Exercise

Technique

1 A straight line N passes through the point $(2, -1, 7)$ and is parallel to the vector $\mathbf{i} - \mathbf{j} + 2\mathbf{k}$.

a Find the vector equation of the straight line, N.
b Which of points R $(6, -5, 14)$ and S $(0, 1, 3)$ lies on line N?

2 The straight line L_1, has vector equation $\mathbf{r}(\lambda) = (\mathbf{i} + 3\mathbf{j} - \mathbf{k}) + \lambda(3\mathbf{i} - 2\mathbf{j} + \mathbf{k})$.

$$\mathbf{r}(\lambda) = \begin{pmatrix} 1 \\ 3 \\ -1 \end{pmatrix} + \lambda \begin{pmatrix} 3 \\ -2 \\ 1 \end{pmatrix}$$

a Write down a vector that is parallel to this line.
b Find the vector equation of the line that is parallel to L_1 and passes through Q $(-5, 1, -3)$.

3 The vector equation of a straight line L is $\mathbf{r} = (2\mathbf{i} - \mathbf{j} + 5\mathbf{k}) + \lambda(\mathbf{i} - \mathbf{j} + \mathbf{k})$. Find the value of m if the point P $(1, 0, m)$ lies on the line L.

4 The points A, B and C have position vectors $\begin{pmatrix} -3 \\ 8 \\ 1 \end{pmatrix}$, $\begin{pmatrix} 0 \\ 7 \\ 5 \end{pmatrix}$ and $\begin{pmatrix} -4 \\ 2 \\ 1 \end{pmatrix}$ respectively.

a Find the vector $\overrightarrow{AB}$.
b Find the vector equation of the straight line parallel to $\overrightarrow{AB}$ that passes through C.

5 The straight line M passes through A $(1, -1, -1)$ and is parallel to vector $\mathbf{b} = \begin{pmatrix} 2 \\ 2 \\ -1 \end{pmatrix}$.

a Find the magnitude of $\mathbf{b}$.
b Find the position vectors of points C and D, which lie on the line M, but are 6 units from A.

6 Find the vector equation of the straight line passing through the points R and S, which have position vectors $2\mathbf{i} - \mathbf{j} + 2\mathbf{k}$ and $7\mathbf{i} + \mathbf{k}$, respectively. Find also the value of p such that P $(-33, p, 9)$ lies on this line.

7 The straight line L_1 is given by $\mathbf{r}(s) = (3\mathbf{i} - \mathbf{k}) + s(\mathbf{i} + \mathbf{j} + \mathbf{k})$. The straight line L_2 passes through A $(6, 2, 0)$ and B $(6, 6, 8)$.

a Find the vector equation of L_2.
b Find the coordinates of the point where the two lines intersect.
c Find the angle between the two lines.

8 The straight lines L and M have vector equations $\mathbf{r}(\lambda) = (2-\lambda)\mathbf{i} + \lambda\mathbf{j} + (3+\lambda)\mathbf{k}$ and $\mathbf{r}(\mu) = (1+\mu)\mathbf{i} + (3-\mu)\mathbf{j} + (-1+3\mu)\mathbf{k}$, respectively.

$\mathbf{r}(\lambda) = \begin{pmatrix} 2-\lambda \\ \lambda \\ 3+\lambda \end{pmatrix}$

$\mathbf{r}(\mu) = \begin{pmatrix} 1+\mu \\ 3-\mu \\ -1+3\mu \end{pmatrix}$

a Show that the lines L and M are skew.

b Find the angle between these two lines.

9 The straight line L passes through A $(-16, 27, 0)$ and B $(8, -5, 8)$.

a Find the vector equation of L.

b Find the shortest distance from the origin to L.

c Find the perpendicular distance from C $(-9, 20, 3)$ to this line L.

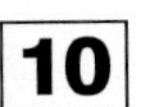

10 The straight line N has vector equation $\mathbf{r}(t) = (8\mathbf{i} + 9\mathbf{j} + 4\mathbf{k}) + t(3\mathbf{i} + \mathbf{j} - 2\mathbf{k})$ and Q $(1, 12, 9)$ is a point not on N.

$\mathbf{r}(t) = \begin{pmatrix} 8+3t \\ 9-t \\ 4-2t \end{pmatrix}$

a Find the point P, on N, such that $\overrightarrow{QP}$ is perpendicular to the line N.

b Find the perpendicular distance of Q from N.

c Q$'$ is the reflection of Q in the line N. Find the coordinates of Q$'$.

Contextual

1

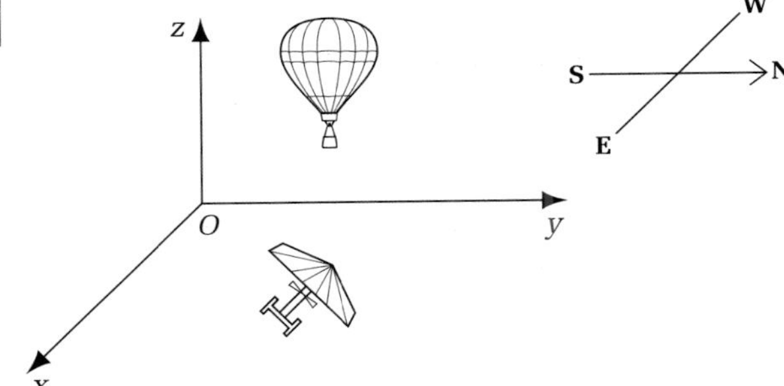

A hot air balloon takes off from point O. At t seconds after take-off, the position of the balloon is given by $\mathbf{r}_1 = \begin{pmatrix} 0 \\ 2t \\ 2t \end{pmatrix}$. At the same time as the balloon takes off a microlight is spotted flying over the point $(500, 500, 0)$. It has a constant height of 200 metres and is flying due west at $8\,\text{m}\,\text{s}^{-1}$.

a Find the position vector $\mathbf{r}_2$ of the microlight t seconds after the balloon takes off from O.

b Explain the meaning of the vector $(\mathbf{r}_2 - \mathbf{r}_1)$.

c Find an expression, in terms of t, for the distance between the balloon and the microlight.

d Find the minimum distance between the balloon and the microlight.

2

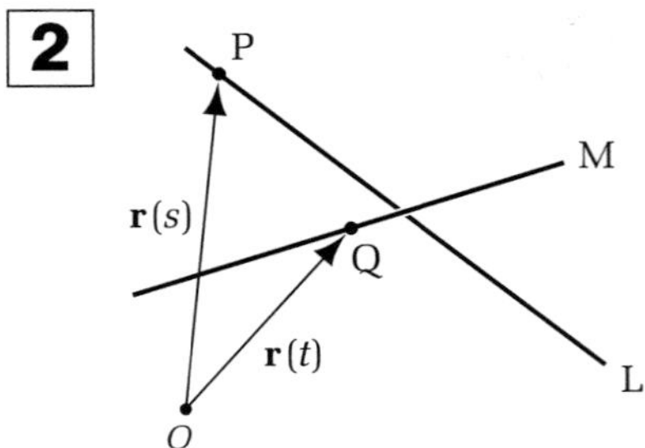

The straight lines L and M are skew and have vector equations

$\mathbf{r}(s) = \begin{pmatrix} 7 \\ 7 \\ 10 \end{pmatrix} + s\begin{pmatrix} 3 \\ 4 \\ 1 \end{pmatrix}$ and $\mathbf{r}(t) = \begin{pmatrix} 3 \\ -5 \\ 3 \end{pmatrix} + t\begin{pmatrix} 2 \\ 2 \\ 1 \end{pmatrix}$ respectively.

a P is a point on L and Q is a point on M. Find an expression, in terms of s and t, for the vector $\overrightarrow{PQ}$.

b Find the coordinates of P and Q if the vector $\overrightarrow{PQ}$ is perpendicular to both L and M.

c Find the shortest distance between L and M.

14.5 The Vector Equation of a Plane

A **plane** can be thought of as a flat surface. In the diagram Luke is standing on the x–y plane. This can also be called the plane $z = 0$, because the z-coordinate of all points on this plane is zero. Luke is leaning against the y–z plane. The x-coordinates of all the points on this plane are zero. This means that the y–z plane can also be called the plane $x = 0$.

The brush is leaning on the x–z plane. Every point on this plane has a y-coordinate of zero. It can be called the plane $y = 0$. Notice that there is also a cube with side 1 unit resting on the plane $z = 0$. The side labelled A is part of the plane $z = 1$ because each point on this side has a z-coordinate of 1. All the points on the side labelled B have an x-coordinate of 4 and every point on the side C has a y-coordinate of 4.

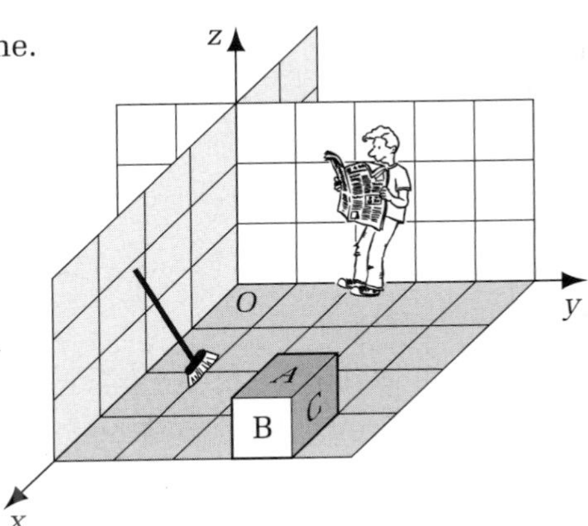

Therefore, side B is part of the plane $x = 4$ and side C is part of the plane $y = 4$. There are other ways to describe planes.
Consider two parallel planes π_1 and π_2.

The Greek letter π is often used to represent a plane.

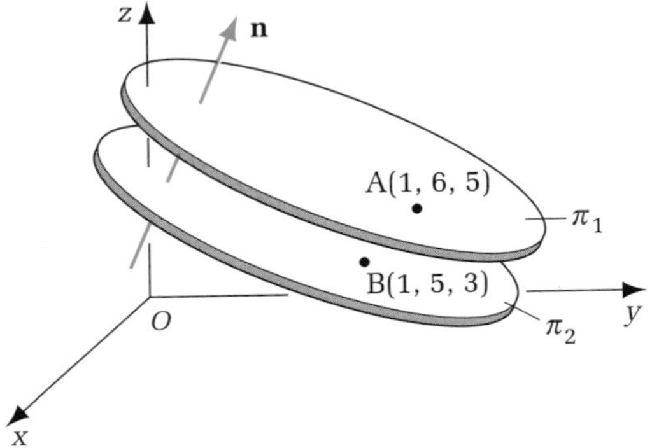

The diagram shows two planes, π_1 and π_2. A plane is infinitesimally thin, but thickness has been shown here to give a 3D effect. Remember that the diagrams only show part of the plane; both planes spread out indefinitely.

Notice that the vector **n** is perpendicular to both planes. The planes π_1 and π_2 can therefore be identified as:

- π_1 is the plane perpendicular to **n** that passes through A $(1, 6, 5)$.
- π_2 is the plane perpendicular to **n** that passes through B $(1, 5, 3)$.

So one way of identifying a particular plane is to:

- state a vector that is perpendicular to the plane and
- state a point on the plane.

This is not the only method. Another is to state three points that lie on the plane; this will be considered later.

We can find the vector equation of a plane when a vector perpendicular to the plane and a point on the plane are known. Let **n** be the vector perpendicular to the plane, and **a** be the position vector of some point A on the plane. Then **r** is the position vector of some other point on the plane.

n is also known as the vector normal to the plane.

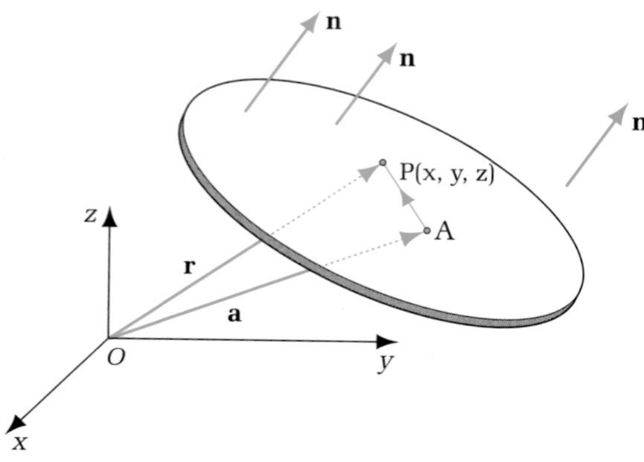

If P is a point on the plane, then the vector $\overrightarrow{AP}$ lies in the plane because if A and P both lie on the same surface, then the line joining them will also lie on the same surface.

$$\begin{aligned} \text{So} \quad \overrightarrow{AP} &= \overrightarrow{AO} + \overrightarrow{OP} \\ &= -\mathbf{a} + \mathbf{r} \\ &= \mathbf{r} - \mathbf{a} \end{aligned}$$

We know that **n** is also perpendicular to $\overrightarrow{AP}$ (because **n** is perpendicular to the plane), so we can use the scalar product with these perpendicular vectors.

Recall that if vectors **a** and **b** are perpendicula then $\mathbf{a}.\mathbf{b} = 0$.

$$\begin{aligned} & \mathbf{n}.\overrightarrow{AP} = 0 \\ \Rightarrow \quad & \mathbf{n}.(\mathbf{r} - \mathbf{a}) = 0 \\ \Rightarrow \quad & \mathbf{n}.\mathbf{r} - \mathbf{n}.\mathbf{a} = 0 \\ \Rightarrow \quad & \mathbf{n}.\mathbf{r} = \mathbf{n}.\mathbf{a} \end{aligned}$$

By the distributive law, $\mathbf{a}.(\mathbf{b} - \mathbf{c}) = \mathbf{a}.\mathbf{b} - \mathbf{a}.\mathbf{c}$.

Since **n** and **a** are both fixed, **n.a** will be some constant. Call this constant d.

Recall that **n.a** is a scalar.

So $\mathbf{n}.\mathbf{r} = d$

or $\mathbf{r}.\mathbf{n} = d$ ◀ **Learn this important result.**

$$\begin{pmatrix} \text{position vector of} \\ \text{a point on the plane} \end{pmatrix} . \begin{pmatrix} \text{vector perpendicular} \\ \text{to the plane} \end{pmatrix} = \text{constant}$$

Once the vector **n** has been determined the value of d will remain constant for that plane.

$\mathbf{r}.\mathbf{n} = d$ is called the **vector equation of the plane.**

Remember that **r** is the position vector of a general point P (x, y, z) on the plane and **n** is a vector perpendicular to the plane.

Let $\mathbf{r} = \begin{pmatrix} x \\ y \\ z \end{pmatrix}$ and let $\mathbf{n} = \begin{pmatrix} a \\ b \\ c \end{pmatrix}$. The vector equation of the plane can then be written as

$$\begin{pmatrix} x \\ y \\ z \end{pmatrix} . \begin{pmatrix} a \\ b \\ c \end{pmatrix} = d$$

The scalar or dot product gives

$$ax + by + cz = d$$

which no longer involves any vectors.
The symbols x, y and z represent coordinates in relation to the Cartesian axes. This equation is called the **Cartesian equation of the plane**. So if the vector equation of the plane is known, the Cartesian equation of the plane can always be found and vice versa.

If $ax + by + cz = d$ is the Cartesian equation of a plane then a vector normal to the plane will be $\begin{pmatrix} a \\ b \\ c \end{pmatrix}$.

Example 1

A plane crosses the axes at A $(2, 0, 0)$, B $(0, 0, 2)$ and C $(0, 2, 0)$. Find the vector equation of the plane ABC.

Solution

We need to know a vector normal to the plane. Since the plane cuts each axis at the same value, try $\mathbf{n} = \mathbf{i} + \mathbf{j} + \mathbf{k}$. Check that $\mathbf{n}$ is perpendicular to any two non-parallel vectors in the plane, as this means $\mathbf{n}$ is perpendicular to the plane. Check that $\mathbf{n}$ is perpendicular to $\overrightarrow{BC}$ and $\overrightarrow{BA}$.

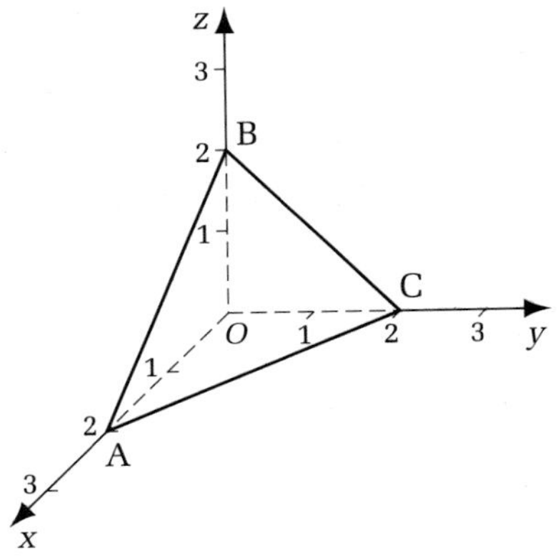

$$\mathbf{n}.\overrightarrow{BC} = \begin{pmatrix} 1 \\ 1 \\ 1 \end{pmatrix} . \begin{pmatrix} 0 \\ 2 \\ -2 \end{pmatrix} = 0$$

$$\mathbf{n}.\overrightarrow{BA} = \begin{pmatrix} 1 \\ 1 \\ 1 \end{pmatrix} . \begin{pmatrix} 2 \\ 0 \\ -2 \end{pmatrix} = 0$$

So $\mathbf{n}$ is perpendicular to the plane ABC.
Now the vector equation of the plane ABC is of the form $\mathbf{r}.\mathbf{n} = d$ so $\mathbf{r}.\begin{pmatrix} 1 \\ 1 \\ 1 \end{pmatrix} = d$.
This is true for any point on the plane, so it is true for A $(2, 0, 0)$.

Then it is true for $\mathbf{r} = \begin{pmatrix} 2 \\ 0 \\ 0 \end{pmatrix}$ and $\begin{pmatrix} 2 \\ 0 \\ 0 \end{pmatrix} . \begin{pmatrix} 1 \\ 1 \\ 1 \end{pmatrix} = d.$

Verify that $d = 2$ using the point B (0, 0, 2), or the point C (0, 2, 0).

That is,

$$(2 \times 1) + (0 \times 1) + (0 \times 1) = d$$
$$2 = d$$

The vector equation of the plane ABC is therefore

$$\mathbf{r}.\begin{pmatrix} 1 \\ 1 \\ 1 \end{pmatrix} = 2 \quad \text{or} \quad \begin{pmatrix} x \\ y \\ z \end{pmatrix} . \begin{pmatrix} 1 \\ 1 \\ 1 \end{pmatrix} = 2$$

Any point satisfying $\mathbf{r}.\begin{pmatrix} 1 \\ 1 \\ 1 \end{pmatrix} = 2$ or $x + y + z = 2$ lies on the plane ABC.

From the second form,

$$x + y + z = 2$$

This is the Cartesian equation of the plane ABC.

Example 2

The plane π passes through the point $(7, 2, -3)$ and is perpendicular to the vector $2\mathbf{i} - \mathbf{j} + 6\mathbf{k}$.

a Find the vector equation of the plane π.

b Which of the points B $(4, 8, -1)$ and C $(1, 2, 2)$ lie on the plane?

c Find the Cartesian equation of the plane π.

Solution

a The vector equation of the plane is of the form $\mathbf{r}.\mathbf{n} = d$.
So the vector equation of the plane π is

$$\mathbf{r}.(2\mathbf{i} - \mathbf{j} + 6\mathbf{k}) = d \quad \text{or} \quad \mathbf{r}.\begin{pmatrix} 2 \\ -1 \\ 6 \end{pmatrix} = d$$

This is true for all points on π, so d can be found by using the point $(7, 2, -3)$.
Let $\mathbf{r} = 7\mathbf{i} + 2\mathbf{j} - 3\mathbf{k}$ be the position vector of this point. Then

$$\begin{pmatrix} 7 \\ 2 \\ -3 \end{pmatrix} . \begin{pmatrix} 2 \\ -1 \\ 6 \end{pmatrix} = d$$

$$\Rightarrow \quad -6 = d$$

So the vector equation of the plane π is

$$\mathbf{r}.(2\mathbf{i} - \mathbf{j} + 6\mathbf{k}) = -6 \quad \text{or} \quad \mathbf{r}.\begin{pmatrix} 2 \\ -1 \\ 6 \end{pmatrix} = -6$$

b B $(4, 8, -1)$ lies on the plane if $\mathbf{r} = 4\mathbf{i} + 8\mathbf{j} - \mathbf{k}$ satisfies $\mathbf{r}.\begin{pmatrix} 2 \\ -1 \\ 6 \end{pmatrix} = -6$.

$$\begin{pmatrix} 4 \\ 8 \\ -1 \end{pmatrix}.\begin{pmatrix} 2 \\ -1 \\ 6 \end{pmatrix} = -6$$

So B lies on the plane π.

The position vector of C is $(\mathbf{i} + 2\mathbf{j} + 2\mathbf{k})$ so C lies on the plane π only if $\begin{pmatrix} 1 \\ 2 \\ 2 \end{pmatrix}.\begin{pmatrix} 2 \\ -1 \\ 6 \end{pmatrix} = -6$. But $\begin{pmatrix} 1 \\ 2 \\ 2 \end{pmatrix}.\begin{pmatrix} 2 \\ -1 \\ 6 \end{pmatrix} = 12$.

So C does not lie on the plane π.

c Putting $\mathbf{r} = x\mathbf{i} + y\mathbf{j} + z\mathbf{k}$ in the vector equation of the plane,

$$\begin{pmatrix} x \\ y \\ z \end{pmatrix}.\begin{pmatrix} 2 \\ -1 \\ 6 \end{pmatrix} = -6$$

$\Rightarrow \quad 2x - y + 6z = -6$

This is the Cartesian equation of the plane π.

Check that B (4, 8, −1) satisfies this Cartesian equation but C (1, 2, 2) does not.

Example 3

The plane π_1 is given by the Cartesian equation $x - 3y + 4z = 16$

a Find the vector equation of the plane π_1.

b Find the vector equation of another plane π_2, which is parallel to π_1 but passes through the point $(3, 2, -1)$.

Solution

a $x - 3y + 4z = 16$

The vector equation of the plane is in the form $\begin{pmatrix} x \\ y \\ z \end{pmatrix}.\begin{pmatrix} a \\ b \\ c \end{pmatrix} = d$. It is clear that for this vector equation to produce the Cartesian equation $x - 3y + 4z = 16$, $a = 1$, $b = -3$, $c = 4$ and $d = 16$.

The vector equation of the plane is

$$\begin{pmatrix} x \\ y \\ z \end{pmatrix}.\begin{pmatrix} 1 \\ -3 \\ 4 \end{pmatrix} = 16 \quad \text{or} \quad \mathbf{r}.\begin{pmatrix} 1 \\ -3 \\ 4 \end{pmatrix} = 16$$

b π_1 has equation $\mathbf{r}.\begin{pmatrix} 1 \\ -3 \\ 4 \end{pmatrix} = 16$.

If π_2 is parallel to π_1 then the vector $\begin{pmatrix} 1 \\ -3 \\ 4 \end{pmatrix}$ must also be perpendicular to the plane π_2.

So the vector equation of π_2 is of the form

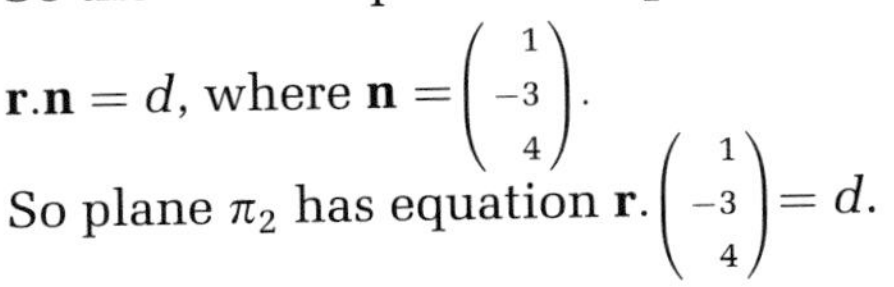

$\mathbf{r}.\mathbf{n} = d$, where $\mathbf{n} = \begin{pmatrix} 1 \\ -3 \\ 4 \end{pmatrix}$.

So plane π_2 has equation $\mathbf{r}.\begin{pmatrix} 1 \\ -3 \\ 4 \end{pmatrix} = d$.

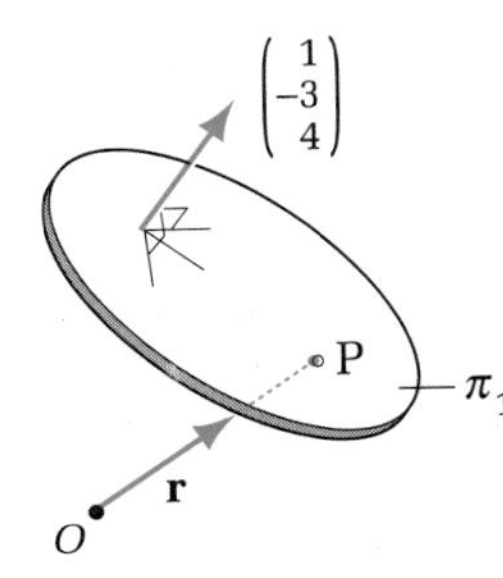

Point $(3, 2, -1)$ is on plane π_2, so to find d let $\mathbf{r} = \begin{pmatrix} 3 \\ 2 \\ -1 \end{pmatrix}$.

$$\begin{pmatrix} 3 \\ 2 \\ -1 \end{pmatrix} . \begin{pmatrix} 1 \\ -3 \\ 4 \end{pmatrix} = d$$

$$(3 \times 1) + (2 \times -3) + (-1 \times 4) = d$$

$$3 - 6 - 4 = d$$

$$-7 = d$$

The vector equation of the plane π_2 is therefore $\mathbf{r}.\begin{pmatrix} 1 \\ -3 \\ 4 \end{pmatrix} = -7$.

Example 4

The straight line M has vector equation $\mathbf{r} = (\mathbf{i} + \mathbf{j} + \mathbf{k}) + \lambda(2\mathbf{i} - \mathbf{j} + 3\mathbf{k})$. Find the equation of the plane that is perpendicular to the line M and passes through Q $(-5, 4, -8)$.

Given $\mathbf{r} = \begin{pmatrix} 1 \\ 1 \\ 1 \end{pmatrix} + \lambda\begin{pmatrix} 2 \\ -1 \\ 3 \end{pmatrix}$ we know that $\begin{pmatrix} 2 \\ -1 \\ 3 \end{pmatrix}$ is a vector parallel to the line M.

Solution

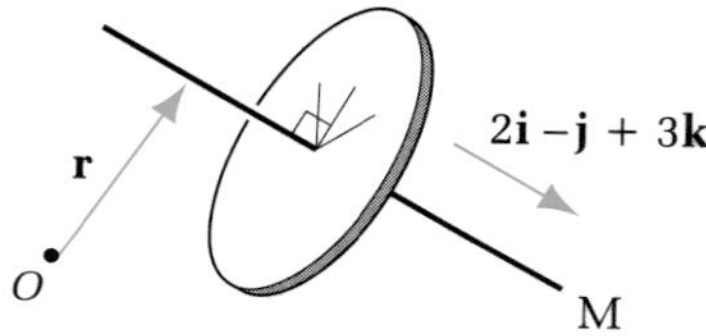

The vector equation of a plane that is perpendicular to $\mathbf{n}$ is $\mathbf{r}.\mathbf{n} = d$, where d is some constant. If the plane is perpendicular to the line M then

$$\mathbf{n} = 2\mathbf{i} - \mathbf{j} + 3\mathbf{k}$$

Now $\quad \mathbf{r}.(2\mathbf{i} - \mathbf{j} + 3\mathbf{k}) = d$

To find the value of d, a point on the plane is required. The plane passes through Q $(-5, 4, -8)$, so let $\mathbf{r} = -5\mathbf{i} + 4\mathbf{j} - 8\mathbf{k}$. Substituting this into the vector equation of the plane,

$$(-5\mathbf{i} + 4\mathbf{j} - 8\mathbf{k}).(2\mathbf{i} - \mathbf{j} + 3\mathbf{k}) = d$$

$$-10 - 4 - 24 = d$$

$$-38 = d$$

So the vector equation of the plane is

$$\mathbf{r}.(2\mathbf{i} - \mathbf{j} + 3\mathbf{k}) = -38$$

The angle between a straight line and a plane

The angle α between a straight line and a plane can be found by first considering the angle between the line and the vector perpendicular to the plane. Let the equation of the plane be $\mathbf{r}.\mathbf{n} = d$ and the equation of the line be $\mathbf{r}(\lambda) = \mathbf{a} + \lambda\mathbf{b}$.

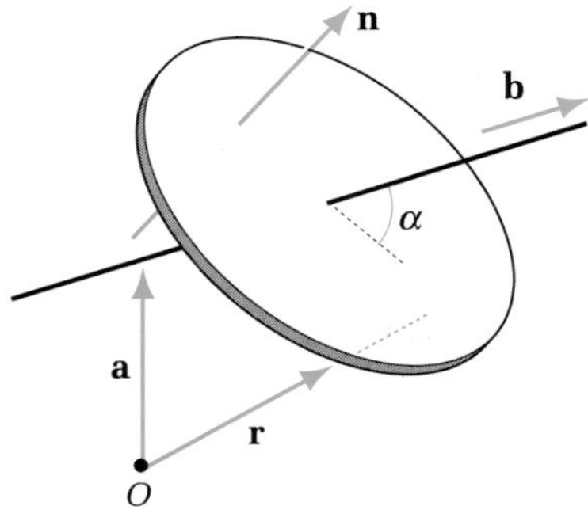

Imagine taking a view from the edge of the plane. If θ is the angle between $\mathbf{b}$, the vector parallel to the line, and $\mathbf{n}$, the vector perpendicular to the plane, then the angle between the plane and the line is

$$\alpha = \frac{\pi}{2} - \theta \quad \text{or} \quad \alpha = 90° - \theta$$

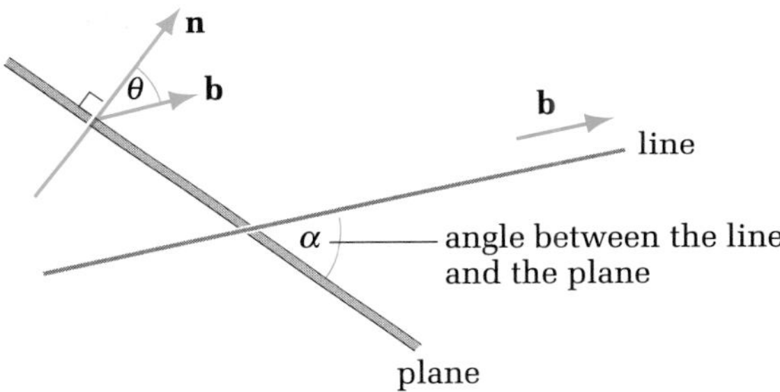

This assumes that θ is an acute angle. If θ is an obtuse angle then the angle between the line and the plane is

$$\alpha = \theta - \frac{\pi}{2}, \quad \text{or} \quad \alpha = \theta - 90°$$

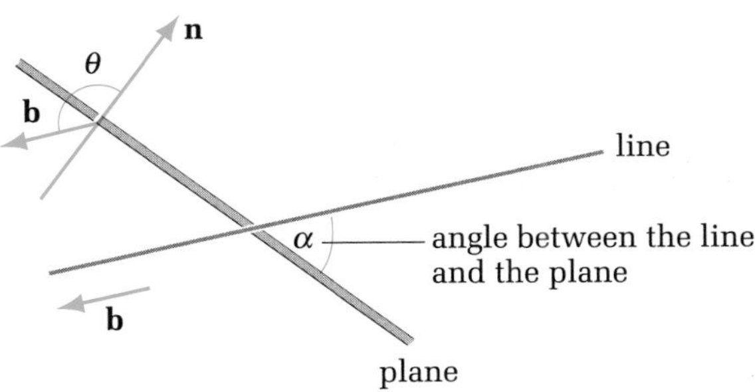

Example 5

Find the angle between the straight line $\mathbf{r} = \begin{pmatrix} 6 \\ 5 \\ 3 \end{pmatrix} + t\begin{pmatrix} 4 \\ 0 \\ 1 \end{pmatrix}$ and the plane $x + y - 3z = 2$.

Solution

Notice that the vector $\begin{pmatrix}4\\0\\1\end{pmatrix}$ is parallel to the line.

The Cartesian equation of the plane $x + y - 3z = 2$ can be written in the vector form $\mathbf{r}.\mathbf{n} = d$ as

$$\mathbf{r}.\begin{pmatrix}1\\1\\-3\end{pmatrix} = 2$$

So a vector perpendicular to the plane is $(\mathbf{i} + \mathbf{j} - 3\mathbf{k})$. Now use the scalar or dot product to find the angle between the vectors normal to the plane and parallel to the line.

$$\cos\theta = \frac{\begin{pmatrix}4\\0\\1\end{pmatrix}.\begin{pmatrix}1\\1\\-3\end{pmatrix}}{\sqrt{17}\times\sqrt{11}} \Rightarrow \cos\theta = \frac{1}{\sqrt{187}}$$

Recall that $\mathbf{a}.\mathbf{b} = ab\cos\theta$ so $\cos\theta = \dfrac{\mathbf{a}.\mathbf{b}}{ab}$.

$$\text{So} \quad \theta = \cos^{-1}\left(\frac{1}{\sqrt{187}}\right) \Rightarrow 1.5\,\text{rad} \quad \text{or} \quad 85.8^\circ$$

Check that $\theta = 85.8^\circ$, so θ is acute.

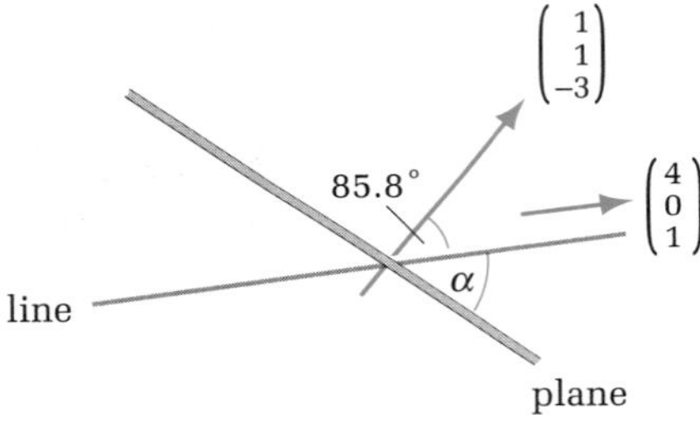

Now the angle between the line and the plane is

$$\frac{\pi}{2} - \theta = 0.07\,\text{rad (2 d.p.) or } 4.2^\circ$$

The angle between two planes

The angle between two planes is the same as the angle between the two vectors perpendicular to the planes.

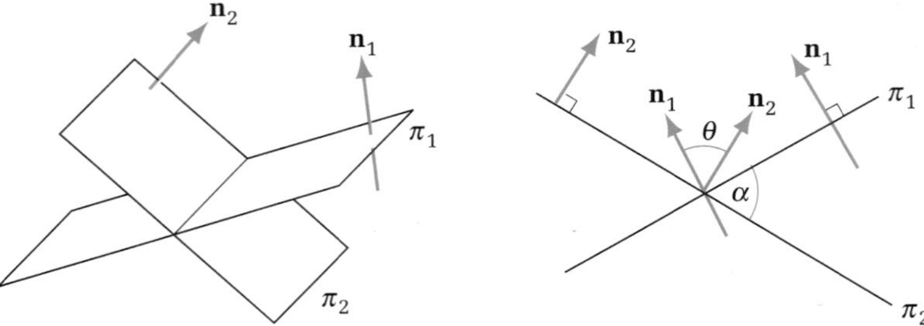

The end view diagram shows that θ, the angle between $\mathbf{n}_1$ and $\mathbf{n}_2$, is the same as α, the angle between the planes.

Check this by considering the angles in the triangles formed by $\mathbf{n}_1$, $\mathbf{n}_2$ and π_1 and $\mathbf{n}_1$, $\mathbf{n}_2$ and π_2.

Example 6

Find the acute angle between the two planes $x + 5y + z = 0$ and $2x - y + 2z = 3$.

Solution

First express both planes in the form $\mathbf{r}.\mathbf{n} = d$. The vectors that are perpendicular to the planes can then be identified quickly.

$$x + 5y + z = 0 \text{ can be written as } \begin{pmatrix} x \\ y \\ z \end{pmatrix} . \begin{pmatrix} 1 \\ 5 \\ 1 \end{pmatrix} = 0$$

$$2x - y + 2z = 3 \text{ can be written as } \begin{pmatrix} x \\ y \\ z \end{pmatrix} . \begin{pmatrix} 2 \\ -1 \\ 2 \end{pmatrix} = 3$$

So the vectors perpendicular to the planes are $\begin{pmatrix} 1 \\ 5 \\ 1 \end{pmatrix}$ and $\begin{pmatrix} 2 \\ -1 \\ 2 \end{pmatrix}$ respectively.

Using the scalar product, the angle between the vectors perpendicular to the planes, θ, is given by

$$\mathbf{a}.\mathbf{b} = ab\cos\theta$$

$$\begin{pmatrix} 1 \\ 5 \\ 1 \end{pmatrix} . \begin{pmatrix} 2 \\ -1 \\ 2 \end{pmatrix} = \sqrt{1 + 25 + 1} \times \sqrt{4 + 1 + 4} \times \cos\theta$$

$$2 - 5 + 2 = \sqrt{27} \times \sqrt{9} \times \cos\theta$$

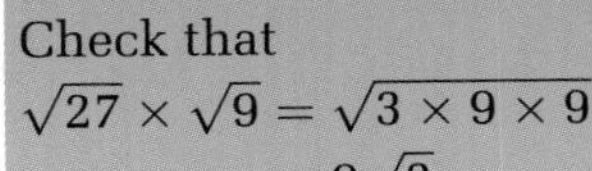

Check that $\sqrt{27} \times \sqrt{9} = \sqrt{3 \times 9 \times 9} = 9\sqrt{3}$

$$-1 = 9\sqrt{3}\cos\theta$$

$$-\frac{1}{9\sqrt{3}} = \cos\theta$$

$$\theta = \cos^{-1}\left(-\frac{1}{9\sqrt{3}}\right) = 1.63 \text{ rad (2 d.p.)}$$

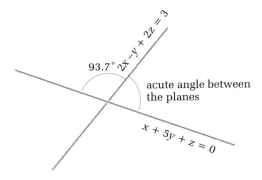

93.7°
$2x - y + 2z = 3$
acute angle between the planes
$x + 5y + z = 0$

Verify that the angle between the planes is 93.7°. Since this angle is obtuse, the acute angle between the planes is

$$\pi - 1.63 = 1.51 \text{ rad}$$

Check that this angle is equivalent to 86.3°.

The intersection of a straight line and a plane

If the angle between a straight line and a plane is not zero, the line should cut the plane at one point only.

Example 7

Find the point where the straight line $\mathbf{r} = (-4\mathbf{i} + \mathbf{j} + 9\mathbf{k}) + \lambda(-2\mathbf{i} + 4\mathbf{k})$ intersects the plane $\mathbf{r}.(2\mathbf{i} + 2\mathbf{j} - \mathbf{k}) = 5$.

$\mathbf{r} = \begin{pmatrix} -4 \\ 1 \\ 9 \end{pmatrix} + \lambda \begin{pmatrix} -2 \\ 0 \\ 4 \end{pmatrix}$

The plane is $\mathbf{r}.\begin{pmatrix} 2 \\ 2 \\ -1 \end{pmatrix} =$

Solution

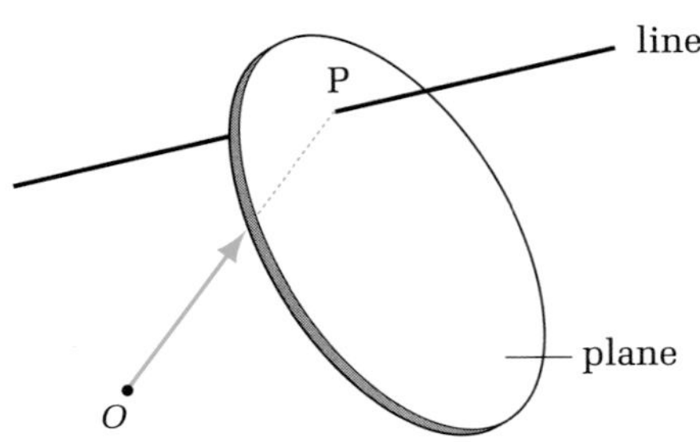

At the point of intersection, because the point lies on the line it can be expressed as

$$\begin{aligned} \mathbf{r} &= (-4\mathbf{i} + \mathbf{j} + 9\mathbf{k}) + \lambda(-2\mathbf{i} + 4\mathbf{k}) \\ &= (-4 - 2\lambda)\mathbf{i} + \mathbf{j} + (9 + 4\lambda)\mathbf{k} \end{aligned}$$

$\mathbf{r}(\lambda) = \begin{pmatrix} -4 - 2\lambda \\ 1 \\ 9 + 4\lambda \end{pmatrix}$

It also lies on the plane so it must satisfy

$$\mathbf{r}.(2\mathbf{i} + 2\mathbf{j} - \mathbf{k}) = 5$$

$$\begin{aligned} \text{So} \quad [(-4 - 2\lambda)\mathbf{i} + \mathbf{j} + (9 + 4\lambda)\mathbf{k}].(2\mathbf{i} + 2\mathbf{j} - \mathbf{k}) &= 5 \\ [(-4 - 2\lambda) \times 2] + [1 \times 2] + [(9 + 4\lambda) \times -1] &= 5 \\ -8 - 4\lambda + 2 - 9 - 4\lambda &= 5 \\ -15 - 8\lambda &= 5 \\ -8\lambda &= 20 \\ \lambda &= -\tfrac{20}{8} = -\tfrac{5}{2} \end{aligned}$$

That is, $\begin{pmatrix} -4 - 2\lambda \\ 1 \\ 9 + 4\lambda \end{pmatrix} . \begin{pmatrix} 2 \\ 2 \\ -1 \end{pmatrix} = 5.$

At P, $\lambda = -\frac{5}{2}$. Substituting this value back into the equation of the line to locate P,

$$\begin{aligned} \mathbf{r}(\lambda) &= (-4 - 2\lambda)\mathbf{i} + \mathbf{j} + (9 + 4\lambda)\mathbf{k} \\ \mathbf{r}(-\tfrac{5}{2}) &= (-4 - 2 \times (-\tfrac{5}{2}))\mathbf{i} + \mathbf{j} + (9 + 4 \times (-\tfrac{5}{2}))\mathbf{k} \\ &= (-4 + 5)\mathbf{i} + \mathbf{j} + (9 - 10)\mathbf{k} \\ &= \mathbf{i} + \mathbf{j} - \mathbf{k} \end{aligned}$$

So the point of intersection, P, has position vector $\mathbf{i} + \mathbf{j} - \mathbf{k}$.

The perpendicular distance between a point and a plane

The scalar product can be used to find the perpendicular distance from a point B, with position vector $\mathbf{b}$, to the plane $\mathbf{r}.\mathbf{n} = d$.

Look closely at the diagram. First find the perpendicular distance of the plane from the origin, denoted by ON. Remember that $\mathbf{r}$ is the position vector of any point on the plane.

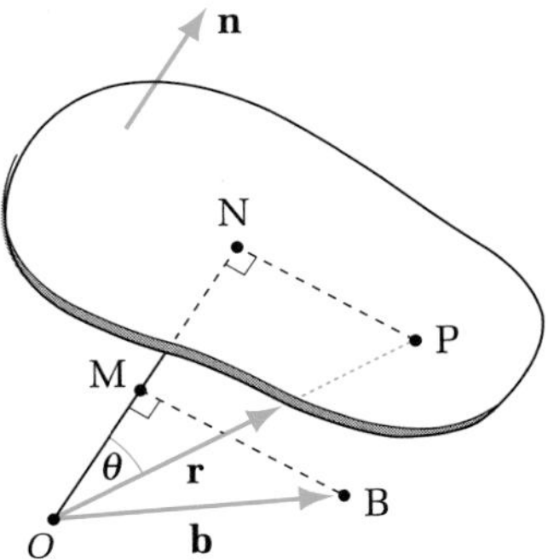

Using trigonometry, an expression for ON is

θ is the angle between $\mathbf{r}$ and $\overrightarrow{ON}$.

$$ON = |\mathbf{r}|\cos\theta$$

But consider $\mathbf{r}.\hat{\mathbf{n}}$ where $\hat{\mathbf{n}}$ is a unit vector (so $|\hat{\mathbf{n}}| = 1$) in the direction of $\mathbf{n}$.

$\overrightarrow{ON}$ must be parallel to $\mathbf{n}$ because both are perpendicular to the plane.

$$\begin{aligned}\mathbf{r}.\hat{\mathbf{n}} &= |\mathbf{r}|\,|\hat{\mathbf{n}}|\cos\theta\\ &= |\mathbf{r}| \times 1 \times \cos\theta\\ &= |\mathbf{r}|\cos\theta\end{aligned}$$

This means $ON = \mathbf{r}.\hat{\mathbf{n}}$.
Now using trigonometry in the triangle OMB,

α is the angle between $\overrightarrow{OB}$ and $\overrightarrow{OM}$.

$$OM = |\mathbf{b}|\cos\alpha$$

And by the same reasoning as above,

$$\mathbf{b}.\hat{\mathbf{n}} = |\mathbf{b}|\cos\alpha$$

So $OM = \mathbf{b}.\hat{\mathbf{n}}$.
From the geometry of the diagram, notice that the perpendicular distance between B and the plane $\mathbf{r}.\mathbf{n} = d$ can be written as $ON - OM$. From the above, we have

$$\begin{aligned}ON - OM &= \mathbf{r}.\hat{\mathbf{n}} - \mathbf{b}.\hat{\mathbf{n}}\\ &= (\mathbf{r} - \mathbf{b}).\hat{\mathbf{n}}\end{aligned}$$

So, providing a point can be found on the plane, the perpendicular distance from a point B to the plane can be found.

Example 8

The Cartesian equation of a plane is $3x + y - 2z = 3$.

a Find the perpendicular distance of the plane from the origin.

b Find the perpendicular distance of the point $(1, 3, -1)$ from the plane.

Solution

a First write the equation of the plane in the form $\mathbf{r}.\mathbf{n} = d$.

$$\begin{pmatrix} x \\ y \\ z \end{pmatrix} . \begin{pmatrix} 3 \\ 1 \\ -2 \end{pmatrix} = 3$$

Therefore $\mathbf{r}.\begin{pmatrix} 3 \\ 1 \\ -2 \end{pmatrix} = 3$

So a vector perpendicular to a plane is $\mathbf{n} = \begin{pmatrix} 3 \\ 1 \\ -2 \end{pmatrix}$.

From the diagram,

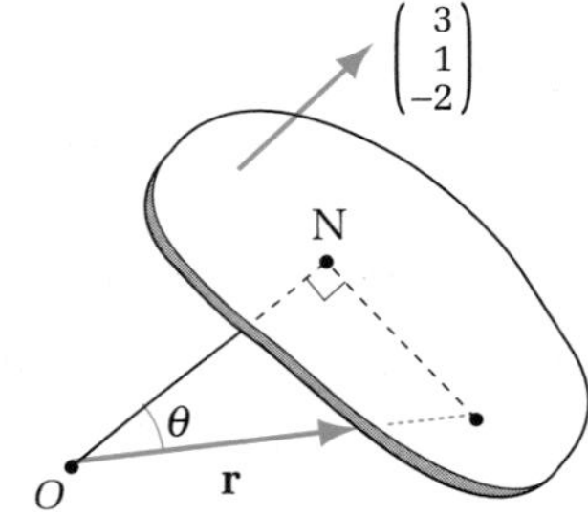

$ON = r\cos\theta$

$ON = \mathbf{r}.\hat{\mathbf{n}}$ [1]

where $\hat{\mathbf{n}}$ is a unit vector in the direction of $\mathbf{n}$.

Now $|\mathbf{n}| = \sqrt{3^2 + 1^2 + (-2)^2} = \sqrt{14}$

So $\hat{\mathbf{n}} = \frac{1}{\sqrt{14}}\mathbf{n} = \frac{1}{\sqrt{14}}\begin{pmatrix} 3 \\ 1 \\ -2 \end{pmatrix}$

Remember that $\mathbf{r}$ is the position vector of any point on the plane. A point on the plane satisfies the equation $3x + y - 2z = 3$, so putting $x = 0$ and $z = 0$, the point $(0, 3, 0)$ is on the plane. Using the position vector of that point in equation [1],

The point (2, 1, 2) also lies on the plane. Chec that this point gives th same value for *ON*.

$$ON = \begin{pmatrix} 0 \\ 3 \\ 0 \end{pmatrix} . \frac{1}{\sqrt{14}}\begin{pmatrix} 3 \\ 1 \\ -2 \end{pmatrix}$$

$$= \frac{1}{\sqrt{14}}\begin{pmatrix} 0 \\ 3 \\ 0 \end{pmatrix} . \begin{pmatrix} 3 \\ 1 \\ -2 \end{pmatrix}$$

$$= \frac{3}{\sqrt{14}}$$

b The perpendicular distance of the point $(1, 3, -1)$ from the plane can be calculated using the result for the distance between a point and a plane.

Here, $\mathbf{r} = \begin{pmatrix} 0 \\ 3 \\ 0 \end{pmatrix}$ and and $\mathbf{b} = \begin{pmatrix} 1 \\ 3 \\ -1 \end{pmatrix}$.

Substituting these vectors into the equation gives

$$\begin{aligned}
(\mathbf{r} - \mathbf{b}).\hat{\mathbf{n}} &= \left(\begin{pmatrix} 0 \\ 3 \\ 0 \end{pmatrix} - \begin{pmatrix} 1 \\ 3 \\ -1 \end{pmatrix} \right) . \frac{1}{\sqrt{14}} \begin{pmatrix} 3 \\ 1 \\ -2 \end{pmatrix} \\
&= \frac{1}{\sqrt{14}} \begin{pmatrix} -1 \\ 0 \\ 1 \end{pmatrix} . \begin{pmatrix} 3 \\ 1 \\ -2 \end{pmatrix} \\
&= \frac{1}{\sqrt{14}} \times (-3 + 0 - 2) \\
&= \frac{-5}{\sqrt{14}}
\end{aligned}$$

So the distance of $(1, 3, -1)$ from the plane is $\frac{5}{\sqrt{14}}$.
The minus sign in the calculation indicates that the point is on the opposite side of the plane from the origin.

A plane passing through three points

Another way of describing a plane is to state three points that lie on it. Many planes pass through any given pair of points, A and B.

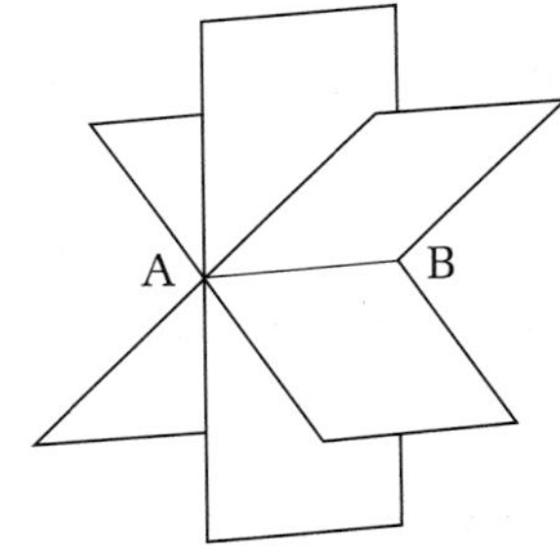

However, providing the points do not lie in a straight line only one plane can pass through three given points. Consider, for example, A $(1, 3, 3)$, B $(-2, -4, 1)$ and C $(3, 8, 5)$.

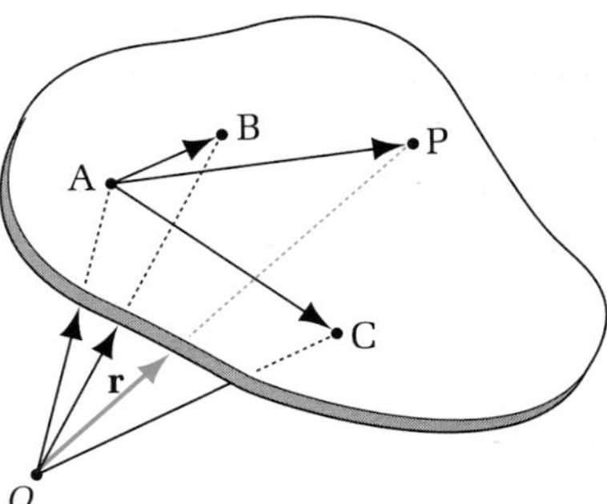

If one point is chosen, for example A, then two vectors $\overrightarrow{AB}$ and $\overrightarrow{AC}$ can be found that lie on the plane. Use vector addition to check that, for the points above, $\overrightarrow{AB} = -3\mathbf{i} - 7\mathbf{j} - 2\mathbf{k}$ and $\overrightarrow{AC} = 2\mathbf{i} + 5\mathbf{j} + 2\mathbf{k}$. Now the position vector of a general point on the plane can be determined.

$\overrightarrow{AP}$ will be a multiple of $\overrightarrow{AB}$ plus a multiple of $\overrightarrow{AC}$.

$$\mathbf{r} = \overrightarrow{OP}$$
$$= \overrightarrow{OA} + \overrightarrow{AP}$$

But since $\overrightarrow{AP}$ lies in the plane, it can be expressed in terms of the vectors $\overrightarrow{AB}$ and $\overrightarrow{AC}$. As P is an arbitrary point on the plane the vector $\overrightarrow{AP}$ will always be in the form $\lambda\overrightarrow{AC} + \mu\overrightarrow{AB}$ where λ and μ are two real numbers.

So $\quad \mathbf{r} = \overrightarrow{OA} + (\lambda\overrightarrow{AB} + \mu\overrightarrow{AC})$

$$\Rightarrow \mathbf{r} = (\mathbf{i} + 3\mathbf{j} + 3\mathbf{k}) + \lambda(-3\mathbf{i} - 7\mathbf{j} - 2\mathbf{k}) + \mu(2\mathbf{i} + 5\mathbf{j} + 2\mathbf{k})$$

The position vector of a[n] arbitrary point on the plane is given by the position vector of a poi[nt] on the plane plus scala[r] multiples of two vecto[rs] that lie in the plane.

$$\mathbf{r} = \begin{pmatrix}1\\3\\3\end{pmatrix} + \lambda\begin{pmatrix}-3\\-7\\-2\end{pmatrix} + \mu\begin{pmatrix}2\\5\\2\end{pmatrix}$$

This equation is the vector equation of the plane when the plane passes through three distinct points.

By writing $\mathbf{r} = \begin{pmatrix}x\\y\\z\end{pmatrix}$ it is possible to eliminate the parameters λ and μ.

This will give the Cartesian equation of the plane. Writing the equation in column vector form,

$$\begin{pmatrix}x\\y\\z\end{pmatrix} = \begin{pmatrix}1\\3\\3\end{pmatrix} + \lambda\begin{pmatrix}-3\\-7\\-2\end{pmatrix} + \mu\begin{pmatrix}2\\5\\2\end{pmatrix}$$
$$= \begin{pmatrix}1 - 3\lambda + 2\mu\\3 - 7\lambda + 5\mu\\3 - 2\lambda + 2\mu\end{pmatrix}$$

Equating the components in each direction,

$$x = 1 - 3\lambda + 2\mu \qquad [1]$$
$$y = 3 - 7\lambda + 5\mu \qquad [2]$$
$$z = 3 - 2\lambda + 2\mu \qquad [3]$$

Subtracting equation [1] from equation [3],

$$z - x = 2 + \lambda$$
$$z - x - 2 = \lambda$$

Substituting $\lambda = z - x - 2$ in equation [1],

$$x = 1 - 3\lambda + 2\mu$$
$$= 1 - 3(z - x - 2) + 2\mu$$
$$= 1 - 3z + 3x + 6 + 2\mu$$
$$-2x + 3z - 7 = 2\mu$$
$$\tfrac{1}{2}(-2x + 3z - 7) = \mu$$

Now substituting for μ and λ in equation [2],

$$y = 3 - 7\lambda + 5\mu$$
$$y = 3 - 7(-2 - x + z) + 5 \times \tfrac{1}{2}(-2x + 3z - 7)$$

Multiplying by 2 to remove the fraction,

$$2y = 6 - 14(-2 - x + z) + 5(-2x + 3z - 7)$$

$$2y = 6 + 28 + 14x - 14z - 10x + 15z - 35$$

$$2y = 4x + z - 1$$

This can be rearranged to give the Cartesian equation $4x - 2y + z = 1$. The Cartesian equation can then be expressed in the vector form $\mathbf{r}.\mathbf{n} = d$.

$$\begin{pmatrix} x \\ y \\ z \end{pmatrix} . \begin{pmatrix} 4 \\ -2 \\ 1 \end{pmatrix} = 1$$

The algebraic manipulation involved in going from parametric form to the Cartesian equation can be time consuming. If the vector equation of the plane is required in the form $\mathbf{r}.\mathbf{n} = d$, an alternative approach is to find a vector that is perpendicular to the plane.

Example 9

The straight lines L_1 and L_2 have vector equations $\mathbf{r}(s) = (\mathbf{i} + 3\mathbf{k}) + s(2\mathbf{i} + 3\mathbf{j} + \mathbf{k})$ and $\mathbf{r}(t) = (-7\mathbf{i} - 5\mathbf{j} - 14\mathbf{k}) + t(3\mathbf{i} + \mathbf{j} + 8\mathbf{k})$. The lines intersect at point T $(-1, -3, 2)$. Find the vector equation of the plane containing the two lines.

$$\mathbf{r}(s) = \begin{pmatrix} 1 \\ 0 \\ 3 \end{pmatrix} + s\begin{pmatrix} 2 \\ 3 \\ 1 \end{pmatrix}$$

$$\mathbf{r}(t) = \begin{pmatrix} -7 \\ -5 \\ -14 \end{pmatrix} + t\begin{pmatrix} 3 \\ 1 \\ 8 \end{pmatrix}$$

Solution

To find the vector equation of the plane it is important to realise that T is a point on the plane containing the lines. Let P be an arbitrary point on the plane. Then $\overrightarrow{TP}$ is a vector parallel to L_1 plus a vector parallel to L_2.

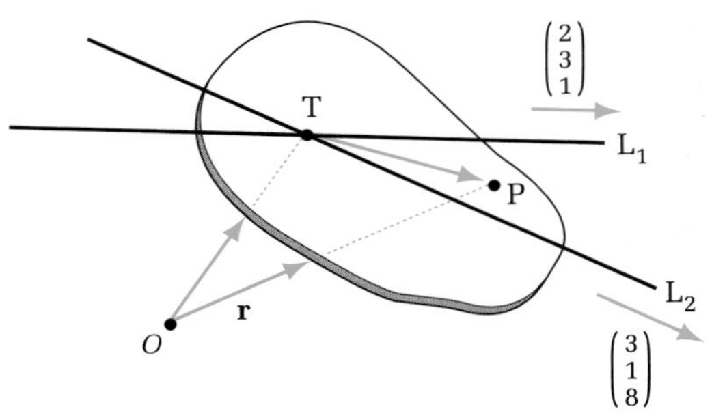

$$\overrightarrow{TP} = \lambda(2\mathbf{i} + 3\mathbf{j} + \mathbf{k}) + \mu(3\mathbf{i} + \mathbf{j} + 8\mathbf{k}) = \lambda\begin{pmatrix} 2 \\ 3 \\ 1 \end{pmatrix} + \mu\begin{pmatrix} 3 \\ 1 \\ 8 \end{pmatrix}$$

Therefore the vector equation of the plane is

$$\begin{aligned}\mathbf{r} &= \overrightarrow{OT} + \overrightarrow{TP} \\ &= (-\mathbf{i} - 3\mathbf{j} + 2\mathbf{k}) + \lambda(2\mathbf{i} + 3\mathbf{j} + \mathbf{k}) + \mu(3\mathbf{i} + \mathbf{j} + 8\mathbf{k}) \\ &= \begin{pmatrix} -1 \\ -3 \\ 2 \end{pmatrix} + \lambda\begin{pmatrix} 2 \\ 3 \\ 1 \end{pmatrix} + \mu\begin{pmatrix} 3 \\ 1 \\ 8 \end{pmatrix}\end{aligned}$$

14.5 The Vector Equation of a Plane

Exercise

Technique

1 a

1 A plane is perpendicular to the vector $\mathbf{i} - \mathbf{j} + 2\mathbf{k}$ and passes through the point $(2, -1, 10)$.

a Find the vector equation of the plane.

b Which of points A $(15, 8, 7)$ and B $(13, 2, 6)$ lies on the plane?

c Find the Cartesian equation of the plane.

2 A plane π_1 has equation $\mathbf{r}.\begin{pmatrix} 1 \\ 0 \\ 3 \end{pmatrix} = 2$.

a Explain why the point A $(2, 1, -1)$ does not lie on the plane.

b Find the vector equation, and the Cartesian equation, of the plane π_2, which passes through A and is parallel to π_1.

3 For each diagram write down a vector perpendicular to the plane. Then write down the vector equation of the plane.

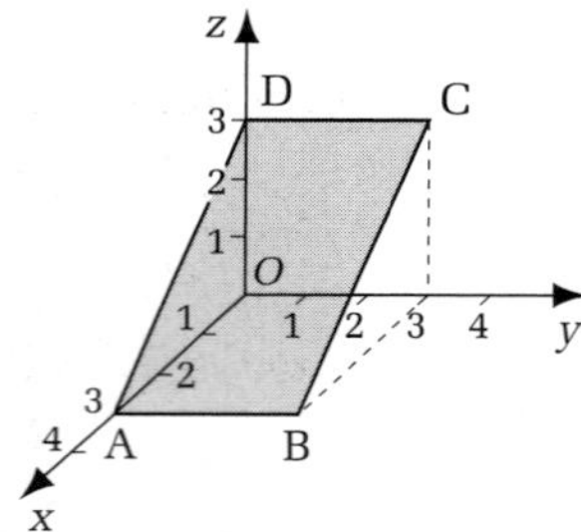

Plane ABCD

Plane OABC

4 The Cartesian equation of a plane is $x - y + 2z = 5$.

a Write the equation of this in the form $\mathbf{r}.\mathbf{n} = d$.

b Find the value of p if the point $(2, p, -3)$ lies on the plane.

5 The triangle ABC has vertices at coordinates

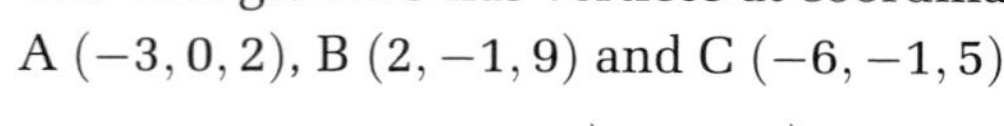

A $(-3, 0, 2)$, B $(2, -1, 9)$ and C $(-6, -1, 5)$.

a Find the vectors $\overrightarrow{AB}$ and $\overrightarrow{BC}$.

b Show that the vector $-\mathbf{i} + 9\mathbf{j} + 2\mathbf{k}$ is perpendicular to $\overrightarrow{AB}$ and $\overrightarrow{BC}$

c Find the vector equation of the plane ABC in the form $\mathbf{r}.\mathbf{n} = d$.

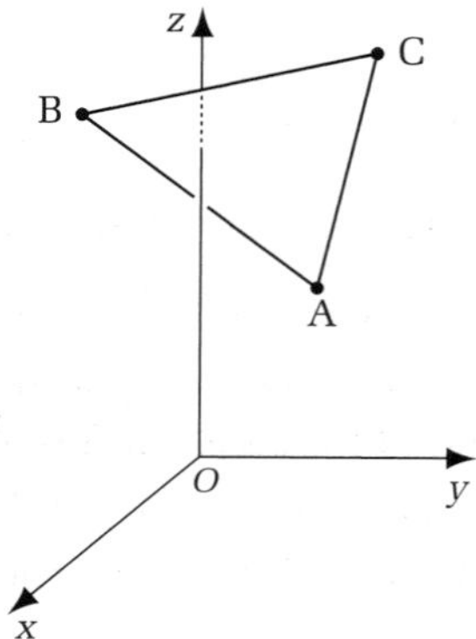

6 The straight line L passes through the point Q $(1, 2, 3)$ and is in the direction of $2\mathbf{i} - \mathbf{j} + 2\mathbf{k}$.

$2\mathbf{i} - \mathbf{j} + 2\mathbf{k} \equiv \begin{pmatrix} 2 \\ -1 \\ 2 \end{pmatrix}$

a Find the vector equation of the straight line L.
b Show that the point A $(5, 0, 7)$ lies on the line L.
c Find the vector equation of the plane perpendicular to L that passes through A.

7 The straight line M has vector equation $\mathbf{r}(\lambda) = \begin{pmatrix} 9 \\ -1 \\ -1 \end{pmatrix} + \lambda \begin{pmatrix} 3 \\ -1 \\ 1 \end{pmatrix}$ and the plane π is given by $\mathbf{r}.\begin{pmatrix} 5 \\ 3 \\ -1 \end{pmatrix} = 10$.

a Find the angle between the line and the plane.
b Find the point where the line cuts the plane.

8 Find the angle between the planes with Cartesian equations $x + y + z = 2$ and $2x - y + 6z = 1$.

9 The Cartesian equation of a plane is $2x - 6y + 3z = 17$.

a Find the perpendicular distance of the plane from the origin.
b Find the perpendicular distance from the point A $(3, 1, 1)$ to the plane.

10 Points A, B and C have position vectors $(\mathbf{i} + \mathbf{j} + \mathbf{k})$, $(5\mathbf{i} + 3\mathbf{j})$ and $(6\mathbf{j} + 7\mathbf{k})$ respectively.

In column form, $\overrightarrow{OA} = \begin{pmatrix} 1 \\ 1 \\ 1 \end{pmatrix}$, $\overrightarrow{OB} = \begin{pmatrix} 5 \\ 3 \\ 0 \end{pmatrix}$, and $\overrightarrow{OC} = \begin{pmatrix} 0 \\ 6 \\ 7 \end{pmatrix}$,

a Find the vectors $\overrightarrow{AB}$ and $\overrightarrow{AC}$.
b Find the vector equation of the plane passing through A, B and C.
c Find the Cartesian equation of the plane, by eliminating parameters.

11 Two straight lines $\mathbf{r} = (13\mathbf{i} - 5\mathbf{j} + 4\mathbf{k}) + \lambda(\mathbf{i} - \mathbf{j} + \mathbf{k})$ and $\mathbf{r} = (14\mathbf{i} - 8\mathbf{j} - 13\mathbf{k}) + \mu(-3\mathbf{i} + 4\mathbf{j} + 6\mathbf{k})$ intersect at point A.

$\mathbf{r}(\lambda) = \begin{pmatrix} 13 \\ -5 \\ 4 \end{pmatrix} + \lambda \begin{pmatrix} 1 \\ -1 \\ 1 \end{pmatrix}$

$\mathbf{r}(\mu) = \begin{pmatrix} 14 \\ -8 \\ -13 \end{pmatrix} + \mu \begin{pmatrix} -3 \\ 4 \\ 6 \end{pmatrix}$

a Find the position vector of A.
b Find the vector equation of the plane containing the two lines.

Contextual

1 Points A, B, C and D have coordinates $(1, 0, -1)$, $(2, -1, 2)$, $(0, 1, 0)$ and $(-1, 0, 1)$ respectively. Find the values of λ and μ if the vector $\begin{pmatrix} \lambda \\ \mu \\ 1 \end{pmatrix}$ is perpendicular to both $\overrightarrow{AB}$ and $\overrightarrow{CD}$. Hence find, in the form $\mathbf{r}.\mathbf{n} = k$, the equation of the plane through $\overrightarrow{CD}$ parallel to $\overrightarrow{AB}$. Write down the vector parametric equation of the line through A normal to this plane, and hence find the perpendicular distance from A to the plane. Explain why your answer gives the length of the common perpendicular to the lines $\overrightarrow{AB}$ and $\overrightarrow{CD}$.

(SMP)

2 The diagram shows a right triangular prism of length 12 units. The points R, S and T have coordinates $(13, 3, 13)$, $(4, 3, 12)$ and $(1, 3, 8)$ respectively.

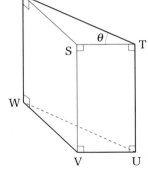

a Find $\overrightarrow{TS}.\overrightarrow{TR}$ and find the exact value for $\cos\theta$.

b Use $\sin^2\theta + \cos^2\theta = 1$ to find the exact value for $\sin\theta$ and then find the area of the triangle RST.

c Use your answer to part **b** to calculate the exact value of the volume of the prism.

d The vector equation of the line through TU is $\mathbf{r}(\lambda) = \begin{pmatrix} 1 \\ 3 \\ 8 \end{pmatrix} + \lambda\begin{pmatrix} 1 \\ -2 \\ -2 \end{pmatrix}$. Use this to find the coordinates of U.

e Show that the vector $\begin{pmatrix} 4 \\ 5 \\ -3 \end{pmatrix}$ is perpendicular to $\overrightarrow{TS}$ and $\overrightarrow{TU}$. Hence find the equation of the plane STUV.

3

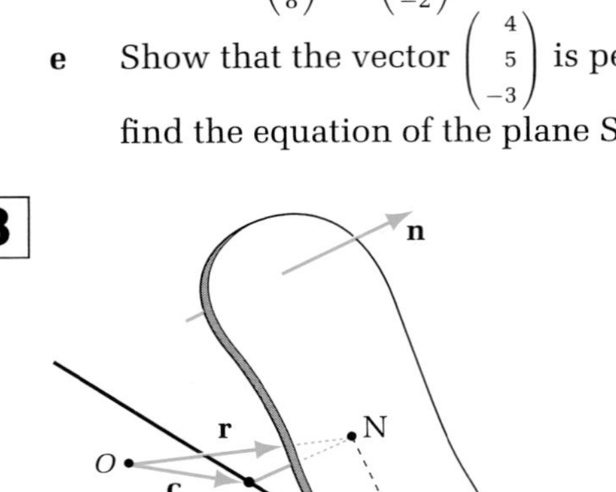

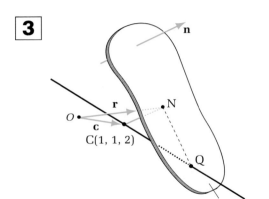

The diagram shows part of the plane π given by $\mathbf{r}.\begin{pmatrix} 2 \\ 2 \\ 1 \end{pmatrix} = 24$ and the straight line L given by $\mathbf{r} = \begin{pmatrix} 1 \\ 1 \\ 2 \end{pmatrix} + s\begin{pmatrix} 1 \\ 0 \\ 16 \end{pmatrix}$. The line intersects the plane at the point Q. C is a point on the line with position vector **c**. The vector **n** is perpendicular to the plane.

a Find the coordinates of Q.

b N is the point on the plane such that $\overrightarrow{CN}$ is perpendicular to the plane. Explain why $\overrightarrow{CN} = \lambda\mathbf{n}$ where λ is a constant.

c If **r** is the position vector of N show that $\mathbf{r} = \mathbf{c} + \lambda\mathbf{n}$.

d **r** also satisfies the equation $\mathbf{r}.\begin{pmatrix} 2 \\ 2 \\ 1 \end{pmatrix} = 24$. Use this to find the value of λ.

e Find the coordinates of C′, the image of C under a reflection in the plane π.

f Find the vector equation of the line L′, where L′ is the image of L under a reflection in the plane π.

Consolidation

Exercise A

1 Four vectors **P**, **Q**, **R** and **S** satisfy the relation $\mathbf{P} + \mathbf{Q} = \mathbf{R} + \mathbf{S}$. Lines representing these vectors form the sides of the quadrilateral shown in the diagram. Make a freehand copy of the diagram and:

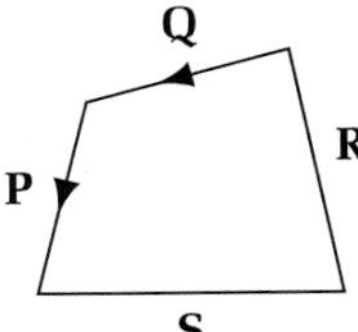

a draw in a directed line representing the vector $\mathbf{P} + \mathbf{Q}$;

b place arrows in the appropriate directions on the sides **R** and **S**;

c draw in a directed line representing the vector $\mathbf{P} - \mathbf{S}$.

(SMP)

2 Points A and B have position vectors $\mathbf{i} - 3\mathbf{j} + 8\mathbf{k}$ and $5\mathbf{i} + 3\mathbf{j} - 4\mathbf{k}$ respectively.

a Find the vector $\overrightarrow{AB}$.

b Find a unit vector in the direction of $\overrightarrow{AB}$.

c Find the position vector of the point C, where C divides the line AB in the ratio $2:5$.

3 The angle between the vectors $(\mathbf{i} + \mathbf{j})$ and $(\mathbf{i} + \mathbf{j} + p\mathbf{k})$ is $\frac{\pi}{4}$. Find the possible values of p.

(ULEAC)

4 The position vectors of A and B are defined by $\overrightarrow{OA} = \begin{pmatrix} 4 \\ -3 \\ 2 \end{pmatrix}$ and $\overrightarrow{OB} = \begin{pmatrix} 2 \\ -2 \\ -7 \end{pmatrix}$.

a Show that $\overrightarrow{OA}$ and $\overrightarrow{OB}$ are perpendicular.

b Find a vector equation for the line AB. Show that this line intersects the line $\mathbf{r} = \begin{pmatrix} 3 \\ -1 \\ 2 \end{pmatrix} + s\begin{pmatrix} -1 \\ 1 \\ -3 \end{pmatrix}$ and find the coordinates of the point of the intersection.

(NEAB)

5 The foot A of a vertical television mast is situated on horizontal ground. Relative to axes *Oxyz*, with *Oz* vertically upwards, the coordinates of A are $(-3, 6, 0)$, where the units are metres. Two straight steel cables are attached to the mast at the point B, 12 m above A. The other end of the cables are attached to the ground at the points C $(1, 3, 0)$ and D $(-2, 1, 0)$.

a Write down the coordinates of B.

b Show that the angle of elevation of B from O is approximately 61°.

c Write down the vectors $\overrightarrow{BC}$ and $\overrightarrow{BD}$, and show that $\overrightarrow{BC}.\overrightarrow{BD} = 163$.

d Calculate, to the nearest degree, the angle between the two cables.

(NEAB)

6

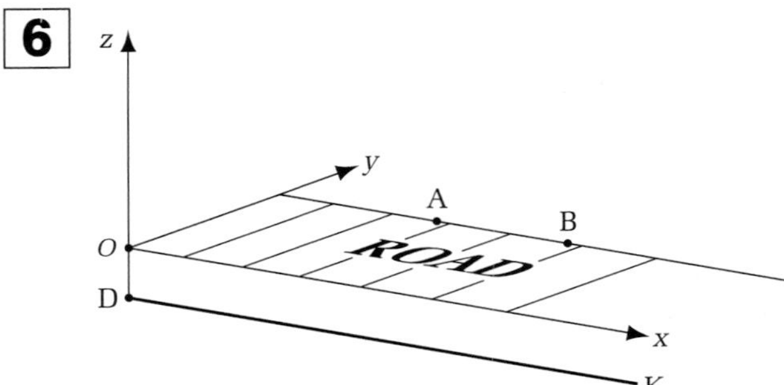

The diagram shows a road in the horizontal plane with one edge along the x-axis. The axis Oy is taken so that it lies in the plane of the road, while the axis Oz is vertically upwards. The unit of length is the metre.
A power cable K runs directly below and parallel to the x-axis at a depth of 1 metre below ground level. A second straight cable L links the point A $(5, 5, 0)$ to a point C on K. Given that the vector equation of L is
$\mathbf{r} = \begin{pmatrix} 5 \\ 5 \\ 0 \end{pmatrix} + t\begin{pmatrix} 5 \\ -5 \\ -1 \end{pmatrix}$, where t is a parameter, find the coordinates of C.
It is intended to lay a third cable M joining the point B $(10, 5, 0)$ to the point D $(0, 0, -1)$. Find a vector equation for the straight line BD. Determine whether the cable M can be laid along the line BD without meeting the line occupied by the cable L. Calculate the acute angle between the lines AC and BD, giving your answer to the nearest degree.

(NEAB)

7 The line L passes through points A $(-1, -3, -3)$ and B $(5, 0, 6)$. Write down in terms of a single parameter, the position vector of a general point P on L relative to the origin O. Find the position of P for which OP is perpendicular to L. Hence find the minimum distance from the origin to the line L.

(SMP)

8 One of the planes of a crystal structure has equation $2x - 3y + z = 5$. An X-ray beam passes through the crystal along the line with vector equation
$\mathbf{r} = \begin{pmatrix} 1 \\ 1 \\ 2 \end{pmatrix} + \lambda\begin{pmatrix} 3 \\ 1 \\ 1 \end{pmatrix}$. Find the angle between the X-ray beam and the given plane.

(SMP)

9 In the triangular prism ABCDEF, the parallel edges AD, BE and CF are each of length 14 units and are at right angles to the plane ends ABC and DEF. The points A, B, C, have coordinates $(2, 3, 5)$, $(4, 3, 4)$ and $(6, -3, 1)$ respectively, and the angle ABC is θ.
Calculate $\overrightarrow{BA}.\overrightarrow{BC}$ and find $\cos\theta$ in surd form. Deduce the value of $\sin\theta$.
Calculate the exact volume of the prism.

The equation of AD is $\mathbf{r} = \begin{pmatrix} 2 \\ 3 \\ 5 \end{pmatrix} + t\begin{pmatrix} 3 \\ -2 \\ 6 \end{pmatrix}$.

a Given that $t > 0$, find the position vector of D.

b Given that $\mathbf{n} = \begin{pmatrix} 2 \\ 15 \\ 4 \end{pmatrix}$, verify that $\mathbf{n}$ is at right angles to both AB and AD. Find the equation of the plane ABED.

(JMB)

10 Prove that the lines with equations $\mathbf{r} = \begin{pmatrix} 0 \\ 2 \\ -3 \end{pmatrix} + s\begin{pmatrix} 1 \\ -1 \\ -1 \end{pmatrix}$ and $\mathbf{r} = \begin{pmatrix} -1 \\ 6 \\ -1 \end{pmatrix} + t\begin{pmatrix} 2 \\ 1 \\ -1 \end{pmatrix}$ have a point in common. Find, in parametric form, an equation for the plane containing the two lines.

(SMP)

Exercise B

1 State a vector equation of the straight line passing through the points A and B whose position vectors are $\mathbf{i} - \mathbf{j} + 3\mathbf{k}$ and $\mathbf{i} + 2\mathbf{j} + 2\mathbf{k}$ respectively. Determine the position vector of the point C which divides the line's line segment AB internally such that $AC = 2CB$.

(ULEAC)

2 A pipe runs from point A $(2, 1, 5)$ to the point B $(6, 0, 6)$. At B the pipe bends, and then runs to the point C $(7, 0, 3)$.

a Find the vector equation for the line AB.

b Find the angle between the vectors $\begin{pmatrix} 4 \\ -1 \\ 1 \end{pmatrix}$ and $\begin{pmatrix} 1 \\ 0 \\ -3 \end{pmatrix}$.

c Find the angle ABC formed by the pipe.

(SMP)

3 Three vectors **a**, **b** and **c** are such that $\mathbf{a} = \mathbf{i} + 3\mathbf{j}$, $\mathbf{b} = 2\mathbf{i} + \mathbf{j}$ and $\mathbf{c} = \mathbf{i} + 13\mathbf{j}$. Find:

a the angle between **a** and **c**.
b the vector that is parallel to $\mathbf{a} + \mathbf{b}$ with magnitude 20 units.
c the values of p and q for which $p\mathbf{a} + q\mathbf{b} = \mathbf{c}$.
d the value of m which $\mathbf{a} + m\mathbf{b}$ is perpendicular to **c**.

(UCLES)

4 The unit vectors **i**, **j** and **k** are parallel to the x-, y- and z-axes of a Cartesian frame of reference $Oxyz$, where O denotes the origin.

a Show that the point C $(1, 3, 2)$, on the straight line joining A $(2, 4, -1)$ and B $(-1, 1, 8)$, divides AB in ratio 1:2.

b Find the vector equation of the straight line through C and D where D is the point$(3, -4, 0)$.

c Find the angle, in degrees (correct to one decimal place), between the straight line CD and the straight line CB.

(NICCEA)

A plane passes through A $(2, 2, 1)$ and is perpendicular to the line joining the origin to A. Write down the vector equation of the plane in the form $\mathbf{r}.\mathbf{n} = p$, where $\mathbf{n}$ is a unit vector.

(ULEAC)

The lines L and M have the equations $\mathbf{r} = \begin{pmatrix} 3 \\ 2 \\ 4 \end{pmatrix} + s\begin{pmatrix} 1 \\ 3 \\ -5 \end{pmatrix}$ and $\mathbf{r} = \begin{pmatrix} -3 \\ 4 \\ 6 \end{pmatrix} + t\begin{pmatrix} 1 \\ -2 \\ 2 \end{pmatrix}$ respectively. The plane π has the equation $\mathbf{r}.\begin{pmatrix} 2 \\ 0 \\ -1 \end{pmatrix} = 16$.

a Verify that the point A with coordinates $(1, -4, 14)$ lies on L and on M but not on π.

b Find the position vector of the point of intersection B of L and π.

c Show that M and π have no common point.

d Find the cosine of the angle between the vectors $\begin{pmatrix} 1 \\ 3 \\ -5 \end{pmatrix}$ and $\begin{pmatrix} 2 \\ 0 \\ -1 \end{pmatrix}$.

Hence find, to the nearest degree, the angle between L and π.

(JMB)

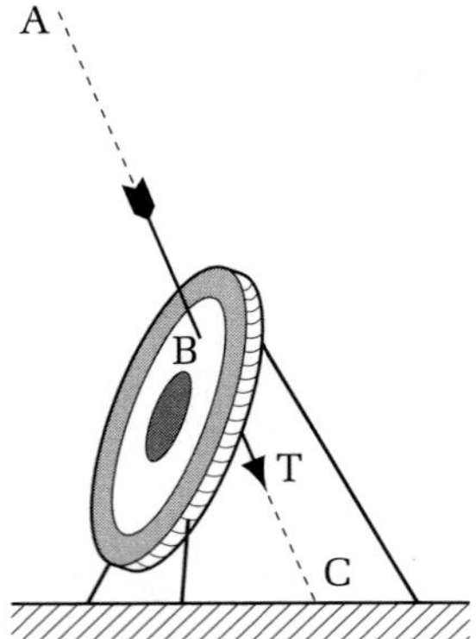

The diagram shows an arrow embedded in a target. The line of the arrow passes through the point A $(2, 3, 5)$ and has direction vector $3\mathbf{i} + \mathbf{j} - 2\mathbf{k}$. The arrow intersects the target at point B. The plane of the target has equation $x + 2y - 3z = 4$. The units are metres.

a Write down the vector equation of the line of the arrow in the form $\mathbf{r} = \mathbf{p} + \lambda\mathbf{q}$.

b Find the value of λ that corresponds to B. Hence write down the coordinates of B.

c The point C is where the line of the arrow meets the ground, which is the plane $z = 0$. Find the coordinates of C.

d The tip, T, of the arrow is one-third of the way from B to C. Find the coordinates of T and the length of BT.

e Write down a normal vector to the plane of the target. Find the acute angle between the arrow and this normal.

(MEI)

Applications and Activities

1 ABC is a triangle and P, Q and R are the mid-points of the sides AB, BC and AC respectively.

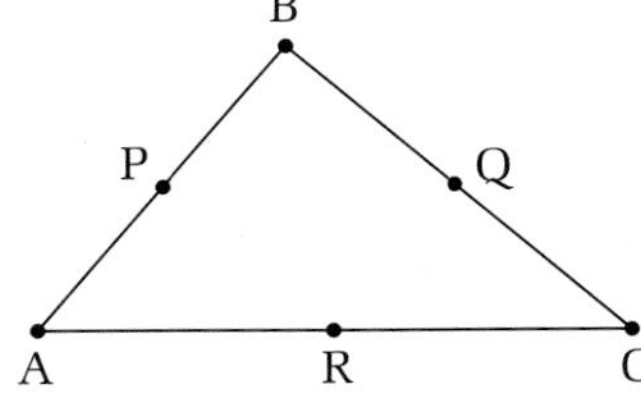

a Select a set of coordinates for each of the points A, B and C.

b Find the vector equation of the lines L_1, L_2 and L_3 where the line L_1 passes through A and Q, the line L_2 passes through B and R and the line L_3 passes through C and P.

c Find the point of intersection between the lines L_1 and L_2 and between L_1 and L_3.

d Comment on your findings.

2 A particle has position vector $\mathbf{r} = \begin{pmatrix} \cos t \\ \sin t \end{pmatrix}$, where t is the time in seconds.

a Plot the path of the particle by finding $\mathbf{r}$ when $t = 0, 0.5, 1, 1.5, 2, 2.5, 3, 3.5$.

b Explain why $\dot{\mathbf{r}} = \begin{pmatrix} -\sin t \\ \cos t \end{pmatrix}$, where $\dot{\mathbf{r}} = \frac{d}{dt}(\mathbf{r})$.

c Find $\dot{\mathbf{r}}.\mathbf{r}$ and comment on your answer.

Summary

- In books and examination papers a vector is commonly shown as a bold, lower case letter; **a**. The **magnitude**, or length of the vector, is indicated by a or $|\mathbf{a}|$.

- When handwritten the same vector is more commonly denoted by $\underline{a}$; the same lower case letter but with a line underneath indicating that it represents a vector. The magnitude of $\underline{a}$ is $|\underline{a}|$.

- The third way is to label its initial point and its terminal point by two capital letters. If the capital letters A and B are chosen the vector is then denoted $\overrightarrow{AB}$. The magnitude of the vector $\overrightarrow{AB}$ is denoted by AB or $|\overrightarrow{AB}|$.

- The **base vectors** in three dimensions are **i**, **j**, and **k**. These are mutually perpendicular unit vectors.

- If $\mathbf{a} = a_1\mathbf{i} + a_2\mathbf{j} + a_3\mathbf{k}$ then the **magnitude** of **a**, $|\mathbf{a}| = \sqrt{a_1^2 + a_2^2 + a_3^2}$.

- A unit vector $\hat{\mathbf{a}}$ in the direction of $\mathbf{a}$ is $\frac{\mathbf{a}}{|\mathbf{a}|}$.
- The **scalar product** (or dot product) of two vectors $\mathbf{a} = a_1\mathbf{i} + a_2\mathbf{j} + a_3\mathbf{k}$ and $\mathbf{b} = b_1\mathbf{i} + b_2\mathbf{j} + b_3\mathbf{k}$ is given by

  $\mathbf{a} = \begin{pmatrix} a_1 \\ a_2 \\ a_3 \end{pmatrix}$ and $\mathbf{b} = \begin{pmatrix} b_1 \\ b_2 \\ b_3 \end{pmatrix}$

  $$\mathbf{a}.\mathbf{b} = ab\cos\theta = a_1b_1 + a_2b_2 + a_3b_3$$

- $\mathbf{a}.\mathbf{b} > 0$ for $0 \leq \theta < \frac{\pi}{2}$ (θ is acute)

  $\mathbf{a}.\mathbf{b} = 0$ for $\theta = \frac{\pi}{2}$ (perpendicular or orthogonal vectors)

  $\mathbf{a}.\mathbf{b} < 0$ for $\frac{\pi}{2} < \theta \leq \pi$ (θ is obtuse)
- $\mathbf{a}.\mathbf{b} = \mathbf{b}.\mathbf{a}$
- $\lambda\mathbf{a}.\mathbf{b} = \mathbf{a}.\lambda\mathbf{b} = \lambda(\mathbf{a}.\mathbf{b})$
- $a.(\mathbf{b} + \mathbf{c}) = \mathbf{a}.\mathbf{b} + \mathbf{a}.\mathbf{c}$, where $\mathbf{c}$ is a third vector.
- Two non-zero vectors $\mathbf{a}$ and $\mathbf{b}$ are perpendicular if $\mathbf{a}.\mathbf{b} = 0$.
- The vector equation of a straight line has the form $\mathbf{r} = \mathbf{a} + \lambda\mathbf{b}$, where $\mathbf{a}$ is the position vector of a point on the line, $\mathbf{b}$ is a vector parallel to the line, and λ is a scalar.
- The equation of a plane passing through three points can be expressed in three ways.
  - using parameters, $\mathbf{r} = \mathbf{a} + \lambda\mathbf{b} + \mu\mathbf{c}$
  - using the Cartesian equation form, $ax + by + cz = d$
  - using the vector equation form, $\mathbf{r}.\mathbf{n} = d$

15 Proof and Mathematical Argument

What you need to know

- How to use sigma notation and sum series.
- What is meant by a 'prime number'.
- How to factorise numbers into their prime factors.
- What is meant by 'integration notation'.

Review

1 Write each of the following mathematical statements using sigma notation and find an expression for the total:

a $a + ab + ab^2 + ab^3 + \cdots + ab^n$
b $\log a + \log a^2 + \log a^3 + \log a^4 + \cdots + \log a^n$
c $1^3 + 2^3 + 3^3 + \cdots + n^3$

2 What is a prime number?

3 Factorise the following numbers into their prime factors:

a 76 **b** 120 **c** 227
d 438 **e** 579 **f** 1591

4 Use integration notation to write an expression for each of these shaded areas:

a

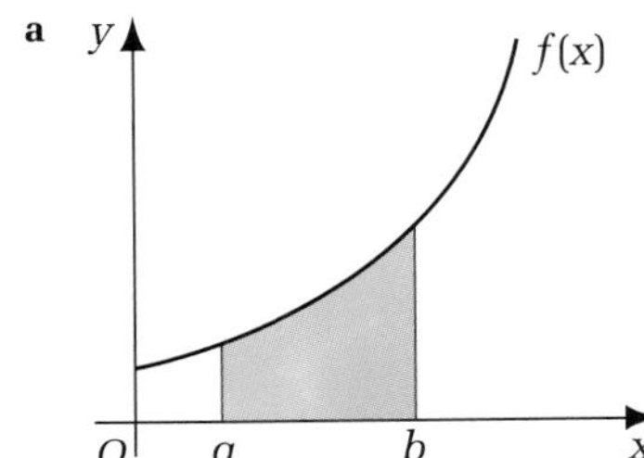

b

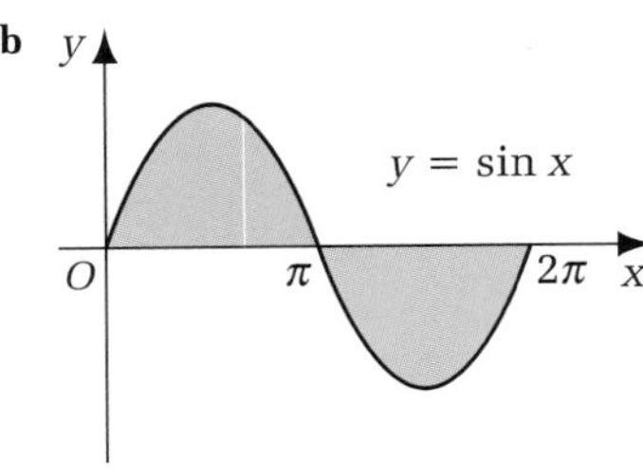

15.1 Mathematical Argument

Mathematics is a human activity that has developed in many different cultures throughout history. Many mathematical statements have been proved by establishing a chain of reasoning. A statement, or **theorem**, is shown to follow from previously proved statements. Sometimes initial assumptions, called *premises*, *axioms* or *postulates* are used to build a proof. This process is called **deductive reasoning** (or deduction).

Euclid of Alexandri (c. 365–300 BC) wrote thirteen books, chapters, collectively called 'The Elements'. them he gave a synops the mathematical knowledge of his time, covering plane geomet the theory of numbers solid geometry. The theorems were proved purely by logical deduc from a set of axioms. M of the proofs depended on triangles being cong Euclidean style proofs remained in British scho text books well into the 20th century and are sti being used in schools.

Example 1

Prove that the angle subtended at the centre of a circle by a chord AB is twice the angle at the circumference.

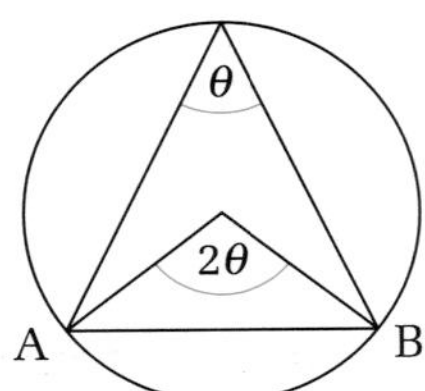

Solution

This Euclidean style proof is easier to follow if supported by a second diagram.

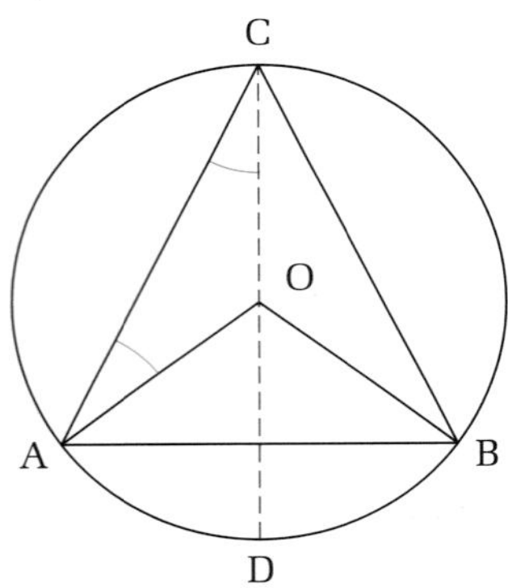

Let O be the centre of the circle and C be the point on the circumference. Join CO and produce (that is, extend) it to D (also on the circumference).

$OA = OC$ ◀ OA and OC are both radii.

$\therefore \quad \angle OAC = \angle OCA$ ◀ OAC is an isosceles triangle.

Also $\angle AOD = \angle OAC + \angle OCA$ ◀ AOD is the exterior angle on the isosceles triangle.

Since $\angle OAC = \angle OCA$,

$\angle OAC + \angle OCA \equiv \angle AOD$

$\therefore \quad \angle AOD \equiv 2\angle OCA$

Using a similar argument for triangle OBC, $\angle BOD = 2\angle OCB$

$$\begin{aligned} \text{So} \quad \angle AOB &= \angle AOD + \angle DOB \\ &= 2\angle OCA + 2\angle OCB \\ &= 2(\angle OCA + \angle OCB) \\ &= 2\angle ACB \end{aligned}$$

This proof was one that students were expected to learn. Familiarity with the notation is essential if the mathematical argument is to be understood. In this example $\therefore$ means 'therefore', and $\angle OAC$ means 'the angle at A, formed by OA and AC'.

Arguments that appear to be logical can be invalid. This is often because the axioms, or assumed knowledge, on which they are based, are broken. Consider the following proof that $2 = 1$.

Let $x = y$ ◀ **This is an assumption.** [1]

Then $x^2 = xy$ [2] Multiply both sides by x.

and $x^2 - y^2 = xy - y^2$ [3] Subtract y^2 from both sides.

So $(x + y)(x - y) = y(x - y)$ [4] Factorise both sides.

$(x + y) = y$ [5] Divide by $(x - y)$.

Now let $x = y = 1$

Statement [5] becomes

$1 + 1 = 1$ [6]

i.e. $2 = 1$ [7]

Notice how each of statements [2]–[7] appear to follow logically from the preceding statement. Statement [7] is absurd, but where is the error? Careful checking shows that the error is in statement [5]. This is produced from statement [4] by dividing both sides by $(x - y)$. However, statement [1] tells us that $x = y$ so $x - y = 0$, and we know that we cannot divide by 0. It is this division by zero that has created the inconsistency.
This type of mathematical argument is sometimes called a **paradox**. To find the incorrect line of reasoning requires understanding of the whole problem.

Example 2

The following deduction that $1 = 2$ is invalid. Find the statement that produces the paradox.

$$\cos^2 x \equiv 1 - \sin^2 x \qquad \text{◀ Pythagorean identity.} \qquad [1]$$

$$(\cos^2 x)^{3/2} = (1 - \sin^2 x)^{3/2} \qquad [2]$$

Raise each side to the same power.

$$\cos^3 x = (1 - \sin^2 x)^{3/2} \qquad [3]$$

Use the laws of indices.

$$\cos^3 x + 3 = (1 - \sin^2 x)^{3/2} + 3 \qquad [4]$$

Add 3 to both sides.

$$(\cos^3 x + 3)^2 = [(1 - \sin^2 x)^{3/2} + 3]^2 \qquad [5]$$

Square both sides.

Statement [1] is an identity so it is true for all angles, in particular $x = \frac{\pi}{2}$ and $x = \pi$ (angles in radians). When $x = \frac{\pi}{2}$, $\cos(\frac{\pi}{2}) = 0$ and $\sin(\frac{\pi}{2}) = 1$. Statement [5] now gives

$$(0 + 3)^2 = [(1 - 1)^{3/2} + 3]^2$$

$$\Rightarrow \quad 9 = 9 \qquad \text{This is true!}$$

Recall that $\Rightarrow$ means 'implies'.

When $x = \pi$, $\cos \pi = -1$ and $\sin \pi = 0$. Statement [5] now gives

$$(-1 + 3)^2 = [(1 - 0)^{3/2} + 3]^2$$

$$\Rightarrow \quad 2^2 = 4^2$$

$$\Rightarrow \quad 2 = 4$$

$$\Rightarrow \quad 1 = 2$$

Solution

Notice that the power $\frac{3}{2}$ can be thought of as $3 \times \frac{1}{2}$. Power 3 is equivalent to cubing, in which algebraic terms keep their sign (positive or negative). Power $\frac{1}{2}$ is equivalent to taking the square root, and a square root has both positive and negative values. But the application of the indices rules in statement [3] has the effect of removing the power $\frac{1}{2}$. Once the square root term has been removed from the left-hand side of the equation, the positive *and* negative values are reduced to positive values only *or* negative values only.
So the error is in statement [3]. The $\cos^3 x$ term should have both positive *and* negative values. This inconsistency creates the paradox.

If the mathematical argument is convincing then it can be considered a **proof**. Each statement, or conjective, is logically deduced and removes all doubt about whether it is true or not. There are many types of proof, some of which are developed further in the next three sections.

15.1 Mathematical Argument

Exercise

Technique

1 The following mathematical arguments are invalid. In each case identify the statement that produces the paradox and explain the inconsistency.

a Showing that any two unequal numbers are actually equal:

a, b and c are positive real numbers.

Let $a = b + c$	[1]	
$a(a - b) = (b + c)(a - b)$	[2]	Multiply by $(a - b)$.
$a^2 - ab = ab + ac - b^2 - bc$	[3]	
$a^2 - ab - ac = ab - b^2 - bc$	[4]	Subtract ac from both sides.
$a(a - b - c) = b(a - b - c)$	[5]	Factorise.
$a = b$	[6]	Divide by $(a - b - c)$.

b Deducing that $\frac{1}{8} > \frac{1}{4}$:

$3 > 2$	[1]	
$3\log(\frac{1}{2}) > 2\log(\frac{1}{2})$	[2]	Multiply both sides by $\log(\frac{1}{2})$.
$\log(\frac{1}{2})^3 > \log(\frac{1}{2})^2$	[3]	$n\log a = \log a^n$
$(\frac{1}{2})^3 > (\frac{1}{2})^2$	[4]	Remove the logarithms.
$\frac{1}{8} > \frac{1}{4}$	[5]	

c Showing that $-1 = +1$:

$\int \frac{1}{x}\,dx = \int -\frac{1}{(-x)}\,dx$	[1]	Integrate both sides.
$\ln(x) = \ln(-x)$	[2]	Remove the logarithms.
$x = -x$	[3]	Divide both sides by x.
$1 = -1$	[4]	

d Showing that if two numbers add together and give an answer greater than zero, then the sum of these numbers is also greater than the second number:

$a + b > 0$	[1]	
$a^2 + ab > 0$	[2]	Multiply by a.
$a^2 + 2ab + b^2 > ab + b^2$	[3]	Add $ab + b^2$ to both sides.
$(a + b)^2 > (a + b)b$	[4]	Factorise.
$a + b > b$	[5]	Divide by $(a + b)$.

If $a + b > 0$ then $a + b > b$

That is, if two numbers add to give a total greater than zero then they also add to a total greater than the second number.

Contextual

1 Construct a Euclidean-style proof to show that:

a opposite angles in a **cyclic quadrilateral** are **supplementary** (that is they add to give $180°$)

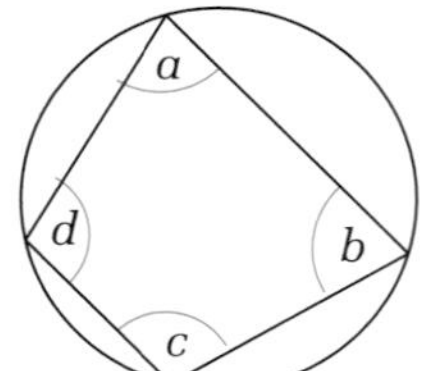

$a + c = 180°$

$b + d = 180°$

b the angle in a semi-circle is a right angle.

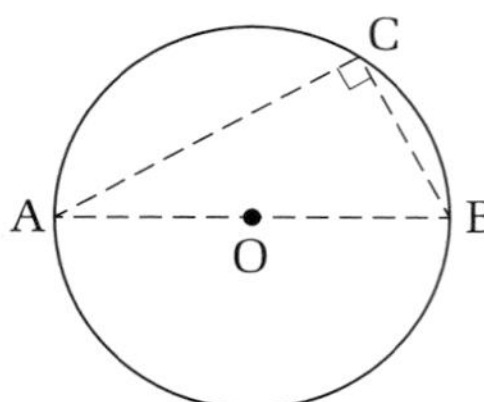

2 Without using a calculator find the units digit of 14!.

Recall the factorial notation from Chapter (Sequences and Series

15.2 Proof by Exhaustion and Disproof by Counter Example

One method of proving a statement or conjecture in mathematics is to list every possibility systematically and check the results. If the statement is true for every case then it can be considered proved. A proof where every possibility is considered is called **proof by exhaustion**.

Example 1

Prove that a three-digit number is divisible by 3 if the sum of its digits is divisible by 3.

Solution

This statement, or conjecture, could be proved using proof by exhaustion. Start with 100 and check every possibility up to and including 999.
We can introduce the notation $3 \nmid 100$ to mean 3 is not a divisor of 100 and $3|102$ to mean 3 is a divisor of 102. The results of checking every possibility can then be written as:

$3 \nmid 100$

$3 \nmid 101$

$3 \mid 102 \quad \Leftrightarrow \quad 102 = 3 \times 34$

$3 \nmid 103$

$3 \nmid 104$

$3 \mid 105 \quad \Leftrightarrow \quad 105 = 3 \times 35$

and so on until we reach

$3 \mid 999 \quad \Leftrightarrow \quad 999 = 3 \times 333$

The symbol $\Leftrightarrow$ is denoting the fact that the statement on one side of it implies the statement on the other side.

Now the process has identified all three-digit numbers that are divisible by 3. The next check is to see that the sum of the digits in each case is also a multiple of 3.

$102: \quad 1 + 0 + 2 = 3 \quad \text{and} \quad 3|3$

$105: \quad 1 + 0 + 5 = 6 \quad \text{and} \quad 3|6$

and so on to

$999: \quad 9 + 9 + 9 = 27 \quad \text{and} \quad 3|27$

Notice how the 'exhaustion-method' is very time-consuming.

Mathematicians would look for a quicker way. In this case it can be shown directly using an algebraic method.

Let the three-digit number be abc [1]

This means there are a hundreds, b tens and c units

$$abc = 100a + 10b + c \quad [2]$$

$$100a + 10b + c = 99a + 9b + (a + b + c) \quad [3]$$

Statement [3] is a rearrangement of statement [2], creating the term $(a + b + c)$, which is simply the sum of the digits in the original number. If the sum of the digits is divisible by 3 then

$$a + b + c = 3d \quad \text{for some number } d. \quad [4]$$

$$100a + 10b + c = 99a + 9b + 3d \quad [5]$$

$$100a + 10b + c = 3(33a + 3b + d) \quad [6]$$

Statement [6] shows that $100a + 10b + c$ can be written as a multiple of 3. This means $3|(100a + 10b + c)$. If this is true then $3|abc$, provided $a + b + c = 3d$ for some number d (statement [4]). That is, a three-digit number is divisible by 3 provided the sum of the digits is divisible by 3. Notice that the deduction of statements [2]–[7] from statement [1] is much quicker than considering the division of every possible three-digit number.

Disproof by counter example

Sometimes it can be much quicker to disprove a conjecture by finding one case for which the statement is false than to use the exhaustion method until it fails. To disprove a statement it is sufficient to find one example for which the conjecture is false. This is called a **counter example**. Many conjectures in the theory of numbers have been disproved by counter example, particularly those relating to the search for prime numbers.

Example 2

Prove by counter example that the following statement is false:
'The function $f(x) = x^2 + x + 41$ produces prime numbers for $x \in \mathbb{N}$.'

$x \in \mathbb{N}$ means x is a natural number.

Solution

Testing this statement by substituting the first few natural numbers into the function it appears to be true.

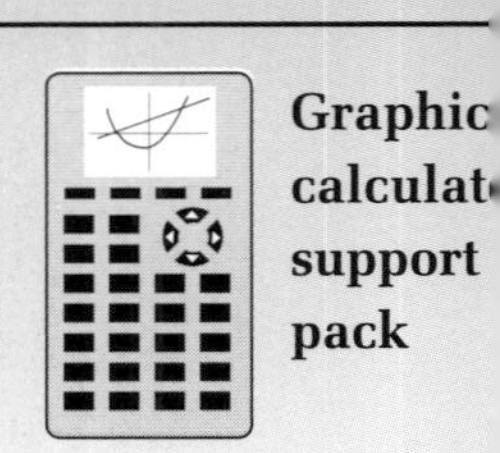

$f(1) = 1^2 + 1 + 41 = 43$ (prime)

$f(2) = 2^2 + 2 + 41 = 47$ (prime)

$f(3) = 3^2 + 3 + 41 = 53$ (prime)

...

$f(10) = 10^2 + 10 + 41 = 151$ (prime)

...

But $f(40) = 40^2 + 40 + 41 = 1681$ (composite)

A composite number i one that will factorise it isn't prime.

Since $1681 = 41^2$, it is not a prime number and so the conjecture can be disproved by the value, or *counter example*, $x = 40$. Had the proof by exhaustion method been adopted it would have failed at the 40th step.

This example illustrates the usefulness of technology to mathematicians. A computer or calculator can process information very quickly, so searching for counter examples can now be done faster than ever before.

The 4-colour conjecture

When colouring maps it is useful to use different colours for countries or counties with common borders. In 1852, Augustus de Morgan (1806–1871) proposed that no matter how complicated the map, at most four colours are needed. In 1976, Kenneth Appel and Wolfgang Haken provided a proof that a **minimal counter example** did not exist. This proof relied upon computer testing of possibilities for a supposed counter example.

A proof of this conjecture was proposed by Alfred Kempe in 1879, but a flaw was found by Percy Heawood in 1890.

A minimal counter example is a counter example with the smallest possible number of countries.

This example highlights the fact that there are many conjectures in mathematics that are unproven for long periods of time. The following problems have created much interest since the conjectures were first made.

1. **The Goldbach conjecture**
   Every even number greater than 4 can be written as the sum of two prime numbers. Use a calculator to investigate this problem.

2. **Fermat's last theorem**
   There are no positive integers a, b and c such that $a^n + b^n = c^n$ where n is an integer greater than 2. This theorem has been worked on by many notable mathematicians. Andrew Wiles has been credited with the first formal proof in 1994.

There is no record of Pierre de Fermat's (1601–1665) proof to this conjecture. He wrote in the margin of his copy of the *Arithmetica*, written by the Greek mathematician Diophantus in AD 275, that he had found a remarkable proof but didn't have enough space to write it.

15.2 Proof by Exhaustion and Disproof by Counter Example

Exercise

Technique

1 Prove that a three-digit number abc is divisible by 4 if the related two digit number bc is divisible by 4.

2 Find a counter example for the following propositions:

a $n^2 - n + 41$ produces prime numbers for all $n \in \mathbb{N}$.
b $n^2 - 79n + 1601$ produces prime numbers for all $n \in \mathbb{N}$.
c Any number of the form $4k + 1$ is the square of an odd number.
d The numbers 7, 37, 337, 3337, . . . are all prime.

3 Is there a two-digit number ab such that the difference between ab and ba is a prime number?

4 Prove that if a^2 is even, then a must be an even number.

Contextual

1 **Mersenne primes**
Father Marin Mersenne (1588–1648) conjectured that all numbers of the form $2^n - 1$ are prime when n is prime. Prove, or disprove by counter example, this conjecture.

2 **The Levy conjecture**
In 1964 Paul Levy (1886–1971) conjectured that every odd number greater than 5 can be written in the form $2P + Q$ where P and Q are prime numbers. Investigate this conjecture.

15.3 Proof by Contradiction

The idea of proof by contradiction is to first assume the opposite of what you are trying to prove. Then show via a mathematical argument that a false conclusion or an absurd result is reached. If all reasoning or deduction is correct then the only incorrect statement must be the initial one. This means the original conjecture you are trying to prove must be true.

Archimedes of Syracuse (287?–212 BC)
Generally considered to be one of the greatest mathematicians of all time. In his work on the 'Quadrature of the Parabola' he used a method of *reductio ad absurdum*, which is now called proof by contradiction and was used by Euclid, amongst others.

Example 1

Prove that $\sqrt{2}$ is an irrational number.

Solution

To prove this conjecture by contradiction, first assume the opposite; that is, that $\sqrt{2}$ is rational. Then

$$\sqrt{2} = \frac{a}{b}$$

where a and b are integers with no common factors; a and b are **co-prime**. So $\frac{a}{b}$ is in its lowest form and *cannot* be cancelled down. Multiplying both sides by b,

$$\sqrt{2}b = a$$

$$\Rightarrow \quad 2b^2 = a^2$$

Now the LHS is even (2 multiplied by any integer is even) so a^2 must be even, and if a^2 is even then a must also be even. Hence a can be re-written $a = 2c$ for some integer c.

You should have proved that if a^2 is even then a is even as part of 15.2 Technique, Exercise 4.

$$\text{Now} \quad 2b^2 = a^2 = (2c)^2 = 4c^2$$

$$\text{Then} \quad b^2 = 2c^2 \Rightarrow b^2 \text{ is even.}$$

If b^2 is even then so is b, but this contradicts our assumption that a and b are co-prime and have no common factors. Since all steps in the mathematical argument are logical, the assumed statement must be false, so $\sqrt{2}$ cannot be rational.

Therefore $\sqrt{2}$ is irrational

Euclid used this method of proof by contradiction to show that there are an infinite number of prime numbers.

Example 2

Prove that the set of prime numbers is infinite (that is that there is no such thing as the largest prime number).

Solution

To prove this conjecture by contradiction, first assume the opposite. Assume that there is a last, and largest, prime number, p. Now consider the product of all existing prime numbers.

$$\text{Let} \quad N = 2 \times 3 \times 5 \times 7 \times 11 \times \ldots \times p.$$

Clearly the number $(N + 1)$ is not divisible by any of these prime numbers, since there would always be a remainder of 1. If $(N + 1)$ isn't divisible by any of the primes $2, 3, \ldots, p$ then it must be prime (and consequently larger than p) or composite and divisible by a prime larger than p. But this is a contradiction. Since the mathematical argument contains only logical steps the original conjecture must be false. This means there cannot be a largest prime number. So the prime numbers must go on forever!

15.3 Proof by Contradiction

Exercise

Technique

1 Prove that $\sqrt{3}$ is an irrational number.

2 Prove that $\sqrt{7}$ is an irrational number.

3 Prove that if p is odd, p^2 must also be odd.

4 Prove there is no largest integer. Is there a smallest integer?

Contextual

1

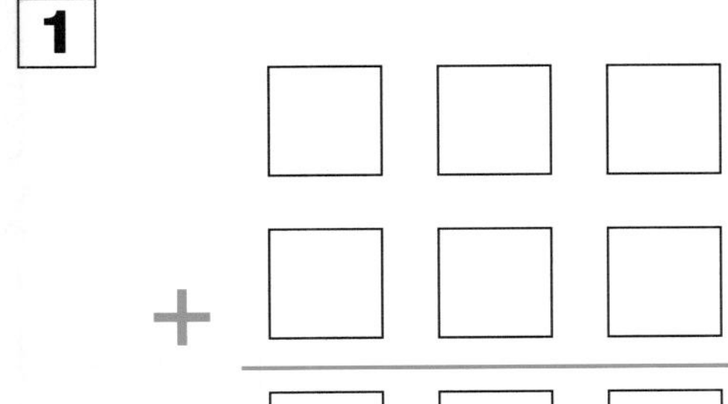

A Maths Club challenge is to place the integers $1, 2, \ldots, 9$ in the squares to create a correct sum. Members of the club produce over 200 solutions. Prove that this can only be done if 'carrying' from one column to another happens.
[Hint: Let a–i be the integers 1–9, and assume that

$$\begin{array}{r} a\ \ b\ \ c \\ +\ d\ \ e\ \ f \\ \hline g\ \ h\ \ i \\ \hline \end{array}$$

can be done without carrying. Show that this leads to a contradiction.]

15.4 Proof by Induction

The principle of **mathematical induction** is a simple three-step proof.

Step ① Show that the result is true for the natural number 1.
Step ② Assume that the result is true for some other natural number $n = k$, where $k > 1$.
Step ③ Show that the result is also true for the next natural number $n = (k + 1)$, given that it is true for $n = k$.

This method is useful for proving a variety of results that are true for all positive integers. One problem with it is that the correct formula, or conjecture, needs to be identified first.

Pierre Fermat (1601–1665)
Used a form of proof that he called 'the method of infinite descent'.

Blaise Pascal (1623–1662)
Used a similar form of proof to Fermat that is close to the modern form induction. It is known tha the two men corresponde In 1654 they jointly developed the fundamen concepts of the theory c probability.

Example 1

Prove that the sum of the first n positive integers is $\frac{1}{2}n(n+1)$.

That is, prove that $\sum_{r=1}^{n} r = \frac{1}{2}n(n+1)$.

Solution

Substitute $n = 1$ into the quoted formula

$$\tfrac{1}{2} \times 1 \times (1+1) = 1$$ ◀ ① True for $n = 1$.

So the result is true for $n = 1$.

Assume $\sum_{r=1}^{k} r = \frac{1}{2}k(k+1)$ ◀ ② Assume true for $n = k$.

If $\sum_{r=1}^{k} r = \frac{1}{2}k(k+1)$ then we require that ◀ ③ Prove true for $n = k + 1$.

$$\sum_{r=1}^{k+1} r = \tfrac{1}{2}(k+1)[(k+1)+1]$$

Replacing k with $k + 1$

$$= \tfrac{1}{2}(k+1)(k+2)$$

Now,

$$\sum_{r=1}^{k+1} r = 1 + 2 + 3 + 4 + \ldots + k + (k+1)$$

$$= \sum_{r=1}^{k} r + (k+1)$$

$$= \tfrac{1}{2}k(k+1) + (k+1)$$

Note the common facto of $k + 1$.

$$= (k+1)\left(\tfrac{1}{2}k + 1\right)$$

$$= (k+1) \times \tfrac{1}{2}(k+2)$$

$$= \tfrac{1}{2}(k+1)(k+2)$$

Since this is the required result the original statement can be considered proved by induction. It has been shown that whenever it is true for $n = k$, it is also true for $n = (k + 1)$. Since we know that it is true for $n = 1$, it is true for $n = 2$ and $n = 3$ and so on. Hence it is true for all positive integer values of n.

Example 2

Prove by induction that, for all positive integers, n,

$$\frac{1}{(1 \times 2)} + \frac{1}{(2 \times 3)} + \frac{1}{(3 \times 4)} + \dots + \frac{1}{n(n+1)} = \frac{n}{n+1}$$

Solution

Taking $n = 1$, $\frac{1}{1 \times 2} = \frac{1}{1+1}$, which is true. ◀ ① **True for $n = 1$.**

When $n = k$ ◀ ② **Assume true for $n = k$.**

$$\frac{1}{(1 \times 2)} + \frac{1}{(2 \times 3)} + \frac{1}{(3 \times 4)} + \dots + \frac{1}{k(k+1)} = \frac{k}{k+1}$$

The proof now requires that when the next term is added to both sides, the new total is of the same form.
The next term is $\frac{1}{(k+1)(k+2)}$.
Adding $\frac{1}{(k+1)(k+2)}$ to both sides, ◀ ③ **Prove true for $n = k + 1$.**

$$\frac{1}{(1 \times 2)} + \frac{1}{(2 \times 3)} + \frac{1}{(3 \times 4)} + \dots + \frac{1}{k(k+1)} + \frac{1}{(k+1)(k+2)}$$

$$= \frac{k}{k+1} + \frac{1}{(k+1)(k+2)}$$

$$= \frac{1}{(k+1)}\left[k + \frac{1}{(k+2)}\right]$$

$$= \frac{1}{(k+1)}\left[\frac{k(k+2)+1}{(k+2)}\right]$$

$$= \frac{k^2+2k+1}{(k+1)(k+2)}$$

$$= \frac{(k+1)^2}{(k+1)(k+2)}$$

$$= \frac{k+1}{k+2}$$

Note the common factor of $\frac{1}{(k+1)}$.

This result is of the correct form with $n = (k + 1)$. So if the result is true for $n = k$, it is also true for $n = (k + 1)$. So by induction the original statement must be true.

Example 3

Prove that $5^n + 3$ is divisible by 4 for all positive integers n.

Solution

If $n = 1$, $5^n + 3 = 5^1 + 3 = 8$ ◀ ① **True for $n = 1$.**

Since $4 \mid 8$ the result is true for $n = 1$.

Recall that $4 \mid 8$ means that 4 is a divisor of 8.

Assume that $5^k + 3 = 4s$, for some integer s. ◀ ② **Assume true for $n = k$.**
That is, $5^k + 3$ is divisible by 4.
If $5^k + 3 = 4s$, the proof requires that $5^{(k+1)} + 3 = 4t$, for some integer t.

$$\begin{aligned} 5^{(k+1)} + 3 &= 5 \times 5^k + 3 \\ &= 5 \times (4s - 3) + 3 \\ &= 20s - 15 + 3 \\ &= 20s - 12 \\ &= 4(5s - 3) \end{aligned}$$

◀ ③ **Prove true for $n = k + 1$.**

Since $5s - 3$ is an integer, t say, we can write

$$5^{(k+1)} + 3 = 4t$$

Since this is the required result the original statement has proved to be true by induction.

Example 4

Prove that $2^n > n$ for $n \in \mathbb{N}$ (that is, for every natural number n).

Solution

If $n = 1$, $2^n = 2^1 > 1$ ◀ ① **True for $n = 1$.**

Clearly $2 > 1$ and so the inequality is true for $n = 1$.

Assume that $2^k > k$. ◀ ② **Assume true for $n = k$.**
If $2^k > k$, the proof requires $2^{k+1} > k + 1$. ◀ ③ **Prove true for $n = k + 1$.**

If $2^k > k$, then multiplying both sides by 2 gives $2^{k+1} > 2k$.

So we now need to show that $2k > k + 1$.

Clearly $2k > k + 1$ provided $k \in \mathbb{N}$ and $k > 1$.

So $\quad 2^{k+1} > k + 1$.

So whenever it is true for $n = k$ it is also true for $n = (k + 1)$. It is true for $n = 1$, so it must be true for $n = 2, 3, \ldots$

So $2^n > n$ for $n \in \mathbb{N}$ has been proved by induction.

15.4 Proof by Induction

Exercise

Technique

1 Prove that the sum of the first n odd numbers is n^2.

2 Prove that $\sum_{r=1}^{n} r^2 = \frac{1}{6}n(n+1)(2n+1)$

3 Prove the following by induction, where n is a positive integer in each case:

a $4^n + 2$ is divisible by 6.

b $6^n + 4$ is divisible by 10.

c $3^n + 3^{n+1} + 3^{n+2}$ is divisible by 13.

Contextual

1 ***The Tower of Hanoi***

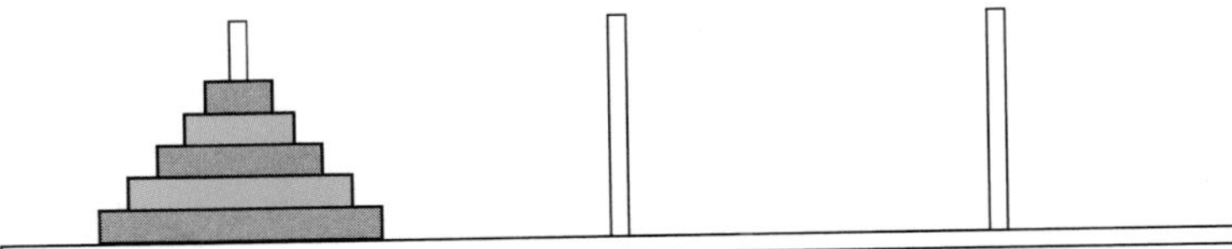

This is a puzzle based on a legend. It involves an ancient monastery, where Buddhist monks moved discs from one spike to another in such a way that no disc was placed on top of a smaller disc. The legend said the monks could move one disc per minute, and that the end of the world would occur before they had moved 100 discs from one spike to another completely.

a Prove by induction that the number of moves required for n discs is $2^n - 1$.

b How long would the monks in the legend take to move 100 discs if they were not to break the rules?

Consolidation

Exercise A

1 Which statement of the following mathematical argument is invalid?

$$1 = 1 \quad [1]$$
$$x = x \quad [2]$$
$$x^2 = x^2 \quad [3]$$
$$x^2 - x^2 = x^2 - x^2 \quad [4]$$
$$x(x - x) = (x + x)(x - x) \quad [5]$$
$$x = (x + x) \quad [6]$$
$$1 = 2 \quad [7]$$

2 Prove that all prime numbers above 3 are of the form $6n \pm 1$, where n is an integer.

3 Comment on the conjecture that $2n^2 + 5$ is prime if n is an integer.

4 Prove by induction the formula for the sum of an arithmetic progression:

$$a + (a + d) + (a + 2d) + \cdots + [a + (n - 1)d] = \tfrac{1}{2}n[2a + (n - 1)d]$$

5 Decide whether the following mathematical statement is true or false.

$$\text{If } 0 < p < q, \text{ then } \int_0^p f(x)\,dx < \int_0^q f(x)\,dx.$$

If it is true prove it. If it is false give a counter example.

Exercise B

1 Prove, or disprove by counter example, the statement: 'the difference between the cubes of any pair of consecutive integers is a prime number'.

2 Show that $2^{4n} - 1$ is always divisible by 3 and by 5 provided n is a positive integer.

3 Use the induction method to prove the following summation.

$$\frac{1}{1 \times 3} + \frac{1}{3 \times 5} + \frac{1}{5 \times 7} + \ldots + \frac{1}{(2n - 1)(2n + 1)} = \frac{n}{2n + 1}$$

4 Find a counter example for the proposition: 43, 433, 4333, . . . are all prime.

5 **a** Use mathematical induction to show that $\sum_{r=1}^{n} r^3 = \dfrac{n^2(n+1)^2}{4}$.

b Use the above result to show that

$$1^3 + 3^3 + 5^3 + \cdots + (2n-1)^3 = n^2(2n^2-1)$$

(WJEC)

Applications and Activities

1 Investigate the following conjecture: 'Every odd number greater than 5 can be expressed in the form $P + 2Q$ where P and Q are prime numbers'. For example:

$7 = 3 + (2 \times 2)$ $\quad$ $11 = 5 + (2 \times 3)$

$9 = 3 + (2 \times 3)$ $\quad$ $13 = 3 + (2 \times 5)$

2 ***Perfect numbers***

A Mersenne number is a prime number of the form $2^n - 1$, where $n \in \mathbb{N}$; that is, one less than a power of 2. Investigate the conjecture: 'If a Mersenne prime is multiplied by the next consecutive whole number, and the result divided by 2, a perfect number is formed'.

A perfect number is a number equal to the su of its proper divisors (excluding the number itself).

Summary

- Mathematical arguments follow a chain of reasoning in which statements follow, or can be deduced from, previous proved results.
- Proof can sometimes be established by exhausting every possibility; this is called **proof by exhaustion**.
- One example is sufficient to show that a statement isn't true; this is called **disproof by counter example**.
- To assume the opposite and show that deduction leads to an absurd result is an acceptable form of mathematical proof; this is called ***reductio ad absurdum*** or **proof by contradiction**.
- If a result is identified it can sometimes be **proved by induction**. If it is shown to be true for $n = 1$, and on the assumption it is true for $n = k$, deduction gives truth with $n = (k + 1)$, it is true for all positive integer values of n.

Answers

1 Algebra I

Review (p. 1)

1 a x^2 b 7^3 c x^3
d a^2b^3 e $4x^2$ f $12a^3$

2 a 36 b 4 c 9
d 16 e a f x

3 a $5x$ b $10x^2$ c $3y + 4x$
d $7xy$ e $2x^2 - 3x + 4$ f $8x$

4 a $3x + 6$ b $2x - 6$ c $-2x - 4$ d $-3x + 9$ e $-5x - 10y + 15$ f $12x - 12y - 72$
g $x^2 + 3x + 2$ h $x^2 + x - 6$ i $x^2 + 3x - 4$ j $x^2 + 8x + 15$ k $x^2 - 5x + 6$ l $x^2 - 8x + 16$

5 a $x = 5$ b $x = 5$ c $x = 5$
d $x = 5$ e $x = 8$ f $x = 11$

6 a $2(x + y)$ b $3(x - y)$ c $7(x + 2y)$
d $4(2x - 3y)$ e $6x(3x - y)$ f $6x^2y^2(2x + y)$

7 a 125 b 127 c $182\frac{2}{17}$
d $461\frac{4}{13}$ e $324\frac{3}{14}$ f $567\frac{5}{16}$

1.1 Technique (p. 7)

1 a $3\sqrt{2}$ b $3\sqrt{3}$ c $4\sqrt{3}$
d $2\sqrt{11}$ e $5\sqrt{5}$ f $3\sqrt{17}$
g 15 h $6\sqrt{2}$

2 a $3\sqrt{3}$ b $9\sqrt{2}$ c $5\sqrt{2}$
d $10\sqrt{2}$ e $7\sqrt{3}$ f $11\sqrt{5}$

3 a 1 b $5 - 2\sqrt{6}$ c $8 - 2\sqrt{15}$
d 2 e $9 - \sqrt{5}$ f $41 - 6\sqrt{5}$
g 5 h 2

4 a $\dfrac{\sqrt{3}}{3}$ b $\dfrac{3\sqrt{5}}{5}$ c $\dfrac{\sqrt{5} - 1}{4}$ d $\sqrt{2} + 1$
e $\dfrac{7(\sqrt{13} + \sqrt{11})}{2}$ f $2(\sqrt{7} - 2)$ g $\dfrac{7 - 2\sqrt{10}}{3}$ h $\dfrac{9 - \sqrt{77}}{2}$

1.2 Technique (p. 13)

1 a 4^6 b 5^5 c $5^0 = 1$
d 7^4 e $2x^2y$ f $2x^2y$

2 a x^{12} b x^6 c $2x^6$
d $3x^{15}$ e $8x^{12}$ f $27x^6$

3 a $3x^{-7}$ b $\frac{1}{3}x^{-7}$ c 4^{-3}
d 5^{-2} e $\frac{1}{2}x^{-2}y^{-4}$ f $\frac{1}{3}x^3y^{-2}$

4 a $x^0 = 1$ b $x^0 = 1$ c $3x^2y^{-1}$
d $\frac{1}{2}x^2$ e $2x^2$ f x^2

5 a 64 b $\frac{1}{16}$ c $\frac{1}{9}$
d 9 e $\frac{5}{3}$ f $\frac{8}{3}$
g $\frac{3}{2}$ h $\frac{8}{27}$

6 a $x = 3$ b $x = 2$ c $x = -1$
d $x = 0$ e $x = 2$ f $x = \frac{4}{3}$
g $x = 8$ h $x = 7$

1.3 Technique (p. 19)

1 a i 3 ii 2
b i 4 ii -2
c i 5 ii -7
d i 2 ii 3
e i 3 ii 0
f i 2 ii 8

2 a $8x^2 + 5x + 5$
b $12x^2 + 9x + 1$
c $7x^3 + 2x^2 + 10x + 3$
d $9x^5 + 2x^4 + 7x^3 + 7x^2 + 4x + 9$

3 a $2x^2 + 5x + 7$
b $5x^2 + 17x - 9$
c $-2x^4 + 5x^3 + 6x + 5$
d $-8x^3 + x^2 + x + 1$

4 a $6x^2 + 7x + 2$
b $4x^3 + 6x^2 + 2x + 3$
c $2x^3 + 5x^2 - x - 1$
d $3x^3 - 7x^2 + 5x - 1$
e $-x^3 + 11x - 6$
f $-2x^3 + 13x^2 - 27x + 28$

5 a $7x^3 + 9x^2 + 15x + 26$
b $12x^3 + 23x^2 + 16x - 11$
c $-2x^3 + x^2 + 16x - 11$
d $-7x^3 + 18x^2 + 16x - 20$
e $4x^3 + 7x^2 + 8x + 1$
f $5x^4 - 3x^3 + 24x^2 - 34x + 12$

6 a $4x^2 + 12x + 9$
b $8x^3 + 36x^2 + 54x + 27$
c $16x^4 + 96x^3 + 216x^2 + 216x + 81$
d $16x^4 + 32x^3 + 24x^2 + 8x + 1$
e $x^4 + 4x^3 + 6x^2 + 4x + 1$
f $x^4 - 4x^3 + 6x^2 - 4x + 1$

7 a $1 - \dfrac{3}{x + 5}$ b $2 - \dfrac{8}{x + 5}$ c $4 + \dfrac{14}{x - 1}$
d $3 + \dfrac{10}{2x - 1}$ e $3 - \dfrac{8}{x + 2}$ f $2 + \dfrac{7}{x - 2}$

1.4 Technique (p. 25)

1 a $(x + 1)(x + 2)$ b $(x + 5)(x + 2)$ c $(x + 4)(x - 5)$ d $(x - 9)(x + 2)$
e $(x - 3)(x + 6)$ f $(x - 3)(x + 4)$ g $(x - 2)(x + 8)$ h $(x - 2)(x + 3)$

2 a $(x-4)(x+4)$
b $(y-3)(y+3)$
c $(3x-1)(3x+1)$
d $(4y-1)(4y+1)$
e $(\cos\theta-1)(\cos\theta+1)$
f $(\sin\theta-1)(\sin\theta+1)$
g $(2x-5y)(2x+5y)$
h $(9x-6y)(9x+6y)$

3 a $2(x+4)(x-4)$
b $3(y+3)(y-3)$
c $5(2x+1)(2x-1)$
d $50(y+2)(y-2)$
e $2t(t+15)(t-15)$
f $2(\cos\theta+1)(\cos\theta-1)$

4 a $(3x-2)(x+1)$
b $(2x-3)(x-1)$
c $(7x+1)(x+3)$
d $(2x-1)(2x-5)$
e $(x-5)(10x+9)$
f $(8x+3)(x-3)$
g $(8x-9)(x-1)$
h $(3x+1)(2x-3)$

5 a $2(2x-3)(x-1)$
b $(x+4y)(x-2y)$
c $(x-4y)(x+9y)$
d $2(5x+1)(x-2)$
e $3(4x-1)(3x-2)$
f $2(4x-15)(2x-5)$
g $y(2x-1)(x-3)$
h $5y(3x+1)(4x-5)$

1.5 Technique (p. 37)

1 a $x=3$ or $x=-2$
b $x=3$ or $x=4$
c $x=1$ or $x=-3$
d $x=-5$ or $x=-1$
e $x=-\frac{5}{2}$ (twice)
f $x=0$ or $x=-2$
g $x=-3$ or $x=-\frac{1}{2}$
h $x=7$ or $x=-\frac{4}{3}$

2 a $x=-4$ or $x=-1$
b $x=-5$ or $x=3$
c $x=5$ or $x=1$
d $x=3$ or $x=-2$
e $x=4$ or $x=\frac{3}{4}$
f $x=-\frac{4}{3}$ (twice)

3 a $x=8$ or $x=-2$
b $x=2$ or $x=-4$
c $x=3$ or $x=-1$
d $x=3\pm\sqrt{8}$
e $x=\dfrac{1\pm\sqrt{3}}{2}$
f $x=\dfrac{4\pm\sqrt{37}}{3}$

4 a $x=2$ or $x=-1\frac{1}{3}$
b $x=\frac{2}{3}$ or $x=-4$
c $x=\dfrac{-1\pm\sqrt{33}}{4}$
d $x=6\pm\sqrt{41}$
e $x=\dfrac{-15\pm\sqrt{177}}{4}$
f $x=3\pm\frac{1}{3}\sqrt{51}$

5 a $x=\dfrac{3\pm\sqrt{6}}{2}$
b $x=2\pm\frac{1}{3}\sqrt{3}$
c $x=3\pm\frac{1}{3}\sqrt{87}$
d $x=-3\pm\sqrt{5}$
e $x=\dfrac{-3\pm\sqrt{5}}{2}$
f $x=3\pm\sqrt{6}$

6 a $(x-1)^2+2$
b $(x+2)^2-3$
c $-(x-1)^2+3$
d $-(x-4)^2-3$
e $-2(x-\frac{5}{4})^2+\frac{1}{8}$
f $2(x-\frac{3}{4})^2-3\frac{1}{8}$

1.5 Contextual (p. 38)

1 $t=0.43$ or 2.83. We are solving to find the time t at which the object is at a certain height. There are two answers because the object is at this height going up and coming down.

2 3.6π

3 12

4 13 sides

5 1

6 $d=30+10\sqrt{5}$ or $d=30-10\sqrt{5}$
($d=52.36$ or $d=7.639$) $d=7.64$ cm (3 s.f.)

1.6 Technique (p. 43)

1 a $(2,4)$ b $(2,3)$ c $(3,5)$
d $(1,8)$ e $(-1,3)$ f $(-\frac{1}{2},-\frac{3}{2})$

2 a $(2,0),(3,2)$
b $(1,-2),(2,-1)$
c $(2,12),(-2,-8)$
d $(-3,18),(4,11)$
e $(5,3),(-3,-5)$
f $(-\frac{1}{4},-3\frac{1}{4}),(4,1)$

3 a $T=52.5$, $a=2.5$
b $x=3$, $y=6$
c $(2.35,1.85),(-1.60,-2.10)$
d $(1.36,5.86),(-5.86,-1.36)$

1.6 Contextual (p. 43)

1 $(-1,-4),(3,12)$

2 32 000 paid the higher price ($x=32\,000$, $y=12\,000$)

3 A CD costs £21 and a tape costs £14

4 $m=2$, $c=3$

5 Callum is 17, Lydia is 15

Consolidation A (p. 44)

1 $t=0.53$ seconds or 2.33 seconds

2 A $(-2,12)$, B $(5,5)$

3 a $x+y=240$, $31x+16y=5595$
b 117 people pay £31 (123 people pay £16)

4 area of outer circle with radius R is πR^2
area of inner circle with radius r is πr^2
cross-sectional area $=\pi R^2-\pi r^2=\pi(R^2-r^2)=\pi(R-r)(R+r)$
volume $=117\pi\,m^3$

5 $\tan\theta=1$, $\theta=45°$ or $\tan\theta=3$, $\theta=71.6°$

6 $N_1=88$, $N_2=22$

7 $(3,1)$ and $(-2\frac{1}{5},-1\frac{3}{5})$

Consolidation B (p. 45)

1 $t = 0.99$ seconds or 2.69 seconds

2 A $(-2, 5)$, B $(1, -4)$

3 **a** $x + y = 600$, $22x + 17y = 11\,400$
b $x = 240$; 240 people paid at the door
$y = 360$; 360 people bought tickets in advance

4 area of outer circle with radius R is πR^2
area of inner circle with radius $r = \pi r^2$
cross-sectional area $= \pi R^2 - \pi r^2 =$
$\pi(R^2 - r^2) = \pi(R - r)(R + r)$
volume $= 0.32\pi\,\text{m}^3$ (or $320\,000\pi\,\text{cm}^3$)

5 $\tan\theta = 2$, $\theta = 63.4°$ or $\tan\theta = 3$, $\theta = 71.6°$

6 **a** $(-1, 5)$; when $x = 0$, $y = 2$
b $a = -3$, $b = 5$

7 **a** 1, 64 **b** 0, -1

2 Coordinate Geometry

Review (p. 49)

1 **a** $y = x + 7$ **b** $y = -x + 5$ **c** $y = 2x + 2$ **d** $y = 3x - 1$ **e** $y = 4x - 14$ **f** $y = \frac{1}{2}x + 4$

2 **a** $x = 2\sqrt{5}$ **b** $x = \sqrt{5}$ **c** $x = 7$

3 **a** $x^2 + 4x + 4$ **b** $x^2 + 6x + 9$ **c** $x^2 + 10x + 25$ **d** $a^2 + 2ab + b^2$ **e** $4x^2 + 4x + 1$ **f** $9x^2 + 12x + 4$

4 **a** $x^2 - 6x + 9$ **b** $x^2 - 2x + 1$ **c** $a^2 - 2ab + b^2$ **d** $9x^2 - 12x + 4$ **e** $4x^2 - 12x + 9$ **f** $25x^2 - 10x + 1$

2.1 Technique (p. 58)

1 **a** $\sqrt{5}$ **b** $\sqrt{5}$ **c** 5 **d** $\sqrt{65}$ **e** $\sqrt{29}$ **f** 15 **g** 13 **h** 15

2 **a** $\sqrt{117}$ **b** $\sqrt{10}$ **c** $\sqrt{65}$ **d** $\sqrt{20} = 2\sqrt{5}$ **e** $\sqrt{212} = 2\sqrt{53}$ **f** $\sqrt{29}$ **g** 15 **h** 7

3 **a** 5 **b** 4 **c** -1 **d** -1 **e** 0 **f** -5

4 **a i** $\frac{1}{2}$ **ii** -2
b i $\frac{5}{8}$ **ii** $-1\frac{3}{5}$
c i -1 **ii** 1
d i $-4\frac{1}{2}$ **ii** $\frac{2}{9}$
e i $-\frac{4}{9}$ **ii** $2\frac{1}{4}$
f i $\frac{2}{9}$ **ii** $-4\frac{1}{2}$

5 **a** parallel **b** perpendicular **c** parallel **d** parallel **e** perpendicular **f** perpendicular

2.1 Contextual (p. 59)

1 **a** $3\sqrt{2}$ cm **b** 0.424 km

2 13

3 23.1 cm; 5.77 km

4 Distance from ash tree to cottage $= \sqrt{53}$
Distance from beech tree to cottage $= \sqrt{53}$

5 **a** S $(-3, -2)$
b Show that all sides are equal in length, then show that the gradients of PS and SR multiplied together do not come to -1.

6 AF $= \sqrt{34}$

2.2 Technique (p. 63)

1 **a** $y = -3x - 7$ **b** $y = -4x + 3$ **c** $y = 4x - 10$ **d** $y = 2x - 12$ **e** $y = -x - 3$ **f** $y = 2x - 5$ **g** $y = 8x + 7$ **h** $y = -2x + 3$

2 **a** gradient, 5; intercept, $(0, -3)$
b gradient, -2; intercept, $(0, 3)$
c gradient, -2; intercept, $(0, 7)$
d gradient, $\frac{1}{2}$; intercept, $(0, 5)$

3 **a** gradient, -2; intercept, $(0, -8)$
b gradient, $\frac{2}{3}$; intercept, $(0, \frac{2}{3})$
c gradient, $-\frac{1}{2}$; intercept, $(0, 1)$
d gradient, 2; intercept, $(0, 3)$
e gradient, $\frac{3}{7}$; intercept, $(0, 2)$
f gradient, $-\frac{a}{b}$; intercept, $(0, -\frac{c}{b})$

4 gradient $= -3$; A $(0, 6)$, B $(2, 0)$

5 $y = \frac{1}{2}x + 7$

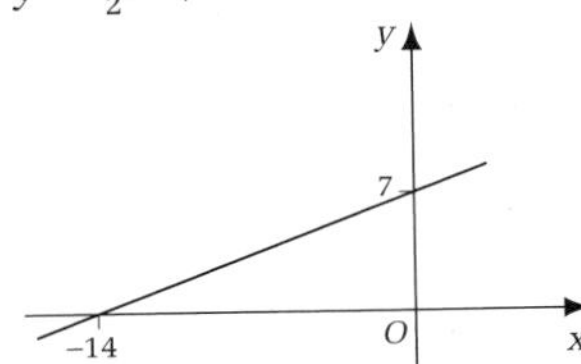

6 $x = 1$, $y = 5$.

2.3 Technique (p. 69)

1 **a** $y = 3x - 7$ **b** $y = 6x + 8$ **c** $y = 5x - 17$ **d** $y = -3x + 4$ **e** $y = \frac{1}{2}x - 4$ **f** $y = -\frac{1}{3}x + 3\frac{2}{3}$

2 **a** $y = 2x$ **b** $y = -\frac{1}{2}x + 2\frac{1}{2}$ **c** $y = 5x + 6$ **d** $y = 2x - 2$ **e** $y = -x + 14$ **f** $y = \frac{1}{2}x - \frac{1}{2}$

3 **a** $(2, 3)$; $y = -\frac{1}{4}x + 3\frac{1}{2}$
b $(\frac{9}{2}, \frac{1}{2})$; $y = x - 4$
c $(-1, 4)$; $y = x + 5$
d $(0, 2)$; $y = -\frac{1}{4}x + 2$

2.3 Contextual (p. 69)

1 5; $y = 2x + 3$

2 **a** $(3, 10)$
b 3
c $-\frac{1}{3}$
d $x + 3y - 33 = 0$

3 M $(2, 1)$; $y = 2x - 3$

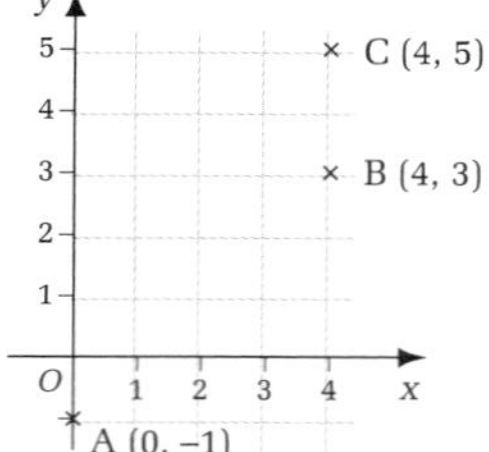

4 **a** $x - 2y + 6 = 0$
b gradient AB $= -2$
gradient of $x - 2y - 4 = 0$ is $\frac{1}{2}$
Multiplying these gradients gives -1, so the lines are perpendicular.
c Distance $= 2\sqrt{5}$

2.4 Technique (p. 76)

1 **a** $x > 5$ **b** $x \leq 2$ **c** $x \geq 3$ **d** $x > -5$

2 **a** $x < -3, x > 3$ **b** $-5 \leq x \leq 5$
c $x < -7, x > 7$ **d** $-8 < x < 8$

3 **a** $x < -5, x > -3$ **d** $-3 < x < 5$
b $x \leq -6, x \geq 1$ **e** $2 \leq x \leq 3$
c $-5 < x < -2$ **f** $x < -4, x > 1$

4 **a** $x \leq -2, x \geq 12$
b $x < -3, x > 2$
c $3 \leq x \leq 8$
d all values of x except $x = -3$
e $-7 < x < 11$
f $x = 2$

5 **a** $x < -2, x > -\frac{1}{3}$ **d** $x < \frac{1}{3}, x > 1$
b $-3 \leq x \leq -\frac{1}{7}$ **e** $x \leq -\frac{1}{2}, x \geq 3$
c $-1 < x < -\frac{2}{3}$ **f** $x < -1, x > \frac{2}{3}$

2.4 Contextual (p. 76)

1 $\frac{1}{2} - \frac{1}{2}\sqrt{13} < x < \frac{1}{2} + \frac{1}{2}\sqrt{13}$

2 $6 - x - x^2 \geq 0$

3 $-1 < x < 2$

4 $x = 3\sqrt{2}$ or $x = 2\sqrt{2}$; $2\sqrt{2} < x < 3\sqrt{2}$

2.5 Technique (p. 82)

1 **a** centre $(5, 3)$, radius 7
b centre $(-6, -1)$, radius 5
c centre $(0, -7)$, radius 11
d centre $(-1, 2)$, radius $\sqrt{11}$

2 **a** $x^2 + y^2 + 2x - 6y + 6 = 0$
b $x^2 + y^2 - 4x + 2y - 4 = 0$
c $x^2 + y^2 + 4x - 1 = 0$
d $x^2 + y^2 - 6x + 6y = 0$

3 **a** centre $(3, 1)$, radius 2
b centre $(-1, 2)$, radius 2
c centre $(-1, -4)$, radius 3
d centre $(0, -2)$, radius $\sqrt{3}$

2.5 Contextual (p. 82)

1 $k = -6$ or 10

2 $k = 1$ or 7

3 $(0, 1)$, $(0, 5)$

4 tangent $4y + 3x - 19 = 0$; normal $3y - 4x - 8 = 0$

5 tangent $y = \frac{3}{4}x - 9$;
perpendicular $4x + 3y - 25 = 0$

6 $x^2 + y^2 + 6x - 8y = 0$

7 8

Consolidation A (p. 83)

1 **a** $AB = \sqrt{50}$, $AC = \sqrt{40}$, $BC = \sqrt{50}$: therefore isosceles
M $(5, 4)$; area $= 20$
b $x - 3y + 7 = 0$
c $7x - y - 21 = 0$
d H $(3\frac{1}{2}, 3\frac{1}{2})$, gradient CH $= -1$, gradient AB $= 1$

2 length $AB = 2\sqrt{10}$, mid-point $(3, 0)$

3 **a** perpendicular to PQ, $3x - 4y - 15 = 0$
perpendicular to PR, $3x + y - 30 = 0$
b C $(9, 3)$
c $x^2 + y^2 - 18x - 6y + 40 = 0$

4 $1 < m < 7$

5 $\sqrt{43}$

6 $x < 1$ and $x > 9$

Consolidation B (p. 84)

1 $(3\frac{1}{2}, -1\frac{1}{2})$, gradient $= -7$; $x - 7y - 14 = 0$

2 $x - 2y - 8 = 0$; $(2, -3)$; $4\sqrt{5}$

3 $2\sqrt{14}$

4 $20x + y - 70 = 0$

5 $-8 < x < -4$

6 **a** $3x - y + 3 = 0$
b $x + y + 5 = 0$
c P $(-2, -3)$
d $AP = 5$
e $x^2 + y^2 + 4x + 6y - 12 = 0$

3 Trigonometry I

Review (p. 87)

1 **a** 10 **b** 10
c 6 **d** $2\sqrt{2} = 2.83$

2 **a** $(a-b)(a+b)$ **b** $(c+2)(c+1)$ **c** $(h+4)(h-3)$ **d** $(k-3)(k-4)$ **e** $p=2,6$ **f** $p=-5,\frac{1}{3}$

3 **a** $\frac{12}{13},\frac{5}{13},\frac{12}{5}$ **b** $\frac{11}{61},\frac{60}{61},\frac{11}{60}$ **c** $\frac{1}{2},\frac{\sqrt{3}}{2},\frac{1}{\sqrt{3}}$

4 **a** $45.5\,\text{m}^2$ **b** $7.22\,\text{m}^2$ **c** $60.0\,\text{cm}^2$

5 **a** $A=60°, a=6.93\,\text{cm}, c=4\,\text{cm}$
b $A=53.1°, B=36.9°, c=10\,\text{cm}$
c $C=30°, a=8.66\,\text{m}, b=10\,\text{m}$
d $A=79.6°, B=79.6°, C=20.8°$

6 **a** 060° **b** 120° **c** 210° **d** 340°

3.1 Technique (p. 97)

1 **a** sin 60° **b** − cos 15° **c** tan 40° **d** cos 55° **e** tan 40° **f** − cos 43° **g** − sin 29° **h** sin 23°

2 **a** $-\frac{\sqrt{3}}{2}$ **b** $-\frac{1}{\sqrt{2}}$ **c** $-\sqrt{3}$ **d** $-\frac{1}{2}$ **e** $-\frac{1}{2}$ **f** $\sqrt{3}$ **g** $\frac{1}{2}$ **h** $-\frac{\sqrt{3}}{2}$

3 **a** 18.3°, 161.7° **b** 121.3°, 238.7° **c** 68.7°, 248.7° **d** 25.2°, 205.2° **e** 45°, 225° **f** 56.3°, 236.3°

4 **a** 1.589 **b** 1.325 **c** −0.05241 **d** −1.589 **e** 2.747 **f** −1.252 **g** 0.5774 **h** −3.864

5 **a** −36.9° **b** −84.3° **c** 75.5° **d** 33.7° **e** −66.8° **f** 41.8°

6

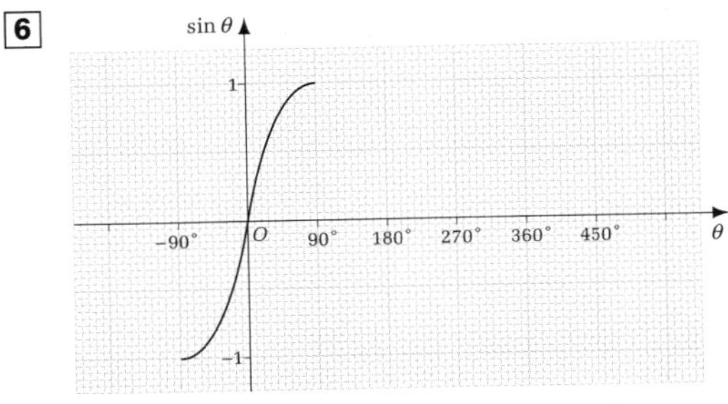

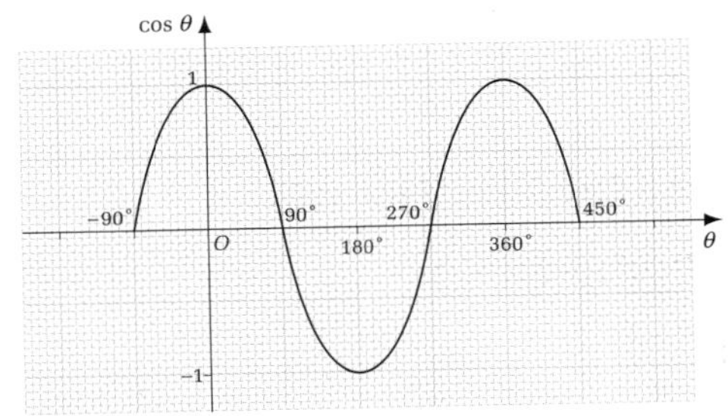

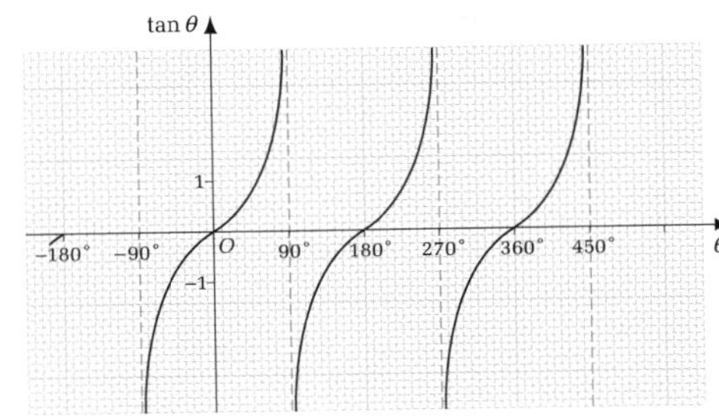

a −30°, 210°, 330°
b −36.9°, 36.9°, 323.1°, 396.9°
c 71.6°, 251.6°, 431.6°

7 **a** −30° **b** 45°

3.1 Contextual (p. 98)

1 **a**

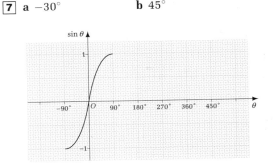

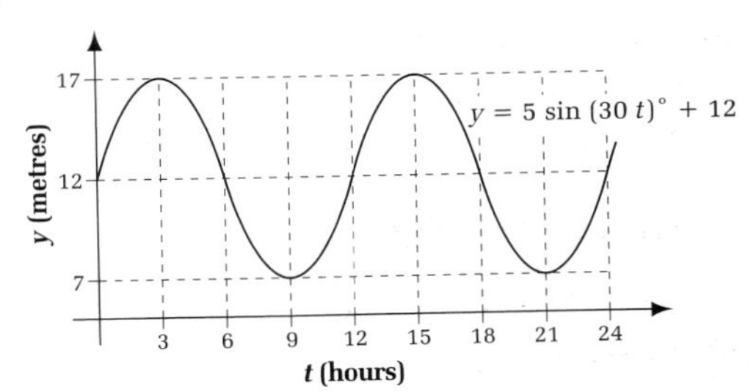

b high tides at 0300, 1500; low tides at 0900, 2100
c From 0114 to 0446 (3 hours, 32 mins), and 1314 to 1646 (3 hours, 32 mins), that is in one day the harbour is deeper than 15 m for 7 hours 4 mins.

2 $a=5, b=30$ and $c=7$ (so $h=5\cos(30t)°+7$)

3 **a** 13 hours, 3 mins
b longest day is day 170 (19 June); shortest day is day 350 (16 December)
c No account taken of leap years. True results are 21 December (day 355) and 21 June (day 172). Model loses accuracy as time (year) progresses.
d Try $n=13-5\cos(x+10°)$ and repeat **a** and **b**.

3.2 Technique (p. 105)

1 **a** $\theta = 53.1°, 233.1°$
b $\theta = 116.6°, 296.6°$
c $\theta = 161.6°, 341.6°$
d $\theta = 14.0°, 194.0°$
e $\theta = 45°, 135°, 225°, 315°$
f $\theta = 30°, 150°, 210°, 330°$

2 **a** $\theta = -135°, -116.6°, 45°, 63.4°$
b $\theta = 19.5°, 90°, 160.5°$
c $\theta = \pm 60°, \pm 180°$
d $\theta = \pm 30°, \pm 150°$
e $\theta = 14.5°, 30°, 150°, -165.5°$
f $\theta = \pm 30°, \pm 150°$

3 **a** $\theta = 15°, 75°, 195°, 255°$
b $\theta = 58.7°, 238.7°$
c $\theta = 48.9°, 151.1°, 228.9°, 331.1°$
d $\theta = 40.2°, 100.2°, 160.2°, 220.2°, 280.2°, 340.2°$
e $\theta = 138.6°, 221.4°$
f $\theta = 22.5°, 112.5°, 202.5°, 292.5°$

4 **a** $\theta = -160.5°, -19.5°, 30°, 150°$
b $\theta = \pm 120°$
c $\theta = -135°, -63.4°, 45°, 116.6°$
d $\theta = -153.4°, -116.6°, 26.6°, 63.4°$
e $\theta = -153.4°, -135°, 26.6°, 45°$
f $\theta = \pm 70.5°, \pm 109.5°$

3.2 Contextual (p. 106)

1 68.2° (3 s.f.)

2 Quadratic equation in $\tan\theta$ is $x^2\tan^2\theta - 50x\tan\theta + (50y + x^2) = 0$. For distinct, real solutions we require $b^2 - 4ac > 0$, that is $(-50X)^2 - 4X^2(50Y + X^2) > 0$. The golfer should understand that it is possible for the ball to pass through a given point (X, Y) in more than one way. Using one club the ball would stay low and another club would pitch the ball higher. The stroke used (and so the speed of the ball) would stay the same at the tee.

3.3 Technique (p. 112)

1 **a** $\frac{\sqrt{2}}{4}(1 + \sqrt{3})$
b $\frac{\sqrt{2}}{4}(1 - \sqrt{3})$
c $\frac{\sqrt{3}-1}{\sqrt{3}+1} = 2 - \sqrt{3}$
d $\frac{\sqrt{2}}{4}(\sqrt{3} + 1)$
e $\frac{\sqrt{2}}{4}(1 + \sqrt{3})$
f $\frac{1+\sqrt{3}}{1-\sqrt{3}} = -(2 + \sqrt{3})$

2 **a** $\cos 90° = 0$ **d** $\sin 60° = \frac{\sqrt{3}}{2}$
b $\sin 45° = \frac{\sqrt{2}}{2}$ **e** $\cos 60° = \frac{1}{2}$
c $\tan 30° = \frac{1}{\sqrt{3}}$ **f** $\tan 120° = -\sqrt{3}$

3 **a** 60°, 240° **b** 85.9°, 265.9°
c 126.2°, 306.2° **d** 104.6°, 284.6°

5 **a** $\frac{63}{65}$ **e** $-\frac{63}{16}$ **i** $\frac{24}{7}$
b $-\frac{16}{65}$ **f** $-\frac{33}{56}$ **j** $\frac{120}{169}$
c $-\frac{33}{65}$ **g** $\frac{24}{25}$ **k** $-\frac{119}{169}$
d $\frac{56}{65}$ **h** $\frac{7}{25}$ **l** $-\frac{120}{119}$

3.3 Contextual (p. 113)

1 **a** **ii** $\theta \le 31.6°$.
iii When $\theta = 31.6°$ point B is 1.57 m above ground; not necessarily an ideal height for a handle to be lifted.
b **i** $\sin(\theta + 13.5°) \le 0.778$
ii $\theta \le 37.6°$
iii Now point B is 1.52 m above the ground (which is only 5 cm lower than it was before).

3.4 Technique (p. 121)

1 **a** $b = 11.9$ cm
b $b = 22.6$ cm
c $b = 10.6$ cm

2 **a** $A = 82.8°, B = 41.4°, C = 55.8°$
b $A = 42.5°, B = 38.6°, C = 98.8°$
c $A = 19.6°, B = 22.6°, C = 137.8°$

3 **a** 6.09 cm **b** 3.80 cm
c 5.33 cm **d** 6.87 cm

4 **a** $A = 85.9°, B = 39.4°, C = 54.7°$
b $A = 112.3°, C = 25.7°, a = 26.3$ cm
c $B = 26.1°, C = 22.9°, a = 44.6$ cm
d $B = 44°, C = 126°, c = 116.5$ m
or $B = 136°, C = 34°, c = 80.5$ m

3.4 Contextual (p. 122)

1 $AC = 8.03$ nautical miles, 121°

2 17.5 miles, 288°

3 4.58 km, 229°

4 36.8 m

3.5 Technique (p. 126)

1 **a** 6 m^2 **b** 6 m^2 **c** 6 m^2

2 **a** 17.1 m^2 **b** 63.2 m^2
c 42 m^2 **d** 204 cm^2

3.5 Contextual (p. 126)

1 6 cm

2 6 km^2

3 yes

3.6 Technique (p. 130)

1 a $\frac{\pi}{12}$ b $\frac{5\pi}{6}$ c $\frac{5\pi}{12}$
d π e $\frac{5\pi}{4}$ f $\frac{7\pi}{4}$

2 a 0.349 b 1.36 c 2.25
d 3.87 e 4.69 f 6.13

3 a 180° b 135° c 540°
d 48° e $22\frac{1}{2}°$ f $157\frac{1}{2}°$

4 a $s = 5$ cm, $A = 12.5$ cm^2
b $s = 12$ cm, $A = 48$ cm^2
c $s = 22$ cm, $A = 121$ cm^2
d $s = 23.4$ cm, $A = 105.3$ cm^2

5 $r\theta = 20$, $\frac{1}{2}r^2\theta = 100$, $r = 10$, $\theta = 2$

6 9.13 cm

7 **1** a $\theta = 0.927, 4.07$
b $\theta = 2.04, 5.18$
c $\theta = 2.82, 5.96$
d $\theta = 0.244, 3.39$
e $\theta = 0.785, 2.36, 3.93, 5.50$
f $\theta = 0.524, 2.62, 3.67, 5.76$

2 a $\theta = -2.36, 2.04, 0.785, 1.12$
b $\theta = 0.34, 1.57, 2.8$
c $\theta = \pm 1.05, \pm 3.14$
d $\theta = \pm 0.524, \pm 2.62$
e $\theta = 0.253, 0.524, 2.62, -2.89$
f $\theta = \pm 0.524, \pm 2.62$

4 a $\theta = -2.80, -0.34, 0.524, 2.62$
b $\theta = \pm 2.09$
c $\theta = -2.36, -1.11, 0.785, 2.04$
d $\theta = -2.68, -2.04, 0.464, 1.11$
e $\theta = -2.68, -2.36, 0.464, 0.785$
f $\theta = \pm 1.23, \pm 1.91$

3.6 Contextual (p. 131)

1 5 cm^3

2 a $\theta = \frac{9}{4}$ d 622 cm^2
b 1800 cm^2 e 141 000 cm^3 (3 s.f.)
c 72.2 cm

3 sector angle is $\frac{2\pi r}{l}$

5 5175 cm^2

Consolidation A (p. 132)

1 27°, 90°, 207°, 270°

2 $x = 6$

3 a 11.4 km b 161°

4 198°, 342°

5 45°, 135°, 225°, 315°

6 b $y > 67\frac{1}{2}°$
c i negative ii positive

7 b 0, 0.464, 3.14 rad.

9 a 8.4 cm b 21.2 cm^2

10 a 78.7°, 258.7° b 3.48, 5.94

Consolidation B (p. 133)

1 a 88.9°, 271.1°
b 24.1°, 155.9°, 204.1°, 335.9°
c 0°, 53.1°, 180°, 306.9°
d 90°, 180°, 270°

2 a $\sin^2 2\theta + \sin 2\theta - 1 = 0$
c $2\theta = 38.2°, 141.8° \Rightarrow \theta = 19.1°, 70.9°$
smallest positive value of θ is 70.9° if **a** is to be satisfied

3 a 18.67 m b 12.77 m c 53.05°

4 a A = 75°, B = 35°, O = 70°
b 1.68 km
c 2.75 km, 114°

5 $\sin 4\theta = 2\sin 2\theta \cos 2\theta$

$$\frac{\sin 4\theta}{\sin \theta} = 4\cos\theta(2\cos^2\theta - 1)$$
$$= 8\cos^3\theta - 4\cos\theta$$

6 a 53.1°, 120°, 233.1°, 240°; $a = 4$, $b = -3$
b $\tan\alpha = \frac{84}{13}$, $\cos\alpha = \frac{13}{85}$, $BC = 28$ cm

4 Functions

Review (p. 139)

1 a $x = \dfrac{1-2y}{5}$ d $x = (y-7)^3$
b $x = \sqrt{\dfrac{y+2}{3}}$ e $x = \dfrac{10}{3-y}$
c $x = 1 + \dfrac{y^2}{16}$ f $x = \dfrac{1}{y-2}$

2 a $(x+4)^2 - 11$ d $(x - \frac{3}{2})^2 - \frac{29}{4}$
b $(x-2)^2 - 1$ e $2(x+3)^2 - 18$
c $(x + \frac{1}{2})^2 + \frac{3}{4}$ f $3(x-1)^2 + 4$

3 a $x = -8$ or 3 d $x = -2 \pm \sqrt{7}$
b $x = \pm\sqrt{5}$ e $x = -3 \pm \sqrt{10}$
c $x = 2$ or 5 f $x = \frac{3}{2} \pm \frac{\sqrt{7}}{2}$

4 a $1 + \dfrac{1}{x+1}$ d $2 + \dfrac{1}{x+3}$
b $1 - \dfrac{1}{x+2}$ e $2 + \dfrac{7}{2x-1}$
c $1 + \dfrac{8}{x-5}$ f $-3 + \dfrac{3}{1-x}$

4.1 Technique (p. 145)

1 a i

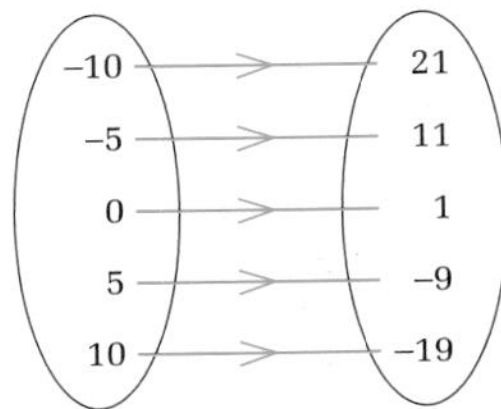

ii range is $\{-19, -9, 1, 11, 21\}$
iii one-to-one function.

b i

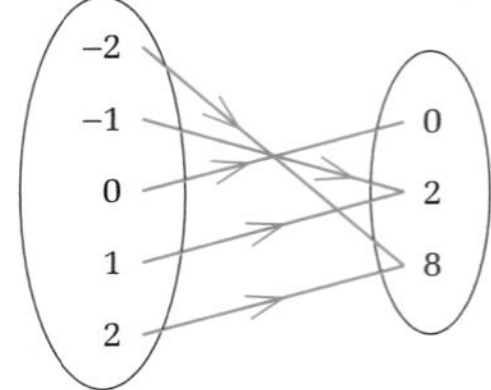

ii range is $\{0, 2, 8\}$
iii many-to-one function.

c i

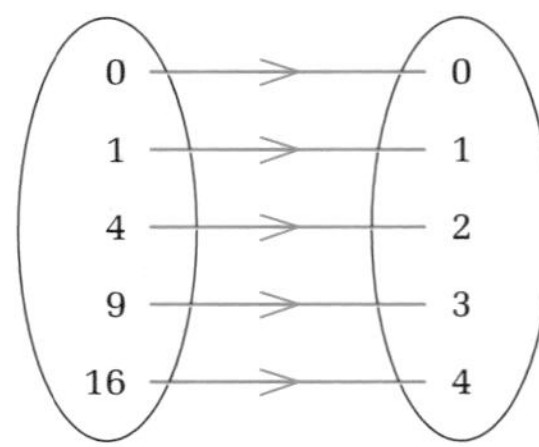

ii range is $\{0, 1, 2, 3, 4\}$
iii one-to-one function.

d i

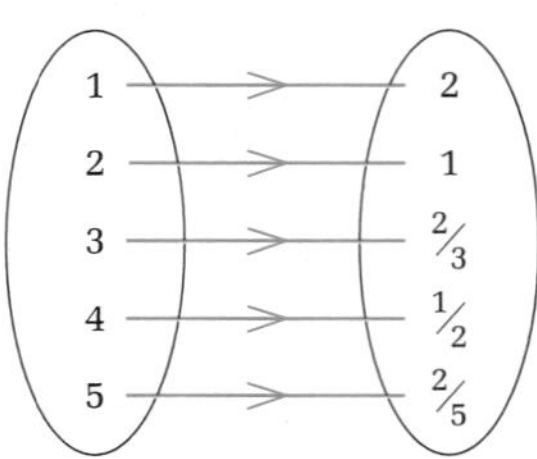

ii range is $\{\frac{2}{5}, \frac{1}{2}, \frac{2}{3}, 1, 2\}$
iii one-to-one function.

2 **a i**

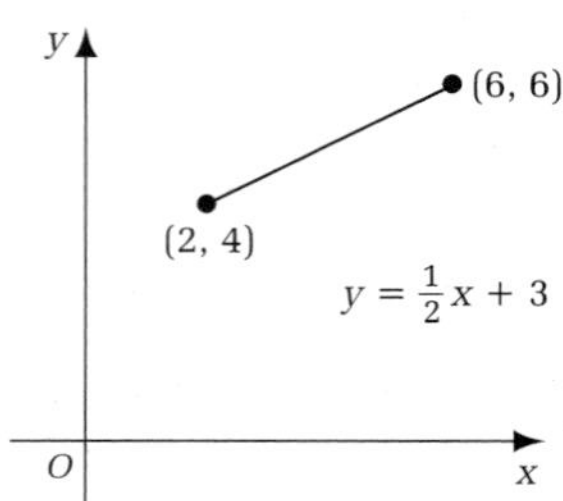

ii range is $\{y \in \mathbb{R}: 4 \leq y \leq 6\}$
iii one-to-one function.

b i

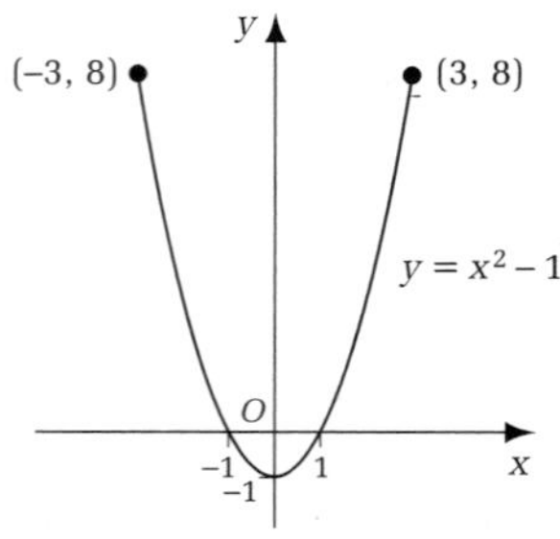

ii range is $\{y \in \mathbb{R}: -1 \leq y \leq 8\}$
iii many-to-one function.

c i

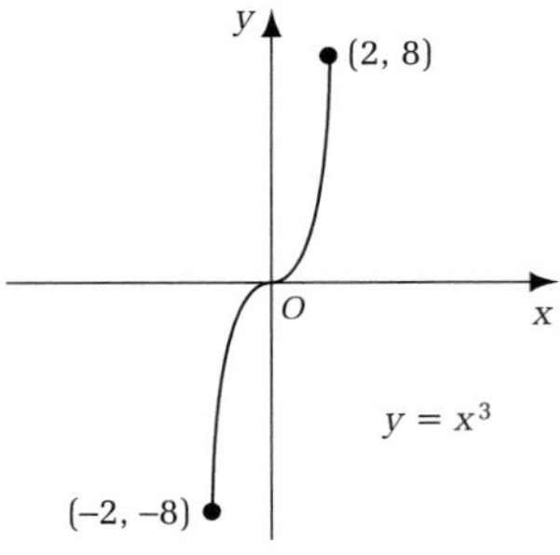

ii range is $\{y \in \mathbb{R}: -8 \leq y \leq 8\}$
iii one-to-one function.

d i

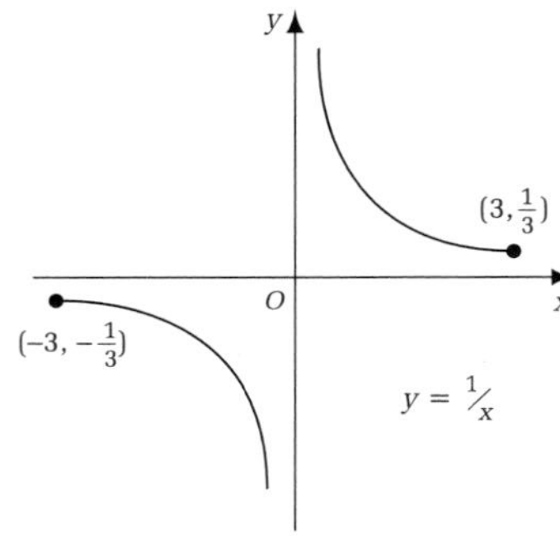

ii range is $\{y \in \mathbb{R}: y \leq -\frac{1}{3}$ and $y \geq \frac{1}{3}\}$
iii one-to-one function.

3 **a** Not a function; the relationship is many-to-many.
b A function; the relationship is many-to-one.
c A function; the relationship is one-to-one.
d Not a function; the relationship is many-to-many.

4 g is a function because it is a one-to-one mapping throughout the domain.
f is not a function because $5 - x = 3$ and $\frac{1}{2}x^3 = 4$ when $x = 2$. Therefore f is not uniquely defined for all values of x in its domain.

5 **a** $a = 3$ **b** $b = -2$ or $b = 2$
c $c = \frac{1}{4}$ or $c = 3$

6 $a = -2, b = 7, c = \frac{7}{2}$

7 $a = 2, b = 5, c = -3, d = -3$ or $\frac{1}{2}$

4.2 Technique (p. 157)

1 **i** Inverse functions exist for **a**, **c** and **d** because these functions are all one-to-one. No inverse function exists for **b**, because it is a many-to-one function.
ii a

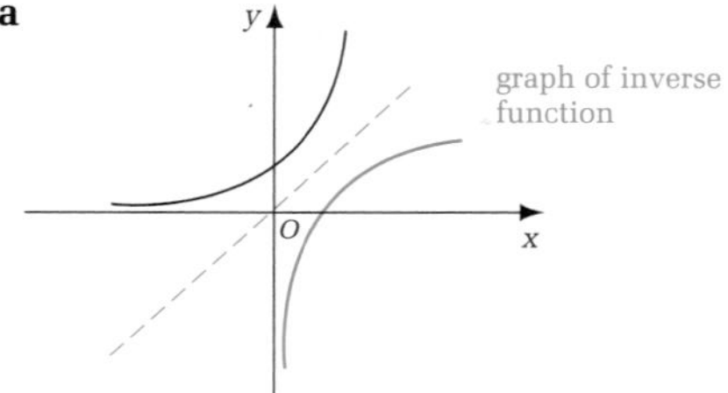

c

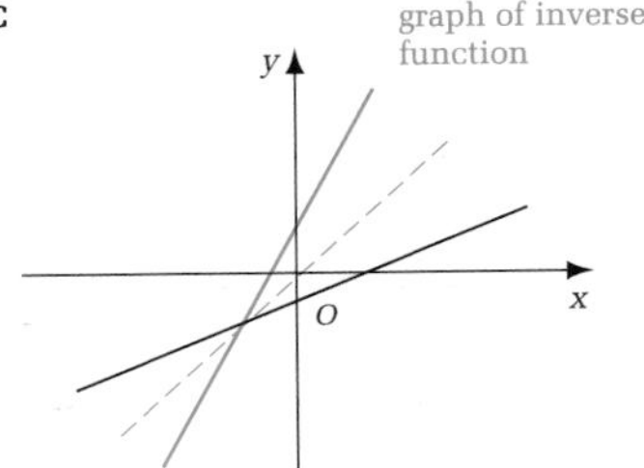

d

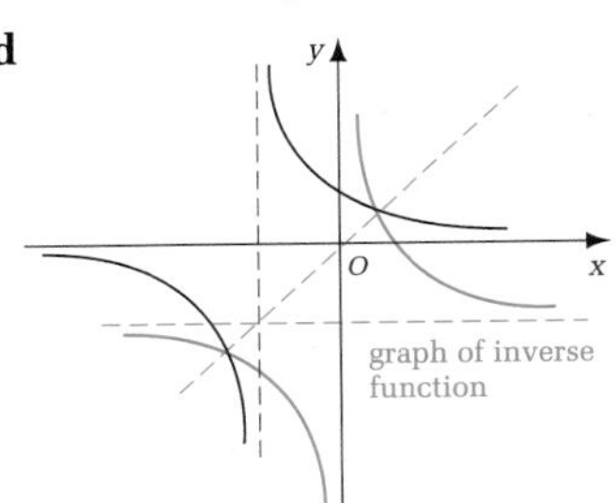

2 **a** $f^{-1}: x \to \frac{x+8}{3}$ **d** $f^{-1}: x \to \sqrt{4x^2 - 5}$

b $f^{-1}: x \to \frac{4}{x} - 3$ **e** $f^{-1}: x \to \frac{2}{x-3}$

c $f^{-1}: x \to \sqrt{\frac{x-7}{2}}$ **f** $f^{-1}: x \to \frac{2}{\sqrt{x}}$

3 **a** $f(x)$ is undefined for $x = 4$
$g(x)$ is undefined for $x = -1$
$h(x)$ is undefined for $x = 5$

b $f^{-1}(x) = \frac{3}{x} + 4$; domain is $\{x \in \mathbb{R}: x \neq 0\}$

$g^{-1}(x) = \frac{x}{2-x}$; domain is $\{x \in \mathbb{R}: x \neq 2\}$

$h^{-1}(x) = \frac{5x+3}{x-2}$; domain is $\{x \in \mathbb{R}: x \neq 2\}$

4 **a** $f^{-1}(x) = \frac{3x+2}{x-a}$, $g^{-1}(x) = -\frac{bx+1}{2x-5}$

b $a = 3, b = -5$

5 **a** $(x-1)^2 - 5$, $a = -1$, $b = -5$
b $q = 1$
c range of f is $f(x) \geq -5$
d $f^{-1}(x) = 1 + \sqrt{x+5}$
e $x = 4$

6 **a** $f^{-1}(x) = \frac{1}{3}\cos^{-1} x$; domain is $\frac{1}{2} \leq x \leq 1$
b $f^{-1}(\frac{\sqrt{3}}{2}) = \frac{\pi}{18}$

7 **a** $-\frac{\pi}{4} \leq x \leq \frac{\pi}{4}$
b i $f^{-1}(x) = \frac{1}{2}\sin^{-1} x$
ii domain $-1 \leq x \leq 1$
iii

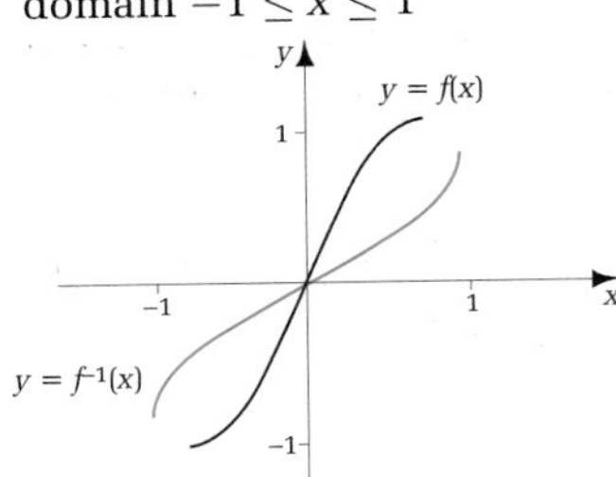

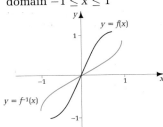

c $-\frac{\pi}{2a} \leq x \leq \frac{\pi}{2a}$

4.3 Technique (p. 165)

1 **a** $fg(x) = \frac{9}{x^2}$ **f** $hg(x) = 2 - \frac{3}{x}$

b $gf(x) = \frac{3}{x^2}$ **g** $g^2(x) = x$

c $fh(x) = (2-x)^2$ **h** $h^2(x) = x$

d $hf(x) = 2 - x^2$ **i** $ghf(x) = \frac{3}{2-x^2}$

e $gh(x) = \frac{3}{2-x}$ **j** $hgf(x) = 2 - \frac{3}{x^2}$

2 **a** $gf(x)$ **b** $hg(x)$ **c** $gh(x)$
d $fgh(x)$ **e** $g^2(x)$ **f** $hfg(x)$

3 **a** $fgh(x) = \frac{10}{x} - 3$ **b** $x = -5$ or $x = 2$

4 **a** $f^2(x) = 9x + 20$, $g^2(x) = \frac{x-20}{9}$

c Since $fg(x) = x$ and $gf(x) = x$, then g and f are the inverse of one another.

5 **a** range of f is $f(x) \leq 4$
range of g is $g(x) \geq 0$
b $fg(x) = 4 - x$; domain of fg is $x \geq 0$
c $gf(x) = \sqrt{4 - x^2}$; domain of gf is $-2 \leq x \leq 2$

6 **a** $fg(x) = \frac{1}{(x-1)^2}$, undefined for $x = 1$

b $gf(x) = \frac{8}{x^2 - 4}$, undefined for $x = -2$ and $x = 2$

c $f^2(x) = \frac{x^4}{64}$, defined for all values of x.

d $g^2(x) = \frac{2(x-1)}{3-x}$, undefined for $x = 3$ and $x = 1$

7 **a** $f^{-1}(x) = \sqrt[3]{x}$, $g^{-1}(x) = \frac{1-x}{3}$, $h^{-1}(x) = \frac{2}{x}$

b $fg(x) = (1-3x)^3$,
$(fg)^{-1} = g^{-1}f^{-1} = \frac{1 - \sqrt[3]{x}}{3}$

c $hg(x) = \frac{2}{1-3x}$, $(hg)^{-1} = g^{-1}h^{-1} = \frac{x-2}{3x}$

d $fh(x) = \frac{8}{x^3}$, $(fh)^{-1} = h^{-1}f^{-1} = \frac{2}{\sqrt[3]{x}}$

4.4 Technique (p. 175)

1 **a i** translation of +2 units parallel to y-axis
ii $y = x^2 - 2x + 2$
iii

y
y = f (x) + 2
2
(1, 1)
O
x

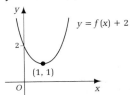

b i translation of +3 units parallel to x-axis
ii $y = x^2 - 8x + 15$

iii

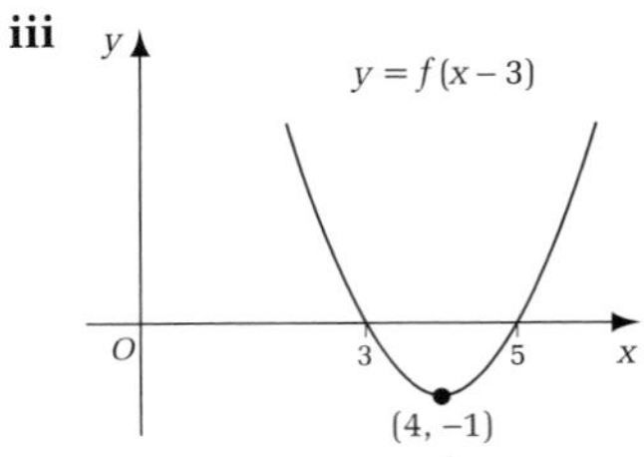

c i stretch factor $\frac{1}{2}$ parallel to the x-axis

ii $y = 4x^2 - 4x$

iii

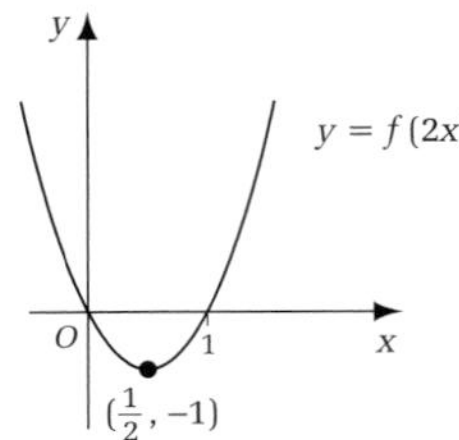

d i reflection in the x-axis, and stretch factor 3 parallel to the y-axis

ii $y = 6x - 3x^2$

iii

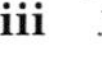

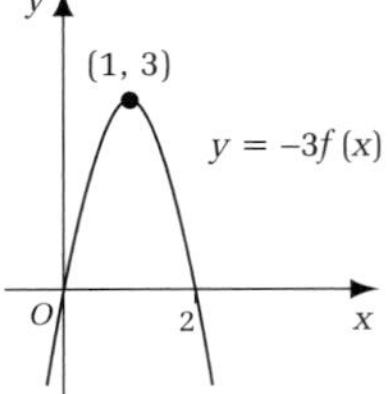

e i reflection in the y-axis, and stretch factor 3 parallel to the x-axis

ii $y = \dfrac{x^2}{9} + \dfrac{2x}{3}$

iii

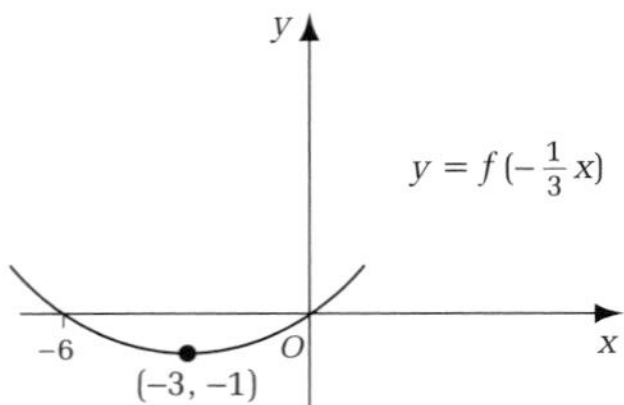

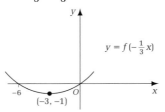

f i translation by +4 units parallel to the y-axis and translation by –1 units parallel to the x-axis

ii $y = x^2 + 3$

iii

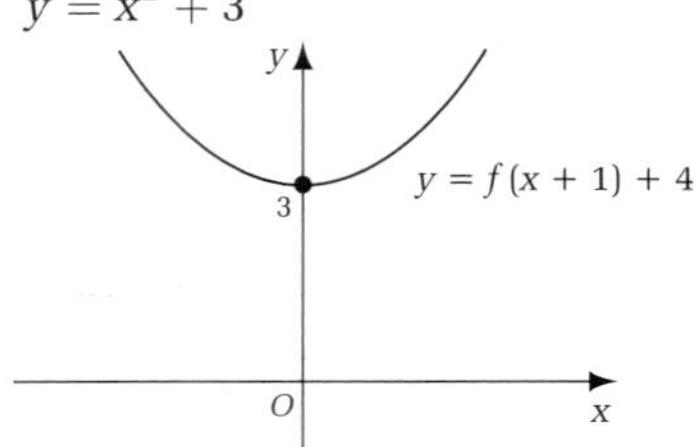

2 **a** $f(x) = (x + 3)^2 - 1$

b translations of –3 units parallel to the x-axis and –1 parallel to the y-axis

3 **a** $g(x) = 2(x - 3)^2 + 1$

b translation of +3 units parallel to the x-axis and a stretch of factor 2 parallel to the y-axis, followed by a translation of +1 units parallel to the y-axis

4 **a** translation of +3 units parallel to the y-axis

b stretch factor 4 parallel to the y-axis or stretch factor $\frac{1}{2}$ parallel to the x-axis

c translation of +2 units parallel to the x-axis

d translations of –1 units parallel to the x-axis and +4 units parallel to the y-axis

e stretch factor $\frac{1}{2}$ parallel to the y-axis followed by translation of +1 units parallel to the y-axis

f translations of +3 units parallel to the x-axis and +1 unit parallel to the y-axis

g translations of –2 units parallel to the x-axis and –4 units parallel to the y-axis

h translation of +1 unit parallel to the x-axis and stretch factor 2 parallel to the y-axis, followed by translation of +1 unit parallel to the y-axis

5 **a i** translations of –3 units parallel to the x-axis and +2 units parallel to the y-axis

ii $y = x^3 + 6x^2 + 9x + 2$

b i reflection in the x-axis and stretch factor 2 parallel to the y-axis

ii $y = 6x^2 - 2x^3$

c i reflection in the y-axis followed by translation of +1 unit parallel to the x-axis; or translation of –1 unit parallel to the x-axis followed by reflection in the y-axis

ii $y = -x^3 + 3x - 2$

d i stretch factor $\frac{1}{2}$ parallel to the x-axis

ii $y = 8x^3 - 12x^2$

6 **a i** translation by –90° parallel to the x-axis

ii

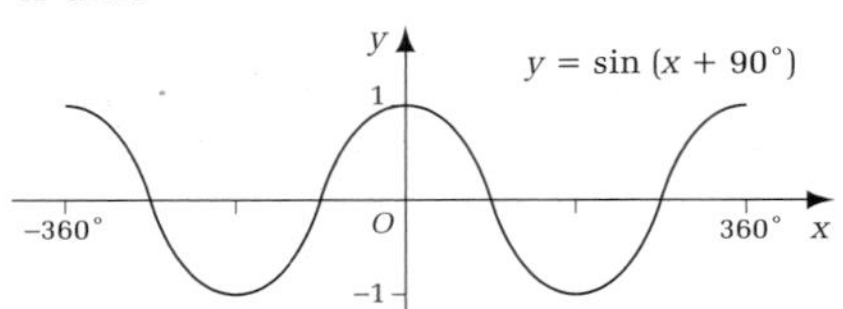

b i stretch factor 2 parallel to the x-axis

ii

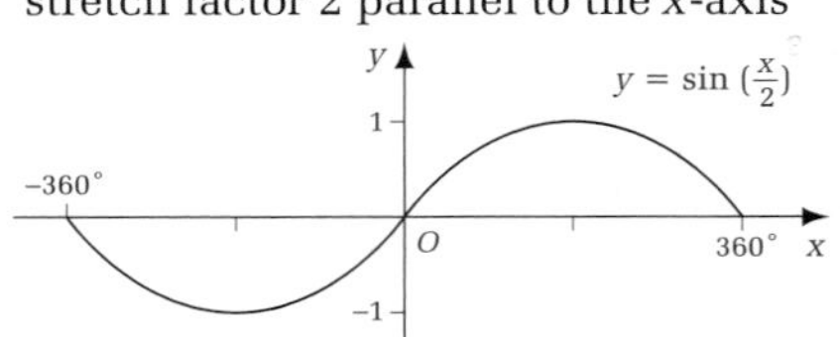

c i reflection in the x-axis and stretch factor 2 parallel to the y-axis

ii

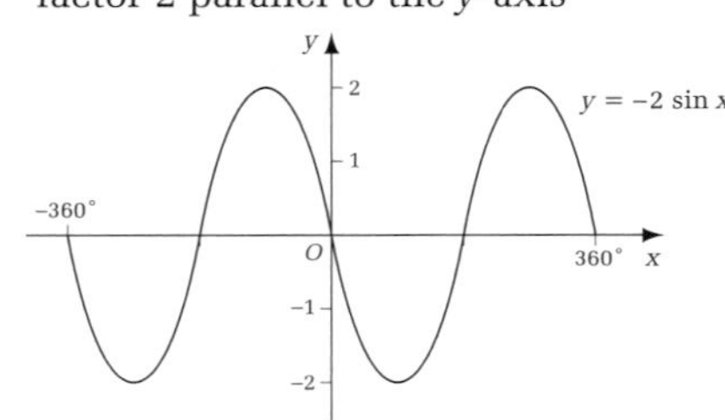

d i translation by +3 units parallel to the y-axis

ii

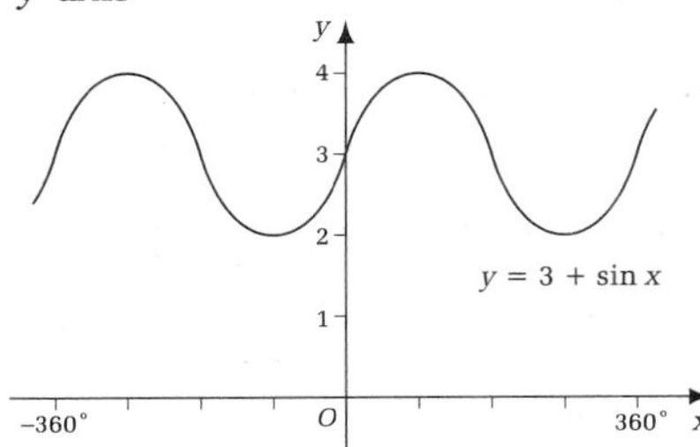

7 **a i** $g: x \to \frac{3}{x}$

ii undefined for $x = 0$

b i $g: x \to \frac{1}{x-2}$

ii undefined for $x = 2$

c i $g: x \to \frac{1}{2x} - 4$

ii undefined for $x = 0$

d i $g: x \to \frac{12}{x+5}$

ii undefined for $x = -5$

4.5 Technique (p. 183)

1 **a** neither **b** odd **c** neither
d even **e** even **f** neither

2 **a** odd **d** neither **g** neither
b neither **e** neither **h** even
c even **f** neither

3 **a**

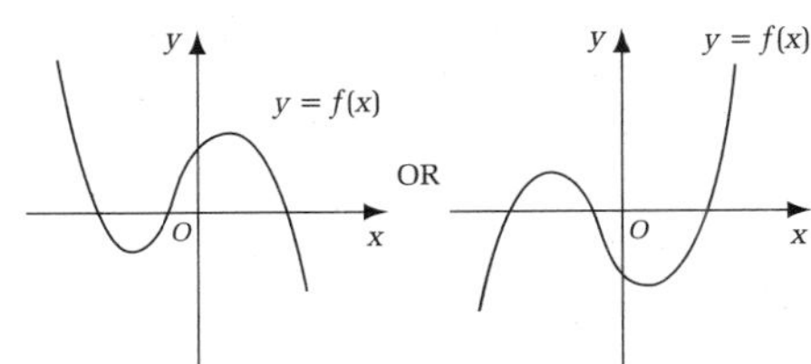

b Since $f(x)$ is a cubic function, distinguish between the two possible graphs by considering the x^3 coefficient
If this coefficient is negative, $f(x)$ is represented by the left graph
If the x^3 coefficient is positive, $f(x)$ is represented by the right graph

4 **a**

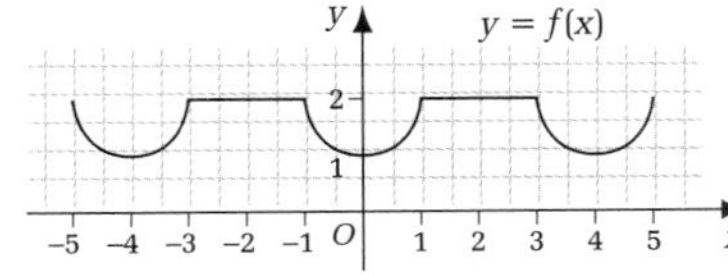

b $f(4.5) = 1.25; f(10) = 2$

Consolidation A (p. 184)

1 **a i** no **ii** yes **iii** yes

b

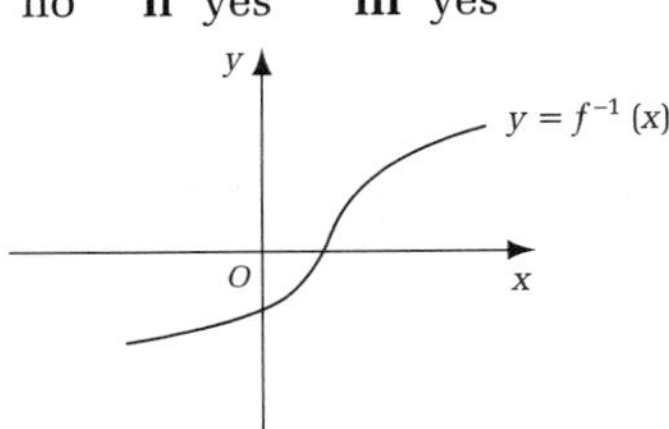

2 **a** $gf(x) = 4 - 9x^2$

b

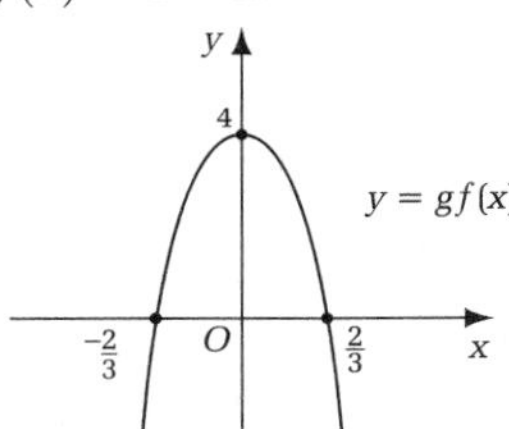

c $gf(x) \leq 4$ **d** $x = \frac{2}{5}$

3 **a** $f(x) \geq -4$

b $f^{-1}(x) = \sqrt{\dfrac{x+4}{9}}$; domain is $x \geq -4$

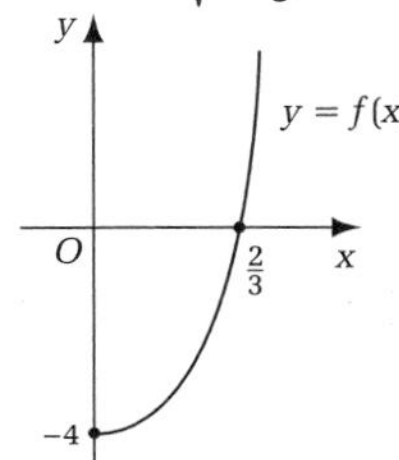

c i $f \circ g(x) = 9x + 5$

ii $x = \frac{1}{2}(1 + \sqrt{5})$

4

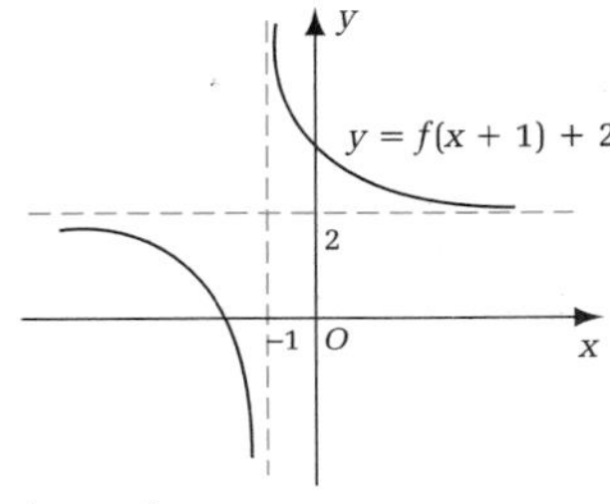

$(-1, 2)$

5 $f^{-1}(x) = \frac{1}{2}\tan^{-1} x$;
domain of f^{-1} is $0 \leq x \leq 1$.

6 **a** $g(x) \geq 0$ **b** $x = 0$ or $x = 8$
c $x = 2$ or $x = 6$

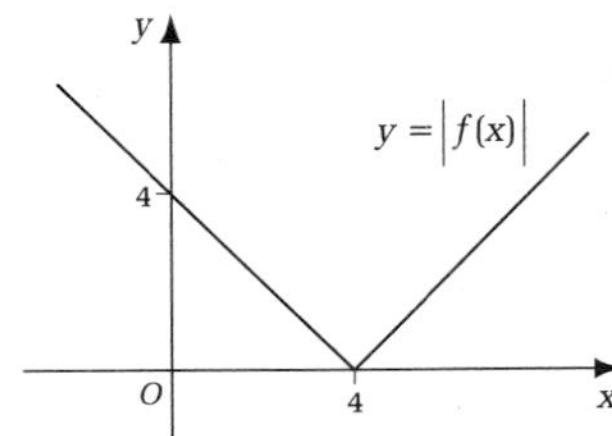

7 **a** $g(x) \geq 1$ **b** $x = 0$ and $x = 1$
c $x = 3$ or $x = -\frac{7}{3}$ **d** $q = -\frac{3}{2}$

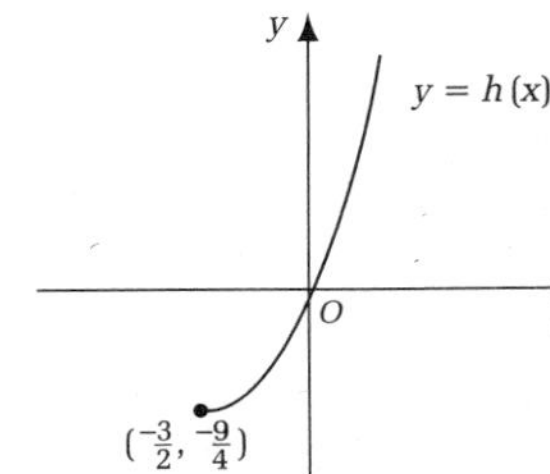

8 **a** max $(0, 3a)$, min $(2a, 0)$

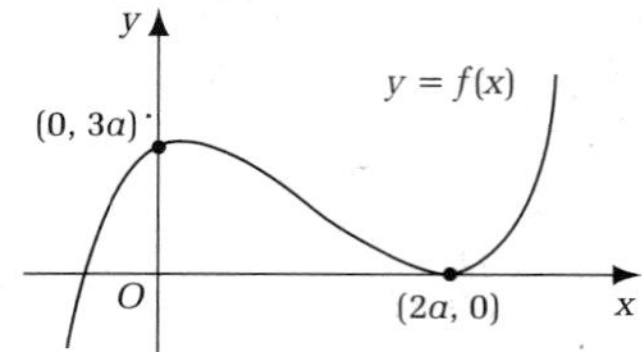

b max $(a, 0)$, min $(-a, -6a)$

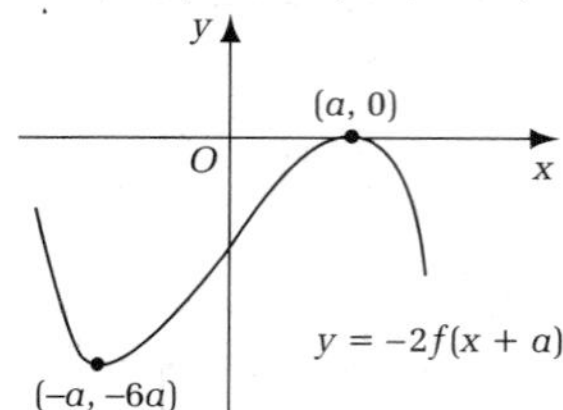

9 **a i** $f^{-1}(x) = \dfrac{2}{x-1}$

ii $x > 1$

b i $g(x) = \dfrac{3x+2}{x+2}$

ii $1 < g(x) < 3$

10 **a** $a = 5, b = 1$
c $(0, 0)$ and $(3, -9)$
d

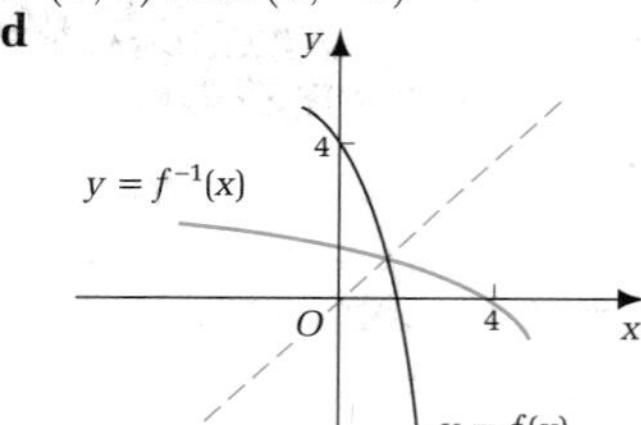

e $x = 1$

Consolidation B (p. 186)

1 **a** translation of $+50$ units parallel to the y-axis
b translation of -50 units parallel to the x-axis
c reflection in the x-axis
d reflection in the line $y = x$
e stretch of factor 30 parallel to the y-axis

2 **a** $fg(x) = 1 + \tan^2 x$
domain of fg is $-\frac{\pi}{2} < x < \frac{\pi}{2}$
b $g^{-1}(\sqrt{3}) = \frac{\pi}{3}$
c function f does not have an inverse because it is not a one-to-one function in the domain for which it is defined

3 **a** $gh(x) = \frac{2}{\sqrt{x}}$
b $fgh(x) = \frac{4}{x}$
functions f and h are the inverse of each other

4 **a** $f(x) = x$ for $x = -1$ and $x = \frac{3}{2}$
b range of g is $g(x) \geq 1$
c $f \circ g(x) = \dfrac{3}{2x^2+1}$
range of $f \circ g$ is $0 < f \circ g \leq 3$.

5 **a**

y
(5, 9)
y = g(x)
(3, 5)
(2, 4)
y = f(x)
O
x

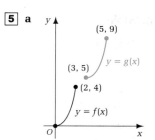

b domain of g is $3 \leq x \leq 5$
range of g is $5 \leq g(x) \leq 9$
c $g(x) = (x-3)^2 + 5$
d $g^{-1}(x) = 3 + \sqrt{x-5}$
e domain of g^{-1} is $5 \leq x \leq 9$
range of g^{-1} is $3 \leq g^{-1}(x) \leq 5$

6 $a = 2, b = -4$
b domain of f^{-1} is $x \geq -4$
c $f^{-1}(x) = -2 + \sqrt{x+4}$
d

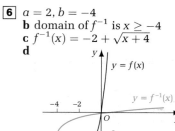

y
y = f(x)
y = f⁻¹(x)
−4 −2
O
x
−2
−4

7 **a**

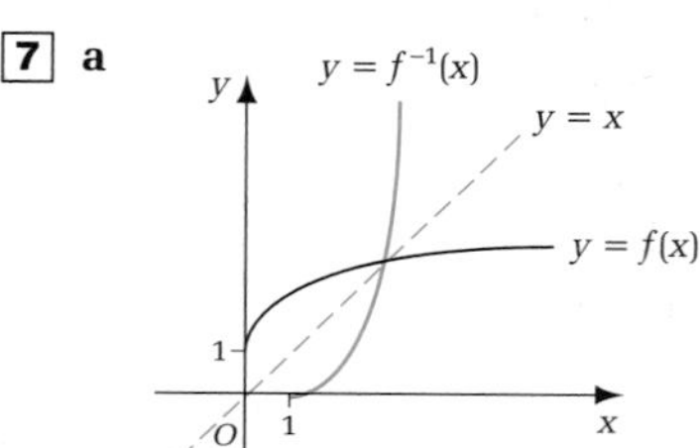

b $f^{-1}(x) = (x-1)^2$
domain of f^{-1} is $x \geq 1$
c The graphs of $y = f(x)$ and $y = f^{-1}(x)$ intersect at the point where $y = f(x)$ intersects with $y = x$. This value of x is therefore found by solving $1 + \sqrt{x} = x$

5 Differentiation I

Review (p. 190)

1 **a** 2 **b** -2
c -6 **d** 3

2 **a** 2 **b** $\frac{11}{2}$ **c** 0

3 **a** $y = 6x - 2$ **b** $y = -3x - 2$
c $y = -\frac{1}{4}x + \frac{3}{4}$ **d** $y = \frac{2}{3}x + \frac{5}{3}$

4 **a** $\frac{\pi}{6}, \frac{2\pi}{3}, \frac{7\pi}{6}, \frac{5\pi}{3}$ **b** $\frac{3\pi}{4}, \frac{7\pi}{4}$
c $\frac{\pi}{6}, \frac{\pi}{2}, \frac{5\pi}{6}, \frac{3\pi}{2}$ **d** $\frac{\pi}{3}, \pi, \frac{5\pi}{3}$

5 **a** $2x^{-3}$ **b** $x^{3/2}$ **c** $(x+5)^{-1}$
d $10x^{-1/2}$ **e** $x^{4/3}$

5.1 Technique (p. 203)

1 **a** $\frac{dy}{dx} = 3x^2$ **b** $\frac{dy}{dx} = 6x - 9$
c $\frac{dy}{dx} = -\frac{1}{x^2}$

2 **a** $\frac{dy}{dx} = 8x^7$ **e** $\frac{dy}{dx} = \frac{12}{x^4}$
b $\frac{dy}{dx} = 1 - 6x - x^2$ **f** $\frac{dy}{dx} = -\frac{4}{x^3} - 1$
c $\frac{dy}{dx} = 12x - 7$ **g** $\frac{dy}{dx} = -\frac{3}{\sqrt{x^3}}$
d $\frac{dy}{dx} = \frac{1}{4x^{3/4}}$ **h** $\frac{dy}{dx} = \frac{9x-2}{2\sqrt{x}}$

3 **a** $f'(x) = \frac{1}{2}x - \frac{1}{2}$
b $f'(t) = 1 - 2t$
c $f'(s) = 3s^2 - 14s - 2$
d $h'(p) = 2 + \frac{10}{p^3}$
e $\theta'(t) = \frac{2}{\sqrt[3]{t^2}}$

4 **a** 10 **b** −1 **c** 0 **d** 19

5 **a** $(1, 2)$ and $(3, -6)$ **b** $(-2, 5)$ and $(2, 1)$
c $(-2, -4)$ **d** $(-\frac{3}{2}, -\frac{2}{3})$ and $(\frac{3}{2}, \frac{2}{3})$

6 **a** $\frac{dy}{dx} = -4$ at $(-3, 0)$ **b** $\frac{dy}{dx} = -5$ at $(-\frac{3}{2}, 0)$
$\frac{dy}{dx} = 4$ at $(1, 0)$ $\frac{dy}{dx} = 5$ at $(1, 0)$
$\frac{dy}{dx} = 2$ at $(0, -3)$ $\frac{dy}{dx} = 1$ at $(0, -3)$

7 **a** $\frac{dy}{dx} = 20x^3 + 6x^2 - 14x - 9$
$\frac{d^2y}{dx^2} = 60x^2 + 12x - 14$
$\frac{d^3y}{dx^3} = 120x + 12$
b $f'(x) = -\frac{4}{x^2} + \frac{2}{x^3}$
$f''(x) = \frac{8}{x^3} - \frac{6}{x^4}$
$f'''(x) = -\frac{24}{x^4} + \frac{24}{x^5}$

5.2 Technique (p. 214)

1 **a i** $(-2, 0)$, $(4, 0)$ and $(0, -8)$
ii $(1, -9)$; minimum point
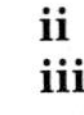
iii
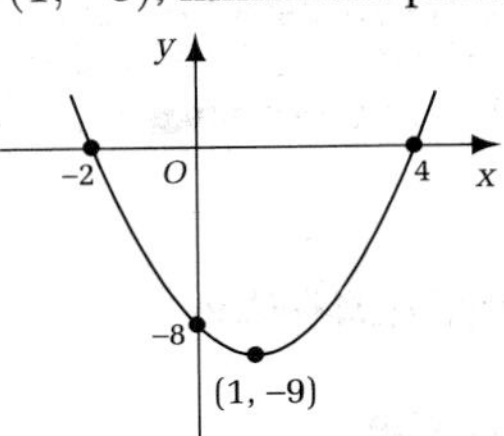

b i $(-5, 0)$, $(7, 0)$ and $(0, 35)$
ii $(1, 36)$; maximum point

iii
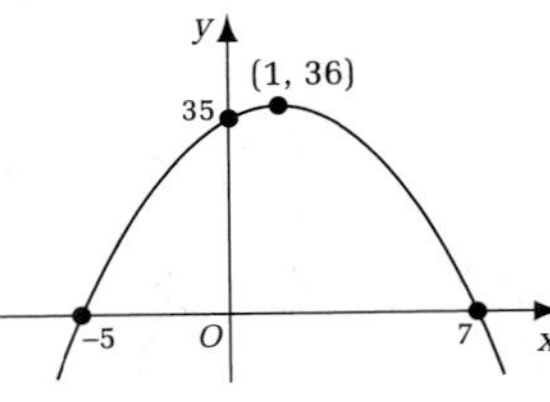

c i $(-\frac{1}{2}, 0)$, $(\frac{9}{2}, 0)$ and $(0, -9)$
ii $(2, -25)$; minimum point

iii
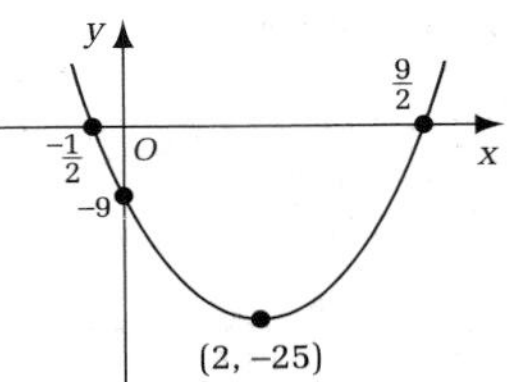

d i $(0, 28)$; graph does not cross x-axis
ii $(-4, 12)$; minimum point
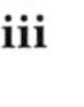
iii
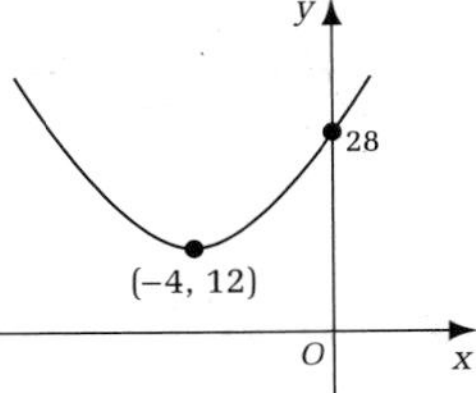

2 **a** point of inflexion at $(-2, -1)$
b maximum point at $(1, 3)$
minimum point at $(3, -5)$
c no stationary points
d maximum point at $(0, 1)$
minimum point at $(\frac{2}{3}, \frac{5}{9})$

3 **a** $(0, 0)$ and $(12, 0)$
b $4x^3 - 36x^2$; $(0, 0)$ is a point of inflexion
$(9, -2187)$ is a minimum point

c
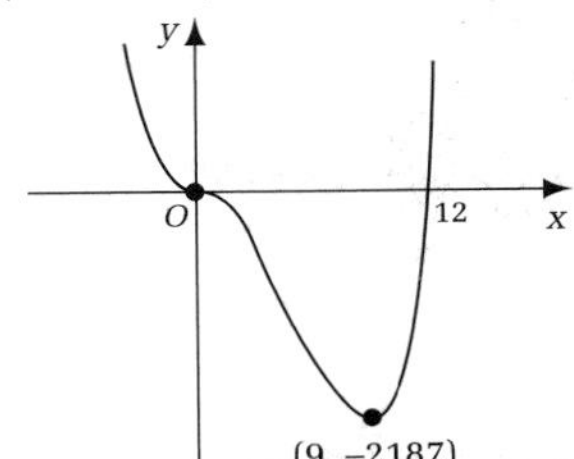

4 **a** $1 - \frac{4}{x^2}$; $(-2, -4)$ is a maximum point
$(2, 4)$ is a minimum point
b $-\frac{50}{x^2} - \frac{2x}{5}$; $(-5, -15)$ is a maximum point
c $-\frac{16}{x^3} - \frac{1}{4}$; $(4, \frac{3}{2})$ is a minimum point
d $-\frac{3}{x^2} + \frac{18}{x^3}$; $(6, \frac{1}{4})$ is a maximum point

5 $s = -\frac{7}{3}$ when $t = \frac{4}{3}$

6 $v = 56\frac{1}{4}$ when $r = 5\frac{1}{2}$

7 $x > 4$

8 $t < -3$ and $t > 1$

5.2 Contextual (p. 215)

1 **a** $V = 4x^3 - 380x^2 + 8400x$
b $\frac{dV}{dx} = 12x^2 - 760x + 8400$; $x = 14.3$ cm or 49.1 cm
c 54 111 cm^3, when $x = 14.3$ cm

2 **a** $A = 3xy$, $L = 6x + 4y$
b $L = 6x + \frac{384}{x}$
c $x = 8$ m, $y = 12$ m
d 96 metres

3 **a** 4011.3
b 4183.9 at 3.19 pm
c Risen 102.0 points
d Between 9 am and 10.41 am; and between 3.19 pm and 4.30 pm

4 **b** $S = 4x^2 + \frac{2100\,000}{x}$
c width = 64 cm; length = 128 cm; height = 85 cm

5 **a** $a = 3000$, $b = -20$
c $s = 76$ pence; maximum profit = £945.20 with 1480 tickets sold.

5.3 Technique (p. 224)

1 **a** tangent $7x - y - 35 = 0$, normal $x + 7y - 55 = 0$
b tangent $5x + y + 7 = 0$, normal $x - 5y - 61 = 0$
c tangent $6x + y - 1 = 0$, normal $x - 6y - 105 = 0$
d tangent $x - 4y + 12 = 0$, normal $8x + 2y - 23 = 0$
e tangent $x - 6y + 9 = 0$, normal $6x + y - 57 = 0$
f tangent $5x - 4y - 1 = 0$, normal $32x + 40y + 51 = 0$

2 $y = -2x + 2$ at $(1, 0)$
$y = 2x - 6$ at $(3, 0)$

3 $(4, -10)$; $y = 3x - 22$

4 $y = -\frac{3}{5}x + \frac{14}{5}$ or $3x + 5y - 14 = 0$; $(-1.25, 3.55)$

5.3 Contextual (p. 224)

1 **a** 8 seconds **b** 4 seconds; 80 metres

2 **a** $v = 3t^2 - 6t + 4\ \text{m s}^{-1}$
$a = 6t - 6\ \text{m s}^{-2}$
c $4\ \text{m s}^{-1}$

3 **a** $32\pi\ \text{cm}^3$ **b** $7.2\pi\ \text{cm}^2$

4 1.5%

5.4 Technique (p. 234)

1 **a** $4(x + 2)^3$
b $-5(3 - x)^4$
c $12(4x - 5)^2$
d $12x(x^2 + 1)^5$
e $5(6x^2 - 1)(2x^3 - x + 1)^4$
f $-\dfrac{5}{(5x + 9)^2}$
g $\dfrac{1}{\sqrt{2x + 3}}$
h $10x^3(x^4 + 2)^{3/2}$
i $\dfrac{12}{(7 - 6x)^3}$
j $\dfrac{x}{(25 - x^2)^{3/2}}$

2 **a** $14(2t + 5)^6$
b $-18(9r - 4)^{-3}$
c $\dfrac{t}{\sqrt{t^2 - 2}}$
d $\dfrac{2}{(6\theta + 2)^{2/3}}$
e $\dfrac{3}{2(1 - t)^{3/2}}$
f $-\dfrac{12(3x^2 + 2)}{(x^3 + 2x)^2}$
g $1 - \dfrac{1}{s^2}$
h $\dfrac{3(1 + \sqrt{u})^2}{2\sqrt{u}}$

3 **a** 80 **b** 8 **c** -60
d $-\frac{3}{5}$ **e** $\frac{8}{5}$

4 **a** $(-7, 1)$ **b** $(3, -8)$, $(5, 8)$ **c** $(16, 3)$

5 $\frac{dp}{ds} = 2s + 3$; $\frac{ds}{dt} = 5$; $\frac{dp}{dt} = 50t + 25$

6 $\frac{dV}{dx} = 24(1 + x)(3x^2 + 6x + 1)^3$

5.4 Contextual (p. 235)

1 $2\pi\ \text{m h}^{-1}$; $40\pi\ \text{m}^2\ \text{h}^{-1}$

2 **a** $0.4\ \text{cm s}^{-1}$ **b** 33.5 litres

3 $(-2, -\frac{5}{2})$, maximum point, $(-1, -\frac{1}{2})$, minimum point

4 **a** $V = 8\pi r^3$, $\frac{dV}{dr} = 24\pi r^2$
b $0.08\ \text{cm s}^{-1}$
c $S = 18\pi r^2$; $45.2\ \text{cm}^2\ \text{s}^{-1}$

5 **a** $V = \dfrac{4\pi h^3}{75}$
b $\dfrac{dV}{dh} = \dfrac{4\pi h^2}{25}$; $0.27\ \text{cm s}^{-1}$
c 151 seconds

5.5 Technique (p. 247)

1 **a** $-\sin 2x$
b $4\cos 4x + 2\cos 2x$
c $-\frac{3}{4}\sin\frac{3x}{4}$
d $10\cos 2x$
e $\sin(5 - x)$
f $3\sin^2 x\cos x$
g $-6\cos 3x\sin 3x$ or $-3\sin 6x$
h $2x\cos(x^2 + 5)$
i $-4\cos\frac{x}{2}\sin\frac{x}{2}$ or $-2\sin x$
j $ap\cos(px) - bq\sin(qx)$

2 **a** -3 **b** 1 **c** $+3$ **d** $\pi + 1$

3 **a** $(0, 0)$ and $(2\pi, 0)$
b $(\frac{3\pi}{4}, \frac{1}{2})$
c $(\frac{\pi}{3}, 1 - \sqrt{3})$ and $(\frac{5\pi}{3}, 1 + \sqrt{3})$
d $(\frac{\pi}{8}, \frac{1}{\sqrt{2}})$ and $(\frac{7\pi}{8}, -\frac{1}{\sqrt{2}})$

4 **a** $f'(x) = \frac{3}{2}\cos\frac{3}{2}x$
maximum point at $(\frac{\pi}{3}, 1)$
minimum point at $(\pi, -1)$
maximum point at $(\frac{5\pi}{3}, 1)$
b $f'(x) = \frac{1}{2} + \sin x$
maximum point at $(\frac{7\pi}{6}, \frac{7\pi}{12} + \frac{\sqrt{3}}{2})$
minimum point at $(\frac{11\pi}{6}, \frac{11\pi}{12} - \frac{\sqrt{3}}{2})$

c $f'(x) = 2 + 2\cos 2x$
points of inflexion at $(\frac{\pi}{2}, \pi - 5)$ and $(\frac{3\pi}{2}, 3\pi - 5)$

5 **a i** $(\frac{\pi}{4}, 0)$, $(\frac{5\pi}{4}, 0)$ and $(0, 1)$
ii minimum point at $(\frac{3\pi}{4}, -\sqrt{2})$
maximum point at $(\frac{7\pi}{4}, \sqrt{2})$
iii

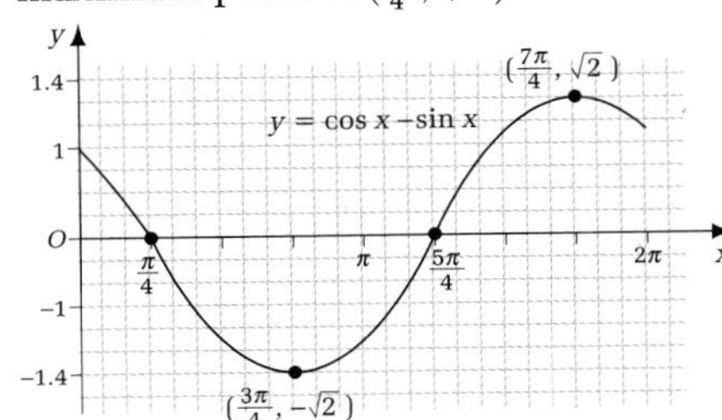

b i $(\frac{2\pi}{3}, 0)$, $(\frac{5\pi}{3}, 0)$ and $(0, \sqrt{3})$
ii maximum point at $(\frac{\pi}{6}, 2)$
minimum point at $(\frac{7\pi}{6}, -2)$
iii

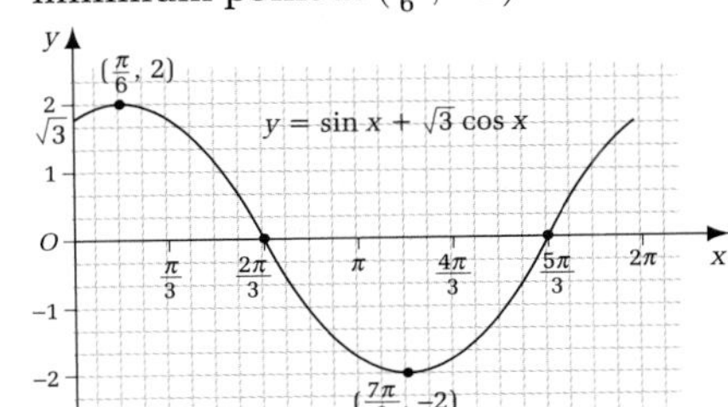

c i $(0.322, 0)$, $(3.463, 0)$ and $(0, -1)$
ii maximum point at $(1.893, 3.162)$
minimum point at $(5.034, -3.162)$
iii

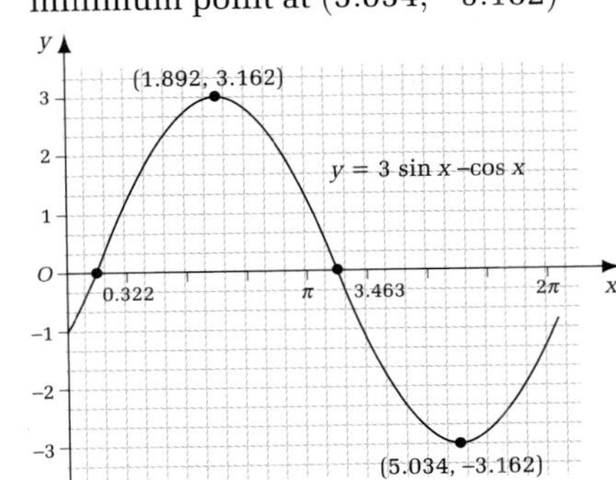

6 **a** tangent: $y = -3x + 2$
normal: $y = \frac{x}{3} + 2$
b tangent: $y = 3x - 3\pi - 2$
normal: $y = -\frac{x}{3} + \frac{\pi}{3} - 2$

5.5 Contextual (p. 248)

1 **a** 14 hours 21 minutes on 1 June ($t = 152$)
13 hours 3 minutes on 26 August ($t = 238$)

b $\frac{dh}{dt} = -\frac{\pi}{73}\sin\left[\frac{2\pi(t-172)}{365}\right]$

c Summer solstice on 21 June ($t = 172$)
Winter solstice on 21 December ($t = 355$)

d increasing at 1 minute 35 seconds per day on 28 January
decreasing at 1 minute 55 seconds per day on 2 November

2 **a** $\frac{dx}{dt} = -8\pi\sin(\pi t) - 5\pi\cos(\pi t)$; $15.7\ \text{cm s}^{-1}$ upwards
b 0.82 seconds, 1.82 seconds
c $29.6\ \text{cm s}^{-1}$ upwards when $t = 0.32$ s

Consolidation A (p. 250)

1 **a** 39, 164
b $6x^2 - 6x - 36$
c $(-2, 164), (3, 39)$
d $(-2, 164)$ is a maximum point; $(3, 39)$ is a minimum point
e $39 < h < 164$

2 $2.55\ \text{cm s}^{-1}$

3 **a** $-12x(3 - x^2)^5$ **b** $x + 24y - 26 = 0$

4 **a** $\frac{3}{10}(4 - 3t - t^2)\ \text{km min}^{-1}$
b 11.56 am, 12.01 pm
c 6.25 km
d $1.25\ \text{km min}^{-1}$ or $75\ \text{km h}^{-1}$
e $1.875\ \text{km min}^{-1}$ or $112.5\ \text{km h}^{-1}$

5 **a** $-4\sqrt{3}$
b $y = -4\sqrt{3}x + \frac{4\pi\sqrt{3}}{3} + 1$

6 **a** $3 + \frac{4}{x^2}$ **b** $4p$

7 **b** $\frac{10}{3}$
d $\frac{2300}{27}\pi\ \text{cm}^3$ or $267.62\ \text{cm}^3$ (2 d.p.)
e 22.2%

8 **a** $3x^2 - 12x$
b $y = -12x + 16$
c $x - 9y - 174 = 0$

9 **a** $\frac{60}{v}$ hours **c** $40\ \text{km h}^{-1}$

10 **a** $c = 250n + 5000$
b $a = 13\,500$, $b = -20$
d $s = £462.50$, 4250 machines, £898 125 profit.

Consolidation B (p. 251)

1 $y = 20x + 11$

2 $\frac{168}{25\pi}$ feet min^{-1} or 2.1 feet min^{-1} (1 d.p.)

3 **b** $36\ \text{m}^3$

4 $(-1, -11)$

5 $T = 3$ s
a $1\frac{1}{3}$ m **b** $2\ \text{m s}^2$

6 a $V = \pi x^2 h$
b $A = 2\pi x h + \pi x^2$
$A = \frac{144}{x}$
d $x = 1.97$ cm, $h = 5.91$ cm (2 d.p.)

7 a i $\frac{dV}{dx} = 0.45(3x+2)^2$
ii $0.02\,\text{m}\,\text{s}^{-1}$
b i $\frac{-3p}{32}$
ii $\frac{2p}{3}$

6 Algebra II

Review (p. 255)

1 a $607\frac{2}{7}$ b $18428\frac{4}{5}$ c $2628\frac{5}{12}$ d $5018\frac{1}{13}$

2 a $\frac{9}{20}$ b $\frac{5}{9}$ c $\frac{22}{35}$ d $\frac{1}{36}$

3 a $1 + \dfrac{7}{x-4}$ b $1 + \dfrac{3}{x+1}$ c $2 - \dfrac{1}{x+2}$ d $-4 + \dfrac{4}{1-x}$

4 a [4] b [5] c [2] d [1] e [3]

6.1 Technique (p. 264)

1 a $x^2 + 2x + 3$ b $x^2 + 3x + 5$ c $x^2 - 3x - 3$ d $x^2 - 2x + 5$

2 a 3 b 3 c -4 d 11

3 a $(x-1)(x-2)(x+2)$
b $(x-1)(x-2)(x-3)$
c $(x+1)(x-1)(x-4)$
d $(x+1)(x-2)(x+6)$
e $(2x+1)(x+2)(x+4)$
f $(x+1)(x+2)(2x-1)$

4 a $1 < x < 4, x > 7$
b $x < -2, 5 < x < 7$
c $x \le -3, 2 \le x \le 7$
d $-5 \le x \le 0, x \ge 6$
e $x < -4, 0 < x < 3$
f $-3 < x < -\frac{1}{2}, x > 7$

6.1 Contextual (p. 264)

1 a $(x-2)(x-2)(x-2)(x+4) = (x-2)^3(x+4)$
b $x > 2, x < -4$

2 $a = 2, b = -5, (x+3)$

3 $(-2, 0), (-1, 0), (6, 0)$

4 $a = 4, b = 2$

5 $x = -\frac{1}{2}, -\frac{1}{3}, 2$ $[y = (x-2)(3x+1)(2x+1)]$

6 $x \le -\frac{1}{4}, 2 \le x \le 3$

6.2 Technique (p. 269)

1 a $\dfrac{8x+1}{(x-1)(x+2)}$ b $\dfrac{2(5x-2)}{(x-2)(x+2)}$ c $\dfrac{18}{(x-2)(x+1)}$ d $\dfrac{x+5}{(x-1)(x+1)}$ e $\dfrac{2(2x-5)}{(x-1)(x+1)}$ f $\dfrac{5x+6}{(x+1)(x+2)}$

2 a $\dfrac{10x-7}{(3-2x)(2x+1)}$ b $\dfrac{13x+1}{(x-1)(4x+3)}$ c $\dfrac{10}{(2-x)(2x+1)}$ d $\dfrac{23x-1}{(x-2)(7x+1)}$ e $\dfrac{5x-4}{(3x-2)(x-1)}$ f $\dfrac{12x-7}{(2x-1)(3x-2)}$

3 a $\dfrac{4x^2-6x-11}{(x-3)(x-2)(x+4)}$
b $\dfrac{5x^2+8x-6}{(x+1)(x+2)(1-2x)}$
c $\dfrac{x+4}{(x+1)^2}$
d $\dfrac{2x+3}{9-x^2}$
e $\dfrac{2x^2-7x-1}{(1-3x)(x-1)(x+2)}$
f $\dfrac{2(x+5)}{3(x+2)^2}$

4 a $\frac{3}{4}$ b $\dfrac{2(x-1)}{9x}$ c $\dfrac{1}{2(x+7)}$ d $\dfrac{x}{7(x+3)}$ e $\dfrac{1}{7(x-3)}$ f $\dfrac{x+2}{2x}$

5 a $\frac{1}{20}$ b $\dfrac{x}{12(x+1)}$ c $\dfrac{1}{5(x+1)}$ d $\dfrac{x}{4(x+2)}$ e $\dfrac{1}{3(x-1)}$ f $\dfrac{x(x-1)}{2}$

6.3 Technique (p. 280)

1 a $\dfrac{1}{(x-5)} - \dfrac{1}{(x+1)}$
b $\dfrac{3}{2(x+3)} + \dfrac{1}{2(x-1)}$
c $\dfrac{7}{(x-4)} - \dfrac{2}{(x+3)}$
d $\dfrac{2}{(x+3)} + \dfrac{4}{(x-1)}$

e $\dfrac{5}{(x-1)}+\dfrac{2}{(x-2)}$

f $\dfrac{2}{(x-3)}+\dfrac{3}{(x-4)}$

2 a $\dfrac{3}{x-2}-\dfrac{2}{x^2+1}$

b $\dfrac{5}{x}-\dfrac{2}{x^2+3}$

c $\dfrac{2}{x-3}+\dfrac{4}{x^2+2}$

d $\dfrac{2}{x+1}+\dfrac{2x+1}{x^2+x+4}$

e $\dfrac{5}{x-2}-\dfrac{2x-1}{x^2+3x+1}$

f $\dfrac{3}{x+1}+\dfrac{2}{x^2+x+4}$

3 a $\dfrac{1}{(x+4)}-\dfrac{2}{(x+4)^2}$

b $\dfrac{1}{(x-2)}+\dfrac{3}{(x-2)^2}$

c $\dfrac{2}{(x+5)}-\dfrac{5}{(x+5)^2}$

d $\dfrac{4}{(x+3)}-\dfrac{6}{(x+3)^2}$

e $\dfrac{4}{(x-1)^2}+\dfrac{3}{(x-1)^3}$

f $\dfrac{-5}{(x+2)}+\dfrac{5}{(x-1)}+\dfrac{3}{(x-1)^2}$

4 a $2x+3+\dfrac{1}{x+2}+\dfrac{3}{x-4}$

b $5x-5+\dfrac{24}{x+3}+\dfrac{11}{x-2}$

c $3+\dfrac{5}{x-1}-\dfrac{2x+8}{x^2+2}$

d $10+\dfrac{29}{x-3}+\dfrac{x-7}{x^2+1}$

e $1-\dfrac{1}{(x+1)^2}$

f $2x+\dfrac{3}{x+1}-\dfrac{8}{(x+1)^2}$

5 a $\dfrac{2}{(x-3)}+\dfrac{3}{(x-4)}-\dfrac{2}{(x+1)}$

b $\dfrac{1}{(x-3)}+\dfrac{4}{(x-2)}+\dfrac{3}{(x-1)}$

c $\dfrac{3}{(x+1)}+\dfrac{2}{(x+5)}-\dfrac{1}{(x-5)}$

d $\dfrac{1}{x+1}+\dfrac{2x+3}{x^2+3}$

e $\dfrac{4}{x-1}-\dfrac{3}{x+1}+\dfrac{3}{(x+1)^2}$

f $\dfrac{2}{x-2}+\dfrac{2x+3}{x^2+x+2}$

6.4 Technique (p. 289)

1

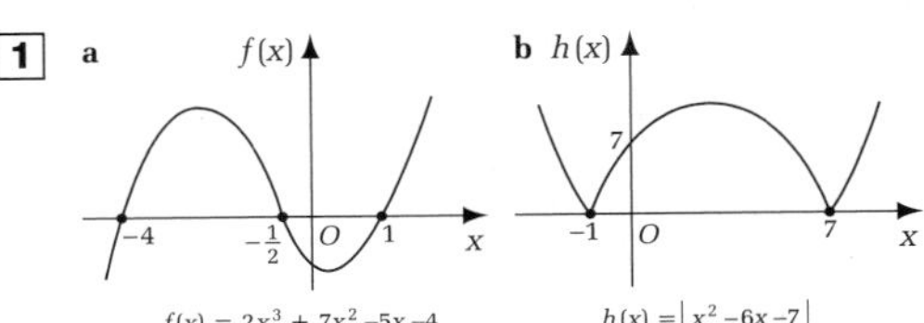

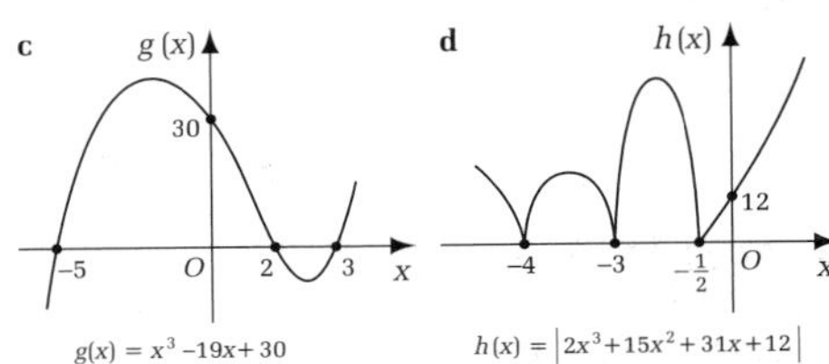

2

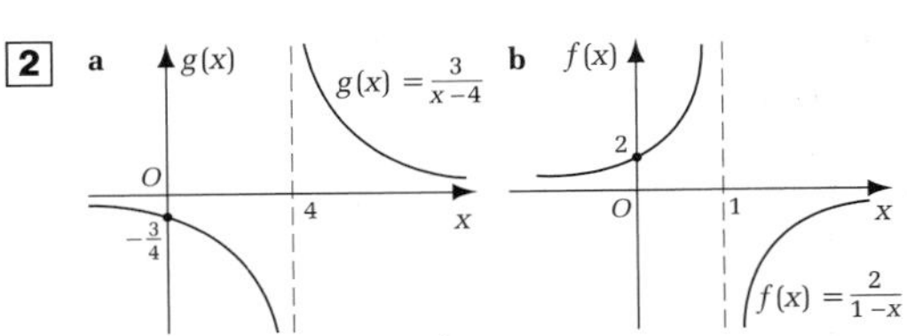

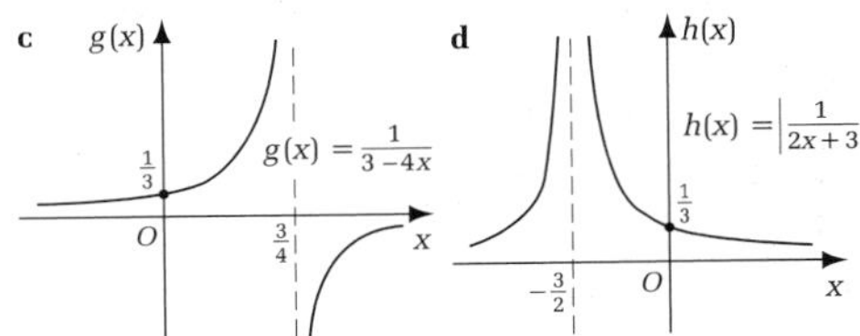

3

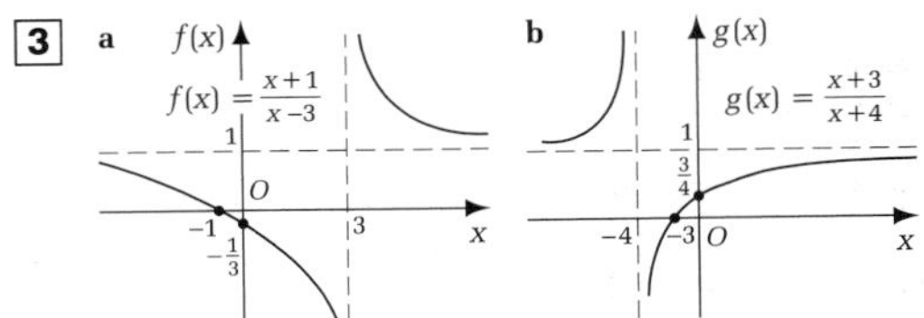

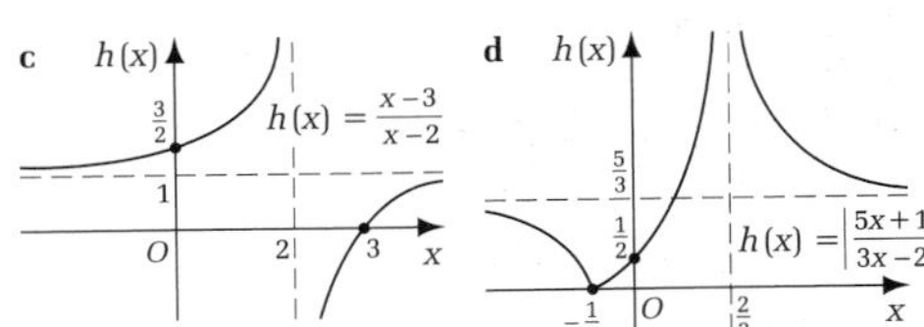

4

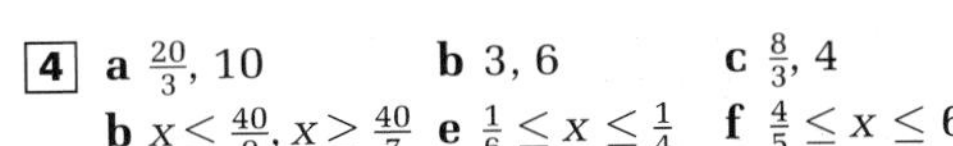

a $\frac{20}{3}$, 10 b 3, 6 c $\frac{8}{3}$, 4

b $x\le\frac{40}{9}$, $x\ge\frac{40}{7}$ e $\frac{1}{6}\le x\le\frac{1}{4}$ f $\frac{4}{5}\le x\le 6$

6.4 Contextual (p. 289)

1 $f(x)=(3x-1)(x-3)(x+1)$

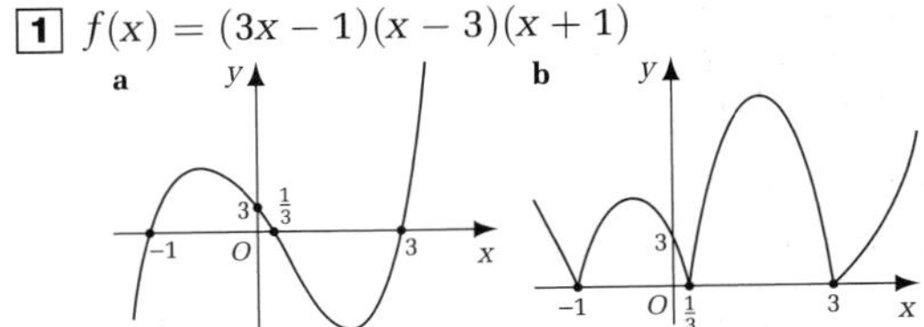

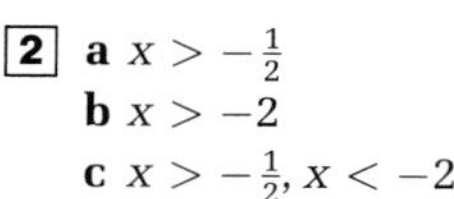

2 **a** $x > -\frac{1}{2}$
b $x > -2$
c $x > -\frac{1}{2}, x < -2$

3

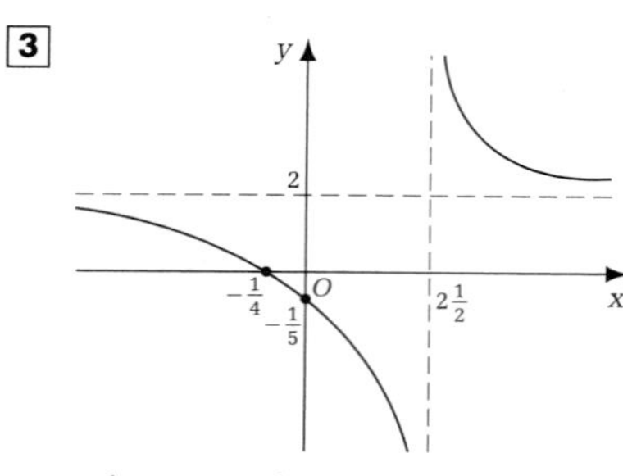

$-\frac{1}{4} < x < 2\frac{1}{2}$

4

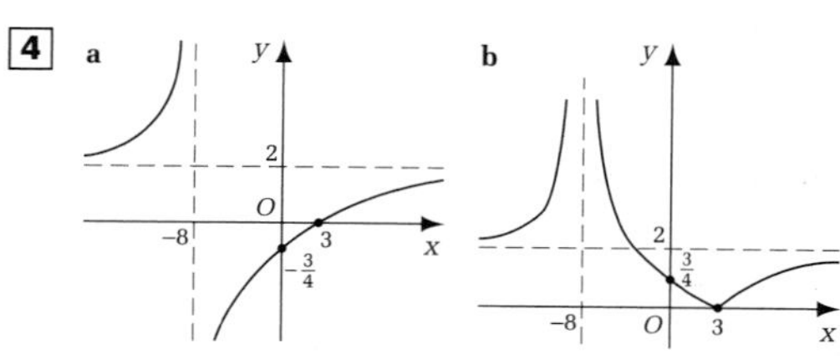

Consolidation A (p. 290)

1 $(x-2)$ is linear factor
$(x-2)(x^2+2x+3)$

2 **a** A = 2; B = −3; C = −11; D = 6
b $a = -14$
c $\dfrac{x-3}{g(x)} = \dfrac{2}{5(2x-1)} - \dfrac{1}{5(x+2)}$
d $x < -2,\ -1 < x < 3$

3 **a** $a = 3$
b $(x-5)(x+5)(3x-1)$

4 **a** $c = 9, d = -14$
b roots are $-2, \frac{1}{2}(-7+\sqrt{77})$,
$\frac{1}{2}(-7-\sqrt{77})$

5 A = 1; B = −3; C = 3; D = −1

6 $y = \dfrac{1}{x} - \dfrac{2}{2x-1} + \dfrac{4}{(2x-1)^2}$

7 $f(3) = 0$
$f(x) = (x-3)(x^2+x+2)$
One real root; quadratic does not factorise the discriminant is negative, $b^2 < 4ac$.
One point of intersection.

8 **a** $(x+3)(2x-1)(x-5)$
b $x = -3, \frac{1}{2}$ or 5
c

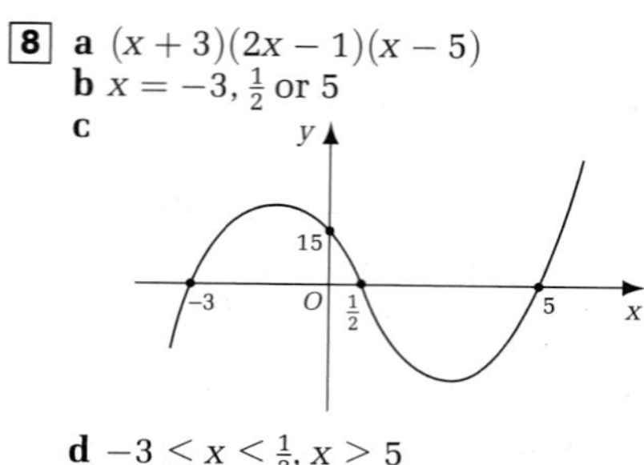

d $-3 \le x \le \frac{1}{2}, x \ge 5$

9 $x < -3, x > 5$

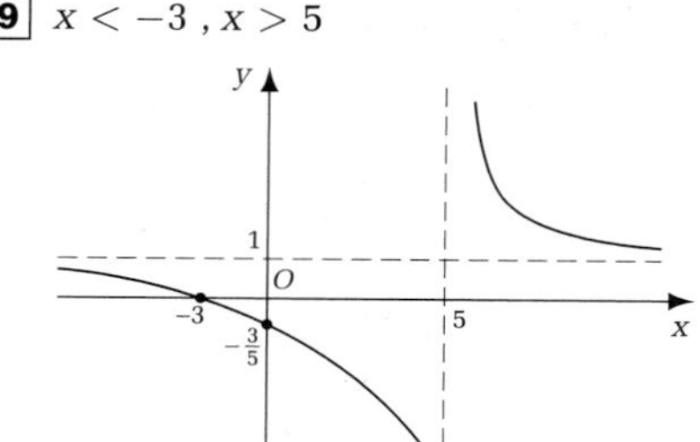

10

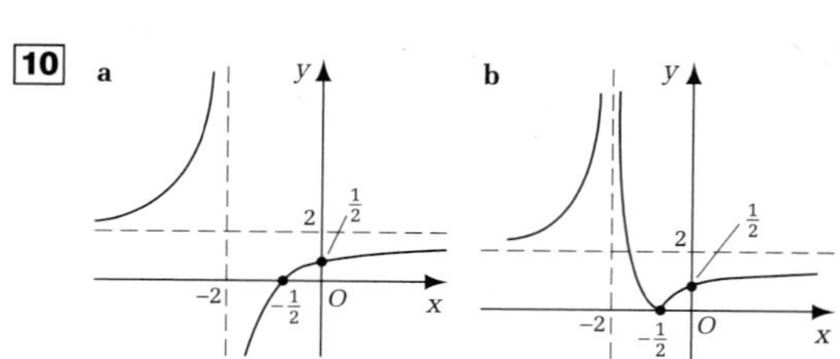

Consolidation B (p. 291)

1 **a** $a = 2$
b $(x+6)(x-2)^2$

2 $p = \frac{1}{2}, q = -\frac{1}{2}$

3 **a** $3x^3 - 2x^2 - 3x + 2$
b $\dfrac{1}{(x-1)} - \dfrac{3}{(3x-2)}$
c $x \ge 2,\ -1 \le x \le 1$

4 **a** $p = -12; q = 6$
b $(5x-2)(x-3)(x+1)$
c $x < -1, \frac{2}{5} < x < 3$

5 **a** $\dfrac{2}{(x-2)} - \dfrac{1}{(2x+1)}$
b when $x = -3, \frac{dy}{dx} = 0$
$x = \frac{1}{3}$

7 Exponentials and Logarithms

Review (p. 294)

1 **a** 9.3×10^7 **b** 6.25×10^{-3}
c 1×10^7 **d** 3×10^{-2}

2 **a** a^{12} **b** a^4 **c** m^{18}
d 1 **e** a^{m+n} **f** a^{m-n}

3 **a** 4 **b** 3 **c** $\frac{1}{64}$
d $\frac{1}{2}$ **e** 16 **f** $\frac{1}{5}$

4 **a** 2.15 **b** 0.246
c 0.579 **d** −0.171

7.1 Technique (p. 298)

1 a 7.39 b 0.368 c 0.318 d 1.65

2 a translation by the vector $\binom{-1}{0}$ (one unit parallel to the x-axis in the negative x direction)
b translation by the vector $\binom{0}{1}$
c translation by the vector $\binom{2}{0}$
d translation by the vector $\binom{0}{-2}$

3 a 2.8 (3) b 1.2 (3) c 0.7 (1) d 0.09

4 a 1.79 b 2.09 c −0.693 d 1.14

7.1 Contextual (p. 298)

1 initial mass is 7.0 g, exceeds 500 g after 7 days.

2 a $M_0 = 120$ g b $k = 0.0693$
c 15 g d 24 days

3 a 70°C
b $k = 0.334$
c approx $7\frac{1}{2}$ minutes

4 a 0.327% b 1.98% c 21.7%
cost of living will double in about 18 years at this rate

5 a

b i after 3 years (approx)
ii after 11 years (approx)

7.2 Technique (p. 302)

1 a 3 b −2 c 7 d −4

2 a 1.70 b 0.301 c −0.477 d −0.176

3 a 6 b 3 c −1 d −4

4 a 5 b 36 c 5 d 625

5 a 0.693 b 3.91 c 4.61 d 3.22

6 a 2 b $\frac{1}{2}$ c $-\frac{1}{3}$ d $-\frac{3}{2}$

7

Exponent form	Logarithmic form
$2^4 = 16$	$\log_2 16 = 4$
$2^{-1} = \frac{1}{2}$	$\log_2 \frac{1}{2} = -1$
$2^5 = 32$	$\log_2 32 = 5$
$2^6 = 64$	$\log_2 64 = 6$
$3^2 = 9$	$\log_3 9 = 2$
$3^{-2} = \frac{1}{9}$	$\log_3(\frac{1}{9}) = -2$
$4^{1/2} = 2$	$\log_4 2 = \frac{1}{2}$

7.2 Contextual (p. 303)

1 a Richter value of 8 is '10 000 times as intense' as a Richter value of 4

2 a $10\log_{10}(\frac{200}{100}) = 10\log_{10} 2 = 10 \times 0.301 \approx 3$
b 10 times
c 7 dB

3 a 8.6 b 316 times

7.3 Technique (p. 307)

1 a ln 14 d log 2
b log 24 e ln 12
c ln 9 f $\log(\frac{1}{3}) = -\log 3$

2 a 0.602 b 1.431 c 1.255
d 1.556 e 2.158 f 0.176

3 a $\log(xy^2z)$ b $\ln(\frac{x^3}{y^2})$ c $\log(\frac{a}{b^2c^3})$
d $\ln(x^{3/2})$ e $\log(x^3z^2)$ f $\ln(\frac{xz}{y^2})$

4 a $\ln x + \ln y + \ln z$
b $3\ln x + 2\ln y - \ln z$
c $\ln x + \frac{1}{2}\ln y - \ln z$
d $\frac{1}{3}\ln x + \frac{1}{3}\ln y$
e $\frac{1}{2}\ln x + \frac{1}{2}\ln y - \frac{1}{2}\ln z$
f $\ln x + \frac{1}{2}\ln y + \frac{3}{2}\ln z$

5 a $x = 81$ b $x = \frac{1}{2}$
c $x = 3.32$ d $x = \frac{2}{3}$

7.3 Contextual (p. 307)

1 $xy = 100$
$\log(xy) = \log(100)$
$\log x + \log y = \log 10^2$
$\log x + \log y = 2$

2

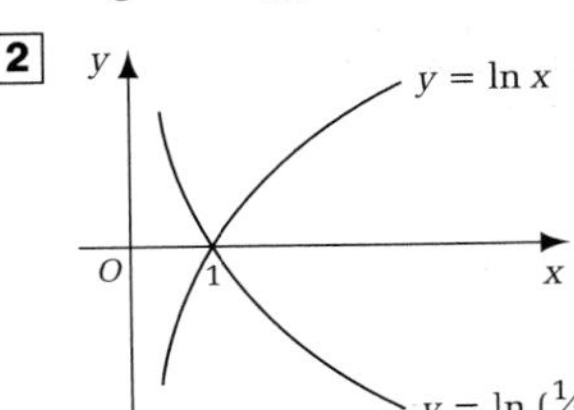

transformation is reflection in x-axis, inverse function is e^{-x}

3 b 2

4 $g(x) = \ln x$

7.4 Technique (p. 314)

1 a 11.966 (3 d.p.) b 3.86
c 2.09 d 2.04

2 a 1.93 b 5.45
c −0.279 d 2.03

3 a −1.35 b 1.71
c −9.48 d 33.867 (3 d.p.)

4 a $x = \ln 2$ or $\ln 3$ (0.693 or 1.10)
b $x = \ln(\frac{1}{2})$ or $\ln 4$ (-0.693 or 1.39)
c $x = \ln 2$ (0.693)
d $x = \frac{1}{2}\ln(\frac{5}{2})$ (0.458)

5 a $p = 10$ b $p = 7$ c $p = 88$ d $p = 10$

6 a $y = 3 \times 5^x$ b $y = 3x^5$
c $y = 2 \times 3^x$ d $y = 3e^{-2x}$

7 a $\log 2, \log 8$ b $\log 3, \log 7$
c $\log 4, \log 6$ d 1

7.4 Contextual (p. 315)

1 $a = 7.96$, $b = 1.52$ (3 s.f.)
population exceeds 500 000 after 10 years

2 second solution is not possible because the exponential function cannot be negative

3 $a = 5.46 \times 10^{-4}$, $b = 1.5$
model is very accurate; error of less than 1%

4 $k = \ln 10 = 2.30$ (3 s.f.)

Consolidation A (p. 316)

2 a $x < 18.1$ (3 s.f.) b $x < -3.08$ (3 s.f.)

3 a £8500 b $\lambda = 0.128$
c £5800 d $5\frac{1}{2}$ years

4 a $A_n = (1.07)^n \times 100$
b interest rate of 7%
c 11 years

5 c $10y^2 - 10\,001y + 1000 = 0$
d $-1, 3$

6 a 1.05×10^7
c 4.99×10^{-3}
d 11 million

7 $y = \log_b(\frac{1}{5}) = -\log_b 5$
when $b = 5$, $y = -1$

8 $A = 5.4 \times 10^{-4}$, $n = 1.5$
distance of Earth from the Sun is 150 million km (2 s.f.)

9 $x = \sqrt{\ln\left(\frac{1}{y^2}\right)}$

$f^{-1}(x) = \sqrt{\ln\left(\frac{1}{x^2}\right)}$

10 a 3 m and 16.9 cm b 60.2 cm

Consolidation B (p. 318)

1 log 150

2 a $x < 74.2$ (3 s.f.) b $x < -41.5$ (3 s.f.)

3 a £14 000 b 0.0289 (3 s.f.)

4 b 28 years

5 $x = \ln 2$ or $x = \ln 3$

6 a 7.97×10^{-3} (3 s.f.) b 2076

7 a $y = \frac{1}{2}$ b $x = \dfrac{4y^2 + 5}{3}$

8 Sequences and Series

Review (p. 321)

1 a $2a + 2d$ b $2a + (n-1)d$
c $a + 2ar$ d $1 + \frac{1}{2}x^2 + \frac{1}{2}x^3$

2 a $n^2 + 7n + 12$ b $r^2 + r - 2$
c $r^2 + r$ d $1 + 2x + x^2$

3 a 9 b 14 c 15
d 3 e 8 f 18.75

4 a $\frac{5}{r} - \frac{5}{r+1}$ b $\frac{6}{r+1} - \frac{6}{r+2}$
c $\frac{7}{n+1} - \frac{7}{n+2}$ d $\frac{12}{n} - \frac{12}{n+1}$

8.1 Technique (p. 327)

1 a 7, 10, 13, 16 d 20, 30, 42, 56
b 3, 7, 11, 15 e 1, 2, 4, 8
c 5, 11, 17, 23 f 2, 9, 28, 65

2 a $2n + 4$ e $-2n - 1$
b $3n + 11$ f $n^2 - 1$
c $5n - 4$ g $\frac{n+1}{n+2}$
d $-2n + 14$ h $\frac{n-1}{n^2}$

3 a 4, 7, 10, 13 d 3, 4, 5, 6
b 3, 7, 15, 31 e 5, 12, 29, 70
c 5, 14, 41, 122 f 3, $2\frac{1}{2}$, $2\frac{1}{4}$, $2\frac{1}{8}$

4 a $\sum_{r=1}^{4} r^2$ d $\sum_{r=1}^{6} (2r+1)$
b $\sum_{r=1}^{4} (r^2+2)$ e $\sum_{r=1}^{7} r(r-1)$
c $\sum_{r=1}^{6} (r+3)$ f $\sum_{r=1}^{7} r(r+1)$

5 a 36 b 32 c 216
d 69 e 104 f 92

6 a $\sum_{r=3}^{6} (3r-4)$ d $\sum_{r=4}^{7} (6r-15)$
b $\sum_{r=3}^{8} (3r-4)$ e $\sum_{r=2}^{6} (3r+1)$
c $\sum_{r=2}^{5} (2r+5)$ f $\sum_{r=3}^{9} 2r$

8.2 Technique (p. 333)

1 a i 21, 23 ii $2n + 11$
b i 32, 38 ii $6n + 2$
c i 22, 19 ii $-3n + 37$
d i $-14, -17$ ii $-3n + 1$

2 a 23 b 119 c 56
d 501 e 38 f -46

3 a 231 b 140 c 116 d 207

4 a 72 b 126 c 308
d 270 e 18 f −120

5 a 185 b 195 c 480 d 253

8.2 Contextual (p. 333)

1 $2n+1$

2 106

3 600

4 1016

5 a $a=10$ b 4

6 351

7 $x=-7$

8 a 19 weeks b 62 weeks; £3.15

9 5, 11, 17

10 16

8.3 Technique (p. 339)

1 a i 16, 32 ii $u_n = 2^{n-1}$
b i 162, 486 ii $u_n = 2 \times 3^{n-1}$
c i $20\frac{1}{4}$, $30\frac{3}{8}$ ii $u_n = 4 \times 1.5^{n-1}$
d i 8.1, 24.3 ii $u_n = 0.1 \times 3^{n-1}$

2 a 1250 b 156 250 c 0.75
d 0.094 e 243 f 6561

3 a 126 b 5470 c 15.75 d 4.62

4 a $S_8 = 510$ d $S_{10} = -29524$
b $S_9 = 9842$ e $S_8 = -197.03$
c $S_7 = 514.75$ f $S_6 = 390.6$

8.3 Contextual (p. 339)

1 0.468

2 $r = \pm 3$

3 $1534\frac{1}{2}$

4 $20+16+12.8$
a 20 b $\frac{4}{5}$ c 89.3

5 a 1343 b 238.7

8.4 Technique (p. 344)

1 a 400
b $73\frac{1}{7}$
c 1500
d does not exist; $r > 1$
e $1666\frac{2}{3}$
f $1111\frac{1}{9}$

2 a oscillates, [10, 2, 6, 2, 6, 2, 6, . . .]
b oscillates
c diverges; $r > 1$
d converges; $r < 1$
e converges; limit $\frac{5}{3}$
f converges; limit 10

3 a $364\frac{1}{2}$ b $182\frac{1}{4}$ c 18
d 500 e $14\frac{2}{7}$ f $10\frac{10}{19}$

4 a 30 b $\frac{5}{8}$ c 18
d $\frac{2}{3}$ e $\frac{1}{10}$ f 30

8.4 Contextual (p. 344)

1 60

2 16

3 $\frac{4}{5}$

4 20

5 $\frac{9}{10}$

6 $a = 135; r = -\frac{2}{3}$ or $a = 27; r = \frac{2}{3}$

7 a r is greater than 1 so no sum to infinity
b $\frac{3}{4}$

8.5 Technique (p. 353)

1 a $1+6x+15x^2+20x^3+15x^4+6x^5+x^6$
b $81-108x+54x^2-12x^3+x^4$
c $625-500x+150x^2-20x^3+x^4$
d $32+80x+80x^2+40x^3+10x^4+x^5$

2 a 6 b 35 c 10 d 190

3 a $1+7x+21x^2+35x^3+35x^4+21x^5+7x^6+x^7$
b $256-256x+96x^2-16x^3+x^4$
c $64-576x+2160x^2-4320x^3+4860x^4-2916x^5+729x^6$
d $x^4-12x^2+54-\frac{108}{x^2}+\frac{81}{x^4}$

4 a $1-20x+190x^2-1140x^3$
b $243-405x+270x^2-90x^3$
c $y^7+7y^6x+21y^5x^2+35y^4x^3$
d $32-240x+720x^2-1080x^3$

5 a $|x|<1$ b $|x|<\frac{3}{2}$ c $|x|<5$ d $|x|<\frac{4}{3}$

6 a $1-8x-36x^2-120x^3+\ldots$
b $1+\frac{2}{3}x-\frac{4}{9}x^2+\frac{40}{81}x^3+\ldots$
c $1-x-\frac{1}{2}x^2-\frac{1}{2}x^3+\ldots$
d $1+4x+11x^2+24x^3+\ldots$

8.5 Contextual (p. 353)

1 $4096+6144x+3840x^2+1280x^3+240x^4+24x^5+x^6$; valid for all x

2 $28160x^9$

3 −14 073 345

4 seventh term = 673 596

5 1.0721

6 $1-2x-2x^2-4x^3$; $|x|<\frac{1}{4}$

Consolidation A (p. 254)

1 $n=133$; $S_{133} = 26\,600$

2 $a=3$; $d=-\frac{1}{3}$; nine more

3 **b** $a = 60.75$ **c** 182.25 **d** 3.16

4 1504.5

5 **a** $u_1 = 76$; $u_2 = 60.8$
b $u_{21} = 0.876$
c 367
d 380

6 $1 + 2t - t^2 + \dots$

7 **a** A: 2, 1, 2, 1, 2; B: 2, $2\frac{1}{2}$, $2\frac{3}{4}$, $2\frac{7}{8}$, $2\frac{15}{16}$
b A oscillates; B converges

8 $1 + x - \frac{1}{2}x^2 + \frac{1}{2}x^3 - \dots$

9 $180x^{12}$

10 **a** $x^4 + 4x^3y + 6x^2y^2 + 4xy^3 + y^4$
b $x^4 + 8x^2 + 24 + \frac{32}{x^2} + \frac{16}{x^4}$
c 32

Consolidation B (p. 355)

1 820

2 **b** debt $= 30(360 - 18n - n^2)$

3 **a** **i** $\dfrac{2}{2r-1} - \dfrac{2}{2r+3}$

ii $2\frac{2}{3} - \dfrac{2}{2n+1} - \dfrac{2}{2n+3}$

b $u_2 = 13$; $u_3 = 35$

4 **a** **i** $r = 1.5$
ii $a = 0.8$
iii 102 000
b divergent; $r = \ln 3 \approx 1.099$, hence $r > 1$
c $S = \ln 3 + 2\ln 3 + 3\ln 3 + \dots + 30\ln 3$
$a = \ln 3$; $d = \ln 3$; $S_{30} = 15[2\ln 3 + 29\ln 3]$
$= 510.85$

5 **a** $d = 6$; $S_{32} = 3264$ **b** $r = \frac{2}{3}$; $S_\infty = 243$

6 **a** $u_1 = 2$; $u_2 = 4$; $u_3 = 8$; $u_4 = 6$; $u_5 = 2$;
$u_6 = 4$
b periodic
c 4

7 **a** divergent to $+\infty$
b convergent to 5
c oscillates
d convergent, limit 3 (as $n \to \infty$)

9 Integration I

Review (p. 359)

1 **a** $2x$ **d** $-\sin x$
b $x - 6$ **e** $2\cos 2x$
c $\frac{1}{2}x^{-1/2} + x^{-2}$ **f** $-2x - 15\sin 5x$

2 **a** x^{-2} **b** $3x^{-3}$ **c** $7x^{-4} - x^{-3}$
d $2x^{1/2}$ **e** $5x^{-1/2}$ **f** $x^{1/2} + x$

3 **a** 46 **b** 14 **c** $\frac{20}{3}$ **d** 4

4 **a** $y = 1$

b

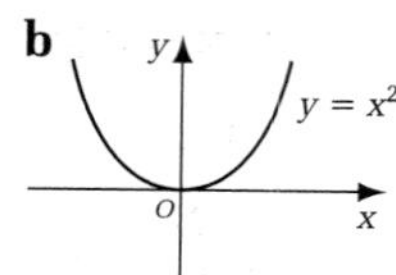

c $y = x^3$

d $y = \sin x$

e

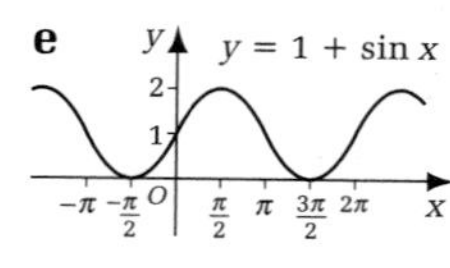

f

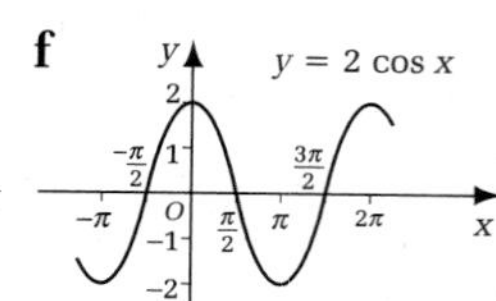

5 **a** $\sum_{i=1}^{3} i$ **b** $\sum_{i=1}^{5} i^2$
c $\sum_{i=1}^{4} 2i$ **d** $\sum_{i=1}^{4} (3i + 1)$

9.1 Technique (p. 365)

1 **a** $\int (2x^2 - 3x + 1)\,dx$
b $\int e^{2t}\,dt$
c $\int \cos\theta\,d\theta$

2 **a** $3x + c$
b $x^2 - 5x + c$
c $\frac{1}{3}x^3 + \frac{1}{2}x^2 - 7x + c$
d $x^2 - x^3 + c$
e $\frac{1}{3}x^3 + x^2 - 15x + c$
f $\frac{1}{3}x^3 + x^2 + x + c$

3 **a** $x + c$ **g** $\frac{1}{2}r^{10} + c$
b $10r + c$ **h** $-\frac{1}{t^2} + c$
c $\frac{1}{4}t^4 + t + c$ **i** $\frac{500}{11}x^{2.2} + c$
d $\frac{2}{3}x^{3/2} + c$ **j** $2\sqrt{r} + c$
e $-\frac{1}{t} + c$ **k** $-9x^{-1/3} + c$
f $\frac{3}{5}x^{5/3} + c$

4 **a** $\frac{1}{3}x^3 - \frac{3}{2}x^2 + 2x + c$
b $\frac{4}{3}t^3 - 10t^2 + 25t + c$
c $x^2 + \frac{1}{3}x^3 + c$
d $\frac{1}{2}t^2 - \frac{1}{2}t^4 + \frac{1}{6}t^6 + c$
e $\frac{1}{3}x^3 - x^2 - 3x + c$
f $4x^{7/2} + c$

5 **a** $\frac{1}{2}x^2 - \frac{1}{x^2} + c$
b $\frac{2}{3}x^{3/2} + 6x^{1/2} + c$
c $-\frac{1}{2t^2} - \frac{2}{t} + \frac{3}{2}t^2 + c$
d $\frac{1}{2}x^2 - \frac{4}{3}x^{3/2} + x + c$
e $2x^{1/2} - \frac{6}{5}x^{5/2} + c$
f $4x^{3/2} + \frac{2}{5}x^{5/2} + c$

6 $f(x) = 4x^2$

7 $g'(x) = f(x)$

9.1 Contextual (p. 365)

1 $S = \frac{1}{2}t^2 + 3t$

2 **a** $\int(2x^3 - 10x^2 - x + 3)\,dx = \frac{1}{2}x^4 - \frac{10}{3}x^3 - \frac{1}{2}x^2 + 3x + c$
b $\int(10 - 15t)\,dt = 5\int(2 - 3t)\,dt = 5(2t - \frac{3}{2}t^2) + c$
c $\int dy = y + c$
d $\int d\theta = \theta + c$
e $\int(2x^{1/2} - x + 1)dx = \frac{4}{3}x^{3/2} - \frac{1}{2}x^2 + x + c$
f $\int(5t - 3t^2 + t^5)\,dt = \frac{5}{2}t^2 - t^3 + \frac{1}{6}t^6 + c$
g $\int(2u - 3)\,du = u^2 - 3u + c$

3 **a** $g'(x) = 6x(x+1)$; $x = 0$ and $x = -1$
b $g(x) = 2x^3 + 3x^2 + 4$

4 **a** Maximum when $\frac{dy}{dx} = 0$. Then $4 - 2x = 0$ and $x = 2$. Maximum because $\frac{dy}{dx} > 0$ when $x < 2$ and $\frac{dy}{dx} < 0$ when $x > 2$.
b $y = 4x - x^2 - 3$

5 $g(x) = x - x^4 + 1$

6 $y = \frac{2}{x^2} + 3$

7 **a** $s = 0.3t^2 - \frac{0.004}{3}t^3$ **b** 2.25 km

8 **a** $v = 14t - 4t^2 + 20$ **b** $s = 7t^2 - \frac{4}{3}t^3 + 20t$

9.2 Technique (p. 373)

1 **a** $[\frac{1}{2}x^2 + 3x]_a^b$ **d** $[r]_a^b$
b $[\frac{1}{4}t^4 + \frac{2}{3}t^3 - t]_a^b$ **e** $[10r]_a^b$
c $[x]_a^b$ **f** $\int_a^b(x^2 - 6x + 9)\,dx$

2 **a** $\int_{-1}^{2}(2 + x - x^2)\,dx$ **b** $\int_0^1(x-1)^2\,dx$

3 $6\frac{2}{3}$

4 **a** 8 **b** $2\sqrt{3}$
c $\frac{27}{4}$ **d** $\frac{46}{15}$

5 **a** 11 **b** $-\frac{125}{6}$
c 104 **d** -63

6 **a** P (2, 0), Q (4, 0)
b Integral negative between $x = 0$ and $x = 2$ and positive between $x = 2$ and $x = 4$.
c Total area = 8 units square

7 **a** $7\frac{1}{2}$ **b** 12 **c** $4\frac{1}{2}$

8 $\frac{4}{3}$; $10\frac{2}{3}$

9 **a** 4 **b** $\frac{80}{3}$ **c** $\frac{4}{9}$ **d** 62

9.2 Contextual (p. 374)

1 **a** $\frac{17}{6} + \frac{22}{3} = \frac{61}{6}$ **b** $8 - \frac{16}{3} = \frac{8}{3}$

2 **a** 52.58 m^2 **b** 736 m^3

3 3948.75 m

4 **a** $p = 1000v^{-1.2}$ **b** 986.29

5 $\sqrt[3]{6} = 1.817$

9.3 Technique (p. 379)

1 **a** $x = y - 1$ **b** 1.5

2 $\pm 2\sqrt{y} = x$; $\frac{56}{3}$

3 $x = \sqrt[3]{y}$; 1.14

4 $x = y^3 + 1$; $\frac{27}{4}$

9.4 Technique (p. 382)

1 9

2 $\frac{64}{3}$

3 $\frac{5}{12}$

9.4 Contextual (p. 382)

1 **a** P (2, 5) **b** $\frac{8}{3}$

2 **a** A (3, 0) **b** 9

3 **a** P (3, 3), Q (−2, −2) **b** $\frac{125}{6}$

4 Cut at the points (−3, 9) and (3, 9). Area between curves is 36 square units

5 **a** $\frac{16}{5}$ **b** $\frac{8}{3}$

9.5 Technique (p. 388)

1 **a** 756.5 cubic units **b** $\frac{25}{2}\pi$
c $\frac{1000}{3}\pi$ **d** $\frac{31}{5}\pi$

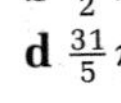

2

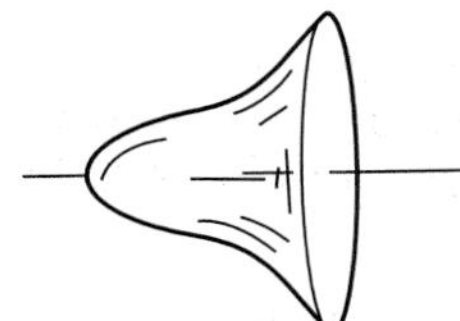

$\frac{405}{14}\pi$ cubic units

3 $\frac{1}{2}\pi$

9.5 Contextual (p. 389)

1 18π; 36π

2 $\frac{7783}{120}\pi$ or 203.76 cubic units

3 $\frac{124}{3}\pi$ cubic units

9.6 Technique (p. 394)

1 **a** $\int \sin x\,dx = -\cos x + c$ and $\int \cos x\,dx = \sin x + c$
b $\int(1 + \cos x + 2\sin x)\,dx$
$= x + \sin x + 2(-\cos x) + c$
$= x + \sin x - 2\cos x + c$
c $\int(t - 5 - 7\sin t - 2\cos t)\,dt$
$= \frac{1}{2}t^2 - 5t - 7(-\cos t) - 2\sin t + c$
$= \frac{1}{2}t^2 - 5t + 7\cos t - 2\sin t + c$

2 **a** $-2\cos x + c$ **b** $3\cos x + c$
c $5\sin x + c$ **d** $-2\sin x + c$

3 **a** $\theta + 3\sin\theta + c$
b $t - \sin t - 3\cos t + c$
c $\frac{1}{4}\theta^2 + a\sin\theta + b\cos\theta + c$
d $10t - t^3 + 2\sin t + \frac{1}{2}\cos t + c$

4 **a** $-\frac{1}{2}\cos 2x + c$
b $\frac{1}{4}\sin 4x + c$
c $x + \frac{1}{3}\sin 3x + c$
d $-5\cos 3x + c$
e $3x + 2\sin 2x + c$
f $10x - 3\sin x + 2\cos 4x + c$

5 **a** $2 - \sqrt{2}$ **b** $\sqrt{2}$

6 3.60

7 **a** 1 **b** π **c** $\frac{2}{3}$ **d** $\frac{1}{4}\pi + \frac{3}{2}$

8 **a** $\frac{1}{2}x - \frac{1}{4}\sin 2x + c$ **b** $\frac{1}{4}\sin 2x + \frac{1}{2}x + c$

9.6 Contextual (p. 395)

1 **a** $\int_0^{2\pi} \sin x \, dx$ gives the total area
The area between 0 and π is positive and the area between π and 2π has the same value but is negative. These cancel each other out giving an answer of zero.
b Area under the curve between $x = 0$ and $x = \frac{\pi}{2}$. Value = 1.
c 4 square units

2 $s = 4\sin 3t$

3 **a** $y = 3\cos x; \frac{3\sqrt{2}}{2}$
b $y = 2\sin x + 2; 2 + 3\pi$
c $y = 1 + \sin x; \frac{\pi}{2} + 1$

4 **a** When $x = \frac{2\pi}{3}$, $y = \sin\frac{2\pi}{3} + \sin\frac{4\pi}{3}$
$= \frac{\sqrt{3}}{2} + (-\frac{\sqrt{3}}{2}) = 0$
b $\frac{9}{4}$

5 **a** $y = \cos\frac{\pi}{3} + \cos\frac{2\pi}{3} = \frac{1}{2} + (-\frac{1}{2}) = 0$
b $\frac{3\sqrt{3}}{4}$

6 π^2 cubic units

7 **b** $\frac{\pi}{4}(3\pi + 2)$ cubic units

Consolidation A (p. 397)

1 **a** $\frac{4}{3}x^3 - 6x^2 + 9x + c$
b $y = 3x^2 - x + 7$

2 **a** $\frac{3}{2}x^2 - \frac{1}{3}x^3 + c$ **b** $\frac{9}{2}$

3 **a** $\frac{dy}{dx} = 20x^3 - 5x^4$, $(0, 0)$ and $(4, 256)$
b 520.8 (1 d.p.)
c 0. Area between $x = 0$ and $x = 5$ is above axis and positive. Area between $x = 5$ and $x = 6$ is below the x-axis, negative in sign but equal in magnitude to the first area.

4 **a** P $(7, 0)$, Q $(-1, 0)$, R $(0, 7)$, S $(6, 7)$
b Starting from the left-hand side the areas are $\frac{13}{3}$, $\frac{11}{3}$ and 36 square units respectively.

5 **a** $y = 2x - 2$ **b** $\frac{27}{4}$

6 **a** 8 **b** $a = 5$

7 6π cubic units

8 **a** $2\sin x + 3\cos x + c$
b $x + 2\cos 3x + c$
c 0
d area = π square units

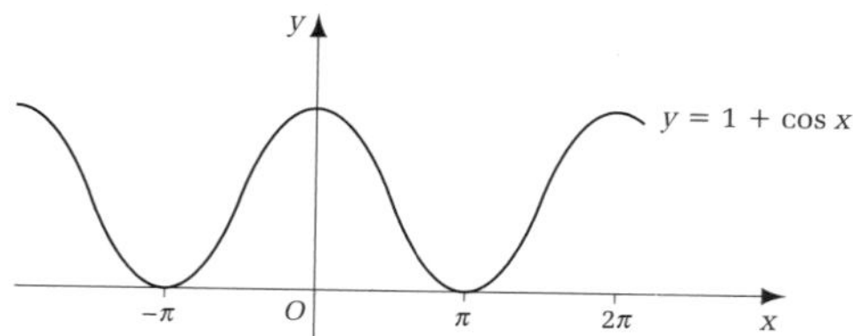

9 **b** $\frac{896\pi}{9}$ cubic units

10 **b** volume $= \frac{\pi(\pi - 2)}{4} = 0.8966$ cubic units (4 d.p.)

Consolidation B (p. 399)

1 **a** $\frac{2}{3}x^{3/2} - \frac{12}{x} + c$ **b** $\frac{43}{3}$

2 **a** $y = 3x^3 - 3x^2 + x + 3$
b $s = \frac{1}{3}t^3 - 2t^2 + 3t$

3 $\sqrt{2}$

4 **a** $(2,4)$ **b** $\frac{44}{3}$

5 **a**

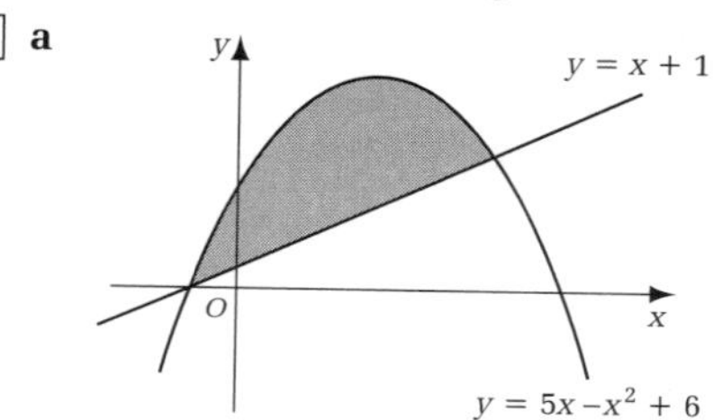

b $(-1, 0)$; $(5, 6)$
c 36

6 $\frac{3\pi}{2}$ cubic units

7 $\frac{9\pi^2}{4}$ cubic units

10 Trigonometry II

Review (p. 403)

1 **a** $\sin A\cos B + \cos A\sin B$
b $\cos A\cos B + \sin A\sin B$
c $\frac{2\tan A}{1 - \tan^2 A}$
d $\frac{1}{2}(\cos x - \sqrt{3}\sin x)$
e $\frac{1}{2}(\sqrt{3}\sin x - \cos x)$
f $\frac{\tan x - 1}{1 + \tan x}$

2 **a** **i** $\frac{\pi}{4}$ **ii** $\frac{2\pi}{3}$ **iii** $\frac{7\pi}{4}$ **iv** $\frac{11\pi}{9}$ **v** $\frac{20\pi}{9}$ **vi** $-\frac{2\pi}{9}$
b **i** 30° **ii** 90° **iii** 225° **iv** 9° **v** 220° **vi** −126°

3 **a** $\frac{\sqrt{3}}{2}$ **b** $\frac{1}{\sqrt{3}}$ **c** 0
d $\frac{\sqrt{3}}{2}$ **e** 0 **f** $-\frac{1}{2}$

10.1 Technique (p. 410)

1 **a** 0°, 90°, 120°, 180°, 240°, 270°, 360°
b 0°, 30°, 90°, 150°, 180°, 210°, 270°, 330°, 360°
c 30°, 60°, 90°, 120°, 150°, 210°, 240°, 270°, 300°, 330°
d 30°, 45°, 135°, 150°, 225°, 315°,

2 **a** $\frac{2\pi}{3}, \pi$ **b** $0, \frac{\pi}{2}, \pi$
c $0, \frac{\pi}{6}, \frac{\pi}{3}, \frac{2\pi}{3}, \frac{5\pi}{6}, \pi$ **d** $0, \frac{\pi}{3}, \frac{\pi}{2}, \frac{2\pi}{3}, \pi$

4 **a** $\sin 6\theta + \sin 2\theta$ **d** $\cos 7\theta - \cos\theta$
b $\sin 6\theta - \sin 4\theta$ **e** $\cos 2\theta - \cos 6\theta$
c $\cos 7\theta + \cos\theta$ **f** $\cos 3\theta - \cos 9\theta$

5 **a** $-\frac{\sqrt{6}}{2}$ **b** $\frac{\sqrt{6}}{2}$
c $\frac{\sqrt{3}-\sqrt{2}}{2}$ **d** $\frac{\sqrt{2}+1}{4}$

10.2 Technique (p. 419)

1 **a** $13\sin(x + 67.4°)$
b $25\sin(x + 73.7°)$
c $61\sin(x + 79.6°)$
d $\sqrt{29}\sin(x + 68.2°)$

2 **a** $2\sin(x - \frac{\pi}{6})$
b $\sqrt{8}\sin(x - \frac{\pi}{4}) = 2\sqrt{2}\sin(x - \frac{\pi}{4})$
c $2\sin(x - \frac{\pi}{3})$
d not possible

3 **a** $10\cos(x + 36.9°)$
b $5\cos(x + 53.1°)$
c $\sqrt{13}\cos(x + 33.7°)$
d $\sqrt{74}\cos(x + 35.5°)$

4 **a** $13\cos(x - 0.395)$
b $10\cos(x - 0.644)$
c $2\cos(x - \frac{\pi}{3})$
d $\sqrt{61}\cos(x - 0.695)$

5 **a** $\sqrt{2}, x = 45°; -\sqrt{2}, x = 225°$
b $61, x = 100.4°; -61, x = 280.4°$
c $25, x = 343.7°; -25, x = 163.7°$
d $\sqrt{34}, x = 31°; -\sqrt{34}, x = 211°$

6 **a** 90°, 180° **b** 30°, 90°
c 195°, 255° **d** 90°, 330°

7 **a** $0, \frac{\pi}{2}$ **b** $-\frac{\pi}{2}, \frac{\pi}{6}$
c −2.95, 0.89 **d** 0.52, −1.80 (2 d.p.)

8 **a** $1, \frac{1}{35}$ **b** $1, \frac{1}{27}$
c $\frac{3}{13}, \frac{1}{13}$ **d** $1, \frac{1}{11}$

10.2 Contextual (p. 420)

1 **a** 6 cm, 14 cm
b 0730 Monday ($7\frac{1}{2}$ hours)
0430 Wednesday ($52\frac{1}{2}$ hours)

2 **a** 13 cm ,33 cm
b $\frac{\pi}{9}$ s (0.349), $\frac{4\pi}{9}$ s (1.40)

10.3 Technique (p. 425)

1 **a** $360°n \pm 25.8°$
b $360°n \pm 104.5°$
c $180°n + (-1)^n 11.5°$
d $180°n + (-1)^n(-36.9°)$
e $180°n + 26.6°$
f $180°n - 56.3°$

2 **a** $2\pi n \pm \frac{\pi}{3}$ **b** $2\pi n \pm \frac{5\pi}{6}$
c $\pi n + (-1)^n \frac{\pi}{3}$ **d** $\pi n + (-1)^n(-\frac{\pi}{2})$
e $\pi n + \frac{\pi}{4}$ **f** πn

3 **a** $90°n + (-1)^n 15°$ **b** $\frac{n\pi}{2}$
c $n\pi$ and $\frac{n\pi}{2} + \frac{\pi}{4}$ **d** $\frac{\pi n}{2} \pm \frac{\pi}{6}$

4 $\theta = 360°n + 122.3°, 360°n + 20.8°$

5 $\pi n \pm \frac{\pi}{3}, \frac{2\pi n}{3} \pm \frac{\pi}{6}$

6 $180°n + 7.5°$

Consolidation A (p. 426)

1 $0, \frac{\pi}{4}, \frac{2\pi}{3}, \frac{3\pi}{4}, \frac{5\pi}{4}, \frac{4\pi}{3}, \frac{7\pi}{4}, 2\pi$

2 $65\sin(x + 0.249)$
a 0.629 **b** 2.89

3 $5\sin(\theta - 0.644); \frac{1}{5}, \frac{1}{15}$

4 $\cos 36° = \frac{1}{4} + \frac{\sqrt{5}}{4}; a = \frac{1}{4}, b = \frac{1}{4}$

5 $5\sin(\theta - 0.927)$
a greatest value, 25; least value, 0
b greatest value, 1; least value $\frac{1}{26}$ (when $\theta = 2.50$)

6 **a** $R = 5, \alpha = 36.9°$
b 5
c 143.1° and 323.1° (1 d.p.)

7 $2\sin(\theta - 30°), \theta = 75°, 165°$

8 $60°n + 10°[1 + (-1)^n]$

9 **a** $R = \sqrt{5}, \alpha = 0.464$
b $2n\pi + 0.643, 2n\pi - 1.571$

Consolidation B (p. 427)

1 $0, \frac{\pi}{10}, \frac{3\pi}{10}, \frac{\pi}{3}, \frac{\pi}{2}$

2 132°, 335°

3 $R = 5, \alpha = 36.9°$
a i 103.3°, 330.5° **ii** 36.9°, 132.3°
b $1, \theta = 216.9°; \frac{1}{11}, \theta = 36.9°$

4 **a** $k = 12$
b $R = 13, \alpha = 1.176$
c greatest value = 3, least value = 1
greatest value occurs when $x = 0.983$

5 $R = \sqrt{8} = 2\sqrt{2}, \alpha = \frac{\pi}{4}$
other angle is $\frac{\pi}{12}$

6 **a** $180°n \pm 26.6°$
b i 60° **ii** 28.1°, 90°

7 $\pi n \pm \frac{\pi}{4}, \pi n \pm \frac{\pi}{3}$

11 Differentiation II

Review (p. 431)

1 **a** $2x - 9$
b $\frac{5}{\sqrt{x}}$
c $\frac{7}{2}x^{5/2} - \frac{5}{2}x^{3/2}$
d $3 - \frac{1}{2x^2}$
e $4\cos 4x$
f $3\sin 2x$
g $-\frac{1}{2}\sin(\frac{1}{2}x + \frac{\pi}{4})$
h $2 + 2\sin 2x$

2 **a** $4(x+11)^3$
b $32(4x-1)^7$
c $\frac{1}{2\sqrt{x+5}}$
d $-\frac{x}{\sqrt{2-x^2}}$
e $-\frac{18}{(3x+1)^2}$
f $-\frac{2}{(x+2)^{3/2}}$

3 minimum point at $(-2, -13)$
maximum point at $(1, 7.25)$
minimum point at $(4, -13)$

4 tangent: $y = -x + 4$
normal: $y = x$

5 **a** $3 + 2\ln 2$
b $\frac{1}{5e^3}$
c $\frac{1}{4}\ln 10$
d $e^6 + 1$

6 **a** $x^2 + y^2 = 16$
b $x^2 + (y-3)^2 = 36$
c $(x-4)^2 + (y+2)^2 = 49$
d $(x+1)^2 + (y-6)^2 = 3$

7 **a** $1 - 2x + 3x^2 - 4x^3$
b $1 - \frac{1}{3}x - \frac{1}{9}x^2 - \frac{5}{81}x^3$
c $1 + 3x + 9x^2 + 27x^3$
d $1 + 2x - 2x^2 + 4x^3$

11.1 Technique (p. 437)

1 **a** $(7x+4)(x+4)^5$
b $4(5x+4)(x+1)^3$
c $\frac{3x-8}{2\sqrt{x-1}}$
d $x^2(2x\cos 2x + 3\sin 2x)$
e $-\frac{7}{(x-3)^2}$
f $-\frac{3(x+2)}{(x-2)^3}$
g $\frac{x\cos x - \sin x}{2x^2}$
h $\frac{3\cos 2x\cos 3x + 2\sin 2x\sin 3x}{\cos^2 2x}$

2 **a** 48
b 25
c $-\frac{1}{27}$
d $-\frac{5}{2}$
e 2
f $-\frac{23}{4}$

11.1 Contextual (p. 437)

1 **a** tangent: $y = -9x + 14$
normal: $x - 9y = 38$ or $x - 9y - 38 = 0$
b tangent: $y = -14x - 47$
normal: $x - 14y = 67$ or $x - 14y - 67 = 0$
c tangent: $y = -2\pi x + \pi^2$
normal: $x - 2\pi y = 2\pi^3 + \pi$ or
$x - 2\pi y - 2\pi^3 - \pi = 0$
d tangent: $3x + 8y = -1$ or $3x + 8y + 1 = 0$
normal: $12y - 32x = 35$ or
$32x - 12y - 35 = 0$

11.2 Technique (p. 446)

1 **a** $2e^{2x-3}$
b $3x^2 e^{x^3}$
c $-5e^{1-5x}$
d $-\sin x e^{\cos x}$
e $-4^{-x}\ln 4$
f $(2-x)xe^{-x}$
g $e^{-x/2}(\cos x - \frac{1}{2}\sin x)$
h $\frac{xe^x - 2e^x - 2}{x^3}$
i $e^x(\sin 2x + 2\cos 2x)$
j $\frac{-\cos x(2\sin x + \cos x)}{e^x}$

2 **a** $\frac{1}{x}$
b $\frac{4}{x}$
c $\frac{5}{x}$
d $\frac{4}{4x+1}$
e $\frac{4x^3}{x^4+1}$
f $\cot x$
g $x(2\ln x + 1)$
h $\frac{1-2\ln x}{x^3}$
i $\frac{2}{1-x^2}$
j $\frac{3}{(3x-4)\ln 10}$

3 **a i** $\frac{dy}{dx} = (2x+3)e^x$, $\frac{d^2y}{dx^2} = (2x+5)e^x$
ii $(\frac{-3}{2}, \frac{-2}{e^{3/2}})$ is a minimum point
b i $\frac{dy}{dx} = \frac{x+1}{(x+2)^2}$, $\frac{d^2y}{dx^2} = \frac{-x}{(x+2)^2}$
ii $(-1, 1)$ is a minimum point
c i $\frac{dy}{dx} = e^x(\sin x + \cos x)$, $\frac{d^2y}{dx^2} = 2e^x\cos x$
ii $(\frac{-\pi}{4}, \frac{-1}{\sqrt{2}\,e^{\pi/4}})$ is a minimum point
$(\frac{3\pi}{4}, \frac{e^{3\pi/4}}{\sqrt{2}})$ is a maximum point
d i $\frac{dy}{dx} = -(x-2)(x+1)^2e^{-x}$,
$\frac{d^2y}{dx^2} = (x+1)(x^2 - 4x + 1)e^{-x}$
ii $(-1, 0)$ is a point of inflexion
$(2, \frac{27}{e^2})$ is a maximum point

11.2 Contextual (p. 446)

1 **a** tangent: $y = \frac{3}{4}x - \frac{3}{4} + 2\ln 2$
normal: $y = -\frac{4}{3}x + \frac{4}{3} + 2\ln 2$
b tangent: $y = \frac{6}{e}x + \frac{9}{e}$
normal: $y = -\frac{e}{6}x - \frac{e}{6} + \frac{3}{e}$
c tangent: $y = 3ex - 2e^2$
normal: $y = -\frac{1}{3e}x + \frac{1}{3} + e^2$
d tangent: $y = -\frac{2}{e^2}x + \frac{7}{e^2}$
normal: $y = \frac{e^2}{2}x - e^2 + \frac{3}{e^2}$

2 **a** 1200
b 1734; 3693
c $\frac{dP}{dt} = 26e^{0.13t}$
95 people per year
350 people per year
d 15 years and 8 months

3 **a** 9.1 cm, 15.8 cm, 22.0 cm
b $v = 6 + 6e^{-1.5t}$ cm s^{-1}
$a = -9e^{-1.5t}$ cm s^{-2}
c $v = 8.8$ cm s^{-1}
$a = -4.3$ cm s^{-2}

4 **a** 8 weeks, £1054.92
b £1078.03; increasing at £1.93 per week

11.3 Technique (p. 454)

1 **a** $7\sec^2 7x$
b $3\sec 3x\tan 3x$
c $-2x\,\mathrm{cosec}^2(x^2)$
d $-10\,\mathrm{cosec}^2 5x\cot 5x$

e $-\frac{9}{\sqrt{1-81x^2}}$
f $-\frac{1}{\sqrt{x(2-x)}}$
g $\frac{2x}{1+x^4}$
h $\frac{1}{2x^2+6x+5}$

2 **a** $x(2\tan x + x\sec x)$
b $5\sec x(1 + x\tan x)$
c $2\sin^{-1}x + \frac{2x}{\sqrt{1-x^2}}$
d $3x^2\tan^{-1}x + \frac{x^3}{1+x^2}$

11.3 Contextual (p. 454)

1 **a** $\frac{4}{3}$; tangent: $y = \frac{4}{3}x - \frac{4\pi}{3} + \sqrt{3}$
normal: $y = -\frac{3}{4}x + \frac{3\pi}{4} + \sqrt{3}$
b $\frac{2\sqrt{3}}{3}$; tangent: $y = \frac{2\sqrt{3}}{3}x + \frac{\sqrt{3}}{3} + \frac{\pi}{6}$
normal: $y = \frac{\sqrt{3}}{2}x + \frac{\sqrt{3}}{4} + \frac{\pi}{6}$
c -1; tangent: $y = -x$
normal: $y = x - 2\pi$

11.4 Technique (p. 463)

1 **a i** $f'(x) = 3x^2 - 24x + 45$
$f''(x) = 6x - 24$
ii $(3, 14)$ is a maximum point
$(5, 10)$ is a minimum point
iii

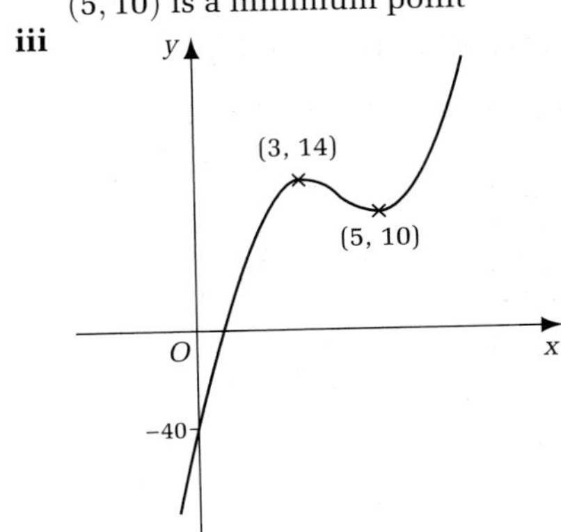

b i $f'(x) = -12 + 12x - 3x^2$
$f''(x) = 12 - 6x$
ii $(2, -1)$ is a point of inflexion
iii

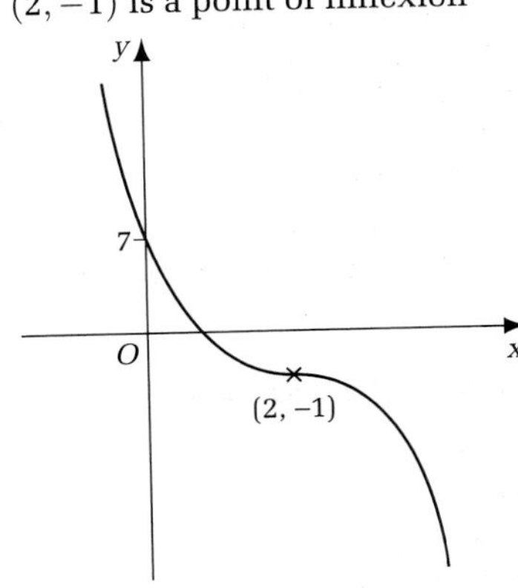

c i $f'(x) = 6x^2 - 18x - 108$
$f''(x) = 12x - 18$
ii $(-3, 229)$ is a maximum point
$(6, -500)$ is a minimum point
iii

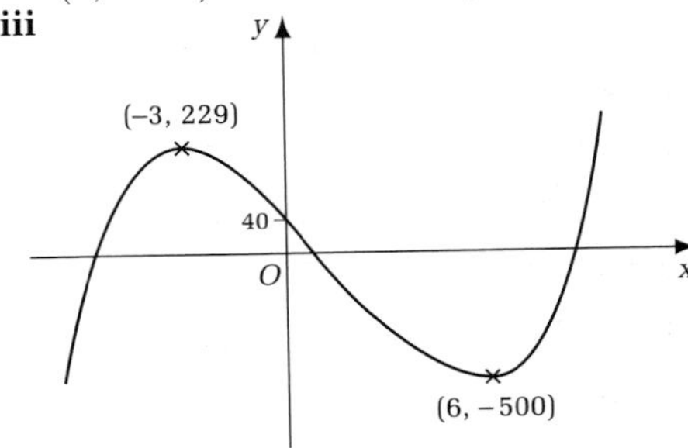

2 **a** $(-3, 0)$, $(5, 0)$, $(0, -135)$
b $(-3, 0)$ is a point of inflexion
$(3, -432)$ is a minimum point
c $(1, -256)$; $\frac{dy}{dx} < 0$ and $\frac{d^3y}{dx^3} > 0$
d

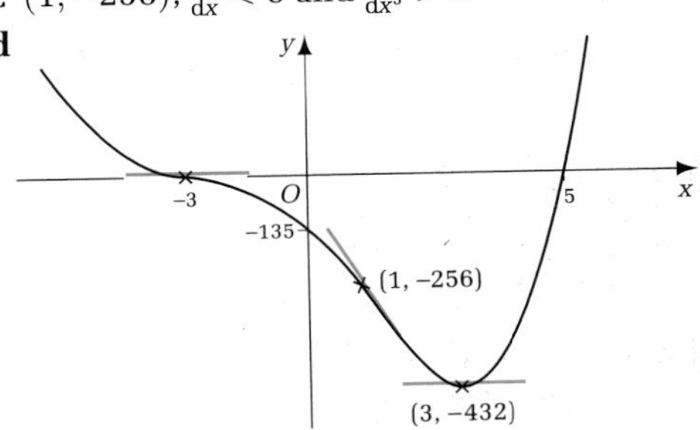

3 minimum points at $(-2\sqrt{3}, -112)$ and $(2\sqrt{3}, -112)$; maximum point at $(0, 32)$
$a = 2$

4 **a** maximum points at $(-\frac{11}{6}\pi, \sqrt{3} - \frac{11}{6}\pi)$ and $(\frac{\pi}{6}, \sqrt{3} + \frac{\pi}{6})$
minimum points at $(-\frac{7}{6}\pi, -\sqrt{3} - \frac{7}{6}\pi)$ and $(\frac{5}{6}\pi, -\sqrt{3} + \frac{5}{6}\pi)$
b $(-\frac{3}{2}\pi, -\frac{3}{2}\pi)$, $(-\frac{\pi}{2}, -\frac{\pi}{2})$, $(\frac{\pi}{2}, \frac{\pi}{2})$, $(\frac{3}{2}\pi, \frac{3}{2}\pi)$
c

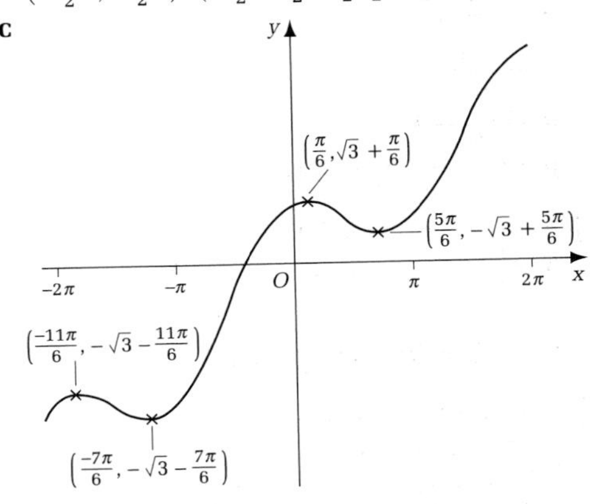

5 **a i** $(0, 0)$ and $(1, 0)$
ii none
iii $\frac{dy}{dx} = (5x - 1)(x - 1)^3$
iv $(\frac{1}{5}, \frac{256}{3125})$ is a maximum point
$(1, 0)$ is a minimum point

v

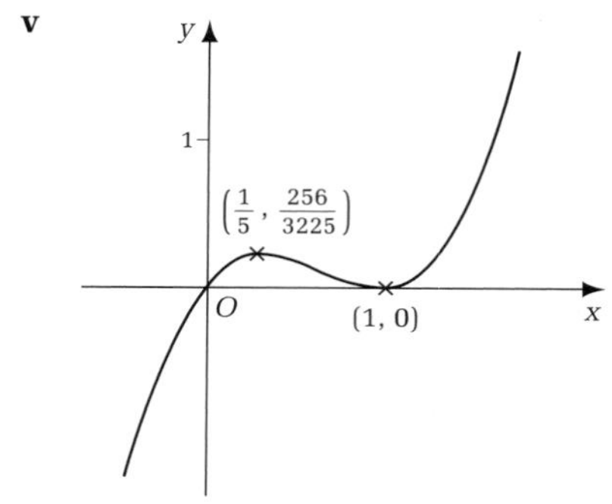

b i $(-4, 0)$, $(2, 0)$, $(0, 64)$
ii none
iii $\frac{dy}{dx} = 4(x-2)(x+1)(x+4)$
iv $(-4, 0)$ is a minimum point
$(-1, 81)$ is a maximum point
$(2, 0)$ is a minimum point
v

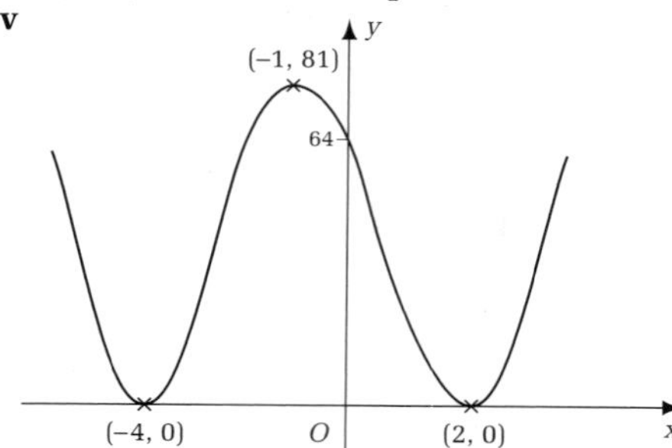

c i $(0, 0)$
ii $x = -3$
iii $\frac{dy}{dx} = \frac{x(x+6)}{2(x+3)^2}$
iv $(-6, -6)$ is a maximum point
$(0, 0)$ is a minimum point
v

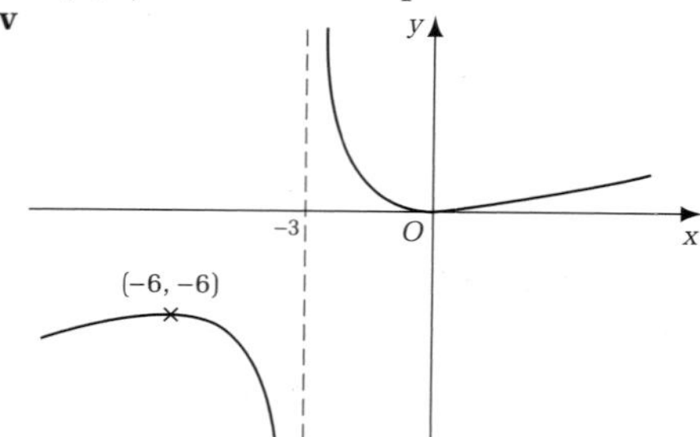

6 **a i** $\frac{dy}{dx} = (2x+3)\,e^x$
$\frac{d^2y}{dx^2} = (2x+5)\,e^x$
ii $\left(-\frac{3}{2}, -\frac{2}{e^{3/2}}\right)$ is a minimum point
b i $\frac{dy}{dx} = \frac{x+1}{(x+2)^2}$
$\frac{d^2y}{dx^2} = -\frac{x}{(x+2)^3}$
ii $(-1, 1)$ is a minimum point
c i $\frac{dy}{dx} = e^x(\sin x + \cos x)$
$\frac{d^2y}{dx^2} = 2e^x \cos x$
ii $\left(-\frac{\pi}{4}, \frac{1}{\sqrt{2}e^{\pi/4}}\right)$ is a minimum point
$\left(\frac{3\pi}{4}, \frac{e^{3\pi/4}}{\sqrt{2}}\right)$ is a maximum point

d i $\frac{dy}{dx} = -(x-2)(x+1)^2e^{-x}$
$\frac{d^2y}{dx^2} = (x+1)(x^2-4x+1)e^{-x}$
ii $(-1, 0)$ is a point of inflexion
$\left(2, \frac{27}{e^2}\right)$ is a maximum point

11.4 Contextual (p. 464)

1 **a** $\frac{dh}{dx} = -\frac{5}{2}x\,e^{-x/2}$
$\frac{d^2h}{dx^2} = \frac{5}{4}(x-2)\,e^{-x/2}$
b $x = 2$ m; $h = 7.36$ m
c -1.84; $61°$

11.5 Technique (p. 471)

1 **a i** $(x-1)^2 + (y-2)^2 = 25$
ii $\frac{dy}{dx} = \frac{x-1}{2-y}$
iii $-\frac{4}{3}$
b i $(x-3)^2 + (y+4)^2 = 169$
ii $\frac{dy}{dx} = \frac{3-x}{4+y}$
iii $\frac{5}{12}$
c i $(x-5)^2 + y^2 = 39$
ii $\frac{dy}{dx} = \frac{5-x}{y}$
iii $2\sqrt{3}$

2 **a** $\frac{dy}{dx} = \frac{6x+y}{4y-x}$
b $\frac{dy}{dx} = \frac{3(x^2-y)}{3x-4}$
c $\frac{dy}{dx} = \frac{12x}{1-4y}$
d $\frac{dy}{dx} = \frac{5-2y}{2(6y^2+x)}$
e $\frac{dy}{dx} = \frac{2(3xy-1)}{7-3x^2}$
f $\frac{dy}{dx} = \frac{2y^2+5}{2y(3-2x)}$

3 **a** 8 **b** -2 **c** $-\frac{5}{23}$

4 **a i** $\frac{dy}{dx} = \frac{6x-3y}{3x-2y}$
ii $(-3, -6)$ and $(3, 6)$
iii $\frac{d^2y}{dx^2} = \frac{6 - 6\frac{dy}{dx} + 2\left(\frac{dy}{dx}\right)^2}{3x-2y}$
iv $(-3, -6)$ is a minimum point
$(3, 6)$ is a maximum point
b i $\frac{dy}{dx} = \frac{5x}{1-2y}$
ii $(0, -2)$ and $(0, 3)$
iii $\frac{d^2y}{dx^2} = \frac{5 + 2\left(\frac{dy}{dx}\right)^2}{1-2y}$
iv $(0, -2)$ is a minimum point
$(0, 3)$ is a maximum point
c i $\frac{dy}{dx} = -\frac{1+2xy}{12+x^2}$
ii $\left(2, -\frac{1}{4}\right)$ and $\left(-6, \frac{1}{12}\right)$
iii $\frac{d^2y}{dx^2} = -\frac{2\left(y + 2x\frac{dy}{dx}\right)}{12+x^2}$
iv $\left(2, -\frac{1}{4}\right)$ is a minimum point
$\left(-6, \frac{1}{12}\right)$ is a maximum point

5 **a** tangent: $y = -2x - 4$
normal: $y = \frac{1}{2}x - \frac{3}{2}$, or $2y - x + 3 = 0$
b tangent: $y = -\frac{1}{4}x + \frac{3}{2}$
normal: $y = 4x - 7$
c tangent: $7x + 33y + 57 = 0$
normal: $33x - 7y - 219 = 0$

11.6 Technique (p. 480)

1 **a** $y = \frac{x^2}{9}$ **d** $\frac{x^2}{16} + \frac{y^2}{9} = 1$
b $y = \frac{x^3}{8} + 1$ **e** $\frac{(x-1)^2}{4} + \frac{(y-3)^2}{16} = 1$
c $x^2 + y^2 = 25$ **f** $\frac{x^2}{a^2} + \frac{y^2}{b^2} = 1$

2 **a** $\frac{dy}{dx} = -\frac{3}{t}$ **b** $\frac{dy}{dx} = \frac{1}{2\sin\theta}$ **c** $\frac{dy}{dx} = \left(\frac{t+1}{t-1}\right)^2$

3 **a** $(2, 5)$ and $(-2, -3)$
b $(2, 9)$
c $(\sqrt{3}, 2 + \frac{\sqrt{3}}{2})$ and $(-\sqrt{3}, 2 - \frac{\sqrt{3}}{2})$

4 tangent: $y = 2ex - e^2 + 1$
normal: $y = -\frac{1}{2e}x + e^2 + \frac{3}{2}$

5 $y = \frac{x}{2t^3} + \frac{3}{2}t - 1$ $y = \frac{x}{16} + 2$

6 **a** $\frac{d^2y}{dx^2} = \frac{2t-4}{3}$
maximum point at $(1, 0)$
minimum point at $(13, -32)$
b $\frac{d^2y}{dx^2} = -\frac{2(t+1)}{9t^5}$
minimum point at $(\frac{7}{8}, -\frac{1}{4})$

11.7 Technique (p. 487)

1 **a** $1 - \frac{1}{32}x^2 + \frac{1}{6144}x^4$ **d** $x + \frac{1}{3}x^3 + \frac{2}{15}x^5$
b $x^2 + 5x^3 + \frac{25}{2}x^4$ **e** $x - \frac{1}{3}x^3 + \frac{1}{5}x^5$
c $3x - \frac{9}{2}x^2 + 9x^3$ **f** $1 + x - \frac{1}{3}x^3$

2 0.28

3 $2x - 2x^2 + \frac{8}{3}x^3$; $-2x - 2x^2 - \frac{8}{3}x^3$; $4x + \frac{16}{3}x^3$; 0.405

Consolidation A (p. 488)

1 $(1 - 3x)e^{-3x}$; $(\frac{1}{3}, \frac{1}{3e})$

2 **a** $\frac{2-2t}{2t+3}$ **b** $(0, -15)$

3 **a** $\frac{dy}{dx} = \frac{13-3x}{2\sqrt{6-x}}$ **b** greater than 4

4 **a** $\frac{dx}{dt} = 2\cos 2t - 2\sin t$
$\frac{dy}{dt} = -\sin t - 4\cos 2t$
b $\frac{1}{2}$
c $y = -2x + \frac{5\sqrt{2}}{2}$

6 **b** $(-1, 0)$ **c** $-\frac{1}{5}$ **d** $y = 5x - 3$

7 $\frac{dy}{dx} = \frac{2e^{2t}-2}{2e^{2t}-5}$; $\ln 2$

8 **a** $x = -1$ and $x = 2$
b $\frac{dy}{dx} = -\frac{3(x^2-6x+5)}{(x^2-x-2)^2}$
A $(5, \frac{1}{3})$, B $(1, 3)$

9 $1 - 2x + 4x^2$
a 0.2027 (4 d.p.)
b $-2 + 8x$

10 $\frac{d^2C}{dx^2} = \frac{500}{(x^2+100)^{3/2}}$; minimum

Consolidation B (p. 490)

1 $\frac{dy}{dx} = 2x + \frac{54}{x^2}$ $\frac{d^2y}{dx^2} = 2 - \frac{108}{x^3}$
$(-3, 27)$; minimum

2 **a** $1 - \frac{1}{2}x^2 + \frac{1}{24}x^4$
b **i** $1 - 2x^2 + \frac{2}{3}x^4$
ii $1 - x^2 + \frac{1}{3}x^4$

3 **a** $\frac{dy}{dx} = \frac{t^2+1}{t^2-1}$
b **ii** $3x + 5y = 60$

4 **a** 3 hours
b 1 215 463 bacteria per hour

5 $y = -x + \frac{\pi}{2} + 2$

6 -1 and 4

7 $\frac{dy}{dx} = -\frac{3x^2+2}{3y^2+5}$

12 Integration II

Review (p. 494)

1 **a** $\frac{1}{4}x^4 + \frac{5}{3}x^3 - \frac{1}{2}x^2 + 10x + c$
b $\frac{1}{3}x^3 - 4x^2 + 16x + c$
c $-\cos x + c$
d $\frac{1}{3}\sin 3x + c$
e $\frac{x^{n+1}}{n+1} + c$, if $n \neq -1$
f $-\frac{1}{k}\cos kx + c$

2

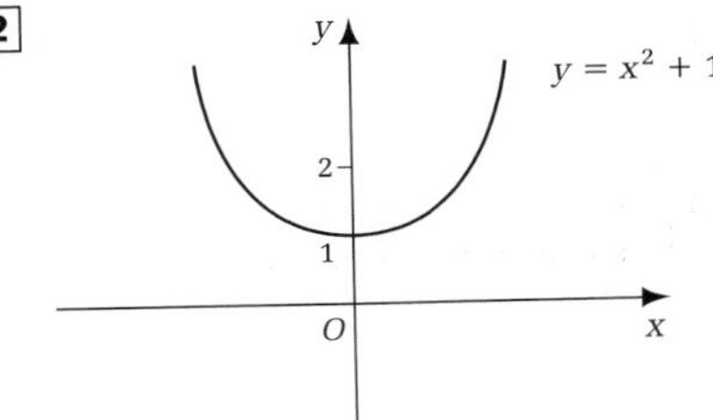

a $\frac{4}{3}$ **b** $\frac{28\pi}{15}$

3 **a** $4\cos(4x + 1)$ **f** $\frac{1}{x}$
b e^x **g** $\frac{2}{2x+13}$
c ke^{kx} **h** $\frac{2x}{x^2+7}$
d $3e^{1+3x}$ **i** $(1 + x)e^x$
e $\frac{1}{x}$ **j** $2x\cos 2x + \sin 2x$

4 **a** $1 + \frac{2}{x-1}$ **b** $1 - \frac{1}{x+1}$

5 **a** $\frac{5}{x+3} - \frac{4}{x+1}$
b $-\frac{2}{x+1} + \frac{2x+1}{x^2+1}$
c $2 + \frac{8}{x-2} - \frac{1}{x-5}$

6 **a** $2y\frac{dy}{dx} = 1$
$\frac{dy}{dx} = \frac{1}{2y}$
b $2y\frac{dy}{dx} = 2x + 2$
$\frac{dy}{dx} = \frac{2x+2}{2y} = \frac{x+1}{y}$

12.1 Technique (p. 504)

1 **a** $-\frac{1}{3}\cos 3x + c$ **d** $\frac{1}{2}\sin(1+2x) + c$
b $\frac{1}{4}\sin 4x + c$ **e** $\frac{1}{3}\tan 3x + c$
c $-\frac{1}{2}\cos(2x-1) + c$ **f** $x + \frac{1}{2}\tan 2x + c$

2 **a** $\frac{1}{2}$
b $\frac{1}{2}(\sin 4 - \sin 1) = -0.799$
c 1
d $\frac{\sqrt{3}}{2}$

3 **a** $-\frac{1}{6}\cos 3x - \frac{1}{2}\cos x + c$
b $\frac{1}{6}\sin 3x + \frac{1}{2}\sin x + c$
c 0
d $-\frac{2}{3}$

4 **a** $\frac{1}{5}e^{5x} + c$ **f** $-4e^{-x/4} + c$
b $-e^{-x} + c$ **g** $e^{2x} + c$
c $-\frac{1}{3}e^{-3x} + c$ **h** $-\frac{1}{12}e^{-6x} + c$
d $3e^{x/3} + c$ **i** $-30e^{-0.1x} + c$
e $\frac{3}{2}e^{2x/3} + c$

5 **a** $x^2 + \frac{3}{2}e^{2x} + c$ **e** $\frac{1}{2}(e^4 - 1)$ or 26.799
b $x + e^{-x} + c$ **f** $3e^{-2} - 1$ or -0.594
c $x + 2e^x + \frac{1}{2}e^{2x} + c$ **g** $\frac{1}{2}e(e-1)$ or 2.335
d $x + \frac{1}{2}e^{1-2x} + c$

6 **a** $4\ln|x| + c$ **e** $2\ln|2x+1| + c$
b $\frac{1}{2}\ln|x| + c$ **f** $\frac{1}{2}\ln|7+6x| + c$
c $x + \ln|x| + c$ **g** $-\frac{5}{3}\ln|2-3x| + c$
d $\ln|x+2| + c$ **h** $-\frac{1}{7}\ln|1-7x| + c$

7 **a** $\ln(1+x^2) + c$ **d** $-\frac{1}{2}\ln|1-x^2| + c$
b $\frac{1}{6}\ln(4+3x^2) + c$ **e** $\frac{1}{2}\ln 3$
c $\ln|x^2+x| + c$ **f** $\frac{1}{2}\ln 2$

8 **a** $\ln|\sin x| + c$
b $-\ln|1+\cos x| + c$
c $\ln|1+\sin x| + c$

9 **a** $\sin^{-1}x + c$ **d** $\frac{2}{\sqrt{3}}\tan^{-1}(\frac{x}{\sqrt{3}}) + c$
b $\sin^{-1}(\frac{x}{3}) + c$ **e** $4\sin^{-1}(\frac{x}{\sqrt{2}}) + c$
c $\frac{1}{3}\tan^{-1}(\frac{x}{3}) + c$ **f** $\frac{1}{\sqrt{7}}\tan^{-1}(\frac{x}{\sqrt{7}}) + c$

12.1 Contextual (p. 505)

1

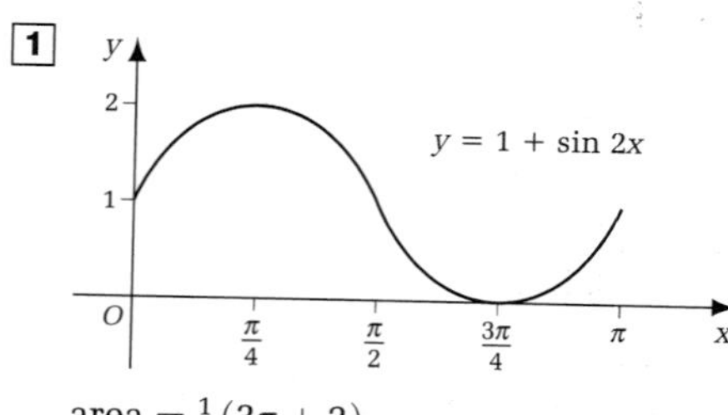

area $= \frac{1}{4}(3\pi + 2)$

2 **a** $\sin(1-1) = \sin 0 = 0$; when $x = 1, y = 0$
b $1 - \cos 1 = 0.46$ (2 d.p.)

3 π

4 **a** $\tan^2 2x = \sec^2 2x - 1$
b $\frac{1}{2}\tan 2x - x + c$

5 $g(x) = 6\sin(1+2x) + 1$

6 $2(e-1)$

7 $\frac{\pi}{16}(e^4 - 1)$

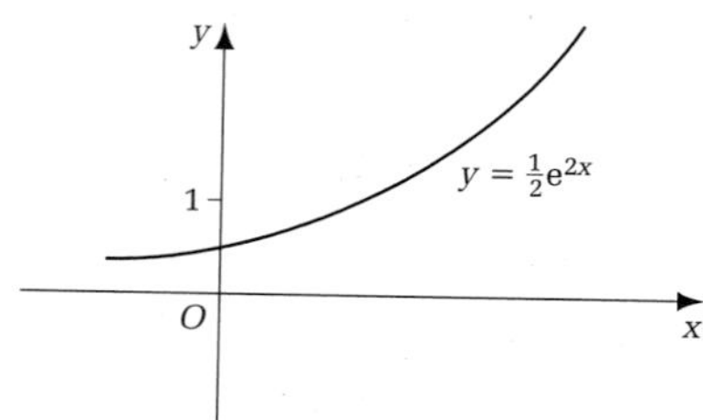

8 $m = x\ln 2$
$2^x = e^{x\ln 2}$
$\int_0^1 2^x\,dx = \frac{1}{\ln 2}$ or 1.44 (2 d.p.)

9

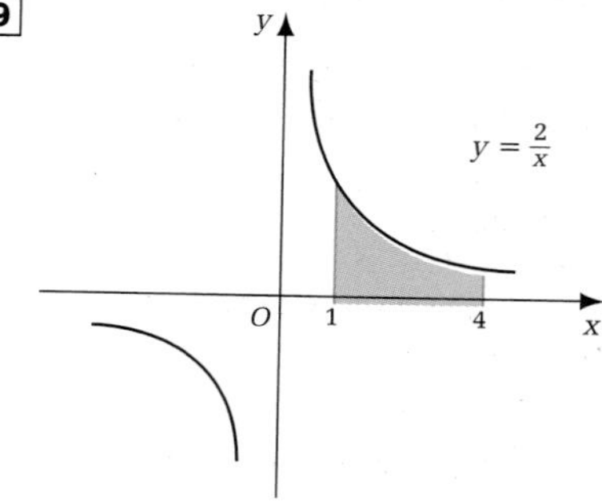

area $= 4\ln 2$

10 **a** $\frac{1}{4}\ln 7$ **b** $2\ln 5$

11 **a** $\frac{5\pi}{3}$ **b** π

12.2 Technique (p. 512)

1 **a** $x - \ln|x+1| + c$
b $x - 2\ln|x+1| + c = x - \ln(x+1)^2 + c$
c $\frac{1}{2}x + \frac{1}{4}\ln|2x-1| + c$
d $\frac{1}{2}x^2 + x + \ln|x-1| + c$

2 **a** $1 - \ln 2$ **b** $1 - \frac{\pi}{2}$

3 **a** 1.49 **b** 2.92

4 **a** $3\ln|x+1| + \ln|x+2| + c$
b $5\ln|x| + \frac{1}{2}\ln|1-2x| + c$
c $3\ln|x-1| - 2\ln|x+1| + c$
d $\ln|x-2| + 3\ln|x+1| + c$

5 **a** $\ln(\frac{4}{3})$ **d** $-\ln 2$
b $-\ln 65$ **e** $-2\ln 2$
c $-\frac{1}{2}\ln 5$ **f** $-2\ln(\frac{3}{2})$

6 **a** $-3\tan^{-1}x - \frac{1}{2}\ln(x^2+1) + \ln|x| + c$
b $\ln|(x+1)(x^2+4)| + c$

7 $\frac{1}{2}\ln 11 - \frac{\pi}{20}$

8 $2 + \frac{3x}{(x+1)(x-2)}$; $2 - \ln 2$

9 **a** $\frac{2}{x+1} + \frac{2-2x}{x^2+3}$ **b** $a = 3$

12.2 Contextual (p. 513)

1 **a** $1 - \frac{1}{x+2}$ **b** $1 - \ln(\frac{3}{2})$

2 **a** $1 - \frac{4}{x^2+4}$ **b** $4 - 2\tan^{-1}(2)$

3 $\frac{1}{7}\ln(\frac{9}{2})$

4 **a** $\frac{1}{x} - \frac{1}{2x+1}$ **b** $\frac{1}{2}\ln\frac{16}{3}$

6 $a = 9$ and $b = 2$

7 $\frac{2}{x^2} - \frac{3}{x} + \frac{12}{1+4x}$; 0.68

8 **a** $1 + \frac{2}{x+1} + \frac{3}{x+2}$ **b** $3 + \ln 50$

9 $\ln|x+3| - 3\ln|x+1| + 2\ln|x|$

10 $\ln 3 - \frac{4}{3}\ln 2$

12.3 Technique (p. 519)

1 **a** $\frac{1}{4}(2x-1)e^{2x} + c$ **b** $\frac{x^4}{16}(4\ln x - 1) + c$
c $-x\cos x + \sin x + c$ **d** $-(1+x)e^{-x} + c$

2 **a** $(2x-1)\sin x + 2\cos x + c$
b $x\tan x + \ln|\cos x| + c$
c $\cos 2x + 2x\sin 2x + c$
d $x(\sin x - \cos x) + \cos x + \sin x + c$
e $\frac{1}{2}x^2\ln 3x - \frac{1}{4}x^2 + c$
f $-\frac{1}{8}(4x+1)e^{-4x} + c$

3 **a** $-(2t+3)e^{-t} + c$ **b** $\frac{2}{3}t^{\frac{3}{2}}(\ln t - \frac{2}{3}) + c$

4 **a** $\frac{1}{6}(\pi\sqrt{3} - 3)$ **b** $\frac{1}{4} - \frac{5}{4}e^{-4}$ **c** $-\frac{2}{3}(\ln 2 + \frac{1}{3})$

5 **a** $(x^2 - 2x + 2)e^x + c$
b $\frac{1}{4}(1 - 2x^2)\cos 2x + \frac{1}{2}\sin 2x + c$
c $\frac{1}{5}(\sin 2x - 2\cos 2x)e^x + c$

12.3 Contextual (p. 519)

1 **a** She let $u = e^{-6x}$ and $\frac{dv}{dx} = x$
b Use integration by parts but let $u = x$ and $\frac{dv}{dx} = e^{-6x}$
c $-\frac{1}{36}(1+6x)e^{-6x} + c$

2 $a = 4, b = 3$

3 **a** $(\frac{\pi}{2}, 0)$ **b** $\frac{\pi}{4}$

4 **a** $\frac{1}{2}(\sin x - \cos x)e^{-x} + c$
b $\frac{1}{2}$

12.4 Technique (p. 528)

1 **a** $\frac{1}{6}(2x+1)^3 + c$ **d** $-\frac{3}{2(1+4x)} + c$
b $\frac{1}{16}(3+4x)^4 + c$ **e** $-\frac{2}{3\sqrt{1+3x}} + c$
c $\frac{1}{3}(2x+1)^{3/2} + c$ **f** $\frac{1}{8}(6x-1)^{4/3} + c$

2 **a** -5 **b** $\frac{8}{3}$

3 **a** $\frac{1}{15}$
b $\sqrt{5+4x} + c$
c $-\frac{1}{8(3+8x)} + c$

4 **a** $\frac{9}{80}$ **f** $\frac{1}{6}e^{2x^3} + c$
b $-x - 2\ln|x-2|$ **g** $\frac{1}{3}\sin^3\theta + \sin\theta + c$
c $\frac{8}{27}$ **h** $x - \ln(1+e^x) + c$
d $\frac{2(x+8)}{\sqrt{4+x}} + c$ **i** $\frac{1}{2}\tan^{-1}(x^2) + c$
e $\frac{3}{5}$

5 **a** $\frac{1}{4}$ **b** $-e^{-\frac{1}{2}x^2} + c$
c $\frac{3}{8}$ **d** $\frac{\pi}{4}$
e $2\ln(2+e^x) - x + c$
f $\frac{2}{3}\sqrt{3x+8} + c$
g $\frac{2}{15}(3x-4)(x+2)^{3/2} + c$
h $\sqrt{x^2-1} + c$
i $\frac{2}{3}\sqrt{1+x^3} + c$

12.4 Contextual (p. 529)

1 $\frac{3\pi}{2}$

2 **a** $\frac{2}{x} - \frac{2}{x+1} - \frac{2}{(x+1)^2}$
$A = 2, B = -2, C = -2$
b $2\ln(\frac{3}{2}) - \frac{1}{2}$

3 $\tan^{-1}(e^x) + c$

4 If c is a constant, $\frac{1}{2} + c$ is also a constant

5 **a** $\frac{1}{2}(\ln x)^2 + c$ **b** $\frac{1}{2}(\ln 2)^2$

6 $x - \ln(1+e^x) + c$

7 π

8 $\frac{1}{x+2} - \frac{2}{2x-1} + \frac{10}{(2x-1)^2}$ $\frac{10}{3} - 2\ln(\frac{3}{2})$

12.5 Technique (p. 535)

1 6π

2 $\frac{15\pi}{2}$

3 **a** $\frac{23}{3}$ **b** $\frac{119\pi}{6}$

4 **a** 9 **b** 12π

12.6 Technique (p. 544)

1 **a** $y = x^3 + \ln|x| + c$
b $y = \frac{1}{2}x^2 - \ln|x| + e^x + c$
c $y = \frac{1}{2}x^2 + e^x + c$
d $y = \frac{2}{3}x^{\frac{3}{2}} + 2e^x + c$
e $y = \frac{3}{4}x^{\frac{4}{3}} - \cos x + c$
f $y = \ln|x| - e^x + c$
g $y = -\frac{2}{x} + \ln|x| + c$
h $y = \frac{1}{3}x - \frac{1}{6}e^x + c$
i $y = \frac{2}{35}x^{\frac{7}{4}} + 2\ln|x| + c$

2 **a** $y = 4x^3 + c$ **g** $y = \frac{(x+c)^3}{27}$
b $y = \sin x + c$ **h** $y = \ln(\frac{1}{2}x^2 + c)$
c $y^2 = x^2 + 2x + c$ **i** $y = Ae^x - 1$
d $y^2 = 2x + c$ **j** $y = A(x+1)^2$
e $y = Ae^{2x}$ **k** $y^2 = \frac{2}{3}x^3 + c$
f $y = Ae^{2x^3}$ **l** $y = A\sqrt{x^2+1}$

3 **a** $(x-1)e^x + c$ **b** $y^2 = 2e^x(x-1) + c$

4 **a** $y = A\cos x$ **b** $y = 2\cos x$

5 **a** $y - 1 = Ax^2$ **b** $y = 3x^2 + 1$

12.6 Contextual (p. 544)

1 **a** rate of change of temperature is proportional to the difference between its temperature and that of its surroundings
b $\frac{dT}{dt} = -k(T-20)$
c $T = Ae^{-kt} + 20$
$t = 0$, $T = 100°C$ gives $T = 80e^{-kt} + 20$
$t = 34$, $T = 70°C$ gives $T = 80e^{-0.014t} + 20$
$t = 45$, $T = 63°C$
d 71 min

2 **a** $\frac{dN}{dt} = kN$ **c** $k = 0.17$ **d** $t = 6.46$ h

3 **a** $\frac{dV}{dt} = -k\sqrt{h}$, $k > 0$
b $V = l \times b \times h = 2 \times 2 \times h = 4h$;
$\frac{dh}{dt} = \frac{-k}{4}\sqrt{h}$
c $\sqrt{h} = 1 - \frac{1}{20}t$, or $h = (1 - \frac{1}{20}t)^2$
empty in 20 min

4 $\frac{dx}{dt} = -kx$
$x = x_0 e^{-kt}$, where $k = 0.19$
time to decay to $\frac{1}{3}$ original value is 5.78 days

5 **a** $\frac{dy}{dx} = \frac{k}{y}$ **b** $y^2 = -5x + 9$

Consolidation A (p. 546)

1 **a** $-\frac{1}{x} + c$
b $2\sin(2x+7) + c$
c $-\frac{1}{2}\cos 2x + 2\sin\frac{1}{2}x + c$
d $\frac{1}{4}\tan 4x + c$
e $\frac{1}{8}\sin 4x - \frac{1}{12}\sin 6x + c$
f $x + \frac{1}{3}e^{3x} + c$
g $-\frac{1}{5}e^{-5x} + c$
h $2\ln|x^2 + 3x| + c$
i $\frac{1}{3}\ln|\sin 3x| + c$
j $\frac{1}{5}\tan^{-1}(\frac{x}{5}) + c$
k $\sin^{-1}(\frac{x}{5}) + c$
l $x - 3\ln|x+3| + c$

2 $\frac{1}{5}x^5\ln x - \frac{1}{25}x^5 + c$

3 $\frac{1}{9}(1 + 2e^3)$

4 $a = \frac{3}{2}$

5 $a = 2, b = 5$

6 $\frac{2}{3}$

7 $\frac{25}{114}$

8 $e^{e^x - 1}$

9 **b** $s^{\frac{3}{2}} = 2700t + 8000$
c $t = 7$ s

10 **b** $t = 6.31$

Consolidation B (p. 547)

1 $\frac{20}{2}(\sqrt{3} - \frac{\pi}{3}) = 10(\sqrt{3} - \frac{\pi}{3})$

2 **a** $-\frac{1}{2}$ **b** $\frac{\pi}{6}$

3 **a** $-(x+1)e^{-x} + c$ **b** 1.22

4 **a** $2 + \frac{3}{(x+1)(2x-1)}$
$2x + \ln|\frac{2x-1}{x+1}| + c$
b $\frac{1}{x} + \frac{2x+3}{x^2+4}$
$\frac{3}{2}\tan^{-1}(\frac{x}{2}) + \ln|x(x^2+4)| + c$
c $2 + \ln 3$

5 **c** $t = \frac{3}{4}\ln|\frac{6}{6-x}|$
when $x = 4$, $t = \frac{3}{4}\ln 3$
speed $= \frac{8}{3}$ km h^{-1}
d model predicts an infinite number of hours; only realistic for early part of jog

6 **a** $T = 20$ min
b **ii** $2x^{1/2} = -kt + c$
iii 21.9 min

7 **b** $x = 4.8e^{0.015t}$
c 5.02 million
d 2010

13 Numerical Methods

Review (p. 551)

1 **a** $e^x - x^2 - 2 = 0$
b $\frac{7}{x-3} - x = 0$ or $x^2 - 3x - 7 = 0$
c $\sqrt{x+5} - x = 0$ or $x^2 - x - 5 = 0$

3 **a** $x = \frac{1}{2}(1 - e^x)$ or $x = \ln(1-2x)$
b $x = 5 - \ln x$ or $x = e^{5-x}$
c $x = \frac{1}{4}(x^2 - 7)$ or $x = \pm\sqrt{4x+7}$ or $x = \frac{7}{x-4}$
or $x = 4 + \frac{7}{x}$

4 **a** $f'(x) = 3x^2 - 2\sin x$
b $f'(x) = 10x - e^{-x}$
c $f'(x) = \frac{1}{x+1} + \frac{4}{x^2}$
d $f'(x) = x\cos x + \sin x$

5 **a** 44 **b** $\frac{\sqrt{3}}{2} - \frac{\pi}{6}$ **c** $e - 2$

13.1 Technique (p. 569)

1 **b** 2.1875, $2.1875 < x < 3$

2 **a** -2 and -1 **b** -1.4 **c** -1.3520

3 3.486; $x^3 - 9x - 11 = 0$ or $x = \sqrt[3]{9x + 11}$

4 **a** $f'(x) = xe^x + e^x - 5$
b $a = 2, b = 3$
c -1.2713
d 2.03

5 **b** $x_{n+1} = \sqrt[3]{\frac{1}{2}(3x_n - 17)}$ and $x_{n+1} = \frac{17}{3-2x_n^2}$
c $x_{n+1} = \sqrt[3]{\frac{1}{2}(3x_n - 17)}$; -2.285

13.1 Contextual (p. 570)

1 **b i** 4.51
ii 4.5052

2 **b** -1.479
c B $(-0.466, 3.511)$
d C $(1.274, 0.397)$

3 **c** 3.50 p.m.

13.2 Technique (p. 581)

1 **a** 0.597 **b** 0.594

2 **a** 13.86 square units
b 13.99 square units

3 **a** 0.9031 **b** 0.9045

4 **a** 1.16 square units
b 1.15 square units

5 **a** 4.3061 **b** 4.2965

6 **a** 11.8595 **b** 11.8423 **c** 0.15%

13.2 Contextual (p. 581)

1 1728.5 cm^3

2 **a**

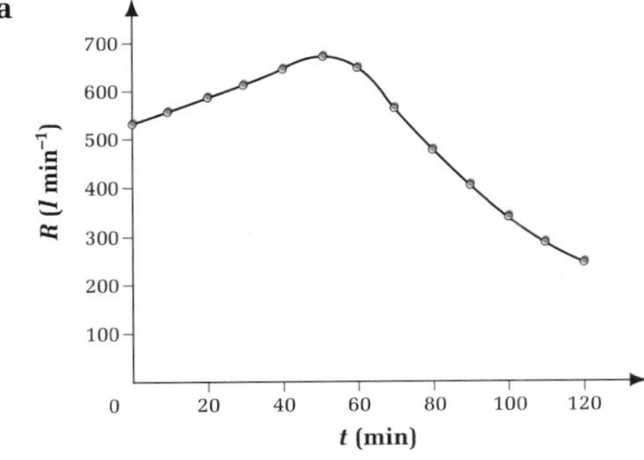

b 60 070 litres

3 **a**

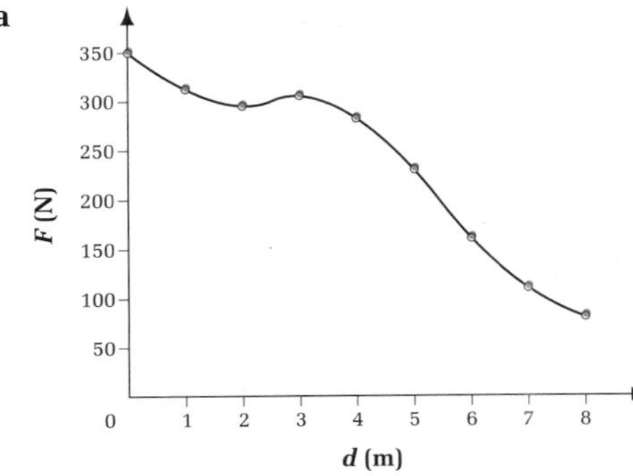

b i 1893.5 J
ii 1897.7 J

Consolidation A (p. 583)

1 1.57 (2 d.p.)

2 1.247 (3 d.p.)

3 2 roots
$x_0 = -1$
$x_1 = -1.1$
$x_2 = -1.115\,394$
$x_3 = -1.120\,045$
$x_4 = -1.121\,549$
$x_5 = -1.122\,045$
$x_6 = -1.122\,209$
$x_7 = -1.122\,264$
root is -1.12 (2 d.p.)

4 0.677 (3 d.p.) 2.1 cubic units (2 s.f.)

5 **b** $\alpha = 0.792$ (3 d.p.)
c $x_1 = 0.788$
$x_2 = 0.794$

6 **a**

x	0	3	6	9	12	15	18
d	0	1.708	2.309	2.598	2.582	2.141	0

b 34.0 m^2
c 3400 $m^3\ min^{-1}$

7 $p = 5, q = 6, r = 5$ 1.708 (3 d.p.)

8 8.6 (1 d.p.)

9 **a** $\int_0^{\pi/2} \sin x \, dx = 1$
b $B = 1$
c i $C \approx 0.954$ (3 d.p.)
ii $C \approx 0.984$ (3 d.p.)

10 **a iii** $x_0 = 2.2$
$x_1 = 2.236\,564$
$x_2 = 2.216\,139$
$x_3 = 2.227\,461$
$x_4 = 2.221\,158$
$x_5 = 2.224\,659$
$m = 2.22$ (2 d.p.)

Consolidation B (p. 585)

1 0.78

2 **b** $x_1 = 3.072\,316\,83$
$x_2 = 3.079\,959\,19$
$x_3 = 3.080\,764\,61$
$x_4 = 3.080\,849\,47$

3 35.77

4 0.35

5 5.2

6 **b** $x_1 = -1.965\,875$
$x_2 = -1.964\,680$
$x_3 = -1.964\,637$
$x_4 = -1.964\,636$
root is -1.9646 (4 d.p.)
c fails to converge

7 $x_0 = 0$
$x_1 = 0.5$
$x_2 = 0.369\,398$
$x_3 = 0.383\,468$
$x_4 = 0.381\,789$
$x_5 = 0.381\,987$
$\alpha = 0.38$ (2 d.p.)

14 Vectors

Review (p. 590)

1 A $(3, 0, 1)$ B $(3, 1, 1)$ C $(3, 1, 0)$ D $(2, 1, 0)$ E $(2, 2, 1)$ F $(1, 1, 1)$ G $(1, 1, 2)$ H $(0, 2, 0)$ J $(0.5, 1.5, 1)$

2 **a** $33.6°$ **b** $129.8°$

3 **a** 34.6 cm^2 **b** 27.6 cm^2

14.1 Technique (p. 598)

1 **a** $\mathbf{w}$
b $-\mathbf{w}$
c $\mathbf{v}$
d $\mathbf{w} - \mathbf{v}$
e $2\mathbf{w}$
f $-2\mathbf{v}$
g $-\mathbf{v}$
h $2(\mathbf{w} - \mathbf{v})$
i $2\mathbf{w} - \mathbf{v}$
j $\mathbf{v} + \mathbf{w}$

2 **a**

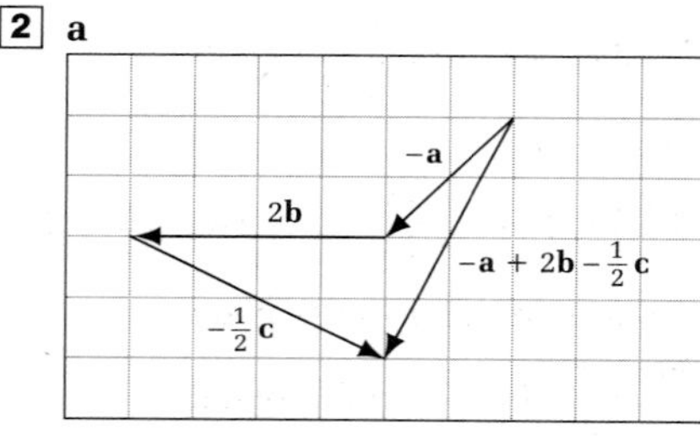

b $2\mathbf{a} + 6\mathbf{b}$

3 *AB* represents the length *AB* or the magnitude of a vector $\overrightarrow{AB}$
$\overrightarrow{AB}$ represents a vector starting at some point A and finishing at the point B.

4 $\overrightarrow{BC} = \mathbf{a}$
$\overrightarrow{DC} = \mathbf{b}$
$\overrightarrow{AC} = \mathbf{a} + \mathbf{b}$
$\overrightarrow{CA} = -\mathbf{a} - \mathbf{b}$ or $-(\mathbf{a} + \mathbf{b})$

5 $\overrightarrow{OM} = \frac{1}{3}\mathbf{a}$
$\overrightarrow{ON} = \frac{1}{3}\mathbf{b}$
$\overrightarrow{AB} = \mathbf{b} - \mathbf{a}$
$\overrightarrow{MN} = \frac{1}{3}\mathbf{b} - \frac{1}{3}\mathbf{a}$ or $\frac{1}{3}(\mathbf{b} - \mathbf{a})$
$\overrightarrow{AB}$ is parallel to $\overrightarrow{MN}$ and *MN* is $\frac{1}{3}$ of *AB*

6 **a** $\overrightarrow{OP} = \frac{1}{2}\mathbf{a} + \frac{1}{2}\mathbf{b}$ or $\frac{1}{2}(\mathbf{a} + \mathbf{b})$
$\overrightarrow{OQ} = \frac{1}{2}\mathbf{b} + \frac{1}{2}\mathbf{c}$ or $\frac{1}{2}(\mathbf{b} + \mathbf{c})$
$\overrightarrow{OR} = \frac{1}{2}\mathbf{a} + \frac{1}{2}\mathbf{c}$ or $\frac{1}{2}(\mathbf{a} + \mathbf{c})$
b $\overrightarrow{OP} + \overrightarrow{OQ} + \overrightarrow{OR} = \mathbf{a} + \mathbf{b} + \mathbf{c}$

14.2 Technique (p. 612)

1 **a** $\mathbf{v} = \mathbf{i} + 3\mathbf{j}$, $\mathbf{w} = 3\mathbf{i} - 2\mathbf{j}$, $\overrightarrow{PQ} = -\mathbf{i}$
b $\mathbf{v} = \binom{1}{3}$, $\mathbf{w} = \binom{3}{-2}$, $\overrightarrow{PQ} = \binom{-1}{0}$
c $\binom{3}{1}$, $\binom{-1}{-2}$
d $|\mathbf{v}| = \sqrt{10}$
e $\hat{\mathbf{w}} = \frac{1}{\sqrt{13}}\binom{3}{-2}$ or $\begin{pmatrix} \frac{3}{\sqrt{13}} \\ \frac{-2}{\sqrt{13}} \end{pmatrix}$
f $2\mathbf{v} = \binom{2}{6}$
$\mathbf{v} + \mathbf{w} = \binom{4}{1}$
$\mathbf{v} - \mathbf{w} = \binom{-2}{5}$
$\frac{1}{2}\mathbf{w} = \begin{pmatrix} \frac{3}{2} \\ -1 \end{pmatrix}$

2 **a** $\mathbf{a} = \begin{pmatrix} 0 \\ 0 \\ 3 \end{pmatrix}$ $\mathbf{d} = \begin{pmatrix} 0 \\ 3 \\ 0 \end{pmatrix}$ $\mathbf{t} = \begin{pmatrix} 3 \\ -3 \\ 9 \end{pmatrix}$
$\mathbf{b} = \begin{pmatrix} 0 \\ 3 \\ -2 \end{pmatrix}$ $\mathbf{e} = \begin{pmatrix} 2 \\ 4 \\ 2 \end{pmatrix}$ $\mathbf{u} = \begin{pmatrix} 2 \\ 4 \\ -2 \end{pmatrix}$
$\mathbf{c} = \begin{pmatrix} -2 \\ 0 \\ 0 \end{pmatrix}$ $\mathbf{s} = \begin{pmatrix} 4 \\ -3 \\ 1 \end{pmatrix}$ $\mathbf{v} = \begin{pmatrix} 8 \\ 0 \\ 4 \end{pmatrix}$
b $\begin{pmatrix} 2 \\ 4 \\ 9 \end{pmatrix}, \begin{pmatrix} 7 \\ 3 \\ 0 \end{pmatrix}, \begin{pmatrix} 2 \\ 4 \\ 2 \end{pmatrix}, \begin{pmatrix} 10 \\ 14 \\ -4 \end{pmatrix}, \begin{pmatrix} 0 \\ -3 \\ 14 \end{pmatrix}, \begin{pmatrix} 7 \\ 0 \\ 9 \end{pmatrix}$
c S $(0, -3, 14)$; T $(7, 0, 9)$; U $(5, 11, 2)$; V $(7, 7, 2)$; W $(2, 11, 6)$ position vectors and coordinates have the same components
d $|\mathbf{a}| = 3$; $|\mathbf{b}| = \sqrt{13}$; $|\mathbf{c}| = 2$; $|\mathbf{d}| = 3$; $|\mathbf{t}| = \sqrt{99} = 3\sqrt{11}$
e $\frac{1}{7}\begin{pmatrix} -2 \\ -3 \\ 6 \end{pmatrix}$
f $\begin{pmatrix} 7 \\ \frac{3}{2} \\ \frac{9}{2} \end{pmatrix}$

3 **a** $\begin{pmatrix} -14 \\ 4 \\ -10 \end{pmatrix}$ **b** $\begin{pmatrix} 2 \\ 2 \\ -1 \end{pmatrix}$ **c** 3

4 **a**

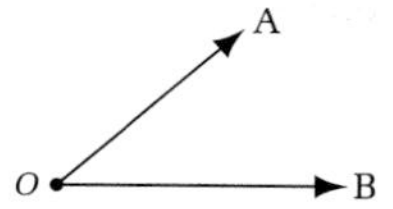

b $-2\mathbf{i} + 3\mathbf{j} + 6\mathbf{k}$
c $\frac{2}{7}(-2\mathbf{i} + 3\mathbf{j} + 6\mathbf{k})$ or $-\frac{4}{7}\mathbf{i} + \frac{6}{7}\mathbf{j} + \frac{12}{7}\mathbf{k}$
d $(-6, 4.5, 3)$

5 **a**

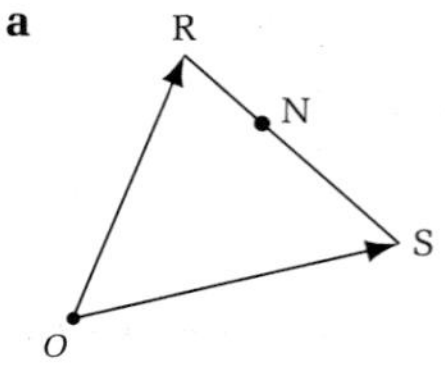

b $2\mathbf{i} - 2\mathbf{j} + 2\mathbf{k}$

6 **a** $\begin{pmatrix} 2 \\ -7 \\ 3 \end{pmatrix}, \begin{pmatrix} 1 \\ -4 \\ 7 \end{pmatrix}, \begin{pmatrix} 3 \\ -7 \\ -2 \end{pmatrix}$
b $\begin{pmatrix} -1 \\ 3 \\ 4 \end{pmatrix}, \begin{pmatrix} 1 \\ 0 \\ -5 \end{pmatrix}, \begin{pmatrix} 2 \\ -3 \\ -9 \end{pmatrix}$

c $|\overrightarrow{AB}| = \sqrt{26}$;
$|\overrightarrow{AC}| = \sqrt{26}$;
$|\overrightarrow{BC}| = \sqrt{94}$

d isosceles

14.3 Technique (p. 623)

1 a 135° or $\frac{3\pi}{4}$ b $|\mathbf{u}| = 2\sqrt{2}$; $|\mathbf{v}| = 3$
c -6 d -6

2 a $\begin{pmatrix} 6 \\ -7 \\ 1 \end{pmatrix}$
b 31
c 6
d 37
e 37
The dot product follows the distributive law.

3 a 6 b -6 c -6 d 0

4 a obtuse
b right angle
c acute

5 a $\lambda = -9$ b $\lambda = 5$

6 a 1.38 rad or 79°
b $\frac{\pi}{2}$ rad or 90°
c 2.06 rad or 118.1°

7 0.955 rad or 54.7°

8 $\lambda = 1$ or $\lambda = -3$

9 a 1.37 rad or 78.5° b 9.86 square units

10 a 10, 7 b $\frac{18}{35}$ c $\sqrt{901}$

11 $\pm\sqrt{6}$

12 $-\mathbf{i} + 19\mathbf{j} + 7\mathbf{k}$ or $\mathbf{i} - 19\mathbf{j} - 7\mathbf{k}$

14.3 Contextual (p. 625)

1 0.955 rad or 54.7°

2 1.89 rad or 108.4°

14.4 Technique (p. 640)

1 a $\mathbf{r} = (2\mathbf{i} - \mathbf{j} + 7\mathbf{k}) + \lambda(\mathbf{i} - \mathbf{j} + 2\mathbf{k})$
b S

2 a $\begin{pmatrix} 3 \\ -2 \\ 1 \end{pmatrix}$ b $\mathbf{r} = \begin{pmatrix} -5 \\ 1 \\ -3 \end{pmatrix} + \lambda\begin{pmatrix} 3 \\ -2 \\ 1 \end{pmatrix}$

3 4

4 a $\begin{pmatrix} 3 \\ -1 \\ 4 \end{pmatrix}$ b $\mathbf{r} = \begin{pmatrix} -4 \\ 2 \\ 1 \end{pmatrix} + \lambda\begin{pmatrix} 3 \\ -1 \\ 4 \end{pmatrix}$

5 a $|\mathbf{b}| = 3$
b $\begin{pmatrix} -3 \\ -5 \\ 1 \end{pmatrix}$ and $\begin{pmatrix} 5 \\ 3 \\ -3 \end{pmatrix}$

6 $\mathbf{r} = (2\mathbf{i} - \mathbf{j} + 2\mathbf{k}) + \lambda(5\mathbf{i} + \mathbf{j} - \mathbf{k})$
$p = -8$

7 a $\mathbf{r} = (6\mathbf{i} + 2\mathbf{j}) + \lambda(4\mathbf{j} + 8\mathbf{k})$
b $(6, 3, 2)$
c 0.685 rad or 39.2°

8 a no common point/not parallel
b 1.40 rad or 80°

9 a $\mathbf{r} = (-16\mathbf{i} + 27\mathbf{j}) + \lambda(3\mathbf{i} - 4\mathbf{j} + \mathbf{k})$
b $\sqrt{7}$
c $\sqrt{3}$

10 a $(2, 7, 8)$ b $3\sqrt{3}$ c $(3, 2, 7)$

14.4 Contextual (p. 641)

1 a $\mathbf{r}_2 = (500 - 8t)\mathbf{i} + 500\mathbf{j} + 200\mathbf{k}$
or $\begin{pmatrix} 500 - 8t \\ 500 \\ 200 \end{pmatrix}$
b the vector joining the balloon to the microlight (position vector of microlight relative to balloon)
c $\sqrt{(500 - 8t)^2 + (500 - 2t)^2 + (200 - 2t)^2}$
d $\sqrt{135\,000}\,\text{m} \approx 367.4\,\text{m}$

2 a $\begin{pmatrix} -4 - 3s + 2t \\ -12 - 4s + 2t \\ -7 - s + t \end{pmatrix}$
b P $(1, -1, 8)$, Q $(5, -3, 4)$
c 6

14.5 Technique (p. 658)

1 a $\mathbf{r}.(\mathbf{i} - \mathbf{j} + 2\mathbf{k}) = 23$ or $\mathbf{r}.\begin{pmatrix} 1 \\ -1 \\ 2 \end{pmatrix} = 23$
b B
c $x - y + 2z = 23$

2 a $\begin{pmatrix} 2 \\ 1 \\ -1 \end{pmatrix}.\begin{pmatrix} 1 \\ 0 \\ 3 \end{pmatrix} \neq 2$ b $\mathbf{r}.\begin{pmatrix} 1 \\ 0 \\ 3 \end{pmatrix} = -1, x + 3z = -1$

3 a $\mathbf{i} + \mathbf{k}$ is perpendicular to the plane $\mathbf{r}.(\mathbf{i} + \mathbf{k}) = 3$
b $\mathbf{i} - \mathbf{j}$ is perpendicular to the plane $\mathbf{r}.(\mathbf{i} - \mathbf{j}) = 0$

4 a $\mathbf{r}.(\mathbf{i} - \mathbf{j} + 2\mathbf{k}) = 5$ b $p = -9$

5 a $\overrightarrow{AB} = 5\mathbf{i} - \mathbf{j} + 7\mathbf{k}$ $\overrightarrow{BC} = -8\mathbf{i} - 4\mathbf{k}$
b $(5\mathbf{i} - \mathbf{j} + 7\mathbf{k}).(-\mathbf{i} + 9\mathbf{j} + 2\mathbf{k}) = 0$
$(-8\mathbf{i} - 4\mathbf{k}).(-\mathbf{i} + 9\mathbf{j} + 2\mathbf{k}) = 0$
c $\mathbf{r}.(-\mathbf{i} + 9\mathbf{j} + 2\mathbf{k}) = 7$

6 a $\mathbf{r} = (\mathbf{i} + 2\mathbf{j} + 3\mathbf{k}) + \lambda(2\mathbf{i} - \mathbf{j} + 2\mathbf{k})$
b $\mathbf{r}(2) = 5\mathbf{i} + 7\mathbf{k}$
c $\mathbf{r}.(2\mathbf{i} - \mathbf{j} + 2\mathbf{k}) = 24$

7 a 0.595 rad or 34.1° b $(0, 2, -4)$

8 0.888 rad or 50.9°

9 a $\frac{17}{7}$ b 2

10 a $\overrightarrow{AB} = 4\mathbf{i} + 2\mathbf{j} - \mathbf{k}$ $\overrightarrow{AC} = -\mathbf{i} + 5\mathbf{j} + 6\mathbf{k}$
b $\mathbf{r} = (\mathbf{i} + \mathbf{j} + \mathbf{k}) + \lambda(4\mathbf{i} + 2\mathbf{j} - \mathbf{k})$
$+ \mu(-\mathbf{i} + 5\mathbf{j} + 6\mathbf{k})$
c $17x - 23y + 22z = 16$

11 a $8\mathbf{i} - \mathbf{k}$
b $\mathbf{r} = (8\mathbf{i} - \mathbf{k}) + s(\mathbf{i} - \mathbf{j} + \mathbf{k})$
$+ t(-3\mathbf{i} + 4\mathbf{j} + 6\mathbf{k})$

14.5 Contextual (p. 659)

1 $\lambda = -1$; $\mu = 2$
$\mathbf{r}.(-\mathbf{i} + 2\mathbf{j} + \mathbf{k}) = 2$
$\mathbf{r} = (\mathbf{i} - \mathbf{k}) + t(-\mathbf{i} + 2\mathbf{j} + \mathbf{k})$
$\frac{2}{3}\sqrt{6}$; line AB is parallel to plane through CD.

2 **a** 56; $\frac{56}{65}$
b $\frac{33}{65}, \frac{33}{2}$
c 198
d $(5, -5, 0)$
e $\mathbf{r}.\begin{pmatrix} 4 \\ 5 \\ -3 \end{pmatrix} = -5$

3 **a** $(2, 1, 18)$
c by vector addition, $\mathbf{r} = \overrightarrow{ON} = \overrightarrow{OC} + \overrightarrow{CN}$
d $\lambda = 2$
e $(9, 9, 6)$
f $\mathbf{r} = \begin{pmatrix} 9 \\ 9 \\ 6 \end{pmatrix} + t\begin{pmatrix} -7 \\ -8 \\ 12 \end{pmatrix}$

Consolidation A (p. 661)

1
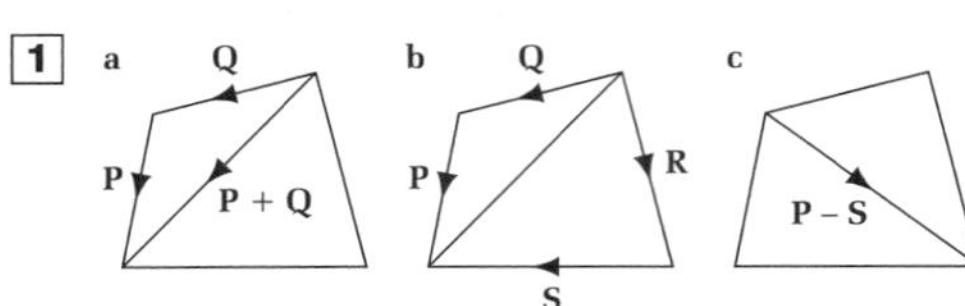

2 **a** $4\mathbf{i} + 6\mathbf{j} - 12\mathbf{k}$
b $\frac{1}{7}(2\mathbf{i} + 3\mathbf{j} - 6\mathbf{k})$
c $\frac{1}{7}(15\mathbf{i} - 9\mathbf{j} + 32\mathbf{k})$

3 $p = \pm\sqrt{2}$

4 **b** $\mathbf{r} = \begin{pmatrix} 4 \\ -3 \\ 2 \end{pmatrix} + t\begin{pmatrix} -2 \\ 1 \\ -9 \end{pmatrix}$
intersection at $(6, -4, 11)$

5 **a** $(-3, 6, 12)$
c $\overrightarrow{BC} = 4\mathbf{i} - 3\mathbf{j} - 12\mathbf{k}$
$\overrightarrow{BD} = \mathbf{i} - 5\mathbf{j} - 12\mathbf{k}$
d $16°$

6 C $(10, 0, -1)$
line BD has equation $\mathbf{r} = \begin{pmatrix} 10 - 10\lambda \\ 5 - 5\lambda \\ -\lambda \end{pmatrix}$
cables intersect, $73°$

7 $\mathbf{r} = (-\mathbf{i} - 3\mathbf{j} - 3\mathbf{k}) + \lambda(2\mathbf{i} + \mathbf{j} + 3\mathbf{k})$
$\overrightarrow{OP} = \mathbf{i} - 2\mathbf{j}$
minimum distance $\sqrt{5}$

8 $18.8°$

9 $\overrightarrow{BA}.\overrightarrow{BC} = -7$
$\cos\theta = -\frac{1}{\sqrt{5}}$
$\sin\theta = \frac{2}{\sqrt{5}}$
volume = 98 cubic units
a $\overrightarrow{OD} = \begin{pmatrix} 8 \\ -1 \\ 17 \end{pmatrix}$ **b** $\mathbf{r}.\begin{pmatrix} 2 \\ 15 \\ 4 \end{pmatrix} = 69$

10 common point $(-3, 5, 0)$
$\mathbf{r} = \begin{pmatrix} -3 \\ 5 \\ 0 \end{pmatrix} + \lambda\begin{pmatrix} 1 \\ -1 \\ -1 \end{pmatrix} + \mu\begin{pmatrix} 2 \\ 1 \\ -1 \end{pmatrix}$

Consolidation B (p. 663)

1 $\mathbf{r} = (\mathbf{i} - \mathbf{j} + 3\mathbf{k}) + t(3\mathbf{j} - \mathbf{k})$
$\overrightarrow{OC} = \mathbf{i} + \mathbf{j} + \frac{7}{3}\mathbf{k}$

2 **a** $\mathbf{r} = \begin{pmatrix} 2 \\ 1 \\ 5 \end{pmatrix} + \lambda\begin{pmatrix} 4 \\ -1 \\ 1 \end{pmatrix}$
b 1.50 rad or $85.7°$
c 1.65 rad or $94.3°$

3 **a** 0.245 rad or $14.0°$
b $12\mathbf{i} + 16\mathbf{j}$
c $p = 5$; $q = -2$
d $-\frac{8}{3}$

4 **b** $\mathbf{r} = (\mathbf{i} + 3\mathbf{j} + 2\mathbf{k}) + \lambda(2\mathbf{i} - 7\mathbf{j} - 2\mathbf{k})$
c $92.3°$

5 $\mathbf{r}.(\frac{2}{3}\mathbf{i} + \frac{2}{3}\mathbf{j} + \frac{1}{3}\mathbf{k}) = 3$

6 **a** $s = -2, t = 4$
b $\begin{pmatrix} 5 \\ 8 \\ -6 \end{pmatrix}$
d $\frac{\sqrt{7}}{5}$; $32°$

7 **a** $\mathbf{r} = (2\mathbf{i} + 3\mathbf{j} + 5\mathbf{k}) + \lambda(3\mathbf{i} + \mathbf{j} - 2\mathbf{k})$
b $\lambda = 1$; $(5, 4, 3)$
c $(9.5, 5.5, 0)$
d $(6.5, 4.5, 2)$; $\sqrt{(\frac{7}{2})}$
e $\mathbf{i} + 2\mathbf{j} - 3\mathbf{k}$; $38.2°$

15 Proof and Mathematical Argument

Review (p. 667)

1 **a** $a\sum_{r=0}^{n} b^r = \dfrac{a(1 - b^{n+1})}{1 - b}$
b $\log a + 2\log a + 3\log a + \cdots + n\log a$
$= \log a \sum_{r=1}^{n} r$
$= \frac{1}{2}n(n+1)\log a$
c $1^3 + 2^3 + \cdots + n^3 = \sum_{r=1}^{n} r^3 = \frac{1}{4}n^2(n+1)^2$

2 A positive integer that has exactly two factors: 1 and itself.

3 **a** $2^2 \times 19$ **b** $2^3 \times 3 \times 5$ **c** 227
d $2 \times 3 \times 73$ **e** 3×193 **f** 37×43

4 **a** area $= \int_a^b f(x)\,dx$
b area $= \int_0^{\pi} \sin x\,dx + |\int_{\pi}^{2\pi} \sin x\,dx|$

15.1 Technique (p. 671)

1 **a** Statement [6]. This is produced using division by zero $(a - b - c)$

b Statement [2]. $\log(\frac{1}{2}) < 0$ so the inequality should be reversed
c Statement [2]. The constant of integration has been omitted. This causes the paradox
d Statement [2] is only true if a is positive.

15.1 Contextual (p. 672)

2 0, because $14! = 1 \times 2 \times 3 \times \cdots \times 10 \times \cdots \times 14$, and multiplying any integer by 10 gives a unit digit of 0.

15.2 Technique (p. 676)

2 **a** $n = 41$; $n^2 - n + 41 = 1681$ is composite
b $n = 80, 81, 84, 89$ or 96.; these are the only values below 100 for which primes are not produced
c $k = 3$ gives 13, which isn't the square of an odd number
d $33337 = 37 \times 901$

3 No; $(ab) - (ba) = (10a + b) - (10b + a) = 9(a - b)$, which is always a multiple of 9, and therefore not prime.

15.2 Contextual (p. 676)

1 A counter example is $n = 11$; $2^{11} - 1 = 2047 = 23 \times 89$

2 Like the Goldbach conjecture no proof has yet been made and no counter example found. This conjecture has also been thoroughly checked by computer

15.4 Contextual (p. 683)

1 **b** $2^{100} - 1$ minutes is 1 267 650 600 228 229 401 496 703 205 375 minutes, which is approximately 2.4×10^{24} years

Consolidation A (p. 684)

1 line [6]; division by zero

3 false; $n = 5$ is a counter example

5 false; let $f(x) = \cos x$ and $p = \frac{\pi}{2}$, $q = \pi$

Consolidation B (p. 684)

1 $8^3 - 7^3 = 169$
$169 = 13^2$, composite

4 $4333 = 7 \times 619$, so is composite not prime.

Formulas

This is a list of formulas you should **remember.** None of these appear in formula booklets. Each formula has been referenced to the chapter in which it **first appears** in the text.

TOPIC	FORMULA	CHAPTER
Quadratic equations	$ax^2 + bx + c = 0$ has solutions $x = \dfrac{-b \pm \sqrt{b^2 - 4ac}}{2a}$	**1**
Sine rule	In the triangle ABC $\dfrac{a}{\sin A} = \dfrac{b}{\sin B} = \dfrac{c}{\sin C}$	**3**
Cosine rule	In the triangle ABC $a^2 = b^2 + c^2 - 2bc\cos A$	**3**
Area of a triangle	In the triangle ABC area $= \frac{1}{2}ab\sin C$	**3**
Pythagorean identities	$\sin^2 A + \cos^2 A \equiv 1$ $1 + \tan^2 A \equiv \sec^2 A$ $1 + \cot^2 A \equiv \operatorname{cosec}^2 A$	**3**
Double angles	$\sin 2\text{A} \equiv 2\sin A\cos A$ $\cos 2\text{A} \equiv \cos^2 A - \sin^2 A$ $\tan 2A \equiv \dfrac{2\tan A}{1 - \tan^2 A}$	**3**
Differentiation of polynomials	$\dfrac{\mathrm{d}}{\mathrm{d}x}(x^n) = nx^{n-1}$	**5**
Differentiation of trigonometric functions	$\dfrac{\mathrm{d}}{\mathrm{d}x}(\sin kx) = k\cos kx$ $\dfrac{\mathrm{d}}{\mathrm{d}x}(\cos kx) = -k\sin kx$	**5**
Differentiation of sums of functions	$\dfrac{\mathrm{d}}{\mathrm{d}x}[f(x) + g(x)] = f'(x) + g'(x)$	**5**
Chain rule	$\dfrac{\mathrm{d}}{\mathrm{d}x}[f(g(x))] = f'(g(x))g'(x)$	**5**
Laws of logarithms	$\log_a x + \log_a y \equiv \log_a(xy)$ $\log_a x - \log_a y \equiv \log_a(\frac{x}{y})$ $k\log_a x \equiv \log_a(x^k)$	**7**
Arithmetic series	$u_n = a + (n-1)d$ $S_n = \frac{1}{2}n(a + l)$ $= \frac{1}{2}n[2a + (n-1)d]$	**8**

TOPIC	FORMULA	CHAPTER
Geometric series	$u_n = ar^{n-1}$ $S_n = \dfrac{a(1-r^n)}{1-r}$ $S_\infty = \dfrac{a}{1-r}$ for $\lvert r\rvert < 1$	8
Integration of polynomials	$\int x^n \, dx = \dfrac{1}{n+1}x^{n+1} + c$ where $n \neq -1$	9
Integration of trigonometric functions	$\int \cos kx \, dx = \dfrac{1}{k}\sin kx + c$ $\int \sin kx \, dx = -\dfrac{1}{k}\cos kx + c$	9
Area under a curve	$\text{area} = \int_a^b y \, dx \quad y \geq 0$	9
Differentiation of other standard mathematical functions	$\dfrac{d}{dx}(e^{kx}) = k e^{kx}$ $\dfrac{d}{dx}(\ln x) = \dfrac{1}{x}$ $\dfrac{d}{dx}(\tan kx) = k \sec^2 kx$	11
Product and Quotient rules	$\dfrac{d}{dx}[f(x)g(x)] = f'(x)g(x) + f(x)g'(x)$ $\dfrac{d}{dx}\left[\dfrac{f(x)}{g(x)}\right] = \dfrac{f'(x)g(x) - f(x)g'(x)}{[g(x)]^2}$	11
These rules are also written as:	$\dfrac{d}{dx}(uv) = uv' + vu'$ $\dfrac{d}{dx}\left(\dfrac{u}{v}\right) = \dfrac{vu' - uv'}{v^2}$	11
Integration of other standard mathematical functions	$\int \sec^2 kx \, dx = \dfrac{1}{k}\tan kx + c$ $\int e^{kx} \, dx = \dfrac{1}{k} e^{kx} + c$ $\int \dfrac{1}{x} \, dx = \ln \lvert x\rvert + c \quad x \neq 0$	12
Scalar or dot product of two vectors	$\begin{pmatrix} x \\ y \\ z \end{pmatrix} \cdot \begin{pmatrix} a \\ b \\ c \end{pmatrix} = xa + yb + zc$	14

Index